The Expanding Sphere of Travel Behaviour Research: Selected Papers from the 11th International Conference on Travel Behaviour Research

Related books

HENSHER	Traffic Safety and Human Behavior
HENSHER & BUTTON	Handbooks in Transport-6 Volume Set
BONNEL, LEE-GOSSELIN, ZMUD & MADRE	Transport Survey Methods: Keeping up with a Changing World
AXHAUSEN	Moving Through Nets: The Physical and Social Dimensions of Travel – Selected Papers from the 10th International Conference on Travel Behaviour Research
TIMMERMANS	Pedestrian Behaviour: Models, Data Collection and Application

The Expanding Sphere of Travel Behaviour Research: Selected Papers from the 11th International Conference on Travel Behaviour Research

EDITED BY

Ryuichi Kitamura†
Kyoto University, Japan

Toshio Yoshii
Kyoto University, Japan

Toshiyuki Yamamoto
Nagoya University, Japan

Emerald

United Kingdom • North America • Japan
India • Malaysia • China

Emerald Group Publishing Limited
Howard House, Wagon Lane, Bingley BD16 1WA, UK

First edition 2009

British Library Cataloguing in Publication Data
A catalogue record for this book is available from the British Library

ISBN: 978-1-84855-936-3

Certificate number 1985

Awarded in recognition of Emerald's production department's adherence to quality systems and processes when preparing scholarly journals for print

INVESTOR IN PEOPLE

Contents

List of Contributors xi

Preface
Ryuichi Kitamura[†], *Toshio Yoshii and Toshiyuki Yamamoto* xv

Tribute
Toshio Yoshii and Toshiyuki Yamamoto xvii

PART 1: Keynote Speeches **1**

Chapter 1.
The Sociabilities of Travel
John Urry 3

Chapter 2.
Knowledge Interactions and Travel Behavior
Masahisa Fujita 17

PART 2: Resource and Synthesis Papers **41**

2.1 Social Networks and Telecommunications

Chapter 3.
ICT and Social Networks: Towards a Situational Perspective on the Interaction Between Corporeal and Connected Presence
Martin Dijst 45

Chapter 4.
Connected Anytime: Telecommunications and Activity–Travel Behavior from an Asian Perspective
Nobuaki Ohmori 77

2.2 Behavioral Modification

Chapter 5.
Travel Behavior Modification: Theories, Methods, and Programs
Tommy Gärling and Satoshi Fujii 97

2.3 Experimental Approaches

Chapter 6.
Learning from Interactive Experiments: Travel Behavior and Complex System Dynamics
Hani S. Mahmassani 131

2.4 Group Behavior

Chapter 7.
Household Decision Making in Travel Behaviour Analysis
Harry Timmermans 159

Chapter 8.
Models of Household Activity and Travel Behavior with Group Decision-Making Mechanisms in Japan
Junyi Zhang and Akimasa Fujiwara 187

2.5 Advances in Data Acquisition

Chapter 9.
Tracking Individual Travel Behaviour Using Mobile Phones: Recent Technological Development
Yasuo Asakura and Eiji Hato 207

2.6 Advances in Econometric Methods

Chapter 10.
Selective Developments in Choice Analysis and a Reminder about the Dimensionality of Behavioral Analysis
David A. Hensher, John M. Rose and Sean M. Puckett 237

Chapter 11.
Advances in Choice Modeling and Asian Perspectives
Toshiyuki Yamamoto, Tetsuro Hyodo and Yasunori Muromachi 277

2.7 Advances in Activity Analysis

Chapter 12.
Challenges and Opportunities in Advancing Activity-Based Approaches for Travel Demand Analysis
Ram M. Pendyala 303

Chapter 13.
Synthesis Report for the Workshop for Advances in Activity Analysis—Approaches for Advanced Activity Analysis in Japan
Kuniaki Sasaki and Kazuo Nishii 337

2.8 Integrated Models

Chapter 14.
Integrated Urban Models: Theoretical Prospects
Eric Miller 351

2.9 Application to Policy Analysis and Planning

Chapter 15.
Application to Policy Analysis and Planning
Konstadinos G. Goulias 387

PART 3: Workshop Reports **421**

Chapter 16.
Behaviour Under Uncertainty
André de Palma and Nathalie Picard 423

Chapter 17.
Social Networks and Telecommunications
Patricia L. Mokhtarian 429

Chapter 18.
Retrospectives and Perspectives on Travel Behavioral Modification Research: A Report of the "Behavior Modification" Workshop
Satoshi Fujii 439

Chapter 19.
Advances in Data Acquisition
Juan de Dios Ortúzar and Piotr Olszewski 447

Chapter 20.
Advances in Activity Analysis
Kay W. Axhausen 457

Chapter 21.
Group Behavior Modeling
Junyi Zhang and Andrew Daly 465

Chapter 22.
Seven Critical Directions for Integrated Land Use–Transport Models
Joan L. Walker and Sarah Bush 475

Chapter 23.
Application to Policy Analysis and Planning
Yoram Shiftan 481

Chapter 24.
Advances in Econometric Methods
Chandra Bhat 491

PART 4: Session Papers **495**

4.1 Measurement and Quantification

Chapter 25.
Designing Stated Choice Experiments: State of the Art
Michiel C.J. Bliemer and John M. Rose 499

Chapter 26.
Modelling Interdependent Behaviour as a Sequentially Administered Stated Choice Experiment: Analysis of Variable User Charging and Agent Influence in Freight Distribution Chains
Sean M. Puckett and David A. Hensher 539

Chapter 27.
Choice Models Using Matching Data
Nobuhiro Sanko and Takayuki Morikawa 571

4.2 Behavioral Change

Chapter 28.
Location Choice vis-à-vis Transportation: The Case of Recent Home Buyers
Michelle Bina and Kara M. Kockelman 597

Chapter 29.
Does the Release from Household Responsibilities Lead to More Out-of-home Activities? The Case of Hiring Live-in Maids in Hong Kong
Donggen Wang 621

Chapter 30.
Role of Minority Influence on the Diffusion of Compliance with a Demand Management Measure
Yos Sunitiyoso, Erel Avineri and Kiron Chatterjee 643

4.3 Behavior and Values

Chapter 31.
The Influence of Trip Length on Marginal Time and Money Values: An Alternative Explanation
Andrew Daly and Juan Antonio Carrasco 673

Chapter 32.
Controlling for Sample Selection in the Estimation of the Value of Travel Time
Stefan L. Mabit and Mogens Fosgerau 703

Chapter 33.
Social Value Orientation and the Efficiency of Traffic Networks
Erel Avineri 725

Chapter 34.
Towards a Multi-Activity Multi-Person Accessibility Measure: Concept and First Tests
Joyce K.L. Soo, Dick Ettema and Henk F.L. Ottens 745

4.4 Decision Dynamics

Chapter 35.
Schedule-based Dynamic Assignment Models for Air Transport Networks
Umberto Crisalli and Fiorella Sciangula 771

Chapter 36.
Learning and Risk Attitudes in Route Choice Dynamics
Roger B. Chen and Hani S. Mahmassani 791

Chapter 37.
Stress Triggered Household Decision to Change Dwelling:
A Comprehensive and Dynamic Approach
Khandker M. Nurul Habib, Eric J. Miller and Ilan Elgar 819

4.5 Prediction and Application

Chapter 38.
The Option Value of Public Transport Services: Empirical Evidence from the Netherlands
Karst Geurs, Rinus Haaijer and Bert van Wee 849

Chapter 39.
Longitudinal Simulation of Travel Under Budget Constraints
Dirk Zumkeller, Tobias Kuhnimhof and Christoph Gringmuth 877

Chapter 40.
A Tour-Based Model for the Simulation of a Distributive Freight System
Armando Cartenì and Francesco Russo 901

List of Contributors

Yasuo Asakura	Graduate School of Science and Technology, Kobe University, Japan
Erel Avineri	Centre for Transport & Society, University of the West of England, Bristol, UK
Kay W. Axhausen	IVT, ETH Zürich, Switzerland
Chandra R. Bhat	Department of Civil, Architectural and Environmental Engineering, The University of Texas, Austin, TX, USA
Michelle Bina	Cambridge Systematics, Inc., Cambridge, MA, USA
Michiel C.J. Bliemer	Faculty of Civil Engineering and Geosciences, Delft University of Technology, The Netherlands and Institute of Transport and Logistics Studies, University of Sydney, Australia
Sarah Bush	Center for Transportation and Logistics, Massachusetts Institute of Technology, Cambridge, MA, USA
Juan Antonio Carrasco	Department of Civil Engineering, Universidad de Concepción, Chile
Armando Cartenì	Department of Civil Engineering, University of Salerno, Italy
Kiron Chatterjee	Centre for Transport & Society, University of the West of England, Bristol, UK
Roger B. Chen	Transportation Center, Northwestern University, Evanston, IL, USA
Umberto Crisalli	Department of Civil Engineering, "Tor Vergata" University of Rome, Italy
Andrew Daly	RAND Europe; Institute for Transport Studies, University of Leeds, UK
André de Palma	Ecole Normale Supérieure de Cachan and Ecole Polytechnique, France
Martin Dijst	Urban and Regional Research Centre Utrecht (URU), Faculty of Geosciences, Utrecht University, The Netherlands
Ilan Elgar	Department of Civil Engineering, University of Toronto, Canada

Dick Ettema	Urban and Regional Research Utrecht, The Netherlands
Mogens Fosgerau	DTU Transport, Technical University of Denmark, Denmark
Satoshi Fujii	Department of Urban Management, Graduate School of Engineering, Kyoto University, Japan
Masahisa Fujita	Professor, Konan University, Japan
Akimasa Fujiwara	Graduate School for International Development and Cooperation, Hiroshima University, Japan
Tommy Gärling	Department of Psychology, University of Gothenburg, Göteborg, Sweden
Karst Geurs	Netherlands Environmental Assessment Agency, The Netherlands
Konstadinos G. Goulias	Department of Geography & GeoTrans Laboratory, University of California, Santa Barbara, CA, USA
Christoph Gringmuth	Institute for Economic Policy Research, University of Karlsruhe, Germany
Rinus Haaijer	MuConsult, Amersfoort, The Netherlands
Eiji Hato	Department of Urban Engineering, The University of Tokyo, Japan
David A. Hensher	Institute of Transport and Logistics Studies, Faculty of Economics and Business, The University of Sydney, Australia
Tetsuro Hyodo	Department of Logistics and Information Engineering, Tokyo University of Marine Science and Technology, Japan
Kara M. Kockelman	Department of Civil, Architectural and Environmental Engineering, The University of Texas, Austin, TX, USA
Tobias Kuhnimhof	Institute for Transport Studies, University of Karlsruhe, Germany
Stefan L. Mabit	DTU Transport, Technical University of Denmark, Denmark
Hani S. Mahmassani	Transportation Center, Northwestern University, Evanston, IL, USA
Eric J. Miller	Department of Civil Engineering, Cities Center, University of Toronto, ON, Canada
Patricia L. Mokhtarian	Department of Civil & Environmental Engineering and Institute of Transportation Studies, University of California, Davis, CA, USA

Takayuki Morikawa	Graduate School of Environmental Studies, Nagoya University, Japan
Yasunori Muromachi	Department of Built Environment, Tokyo Institute of Technology, Japan
Kazuo Nishii	Department of Information Science, University of Marketing and Distribution Science, Japan
Khandker M. Nurul Habib	Department of Civil & Environmental Engineering, University of Alberta, Canada
Nobuaki Ohmori	Department of Urban Engineering, The University of Tokyo, Japan
Piotr Olszewski	Department of Civil Engineering, Warsaw University of Technology, Warsaw, Poland
Juan de Dios Ortúzar	Department of Transport Engineering and Logistics, Pontificia Universidad Católica de Chile, Santiago, Chile
Henk F.L. Ottens	Urban and Regional Research Utrecht, The Netherlands
Ram M. Pendyala	School of Sustainable Engineering and the Built Environment, Arizona State University, Tempe, AZ, USA
Nathalie Picard	Université de Cergy-Pontoise, Ecole Polytechnique and INED, France
Sean M. Puckett	Institute of Transport and Logistics Studies, Faculty of Economics and Business, The University of Sydney, Australia
John M. Rose	Institute of Transport and Logistics Studies, Faculty of Economics and Business, The University of Sydney, Australia
Francesco Russo	Department of Computer Science, Mathematics, Electronics and Transport, University of Reggio Calabria, Italy
Nobuhiro Sanko	Graduate School of Business Administration, Kobe University, Japan
Kuniaki Sasaki	Institute of Materials and Environmental Technology, University of Yamanashi, Japan
Fiorella Sciangula	Department of Civil Engineering, "Tor Vergata" University of Rome, Italy
Yoram Shiftan	Technion-Israel Institute of Technology, Haifa, Israel
Joyce K.L. Soo	Urban and Regional Research Utrecht, The Netherlands

Yos Sunitiyoso	Transportation Research Group, University of Southampton, UK
Harry Timmermans	Urban Planning Group, Eindhoven University of Technology, The Netherlands
John Urry	Department of Sociology, Lancaster University, Lancaster, UK
Bert van Wee	Faculty of Technology, Policy and Management, Delft University of Technology, The Netherlands
Joan L. Walker	Civil and Environmental Engineering, University of California, Berkeley, CA, USA
Donggen Wang	Department of Geography, Hong Kong Baptist University, Hong Kong
Toshiyuki Yamamoto	Department of Civil Engineering, Nagoya University, Japan
Junyi Zhang	Graduate School for International Development and Cooperation, Hiroshima University, Japan
Dirk Zumkeller	Institute for Transport Studies, University of Karlsruhe, Germany

PREFACE

Ryuichi Kitamura[†], *Toshio Yoshii and Toshiyuki Yamamoto*

Our travel behaviour manifests as the resolution of internal needs and desires with the rapidly changing external travel environment. This volume of the 11th International Conference on Travel Behaviour Research examines key issues in this expanding field, and emerging trends in travel behaviour resulting from these changes.

Advances in information and communication technologies (ICT) have spurred drastic changes in our lifestyles and consequently our travel needs and desires, thus impacting travel behaviour. The fax machine and Federal Express have certainly changed the way we collaborate over distances. The cellular phone has reduced many of the constraints and needs for advance planning. Tremendous capabilities in the exchange of information became available over the Internet in the forms of e-library, electronic magazines, and newspapers. The PDF format, other software and hardware developments, and standardization have helped to make this exchange possible. Chat rooms, blogs, and bulletin boards facilitate the formation of social networks, although transient they may be. As anticipated by Gore, and utilized by the Obama campaign, these networks are real and can wield tremendous political power.

Emerging economic factors are challenging the assumptions implicit in the form of our external travel environment, namely that of cheap transportation. Rising oil prices have impacted many aspects of our travel environment. For example, urban structure has taken for granted a low cost of transportation. As a result, households have chosen homes at the fringe of a metropolitan area to start their suburban (or exurban) living. Suburban shopping malls depend on attracting market share from a huge geographical expanse, which can be economically justified only when transportation costs are negligibly small—at least in the minds of consumers.

To meet the needs of the future, we need to broaden our approach toward mitigating the problems of traffic congestion. Although we have made efforts to provide useful road networks that facilitate convenient mobility at low cost, we still moan about traffic congestion. The ranking of the most congested cities is still a favorite subject. Although we have constructed new highways, widened streets, and made improvements in traffic controls, we realize now that these measures have almost reached their limits. We must now consider how to mitigate traffic congestion by other means—by demand or behavioural modification. Policy measures are now aiming for sustainability of sound development. The issues of the built environment and travel, travel of children and seniors, and safety and health must be addressed together. We must also consider social networks and social capital in our digital age, and the role of travel to support such social activities.

Future application of ICT will improve the acquisition of data and enable more accurate modeling of complex systems. Investigating the impacts of new technologies on travel behaviour is essential for evaluating the value of new policy measures. Simulation is one method of investigating complex systems such as an urban transportation network. However, every model needs traffic data for verification, and data availability has been a serious limitation in the past. We anticipate new applications of ICT to enable the acquisition of new data, the creation and validation of more advanced models, and ultimately yield a new framework for travel behaviour analysis.

In this 11th International Conference on Travel behaviour Research, Kyoto, we have had valuable discussions on these issues relating to the expanding sphere of travel behaviour analysis, comprising of keynote speeches, workshops, and paper sessions. These proceedings contain the keynote speeches of Professor John Urry of Lancaster University (sociology) and Professor Masahisa Fujita of Kyoto University (economics), workshop resource papers by the most distinguished authors in nine subject areas, four synthesis papers (focus on Asian developments), nine workshop reports, and 17 papers selected from presentation sessions. This is one in a series of IATBR conference proceedings that comprehensively reviews, synthesizes, and offers future directions for the respective subareas of the travel behaviour research field. We hope this book will be used by many researchers, practitioners, and students.

Tribute

Toshio Yoshii and Toshiyuki Yamamoto

Professor Ryuichi Kitamura, known affectionately as "Kitamura-sensei," Chair of the Local Organizing Committee of the 2006 IATBR Kyoto Conference, passed away on February 19, 2009. He bravely struggled with cancer for more than 6 years.

He contributed toward the advance of travel behaviour research as well as the whole field of transportation research. After working in the United States from 1975 to 1993, he became a professor in Kyoto University, Japan, where he continued for 16 years. He was proud of Japanese and Asian cultures and made efforts to share them with others. He organized the 2006 IATBR Kyoto Conference, which was the first conference of its kind held in an Asian city. He introduced the participants to Japanese-style hospitality so as to let them come in contact with Japanese culture.

He published a collection of remarkable papers, and filled a variety of important posts, such as Chair of the International Association for Travel Behaviour Research from 1992 to 1995. In addition to other prizes, he received the Lifetime Achievement Award from IATBR. He also made extraordinary efforts in education. As a result, there is now a thriving community of talented researchers who got their start from Kitamura-sensei, and they carry on his legacy.

This book is the last one to which Kitamura-sensei contributed directly. On behalf of all of us who were influenced by Kitamura-sensei and who have grieved his death, we want to record a tribute of admiration for him, to express sincere thanks, and to pray for the repose of sensei's soul.

PART 1

Keynote Speeches

The Expanding Sphere of Travel Behaviour Research
Selected Papers from the 11th International Conference on Travel Behaviour Research

1

The Sociabilities of Travel ☆

John Urry

Thank you very much for inviting me. As well, thank you for all the hospitality that I have been shown since arriving here. I'm very pleased to be here and I suppose this hospitality illustrates one of the points that I am going to make today, namely, the "sociabilities of travel."

However, in this talk I'm going to, as we say in English, "bite the hand that feeds me," because one of things that I want to show is that the very term "travel behavior" is not a very helpful term. There is, I suggest, no such thing as "travel behavior." What there are, are various forms of social practices and some of these social practices from time to time contingently demand various forms of traveling. Decisions about traveling are thus highly relational and depend upon multiple social practices. Especially the practices of work, but I shall particularly focus on friendship and family life.

Moreover, travel itself is not merely behavioral but on occasions contingently consists of meaningful actions tied into and interconnected with people's social practices. I particularly want to link this set of questions to issues of people's social networks. People meet up intermittently to cement their social networks; to enjoy each other's company, and carry out certain obligations. As societies appear to have become more

☆ Keynote speech at The International Association for Travel Behaviour Research (IATBR), Kyoto, Japan (2006).

distributed, as people's links are spread out more geographically, people are less likely to bump into their social contacts and hence scheduled meetings and various kinds of "meetingness" become highly significant. Thus, we might say transport and meetings at a distance are increasingly necessary and obligatory to social life, particularly for leisure activities or through attendance at peoples' birthdays, weddings, funerals, or visits.

So-called travel demand thus seems to stem from a "compulsion to proximity," to feel the need to be physically copresent with others and to fill certain cultural and social obligations with significant others.

This talk explores the social obligations that result in various kinds of physical travel. In a way, one of the things that I'm going to say is that conversation, or more prosaically talk, is central to thinking about how and why and when people are physically copresent and thus physically travel. I also try to link these issues to a more general consideration as to the significance of movement to social life. In general, I think issues of movement, of too little movement for some, or of too much movement for others, or of the wrong sort of movement, or at the wrong time are central to many people's everyday lives, and to the operation of countless operations from SARS to plane crashes, from airport expansion controversies to SMS texting, from refugees to global terrorism, from obesity to oil wars in the Middle East, from global warming to slave trading, issues to what I term mobility are center stage on countless policy and academic agendas. Consequently there is what I like to call a mobility "structure of feeling" in the air and it is that which I'm very keen to try to develop.

One of the ways that I've sought to develop this is through the "mobilities paradigm." This has a number of features. First, all social relations involve diverse connections. I'm using "connections," rather than the more specific term "travel," as all sorts of social relations, social travel practices, are more or less at a distance and they are never simply fixed or located in place, but are to varying degrees constituted through circulating entities.

Secondly, these processes stem from and are reproduced by "five interdependent mobilities": the physical travel of people; the physical movement of objects; imaginative travel perfected through images of places; virtual travel; and communicative travel. One of things that I'm interested in exploring is how different sorts of travel practices depend upon particular and changing combinations, or "assemblage" of those different forms of mobility.

But thirdly, there's something very specific about face-to-face connections. From time to time people feel the need to come face-to-face. That somehow, connections at a distance have to be embodied. We have to be physically in the same place and, to see each other, meet face-to-face. I term this "contingent meetingness."

These patterns of contingent meetingness come about through a very complex process in which various kinds of environments, technologies, and machines are put together with social life, with human life, and various kinds of human actions. Examples include the actions that constitute itself within a conference, but also constitute itself within a family meeting, or a friendship group meeting up.

These are organized through "mobility systems," such as automobility but also the pedestrian system, the cycle system, and so on. These mobility systems endure through patterns of path dependency, such as the awesome path dependency of the automobility system. Further, these systems are involved in highly expert forms of knowledge that make those systems often difficult to monitor, change, or transform. These systems I also see as self-organizing and coevolving within each other as well as being interdependent.

Sixth, these systems have the effect of producing various kinds of movement and those movements are highly significant for the ways in which contemporary societies are governed. The governing of mobile populations, becomes, has become, and is becoming an incredibly significant feature of the governance of contemporary societies. This is another way in which issues of mobility are sort of centered—have come to occupy center stage. The governing of mobile populations that move across so-called territories is utterly central.

Seventh, some of the time mobilities are not just something to enable other activities, but are in part meaningful activities in their own right.

That's a very brief account of what I like to call the "mobilities paradigm."

I now want to turn to specifically say something about meetings. I use the term meetings, as a very general or generic notion, to capture what happens not only in relatively formal meetings but also in informal contingent meetings that happen in all sorts of more informal practices around friendship and family.

I think the significance of meetings is highly important in relationship to the distribution of social networks across space. The literature on small worlds demonstrates the ways in which there are relatively limited connections that link people across the world. Networks demonstrate the combination of tight clumps with a few random long-term connections through weak ties. These weak ties based on intermittent travel connect people to the outside world, and central to the connections are various kinds of intermittent meetings. I think the social network literature, which has a more formal notion, has ignored the significance of meetings. Meetings seem to be everywhere, and one of the things we might note is that for all the growth of the Internet and mobile telephony over the last 15 years, there also seems to be overwhelming evidence that meetings are empirically more significant.

In relationship to business meetings or professional meetings, we can note the way in which, as the Henley Centre says, we increasingly live in a connecting economy. Since few of us actually make anything, what we really do is to make meetings, and those meetings are crucial to the influence that we might have over social networks. Over almost 20 years ago, the United States' major 500 companies were said to have had 11–15 million formal meetings each day, and 3–4 billion meetings each year.

One key thing about meetings is that often people have to travel to get there. Maybe it is walking down the corridor, but a lot of the time it is traveling substantial distances. One of the things that I think is much under-researched within organizations is the significance of meetings. One piece of work by Strassmann describes how there are meetings about meetings. There are meetings to plan reports and meetings to review the status of reports. What these meetings are about is people trying to figure out what they are doing.

One of things that is also interesting about meetings is that invariably at those meetings are various technologies that enable future meetings to be planned and arranged. Therefore, the cycle of meetings is self-sustaining. They are not simply a one-off event. What can be said more specifically about what happens in meetings?

My late colleague Dede Boden wrote very interestingly about the business of talk. She writes, "the drums beat, from far and near the chosen gather, face-to-face across the shiny table, the shiny podium." Meetings are complex encounters and as she says, "(w)hen in doubt, call a meeting. And when one meeting isn't enough, schedule another."

The English novelist David Lodge writes about academic conferences. This can be generalized, and I thought this quote might help us to understand what we're all doing here. "You journey to new and interesting places, meet new and interesting people, and more new interesting relationships with them, exchange gossip, exchange confidences, eat drink and make merry and return home with an enhanced serious of mind."

There is something important about the pleasures, the routines, and the rituals. This is a topic for anthropological study, namely the rituals of meetings, such as a plenary address. There is something about different kinds of meetings and their pleasures. What David Lodge brings out is the consequences that are beyond the formal events, namely, the informal kinds of relationships, the distributions of power and authority, gossip, and the building up or dissolving of trust relationships between people.

Central here, it is argued, is eye contact which enables certain things to be done face-to-face which could not be done at a distance—or so far cannot be done as effectively at a distance. The German sociologist Simmel writing in the early part of this century talked about the significance of the eye as a significant achievement, since looking at one another is what affects the connections and interactions of individuals.

Simmel terms this the most direct and purest of interactions which are moments of intimacy, since one cannot take through the eye without at the same time giving through the eye. There's a kind of mutual interdependence that eye contact, or face-to-face contact, can establish. He calls this "the most complete reciprocity of person-to-person." The face-to-face look is returned and trust relationships can get established and reproduced.

Many other writers in the social sciences have explored other aspects of these properties of face-to-face interaction. I argue that this is utterly central to why travel takes place. Eye-to-eye contact enables people to develop encounters, to display attentiveness, and commitment and detecting where a lack of trustful commitment is with others. One thing that happens in all of this is that the eyes get "joined."

Conversations themselves are completely central to explaining travel in travel behavior because conversations are a complex kind of performance and achievement. Conversations are often necessary to talk through problems—"we have to meet to talk this through," is a common refrain.

Through the centrality of those face-to-face conversations, topics can come and go, trust can be built up, misunderstandings can be quickly corrected, and commitment and sincerity can be quickly assessed. Often those conversations take time and they have to take that time in particular places. They are therefore occasioned in time and place. As well, they are often rich, multilayered, and dense.

Conversations are not just made up of words, but they also consist of other things such as body language, facial gestures, intonation, status, and silences — the processes of talking, talking when you have met because of the fact that some or all have traveled significant distances. Particular characteristics of talk can mean that one has a good conference, a good family meal, or a good meet-up with friends or acquaintances.

One thing that is central to these conversations is turn taking. There's a whole social science literature on turn taking, "turn taking works like a revolving door, demanding and facilitating entry, and exit, and effectively managing the flow of talk by spacing speakers and pacing topics."

How will these conversations or this talk develop over time? In some research, it is argued that such talk, such copresent talk (being with others to talk), will interestingly become particularly significant. Boden argues that workplaces will become highly interactive, not just with technology, but with people.

The pacing and sequencing of work tasks may become even more talk based. According to Weber and Chon, "since much more information can now be exchanged by various technologies," technologies that produce instantaneous information flow, "there is a greater need to build relationships when getting together," for face-to-face meetings. "Consequently," they continue, "meetings in the future will focus more on the social aspects rather than on the business." To put it another way, they mean the exchange of cognitive information can be done mainly by technology. However, it is the social aspects that will be central to meetings of the future.

Meetings of the future are not just work meetings. In fact, the most interesting meetings are probably not those which are principally work meetings. In some research on architects in the UK, Kennedy argues, the significance of meetings and networks, "friends move and or form other networks, with more like-minded individuals, in the next host country, and because previous contacts are maintained, yet more friends get added to." He refers to this as, "the revolving circuits of trans-national social life." This study is based on architects, but it became a study of friendship and of the "transnational social life" that people working within the same occupation developed and extended.

An interesting Rowntree report in the UK talks about the kinds of things that people feel they must do. It asked people what are the social customs, obligations, activities that they feel they have to do. It was a study of poverty and social deprivation, and the top necessities of life were thought to be celebrations and special occasions, attending weddings and funerals, visits to friends and families, including those who are in hospital and so on.

That was rather interesting because the ways in which these were thought to be obligatory. People, if they had the money and time would necessarily want to do those things. Over four-fifths of the population sees those celebrations as matters of obligation. I use the term obligation quite often in the rest of this talk. One example of such an obligation is certain kinds of meals. Travel behavior research might study more meals and eating out, and who to eat with. As well, what are the kinds of obligations that were necessary to make a person be present at that meal, at that time? A UK study regarding eating out argues that it is important to be present, because the meal symbolizes a socially significant occasion. The authors say that to have eaten the same meal the day before, or the day after, would not have been a satisfactory substitute, even if the same people were present. It is to eat that meal, at that time, on that occasion that is significant. Therefore, there is a kind of ritual involved in being present at that meal.

Social networks are extremely complex and difficult to research. There is an interesting website, wheresgeorge.com, which tracks the movement of dollar bills in the United States. Dollar bills are normally physically carried in people's wallets or purses. The authors of this report use this to demonstrate the incredibly far-flung character of those notes. They suggest that this shows something about the ways that people have traveled and physically carried those notes and therefore had to travel. This travel was probably linked to their changing social networks. That is just one way of tracking people's movement.

People's movements are significant. I've tried to encapsulate this in a concept called "network capital." In a mobile society, that is the way that people make or remake their social networks. In relationship to the social sciences, it would be another basis of social stratification. Societies are often seen as stratified by income, political power, or social status. I argue that "network capital" would be another basis of social stratification. Many different sorts of things constitute such network capital: the possession of various kinds of competences, to physically move all sorts of things, including the capacity to walk distances within different environments, to board different means of mobility, to carry or move baggage, to read timetable information, to access computerized information, to arrange and rearrange connections and meetings, the competence to use mobile phones to perform text messaging, e-mail, Internet, Skype, and so on.

Second, there are various kinds of information and contact points. There are sites where information and communications can arrive, be stored, and be received. Once upon a time, they had to be physically located. Now, through mobile systems, they can be on the move.

Third, there is possession or access to various kinds of communication devices to make and remake engagements, especially on the move. This is increasingly in conjunction with others who are also on the move.

The availability of appropriate safe and secure meeting places, while on route and at the destination. The destinations can include offices, club spaces, hotels, public spaces, or university campuses.

Fifth, the physical and financial access to a such things as a car, road space, fuel, lifts, aircrafts, trains, ships, taxis, buses, trams, or minibuses.

Finally, there is the time, money, and resources to manage and coordinate points one to five and to manage and coordinate them when, from time to time, there is a system failure.

This produces a highly significant set of social inequalities in the contemporary world. There is huge variation in access to network capital and network capital is a major source of social stratification, or social inequality. This is over and above inequalities of income and wealth.

I turn now to report on some research that Kay Axhausen, myself, and a researcher Jonas Larsen were engaged funded by the Department for Transport in the United Kingdom. This is reported in the book *Mobilities, Networks, Geographies* (published by Ashgate, 2006).

I am going to talk only about some of the more general findings and arguments that we put together in that book.

First of all, we were interested in how meetings and visits are becoming more significant as societies are becoming more geographically spread out (according to the empirical evidence). Those meetings and visits are part of the ways in which social networks are accomplished. "Accomplishment" is a social science term that describes the performances that are necessary in order that a social network has an existence over time and intermittently across space.

Social networks involve a lot of work. In particular, social networking involves some intermittent long distance travel by some or all of the people in such a network. In this project we were particularly interested in this intermittent, longer distance travel as opposed to shorter commuting patterns.

We were also interested in the relational commitments that people have to their social networks of work, friendship, and family life, both domestically and especially overseas. We argue that those social networks are crucial to emergent travel patterns.

We were also interested in pointing out that people both visit and receive visits. The receiving of visits has been less examined. People receive the hospitality of close friends, workmates, and family members when they travel elsewhere. Or they provide hospitality to visitors. There are complicated relationships of reciprocity. This reciprocity over time is the sort of thing anthropologists discuss; it involves the giving of time, because you've taken some time to travel somewhere, and also the giving of hospitality to others.

Let me say a little more specifically, drawing on some of the more qualitative data. We described the way that people are enmeshed in social dramas where travel is not something that is simple and direct, but depends upon negotiation, approval, and guilt.

We thought guilt was fairly important in explaining how and why people intermittently travel. We came up with the idea that guilt trips set in motion physical trips. One respondent described how he does not like going to visit his family in Italy. This respondent was a relatively poorly paid person in the security industry in the UK. "I didn't particularly like going to Italy, I must admit, I'm not a massive fan, but I did. My mum wanted me to go there, so I got the old guilt trip, and then I felt like, I have to go."

In that description there is moral work, the use of emotions, indeed of emotional blackmail, to encourage, force, or coerce the person into going. Another respondent comments about their wedding, "I think my father probably put a lot of pressure on his brothers and sisters, my aunts and uncles, to come over from Ireland, because they were all there."

That demonstrates the role of social pressure—how it enforces, coerces, or makes it impossible for people not to travel. If you happen to be absent, then this may well be remembered. Your "social face" could well be damaged if you are not present. Another respondent described how, "my partner's family are very rigid in that there are certain days of the year when it's kind of compulsory family get together." Note how they say, "kind of compulsory." The significance again is that there are certain dates in the year where your absence would be noted if you weren't there. You would lose "face."

I think these quotes bring out some of the powerful emotions and moral work involved in being present on certain occasions. If you're not there, you'll have to make up for it in all sorts of other ways. You haven't given, as Glenn Lyons describes it, "the gift of travel time" to those other people.

We also found that being in relationships means a lot of traveling, whether that's being in a marriage or having a regular partner. This particular respondent describes how they had lots of different groups of friends, "her friends and my friends." He explained that, "there's this terrible burden" that he has when he goes to London. He has many people that he feels obliged to go and see. "You have to try and see everybody and at the end you have to come back on a Sunday and you wish you had another couple of days off." He found the burden of having to travel a lot of work. It was a lot of pressure and a lot of work to have to do. "It just never feels like a weekend when you go down there."

"There will always be arguments because someone will find out you'd been down to London, but you didn't tell them purposefully because you'd have to fit them in to your busy schedule." This again brings out the obligatory and complex overlapping networked character of these patterns of traveling.

The second quote brings out the significance of particular key events in people or families' calendars. I love this quote, "this year I've got seven weddings to go to, and I'm going to have to take out a mortgage." This reminded us while we were doing this research of the film *Four Weddings and a Funeral*.

That's an example of how obligations are part of the ways in which relationships organize and structure people's patterning of sociability. In that patterning of sociability, people may have to travel.

We were also interested in how this related to tourist travel. We came to the view that a lot of what is called tourist travel (and this begs the question what is meant by tourism here) is actually as much about sociability and meeting-up as it is a search for what we might loosely call the exotic, or the tourist gaze.

Thus, tourist-type travel essentially enters many peoples' lives including otherwise relatively immobile people. That is, meetings with friends and family have often what we might call a tourist-type element to it. So tourism is less the privilege of a rich few but more something involving and affecting very many people. Thus, tourists can be found in city flats, suburban homes, local supermarkets, and other everyday places. The obligations to engage in such tourist-type travel can be as persuasive and as demanding as other kinds of travel.

To illustrate these points, I consider a couple of more quotations. First, "it's usually a combination. Obviously with the cost of travel and the cost of staying somewhere, it would be better if we can get the best out of the trip. So if we can get in doing the tourist thing, doing the relaxation thing, and doing the family thing all in one go, then that's a convenient bonus."

They put together in their patterns of family and friendship travel, a kind of tourist travel, or what this person calls "the tourist thing." Then he goes on to say, "if my friend's in Berlin, then that's great because I've never been to Berlin before so I'm killing two birds with one stone. I'm looking forward to going to Berlin." This shows a highly complex combination of both the sociabilities and "the tourist thing," as this person puts it.

Another person describes, "I'm organizing a trip to Mexico because I know he," this particular friend, "is only there for another year, so there's no point on missing out on free accommodation." So again there is this so-called tourist who will be in free probably modest accommodation in a suburban street and not in a hotel. He continues, "you know, say it was somewhere like Azerbaijan, I don't think I would be that keen on going, but you know Mexico, I'd quite like to go there." This once more brings up the combination of practices of friendship and tourism.

We were also struck how these youngish people in this research were extremely effective at describing the systems of coordination in order to do their traveling. Going out, they described, involves continuous coordination, negotiation, and movement, a bit like a swarm of birds moving through the air. "It's usually a loose arrangement, say meet up roughly," not exactly, but roughly, "8 o'clock in this bar, but most of the time that gets changed. Because you've got mobiles, you can do that ... I'm running late, or we've decided to go a different bar, meet us in that bar or whatever." We suggest what that does is produce a shift in the forms of coordination away from strict punctuality, to a more fluid coordination process in which certain kinds of places, such as bars or cafes, conference centers, hotel lounges, and so on become crucial. We refer to these as "interspaces," which are spaces in-between spaces to work or home places and so on.

There seems to be a shifting from punctuality to a more indeterminate, fluid, meeting culture where there are these interspaces. In this sort of fluid negotiation, mobile phones, messages, and texting were particularly significant. However, e-mail seemed much more significant, from this research, with increasing distance. E-mail seemed to be a substitute for face-to-face sociality when distance makes frequent travel too time-consuming and expensive.

Using this data we mapped the local, national, and international ties of some of our respondents. I'm just going to mention just two of them that bring out one or two points.

The first is a man working as a university porter in the UK. On the face of it, this man has a large number of local ties from Lancaster down to Manchester and further down to Preston and Southport. These are all in the northwest of England and are about a 30 mile distance apart. These connections bring out the patterns of connection with those people who are most important in his life.

If you look on the map to the left of the UK, it would appear that he has rather localized traveling, but in fact he has a number of friends and family members who live abroad. E-mail is particularly significant in maintaining the links that he has with them. He says, "I've got an uncle who lives in America, so I e-mail him a lot, as it's a lot cheaper. I've also got former friends," from Preston, "who also now live abroad." What's significant here is how he combines highly localized networks with highly far-flung networks. In maintaining the far-flung networks, e-mail is particularly significant, but in which a certain amount of physical travel takes place. However, much of the physical travel that he does with his far-flung networks is because those people travel to the UK partly to see him. This shows how he provides hospitality. He does not do the traveling so much, but he still has a very strong sense of the importance of these far-flung, intermittent links in his social network.

A different pattern is somewhat found in a woman who is working as a personal trainer. She seems to have a more distributed pattern of local ties between Manchester and Liverpool, some ties nationally, linking Manchester and London, but also a significant number of international ties. The text here describes how she keeps in touch with those. One thing that this person demonstrates is how this person's previous working practices produced friendship patterns. For this person, the three most important people in her life all live in the United States and they were all met through various workplace mobilities.

This person organizes her network through weekly e-mails and phone calls flowing between Manchester and the USA. At least once a year she meets up with these friends in the United States. They travel to see her or she travels to see them. This brought home to us the significance of reunions—the importance of reunions in academic conferences, within workplace groups, but especially within family groups, and friendship groups. That is, how often should you have a reunion of that group or of that network? This particular person, in her description of the social dynamics of her life was incredibly insistent on the importance of reunions.

I come now to the conclusion. What I tried to demonstrate through variety of arguments and some evidence are the ways in which the understanding of physical travel should significantly shift from an individualistic homo-economicus to a network actor engaging in sets of social practices often involving many far-flung networks. These networks in work, family, and friendship are a key feature of contemporary life. Hence, much work is undertaken to establish and to sustain those networks within these different domains.

Central to these networks are travel and communication practices. They extend and strengthen such networks. All these networks more or less depend upon intermittent meetings involving travel and communications. Such travel and communications generates network capital which is a major source of social stratification in contemporary societies. Therefore, it gives a significance to traveling that makes it much less a very specific thing, studied by specific groups to being something that is a much more generically important feature that structures and organizes the distribution of opportunities around the world.

But also significant to the understanding of that travel is the understanding of meetings and the character, properties, and consequences of those meetings. Studying people's meetings is a methodological challenge. Some of the time, you have to be present at those meetings in order to do the research which implies that there are significant methodological challenges in this. In the research that I reported we had to reply upon people's accounts of what happened in the meetings with their friends or family. We were not present at all of those meetings and yet in order to conduct more in-depth research, this would entail being present at some of those meetings.

I have also suggested that there is something interesting in the shift in the nature of meetings from punctuality and specific spaces of movement to a more informal, fluid meeting-up culture, and also "interspaces." And thus I have tried to say that the sociabilities before, during, and after the travel are utterly central to understanding contemporary patterns of a networked life that is partly conducted on the move. The sociabilities therefore of talk, meetings, guilt, emotions, and so on are thus central topics to researching how and why people are intermittently and contingently on the move.

Thank you.

Andre: Thank you very much for your very nice talk. I have two questions. The first question is concerning the theory that says that people travel 1.1 hours and that this is rather constant over time and space. Can you explain this constant law, which seems to be true on average? But, my second question is concerning another theory by Marshall McLuhan that says, "the medium is the message" and the idea is that the type of media that you are using conveys information about what you want to say. I was wondering, when I was listening to you, if this might explain partially this face-to-face interaction. We are surrounded by a lot of information, so you must compete for the attention of people. To prove that you have something important to tell someone, you go to see them, rather than sending an e-mail. Thank you very much.

Urry: Thank you very much. Those are interesting questions. On the second one first, I think it's very interesting the way you put it there, that is, the significance of the medium of face-to-face that you've captured very well. There's obviously an interesting question, as to whether it will be possible, in some future time, that the medium of virtual electronic communications so changes that it can simulate the properties and characters of this physical copresence.

I think that this electronic substitution effect of virtual communications for physical copresence will only occur if it is able to reproduce those very properties of the medium. Actually, the way you put it, in terms of "the medium is the message," from McLuhan, helpfully clarifies that for me. Thank you for that comment.

On the first point about travel time and its supposed constancy, I know there's a big debate about that. One of the things I suppose I was pointing to, and I don't know quite what implications this will have, is that quite a lot of what we might call travel time is now spent engaging in activities, including the activities of making and remaking your social networks on the move. Whether that means the amount of travel time might extend because less of it is now "pure travel time" and more of it is a kind of travel time and the activity of maintaining one's social networks.

I know there's some suggestion that there are some increases in travel time, in some studies, and if that were the case then what I pointed out here might be part of that process. Certainly there is something of a dissolving of a distinction of travel time and activity time through the sorts of processes I've been talking about.

The Expanding Sphere of Travel Behaviour Research
Selected Papers from the 11th International Conference on Travel Behaviour Research

2

Knowledge Interactions and Travel Behavior ☆

Masahisa Fujita

Thank you for the very kind introduction. I am especially pleased to be invited today as I graduated from the Department of Civil Engineering in the University of Kyoto almost exactly 40 years ago. However, after graduating I moved over to economics. I moved over to economics because, as you may know, Civil Engineering is a very serious science, but in economics, we can assume almost anything. That is very convenient sometimes. For instance, if I were to design a bridge without accounting for gravity, my professor would probably kill me. But in economics, we almost never assume gravity.

My talk today is about "knowledge interactions and travel behavior." My knowledge about travel behavior is virtually nothing, but I shall present a simple model of knowledge interactions—without assuming "gravity." It would surpass my objective today if I could give some kind of idea to future research on travel behavior.

To begin, many people say that we are moving from an industrial society based on mass production of commodities to a "brain power society" or "C-society" that is based on the brain power or creativity of people. My ultimate objective is to develop a

☆ Key Note Speech at The International Association for Travel Behaviour Research (IATBR), Kyoto, Japan, 2006.

comprehensive theory of spatial economics or an "economic theory of space." In a brain power society, what you need to incorporate are dual linkages. One type of linkage is the traditional economic linkage that connects production and transaction of traditional goods and services. These are well studied, but I feel that within a brain power society the knowledge linkages or "k-linkages" are an important aspect of spatial economic theory. I use the term knowledge in a very broad sense, incorporating ideas, information, and knowledge. Economic activity consists of dual linkages, but I believe that research about k-linkages is still rather weak.

In my presentation today, I will introduce a very simple model of knowledge interaction—without "gravity." Knowledge interaction means human interaction for the creation and transfer or learning of knowledge. I will initially present a simple model, without expressly considering travel. I will then introduce a little bit of gravity in the form of travel behavior into the knowledge interaction.

There are three basic characteristics of knowledge interaction. The first is the basic creation of knowledge through using the brain. However, the brain is a very complex thing, so I am just taking the brain very superficially to mean a state of knowledge for a person.

In order to create knowledge or to transfer knowledge, it is essential that there be heterogeneity between brains. Through coming here and discussing things, you create a synergy through interaction.

However, I want to emphasize that the heterogeneity of people's brains, of their state of knowledge, is endogenous. It will change through interaction. Take this conference, for example. You have come here and over a course of several days, if your brain does not change then you are probably sleeping. But as long as you are awake, your brain will have changed by the end of the conference as a matter of course through developing friendships or being social. As well, the purpose of this conference is to get some new inspirations, ideas, or to transfer them. As a result, the endogenous dynamics of heterogeneity must be included in the model.

Speaking of the brain, I came across an interesting advertisement while traveling in Finland a few years ago. It is an advertisement to attract high-tech companies to an area in Sweden. The advertisement read, "The bad news is, the brain is the only natural resource in the region. The good news is, the brain is the only natural resource that expands with use." I think this characterizes an important aspect of the brain. A university is, as well, a concentration of brains, and high-tech firms often locate near one.

Individual brains are also important. In the cooperation of many different brains for the creation of new ideas or new knowledge, heterogeneity among people is essential. Let me further explain.

Suppose we have two people, person *i* and person *j*. Imagine that this (*editor*: raising left hand) is the state of knowledge of person *i*, and that this (*editor*: raising right hand) is the state of knowledge for person *j*. If the two states of knowledge are exactly the same, then there is no need to join together (*editor*: joins hands). Conversely, if the states of knowledge are completely disjointed, then they cannot effectively communicate (*editor*: crossing arms in air).

This means that we need some basic common knowledge in order to communicate. When you are writing a paper with a friend or colleague, you need some common knowledge to facilitate communication, but you also need differential knowledge so you can create a new idea. That is the essence of cooperation here.

It is essential to have the right mix of commonality and difference between two people's brains. I found an article by Joe Klein of the *Guardian* in London that read, "Heterogeneity is a tonic; it adds an energy of unexpected combination."

This idea of heterogeneity, being important in the creation of new ideas, is very well known in history. As shown in Figure 1, in an old Chinese saying, "San ge chou pi jian. Di ge zhu ge liang." So what does this say in Japanese? Here is the Japanese translation (*editor*: on slide). On a side note, the Japanese government recently complained to the Chinese government that China was not respecting intellectual property rights. The Chinese government responded, "You're kidding. You've been using Chinese characters for the entire history of Japan." You can see here (*editor*: gesturing to Japanese translation) that it is mostly Chinese characters. "But you never paid us!" Now, the English translation roughly says, "Bring three ordinary people together and a splendid idea will come out." This is the essence of knowledge creation. The question remains though: "Is this true in the long run?" And to every good saying, there is always an antinomy.

"三 个 臭 皮 匠、

抵 个 渚 葛 亮"

"三人寄れば、文殊の知恵"

With three ordinary persons together,
splendid ideas will come out.

But,
Question: Is it true in the long-run?

Figure 1
Old Chinese Saying

Let us look at "Bring three ordinary people together and a splendid idea will come out." We could also say, "But after three ordinary people have been meeting for three years, no splendid idea will come out." Consider Joe Klein's sentence, "Heterogeneity is a tonic: it adds energy of unexpected combinations." To this we could respond, "But after three glasses of tonic, it will just taste like plain water."

I think that an important antinomy for knowledge work is, "In the short run, through close communication, synergy increases." But in the long run, through close communication, common knowledge will expand too much and the heterogeneity will diminish along with synergy.

An example of this is "nominication" in Japan (*editor*: "nomi" means "to drink"). I was teaching in Pennsylvania in the 1980s and many people asked me what the secret was behind the Japanese companies' strong performances. For some, the explanation was: "It's our nominication." This does not occur during work hours, but after work finishes, many people do not return home immediately in Japan. They go somewhere to drink and socialize in places like Ginza. Through this socializing, they continue, to some extent, to discuss work and develop close communication. That may have been the secret of Japanese economic strength, but I think that recently the Japanese economy is not doing well, and perhaps the antinomy is working. I think that Japanese people may be becoming too close through their communication, as well as through media, and that people are becoming too similar in their thoughts. This is why the synergy for the creation of new ideas might be diminishing.

The important thing is thus to retain heterogeneity in the creation of knowledge. In the rest of my presentation, I will present a simple model of knowledge interaction without expressly considering space. However, I will introduce location and distance with some implications for travel behavior.

My presentation is based on my recent paper (Berliant and Fujita, 2008) with Berliant, "Knowledge Creation as a Square Dance on the Hilbert Cube." There is actually a second paper because the original became too large. Even with this, the first paper is more than 40 pages.

I am going to model the dynamic process of knowledge creation as a square dance on the Hilbert Cube. I will explain "square dance" later. Our main question is, "How does heterogeneity change over time?" As well we consider, "How is the productivity of knowledge creation affected?"

But before I get to the modeling, let me explain what a square dance is. It is a type of dance composed of eight dancers, broken into pairs as shown in Figure 2. However, these pairs sequentially change partners. Likewise, academics often pair up when writing a paper. There are often many names on a paper, but I believe that there are

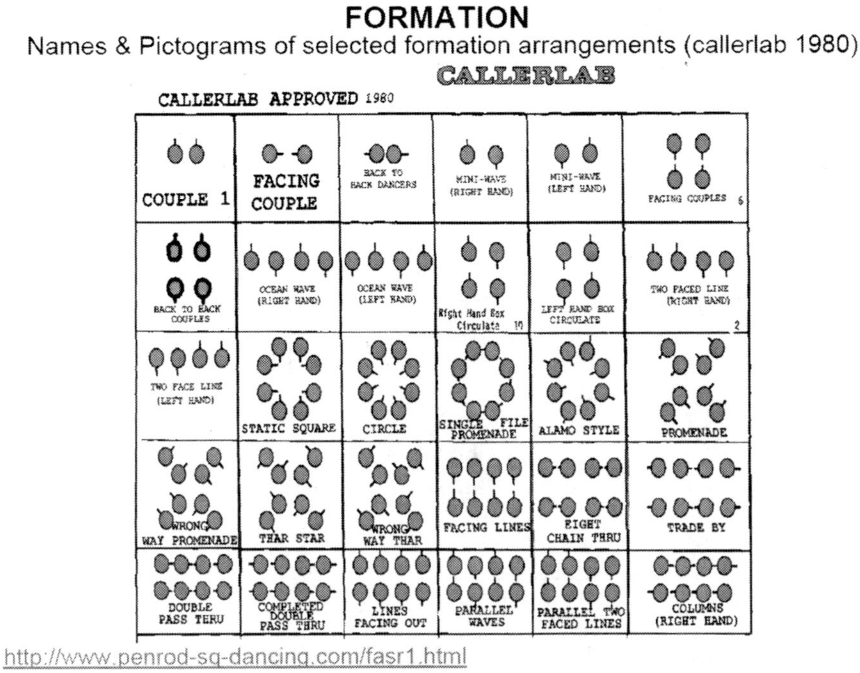

Figure 2
Square Dance

usually only two main writers. Through the course of writing papers, you will probably change partners. Thus, I use the same terminology from square dancing to describe how people change partners in knowledge creation.

Anyway, this is the Hilbert Space or Cube as shown in Figure 3. A Hilbert Space is an infinite-dimensional space, and what I am concerned about is the process of knowledge creation as the movement along the edge of a Hilbert Cube. The cube actually has infinite space, but I will represent it as a three-dimensional cube. In this chapter, I am concerned with the creation of knowledge and the first idea is represented by alpha, the second by beta, then gamma, and continuing on. If this stops, then the space is finite. However, I feel that new ideas are limitless, so we need infinite space.

In order to describe the infinite directional vector, I number the potential ideas from one to infinity as shown in Figure 4. For example, we have many journals, the transportation journals, etc. If we were to order the titles of each paper, or potential paper, without considering the contents, we would have an infinite list. Merely reading a title is effortless, but really reading and understanding the contents requires a lot of effort. But that is basically similar to the creation of new ideas. So we consider our list

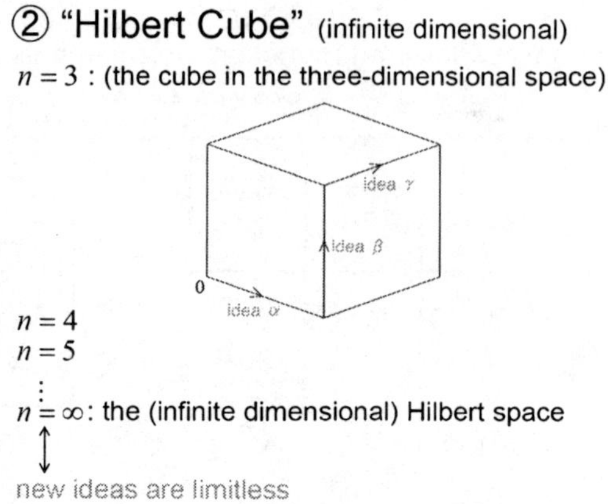

Figure 3
Hilbert Cube

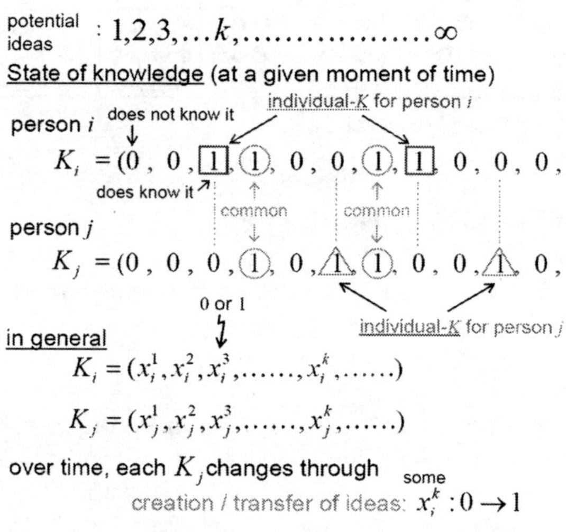

Figure 4
State of Knowledge

of titles as a list of sequentially labeled potential ideas. We also consider the state of knowledge of person i at a given point in time as a string of ones and zeros, where each binary digit indicates whether or not person i grasps the corresponding idea. The state of knowledge of person j is represented the same way, as an infinite sequence comprising of zeros and ones. Now the important thing in this model is that we require two persons to meet. When they meet, I assume they can recognize differential knowledge, for example, when person *i* knows something that person *j* does not.

In Figure 4, a square in the knowledge vector represents person *i*'s differential knowledge and the triangle represents that of person *j*'s. A circle in the knowledge vector indicates common knowledge shared by the two people. I always consider people in pairs. As well, I do not consider the loss of knowledge by forgetting something, but only the addition of knowledge. We must soon define the knowledge creation function.

But before that, I will introduce two ways of creating new knowledge. I initially only consider the basic case of two people working together, or in isolation. When you write a paper, you can either write with someone or you can go to a mountain, seek out a cave, and write in isolation. As shown in Figure 5, at each moment of time, knowledge creation can take place by choosing strategy 1 or 2. When 1 is chosen, which means each person chooses a partner, it must be chosen by both persons. This choice is made so as to maximize the desired objective function. But before going into the objective function, I assume each person to maximize his income rate at each moment of time. This I express by simply taking the amount of knowledge in that infinite vector, that is, how many ones there are in it. I consider that to be the level of knowledge for that person. Now at every given moment of time, a person wishes to maximize the rate of increase in his income, or in this case, the rate of increase in his amount of knowledge. This value is equal to the creation rate of new ideas, that is, the ideas person *i* creates at time *t* plus ideas transferred from the other at time *t*. So, each person tries to maximize income by choosing a strategy, either 1 or 2, and in case of 1, chooses a person with whom to cooperate so as to maximize the rate of growth of his own knowledge.

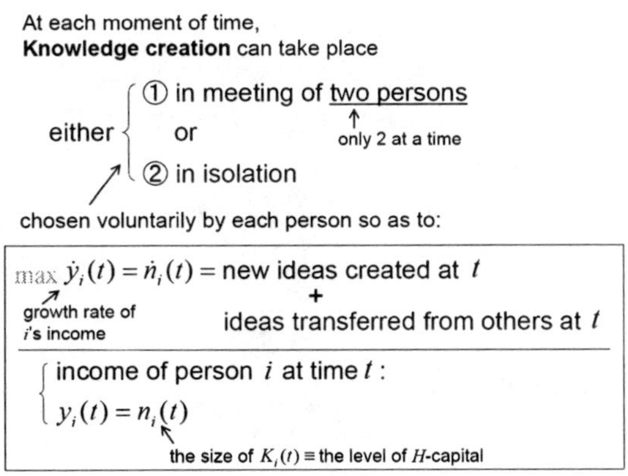

Figure 5
Knowledge Creation

When two people, *i* and *j*, meet, one objective may be to create new knowledge and write a paper. Now, creation usually occurs when people are together; you are working to write a paper for a transportation conference, and you are working together while creating new ideas. Let us consider continuous time and take a continuous variable for the rate of increase in knowledge per unit time when *i* and *j* work together. Now what is the production function in this case? The two persons' collective state of knowledge, as shown in Figure 6, is simply represented by three subsets. Common knowledge is the intersection of K_i and K_j, with size n^{c}_{ij}. The differential knowledge of person *i* from person *j* is the set difference K_i minus K_j, with size n^{d}_{ij}. The differential knowledge of *j* from *i* is the set difference K_j minus K_i, with size n^{d}_{ji}. I carry out simple multiplication and normalize results by taking the product to the one-third power. Multiplication is based on common sense; I would say in order to be productive we need appropriate balance of common knowledge and differential knowledge, and a simple way to balance them, I think, is to multiply them. So that is simple thinking. You may not necessarily agree, but let us accept this for now.

I assume when two people get together to write a paper, they learn from each other, and there is mutual knowledge transfer. This knowledge transfer occurs through some initial common knowledge. To present an example, a student needs common knowledge to learn from a teacher. There must be a base of knowledge upon which to build. Through this, *i* and *j* each learn from each other and this is a very simple production function of knowledge creation and transfer. In contrast, when you go to your mountain cave to write, you may also develop new ideas and I take this as a

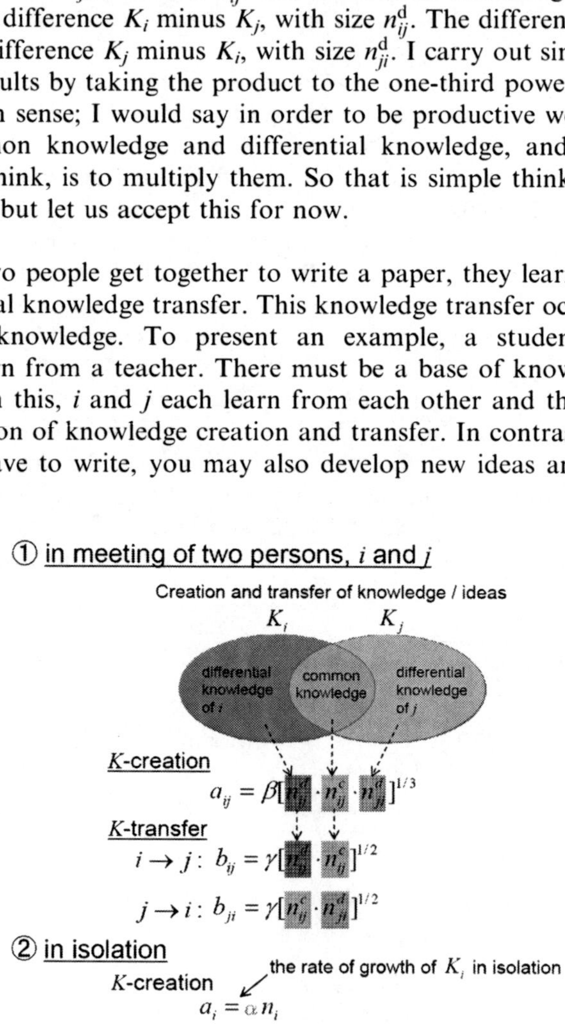

Figure 6

Production Function of Knowledge Creation

Index for meeting / not meeting

at each time t:

$$\delta_{ij}(t) = \begin{cases} 1 & \text{if person } i \text{ wants to meet person } j \\ 0 & \text{otherwise} \end{cases}$$

$$\delta_{ji}(t) = \begin{cases} 1 & \text{if person } j \text{ wants to meet person } i \\ 0 & \text{otherwise} \end{cases}$$

when the meeting of i and j occurs at time t,

$$\delta_{ij}(t) = \delta_{ji}(t) = 1$$

Figure 7
Index for Meeting

constant rate of growth of knowledge. Any new ideas are proportional to the size of your current knowledge.

People must decide to meet, or not to meet, each other. As shown in Figure 7, δ_{ij} is an indicator function that is set to one when person i wants to meet person j, otherwise it is zero. Both δ_{ij} and δ_{ji} must have a value of one in order for persons i and j to meet.

When do two people meet? We will focus on only two people for now. The question is whether they will be working in isolation or working together to create and write a new paper. Now because our production function is linearly homogeneous, I can normalize everything by the total knowledge of persons i and j, which is the sum of these components. And I divide each component by the total size and represent it now by m, as shown in Figure 8. And the first variable is m_{ij}^{d}, which represents the proportion of differential knowledge of person i; the next variable represents the proportion of common knowledge; and the last variable represents the proportion of differential knowledge of person j. So they add up to one. The possible states of the system are contained in a two-dimensional triangle. The vertical axis is the proportion of differential knowledge of person i, and the horizontal axis is the proportion of differential knowledge of person j.

When both δ_{ij} and δ_{ji} are equal to one, a meeting is set. In this case both i's and j's rate of knowledge growth will be greater than α, the growth rate in isolation. For example, let $\alpha = 0.6$; then the region where a meeting will occur takes the shape of a heart as shown in the shaded area in Figure 8.

The evolution of the system is described by a differential equation and any particular trajectory will depend on the initial conditions.

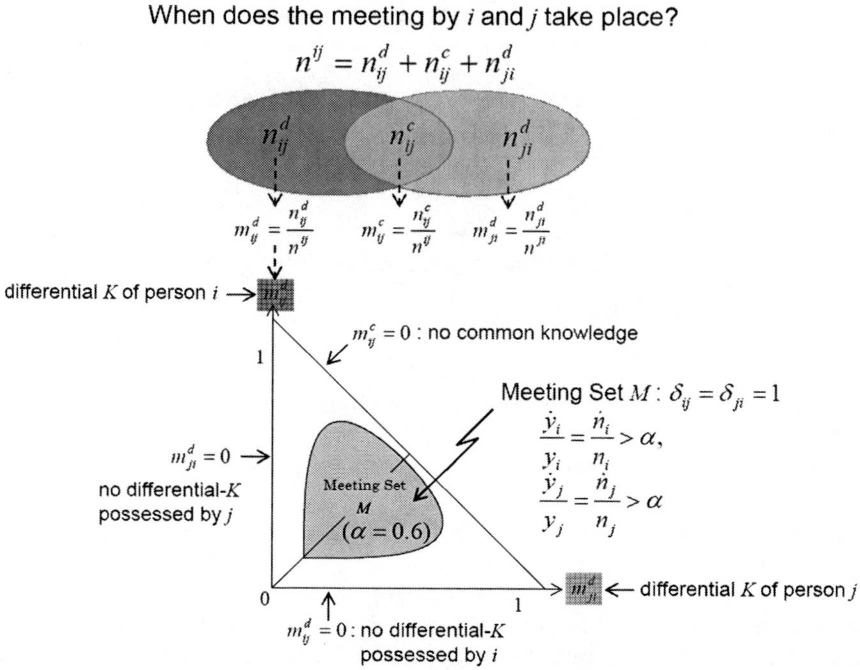

Figure 8
Meeting Set in a Two-Dimensional Space

Let us assume the two people work in isolation. In this case, δ equals zero for both. Each person goes to a different cave in the mountain to write and to develop new ideas separately. I assume they have no communication and no knowledge transfer, so they are accumulating differential knowledge. Differential knowledge increases for both, and that means that the state of the system will move toward the diagonal line shown in Figure 9. Since they do not meet, they both create differential knowledge at rate α.

Now let us fix δ equal to one for the two persons, thus forcing them to meet. New ideas are shared and become common knowledge. We also have knowledge transfer, increasing common knowledge and decreasing differential knowledge. When continuously meeting, differential knowledge shrinks and common knowledge increases, moving the state of the system toward the origin. Of course, in actuality each person can choose freely to set his δ equal to one, zero, or back to one. What are the actual dynamics of this system?

When the initial state is inside the heart shape, then people meet. The system moves along a trajectory inside the heart until hitting the edge, and then the state moves along the edge until hitting point J, which is located at the vertex of the heart. Starting from

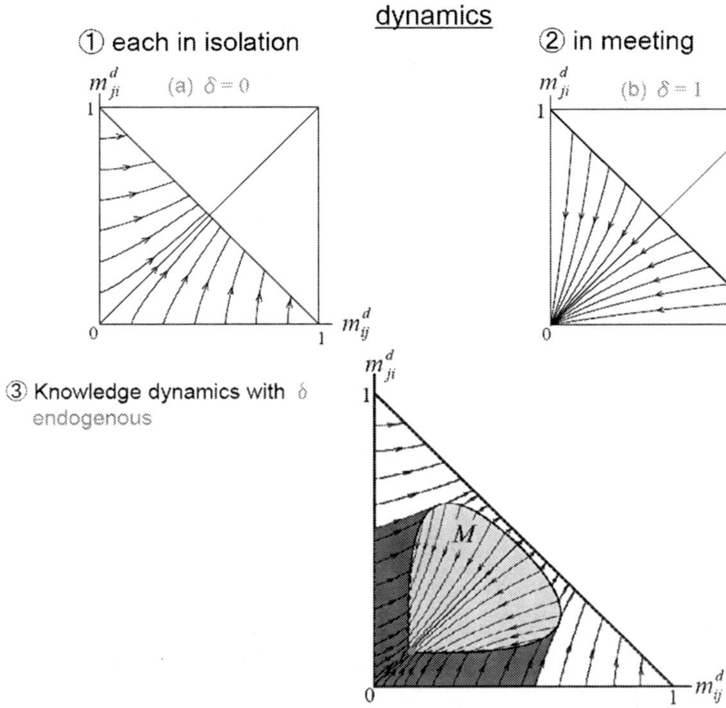

Figure 9
Dynamics of the Two-Person Case

the darkly shaded area, trajectories eventually hit the heart, and then move along the edge to the vertex. Starting from the lightly shaded area, no one ever meets. The important thing is that for this two-person case and a broad range of initial conditions, the final state approaches a single equilibrium point J.

Now, in order to explain a little bit more, let me focus on the symmetric case along the 45° line, where the proportions of differential knowledge of *i* and *j* are the same as illustrated in Figure 10. In this case, I can represent the state of the system with one coordinate on the horizontal axis. The vertical axis is now the rate of income growth, which is equal to the rate of knowledge growth for *i* and *j*. Because it is symmetric, both rates are equal.

Now if each person is in isolation then the rate of growth is α, but if in cooperation, the rate of growth is dependent on the proportion of differential knowledge, which has the concave shape shown in the figure, and of course the point of maximum growth rate is point B; I call it the bliss point. Now the dynamics depend on the starting point. Let us take a simple case first.

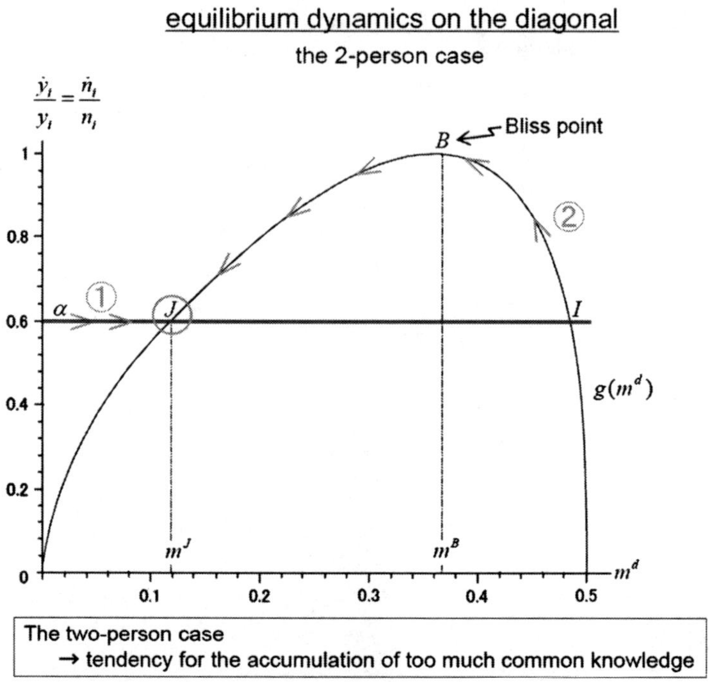

Figure 10
Equilibrium Dynamics on the Diagonal

If starting from point 1, where individual and differential knowledge is very small, people have so much common knowledge that they do not bother to cooperate. This results in isolation, and the increase of differential knowledge. The state of the system gradually moves toward the right of point 1. Now if we start from point 2, where the two people have much differential knowledge, then we can see it is better for them to cooperate. What will happen next?

If they continue to cooperate, then the proportion of differential knowledge will necessarily decrease as new ideas are shared, and knowledge is transferred. As long as they keep cooperating, productivity will eventually start diminishing. You might ask, "Why can't people stop at B, the best point?" If they stop cooperating suddenly and work in isolation, their productivity will immediately be reduced to the horizontal line at α. So the best they can do is to continue to cooperate. Eventually the state moves down to point J; I call it the Japanese point. Anyway, in the two-person case, the conclusion is that there is a tendency for the accumulation of too much common knowledge. Sometimes I observe some of my friends in the United States who are always working together with the same people. Initially they come out with an exciting paper, but as they continue to work together, their papers become gradually less exciting, and I do not feel inspired to read their papers anymore. So, I feel you had better not keep to the same person for too long, otherwise productivity diminishes. Anyway that is two-person case, and it is extreme. There are always alternatives.

Let us take the simple case of four people. Afterwards, I will introduce the general case of *N* persons. Of course, the four-person case is much richer than the two-person case because you can change partners. That is why the four-person case is called the square dance. Possible configurations in the four-person case are shown in Figure 11. One possible configuration at any given moment is that each person goes to separate caves on a mountain and thinks in isolation.

Another possible configuration is that persons one and two get together to write a new paper, while persons three and four get together and do the same. Other configurations include one–three and two–four cooperation, and one–four and two–three cooperation.

In addition to the basic configurations, I introduce a kind of mixed strategy involving a kind of quick rotation. In this case, persons one, two, three, and four are connected. For example, suppose each week has 6 working days, and person one can work for 2 days with person two, and for 4 days with person three. I assume that people can, as long as they agree, alternate partners as shown in Figure 11(c-1), (c-2), or (c-3).

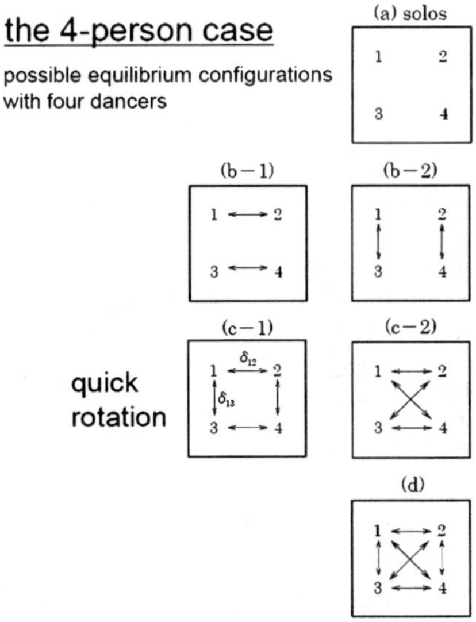

Figure 11
Possible Equilibrium Configurations with Four Persons

They can also perform a full rotation as shown in Figure 11(d). Suppose we have 6 days a week, and person one works 2 days with person two, 2 days with person three, and 2 days with person four. Here I am assuming no switching cost, which means I am not accounting for "gravity." Over time, this pattern will change. Now we investigate how and why.

Starting with the configuration shown in Figure 11(b-1), we have persons one and two working together and developing a new idea, while persons three and four are together developing their own idea. Let us assume the two groups are not communicating. Therefore, persons one and two are increasing their common knowledge while persons three and four are doing the same. However, each individual in a group is increasing his differential knowledge with those in the other group because they are not communicating.

If this configuration persists for too long, then each individual in the group accumulates too much common knowledge, and productivity diminishes. However, individuals in different groups increase their differential knowledge, so partner switching might happen.

Now, the configuration in Figure 11(d) is the case of a quick rotation among all four. In order to understand the reason for the rotation, let us focus on one pair only. We focus on persons one and two. Now, persons one and two are meeting one-third of the time, and they are not meeting for two-thirds of the time each week. Therefore, we have 2 days of meeting and 4 days of not meeting, so that one and two can build differential knowledge between each other on the days they are not meeting. With this quick rotation, they can build a net increase in their proportion of differential knowledge while cooperating closely with each other part-time. The way to increase (or maintain) differential knowledge is through rotation.

In the following, in order to express the solution for dynamics, though it looks simple, we have solved every pair of differential equations. Let us forget about knowledge transfer while people are working. Basically we are talking about very sticky knowledge when they develop together, which becomes common knowledge, and never move out. That is why it is a very sticky situation. It happens very often that small firms, each one as small group, are very much specialized in very specific manufacturing services. Also, you engage in the activities at many places.

In order to explain the dynamics in a two-dimensional graph, let us take a simple case. Suppose that for each pair, the initial proportion of differential knowledge is the same. You can see that for every pair, common knowledge is always symmetric, though not necessarily the same absolute value, but initially everyone has the same proportion of common knowledge. Assuming symmetry, we can represent everything in a two-dimensional space as shown in Figure 12. In the figure, the horizontal axis is

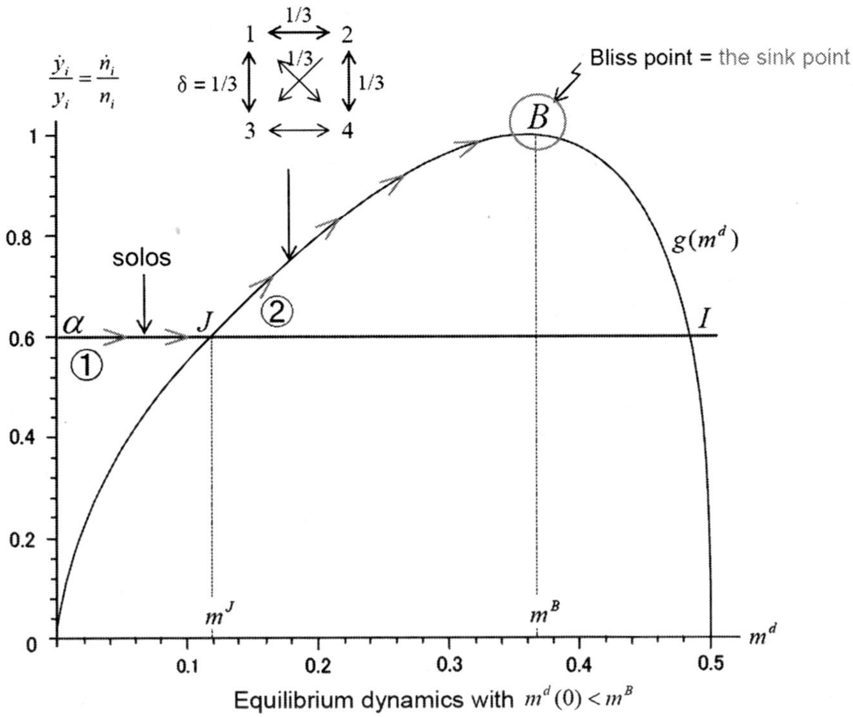

Figure 12
Equilibrium Dynamics with Symmetric Initial Differential Knowledge

differential knowledge, which is symmetric and the same size for each pair. The vertical axis is the knowledge growth rate for each person, which is the function g, and of course B is the best point.

Now, let me explain the dynamics. Consider the initial state at point 1 in the figure. Again, this is the four-person case, but for each pair, common knowledge is so large that people do not bother to cooperate, and so each works in isolation, gradually building up differential knowledge. So the state moves toward the right.

Starting from an initial state at point 2, if people formed into pairs, the state would move to the point J. However, it is possible to do better. In the two-person case, they can only form one pair, but in the four-person case they can rotate. This rotation allows the state to move toward point B. The quick rotation makes it possible for people to alternately build up common and differential knowledge. Now, in solving the differential equation, it turns out that point B is the stable equilibrium. This is rather surprising. In this case, the final state is the best possible as long as they start from a state having fairly large common knowledge. We have high school, media, and lots of common education. When we talk about professional people working, this initial condition of large common knowledge occurs just before graduating college or high school.

However, things do not always work out so well. Figure 13 shows the case that results when differential knowledge is initially too large. They would like to cooperate, as it is better than working in isolation. But because there is too much differential knowledge, it is quite difficult. In order for them to move to the bliss point, they need to increase their common knowledge. It is fastest to do this in pairs. However, in this case, they cannot stop at the bliss point. Let us say that initially persons one and two are partners, and persons three and four are also partners. Now persons one and three are potential partners, or "shadow partners." In this case, persons one and three will not meet, so proportionally their differential knowledge increases. What happens here is that the two can never meet as their differential knowledge has become too large. This is similar to a situation at the University of Kyoto. There are actually two schools of economics, Marx's and the modern economics school. When we meet we say, "Good morning. How are you?" But that is all. We never cooperate together. There is too little common knowledge, so we cannot communicate effectively. Therefore, there will always be two schools.

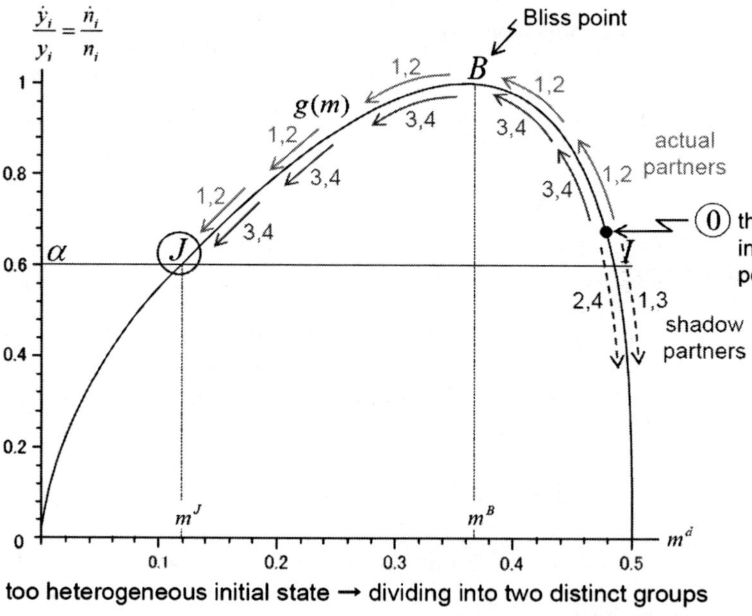

Figure 13
The Case for Too Large Initial Differential Knowledge

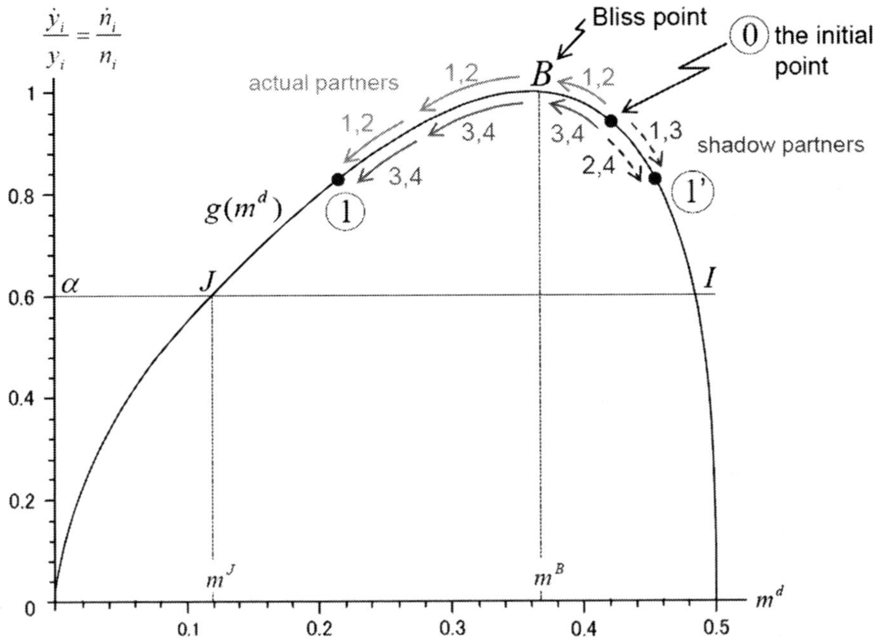

Figure 14
The Case where the Initial Point is in the Middle

We now take the case where the initial point is to the right of the bliss point as shown in Figure 14. To maximize their knowledge growth rate, they should start in pairs. As before, they cannot stop at the bliss point. Once beyond B, they may want to switch, but what will be the productivity if they do? Once again, there will be a shadow partner created if they switch where the differential knowledge will increase. As the common knowledge grows between the new pairs, they will reach a point where they want to switch again and their previous partner becomes the potential partner. All four will actually work together.

If there is initially too much differential knowledge, a pair cannot be productive. But if there are four people, they can effectively change partners to balance common knowledge and retain enough differential knowledge.

What about the case of more than four people? Let us take *N* as a multiple of four as this allows for groups of two pairs to be formed. This is essentially the same as the four-person case. The members are initially in isolation, and then they can perform the rapid square dance involving all members. I again assume that there is no friction in their cooperation. Once again, they will approach the bliss point. Through rotation, they can maintain the highest growth rate. This equilibrium process is based on the continuation of the myopic core.

It seems that as long as we start from the left (initial points with large common knowledge), then the final equilibrium ends up at the most productive state. This was not initially expected. At this point, I should emphasize that I have not yet introduced any information flow such as public media.

Why is the fastest rate of growth realized when we have multiples of four? In order to find a magic number, I must generalize our model, which so far is very simple. To generalize, I place different exponential weights on common knowledge and differential knowledge. In Figure 15, θ is the exponent applied to common knowledge and $(1-\theta)/2$ the exponent applied to differential knowledge. In the simple case, θ is one-third, and therefore the weights for both common and differential knowledge are one-third. In the production of differential knowledge, we have obtained an optimal partnership size equal to $1 + 1/\theta$. When θ is one-third, the optimal partnership size is four. As θ decreases, the optimal partnership size increases.

We might expect that the appropriate exponential weight on common knowledge is different for different sorts of activities. Figure 16 shows optimum partnership size as a function of the exponential weight on common knowledge, which represents how important common knowledge is when cooperating together. When the weight on common knowledge is larger, the optimum partnership size becomes smaller and

why 4 ?

dividing into $N = 4$ at $m^B = \frac{2}{5}$ (Bliss point)

↓ the fastest growth rate of K

Where does this magic number come from?

so far : $a_{ij} = \beta[n_{ij}^c \cdot n_{ij}^d \cdot n_{ji}^d]^{1/3}$

↓ the weight on the common knowledge

generalization : $a_{ij} = \beta(n_{ij}^c)^\theta (n_{ij}^d \cdot n_{ji}^d)^{\frac{1-\theta}{2}}$

↓

$$N^B = 1 + \frac{1}{\theta} \quad \text{at } m^B = \frac{1-\theta}{2-\theta}$$

↑ the size of partnership, achieving the fastest growth rate of K

Figure 15
Optimal Size of Partnership

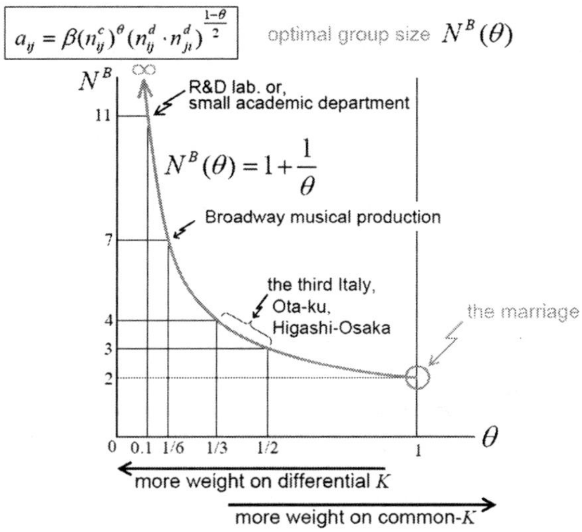

Figure 16
Optimal Group Size by the Weight on Common Knowledge

smaller. If we look at Osaka, there is an area called Higashi-Osaka where there are many small, specialized companies and factories. As well, there is Ohtaku-Tokyo where there are small, very specialized companies that have only three or four people working in them. If we assume these companies have evolved to an optimal configuration, and the model is right, then for those business environments, common knowledge must be very important. I read an interesting, related paper about Broadway musical productions. Apparently there are only around seven people in a group that creates the shows. Why is it seven? Perhaps, it is because the exponential weight θ is 1/6 for this activity. However, for an academic laboratory, differential knowledge is very important and the optimal partnership size appears to get bigger and bigger.

If the weight of common knowledge is high enough, then a two-person partnership becomes optimal. When is this the case? When is common knowledge essential? When can you never switch partners? This case is marriage. If you are married and you try to switch partners, you will have a lot of trouble.

So far I have not introduced the importance of location in space. I will introduce it only in a minimal way. We will introduce a little "gravity." Suppose that two people, i and j, are at a distance d. Here I use the term "distance" to mean the friction of communication through organizational distance or geographical distance.

The simplest way to do this is through the knowledge productivity parameter β. As distance d increases, the production function decreases proportionately.

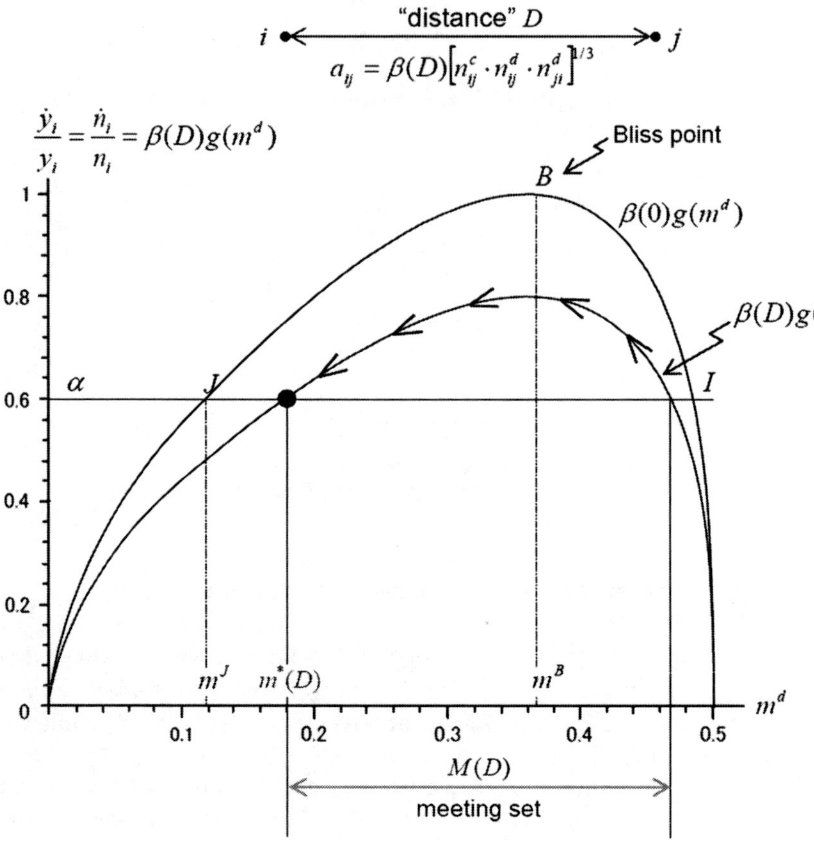

Figure 17
The Effect of the Distance

Again, let us consider the two-person symmetric case. In Figure 17, the upper curve is the rate when the distance is zero and the shape of the curve is only dependent on the differential knowledge of the people involved. As distance increases, the meeting set—the range of values of differential knowledge for which it is fruitful for people to cooperate—shrinks.

An equilibrium point still exists at which productivity is α. However, the new equilibrium point occurs when differential knowledge is equal to $m^*(D) > m^J$. In other words, it takes a greater amount of differential knowledge incentive to entice people to overcome the distance barrier in order to meet.

If we consider four different distances (zero distance, D_1, D_2, and some critical distance), then we obtain the graph in Figure 18. What we can see here is that as

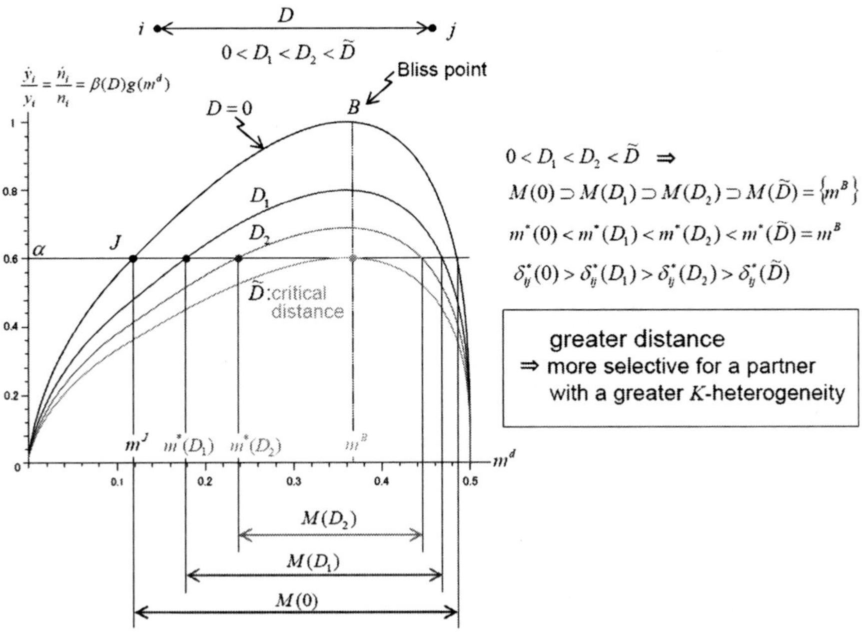

Figure 18

The Relationship between Distance and the Meeting Set

distance increases, the meeting set shrinks, and at some critical distance, point B meets the line of constant α. Observe the trend of the equilibrium point and the required proportion of differential knowledge, $m^*(D)$, at that equilibrium point. Clearly, the value of m^* increases with distance, D. This result seems intuitively true. When many people are near you, you can choose anyone with whom to build common knowledge, but when they are at an extreme distance you must carefully choose your partner.

Let us look at a four-person case in abstruct space in Figure 19. There are four people at two different places, A and B. Let us initially assume that their common knowledge is pair-wise identical. Initially one pair, persons one and two, is at location A and the other pair, persons three and four, is at location B. Through cooperating, their common knowledge will increase within each pair and their productivity will diminish. However, the differential knowledge between groups is increasing. If the four people then start to switch partners and cooperate at different rates, they will retain enough differential knowledge to be optimal.

In the case where we have two regions with many people, they may have infrequent inter-regional interaction, and eventually one member may move from one region to

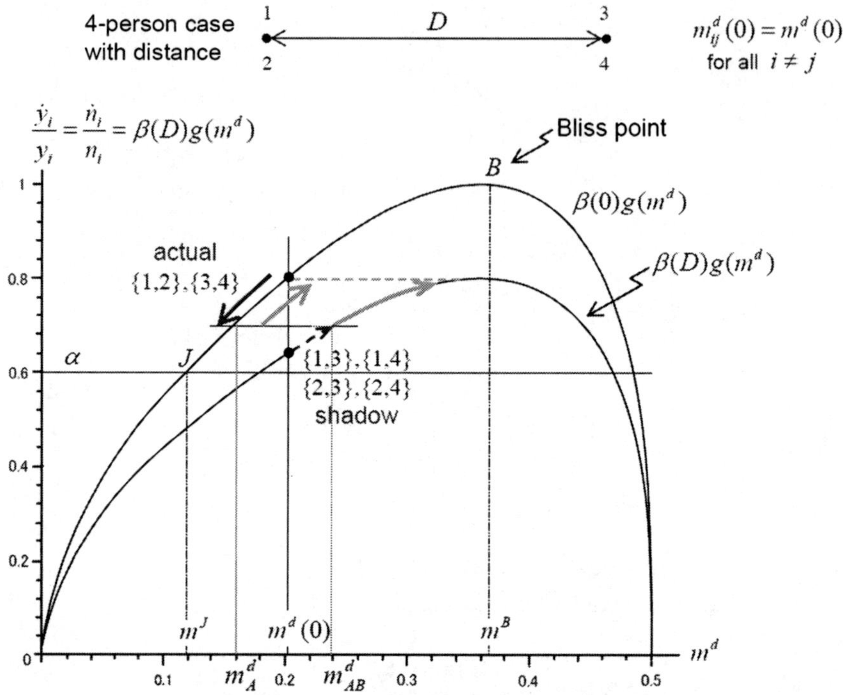

Figure 19
Four-Person Case with Distance

the other. How can we explain this migration? Within the region, common knowledge may increase too much, causing productivity to become too low. However, what is the optimal distance or separation of these two regions, A and B? If A and B are too close, then their knowledge may become too homogenous over time. In Japan, this may have already happened. When I was a graduate student, students from Osaka would go to Tokyo a few times a year. Now I commute there every week. If you look at Kyoto, before the Shinkansen (*editor*: Japan's bullet train) there were several Noble Prize winners, but since it has been built, there have been none. The reduction of travel cost may have led to an increase in face-to-face interactions, which has diminished the differential knowledge too significantly. However, this is just a joke.

The ability to transfer knowledge at high speed is good in the short run, but over the long run it may create too much homogeneity. The important thing for creativity is heterogeneity, and so an interesting question emerges. What is the optimum distance?

In order to investigate this question, we will have to introduce more realistic notions of "gravity." One notion is the ability to transfer knowledge through many modes.

Currently, I have only considered face-to-face knowledge transfer, but there are other modes such as the media and the Internet.

As well, there are multiple types of meetings. There are 10-person meetings, or extreme meetings such as this conference. These meetings are organized in order to share and build knowledge.

Further, as Professor John Urry said (*editor*: reference to preceding speech), there must be travel to have these face-to-face meetings. Right now, I only consider periodic travel, but eventually we must consider infrequent travel and migration. In addition, travel may have other purposes such as tourism or socializing.

Knowledge also has a very complex structure and the current model considers only common and differential knowledge. In addition, there is no uncertainty or error in estimating differential knowledge when searching for partners in this model. As such, there are a number of refinements left for the future.

Linkages between traditional economics, social interaction, and knowledge interaction are crucial to more completely understand the theory of social systems in this age of brain power.

However, I am too old now and cannot do any more. I hope that some of the young people here today will take an interest in this type of research. That would greatly please me.

Thank you very much for listening.

Reference

Berliant, M. and M. Fujita (2008). Knowledge creation as a square dance on the Hilbert cube. *International Economic Review* 49(4), 1251–1295.

PART 2

Resource and Synthesis Papers

2.1 Social Networks and Telecommunications

The Expanding Sphere of Travel Behaviour Research
Selected Papers from the 11th International Conference on Travel Behaviour Research

3

ICT and Social Networks: Towards a Situational Perspective on the Interaction Between Corporeal and Connected Presence

Martin Dijst

Abstract

Although the relationship between information and communication technologies (ICT) and social networks has been acknowledged in seminal publications, knowledge on this subject is inconclusive and sometimes even contradictory. This paper maps out some of the main empirical results on the relationship between ICT and social networks and puts forward some ideas for future research.

It has been shown that a distinction can be drawn between the role of mobile and fixed communication devices and services in social networks. The use of the mobile phone fulfils the need for *instantaneous social contacts*, which are short in duration, smooth coupling constraints in daily life and provide short signs of affection. *Prolonged social contacts* are served by fixed devices and networks at home, at work or elsewhere, offering ample opportunities to make long phone calls, send elaborate e-mails and to chat at length.

The empirical studies reviewed give the impression that a *complementary* relationship prevails for the *size of the social network* and *frequency of contacts*. Electronic communication means offer the opportunities to maintain a large social network. However, as for face-to-face contacts, the frequency of these electronic means decrease with increasing geographical distance between members of a social network. Because of its relatively low cost, e-mail seems to be the exception to this rule. In terms of the *time budget* spent on social ties, the impression is given that the relationship with the use of ICT means is more *substitutive*.

The paper shows that, in empirical studies on the use of ICT and its interaction with social networks, explanatory factors such as cost structures, the technological capabilities of communication modes, attitudes towards relations and the characteristics of social networks explaining the use of communication modes and services are often studied in isolation from each other and not in connection with the concrete situations in which interactions take place. To meet this deficiency, a *tripartite situatedness* composed of corporeal, connected and mental presence is proposed as an alternative analytical framework.

Introduction

Entering into relationships, consciously or unconsciously, with human beings, animals and non-living elements, is fundamental in human life, but also for other living organisms. From a hunter-gatherer to post-industrialist way of life, human beings have never lived in isolation from others, if only for reproductive reasons. Even a hermit's existence is at least indirectly dependent on the fellow human beings who supply the elementary materials and equipment or other opportunities to be left alone. The relationships between human beings in this 'living togetherness' have been studied for a long time in the domains of various social sciences. The structural expressions of social relationships in the form of social networks have received particular attention (Latour, 2005). However, until recently social networks have been largely ignored in the realm of transportation research (Urry, 2000, 2003; Axhausen, 2005; Larsen et al., 2006; Carrasco and Miller, 2006). This is remarkable, since (physical) encounters between family members, colleagues and friends are crucial for joint work, maintenance and leisure activities (Hägerstrand, 1970; Axhausen, 2002).

Face-to-face interaction with a person is the oldest form of interpersonal communication and sociability. Cultural change and the transformation of work and technology have induced in modern societies the rise of individualism in behavioural patterns (Castells, 2002). In the past, the use of faster transportation modes stimulated the decoupling of activity and travel patterns and the built environment, which reduced the significance of the dwelling and local community as the focus of daily life (Graham and Marvin, 1996; Dematteis, 1998; Urry, 2002; Bertolini and Dijst, 2003). The introduction and spread of modern information and communication technologies (ICT), such as the personal computer (PC) and mobile phone and various information and communication services, further encourage the decoupling of places and activities. The new communication modes together with the spread of innovative transportation modes can be expected to transform post-industrial society from a place-based to a person-based society (Castells, 1996, 2002; Couclelis, 1998; Haythornthwaite and Wellman, 2002; Fortunati et al., 2003; Dijst, 2006). The expected shift from micro-electronics to nano-electronics that allow the development of miniaturized ICT devices might further stimulate this development (Somalvico, 2003). The decoupling processes will not, however, lead to the often-discussed 'death of distance' (Cairncross, 1997), but rather to the continuous reconfiguration of the locations where physical and electronic encounters take place (Boden and Molotoch, 1994).

Although the relationship between ICT and social networks has been acknowledged in seminal books and journal publications, the knowledge on this subject is highly inconclusive and even contradictory. Boden and Molotoch (1994), for example, hypothesize that using new communication technologies will only lead to a limited adjustment of the distribution of face-to-face contacts. Putnam (2000), however, combats this view. He claims that the widespread use of technological devices such as the private car, telephone, television and computer in past decades have already diminished face-to-face contacts at the local level. In order to clarify our understanding of the relationship between ICT and social networks, in this paper I discuss some of the main results from empirical studies of the use of ICT services, in particular, PCs and mobile phones and the interaction of ICT with social networks. For that purpose, in the next section I introduce an inventory of the various forms of associations of relationships of which social networks is just one manifestation. In the section thereafter, I describe and explain the use of communication modes and services. In Interaction Between Corporeal and Connected Presence in Social Networks and Interaction Between Connected and Corporeal Presence in Fluids sections, I discuss the interactions between the use of electronic communication modes and services and face-to-face contacts in social networks and in public places. The empirical evidence on the relationship between ICT and social networks will be seen to be fragmented and too general in nature. A comprehensive situational approach to the analysis of the interaction between electronic and face-to-face communications could generate additional insights. A framework for such an approach is presented in Towards a Situational Perspective on Interaction Between Corporeal and Connected Presence section. Finally, the Conclusions section draws the paper to a close.

Social Networks Between Regions and Fluids

Human life is in essence a social life in which persons interact with each other. Boden and Molotoch (1994, p. 277) see corporeal co-present interaction as the fundamental mode of human interaction and socialization: '*Through the trust, commitment and detailed understandings made possible in situations of copresence the essential space–time distantiation of modern society is achieved.*' Urry (2002, 2004) also takes the normative position that co-presence is a fundamental right for every social group in society. Co-presence is obligatory in many situations, such as face-to-face meetings (legal, economic, family and social obligations), face-the-place (sensing the place) and face-the-moment (spending quality time with dear ones and experiencing live events) (Urry, 2002, 2004).

(Co)presence can take various forms or social typologies, namely, regions, networks and fluids (Mol and Law, 1994). In a *region*, objects are clustered together and clear boundaries are drawn around them. This type is characteristic of a sedentary, pre-industrial or industrial society in which most activities took place in the proximity of the dwelling at fixed locations (Couclelis, 1998, 2000). A region is in line with the concept of *community*, which entails strong ties, a shared geographic territory and a common history and value system (Wittel, 2001). In such a 'space of places', interactions usually take place through personal encounters (Castells, 1996).

However, facilitated by technological developments in transportation, data processing and communication, '*social life at least for many in the "west" and "north" is increasingly networked*' (Urry, 2003, p. 170). In a *network*, distance is a function of the relationships between their elements (Mol and Law, 1994). This can be illustrated for a social network. In such a network, these elements or 'nodes' are individuals or collectives and 'ties' represent the relationships between the nodes (Wellman and Berkowitz, 1988). These ties can be divided into various social circles (Harvey and Taylor, 2000) namely *intimate* or *core* ties and at larger relational distance *active* or *significant* ties (Wellman, 1996; Boase et al., 2006). Physical travel enables corporeal encounters in these social networks, while communication means can substitute for these face-to-face contacts. The use of communication means for social interaction is called *absent presence* (Licoppe, 2004; Sheller, 2004), *tele-presence* (Wellman, 2001) or *connected presence* (Licoppe and Smoreda, 2005). In this form of presence, people make use of various forms of mediation or artefacts, such as letters, phone calls, e-mails, short message service (SMS) and instant messenger (IM).

The network concept has often been criticized for assuming a structure that is unchangeable (Mol and Law, 1994; Callon and Law, 2004; Kakihara et al., 2002; Sheller, 2004). However, relationships can come and go, or become transformed from weak to strong ties or vice versa. To meet this concern, other metaphors, such as *fluid* (Mol and Law, 1994) or *gel* (Sheller, 2004) have been introduced that can be associated with fragmented, temporary, messy, but sometimes intense relationships (Sheller and Urry, 2003; Wittel, 2001). In a fluid, a continuous process takes place of the coupling and decoupling of relationships, referring to the strengthening or weakening of ties, respectively (Sheller, 2004).

The sequence of the presentation of the social typologies might give the impression that each type has been—or soon will be—replaced by its successor. However, although the people will show differences in the mix and relative weight, in reality the various typologies of human interactions, regions, networks and fluids will coexist. People are members of a family at home and have contacts with members of their local community, but they will also have strong ties with friends and relatives living further away and weak ties with the relative strangers they meet in a post office, a department store, on public transport or in the street. Latour (2005) states that social categories, ties, networks and processes can be studied in stable situations, but that in situations where innovations proliferate, the actors should be followed in order to trace an actor's new associations of relationships between humans and non-humans. In an era in which the use of various forms of ICT is spreading rapidly and changing interaction patterns, the identification of these new associations could be at least as important an aim as studying social networks.

Use of Communication Modes and Services

In this section, I first discuss the use of various communication modes and services in general and by various socio-demographics. Next, I explore the factors by which the use of these modes can be understood. Finally, this is repeated for the communication services.

Penetration in General and by Socio-Demographics

In order to get an impression of the penetration rates of ICT in various countries, I have compiled Table 1, which shows for the year 2004 the access to PCs, Internet and phones for countries ordered by broadband penetration rate.

Table 1 clearly shows the gaps in opportunities for individuals to use the Internet, voice or other ICT services at home or on the road. South Korea, Hong Kong and Canada with approximately 20–25 subscribers per 100 inhabitants form the top 3 countries in broadband connections, while with 15 and 13, respectively, Japan and the USA take up the lower levels. The leading countries in access to PCs at home are Switzerland, followed at a distance by the USA, Sweden and Israel. The penetration rates for broadband and PCs at home is not the only condition for use of the Internet. The top positions of Iceland and Sweden in Internet use show that, besides facilities at home, connections offered elsewhere also offer ample opportunities to use this network. The Internet can also be accessed on the newest generation of mobile phones, which are used in Japan and South Korea in particular (Ministry of Public Management, Home Affairs, Posts and Telecommunications, Japan, 2004).

The ownership and use of mobile phones has increased enormously. In 1991, the world counted 16 million mobile phone subscribers; in 2004 this figure had risen to 1,758 million. In the year 2002, for the first time the number of mobile phone subscribers was larger than the number of mainline phones (International Telecommunications Union, 2006). Table 1 shows that the number of mobile subscribers is largest in Hong Kong, Sweden, Israel, Norway, the United Kingdom and Taiwan with more than 100 subscribers per 100 inhabitants. Japan and the USA have 72 and 62 subscribers, respectively. In general, the number of mainline subscribers decreases as the number of mobile subscribers increases. However, this relationship only shows up for countries with fewer than 90 mobile subscribers. Above this figure the relationship is unclear.

Table 1
ICT Connections in Top 20 Broadband Countries in 2004 (per 100 inhabitants)*

	Broadband penetration rate	Number of PCs	Number of Internet users	Number of mainline subscribers	Number of mobile subscribers
Korea (Republic)	24.8	54.49	65.68	55.31	76.09
Hong Kong (China)	22.0	60.54	50.32	54.42	118.77
Canada	22.0	69.82	62.36	64.27	46.72
Netherlands	19.8	68.47	61.63	48.44	91.21
Denmark	19.1	65.48	60.41	64.46	95.51
Iceland	18.8	47.10	77.00	65.01	99.00
Taiwan (China)	16.5	52.78	53.81	59.63	100.31
Switzerland	16.4	82.33	47.20	70.97	84.63
Belgium	15.6	35.08	40.62	46.44	88.32
Finland	15.3	48.22	63.00	45.40	95.63
Japan	15.3	54.15	50.20	46.00	71.58
Norway	14.9	57.78	39.37	47.24	103.60
Israel	14.0	73.40	46.63	43.72	105.25
Sweden	13.7	76.14	75.46	71.54	108.47
United States	12.9	76.22	63.00	60.60	62.11
United Kingdom	11.9	60.02	62.88	56.35	102.16
Singapore	11.9	62.20	56.12	43.20	89.47
France	11.2	48.66	41.37	56.04	73.72
Austria	10.0	57.63	47.52	46.20	97.36

Source: International Telecommunications Union (2006).
*Excluding Liechtenstein.

Countries use widely varying definitions, units of analysis and data-collecting methods, hence meaningful comparisons are difficult to make. Nevertheless, an impression of the digital divide in the use of the Internet and mobile phones by individuals in various countries is still worth considering. Instead of one divide, there is a multiplicity of digital divides in Internet access and use within countries based on socio-economic status, gender, life stage and ethnicity (Chen and Wellman, 2003; Nie and Erbring, 2000; Miyata et al., 2002; Haythornthwaite and Wellman, 2002). In general, one could say that Internet users have a high level of education and income, are male and young, and in the USA are Asian or white. In most countries we see these gaps diminish as the penetration rate of the Internet increases. However, in spite of increasing penetration rates, it seems that in some countries the gaps are widening. For example, there is a gap with respect to gender for Germany and Italy; for socio-economic status for the UK, Germany and South Korea; and for life stage for South Korea (Chen and Wellman, 2003).

In countries such as Finland (Puro, 2002), Norway (Skog, 2002) and South Korea (Kim, 2002) the ownership of mobile phones is relatively large among people of young and middle ages. The penetration rate drops dramatically above the age of 60 in Finland or above 50 in South Korea. Although men are more likely to possess a mobile phone, the difference from women is rather small in Finland and Norway (Puro, 2002; Skog, 2002) and probably in most western countries also. However, in 1999 in South Korea the gender division was still large: 77% of men owned a mobile compared with just 43% of women (Kim, 2002).

Use of Communication Modes Explored

The ownership and use of communication modes can be explained by the cost structure of the modes and the attitudes towards and characteristics of social networks. In Scandinavia (Roos, 1993), and also in Japan (Hashimoto, 2005), the rapid rise of the mobile phone can largely be explained by its favourable price structure compared with the mainline telephone. Internet use is dependent on the availability of high-speed broadband connections. It has been shown that the relatively low fees for these connections in South Korea, Hong Kong and Canada partly explain their high penetration rate in these countries (Ministry of Internal Affairs and Communications, Japan, 2005).

From a social network perspective, the mobile phone is used to build up and to maintain social relationships. Adolescents embrace particularly the mobile phone to build up new networks. They use mobile phones to free themselves from parental control (Hashimoto, 2005; Rössler and Höflich, 2005; Ito, 2004; Green, 2002; Ling and Yttri, 2002). The mainline phone at home is seen as a household device with multiple users, associated with supervision by parents and other family members. The mobile phone offers more privacy (Kopomaa, 2000) and requires less psychological effort, since the device reaches the person the caller wishes to contact directly and avoids unnecessary and unwanted communication with other household members (Rivière and Licoppe, 2004). The need for a mobile phone seems particularly great in Japan where people's homes, especially in urban areas, are usually too small to allow children to meet their friends at home, which hinders face-to-face contacts in a private sphere. The virtual space created by the use of the mobile phone is seen as a compensation for the lack of physical space (Hashimoto, 2005).

The general trend of increasing mobile phone ownership among adolescents, but also among adults, fits very well in the general individualization process caused by economic, cultural and technological developments in post-industrial society. Traditional institutions such as neighbourhoods, church and family have lost their constraining character (Wittel, 2001). On the other hand, the disintegration of these traditional institutions and social networks will also feed the need for the development of new social ties to establish identity vis-à-vis others, such as adolescents who associate with fellows in their generation (Ling and Yttri, 2002). In line with this desire, Hashimoto (2005) states that young Japanese have a fear of feeling excluded from the groups to which they would like to belong. This fear of loneliness or even a feeling of loss of the self feeds the desire to possess a mobile phone that can increase the frequency and intensification of contacts between friends (op. cit.). Ling and Yttri (2002) found similar results for Norway: '*. . . the teens thrive on access and interaction. To receive a message is a confirmation of one's membership in the group.*' Korean undergraduates also strive for 'emotional connectedness' (Lee, 2005). According to Kim (2002), this need for belonging to a group and maintaining connections is a general characteristic of Korean society.

Not only does the mobile phone offer the opportunity to make contact with those in a social network with whom their owners want to identify; it is also an expression of identity in itself. Some researchers state that the mobile phone could be treated as an extension of the body (Townsend, 2002; Fortunati and Contarello, 2005). The manifestation of the device confirms the membership of one's social network and offers the opportunity to associate with (still) unknown others in more fluid relationships. This identity feature of mobile phones has been found amongst teenagers in particular (Gaglio, 2005; Kasvio, 2001). Mobile phone owners try to personalize and customize their devices through their choice of brand, ring tones, wallpapers, flashes, form, colours, services and so forth (Ito, 2004; Green, 2002; Meizhi and Shim, 2004). A study from South Korea shows that women are more keen to decorate their mobile phones than men are (Lee and Sohn, 2004). However, Finnish teenage boys were also found painting their phones to match them with their motors and snowboards (Kasvio, 2001).

The mobile phone is useful not only for maintaining social relationships, but also for the coordination and rescheduling of activities within social networks. Individualization processes have led to the diversification of activity and travel patterns. Breaking down common social rhythms (Castells, 1996) makes the synchronization and synchorization of activities between individuals less easy. Mobile phones can lighten these coupling constraints, especially when the individuals concerned are faced with uncertain and modified schedules (Katz, 1997; Ling and Yttri, 2002; Schwanen, 2006). By using a mobile phone for killing dead time between activities, time efficiency can also be improved (Katz, 1997).

The use of mobile devices such as mobile phones and laptops, but also the spread of home-based computers and fast connections at affordable tariffs, has stimulated the mobilization of work activities. These ICTs offer the potential to free workers from their traditional fixed and formal workplace and working time. Work can be carried out in a car, in public transport, at a client's place, in a public place, at home and so forth and at times chosen by the employee (Kakihara et al., 2002; Vilhelmson and Thulin, 2001). This relationship between ICT and work activities is reciprocal: ICTs offer the opportunity for restructuring work activities, but at the same time also make work more dependent on ICT devices and network (Laurier and Philo, 2003).

As mentioned above, the penetration rate of mobile phones amongst the elderly is less than for other age groups. This could be the result of a lack of the skills needed to use such a device, relatively high costs for low-income categories and entrenched habits that are difficult to change. The low take-up level is probably the reason why studies of the use of mobile phones by the elderly are not numerous. Based on group interviews in Norway, Ling and Yttri (2002) found that the main reasons why this age group owned a mobile phone were safety and security.

Use of Communication Services Explored

The PC also offers various services for contacting other people. On thePC, e-mail and IM are well-known communication modes. Depending on the type of device, the mobile phone also can offer a large variety in choice including voice call, SMS, e-mail and IM. The choice between synchronous or asynchronous services can be explained by a combination of the comparative costs of the services, the technical capabilities of the mode used for these services and the attitudes towards and characteristics of the social network.

Direct or synchronous contacts, such as phone calls, often require larger investments of money, time and effort than do indirect or asynchronous communication services (Licoppe and Smoreda, 2005; Rivière and Licoppe, 2004; Pertierra, 2005; Larsen et al., 2006). This cost argument can explain why SMS or e-mail on a mobile phone is in general used more by young people than by other age categories. For example, adolescents in Germany and Japan usually send SMS or e-mail by mobile phone (Rössler and Höflich, 2005; Hashimoto, 2005). Besides choice of service, high costs can also lead to a reduction in the length of phone calls and text messages (Hashimoto, 2005). For example, for young people in the UK, it has been shown that increasing costs are leading to a reduction in the use not only of the (mainline and mobile) phone, but also of SMS with increasing geographical distance (Larsen et al., 2006). The tariff structure for various services is not the same in every country. For example, the relatively high costs for SMS compared with phone calls in Hong Kong make these text messages less popular than in other economically developed Asian countries such as Singapore and South Korea (Lin and Lo, 2004).

The technological capabilities of communication modes such as the networks offered and the ergonomics of the device also have an impact on the choice of communication service. Japanese people (between 15 and 39 years) consider computer e-mail via the Internet to be less attractive than SMS, because the effective use of e-mail on a home-based PC is dependent on continuous fast connections, which Table 1 shows is still limited in Japan. On the other hand, at 90% the penetration rate of mobile Internet in Japan is the highest in the world (Ministry of Public Management, Home Affairs, Posts and Telecommunications, Japan, 2004), which may encourage the use of e-mail over the wireless network. The presence of a large keyboard and screen makes the writing and reading of long e-mails much more pleasant on a PC than on the miniaturized mobile phones (Miyata et al., 2002). As a consequence, e-mails sent by a home-based PC can be expected to contain longer messages than those sent by mobile phone.

Various communication services could be chosen to expand or maintain social ties in networks. The interaction between Internet use and social networks has been studied by Wellman's group in Canada. In the context of the Pew Internet & American Life Project, they studied the association for adults of 18 years and older between Internet use and core (family and close friends) and significant (colleagues and less close friends) ties in the social network (Boase et al., 2006). In general, Americans rely heavily on face-to-face encounters and mainline phones to contact core and significant members of their network. The mobile phone and e-mail rank third and fourth. All these communication means are used more for core than for significant ties. This difference can be explained by the fact that phone numbers and e-mail addresses for significant ties are often unknown and that their weaker ties make people more reluctant to disturb them with their mobile phone. IM is used much less widely than the other communication modes in maintaining existing social networks.

In France, as in many other European countries, SMS messages are mainly sent to the most intimate members of close circles, independent of age and not to acquaintances or professional members of their networks. As in the USA (Boase et al., 2006) and in Toronto, Canada (Carrasco and Miller, 2006), a personal phone call for maintaining interpersonal relationships is also more usual in France (Rivière and Licoppe, 2004). In Japan, more than in Europe, text messages could serve emotional as well as instrumental purposes. As a consequence, these messages are sent by mobile phone to all persons, independent of relational distance. In Japan, only the very close, like parents, boy- or girlfriend receive (relatively) expensive phone calls (Rivière and Licoppe, 2004; Carrasco and Miller, 2006). Sending the indirect communication services also liberates the user from relatively strict values and norms in personal contact expressed in, for example feelings of embarrassment when one disturbs another person (Rivière and Licoppe, 2004).

This interaction between relational distance and choice of communication service has also been shown by Licoppe (2004) and Licoppe and Smoreda (2005) for placing an announcement of an important change in one's life, such as marriage, moving house, the birth of a child or a death. Those who belong to the close social circle would receive the announcement by phone, offering immediate contact and interaction. However, those at a greater relational distance were informed with some delay by a communication medium without immediate contact, such as a postcard or e-mail. It seems that the choice of mode produces and reproduces the social structure.

These results for choice of communication service might hide a gender difference. Boneva and Kraut (2002; see also Kennedy et al., 2003) state that women can be characterized by an expressive relational style that means that they like to share thoughts and feelings with others. In contrast, most men have an instrumental perspective on relationships. They like to do things together with others. This difference in preference for relational styles has implications for the use of electronic communication means. For example, in general, women have more extensive social networks and use the phone and e-mail more often to sustain their network (op. cit.). However, men's preference for joint activities is hard to accomplish far away from home. They probably prefer to meet others face-to-face. As a consequence, men use electronic communication means mostly for instrumental purposes, such as logistics and information-seeking (Wei and Lo, 2006; Igarashi et al., 2005; Oksman and Rautiainen, 2003) and exchange of more specific information (Rössler and Höflich, 2005; Rivière and Licoppe, 2004; Sung, 2005; Katz, 1997).

Not only the strength of the social ties, but also the activity patterns of the members of social networks influence the choice of a direct or indirect communication service. As for mode choice, individualization in individual activity and travel patterns also has an impact. The relatively small chance to be in direct contact with others leads to a preference for asynchronous communication services, like SMS or e-mail (Rivière and Licoppe, 2004). The reluctance to interrupt somebody's daily activities, such as eating, working, childcare, could also feed the preference for this type of service (Rössler and Höflich, 2005).

Interaction Between Corporeal and Connected Presence in Social Networks

Communication between people by ICT does not take place independent of face-to-face contacts. Larsen and colleagues (2006) noticed that most research on the use of communication modes and services fail to take into account the opportunities people have for travelling, which could influence their use of communication means. In this section I consider further the relationships between face-to-face contacts and the use of technical communication modes and services, especially the Internet. In this respect I draw a distinction between size of the social network and contact frequency and time spent on corporeal and connected presence. With these explorations it is good to keep in mind that the relationships between size of social network and Internet use could indicate a self-selection mechanism: people who already have a large network of close friends and relatives use the Internet to maintain these relationships (Nie, 2001). First, let us consider the relationship between geographical distance and communication at the aggregate level.

Geographical Distance

The choice of a communication mode and service seems to depend on the interaction between the geographical distances between members of a social network. For the USA (Boase et al., 2006) and for the UK (Larsen et al., 2006), face-to-face contacts have been shown to diminish with increasing geographical distance (Figure 1). While in the USA, phone calls (mainline and mobile phone) show no relationship with geographical distance, for the UK the relationship is negative. This difference might be explained by the operationalization of the variable 'distance' in the two studies. For the USA, the most distant category is specified as 'more than 1 hour travelling', while in the UK a continuous variable up to 400 km is used. It is feasible that after a distance of 100 km phone calls reduce in frequency because of the financial costs. In both studies, the frequency of e-mail use increases with geographical distance, because of the relatively

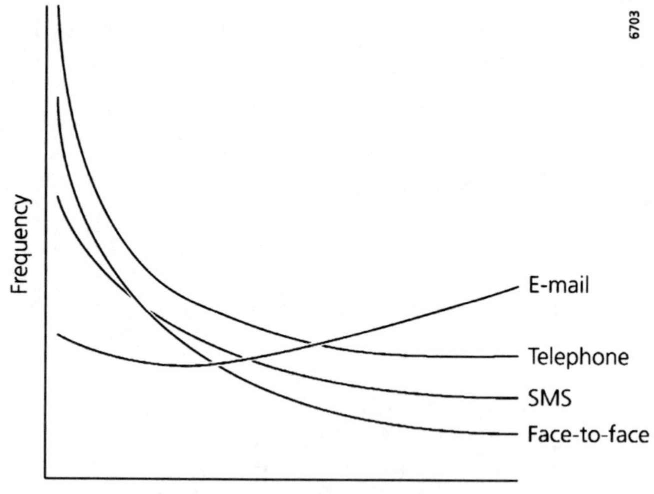

Figure 1
Hypothetical Relationship Between Contact Frequency, Geographical Distance and Communication Modes and Services

low costs. The same result has been found in Japan for e-mails sent by mobile phone (Miyata et al., 2002).

Although Chen and colleagues (2002) and Quan-Haase and colleagues (2002) have found in a World Wide Web survey that, in general, e-mail is supplementing, not substituting for face-to-face and telephone contacts, Figure 1 shows that this relationship is highly dependent on the situation. E-mail is more often used than telephone and corporeal contacts, probably because of the difference in financial costs between face-to-face contacts, e-mail and other electronic communication services, and also possibly because of individualized activity patterns; both factors constrain opportunities for co-presence at large distances. The low popularity of SMS could be a combined effect of the need to compensate a lower frequency of corporeal presence with longer connected presence by e-mail or phone call (Licoppe and Smoreda, 2005) and the limited capabilities of mobile devices to send long texts.

These aggregate results on the relationship between geographical distance and communication service might hide a gender difference. It can be hypothesized that women's more expressive relational style and extensive social networks (Boneva and Kraut, 2002) influence positively not only the frequency but also the length of their communications. In contrast, however, men's preference for joint activities could stimulate the use of electronic communication means in the frequency and length of their face-to-face contacts.

Size of Social Network and Frequency of Contacts

Based on my literature review, I have found that in general Internet use seems to have a neutral or positive effect on the *size of the social network* or *frequency of contacts*. Based on an international Web survey, the use of the Internet increased the frequency of contacts with friends and family in the USA and Japan (Ministry of Internal Affairs and Communications, Japan, 2005). The same result has been found for the impact of the use of mainline and mobile phone and e-mails on the amount of members of the social network in a multivariate study from Toronto, Canada (Carrasco and Miller, 2006). Täube (2004) gives more detailed findings from an analysis of data from the Swiss Household Panel for the years 1999 and 2000 to determine the effect of Internet use, categorized by minutes per week, on the number of contacts with neighbours and friends. After correcting for possible influences of socio-demographics his conclusion is that Internet use has no substantial effect on this social capital either for the population as a whole or for men or women separately. The direction of the effect is positive for the number of contacts with friends. However, for contacts with neighbours, the results are mixed: non-users of the Internet have more contacts than do Internet users, but intensive Internet users have more contacts than do the non-users. His conclusions seem to contradict the findings of Putnam (2000).

Kraut and colleagues (1998) have found in a longitudinal study in the USA amongst new Internet users that Internet use, measured by time investment, e-mail volume and number of websites visited reduces the number of contacts with local and distant social circles and the time spent on family communication. However, after 3 years and controlling for socio-demographics, they concluded that this negative impact had disappeared (Kraut et al., 2002). This result can be attributed to the enormous increase in the number of people who are using the Internet, which has made it easier to communicate online, to expand social networks and maintain contact with people with whom they also have corporeal contact. However, Katz and Rice (2002) found in a survey for the USA that Internet use, measured by the number of years of Internet use, is associated with sociability positively, but also negatively in some respects. Those who can be qualified as long-time or short-time users of the Internet had more face-to-face contacts with friends in the week before the survey than former and non-users of the Internet. On the other hand, the use of the Internet did harm the number of encounters with neighbours.

Boase and colleagues (2006) show that the size of the social network for core and significant ties has an impact on connected and corporeal presence. They found at the network level a negative relationship between the size of the social network and the total number of face-to-face and mediated encounters. By reducing the frequency of (and time spent on) contacts, people seem to be capable of maintaining large networks. The only exception to this rule is e-mail, which seems to be independent of network size. The asynchronous character of e-mail makes this communication service very flexible and time efficient in maintaining contacts, especially for people with busy time schedules (op. cit.). As mentioned before, this relationship between size of social network and Internet use could also indicate a self-selection mechanism (Nie, 2001).

Duration of Contacts

In contrast with the number of members of ones social network and frequency of face-to-face encounters, it seems that the impact of Internet use on *time spent* on these members is negative or neutral. In his studies, Nie (Nie and Erbring, 2000; Nie and Hillygus, 2002) suggests a substitution effect of Internet use on time spent on family and friends. This result was also found in a Web survey in Japan and the USA (Ministry of Internal Affairs and Communications, Japan, 2005, p. 20). These findings seem to be confirmed by a study by Gershuny (2002) in the UK. He analysed full-week diaries of 1,000 participants in The British Household Panel Survey for the years 1999 and 2000. He analyses the effect of Internet use on the home computer by new users, old users and non-users on time spent on social life (going out), visiting and phone calls. Table 2 shows the average time spent on social activities by respondents who did not change category in both years. In view of the relative short time span between both years it is highly unlikely that the changes in duration are caused by changes in socio-demographics. Nevertheless, these results should be treated carefully.

Table 2

Impact of the Use of the Home Computer on Hours Spent per Week on Social Activities in the UK in 2000 and Changes in the Years 1999 and 2000

Activity	Non-users		New users		Old users	
	Time	Change	Time	Change	Time	Change
Social life	4.2	0.1	4.6	0.5	5.0	0.5
Visiting	6.0	−0.5	6.4	0.4	4.7	−0.9
Phone calls	11.5	−0.1	1.0	−0.1	10.9	0.1
Internet	0.0	0.0	1.3	1.3	1.7	1.1

Source: Gershuny (2002).

The table shows how time spent on social life increases with use of the Internet. However, the converse applies to meeting relatives and friends. People who have used the Internet for a long time and also more intensively spend less time on visits than new users do. The reduction of time spent on visits by the old users might indicate that, after a couple of years, e-mail contacts may substitute for face-to-face meetings with friends. As reported previously, other factors such as the size of the social network and the geographical distance between friends might influence this result. In Table 2, the relationship between telephoning and Internetting is unclear. While the time spent on phone calls is low for new users, for non-users and old users it remains much the same.

Teleworking or telecommuting, for which the PC and Internet are indispensable, might be a special case. Harvey and Taylor (2000) showed for Canada in the early 1990s that working at home changed the time budget for social activities in favour of the family and at the expense of others. People with low levels of local social interaction can fulfil their need for social contact by travelling more (see also Nilles, 1996).

It is feasible that the impact of Internet use on time spent on social ties can be explained by the fact that the researchers did not take socio-demographics into account. Kestnbaum and colleagues (2002) used time-diary results for the USA to show that Internet use diminishes the time spent on socializing and visiting non-family members; however, after controlling for socio-demographics, this result was no longer statistically significant.

Expanding Size of Social Network

The Internet can be used not only to maintain existing contacts with family and friends but also to expand their social network. People use newsgroups, mailing lists, chat rooms and other forms of online groups to communicate synchronously or asynchronously through e-mailing, messaging and file sharing for both work and private reasons (Lin and Chen, 2004; Girgensohn and Lee, 2002). Baym (1998) concludes from a review of research on online groups that they are often interwoven with offline groups. Participants in online groups can have pre-existing face-to-face relationships, as with colleagues and friends. In other cases, they may know each other from other online groups. People who construct new relationships in online groups usually communicate with them after a while by phone or face-to-face. Whether this communication occurs and the degree and communication mode chosen depend on such factors as the geographical distance between the participants.

Not only people but also devices communicate with each other in an ubiquitous network society in which each person can connect to networks at any time, from anywhere and from any appliance (Ministry of Public Management, Home Affairs, Posts and Telecommunication, Japan, 2004). Some location-based technologies might impact on social networking by allowing their users to meet family, friends and acquaintances on the 'buddy list' showed on their mobile phone or PDA (Consolvo et al., 2005) or expand their social networks by using electronic badges or bracelets. The software on these devices store, display and exchange information with other devices of the same kind about its users and their relationships (Kanis et al., 2005; Counts and Geraci, 2005). In the last case this might lead to fluid contacts when the persons only meet by incident or more durable relationships. The impact of these techniques on social networking is hardly known as yet, since these social technologies are still in their infancy and the market for these devices has not stabilized.

Interaction Between Connected and Corporeal Presence in Fluids

In the previous section, I described the use of communication modes and services and the interaction between connected and corporeal presence. As indicated in Social Networks Between Regions and Fluids section, not only is the social network a relevant form of association of people, but also are more fluid types. These fluid associations stand out in particular in public places. For that reason, I focus in this section on the use of mobile devices, predominantly the mobile phone, in public places such as public transport and the street.

While the mainline phone is fixed in a geographical situation, this is not the case for the mobile phone, which is placeless by intention (Ling, 2005). Does that mean that mobile phones are only used outside such locations as the home and the fixed workplace? Fortunati (2002) asked herself this question and searched for some answers in the data of a telephone survey in five European countries. A summary of her findings is shown in Table 3. This table indicates that mobile phones are predominantly used in temporary places such as transport modes and the street. However, it can also be seen

Table 3
The Use of Mobile Phones at Fixed and Temporary Places in Selected European Countries (%)

	France	Germany	Italy	Spain	UK	Europe
Fixed places						
At home	33.3	10.0	6.6	5.6	5.6	10.1
At work	3.3	7.5	10.7	8.3	9.7	8.7
Temporary places						
In a vehicle	27.8	58.3	27.9	25.0	64.1	42.4
In the street	20.0	5.0	35.7	22.2	7.7	19.7
Elsewhere	11.1	10.9	10.2	20.9	6.1	10.4
No response	4.4	8.3	9.0	18.1	6.7	8.6

Source: Fortunati (2002).

that a fifth of those surveyed also use their mobile at a fixed place, at home or at work. This figure is particularly high for France. These results show that the mobile phone has become an integral part of an individualized lifestyle that could give rise to personalized networking (Wellman, 2001). Referring to Use of Communication Modes and Services section, not only cultural, but also tariff-structure differences could explain the differences between countries.

Various countries show differences in the manner in which mobile phones are used in public. In Japan, social behaviour in public places is highly regulated. Although a few people pay no attention to the norms, in Japanese public places crowded with people, mobile phones are usually put in 'silent mode' and their use is restricted to text messaging services or the Internet (Hashimoto, 2005; Ito, 2004). Ito (op. cit.) observed mobile phone use in Japanese trains and noticed that the overall average of voice calls in 30 minutes was 1–2 calls. It seems that, even at home, Japanese youngsters use silent modes in order not to attract the attention of their parents. Comparative studies show that Italians and Israelis are more inclined than the Japanese to switch on their mobile phone in public places and the French are more reluctant to make mobile phone calls in public than are the English or Spanish (Haddon, 2004).

The use of a mobile device can often be seen to lead to the creation of a private sphere in a public space; as Cooper (2002) puts it, the mobile phone is: '*... a resource for personalizing one's existence in public spaces, a resource for achieving privacy*'. By using the mobile phone or other mobile device, individuals can occupy themselves with their own private activities, strengthening their ties with close social circles, but at the same time avoiding encounters with strangers. As a consequence, Katz (1997) expects that on public transport contact with seatmates will be substituted for contact with callmates. Hashimoto (2005) characterizes this development in public space as the 'mosaicking of communication space'.

This personalization of public space could produce public obstructiveness or even embarrassment and annoyance (Murtagh, 2002; Rössler and Höflich, 2005; Ling, 2005; Roos, 1993; Hashimoto, 2005). These reactions can be caused by the phone ring (length, volume and tune), the length of the phone call and the discussion of private matters in public. The norms for appropriate use of mobile devices are negotiated with others who are corporeally present in these situations (Ling, 2005). The display of norms for mobile use can be in the form of vocal, non-vocal (eye contact) and body movements (turning of the head or upper body) (Ito, 2004; Murtagh, 2002). The outcomes of these negotiations can depend on the duration of presence in the public place and individual and situational characteristics. These outcomes can be expressed in persistent annoyance, searching for another place in public space or, in the long term after frequent unpleasant experiences, avoiding public transport and particular urban places. Although the use of text instead of voice services may reduce the annoyance of others, the use of these text services is not always free from reactions from the public. Managing these messages might have an impact on participation in co-located activities in public places (Ling, 2005) and can strengthen the 'mosaicking' of space. Instead of negotiating norms of behaviour, authority constraints could be applied through 'mobile phone free area' signs or oral announcements to limit the negative effects of mobile phone use (Ito, 2004).

Towards a Situational Perspective on Interaction Between Corporeal and Connected Presence

So far we have discussed the factors which influence the use of communication modes and services and the interaction between these communications forms and face-to-face encounters in social networks. In general we can conclude that the explanations given are highly fragmented and too generalized: the various factors have been discussed in relative isolation from each other and their contexts, while they ought to be considered together in concrete situations if we are to improve our understanding of the use of electronic communication modes and services. Referring to the use of the Internet, Nie and colleagues (2002, p. 227) state: '*It is overly simplistic to look for one effect for all Internet use. Where and when an individual uses the Internet is as important as how he or she uses it*'.

In general in studies on communication activities three dimensions are considered in mutual relationship. These are *corporeal presence* (face-to-face interaction between people, tools and materials), *connected presence* (mediated interaction) and *mental presence* (referring to cognitive, affective and unconscious processes, which mediate between the experience of interactions and individuals' aspirations, attitudes, values, norms, goals and desires). Most studies reviewed in this paper search for universal, that mean non-situation specific, general behavioural rules and processes. These studies do not take into account the possibility that behaviours vary across time and place. In the case authors contextualize communication activities they are selective in their choice for the three 'presence dimensions' or operationalize these dimensions in a very rudimentary way. For example, classical time geography in studying face-to-face interactions in spatio-temporal situations largely ignored connected and mental presence (Dijst, 2009). However, in studies on electronic communication modes discussed in this paper (e.g. Boase et al., 2006; Licoppe and Smoreda, 2005; Nie et al., 2002) these spatio-temporal situations do not exist. As far as differences in contexts are operationalized these refer to countries or cultures (e.g. Chen and Wellman, 2003; Fortunati, 2002; Haddon, 2004; Rivière and Licoppe, 2004) and not to concrete, local situations in which communication activities occur. An exception is perhaps the study of Fortunati (2002) in which she makes a distinction between various types of fixed and temporary places and its impact on mobile phone use (Table 3). Unfortunately, the other two dimensions are hardly operationalized since we do not know, for example whether persons have the opportunity to use other communication modes and their motivation for communicating.

In this section I will sketch the contours of a contextual or situational approach for studies on the relationships between ICT use and social networks. This approach is highly influenced by theories which are based on the principle that behaviour is in essence contextualized (Dijst et al., 2008). In this respect we can think of time geography (Hägerstrand, 1970), non-representational theory (Thrift, 1996), actor-network theory (Latour, 2005), post-structuralist geography (Murdoch, 2006) and the new mobilities paradigm (Sheller and Urry, 2006). In this paper, contexts or situations are concrete and local spatio-temporal assemblages of dynamic, constraining and enabling relationships between human beings, electronic communication modes and other material entities. Since in these assemblages all three 'presence dimensions' are at work we can talk about a 'tripartite situatedness' (Figure 2). In the remainder of this section I will elaborate each dimension and provide some examples of how the analytical framework might be applied.

In Social Networks Between Regions and Fluids section, I have stated that corporeal presence means that human beings and other organisms and material elements are linked together for the purpose of carrying out an activity. A situational theory of corporeal presence is classical time geography as developed in Sweden by Hägerstrand and his colleagues in the 1960s and 1970s. The basic idea of this well-known theory among geographers and transportation researchers is that each individual, but also other organisms and material objects follow an uninterrupted path through time and across space, which together form various webs or networks. The course of these individual paths is related to capability (biological, mental and instrumental restrictions), coupling (synchronization and synchorization of individuals, instruments

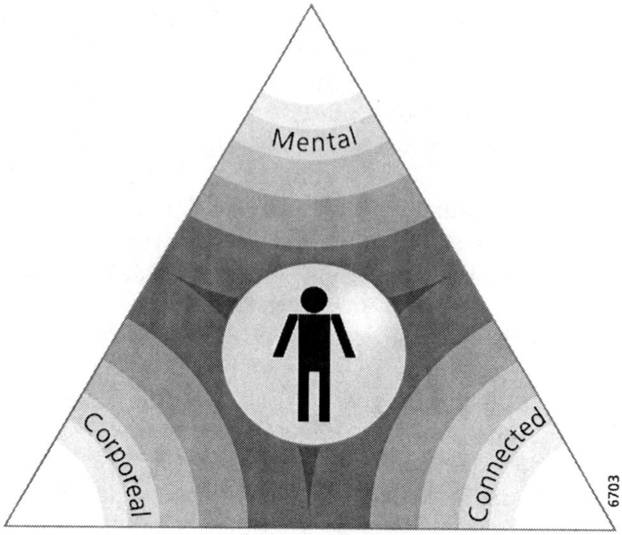

Figure 2
Tripartite Situatedness

and materials) and authority constraints (regulation of access to space). Operationalization of these constraints can be found in, for example Dijst and colleagues (2002).

These constraints define a three-dimensional prism that embraces the set of opportunities for corporeal presence in time and space. The projection of this prism in a two- or three-dimensional space is called *potential action space* (Dijst, 1995; Dijst and Vidakovic, 1997) (Figure 3: left). Over the day, people participate in various action spaces. Each individual carries this enveloping action space, which expands and contracts like a balloon under the influence of changes in the three constraints mentioned and behavioural decisions concerning the course of the daily path (Figure 3, right). These action spaces have not only a plastic but also a fluid character. As one moves across space, one notices that people and material objects move in and out of one's potential action space because of one's change in spatial position. Conversely, when one is fixated in space, others with their own potential action spaces move in and out of one's action space. In other words, the size and social composition of people *physically* present in potential action spaces and with whom one can interact are dependent on temporal but also spatial locations of people.

People whom one could contact by use of ICT devices and networks available in a potential action space represent 'connected presence'. Increasing use of ICT could give the impression that daily life is becoming footloose. However, although the use of ICT

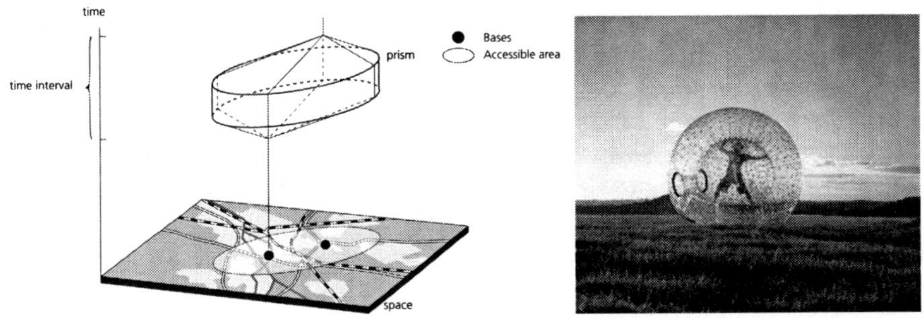

Figure 3
Corporeal Spatio-Temporal Situation Defined by Prism and Potential Action
Source: Dijst (2009) (left), Dijst (2006)/ www.truenz.co.nz/ (right)

relieves some capability constraints, they are still at work (Dijst, 2004). Concerning the relationship between ICT and social networks, we see in this paper that the PC offers faster connections, a more user-friendly keyboard and a large screen, which invite their owners to engage in writing lengthy e-mails to friends and relatives who live at a distance. In addition to these capability constraints, coupling constraints also influence the choice of communication mode. Busy activity and travel patterns stimulate the preference for a flexible, asynchronous and time-efficient communication service. As the geographical distance between individuals increases, corporeal presence is substituted by telephone, which after a certain further distance is overtaken by e-mail. Finally, authority constraints can forbid the use of mobile phones, as Japanese experiences show. Installing intelligent filters and agents on a mobile phone, which identify a group of callers by a specific ring tone (Weilenmann, 2003; Katz, 1997), can also be treated as authority constraints. In other words, the size and social composition of people *virtually* present in potential action spaces and with whom one can interact are dependent on temporal, spatial and other characteristics of electronic devices and people.

As mentioned before the mental presence mediates between individuals' perceptions, attitudes, emotions, values, norms, desires and objectives, and the opportunities offered by corporeal and connected presence. These mental characteristics do apply to all individuals physically and/or virtually present in potential action spaces. One could say that mental presence glues the various elements of the potential action space together as meaningful. This mental presence will impact, for example the perception and weighing of constraints on the use of communication modes and the choice for people to communicate face-to-face or virtually.

An illustration of this situational approach is a journey in the train. The choice for the use of a mobile phone while travelling in a train is dependent on the interrelationships between various aspects of the situation. The morning commute can be crowded which might reduce the use of the mobile phone in order to avoid public obstructiveness, embarrassment and annoyance. However, this choice is also dependent on the characteristics of the communication activity. An individual with a mobile phone who wants to make an appointment with a hairdresser is maybe less annoying than a caller who is discussing very intimate and delicate issues. In addition, public opinion is highly dependent on the social composition of the train compartment. Based on the review in this paper one can hypothesize that compared to Italians the Japanese will react differently in such a situation. Those passengers who bear in mind the feelings and opinions of others will probably postpone the call until another situation. However, the situation can change substantially when passengers are travelling outside rush hours. A lower density of people in this situation increases on the average the physical distance between passengers and by that can lower the nuisance.

Situational effects can also be expected for less fluid social networks. For example, a woman's choice for a communication mode to discuss an important and urgent issue with a good friend is highly dependent on her situation. When she is at her workplace she might choose the land line phone to make an appointment for a face-to-face meeting later that day. However, when she has other activities planned for that evening she could decide to contact her good friend over the break by mobile phone. This choice is dependent on her impression of the relation style of the other. We know from literature that in general men have an instrumental perspective on relationships which will temper their inclination to use the phone for emotional issues. The situation will change when both friends are not working and could meet in daytime. On the other hand, a large geographical distance between both friends could limit the attractiveness of this option. In this respect a special case is the situation in which the friends are separated by many time zones which might render e-mail communication from a financial and logistic perspective a better alternative.

The basic idea behind a situational approach is that these and other types of situations mentioned above will influence the use of electronic communication means for the purpose of a social activity. The behavioural variance across time and space cannot be caught by research in which only the impact of socio-demographics is analysed, as in most studies on ICT and social networks reviewed in this paper. These analyses result in the formulation of universal behavioural rules concerning the meaning of socio-demographics for the use of communication modes. In contrast a situational approach can lead to a better understanding of these behavioural choices.

Conclusions

Although the spread of ICT in the form of PC, mobile phone, broadband networks and communication services is progressing smoothly, knowledge about the use of these electronic communication means and its relationship with social networks is fragmented and generalized. This situation is in part a consequence of the fast successive development and distribution of ICT innovations and the necessary time it takes for individuals to integrate the new communication modes and services into their daily lives. Another reason for our lack of knowledge is the incoherence of the research on the implications of ICT for social networks. Differences in definitions, data collection and analytical methods lead inevitably to inconclusive evidence that cannot be compared across countries. This paper has mapped out some of the main empirical results on the relationship between ICT and social networks.

We have seen that, for networks and more flexible types of relationships (fluids) a combination of cost structures, technological capabilities of communication modes and attitudes towards the relationships and characteristics of social networks is capable of explaining the use of communication modes and services. In general, these factors explain the distinction drawn between the use of mobile and of fixed devices and services. The mobile phone fulfils the need for *instantaneous social contact*, which is short in duration, smoothes coupling constraints in daily life and serves to convey brief signs of affection. *Prolonged social contacts* are served by fixed devices and networks at home, at work or elsewhere; they offer ample opportunities to make long phone calls, send elaborate e-mails and chat at length.

Concerning the relationship between ICT and social networks, it has been shown that corporeal and connected presence could be complementary as well as substitutive to each other. The empirical studies reviewed give the impression that a *complementary* relationship dominates for the *size of their social networks and frequency of contacts.* Electronic communication means in particular offer the opportunities to maintain frequent contact with a relatively large social network. However, as for face-to-face contacts, the frequency of these electronic means decrease with increasing geographical distance between members of a social network. The exception to this rule seems to be e-mail, which is a relatively cheap communication service. In terms of *time budget* spent on social ties, the impression is given that the relationship with use of ICT means is more *substitutive.*

As I stated at the outset, empirical studies have investigated the various factors that influence the use of ICT and its interaction with social networks in isolation from each other and not in connection with the concrete local situations in which interactions take place. To meet this objection, I have proposed a tripartite situatedness, composed of corporeal, connected and mental presence, as an alternative analytical framework. This situatedness offers individuals the concrete opportunities to expand, maintain and terminate their social relationships. This situational approach, together with the application of multivariate analytical methods and adjustments in data collections between countries, could lead to a better understanding of the interaction between the use of ICT and social networks.

References

Axhausen, K. W. (2002). *A dynamic understanding of travel demand: a sketch.* Zurich: Institut für Verkehrsplanung, Transporttechnik, Strassenund Eisenbahnbau (IVT), ETH Zurich (Arbeitsberichte Verkehrs- und Raumplanung, 119).

Axhausen, K. W. (2005). Social networks and travel: some hypotheses. In K. P. Donaghy, S. Poppelreuter and G. Rudinger (Eds.), *Social Dimensions of Sustainable Transport: Transatlantic Perspectives*, Aldershot, Ashgate, pp. 90–108.

Baym, N. K. (1998). The emergence of on-line community. In S. G. Jones (Ed.), *Cybersociety 2.0*, Newbury Park, CA, Sage, pp. 35–68.

Bertolini, L. and M. Dijst (2003). Mobility environments and network cities. *Journal of Urban Design* 8, 27–43.

Boase, J., J. B. Hoorigan, B. Wellman and L. Rainie (2006). *The Strength of Internet ties: The Internet and Email Aid Users in Maintaining Their Social Networks and Provide Pathways to Help When People Face Big Decisions*. Washington, DC: Pew Internet & American Life Project. Available at: http://www.pewinternet.org/

Boden, D. and H. L. Molotoch (1994). The compulsion of proximity. In R. Friedland and D. Boden (Eds.), *Nowhere Space, Time and Modernity*, London, University of California Press, pp. 257–286.

Boneva, B. and R. Kraut (2002). Email, gender and personal relationships. In B. Wellman and C. Haythornthwaite (Eds.), *The Internet in Everyday Life*, Malden, Blackwell, pp. 372–403.

Cairncross, F. (1997). *The Death of Distance: How the Communications Revolution will Change Our Lives*. Boston, MA, Harvard Business School Press.

Callon, M. and J. Law (2004). Guest editorial. *Environment and Planning D* 32, 3–11.

Carrasco, J. and E. J. Miller (2006). Exploring the propensity to perform social activities: a social networks approach. Presented at *85th Annual Transportation Research Board Meeting*, January 2006, Washington, DC.

Castells, M. (1996). *The Rise of the Network Society*. Oxford, Blackwell Publishers.

Castells, M. (2002). The internet and the network society. In B. Wellman and C. Haythornthwaite (Eds.), *The Internet in Everyday Life*, Malden, Blackwell, pp. xxix–xxxi.

Chen, W., J. Boase and B. Wellman (2002). The global villagers: comparing Internet users and uses around the world. In B. Wellman and C. Haythornthwaite (Eds.), *The Internet in Everyday Life*, Malden, Blackwell, pp. 74–113.

Chen, W. and B. Wellman (2003). *Charting and Bridging Digital Divides: Comparing Socio-Economic, Gender, Life Stage, and Rural–Urban Internet Access and Use in Eight Countries*. Toronto, University of Toronto, Centre for Urban and Community Studies.

Consolvo, S., I. E. Smith, T. Matthews, A. LaMarca, J. Tabert and P. Powledge (2005). *Location disclosure to social relations: why, when & what people want to share.*

CHI, April 2–7, Portland, Oregon, USA. Available at: guir.berkeley.edu/pubs/chi2005/p486-consolvo.pdf

Cooper, G. (2002). The mutable mobile: social theory in the wireless world. In B. Brown, N. Green and R. Harper (Eds.), *Wireless World: Social and Interactional Aspects of the Mobile Age*, London, Springer-Verlag, pp. 19–31.

Couclelis, H. (1998). Editorial: the new field workers. *Environment and Planning B* 25, 321–323.

Couclelis, H. (2000). From sustainable transportation to sustainable accessibility: can we avoid a new tragedy of the commons? In D. G. Janelle and D. C. Hodge (Eds.), *Information, Place and Cyberspace: Issues in Accessibility*, Berlin, Springer-Verlag, pp. 341–356.

Counts, S. and J. Geraci (2005). *Incorporating physical co-presence at events into digital social networking. CHI, April 2–7, Portland, Oregon, USA*. Available at: portal.acm.org/citation.cfm?id = 1056903&dl = ACM&coll = ACM&CFID = 15151515&CFTOKEN = 6184618

Dematteis, G. (1998). The weak metropolis. In L. Mazza (Ed.), *World Cities and the Future of the Metropolis*, Milano, Electa-XVII Triennale, pp. 121–133.

Dijst, M. (1995). *Het Elliptisch Leven: Actieruimte als Integrale Maat voor Bereik en Mobiliteit*. Utrecht: KNAG (NGS 196) [The elliptical life: action space as integral measure for accessibility and mobility]. Copy available from http://igitur-archive.library.uu.nl/search/search.php?m = simple&p = 2&qry = dijst&language = nl

Dijst, M. (2004). ICT and accessibility: an action space perspective on the impact of new information and communication technologies. In M. Beuthe, V. Himanenen, A. Reggiani and L. Zamparini (Eds.), *Transport Developments and Innovations in an Evolving World*, Berlin, Springer, pp. 27–46.

Dijst, M. (2006). Stilstaan bij beweging: over veranderende relaties tussen steden en mobiliteit. Utrecht: Faculteit Geowetenschappen, Universiteit Utrecht (inaugural lecture). [Dwelling on motion: changing relationships between cities and mobility]. Copy available from http://igitur-archive.library.uu.nl/search/search.php?m = simple&p=2&qry=dijst&language=nl

Dijst, M. (2009). Time geographical analysis. In R. Kitchin and N. Thrift (Eds.), *International Encyclopaedia of Human Geography*. Oxford, Elsevier (forthcoming).

Dijst, M., T. de Jong and J. Ritsema van Eck (2002). Opportunities for transport mode change: an exploration of a disaggregated approach. *Environment and Planning B* 29, 413–430.

Dijst, M., S. Farag and T. Schwanen (2008). *A comparative study of attitude theory and other theoretical models for in-store and online shopping. Environment and Planning A* 40, 831–847.

Dijst, M. and V. Vidakovic (1997). Individual action space in the city. In D. F. Ettema and H. J. P. Timmermans (Eds.), *Activity-Based Approaches to Travel Analysis*, Oxford, Elsevier, pp. 117–134.

Fortunati, L. (2002). Italy: stereotypes, true and false. In J. E. Katz and M. Aakhus (Eds.), *Perpetual Contact*, Cambridge, University Press, pp. 42–62.

Fortunati, L. and A. Contarello (2005). Social representation of the mobile: an Italian study. In S. D. Kim (Ed.), *When Mobile Came: The Cultural and Social Impact of Mobile communication*, Seoul, Korea, Communication Books, pp. 45–61.

Fortunati, L., J. E. Katz and R. Riccini (2003). Introduction. In L. Fortunati, J. E. Katz and R. Riccini (Eds.), *Mediating the Human Body: Technology, Communication, and Fashion*, Mahwah, NJ, Lawrence Erlbaum Associates, pp. 1–11.

Gaglio, G. (2005). Are ostentation and distinction relevant concepts for dealing with material culture? Illustration through the mobile phone and its social trajectory. In S. D. Kim (Ed.), *When Mobile Came: The Cultural and Social Impact of Mobile Communication*, Seoul, Korea, Communication Books, pp. 81–103.

Gershuny, J. (2002). Mass media, leisure and home IT: a panel time-diary approach. *IT&Society* 1(1), 53–66.

Girgensohn, A. and A. Lee (2002). *Making web sites be places for social interaction. CSCW, November 16–20, New Orleans, Louisiana, USA*. Available at: www.webcollab.com/alee/papers/cscw02.htm

Graham, S. and S. Marvin (1996). *Telecommunications and the City. Electronic Spaces, Urban places*. London, Routledge.

Green, N. (2002). Who's watching whom? Monitoring and accountability in mobile relations. In B. Brown, N. Green and R. Harper (Eds.), *Wireless World: Social and Interactional Aspects of the Mobile Age*, London, Springer-Verlag, pp. 32–45.

Haddon, L. (2004). Cultural differences in communication: examining patterns of daily life. In S. D. Kim (Ed.), *Mobile Communication and Social Change, 2004 International Conference on Mobile Communication*, October 18–19, 2004, Seoul, Korea, pp. 18–30.

Hägerstrand, T. (1970). What about people in regional science?. *Papers of the Regional Science Association* 24, 7–21.

Harvey, A. S. and M. E. Taylor (2000). Activity settings and travel behaviour: A social contact perspective. *Transportation* 27, 53–73.

Hashimoto, Y. (2005). The spread of cellular phones and their influence on young people in Japan. In S. D. Kim (Ed.), *When Mobile Came: The Cultural and Social Impact of Mobile Communication*, Seoul, Korea, Communication Books, pp. 198–211.

Haythornthwaite, C. and B. Wellman (2002). The Internet in everyday life: an introduction. In B. Wellman and C. Haythornthwaite (Eds.), *The Internet in Everyday Life*, Malden, Blackwell, pp. 3–44.

Igarashi, T., J. Takai and T. Yoshida (2005). Gender differences in social network development via mobile phone text messages: a longitudinal study. *Journal of Social and Personal Relationships* 22, 691–713.

International Telecommunications Union (2006). Available at: http://www.itu.int/ITU-D/ict/statistics/at_glance/KeyTelecom99.html

Ito, M. (2004). Personal portable pedestrian: lessons from Japanese mobile phone use. In S. D. Kim (Ed.), *Mobile Communication and Social Change, 2004 International Conference on Mobile Communication*, October 18–19, 2004, Seoul, Korea, pp. 31–37.

Kakihara, M., C. Sørensen and M. Wiberg (2002). Fluid interaction in mobile work practices. Paper presented at the First Global Mobile Roundtable, Tokyo, Japan, May 29–30, 2002. Institute of Innovation Research, Hitotsubashi University. Available at: www.kakihara.org/papers/Kakihara_EtAl_TMR.pdf

Kanis, M., N. Winters, S. Agamanolis, A. Gravin and Cullinan C. (2005). *Toward wearable social networking with iBand. CHI, April 2-7, Portland, Oregon, USA.* Available at: web.media.mit.edu/~stefan/hc/publications/Kanis05iBandCHI.pdf

Kasvio, A. (2001). *Consumption, Everyday Life and Culture.* Tampere, Tampere University.

Katz, J. E. (1997). Social and organizational consequences of wireless communications: a selective analysis of residential and business sectors in the United States. *Telematics and Informatics* 14(3), 233–256.

Katz, J. E. and R. E. Rice (2002). Syntopia: access, civic involvement and social interaction on the net. In B. Wellman and C. Haythornthwaite (Eds.), *The Internet in Everyday Life*, Malden, Blackwell, pp. 114–138.

Kennedy, T., B. Wellman and K. Klement (2003). Gendering the digital divide. *IT&Society* 1(5), 72–96.

Kestnbaum, M., J. P. Robinson, A. Neustadl and A. Alvarez (2002). Information technology and social time displacement. *IT&Society* 1(1), 21–37.

Kim, S. D. (2002). Korea: personal meanings. In J. E. Katz and M. Aakhus (Eds.), *Perpetual Contact*, Cambridge, University Press, pp. 63–79.

Kopomaa, T. (2000). *The City in Your Pocket: Birth of the Mobile Information Society.* Helsinki, Gaudeamus.

Kraut, R., S. Kiesler, B. Boneva, J. Cummings, V. Helgeson and A. Crawford (2002). Internet paradox revisited. *Journal of Social Issues* 58, 49–74.

Kraut, R., M. Patterson, V. Lundmark, S. Kiesler, T. Mukopadhyay and W. Scherlis (1998). Internet paradox: a social technology that reduces social involvement and psychological well-being? *American Psychologist* 53, 1017–1032.

Larsen, J., J. Urry and K. Axhausen (2006). Social networks and future mobilities. Report to the Horizons Programme of the Department for Transport. Kancaster/Zurich: Department of Sociology, University of Lancaster/IVT, ETH Zürich.

Latour, B. (2005). *Reassembling the Social: An Introduction to Actor-Network-Theory.* Oxford, Oxford University Press.

Laurier, E. and C. Philo (2003). The region in the boot: mobilizing lone subjects and multiple objects. *Environment and Planning D* 21, 85–106.

Lee, D. and S. Sohn (2004). Is there a gender difference in mobile phone usage? In Kim, S. D. (Ed.), *Mobile Communication and Social Change, 2004*

International Conference on Mobile Communication, October 18–19, 2004, Seoul, Korea, pp. 243–259.

Lee, M. (2005). Construction of differences in cellular phone usage between Koreans and Americans. In S. D. Kim (Ed.), *When Mobile Came: The Cultural and Social Impact of Mobile Communication*, Seoul, Korea, Communication Books, pp. 273–287.

Licoppe, C. (2004). 'Connected' presence: the emergence of a new repertoire for managing social relationships in a changing communication technoscape. *Environment and Planning D* 22, 135–156.

Licoppe, C. and Z. Smoreda (2005). Are social networks technologically embedded? How networks are changing today with changes in communication technology. *Social Networks* 27, 317–335.

Lin, F. and C. Chen (2004). Developing and evaluating the social network analysis system for virtual teams in cyberspace communities. *Proceedings of the 37th Hawaii International Conference on System Sciences – 2004*. Available at: csdl.computer.org/comp/proceedings/hicss/2004/2056/08/205680249c.pdf

Lin, R. and J. Lo (2004). New youth digital literacies and mobile connectivity: text-messaging among Hong Kong College Students. In S. D. Kim (Ed.), *Mobile Communication and Social Change, 2004 International Conference on Mobile Communication*, October 18–19, 2004, Seoul, Korea, pp. 297–304.

Ling, R. (2005). The social juxtaposition of mobile telephone conversations and public spaces. In S. D. Kim (Ed.), *When Mobile Came: The Cultural and Social Impact of Mobile Communication*, Seoul, Korea, Communication Books, pp. 13–44.

Ling, R. and B. Yttri (2002). Hyper-coordination via mobile phones in Norway. In J. E. Katz and M. Aakhus (Eds.), *Perpetual Contact*, Cambridge, University Press, pp. 139–169.

Meizhi, L. and D. Shim (2004). The mobile phone as a cultural artifact in Singapore. In S. D. Kim (Ed.), *Mobile Communication and Social Change, 2004 International Conference on Mobile Communication*, October 18–19, 2004, Seoul, Korea, pp. 569–577.

Ministry of Internal Affairs and Communications, Japan (2005). Information and communications in Japan: Stirrings of u-Japan. White Paper, Tokyo, Japan.

Ministry of Public Management, Home Affairs, Posts and Telecommunication, Japan (2004). Information and communications in Japan. White paper, Tokyo, Japan.

Miyata, K., J. Boase, B. Wellman and K. Ikeda (2002). *The mobile-izing Japanese: connecting to the Internet by PC and web phone in Yamanashi*. Available at: www.chass.utoronto.ca/|wellman/netlab/publications/frames.html (working paper).

Mol, A. and J. Law (1994). Regions, networks and fluids: anaemia and social topology. *Social Studies of Science* 26, 641–671.

Murdoch, J. (2006). *Post-Structuralist Geography: A Guide to Relational Space*. London, Sage.

Murtagh, G. M. (2002). Seeing the "rules": preliminary observations of action, interaction and mobile phone use. In B. Brown, N. Green and R. Harper (Eds.), *Wireless World: Social and Interactional Aspects of the Mobile Age*, London, Springer-Verlag, pp. 81–91.

Nie, N. H. (2001). Sociability, interpersonal relations, and the internet. *American Behavioral Scientist* 45, 420–435.

Nie, N. H. and L. Erbring (2000). *Internet and Society: A Preliminary Report*. Stanford, Stanford Institute for the Quantitative Study of Society (SIQSS), Stanford University, and InterSurvey, Inc.

Nie, N. H. and D. S. Hillygus (2002). Where does Internet time come from?: a reconnaissance. *IT&Society* 1(2), 1–20.

Nie, N. H., D. S. Hillygus and L. Erbring (2002). Internet use, interpersonal relations and sociability. In B. Wellman and C. Haythornthwaite (Eds.), *The Internet in Everyday Life*, Malden, Blackwell, pp. 215–243.

Nilles, J. M. (1996). What does telework really do to us? *World Transport Policy & Practice* 2(1–2), 15–23.

Oksman, V. and P. Rautiainen (2003). Extension of the hand: children's and teenagers' relationship with the mobile phone in Finland. In L. Fortunati, J. E. Katz and R. Riccini (Eds.), *Mediating the Human Body: Technology, Communication, and Fashion*, Mahwah, NJ, Lawrence Erlbaum Associates, pp. 103–112.

Pertierra, R. (2005). Mobile phones, identity and discursive intimacy. *Human Technology* 1(1), 23–44.

Puro, J. (2002). Finland: a mobile culture. In J. E. Katz and M. Aakhus (Eds.), *Perpetual Contact*, Cambridge, University Press, pp. 19–29.

Putnam, D. R. (2000). *Bowling Alone: The Collapse and Revival of American Community*. New York, Simon & Schuster.

Quan-Haase, A. and B. Wellman (2002). Capitalizing on the net: social contact, civic engagement and sense of community. In B. Wellman and C. Haythornthwaite (Eds.), *The Internet in Everyday Life*, Malden, Blackwell, pp. 291–324.

Rivière, C. A. and C. Licoppe (2004). From voice to text: continuity and change in the use of mobile phones in France and Japan. In S. D. Kim (Ed.), *Mobile Communication and Social Change, 2004 International Conference on Mobile Communication*, October 18–19, 2004, Seoul, Korea, pp. 488–503.

Roos, J. P. (1993). Sociology of cellular telephone: the Nordic model (300 000 yuppies? Mobile phones in Finland). *Telecommunications Policy* 17, 446–458.

Rössler, P. and J. R. Höflich (2005). More than a telephone: mobile phone and the usage of the short message service (SMS) by German adolescents.

In S. D. Kim (Ed.), *When Mobile Came: The Cultural and Social Impact of Mobile Communication*, Seoul, Korea, Communication Books, pp. 104–134.

Schwanen, T. (2006). On arriving on time, but what is time? *Geoforum* 37, 882–894.

Sheller, M. (2004). Mobile publics: beyond the network perspective. *Environment and Planning D* 22, 39–52.

Sheller, M. and J. Urry (2003). Mobile transformations of 'public' and 'private' life. *Theory, Culture & Society* 20, 107–125.

Sheller, M. and J. Urry (2006). The new mobilities paradigm. *Environment and Planning A* 38, 207–226.

Skog, B. (2002). Mobiles and the Norwegian teen: identity, gender and class. In J. E. Katz and M. Aakhus (Eds.), *Perpetual Contact*, Cambridge, University Press, pp. 255–273.

Somalvico, M. (2003). Bodies and robots. In L. Fortunati, J. E. Katz and R. Riccini (Eds.), *Mediating the Human Body: Technology, Communication, and Fashion*, Mahwah, NJ, Lawrence Erlbaum Associates, pp. 31–38.

Sung, D.-K. (2005). Mobile internet and changing communication means: a Korean case. In S. D. Kim (Ed.), *When Mobile Came: The Cultural and Social Impact of Mobile Communication*, Seoul, Korea, Communication Books, pp. 288–298.

Täube, V. G. (2004). Connected and disconnected? On the impact of internet use on social connectedness. *Computational & Mathematical Organization Theory* 10, 227–241.

Thrift, N. (1996). *Spatial Formations*. London, Sage.

Townsend, A. M. (2002). Mobile communications in the twenty-first century city. In B. Brown, N. Green and R. Harper (Eds.), *Wireless World: Social and Interactional Aspects of the Mobile Age*, London, Springer-Verlag, pp. 62–77.

Urry, J. (2000). *Sociology Beyond Societies: Mobilities for the Twenty-First Century*. London, Routledge.

Urry, J. (2002). Mobility and proximity. *Sociology* 36, 255–274.

Urry, J. (2003). Social networks, travel and talk. *British Journal of Sociology* 54, 155–175.

Urry, J. (2004). Connections. *Environment and Planning D* 22, 27–37.

Vilhelmson, B. and E. Thulin (2001). Is regular work at fixed places fading away? The development of ICT-based and travel-based modes of work in Sweden. *Environment and Planning A* 33, 1015–1029.

Wei, R. and V.-H. Lo (2006). Staying connected while on the move: cell phone use and social connectedness. *New Media & Society* 8, 53–72.

Weilenmann, A. (2003). "I can't talk now, I'm in a fitting room": formulating availability and location in mobile-phone conversations. *Environment and Planning A* 35, 1589–1605.

Wellman, B. (1996). Are personal communities local? A Dumptarian reconsideration. *Social Networks* 18, 347–354.

Wellman, B. (2001). Physical place and cyberplace: the rise of personalized networking. *International Journal of Urban and Regional Research* 25, 227–252.

Wellman, B. and S. D. Berkowitz (1988). Introduction: studying social structures. In B. Wellman and S. D. Berkowitz (Eds.), *Social Structures: A Network Approach*, Cambridge, Cambridge University Press, pp. 1–14.

Wittel, A. (2001). Toward a network sociality. *Theory, Culture and Society* 18, 51–76.

The Expanding Sphere of Travel Behaviour Research
Selected Papers from the 11th International Conference on Travel Behaviour Research

4

Connected Anytime: Telecommunications and Activity–Travel Behavior from an Asian Perspective

Nobuaki Ohmori

Abstract

Over the past decade, the prevalence of information and communications technology (ICT), such as the Internet and mobile phones, has dramatically changed our daily lives and activity–travel patterns. Virtual mobility and accessibility in cyberspace enable people to engage in a variety of activities at anytime and in any location. This chapter introduces the current trends of ICT use and social interaction in Japan and other Asian countries, and briefly reviews the progress of research on telecommunications and travel in Japan. It also discusses some future research topics regarding travel behavior.

Introduction

Over the past decade, the rapid development and diffusion of information and communications technology (ICT), exemplified by mobile phones and the Internet, has provided people with a variety of activity opportunities for communications in cyberspace. The penetration of ICT into daily life can be considered as one of the greatest changes in lifestyle since motorization. The use of ICT has affected individual activity–travel behavior and facilitated dramatic changes in our lifestyles and activity–travel patterns. In particular, mobile communications that are not tied to a specific place or time have made personal decisions about activity scheduling more flexible.

Interactions between telecommunications and travel are varied, and can be classified into four types: substitution, complementarity, modification, and neutrality (Salomon, 1985, 1986). By reviewing roughly 100 studies related to the impacts of ICT on personal activities and on travel, Andreev et al. (2006) found substitution to be the most prevailing ICT factor in telecommuting, while complementarity is a major ICT factor in teleshopping and teleleisure. Although many new concepts have been proposed to better understand human activity–travel behavior in the information age, the most important could be "virtual mobility" and "virtual accessibility" (Golob, 2001; Kenyon et al., 2002). As Golob (2001) suggested, the three space–time constraints proposed by Hägerstrand (1970), the capability constraint, the coupling constraint, and the authority constraint, can be adapted to the modern world of ICT. Automobiles have enhanced physical accessibility, whereas ICT has enhanced virtual accessibility (physical accessibility has also been improved through intelligent transport system (ITS), global positioning systems (GPS), and other technologies that improve system operation). As travel is considered a demand derived from participating in activities in real space, telecommunications is also considered a demand derived from participating in activities in cyberspace. To better understand human activity–travel behavior in the information age, we have to explicitly consider the relationships between activity, travel, and telecommunications.

Although travel has generally been regarded as a disutility, some researchers argue the positive utility of traveling (Mokhtarian and Salomon, 2001; Redmond and Mokhtarian, 2001). They discuss three elements of travel utility: activities conducted at the destination, activities that can be conducted while traveling, and the activity of traveling itself. Of these, the second element will probably be the most important due to increasing opportunities for conducting activities in cyberspace via ICT while traveling. For example, mobile phones equipped with a variety of functions, miniaturized electronic devices, and portable computers and music players will contribute to providing activity opportunities in real space while traveling (Lyons and Urry, 2005).

The following sections introduce ICT's use in social interaction in Japan and other Asian countries, and briefly review the progress of research on telecommunications and travel in Japan. The next section introduces a short history of mobile communications in Japan, and describes the characteristics of ICT use in Japan and compares them with those of other Asian countries. The section "Progress of Research on Telecommunications and Travel in Japan" reviews the progress of research on telecommunications and travel, and on other related research fields. The last section discusses some future research topics for activity–travel behavior from an Asian perspective.[1]

[1]Research on telecommunications and travel also relates to group behavior. In another workshop in the IATBR-Kyoto conference "Group Behavior," Fujiwara and Zhang (2006) reported research progress of group behavior analysis in Japan.

ICT Use and Social Interaction in Japan and other Asian Countries

Supply of Mobile Communications in Japan

By the end of 2007, the number of Internet users in Japan had reached 88 million and its penetration rate in the general population was 69% (Ministry of Internal Affairs and Communications, Japan, 2008). Other Asian countries with relatively high penetration rates as of 2007 were South Korea (76%), Singapore (68%), Taiwan (64%), and Hong Kong (55%) (see International Telecommunications Union). The number of mobile phone subscriptions in Japan had also reached about 105 million (including 4.8 million personal handy-phone system (PHS) subscriptions) by the end of 2007 (see Telecommunications Carriers Association). The penetration rate in the general population was about 82%. The penetration rates of mobile phones in the other four Asian countries in 2007 were 90% in South Korea, 134% in Singapore, 106% in Taiwan, and 149% in Hong Kong (see International Telecommunications Union). Furthermore, Japan was also the largest provider of Internet connection services via mobile phones. About 83% of the total number of mobile phone subscribers were also mobile Internet subscribers (including *i-mode*, *EZweb*, and *Yahoo! keitai* services), which is fairly high in comparison with other major countries and regions (see Telecommunications Carriers Association). In response to this trend, the Japanese government began promoting "ubiquitous" networks that are characterized by the realization of easy "person-to-person," "person-to-goods," and "goods-to-goods" communications (Ministry of Internal Affairs and Communications, Japan, 2005).

Before moving on, a short history of mobile communications in Japan from pagers to mobile phones and brief introduction of cyberspace social networks is necessary. Modes and services for mobile communications have changed drastically over the past decade. Pager services originally started in 1968, but spread in the second half of the 1980s. When a person called the number of a pager, the pager vibrated or rung to inform the user of a call. Using a pager, one could also receive a series of numbers from a telephone. This style spread wildly in the mid-1990s, especially among high-school girls. They sent communications as a series of numbers like a coded message. For example, "0906," which is pronounced "okureru" in Japanese, meant "I will be late," and "14106," which is pronounced "aishiteru," meant "I love you." A pager which could receive messages in Japanese characters was also developed. In 1996, the number of pager subscriptions peaked at about 10 million. On the other hand, cellular phone service started in 1987 and rapidly spread thereafter. PHS service, starting in 1995, was regarded as a low-cost mobile phone system and spread especially among young people. PHS service also spread in other Asian countries, such as China, Taiwan, Thailand, and Vietnam. Today, 95% of mobile phone users in Japan use cellular phones (popularly called *keitai*).

Functions other than voice calls and e-mails have been added to mobile phones over the years, such as cameras, software applications (e.g., games), two-dimensional bar-code readers, video players, music players, video phones, GPS, navigation tools, PC website viewers, TV receivers, electronic wallets, and FM radio receivers. Recently, digital font styles, such as *emoji*, that represent a variety of emotions using facial symbols and *gyarumoji* that rely on unconventional combinations of existing characters and symbols can be sent by mobile e-mail. They are popularly used among young girls, in particular *kogyaru* (street-savvy high-school girls). In this way, teenagers have created new trends and cultures out of the use of mobile phones (Ito et al., 2006).

The mobile number portability (MNP) system was introduced in October 2006 in Japan. Mobile phone users can continue to use the same phone number even if they change mobile phone carriers. This system was designed to stimulate more competition among the various mobile phone carriers. Since the new carrier *EMOBILE* started mobile communication service in March 2007, a total of four carriers, *NTT DoCoMo*, *KDDI*, *SOFTBANK MOBILE*, and *EMOBILE*, have begun providing cellular phone service, and only one carrier, *WILLCOM*, provides PHS voice service in Japan.

Recently, social networks created through bulletin board systems (BBS), Weblogs (Blog), and social networking services (SNS) have come to play an important role in communicating in cyberspace. The most famous BBS in Japan is *2 channel*. Over the past several years, Blogs and SNSs have spread rapidly in Japan. Blogs are regarded as private diaries open to the public, whereas participating in some SNS groups requires an invitation from a current member of the group. The number of Blog and SNS users has grown rapidly. For example, between September 2005 and March 2006, the numbers of Blog users (53 service providers) and SNS users (21 service providers) increased from 4.73 million to 8.68 million and from 3.99 million to 7.16 million, respectively (Ministry of Internal Affairs and Communications, Japan, 2006). *Mixi* is the most popular SNS among a total of more than 200 SNS services in Japan and the number of users had reached 16 million by the end of 2008 (see Mixi). Accessing SNS using mobile phones has become a growing trend.

Characteristics of ICT Use in Japan

This section briefly introduces some important characteristics of ICT use in Japan. The first aspect of which is Japanese characters. In countries where people use only one type of character, such as in Europe, it is relatively easy to write sentences on mobile phones. However, in countries such as Japan where people use more than one type of character, they have to change character sets. Basically, in Japanese, when inputting words and sentences on mobile phones for writing e-mails, one first inputs *hiragana* characters and if necessary converts the *hiragana* into *katakana* or *kanji* characters by pushing a conversion button several times. Mobile phones in Japan have a function that allows them to learn words that are used frequently by the individual user to facilitate writing. When a character is input, candidates for words appear based on this function and one of them can be selected, saving time. For Korean mobile phones, people input a character by combining two or three parts of a character using vowels and consonants. In this way, different original input methods are developed and used in Asian countries. This difference in input styles might affect the required time and effort needed to input the same amount of information. In other words, it might affect the level of "virtual mobility" and "virtual accessibility."

The use of mobile phone outside of "digital boxes" is restricted by space–time and authority constraints (Dijst, 2004). Using mobile phones (both for voice and e-mail) while driving vehicles and motorcycles has been prohibited by Japanese law since November 2004 (hands-free calling is not prohibited). Prior to the law's enactment, though, an observation survey reported that about 5% of drivers were using mobile phones while driving (Yamada et al., 2004). Talking on mobile phones inside public transport vehicles is basically prohibited by public transport companies. Other institutional constraints also restrict the use of mobile phones, for example, using mobile phones is forbidden in hospitals, airplanes, and priority zones inside train cars. However, compared with other countries, more people in Japan seem to engage in activities using some function or other on their mobile phones while traveling. This is evidenced by a marketing company's survey for *NTT DoCoMo* mobile phone users in October 2005 which asked what activities they performed while traveling by train (see IT media news). The survey showed that many activities were conducted in the train, such as sleeping (66.2%), surfing *i-mode* sites (59.5%), viewing advertisements (58.4%), and e-mailing by mobile phones (51.9%) for males, and sleeping (71.3%), e-mailing by mobile phones (70.3%), talking with companions (67.2%), viewing advertisements (64.2%), and surfing *i-mode* sites (58.1%) for females. In addition to using mobile phones inside the train, people also use them while waiting for the train at train stations and buses at bus stops. It has also been found that the dominant purpose of telecommunications by mobile phones is "making appointments and communications for meeting people" (Institute of Socio-Information and Communication Studies, The University of Tokyo, 2001); methods for making appointments and waiting behavior have also dramatically changed (Ohmori et al., 2006a).

Another major characteristic in Japan is the prevalence of mobile phones equipped with GPS. Positioning technologies installed in mobile phones are used for convenience and safety and security matters. For convenience matters, mobile phones with GPS can provide the user with information on their current location, multimodal route navigation, and information on shops and restaurants around their current location. For safety and security matters, mobile phones with GPS provide specific persons with the current location of the user, which prevents children from being victims of crime and helps locating elderly people suffering from dementia. From April 2007, all 3G mobile phone devices shall be equipped with GPS as a regulation of the Ministry of Internal Affairs and Communications, Japan. In addition, GPS mobile phones with specific application software can also be used for activity–travel diary surveys (Itsubo and Hato, 2006; Ohmori et al., 2006b).

Comparisons with Other Asian Countries

This section discusses past research on telecommunications that compare Japan and other Asian countries. Yoshii (2005), for example, compared the use of mobile phones and their social impacts on Japan, South Korea, and Taiwan. In Japan, mobile phones are often used for communications with close friends. In particular, mobile e-mails are used more frequently than voice calls. One reason for this trend is that Japanese people tend to consider their partners' current situation and refrain from interrupting their activities even if they are very close friends, a characteristic of the Japanese culture. On the other hand, in South Korea, voice calls are the dominant use of mobile phones among members of a family group or among close friends, called *oori* (sometimes translated into *we-ness*) (Kim, 2006). In the South Korean culture, reserve among these groups is not expected regardless of the circumstances. This promotes voice calls rather than e-mails. There is also a difference in using mobile phones in public spaces. Japanese people care about the opinions of the public very much. However, South Korean people take little account of relative strangers called *nam*. Moreover, South Korean people consider that replying to e-mails as soon as possible is proper when receiving e-mails from their friends. In Taiwan, however, mobile e-mails and mobile Internet are rarely used. One reason is that the number of characters used in daily communication is very large, making inputting sentences cumbersome. Another reason is that frequent voice calls are allowed in the Taiwanese culture. Compared with Japan, voice communications by mobile phones among family members are frequently conducted because the family has a more important position in society. In short, the use of mobile phones in various Asian countries reflects the cultural characteristics of that society; the use of mobile phones might strengthen the connection and relationships between daily and close friends in Japan, members of *oori* in Korea, and family members in Taiwan.

Oya and Kondo (2005) compared the use of mobile phones among Japanese and Chinese university students. In China, mobile phones are very expensive commodities. The price of mobile phones can be as much as the starting monthly salary that Chinese people graduating from universities draw. In China, people can use only short message services (SMS) between mobile phones (no e-mails to any e-mail addresses) and SMS is used more frequently than voice calls. However, the frequency of sending SMS in China is less than that of mobile e-mails sent in Japan. The main purposes of using SMS are for chatting with friends and making appointments to get together, which is similar to Japan. The main purposes of voice calls in China are for urgent business and making appointments to get together, which is also similar to Japan. SMS and voice calls are used differently, however, depending on the purpose of the communication.

People can also use graphical characters in SMS in China and often use abbreviated sentences to reduce the number of characters to be input, for example, "U (you)," "IC (I see)," and "39 (thank you)."

Progress of Research on Telecommunications and Travel in Japan

Transportation and Travel Behavior Research

The Eastern Asia Society for Transportation Studies (EASTS) is an academic institute from Asia established in 1994. It holds a conference every two years and many researchers from Asian countries participate to make presentations and exchange information. In Japan, there are academic institutes associated with transportation planning and travel behavior research, such as the Infrastructure Planning Committee of the Japan Society of Civil Engineers (JSCE), the Japan Society of Traffic Engineers (JSTE), the City Planning Institute of Japan (CPIJ), and the International Association of Traffic and Safety Sciences (IATSS). This section briefly introduces the progress of research on telecommunications and travel in Japan made by some of these institutes.

In Japan, interactions between telecommunications and travel have been discussed for more than 20 years. The IATSS 633 Project Team (1982) investigated the possibility of the substitution effect of telecommunications on travel for solving transportation-related problems, one of the earliest research projects in Japan on this subject. The project conducted a questionnaire survey of office workers in Tokyo and collected information on attitudes toward teleworking and the impacts of telecommunications on travel. Most of the respondents considered that it would be unlikely that telecommunications could substitute for travel. However, if telecommunications could substitute for travel, they felt the effects of substitution would lead to an increase in work efficiency, energy savings, traffic mitigation, and an increase in time for discretionary activities. The project suggested that analysis of both individual behaviors and attitudes as well as of macro-scale data on travel and telecommunications would be necessary in order to reveal the impacts of telecommunications on travel.

Telecommuting and teleworking, which can substitute for commuting, have been expected to solve various urban problems. In the 1980s, thc Japanese government actively promoted teleworking. However, after the collapse of the "bubble economy," teleworking was mostly abandoned, although about 10% of workers could be considered teleworkers (more than 8 hours per week) in 2005 (Ministry of Land, Infrastructure and Transport, 2006). Research on the impacts of telecommuting and teleworking on workers and urban systems is prevalent. For example, Mitomo and Jitsuzumi (1999) investigated the impacts of telecommuting on mass transit congestion in Tokyo. They estimated that about 9–14 million employees would telecommute by

2010, which would result in a 6.9–10.9% reduction in mass transit congestion in Tokyo. Associated cost savings were estimated to be equivalent to between 7.9 and 26.4% of annual spending on public transportation. Sato and Ota (2000) showed that the prevalence of telecommuting could promote suburbanization and mitigate congestion in central city areas from an analysis using urban economic models. On the other hand, since Japan has been facing a rapidly aging society (19.5% of the population was 65 years and over in the 2005 census and the ratio is estimated to reach 40.5% by 2055 (see National Institute of Population and Social Security Research)), maintaining the work force is an important policy issue. From this point of view, teleworking, which would mitigate long commutes, could provide the elderly and handicapped persons with more opportunities for work. Kanbara and Mihoshi (1999) examined the possibility of handicapped persons' teleworking. They pointed out that some of the problems when handicapped persons engage in teleworking might be the speed of completing tasks, communication problems, and the level of completeness of the task. In 1999, an academic institute of the Japan Telework Society (J@TS) was established and has promoted research on teleworking.

As the Internet and e-mails gradually spread among office workers, the possibility of substitution by these new media for travel became a research interest in Japan as well. The communications media choice of office workers has been researched using data on individual behavior. Takita et al. (1995) developed logit models for office workers' communication media choice behavior: face-to-face contacts, telephone, facsimile, and TV conference systems. The explanatory variables of the models that were introduced were: access time and cost, and attitudes toward communication media such as reliability, the volume of information, secrecy, and the ease of use of the media. They found that the types of information to convey, such as the purpose of the contact, the volume of the information, and the number of persons to communicate with, affected the choice of communications media. Doi et al. (1998) conducted a diary survey of business communications of office workers in Tokyo and found that the time required for meeting and travel affected the behavior of choosing between face-to-face contacts and telecommunications. They also found that face-to-face contacts were substituted by facsimile and complemented by (mobile) telephone. Baba (1998) conducted a questionnaire survey on business communications and revealed the existence of substitution effects among different telecommunications devices. He found that e-mails often substituted for telephones and facsimile, but rarely substituted for postal mail and home delivery services. He also concluded that e-mails substituted more for intra-office business communications than business communications with persons outside the office. In another study, Baba (2000) investigated relationships between face-to-face contacts and prior related communications. He found that e-mails were mostly used for arranging meetings and sending related materials in advance of face-to-face meetings. According to his analysis, in order to substitute for face-to-face meetings using an electric meeting system (EMS), it is important not only to improve the user-friendliness of the environment, but also to educate office workers of its advantages.

As for a similar analysis at the national level, Tsukai and Okumura (1999) investigated relationships of inter-regional business trips and telephone call flows by developing gravity models. They found that the volume of employment in a region, geographical distance, travel cost, and telecommunications cost between two regions affected the frequency/time of telephone calls, and the number of business trips between two regions. They concluded that a reduction in telephone costs could increase the frequency/time of telephone calls but decrease the number of trips, whereas a reduction in travel cost could increase both the number of trips and the frequency/time of telephone calls. Taniguchi et al. (2000) investigated how the distribution patterns of urban activities have changed to evaluate regional equalization brought on by the improvement in the transportation and communication systems infrastructures. They found that the distribution pattern of manufacturing industries has balanced out, whereas that of service industries has grown unbalanced and the concentration rate of specific service industries in the Tokyo region has become very high.

The impacts of the Internet and mobile phones on daily life are also reflected in consumer behavior. However, research on the effects of ICT on consumer behavior and shopping travel does not seem to have made much progress in the transportation field in Japan. Taniguchi et al. (2003) observed individual shopping behavior both in real space and in cyberspace. They developed gravity models for shopping destination choice in real and cyberspace that revealed that even in cyberspace there was resistance stemming from physical distances between geographical locations. Analysis of preferences toward shopping in real and cyberspace revealed both substitution and complementarity effects. Oya (2003) explored trade-offs in consumption between telecommunications and other commodities, and found that some people tended to spend more money for mobile communications and less money for other commodities after starting to use mobile phones. Oya (2004, 2006) recognized that consumer behavior for amusement, recreation, and entertainment during both the daytime and night time has changed. He suggests that rapid increase in sexual service delivery has been promoted by mobile phones and the Internet. He and I organized a session called "City Planning for Night Time" at the Conference on Infrastructure Planning and discussed the impacts of telecommunications on personal activity–travel behavior at night time.

Especially over the past five years, some researchers have been deeply interested in the impact of the Internet and mobile phones on travel behavior from an activity-based approach (e.g., Ohmori et al., 2001; Ohmori, 2003; Nishii et al., 2003, 2004, 2005; Senbil and Kitamura, 2003a, b, c). Research has investigated the effects of the use of telecommunications on activity scheduling and travel behavior using information obtained through activity and telecommunications diary surveys. Nishii et al. (2004) analyzed the effects of telecommunications on joint activities among household members. They found that the frequency of telecommunications between household members decreased as the life cycle stage of the household progressed, whereas there was not a clear relationship between the number of joint activities and the life cycle stage. Sasaki et al. (2003) proposed data mining methods for analyzing complicated relationships between activities, travel, and telecommunications. Niwa and Ohmori (2003, 2006) observed young couples' communication behavior to investigate differences between face-to-face and telecommunications-based interactions. The study in Tokyo shows variability in activity duration and locations for face-to-face meetings, variations in the frequency of telecommunications with the partner, and differences among couples with different living styles: living together, alone, or with family members. As described in the previous section, Ohmori et al. (2006a) investigated the meeting appointment and waiting behavior of young people making mobile communications in Tokyo. It was found that about half of the first persons to arrive at the meeting point participated in some activity at other opportunities around the meeting place, not necessarily at the pre-decided meeting location itself. The waiting activity choice behavior of the first person to arrive was affected by the frequency of his or her visits to the town, by considering the possible opportunities around the meeting place, and by the length of the expected waiting time and additional expected waiting time.

New concepts and frameworks to better understand relationships between activity, travel, and telecommunications have also been proposed. Kondo (2003) has proposed a concept of dynamics between the three "tsu"; "kou-tsu," which means "travel" and "transportation," "ryu-tsu," which means "distribution," and "tsu-shin," which means "telecommunications." He suggests that automobile and public transport have changed from "travel modes" into "travel spaces" where various activities can be conducted. This shift has created the "mobile market." Nishii (2006a, b) has proposed a new framework of "transportation and communications systems analysis" that extends Manheim's (1979) "transportation systems analysis" by introducing ICT systems to the activity system and the transportation system. He also argues for the importance of an interdisciplinary approach using time geography, marketing science, and urban sociology to better understand the impacts of telecommunications on our lifestyles.

Other Important Progress

Two large-scale national time use surveys have been conducted in Japan. Every five years, beginning in 1960, the NHK Broadcasting Culture Research Institute has conducted a national time use survey where the number of samples ranges from 10,000 to 100,000 individuals all over Japan (see NHK Broadcasting Culture Research Institute, 1996, 2002). The 2000 survey included "using the Internet" and "e-mailing" as new activity categories for the first time. Since 1976, the Survey on Time Use and Leisure Activities has been conducted on more than 200,000 individuals every five years by the Statistics Bureau in the Ministry of Internal Affairs and Communications (see Statistics Bureau in Ministry of Internal Affairs and Communications). In the 2001 survey, "using the Internet" and "e-mailing" were explicitly added as survey categories. The time series data obtained by these surveys are very useful in understanding the impacts of ICT on our daily time use.

In the field of sociology, social impacts of ICT are a major research concern. The Institute of Socio-Information and Communication Studies, The University of Tokyo (2001) has conducted diary-type surveys on information use on more than 2,000 individuals in Japan. The research group conducted the surveys in 1995, 2000, and 2005. Their work published in 2001 contains information on the use of ICT, comparisons between 1995 and 2000 data, and specific topics such as the digital divide, information literacy, multitasking, and communication habits. In the work, Hashimoto (2001) discusses the digital divide. He argues that activity opportunities provided by the Internet help the elderly, handicapped persons, people living in suburban areas, and child-rearing women. However, these groups use the Internet less than other groups. In this way, the digital divide enhances inequality and social exclusion problems. Suzuki (2001) argued the difficulty of measuring information literacy and discussed the gap in information literacy. From an international perspective, he found that similar trends existed in Japan, the US, and Italy, such as that male and younger people had higher literacy and educational backgrounds which affected their information literacy level. Nakamura (2001) investigated mobile e-mail communications and discussed that a "full-time intimate community" was strengthened more by mobile e-mails rather than by mobile voice-calls. Their research interests are mainly in the social impacts and psychological aspects of these changes, but they do not seem to explicitly consider concrete geographical locations, such as real urban space, wherein the activities and communications take place. However, their research gives transportation researchers fruitful information for better understanding human communications behavior.

Another group that is interested in this subject is the Advanced Institute of Wearable Environmental Information Networks (WIN) established in 2000, which has promoted research on "wearable computers." One of their projects is the development of services for "wearable information networks" to wirelessly monitor plants, animals, humans, and objects on which the miniaturized terminals are attached. Through the fusion of micro-machines, micro-sensors, and network technologies, they aim to positively contribute to the development of human health and wealth, as well as the preservation of the natural environment. The wearable computers can provide people with more activity opportunities at any given time and any given place. This approach presents the possibility to change our lifestyles even more dramatically.

Discussion on Future Research

Lastly, I would like to discuss some research topics regarding the impacts of telecommunications on activity–travel behavior from the Asian perspective. As described in the previous section, the disutility of traveling could be reduced by the increasing of activity opportunities through ICT use while traveling (Lyons and Urry, 2005; Lyons et al., 2007). Activity alternatives while traveling, however, depend on different travel modes. In this way, there is the possibility that public transport may become more attractive than driving a car because travelers can engage in activities more comfortably during both in-vehicle time and during waiting and transferring time. A recent trend, seen especially in Tokyo, is that more people are preferring to live in the downtown areas near their working places. On the other hand, some people live far from their working places and enjoy long commute times by high-quality trains, in which they can engage in a variety of activities while traveling. In this way, understanding the relationship between activity opportunities while traveling and individual decisions about travel behavior, daily activity scheduling, and residential/job location choice is necessary. To accomplish this, activity diary surveys which include activities while traveling might be useful. There is also the possibility of directly observing activities while traveling by train or bus (Ohmori and Harata, 2008).

Furthermore, it is important to explicitly consider the "digital divide." As described in the previous section, people with lower physical mobility tend to have lower virtual mobility because most of them are elderly and are without access to a car or living in suburban areas where the level of service for both public transport and telecommunications is relatively low. This divide could lead to problems of "social exclusion." Recently, for example, airline tickets booked via the Internet have become cheaper than conventional booking methods, resulting in disadvantages for those people without Internet access. In some cases, people with specific characteristics cannot communicate with each other and cannot join social networks. For example, a blind person cannot communicate with a deaf person without the help of another person who can use sign language. New applications and terminologies for ICT appear frequently. ICT users must understand what the new applications are and how they work. Most of the new words used in ICT come from English and the primary language used for websites throughout the world is English. This could cause lower levels of virtual accessibility to activity opportunities in cyberspace for Asian people. As Kenyon et al. (2002) suggest, virtual mobility should be able to contribute to a solution for social exclusion problems. To realize this solution, though, it is important to provide every person with equal opportunities to participate in activities in both real space and cyberspace.

As described in this report, ICT has had a major impact on the daily lives and activity–travel patterns of everyone, including in Japan, and research on telecommunications and travel has made progress. In the future, ICT will continue to change social interactions and human communication behavior. As a result, human activity–travel behavior will also continue to evolve. In this way, I believe that research on telecommunications and travel is one of the most important and intriguing topics in travel behavior research today. I hope that more transportation researchers become involved in this topic and research on telecommunications and travel continues to make progress.

ACKNOWLEDGMENTS

The author is grateful to the members of the "mobile marketing research group," Prof. Katsunao Kondo, Prof. Ryuichi Kitamura, Prof. Kazuo Nishii, Prof. Zhang Junyi, Prof. Kuniaki Sasaki, Mr. Masaki Oya, and Prof. Noboru Harata, for their valuable comments. I also thank Prof. Yoshiaki Hashimoto and Dr. Kim In Bae for providing me with useful information in the field of sociology and Dr. Sangho Choo for useful points of discussion.

REFERENCES

Andreev, P., I. Salomon and N. Pliskin (2006). Review: the state of tele-activities. Paper presented at the 11th International Conference on Travel Behaviour Research. Kyoto, August.

Baba, K. (1998). An impact of new information infrastructure on office communication behavior. *Infrastructure Planning Review* 15, 121–126 (in Japanese).

Baba, K. (2000). Complementarity and substitutability of information & communication technology on travel-communication behavior: a case study on office meetings concerning process. *Infrastructure Planning Review* 17, 163–168 (in Japanese).

Dijst, M. (2004). ICTs and accessibility: an action space perspective on the impact of new information and communication technologies. In M. Beuthe, V. Himanen and A. Reggiani (Eds.), *Travel Demand and Organization in an Evolving World*, Berlin, Springer, pp. 27–46.

Doi, K., K. Takahashi and S. Morimoto (1998). A study on communication media choice of office workers and inter-media relationship. *Infrastructure Planning Review* 15, 481–487 (in Japanese).

Fujiwara, A. and J. Zhang (2006). Research progress of group behavior analysis in Japan. Paper presented at the 11th International Conference on Travel Behaviour Research. Kyoto, August.

Golob, T. (2001). Travel Behavior.Com: activity approaches to modeling the effects of information technology on personal travel behavior. In D. Hensher (Ed.), *Travel Behaviour Research: The Leading Edge*, Oxford, Pergamon, pp. 145–183.

Hägerstrand, T. (1970). What about people in regional science? *Papers of the Regional Science Association* 24, 7–21.

Hashimoto, Y. (2001). Digital divide in Japan. In Institute of Socio-Information and Communication Studies, The University of Tokyo (Ed.), *Information Behavior 2000 in Japan*. University of Tokyo Press, Tokyo, pp. 173–192 (in Japanese).

IATSS 633 Project Team. (1982). The relationship between substitution and complementary function of traffic and communication. *IATTS Review* 8(3), 36–41 (in Japanese).

Institute of Socio-Information and Communication Studies, The University of Tokyo. (2001). *Information Behavior 2000 in Japan.* Tokyo, University of Tokyo Press (in Japanese).

International Telecommunications Union. Available at: http://www.itu.int/ITU-D/ict/statistics/

IT media news. Available at: http://www.itmedia.co.jp/enterprise/mobile/articles/0511/01/news128.html (in Japanese).

Ito, M., D. Okabe and M. Matsuda (2006). *Personal, Portable, Pedestrian: Mobile Phones in Japanese Life*. Cambridge, MA, MIT Press.

Itsubo, S. and E. Hato (2006). Effectiveness of household travel survey using GPS-equipped cell phones and Web diary: comparative study with paper-based travel survey. *TRB 2006 Annual Meeting*. Washington, DC (CD-ROM).

Kanbara, T. and A. Mihoshi (1999). A study of tele-work on general people and handicapped people: in commute and service environment. *Proceedings of Infrastructure Planning* 22(1), 555–558 (in Japanese).

Kenyon, S., G. Lyons and J. Rafferty (2002). Transport and social exclusion: investigating the possibility of promoting inclusion through virtual mobility. *Journal of Transport Geography* 10(4), 207–219.

Kim, I. B. (2006). The use of mobile phones and its social impact: comparing Japan and Korea. Paper presented at the 33rd Conference on Infrastructure Planning. Sendai, June (in Japanese).

Kondo, K. (2003). Telecommunications, time use and travel: making the connection among the three T's. *Proceedings of Infrastructure Planning* 27 (CD-ROM, in Japanese).

Lyons, G., J. Jain and D. Holley (2007). The use of travel time by rail passengers in Great Britain. *Transportation Research A* 41, 107–120.

Lyons, G. and J. Urry (2005). Travel time use in the information age. *Transportation Research A* 39, 257–276.

Manheim, M. (1979). *Fundamentals of Transportation Systems Analysis*. Cambridge, MA, MIT Press.

Ministry of Internal Affairs and Communications, Japan (2005). Information and communications in Japan: White paper 2005. Available at: http://www.johotsusintokei.soumu.go.jp/whitepaper/whitepaper01.html

Ministry of Internal Affairs and Communications, Japan (2006). The number of registration for blog and SNS in March 2006. Available at: http://www.soumu.-go.jp/s-news/2006/060413_2.html

Ministry of Internal Affairs and Communications, Japan (2008). Information and communications in Japan: White paper 2008. Available at: http://www.johotsusintokei.soumu.go.jp/whitepaper/whitepaper01.html

Ministry of Land, Infrastructure and Transport, Japan (2006). The estimated number of teleworkers in 2005. Available at: http://www.mlit.go.jp/kisha/kisha06/04/040614.html

Mitomo, H. and T. Jitsuzumi (1999). Impact of telecommuting on mass transit congestion: the Tokyo case. *Telecommunications Policy* 23, 741–751.

Mixi, Inc. Available at: http://mixi.co.jp/

Mokhtarian, P. and I. Salomon (2001). How derived is the demand for travel? Some conceptual and measurement considerations. *Transportation Research A* 35, 695–719.

Nakamura, I. (2001). Human relations by mobile e-mails. In Institute of Socio-Information and Communication Studies, The University of Tokyo (Ed.), *Information Behavior 2000 in Japan*. University of Tokyo Press, Tokyo, pp. 285–303 (in Japanese).

National Institute of Population and Social Security Research. Available at: http://www.ipss.go.jp/index-e.html

NHK Broadcasting Culture Research Institute. (1996). *Japanese Time Use 1995*. Tokyo, Japan Broadcast Publishing Co. Ltd. (in Japanese).

NHK Broadcasting Culture Research Institute. (2002). *Japanese Time Use 2000*. Tokyo, Japan Broadcast Publishing Co. Ltd. (in Japanese).

Nishii, K. (2006a). ICT and travel behavior. Paper presented at the 17th Meeting of the Japanese Association of Sociolinguistic Sciences. Tokyo, March (in Japanese).

Nishii, K. (2006b). Mobile communications and activity behavior. Paper presented at the 35th Conference on Infrastructure Planning. Sendai, June (in Japanese).

Nishii, K., K. Sasaki and S. Akasawa (2004). An analysis of relationship between household members' joint-activity patterns and their telecommunication. *Proceedings of Infrastructure Planning* 29 (CD-ROM, in Japanese).

Nishii, K., K. Sasaki, R. Kitamura and K. Kondo (2005). Recent developments in activity diary-based surveys and analysis: some Japanese case studies. In H. Timmermans (Ed.), *Progress in Activity-Based Analysis*, Oxford, Elsevier, pp. 335–354.

Nishii, K., K. Sasaki and M. Yamada (2003). Effect of mobile telecommunication on activity and travel patterns. *Proceedings of Infrastructure Planning* 27 (CD-ROM, in Japanese).

Niwa, Y. and N. Ohmori (2003). Communication of long-distant couples. *Proceedings of Infrastructure Planning* 27 (CD-ROM, in Japanese).

Niwa, Y. and N. Ohmori (2006). Communications behavior of young couples—through four-week activity-telecommunications diary and depth interview surveys. *Papers on City Planning* 41(3) (CD-ROM, in Japanese).

Ohmori, N. (2003). Change of travel behavior after introduction of ICT: Results from focus group interviews. *Proceedings of Infrastructure Planning* 27 (CD-ROM, in Japanese).

Ohmori, N. and N. Harata (2008). How different are activities while commuting by train: a case in Tokyo. *Journal of Economic and Social Geography (TESG)* 99(5), 547–561.

Ohmori, N., N. Harata and K. Ohta (2001). The effects of using telecommunications on individual activity schedule. *Infrastructure Planning Review* 18(4), 587–594 (in Japanese).

Ohmori, N., T. Hirano and N. Harata (2006a). Meeting appointment and waiting behavior using mobile communications. *Transportation Research Record* 1977, 250–257.

Ohmori, N., M. Nakazato, N. Harata, K. Sasaki and K. Nishii (2006b). Activity diary surveys using GPS mobile phones and PDA. *TRB 2006 Annual Meeting*. Washington, DC (CD-ROM).

Oya, M. (2003). Thoughts for the influence of cellular phone on consumer behavior. *Proceedings of Infrastructure Planning* 27 (CD-ROM, in Japanese).

Oya, M. (2004). Thoughts for the influence of cellular phone on popular night entertainment area. *Proceedings of Infrastructure Planning* 29 (CD-ROM, in Japanese).

Oya, M. (2006). Thoughts for the relationship between obscene facilities and popular night entertainment area. *Proceedings of Infrastructure Planning* 33 (CD-ROM, in Japanese).

Oya, M. and K. Kondo (2005). Daily activities and mobile communications of Chinese university students. Paper presented at the 31st Conference on Infrastructure Planning. Hiroshima, 2005.6. (in Japanese).

Redmond, L. and P. Mokhtarian (2001). The positive utility of the commute: modeling ideal commute time and relative desired commute amount. *Transportation* 28, 179–205.

Salomon, I. (1985). Telecommunications and travel: substitution or modified mobility? *Journal of Transport Economics and Policy* 19(3), 219–235.

Salomon, I. (1986). Telecommunications and travel relationships: a review. *Transportation Research A* 20(3), 223–238.

Sasaki, K., K. Nishii and A. Suzuki (2003). Data mining analysis on the relations between telecommunication and activity scheduling. *Proceedings of Infrastructure Planning* 27 (CD-ROM, in Japanese).

Sato, H. and M. Ota (2000). A study on the effect of the spread of telecommuting in the metropolitan area. *Papers on City Planning* 35, 1051–1056 (in Japanese).

Senbil, M. and R. Kitamura (2003a). Scheduling through ICT: what are the travel implications? *Proceedings of Infrastructure Planning* 27 (CD-ROM).

Senbil, M. and R. Kitamura (2003b). The use of telecommunications devices and individual activities relationships. *The 82nd TRB Annual Meeting*. Washington, DC (CD-ROM).

Senbil, M. and R. Kitamura (2003c). Simultaneous relationships between telecommunications and activities. Paper presented at the 10th International Conference on Travel Behaviour Research. Lucerne, August.

Statistics Bureau, Ministry of Internal Affairs and Communications, Japan. Available at: http://www.stat.go.jp/index.htm

Suzuki, H. (2001). Information literacy. In Institute of Socio-Information and Communication Studies, The University of Tokyo (Ed.), *Information Behavior 2000 in Japan*. University of Tokyo Press, Tokyo, pp. 193–200 (in Japanese).

Takita, T., A. Yuzawa and H. Suda (1995). Communication media choice model considering substitution between new telecommunication media and transportation. *Infrastructure Planning Review* 12, 93–98 (in Japanese).

Taniguchi, M., H. Abe and A. Hasumi (2003). The cyber-walk: its space resistance and the potentiality to supplant the town-walk. *Infrastructure Planning Review* 20(3), 477–484 (in Japanese).

Taniguchi, M., S. Takeshima and H. Abe (2000). How regional equalization policy based on transportation and communication infrastructure improvement changed the distribution pattern of urban activities? *Infrastructure Planning Review* 17, 211–218 (in Japanese).

Telecommunications Carriers Association (TCA). Available at: http://www.tca.or.jp/english/database/.

Tsukai, M. and M. Okumura (1999). Gravity models of business trips and telephone calls considering substitutability and complementarity. *Papers on City Planning* 34, 85–90. (in Japanese)

Yamada, K., Y. Fukuoka, S. Ueno and T. Mitani (2004). Investigation about use of a mobile phone in driving. *Koutsukagaku* 35(1), 39–44 (in Japanese).

Yoshii, H. (2005). *International Comparison of the Use of Mobile Phones and the Impacts* (in Japanese).

2.2 Behavioral Modification

The Expanding Sphere of Travel Behaviour Research
Selected Papers from the 11th International Conference on Travel Behaviour Research

5

Travel Behavior Modification: Theories, Methods, and Programs

Tommy Gärling and Satoshi Fujii

Abstract

Various policy measures that aim at reducing the levels of car-use related congestion, noise, and air pollution have been proposed and implemented. Some of these, referred to as either mobility management or travel demand management measures, target changing or reducing demand for private car use. A distinction relevant to the chapter is that between measures that aim at changing available travel options (e.g., road or congestion pricing that increases monetary costs and decreases congestion) and those aimed at changing car users (e.g., information and education measures) without any changes in travel options. The chapter focuses on the latter highlighting underlying behavioral constructs and theories as well as their potential and actual implementation in travel behavior modification programs. It is concluded that informational and educational measures (travel feedback programs) may have large impacts on travel behavior but that evaluations are needed to disentangle the most cost-effective techniques, procedures, and target groups. Methods for such evaluations are discussed.

Introduction

The urgent economic, social, and environmental problems being experienced worldwide due to increasing trends in car ownership and use have been frequently noted and documented (e.g., Black, 2001; Crawford, 2000; Goodwin, 1996; Hine and Grieco, 2003; Whitelegg, 2003). Various policy measures that aim at reducing the levels of car-use related congestion, noise, and air pollution have been proposed and implemented. Some of these policy measures focus on changing or reducing demand for private car use. They are generally referred to as either *mobility management* or *travel demand management* (TDM) measures (Kitamura et al., 1997; Pas, 1995).

Table 1 presents a list of major TDM measures that are considered to be or are being implemented in many urban areas around the world. Several distinctions can be made based on classifications that have been proposed (Steg, 2003; see Loukopoulos, 2007, for another overview). One distinction is between pull measures that make alternative modes relatively more attractive and push measures that make a chosen mode relatively less attractive or even prohibited. Another distinction important for this chapter is that between measures that aim at changing available travel options (e.g., road or congestion pricing that increases monetary costs and decreases congestion) and those aimed at changing car users (e.g., informational and educational measures) without any changes in travel options. The goal is in both cases *a change in travel behavior*, for instance, a reduction of car use, totally or limited to peak hours, or a switch to other modes such as mass transit, biking, or walking.

A chapter in the published edited volume from the previous IATBR conference (Jones and Sloman, 2006) thoroughly reviewed implementation of marketing and management methods to change travel behavior, with many application examples, mainly from the UK. In contrast, the present chapter highlights underlying behavioral constructs and theories, drawing widely on psychological research, as well as their potential and

Table 1
Travel Demand Management Measures

TDM measure	Examples
Physical change measures	Improving public transport
	Improving infrastructure for walking and cycling
	Park and ride schemes
	Land use planning to encourage shorter travel times
	Technical changes to make cars more energy-efficient
Legal policies	Prohibiting car traffic in city centers
	Parking control
	Decreasing speed limits
Economic policies	Taxation of cars and fuel
	Road or congestion pricing
	Kilometer charging
	Decreasing costs for public transport
Information and education measures	Individualized marketing
	Public information campaigns
	Giving feedback about consequences of behavior
	Social modeling

actual implementation in travel behavior modification programs. In the next section, we introduce some basic conceptual issues. This is followed by a presentation of several theoretical perspectives and how these address the different conceptual issues. A following section describes and discusses in more depth the four classes of travel behavior modification (TDM measures) listed in Table 1. A section is then devoted to a discussion of methods for evaluation. The last section before the concluding section provides an overview of existing programs of travel behavior modification.

Conceptual Issues

It may seem self-evident that the target of a car-use change policy measure should be a change in *actual car use* such as the number of car trips or distance traveled per person, or more specific targets involving also other travel choices than mode choice, for instance, a change in car use depending on type of road, area, or time of day. Although observable changes in travel behavior or choice obviously is an ultimate criterion in most applications, an effective method is frequently to change beliefs, attitudes, and values.[1] The reason is that unless forced by social, monetary, or physical means, a change in travel behavior is determined by a change in beliefs, attitudes, and/or values (Fishbein and Ajzen, 1975). A caveat is that the correspondence to behavior is not perfect. An in-depth analysis of this issue is found in Eagly and Chaiken (1993). Fujii and Gärling (2003) and Gärling et al. (1998) applied this analysis to travel behavior.

If actual travel behavior to some extent depends on beliefs, attitudes, and values, it is obviously important to also target changes in these respects. Some would argue (e.g., Golob, 2001) that a forced change of travel behavior causes a change in beliefs, attitudes, and/or values. This is only likely, however, to be true if the outcome is positive (Fujii and Gärling, 2006); in other cases a forced change has been shown to result in increased resistance (called reactance, see Brehm and Brehm, 1981; cf. also evidence of negative effects of payment or "crowding out," Deci et al., 1999; Frey, 1993).

A change in actual travel behavior depending on, for instance, a monetary payoff is possibly maintained by this payoff. However, as demonstrated by many attempts at changing people's behavior by monetary payoffs (response-contingent reinforcement, see Dwyer et al., 1993, for overview; see Jakobsson et al., 2002, for a recent travel

[1]These concepts will be more precisely defined in the next section. Suffice here to say that both behavior and choice refers to *observable actual behavior* although the latter in contrast to the former implies that a choice is made among available alternatives. Preference or utility is assumed to determine this choice. Attitude and values are concepts similar to preference but is assumed to be more general and enduring dispositions to choose or behave in certain ways. Beliefs are defined as perceived likelihood of properties of objects (e.g., outcomes of choices).

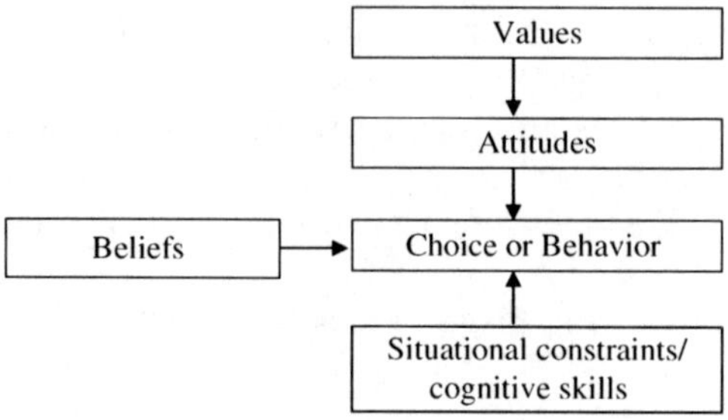

Figure 1
How Behavior or Choice is Related to Beliefs, Attitudes, and Values

behavior example), the behavioral change is often only temporary and does not remain after the monetary payoff is discontinued. Thus, it is implied that some internal changes, in cognitive skills, beliefs, attitudes, or values are necessary for achieving a permanent behavioral change.

Figure 1 illustrates how behavior is assumed to depend on beliefs (perceived likelihood of the behavioral outcome), choice (or preference, see Footnote 1), attitudes, and values. The tenet is that cognitive skills, beliefs, preference or choice, and situational constraints are proximal determinants of mundane routine behavior such as daily travel. However, it is plausible to assume that a permanent behavioral change requiring sacrifices (such as effort invested to acquire cognitive skills needed to overcome situational constraints as well as breaking resistance to changing beliefs) is mediated (motivated) by changes in enduring dispositions such as attitudes that in turn are related to values (defined as higher-order abstract attitudes closely connected to "self-identity"). Examples of relevant values include moral, environment-protective, and pro-societal or collective (see Schwartz, 1992; Stern and Dietz, 1994). Conversely, a change in beliefs, attitudes, and values has some likelihood to result in changes in travel behavior.

Feedback is an important concept that needs to be defined in this context. A distinction can be made between hedonic feedback or incentive and informational feedback. In both cases, the terms positive and negative are used but with different meanings. The effect of a monetary payoff is generally believed to be effective because it increases (or reduces if negative) a person's well-being (hedonic positive or negative feedback). At the same time, if the payoff is predictable, the payoff provides informational feedback that strengthens beliefs about situation-outcome contingencies.

In more recent theoretical analyses of behavior (pioneered by, e.g., Miller et al., 1960; Powers, 1973), informational feedback has been given the most prominent role (e.g., Carver and Scheier, 1998). These analyses replace obsolete approaches grounded in conceptualizations of behavior as largely, or even exclusively, controlled by reinforcement (hedonic feedback) (Dwyer et al., 1993). The tenet is that behavior is goal-directed. A behavioral change is, therefore, mediated by a change in goal (or intention) related to attitudes and values. Negative feedback informs about the discrepancy between the current state (e.g., frequency of car travel) and the change goal (e.g., reduction of car use). Positive feedback informs about the distance from an undesirable goal (e.g., costs exceeding the household budget).

Even though evidence from many areas of human behavior documents the essential role played by nested negative and positive feedback loops in the regulation of human behavior (see Carver and Scheier, 1998, for a review), paradoxically evidence also indicates that feedback frequently has no effect (Brehmer, 1995). Reasons include that the goal and/or the feedback is too vague or that the feedback is delayed, intermittent, or probabilistic. People may also misperceive feedback; a case in point is that feedback is often falsely interpreted to confirm expectations (Klayman and Ha, 1987). Behavior may still be controlled by *feedforward*. Thus, a goal (of changing travel behavior) is likely to be followed by that a plan is formed for how to change behavior (Gollwitzer, 1993; Gollwitzer et al., 1990). This plan (e.g., "never use the car for the work commute") may lead to a change in behavior despite that feedback is lacking.

In applications focusing on methods of modification of travel behavior, the concept of *influence* is clearly in need of some clarification. It seems to be common to equate influence with changes in payoffs. Although this is one type of influence, there are also others, primarily different forms of social influence or persuasion (Eagly and Chaiken, 1993, 1998). Social influence includes pressure from family, peers, or society as well as internalized social norms formed in a society as the outcome of a socialization process. It is important to note that influences may also be indirect resulting in changes (e.g., a worse household economy because of increased spending) that in turn leads to influences on the targeted behavior (i.e., travel behavior).

Humans are distinguished from other species in their outstanding ability to adapt to changing circumstances. *Learning* is a major factor making this possible. Some learning is explicit and effortful, sometimes requiring extended practice. Other learning is implicit, automatic (effortless), and immediate. Learning would result in changes in attitudes after hedonic feedback and, based on informational feedback, in changes in cognitive skills and beliefs. Changes in beliefs would in turn result in attitude changes. These internal changes may or may not result in changes in actual behavior depending on situational factors.

Theoretical Perspectives

In the following we identify a number of *prototypical* theoretical perspectives. Note that any specific theory or model derived to test the theory may in some respects differ from the prototype. Our aim is to disentangle how the theoretical perspectives address the conceptual issues discussed in the last section. From this follows an assessment of when and why a particular theoretical perspective is more valuable than another one.

Choice Theories

Discrete mode choice has for decades been statistically modeled within a micro-economic utility-maximization theoretical framework (random utility or multiattribute utility; see Ben-Akiva and Lerman, 1985; Hensher, 1994; Keeney and Raiffa, 1993; McFadden, 2001). Thus, the likelihood (p) of choosing a specific mode j is

$$p = p(j \in \Omega | X)$$

where Ω is the choice set and X a vector of attributes of alternative modes and characteristics of the decision maker. This formalism has then been extended to other, both discrete and continuous, travel choice such as choices of destination, departure time, and route (e.g., Fujii et al., 1998; Kitamura and Fujii, 1998). Based on the insight that such choices frequently are linked, a target of modeling has also been the nesting relations between different choices, for instance, how car users' choices of departure time depend on choice of route or mode (e.g., Hamed and Mannering, 1993; Yamamoto et al., 2000).

A behavioral change is within this theoretical perspective conceived of as that a change in determinants (e.g., higher cost, shorter travel time) leads to different choices (of, e.g., mode). Thus, if the theory is valid, for a TDM measure that changes travel options, it would be possible to forecast changes in choices.[2] If persons change their attitudes or values leading to differences in choices (e.g., a different weighing of mode attributes), a correct forecast would no longer be possible. Furthermore, the behavioral change is assumed to be instantaneous.

In the activity-based approach (Axhausen and Gärling, 1992; Bhat and Koppelman, 1999; Kitamura, 1988), travel choice is assumed to depend on biological needs, obligations, or desires to engage in various activities at different places. Changes in activity engagement (e.g., a compressed work week) would therefore presumably indirectly change travel behavior.

[2]It is important here to maintain the distinction between choice and behavior, since choice theories are limited to choices among alternatives.

Attitude Theories

Fishbein and Ajzen's (1974, 1975) theory of reasoned action was introduced in travel behavior research not a long time after it was published (e.g., Golob et al., 1979). Although choice theories have tended to dominate the scene in recent years, there are still examples of applications based on this attitude theory or its successor The Theory of Planned Behavior (TPB) (Ajzen, 1991). In TPB, the attitude (A) toward performing a behavior is

$$\mathrm{A} = \Sigma be$$

where e represents salient positive or negative outcomes of the behavior and b their perceived likelihood. Intention (I) to perform the behavior is defined as

$$I = w_{\mathrm{A}}\mathrm{A} + w_{\mathrm{SN}}\mathrm{SN} + w_{\mathrm{PCB}}\mathrm{PCB}$$

where SN is subjective norm (the belief that significant others will or will not approve) and PBC perceived behavioral control (the perceived degree to which situational constraints and available resources facilitate or prevent performance of the behavior). The w_{SN} represents empirically determined weights.

Applications of the TPB have increased in recent years due to a number of behavioral scientists studying how travel behavior can be changed (see Gärling and Steg, 2007). Unfortunately, such applications tend to ignore three problems: (1) TPB may not apply when moral motives are the primary drivers of behavioral change (Stern, 2000); (2) TPB does not go far enough in explaining the reasons for noncorrespondence between attitudes and behavior (Fujii and Gärling, 2003; Gärling et al., 1998); (3) TPB does not satisfactorily model the *process* of behavioral change (Gärling et al., 2002).

Other theories based on Schwartz' (1977) norm-activation theory have been proposed to account for the fact that moral motives drive intentions to engage in sustainable behavior. An example is the value–belief–norm theory proposed by Stern (2000) that has been shown to successfully account for intentions to reduce car use (Bamberg and Schmidt, 2003; Nordlund and Garvill, 2003).

Self-Regulation Theories

Gärling et al. (2002) (see also Gärling, 2005) introduced a new conceptual framework to understand the process of behavioral change. This framework draws on self-regulation theories in social and cognitive psychology (e.g., Carver and Scheier, 1998). In the proposed framework (see Figure 2), setting of goals (Austin and Vancouver, 1996; Locke and Latham, 1990) is posited to be the outcome of a deliberation process. If road pricing is implemented, a set goal may be a certain degree of car-use reduction

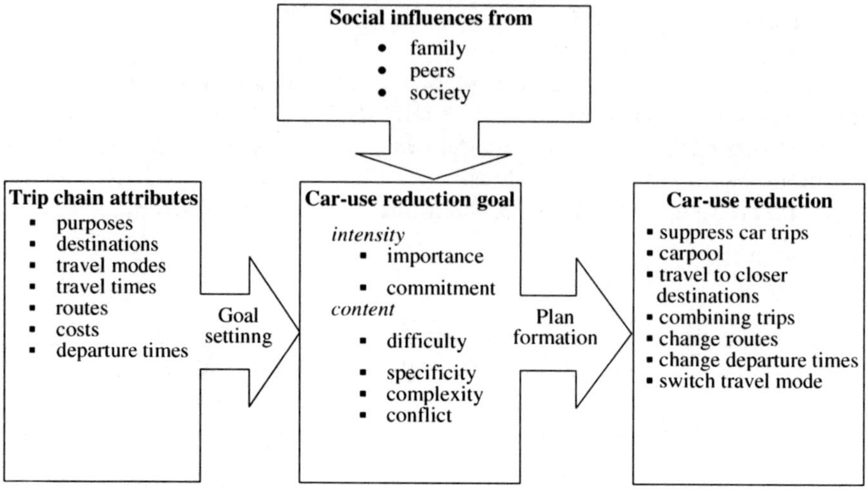

Figure 2
A Conceptualization of Behavioral Change

but it may also be some other change (e.g., minimizing spending on other things). A high degree of commitment and a large specific goal are known to increase the likelihood that the goal is attained. Whether the goal is forced on the car user or self-imposed does not seem to be important however (Locke et al., 1988). Furthermore, as demonstrated by Loukopoulos et al. (2004, 2005, 2006), attainment of car-use change goals is a process entailing choices of adaptation alternatives such as car pooling, trip chaining, trip suppressing, and mode switching on the basis of subjective assessments of psychological costs and effectiveness (degree of goal attainment). Of importance here is that car users (like, people in general) are unwilling to change activities they like and have become used to. A number of well-known phenomena such as status quo or inaction bias (Samuelson and Zeckhausen, 1988) as well as habit formation (Ouellette and Wood, 1998) witness to this. Car users are according to a "minimal cost of change" principle likely to start by making the less costly changes. If these changes are insufficient as determined by negative feedback, more costly changes are chosen. In this process several things may go wrong. First, the more costly changes may be too costly in which case the change goal is abandoned or reduced. Second, feedback about effectiveness is generally delayed and likely to be imprecise. In contrast, cost is directly felt and may, therefore, dominate effectiveness, leading to short-sightedness.

Habit-Formation Theories

In particular implicit learning has been a focus of research on travel habits (Fujii and Gärling, 2006). A repeated choice is referred to as a habit (Ronis et al., 1989).

Recent research suggests that the formation of habits is adaptive in that it prevents overload on information processing (Bargh, 1997). Furthermore, habits are strengthened by positive and weakened by negative hedonic feedback. Thus, habits are also adaptive in that they attain set goals (Verplanken et al., 1997). Habits are assumed to depend on storage in long-term memory of scripts (Abelson, 1981) or ready-made choice rules that can be retrieved, thus choices require minimal search for external information. An illustration (see Gärling, 2004; Gärling et al., 2001) is that distance information is processed less thoroughly after repeated choices of driving a car. Scripts may also represent in memory predetermined sequences of linked choices or travel plans, thus simplifying complex multistage decision making (Arentze and Timmermans, 2003).

Based on habit-formation theories, it follows that changes in travel behavior are not likely to occur unless changes in travel options are very salient and have positive outcomes. Methods making habitual car drivers aware of changes are required (e.g., Fujii and Gärling, 2005; Garvill et al., 2003).

Overview

Table 2 gives an overview of the theoretical perspectives discussed above. For each one a rough categorization has been made with respect to *targeted change*, *type of influence*, *type of regulation*, and what *type of learning* (permanent change) is assumed to occur.

The different theoretical perspectives are to some extent complementary. The choice theories underpinning travel demand modeling may be applied to understand and forecast effects on choice of changes in travel options (time, cost). However, attitude

Table 2
Overview of Theories for Understanding Changes in Travel Behavior

Theoretical perspective	Targeted change	Type of influence	Type of regulation	Type of learning
Choice theories	Choice (optional travel behavior)	Changes in travel options	Hedonic feedback	None
Attitude theories	Beliefs, attitudes, values, intentions, travel behavior	Changes in travel options, social influence	Hedonic feedback, informational feedback	Implicit, explicit
Self-regulation theories	Goal setting, plan formation, travel choice	Changes in travel options, social influence	Feedforward, informational feedback	None
Habit-formation theories	Travel choice, travel behavior	Repeated travel choice or behavior	Hedonic feedback	Implicit

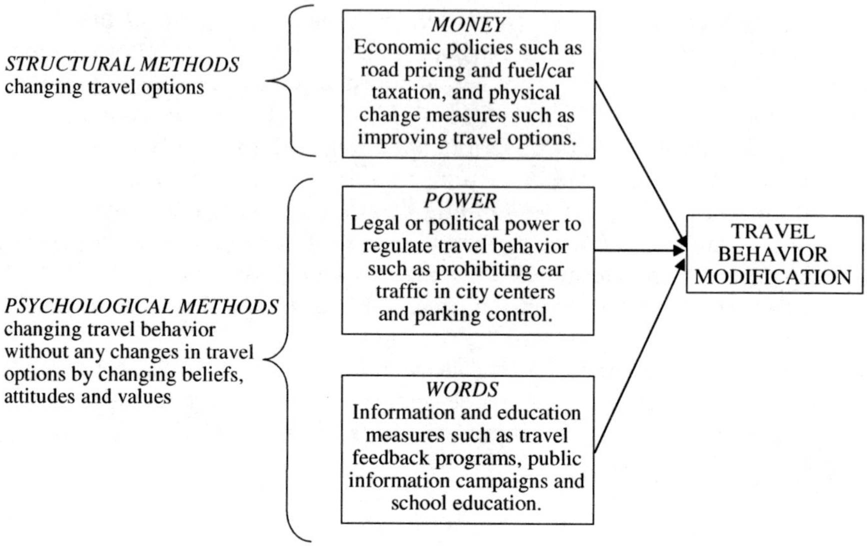

Figure 3
Three Ingredients (Money, Power, and Word) in Structural and Psychological Methods of Travel Behavior Modification

theories may alternatively be used since these are not confined to choice (e.g., a reduction of car use is not necessarily the outcome of a choice among modes unless the definition of choice is stretched). Furthermore, social influence as well as effects of learning (changes in beliefs, attitudes, and values) are accommodated. Self-regulation theories have many elements in common with attitude theories. Still, whereas attitude theories tend to be mute about the implementation of intentions, this phase is specified in self-regulation theories. Neither choice theories nor self-regulation theories address the issue of learning. In both cases it would be possible to augment the theories by drawing on habit formation theories.

In a later section (see Figure 3), we indicate how choice and attitude theories (TPB) can be integrated with self-regulation and habit-formation theories to be useful for understanding changes in travel behavior as a result of individualized communication.

Methods of Travel Behavior Modification

It is common wisdom that essential ingredients in any method of changing behavior are "money," "power," and "words" (see Table 1 and Figure 3). Money refers to economic factors including money as well as goods and services that can be traded for money. Economic policies exemplify the method of money. Physical change measures such as improving travel modes can also be categorized as such since benefits such as reduced travel time are measured in monetary terms. "Power" refers to physical power (barriers) as well as political power (regulation). Legal policies such as prohibiting car traffic in city centers and parking control exemplify the method of power. "Words" refer to various types of communication such as information and education measures.

These three methods can be further categorized according to whether they aim at changing the travel environment that influences travel behavior, thus indirectly changing travel behavior, or directly changing travel behavior without any changes of the travel environment. "Methods of power" (e.g., legal policies) and "methods of money" (e.g., economic policies) can be regarded as changes of the travel environment, "methods of words" as changes of travel behavior by changing beliefs, attitudes, and values or norms without any changes of the travel environment. The former is referred to as "structural methods," while the latter is referred to as "psychological methods." This categorization has been applied to behavior modification methods in previous research (e.g., Dawes, 1980; Messick and Brewer, 1983; Yamagishi, 1986).

Structural Methods

There are two types of structural methods for changing car use to nonautomobile travel modes: pull measures and push measures (Steg, 2003; Vlek and Michon, 1992). Pull measures increase benefits from using other travel modes than the car. Examples include increases of service level of public transport (such as reduction of travel time, increases in the number of seats, or improved air conditioning), rebates on fares for public transport, or construction of new bicycle and pedestrian roads.

It should be noted that pull measures always incur monetary costs which may sometimes go beyond a feasible public budget. Due to such budget constraints, pull measures could not always be implemented even if desirable.

Even if pull measure that might be effective in attracting car users to use nonautomobile travel modes could be implemented, car users would not always become aware of the increases in attractiveness of the nonautomobilized modes. This would in particular occur when car users have developed a strong car-use habit since they would then have no or little motivation to acquire information about nonautomobile modes (Fujii and Gärling, 2006). Therefore, such measures are not alone likely to be effective for travel behavior modification, in particular not when applied to habitual car users.

Push measures imply decreasing benefits associated with car use. Examples are economic policies including road pricing and gasoline taxation, legal policies to regulate car use, and physical measures such as reduction of road capacity. Any car users, including even those with strong car-use habits, will perceive the change since it directly affects their behavior. For this reason push measures may be more effective than pull measure. However, the public attitude toward these measures is generally negative (Jakobsson et al., 2000; Jones, 1991, 1995, 2003). Such a negative public attitude may prevent politicians to endorse push measures (Gärling and Schuitema, 2007).

In sum, structural methods including pull and push measures are expected to be effective in modifying travel behavior. However, it may be difficult to implement pull measures due to budget constraints and push measures due to negative public attitudes. Furthermore, if such measures are implemented, there may be undesirable side effects. Deci et al. (1999) and Frey (1993) make a distinction between intrinsic motivation and extrinsic motivation for behavioral change. Extrinsic motivation is triggered by external incentives or disincentives that would be provided to travelers in structural methods. Intrinsic motivation originates in internal psychological factors such as beliefs, attitudes, values, or norms (e.g., moral obligation). It is hypothesized that intrinsic motivation would be "crowded out" by incentives or disincentives. Based on this hypothesis, people's intrinsic motivation to use socially or environmentally desirable travel modes may be reduced by structural methods. Thus, it is implied that structural methods, even if possible to implement, would not always be cost-effective in modifying travel behavior.

One way to avoid or minimize undesirable side effects is to implement a temporary structural change. Examples include freeway closures, offering free public transport on selected days, distributing free public transport tickets to frequent drivers, or road pricing on a temporary basis. In several studies, it has been found that temporary changes in payoffs and regulations that force car users to use alternative travel modes lead to lasting changes in car use (Fujii et al., 2001; Fujii and Gärling, 2003, 2005; Fujii and Kitamura, 2003). The impacts of temporary changes are particularly strong on habitual car users who have no or little previous experience of using other modes. Thus, temporarily changing payoffs and regulations may break car-use habits by affecting habitual car users' beliefs about and attitudes toward alternative modes. Because the objective of a temporary structural change is changing beliefs and attitudes that would result in lasting travel behavior changes, it is a bridge between structural and psychological methods. The latter is focused in the following.

Psychological Methods

Psychological methods aim at modifying travel behavior through changing psychological factors such as cognitive skills, beliefs, attitudes, and values or norms. Although one way to change psychological factors is to implement temporal structural changes, psychological methods are typically "methods of words," that is communication measures (see Figure 3).

There are two types of communication measures that potentially can lead to travel behavior modification: individualized communication and mass communication. Individualized communication includes personal conversation, workshops, education, and travel feedback programs (TFPs, see Fujii and Taniguchi, 2005) such as individualized marketing (Brög et al., 2003), travel blending (Rose and Ampt, 2001), and personal travel planning (Jones and Sloman, 2006). Unlike mass communication, individualized communication provides car users with information or messages that are customized based on their attitude toward or actual current travel behavior. Car users cannot as easily ignore individualized communication as they can ignore mass communication if the message is well designed to make them feel it is socially desirable and easy to respond. For example, a telephone call from the city government with a request to answer a few simple questions, made at the beginning of a program of individualized communication, would more likely be attended than comparable messages on TV or in newspapers. Thus, individualized communication has the potential of being more effective for travel behavior modification than mass communication.

The main reason why communication would be effective for travel behavior modification is that it directly affects psychological factors that are determinants of the behavior change. This is illustrated in Figure 4 that integrates TPB (Ajzen, 1991), value–belief–norm theory (Stern, 2000), the theory of implementation intention (Gollwitzer, 1993; Gollwitzer et al., 1990) which is part of self-regulation theories

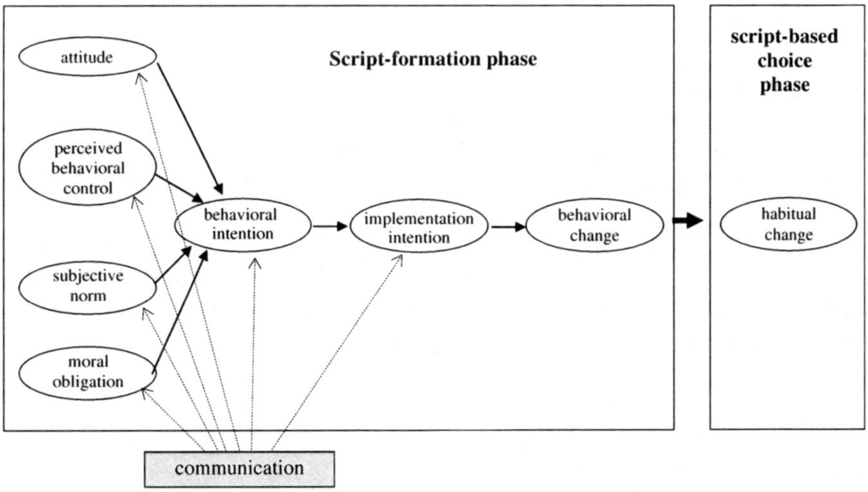

Figure 4

A Process Model of the Effects of Individualized Communication on Travel Behavioral Modification

(Carver and Scheier, 1998), and the process model of acquisition of script-based choice (Gärling et al., 2001). As can be seen, intention ("I will change to bus instead of car") is influenced by attitude toward change ("I like to change to bus instead of car"), perceived control ("I think it is not difficult to change to bus instead of car"), subjective norm ("I think others expect that I will change to bus instead of car"), and moral obligation ("I feel a moral obligation to change to bus instead of car"). These determinants of intention to change would be strongly influenced by individualized communication (see Taniguchi and Fujii, 2004). Attitudes toward behavioral change may become more positive by messages informing about the positive aspects of the behavior modification (such as reducing health hazards and prevalence of accidents). Perceived control may be enhanced by information about how to use alternative travel modes. Subjective norm may be enhanced by providing feedback about others' attitudes toward behavioral change. Norms (i.e., moral obligation) may be indirectly activated by messages informing about negative consequences of car use.

Intention may also be directly strengthened by persuasive messages in order to make car users thoroughly deliberate their travel mode choice. Another way of accomplishing the same thing would be to make car users form an intention to implement choices of alternative travel modes. Implementation intentions are formed through planning how to implement the behavior (Gollwitzer, 1993; Gollwitzer et al., 1990). Individualized advice for how to use alternative modes may therefore be given. Bamberg (2002) and Taniguchi and Fujii (2004) observed positive effects of such advice on changes from habitual car use to other travel modes.

It can be noted that the cost per driver or household of individualized communication is in general higher than the cost of mass communication. Still, the cost for individualized communication is likely to be much less than infrastructure investments in new railway or bicycle road construction (Brög et al., 2003). Furthermore, unlike push measures such as changing payoffs and regulations, policy makers would not meet with public opposition when they implement communication measures.

Education in schools may have stronger impacts than any other type of communication method because youngsters are likely to have a less positive attitude toward car use and have not yet developed a car-use habit. In line with this, Taniguchi and Fujii (2004) found that the impacts of educational programs in elementary schools were larger on the young pupils than impacts of similar programs on adults.

Combination of Methods

An appropriate combination of several types of information may be more influential than a single type of information. This is because travel behavior modification would be achieved through the activation of several psychological variables assumed in

Figure 4 to cause travel behavior change, and different psychological variables would be activated by different types of information. Communication programs for travel behavior modification that includes many types of information have been proposed and implemented. This applies to TFPs such as individualized marketing (Brög et al., 2003), travel blending (Ampt and Rooney, 1999; Rose and Ampt, 2001; Taylor and Ampt, 2003), and personalized travel plans (Department for Transport, UK, 2004a, b).

It would probably be even more effective to include pull measures such as infrastructure investments in alternative, more sustainable travel modes. Such measures are sometimes necessary because the availability of attractive alternatives is essential. On the other hand, as noted, infrastructure investments may not lead to changes in car use, because car users do not perceive the improved alternatives. Therefore, a psychological method making car users aware of the more attractive alternatives should increase effectiveness. As an example, a TFP recently implemented to promote public transport 3 months after building a public transport system resulted in approximately a 50% increase in the number of passengers (Taniguchi and Fujii, 2007). In a similar vein, push measures such as regulation or road pricing may not be sufficient to break car-use habits if these induce "rat running" (Emmerink et al., 1995), that is, drivers continue to use the car during periods or in areas without any regulations or pricing. If communication succeeds in conveying that (possibly) "rat running" is less attractive than the use of some alternative travel mode, car users should be more likely to abandon their car use.

Another type of combination between psychological and structural methods is to incorporate small incentives into a communication program. Although such small incentives would not continuously support a behavior change, they may nevertheless induce car users to change despite that they would otherwise not do. Small incentives may consequently be expected to work as a temporary structural change (Fujii and Gärling, 2005) and thus increase the effectiveness of TFPs (see Brög, 1998; Taniguchi and Fujii, 2007).

Methods of Evaluation

Internal, External, and Construct Validity

A number of concepts have been used to characterize the adequacy of a research design (Campbell and Stanley, 1966; Cook and Campbell, 1979). *Internal validity* refers to the possibility to make valid causal inferences. If a travel behavior modification program is implemented, how should an evaluation be designed to make possible to establish that the program (or components of the program) causes the observed change in travel behavior? A basic requirement of any evaluation is that internal validity is achieved. Some well-known general threats to internal validity include experimenter-expectancy effects, that is, that experimenters unwittingly influence participants. This is augmented by demand characteristics: Participants are generally willing to cooperate with and to gain a positive evaluation from the experimenter. This may in particular be a problem with travel behavior modification programs employing psychological methods since cooperation is a requirement. An unbiased evaluation is, therefore, particularly difficult to achieve. Double-blind procedures are recommended where experimenter and participants are unaware of the hypotheses and the treatment conditions.

The generalizability of the results is referred to as *external validity*. Statistical sampling theory specifies when, how, and the certainty with which it is feasible to generalize to a population of individuals. In an evaluation of a travel behavior modification program, it may be difficult to do this when the population is not well specified due to self-selection or attrition. Even harder to answer is the question of whether the results of an implementation in one geographical area can be transferred to another geographical area where the conditions may differ in several respects. Another threat is obtrusive or reactive measurements, that is, measurements that affect what is measured.

Some travel behavior modification programs are grounded in theory. This raises the issue of *construct validity* referring to whether the theory's constructs are properly operationalized. Failure in this respect means that the application is not based on the theory and may be less effective than believed. Generalizability may also be less.

Before–After Research Designs

Measuring travel behavior before and after the implementation of a travel behavior modification program may seem to be an adequate evaluation design. However, the design fails to eliminate a number of known threats to internal validity such as spontaneous changes over time (e.g., increased experience, attitude, or value changes), external factors (seasonal factors, changes in household economy), reactive effects of repeated measurements, and systematic changes in measuring instruments. If the sample is selected to include only an extreme group (as may be the case with habitual car drivers), regression toward the mean is expected when a repeated, not perfectly reliable measurement is made. Thus, a spurious regression effect may threaten valid conclusions.

A before-measurement could actually increase the effect of a travel behavior modification program if the measurement primes a positive attitude or informs the participants what is expected from them. This is a threat to external validity. Differential mortality is another such threat.

Research Designs with Control Groups

Including control groups alleviates some of the threats to internal validity pertaining to before–after evaluation designs at the same time as it introduces other threats.

The worst threat to internal validity in experimental-control group designs is that participants are not randomly assigned to experimental and control groups. Comparisons between intact groups are still an alternative if the groups are large and there is no bias in the selection of participants to the groups. The experimental and control groups must furthermore be treated in identical ways except with respect to the critical components of the travel behavior modification program. Differential mortality is another serious threat if it has the effect of making the groups nonequivalent.

In an experimental-control group design, no before-measurement is needed. However, if intact groups are compared, before-measurements may be used to establish that the groups do not differ before a travel behavior modification program starts. Some of the threats to internal and external validity due to repeated measurements will then remain. Other threats to external validity is communication between experimental and control groups or simply knowledge of each other that compromises the treatment effect. A double-blind procedure is essential.

Effect and Process Measures

In most experimental research only one or a few effect measures are employed. This may not be cost-effective in an extensive evaluation of a travel behavior modification program that perhaps employ a large sample randomized to several experimental and control groups. Process measures should, therefore, be considered. For instance, in addition to observing actual travel behavior changes, travel diaries and subjective reports secured in interviews or survey questionnaires are useful. Such data can be used to model how repeated choices change over time or how beliefs and attitudes change at the same time as behavior changes. Necessary precautions must still be undertaken to counteract undue influences of the multiple measurements.

Evaluation of Large-Scale Travel Behavior Modification Programs

In a large-scale travel behavior modification program targeting perhaps many hundreds of individuals or households, evaluation of all the participants' attitude and behavior changes requires a large budget, therefore, this may not always be feasible. A sample-based evaluation may need to be sufficient for assessing effects of the program in terms of a disaggregated-level evaluation. For designing the disaggregated-level evaluation scheme of such programs, the recommendations in the preceding section are essential.

In a large-scale program aggregated-level evaluations are also important, including observations of traffic volumes, regional modal shares of car and public transport, frequency and duration of traffic congestion, and number of passengers in bus or trains. To ensure internal validity in aggregated-level evaluations, before and after changes in the aggregated variables could be compared to observations made in previous years. It is also advisable to make observations in different areas where travel behavior modification programs are not implemented. Such control areas need to be enough similar to the target area in important respects to make possible the isolation of the effect of the travel behavior modification program from other changes.

A program proved to be effective in one area may not be effective in another area, and conversely, a program proved not be effective in an area may be effective in another area. For the assessment of external validity, meta-analyses[3] of several behavioral modification programs would be useful. A program that has proved to be effective in several areas would more likely be externally valid than a program that is shown to only be effective in a specific area. In addition, such meta-analyses may indicate the conditions under which a specific program is effective. In the next section, we will review travel behavior modification programs that have been implemented in many cities in European countries, Japan, and Australia, and that meta-analyses have proved to be effective.

Review of Travel Behavior Modification Programs

Psychological methods for behavior modification usually take the form of a "program." This is because psychological methods are composed of several types of information targeting changes in different psychological factors (see Figure 4). As there are two types of communication, individualized communication and mass communication, travel behavior modification programs may likewise be categorized in two types, mass communication programs and travel feedback (individualized communication) programs.

Mass Communication Programs

Examples of mass communication programs include travel awareness campaigns such as "TravelWise" in the UK (Jones and Sloman, 2006), "Cycle-Friendly Employers' Project" in Nottingham, UK (Thøgersen, 2007), the travel awareness campaign for promotion of public transportation in Madrid, Spain (INPHORMM, 1998), and the travel awareness campaign for sustainable transport in Kassel, Germany (INPHORMM, 1998). All these programs attempt to influence public attitudes toward travel modes and individuals' travel behavior through the mass media including

[3]Meta-analysis is a statistical technique that is applied for the purpose of synthesizing the results of many studies (see, e.g., Cooper and Hedges, 1994).

newspapers and radio, through leaflets and newsletters distributed to the public, and through posters displayed in public places. It is not easy to evaluate these mass communication programs because of difficulties with isolating their effects from other effects. Still, some changes in attitudes are reported. For example, those who prioritize car over public transport decreased from 27 to 9% in Kassel. Similar changes in public attitudes were reported in Madrid.

Travel Feedback Programs

Although mass communication programs may be effective in modifying public attitudes, they may be less effective in changing travel behavior. Is individualized communication programs more effective in this respect? Among several types of individualized communication programs such as personal conversation, workshops, school education, and TFPs, the latter (e.g., individualized marketing and travel blending) seems to be the most effective as judged from aggregated effects such as regional modal share, regional amount of CO_2 emission reduction, and the number of passengers of public transport. This is probably because if the budget is sufficient, TFBs can target all the households or individuals in a specific area or organization. It would not be feasible to invite this many people to workshops or having conversations with all of them. Education in schools is another important approach, but it takes tens of years until the pupils have reached the age where they can drive a car and when the program has an effect at the aggregated level.

All TFPs share the common feature that participants receive feedforward and feedback information. Feedforward includes travel information (e.g., time tables, maps informing about alternative travel options for commuting or shopping). Feedback refers to information about behavioral consequences, for instance, CO_2 emissions caused by car use.

TFPs differ with respect to location, technique, and procedure (Fujii and Taniguchi, 2006) (see Table 3). There are three types of locations where TFPs have been implemented: residential areas, schools, and workplaces. TFPs in residential areas typically target daily travel behavior of any household member, whereas TFPs in schools and workplaces are typically confined to commuting trips. TFPs in schools may be implemented as part of the school curriculum.

TFPs use several different techniques. These techniques differ with respect to whether they motivate travel behavior change, whether they provide customized information, whether they request setting goals of changing travel behavior, and whether they request plans for how to change travel behavior. For example, individualized marketing does not provide motivational support (Brög, 1998), while travel blending does (Ampt and Rooney, 1999; Rose and Ampt, 2001). A TFP that involves planning

Table 3
Common Features of Travel Feedback Programs (TFPs) and Features on Which They May Differ

Location	Technique	Procedure
Residential area (all trips)	Motivational support	Single stage
Workplace (commute)	Customized information	Multistage (travel diary survey, feedback)
School (commute)	Request goal setting	
	Request plan formation	

includes a request that participants make plans for how to change their travel behavior. As an example, Fujii and Taniguchi (2005) proposed a TFP, implemented in several cities in Japan (see Fujii and Taniguchi, 2006), that required participants to form a behavioral plan for changing their travel behavior. A final issue is whether the TFP provides customized information. Typical TFPs such as travel blending and individualized marketing do this, but some less elaborated TFPs do not. For example, a TFP implemented in Obihiro, Japan provided participants with noncustomized information about the bus service and requested that they made a behavioral plan for how to use the bus (Taniguchi and Fujii, 2007).

TFP procedures also differ. For instance, individualized marketing involves two or three contacts to conduct a survey of travel as well as of intentions to change travel behavior, to provide customized information, and to provide further customized information if necessary (Brög, 1998). Travel blending involves four contacts (Ampt and Rooney, 1999; Rose and Ampt, 2001): to motivate a travel behavior change, to conduct a travel diary survey, to provide customized comments, and to provide additional customized comments. The less elaborated TFP includes a single contact. For instance, a TFP in Obihiro, Japan (Taniguchi and Fujii, 2007) provided participants with a single questionnaire and noncustomized information. The questionnaire included a request that participants formulate a behavioral plan for how to change their travel behavior.

TFPs have been implemented in several cities in Australia, Germany, Sweden, the UK, the United States, and Japan (see reviews in Department for Transport, UK, 2004a, b; Fujii and Taniguchi, 2006). Individualized marketing has produced a reduction in car use up to 14% (South Perth, Australia) and not less than 2% (Breisgau-Hochschwartwald, Germany). Travel blending implemented in Australia and the United States produced a reduction in car use up to 15% (Adelaide, Australia) and not less than 9% (Brisbane, Australia). TFPs implemented in UK cities such as Gloucester, Bristol, and Nottingham have reduced car use by 7 to 15% in urban areas, and by 2 to 6% in rural areas. Transport for London implemented four different pilot TFPs, called "personalized journey planning" under the brand name TravelOptions, which reduced car use by 5–11% (Transport for London, UK, 2004a, b). Note that the above percentage of car-use reduction is regional-based total reduction of car use.

The effectiveness of TFPs implemented in Japan until 2003 was reported in Fujii and Taniguchi (2006). Thirteen Japanese TFPs reduced car use or CO_2 emissions by 0 to 40% with an average of 18%. Note that the reported percentages were based on the targeted sample, thus these differ from those presented in the reports from Department for Transport, UK (2004a, b) that were based on aggregated data.

To disentangle determinants of the effectiveness of TFBs, Japanese cases are focused to avoid possible confounding with cultural differences. Tables 4 and 5 show brief summaries of TFPs for residential areas and workplaces implemented in Japan that has been reported until 2005. Although other TFPs also have been implemented in Japan, the tables only summarize the TFPs that assessed car-use reduction and whose sample sizes were adequate. Note also that TFPs in schools are not included. The percentage of car-use change and public transport use change reported in these tables are for the sample assigned to experimental groups.

As can be seen in Table 4, residential area TFPs reduced car use by 6 to 27% (average 18%) and increased public transport use by 4 to 257% (average 58%). Workplace TFPs shown in Table 5 reduced car use by 0.1 to 17% (average 9%) and increased public transport use by 15 to 44% (average 29%). Although there is not enough cases to warrant firm conclusions, these results suggest that residential area TFPs are more effective than workplace TFPs. The reason may be that modifying commuting trips that workplace TFPs typically target are more difficult than changing other trips such as for shopping and leisure that residential area TFPs target.

All 14 TFPs in Tables 4 and 5 provided information to motivate behavior modification. Almost all TFPs (11) adopted a technique to provide customized information. In addition, again almost all TFPs (11) requested participants to make a behavioral plan for how to change travel behavior. Its effectiveness was empirically proved in a TFP experiment in Japan (see Fujii and Taniguchi, 2005). The average car-use reduction of 18% for residential area TFPs and 9% for workplace TFPs depended on motivation support, customized information, and a request to form a behavioral plan.

In 7 of 14 TFPs, participants were requested to set a goal of behavioral change (Himeji in 2004; Kawanishi-Inagawa in 2003; Keihanshin in 2004; Miki in 2004; Osaka in 2004; Suita in 2003; Suzurandai in 2004). Before making the behavioral plan, participants filled out a questionnaire specifying the percentage by which they would reduce their car use. In two cases (Miki in 2004; Suzurandai in 2004), participants were also requested to specify the percentage by which they would increase public transport use.

Table 4
Summary of Residential Area TFPs Implemented in Japan

Place	Year	Sample size	Technique	Procedure	Method of measurement	Car use change (%)	Public transport use change (%)
Sapporo (Ainosato)	2000	120	(a) Motivation (b) No plan (c) Provide individualized information	(1) Travel diary survey (2) Feedback on travel behavior (3) Travel survey (4) Feedback on travel behavior change	Before–after design without control group	−26.08	9.93
Sapporo (Ebetsu)	2000	349	(a) Motivation (b) No plan (c) Provide individualized information	(1) Travel diary survey (2) Feedback on travel behavior (3) Travel survey (4) Feedback on travel behavior change	Before–after design without control group	−8.95	6.06
Kawanishi-Inagawa area	2003	312	(a) Motivation (b) Plan with goal setting (c) Provide individualized information	(1) Simple travel survey (2) Individualized information with behavioral plan	Before–after design with control group	−27.02	68.97
Sapporo	2003	50	(a) Motivation (b) Plan (c) Provide individualized information	(1) Simple travel survey (2) Individualized information with behavioral plan	Before–after design with control group	−11.78	72.01

Suzurandai (Hyogo-prefecture)	2004	210	(a) Motivation (b) Plan with goal setting (c) Provide nonindividualized information	(1) Area specific information with behavioral plan	Before–after design with control group	−18.74	50.79
Miki city	2004	48	(a) Motivation (b) Plan with goal setting (c) Provide nonindividualized information	(1) Area specific information with behavioral plan	Before–after design with control group	−26.09	31.61
Himeji city	2004	103	(a) Motivation (b) Plan with goal setting (c) Provide individualized information	(1) Simple travel survey (2) Individualized information with behavioral plan	Before–after design with control group	−12.80	3.77
Keihanshin area	2004	1,560	(a) Motivation (b) Plan with goal setting (c) Provide nonindividualized information	(1) Simple travel survey (2) Feedback on travel behavior with behavioral plan	Before–after design with control group	−26.92	257.28
Ryugasaki city	2005	153	(a) Motivation (b) Plan (c) Provide individualized information	(1) Simple travel survey (2) Individualized information with behavioral plan	Before–after design with control group	−6.00	20.60

Table 5

Summary of Workplace TFPs Implemented in Japan

Place	Year	Sample size	Technique	Procedure	Method of measurement	Car use change (%)	Public transport use change (%)
Kanazawa city (several workplaces)	2001	106	(a) Motivation (b) No plan (c) Provide individualized information	(1) Travel diary survey (2) Feedback on travel behavior (3) Travel survey (4) Feedback on travel behavior change	Before–after design without control group	−0.10	29.00
Toyonaka city (one workplace)	2003	79	(a) Motivation (b) Plan (c) Provide individualized information	(1) Simple travel survey (2) Individualized information with behavioral plan (3) Travel survey (4) Feedback on travel behavior change	Before–after design without control group	−6.10	–
Suita city (one university)	2003	133	(a) Motivation (b) Plan with goal setting (c) Provide individualized information	(1) Travel diary survey (2) Individualized information with behavioral plan	Before–after design without control group	−16.50	–
Himeji city (three workplaces)	2004	99	(a) Motivation (b) Plan (c) Provide individualized information	(1) Simple travel survey (2) Individualized information with behavioral plan	Before–after design with control group (measuring commuting trips)	−8.80	14.81
Osaka prefecture (several workplaces)	2004	500	(a) Motivation (b) Plan with goal setting (c) Provide individualized information	(1) Simple travel survey (2) Individualized information with behavioral plan (3) Travel survey (4) Feedback on travel behavior change	Before–after design with control group	−15.06	43.76

The average of car-use reduction for the TFPs with a request of setting a goal was 20% compared to 10% for TFPs without such a request. The average of public transport use increase for six TFPs with a request to set a goal was 76%, and only 25% for six TFPs without such request. These results imply that the technique of asking participants to set goals of behavioral change is promising.

Summary and Conclusions

Various policy measures have been proposed and implemented that aim at reducing the levels of car-use related congestion, noise, and air pollution. This chapter has primarily focused on measures aimed at changing *car users* (e.g., informational and educational measures) without any changes in travel options. Although in practice several measures are implemented in concert (and we argue they should), it is still essential to disentangle and theoretically understand the effects of different components entailed by the measures. This is necessary in the shorter run in order to develop cost-effective policy measures. Furthermore, theoretical understanding is crucial since applications and their generalizations to other conditions would otherwise never improve in the longer run.

Our treatment in this chapter of the important issue, today and in the future, of how to modify travel behavior is a complement to the detailed review some years ago (Jones and Sloman, 2006). In that previous chapter, the theoretical underpinnings in behavioral research was largely lacking. In contrast, we have discussed and hopefully clarified some important conceptual issues as well as identified the potential theoretical foundations of travel behavior modification. Perhaps the most important conclusion emerging from this is that social influences may be very important in driving changes in travel behavior. Furthermore, information is probably more important than hedonic factors. Thus, an important insight is that both social and psychological processes mediate the relationship between changes in travel options (cost and time) and travel behavior. Given this insight, it should not come as a surprise that TFPs (usually featuring both customized feedback and feedforward information) are at least as effective as push measures (such as road pricing) changing the travel options. It is of course still the case that combinations of these measures may be even more effective.

It should also be asked whether TFPs can be made even more effective. Not only providing customized information but requiring participants to set behavioral change goals and forming plans for how to attain the set goals appear to be particularly promising. In fact, it may even be argued that customized information does not have any effect if participants do not actively engage in these processes of goal setting and plan formation. Current research in several other areas of behavioral modification (e.g., Geller, 2002) appears to confirm this. Thus, further refinement and evaluation of TFPs, both their effectiveness and their cost-effectiveness, are called for, drawing more closely on relevant behavioral theories that have proved useful.

For a long time daily travel has been considered to be habitual (e.g., Gärling and Axhausen, 2003). However, it is seldom made explicit that this in fact constitutes an impediment to behavioral modification. A habit is executed based on minimal information search (Gärling et al., 2001). Changes in travel options are, therefore, frequently not noted. This is an additional argument for that changes in travel options are in themselves insufficient to change travel behavior.

Evaluation is crucial for progress. This applies to participants in a TFP. If they lack (informational and hedonic) feedback, the change in behavior may be insufficient or not sustained. It also applies to the TFP. If feedback is lacking from an evaluation, a program may not be discontinued despite being ineffective or the reverse. In this chapter, we have highlighted many problems with evaluations. It may be worth repeating that, in general, straightforward before–after effect measures are not fully adequate. Control groups should be employed. Also, it is essential to use broadband measurement approaches focusing both on effects on the targeted sample as well as spillover effects on others, the process leading to the change, and following up by monitoring the effects after abortion of the program. Any such evaluation promises to be expensive. However, the alternative of doing the wrong thing is probably almost always more expensive.

ACKNOWLEDGMENT

Our own research referred to in this chapter was financially supported by grant no. 2002-00434 from the Swedish Agency for Innovation Systems and grant no. 25.9/2001-1763 from the Swedish Research Council for Environment, Agricultural Sciences, and Spatial Planning to Tommy Gärling, and by a grant for mobility management studies from Japanese National Institute for Land and Infrastructure Management to Satoshi Fujii.

We would like to thank our collaborators Cecilia Jakobsson, Peter Loukopoulos, Ayako Tniguchi, and Haruna Suzuki for their valuable contributions.

REFERENCES

Abelson, R. P. (1981). Psychological status of the script concept. *American Psychologist* 36, 715–729.

Ajzen, I. (1991). The theory of planned behavior. *Organizational Behavior and Human Decision Processes* 50, 179–211.

Ampt, E. and A. Rooney (1999). Reducing the impact of the car—a sustainable approach. Travel Smart Adelaide, 23rd Australasian Transport Forum, Perth, 29 September–1 October.

Arentze, T. and H. P. J. Timmermans (2003). Modeling learning and adaptation processes in activity-travel choice: A framework and numerical experiments. *Transportation* 30, 37–62.

Austin, J. T. and J. B. Vancouver (1996). Goal constructs in psychology: structure, process, and content. *Psychological Bulletin* 80, 286–303.

Axhausen, K. and T. Gärling (1992). Activity-based approaches to travel analysis: conceptual frameworks, models, and research problems. *Transport Reviews* 12, 323–341.

Bamberg, S. (2002). Effects of implementation intentions on the actual performance of new environmentally friendly behaviors: results of two field experiments. *Journal of Environmental Psychology* 22, 399–411.

Bamberg, S. and P. Schmidt (2003). Incentives, morality, or habit? Predicting students' car use for university routes with the models of Ajzen, Schwartz and Triandis. *Environment and Behavior* 35, 264–285.

Bargh, J. A. (1997). The automaticity of everyday life. In R. S. Wyer (Ed.), *The Automaticity of Everyday Life: Advances in Social Cognition*, Vol. 10. Mahwah, NJ, Erlbaum, pp. 1–61.

Ben-Akiva, M. and S. R. Lerman (1985). *Discrete Choice Analysis*. Cambridge, MA, MIT Press.

Bhat, C. R. and F. S. Koppelman (1999). A retrospective and prospective survey of time-use research. *Transportation* 26, 119–139.

Black, W. R. (2001). An unpopular essay on transportation. *Journal of Transport Geography* 9, 1–11.

Brehm, S. and J. W. Brehm (1981). *Psychological Reactance: A Theory of Freedom and Control*. New York, Academic Press.

Brehmer, B. (1995). Feedback delays in complex dynamic decision making. In P. A. Frensch and J. Funke (Eds.), *Complex Decision Making: The European Perspective*, Hillsdale, NJ, Erlbaum, pp. 103–130.

Brög, W. (1998). Individualised marketing: implications for TDM. *Proceedings of 77th Annual Meeting of Transportation Research Board*. Washington, DC.

Brög, W., E. Erl and N. Mense (2003). Individualised marketing: changing travel behaviour for a better environment. Paper presented at the TRIP research conference: The economic and environmental consequences of regulating traffic, Hillerød, 2–3 February.

Campbell, D. T. and J. C. Stanley (1966). *Experimental and Quasi-Experimental Design for Research*. Chicago, Rand McNally.

Carver, C. S. and M. F. Scheier (1998). *On the Self-Regulation of Behavior*. Cambridge, Cambridge University Press.

Cook, T. D. and D. T. Campbell (1979). *Quasi-Experimentation: Design and Analysis for Field Settings*. Chicago, Rand McNally.

Cooper, H. and L. V. Hedges (Eds.) (1994). *Handbook of Research Synthesis*. New York, Russell Sage Foundation.

Crawford, J. H. (2000). *Carfree Cities*. Utrecht, The Netherlands, International Books.

Dawes, R. M. (1980). Social dilemmas. *Annual Review of Psychology* 31, 169–193.

Deci, E. L., R. Koestner and R. M. Ryan (1999). A meta-analytic review of experiments examining the effects of extrinsic rewards on intrinsic motivation. *Psychological Bulletin* 125, 627–668.

Department for Transport, UK (2004a). Smarter choices: changing the way we travel. Final Report, London, UK.

Department for Transport, UK (2004b). Personalised travel planning demonstration programme. Presented at Personalised Travel Planning: End of Programme Conference 2004. Bristol, UK.

Dwyer, W. O., F. C. Leeming, M. K. Cobern, B. E. Porter and J. M. Jackson (1993). Critical review of behavioral interventions to preserve the environment: Research since 1980. *Environment and Behavior* 25, 275–321.

Eagly, A. H. and S. Chaiken (1993). *The Psychology of Attitudes*. Fort Worth, FL, Harcourt Brace Jovanovich.

Eagly, A. H. and S. Chaiken (1998). Attitude structure and function. In D. T. Gilbert, S. T. Fiske and G. Lindzey (Eds.), *Handbook of Social Psychology*, 4th edn., Vol. 1. Englewood Cliffs, NJ, McGraw-Hill, pp. 269–322.

Emmerink, R. H. M., P. Nijkamp and P. Rietveld (1995). Is congestion pricing a first-best strategy in transport policy? A critical review of arguments. *Environment and Planning B* 22, 581–602.

Fishbein, M. and I. Ajzen (1974). Attitudes towards objects as predictors of single and multiple behavior criteria. *Psychological Review* 81, 59–74.

Fishbein, M. and I. Ajzen (1975). *Belief, attitude, intention, and behavior: an introduction to theory and research*. Reading, MA, Addison-Wesley.

Frey, B. S. (1993). Motivation as a limit to pricing. *Journal of Economic Psychology* 14, 635–664.

Fujii, S. and T. Gärling (2003). Application of attitude theory for improved predictive accuracy of stated preference methods in travel demand analysis. *Transportation Research A* 37, 389–402.

Fujii, S. and T. Gärling (2005). Temporary structural change: a strategy to break car-use habit and promote public transport. In G. Underwood (Ed.), *Traffic and Transport Psychology*, Amsterdam, Elsevier, pp. 585–592.

Fujii, S. and T. Gärling (2006). Role and acquisition of car-use habit. In T. Gärling and L. Steg (Eds.), *Threats to the Quality of Urban Life from Car Traffic: Problems, Causes, and Solutions*. Amsterdam, Elsevier.

Fujii, S., T. Gärling and R. Kitamura (2001). Changes in drivers' perceptions and use of public transport during a freeway closure: Effects of temporary structural change on cooperation in a real-life social dilemma. *Environment and Behavior* 33, 796–808.

Fujii, S. and R. Kitamura (2003). What does a one-month free bus ticket do to habitual drivers? An experimental analysis of habit and attitude change. *Transportation* 30, 81–95.

Fujii, S., R. Kitamura and T. Monma (1998). A utility-based micro-simulation model system of individual's activity-travel patterns. *Proceedings of Transportation Research Board 77th Annual Meeting*. Washington, DC, USA.

Fujii, S. and A. Taniguchi (2005). Reducing family car use by providing travel advice or requesting behavioral plans: an experimental analysis of travel feedback programs. *Transportation Research D* 10, 385–393.

Fujii, S. and A. Taniguchi (2006). Determinants of the effectiveness of travel feedback programs—a review of communicative mobility management measures for changing travel behavior in Japan. *Transport Policy* 13, 339–348.

Gärling, T. (2004). The feasible infeasibility of activity scheduling. In M. Schreckenberg and R. Selten (Eds.), *Human Behavior in Traffic Networks*, Berlin, Springer, pp. 231–250.

Gärling, T. (2005). Changes in private car use in response to travel demand management. In G. Underwood (Ed.), *Traffic and Transport Psychology*, Amsterdam, Elsevier, pp. 551–571.

Gärling, T. and K. Axhausen (2003). Habitual travel choice (introduction to special issue). *Transportation* 30, 1–11.

Gärling, T., D. Eek, P. Loukopoulos, S. Fujii, O. Johansson-Stenman, R. Kitamura, R. Pendyala and B. Vilhelmson (2002). A conceptual analysis of the impact of travel demand management on private car use. *Transport Policy* 9, 59–70.

Gärling, T., S. Fujii and O. Boe (2001). Empirical tests of a model of determinants of script-based driving choice. *Transportation Research F* 4, 89–102.

Gärling, T., R. Gillholm and A. Gärling (1998). Reintroducing attitude theory in travel behavior research: the validity of an interactive interview procedure to predict car use. *Transportation* 25, 129–146.

Gärling, T. and G. Schuitema (2007). Effectiveness, public acceptability, and political feasibility of policy measures to change demand for private car use. *Journal of Social Issues* 63(1), 139–153.

Gärling, T. and L. Steg (Eds.) (2007). *Threats from Car Traffic to the Quality of Urban Life: Problems, Causes, and Solutions*. Amsterdam, Elsevierm.

Garvill, J., A. Marell and A. Nordlund (2003). Effects of awareness on choice of travel mode. *Transportation* 30, 63–79.

Geller, E. S. (2002). The challenge of increasing proenvironmental behavior. In R. B. Bechtel and A. Churchman (Eds.), *Handbook of Environmental Psychology*, 2nd edn. New York, Wiley, pp. 525–540.

Golob, T. F. (2001). Joint models of attitudes and behavior in evaluation of the San Diego I-15 Congestion Pricing Project. *Transportation Research A* 35, 495–514.

Golob, T. F., A. D. Horowitz and M. Wachs (1979). Attitude-behavior relationships in travel demand modeling. In D. A. Hensher and P. R. Stopher (Eds.), *Behavioral Travel Demand Modelling*, London, Croom Helm, pp. 739–757.

Gollwitzer, P. M. (1993). Goal achievement: the role of intentions. *European Review of Social Psychology* 4, 141–185.

Gollwitzer, P. M., H. Heckhausen and B. Steller (1990). Deliberative and implemental mind-sets: cognitive tuning toward congruous thoughts and information. *Journal of Personality and Social Psychology* 59, 1119–1127.

Goodwin, P. B. (1996). Simple arithmetic. *Transport Policy* 3, 79–80.

Hamed, M. M. and F. L. Mannering (1993). Modeling travelers' postwork activity involvement: toward a new methodology. *Transportation Science* 27, 381–394.

Hensher, D. A. (1994). Stated preference analysis of travel choices: the state of practice. *Transportation* 21, 107–133.

Hine, J. and M. Grieco (2003). Scatters and clusters in time and space: implications for delivering integrated and inclusive transport. *Transport Policy* 10, 299–306.

INPHORMM (1998). Case studies of transport information and publicity/marketing campaigns to reduce car use and promote cycling, walking and public transport. *INPHORMM Deliverable D2 to the European Commission. Transport Studies Group.* University of Westminster, and Partners.

Jakobsson, C., S. Fujii and T. Gärling (2000). Determinants of private car users' acceptance of road pricing. *Transport Policy* 7, 153–158.

Jakobsson, C., S. Fujii and T. Gärling (2002). Effects of economic disincentives on private car use. *Transportation* 29, 349–370.

Jones, P. (1991). Gaining public support for road pricing through a package approach. *Traffic Engineering and Control* 32, 194–196.

Jones, P. (1995). Road pricing: the public viewpoint. In B. Johansson and L.-G. Matsson (Eds.), *Road Pricing: Theory, Empirical Assessment and Policy*, Dordrecht, The Netherlands, Kluwer, pp. 159–179.

Jones, P. (2003). Acceptability of transport pricing strategies: meeting the challenge. In J. Schade and B. Schlag (Eds.), *Acceptability of Transport Pricing Strategies*, Amsterdam, Elsevier, pp. 27–62.

Jones, P. and L. Sloman (2006). Encouraging behavioral change through marketing and management: what can be achieved? In K. W. Axhausen (Ed.), *Moving Through Nets: The Physical and Social Dimensions of Travel*, Oxford, Elsevier, pp. 189–218.

Keeney, R. L. and H. Raiffa (1993). *Decisions with Multiple Objectives*. Cambridge, Cambridge University Press.

Kitamura, R. (1988). An evaluation of activity-based travel analysis. *Transportation* 15, 9–34.

Kitamura, R. and S. Fujii (1998). Two computational process models of activity-travel behavior. In T. Gärling, T. Laitila and K. Westin (Eds.), *Theoretical Foundations of Travel Choice Modeling*, Amsterdam, Elsevier, pp. 251–279.

Kitamura, R., S. Fujii and E. I. Pas (1997). Time-use data, analysis and modeling: toward the next generation of transportation planning methodologies. *Transport Policy* 4, 225–235.

Klayman, J. and Y.-W. Ha (1987). Confirmation, disconfirmation, and information in hypothesis testing. *Psychological Review* 94, 211–228.

Locke, E. A. and G. P. Latham (1990). *A Theory of Goal-Setting and Task Performance*. Englewood Cliffs, NJ, Prentice-Hall.

Locke, E. A., G. P. Latham and M. Erez (1988). The determinants of goal commitment. *Academy of Management Review* 13, 23–39.

Loukopoulos, P. (2007). A classification of travel demand management measures. In T. Gärling and L. Steg (Eds.), *Threats to the Quality of Urban Life from Car Traffic: Problems, Causes, and Solutions*, Amsterdam, Elsevier, pp. 275–292.

Loukopoulos, P., T. Gärling, C. Jakobsson, S. Meland and S. Fujii (2005). Choices of activity- and travel-change options for reduced car use. In H. P. J. Timmermans (Ed.), *Progress in Activity-Based Analysis*, Amsterdam, Elsevier, pp. 489–501.

Loukopoulos, P., C. Jakobsson, T. Gärling, C. M. Schneider and S. Fujii (2004). Car user responses to travel demand management measures: goal setting and choice of adaptation alternatives. *Transportation Research D* 9, 263–280.

Loukopoulos, P., C. Jakobsson, T. Gärling, S. Meland and S. Fujii (2006). Understanding the process of adaptation to car-use reduction goals. *Transportation Research F* 9, 115–127.

McFadden, D. (2001). Disaggregate behavioral travel demand's RUM side—a 30 years retrospective. In D. A. Hensher (Ed.), *Travel Behavior Research*, Amsterdam, Elsevier, pp. 17–63.

Miller, G. A., E. Galanter and K. H. Pribram (1960). *Plans and the Structure of Behavior*. New York, Holt, Rinehatr, & Winston.

Messick, D. M. and M. B. Brewer (1983). Solving social dilemmas: a review. In L. Wheeler and P. Shaver (Eds.), *Review of Personality and Social Psychology*, Vol. 4. Beverly Hills, CA, Sage, pp. 11–44.

Nordlund, A. M. and J. Garvill (2003). Effects of values, problem awareness, and personal norm on willingness to reduce personal car use. *Journal of Environmental Psychology* 23, 339–347.

Ouellette, J. A. and W. Wood (1998). Habit and intention in everyday life: the multiple processes by which past behavior predicts future behavior. *Psychological Bulletin* 124, 54–74.

Pas, E. I. (1995). The urban transportation planning process. In S. Hanson (Ed.), *The Geography of Urban Transportation*, Amsterdam, Elsevier, pp. 53–77.

Powers, W. T. (1973). Feedback: beyond behaviorism. *Science* 179, 351–356.

Ronis, D. L., J. F. Yates and J. P. Kirscht (1989). Attitudes, decisions, and habits as determinants of repeated behavior. In A. R. Pratkanis, S. J. Breckler and A. G. Greenwald (Eds.), *Attitude Structure and Function*, Hillsdale, NJ, Erlbaum, pp. 213–239.

Rose, G. and E. Ampt (2001). Travel blending: An Australian travel awareness initiative. *Transportation Research D* 6, 95–110.

Samuelson, W. and R. Zeckhausen (1988). Status quo bias in decision making. *Journal of Risk and Uncertainty* 1, 7–59.

Schwartz, S. H. (1977). Normative influences on altruism. *Advances in Experimental Social Psychology* 10, 221–279.

Schwartz, S. H. (1992). Universals in the content and structure of values: Theoretical advances and empirical tests in 20 countries. *Advances in Experimental Social Psychology* 25, 1–65.

Steg, L. (2003). Factors influencing the acceptability and effectiveness of transport pricing. In J. Schade and B. Schlag (Eds.), *Acceptability of Transport Pricing Strategies*, Amsterdam, Elsevier, pp. 187–202.

Stern, P. C. (2000). Toward a coherent theory of environmentally significant behavior. *Journal of Social Issues* 56, 407–424.

Stern, P. C. and T. Dietz (1994). The value basis of environmental concern. *Journal of Social Issues* 50, 55–84.

Taniguchi, A. and S. Fujii (2004). A process model of voluntary travel behavior modification and effects of the Travel Feedback Program (TFP). *Proceedings of 3rd International Conference on Traffic & Transport Psychology*. Nottingham, UK.

Taniguchi, A. and S. Fujii (2007). Promoting public transport using marketing techniques in mobility management and verifying quantitative effects: a case study of a community bus in Obihiro City, Japan. *Transportation* 34(1), 37–49.

Taylor, M. A. P. and E. S. Ampt (2003). Travelling smarter down under: policies for voluntary travel behavior change in Australia. *Transport Policy* 10, 165–177.

Thøgersen, J. (2007). Social marketing of alternative transportation modes. In T. Gärling and L. Steg (Eds.), *Threats from Car Traffic to the Quality of Urban life: Problems, Causes, and Solutions*. Amsterdam, Elsevier.

Verplanken, B., H. Aarts and A. Van Knippenberg (1997). Habit, information acquisition, and the process of making travel mode choices. *European Journal of Social Psychology* 27, 539–560.

Vlek, C. A. J. and J. A. Michon (1992). Why we should and how we could decrease the use of motor vehicles in the near future. *IATSS Research* 15, 82–93.

Whitelegg, J. (2003). Transport in the European Union: time to decide. In N. Low and B. Gleeson (Eds.), *Making Urban Transport Sustainable*, Basingstoke, UK, Palgrave Macmillan, pp. 115–131.

Yamagishi, T. (1986). The structural goal/expectation theory of cooperation in social dilemmas. In E. Lawler and B. Morkovsky (Eds.), *Advances in Group Processes*, Vol. 3. Greenwich, CT, JAL, pp. 52–87.

Yamamoto, T., S. Fujii and R. Kitamura (2000). An analysis of departure time and route choice behavior under congestion pricing using stated preference data. *Transportation Research Record* 1725, 95–101.

2.3 Experimental Approaches

The Expanding Sphere of Travel Behaviour Research
Selected Papers from the 11th International Conference on Travel Behaviour Research

6

Learning from Interactive Experiments: Travel Behavior and Complex System Dynamics

Hani S. Mahmassani

Abstract

Experimental methods have an increasing role to play in the study of complex activity and travel behavior dynamics, especially as information and communication technologies increase the realm of spatiotemporal opportunities available for individual and household activity engagement. This paper is concerned with the use of experiments and gaming situations to study travel and activity behavior, for the purpose of understanding and modeling the underlying decision, judgment and learning processes, and/or exploring the collective properties resulting from the interaction of multiple decision agents in a transportation context. The scope is specifically targeted at methods where (1) respondents engage in a repeated game situation, in an iterative, interactive process; and (2) respondents experience some kind of payoff as a consequence of the response provided. In addition, the primary interest is in situations where the outcome or payoff experienced by a subject depends specifically on the decision/response supplied by that subject, individually or in interaction with those of other respondents.

Why Conduct Experiments?

When approaching a complex sociotechnical system, with many interacting elements, or considering the impact of a new policy or technology, several approaches may be applied, generally reflecting a sequence with increasing involvement of resources (Mahmassani and Herman, 1990):

1. Formulate analytical models of idealized situations, to derive basic insight about major elements of the problem.
2. Construct and conduct computer simulations of more realistic situations under assumed behavior and interaction rules, to capture the effect of interactions that are beyond the tractability of simplified idealizations.
3. Design and conduct laboratory experiments, which enable observation of behavior under controlled conditions, with a limited number of subjects.
4. Conduct field experiments and/or demonstration projects, to observe the performance of the system and associated user behavior in actual operation.

Laboratory experiments are called for when:

1. Complex dynamics and collective effects are essential aspects of the system under consideration, making joint measurement in the real world considerably complicated or costly.
2. Situations or policies of interest are not available in the real world (e.g., new technologies), or may be mutually inconsistent in the same system.
3. Control for extraneous factors is desired.
4. Understanding of dynamics and learning processes is of concern.

Of course, observing users is a fundamental ingredient of travel and activity behavior research. Surveys and passive measurement techniques in actual conditions have always provided the foundation for the field, yielding so-called revealed preference information in the form of travelers' actual decisions. Recognizing the limitations of the latter with regard to conditions that do not exist in the system of interest, and the inability to yield information on user trade-offs for attribute values outside of the range readily observable in the actual system (or insufficient observed variation within the system to support parameter estimation), stated preference techniques have seen an explosion of interest in travel behavior analysis and demand forecasting practice (Hensher et al., 2005). Stated preference elicitation techniques have undergone considerable sophistication in the past decade, especially with regard to interactive delivery and situation presentation in computer-assisted environments.

Stated preference techniques have followed conventional statistical experiment design techniques, namely (1) define factors of interest; (2) determine factor levels for factors that are fixed, and/or range when factors are random; (3) design treatments, or factor combinations to be administered to users; (4) assign treatments to users; (5) administer experiments, generally with multiple treatments per subject and measure responses; and (6) analyze responses. As such, respondents do not typically experience a consequence or receive a payoff as a result of their response(s), and the set of stimuli to which subjects are responding does not depend on interaction among the responses provided by users.

Experiments that entail varying degrees of sophistication in context design, task design, and delivery environment, and different scales of experimentation in terms of number of participants and environmental perturbation, are common in many disciplines concerned with the study of human systems. Leaving aside clinical experiments in the biological and life sciences, psychologists, economists, sociologists, anthropologists, and increasingly physicists are following experimental approaches within those disciplines as a companion to support theoretical development. Applied professional disciplines such as education, political science, and marketing have also taken to experimental approaches and games to study the effectiveness of proposed solutions, measures, products/services prior to their introduction.

In certain areas of the transportation field, such as safety, human factors, and traffic control, both field as well as laboratory experimentation are commonplace, albeit following traditional statistical experimental designs and precepts. Transportation planning professionals, and travel behavior–activity researchers have been slower to adopt experimental methods in either research or practice (with the exception of stated response methods noted above, and full-scale operational tests). However, from modest beginnings in the early 1980s, there appears to be growing interest in experimental methods for the study of human behavior in transportation decision situations. Several reasons can be surmised for this phenomenon: (1) growing interest in experimental economics as an approach for the study of economic systems; (2) related development in complexity science and its application to human, economic, and sociotechnical systems; (3) explosion in computing capabilities and networked environments, and interest in large-scale collective phenomena in networks; (4) continued development of travel behavior as a focus of interdisciplinary research, with entry of professionals with varying disciplinary backgrounds; (5) increased sophistication in methods, theories, and intellectual constructs in travel and activity behavior research; (6) significance of policy questions and concerns that require better understanding of behavioral dynamics and multi-agent interactions (e.g., environmental sustainability, vehicle use, congestion mitigation, etc...); and (7) technological advances in information and communication technologies that enable improved simulation/gaming environments, delivery platforms, and multiplayer interactions.

The present paper is concerned with the use of experiments and gaming situations to study travel and activity behavior, for the purpose of understanding and modeling the underlying decision, judgment and learning processes, and/or exploring the collective properties resulting from the interaction of multiple decision agents in a transportation context. The scope is specifically targeted at methods where (1) respondents engage in a repeated game situation, in an iterative, interactive process; and (2) respondents experience some kind of payoff as a consequence of the response provided. In addition, the primary interest is in situations where the outcome or payoff experienced by a subject depends specifically on the decision/response supplied by that subject, individually or in interaction with those of other respondents.

The paper is organized as follows. In the next section, we discuss methods that have evolved primarily for the study of activity engagement and scheduling behavior. Next, we review experimental approaches that have been applied to the study of commuter behavior, particularly route and departure time decision dynamics, within the travel behavior community. This is followed in ATIS Simulators and Experiments section by the discussion of simulators and experiments conducted to study user responses to traffic information delivered in real time through various communication devices. In Route Choice Games and Experimental Economics section, we review concepts of experimental economics and recent applications to study route choice as an example of noncooperative game situation. In Prediction Markets section, recent developments with the use of virtual marketplaces as a mechanism to study user decisions and for forecasting future events are discussed, along with their potential transportation applications. Last section concludes the paper with a discussion of limitations, issues, and opportunities.

Key Elements of Experiments

Interactive experiments for the study of traveler behavior, and more generally complex human decision systems, entail the following principal elements, illustrated in Figure 1:

1. A *decision situation*, describing the hypothetical situation faced by the respondent, or more generally the problem context that the respondent is asked to consider.
2. *Experimental task(s)* for subjects to perform; these need to be well defined, and unambiguous to the participants. These tasks may involve simple single activities (e.g., choose one of a given set of routes), a sequence of conditional decisions (e.g., choose a mode and then a specific path within that mode), and/or a combination of response types (e.g., rate quality of several alternatives, and choose one, or provide estimate of expected arrival time for a given chosen route).
3. An *interaction "box,"* which determines payoffs given decisions; this ranges from determining a winning bid in a spot market auction game, to solving an optimization problem in a combinatorial auction; from applying a simple analytic function to determine delay on a road given associated flow, to elaborate simulations of traffic in a road network. In some instances, payoffs may be drawn at random from certain distributions that may or may not depend on the users' decisions.
4. A *currency*, for the payoff, to each participant, resulting from the interaction among the supplied responses. This is how the "score" is kept for each participant. In experimental economics, the payoff is typically in monetary terms, and may be accumulated and/or traded across several games or game trials. In certain

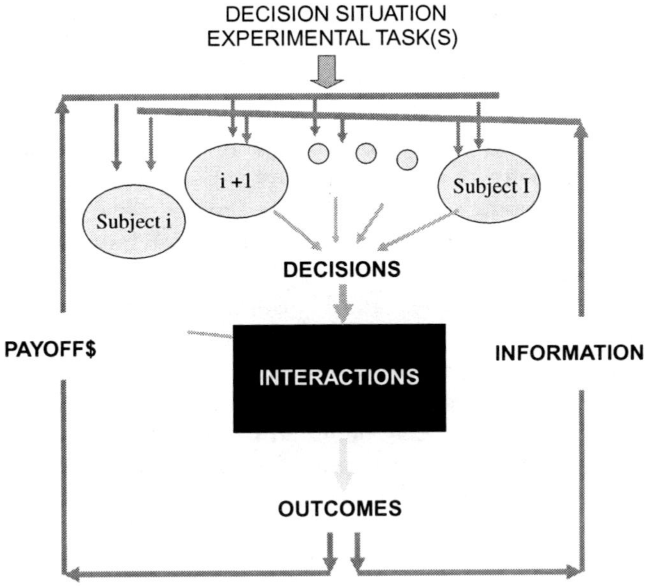

Figure 1
Key Elements of Experimental Procedure

market-oriented games, the participant is typically given some initial allocation of that currency to trade. The nature of the currency and its tradability is a key difference between classical experimental economics and many transportation games. In the latter, motivated partly by the belief that small monetary payoffs may not be adequate to incentivize or induce realistic behavior in transportation contexts, payoffs are in the currency in which they are experienced in the real world. For instance, commuter behavior experiments have considered travel time or delay as the primary currency for the experiments. In this regard, travel time cannot be stored and explicitly traded in actual situations.

5. *Feedback mechanism*, to provide information to the user at the end of a given game, on the performance of his/her strategy. This is a critical element of the experimental apparatus, which allows specification of the levels of certain experimental factors, especially with regard to information availability to the user. Specification of feedback mechanisms includes the content of the feedback (naturalistic outcome vs. monetary payoff), the timing of the feedback relative to the simulated decision process, and the manner in which it is displayed.
6. *Stopping rule*, for stopping the interactive process; this may be a predetermined number of iterations or a rule that depends on the state of the system (e.g., if some form of convergence is attained).

Activity Simulators and Stated Adaptation

One of the earliest applications of gaming situations in travel behavior research is the HATS activity–travel simulator, developed at the Transport Studies Unit (Oxford) to aid in understanding individual and household activity and travel decision processes in an effort to predict responses to constraints and various travel- and activity-impacting policy measures (Jones et al., 1983). There are several other examples of interactive board-based tools and protocols designed to interact with travelers and households for the purpose of exploring changes in activity–travel patterns associated with various scenarios and policies (e.g., Burnett and Hanson, 1982; Lee-Gosselin and Turrentine, 1997). Two main novelties have entered this realm in the past decade: (1) GIS platforms for computer-supported interaction, thereby improving on the tools' representation of space (Golledge et al., 1994; Kwan, 1997; Ohmori et al., 2004); and (2) coupling GPS and/or cell phone tracking with activity diaries, enabling accurate spatial data on individual trajectories in the physical world (Doherty and Miller, 2000; Lee and McNally, 2001; Ohmori et al., 2005).

Interactive gaming situations and related tools for activity and travel planning have evolved from being an experimental approach for small-scale, mostly qualitative exploration in the spirit of a focus group, of household behavior processes, to assuming more ambitious roles. We identify five main uses of these tools:

1. Exploration for the purpose of gaining insight and understanding into the processes and mechanisms underlying activity and travel choices;
2. Prediction of responses to contemplated policies, incentives, or anticipated future scenarios, through interaction with a facilitator and consideration of hypothetical scenarios;
3. Decision-support systems to aid the traveler or household in activity scheduling and travel planning (Kwan, 1997);
4. Policy intervention, to affect behavior change, for example, through travel blending strategies (Rose and Ampt, 2001);
5. Data collection, primarily of activity–travel diaries, as a substitute or complement to traditional surveys.

The last three uses depart somewhat from the original purpose of experimental tools, though they also reflect greater comfort with and confidence in the ability of these tools to contribute directly to analysis and prediction.

These methods can be viewed as variants of interactive stated response methods. They are usually specific to a responding individual or household, and self-contained, in that the payoff does not result from some interaction process involving multiple respondents (other than members of the same household or other joint decision unit, such as a firm). Furthermore, the "rules of the game" tend to be less structured than experimental games and simulations conducted in experimental economics or commuter choices in congested traffic systems.

Yet another semi-structured variant used to explore the processes by which users plan their activity patterns is referred to as *stated adaptation*. According to Lee-Gosselin (1996), in stated adaptation, the possible behaviors in the hypothetical setting under consideration are left completely undefined, unlike standard stated response techniques. Stated adaptation methods also generally engage participants in observing their own behaviors in novel situations, and are thus referred to as "reflexive" methods (Turrentine and Kurani, 1998). The success of such exercises will depend in large part on the skill of the facilitator/interviewer, who guides the interaction process toward its intended goal.

While stated adaptation methods may take many forms, most procedures have in common the following elements (Doherty and Lee-Gosselin, 2000):

1. *Framing* of the hypothetical situation, especially the manner in which the (policy-related) constraints which are the motivation for the study are presented. Framing has long been recognized as playing an important, and sometimes determining effect on user response (Einhorn and Hogarth, 1981).
2. *A base of revealed data*, on respondents' actual behavior over a base period, for example, using a travel or activity diary (Doherty and Lee-Gosselin, 2000).
3. An *experimental "currency" for change* to allow respondents to reflect on the consequences of stated responses. However, unlike experimental economics approaches, the currency is only used to assist participants to visualize consequences of contemplated actions, and not as the primary means of response elicitation.
4. *A "game" with rules and feedbacks*, intended to provide ground rules for interaction between respondents and interviewer, though much less formally structured than laboratory experiments.
5. *Criteria for deciding when decisions have been made*, which are not well delineated in a semi-structured and possibly unstructured interaction process (Doherty and Lee-Gosselin, 2000).

These methods have been applied primarily to study individual and household adaptation to shortfalls in energy or in response to environmental measures, and more generally in the realm of sustainable transportation. In addition, a related strand of work has focused on interactive agency choice behavior, for example, in the area of telecommuting adoption by employers (Brewer and Hensher, 2000; Rose and Hensher, 2004).

Early Commuter Behavior Experiments

In the mid- to late 1980s, Mahmassani, Herman, and coworkers conducted a series of three experiments involving actual commuters in a simulated congested traffic corridor

(Mahmassani and Herman, 1990). Those experiments were conducted before the widespread availability of personal computers and the Internet, and entailed overcoming significant logistical challenges. The participants are all actual daily commuters who respond to traffic conditions with their selection of a particular time to depart and/or route to use in a typical commuting corridor, shown in Figure 2. The general experimental procedure is summarized in Figure 3. Given respondents' choices of departure time and/or route, the interaction "box" consists of a special-purpose macroparticle traffic simulation model (Mahmassani et al., 1986). The model simulates the resulting system performance and provides the travel time corresponding to each departure time and route choice. A (paper and pen) questionnaire, administered on a daily basis, communicates and interfaces between the system performance and commuters' response. It also provides each commuter with the simulation outcome, and accordingly seeks their response to this information (Mahmassani and Tong, 1988).

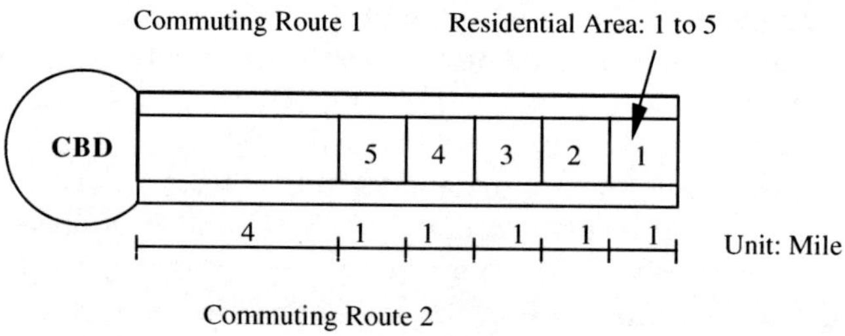

Figure 2
Hypothetical Commuting System

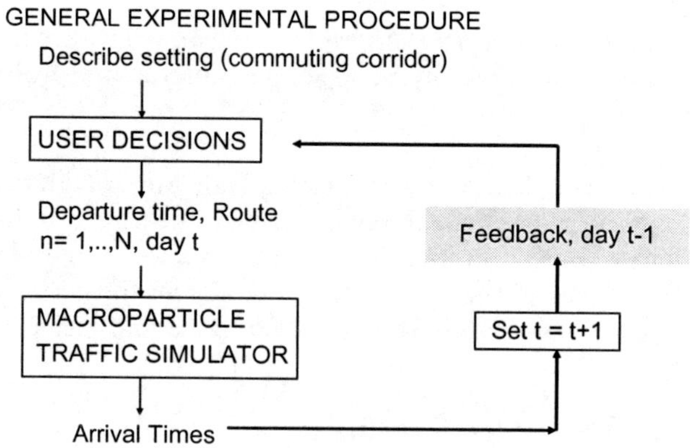

Figure 3
Summary of Experimental Procedure

The hypothetical commuting system in Figure 2 consists of two major roadways, each nine miles long and connecting a residential area (sectors 1–5) with the CBD. Only the inbound trip (home-to-work) was considered. The two roadway facilities serving the corridor consist of: (1) Route 1, a four-lane highway (two lanes in each direction) with a speed limit of 50 mph, and (2) Route 2, a two-lane arterial street (one lane in each direction) with a speed limit of 40 mph. The decisions of each participant were treated as decisions of 20 identical tripmakers for traffic simulation purposes (Mahmassani and Stephan, 1988).

The experiment was administered on weekdays only, with each participant supplying the decision for the given day, consistently with the natural time frame of actual commuter behavior. The departure time on each day was assumed to be in 1 of the 11 five-minute intervals from 7:00 am to 7:50 am. On each day, users' responses including the departure time and the route decisions, and the anticipated arrival time were collected. Using these data, the arrival time, travel time, schedule delay, and other performance measures were obtained from the traffic simulation program. The feedback mechanism in this experiment allows experimental control over the information available to participants. As such, information availability was a key experimental factor in the investigation. Two levels of this factor were considered: full vs. limited information. Participants selected to receive complete information (full-information users) were shown arrival times corresponding to all departure times, whereas the limited-information users were only told about their own arrival time.

Three sets of experiments were performed using this general procedure, summarized in Table 1. The experiments differed in terms of number of route alternatives (and hence available choice dimensions), as well as the feedback information provided to the participants. An initial result of considerable interest regarding the effect of information on commuter switching decisions was obtained by contrasting the evolution of the system under experiments 1 (limited information) and 2 (full information), which otherwise offered near-identical experimental conditions (especially similar levels of

Table 1

Characteristics of the Three Sets of Early Experiments

Experiment 1: 100 subjects
Single route corridor → departure time only
Feedback: Individual performance only (limited information)
Experiment 2: 100 subjects
Same as 1; feedback on overall system performance (full information)
Experiment 3: 200 subjects
Two routes: Not identical
Two information availability groups: *full* vs. *limited*
More congestion

overall congestion, in terms of number of users and traffic system parameters). It was found that the system took significantly longer to converge when all users were provided with previous-day information on arrival times corresponding to all departure times than when they only received information on their own arrival time. The interpretation is that provision of information raised tripmakers' expectations, as they switched decisions in search of a better outcome. They eventually succeeded, in that the overall system performance measures of average trip time and user schedule delay were both lower under full information. In the third experiment, in which two information groups were essentially competing in the same traffic system, not only did the full-information group outperform the limited-information group, on average, in terms of travel time and schedule delay, but they appeared to require less experimentation (switching) to reach this outcome (though no steady state was reached in this particular experiment, which had greater congestion level than the preceding ones; Mahmassani and Herman, 1990). These results are illustrated in Figure 4, which summarizes the daily percentage of users changing departure time, route, or both, under each experiment.

The experiments provided a basis for articulating a theory of departure time and route-switching decision mechanisms in repeated decision situations, such as work

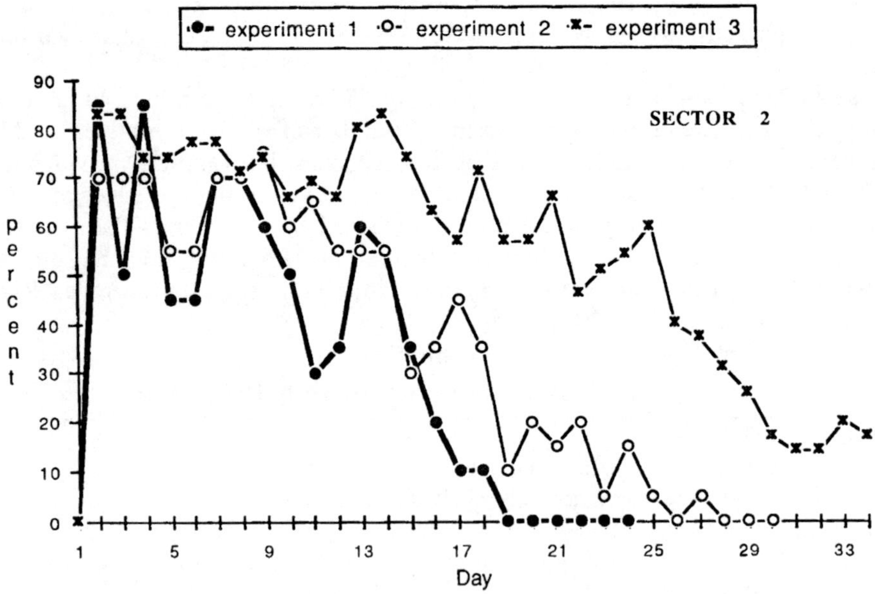

Figure 4

Day-to-Day Evolution of Fraction of Users Who Switch Departure Time or Route in Sector 2 (All Three Experiments)

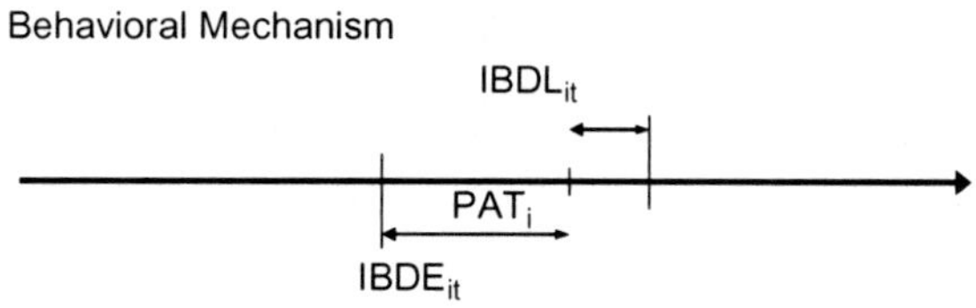

Figure 5
Late (IBDL) and Early (IBDE) Indifference Bands for Day-to-Day Switching of Departure Time

commuting. Drawing on Simon's (1955) notion of bounded rationality, individual day-to-day decisions were viewed as a boundedly rational search, for an acceptable outcome, in this case a time of arrival at the workplace. The satisfying decision mechanism is thus operationalized in the form of an indifference band of schedule delay (defined vis-à-vis the user's preferred arrival time), shown graphically in Figure 5 for departure-time-switching decisions. The experimental results confirmed asymmetries in user preferences for early vs. late arrival (relative to the preferred arrival time) at the workplace, with significantly wider bands on the early side than on the late side (IBDE and IBDL, respectively, in Figure 5). The bands are distributed across the population, reflecting differences in sociodemographic characteristics; the bands also vary dynamically in response to prior experience as well as information availability (Mahmassani, 1990).

A similar indifference band mechanism was formulated for route-switching decisions; estimation results from the third experiment clarified the relation between the departure time and route bands. On average, the route indifference band was found to be larger than the corresponding departure time band, which explains the greater propensity of users to switch departure time than route. These mechanisms were formalized through specification of dynamic indifference bands for route and departure time, for both early and late arrivals, jointly calibrated using a multinomial probit econometric model framework that captures state dependence and heterogeneity (Mahmassani, 1990).

The experiments also formed the basis for process models of departure time adjustment, conditional upon the decision to switch. These adjustment processes include models of travel time learning and prediction by commuters (Mahmassani and Tong, 1988). Because of the inherently latent nature of the quantities of interest, and consequent inability to directly observe or measure perceptions, this aspect has been particularly challenging to investigate and model. The perception process must be inferred indirectly through choices made by tripmakers. That work appears to be one of a very limited number of studies of this aspect of tripmaker decision dynamics.

The experiment results were indirectly validated with 2-week diary surveys of actual commuters in Austin and Dallas (Mahmassani et al., 1993; Mahmassani and Jou, 2000). Of course, direct comparison is not possible given the large number of factors that cannot be controlled in actual commuting. In particular, day-to-day variation in actual systems is not only dependent on traffic conditions and experience but also on activity patterns (trip chaining), which are not constant for commuters. For this reason, the boundedly rational model was extended to incorporate activity chaining, though still within a dynamic indifference band model framework (Mahmassani and Jou, 1998). An important methodological question is the extent to which behavioral findings from laboratory experiments are indeed representative of actual behavior in real traffic systems. The main conclusion in this regard from the comparative analyses performed is that behavioral mechanisms developed on basis of laboratory experiments provided good explanation of observed behavior: essentially similar model specification, correct signs, but different coefficient magnitudes (Mahmassani and Jou, 2000).

Other laboratory experiments to investigate route choice dynamics were conducted in the late 1980s and early 1990s by Iida et al. (1992). The focus of those experiments was on the route choice dimension alone, not considering departure time. Methodologically, those experiments differed in two marked ways from the simulation-based experiments discussed above: (1) the experiment was administered on an accelerated basis, with repeated decisions corresponding to different days administered sequentially; and (2) the interaction box was considerably simpler, relying on analytic link performance functions of the well-known BPR form used for static planning applications. With these simplifications, it was possible to accelerate these experiments, at lower cost, and over a larger number of iterations. This approach is more in line with the experimental economics approaches that have appeared more recently, discussed in Route Choice Games and Experimental Economics section.

ATIS Simulators and Experiments

The advent of Advanced Traveler Information Systems (ATIS) provided considerable impetus and motivation for the development of simulators and use of laboratory experiments to investigate the effect of real-time information on individual decision processes and system dynamics, and support the design of such information systems as well as the evaluation of their impact on traffic network performance. Several simulators with varying degrees of fidelity and complexity were developed, and used for experiments with varying degrees of interactivity. An authoritative review of tripmaker simulators for the study of user behavior under ATIS is provided by Bonsall (2004). That review identified several advantages of route choice simulators over questionnaire-based methods, including providing "a means of allowing the perception of key attributes to be part of the choice process rather than artificially excluded from it," and "a mechanism for including a very wide range of potential behavioral stimuli," along with various bias-reduction advantages. Compared to full-scale driving simulators, cost is of course a major advantage of tripmaker route choice simulators, in addition to ability to recruit a wider range of subjects and "more rapid collection of data (and hence an enhanced ability to design experiments incorporating learning effects)." Bonsall (2004) also highlights the potential for virtual-reality environments to blur the distinction between full-scale driving simulators and route choice simulators.

Many applications of route choice simulation experiments have been more in line with standard stated response techniques, with predetermined stimuli and payoffs that do not depend on the individual and collective choices of participants. Nonetheless, the prevalence of this approach signaled the mainstream acceptance of simulation-based experiments as a preferred method for the study of user response dynamics in situations where new technologies had not yet become sufficiently available in actual systems.

An extensive set of experiments was conducted by Mahmassani and coworkers to investigate user dynamics under real-time information of varying types. In contrast to the early experiments described in the previous section, which addressed only the day-to-day dynamics of user decisions, the ATIS investigation address both real-time and day-to-day dynamics of user decisions. As such, these experiments required a special-purpose simulator that allows real-time interaction between respondents and the traffic system. The interactive simulator provides ATIS information that is consistent with the traffic conditions on the network. The prevailing traffic conditions, in turn, are the result of collective decisions of tripmakers on the network, whose interactions in traffic are modeled using a dynamic traffic simulation model. Thus, the simulator ensures mutual consistency between user behavior, experienced traffic network conditions, and real-time information (Chen and Mahmassani, 1993).

Three sets of experiments were performed over a 3-year period: (1) en route path choice and day-to-day departure decisions under given overall congestion level (Mahmassani and Liu, 1999); (2) effect of congestion and experimental exposure sequence (Srinivasan and Mahmassani, 1999); and (3) effect of information type, quality, and feedback (to users) on user decision processes (Srinivasan and Mahmassani, 2002). An overview is presented in Mahmassani and Srinivasan (2004). All three sets of experiments use the same basic simulator, suitably modified for the particular requirements of each case. The third set of experiment is briefly described below, as the design was considerably more intricate and ambitious than previously attempted.

In the experiments, actual commuters selected route and departure time decisions in a simulated commuting corridor. The simulated corridor consists of three parallel facilities (Figure 6), with speed limits of 89 km/hour (55 mph), 72 km/hour (45 mph), and 56 km/hour (35 mph) on Highway 1, 2, and 3, respectively. Each of the three highways is nine miles long, and is discretized into nine one-mile segments. The cross-over links at the end of the third, fourth, fifth, and sixth miles enable travelers to switch

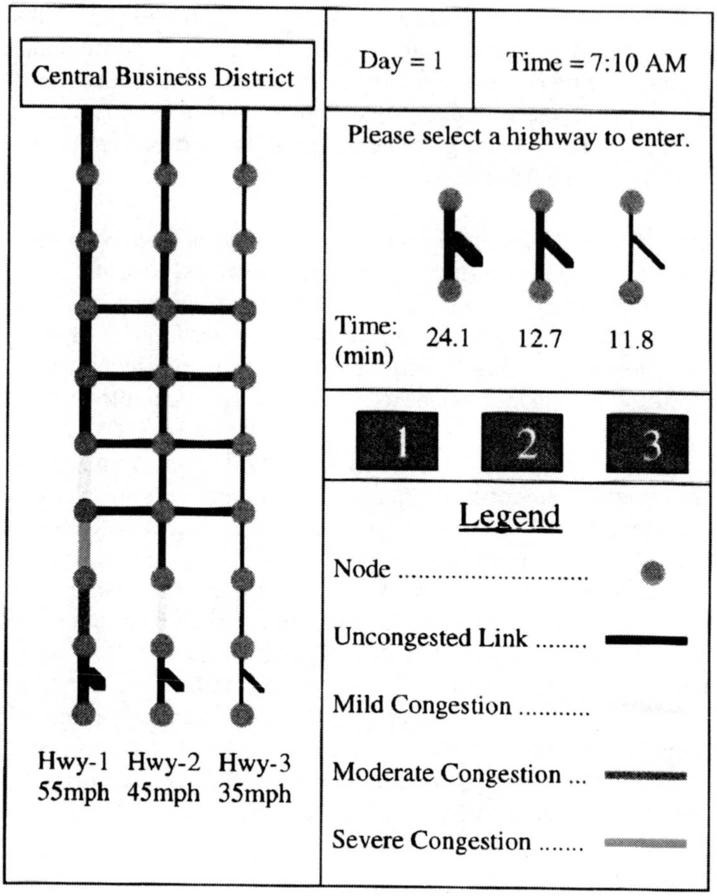

Figure 6
Example User Interface for the Pretrip Choice of Route

between the facilities, thus allowing for one pretrip route choice decision, and four en route choice decisions.

Methodologically, a novel feature in these experiments is that actual participants interact not only with one another but also with "agents" or "bots" programmed to follow response rules that have been calibrated on the basis of the observed responses of the actual human participants. Twenty-five percent of the simulated commuters (background traffic) are selected randomly and independently to receive real-time traffic information. Each participant travels from home to work for a series of 12 days. To avoid respondent burden due to fatigue and memory effects, and to avoid attrition and nonresponse biases, the experiments on successive "simulated days" were conducted on a given "actual" day. To reflect work arrival constraints, the work start time (at a work location in the central business district) is set at 8:00 a.m., and lateness is not permitted. The ATIS supplies information to each tripmaker, using three different information strategies (consisting of a combination of treatment levels described below). The strategies and the order in which they are administered are varied across different batches of users to ensure a sufficient number of observations (30+) for each treatment level. The information supplied to the user includes congestion indicated through color coding on network links, trip times on alternative paths, messages when the user is stuck in a queue, and feedback at the end of the trip. Table 2 is a summary of the experimental procedure and tasks. For each of the 12 simulated days, all users' trip decisions (one departure time and five route choice decisions per day), experienced traffic conditions, and information provided to users at each decision location are recorded. Day 1 is discarded as a trial day and the remaining 11 are considered for analysis. The data set, thus, consisted of records of a total of 6,820 route choice decisions for the 124 participants.

The experimental design consists of three experimental factors pertaining to alternative ATIS information strategies, summarized in Table 3. The first relates to the nature of information, and is intended to examine the influence of information format on route

Table 2

Summary of Experimental Procedure, Tasks and Feedback for ATIS Experiments

Setting: Commuting corridor with common destination in CBD
Task: Reach workplace in CBD by 8:00 a.m.
Trip choices: En route path choice, day-to-day departure time choice
ATIS information: Congestion information (color-coded links), trip time, traffic jam message (stuck in queue), feedback (at end of trip)

Table 3

Experimental Treatments for the Third Set of ATIS Experiments

Nature of ATIS information:
Descriptive, prescriptive
Information type:
Prevailing, predicted, perturbed
Differential prevailing, differential predicted
Random
Feedback:
Own trip experience
Recommended path (path with least trip time at each decision node)
Best path (expost, least trip time path for the chosen departure time)

choice behavior. Two levels are considered for this factor—*descriptive* and *prescriptive* information. Under descriptive information, the user is provided with trip times to the destination on all three alternative routes; prescriptive information simulates route guidance information, by advising the user of the highway to follow next, and its trip time. Trip time information is reported on other routes under prescriptive information.

The second factor is information type. Six levels of this factor are considered: *prevailing*, *predicted*, *differential prevailing*, *differential predicted*, *perturbed*, and *random* information. Under prevailing information, the travel times reported to users are based on currently prevailing conditions on downstream links, whereas predictive information reports information based on a prediction mechanism using virtual probe vehicles. Under differential information, no information is available to users on one of the three facilities, randomized on each day. The final two levels (perturbed and random information) are intended to represent inaccurate and highly imperfect information. Under perturbed information, predicted information is perturbed by the addition of an error term, whereas under random information, reported trip times are completely independent of traffic conditions on the network.

The third factor consists of the posttrip feedback provided to users at the end of the commute. Three levels of this factor are considered: (1) the commuter's own trip experience, including the trip time on the chosen path, and the arrival time at work; (2) in addition to their own experience, users receive information on the path recommended by the ATIS and its associated trip time and arrival time; and (3) instead of providing feedback on the recommended path, the information system supplies user feedback on the actual best path and the associated trip time and arrival time (for the chosen departure time). Chen et al. (1999) provide a more detailed discussion of the experimental factors.

These experiments generated a rich set of data on user choice dynamics under real-time information. These data have supported extensive analysis of users' decision mechanisms and judgment. A synthesis of these results is presented in Mahmassani and Srinivasan (2004), and addresses the following aspects: (1) en route and pretrip route-switching behavior, especially the extent of heterogeneity and unobserved structural effects; (2) route choice (selection) behavior mechanisms, particularly the role of inertia vs. compliance effects; (3) day-to-day departure time adjustment, including a comparison of alternative behavioral adjustment mechanisms; and (4) cognitive processes underlying commuter behavior dynamics.

Route Choice Games and Experimental Economics

The past decade has seen the (re)discovery of transportation network problems by researchers in a variety of disciplines, ranging from physicists interested in complexity science, to experimental economists interested in repeated game situation, to computer scientists interested in Braess Paradox and the dichotomy between user and system equilibria and its implications for network design and pricing, to social scientists interested in the interplay between collaboration and competition in human and social dynamic systems.

Experimental economics has gained considerable popularity and interest in the past decade, partly in conjunction with developments in information technology that facilitate the conduct of interactive experiments. A simple definition, according to Wikipedia (http://www.answers.com/topic/experimental-techniques) is as follows:

> Experimental economics is the use of experimental methods to evaluate theoretical predictions of economic behaviour. It uses controlled, scientifically-designed experiments to test economic theories under laboratory conditions. Typical empirical research is limited by the fact that only a subset of the set of all possible influences affect (or can be observed to be affecting) economic decision making; therefore, the ability to control for certain influences is limited or non-existent. With experiments, economists can fix some inputs and measure the effects of other inputs in a way that allows ceteris-paribus comparisons.

Methodologically, the following guidelines are generally followed in experimental economics (Davis and Holt, 1993):

- Use real monetary payoffs to "incentivize" subjects; in other words, the payoffs should be designed so as to induce the same behavioral response as the experienced consequences in a natural context.
- Publish complete experimental instructions.
- Do not use deception, though there is considerable debate regarding this matter in the field; experimental evidence suggests that deception (false consequences to deny participants monetary payoffs) leads to unreliable responses and loss of goodwill.
- Avoid introducing specific, concrete context; that is, keep the decision context stylized and generic, and hence transferable and generalizable.

The precepts of experimental economics differ from prevailing practice in transportation and travel behavior because the latter have generally sought to elicit responses to the actual attributes that influence choices in the real world, rather than some monetary surrogate that may be of questionable realism.

The influence of experimental economics has been most notably felt in the area of route choice behavior. In particular, several research groups have conducted relatively simple route choice experiments that involve the following elements: (1) a simplified two-route context; (2) idealized payoff functions that relate the number of people choosing a route to the payoff, reflecting congestion effects; (3) multiple subjects interacting simultaneously through virtual environment; (4) a large number of iterations; (5) different experimental treatments corresponding to varying information availability/feedback levels.

Compared to the previous line of experimentation conducted in the transportation/travel behavior community, these experiments are considerably simpler in terms of congestion representation or task realism. However, they have allowed somewhat wider and more liberal experimentation with monetary payoffs, which may or may not correspond to realistic settings, and have considered a larger number of iterations (conducted on a highly accelerated basis relative to natural time settings). This is possible because the main stimulus is not time, but money. The key experiment design question then is whether the payoff structure is sufficiently meaningful to induce behavior similar to that that may be obtained in the real world, where the main stimulus is in units of time.

Three main types of questions have been of interest in these experiments:

1. Understand the dynamic properties of the system, with particular focus on convergence:
   a. Does convergence occur?
   b. What does it converge to? (properties of steady state, e.g., is it an equilibrium, what kind of equilibrium . . .)
   c. Does it converge to the same state? (uniqueness)
   d. Is it stable?
   e. Convergence path, and factors that affect convergence
2. Uncover individual choice mechanisms, decision rules and heuristics underlying user behavior; these sometimes form the basis for building agents in agent-based simulations of these systems. These agents could also act as "bots" that may play alongside real human players in experiments where large-population interactions may be desired (Chen and Mahmassani, 1993).
3. Examine potential impact of certain policies or effect of different factors on the decisions of individuals, as well as on properties of the system; for example, effect of information systems, disruptions, new policies, etc . . .

Selten et al. (2004) have conducted laboratory experiments of a highly stylized day-to-day route choice game with two route alternatives (a main road and a side road), and two experimental treatments corresponding to (1) feedback only about one's own travel time, and (2) feedback on the travel times of the alternative route in addition to one's own route. Each experiment consisted of 18 players at a time (equilibrium consisted of 12 players on main road, 6 on side road). Methodologically, the money payoffs increase according to a simple linear formula with decreasing travel time, itself related linearly to the volume ($Tm = 6 + 2\,Nm$; $Ts = 12 + 2Ns$—where Nm, Ns are numbers of players choosing main vs. side and Tm and Ts the corresponding travel times). The researchers ran 200 iterations, but still encountered fluctuations, considered a very long time in experimental economics. The results seemed to converge toward equilibrium, but not perfectly, as fluctuations persisted under both treatments (fluctuations appeared to be smaller under full-information treatment). Both direct and contrarian response modes could be identified among the players, with direct players changing routes after a bad payoff, while contrarians would change roads after a good payoff (Schreckenberg and Selten, 2004).

More experiments that claim findings consistent with a Nash equilibrium are presented by Schneider and Weimann (2004), for a simple route choice situation with a single bottleneck and pricing. The experiment was constructed to test assumptions in the theoretical formulations of Arnott et al. (1990). However, the claim of consistency with a Nash equilibrium is not strongly evident in the reported data. Helbing (2004) conducted multiperson interactive route choice game with two routes, and found evidence of chaotic behavior, failure to converge, and turbulence—that is, changing behavior after periods of stationarity. The results confirmed the earlier finding of Mahmassani and Stephan (1988) that experiments with more people tend to be more chaotic and take longer to converge.

A recent paper by Rapoport et al. (2005) reports on an experimental verification of the well-known Braess Paradox in a simple network route choice game. Two route choice experiments are conducted, on networks that differ by the addition of a link (similar to the classic configuration in the pedagogical presentation of the Braess Paradox). The researchers find that the flow distribution in the augmented network leads to considerably less aggregate payoff for users than in the original network, reflecting the fact that the equilibrium solution in the augmented network incurs higher overall cost than the corresponding solution in the original network.

Denant-Boemont and Petiot (2003) present an interesting example of an experimental economics approach to assess the value of information to tripmakers in a mode and route choice situation. The experiment is more elaborate than the binary route choice problems, and involves participants in the purchase of information as one of the experimental tasks (in addition to the mode and route decisions). They find that players buy information when the variance in payoffs for the route choice is high, confirming previous theoretical results. They also find that players follow different strategies as the game evolves, from relying on external information initially to relying increasingly on one's own experience (as such experience is accumulated).

An important direction in experimental economics, which is of considerable relevance to travel behavior dynamics, is the role of learning and judgment in repeated decision situations, for example, day-to-day adjustment. Psychological studies have examined some of these questions through experiments on individual subjects, though they have typically ignored the effect of other decision makers and different information environments. Information availability plays an important role in determining which theories are feasible in different environments. Economists have investigated learning behavior both experimentally and theoretically, but on a more macroscopic scale, studying how simple information adjustment rules drive equilibrium processes in games under different information environments (Roth and Erev, 1993; Crawford, 1995; Erev et al., 1999; Camerer et al., 2002).

In the context of route choice, a growing number of researchers are focusing on the effect of learning, travel time uncertainty, and risk. Both early and more recent laboratory experiments reveal that learning and uncertainty are important, showing that route-switching behavior does depend on previously experienced travel time differences and their variance (Mahmassani and Liu, 1999; Nakayama et al., 1999; Srinivasan and Mahmassani, 2000; Mahmassani and Srinivasan, 2004; Avineri and Prashker, 2005, 2003). Experimental studies on route choice and learning have revealed that learning plays an important role at the aggregate system level by steering traffic networks toward cooperative states (Helbing et al., 2005) and at the individual level by reducing uncertainty (Avineri and Prashker, 2005; Chancelier et al., 2006). Several theoretical studies have examined some aspect of learning, uncertainty perception, or risk attitudes in the context of route choice. However, the connection between individually perceived uncertainty, risk attitudes, and their aggregate effects in traffic systems where payoffs (travel time savings) are dependent on the decisions of all users has not been fully addressed, and is an area where additional experimental research would be valuable.

Until the late 1990s, there had been few transportation applications of experimental economics approaches in areas other than commuter behavior, with limited examples in the areas of air transport (Grether et al., 1989) and rail deregulation (Brewer and Plott, 1994). Notable among more recent works are applications focused on freight markets and supply chains (Groothedde et al., 2005), and the body of contributions by Hensher and collaborators, which is further advancing the methodological aspects of experimental game design to study choice revelation processes (e.g., Hensher and Puckett, 2007).

Prediction Markets

The spread of information technologies, through near-universal broadband access to the World Wide Web, is enabling a host of developments that offer considerable potential for gaining a deeper understanding of the collective behavior of complex human, economic, and social systems. Essentially, the cost of interactive experimentation drops considerably, enabling simultaneous game situations with possibly large communities of participants at relatively low cost (Hogg and Huberman, 2002). Electronic marketplaces are one manifestation of this virtual community, and the exercise of economic activity through virtually connected communities of individuals and firms.

Coupling the notions of virtual electronic trading with the objectives of experimental study enables the application of experimental economics principles at an unprecedented scale, and through near-instantaneous interactivity. A notable example is the Iowa Elections markets, which has been used to predict the outcomes of elections, and study the opinions and potential behaviors of voters, through their trading activity in an options market (Berg et al., 2000).

Quoting Chen et al. (2003), in their preface to a proposed approach to improve the predictive ability of a small-population information marketplace for the purpose of predicting the future:

> Information markets generally involve the trading of state-contingent securities. If these markets are large enough and properly designed, they can be more accurate than other techniques for extracting diffuse information, such as surveys and opinions polls. There are problems however, with information markets, as they tend to suffer from information traps (Camerer and Weigelt, 1991; Noth et al., 1999), illiquidity (Sunder, 1992), manipulation (Forsythe and Lundholm, 1990; Noth and Weber, 1998), and lack of equilibrium (Anderson and Holt, 1997; Scharfstein and Stein, 1990).

Berg and Rietz (2003), who run the widely acclaimed Iowa Election markets, believe that the information and forecasts produced by such large virtual prediction markets can play an important role in decision-support systems that address decision situations whose outcomes depend on events predicted through the markets. They illustrate how such markets could be used to obtain conditional predictions, given the occurrence of specific events, for example, likelihood of a candidate winning conditional on a specific opponent (Berg and Rietz, 2003).

No applications of these ideas in the area of transportation have been reported, though the potential certainly exists and should be tapped. In particular, it is not difficult to envisage applications to predicting adoption and usage of new transportation services and technologies before and during their introduction. The trader's payoff might then depend on the accuracy of their forecast relative to actual usage, all the while the latter varies dynamically during the introduction period. Such marketplace environments also offer the opportunity to study users' choice processes in a highly interactive environment through repeated trials and carefully constructed sequence of steps. The high degree of interactivity in this type of environment would be particularly useful to study patterns of convergence, bias, and collective vs. individual effects in dynamic transportation environments.

Concluding Comments

The travel behavior field is still in the very early stages of developing and using experimental methods to understand individual behavior processes as well as the collective effects resulting from the interactions of these individual behaviors. Several areas of fundamental investigation in travel and activity behavior can benefit greatly from use of experimental methods. Examples include

(1) Understanding day-to-day evolution;
(2) Effect of information on activity and travel patterns;
(3) Dynamics in activity and travel patterns;
(4) Uncovering decision and learning mechanisms and heuristics (nonutility maximization behaviors);
(5) Learning and judgment processes in dynamic context;
(6) Role of prediction within experiments, and use of experiment results for prediction of behaviors and policy outcomes.

Opportunities for methodological research include

(1) The potential role of virtual field experiments, as an extension and expansion of laboratory methods to include the actual system of interest as a virtual environment.
(2) Measurement opportunities, realizing the promise of cell phones in the era of third-generation wireless networks.
(3) Adaptive experiments—learning from respondent behavior and adjusting system behavior accordingly (e.g., through intelligent adaptive bots).

Nonetheless, there also remain some fundamental questions to address as experimental methods play a greater role in the study and application of travel behavior research:

(1) Heisenberg Principle—can we observe human particles in a game situation without unduly biasing/influencing their behavior?
(2) Experimental economics: can monetary payoffs substitute for other natural environment outcomes in all situations?
(3) Simplicity vs. clutter—many experiments can get so complicated as to lose the basic insight that is desired.
(4) Simple rules, simplistic conclusions?
(5) Finally, there is the perennial question of external validity, or more appropriately the question of how to properly interpret experimental results. This can only be accomplished through systematic validation against field observation, a task that can be facilitated through virtual field experiments.

References

Arnott, R., A. dePalma and R. Lindsey (1990). Economics of a bottleneck. *Journal of Urban Economics* 27, 111–130.

Avineri, E. and J. N. Prashker (2005). Sensitivity to travel time variability. *Transportation Research Part C* 13, 157–183.

Berg, J., R. Forsythe, F. Nelson and T. Rietz (2000). Results from a dozen years of election futures markets research. Working Paper, College of Business Administration, University of Iowa, Iowa City, IA. Available at: http://www.biz.uiowa.edu/iem/

Berg, J. and T. Rietz (2003). Prediction markets as decision support systems. *Information Systems Frontiers* 5(1), 79–93.

Bonsall, P. W. (2004). Route choice simulators. In M. Schreckenburg and R. Selten (Eds.), *Human Behavior and Traffic Networks*. Berlin, Springer-Verlag, pp. 167–192.

Brewer, A. and D. A. Hensher (2000). Distributed work and travel behaviour: the dynamics of interactive agency choices between employers and employees. *Transportation* 27(1), 117–148.

Brewer, P. J. and C. R. Plott (1994). A binary conflict ascending price (BICAP) mechanism for the decentralized allocation of the right to use railroad tracks. Caltech Social Science Working Paper 887.

Burnett, P. and S. Hanson (1982). The analysis of travel as an example of complex human behavior in spatially-constrained situations: definition and measurement issues. *Transportation Research A* 16, 87–102.

Camerer, C., T. Ho and K. Chong (2002). Sophisticated experienced-weighted attraction learning and strategic teaching in repeated games. *Journal of Economic Theory* 104, 137–188.

Chancelier, J.-P., M. De Lara and A. de Palma (2006). Risk aversion, road choice, and the one-armed bandit problem. *Transportation Science* 41(1), 1–14.

Chen, K.-Y., L. R. Fine and B. A. Huberman (2003). Predicting the future. *Information Systems Frontiers* 5(1), 47–61.

Chen, P. S. and H. S. Mahmassani (1993). Dynamic interactive simulator for studying commuter behavior under real-time information supply strategies. *Transportation Research Record* 1413, 12–21.

Chen, P. S., K. K. Srinivasan and H. S. Mahmassani (1999). Effect of information quality on compliance behavior of commuters under real-time traffic information. *Transportation Research Record* 1676, 53–60.

Crawford, V. P. (1995). Adaptive dynamics in coordination games. *Econometrica* 63(1), 103–143.

Davis, D. and C. Holt (1993). *Experimental Economics*. New Jersey, Princeton University Press.

Denant-Boemont, L. and R. Petiot (2003). Information value and sequential decision-making in a transport setting: an experimental study. *Transportation Research Part B* 37, 365–386.

Doherty, S. and M. Lee-Gosselin (2000). Activity scheduling adaptation experiments under vehicle reduction scenarios. *9th International Association for Travel Behaviour Conference*, Gold Coast, Australia, July 2–7, 2000.

Doherty, S. and E. Miller (2000). A computerized household scheduling survey. *Transportation* 27(1), 75–97.

Einhorn, H. and R. Hogarth (1981). Behavioral decision theory: processes of judgment and choice. *Annals of Psychology* 32, 53–88.

Erev, I., Y. Bereby-Meyer and A. Roth (1999). The effect of adding a constant to all payoffs: experimental investigation, and implications for reinforcement learning models. *Journal of Economic Behavior and Organization* 39(1), 111–128.

Golledge, R. G., M.-P. Kwan and T. Gärling (1994). Computational process modeling of household travel decisions using a geographical information system. *Papers of the Regional Science Association* 73(2), 99–117.

Grether, D. M., R. M. Isaac and C. R. Plott (1989). The allocation of scarce resources: experimental economics and the problem of allocating airport slots. In *Underground Classics in Economics* series. Boulder, CO, Westview Press.

Groothedde, B., C. J. Ruijgrok and L. A. Tavasszy (2005). Towards collaborative hub networks, a case study in consumer goods market. *Transportation Research Part E* 41(6), 567–583.

Helbing, D. (2004). Dynamic decision behavior and optimal guidance through information services: models and experiments. In M. Schreckenburg and R. Selten (Eds.), *Human Behavior and Traffic Networks*. Berlin, Springer-Verlag, pp. 47–96.

Helbing, D., M. Schonhof and H.-U. Stark (2005). How individuals learn to take turns: emergence of alternating cooperation in a congestion game and the prisoner's dilemma. *Advances in Complex Systems* 8, 87–116.

Hensher, D. A. and S. M. Puckett (2007). Theoretical and conceptual frameworks for studying agent interaction and choice revelation. *International Journal of Transport Economics* XXXIV(1), 17–47.

Hensher, D. A., J. Rose and B. Greene (2005). *Applied Choice Analysis: A Primer*. Cambridge, UK, Cambridge University Press.

Hogg, T. and B. A. Huberman (2002). Avoiding moral hazards in organizational forecasting. Working Paper, HP Labs, Palo Alto, CA.

Iida, Y., T. Akiyama and T. Uchida (1992). Experimental analysis of dynamic route choice behavior. *Transportation Research Part B* 26B(1), 17–32.

Jones, P. M., M. C. Dix, M. I. Clarke and I. G. Heggie (1983). *Understanding Travel Behavior*. Aldershot, Gower.

Kwan, M.-P. (1997). GISICAS: an activity-based travel decision support system using a GIS-interface computational process model. In D. Ettema and H. Timmermans (Eds.), *Activity-Based Travel Analysis*. Oxford, Pergamon.

Lee, M. S. and M. G. McNally (2001). Experiments with a computerized self-administered activity survey. *Transportation Research Record* 1752, 91–99.

Lee-Gosselin, M. (1996). Scope and potential of interactive stated response data collection methods. In *Household Travel Surveys: New concepts and Research Needs*. National Academy Press, *Transportation Research Board Conference Proceedings* 10: pp. 115–133.

Lee-Gosselin, M. E. and T. S. Turrentine (1997). Investigating past and future choice sets of car-users, with special reference to perceptions of safety. Eighth Meeting of the International Association of Travel Behaviour Research, Austin, TX.

Mahmassani, H. S. (1990). Dynamic models of commuter behavior: experimental investigation and application to the analysis of planned traffic disruptions. *Transportation Research* 24A, 465–484.

Mahmassani, H. S., G.-L. Chang and R. Herman (1986). Individual decisions and collective effects in a simulated traffic system. *Transportation Science* 20, 258–271.

Mahmassani, H. S. and R. Herman (1990). Interactive experiments for the study of tripmaker behaviour dynamics in congested commuting systems (Chapter 13). In P. Jones (Ed.), *Developments in Dynamic and Activity-Based Approaches to Travel Analysis*. Aldershot, Avebury.

Mahmassani, H., T. Joseph and R. C. Jou (1993). A survey approach for the study of urban commuter choice dynamics. *Transportation Research Record* 1412, 80–89.

Mahmassani, H. S. and R. C. Jou (1998). Bounded rationality in commuter decision dynamics: incorporating trip chaining in departure time and route switching decisions (Chapter 9). In T. Gärling, T. Laitila and K. Westin (Eds.), *Theoretical Foundations of Travel Choice Modeling*. Oxford, Pergamon, pp. 201–229.

Mahmassani, H. S. and R. C. Jou (2000). Transferring insights into commuter behavior dynamics from laboratory experiments to field surveys. *Transportation Research* 34A, 243–260.

Mahmassani, H. S. and Y.-H. Liu (1999). Dynamics of commuting decision behaviour under advanced traveler information systems. *Transportation Research* 7C, 91–107.

Mahmassani, H. S. and K. K. Srinivasan (2004). Experiments with route and departure time choices of commuters under real-time information: heuristics and adjustment processes. In M. Schreckenburg and R. Selten (Eds.), *Human Behavior and Traffic Networks*. Berlin, Springer-Verlag, pp. 97–132.

Mahmassani, H. and D. Stephan (1988). Experimental investigation of route and departure time dynamics of urban commuters. *Transportation Research Record* 1203, 69–84.

Mahmassani, H. S. and C.-C. Tong (1988). Availability of information and dynamics of departure time choice: experimental investigation. *Transportation Research Record* 1085, 33–47.

Nakayama, S., R. Kitamura and S. Fujii (1999). Drivers' learning and network behavior: a systematic analysis of the driver-network system as a complex system. *Transportation Research Record* 1493, 30–36.

Ohmori, N., N. Harata and M. Nakazato (2005). GPS mobile phone-based activity diary survey. *Proceedings of the Eastern Asia Society for Transportation Studies* 5, 1104–1115.

Ohmori, N., N. Harata and K. Ohta (2004). Two applications of GIS-based activity-travel simulators. *Proceedings of EIRASS Workshop on Progress in Activity-Based Analysis*, Maastricht, The Netherlands, May 28–31, 2004.

Rapoport, A., T. Kugler, S. Dugar and E. Gisches (2005). Choice of routes in congested traffic networks: experimental tests of the Braess Paradox. Working Paper, Department of Management and Policy, University of Arizona, Tucson.

Rose, G. and E. Ampt (2001). Travel blending: an Australian travel awareness initiative. *Transportation Research Part D* 6D, 95–110.

Rose, J. and D. A. Hensher (2004). Modelling agent interdependency in group decision making: methodological approaches to interactive agent choice experiments. *Transportation Research Part E* 40(1), 63–79.

Roth, A. and I. Erev (1993). Learning in extensive-form games: experimental data and simple dynamic models in the intermediate term. *Games and Economic Behavior* 8, 164–212.

Schneider, K. and J. Weimann (2004). Against all odds: Nash equilibria in a road pricing experiment. In M. Schreckenburg and R. Selten (Eds.), *Human Behavior and Traffic Networks*. Berlin, Springer-Verlag, pp. 133–153.

Schreckenberg, M. and R. Selten (Eds.) (2004). *Human Behavior and Traffic Networks*. Berlin, Springer-Verlag.

Selten, R., M. Schreckenberg, T. Chmura, T. Pitz, S. Kube, S. Hafstein, R. Chrobok, A. Pottmeier and J. Wahle (2004). Experimental investigation of day-to-day route choice behaviour and network simulations of autobahn traffic in North Rhine-Westphalia. In M. Schreckenburg and R. Selten (Eds.), *Human Behavior and Traffic Networks*. Berlin, Springer-Verlag, pp. 1–23.

Simon, H. (1955). A behavioral model of rational choice. *Quarterly Journal of Economics* 69, 99–118.

Srinivasan, K. and H. S. Mahmassani (1999). Role of congestion and information on tripmaker decision processes: an experimental investigation. *Transportation Research Record* 1676, 44–52.

Srinivasan, K. K. and H. S. Mahmassani (2000). Modeling inertia and compliance mechanisms in route choice behavior under real-time information. *Transportation Research Record* 1725, 45–53.

Srinivasan, K. K. and H. S. Mahmassani (2002). *Dynamic decision and adjustment processes in commuter behavior under real-time information*. Research Report SWUTC/02/167204-1. Southwest University Transportation Center, University of Texas at Austin.

Turrentine, T. and K. Kurani (1998). Adapting interactive stated response techniques to a self-completion survey. *Transportation* 25, 207–222.

2.4 Group Behavior

The Expanding Sphere of Travel Behaviour Research
Selected Papers from the 11th International Conference on Travel Behaviour Research

7

Household Decision Making in Travel Behaviour Analysis

Harry Timmermans

Abstract

This chapter provides a review of studies on household decisions in travel behaviour analysis. First, comprehensive models of activity–travel patterns are evaluated. Next, the existing literature is discussed, differentiating between resource allocation and usage, task and time allocation and joint activity participation. A discussion of prospects concludes this chapter.

Introduction

The activity-based approach in transportation research has in part been motivated by the need to bring more consistency in predicting the various choice facets underlying transport decisions, and address the many interdependencies that characterize travel behaviour. Trip generation, destination, mode and route choice are not independent decisions, but represent interdependent choice facets that travellers combine in a particular way when organizing their activities in time and space, given a set of dynamic constraints. Compared to four-step models, all operational comprehensive activity-based models have made significant progress in capturing these interdependencies, although there are still differences in this regard between activity-based models.

Consistency also concerns the coordination and synchronization of activity–travel patterns of individuals belonging to the same household. Modelling such household decisions is important for a variety of reasons. First, some households may face limited resources (e.g. one car in multi-driver households), implying that household-level resource allocation and usage decisions influence individual activity–travel patterns. Second, only a single household member needs to conduct a particular household task. An example is bringing children to school. This means that task and time allocation decisions influence which household member will perform particular household tasks. Finally, being part of the same household means that certain activities such as dining and some leisure activities will be conducted jointly. This means that joint activity participation decisions influence the synchronization of activity–travel patterns in time and space of the household members involved.

Although the relevance of household decision has been acknowledged for quite some time, the earlier models have only implicitly modelled intra-household interactions through household composition and other variables in the utility functions of individual activity/travel patterns. This does however not ensure consistency of model outcomes. Only very recently, research into household decision making has received some interest in transportation research. Much of this research has addressed specific research questions, implying that the travel demand research community is still a long way from fully operational household-level activity-based models that systematically incorporate resource allocation and usage, task allocation and joint activity participation decisions, and particularly their interdependencies.

The purpose of this chapter is to review the literature in transportation research about household decision making. This review should provide an overview of topics that have been adequately addressed and topics that have received only scant attention. In addition, it should allow readers to identify promising lines of future research. The chapter is organized into the three distinctive topic areas: resource allocation and use, task and time allocation, and joint activity participation and travel arrangements. Within each section, I will first discuss the results of analytical studies and then, where appropriate, review modelling attempts, immediately admitting that this distinction is often arbitrary. The chapter is completed with a discussion of potentially promising avenues of future research. First, however, I will summarize to what extent operational, comprehensive activity-based models have incorporated aspects of household decision making.

Household Decisions in Comprehensive Activity-based Models

In this section, existing comprehensive activity-based models will be reviewed in terms of their inclusion and treatment of household decisions. Comprehensive in this context means that the model allows predicting a combination of choice facets, at least compatible with those underlying traditional four-step models: that is, activity generation, destination and transport mode choice. Over the years, many activity-based models have been suggested in the literature, including constraints-based models, micro-simulation models, (nested logit) utility-maximizing models, suites of advanced statistical models and rule-based models (see Timmermans et al., 2002 for a more detailed overview).

Constraints-based Models

These models have primarily been developed to assess the feasibility of a planned activity schedule, given a set of institutional and space–time constraints. These models have a long history in activity-based analysis from the early work of Hägerstrand and co-workers (PESASP, Lenntrop, 1976) to more recent models such as MASTIC (Dijst and Vidacovic, 1997) and GISICAS (Kwan, 1994). Although there are subtle differences between these models, all have individual activity schedules as input. Their purpose is to assess accessibility conditions and the feasibility of activity schedules as opposed to predicting activity–travel patterns. Hence, to the best of our knowledge, these constraints-based models have not dealt with household decision making. However, at least theoretically, it seems straightforward to extend these models to the household level and assess the feasibility of household activity schedules, incorporating synchronizing constraints, possible task allocation and resource allocation. A computational problem is the explosion of possible combinations of patterns that need to be evaluated. If the purpose of the model is to identify the number of feasible household activity–travel patterns, a sophisticated algorithm will be required; if the purpose is to generate a single feasible activity–travel pattern, a simple genetic algorithm will be sufficient (e.g. Charypar and Nagel, 2005; Meister et al., 2005, although the authors did not (yet) account for all types of constraints typically incorporated in constraints-based models).

Simulation Models

In the context of this chapter, this term is used for primarily data-driven models that simulate activity–travel patterns by drawing from relevant statistical distributions. Examples of these models are McNally (1997) and Ramblas (Veldhuisen et al., 2000, 2005). Pribyl and Goulias (2005) are the only ones who suggested an approach to simulate activity patterns that take interactions within the family into account. Their approach consists of six steps. The objective of Step 1 is to find groups of households with similar activity patterns. To that effect, a clustering is applied to the activity patterns of the household, combining the patterns of the adults. Next, in Step 2, the probability that an individual starts a particular activity at a particular time and activity duration are derived. For every cluster and every time step, the relative frequencies of leaving home to conduct a particular activity are derived. In addition, for each time step, activity type, means of travel, average duration and the standard deviation of duration are computed. Then, in Step 3, the identified clusters are linked to personal socio-demographic characteristics and characteristics of their entire household, using a CHAID-based decision-tree algorithm. In Step 4, the decision trees are used to assign households to a cluster. Once households have been assigned to clusters, Step 5 simulates daily activity patterns. The activity patterns consist of the sequence of activities, each with their start time, duration and the within-household interactions. The model is constructed for each time step from the proportion of cluster members who start each particular activity within half an hour on either side of the time step in question. Travel is not treated as a separate activity, but rather as an indivisible part of each activity. A normally distributed random number with the mean and standard deviation obtained from the sample for a particular activity type is used at every time instant. The patterns of all adult household members are simulated sequentially. First, the pattern of the head of the household is simulated. In case an activity is a joint activity with the spouse, the schedule of the spouse defines an exact part of her/his schedule. The remainder of the schedule is simulated, conditionally on the derived probabilities and the joint parts of the schedule. The probability of an activity to start at the end of the joint activity is used.

This approach can be viewed as an effective and straightforward extension of individual-level simulation models. A potential problem of this simulation approach is that by sampling from separate statistical distributions, the simulated schedules may be infeasible within a specific spatial–temporal context. This problem may increase for household activity schedules. Because these simulation models use observed data, they lack the behavioural mechanisms of how individuals and households adjust their preferred schedules in time and space to cope with the various types of constraints they face. These problems may be more severe when repeatedly sampling from distributions, one of the reasons why Veldhuisen et al. (2000) sampled complete activity–travel patterns. Alternatively, one can extract skeletal activity travel patterns (e.g. Janssens et al., 2005), but such an approach should be extended to cope with possible inconsistencies between simulated patterns and space–time constraints. This may not be a major issue when these skeletons are used to predict activity–travel patterns in similar spatial contexts, but the implied assumption of generalizability may be too strong if the space–time characteristics differ dramatically between the two areas. Under such circumstances, one cannot reasonably expect that similar activity–travel patterns will or can be implemented.

Utility-Maximizing Models

Over the years, several activity-based models, founded on the principle of utility maximization, have been suggested in the literature. Most of these have relied on nested or GEV logit models (e.g. Kamakami and Isobe, 1982, 1989; Bowman, 1998; Fosgerau, 1998; Wen and Koppelman, 1999; Bowman and Ben-Akiva, 2001).

This approach has been further elaborated for applications in the United States. Most of these utility-maximizing models are based on the idea of individual utility functions. Recently, some progress has been made in elaborating this modelling approach to incorporate intra-household interactions. An overview of this work is given in Vovsha et al. (2005a).

Vovsha and co-workers consider three principal layers of intra-household interactions: (i) coordinated principal activity pattern (DAP) types at the entire-day level, (ii) episodic joint activity and travel and (iii) intra-household allocation of maintenance activities. DAPs are coordinated to ensure that a particular household member can, for example, take care of the children at home. They distinguish between a mandatory pattern, further sub-divided into work, university and school, and the frequency of tours, a non-mandatory pattern and a stay home pattern. Vovsha et al. (2004a) and Bradley and Vovsha (2005) showed a strong correlation between DAP types of different household members. Joint activity and travel is differentiated between fully joint travel tours for shared activities and partially joint tours, in which household members share transportation without participation in the same activity.

The following categories of out-of-home episodic joint activity and travel are distinguished: joint travel generated by the shared activity, joint travel to synchronized mandatory activities and escorting. This leads to a sequence of five models: (i) coordinated DAP, (ii) joint travel for shared non-mandatory activity, (iii) joint travel (ride-sharing) for mandatory activities, (iv) escorting children and (v) allocation of maintenance tasks. Alternative DAP types are broken down into a group, containing individual mandatory activities, and a group containing non-mandatory and staying at home patterns that potentially can be conducted jointly by several household members. From a modelling perspective, the authors have attempted different structures. First, in several regional travel models in the United States, they adopted a sequential processing of persons according to an intra-household hierarchy (Vovsha et al., 2004a). Second, simultaneous modelling of potentially joint alternatives for all household members with subsequent modelling of individual alternatives was attempted. This involves for each household member a trinary choice (M, NM, H) and modelling the sub-choice of the mandatory alternative by a separate choice model, conditional upon the choice of mandatory alternative in the trinary choice (Bradley and Vovsha, 2005). Finally, a parallel choice structure that considers combinations of joint choices at the upper level and individual sub-choices simultaneously in one choice structure has been applied (Gliebe and Koppelman, 2005). These nests correspond to the combination of activities where joint participation is essential. The structure of these nests captures different levels of intra-household interaction. Under each nest, the correspondent individual choices of mandatory alternatives are considered for each person individually. Episodic joint non-mandatory activities are associated with fully joint travel tours. A frequency-choice model is used to predict the number of joint tours by purpose/activity type at the household level. Subsequently, a person participation choice model predicts the probability of having a certain participation matrix, conditional upon the chosen set of joint tours (Vovsha et al., 2003, 2004a, b). The various structures are modelled using a simple nested logit model or generalized nested structures of the GEV class.

Allocation of maintenance tasks to individual household members is modelled as a two-step process. First, a frequency-choice model predicts the number of maintenance tasks. Next, each task is assigned to a particular household member. Vovsha et al. (2004b) applied a task allocation choice model that predicts the probability of a person most suitable for the task as a function of activity type and person characteristics (person type, residual time window left after mandatory activities, the number of joint and escorting tours in which the person participates, etc.). Next, the resulting fractional matrix of allocation probabilities is discretionized to derive consistent sets of tasks, avoiding illogical allocations with one person overloaded while others may have no tasks.

FAMOS

FAMOS (Pendyala et al., 2005), derived from HAGS/PCATS developed by Kitamura and co-workers in Japan (e.g. Kitamura and Fujii, 1998), is a micro-simulator of individual-level activity–travel patterns. The model system does not include explicit household-level allocation models, but the individual-level models do incorporate 'intra-household interaction' effects. The individual-level activity type choice model, for example, incorporates variables that reflect household demographics and associated activity needs. The individual-level mode choice model considers household vehicle availability and the micro-simulator keeps track of the availability or non-availability of household vehicles at any point in time. There is no explicit model of joint activity engagement; however, household-level activity–travel patterns (including joint travel) can be constructed/deduced from the simulated individual-level activity–travel patterns.

CEMDAP and CEMDAP-2

This model system, developed by Bhat et al. (2004), basically is a suite of loosely connected models, predicting the activity travel patterns of workers and non-workers, and students and non-students. In turn, for some segments, the patterns are further broken down into sub-patterns. For example, the daily pattern of workers is characterized by four different sub-patterns: before-work pattern, commute pattern, work-based pattern and after-work pattern. Within each before-work, work-based and after-work patterns, several tours may exist. Considering practical implementation constraints, certain restrictions are imposed on the maximum number of tours and the maximum number of stops in any tour. A set of 22 different advanced econometric models is used to predict different facets of activity–travel patterns, where the type of model chosen does justice to the properties of the data. This is a strong feature of this model system. On the other hand, where one of the major objectives of developing activity-based models was to improve integrity and better capture the many interdependencies in activity–travel patterns, CEMDAP does not differ that much in a fundamental sense from traditional four-step models. First, activity generation is predicted, much as trip generation is modelled in the four-step models. The explanatory variables are largely socio-demographic data: constraints and characteristics of the daily patterns do not play a major role—pattern-level characteristics are limited in number and level of detail. In terms of household decisions, the model system is primarily based on individual choices. Household characteristics sometimes are used as explanatory variables, but processes such as coordination, synchronization, etc., are not explicitly represented. The new version of CEMDAP considers joint activities, though data constraints did not allow considering all possible joint activities among each sub-set combination of individuals in the household. This is seen as a separate choice and hence, the utility of joint activities against individual activities is not addressed in much detail. Car allocation (if needed) and task allocation are also modelled as part of CEMDAP. Children's activity–travel behaviour is explicitly modelled in CEMDAP now.

Rule-based Models: Albatross and TASHA

An important difference between utility-maximizing models and a rule-based model, such as Albatross (Arentze and Timmermans, 2000, 2004), is that the former models predict the choice probability of activity–travel sub-patterns. In contrast, rule-based models do not a priori assume certain multi-faceted choice alternatives but induce choice rules, based on a process model, for specific choice facets. Activity–travel patterns emerge; they are not a priori given.

Keeping this in mind, Albatross simultaneously generates activity schedules for individual household members, in which activity selection of one household member depends on the activity schedule of the other adult, if any, in the household. In case the number of cars is less than the number of drivers, a decision table, representing choice heuristics, is used to assign the car to a single household member. The result serves as one of the condition variables for other choices. Car use is systematically traced throughout the prediction of activity–travel schedules to create dynamic choice sets/action spaces, which are used to check for any violations of space–time constraints.

Joint activity participation, escorting and chauffeuring are not separately and explicitly modelled. However, bring and get activities (and sub-classifications if so desired) constitute one class of activities, while travel party is a structural choice facet of the model, implying that joint activity participation, ride-sharing, escorting and chauffeuring are endogenously generated by the model. In addition, it means that these household activities are also predicted in terms of all other choice facets (timing, duration, location, trip chaining and transport mode). Having said that, several aspects can be further improved; work along these lines is on its way.

TASHA is another rule-based model (Miller and Roorda, 2003). Although not fully operational yet, a prototype has some unique features to warrant discussion. The model uses a set of rules to generate schedules. Unlike Albatross, these rules are not derived from observations, but primarily based on expert decisions, and involve concepts such as priority and flexibility. In addition, an ad hoc fine-tuning algorithm is used. Activity–travel patterns of household members are generated simultaneously to allow for possible interaction between members. These joint activities require the activity to have the same start time, duration and location for each household member participating in that activity. Thus, a window of opportunity must exist or be created in the schedules of all household members taking part in that activity for it to be a feasible joint activity. The authors acknowledge that several other types of intra-household interaction exist, but leave that for future research.

This brief characterization of operational, comprehensive activity-based models suggests that most of these models have at best only started to look at household decisions and household-level activity–travel patterns. In earlier versions and to some extent also in the latest versions, household characteristics have been incorporated primarily as explanatory variables in individual-level models. Of course, this is quite remote from a model of household decision making. Some improvement in statistical analysis can and should be made by realizing the multi-level nature of this problem (e.g. Goulias, 2002; Miller et al., 2006) but this only implies a marginal adjustment. Incorporating mechanisms of household decision making should substantially improve the consistency and interdependencies of activity–travel patterns compared to a more or less arbitrary breakdown of the decision problem, also typical of the four-step models. However, although the degree of complexity and the sophistication of the econometric analysis have been substantially enhanced, at a more fundamental theoretical level considerably less has happened. Separating out the generation of activities and classifying certain patterns will at best allow us to capture only some aspects of how households cope with the constraints of their physical and social environments and how they organize their activities in time and space in an inherently dynamic context. In other words, a better understanding of this process and the underlying mechanisms and determinants is required. Fortunately, analytical research and research on modelling specific sub-problems has increased rapidly over the last couple of years. The findings of these research efforts make up a good starting point for more elaborate modelling efforts. This research will be summarized in the following sections.

Resource Allocation and Usage Decisions

Descriptors

Activity participation and destination choice often depend on the transport modes that are available to individual household members. Car use often means that more destinations or destinations further away from home can be reached within a given time budget. Especially in multi-person households in which the number of cars is less than the numbers of drivers, resource (car) allocation and usage is a household decision which impacts many other choice facets of individual activity–travel patterns. Golob et al. (1996) analysed how drivers are allocated to vehicles in multi-driver/multi-vehicle households. They found that gender, income, work status, age and the presence of small children in the household influenced vehicle miles travelled with the first and second household vehicles. Using the Atlanta travel survey, Hunt and Petersen (2005) also found evidence of gender differences, but less than they expected.

Models

Petersen and Vovsha (2006) argued that the first activity-based models did not involve any explicit modelling of car allocation and use. One of the few exceptions in this regard is Albatross (Arentze and Timmermans, 2000), which included rules to simulate car allocation to individual household members and explicitly tracked household cars throughout the simulation. Petersen and Vovsha (2005, 2006) modelled car-type choice, in addition to car allocation. First, they simulated which individual and joint activities are conducted and where these activities are conducted. Then, accessibility to the most important activities (work and school) in combination with the household characteristics determines car ownership by vehicle type. Next, generated activities are scheduled and out-of-home activities are distributed by travel tours. Travel needs of the household members are further consolidated through joint travel arrangements. Finally, available household cars are allocated to these tours. The authors argue that numerous feedbacks can be implemented within this framework in order to enhance the integrity of the model system and eliminate possible inconsistencies. Interestingly, they notice that only some of them can be formalized as log-sums in a nested logit model. Other feedbacks are more complicated in nature and require rule-based algorithms. For example, re-scheduling and tour-formation procedures are needed to synchronize tours and enforce joint travel arrangements. If the total time budget proved to be unrealistic in terms of travel time share, adjustment of certain activities and locations is needed.

The actual model is a multinomial model which predicts the choice of household car. A maximum of eight choice alternatives is distinguished, varying in terms of five car types (small auto with four or less cylinders; large auto with six or more cylinders;

van; SUV/jeep; truck, and car age in years). If a household has less than eight cars, unavailable choice alternatives are blocked out. For each tour, assumed known are tour-related attributes (purpose, destination, distance, schedule, number of stops, pure auto tour versus drive-to-transit tour), driver-related attributes (person type, gender, age), joint-travel-related attributes (party type, party size, fully joint versus partially joint tours), household-related attributes (income group) and zonal attributes (area type at the origin, area type at the destination). Purpose, distance, number of stops, driver type, party type, joint activity participation and socio-demographics were used as explanatory variables.

Albatross (Arentze and Timmermans, 2000) has less detail in terms of car-type choice. One of the reasons is that the number of cars per household is rarely more than three and in fact most households only have one car in The Netherlands. However, it includes more variables to capture interactions between household members, deciding who will use the car, given the nature of their activity–travel pattern, and also more variables to model the choice of transport mode for the work activity. Car allocation is not modelled for individual tours. Rather, first car allocation to work is simulated because under the described circumstances if the car is used by one household member to go to work, it will not be available for conducting any other activity by any other household members in case of single-car, multi-person households. Car availability is thus explicitly tracked in the model throughout the day for every simulated household member.

As part of the TASHA model system, Miller et al. (2003) developed a tour-based model of travel mode choice. Unlike Albatross, this model is based on the principle of utility-maximization. In particular, cars are allocated to household members such as to maximize household utility, which is assumed to be the sum of household members' individual utilities. The scope of explanatory variables is largely restricted to travel time and costs of alternative transport modes and trip purpose.

Task and Time Allocation Decisions

Descriptors

There is a substantial amount of empirical evidence in the literature that household characteristics, such as the structure and the number of persons in a household, influence the number and type of activities conducted in the household and therefore task allocation and travel decisions. Household structure also influences where (in-home versus out-of-home) activities are conducted (Gronau, 1977; Lawson, 1999). An interesting study on the relationship between task allocation and aspects of travel patterns was conducted by BGC (1995). In particular, the authors examined the relationship between the number of tasks, defined as paid work, school, volunteer work and in-home maintenance, that are performed and aspects of travel patterns. They concluded that females who combine more tasks have a higher car ownership and car availability rate. There was also evidence that if individuals performed more tasks, their mobility was higher and their travel patterns were more complex. This relationship was especially strong for women.

Many studies involved similar analyses, but for specific type of activities. A major factor that influences the decision to travel relates to the role of paid work within a household. The amount of time spent on paid work strongly influences the available budget for household consumption, the total amount of time and the time of day available for other activities. Lee and Hickman (2004) examined time allocation of households within trip chains using simultaneous doubly censored tobit models. In particular, they compared trip-chaining behaviour, among five types of households: single non-worker households, single-worker households, couple non-worker households, couple one-worker households, and couple two-worker households. Durations of out-of-home subsistence, mandatory and discretionary activities in trip chains were used to examine intra-household interactions with the household types. They found that household types, defined by the number of household heads and work status, strongly influence activity time allocation in trip chains. The presence of children in the household has a positive effect on the duration of all out-of-home activities in household trip chaining, except for the duration of out-of-home discretionary activities of households having children under 5 years of age. This suggests that the presence of children induces more time constraints to the household, resulting in more trip chaining and more time allocated to these trip chains. Finally, they found that flexible work arrangements tend to be correlated with less trip chaining for the work trip.

There is a large body of accumulative evidence that the work commute of women is shorter (e.g. Hanson and Hanson, 1980; Hanson and Johnston, 1985; Singell and Lillydahl, 1986; White, 1986; Fagnani, 1987; Gordon et al., 1989; Hanson and Pratt, 1990; Turner and Niemeier, 1997). It likely reflects the fact that on average working women are less flexible because they need to combine paid work and household activities. Women are able to combine work and domestic duties primarily by working closer to home, but also by trip chaining and relying on social networks (Kwan, 1999a, b; Dowling, 2000). Consequently, accessibility considerations are more important to them, both in terms of accepting a job and also because they need to take care of many other non-work activities. Stopher and Metcalf (1999, 2000) concluded for several cities in the United States that beyond the effects of lifecycle, both gender and working status influence the amount of time allocated to household activities (see also Vadarevu and Stopher, 1996). Likewise, Swanen et al. (2007) argued that if a spouse works longer hours, s/he has less time for domestic tasks. Relegating household activities to one's partner may then be a reasonable strategy to cope with this situation. Alternatively, households may consider an overall reduction of household tasks at the household level (Morris, 1990). However, such effects are gender-specific in the sense that male's household tasks do not change much if women work longer hours as women, irrespective of their employment status, continue to carry prime responsibility for these tasks (Morris, 1990; Pinch and Storey, 1992). There are nonetheless variations. In addition to the impact of class, occupation and lifecycle, gender roles and power differentials among spouses matter (Morris, 1990). Men tend to conduct more household tasks if spouses' role orientations are more egalitarian (Huber and Spitze, 1983), and women have more resources relative to men (Antill and Cotton, 1988). Yet another coping strategy may be task specialization. Men may conduct more tasks in larger households with young children to increase the efficiency of the household or to comply with the prevailing moral climate and gender ideology (Knijn, 2004).

There is also some evidence that good accessibility stimulates out-of-home activity participation and trip making (Boarnet and Crane, 2001; Ettema et al., 2007). In contrast, poor accessibility, either as the result of the non-availability of a car or as the result of the spatial distribution of facilities relative to home, may lead households to assign out-of-home household tasks to one spouse—usually the female—who can combine several tasks in multi-stop activity chains. For example, Strathman et al. (1994) concluded that the likelihood of forming complex commuting chains is higher for women and high-income households, both of which tend to be 'time challenged' groups. If, however, accessibility is better, men may take on more household tasks, because accommodating such activities in their activity schedules is easier (Ettema et al., 2007). Kwan (1999a, b, 2000) found that women's household activities tend to be more fixed in space and time than those by men, suggesting that such tasks are a structural component of their daily schedules, while men conduct such activities on a 'standby/basis'. This interpretation is corroborated by Aitken (2000), who concluded from interviews that fathers responsible for childcare felt they were merely 'helping out' their spouses.

Household tasks also have an effect on other in-home and out-of-home activities. For example, Gronau (1977) looked at the effects of an increase in the number of children and the age cohorts of the children. He found that as the number of children in a household increases, the additional time devoted to children is not spent on work at home and leisure. Similarly, Redman (1980) found that family size had a negative effect on meals being eaten outside the home. Golob and McNally (1997) used a structural equation model to investigate activity participation and travel of couples. Activities were classified into three categories: work, maintenance and discretionary. The total out-of-home duration for these categories was calculated as was total travel time. A series of household and personal characteristics was used as the exogenous variables of the model. They studied four types of direct effects: travel requirements of out-of-home activities, within-person activity interactions, within-person travel interactions and cross-person interactions. One of the interesting results was that if the male increases his participation in work activities, the female's travel for maintenance activities increases more than proportionally to the increase in the female's participation in maintenance activities.

Meka et al. (2002) examined interactions between two adult household members in multi-adult households using a data set derived from a 1999 household travel survey conducted in Southeast Florida. Daily activity and time allocations between two household members were examined and potential trade-offs and complementary effects were modelled simultaneously using a structural equations modelling methodology. In particular, their focus was on causal relationships among work and non-work activity and travel durations and frequencies. The model included six endogenous variables with six significant error co-variances and captured within-person trade-offs between work and non-work activity engagement. For each person, as the amount of work activity or travel increased, the amount of non-work activity or travel decreased. Between persons, the model captured the complementary and joint nature of non-work activity engagement where household members tend to pursue non-work activities together. Thus, when one person's non-work activity or travel increases, so does the other person's non-work activity travel engagement.

Borgers et al. (2001) used a stated choice approach for estimating the probability of certain task allocation profiles. The problem addressed in their paper was that stated choice experiments typically involve a choice between single alternatives and not between portfolios (a specific combination of tasks). The authors therefore explored alternative approaches of how to measure the influence of experimentally varied factors on task allocation. In a sequel, Borgers et al. (2002) estimated a slightly simpler model. They assumed that the presence of children of various ages in the household, the socio-economic status of the household, age, car availability and work status of the spouses influence time allocation decisions. Multinomial logit models, including these variables as contextual effects, were used to predict time allocation of two spouses to a set of activities. First, a multinomial logit model was estimated to predict the amount of time spent together. Next, a conditional choice model was estimated to predict the proportion of time spent by each spouse on conducting a particular activity. Because the total amount of time is known, these proportions can be translated into the number of hours spent on particular activities. Respondents were requested to jointly express the amount of time they typically spend alone and together on 27 different activities, which were later grouped into activity classes. The following activities were distinguished: (1) sleep, eat, drink and personal care; (2) work out of home, including travel time; (3) shopping and services, including travel time; (4) in-home non-leisure; (5) in-home leisure; (6) out-of-home leisure; (7) bring/get activities; and (8) others. Results indicated that if an older child is present in the household, the amount of time spent together significantly increases. The amount of time spent together is less if either spouse works. Time spent on sleeping, eating, drinking and personal care is significantly less when older children belong to the household. The effects of the work status variables were interesting. If men work part-time, they tend to spend more time on in-home work activities, although the effect was not significant. If they work full-time, they allocate significantly less time to in-home work. If their spouses work, men also tend to spend more time on in-home work activities, but this effect is only significant if their spouses work part-time. If their spouses have a full-time or part-time job, women allocate less time to shopping, which is especially true if their spouse works part-time. This result might reflect a shift in the overall activity pattern in the sense that they may spend more time together on other activities. The impact of work status of women is such that working women spend less time on shopping, but this effect is only significant if they work full-time, and then only at the 90% probability level. Overall, the results suggest that task and time allocation in households depends on household type (age, children, number of workers), the utility that is derived from joint versus solo activities, the urgency of conducting particular activities, gender roles and the constraints and possibilities offered by the environment to conduct these activities efficiently in time and space.

Ettema and Van der Lippe (2006) investigated task allocation patterns on a weekly basis. The results of their analyses indicated that specialization is a dominant weekly pattern in dealing with time constraints, that is, each spouse takes primary responsibility for different tasks. The presence of young children and a lower accessibility to jobs and services increase the female's share of household tasks and childcare. This specialization is strongest on Friday and on Wednesday, reflecting school hours and part-time work arrangements in the Netherlands. Non-traditional roles and a highly qualified job increase the females' share of paid labour and decrease their share of household and childcare tasks. However, this effect was not observed on Fridays, suggesting that women still, more than men, work in part-time jobs where Friday is the free day.

Models

Wen and Koppelman (1999, 2000) proposed a prototype activity stop generation and tour scheduling model that includes the daily allocation of household maintenance tasks and automobile use. Their model focuses on travel that is generated from participation in activities undertaken to satisfy needs and desires of the household and its members. The model itself is a nested logit model that differentiates between household subsistence (work and work-related business) needs and mobility decisions, the generation of maintenance (grocery shopping, personal and household business) activities (stops) which serve the household in general and each member of the household and the allocation of stops and autos among household members exclusively or jointly. Finally, individual daily travel/activity patterns are derived through the generation of tours, the assignment of stops to tours and the selection of locations for each stop and travel mode(s) for tours. The highest level is the choice of the number of household maintenance stops. The second level is the allocation of maintenance stops to individuals. The lowest level of the model concerns the allocation of cars to individual household members. The second stage choices, for each adult household member, include the number of tours and the assignment of stops to tours, conditional on the choices of the number of maintenance stops and the allocation of stops and autos. A distinction is made between workers and non-workers. The following workers' tour pattern alternatives are distinguished. If work is out-of-home work, a maintenance stop may be part of the work tour or part of an additional non-work tour. The work or maintenance tours may include one or more leisure stops and the daily pattern may include additional leisure tours. If the maintenance stop is part of a work tour, the maintenance stop can be made before, during or after work or during a later tour. If no maintenance stop is assigned, a simple work tour with or without a leisure stop and with or without additional leisure tours is made. Similarly, the non-worker's tours depend on whether or not a maintenance stop is assigned. If the maintenance stop is assigned to the non-worker, a primary maintenance tour with or without a leisure stop and with or without additional leisure tours is made. If no maintenance stop is assigned to the non-worker, the choice set consists of staying at home or having one or multiple leisure stops and tours. A set of individual and household characteristics, transportation performance and land use is suggested as explanatory variables of the model.

Zhang et al. (2002) developed a more general model of task allocation and time use of household members. They assumed that households allocate their time to activities such that household utility is maximized. In contrast to many other models, household utility is not assumed to be a simple sum of household members' utilities, but also incorporates relative influence and interest. Role patterns within households and more general lifestyle decisions influence the kind of activities that are conducted, the household member primarily responsible for the task, and activity participation and allocation of time across activities (and related travel). Activities are classified into four types, that is, in-home activities, out-of-home independent, allocated and shared (or joint) activities. An independent activity is an activity, not being a household task, that is conducted by an individual household member (e.g. work or attending a football match). Shared activities are those activities that require the presence of more or all household members (e.g. dinner or a family outing). An allocated activity is a household task that is assigned to a specific household member (e.g. daily shopping). Shared activities may be synchronized or non-synchronized. In the former case, household members carry out the activity together. In the latter case, household members share the activity partially. The model was initially estimated for 188 households, who reported their activity–travel patterns in the South-Rotterdam region, the Netherlands. The influence of the male on-time allocation was on average higher than the influence of the females in the sample. In a sequel, Zhang et al. (2005b) also included travel time in the model, which significantly improved model performance.

They also compared weekday versus weekend time allocation (Zhang et al., 2005c), and concluded that the influence of intra-household interaction and interdependency among activities seems invariant across days of the week. Later, Zhang et al. (2004) extended their basic model to also include dependencies among activities. The results suggested that decisions regarding household task and time allocation start with in-home activities of household members and personal and joint out-of-home activities, after which the allocation of time to allocated activities is negotiated. Women seem to regard the allocated activities more important and the in-home activity less important than men do. Zhang and Fujiwara (2004) estimated an iso-elastic household utility function, known from research on social welfare (Atkinson, 1970). Zhang et al. (2005a, b, c) compared these alternative utility functions and found the multi-linear household utility function to have a better goodness-of-fit than the iso-elastic function for data, pertaining to Japan.

Joint Activity Participation Decisions and Travel Arrangements

Joint participation in activities represents a substantial portion of non-work activities, is an important component of travel during certain time periods and affects individual travel schedules. Joint participation in maintenance and leisure activities and the provision of rides to family members constrain individual choice sets and affect the saliency of attributes that contribute to the generalized cost of travel alternatives. Therefore, this choice problem has received relatively most interest.

Descriptors of Joint Activity Participation

The relative importance of joint activity participation is evident in that joint activities tend to have a longer duration than non-work independent activities, and persons tend to stay out later and travel farther from home (Kostyniuk and Kitamura, 1983). Moreover, Fujii et al. (1999) found that time spent on activities jointly with other household members, particularly with children, was incremental to individual feelings of satisfaction and in decisions to allocate time to joint and independent activities.

Several studies have examined the effect of household attributes on joint activity–travel behaviour. Kostyniuk and Kitamura (1983) and Chandraskharan and Goulias (1999) found that joint activities involving household heads are significantly affected by the presence of children. Couples without children living at home are more likely to pursue joint out-of-home non-work activities than couples with children. In households with children, most joint activities between adults are at home. In addition, the employment status of the household heads influences whether a joint activity originated from home or from an out-of-home contact point.

Models of Joint Activity Participation

Research into joint decision structures is less prevalent, although it should be realized that some models of time use include joint activity participation (see previous section), and joint activity participation is also modelled in some comprehensive activity-based models such as Albatross (Arentze and Timmermans, 2000). Fujii et al. (1999) modelled the allocation of an individual decision-maker's time to in-home and out-of-home activities with other family members, with non-family members and alone, using a production function paradigm. Gliebe and Koppelman (2001) argued that at the time of their writing, no researcher has presented a model of household decision making in which the utility of multiple decision makers is represented in both an individual and a collective sense for the purpose of explaining joint activity participation and travel. They assumed that the joint decision is an aggregation of individually formed preferences and that households make activity decisions to maximize collective utility, subject to time constraints. Individual utility is weighted by the importance of that person to the household's total utility. Individual utility is assumed to be a monotonically increasing function of four components: (1) consumption of the products of market work (subsistence activity) and household maintenance activities; (2) satisfaction derived from participation in market work, household maintenance and leisure activities; (3) altruism from the utilities of other household members; and (4) companionship from participation in maintenance and leisure activities with other household members. Overall, different explanatory variables play different roles in the utilities of different activities for different members in the sense that they have different values of estimated parameters and statistical significance.

Scott and Kanaroglou (2002) developed a trivariate-ordered probit model to model the daily number of non-work, out-of-home activity episodes for household heads, accounting for two activity settings: independent and joint activities. They differentiated between different types of households: couple, non-workers; couple, one worker; and couple, two workers. Significant interactions between household heads were found, the nature of which varied by household type. Traditional gender roles were found to persist in couple, one-worker households. In terms of predictive ability, the models incorporating interactions were found to predict more accurately than models excluding interaction.

Srinivasan and Bhat (2006) simultaneously modelled: (1) the male's decision to undertake independent in-home discretionary activities and the corresponding duration, (2) the female's decision to undertake independent in-home discretionary activities and the corresponding duration, (3) the male's decision to undertake independent out-of-home discretionary activities and the corresponding duration, (4) the female's decision to undertake independent out-of-home discretionary activities and the corresponding duration and (5) the household's decision to undertake joint out-of-home discretionary activities and the corresponding duration. The discrete components of the choices (i.e. the decision to undertake activity) are each modelled using the binary logit structure. The continuous components of the choices (i.e. the activity duration) are each modelled using a linear regression structure with the natural logarithm of the corresponding activity duration as the choice variable.

Travel Arrangements

Ride-Sharing for Mandatory Activities

Vovsha et al. (2005a, b) conceptualized ride-sharing for mandatory activities as a pure travel arrangement, where the underlying activity for each participant is assumed to vary between individuals. Thus, they argued that different from joint activities, ride-sharing modelling for mandatory activities does not require a generation model but rather a linking and synchronizing model. This is a limiting conceptualization in that it implicitly assumes that activities are fixed. When modelling ride-sharing, the authors assumed that for each household member, the number and purpose of mandatory tours and their location zone, preferred departure from home and preferred arrival back home are known for each tour. They differentiate between outbound and inbound ride-sharing. Their model involves two stages: (i) linkage and synchronization of outbound and inbound half-tours by means of a partition-choice model that considers all possible partitions of mandatory half-tours into rides (alone and shared); (ii) ordered participation choice model that essentially considers a role of each participant (driver, passenger) and route along which activity locations of all ride participants are visited. To restrict the number of possible linkages, thresholds, including maximum allowable differences in departure/arrival times and maximum deviation from the shortest path to or from the location of activity for the driver are assumed. In addition, the maximum size of travel party was limited to three participants. The person participation role model considers sequences of persons within the ride in such a way that the first person plays the driver role, the second person corresponds to the passenger with the longest route and so forth. The last person is the first passenger dropped off on the outbound half-tour or the last person picked up on the inbound half-tour. The last person does not experience any route deviation. The order of persons from the driver to the shortest leg passenger corresponds to the magnitude of potential deviations from the shortest route.

Another interesting and in some respects more elaborate model was suggested by Roorda et al. (2006). They differentiate between joint trips, serve passenger trip (see also next section), pure joint tours, partial joint tours, pure serve passenger tours and en route serve passenger tour. The model incorporates individual tour mode choice, vehicle allocation, a serve passenger matching procedure and pure serve passenger tours, and optimizes a utility function. In their application, the number of explanatory variables was rather limited, but in principle this could be extended to encompass a wider selection of personal, household, transportation and especially activity–travel pattern characteristics.

Escorting Children

Escorting is a joint travel arrangement that is characterized by different roles of participants. There is always an escorting adult driver and one or several escorted children. Vovsha et al. (2005a, b) argued that the important characteristic that distinguishes escorting from all other joint activity and travel arrangements is that only the escorted persons have a purposed activity to participate while the driver does not participate in any activity and implements a pure chauffeuring function. A dominant share of escorting involves children as passengers. For each tour of a child that demands escorting, they distinguish five possible alternatives: (1) no escort; (2) escort in outbound direction only (from home to activity); (3) escort in inbound direction only (from activity back home); (4) escort in both directions by means of two separate tours of the same driver or by different drivers without waiting; and (5) escort in both directions by means of a single tour of the same driver with waiting. The set of children's tours with all pertinent characteristics of the person tour purpose/activity type, departure-from-home time for outbound half-tour, arrival-back-home time for inbound half-tour and location is assumed known and fixed. The set of adult chauffeurs with all pertinent characteristics of the person and availability to serve child tours within the time window left after scheduling the chauffeur's mandatory and joint activities (they are considered of higher scheduling priority) is also assumed known and fixed. Escorting tours for each chauffer are listed in a chronological order. The first escort tour can take any outbound or inbound child half-tours that fall into the available time window of the chauffeur, while each subsequent escorting tour of the same chauffeur has a narrower window available since the previous tour(s) blocked out some time. Three feasible conditions are adhered to: the bundle of outbound half-tours of children served by the tour should have close departure-from-home times and locations. A threshold was used for bundling outbound half-tours. The bundle of inbound half-tours of children served by the tour should have close arrival-back-home times and locations, and all outbound half-tours start earlier than inbound half-tours served by the same escorting tour. These constraints normally reduce the choice set size significantly. However, further decomposition may be required, for example, by ordering household chauffeurs. Then, the choice model is developed for a single person and includes only residual chauffeuring alternatives left after the choices actually made by the previously modelled chauffeurs. Alternatively, Vovsha and Petersen (2005) suggest an ordering of child tours demanding escort rather than an ordering of chauffeurs. The utility function then consists of some combination of escorting utility for each child half-tour (no escort has zero utility), additional child utility of escorting in both directions, chauffeur suitability and availability for each child half-tour, chauffeur workload saturation effect and chauffeur tour disutility.

Prospects

In this chapter, I have discussed some key publications on household decisions in transportation research. Central to the discussion has been the contention that activity-based analysis in transportation has been stimulated to improve the integrity of models of transport demand. Travel decisions are embedded in much more complex decisions on how to organize one's life in time and space, and therefore are characterized by multiple interdependencies between the various choices involved. The breakdown into four sequential choice facets as done in the four-step model is convenient, but also oversimplified. In addition to interdependencies between choice facets, interdependencies between household members also play an important role. Resource allocation, task and time allocation, and joint activity participation and travel arrangements are key decision problems in this context. Although the importance of household-level analysis has been identified for decades, this review has shown that only some comprehensive activity-based models of travel demand have only just started to pay some attention to household decision making and to incorporate sub-models of resource allocation, task and time allocation, joint activity participation and travel arrangements into the overall model system. Moreover, most efforts have focused on intra-household interactions between household heads.

Some qualifications seem to be in order at the current stage of this line of research. First, the approaches taken are rather ad hoc and do not differ in approach that much from the four-step models. Taking out a particular activity type or tour and modelling household decisions in that context may add some detail, but at best only represents a partial solution because trade-offs with other choice facets are not considered. For example, modelling car allocation and activity participation separately and combining these choice facets only in a micro-simulation fails to recognize that car allocation and activity participation are strongly interconnected. A member in car-deficient households will only consider conducting an activity that preferably requires the car when that car is available and the utility of this person using the car is higher than the utility of any other driver using the car.

Second, the theoretical underpinnings of these models need further consideration. Most research has adopted the GEV class of logit-based models. Regardless of one's opinions about the need of theoretically based models of transport demand and the validity of random utility theory, these models are founded on a theory of *individual* behaviour. Interpretation in terms of household utility is not straightforward. Empirical research has shown that there is little foundation for viewing households as homogeneous decision-making units. Also the assumption that household members are fully or at least well informed and know each other's preferences has been repeatedly invalidated. Hence, currently, these GEV class of models (and that also applies to hazard and other models) are better viewed as statistical tools, and do not have an immediate interpretation in terms of household decision mechanisms.

In this regard, some of the specific models on household time allocation have more to offer, although their theoretical foundations could be articulated in more detail. However, these specific models are still far from fully comprehensive models in the sense that their predictions of time allocation still need to be linked to other choice facets such as the generation of activity episodes, tour and transport mode choices, taking interdependencies into account. On the other hand, this situation is not much different from the state-of-the-art in many comprehensive activity-based models that also lack such integration.

Third, across the chapter, I have implicitly and explicitly argued that (household) decision making in the context of activity–travel decisions is highly context-dependent. The utility of a particular pattern depends on the urgency of the activities, the history of previous behaviour, the activity–travel patterns of other household members and a set of time-varying personal, household, institutional and time–space constraints. The current tendency of identifying a limited set of typical patterns and predicting choice probabilities of such patterns as a function of personal, household and environmental characteristics may be counterproductive in the long run. Households probably entertain a repertoire of activity–travel patterns. The choice of a particular pattern is triggered under certain circumstances. Identifying and modelling those triggers may be more productive to incorporate heterogeneity into our models. In general, identifying context-dependent relations seems a more productive approach, from a predictive perspective, than adding increasingly more parameters, accounting for heterogeneity and unknown dependencies that appear in the data. The assumption of individual weights in specific models of household time allocation is better than assuming a coherent decision-making unit, but does not acknowledge that weights in turn depend on context, preference intensity, etc. If the goal of model application is to assess the need and impact of new infrastructure, such detail may not be necessary. However, when the focus of application shifts to travel demand management, such additional detail will be required to improve the sensitivity and hence usefulness of the model.

Fourth, there is an enormous lack of research on the temporal aspects of household-level activity–travel decision making. Models tend to maximize utility for a particular day, but it may be that households tend to maximize utility across a longer time horizon. Such a perspective would also allow one to examine strategies such as turn-taking behaviour.

Recommendations

This review implies that several topics and lines of research are worth further investigation. I will just mention a few. First, comprehensive activity-based models should take a more fundamental look at household decision making and incorporate more interdependencies between the choices of different household members. It should be realized that (aspects) of morning patterns depend on (aspects) of afternoon patterns, and vice versa; that patterns of one spouse depend on the pattern of the other spouse and patterns of other household members; and that the choice of vehicle or transport mode depends on the characteristics of the pattern and vice versa. The process of breaking down complex decision-making processes is understandable and inevitable, but perhaps in the process too many interdependencies may have got lost.

Second, more theoretical work is required. Developments in other disciplines seem useful in this regard. Especially, the relative influence of household members should be further modelled as it seems to depend on contextual and situation variables. In addition, it seems relevant to estimate models with attribute-specific weights. In addition to the household utility functions that have been tested to date, it would be interesting to examine the performance of alternative specifications.

Third, an analysis of context and situation effects, and how such effect may vary across different types of households with different lifestyles and role structures, seems promising. Examining dynamics and temporal aspects is another topic that requires substantially more research: what is the temporal variability in activity patterns within a week, across seasons but also related to specific social events; to what extent do households apply temporal coping strategies; to what extent have households developed a typical, habitual pattern that allocates tasks across household members, and under what conditions do households fall back to secondary or tertiary learned patterns that together make up a repertoire of interrelated household and individual-specific activity–travel patterns? What are the dynamics of such patterns in light of dynamics in their social network?

Several some more general questions seem interesting. One of the issues in household activity–travel patterns is the issue of uncertainty with respect to on-time arrival to pick up the children. One of the coping strategies to deal with uncertainty in such situations is to rely on other household members and members of the social network. An interesting research question is to what extent this reliance on other household members occurs and to what extent the notion of permanent rescheduling behaviour enabled by modern communication technology has intensified such reliance and reduced flexibility margins in activity–travel scheduling behaviour? A second one concerns the substitution of household members and members of the social network. This would bring in a broader scope, and also requires an investigation on how to deal with decision making in social networks. Even expanding the strong current focus from household heads to all household members constitutes a challenge that needs further attention.

Finally, it goes without saying that the quality of any model and analysis depends on the quality of the data. Unfortunately, valid household-level data are still scarce.

The travel survey community and practitioners seem to have given priority to response rates. Collecting household activity–travel data increases respondent burden and therefore negatively affects response rates. However, it has not been sufficiently realized that confidence rates are not a linear function of sample size and therefore response rates. The overall usefulness of a survey may be better if more household-level data would be collected, even at the expense of lower response rates. Ideally, all household members (beyond a particular age) should complete a diary. At least, it is necessary to explicitly ask questions about individual versus joint activity and travel and about travel party in case of joint activity/travel. New communication technology may perhaps decrease respondent burden and allow easier data collection of activity–travel patterns at the household level. In any case, further analysis and modelling of household decision-making processes in a transportation context seems worth the effort, if not necessary, to improve the integrity and sensitivity of our models of transport demand. We have only scratched the surface!

References

Aitken, S. C. (2000). Fathering and faltering: 'sorry, but you don't have the necessary accoutrements'. *Environment and Planning A* 32, 581–598.

Antill, J. K. and S. Cotton (1988). Factors affecting the division of labour in households. *Sex Roles* 18, 531–553.

Arentze, T. A. and H. J. P. Timmermans (2000). *Albatross: A Learning based Transportation oriented Simulation System*. Eindhoven, The Netherlands, European Institute of Retailing and Services Studies.

Arentze, T. A. and H. J. P. Timmermans (2004). *Albatross 2.0: A Learning based Transportation oriented Simulation System*. Eindhoven, The Netherlands, European Institute of Retailing and Services Studies.

Atkinson, A. B. (1970). On the measurement of inequality. *Journal of Economic Theory* 2, 244–263.

BGC (1995). Taakcombinatie en Mobiliteit. Report prepared for AVV, Deventer.

Bhat, C. R., J. Guo, S. Srinivasan, A. Sivakumar, A. Pinjari and N. Eluru (2004). Activity-based travel-demand modelling for metropolitan areas in Texas: representation and analysis frameworks for population updating and land-use forecasting. Report 4080-6. Prepared for the Texas Department of Transportation.

Boarnet, M. G. and R. Crane (2001). *Travel by Design: The Influence of Urban Form on Travel*. Oxford, Oxford University Press.

Borgers, A. W. J., F. Hofman, M. Ponje and H. J. P. Timmermans (2001). Towards a conjoint-based, context-dependent model of task allocation in activity settings: some numerical experiments. *Journal of Geographical Systems* 3, 347–367.

Borgers, A. W. J., F. Hofman and H. J. P. Timmermans (2002). Conditional choice modelling of time allocation among spouses in transport settings. *European Journal of Transportation and Infrastructure Research* 2, 5–17.

Bowman, J. L. (1998). The daily activity schedule approach to travel demand analysis. Ph.D. Dissertation, MIT.

Bowman, J. L. and M. Ben-Akiva (2001). Activity-based disaggregate travel demand model system with activity schedules. *Transportation Research A* 35, 1–28.

Bradley, M. and P. Vovsha (2005). A model for joint choice of daily activity pattern types of household members. Paper presented at 84th Annual Meeting Transportation Research Board. Washington, DC.

Chandraskharan, B. and K. G. Goulias (1999). Exploratory longitudinal analysis of solo and joint trip making in the Puget sound transportation panel. *Transportation Research Record* 1676, 77–85.

Charypar, D. and K. Nagel (2005). Generating complete all-day activity plans with genetic algorithms. Paper presented at the 10th International Conference on Travel Behaviour Research. Lucerne, Switzerland.

Dijst, M. and V. Vidacovic (1997). Individual action space in the city. In D. F. Ettema and H. J. P. Timmermans (Eds.), *Activity-based Approaches to Travel Analysis*, Oxford, Pergamon, pp. 117–133.

Dowling, R. (2000). Cultures of mothering and car use in suburban Sydney: a preliminary investigation. *Geoforum* 31, 345–353.

Ettema, D. F., T. Schwanen and H. J. P. Timmermans (2007). The effect of location, mobility and socio-demographic factors on task and time allocation in households. *Transportation* 34, 89–105.

Ettema, D. F. and T. Van der Lippe (2006). Weekly rhythms in task and time allocation of household. Paper presented at TRB 85th Annual Meeting. Washington, DC.

Fagnani, J. (1987). Daily commuting time: the stakes for working mothers in France. *Transportation Research Record* 1135, 26–30.

Fosgerau, M. (1998). PETRA: an activity based approach to travel demand analysis. Paper presented at the 8th WCTR Conference. Antwerp.

Fujii, S., R. Kitamura and K. Kishizawa (1999). Analysis of individuals' joint activity engagement using a model system of activity–travel behaviour and time use. *Transportation Research Record* 1676, 11–19.

Gliebe, J. P. and F. S. Koppelman (2001). A model of joint activity participation. Paper presented at the 80th Annual Meeting Transportation Research Board. Washington, DC.

Gliebe, J. P. and F. S. Koppelman (2005). Modelling household activity–travel interactions as parallel constrained choices. Paper presented at 84th Annual Meeting Transportation Research Board. Washington, DC.

Golob, T. F., S. Kim and W. Ren (1996). How households use different types of vehicles. *Transportation Research A* 30, 103–118.

Golob, T. F. and M. G. McNally (1997). A model of household interactions in activity participation and the derived demand for travel. *Transportation Research* 31B, 177–194.

Gordon, P., A. Kumar and H. W. Richardson (1989). Gender differences in metropolitan travel behaviour. *Regional Studies* 23, 499–510.

Goulias, K. (2002). Multilevel analysis of daily time use and time allocation to activity types accounting for complex covariance structures using correlated random effects. *Transportation* 29, 31–48.

Gronau, R. (1977). Leisure, home production, and work—the theory of the allocation of time revisited. *Journal of Political Economy* 85, 1099–1123.

Hanson, S. and P. Hanson (1980). Gender and urban activity patterns in Uppsala, Sweden. *Geographical Review* 70, 291–299.

Hanson, S. and I. Johnston (1985). Gender differences in work-trip length: explanations and implications. *Urban Geography* 6, 193–219.

Hanson, S. and G. Pratt (1990). Geographic perspectives on the occupational segregation of women. *National Geographic Research* 6, 376–399.

Huber, J. and G. Spitze (1983). *Sex Stratification: Children, Housework and Jobs.* New York, Academic Press.

Hunt, K. and E. Petersen (2005). The role of gender, work status and income in auto allocation decisions. *Proceedings of the Annual TRB Meeting*. Washington, DC.

Janssens, D., G. Wets, T. Brijs and K. Vanhoof (2005). Simulating daily activity patterns through the identification of sequential dependencies. In H. J. P. Timmermans (Ed.), *Progress in Activity-based Analysis*, Oxford, Pergamon Press, pp. 67–89.

Kamakami, S. and T. Isobe (1982). Development of a one day travel-activity scheduling model for workers. In S. Carpenter and P. Jones (Eds.), *Recent Advances in Travel Demand Analysis*, Aldershot, Gower, pp. 314–344.

Kamakami, S. and T. Isobe (1989). Development of a scheduling model considering time constraint and temporal transferability test of the model. *Selected Proceedings of the 5th WCTR Conference*. Yokohama, Japan, Vol. IV, pp. 221–233.

Kitamura, R. and S. Fujii (1998). Two computational process models of activity–travel choice. In T. Garling, T. Laitila and K. Westin (Eds.), *Theoretical Foundations of Travel Choice Modelling*, Oxford, Elsevier, pp. 251–279.

Knijn, T. (2004). Challenges and risks of individualisation in the Netherlands. *Social Policy & Society* 3, 57–65.

Kostyniuk, L. P. and R. Kitamura (1983). An empirical investigation of household time space paths. In S. Carpenter and P. Jones (Eds.), *Recent Advances in Travel Demand Analysis*. Aldershot, UK, Gower Publishing Co. Ltd.

Kwan, M.-P. (1994). GISICAS: a GIS-interfaced CPM for activity scheduling in ATIS. Unpublished dissertation, University of California at Santa Barbara, USA.

Kwan, M.-P. (1999a). GISICAS: an activity-based travel decision support system using a GIS-interfaced computational process model. In D. F. Ettema and H. J. P. Timmermans (Eds.), *Activity-based Approaches to Travel Analysis*, Oxford, Pergamon, pp. 263–282.

Kwan, M.-P. (1999b). Gender, the home–work link and space–time patterns of non-employment activities. *Economic Geography* 76, 370–394.

Kwan, M.-P. (2000). Gender differences in space–time constraints. *Area* 32, 145–156.

Lawson, C. T. (1999). Household travel/activity decision: who wants to travel? Paper presented at the 78th Annual Meeting Transportation Research Board. Washington, DC.

Lee, Y. and M. Hickman (2004). Household type and structure, time use pattern, and trip chaining behaviour. Paper presented at the 83rd Annual Meeting Transportation Research Board. Washington, DC.

Lenntrop, B. (1976). Paths in space–time environment. In *Lund Studies in Geography*, No. 44. Royal University of Lund, Lund, Sweden.

McNally, M. G. (1997). An activity-based micro-simulation model for travel demand forecasting. In D. F. Ettema and H. J. P. Timmermans (Eds.), *Activity-based Approaches to Travel Analysis*, Oxford, Pergamon, pp. 37–54.

Meister, K., M. Frick and K. W. Axhausen (2005). A GA-based household scheduler. *Proceedings of the TRB Annual Conference*. Washington, DC (CD-ROM).

Meka, S., R. Pendyala and M. Kumara (2002). A structural equations analysis of within-household activity and time allocation between two adults. *Proceedings of 81st TRB Conference*. Washington, DC (CD-ROM).

Miller, E. J., H. Nurul and M. Kandker (2006). Modelling individuals' frequency and time allocation behaviour for shopping activities considering household level random effects. *Proceedings of TRB Annual Meeting*. Washington, DC (CD-ROM).

Miller, E. J. and M. J. Roorda (2003). A prototype model of household activity–travel scheduling. Paper presented at the 82nd Annual Meeting Transportation Research Board. Washington, DC.

Miller, E., M. J. Roorda and J. Carrasco (2003). A tour-based model of travel choice. *Proceedings of 10th IATBR Conference*. Lucerne, Switzerland (CD-ROM).

Morris, L. (1990). *The Workings of the Household*. Cambridge, Polity Press.

Pendyala, R., R. Kitamura, A. Kikuchi, T. Yamamoto and S. Fujii (2005). Florida activity mobility simulator. *Transportation Research Record* 1921, 123–130.

Petersen, E. and P. Vovsha (2005). Auto allocation modelling in activity-based models. Presented at the *10th Transportation Planning Application Conference*. TRB, Portland, OR.

Petersen, E. and P. Vovsha (2006). Intrahousehold car type choice for different travel needs. Paper presented at 85th Annual Meeting Transportation Research Board. Washington, DC.

Pinch, S. and A. Storey (1992). Who does what, where? A household survey of domestic labour in Southampton. *Area* 24, 5–12.

Pribyl, O. and K. G. Goulias (2005). Simulation of daily activity patterns. In H. J. P. Timmermans (Ed.), *Progress in Activity-based Analysis*, Oxford, Pergamon, pp. 43–66.

Redman, B. J. (1980). The impact of women's time allocation on expenditure for meals away from home and prepared foods. *American Journal of Agricultural Economics* 62, 234–237.

Roorda, M., E. S. Miller and N. Kruchten (2006). Incorporating within-household interactions into a mode choice model using a genetic algorithm for parameter estimation. *Proceedings of the Annual TR Meeting*. Washington, DC.

Scott, D. M. and P. S. Kanaroglou (2002). An activity-episode generation model that captures interactions between household heads: development and empirical analysis. *Transportation Research B* 36, 875–896.

Singell, L. D. and J. H. Lillydahl (1986). An empirical analysis of the commute to work patterns of males and females in two-earner households. *Urban Studies* 2, 119–129.

Srinivasan, S. and C. R. Bhat (2006). A multiple discrete–continuous model for independent- and joint-discretionary-activity participation decisions. *Proceedings of the TRB Conference*. Washington (CD-ROM).

Stopher, P. R. and H. M. A. Metcalf (1999). Household activities, lifecycle, and role allocation: tests on datasets from Boston and Salt Lake City. *Transportation Research Record* 1676, 95–102.

Stopher, P. R. and H. M. A. Metcalf (2000). Allocation time to activities and household members: results from four urban areas. *Proceedings of IATBR Conference*. Gold Coast, Australia (CD-ROM).

Strathman, J. G., K. J. Dueker and J. S. Davis (1994). Effects of household structure and selected travel characteristics on trip chaining. *Transportation* 24, 23–45.

Swanen, T., D. F. Ettema and H. J. P. Timmermans (2007). If you pick up the children, I'll do the groceries: spatial differences in between-partner interactions in out-of-home household activities. *Environment and Planning A*, 39, 2754–2773.

Timmermans, H. J. P., T. A. Arentze and C.-H. Joh (2002). Analysing space–time behaviour: new approaches to old problems. *Progress in Human Geography* 26, 175–190.

Turner, T. and D. Niemeier (1997). Travel to work and household responsibility: new evidence. *Transportation* 24, 397–419.

Vadarevu, R. and P. R. Stopher (1996). Household activities, lifecycle and role allocation. *Transportation Research Record* 1556, 77–85.

Veldhuisen, K., H. J. P. Timmermans and L. L. Kapoen (2000). Ramblas: a regional planning model based on the micro-simulation of daily activity travel patterns. *Environment and Planning A* 32, 427–443.

Veldhuisen, K. J., H. J. P. Timmermans and L. L. Kapoen (2005). Simulating the effects of urban development on activity–travel patterns: an application of Ramblas to the Randstad North Wing. *Planning and Design* 32, 567–580.

Vovsha, P., M. Bradley and J. L. Bowman (2005a). Activity-based travel forecasting models in the United States: progress since 1995 and prospects for the future. In H. J. P. Timmermans (Ed.), *Progress in Activity-based Analysis*, Oxford, Pergamon, pp. 389–414.

Vovsha, P., J. Gliebe, E. Peterson and F. S. Koppelman (2005b). Sequential and simultaneous choice structures for modelling intra-household interactions in regional travel models. In H. J. P. Timmermans (Ed.), *Progress in Activity-based Analysis*, Oxford, Pergamon, pp. 223–258.

Vovsha, P. and E. Petersen (2005). Escorting children to school: statistical analysis and applied approach. *Proceedings of 84th TRB Conference*. Washington, DC (CD-ROM).

Vovsha, P., E. Petersen and R. Donnelly (2003). Explicit modelling of joint travel by household members: statistical evidence and applied approach. *Transportation Research Record* 1831, 1–10.

Vovsha, P., E. Petersen and R. Donnelly (2004a). A model for allocation of maintenance activities to the household members. Paper presented at the 83rd Annual Meeting Transportation Research Board. Washington, DC.

Vovsha, P., E. Petersen and R. Donnelly (2004b). Impact of intra-household interactions on individual daily activity–travel patterns. *Proceedings of 83rd TRB Conference*. Washington, DC. (CD-ROM).

Wen, C. and F. S. Koppelman (2000). A conceptual and methodological framework for the generation of activity–travel patterns. *Transportation* 27, 5–23.

Wen, C.-H. and F. S. Koppelman (1999). An integrated system of stop generation and tour formation for the analysis of activity and travel patterns. *Transportation Research Record* 1676, 136–144.

White, M. J. (1986). Sex differences in urban commuting patterns. *The American Economic Review* 76, 332–368.

Zhang, J. and A. Fujiwara (2004). Representing heterogeneous intra-household interaction in the context of time allocation. Paper presented at the 83rd Annual Meeting of Transportation Research Board. Washington, DC.

Zhang, J., A. Fujiwara, H. J. P. Timmermans and A. W. J. Borgers (2005a). An empirical comparison of alternative models of household time allocation. In H. J. P. Timmermans (Ed.), *Progress in Activity-based Analysis*, Oxford, Elsevier, pp. 259–284.

Zhang, J., H. J. P. Timmermans and A. W. J. Borgers (2002). A utility-maximizing model of household time use for independent, shared and allocated activities incorporating group decision mechanism. *Transportation Research Record* 1807, 1–8.

Zhang, J., H. J. P. Timmermans and A. W. J. Borgers (2004). Model structure kernel for household task and time allocation incorporating household interaction and inter-activity dependency. *Proceedings of 83rd TRB Conference*. Washington, DC (CD-ROM).

Zhang, J., H. J. P. Timmermans and A. W. J. Borgers (2005b). Comparative analysis of married couples' task and time allocation behaviour on weekdays vs. weekends. Paper presented at 84th Annual Meeting Transportation Research Board. Washington, DC.

Zhang, J., H. J. P. Timmermans and A. W. J. Borgers (2005c). A model of household task allocation and time use. *Transportation Research B* 39, 81–95.

The Expanding Sphere of Travel Behaviour Research
Selected Papers from the 11th International Conference on Travel Behaviour Research

8

Models of Household Activity and Travel Behavior with Group Decision-Making Mechanisms in Japan

Junyi Zhang and Akimasa Fujiwara

Abstract

In line with the resource paper for the Workshop "Group behavior" presented by Harry Timmermans at the 11th International Conference on Travel Behaviour Research, this paper reports progress in Japanese research on household activity and travel behavior that explicitly incorporates decision-making mechanisms. Although transportation researchers in Japan have started research on group behavior later than their American and European colleagues, one can observe a rapidly increasing number of relevant studies. The studies reported here cover household time and task allocation, scheduling behavior, car ownership, telecommunication and activity participation, and joint trip-making behavior. Methodologically, general theories of group (household) decision-making have been mainly applied.

Introduction

Many policy issues in transportation are related to the joint decisions of at least two people. To better understand the impact of such policies, it is paramount to study such household decision-making processes. For example, travel patterns are influenced by demographic processes. Decisions about marriage and/or having children are clearly a joint task by at least two people. Parents need to choose appropriate schools/universities for their children, and they may also give some advice about career decisions to their children. Marriage sometimes forces women to give up their jobs or change their work hours (e.g., from full-time to part-time). When children grow up, mothers may wish to find a job again. Women's participation in the labor market and the associated rise of dual-earner households may result in a change of travel patterns. Another example deals with land use. It is obvious that the choice of residential area is a household decision. The couples and/or other household member(s) have to jointly determine the residential area and types of houses by balancing their individual preferences. A third policy area is that of environmental issues in transportation, which is closely related to household car ownership and use behavior. Household car ownership and use usually involves group decision-making process. Employers' environmental attitudes/policies may also influence their employees' commuting and noncommuting travel behavior. These examples show that many decisions relevant to better understand transportation policies are inherently household/group decisions. Ignoring such group decision-making mechanisms may lead to wrong policy decisions.

Studies of group behavior date back to the late 1930s when Thorndike (1938) conducted a pioneer study to examine the relationship between type of task and quality of the group decision. Early studies indirectly related to transportation, which were conducted in the 1960s, included housing choice and car ownership behavior, daily shopping behavior, and tourism behavior (Davis, 1976). For example, it was found that wives did most of grocery shopping with an awareness of products and brands that their families liked, and husbands and teenagers were frequently involved in new or different brands. In case of house-buying behavior, it was also shown that husbands decided whether to move or not, and range of price, and wives decided number of bedrooms and other house features. For car purchase behavior, the influence of husband–wife with respect to specific product attributes (e.g., make, model, color, size, budget consideration including price or when to buy) was empirically examined. An analysis of tourism behavior, it was found that husbands suggested to take a trip and selected an airline, while the decision where to go was a joint decision.

Since 1980s, the importance of group behavior, especially household behavior, has been recognized by some researchers in the context of activity-based analysis. For example, Jones et al. (1983) examined the relationship between household members and the constraints that bind their decision-making processes in the HATS gaming simulator. Their approach provides a wealth of information on intrahousehold interaction and the associated decision-making processes. A recent review of research of household behavior from the perspective of group decision-making in transportation can be found in Timmermans (2009). In Japan, a focus on group behavior research is important for the following reasons.

(1) Due an aging and shrinking population, it is becoming increasingly important to secure the mobility of elderly and disabled in depopulated regions. These persons' participation in out-of-home activities needs the assistance or help of others.

(2) In Japan, urban sprawl is increasing due to the continuing motorization. Simultaneously, it has been observed that population distribution tends to move toward central urban areas because of the fall in land price in urbanized areas. Regeneration of city centers is being urged to overcome the issues caused by the urban sprawl. Promoting residential development in city centers is one policy. Understanding the relationship between residential choice and job location and car ownership/use is essential and requires a household-level perspective.
(3) Because of ever-increasing environmental concerns, public transportation systems are playing an increasingly important role in reshaping urban structures and modifying people's car-use behavior. To avoid the NIMBY problem in the implementation of environmental policies, it seems important to study the feasibility of promoting people's prosocial behavior.
(4) Development of information and communication technologies (ICT) in Japan has been very rapid. Use of ICT has changed people's daily life in various ways. It is expected that nontravel communication induces participation in out-of-home joint activities, which surely involve a group decision-making process.
(5) To enhance the accountability and public acceptance of effective transportation policies, it is necessary to promote the communication between policy makers and the public in order to realize smooth consensus building through the implementation of public involvement. Such research has been quite active in Japan, applying game theory and other group decision-making theories.

Looking at travel behavior analysis, which is the focus of this synthesis report, even though activity-based approaches have been applied since the late 1980s (see Sugie et al., 1988), research on household/group behavior modeling is new. To the authors' knowledge, group behavior research in Japan dates back to the late 1990s. More recently, the topic has gained much interest as reflected by an independent session focusing on group behavior at the semiannual Conference of Infrastructure Planning, organized by the Japan Society of Civil Engineers, in June 2005. This conference is the only conference in Japan to comprehensively deal with the advanced planning issues in civil engineering including transportation.

As discussed above, there are various fields in transportation dealing with group behavior. In this synthesis report, we only focus on the studies of household behavior that explicitly deal with group decision-making mechanisms. These studies can be divided into analyses and modeling of (1) household task and time allocation, (2) household scheduling behavior, (3) group discrete choice models with applications to household car and residential choice behavior, (4) joint trip-making behavior, and (5) research on telecommunication and activity participation.

There are also some interesting relevant studies that will not be mentioned. For example, Yao and Morikawa (2003) conducted an interesting study. They measured the value of travel time saving from collective choice model in their study on integrated intercity travel demand model, where the collective utility is defined as a function of both employer's and employee's preferences. Yamamoto et al. (2007) proposed an interesting approach to calculate maximal potential market for neighborhood car sharing considering optimization of car use within household, using the data collected in Toyota City. It is known that scope of group behavior research is very broad. There are some studies conducted in Japan that address other types of topics related to group behaviors. Such examples include social dilemmas (e.g., Fujii, 2005), consensus building and public involvement (e.g., Terabe and Yai, 1999), social network and telecommunication (e.g., Ohmori, 2006), and network behavior (e.g., Hato, 2001). These days, social capacity building is receiving more and more attention in the field of public policies in both developing and developed countries. Social capacity refers to the capacity that the whole society, composed of three social actors: government, firms, and civil society, makes use of available capital assets to deal with social problems toward sustainable states under the influence of interactions among actors (e.g., Bengston et al., 2003; Zhang and Fujiwara, 2006a). Group behavior research could contribute to the development of social capacity indicators and improvement of social capacity.

Development of Household Task and Time Allocation Models

Motivation

Household task and time allocation behavior could be modeled by integrating group decision-making theories and Becker's (1965) time allocation theory. Gliebe and Koppelman (2000) pioneered research on household time allocation modeling. They proposed a household joint-activity participation model by adopting an *additive*-type household utility function. This function defines each member's utility by introducing other members' utilities and the utilities from participation in joint activities. However, it is assumed that weights (or relative influence/importance) of members or activities during joint decision-making process are the same. They conceptually examined the trade-offs between joint and individual activities. However, they did not derive an operational joint-activity participation model endogenously. To overcome the short-comings of Gliebe and Koppelman's model, Zhang et al. (2002) developed a new household task and time allocation model by applying a multilinear household utility function. As a result, they derived an operational and comprehensive model system to describe household task and time allocation behavior. In the same year, Gliebe and Koppelman (2002) successfully derived their joint-activity participation model by improving their previous research. The *additive*-type utility function adopted by Gliebe and Koppelman is a special case of multilinear utility function. The multilinear function can also include *compromise*-type, *capitulation*-type, and *autocracy*-type utilities as special cases, and incorporates the *Nash*-type intrahousehold interaction. However, Zhang et al.'s (2002) model cannot deal with some extreme cases, such as *max–max* and *max–min* decision rules. Therefore, methodologically, introduction of some more general household utility functions was required.

Modeling Framework with Isoelastic Household Utility

To further explore group decision-making mechanisms in household task and time allocation behavior, Zhang and Fujiwara (2006b) developed another new model, which adopts an *isoelastic* household utility function. They drew on Atkinson's (1970) research on social welfare. An individual member's utility is defined using a multilinear utility function. Different values and signs of the intrahousehold interaction parameter, and different weight parameters of household members represent different household decision-making mechanisms. The *isoelastic* function can include various types of household utility functions as special cases such as, *max–max*, *max–min*, *Nash*-type without reference point, *additive-*, *compromise-*, *capitulation-*, and *autocracy*-type. It is obvious that *isoelastic* and *multilinear* utility functions share some common types of utilities including *additive-, compromise-*, *capitulation-*, and *autocracy*-type. However, *Nash*-type utility is a special case of the *isoelastic* utility function, but it is only a part of *multilinear* utility function. Thus, as a method of representing intrahousehold interaction, the *isoelastic* and *multilinear* utility functions adopt different modeling strategies on one hand, and overlay functionally on the other. The *isoelastic* function seems much more flexible and general. But at this moment, comparison between *multilinear* and *multilinear* utility functions has not confirmed which is superior.

Zhang and Fujiwara (2006b) further classified the activities into four major types: in-home activities, out-of-home independent, allocated and shared activities. To examine the effectiveness of the derived household task and time allocation model, they conducted a 1-week activity diary survey in two small towns: Kakeya (population: 3,422, the ratio of elderly people: 33.3%) and Akagi (population: 4,036, the ratio of elderly people: 33.6%), in Shimane Prefecture near the Sea of Japan. They collected 1-week activity diary data for 153 households. As an initial attempt to examine the model effectiveness, they only extracted the activity data from the households with elderly couples. Consequently, 1-week activity diary data from 38 households with elderly couples, and a total of 255 person-day were adopted as the sample. They empirically confirmed the effectiveness of the proposed model and its applicability to evaluate the influence of elderly transportation policies, based on a simulation analysis. From the same data source, focusing on the analysis of pick-up/deliver choice behavior, Zhang et al. (2005) extracted different samples to compare the multilinear and isoelastic household time and task allocation models and did not find any significant difference in model accuracy. However, they found that the two types of household utility functions, that is, *multilinear* and *isoelastic* functions, lead to different decision-making mechanisms. Zhang and Fujiwara (2009a) reached similar conclusions using a large-scale national time use data set, collected in 2001 by the Ministry of

General Affairs, Japan. Research findings suggest that some new modeling approaches are required to simultaneously incorporate various decision-making rules.

Incorporating Monetary Constraint

The models mentioned above have not incorporated the influence of monetary constraints. Ignoring such constraints is partially due to data availability. In reality, it is quite difficult to collect the data related to monetary consumption. Recognizing this issue, Nepal et al. (2005) conceptually presented some microeconomic models of household time allocation, incorporating both time and monetary constraints. It is assumed that an individual member's total time could be allocated to either independent or joint (shared) activities. Similarly, the household consumption could be either private or shared consumption bundles. It is further assumed that working hours are not allocated together with other daily activities. Travel costs and expenditures related to each activity are also incorporated. Summation of wage and unearned income is the upper limit of monetary consumption.

Nepal et al. classified the household time allocation model into a unitary model and a nonunitary model, where the latter is further grouped into a *Nash*-bargained model and a collective model. The unitary model arbitrarily selects a household member and uses his/her utility to represent total household utility. A difference between the unitary model and the individual-based model is that it introduces household monetary constraints instead of individual constraints. The *Nash*-bargained model adopts a *Nash*-type utility function with threat point (or reference point) as the household utility function, where the threat point is each member's maximized utility derived unconditionally from the influence of the household. In contrast, the collective model adopts the *additive*-type household utility. Unfortunately, Nepal et al. only conceptually discussed the characteristics of the models, and have not shown the detailed model structure. We can imagine that the maximization methods adopted by Zhang and Fujiwara (2006b) could be easily extended to incorporate the above-mentioned monetary constraints.

Interestingly, Fukuda et al. (2006) applied the *additive*-type household utility function to derive an additional household time allocation model with both time and monetary constraints. They further measured the value of activity time. Even though there are some problems with the used expenditure data, their study shows the new potential in policy analysis of household time allocation models.

Kato et al. (2003) applied a structural equation model with latent variables to examine how intrahousehold interaction affects the durations of discretionary activities performed on weekdays and weekends. They collected activity diary data in Tokushima Prefecture between November 2001 and January 2002, and asked the recruited households to report their activity participations on a weekday and a weekend, respectively. As a case study, they extracted 72 households with valid activity data and introduced the partner's working hours to represent intrahousehold interaction. Their established structural equation models are good enough to describe the durations of discretionary activities. They also showed that the unemployed member's durations of discretionary activities on weekdays are not affected by another member's working hours, but the durations on weekends are affected. Matsumoto and Kato (2006) applied 1-week activity diary data from the same survey mentioned above to present a conditional probability model for the generation of discretionary out-of-home activity participation to understand the interactions of time–space, interdependence of household members, and day-to-day variability in a week.

Development of a Household Activity-Travel Scheduling Model

It is known that utility of activity participation and trip-making behavior changes over time, and timing decisions within a given period of time interact across activities/trips because of available time constraints. Such behavioral mechanisms become more complicated in the context of household decisions, where some of household members usually perform some activities and/or make trips jointly. In other words, there exist coupling constraints in household activity-travel scheduling behavior. Zhang et al. (2006a) adopted a gamma probability density function as the utility function of timing and then derived the optimal timing functions for both nonshared and shared activities/trips using the following modeling framework.

Maximize

$$U_h = \sum_n \sum_i U_{hni} = \sum_n \sum_i \int_{t_{hni-1}}^{t_{hni}} u_{hni}(s)\, ds \tag{1}$$

$$u_{hni}(s) = \frac{\beta_{hni}^{\alpha_{hni}}\, s^{\alpha_{hni}-1}}{\Gamma(\alpha_{hni})} \exp(-\beta_{hni}\, s) \tag{2}$$

$$\Gamma(\alpha_{hni}) = \int_0^{\infty} y^{\alpha_{hni}-1} e^{-y} dy,\ \alpha_{hni} > 0,\ \beta_{hni} > 0 \tag{3}$$

Subject to

$$\sum_i \tau_{hni} = \sum_i (t_{hni} - t_{hni-1}) = T_{hn} \tag{4}$$

where, h, n, i indicate household, individual, and activity/trip, respectively; U_{hni} is the utility that individual n from household h performs the ith activity or trip; $U_{hni}(s)$ is timing utility that individual n from household h performs the ith activity or trip at time s; α_{hni}, β_{hni} indicate shape and scale parameters of timing utility $U_{hni}(s)$ that individual n from household h performs the ith activity or trip, respectively; $\Gamma(\cdot)$ is the gamma function; t_{hni-1} is start or departure time that individual n from household h performs the ith activity or trip; t_{hni} is end or arrival time that individual n from household h performs the ith activity or trip; τ_{hni} is duration of individual n from household h performing the ith activity or trip; and T_{hn} is the available time of individual n from household h.

The derived function for nonshared activity/trip timing includes only information of the household member of interest, while that of shared activity/trip includes the information of all involved household members. To incorporate interdependencies among activities/trips over time, Zhang et al. (2006a) further applied the concept of the first-order sequential correlation, which describes the correlation between error terms of consecutive activity/trip timing functions based on a bivariate normal distribution. The derived timing function for the shared activity/trip is used to endogenously represent the household's coupling constraints using sequential correlations related to all relevant members. The model is estimated using activity data collected in the Netherlands. Model estimation results confirm the effectiveness of the proposed model in representing household timing decisions, both in terms of model accuracy and statistical significance of the introduced explanatory variables and parameters related to sequential correlation. Factors to explain shape and scale parameters show inconsistent influences on the timing distribution related to coupling constraints, suggesting the complexity of household timing decisions.

Development of Household Discrete Choice Models with Group Decision-Making Mechanisms

Traditionally, an individual has been regarded as an independent decision maker or a representative agent in transportation. For example, household choice behavior has been analyzed using unitary-type choice models, which regard the household as a single decision maker and ignores each member's roles in and influences on household decisions. Logit-type and probit-type models are the examples, such as multivariate probit, nested logit model, nested covariate heterogeneity logit model, mixed logit model, and latent class (LC) segmentation model (Rich, 2001; Hensher, 2003, 2004; Gliebe and Koppelman, 2005). If one can clearly identify which member makes the decision, these models are acceptable and applicable. However, analysts often do not know exactly who is the decision maker. In such cases, applying these models to represent group decision-making mechanisms is problematic, because all these models assume that decision makers are prespecified. Under such circumstances, Zhang et al. (2006b, 2007, 2009) developed some alternative approaches to represent household discrete choice behavior with group decision-making mechanisms based on the concept of metautility.

Kernel Model Structure

To define household utility function, Zhang et al. (2006b, 2007, 2009) introduced the concept of metautility under the principle of random utility maximization, which is defined below as:

$$U_{gj} = f(u_{g1j}, \ldots, u_{gij}, \ldots, u_{gnj}) = f(v_{g1j}, \ldots, v_{gij}, \ldots, v_{gnj}) + \varepsilon_{gj} \tag{5}$$

where g and i indicate household and its member, U_{gj} refers to the utility that household g derives from choosing alternative j, incorporating the influence of its members' utilities $u_{g1j}, \ldots, u_{gij}, \ldots, u_{gnj}$ and intrahousehold interaction. ε_{gj} is error term of household utility, and $v_{g1j}, \ldots, v_{gij}, \ldots, v_{gnj}$ are determinant terms of members' utilities.

Swait et al. (2004) initially proposed the concept of metautility in the development of dynamic discrete choice model to evaluate temporal welfare impacts. They adopted the metautility to relate previous utilities to current utility and also simultaneously incorporated initial condition, future expectation, state dependence, and temporally changing scale and taste parameters and covariance. McFadden et al.'s (1977) mother logit model and Zhang et al.'s (2004) relative utility choice model can be also regarded as derived from metautility functions.

To derive an operational and logical household discrete choice model, one can assume various distributions of error terms $\{\varepsilon_{gj}\}$. In the case studies, Zhang et al. (2006b, 2007, 2009) simply assumed that error terms $\{\varepsilon_{gj}\}$ follow an independent and identical Gumbel distribution. Then they obtained the following logit-type household discrete choice model with group decision-making mechanisms.

$$P_{gj} = \frac{\exp(f(v_{g1j}, \ldots, v_{gij}, \ldots, v_{gnj}))}{\sum_k \exp(f(v_{g1k}, \ldots, v_{gik}, \ldots, v_{gnk}))} \tag{6}$$

Needless to say, adopting a more general distribution of error term will further strengthen its accountability. Various types of household utilities have been proposed and examined in the context of household time and task allocation. They can be roughly classified into two major types: *multilinear* utility and *isoelastic* utility, as discussed previously.

Representing Heterogeneous Group Choice Rules

It has been pointed out that choice behavior is highly adaptive and context-dependent from a psychological viewpoint (McFadden, 2001), and use of a particular choice rule depends on the situations surrounding the decisions (Wilson et al., 1989). One remarkable difference between individual and group behaviors might be observed in the complexity of choice rules due to the existence of several members in a group. Under such circumstances, instead of exploring a superior and absolutely dominating group choice rule, it might be wise to find some better ways to accommodate various rules in the same modeling framework. In line with such thinking, Zhang et al. (2009) proposed a new household discrete choice model to represent heterogeneous group choice rules across household members (named HCHG model). Model development is realized by using the LC modeling approach. LC modeling approach is used to first specify the LC membership probability that a household belongs to a LC with a specific choice rule and then integrate the choice probabilities conditional on different choice rules using the membership probabilities. A Bayesian approach is used to repeatedly update the LC membership probabilities, and EM algorithm is finally adopted to estimate the parameters.

Applications

Analysis of Household Car Ownership Behavior

To examine the effectiveness of the proposed household discrete choice models, Zhang et al. (2006b, 2007, 2009) used revealed preference data on household car ownership behavior. They collected the data in October 2004 from households living in Hiroshima City (population: about 1.12 millions) and one of its satellite cities, Higashi-Hiroshima City (population: about 0.12 millions). They dealt with choice of car type, which is classified into small-, middle-, and large-sized cars. Zhang et al. (2007) empirically examined and confirmed the effectiveness of *multilinear* type group choice model. Zhang et al. (2006b) compared some alternative household discrete choice models with the *multilinear* model and found that the models do not have significant differences, and consequently suggested the necessity and importance of integrating various group choice rules in the same model structure. To incorporate various choice rules in the same model structure, Zhang et al. (2009) applied the above-described household choice model with heterogeneous group decision-making rules (i.e., HCHG model). As the first case study, they only dealt with the paired combinations of the following three choice rules: *multilinear, max–max* and *max–min* rules, in the context of household car ownership behavior analysis. Estimation results confirmed the effectiveness of the proposed group choice model from both model performance and applicability to analysis of household car ownership behavior. Small variation of LC probabilities across choice rules also supports the adopted modeling strategy in this study, that is, to integrate different choice rules in the same modeling framework.

Analysis of Household Residential Choice Behavior

Focusing on group decision-making mechanisms in household residential choice behavior Zhang and Fujiwara (2009b) conducted a web-based stated preference survey method to investigate households' preferences for moving to residential areas along the Astramline, a transit system in Hiroshima City. They found that joint decisions lead to changes of members' preferences in about 40% of the households. They further empirically confirmed the effectiveness of the multilinear group discrete choice model, and suggested that high-rising housing close to the Astramline could attract more people to live in and consequently contribute to an effective use of the transit system.

Zhang and Fujiwara (2004) conducted a study on the evaluation of living environments and an analysis of household residential attitudes considering intrahousehold interaction. Evaluation of living environments is an important research topic in urban planning, especially from the perspective of promoting residence in local cities. They applied a structural equation model with latent variables to evaluate living environments and analyze household residential attitudes by explicitly incorporating the influence of such collective decision-making mechanisms. Based on the data collected in Higashi-Hiroshima, Japan, they clarified the effectiveness of the proposed methodology.

Development of Joint Trip-Making Behavior Model

Focusing on pick-up/deliver choice behavior in Japan, Kobayashi et al. (1996) proposed a random matching model for joint trip-making behavior in a two-member household. They call the member who provides the pick-up/deliver transport service as *agent* and the member receiving the service as *principal*. The *agent* needs to decide whether to provide the service or not, and the *principal* decides whether to receive the service or not. They further argued that choice behavior is conditional on the consensus between the *agent* and the *principal*. Therefore, they defined the utility of each member (either *agent* or *principal*) as a linear function of another member's utility, as shown below.

$$u_i^p = \sum_k \beta_k x_{ik}^p + \eta_p u_i^a + \varepsilon_i^p \tag{7}$$

$$u_i^a = \sum_m \gamma_m x_{im}^p + \eta_a u_i^p + \varepsilon_i^a \tag{8}$$

where, u_i^p, u_i^a are the utilities of alternative i of the *principal* p and the *agent* a, respectively, x_{ik}^p, x_{im}^a are the explanatory variables with parameters β_k, γ_m, η_p is a parameter indicating the degree of the *principal*'s uneasiness to the *agent*, η_a is a parameter indicating the degree of the *agent*'s kindness to the *principal*, and ε_i^p, ε_i^a are error terms.

In equations (7) and (8), alternative i refers to either receiving the pick-up/deliver service ($i = 1$) or not ($i = 0$) in case of the *principal*, and it refers to either providing the pick-up/deliver service ($i = 1$) or not ($i = 0$) in case of the *agent*. $\eta_a u_i^p$ and $\eta_p u_i^a$ are the partial utilities, which represent the altruistic behavior of the *principal* and the *agent*. To build joint trip-making behavior model, they classified the choice situations into the following four cases.

Q_1: Both the *principal* and the *agent* agree to make a joint trip. In this case, $u_1^p \geq u_0^p$, $u_1^a \geq u_0^a$.
Q_2: The *agent* suggests picking-up/delivering the *principal*, but the *principal* refuses the suggestion. In this case, $u_1^p < u_0^p$, $u_1^a \geq u_0^a$.
Q_3: The *principal* asks for picking-up/delivering, but the *agent* refuses the request. In this case, $u_1^p \geq u_0^p$, $u_1^a < u_0^a$.
Q_4: Both the *principal* and the *agent* disagree to make a joint trip. This means that $u_1^p < u_0^p$, $u_1^a < u_0^a$.

Then, the choice probability for the four cases can be described below.

$$P(Q_1) = \text{Prob}(u_1^p \geq u_0^p,\ u_1^a \geq u_0^a) \tag{9}$$

$$P(Q_2) = \text{Prob}(u_1^p < u_0^p,\ u_1^a \geq u_0^a) \tag{10}$$

$$P(Q_3) = \text{Prob}(u_1^p \geq u_0^p,\ u_1^a < u_0^a) \tag{11}$$

$$P(Q_4) = \text{Prob}(u_1^p < u_0^p,\ u_1^a < u_0^a) \tag{12}$$

Assuming the error terms follow a bivariate normal distribution results in the random matching model. They applied the model to the analysis of pick-up/deliver choice behavior, using travel diary data collected in 1993 Tottori City and its surrounding towns and villages. Since the adopted data is a traditional travel diary data, the only available information is whether case Q_1 applies or not. In other words, the used data cannot distinguish between cases Q_2 and Q_4. Therefore, they had to simplify their model by grouping cases Q_2–Q_4 as a single case. Even though the above random matching model provides a promising modeling approach to represent joint trip-making behavior, however, in reality, it might be difficult to collect the data about consensus building during the joint trip-making process.

Telecommunication and Activity Participation

As discussed by Ohmori (2006), progress in telecommunication technologies gives rise to various changes in people's daily life. Nishii et al. (2004) conducted a survey on communication, activity, and travel (called SCAT) in the Kofu region in November 2003 to investigate the influence of telecommunication on activity participation. Interestingly, the survey consisted of not only a standard activity diary questionnaire, but also a questionnaire of telecommunication history. The relationship between telecommunication and activity participation was also investigated. The respondents were recruited from university students (60 households), employees at governmental offices (55 households), and others (17 households), and asked to report their activity and telecommunication behavior on a weekday and a weekend. They aggregately analyzed the relationship between telecommunication and activity participation. Using the same SCAT data, Sasaki et al. (2005) first clarified the characteristics of joint activity, and then showed that telecommunication between parents and their children influence the joint-activity participation by using a data mining approach. Sasaki et al. (2006) further revealed that joint activities may be activated by mobile communication. Moreover, they found that if members with low-mobility are present in households, joint activities and mobile communication are significantly inter-related.

Summaries and Future Perspectives

Although the Japan transportation researchers were relatively late, recently a considerable amount of research on household decisions can be observed, covering household time and task allocation, car ownership behavior, joint trip-making behavior, and telecommunication and activity participation. Examples of such studies were briefly introduced in this paper. Most of these studies developed household behavior models based on random utility maximization principle and explicitly incorporated the heterogeneous preferences of different household members in joint decision as well as intrahousehold interaction. Applications mainly focused on modeling the joint decisions made by two household members. Even though the adopted modeling approaches are promising, these models should be further improved by adopting more advanced estimation methods to accommodate more complicated and general household decisions. Some innovative survey methods should also be developed to empirically confirm the observed group decision-making mechanisms.

The adopted modeling approaches are promising and could be applied to describe other joint decision issues in transportation. For example, household car ownership and use behavior is an old-fashioned topic, but recently, it is attracting more and more attention in Japan, because of social requirements to reduce environmental loads from car traffic. From such viewpoint, mobility management policies are currently deployed at various cities in Japan. Effective and successful mobility management needs better understanding of car ownership and use behavior, which is usually influenced by both intrahousehold interaction and social interaction. Application of group choice model to the analysis of mobility management policies might be helpful. Compared with the modeling progress of the above-mentioned behavioral aspects, telecommunication and activity participation has not been satisfactorily modeled. This is due to both the behavioral complexity and difficulties in investigating those behaviors. Fortunately, some active research efforts are underway (Ohmori, 2006).

Needless to say, it is necessary to incorporate the group decision-making mechanisms in household behavior into the comprehensive/integrated transportation and land use models. Such modeling efforts could further enhance the accountability of transportation planning and policies.

ACKNOWLEDGMENTS

We appreciate Dr. Kuniaki Sasaki, Dr. Toshiyuki Yamamoto, and Dr. Nobuaki Ohmori who provided their valuable research information to us, and Prof. Harry Timmermans who kindly reviewed the paper. We apologize to those researchers in Japan whose relevant work could not be cited because of space limitations.

References

Atkinson, A. B. (1970). On the measurement of inequality. *Journal of Economic Theory* 2, 244–263.

Becker, G. S. (1965). A theory of the allocation of time. *Economic Journal* 75, 493–517.

Bengston, D. N., J. O. Fletcher and K. C. Nelson (2003). Public policies for managing urban growth and protecting open space: policy instruments and lessons learned in the United States. *Landscape and Urban Planning* 69, 271–286.

Davis, H. L. (1976). Decision making within the household. *Journal of Consumer Research* 2, 241–260.

Fujii, S. (2005). Reducing inappropriate bicycle-parking through persuasive communication. *Journal of Applied Social Psychology* 35(6), 1171–1196.

Fukuda, D., T. Matsumura and T. Yai (2006). Intra-household activity time allocation model for elderly couple with time and budget constraints. *Proceedings of Infrastructure Planning*, Vol. 34, Takamatsu (CD-ROM) (in Japanese).

Gliebe, J. P. and F. S. Koppelman (2000). A model of joint activity participation. Paper presented at the 9th International Association for Travel Behavior Conference, 2–7 July. Gold Coast, Qld, Australia.

Gliebe, J. P. and F. S. Koppelman (2002). A model of joint activity participation between household members. *Transportation* 29, 49–72.

Gliebe, J. P. and F. S. Koppelman (2005). Modeling household activity-travel interactions as parallel constrained choices. *Transportation* 32(5), 449–471.

Hato, E. (2001). Behaviors in network. *Proceedings of Infrastructure Planning* 24(2), 15–29 (invited paper in Japanese)

Hensher, D. A. (2003). Models of organizational and agency choices for passengers and freight-related travel choices: notions of inter-activity and influence. Paper presented at the 8th IATBR Conference Workshop on Models of Organisational Choices (Freight and Passenger), 10–15 August. Switzerland.

Hensher, D. A. (2004). Modeling agent interdependency in group decision making. *Transportation Research Part E* 40, 63–79.

Jones, P., M. C. Dix, M. I. Clarke and I. G. Heggie (1983). *Understanding Travel Behavior*. Aldershot, Gower.

Kato, K., M. Kiuchi and M. Kondo (2003). Analysis of discretionary activity duration on weekdays and weekends considering household members' activity participation behavior. *Selected Proceedings of Annual Meeting of Japan Society of Traffic Engineers* 23, 221–224 (in Japanese).

Kobayashi, K., H. Kita and H. Tatano (1996). A random matching model for joint trips production within households. *Journal of Infrastructure Planning and Management* 536(IV-31), 59–68 (in Japanese).

Matsumoto, S. and Kato, K. (2006). A model of generating out-of-home discretionary activity participation and travel for household members in a week. Paper presented at the 11th International Conference on Travel Behaviour Research, August 16–20. Kyoto.

McFadden, D. (2001). Economic choices. *American Economic Review* 91(3), 351–378.

McFadden, D., K. Train and W. B. Tye (1977). An application of diagnostics tests for the independence from irrelevant alternatives property of the multinomial logit model. *Transportation Research Record* 637, 39–46.

Nepal, K. P., D. Fukuda and T. Yai (2005). Microeconomic models of intra-household activity time allocations. *Journal of Eastern Society for Transportation Studies* 6, 1637–1650.

Nishii, K., K. Sasaki and S. Akazawa (2004). An analysis of relationship between household members' joint-activity patterns and their telecommunication. *Proceedings of Infrastructure Planning*, Vol. 29 Kobe (CD-ROM) (in Japanese).

Ohmori, N. (2006). Connected anytime: telecommunications and activity-travel behavior from Asian perspectives. Synthesis report presented at the 11th International Conference on Travel Behaviour Research, August 16–19, Kyoto.

Rich, J. H. (2001). Modeling two-worker households. Paper presented at the 9th International Association for Travel Behaviour Conference, July 2–7. Gold Coast, Qld, Australia.

Sasaki, K., K. Nishii, R. Kitamura and K. Kondo (2006). The use of mobile communication tools and its influence to joint activities—empirical analysis of personal communication and household activities. *Selected Proceedings of TRANS-TEC (The Transport Science & Technology Congress) 2004*. Athens (in press).

Sasaki, K., K. Nishii and J. Yamamoto (2005). An analysis of joint activity using household activity diary data on weekend. *Proceedings of Infrastructure Planning*, Vol. 31, Hiroshima (CD-ROM) (in Japanese).

Sugie, Y., A. Fujiwara and K. Suenaga (1988). Effectiveness of the activity diary as a travel survey instrument. *Papers on City Planning* 23, 409–414 (in Japanese).

Swait, J., W. Adamowicz and M. van Bueren (2004). Choice and temporal welfare impacts: incorporating history into discrete choice models. *Journal of Environmental Economics and Management* 47, 94–116.

Terabe, S. and T. Yai (1999). Attitudes on public involvement in transportation planning process: comparison between citizens of the United States and Japan. *Journal of the Eastern Asia Society for Transportation Studies* 3(4), 1–6.

Timmermans, H. (2009). Household decision making in travel behaviour analysis. In R. Kitamura, T. Yoshii and T. Yamamoto (Eds.), *The Expanding Sphere of Travel Behaviour Research*. Amsterdam, Emerald.

Thorndike, R. L. (1938). On what type of task will a group do well? *Journal of Abnormal and Social Psychology* 33, 409–413.

Wilson, E. J., G. L. Lilien and D. T. Wilson (1989). Formal models of group choice in organizational buying: toward a contingency paradigm. *Advances in Consumer Research* 16(1), 548–554.

Yamamoto, T., D. Kiuchi and T. Morikawa (2007). A study on possibility of reduction in car ownership by car sharing system. *Journal of Infrastructure Planning and Management* 63(1), 14–23.

Yao, E. and T. Morikawa (2003). A study on integrated intercity travel demand model. Paper presented at the 10th International Conference on Travel Behaviour Research, August 10–15. Lucerne.

Zhang, J. and A. Fujiwara (2004). Basic study on evaluation of living environments and analysis of household residential attitude considering intra-household interaction. *Journal of the City Planning Institute of Japan* 39(3), 619–624 (in Japanese).

Zhang, J. and Fujiwara, A. (2006a). Measuring social capacity for environmental management in transport sector in Beijing based on an attitudinal survey from the perspective of civil society. Paper presented at the 12th International Sustainable Development Research Conference, April 6–8, Hong Kong (CD-ROM).

Zhang, J. and A. Fujiwara (2006b). Representing household time allocation behavior by endogenously incorporating diverse intra-household interactions: a case study in the context of elderly couples. *Transportation Research Part B* 40(1), 54–74.

Zhang, J. and A. Fujiwara (2009a). A comparative modeling analysis of household time allocation behavior using a large-scale national time use data in Japan. *Compendium of Papers CD-ROM, the 88th Annual Meeting of the Transportation Research Board*, January 11–15. Washington, DC.

Zhang, J. and A. Fujiwara (2009b). Representing intra-household interaction in transit-oriented residential choice behavior using stated preference approach. *Transportation Research Record* (in press).

Zhang, J., A. Fujiwara and M. Kuwano (2007). Modeling group decision-making mechanisms in household travel behavior: theories and an application. *Journal of the Eastern Asia Society for Transportation Studies* 7, 654–669.

Zhang, J., A. Fujiwara, H. Timmermans and A. Borgers (2005). An empirical comparison of alternative models of household time allocation. In H. Timmermans (Ed.), *Progress in Activity-Based Analysis*, Amsterdam, Elsevier, pp. 259–283.

Zhang, J., A. Fujiwara, H. Timmermans, B. Lee and T. Arentze (2006a). Multi-dimensional timing decision model of household activity-travel behavior with endogenous coupling constraints. Paper presented at the 11th International Conference on Travel Behaviour Research, August 16–20. Kyoto, Japan.

Zhang, J., M. Kuwano and A. Fujiwara (2006b). Comparative analyses of discrete group choice models: a case study in the context of household choice of vehicle type. *Infrastructure Planning Review* 23(2), 463–472 (in Japanese).

Zhang, J., M. Kuwano, B. Lee and A. Fujiwara (2009). Modeling household discrete choice behavior incorporating heterogeneous group decision-making mechanisms. *Transportation Research Part B* 43, 230–250.

Zhang, J., H. Timmermans and A. Borgers (2002). A utility-maximizing model of household time use for independent, shared and allocated activities incorporating group decision mechanisms. *Transportation Research Record* 1807, 1–8.

Zhang, J., H. Timmermans, A. Borgers and D. Wang (2004). Modeling traveler choice behaviour using the concepts of relative utility and relative interest. *Transportation Research Part B* 38(3), 215–234.

2.5 Advances in Data Acquisition

The Expanding Sphere of Travel Behaviour Research
Selected Papers from the 11th International Conference on Travel Behaviour Research

9

Tracking Individual Travel Behaviour Using Mobile Phones: Recent Technological Development

Yasuo Asakura and Eiji Hato

Abstract

Advanced technologies in location positioning and mobile communication have been recently applied to travel data collection in many countries. There were excellent reviews of the application of travel surveys based on global positioning systems (GPSs). This paper aims to review recent technological developments in travel data collection methods using mobile phones and related communication instruments and to discuss data processing and modelling methods that have been proposed for 'dot' data analysis. Finally, the problems and tasks in travel data collection using mobile communication instruments in the future are discussed.

Introduction

It is evident that travel survey and data collection are essential for travel behavioural studies. Various data collection methodologies have been proposed in recent decades. Two major characteristics can be distinguished when we discuss travel data collection methods: 'virtual or real' and 'active or passive'. The first feature indicates the data collection environment in which a traveller is located. In virtual world, a test subject is requested to travel in an artificial environment such as a laboratory. The second feature means the difference in the relations between the test subject and a surveyor. Active data collection implies that the surveyor requests the test subject to describe his/her travel behaviour. On the other hand, in passive data collection, the test subject is not requested to mention his/her behaviour. This can be reworded as the 'observation' of the test subject by the surveyor. As shown in Martin and Bateson (1985), this is a type of an external measurement of an individual behaviour, which is popular in psychological tests.

Travel data collection methods can be characterized as combinations of these two features. A questionnaire survey that enquires about the travel behaviours under hypothetical situations is a typical 'virtual and active' case. A stated preference (SP) survey in a laboratory can be categorized into this group. Data collection using a travel simulator supported by computer graphics (CG) technology can be categorized into the 'virtual and passive' case. These methods under virtual or hypothetical environments are effective in obtaining the travel behavioural data for various alternative transport policies. The usefulness of a particular method depends on the extent to which the given environment is consistent with the real world.

Real-world travel data collection is primarily performed with the active approach. Questionnaire-type travel surveys such as person trip (PT) surveys have been applied to large-scale travel surveys for many years. Mails with questionnaire sheets, personal telephone interviews and Internet surveys have been used as the survey instruments. In questionnaire-based survey methods, sampled individuals are commonly asked about their travel behaviour during the past day(s). They are required to respond to various aspects of their travel activities such as the places and times of departure and arrival, the purpose of travel, the mode of travel and so on.

When detailed attributes of the travel behaviour are required for travel demand analysis and modelling, the sampled individuals are required to respond to a large number of questions. However, an individual may not be easy to remember his/her past travel activities. In particular, the exact place and time of the activities are difficult to answer. The description of behaviour depends on the individual's memory; therefore, errors and mistakes may occur. Thus, behavioural surveys based on questionnaires are not always sufficient for microscopic travel behaviour measurements. Problems regarding conventional questionnaire-type travel surveys were discussed in Ettema et al. (1996) and Axhausen (1998). They examined the data collection methods with regard to the travel behaviour from the perspective of the validity and quality of the travel and activity data.

Recently, computer-assisted telephone interviews (CATI), computer-assisted personal interviews (CAPI) and computer-assisted self-interviews (CASI) have been developed. They will be useful to reduce the efforts of both the surveyors and respondents and to improve the accuracy of travel data collection. An excellent discussion on the survey methodology considerations for personal travel surveys can be found in Sharp and Murakami (2005).

In comparison with the active approach, the application of the passive approach to real-world travel data collection was limited. For the passive method in the real world, the process in which a surveyor tracks the movement of a sampled individual can be appropriately termed as 'tracking'. Some examples of tracking surveys can be found in transport research. However, they were limited to the observation of the movement of a small number of pedestrians or cyclists in a narrow area. For example, Sasaki and Mastui (1968) performed a tracking survey in the Kyoto Zoological Garden to find the movement of visitors from one spot to the other. Bovy and Stern (1990) discussed tracking methods for collecting way-finding data in networks.

The advantage of tracking surveys is the precise measurement of the space–time attributes of an object if appropriate survey instruments are employed. However, it was true that the time and labour costs were greater than that in the active survey methods. Therefore, tracking surveys have not been frequently used as travel surveys in transport planning and management in which a large number of samples were required.

Recently, mobile communication technologies have rapidly advanced. They demonstrate great potential as survey instruments for tracking individual travel behaviour. Mobile communication systems such as global positioning systems (GPSs), mobile phones and radio-frequency identification (RFID) tag systems are available to determine the accurate place and time of a mobile object. These technologies can be used as core instruments in the tracking survey. They may also compensate for the disadvantages of active-type travel surveys. In addition to the observation of travel behaviour, the level of service (LOS) variables of various transport modes can be measured with the mobile communication instruments of individual travellers.

The objective of this paper is to show the methodologies of using mobile communication instruments for tracking individual travel behaviour. Wolf (2004a) conducted an excellent review of GPS technologies for travel surveys. Thus, this paper mainly focused on the mobile-phone-based location-positioning technologies and their application to tracking-type travel data collection. The other reason why we focus on mobile-phone-based location positioning is the increasing penetration rates and increasing variety in the additional functions of mobile phones. For example, there have been more than 90 million contracts of mobile phones in Japan, and the number of contracts per capita is about 80% in 2006.

The collected travel data using mobile instruments are represented as a set of dots having space–time dimensions. The dot data are managed in different ways that have been used in traditional 'trip'-based analysis. Thus, the other objective of this paper is to discuss data-processing methods that have been proposed for dot data analysis. This includes data transfer and map-matching algorithms in which their original location characteristics are maintained. Finally, the problems and tasks in travel data collection using mobile communication instruments for future research are discussed.

GPS-Based Travel Survey

GPS applications have been extensively used in travel surveys. The *Handbook of Transport Geography and Spatial Systems* (Wolf, 2004b; Stopher, 2004) provides a comprehensive description of GPS and its applicability to household travel surveys. Wolf (2004a) presents an overview of various location collection technologies, their recent applications in travel behavioural surveys and technology trends for the future; it shows that several regional household travel/activity surveys have incorporated a GPS component as a sub-sample in their household diaries between 2001 and 2004. The potential of automatically collected GPS data for travel behavioural studies was also described in Schönfelder et al. (2002). In this section, GPS-based on-board travel surveys and personal surveys are discussed.

On-Board GPS Survey

GPS applications to traffic and transport studies have been conducted since the middle of the 1990s. First, they mainly focused on traffic flow surveys. Zito et al. (1995) and Sermons and Koppelman (1996) applied GPS to the floating surveys of vehicle traffic. D'Este et al. (1999) developed a GPS-based system to measure the traffic system performance. Quiroga and Bullock (1998) described a new methodology for performing travel time studies using GPS and geographic information system (GIS) technologies. They illustrated the capabilities of the GPS/GIS methodology.

Then, GPS-based household travel surveys have been developed as on-board GPS surveys; this implies that a data recorder with a GPS receiver is installed on a sampled household vehicle and the location position data of the vehicle movement are collected. One of the advantages of on-board GPS surveys is that there are almost no battery constraints for the equipment. It is possible to set up a variety of combinations of data recorder and communication devices. On-board GPS household travel surveys are suitable for areas where automobiles are used as the dominant mode of travel. However, it is not sufficient for individual travel behavioural survey of a multimodal area.

Wagner et al. (1997) and Battele (1997) reported a proof-of-concept field test that was conducted from September to December 1996, where the units were installed in 100 household vehicles in Lexington, KY. A personal digital assistant (PDA) was used as the data recorder. Similar experiments were conducted by Andre (1997), who studied the on-board measurements of vehicle use. Murakami and Wagner (1999) studied the results of a GPS-based experiment for 100 households in the United States. Wolf (2004a) mentioned that a survey in Austin conducted in 117 households represented the first generation of the on-board GPS regional travel survey in the United States. The ability to record unreported trips ranges widely from 20% to 80%.

Zmud and Wolf (2003) found that trips lasting for less than 10 minutes are likely to be unreported. Forrest and Pearson (2005) showed that the difference in the trip generation characteristics depends on the purpose of the trip. An interesting on-board GPS survey was conducted in Atlanta with 365 days of GPS data collection for 1 second in over 450 household vehicles. Guensler et al. (2006) showed that the Atlanta data set could be used for analysing the longitudinal variability of travel.

One of the important analyses for on-board GPS travel data is the analysis of the route choice behaviour in a road network. Jan et al. (2000) analysed the Lexington data and found that the path selected on a trip was fairly sensitive to the location of the origin and destination and the selected path was most often considerably different from the shortest path across the network. Li et al. (2005) analysed the data of 182 morning commuters over 10 days. They revealed a strong relationship between the decision of the route choice for the morning commute and the commuters' work schedule flexibility, socio-demographic characteristics and commute route attributes.

GPS for Personal Trip Survey

When an open-sky environment is assumed and the satellite signals are observed, accurate location position data of personal movement can be obtained and seamless data collection becomes possible in multimodal urban areas. However, carrying data collection devices can sometimes be annoying even when the size of the device is compact and wearable. Battery constraints become critical for personal surveys depending on the data collection interval.

In spite of these difficulties, a number of examples of GPS applications to personal travel data collection were available. Draijer et al. (2000) conducted a pilot study involving 151 people in the Netherlands. The data collection package comprises a GPS, antenna and custom-built PDA. The weight of the package was approximately 2 kg, which appeared to be too heavy for the survey participants. Greaves (2006) reported a GPS panel survey comprising 200 households in South Australia. They were requested to use wearable GPS devices for 1 week once a year for a period of almost over 2 years. Pilot surveys for both the odometer and GPS surveys were conducted from March to June 2005.

Doherty et al. (2001) focused on the use of GPS to enhance and extend the travel behaviour survey methods. The paper described the testing of a passive vehicle-based GPS tracking system in Quebec City; then, the development of algorithms using a GIS is described, which can be used to automatically match the GPS data to road segments along a network and identify stops along the way. They explore how GPS-traced routes and stops could be used as a 'memory jogger' for further in-depth explorations of travel behaviour in a home-based survey approach. This paper describes a comprehensive approach that combines GPS and GIS technologies with a computerized activity scheduling survey termed as computerized household activity scheduling survey (CHASE) presented by Doherty and Miller (2000).

Ohmori et al. (1998) performed a fundamental experiment to validate a GPS survey for individual travel behavioural survey in Tokyo. Ohmori et al. (2006) presented the development of a GPS-equipped PDA-based activity diary survey system. By comparing the activity data collected by the PDA/GPS instrument with data collected from a conventional paper-based activity diary survey, it was found that the former was useful in reducing the time lag in data entry and mitigating spatial constraints for the data entry. It was shown that both the number of activities and total activity time recorded were longer in the paper-based survey, particularly for in-home activities.

Sugino and Asakura (2004) studied the field survey of tourists' behaviour in Asuka, Nara. The PDA recorded the information access log of every tourist in addition to the tourist's location-positioning log with GPS. Thus, it was possible to analyse the information access behaviour of the tourist in relation to his/her location. It was found that the information acquisition of a tourist was actually a location- and time-specific behaviour.

Mobile-Phone-Based Travel Survey

GSM Survey in Germany

Global system for mobile communications (GSM) is a second-generation mobile phone system that was standardized in Europe in the 1990s. GSM is available in more than 210 countries and regions of the world. Few studies regarding the use of GSM for personal travel data collection have been conducted. In Germany, a GSM-based location-positioning technology was developed, and its application to travel surveys was studied. The activated unit of GSM is constantly connected with a base station to receive or transmit calls. The communication cell and its surrounding cells are used to locate the approximate position of the mobile unit. The accuracy of GSM-based location positioning is approximately 50–100 m depending on the density of base stations; this value is lower than the GPS-based location positions in an open-sky environment.

In Wermuth et al. (2003), it was mentioned that GSM was used as a method for collecting individual movement data for the first time in Germany in 1999. Along with a variety of computer-assisted data collection (CADAC) methods, the research project termed as 'teletravel system' (TTS) was an important example of using GSM for both location positioning and electronic questionnaires. A small chip card, referred to as the SIM card, was installed in a GSM phone for automatic location positioning and electronic questionnaires. An electronic questionnaire on mobile phone is another function of TTS, which can be classified into CASI surveys. A respondent was required to reply to the purpose of the trip, mode of travel and time when the mode of travel was changed. Wermuth et al. (2003) also presented the results of a field test of this function. It was found that the mobile phone survey was interpreted as 'easy' for over 75% of the respondents; over 80% of them favoured TTS data collection method than the conventional questionnaires. According to the authors, the reasons of this preference were low-input requirements, easy and quick data collection, no need to enter data regarding the time and place and no need to tray and remember the details.

Kracht (2004) revealed that either the parallel and simultaneous use of GPS and GSM tracking technologies or only the use of GSM tracking technology in combination with a historic GPS/GSM tracking database can yield reliable tracking results. He conducted the experiment in Berlin in order to show how the simultaneous use of GPS/GSM tracking technologies increased data availability and accuracy. He proposed GSM tracking with a historic GPS/GSM database that would be established as a longer-period parallel GPS/GSM tracking. He showed that the adapted data collection with electronic questionnaires on mobile electronic devices was expected to reduce the burden of data collection on the survey respondents.

PHS-Based Survey

PHS-Based Location-Positioning Technologies

A personal handy-phone (PHS) system uses smaller signal power than normal cellular phone systems, and it requires densely located base stations (antennas). A service carrier distributes antennas at approximately every 100 m in an urban area. Generally, the signal strength of an antenna decreases in proportion to the distance from the antenna. The most useful characteristic of a PHS handset is that the handset usually measures the signal strength of multiple (up to seven) base stations even if a user does not make a call.

If the exact locations of antennas are known and the signal strength from each antenna is measured, the position of the PHS handset can be calculated by using the triangle survey method. In spite of the effects of reflection and shielding by buildings and obstacles, the system yields location-positioning errors within the range of approximately 20–150 m. The error distance depends on the density of the base stations. When a person's movement is described in a large-scale map, such as a 1/200,000 scale, the magnitude of the error distance appears acceptable as a measurement error of 100 m from the exact location is considered to be negligibly small.

Table 1
Summary of the Field Test Results of Error Distance

Environment	Index number	PHS	GPS	Enhanced GPS
Urban canyon	Mean	39.5	61.7	35.9
	Median	38.7	50.4	36.2
	90 percentile value	61.4	128.6	54.3
	Standard deviation	18.4	42.0	14.8
	Number of data	43	31	21
Central business district	Mean	29.8	38.8	15.3
	Median	23.4	34.3	14.2
	90 percentile value	54.7	75.2	24.8
	Standard deviation	16.2	26.8	7.9
	Number of data	25	74	30
Residential district	Mean	33.3	32.0	20.0
	Median	28.5	30.8	23.2
	90 percentile value	64.5	45.0	31.3
	Standard deviation	15.7	13.0	10.0
	Number of data	35	90	31
Bay area	Mean	107.3	49.6	19.2
	Median	105.9	45.0	17.3
	90 percentile value	129.8	80.6	28.8
	Standard deviation	22.9	23.8	12.4
	Number of data	24	64	30

Asakura et al. (2000b) showed a comparison of the accuracy of location-positioning technologies as Table 1. They compared a PHS-based positioning system and two different types of GPS-based positioning system—conventional GPS and enhanced GPS. The latter uses server-assisted technology, which has been extended to GPS-assisted mobile phones. The test sites include various environments ranging from urban canyons to central business districts, residential districts and the bay area in Osaka City. The mean value of the GPS error distance is 61.7 m in urban canyons that are surrounded by high buildings with 20–40 storeys. The accuracy of enhanced GPS is similar to that of PHS. This shows that the accuracy of GPS in an environment with weaker signal strength and long multi-paths can be improved by the server-assisted technology used in enhanced GPS. In environments such as central business districts and residential districts, the data accuracy of enhanced-GPS-based positioning systems is superior to the other systems. The mean values of the error distance between PHS and GPS are not distinctly different. Among all the environments, the positioning error of PHS in the bay area is the greatest. This is due to the lower density of the base stations.

Asakura and Iryo (2005a) developed a PHS-based location-positioning method that can be applied when the location data of the base stations are not available. This method used the signal strength vectors at different locations (reference sites), which are referred to as reference vectors. When the location of a mobile object is in close proximity to the reference site, the signal strength vector of the mobile object is expected to be identical to the reference vector of the particular site. On the other hand, the target vector of a mobile object differs from the reference vector when the mobile object is located at a faraway distance from the reference site. A similarity index calculated by the signal strength vectors was used as an alternative measurement of the 'distance' between a predetermined reference site and the target object. The average error in the field experiment was 28 m and 80% of the error was less than 40 m. When the signal strength vectors are observed at many reference sites in a narrower area, more accurate location positioning can be achieved. This method is applicable for tracking surveys in narrower areas such as downtown shopping zones.

Online Tracking System

The location information service using PHS was first commercialized by LOCUS—a private company in Osaka—in April 1998. It has been applied to several socio-economic activities such as welfare, security and amusement purposes. The first PHS-based online travel survey was conducted in August 1998, immediately after the location-positioning service was started. A detailed description is provided in Asakura et al. (1999) and Asakura and Hato (2004).

Figure 1 shows the outline of the online tracking system. In order to ensure a traveller's privacy, it is required to agree with the traveller who joins the survey. A registered traveller is only required to switch on his/her PHS handset and carry it along. The

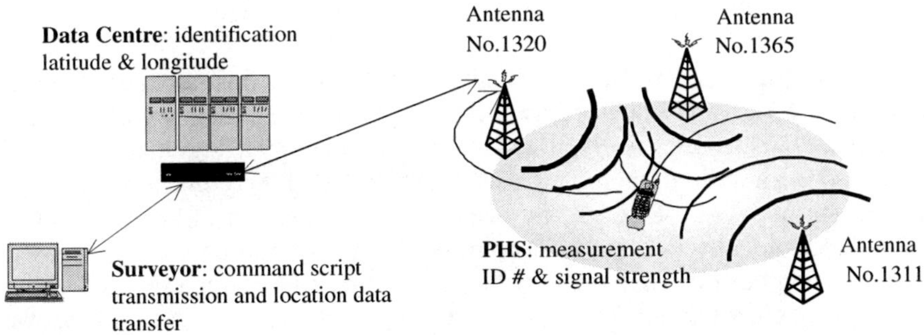

Figure 1
Online Tracking System Using PHS-Based Personal Location Service

observer forwards the start script to the PHS handset of the traveller. When the script is received, the handset transmits the ID number and signal strength of the neighbouring base stations to the LOCUS centre. The geometric coordinates of every base station are known, and the location position of the PHS can be calculated at the centre. The observer obtains the longitude and latitude of each PHS handset for every time interval via the Internet. Consequently, the movement of an individual traveller can be tracked.

Offline Data Logger

An online data collection system was considered to be suitable for real-time monitoring of travel behaviour. However, the cost of data transmission for long-term travel survey is not negligible. The other limitation of the online collection method is that precise location data are not always perfect for identifying the mode of travel. For example, an individual moving along a street with a speed of 30 km/hour may be travelling in a car or bus. Thus, additional information is necessary to determine the mode of travel.

Suzuki et al. (1994) have developed a handy device comprising a three-dimensional (3D) acceleration sensor combined with a gyrocompass. This device was employed to measure the microscopic movements of a person: walking, standing and so on. An analytical method to compute the acceleration wave can be applied to the travel mode classification when a 3D acceleration sensor is combined with a PHS-based location-positioning device. Asakura et al. (2001) described the development of an instrument referred to as a personal activity monitor (PEAMON). The location data are collected via a PHS-based location-positioning system and the acceleration data are simultaneously observed via an acceleration sensor. The dimensions of the unit are as follows: height, 120 mm; width, 70 mm; thickness 12 mm; and weight, 125 g. The instrument can be carried in an individual's pocket or bag.

The signal strength data required to calculate the location position are observed and recorded every 15 seconds. The acceleration data of the unit holder are observed via the 3D sensor every 0.03 seconds during the 4 seconds after the PHS signal is received. These data are stored in an internal memory card. When PEAMON is continuously used, it can be used to monitor for 48 hours. In order to save memory and battery capacity, PEAMON automatically switches to sleep mode if the acceleration signals are weak. The current setting can be effective for more than 200 hours, and this can be used in the diary survey of travel behaviour for 2 weeks. The threshold values for switching between the sleep and active modes can be altered according to the purpose of the survey.

In addition to offline multi-day data collections, PEAMON can identify the mode of travel. Rail travelling can be identified by using route matching since the route involves rail tracks and stops at stations. If the positioning data are not sufficient to identify the mode of travel, the acceleration data are then calculated for estimating the mode of travel. A spectrum analysis is performed to distinguish the different modes of travel. Each mode of travel has individual values for the standard deviation of acceleration and the percentage of power spectrum. Walking can be distinguished since the standard deviation of acceleration is approximately 0.02 for walking, which is one order greater than other modes of travel. When a bus and a passenger car share the same street and travel at the same speed, they cannot be distinguished by using route matching. However, the power spectrums of both these modes are rather different. For a bus, the percentage of power spectrum that is less than 3 Hz is approximately double of a passenger car. Thus, these two modes can be distinguished by using this index if they share a common lane along a road network.

Survey Examples

PHS-Based Online Tracking Survey in Osaka The first online tracking of individuals using PHS was conducted in Osaka during 3–16 November 1998 (Asakura et al., 1999; Hato and Asakura, 2001; Asakura and Hato, 2001). Ten persons joined the 2 weeks survey. The data collection interval was set at 2 minutes. Along with the PHS survey, the participants were also requested to fill in an activity diary form and a conventional PT survey form. The results of these surveys were used to find the differences between the PHS survey and the questionnaire surveys.

Hato and Asakura (2001) compared the total number of trips measured using the different survey methods. The number of observed trips during a day was 76, 80 and 84 for the PT survey, PHS survey and PHS combined with the diary survey, respectively. For PHS, the number of trips was estimated using the data-processing algorithm presented in the next section. For the PHS combined with the diary survey, the number of trips included the trips observed by PHS in addition to those obtained only with the activity diary survey. If we assume that 84 trips were 'true', 95% (82/84) of them would be observed by the PHS survey. On the other hand, conventional PT surveys might lose 9% (8/84) of the trips. This indicates that a PHS survey is sufficient to collect travel data of individuals, and it performs efficiently when combined with a travel diary survey. The consistency of travel data obtained by the PHS survey and data from the dairy survey were examined. It was found that 90% of the trips could be reproduced by the PHS survey, and short-distanced trips and stop-over trips could be observed by the PHS survey.

Asakura and Hato (2001) compared the average number of trips and the average travel time during a day among the individuals. Although they depended on the threshold values of the data-processing algorithm, the results of the PHS survey were fairly consistent with the tendency of those of the diary survey.

Sumo Participants Survey A questionnaire survey might be unsuitable for collecting the unusual travel behaviour such as leisure and recreation trips. It is difficult for respondents to reply about the exact place and time of each activity. Asakura and Hato (2004) presented the results of a PHS-based tracking survey of 100 spectators who watched a sumo wrestling event held in Osaka on 3 April 1999. Before the event, a PHS handset was mailed along with admission tickets to the selected spectators. The tracking survey duration was 7:30 to 24:00 with a data collection interval of 2 minutes.

The results were analysed for understanding the space–time characteristics of recreational travel demand. Figure 2 shows the space–time distribution of the spectators. During the morning hours, the spectators distributed within an area at a distance of almost 60 km from the event hall. During the evening hours, almost all the spectators concentrated within an area at a distance of 5 km from the hall; this is because the sumo tournament was held during 15:00–17:00. After the event, the spectators started to segregate, and the spatial distribution of the spectators spread again with the same speed by which they moved towards the hall.

Asakura and Hato (2001) aggregated the location positions of the spectators at gateway stations near the hall. For the return-to-home demand, different wave patterns were observed for each gateway station. The peak time of the return-to-home demand depended on the characteristics of the gateway stations. The results can be employed to

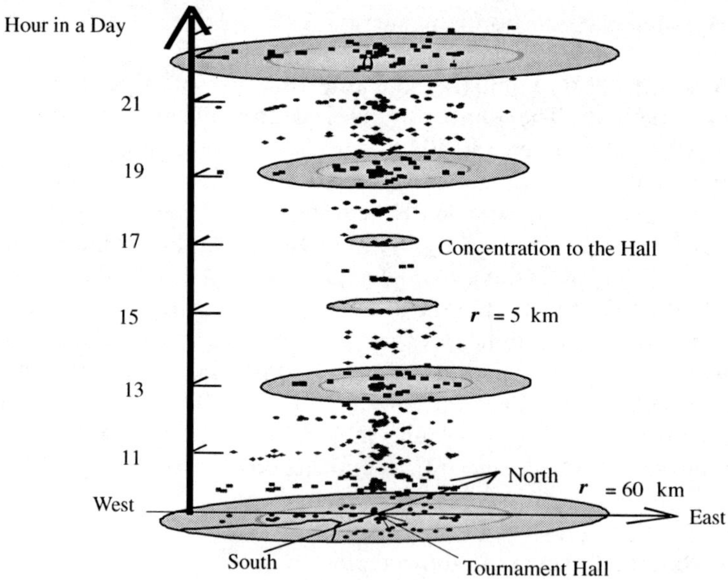

Figure 2
Congregation and Segregation of Event Spectators in a Day

estimate the arrival times of the wave and determine the strategy of information provision and guidance.

Other travel survey examples using PHS are on-board traffic monitoring and travel time estimation on urban expressway networks (Sugino et al., 2000) and sightseeing travel data collection in Kobe (Asakura and Iryo, 2005b).

Internet Mobile Phone

GPS-Assisted Mobile Phones

Two different types of mobile phones with the GPS function are available in the market. One is a server-assisted phone in which the mobile phone handset receives and transmits the GPS signals to the server and the server calculates the location position (longitude and latitude) of the handset. In this phone, the handset frequently communicates with the server to calculate the location positions. Frequent communication involves a considerable amount of time and cost. The minimum data collection interval is approximately 20 seconds.

The other GPS-assisted mobile phone is a quasi-self-standing phone. When tracking begins, the server provides the instrumental information of the GPS satellites to the mobile phone handset. Then, the handset identifies the GPS signals and calculates the location position without the server's assistance. While the initial communication between the server and the handset is necessary, additional communication is not required. The minimum data collection interval is about 10 seconds, which implies that frequent tracking becomes possible. The battery exhaustion time of a quasi-self-standing mobile phone is around 5–6 hours. This is almost double of a server-assisted mobile phone.

The accuracy of location positioning is similar for both the mobile phones. When a GPS mobile phone was placed in an open-sky environment, the average error distance for 50 observations was 28 m. The observation site was a park surrounded by higher buildings in downtown Osaka. The average error distance for 50 observations becomes 188 m in a building where GPS signals are unavailable. It is inevitable that the accuracy of location position depends on the density of the base stations when GPS signals are unavailable.

Internet Mobile Phone Survey System

A GPS-assisted mobile phone is effective for obtaining precise location position data, while a computer-based interview is superior with regard to the collection of travel characteristics such as the purpose of the trip that cannot be externally observed. Hato et al. (2006) described a probe person (PP) survey system—a hybrid travel data collection system for GPS-assisted mobile phones and an Internet web diary for GIS.

In the PP survey, a traveller is requested to hold a mobile phone and operate it a few times. At the origin, the standard operation is to select 'departure' at the mobile phone screen. The location position of the origin and the departure time are automatically recorded in the data collection server. The location position data are collected during the trip. When the traveller arrives at the destination, he/she is requested to operate the mobile phone again and select 'arrival'. Then, the location position of the destination and the arrival time are recorded in the server. The data collection interval of the location position is set to approximately 30 seconds during a trip and 600 seconds in between trips. Even if the traveller forgets to operate the mobile phone, the location data are automatically collected in an interval of approximately 600 seconds. When the traveller is at home, he/she is requested to access the website to confirm the previous trips and respond to a few questions including the purpose of the trip. The trip record is presented in a time sequence of the day with the location-positioning data. The traveller enters the purpose of the trip and other trip characteristics to complete the travel diary.

In addition to the travel data collection and processing function, the PP system is being developed as a comprehensive system for traffic management and transport planning. Various analytical tools have been provided such as data mining, travel behavioural modelling and network simulation. A traffic and travel information provision function is installed in the PP system. Travel time information is generated by using the historical travel time data, which is obtained from the mobile phones. This implies that a mobile phone can be used as a device for information provision as well as behavioural data collector and travel time monitor.

Survey Examples

PP surveys have been applied to real-world travel data collections since 2003. Table 2 summarises the PP survey outlines conducted in Matsuyama during 2003–2005 (Mitani, 2005). Around 100–300 participants were used for a 1-month travel survey. The incentive for each participant was 10,000–15,000 yen (100–150 US dollars) per month. The number of withdrawn samples was very small, and the percentage of effective samples exceeded 95%. The average number of trips per person per day was 3.61 (2003), 3.67 (2004) and 5.31 (2005). The largest figure in 2005 is attributed to the introduction of an 'ecological point' that might have proved as an incentive to generate trips. The number of trips per day per person was 3.06 for a PT survey in Matsuyama

Table 2
Probe Person Survey in Matsuyama, 2003–2005

	MPP2003	MPP2004	MPP2005
Survey period	2003/01/29–02/28 (31 days)	2004/01/28–02/29 (35 days)	2004/01/28–02/29 (28 days)
Time of day	06:00-24:00	24 hours	24 hours
Data collection interval	90 or 120 seconds	40 seconds for trip, 600 seconds for stay	30 seconds for trip, 600 seconds for stay
Monitor recruitment	Mail magazine	Mail magazine Re-recruiting for 2003 monitors Collaborating companies	Mail magazine Re-recruiting for 2004 monitors Collaborating companies Radio broadcasting, advertising flyer, home page
Number of monitors	100	317	384
Incentive	15,000 yen	10,000 yen	10,000–15,000 yen
Drop out	1	6	6
Information provision period	W/o	2004/02/09–2004/02/29	2005/02/08–2005/02/28
Information contents	W/o	Auto travel times	Auto travel times/rail travel times Travel time contour/congestion map
Ecological point	W/o	W/o	Public transport users/off-peak road users
Effective number of samples	98	311	378
Total person–days	3,038	10,885	10,584
Total number of dots	1,114,477	1,137,622	1,564,965
Number of dots/day/person	367	105	148
Number of trips/day/person	3.61	3.67	5.31
Number of dots/trip	102	29	28
Number of car trips/day/person	Nil	3.04	4.05

in 1979 and 2.38 for a PT survey in Tokyo in 1998. When compared with these figures, the number of trips per day per person in the PP survey was fairly large. This can be attributed to the fact that short-distance trips were collected by the PP survey.

As shown in Table 3 (Tanabe and Tange, 2006), more than 20 examples of the field application of the PP survey are available in Japan since 2003. They include a long-distance sightseeing travel survey in Shikoku (Sugino et al., 2005), an intercity rail use survey in Tsukuba (Itsubo and Hato, 2006) and a travel behavioural survey for urban expressway users in Osaka (Yatsumoto et al., 2006). This reveals the potential of PP surveys in travel data collection and analysis.

Methodologies for Processing 'Dot' Data

The travel behavioural data collected using mobile instruments represents sequential 'dots' in space–time dimensions. Each dot has labels of longitude, latitude and time of day. The approach for travel behavioural analysis involves transferring a 'dot' to a 'trip', and then applying conventional analytical tools such as trip-based models. However, the original characteristics of the dot data may be lost in this data transfer process. Therefore, it is necessary to analyse the dot data in their original form. In this section, data-processing technologies are presented for 'dot' data. They are data cleaning, labelling, stay-or-move identification (SMI) and map matching. These technologies are essential whenever dot data are analysed in their original form or once transferred to trip data and then analysed.

Stay-or-Move Identification

Location-positioning errors are inevitable in the data obtained using GPS or mobile phones. The first step in data processing is termed as cleaning or cleansing. A dot can be eliminated if it is extremely isolated from a series of dots along a line. A sudden increase in the distance between two dots is used as the decision criterion. Technological issues in data processing are also discussed in Schönfelder et al. (2002).

When we analyse a set of dot data, it is unknown whether each dot was observed during a trip. If it is possible to identify the dot during a trip, various trip attributes are extracted in time–space dimensions from a series of dots. The most important consideration in this process is the discrimination of an observed point into one of the two categories: moving point or staying point. When one of these two labels is allocated to each dot, it becomes possible to determine additional trip attributes such as the origin and destination. Figure 3 explains the concept of SMI for a series of dots.

Table 3
PP Survey Implementation in Japan

Name of survey	Survey duration		Number of samples	Survey purposes
Matsuyama (2003)	03/01/29–02/28	31 days	100	Evaluation of information provision
Miyoshi (2003)	03/11/01–01/10 04/01/10–02/06	70 days 27 days	20	LOS measurement
Matsuyama (2004)	04/01/26–02/29	35 days	317	Evaluation of information provision
Kochi (2004)	04/10/03–11/30	58 days	192	Evaluation of social experiment
Tokushima (2004)	04/10/03–11/30	58 days	151	Evaluation of social experiment
Matsuyama (2004–2)	04/12/06–12/10	5 days	31	Survey method development
Tokushima (2004–2)	05/01/11–02/28	48 days	61	Evaluation of expressway de-pricing
Matsue (2005)	05/01/24–02/24	31 days	15	LOS measurement
Matsuyama (2005)	05/02/01–02/28	28 days	384	Evaluation of information provision, Ecological point
Hanshin EXP (2005)	05/02/07–02/20	13 days	74	Route choice model
Shikoku (2005)	05/02/–05/05	Nil	20 pairs	Sightseeing travel behaviour
Ozu (2005)	05/06/24–07/08	14 days	10	LOS measurement
Niihama (2005)	05/07/09–07/30	22 days	37	Risk evaluation for natural disaster
Tsukuba (2005)	05/07/04–07/24 05/08/24–09/30	20 days 37 days	74	Impact measurement new rail line
Hanshin Bay (2005)	05/11/18–12/16	29 days	50	Analysis of freight transport
Hanshin EXP (2006)	06/01/16–02/17	33 days	91	Route choice modelling, sensitivity of pricing
W-Meihan (2006)	06/01/23–02/28	37 days	93	Evaluation of social experiment
Nara (2006)	06/03/10–03/31	22 days	196	Impact analysis for access-controlled highway

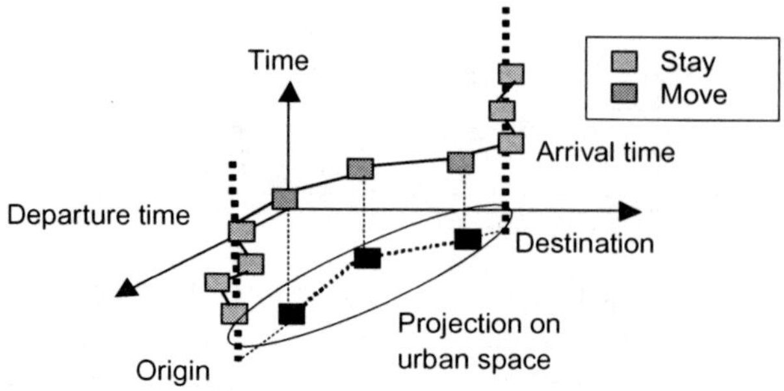

Figure 3
Concept of SMI

The distance between two adjacent points in a time sequence is the key measure in an SMI algorithm. If this distance is sufficiently small, two adjacent points can be identified as staying at the same position. Otherwise, these two points are considered to be moving or provisionally moving (one of the two points is staying and the other is moving). This depends on the state of the preceding points. The SMI algorithm was first proposed by Asakura et al. (1999) and a detailed description of the algorithm is available in Asakura and Hato (2004). In order to improve the performance of the algorithm, practical constraints on staying time and travel time are included. They are effective to eliminate short stops and short trips.

Asakura et al. (2003) examined how the SMI algorithm performs with regard to actual behavioural data and proposed an improved SMI algorithm. The actual location-positioning data collected with PEAMON in Osaka were used for the validation test. The improved SMI algorithm showed better performance with a hit ratio of 85% for the test data set. The number of trips estimated using the identification results was also consistent with the number of trips in the tours. It was found that the optimum combination of the distance threshold and staying time threshold were approximately 80 m and 200 seconds, respectively.

Dot Data Cleaning: Route Matching Algorithm

A sequence of staying dots indicates that an activity was performed at the location position of these dots. In the sequence of dots, the times of the first and last dots correspond to the arrival time and departure time, respectively. When a sequence of moving dots is projected on transport networks, a travel route can be identified; this procedure is referred to as map matching. The map-matching process is used to identify the location of data points on a coded map of a transport network. The output of the map-matching process is an identification of the routes that were originally considered. The development of map-matching algorithms appears really important not only for analysing travel route choice behaviour but also for providing travel time data for network performance evaluation and travel information provision.

A map-matching algorithm was also proposed by Asakura et al. (1999, 2000a) for PHS-based location-positioning data. The first step is the extraction of a sub-network from a complete transport network. The sub-network consists of links that are sufficiently close to the observed dots between the origin and destination pair. The second step is the generation of the *k*th shortest path in the sub-network. When location positioning is accurate, the size of the sub-network is minimized and a few paths are generated. Among these paths, the nearest path from a sequence of dots is selected. This basic algorithm was then improved such that the most likely path weighted by observed points was selected.

Miwa et al. (2004) studied the route identification algorithm for travel time prediction. Morikawa and Miwa (2004) analysed the route choice behaviour of taxis in Nagoya using the results of route identification. Marchal et al. (2005) presented a map-matching algorithm that only employed the GPS coordinates and network topology. They show examples of the Zürich area on a large data set. They demonstrate the efficiency of the algorithm with regard to accuracy and computational speed.

Database Management

In traditional travel behavioural studies, the minimum unit of data collection and analysis was a 'trip'. Several attributes are then allocated to the trip, such as origin, destination, departure and arrival times, mode of travel and purpose of the trip. Database structure and management methods have been established for these trip-based travel behavioural data. On the other hand, the travel data collected from mobile instruments represent a set of 'dot' data. Traditional database management methods are not yet fully applicable for these data. If the dot data are transferred to the trip data, conventional database management schemes can be applied. However, the dot data may lose their location-specific characteristics, which are important for space–time analysis of travel behaviour. Thus, database management methods for dot data should be developed such that location-specific characteristics of the dot data are preserved.

An essential procedure for dot-based data management is referred to as 'labelling' in which various attributes are allocated to each dot (Asakura and Hato, 2001). This is referred to as 'indexing'. Location-positioning attributes are common labels for a dot; they are the observed time, longitude and latitude. The other observed attributes are also used as labels, such as spot speed, acceleration and so on.

In addition to these observed location-specific attributes, secondary labels are allocated after data processing. They include a stay-or-move flag, departure and arrival flag, and map-matching labels such as link number and re-calculated coordinates of the location position of each dot. The selection of labels may depend on the size of data and the purpose of analysis, while the common labels are essential for all the cases.

Conclusions and Recommendations

Recent technological developments in tracking-type travel behavioural data collection methods supported by mobile communication systems have been described in this paper. A key technology is the location positioning of a mobile object. While GPS-based location positioning can be considered as the representative technology, a variety of location-positioning technologies and data collection instruments have been proposed. Recently, a hybrid system comprising GPS-assisted mobile phones along with the Internet has been employed for personal travel data collection in a multimodal environment. It is developing into a more comprehensive travel survey and analysis system for transport planning and management.

The methodologies of processing and analysing dot data have been presented in the latter half of the paper. SMI and map-matching algorithms are essential data-processing methods. It appears fairly important to directly analyse dot data such that the original location characteristics of each dot might be reserved to the maximum extent. A large amount of accurate travel data becomes available as advanced technologies are applied to travel data collection. A data-oriented approach including spatial data-mining methods should be further studied under the environments of substantial amounts of travel data. Remaining research targets and recommendations are shown below.

Further System Developments

Location positioning and communication technologies are expected to further improve in the future. In addition to current technologies such as GPS, various technologies would be applicable to travel data collection. Survey instruments will be more compact and wearable rendering them suitable for tracking personal movements in urban spaces. One of the ways is to extend computer-assisted travel survey systems in combination with wearable communication instruments. An effective assignment of data collection functions between wearable instruments and the central server appears to be important. In other words, a better balance between tracking and self-interviews should be further discussed such that accurate travel data can be collected with a minimum burden on travellers. Stand-alone travel data loggers with minimum communication functions should be developed further as well.

Large-Scale Tracking Survey

It is apparent that travel surveys using mobile instruments can supplement conventional data elements recorded using paper or electronic travel diaries. Wolf et al. (2001) demonstrated that it is feasible to determine the purpose of the trip from the GPS data by using a spatially accurate and comprehensive GIS. Sharp and Murakami (2005) discussed survey methodology considerations for a subsequent series of personal travel surveys in the United States. Tracking-type data collection methods have been applied to longitudinal travel surveys with a limited number of respondents. This is because of the constraint of the number of available data collection instruments. Whether a long-term data collection of smaller samples can yield meaningful information as compared to a conventional large-scale 1-day survey has not been sufficiently discussed. Evidently, it is necessary to validate whether new technologies contribute to an improvement in the survey quality and response rate of large-scale travel surveys within a cost constraint.

Survey Costs

It is true that tracking surveys are expensive in terms of hardware and communication costs, while the labour costs of data collectors could be minimized. Some of the cost factors such as communication costs are now decreasing. The repeated use of data collection devices contributes to a reduction in the survey costs. The number of data collection devices could be minimized if the data collection devices used for a group of samples are reused for the subsequent group of samples. It is evident that tracking surveys are superior in the collection of more accurate data with regard to the time and location of the travel behaviour. The cost of data collection in tracking surveys would become acceptable if it is compensated by the quality of data. A decision needs to be made between either cheaper but low-quality data or expensive but high-quality data.

Survey Participation and Response Rate

Improving the response rate is one of the important issues in personal travel surveys. It is known that the response rate of an in-person survey is the highest than other data collection modes. However, the response rate has been decreasing every year, particularly in urban areas. It has not yet been verified whether tracking surveys contribute to an improvement in the response rate. As an example, the PP surveys in Matsuyama showed that the ratio of withdrawn samples during a survey lasting 1 month was less than 3% of the initial samples. This indicates that once the respondents joined the tracking survey, they might not withdraw from the survey. In order to retain the respondents in the travel survey, it is necessary to provide an additional interesting entity to the survey. Survey respondents in the PP survey can verify their past trajectories on the GIS. A few respondents mentioned that this function was fairly interesting. Gaming sections may be installed within travel survey systems with careful considerations on the mutual dependency between the actual behaviour and the installed game.

Participatory approaches could be included in personal travel surveys. When a travel survey is conducted as the fundamental travel data collection method, the inhabitants of the planning area are essentially sampled as the survey respondents. If a participatory approach is adapted as the transport planning scheme, the inhabitants are requested to join the travel survey at the initial survey design stage. This may increase the motivation of the inhabitants to participate in the travel survey, which might result in a higher response rate. Advanced technologies can be utilized in this participatory approach used for travel data collection.

Statistical Issues

A sampling bias is inevitable in any travel survey. Currently, tracking-type travel surveys with advanced technologies have not overcome this problem. The technological literacy of the respondents may increase the survey bias when mobile communication devices and the Internet are essential elements of the tracking survey. For example, elderly people were less involved in the PP survey, while younger people participated in it without any difficulties. It is necessary to design a universal survey system that requires a minimum operation of the data collection devices. An increase in the number of samples is another statistical issue for tracking surveys. As discussed earlier, it has not been widely applied to large-scale travel surveys. A sufficient number of samples were obtained through the tracking survey if these data were used to understand the travel behaviour and develop a trial model. However, the required number of samples has not been statistically investigated when the tracking data were extended to record the spatial and dynamic interactions in actual urban areas.

Emergency Transport

Conventional travel surveys are aimed to assist in ordinary transport planning and management; they have not targeted emergency transport issues. Location-positioning technologies such as GPS and mobile phones originated from the emergency and rescue requirements of people who could not identify their location positions. Tracking-type travel surveys could be applied to emergency transport issues. For example, it could be applied to know how people change the behaviour if ordinary travel routes and modes are unavailable. Tracking surveys can be used for understanding the travel behaviour under such unusual travel conditions. The results would be useful in discussing evacuation plans and transport plans during the recovery period following a natural disaster.

ACKNOWLEDGMENTS

This study was initiated when both the authors worked together in Ehime University in 1998. Thereafter, many people have collaborated with the development and installation of tracking-type personal data collection methods. The authors are greatly honoured to share history with them. The authors would like to express their sincerest gratitude to all of them.

REFERENCES

Andre, M. (1997). Vehicle uses and operating conditions: on board measurement. In M. Stopher and M. Lee-Gosselin (Eds.), *Understanding Travel Behaviour in Era of Change*, Pergamon, pp. 469–481.

Asakura, Y. and E. Hato (2001). Analysis of travel behaviour using positioning function of mobile communication devices. In D. Hensher (Ed.), *Travel Behaviour Research: The Leading Edge*, Pergamon Press, pp. 885–899.

Asakura, Y. and E. Hato (2004). Tracking survey for individual travel behaviour using mobile communication instruments. *Transportation Research C* 12(3/4), 273–291.

Asakura, Y., E. Hato and M. Kashiwadani (2000a). Monitoring traveller's route choice behaviour using mobile phone system. *Proceedings of the 8th EWGT*, Rome, pp. 483–486.

Asakura, Y., E. Hato, Y. Nishibe, T. Daito, J. Tanabe and H. Koshima (1999). Monitoring travel behaviour using PHS based location positioning service system. *6th ITS World Congress*, Toronto (CD-ROM).

Asakura, Y., E. Hato and Y. Utsunomiya (2003). Verification of stay and move identification algorithm for mobile objects using observed location positioning data. *Journal of Eastern Asia Society for Transport Studies* 5, 1962–1974.

Asakura, Y. and T. Iryo (2005a). Tracking individual travel behaviour using mobile phone without information from base stations. *Journal of Advanced Transportation* 39(1), 105–116.

Asakura, Y. and T. Iryo (2005b). Analysis of tourist behaviour based on the tracking data collected using mobile communication instrument. Paper presented at *Successes and Failures of Traffic Demand Management*. Edinburgh, UK.

Asakura, Y., A. Okamoto, A. Suzuki, Y. H. Lee and J. Tanabe (2001). Monitoring individual travel behaviour using PEAMON: a cellular phone based location positioning instrument combined with acceleration sensor. *8th ITS World Congress*, Sydney.

Asakura, Y., J. Tanabe and Y. H. Lee (2000b). Characteristics of positioning data for monitoring travel behaviour. *7th ITS World Congress,* Turin (CD-ROM).

Axhausen, K. (1998). Can we ever obtain the data we would like to have? In T. Garling, K. Westin and T. Laitila (Eds.), *Theoretical Foundations of Travel Choice Modeling*, Pergamon Press, pp. 305–334.

Battelle Transportation Division (1997). Lexington area travel data collection test: global positioning systems for personal travel surveys. Final Report to FHWA (Federal Highway Administration). Available at: http://www.fhwa.dot.gov/ohim/trb/reports.htm

Bovy, P. H. L. and E. Stern (1990). *Route Choice—Wayfinding in Transport Networks*. The Netherlands, Kluwer Academic Publishers.

D'Este, G. M., R. Zito and M. A. P. Taylor (1999). Using GPS to measure traffic system performance. *Journal of Computer-Aided Civil and Infrastructure Engineering* 14, 273–283.

Doherty, S. T. and E. J. Miller (2000). A computerized household activity scheduling survey. *Transportation* 27, 75–97.

Doherty, S. T., N. Noel, M.-L. Gosselin, C. Sirois and M. Ueno (2001). Moving beyond observed outcomes: integrating global positioning systems and interactive computer-based travel behavior surveys. *Transportation Research Circular*, 449–466.

Draijer, G., N. Kalfs and J. Perdok (2000). Global positioning system as data collection method for travel research. *Transportation Research Record* 1719, 147–153.

Ettema D., H. Timmermans and L. V. Veghel (1996). Effects of data collection methods in travel and activity research. Prepared for *European Institute of Retailing and Services Studies.*

Forrest, T. L. and D. F. Pearson (2005). Comparison of trip determination methods in household travel surveys enhanced by a global positioning system. *Transportation Research Record* 1917, 63–71.

Greaves, S. (2006). A panel approach to evaluating voluntary travel behavior change programs—South Australia Pilot Survey. *Transportation Research Board 85th Annual Meeting.*

Guensler, R., H. Li, J. Ogle, K. W. Axhausen and S. Schönfelder (2006). Analysis of Commute Atlanta Instrumented Vehicle GPS data: destination choice behavior and activity spaces. *Transportation Research Board 85th Annual Meeting.*

Hato, E. and Y. Asakura (2001). New approaches for collecting time–space activity data. *Transportation Research Board 80th Annual Meeting.*

Hato, E., T. Mitani and S. Itsubo (2006). Development of MoALs (Mobile Activity Loggers Supported by GPS-Phones) for travel behavior analysis. *Transportation Research Board 85th Annual Meeting.*

Itsubo, S. and E. Hato (2006). Effectiveness of household travel survey using GPS-equipped cell phones and web diary: comparative study with paper-based travel survey. *Transportation Research Board 85th Annual Meeting.*

Jan, O., A. Horowitz and Z. R. Peng (2000). Using GPS data to understand variations in path choice. *Transportation Research Record* 1725, 37–44.

Kracht, M. (2004). Tracking and interviewing individuals with GPS and GSM technology on mobile electronic devices. *7th International Conference on Travel Survey Methods*, Costa Rica.

Li, H., R. Guensler and J. Ogle (2005). Analysis of morning commute route choice patterns using global positioning system–based vehicle activity data. *Transportation Research Record* 1926, 162–170.

Marchal, F., J. Hackney and K. W. Axhausen (2005). Efficient map matching of large global positioning system data sets: tests on speed-monitoring experiment in Zürich. *Transportation Research Record* 1935, 93–100.

Martin, P. and P. Bateson (1985). *Measuring Behaviour: An Introductory Guide.* Cambridge, Cambridge University Press.

Mitani, T. (2005). Study on the applicability of travel information provision system supported by probe person survey. Ph. D. dissertation, Ehime University.

Miwa, T., T. Sakai and T. Morikawa (2004). Route identification and travel time prediction using probe-car data. *International Journal of ITS Research* 2(1), 21–28.

Morikawa, T. and T. Miwa (2004). Analysis on route choice behavior using probe-vehicle data. *Proceedings of International Workshop on Behavior in Networks.* The University of Seoul, pp. 253–262.

Murakami, E. and D. P. Wagner (1999). Can using global positioning system (GPS) improve trip reporting?. *Transportation Research C* 7, 149–165.

Ohmori, Y., Y. Muromachi, N. Harata and K. Ohta (1998). The study on the availability of GPS to travel behaviour survey. *Proceedings of the 18th Annual Meeting of Japan Traffic Engineers,* pp. 5–8 (in Japanese).

Ohmori, N., M. Nakazato, K. Sasaki, K. Nishii and N. Harata (2006). Activity diary surveys using GPS mobile phones and PDA. *Transportation Research Board 85th Annual Meeting.*

Quiroga, C. A. and D. Bullock (1998). Travel time studies with global positioning and geographic information systems: an integrated methodology. *Transportation Research C* 6, 101–127.

Sasaki, T. and H. Mastui (1968). A stochastic model for traffic in the exposition field. *Proceedings of Japan Society of Civil Engineers*, 159, pp. 90–95 (in Japanese).

Sermons, M. W. and S. Koppelman (1996). Use of vehicle positioning data for arterial incident detection. *Transportation Research C* 4(2), 87–96.

Schönfelder, S., K. W. Axhausen, N. Antille and M. Bierlaire (2002). Exploring the potentials of automatically collected GPS data for travel behaviour analysis—a Swedish data Source. In J. Möltgen and A. Wytzisk (Eds.), *GI-Technologien für Verkehr und Logistik, number 13*, Münster, Universität Münster, pp. 155–179.

Sharp, J. and E. Murakami (2005). Travel survey methods and technologies—related considerations. *Journal of Transportation and Statistics* 8(3). Available at http://www.bts.gov/publications/journal_of_transportation_and_statistics/volume_08_number_03/html/paper_07/index.html

Stopher, P. R. (2004). GPS, location, and household travel. In D. Hensher, K. Button, K. Haynes and P. Stopher (Eds.), *Handbook of Transport Geography and Spatial Systems*, Vol. 5. Amsterdam, Elsevier.

Sugino, K. and Y. Asakura (2004). Analysis of information access behaviour of tourists with mobile instrument. *Infrastructure Planning Review* 23, 593–598 (in Japanese).

Sugino, K., Y. Asakura, T. Daito and T. Matsuo (2000). Traffic information service in road network using mobile location data. *7th ITS World Congress in Turin* (CD-ROM).

Sugino, K., S. Yano, E. Hato and Y. Asakura (2005). Empirical analysis of sightseeing behaviour using probe person survey data. *Proceedings of Infrastructure Planning* 32 (CD-ROM).

Suzuki, A., T. Takahashi and H. Ino-oka (1994). Identification of unconstrained behaviour for pedestrian's route estimation. *ICEIE Annual Meeting* (in Japanese).

Tanabe, J. and M. Tange (2006). Evolution and perspective of probe person system in traffic data acquisition. *33th Meeting of Infrastructure Planning* (in Japanese).

Wagner, D. P., E. Murakami and M. Guindon (1997). Using GPS for measuring household travel in private vehicles. *6th TRB Conference on the Application of Transportation Planning Methods*, Dearborn, Michigan.

Wermuth, M., C. Sommer and M. Kreitz (2003). Impact of new technologies in travel surveys. In P. Stopher and P. Jones (Eds.), *Transport Survey Quality and Innovation*, Pergamon Press, pp. 465–469.

Wolf, J. (2004a). Applications of new technologies in travel surveys. *7th International Conference on Travel Survey Methods*, Costa Rica.

Wolf, J. (2004b). Defining GPS and GPS capabilities. In D. Hensher, K. Button, K. Haynes and P. Stopher (Eds.), *Handbook of Transport Geography and Spatial Systems*, Vol. 5. Amsterdam, Elsevier.

Wolf, J., R. Guensler and W. Bachman (2001). Elimination of the travel diary: experiment to derive trip purpose from global positioning system travel data. *Transportation Research Record* 1768, 125–134.

Yatsumoto, H., T. Kitazawa, S. Nakagawa, A. Okamoto and Y. Asakura (2006). Analysis of route choice behaviour under flexible toll system of urban expressway based on probe person trip survey. *33th Meeting of Infrastructure Planning* (in Japanese).

Zito, R., G. M. D'Este and M. A. P. Taylor (1995). Global positioning systems in the time domain: how useful a tool for intelligent vehicle-highway systems? *Transportation Research C* 3(4), 193–209.

Zmud, J. and J. Wolf (2003). Identifying the correlates of trip misreporting—results from the California Statewide Household Travel Survey GPS Study. *10th IATBR*, Lucerne.

2.6 Advances in Econometric Methods

The Expanding Sphere of Travel Behaviour Research
Selected Papers from the 11th International Conference on Travel Behaviour Research

10

Selective Developments in Choice Analysis and a Reminder about the Dimensionality of Behavioral Analysis ☆

David A. Hensher, John M. Rose and Sean M. Puckett

Abstract

Developments in data and modeling paradigms in choice analysis are occurring at a fast pace. A review of activity leading up to each IATBR conference shows progress on many fronts. This paper takes a selective view of some of these developments, especially those that have been close to the research program of the authors. We focus on information processing strategies, especially in the context of stated choice studies, and developments in the design of choice experiments, centered on expanding the behavioral capabilities of discrete choice models.

Introduction

Choice analysis has become mainstream in transportation research (Hensher et al., 2005b). Beginning with a relatively narrow focus on the development of econometric models to estimate the parameters of discrete choice models, the literature has evolved into a number of streams, all having real potential to be integrated in a *behavioral system of choice and payoff*.

☆ Resource paper for the 2006 International Association of Traveler Behavior Conference, Kyoto, Japan, August 16–20, 2006.

While noting the fast pace of development of model specification, from simple (but still useful) multinomial logit to ever-increasingly detailed closed- and open-form choice models, that account for the sources of observed and unobserved random and systematic heterogeneity and heteroskedasticity in preferences, we are now seeing a growing interest in the choice *process* in complementing the dominant emphasis on the choice *outcome*.[1] Indeed, some researchers with a penchant beyond mainstream economics (notably in behavioral economic psychology, and to a lesser extent in human geography and sociology) have been arguing for many years that the economist's perspective on choice and random utility is limiting, not so much because it is wrong, but more that it imposes bounds that are somewhat narrow in what can be incorporated in the study and modeling of choice. Choice after all has no disciplinary bounds—it is strictly behavioral.

Themes that have emerged in recent years have highlighted the need to refocus the boundaries and to give as much credence to broadened themes as we continue to deliver in extending the econometric niceties of the family of choice models, especially the set of logit derivatives. This paper synthesizes a number of themes that are exercising the minds of a growing number of travel behavior researchers. In one sense, these themes are far from new, but the research effort is growing significantly, and we see very strong signs that the new insights can be relatively easily integrated into a system of choice models that recognize not only outcome, but also process. The intent clearly is to justify the added 'complexity' in terms of an improved understanding of decision-making, and especially in improving our ability to predict behavioral response under conditions of change. Strictly, we promote 'relevancy' instead of 'complexity', since the latter has produced a belief in limiting empirical efforts for (unfounded) fear of cognitive burden (assumed to be highly correlated with the amount of information to report, especially in RP studies, and process—especially in SP studies).

The themes presented in this review promote a greater focus on the way that information is processed in choice making, the link between the amount of information on offer (especially that associated with the attributes within a stated choice (SC) framework) and its relevancy, and whether it is ignored or rearranged for a variety of rational reasons. An additional topic that interweaves, with a capability to embed information processing strategies, is the design of SC experiments, which is now an order of magnitude more sophisticated, and the paths in advanced discrete choice models that are available to capture the role of attribute processing (AP).[2]

---

[1]Designed hopefully to improve forecasting accuracy through an improved understanding on choice making.
[2]An earlier version presented at the IATBR conference in August 2006 included a section of agent interdependency. We have removed this and refer the reader to the chapter by Puckett and Hensher in this volume.

The paper is organized as follows. In the section 'Information Processing', we present a framework within which information processing can be captured, that has a logical interface with choice analysis. This is followed in the section 'The Stated Choice Setting: In need of Revision?' with a way of identifying the power relationship between agents where a cooperative outcome is necessary (often through concession) in order to activate a choice outcome. The section 'Stated Choice Experimental Design Strategies' overviews developments in the design of choice experiments, moving beyond orthogonal designs to designs that permit behaviorally plausible correlation (to some extent), in recognition of the need to deliver asymptotically efficient parameter estimates and cost-justifiable sample sizes. The section 'Conclusions and Future Directions' offers suggestions on continuing research directions.

Information Processing

> "What lies ahead for discrete choice analysis? ... The potentially important roles of information processing, perception formation and cognitive illusions are just beginning to be explored and behavioral and experimental economics are still in their adolescence." (McFadden, 2001)

Decision-making life can be thought of as starting as a set of continuous random variables, and if there is no information added, the outcomes or payoffs are strictly random events. Fortunately, decision-making is assisted by a number of behavioral inputs, often called attributes, but more generally a suite of cues and a set of rules used by individuals to assist them in processing the information centered on the cues in arriving at outcomes that deliver payoffs. Crucially, the payoffs result from the amount of information processed (Berg, 2005). The decision-making environment can be defined as a joint probability distribution over states of nature (i.e. alternatives on offer) and cues and a payoff function[3] that ranks stochastic outcomes conditional on observed cues and actions. Cues are typically a set of attributes and actions are the mechanisms that individuals adopt in processing the attributes to arrive at outcomes that have payoffs.

What we have found in recent years is that these attributes are the centerpiece of information processing and they can be relevant or not relevant (Hensher, 2006a, b). Within the relevant set, they can be processed or ignored, and they can be ignored in the presence or absence of cognitive constraints. Likewise deeming attributes as not relevant can be associated with cognitive and non-cognitive constraints. Importantly, we argue that relevancy and ignoring such information are not contradictions in a

[3]A payoff function refers to the contrast of all costs and benefits linked to information processing in the context of a set of assessable attributes and outcomes. One interpretation, adopted in choice analysis, is that it is a utility function representing a preference ordering over all alternatives in a pre-defined choice set.

behavioral sense. We are of the view that ignoring can be good (e.g. the divided attention syndrome), it can be smart and it aligns with a sentiment that individuals adopt relatively frugal action rules. Herbert Simon in the 1950s made the equivalent case that arguments that tend (in our view too much) to rely on cognitive burden to justify simplistic SC experiments have failed to understand the simple principle that cognitive processes should not be evaluated in a vacuum, and that a context is required to establish how adaptive choice rules are.

Fundamentally, information is relevant if it contributes in a non-marginal way (i.e. beyond the just noticeable difference threshold) to payoff and the benefits perceived to flow through from effort expended in accounting for that attribute exceed the costs. As a corollary, relevant information can be ignored within the context of good choice making for many non-trivial reasons. Within the choice-making context, we distinguish between alternatives in a choice set of outcomes (i.e. what is the common behavioral metric in choice analysis) and the choice set of actions or decision rules on information processing that an individual selects to maximize the expected payoff function conditional on observable information. Central to the selection of a preferred information processing rule (described as an optimal action in behavioral economics) is the treatment of attributes (which we refer as the *attribute processing strategy* (APS)). This is at the heart of the process model, regardless of whether the attributes are pre-specified as in the majority of SC experiments or whether they are elicited through other mechanisms.

Drawing on the experimental findings from psychology, we know that individuals often make incomplete use of available information, which implies that, although expected payoff functions may be influenced by specific attributes, an adopted information processing rule does not depend on these specific attributes. Such information processing rules are incomplete in the sense that human cognition provides filters[4] that result in adaptive responses to specific types of payoff/information environments. This is not the result of bounded rationality per se[5] but the interaction of such rationality with the payoff-probability structure within the choice environment under study. Hence, ignoring attributes is a rational outcome of a choice process.

Cognitive constraints are commonly cited as the generic basis of information processing rules. Such constraints are derivatives of complex phenomena, many of which are unknown and/or poorly understood or articulated by the individual and/or the researcher. There is a large body of research that associates cognitive constraints with memory limitations (Stroop, 1935), bounds on processing speed and pre-attentive

[4]This enables cognitive effort in general and hence selective cognitive responses to be allocated to the important tasks.

[5]Bounded rationality in economics is typically given a narrow interpretation often linked to coping in a negative sense (or sub-optimal sense), whereas a more appealing interpretation credits it as an adaptive mechanism to support enhanced outcomes. We read rationality as the product of behavior *and* reasoning.

capability (i.e. number of channels), all leading to mechanisms to cope or economize on processing resources such as ignoring certain amounts of information. The information ignored (or what is increasingly referred as information suppression—see Erber and Fiske, 1984) can include total exclusion of a specific attribute (with the selection rule being systematic[6] or random),[7] or partial exclusion as a consequence of noting but discounting its presence. Importantly, and almost perceptually self-evident, individuals discount specific information in line with their own payoff-probability function, which processes all opportunities and assigns a probability to each, which is mapped into an expected payoff to arrive at a preferred outcome or choice. The idea of *ignoring* information is complex in that individuals often analyze all attributes (or cues) in order to identify which ones can be excluded from the optimal action plan.[8] Within the setting of a (subjective) utility function, as is the case of SC analysis, the two-stage process applies. However, if we can assume the existence of an adaptive mechanism with a history of evolutionary exposure and (overt) experience, then it is possible to 'go straight to the set' that is used in selecting the optimal action plan (i.e. choice outcome). Another way of stating this is that when the payoff function is defined strictly by adaptation, then the optimal outcome does not depend on a current attribute, and hence the need to know about AP in the current state is of little consequence to the outcome. Unfortunately, the analyst is unlikely to know this and be able to make inferences up to a probability, and will have to rely on an explicit test of information processing involving a mixture of adaptive presence and current state attribute relevance.

The analyst has the task of identifying the components of the process-outcome model that drive individual decision-making and the diversity of such models, as a way of accommodating the heterogeneity existing within a population of decision-makers. Within the travel behavior setting, we are embellishing the SC framework to accommodate such features of decision-making.

The Stated Choice Setting: In need of Revision?

SC experiments are typified by a pre-determined set of attributes and alternatives, with the number of levels and range of each attribute fixed within the design.

[6]For example, the level does not differentiate enough from a reference alternative or accumulated experience on expected gain, as postulated in case-based decision theory which invokes similarity weights (Gilboa and Schmeidler, 2001).

[7]For example, ignore any attributes below the first three listed.

[8]This plan becomes the equilibrium state (at least in the short run), which is often a habit-forming state that is repeated without any further filtering tasks. This accords also with transactions cost theory and search/minimum-regret theory in economics. Any major changes in the context may invoke a review of the equilibrium state, leading to a renewed filtering process.

The experimental design is then developed under a specific set of rules, such as orthogonality or D-efficiency (see the section 'Stated Choice Experimental Design Strategies'), with or without priors on the parameter estimates, and typically under the assumption that the resulting data will be estimated under the multinomial logit IID condition. Although there has been a growing recognition that the design of choice experiments should be conditioned by the specific functional specification of the estimation model, another strand of activity is focusing on the influence that the dimensionality of the choice experiment has on the revelation of preferences and hence on choice responses.

This section discusses ways that the information in a SC experiment is processed, which is attributed in part to the dimensionality of the SC experiment and in part to recognition that there is substantial heterogeneity in the processing strategies of individuals in a sample. In particular, we argue that failure to take into account the *relevancy* of the information offered in the evaluation process leading to a choice outcome, no matter how 'simple' or 'complex' a design is, will contribute to biases in preference revelation. The great majority of researchers and practitioners ignore this aspect of SC methods, assuming that attributes offered are all relevant to some degree (Hensher, 2006b).

In recent years, there has been a growing interest on understanding the processes or rules invoked by respondents in dealing with the information in SC experiments. Although the impetus for this focus appears to have been motivated by an interest in cognitive burden, research by Hensher (among others) found that the real issue is not the amount of information to process, which became associated with 'complexity', but rather the *relevance* of the information. This opened up the possibility that a study of the implications on choice response of the amount of information provided in a choice experiment should be investigated in the context of the broader theme of what rules individuals bring to bear when assessing the information in a choice experiment. These rules may be embedded in prejudices that have little to do with the amount of information in the experiment; rather they may be rational coping strategies that are used in everyday decision-making for a whole host of reasons. There is an extensive literature on information processing, which includes prospect theory (Kahnemann and Tversky, 1979a, b), case-based decision theory (Gilboa and Schmeidler, 2001) and non-expected utility theory (Starmer, 2001).

How does a Respondent Assess a Stated Choice Task?

Imagine that you have been asked to review the choice screen shown in Figure 1 and indicate which alternative is your preferred. There is a lot of information in this screen that you have to *attend to*, in deciding what influences your decision (what we refer as *relevant* information). There are likely to be many implicit and often subconscious rules

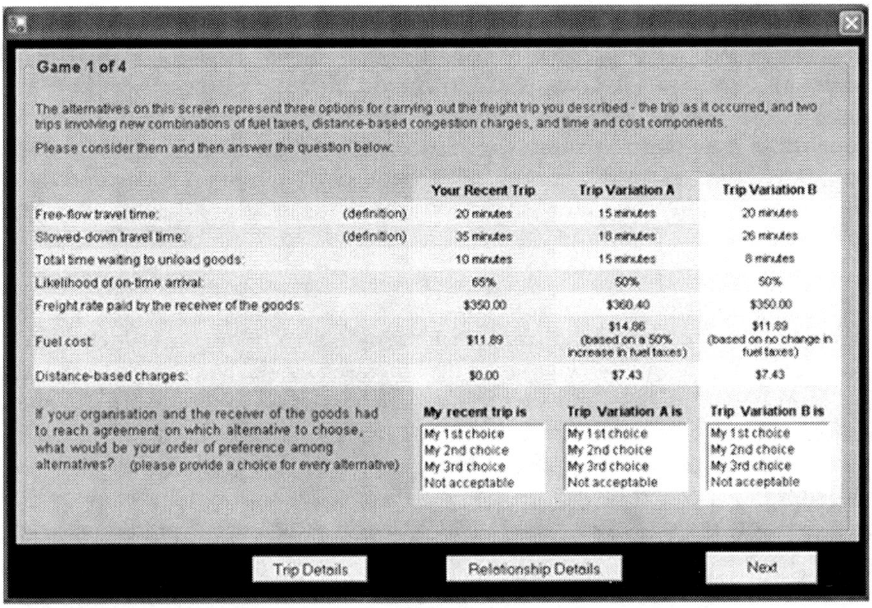

Figure 1
Example of a Stated Choice Screen

being adopted to process the attributes and alternatives that are used, possibly to cope in a constructive way with the amount of information to assess (what we refer as a *coping* strategy). The screen, for example, may be regarded as too *complex* in terms of the amount of information presented and its content. Whether one invokes a specific set of *processing rules* to cope with complexity, or whether these are a sub-set of the rules you have built up over time and draw on from past experiences, may be unclear. What we do suspect is that there are a large number of processing rules (what we call heterogeneity in information processing) being used throughout any sampled population, and that individuals are using them to handle mixtures of relevancy and cognitive burden (including task learning).[9] Indeed, it may be reasonable to suggest that relevancy is in part a natural response to cognitive constraint (as suggested above).

It is reasonable to propose that individuals do have a variety of AP styles, including the *simplifying* strategy of ignoring certain attributes (for whatever reason). Heterogeneity in AP strategies is widely reported in consumer research (see, e.g. Hensher, 2004;

[9]Studies decomposing random parameters by amount of time spent show (1) people spend longer on earlier choice sets and (2) the amount of processing time is a significant decomposition parameter for random parameter distributions.

DeShazo and Fermo, 2002, 2004) and its existence in choice experiments is supported by observation of lexicographic[10] choice behavior in segments of respondents completing SC surveys (see, e.g. Sælendsminde, 1994).[11] When researchers fail to account for such an AP strategy, they are essentially assuming that all designs are comprehensible, all design attributes are relevant (to some degree) and the design has accommodated the relevant amount of 'complexity' necessary to make the choice experiment meaningful (Hensher et al., 2005a, b). Ideas of good and smart choosing appear absent.

Experimental evidence and self-reported decision protocols support the view that heuristic rules are the proximate drivers of most human behavior (McFadden, 2001). The question remains as to whether rules themselves develop in patterns that are broadly consistent with random utility-maximization postulates. If there are preferences behind rules, then it is possible to recover them and correctly evaluate policies in terms of these underlying preferences. If not, economics will have to seek a new foundation for this task. While many psychologists argue that behavior is far too sensitive to context and affect to be usefully related to stable preferences, this is a somewhat pessimistic view. A number of authors have challenged this position (e.g. Hensher, 2006b; McFadden, 2001; Swait and Adamowicz, 2001). Many behavioral deviations from the economist's standard model can be attributed to perceptual illusions, particularly in the way that we process information, rather than a more fundamental breakdown in the pursuit of self-interest. Many of the rules we do use are essentially defensive, protecting us from mistakes that perceptual illusions may induce.

The (implicit) assumption in SC studies that all attributes are processed by all respondents has been challenged by a number of researchers (e.g. DeShazo and Fermo, 2004; Hensher, 2004, 2006b; Hensher et al., 2005a, b) who argue that it is more likely that individuals react to increasingly 'complex' choice situations by adopting one of the two AP strategies, broadly defined by the rival *passive bounded rationality* and *rationally adaptive* behavioral models. Under the passive bounded rationality model, individuals are thought to continue assessing all available attributes; however, they do so with increasing levels of error as choice complexity increases (DePalma et al., 1994). The rationally adaptive model assumes that individuals recognize that their limited

[10]We are of the view that non-compensatory behavior is confounded with attribute processing and that when one conditions the choice outcome on the heterogeneous set of AP rules, that compensatory behavior is a good approximation. The real risk with non-compensatory choice models is that they are placing the 'not relevant' attributes at the lowest level in the EBA hierarchy without assessing whether they should be there at all.

[11]Significant research effort has been expended on how to optimize the outputs derived from respondents completing choice tasks derived from these single design plans, generated using statistical design theory (e.g. Bunch et al., 1996; Huber and Zwerina, 1996; Kanninen, 2002; Kuhfeld et al., 1994; Lazari and Anderson, 1994; Sandor and Wedel, 2001), while minimizing the amount of cognitive effort required of respondents (e.g. Louviere and Timmermans, 1990; Oppewal et al., 1994; Wang et al., 2001; Bliemer and Rose, 2005a, b).

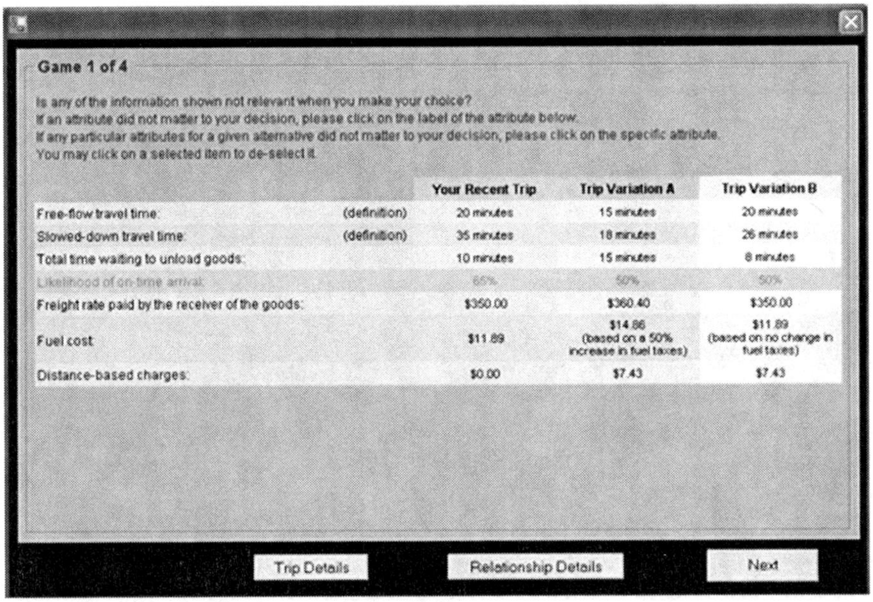

Figure 2
Attribute and Alternative Specific Processing Rules

cognition may have positive opportunity costs and react accordingly. As DeShazo and Fermo (2004) state:

> "Individuals will therefore allocate their attention across alternative-attribute information within a choice set in a rationally-adaptive manner by seeking to minimize the cost and maximize the benefit of information evaluation." (p. 3).

It is important to recognize that simplistic designs may also be 'complex' in a perceptual sense. Individuals may expect more information than was given to them, thinking such information would be relevant in a real market setting.[12] The development of a SC experiment, supplemented with questions on how an individual processed the information, enables the researcher to explore sources of systematic influences on choice. Examples of such questions are shown in Figures 2 and 3.

---

[12]There is widespread evidence in the psychology literature on the behavioral variability, unpredictability and inconsistency regularly demonstrated in decision-making and choices (e.g. González-Vallejo, 2002; Slovic, 1995), reflecting an assumption that goes back at least to Thurstone's law of comparative judgment (1927). One of the particularly important advantages of using a stochastic representation of decision strategies, as promoted herein, is that it enables a more behaviorally realistic analysis of variation in decision strategies.

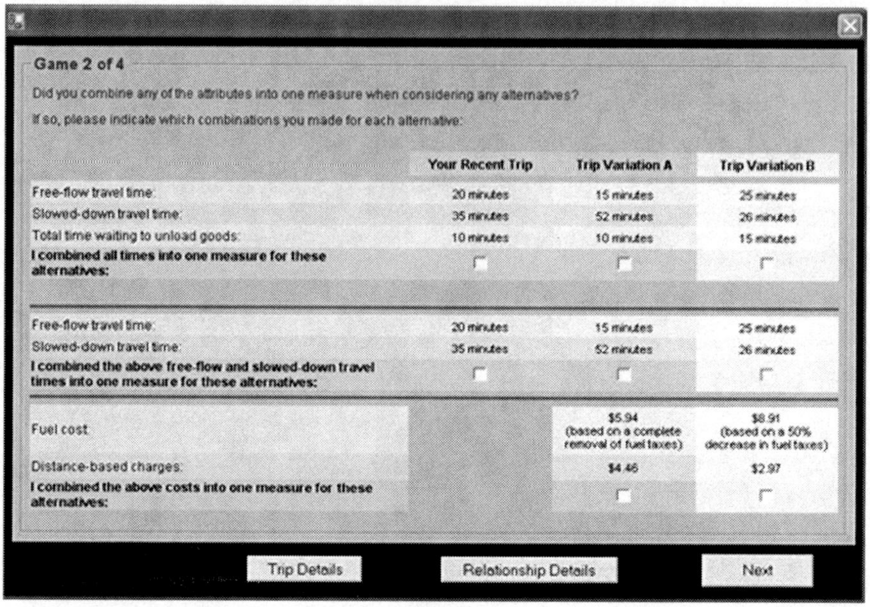

Figure 3
Inter-related Attribute Processing Rules

There is a substantial extant literature in the psychology domain about how various factors affect the amount of information processed in decision tasks. Recent evidence demonstrates the importance of such factors as time pressure (e.g. Diederich, 2003), cognitive load (e.g. Drolet and Luce, 2004) and task complexity (Swait and Adamowicz, 2001). There is also a great deal of variability in decision strategies employed in different contexts, and this variability adds to the difficulties of understanding the behavioral mechanisms. A recent attempt to define a typology of decision strategies (e.g. Payne et al., 1992) has been particularly useful.

Payne et al. (1992) characterized decision strategies along three dimensions: basis of processing, amount of processing and consistency of processing. Decision strategies are said to differ in terms of whether or not many attributes within an alternative are considered before another alternative is considered (*alternative-based* processing) or whether values across alternatives on a single attribute are processed before another attribute is processed (*attribute-based* processing). Strategies are also said to differ in terms of the amount of information processed (i.e. whether any information is ignored or not processed before a decision may be made). Finally, decision strategies can be grouped in terms of whether the same amount of information for each alternative is examined (*consistent* processing) or whether the amount of processing varies depending on the alternative (*selective* processing).

Table 1
Typology of Decision Strategies

Strategy	Attribute or alternative-based	Amount of information	Consistency
EBA	Attribute-based	Depends on values of alternatives and cut-offs	Selective
LEX	Attribute-based	Depends on values of alternatives and cut-offs	Selective
MCD	Attribute-based	Ignores probability or weight information	Consistent
WADD	Alternative-based	All information processed	Consistent
SAT	Alternative-based	Depends on values of alternatives and cut-offs	Selective
EQW	Alternative-based	Ignores probability or weight information	Consistent

On the basis of this typology, Payne et al. (1992) identified six specific decision strategies, three of which are attribute-based and three alternative-based approaches. The attribute-based approaches included the elimination-by-aspects (EBA), lexicographic choice (LEX) and majority of confirming dimensions (MCD) strategies. The alternative-based approaches included the weighted additive (WADD), satisficing (SAT) and equal-weight (EQW) strategies. These strategies are further described in Table 1. The main argument posited by Payne et al. (1992) was that individuals construct strategies depending on the task demands and the information they are faced with.

The status quo in SC modeling is the WADD strategy, since it assumes that all information is processed. EBA (see Starmer, 2001) involves a determination of the most important attribute (usually defined as the attribute with the highest weight/probability) and the cut-off value for that attribute (i.e. a threshold). An alternative is eliminated if the value of its most important attribute falls below this cut-off value. This process of elimination continues for the second most important attribute, and so on, until a final alternative remains. Thus, the EBA strategy is best characterized as a '*threshold*' APS. The LEX strategy, in its strictest sense, involves a direct comparison between alternatives on the *most important* attribute. In the event of a tie, the second most important attribute is used as a comparison, and so on, until an alternative is chosen. The LEX strategy is thus best characterized as a '*relative comparison*' strategy. Thus, we can clearly differentiate two classes of APSs: threshold and relative comparison.

A major deficiency of these strategies is that although they assume selectivity in AP across different decision task contexts, *they assume consistency in attribute strategy within the same decision context*. In other words, once a strategy is selected for a given task (or choice), it does not change within the task. This issue is further complicated by psychological theory which identifies two main stages in the decision process. Differentiation and Consolidation Theory, developed by Svenson (1992), assumes that decision-making is a goal-oriented task which incorporates the pre-decision process of differentiation and the post-decision process of consolidation. This theory is crucial in encouraging a disaggregation of the entire decision process.

The two issues discussed above, namely the *adaptive* nature of strategies and the *disaggregation* of the decision process, are issues that can only be assessed realistically within a paradigm that relaxes the deterministic assumption of most models of decision-making. This is consistent with the payoff-probability structure discussed above. A preferred approach would involve a stochastic specification of AP that is capable of accommodating the widespread consensus in the literature that decision-making is an active process which may require different decision-making strategies in different contexts and at different stages of the process (e.g. Stewart et al., 2003). As the relevance of attributes in a decision task changes, so too must our approach to modeling the strategies individuals employ when adapting to such changes. Specifically we need a flexible framework within which we can accommodate the influence of one or more of the processing strategies on choice making across the sampled population.

How do Analysts Account for Heterogeneous Attribute Processing?

How is the APS of each individual best represented within the SC modeling framework? The editing stage of prospect theory (see Starmer, 2001; Kahnemann and Tversky, 1979a, b) is a useful theoretical setting; in this stage, agents use heuristics to make a decision setting optimally tractable. The APS can be partitioned into: (i) processes associated with decision-making in real markets and (ii) processes invoked to accommodate the information load introduced by the SC survey instrument.

Hensher (2004, 2006b) has shown that the two processes are not strictly independent. The processing of an SC experiment has some similarity to how individuals process information in real markets.[13] The APS may be hypothesized to be influenced by relevant information sources resident in the agent's memory bank, either processing instructions or knowledge sources. Specific processing instructions can include: (i) reference dependency,[14] (ii) event and attribute splitting, (iii) attribute re-packaging, (iv) the degree of information preservation and (v) the role of deliberation attributes. Knowledge sources can include the macro-conditioners.

[13]The main difference is that the SC experiment provides the information to be processed, in contrast to real markets where more effort is required to search for relevant information. We recognize, however, that the amount of information in the SC experiment may be more than what an individual would normally use in making a choice. Yet that is precisely why we have to establish the APS of each individual to ensure that the offered information is represented appropriately in model estimation. For example, if an attribute is ignored, we need to recognize this and not assume it is processed as if it is not ignored.

[14]This is defined empirically by the relative distance between the attribute levels in the SC alternative and levels that an individual is familiar with (i.e. a case-based decision–theoretical memory set that actually has been experienced as defined herein by the base alternative—a recent or a most experienced alternative). Reference dependency is a member of the broader class of the similarity condition of CBDT in which it is suggested that individuals choose acts based on their performance in similar problems in the past. The review and assessment of a choice task is defined as a *problem* in CBDT.

We can view the treatment of process via one or more rules, as a deterministic or stochastic specification. In Hensher et al. (2005a), for example, we treated the exogenous information of attribute inclusion/exclusion deterministically. We assumed that the analyst knows for certain which attributes are used by which respondents. It is probably more realistic, however, for the exogenous information to point to the correct likelihood specification, so that the likelihood for a respondent is a probabilistic mixture of likelihoods (Hensher et al., 2007a). In contrast to a deterministic specification, which assumes knowledge of the respondent-level likelihood of AP with certainty, a stochastic specification relaxes this assumption. One way of defining a stochastic model is to assume that the exogenous covariate is probabilistically related to the structural heterogeneity specification, through an expected maximum utility index derived from a choice of APS model, conditioning the preference heterogeneity distribution for each random parameter associated with the attributes of the SC model.

To illustrate this point, using a sample of car non-commuters in Sydney, we estimated a mixed logit (ML) model in which all attributes are assumed to be attended to, and models which assume that certain attribute(s) are not attended to, based on supplementary information provided by respondents (see Table 2). The supplementary information is accounted for in a deterministic and a stochastic way, the latter in recognition of the analyst's lack of full information on why a specific APS was adopted by each sampled individual. We compare the value of travel time savings (VTTS) distribution under alternative AP regimes (Table 3). As expected, there are significant variations in the mean and standard deviation willingness to pay (WTP) across the three AP strategies.

Defining the choice set of AP strategies is also important and is a little-studied issue. Hensher (2004) investigated one AP strategy, where the alternatives were defined as the number of preserved attributes (0, 1, 2, ...). This is appealing in the sense that an individual, when evaluating alternatives in a choice set, as defined by a set of attributes, has in front of them information from the attributes (number, levels and range) that varies across the alternatives. The individual then processes this information by invoking a series of rules that appear to be linked to the processing instructions given above. Given the central role of a SC experiment in the parameterization of the utility expressions that describe preference formation and equilibrium choices up to a probability of choice, the APS alternatives might reasonably be defined by the dimensionality of each choice task. Parameterization of the APS alternatives will reveal the sources of information brought to bear on the way that individuals establish their preferences for specific alternatives.[15]

---

[15]Importantly, in order to establish the full dimensionality of an agent's APS, we must show them the full attribute design and establish how they choose to process it. This is essential for each choice set if we are to assess the influence of reference dependency as defined by the levels of attributes in each SC alternative relative to the reference alternative (i.e. experienced or memory-based) alternative.

Table 2

Utility Expressions for Attribute Attention Profiles, Estimated as Multinomial Logit

Attribute processing profile	
V_1	All attributes attended to
Attributes not attended to	
V_2	Running cost
V_3	Running and toll cost
V_4	Toll cost
V_5	Slowed-down time
V_6	Free-flow and slowed-down time
V_7	Free-flow time
V_8	Slowed-down time and running cost
V_9	Free-flow and slowed-down time and toll cost

$V_1 = 2.0909 + 0.02872 \times \text{age} - 0.01088 \times \text{income} - 0.03606 \times ff + 0.11071 \times sdt + 0.1969 \times \text{cost} + 0.06767 \times \text{toll}$;
$V_2 = 1.7487 + 0.019159 \times \text{age} - 0.011466 \times \text{income} - 0.03545 \times f + 0.10151 \times sdt + 0.17557 \times \text{cost} + 0.06932 \times \text{toll}$;
$V_3 = -1.49000 + 0.01978 \times \text{age} - .001379 \times \text{income} - \mathbf{0.00194} \times ff + 0.13364 \times sdt + \mathbf{0.07899} \times \mathbf{cost} + \mathbf{0.01865} \times \mathbf{toll}$;
$V_4 = -3.055 + \mathbf{0.01147} \times \mathbf{age} + 0.01349 \times \text{income} - 0.020047 \times ff + 0.1175 \times sdt + 0.20619 \times \text{cost} + 0.07678 \times \text{toll}$;
$V_5 = 0.82309 + 0.03845 \times \text{age} - 0.01994 \times \text{income} - \mathbf{0.01032} \times ff - 0.05525 \times sdt + 0.33109 \times \text{cost} + \mathbf{0.00305} \times \mathbf{toll}$;
$V_6 = 1.68608 + 0.01397 \times \text{age} - 0.02204 \times \text{income} - 0.061966 \times ff + 0.126399 \times sdt + 0.2674 \times \text{cost} + 0.0999 \times \text{toll}$;
$V_7 = 1.5842 - 0.02523 \times \text{age} - \mathbf{0.003078} \times \mathbf{income} - 0.017136 \times ff + 0.07665 \times sdt + 0.14232 \times \text{cost} - \mathbf{0.016056} \times \mathbf{toll}$;
$V_8 = -4.10832 + 0.07469 \times \text{age} - 0.0112178 \times \text{income} - 0.03349 \times ff + 0.12575 \times sdt + 0.23752 \times \text{cost} - \mathbf{0.00806} \times \mathbf{toll}$; $V_9 = 0$.

Pseudo-$R^2 = 0.179$. Bold values: statistically non-significant at 95% confidence level.

Table 3

Values of Travel Time Savings ($ per Person Hour Car Non-Commuter Driver)

Attribute	**All attributes assumed to be attended to**		**Deterministic attribute exclusion**		**Stochastic attribute exclusion**	
	Mean	**Standard deviation**	**Mean**	**Standard deviation**	**Mean**	**Standard deviation**
Free flow time	7.60	0.47	7.81	0.46	7.95	3.59
Slowed down time	9.33	0.57	10.65	0.67	9.91	1.22
Ratio slowed to free flow time	1.23	1.21	1.36	1.46	1.25	0.69
Confidence level (95%)						
Free-flow time	0.02		0.02		0.12	
Slowed-down time	0.02		0.02		0.04	
Sample size	3568		3071/2944*		3568	

Time: random parameter, cost: fixed parameter.
*3,071 relates to free-flow time and 2,944 relates to slowed-down time.

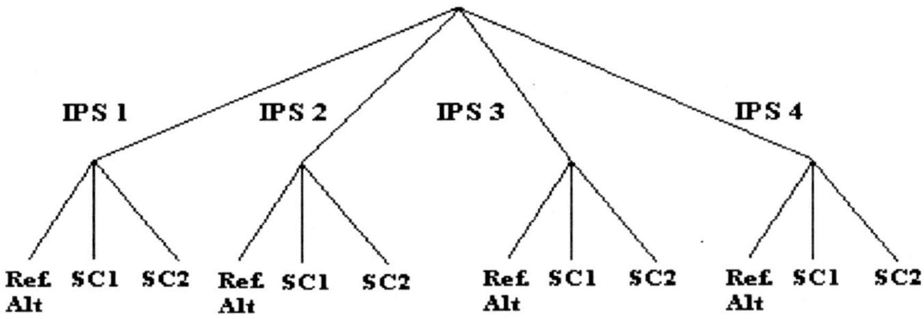

Figure 4
Individual-specific Decision Structure for SC Assessment

Since the choice made by an individual is conditioned on the APS, and given the two-stage decision process promoted in prospect theory, it is desirable to re-specify the choice model as a two-stage processing function, wherein each individual's choice of alternative is best represented by a joint choice model involving the individual's choice conditional of the APS and the (marginal) choice of APS (Figure 4). We then have to decide which set of influences resides in the APS utility expression and in the choice utility expression. We anticipate that it is the processing rules that reside in the APS expressions (e.g. equation (1)) and the attributes of alternatives that reside in the choice utility expressions. The contextual and person-specific interactions may reside in both sets of utility expressions. The APS utility expression might be, in a linear form (although non-linearity should be tested), as follows:

$$U_{\text{aps}\_i} = \alpha + \beta_1 \text{AddAtts}_i + \beta_2 \#\text{IgnAtts}_i + \beta_3 \text{RefDepX}_{1i} + \beta_4 \text{RefDepX}_{2i} + \beta_5 \text{IV}_i \quad (1)$$

where IV_i is the expected maximum utility associated with the choice process at the lower level of the tree structure proposed in Figure 4, similar to the theoretical link established within a nested logit model. This model recognizes that the APS is influenced by the actual information setting within which the preferred contract outcome is selected by an agent.

The approach described above implies a specific experimental design strategy. All individuals are given a single design specification in terms of the constituent attribute dimensions (number of attributes, number of levels of each attribute, attribute range) plus a fixed number of alternatives. For each choice task, a choice is made and then supplementary questions establish how the choice task is processed in terms of the invoking of one or more of the processing instructions listed above.

Alternatively, we might establish the APS more directly through the first stage of a two-stage choice experiment. In stage 1, we might offer a number of pre-designed choice experiments with varying numbers, levels and range of attributes across two alternatives, plus a reference alternative (from the agent's memory bank). These attributes can be structured in each design (in accordance with D-optimality conditions of experimental design—see below) under rules of preservation, attribute re-packaging and relativity to the reference alternative.[16] Individuals would be asked to evaluate each design and to indicate their preferred design in terms of the information that matters to them (i.e. relevancy). We could then identify, across all designs, what information is irrelevant for behavioral processing and what is ignored to avoid cognitive burden. We can also establish the extent to which specific alternatives are seen as similar to prior accumulated experience resident in the memory bank of the individual, which are recalled as an aid in AP (since this links nicely to the notion of similarity-weighted utility in choice-based decision theory).[17]

Hensher et al. (2007a) have implemented the APS choice method in the context of urban freight distribution in a supply chain, where transporters and shippers were interviewed. Identification of the role of different APSs in a model of choices among attribute packages (as shown in Figure 1) is elicited through Figures 2 and 3. Tables 4 and 5 summarize the degree to which attributes in the model were assigned an adjusted value for marginal (dis)utility through the adoption of specific APSs.

To establish the influence that the distribution of APSs has on key behavioral outputs such as the VTTS, we estimated ML models (reported in Hensher et al., 2007a) for the non-APS (Figure 1) and APS (Figures 1–3) data. The estimation sample includes 108 transporters and 102 shippers, yielding 1,248 observations (432 choice sets faced by transporters and 816 choice sets faced by shippers). Table 6 summarizes the variation in VTTS measures across attribute exclusion and aggregation strategies for transporters, to contrast with the findings under a non-APS model for transporters (Table 7).

When taking attribute exclusion and aggregation into account, strong variation in VTTS estimates is found across AP strategies. An assumption of passive bounded rationality assigns a uniform relationship between free-flow and slowed-down time savings across the sample, while the APS model allocates significantly different ratios in VTTS measures for free-flow time and slowed-down time across exclusion and

[16]The range of possible APSs would be established in prior in-depth interviews with stakeholders. The advantage of this two-stage approach is that *each design* (conditioned on the APS) will be D-efficient.

[17]Establishing how similarity from memory is built into the estimation of the choice model is challenging. As a global condition throughout the utility expression, it can be treated as an exogenous adjustment through a discrete–continuous choice specification. For example, we might estimate a similarity model where the dependent variable is some measure of 'similarity', and then use the predicted similarity indicator as a multiplicand of the utility estimate attached to each alternative in the discrete choice model prior to deriving the choice probabilities.

Table 4
Occurrence of Attribute Exclusion

Attribute	Number of times ignored (frequency)
Free-flow time (transporter)	43 (10%)
Free-flow time (shipper)	224 (27%)
Slowed-down time (transporter)	53 (12%)
Slowed-down time (shipper)	268 (33%)
Waiting time (shipper)	324 (40%)
Probability of on-time arrival (transporter)	49 (11%)
Probability of on-time arrival (shipper)	61 (7%)
Freight rate (transporter)	40 (9%)
Freight rate (shipper)	82 (10%)
Fuel cost (transporter)	29 (7%)
Fuel cost (shipper)	242 (30%)
Variable charges (transporter)	25 (6%)
Variable charges (shipper)	246 (30%)

Table 5
Occurrence of Attribute Aggregation

Attribute	Number of times aggregated (frequency)
Time measures (transporter)	292 (68%)
Time measures (shipper)	271 (33%)
Cost measures (transporter)	326 (75%)
Cost measures (shipper)	341 (42%)

Table 6
VTTS Measures (AU$ per hour) for APS Models

	Aggregate time (aggregate cost)	Aggregate time (distance costs)	FF (aggregate cost)	SDT (aggregate cost)	FF (distance costs)	SDT (distance costs)
Proportion of sample (%)	64.4	5.6	18.4	18.4	11.7	11.7
Mean ($)	19.36	37.66	64.38	84.53	134.82	178.41
Standard deviation ($)	18.69	30.83	–	–	82.01	108.42
Minimum ($)	55.63	38.44	–	–	75.92	99.69
Maximum ($)	87.57	102.16	–	–	274.53	360.48
Proportion of negative values (%)	4.8	5.6	0	0	0	0

Note: Exclusion has been accounted for prior to the aggregation condition.

Table 7
VTTS Measures (AU$ per hour) for non-APS model

	Free-flow time	Slowed-down time
Mean ($)	42.48	83.77
Standard deviation ($)	22.95	8.88
Minimum ($)	22.64	55.67
Maximum ($)	99.39	162.42
Proportion of negative values (%)	1.9	0

aggregation strategies. The most straightforward case involves the aggregation of time measures, which, by definition, results in no difference in the valuation of a unit of free-flow time versus a unit of slowed-down time. This lack of variation in VTTS for a given decision-maker across time components is countered by differential WTP between the valuation of free-flow and slowed-down time for those who distinguished between the two measures. For both those who aggregated cost measures and those who kept them separate, the ratio of VTTS for slowed-down time to VTTS for free-flow time is approximately 1.32.

This ratio is tempered relative to that found in the non-APS model (Table 7), in which the VTTS for slowed-down time is almost twice the VTTS for free-flow time. There are two highly significant implications of this discrepancy: (1) the inclusion of APS information into the model results in a lower inferred premium placed by transporters on the mitigation of slowed-down time and (2) heterogeneity in processing strategies for costs does not have an impact on this relationship. In other words, acknowledging the aggregation strategies of transporters with respect to time has a significant impact on the resulting behavioral implications with respect to time savings; furthermore, acknowledging the aggregation strategies of transporters with respect to cost does not obscure this relationship at all.

The utilization of APS information in model estimation identifies sub-groups, each of which holds a distinct distribution of VTTS. The choice not to differentiate between free-flow and slowed-down time results in the presence of no unique disutility of slowed-down time for those who opted to aggregate time measures. However, the link between this aggregation strategy and VTTS goes beyond the direct relationship between free-flow and slowed-down time: transporters who aggregated transit time measures appear to value travel time savings much lower than those who treated free-flow and slowed-down time separately, regardless of cost aggregation strategy. The mean VTTS estimates for those who aggregated time measures are considerably lower than the remainder of transporters, at only $19.36 and 37.66 hour^{-1} when aggregating costs and keeping costs separate, respectively.

These values, which are less than half of the mean estimates in the non-APS model, are in stark contrast to the mean VTTS estimates for those who did not aggregate time measures. The sub-group who aggregated costs but not times has a mean VTTS that is close to the mean estimates from the non-APS model, after considering the difference in ratios of free-flow and slowed-down VTTS across the models. That is, the mean VTTS for slowed-down time is very similar in the two models ($83.77 hour^{-1} in the non-APS model versus $84.53 hour^{-1} in the APS model), while the mean VTTS for free-flow time conforms to the general ratio between free-flow and slowed-down VTTS in each model.

Most strikingly, respondents who attended to all time and cost measures individually demonstrate a high VTTS for free-flow and slowed-down time, with mean values above the corresponding maximum values in the non-APS model. Whereas the non-APS model identified the presence of some VTTS estimates well above the mean, these values could be interpreted as artifacts of the distributional assumptions on the random parameters. However, on including APS information into the modeling process, one finds that a small proportion of transporters (the 11.7% who kept times and costs disaggregate) does have much higher values of travel time savings, relative to the remainder of the sample.

This evidence clearly shows that there are systematic (i.e. AP) forces driving the variation in behavioral measures. Indeed, it may be the case that APSs serve as proxies for factors that may be difficult to otherwise capture, such as the profitability of respondents, or their flexibility in utilizing the efficiency gains offered through variable charges. That is, relatively low or high VTTS measures may be indicative of both the ability of the respondent's organization to take advantage of efficiency gains (e.g. utilizing the truck in an additional task that would not be otherwise possible) and the magnitude of net benefits afforded through these efficiency gains (i.e. the net profitability of any potential subsequent freight task that is made available through gains in travel quality).

Stated Choice Experimental Design Strategies

Conceptually speaking, an experimental design may be viewed as nothing more than a matrix of numbers that are used to assign values to the attributes of the alternatives present within the hypothetical choice situations of SC surveys (such as that shown in Figure 1). Typically, the allocation of the levels shown in these hypothetical choice situations is pre-determined, systematically drawn from some underlying experimental design. For example, the attribute level values shown in Figure 1 are related to the attribute levels of a design, x, associated with each of the alternatives j, which may differ for each individual, n, as well as over each choice situation, s. By using experimental design theory, the assignment of these values occurs in some systematic (i.e. non-random) manner. What determines the systematic processes underlying the assignment of attribute level values to choice situations will be the basis of discussion in this section.

A cursory examination of the transportation literature suggests that the majority of SC studies applied to transportation contexts employ orthogonal fractional factorial designs[18] as opposed to using designs generated using *efficient* design techniques. The two approaches differ in that orthogonal fractional factorial designs are simply designs in which the attribute levels are orthogonal (uncorrelated), whereas efficient design techniques *typically* seek to generate designs which are not necessarily orthogonal but which minimize the asymptotic standard errors (and hence maximize the asymptotic t-ratios) of the parameter estimates to be obtained from a design. Independent of the type of design employed, experimental designs underlying SC studies require that respondents be shown one or more choice situations consisting of alternatives, each defined by a number of attributes which take discrete values called attribute levels.

Efficient Designs

A statistically efficient design is a design that minimizes the elements of the asymptotic (co)variance matrix, Ω, with the aim of producing greater *reliability* in the parameter estimates given a fixed number of choice observations. In order to be able to compare the statistical efficiency of SC experimental designs, a number of alternative approaches have been proposed within the literature (see, e.g. Bunch et al., 1994). The two most commonly used measures found within the literature are those of A-error and D-error, given as follows:

$$\text{A-error} = (\text{trace}\ \Omega)^k = -\frac{1}{N}\left(\text{trace}\left(\frac{(\partial LL(\beta)^2/\partial\beta\ \partial\beta')}{k}\right)\right) \tag{2}$$

$$\text{D-error} = (\det\ \Omega)^{1/k} = -\frac{1}{N}\left(\det\left(\frac{\partial LL(\beta)^2}{\partial\beta\ \partial\beta'}\right)\right)^{-1/k} \tag{3}$$

where k represents the number of parameters for the design, $LL(\beta)$ the log-likelihood function of the discrete choice model under consideration, N the sample size (we discuss the role sample size plays in generating efficient SC experiments below) and β the parameters to be estimated from the design. Given that we are generating designs and not estimating parameters for an already existing design, it is necessary to assume a

[18]Unfortunately, a large number of studies do not provide any information as to the type of design being used, nor the properties of the designs.

set of priors for the parameter estimates. Given uncertainty as to the actual population parameters, it is typical to draw these priors from Bayesian distributions rather than assume fixed parameter values. Typically normal and uniform Bayesian distributions are used (uniform distributions are used if the direction and magnitude of the parameter estimates are unknown, e.g. Kessel et al., 2006). When Bayesian priors are assumed, the A- and D-error measures are referred as A_b-error and D_b-error (where subscript b means Bayesian).

The A_b-error is computed by taking the trace of the asymptotic (co)variance matrix, while the D_b-error is calculated by taking the determinant, with both scaled to take into account the number of parameters to be estimated. The trace of a matrix is calculated as the sum of the diagonals of that matrix. As such, minimizing the trace of the asymptotic (co)variance matrix will minimize the variances (standard errors) of the associated parameter estimates, without consideration being given to the covariances. Given that the trace is calculated as the sum of the diagonal elements, if one of these elements is large in magnitude, then that element will tend to dominate the calculation. For this reason, the A_b-error measure has fallen out of favor. The D_b-error computation is a little more complicated as the determinant of a matrix is calculated as a series of multiplications and subtractions over all the elements of the matrix (see, e.g. Kanninen, 2002). As such, the determinant (and by implication, the D_b-error measure) summarizes all the elements of the matrix in a single 'global' value. Thus, while attempts to minimize the D-error measure, on average, minimize all the elements within the matrix, it is possible that in doing so, some elements (variances and/or covariances) may in fact become larger. Despite this property, the D_b-error measure has become the most common measure of statistical efficiency within the literature.

Whatever measure of statistical efficiency is used by the researcher, the generation of an efficient SC design requires that the attribute levels that are assigned to the design be evaluated as to their influence on the asymptotic (co)variance matrix for the appropriate model to be estimated[19] (the second derivatives of the log-likelihood function). The general form of the log-likelihood function for a model of discrete choice can be expressed as follows:

$$LL(\beta) = \sum_{n=1}^{N} \sum_{s=1}^{S} \sum_{j} y_{njs} \ln(P_{njs}) \tag{4}$$

where N represents the number of respondents, S the number of choice situations faced by each respondent, j the alternatives present in each s and y_{njs} a choice indicator taking the value one if alternative j was chosen or zero otherwise. P_{njs} in equation (4)

[19]This means that the likely model to be estimated (e.g. MNL, NL, ML) be known a priori as the derivation of the asymptotic (co)variance matrices of different model forms requires different considerations.

represents the probability that alternative j will be chosen by respondent n in choice situation s.

The presence of P_{njs} in equation (4) plays an extremely important role in generating efficient SC experiments. The probability that an alternative will be selected is a function not only of the attribute levels and priors (parameters) of that alternative, but also of the attribute levels and priors (parameter) assumed for all other competing alternatives. As such, *changing the existing order* of the attribute levels within a design will generally[20] influence the log-likelihood function, and in turn the asymptotic (co)variance matrix for that design. Similarly, the log-likelihood function and asymptotic (co)variance matrix of a design will be equally influenced by the priors assumed in the design generation process. Whereas an orthogonal design will be orthogonal from one experiment to another, an efficient design will generally be efficient only for the specific experiment for which it was created.

The *trick* in generating an efficient SC design is therefore to manipulate the attribute levels of the design and observe the changes in the asymptotic (co)variance matrix given the manipulations made. Unfortunately, even a slight change in one attribute level will likely influence P_{njs} and hence impact upon the entire asymptotic (co)variance matrix for the design. The *unfortunate* part in the above is that the direction and magnitude of the impact will be *largely* unpredictable a priori to the change made. It is therefore necessary to manipulate *intelligently* the attribute levels in some way; otherwise the analyst may waste a significant amount of time and computing resources evaluating inefficient design manipulations. In the next section, we discuss methods to reduce the computing time required to locating more efficient SC designs.

Design Challenges

There are a number of significant challenges which face those wishing to generate efficient SC experiments. Aside from the lack of available software capable of generating such designs (only a few programs are currently available including SAS, some GAUSS code and ITLS's NGENE, e.g.), the level of expertise and the amount of time necessary to generate such designs are currently significantly prohibitive. The level of expertise in generating such designs will naturally improve over time; however, the amount of time required to generate efficient experimental designs will likely remain a problem given greater complexity in the designs that are being generated, even given increases in the computing power available to today's discrete choice modelers. In the

[20]We use the term generally here as the influence on the asymptotic (co)variance matrix is dependent on a large number of factors, not the least of which are the priors assumed for each of the design-related parameters.

following sections, we outline some of the challenges that those wishing to design efficient SC experiments face and what we believe may be some possible solutions to these challenges.

Reducing Generation Run Times

By and far, the greatest problem in generating efficient SC experiments is the amount of time required to generate such designs. A significant number of available software packages (e.g. SAS, SPSS, NGENE, SPEED, CONSURV, etc.) are capable of generating orthogonal designs of various dimensions. Mostly, these software packages rely on tables of known orthogonal designs (this is how SPSS orthogonal designs are generated), meaning that where such designs exist, the software package can very quickly generate the desired design. However, fewer software packages are currently available that are capable of generating efficient designs. Where such software packages are available, the generation time is generally far greater than for generating orthogonal designs. Indeed, for all but the smallest of SC experiments, the run time required to locate an efficient design can range anywhere from minutes to even days or weeks, with the amount of time required being a function of the type of econometric models the designs are being generated for as well as the dimensions of the designs being considered. In the following sections, we discuss some means that are currently being investigated to reduce the computation times required to locate efficient SC designs.

Independent Random Draws versus Quasi-random

The current literature on the generation of efficient experimental designs using Bayesian methods has tended to rely on independent random *Monte Carlo* draws for priors taken from pre-specified distributions. The results for such methods are highly dependent on the number of draws taken as well as the seed used in generating the draws, a fact that has been well identified and addressed within the mainstream discrete choice modeling literature (Bhat, 2001, 2003; Sandor and Train, 2003). Typically the literature has tended to use only a small number of draws in an effort to reduce software run times. The use of only a small number (with small being undefined) of independent random draws, however, will likely mean that any efficient design generated will be efficient only for the small number of draws made, and different designs may be deemed efficient given different sets of draws. Even with 1,000 or 2,000 independent random draws, the average D_b-error for a design given different starting seeds can vary by as much as 10% and it is not infeasible that over 100,000 random draws may be required to obtain stability in generating efficient designs.

Rather than rely on independent random draws, several researchers working in other related areas of discrete choice modeling (in particular, on ML models) have examined the use of quasi-random draws as a method to reduce the number of draws required to obtain sufficient coverage of distribution space (Bhat, 2001, 2003; Sandor and Train, 2003). These researchers have shown significant efficiency gains in terms of parameter stability and estimation time when using such methods. Nevertheless, with the exception of Sandor and Wedel (2002), a paper which appears to have been largely ignored within the mainstream experimental design literature, the use of quasi-random draws appears to have been overlooked.

Gauss–Hermite Approximation When Bayesian distributions for the priors are assumed normal, stability of selected efficiency measure employed in generating a design may be achieved by using the Gauss–Hermite approximation method. The approximation works as follows. Let the draws, $B_{k,r}$, $r = 1, \ldots, R_k$, be designed draws taken from a series of normal distributions, the number of distributions being equal to k, the number of parameters. Each draw of $B_{k,r}$ is calculated as:

$$B_{k,r} = \mu_k + x_{,k,r} \times \sigma_k \times 2^{0.5} \quad \text{with associated weights } \frac{w_{k,r}}{\Pi^{0.5}} \tag{5}$$

$x_{k,r}$ and $w_{k,r}/\Pi^{0.5}$ are taken from Table 8, depending on the value of R_k specified by the analyst for each prior B_k. It is necessary to evaluate all combinations of draws such that the total number of evaluations is $R = R_1 \times R_2 \times \cdots \times R_k$:

Step 1: The analyst determines the numbers R_k ($=$ 2, 3 or 4 corresponding to sheets $n = 2$, 3 and 4).

Table 8

Gauss–Hermite Approximation Weights and Points

	$w_{k,r}/\Pi^{0.5}$	$x_{k,r}$
$R_k = 2$		
0	0.5	−0.70711
1	0.5	0.70711
$R_k = 3$		
0	0.6667	0
1	0.1667	−1.22474
2	0.1667	1.22474
$R_k = 4$		
0	0.4541	−0.52465
1	0.4541	0.52465
2	0.0459	−1.65068
3	0.0459	1.65068

Step 2: Create a full factorial for R. For this example, if $R_k = 2$ for each attribute, then the full factorial with have four evaluations (2 × 2). If $R_k = 3$ for each attribute, then the full factorial will involve nine evaluations (3 × 3) and if $R_k = 4$ for each attribute, then the full evaluation will involve 16 evaluations (4 × 4). Note that it is possible to allow a different number for R_k for each attribute (e.g. if $R_1 = 2$ and $R_2 = 3$, then the total number of evaluations will be six (2 × 3)). The full factorial is then populated using equation (5), thus providing the full enumeration of R combinations.

Step 3: The total number of draws used in the calculation is equal to R (the full factorial). The R evaluations calculated in Step 2 are used as the priors in Step 3. For each R_k, the efficiency measure (e.g. D_b-error, A_b-error, etc.) is computed as normal.

Step 4: Rather than take the average of the efficiency measure calculated in Step 3, the weighting values $w_{k,r}/\Pi^{0.5}$ are applied to each. The correct weights to apply are also calculated from the full factorial. Multiply each efficiency measure value by W and then sum the total. This value is the efficiency measure for the design (equivalent to the average efficiency measure using the Monte Carlo D_b-error but requiring much less draws).

Halton (Sequences) Draws Halton sequences have been used in the discrete choice literature to provide better coverage of distributional space. Halton sequences are generated in multiple dimensions by selecting an integer, i ($i \geq 2$), and expanding a sequence of integers from one to the desired number of draws, R, using i as the base. The steps in generating Halton sequences are as follows:

Step 1: List the sequence of integers up to R, the total number of draws required (e.g. $\{0, 1, 2, 3, 4, 5, 6, 7, 8, 9, \ldots, R\}$).

Step 2: Select $i \geq 2$.

Step 3: Convert the integers to base i selected in Step 2. For example, the sequence of integers listed above to base 3 would be $\{0, 1, 2, 10, 11, 12, 20, 21, 22, 100, \ldots, R\}$. For $i = 10$, the sequence remains unchanged (i.e. $\{0, 1, 2, 3, 4, 5, 6, 7, 8, 9, \ldots, R\}$).

Step 4: Reverse the order of the values for each digit obtained in Step 3 and reflect the resulting numbers around the decimal point. For the base 3 example shown above, the sequence becomes $\{0 \rightarrow 0.0, 1 \rightarrow 0.1, 2 \rightarrow 0.2, 10 \rightarrow 0.01, 11 \rightarrow 0.11, 12 \rightarrow 0.12, 20 \rightarrow 0.02, 21 \rightarrow 0.12, 22 \rightarrow 0.22, \ldots, R\}$. The same sequence in base 10 is $\{0 \rightarrow 0.0, 1 \rightarrow 0.1, 2 \rightarrow 0.2, 3 \rightarrow 0.3, 4 \rightarrow 0.4, 5 \rightarrow 0.5, 6 \rightarrow 0.6, 7 \rightarrow 0.7, 8 \rightarrow 0.8, \ldots, 12 \rightarrow 0.21, \ldots, R\}$.

Step 5: Convert the values obtained in Step 4 back to base 10. For the first sequence (base 3), the Halton sequence is given as $\{0.0 \rightarrow 0, 0.1 \rightarrow 1/3, 0.2 \rightarrow 2/3, 0.01 \rightarrow 1/9, 0.11 \rightarrow 4/9, 0.12 \rightarrow 7/9, 0.02 \rightarrow 2/9, 0.12 \rightarrow 5/9, 0.22 \rightarrow 8/9, \ldots, R\}$ and the base 10 sequence as $\{0.0 \rightarrow 0, 0.1 \rightarrow 1/2, 0.2 \rightarrow 1/4, 0.3 \rightarrow 3/4, 0.4 \rightarrow 1/8, 0.5 \rightarrow 5/8, 0.6 \rightarrow 3/8, 0.7 \rightarrow 7/8, 0.8 \rightarrow 1/16, \ldots, 0.21 \rightarrow 3/16, \ldots, R\}$.

Figure 5 shows 100, 250 and 1,000 Halton sequence ($i = 0$) and random draws when applied to a normal distribution with mean zero and standard deviation one. The Halton sequence covers the distributional space much better than independent random

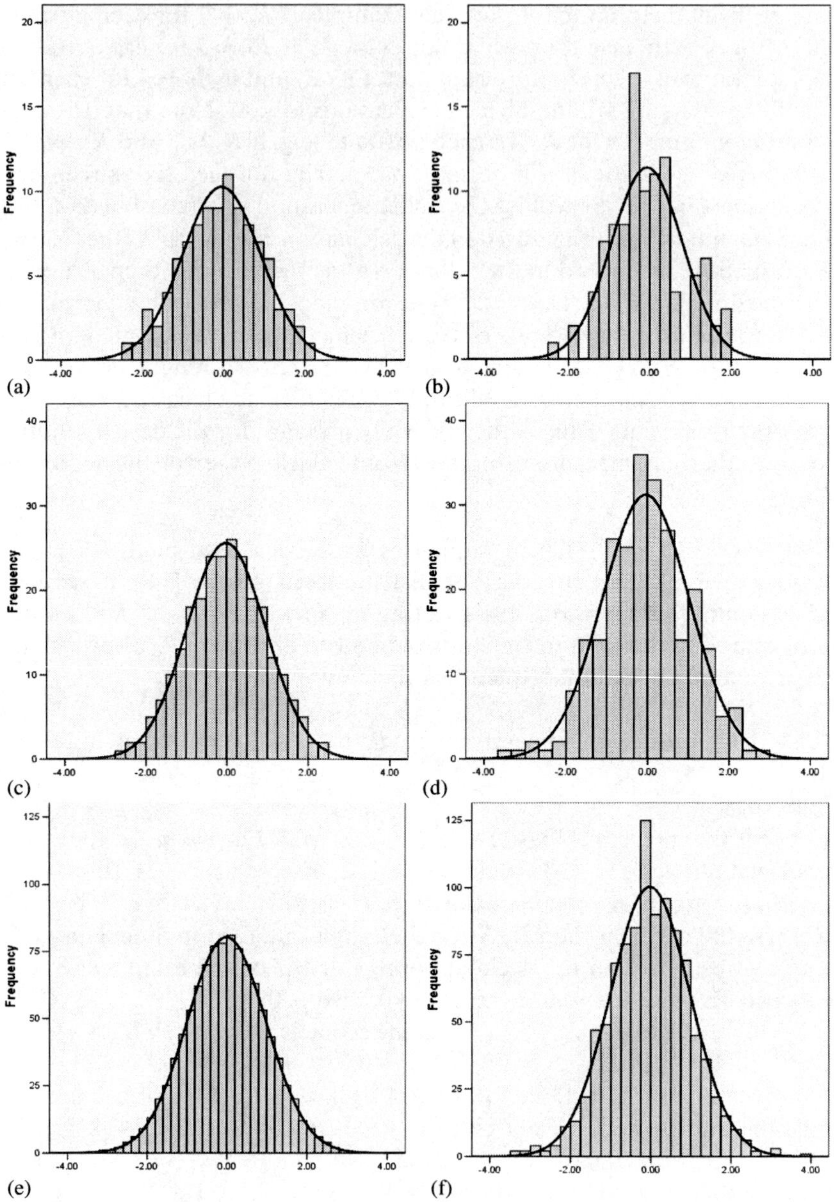

Figure 5

Halton versus Independent Random Draws Assigned to *N*(0, 1): (a) 100 Halton Draws, (b) 100 Independent Random Draws, (c) 250 Halton Draws, (d) 250 Independent Random Draws, (e) 1,000 Halton Draws and (f) 1,000 Independent Random Draws.

draws even at 100 draws, although it should be noted that 1,000 random independent draws could feasibly perform better than shown here.

Bliemer and Rose (2006) have explored the use of Gauss–Hermite approximation and Halton sequences in generating Bayesian SC designs. They found that the use of Gauss–Hermite outperforms both independent random and Halton draws for designs with up to eight parameters, but that for designs with greater than eight parameters, Halton draws are preferred.

The recent interest in generating SC experiments for ML models has increased the need to research the use of intelligent draws in generation of SC designs. Models such as the ML model assume distributions for one or more parameters of the model (each with a mean and standard deviation). Assuming the true mean and standard deviation of the parameter distributions are not known with certainty prior to the generation of the design, the values for these population moments should also be drawn from Bayesian prior distributions. As such, the generation of ML designs requires not only draws for the random parameters of the models, but draws reflecting uncertainty of the population moments for each of the random parameters as well. Clearly, this requires significant computing resources to achieve; hence, there is a need to invest research effort into the effects of using intelligent draws drawn from intelligent draws in designing efficient SC experiments.

Using the Asymptotic Properties of Discrete Choice Models

There exist at least two approaches in generating and evaluating the properties of an efficient design. The first approach involves simulation of a sample of respondents, N, after which Monte Carlo simulations can be used to test the efficiency of the design as applied to the simulated sample. This approach requires that the choice response, the y_{njs} vector in equation (4), be generated for each choice situation. In order to do this, for a given design and known parameters (the priors in this instance), the analyst takes a random draw representing the error component of the model and computes the (dis)utility for each alternative. Once the utilities are known to the analyst, y_{njs} is assigned a value of one for the alternative with the highest (dis)utility or zero otherwise. Once the y_{njs} vector has been simulated for the sample, the desired choice model can be estimated for the design. Given a large enough sample, the level of efficiency for various designs can be evaluated. While relatively straightforward to implement, the use of simulated data requires substantial computation time.

Rather than rely on Monte Carlo simulation methods, it is possible to use the asymptotic properties of the discrete choice models to reduce computation time in evaluating numerous SC experiments. For models of discrete choice, the asymptotic (co)variance matrix is equivalent to the second derivatives of the log-likelihood function for the appropriate model form. For the simple MNL model, it can easily be shown that the choice profile, y_{njs}, in equation (4) disappears when the second derivatives are taken (see Bliemer and Rose, 2005a). As such, knowledge of the vector of the choice profile, y_{njs}, is not necessary in order to evaluate the asymptotic (co)variance matrix for this model form. Nevertheless, the y_{njs} vector in other models of discrete choice do not disappear when the second derivatives are taken from the log-likelihood function, meaning that knowledge of this vector *is* required in order to evaluate the second derivatives of such models.

Fortunately, we are interested in the asymptotic properties of efficient SC designs. As such, the main point of interest lies in the asymptotically limiting case of $N \rightarrow +\infty$. As argued by Bliemer et al. (2009) and Sandor and Wedel (2002), in large samples, the asymptotic properties of discrete choice models allow the substitution of P_{js} (the probability of choosing alternative j in choice situation s) for y_{njs} given that $P_{js} = \lim_{N\rightarrow\infty}(1/N)\sum_{n=1}^{N} y_{njs}$. Following from this substitution, the sub-index n will no longer be present within the second derivatives of the log-likelihood functions, as the summation over the respondents is simply the multiplicand of the value by N.

Given the above, it is therefore possible to generate a single design (or rather a design for a single individual) and substitute the y_{js} vector (subscript $n = 1$, and hence drops out) with the vector of probabilities, P_{js}, which represent the choice probabilities over the entire sample of respondents, N. In this way, there is no need to simulate data, or estimate models in order to obtain the asymptotic (co)variance matrix for a design. As shown in Bliemer and Rose (2005a), once a design is generated for a single individual, the asymptotic (co)variance matrix for the design can be simply divided by N to establish what it would look like at that sample size (this is why N also appears in equations (2) and (3) as $(1/N)$).

Table 9 demonstrates this result precisely. Part (a) of Table 9 shows the asymptotic (co)variance matrix for a design generated using the probability substitution method described above, as applied to a single respondent. Part (b) of the table shows the results of a Monte Carlo simulation for the same design in which 2,500 respondents were simulated using the same parameter priors used in generating the asymptotic (co)variance matrix shown in part (a) of the table. Dividing each element of the asymptotic (co)variance matrix shown in part (a) by 2,500 reproduces exactly the asymptotic (co)variance matrix shown in part (b) of the table. This is shown in part (c) of the table. This result will hold for any sample size.[21]

[21]The literature on the generation of efficient SC designs appears to be wedded to the use of Monte Carlo simulations to test the influence of sample size on the efficiency of experimental designs. Given the above results, this appears to be preposterous, as one can determine the influence of sample size based on a design generated for a single individual (see Bliemer and Rose, 2005b for further information on sample size and efficient SC design generation).

Table 9

Asymptotic (Co)variance Matrix for a Design using Probability Substitution and Monte Carlo Simulations

	β_1	β_2	β_3	β_4	β_5	β_6	β_7
(a) Probability substitution with $N = 1$							
β_1	**0.1245**	0.0691	0.0084	0.1505	−0.3928	0.0873	0.1636
β_2	0.0691	**0.0748**	0.0188	0.1000	−0.2499	0.0528	0.1166
β_3	0.0084	0.0188	**2.1117**	0.0974	6.5426	0.0215	0.0497
β_4	0.1505	0.1000	0.0974	**0.3391**	0.3136	0.1297	0.2527
β_5	−0.3928	−0.2499	6.5426	0.3136	**33.4178**	−1.0807	−1.1862
β_6	0.0873	0.0528	0.0215	0.1297	−1.0807	**0.2942**	0.1257
β_7	0.1636	0.1166	0.0497	0.2527	−1.1862	0.1257	**0.3932**
(b) Sample generation Monte Carlo method with $N = 2{,}500$							
β_1	$\mathbf{4.98 \times 10^{-5}}$	2.76×10^{-5}	3.35×10^{-6}	6.02×10^{-5}	-1.57×10^{-4}	3.49×10^{-5}	6.54×10^{-5}
β_2	2.76×10^{-5}	$\mathbf{2.99 \times 10^{-5}}$	7.52×10^{-6}	4.00×10^{-5}	-9.99×10^{-5}	2.11×10^{-5}	4.67×10^{-5}
β_3	3.35×10^{-6}	7.52×10^{-6}	$\mathbf{8.45 \times 10^{-4}}$	3.89×10^{-5}	2.62×10^{-3}	8.59×10^{-6}	1.99×10^{-5}
β_4	6.02×10^{-5}	4.00×10^{-5}	3.89×10^{-5}	$\mathbf{1.36 \times 10^{-4}}$	1.25×10^{-4}	5.19×10^{-5}	1.01×10^{-4}
β_5	-1.57×10^{-4}	-9.99×10^{-5}	2.62×10^{-3}	1.25×10^{-4}	$\mathbf{1.34 \times 10^{-2}}$	-4.32×10^{-4}	-4.74×10^{-4}
β_6	3.49×10^{-5}	2.11×10^{-5}	8.59×10^{-6}	5.19×10^{-5}	-4.32×10^{-4}	$\mathbf{1.18 \times 10^{-4}}$	5.03×10^{-5}
β_7	6.54×10^{-5}	4.67×10^{-5}	1.99×10^{-5}	1.01×10^{-4}	-4.74×10^{-4}	5.03×10^{-5}	$\mathbf{1.57 \times 10^{-4}}$
(c) Probability substitution with $N = 2{,}500$							
β_1	$\mathbf{4.98 \times 10^{-5}}$	2.76×10^{-5}	3.35×10^{-6}	6.02×10^{-5}	-1.57×10^{-4}	3.49×10^{-5}	6.54×10^{-5}
β_2	2.76×10^{-5}	$\mathbf{2.99 \times 10^{-5}}$	7.52×10^{-6}	4.00×10^{-5}	-9.99×10^{-5}	2.11×10^{-5}	4.67×10^{-5}
β_3	3.35×10^{-6}	7.52×10^{-6}	$\mathbf{8.45 \times 10^{-4}}$	3.89×10^{-5}	2.62×10^{-3}	8.59×10^{-6}	1.99×10^{-5}
β_4	6.02×10^{-5}	4.00×10^{-5}	3.89×10^{-5}	$\mathbf{1.36 \times 10^{-4}}$	1.25×10^{-4}	5.19×10^{-5}	1.01×10^{-4}
β_5	-1.57×10^{-4}	-9.99×10^{-5}	2.62×10^{-3}	1.25×10^{-4}	$\mathbf{1.34 \times 10^{-2}}$	-4.32×10^{-4}	-4.74×10^{-4}
β_6	3.49×10^{-5}	2.11×10^{-5}	8.59×10^{-6}	5.19×10^{-5}	-4.32×10^{-4}	$\mathbf{1.18 \times 10^{-4}}$	5.03×10^{-5}
β_7	6.54×10^{-5}	4.67×10^{-5}	1.99×10^{-5}	1.01×10^{-4}	-4.74×10^{-4}	5.03×10^{-5}	$\mathbf{1.57 \times 10^{-4}}$

The bold are variances in contrast of off-diagonal elements that are covariances.

For models which offer a closed-form solution[22] for the second derivatives of the log-likelihood function (such as the MNL and NL[23] models), the asymptotic (co)variance matrix for a design can be analytically derived. For models with an open-form solution, when taking the second derivatives of the log-likelihood function (such as the ML and probit models), it is necessary to resort to numerical approximations of the first- and second-order derivatives of the model. This is usually accomplished using simulation methods.[24] In terms of the generation of efficient SC designs, the need to numerically derive the asymptotic (co)variance matrix for designs associated with open-form solutions presents a significant problem for the analyst. Most researchers advocate the use of the DFP and BFGS algorithms (see Train, 2003); however, these methods rely on iteratively maximizing the log-likelihood function of some data, and updating the asymptotic (co)variance matrix given the results of the previous iteration. In effect, this necessitates the estimation of the model. The BHHH algorithm, however, does not require that the asymptotic (co)variance matrix be updated over iterations, and as such, possibly offers the best way forward in evaluating efficient SC designs for complex discrete choice models.

Distributed Networks

If, for example, it takes one computer 24 hours to locate an efficient design, then it is feasible that it could take four computers 6 hours to locate the same design, assuming each computer were able to communicate with the other as to what it is doing so as to avoid repetition of effort. Rather than look toward improvements in computing power, one possible way forward in generating statistically efficient SC experiments is to move toward the use of distributed computer networks. Work currently being conducted at the Institute of Transport and Logistics Studies, Sydney (unpublished), has shown remarkable gains in computation time given the use of distributed computer networks in generating efficient SC designs; however, it should be noted that the use of such

[22]Closed form refers to the fact that when taking the (second) derivatives of a function, no integration term remains within the resulting derivative. Open form refers to models in which when taking the (second) derivatives of a function, an integration term remains. In such cases, the (second) derivative cannot be analytically evaluated.

[23]While it is well known that the NL model offers a closed-form solution when deriving the asymptotic (co)variance matrix, an examination of available software capable of estimating such models suggests that numerical approximation of the asymptotic (co)variance matrix is employed in model estimation, as opposed to the analytical derivation of the matrix. For example, Nlogit defaults to the BFGS algorithm to numerically compute the asymptotic (co)variance matrix for NL models. Bliemer et al. (2006) derive the analytical equations for the asymptotic (co)variance matrix for NL models with two levels. The use of analytically derived as opposed to numerically approximated asymptotic (co)variance matrices should generally result in quicker model estimation (or in the case of design generation, quicker and more accurate representation of the asymptotic (co)variance matrix of a design).

[24]Numerous algorithms exist for this, including the BHHH, DFP and BFGS algorithms (see Train, 2003).

networks comes with a barrier of significant upfront programming which may prove prohibitive to many researchers.

Smarter Algorithms

In order to search over the available design space, some form of algorithm is required to manipulate the order of the attribute levels of the design. Within the SC experimental design literature, there appears to exist only a limited number of algorithms in use. Initial studies in the generation of efficient SC designs (Kuhfeld et al., 1994; Zwerina et al., 1996) were limited to the Modified Fedorov exchange algorithm. This algorithm, originally developed for generating efficient designs for linear models (Fedorov, 1972), begins by generating a pre-specified set of candidate choice situations, some of which are initially assigned to the design to be constructed. The choice situations assigned to the design are systematically exchanged for other choice situations from the candidature set, and retained if an improvement in efficiency is observed to be achieved. The Modified Fedorov exchange algorithm, while simple, will generally result in a local efficient design as the total design space explored will be limited to the candidate set generated as part of the algorithm.

Recently, the SC experimental design literature has moved toward the use of an algorithm known as the Relabelling, Swapping and Cycling (RSC) algorithm (or derivations thereof, e.g. the RS algorithm of Huber and Zwerina, 1996). Re-labeling in the RSC algorithm occurs by exchanging the attribute level values within an attribute with each one another (e.g. for attribute A, $1 \rightarrow 3$, $2 \rightarrow 4$, $4 \rightarrow 2$ and $3 \rightarrow 1$). If the exchange yields a more efficient design based on whatever criterion is selected by the researcher, then the corresponding design is retained. One benefit of re-labeling is that for small designs, it is generally possible to explore each possible permutation over all attributes of the design in a relatively small amount of time. This becomes much more difficult for larger designs, however.

Swapping in the RSC algorithm occurs by simply swapping two attribute levels within a choice situation while all other attribute levels remain in place. The algorithm has also been implemented using simultaneous swapping of attribute levels (see Kessel et al., 2006). The design judged best on the efficiency criteria employed represents the final design to be used as part of the analyst's ongoing study. Cycling of a design is a simple process whereby the attribute levels of the design are exchanged in order, one choice situation at a time, such that $1 \rightarrow 2$, $2 \rightarrow 3$, $3 \rightarrow 4$, $4 \rightarrow 1$, etc. This process is continued until the initial design is obtained once more. The best design judged on whatever criteria is then retained.

Combined, the RSC algorithm is generally applied to a design in the order that the name implies. The best design possible is first located using the re-labeling algorithm after which the swapping algorithm is employed to determine if yet a better design can be located. Finally cycling is applied to the most efficient RS design. The resulting design should be at or near optimality (see Kessel et al., 2006; Ferini and Scarpa, 2005 for two excellent reviews of the RSC and Modified Fedorov exchange algorithms).

The RSC and Modified Fedorov exchange algorithms have been used extensively in the literature on the generation of SC experimental designs. Unfortunately, the literature on the generation of experimental designs has been limited to small designs (a maximum of eight parameters is the largest design we are aware of and even then this was as a result of the effects coding of the attributes of the design; Kessel et al., 2006). Further, apart from Bliemer and Rose (2005a), no single study that we are aware of has properly addressed the issue of alternative specific parameter estimates (Ferini and Scarpa (2005) and Carlsson and Martinsson (2003) come closest by allowing for alternative specific constant terms). While Bliemer and Rose (2005a) use a simple swapping method, the feasibility of the RSC and Modified Fedorov exchange algorithms remains an open question when applied to truly alternative specific (i.e. with parameters other than the constant terms being specified as alternative specific) designs as well as to designs much larger than those currently explored within the literature.

A number of other algorithms are currently under investigation. Bliemer (2006) examines the use of a genetic algorithm with promising results, while Collins et al. (2006) compare a number of other potential algorithms, also with promising results. One such algorithm, which Collins et al. (2006) term *targeted swapping*, has been shown to produce impressive results with minimal computation time, even with large designs. This algorithm uses the probabilities of the alternatives to intelligently swap the attribute levels within an attribute. While a perfect utility balanced design (where the utilities are all the same and hence, so to the probabilities of the alternatives; see Huber and Zwerina, 1996) may prove too restrictive (as well as extremely difficult to generate, particularly for designs with alternative specific parameter estimates), and may not necessarily result in the best design, Collins et al. (2006) note that by swapping the attribute levels of a design in a manner that brings the probabilities closer to balance (but not necessarily perfectly balanced) may, under certain circumstances, produce more efficient designs. Rather than naively re-labeling, swapping and cycling through the design permutations, Collins et al. (2006) found that by intelligently swapping the levels of the design to bring about near utility balance, a design at least as efficient as an efficient RSC design can be located in significantly less time, particularly for designs with many more parameters than eight.

Working with Reference Alternatives

In the section 'How do Analysts account for Heterogeneous Attribute Processing?', we briefly introduced the concept of using reference alternatives in SC studies. Indeed, the use of a respondent's knowledge base to derive the attribute levels of the experiment has come about in recognition of a number of supporting theories in behavioral and cognitive psychology, and economics, such as prospect theory, case-based decisions theory and minimum-regret theory (see Starmer, 2001; Hensher, 2004; Kahnemann and Tversky, 1979a, b; Gilboa et al., 2002). The use of reference alternatives in SC tasks, however, is inconsistent with current methodology on the generation of efficient SC experiments, highlighting the need to assess SC designs on both statistical and behavioral criteria.

The common use of a fixed set of attribute levels from which to draw from in generating efficient SC experiments is convenient and allows, when priors are assumed, the estimation of the utility functions for the design as well as the related choice probabilities. These in turn may be used to construct the asymptotic (co)variance matrices necessary for determining the efficiency of different experimental designs. However, when the attribute levels of a SC experiment are pivoted as percentages around some base reference alternative, consisting of the attribute levels reported by individual respondents during the survey task, the precise (absolute) attribute levels will not be known to the analyst prior to conducting the survey. As such, the analyst cannot easily determine the statistical efficiency of different designs before going to field. Nevertheless, there exist a number of different strategies that one may use to derive efficient SC experiments, involving the use of pivoting from reference alternatives.

Given the desirability in using reference alternatives in SC experiments, Rose et al. (2008) examine a number of possible methods to generate efficient reference-based experiments. Strategies examined by Rose et al. (2008) include the use of predicted *average attribute levels*, which may be substituted for the fixed attribute levels used in more traditional design generation processes. However, given that designs that rely on the use of reference alternatives employ percentages to *pivot* the attribute levels of the SC alternatives around the fixed alternative specific reference alternative, the use of *average predicted attribute levels* is used simply to determine the percentage differences for the design that will be applied to the real reference alternative for each respondent. That is, once the actual attribute levels of the reference alternative for a respondent are made known to the researcher, the percentage differences are applied to generate the SC alternatives for the study. In using a single population average for the attribute levels, the percentages applied for each choice situation remain fixed over the sampled population (the absolute values differ, however). Rather than use a single 'population average' to pre-determine the allocation of the pivot percentages over a design, it is also possible to use segment-specific attribute levels (e.g. based on trip length) to generate a number of (percentage) designs which are allocated to respondents based on each respondents' real 'reference alternative' determined by the researcher.

Rose et al. (2008) also examine the possible use of a two-stage process, whereby information is first captured about the reference alternative in a phase one survey, after which either a respondent-specific efficient design is generated or a sample-specific efficient design is generated after all respondents complete phase one of the project. Once generated, the efficient design can be subsequently administered to the respondent during phase two of the study. In reality, such an approach to SC experiments may prove logistically difficult, however, and statistical efficiency may be lost if not all individuals complete the second phase of the survey.

The use of internet or computer-aided personal interviews (CAPI) provides yet another alternative strategy in the generation of statistically efficient SC experiments using reference alternatives. Depending on how the survey is structured, if the information about the reference alternative is captured early in the survey, it may be possible to generate individual-specific efficient SC designs within a single instrument. Nevertheless, we would expect that optimizing designs for each individual would, overall, produce a sub-optimal result in comparison to the proposed two-stage process (assuming zero respondent attrition).

Rose et al. (2008) found that orthogonal designs performed relatively poorly when applied to pivot designs, but surprisingly, that when applied to a numerical example, the generation of pre-defined designs based on population and segment-specific reference alternative averages produced highly reliable parameter estimates, which in some cases were comparable in efficiency to the two-stage and individually optimized designs. Nevertheless, when comparing all asymptotic *t*-ratios of the design methods, the latter two strategies do appear to perform best overall. This is to be expected. The objective of producing statistically efficient designs is to minimize the asymptotic standard errors obtained from models estimated from data collected from sampled individuals. Given that the econometric models used for modeling SC data are typically estimated on data pooled from all sampled individuals, it stands to reason that generating a design that minimizes the asymptotic standard errors for the pooled data rather than minimizing the asymptotic standard errors for individuals, we would expect to achieve better results. Further, we would anticipate that in reality tailoring the design for each sampled individual would produce more efficient designs than the use of assumed averages or even the use of a randomly generated orthogonal design.

Conclusions and Future Directions

Serious efforts are being made to advance the state of econometric tools utilized in the modeling of choice data. The underlying motivation in the development of new statistical techniques is to increase the inferential power available to the analyst, given the predominant methods of both collecting choice data and the general frameworks within which the data are analyzed. That is, researchers seek to minimize the degree to which unobserved effects interfere with the ability of the analyst to make behavioral inference with respect to a given set of choice data.

The inherent limitation of this line of research is that it fails to address sources of misspecification bias that cannot be mitigated without direct methodological approaches. The state of practice tends to abstract from some systematic forces that may influence choice behavior significantly. Failing to incorporate these forces into empirical investigations of choice may lead to misspecification bias that trumps the relative benefits of utilizing advanced statistical techniques. In other words, although it is of merit to advance our statistical toolkit in efforts to account for forces such as preference heterogeneity, it may be of relatively greater merit to seek data collection techniques and general modeling structures beyond the scope of the status quo, in an effort to internalize elements influencing choice behavior that have been generally abstracted from to this point.

This paper promotes one area in which research effort would be particularly well placed: APSs of respondents. The predominant assumption that all decision-makers attend to all information presented to them equally when making all decisions has been violated in empirical studies of the APSs utilized by respondents. Heuristic decision-making theories proposed by cognitive psychologists and behavioral economists have been supported by observed choices, in which respondents indicate, sometimes overwhelmingly, that rational coping strategies were enacted to attend to a sub-set of the information presented when making choices. The divergence in behavioral implications across models incorporating APSs versus those that do not can be staggering. Hence, it is clear that responsible studies of choice behavior cannot reply on assumptions of passive bounded rationality, and should take appropriate steps to internalize APS heterogeneity.

Finally, in terms of ongoing developments in experimental design, we are unaware of any study that has looked at a comparison of efficient versus orthogonal SC designs when applied to real respondents. Current research appears to rely solely on the use of Monte Carlo simulation to predict the efficiency gains obtained in using efficient SC designs. There is plenty more to do despite some notable progress to date.

ACKNOWLEDGMENT

Tony Bertoia provided useful material from the psychology and marketing literature.

REFERENCES

Berg, N. (2005). Decision-making environments in which unboundedly rational decision makers choose to ignore relevant information. *Global Business and Economics Review* 7(1), 59–73.

Bhat, C. R. (2001). Quasi-random maximum simulated likelihood estimation of the mixed logit model. *Transportation Research B* 35(7), 677–693.

Bhat, C. R. (2003). Simulation estimation of mixed discrete choice models using randomized and scrambled Halton sequences. *Transportation Research B* 37(9), 837–855.

Bliemer, M., J. Rose and D. A. Hensher (2009). Efficient stated choice experiments for estimating nested logit models. *Transportation Research B* 43, 19–35.

Bliemer, M. C. J. (2006). Genetic algorithms for generating optimal experimental designs. Working Paper, Delft University.

Bliemer, M. C. J. and J. M. Rose (2005a). *Efficient Designs for Alternative Specific Choice Experiments.* Institute of Transport and Logistics Studies, University of Sydney, February.

Bliemer, M. C. J. and J. M. Rose (2005b). *Efficiency and Sample Size Requirements for Stated Choice Studies.* Institute of Transport and Logistics Studies, University of Sydney, March.

Bliemer, M. C. J. and J. M. Rose (2006). *Quasi-random Bayesian Efficient Stated Choice Designs.* Institute of Transport and Logistics Studies, University of Sydney, February.

Bunch, D. S., J. J. Louviere and D. A. Anderson (1996). A comparison of experimental design strategies for choice-based conjoint analysis with generic-attribute multinomial logit models. Working Paper, Graduate School of Management, University of California, Davis.

Carlsson, F. and P. Martinsson (2003). Design techniques for stated preference methods in health economics. *Health Economics* 12, 281–294.

Collins, A. T., M. C. J. Bliemer and J. M. Rose (2006). *A Comparison of Algorithms for designing Efficient Stated Choice Experiments.* Institute of Transport and Logistics Studies, University of Sydney, February.

DePalma, A., G. M. Meyers and Y. Y. Papageorgiou (1994). Rational choice under an imperfect ability to choose. *American Economic Review* 84, 419–440.

DeShazo, J. R. and G. Fermo (2002). Designing choice sets for stated preference methods: the effects of complexity on choice consistency. *Journal of Environmental Economics and Management* 44, 123–143.

DeShazo, J. R. and G. Fermo (2004). Implications of rationally-adaptive pre-choice behavior for the design and estimation of choice models. Working Paper, School of Public Policy and Social Research, University of California at Los Angeles, August.

Diederich, A. (2003). MDFT account of decision making under time pressure. *Psychonomic Bulletin & Review* 10, 157–166.

Drolet, A. and M. F. Luce (2004). The rationalizing effects of cognitive load on emotion-based trade-off avoidance. *Journal of Consumer Research* 31, 63–77.

Erber, R. and S. T. Fiske (1984). Outcome dependency and attention to inconsistent information. *Journal of Personality and Social Psychology* 47(4), 709–726.

Fedorov, V. V. (1972). *Theory of Optimal Experiments.* New York, Academic Press.

Ferini, S. and R. Scarpa (2005). Experimental designs for environmental evaluation with choice-experiments: a Monte Carlo investigation. Working Paper, Waikato Management School, Hamilton, New Zealand.

Gilboa, I. and D. Schmeidler (2001). *A Theory of Case-based Decisions*. Cambridge, Cambridge University Press.

Gilboa, I., D. Schmeidler and P. Wakker (2002). Utility in case-based decision theory. *Journal of Economic Theory* 105, 483–502.

González-Vallejo, C. (2002). Making trade-offs: a probabilistic and context-sensitive model of choice behavior. *Psychological Review* 109, 137–155.

Hensher, D. A. (2004). Accounting for stated choice design dimensionality in willingness to pay for travel time savings. *Journal of Transport Economics and Policy* 38(2), 425–446.

Hensher, D. A. (2006a). Revealing differences in behavioral response due to the dimensionality of stated choice designs: an initial assessment. *Environment and Resource Economics* 34(1, May), 7–44.

Hensher, D. A. (2006b). How do respondents handle stated choice experiments? Attribute processing strategies under varying information load. *Journal of Applied Econometrics* 21, 861–878.

Hensher, D. A., J. Rose and T. Bertoia (2007a). The implications on willingness to pay of a stochastic treatment of attribute processing in stated choice studies. *Transportation Research E* 43(1), 73–89.

Hensher, D. A., J. M. Rose and W. H. Greene (2005a). The implications on willingness to pay of respondents ignoring specific attributes. *Transportation* 32(2), 203–222.

Hensher, D. A., J. M. Rose and W. H. Greene (2005b). *Applied Choice Analysis: A Primer*. Cambridge, Cambridge University Press.

Hensher, D. A., S. M. Puckett and J. M. Rose (2007b). Agency decision making in freight distribution chains: revealing a parsimonious empirical strategy from alternative behavioural structures. *Transportation Research B* 41(9), 924–949.

Huber, J. and K. Zwerina (1996). The importance of utility balance and efficient choice designs. *Journal of Marketing Research* 33(3), 307–317.

Kahnemann, D. and A. Tversky (1979a). Prospect theory: an analysis of decisions under risk. *Econometrica* 47(2), 263–291.

Kahneman, D. and A. Tversky (1979b). Intuitive prediction: biases and corrective procedures. In S. Makridakis and S. C. Wheelwright (Eds.), *Studies in the Management Sciences: Forecasting*, Vol. 12. Amsterdam, North Holland.

Kanninen, B. J. (2002). Optimal design for multinomial choice experiments. *Journal of Marketing Research* 39(2), 214–217.

Kessel, R., P. Goos and M. Vandebroek (2006). 'Comparing algorithms and criteria for designing Bayesian conjoint choice experiments. *Journal of Marketing Research* 43(3), 409–419.

Kuhfeld, W. F., R. D. Tobias and M. Garratt (1994). Efficient experimental design with marketing research applications. *Journal of Marketing Research* 21(4), 545–557.

Lazari, A. G. and D. A. Anderson (1994). Designs of discrete choice experiments for estimating both attribute and availability cross effects. *Journal of Marketing Research* 31(3), 375–383.

Louviere, J. J. and H. J. P. Timmermans (1990). Hierarchical information integration applied to residential choice behavior. *Geographical Analysis* 22, 127–145.

McFadden, D. (2001). Economic choices: economic decisions of individuals. A set of notes prepared for a lecture at the University of California, Berkeley, 18 March.

Oppewal, H., J. J. Louviere and H. J. P. Timmermans (1994). Modeling hierarchical information integration processes with integrated conjoint choice experiments. *Journal of Marketing Research* 31, 92–105.

Payne, J. W., J. R. Bettman, E. Coupey and E. J. Johnson (1992). A constructive process view of decision making: multiple strategies in judgment and choice. *Acta Psychologica* 80, 107–141.

Rose, J. M., M. C. J. Bliemer, D. A. Hensher and A. T. Collins (2008). Designing efficient stated choice experiments involving respondent based reference alternatives. *Transportation Research B Part B* 42(4), 395–406.

Sælensminde, K. (1994). The impact of choice inconsistencies in stated choice studies. *Environmental & Resource Economics* 23(4), 403–420.

Sandor, Z. and K. E. Train (2003). Quasi-random simulation of discrete choice models. *Transportation Research B* 38(4), 313–327.

Sandor, Z. and M. Wedel (2001). Designing conjoint choice experiments using managers' prior beliefs. *Journal of Marketing Research* 38(4), 430–444.

Sandor, Z. and M. Wedel (2002). Profile construction in experimental choice designs for mixed logit models. *Marketing Science* 21(4), 455–475.

Slovic, P. (1995). The construction of preference. *American Psychologist* 50, 364–371.

Starmer, C. (2001). Developments in non-expected utility theory: the hunt for a descriptive theory of choice under risk. *Journal of Economic Literature* XXXVIII, 332–382.

Stroop, J. R. (1935). Studies of interference in serial verbal reactions. *Journal of Experimental Psychology* 18, 643–662.

Svenson, O. (1992). Differentiation and consolidation theory of human decision making: a frame of reference for the study of pre- and post-decision processes. *Acta Psychologica* 80, 143–168.

Swait, J. and W. Adamowicz (2001). The influence of task complexity on consumer choice: a latent class model of decision strategy switching. *Journal of Consumer Research* 28, 135–148.

Thurstone, L. L. (1927). A law of comparative judgment. *Psychological Review* 23, 273–286.

Train, K. E. (2003). *Discrete Choice Methods with Simulation*. Cambridge, Cambridge University Press.

Wang, D., L. Jiuqun and H. J. P. Timmermans (2001). Reducing respondent burden, information processing and incomprehensibility in stated preference surveys: principles and properties of paired conjoint analysis. *Transportation Research Record* 1768, 71–78.

Zwerina, K., J. Huber and W. F. Kuhfeld (1996). A general method for constructing efficient choice designs. Working Paper, Fuqua School of Business, Duke University, Durham, NC 27708. Available from SAS Institute at: http://ftp.sas.com/techsup/download/technote/ts629.pdf

The Expanding Sphere of Travel Behaviour Research
Selected Papers from the 11th International Conference on Travel Behaviour Research

11

Advances in Choice Modeling and Asian Perspectives

Toshiyuki Yamamoto, Tetsuro Hyodo and Yasunori Muromachi

Abstract

The purpose of this paper is to review recent methodological developments in travel behavior analysis, especially choice modeling, to summarize the particular characteristics of travel behavior in Asia and review research efforts in Asia aimed at taking them into account. Also included is a discussion of inaccuracies in transport demand forecasting. In the section "Recent Developments in Econometric Choice Modeling", recent advances in choice models of the generalized extreme value family and mixed logit (error component) models are reviewed. Other topics, such as the value of travel time saving, are also introduced. The section "Challenges of Choice Modeling in Asia" looks at issues of demand modeling from an Asian perspective. Characteristics that affect model structure are considered in the section "Characteristics of Transport Modeling in Asian Cities" and research on the accuracy of demand models is presented in the section "Inaccuracy in Transport Demand Models". The final section introduces further relevant topics and includes a summary.

Introduction

There have recently been remarkable advances in discrete choice modeling. Several new operational specifications for generalized extreme value (GEV) models have been developed to represent complex error structures among the alternatives in the choice set, while there has been thorough research into the nature of fully flexible mixed multinomial choice models, ranging from work on identification of model structures to efficient estimation techniques for the model. As a result, we now have very powerful tools that can be used to investigate any type of discrete choice behavior.

On contrary, many transport demand forecasts for large projects around the world have attracted criticism recently. The discrepancy between demand forecasts and realized demand does not in most cases result solely from inappropriate modeling, but there is a danger that the theoretical development of transport demand modeling to date will be undervalued because of these inaccurate forecasts. There is a need to go back and look at the circumstances of travel behavior first, and then examine the appropriateness of the transport model used for each situation. In an Asian context, the population density of metropolitan areas is high and metropolises expand rapidly. As a result, the diversity of transportation modes is large and the situation changes quickly. In areas with hot climates, a variety of access and egress modes for short distance exists, while service levels as measured in terms of schedules, frequency, and routes are not stable.

The purpose of this paper is to review recent methodological developments in travel behavior analysis, especially choice modeling, to summarize the particular characteristics of travel behavior in Asia and review research efforts in Asia aimed at taking them into account and to discuss the inaccuracy of transport demand forecasting. We hope this will clarify the need for further research in theoretical, methodological, and practical contexts. The rest of the paper is structured as follows. The section that follows presents recent developments in econometric choice modeling. The section "Challenges of Choice Modeling in Asia" introduces the particularly Asian circumstances of travel choice and means of accommodating them in the modeling of travel choice behavior and demand forecasting. Inaccuracies in demand forecasting are also discussed in this section. Section "Conclusions and Future Studies" concludes the paper with a summary and some recommendations for future studies.

Recent Developments in Econometric Choice Modeling

In this section, recent developments in econometric choice modeling are briefly outlined. This is by no means a complete review of the history, but a mere glance at the fast-growing field of travel behavior analysis. The range of the review is limited to results published since the previous IATBR meeting in 2003. Please refer to the resource paper presented at the previous IATBR meeting (Bhat, 2006) for advances up until 2003. The emphasis here is on discrete choice modeling, and especially mixed logit models, but some other topics are also mentioned.

The Generalized Extreme Value Models

GEV models have flexible error correlations as a result of relaxation of the independence from irrelevant alternatives (IIA) property of the multinomial logit (MNL) model. An appropriate type of GEV model should be selected or, if unavailable beforehand, created in order to capture an error structure representing the assumed choice situation. In fact, any error correlation adopted for a GEV model can be mimicked using a mixed multinomial logit (MMNL) model (also known as a kernel logit model) using error components to represent any types of correlation among alternatives. However, GEV models are preferred whenever feasible because they maintain a closed form in representing choice probability, thus are free from the numerical integrations needed for MMNL models and that are vulnerable to simulation error. Still, the interpretation of the covariance parameters in GEV models remains unclear in some cases, so the structure of these parameters must be carefully examined based on the predetermined behavioral assumptions.

Many types of operational GEV models are available these days and still new types are being generated, including extensions of the cross-nested logit (CNL) and generalized nested logit (GNL) models. Papola (2004) reformulated the CNL model as a generalization of the two-level hierarchical logit model. The CNL model has been shown to be able to reproduce any hypothetical homoscedastic covariance matrix, thus it is possible to derive choice probabilities in a closed analytical form from any hypothetical homoscedastic covariance matrix. Koppelman and Sethi (2005) extended the GNL model to include observational covariance heterogeneity and heteroscedasticity. These models fall within the context of closed-form extensions of MNL and nested logit (NL) models, so the computation is still free from numerical integration.

Daly and Bierlaire (2006) proposed an operationally easy way of generating new GEV models without the need for complex proofs. The proposed technique uses the recursive nested extreme value model by Daly (2001) and the network structure developed by Bierlaire (2002). The basic concept is to represent the correlation of error terms in the utility function using the structure of the network. By using this technique, new GEV models can be easily formulated to best represent the assumed choice situation.

For example, a simple network with six nodes and eight arcs is shown in Figure 1. The alternatives are v_3, v_4, and v_5 and the correlations among alternatives are represented by nodes (nests) v_1 and v_2. Location parameters, α_n, are assigned to each arc and scale parameters, μ_n, are assigned to each node.

The probability of choosing alternative v_3 given by the model associated with node v_1 is:

$$P(v_3|v_1) = \frac{\alpha_{13}\exp(\mu_1 V_3)}{\sum_{j=(3,4,5)}\alpha_{1j}\exp(\mu_1 V_j)} \tag{1}$$

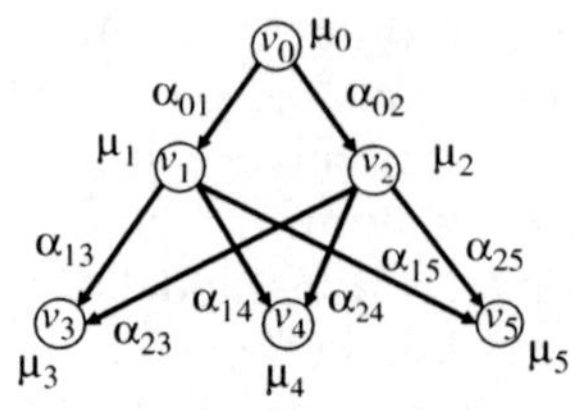

Figure 1
A Simple Network
Source: Modified from Daly and Bierlaire (2006)

where V_3 through V_5 represent the deterministic parts of the utility for alternative v_3 through v_5, respectively. The probability of choosing a nest v_1 is:

$$P(v_1) = \frac{\left\{\sum_{j=(3,4,5)} \alpha_{1j} \exp(\mu_1 V_j)\right\}^{\mu_0/\mu_1}}{\sum_{m=(1,2)} \left\{\sum_{j=(3,4,5)} \alpha_{mj} \exp(\mu_m V_j)\right\}^{\mu_0/\mu_m}} \tag{2}$$

Finally, the probability of choosing alternative v_3 is:

$$P(v_3) = P(v_3|v_1)P(v_1) + P(v_3|v_2)P(v_2) \tag{3}$$

The equation above shows that the probability of choosing an alternative is represented in recursive form, so an arbitrary number of levels can be used. Moreover, the resulting models are proven consistent with random utility theory, thus the remaining task for analysts is to develop meaningful network structures, including the imposition of constraints on the location parameters, α_n, and the scale parameters, μ_n.

Aside from the explorations of new GEV models, new properties of basic GEV models such as the MNL and NL models, have also been revealed. Ivanova (2005) proposed a set of rules allowing the consistent aggregation of alternatives for an NL model. The rule was derived for the joint choice of destination and travel mode. Origins and destinations are usually defined arbitrarily by travel analysis zones, so the zones should be consistently aggregated. A utility function to provide consistent aggregation of zones in the MNL model for destination choice was available already. He extended it to the case where the nested structure of joint destination and mode choice has zones in the upper level and travel mode in the lower level. Aggregation opens the possibility of applying estimated models based on a small zone system to demand forecasting for a larger zone system. However, the utility function becomes nonlinear with this modification and parameter estimates are dependent on the original zone system.

The reliability of alternative specific constants (ASC) in mode choice models estimated using a mixture of revealed preference (RP) and stated preference (SP) data has been examined theoretically and empirically using the MNL model. In the RP/SP model, some attributes may be specified as generic for both RP and SP alternatives and others as specific to each subset even if the same attributes are used in both data. ASC can be also specified as generic or specific based on the assumptions made in the choice situations. There is no consensus regarding the specification of ASC to forecast the market share taken by new alternatives included only in SP choice set. Cherchi and Ortúzar (2006) investigated the forecasting implications of using generic and specific constants for both data sets and offered some guidelines. They suggest that we can rely on estimation results (i.e., using a model that provides the best statistical fit) as long as theoretical underpinnings are satisfied.

Estimation of Mixed Logit Models

As noted above, the estimation of MMNL models includes a process of numerical integration. Simulation techniques are used to achieve the required numerical integrations. Various simulation algorithms have been examined for their applicability to MMNL models in terms of accuracy and computation speed. The available algorithms can be grouped into three categories: pseudorandom sequences, quasirandom sequences, and combinations of these two. Pseudorandom sequences use independent random draws to obtain the numerical integrations. Actually, a pure random draw is not possible and instead a deterministic pseudorandom sequence is used, hence the name pseudorandom. Quasirandom sequences are designed to provide better coverage than independent draws over the density and have the potential to reduce both simulation-induced bias and variance.

Sándor and Train (2004) proposed (*t*, *m*, *s*)-nets and compared them with Halton sequences in an application of maximum simulated likelihood estimation using MMNL. The (*t*, *m*, *s*)-nets include Sobol sequences (Sobol, 1967) and Faure sequences (1982) as special cases; both (*t*, *m*, *s*)-nets and Halton sequences are quasirandom sequences. Sivakumar et al. (2005) examined Halton sequences and Faure sequences, which are a special case of a (*t*, *m*, *s*)-net, as well as their scrambled versions. The scrambled Halton sequences and the scrambled Faure sequences fall into the third category mentioned above. They also compared them against a version of a pseudorandom sequence, the Latin hypercube sampling (LHS) sequence. Hess et al. (2006) proposed modified Latin hypercube sampling (MLHS). MLHS uses the same draw for all elements in each dimension, while LHS uses a different draw for each element in each dimension, thus attaining a sequence that has more uniform coverage in each dimension by using one draw to shift all points.

In addition to the simulation techniques used for numerical integrations, new algorithms have been examined to find an optimization method appropriate for MMNL models. Bastin et al. (2006) proposed basic trust-region with dynamic accuracy

(BTRDA) algorithm. The algorithm uses a variable number of draws in each iteration to estimate the choice probabilities, which gives significant gains in optimization time compared to conventional line search algorithms with a fixed number of draws. The algorithm is shown to be able to handle the nonconcavity of the problem better than the conventional line search algorithm. Bastin et al. (2005) examined BTRDA combined with MLHS, comparing it with the Broyden–Fletcher–Goldfarb–Shanno (BFGS) algorithm and a pure pseudo-Monte Carlo sequence.

Many comparisons of different sequences have been carried out recently as noted here, but there has been no good generalization of the results. Further investigations are required to reach a conclusive understanding of suitable estimation techniques for MMNL.

Distribution of Value of Travel Time Saving

The concept of value of travel time saving (VTTS) has attracted renewed attention in recent years. VTTS is a fundamental factor used in evaluating transportation policy measures related to travel time reduction. VTTS can be calculated from estimated discrete choice models by taking the ratio of the time coefficient to the cost coefficient in the linear-in-variables utility function. MMNL models are capable of considering unobserved heterogeneity in the marginal utility of specific variables among individuals as well as the flexible error structure. The unobserved heterogeneity is represented by random variations of coefficient estimates in MMNL; the distribution of VTTS among individuals can then be calculated from the estimated random coefficient estimates. An important issue is the shape of the VTTS distribution. Usually, normal distributions are used for random coefficients in MMNL models. The normal distribution, however, is unbounded. As a result, a proportion of individuals is assumed to have a negative VTTS when a normal distribution is used to represent the random variations in the time and/or cost coefficient. To avoid such negative VTTS values, several alternative distributions have been examined in recent years as a means of better representing the distribution of VTTS using various types of data.

Cherchi and Polak (2005) examined the use of a truncated normal distribution for the time coefficient using simulated choice data. They found that a mis-specification of the distribution causes biased parameter estimates. Hensher et al. (2005) applied triangular distributions for the time coefficient using SP data and examined the suitability of this approach. Amador et al. (2005) examined the bounded uniform distribution and triangular distribution as well as the normal distribution to obtain the variations in the time coefficient using RP data. They found that the uniform distribution gave the best results. Hess et al. (2005) compared the normal distribution, normal distribution with truncation at zero, lognormal distribution and Johnson's S_B distribution (Train and Sonnier, 2004) for the time coefficient using simulated choice data.

The S_B distribution is given by

$$c = a + (b - a)\frac{\exp(\xi)}{1 + \exp(\xi)} \tag{4}$$

where a and b are the parameters representing the bounds of the distribution and ξ a random variable in the form of a normal distribution with mean μ and standard deviation σ. Based on the results, they suggest the use of a bounded distribution such as the triangular or S_B distribution, where the bounds are estimated from the data used. Cirillo and Axhausen (2006) also examined the censored normal, normal, lognormal, and S_B distributions. They used RP data and applied a random coefficient both to time and cost, finding that 10–15% of individuals have a negative VTTS. Fosgerau (2006) investigated the distributional shape of VTTS by applying nonparametric and semiparametric methods, though the MMNL model was not used. Confirmation of the distribution of VTTS will require more intensive investigations.

Other than the distributional shape, variance heterogeneity in the distribution of VTTS has also been examined. Greene et al. (2006) applied a triangular distribution for the time coefficient using SP data. They also considered variance heterogeneity of the time coefficient. The results suggest that accounting for variance heterogeneity leads to better model fitting as well as behaviorally sensible outputs in terms of VTTS distribution. However, Brownstone and Small (2005) reviewed existing studies of VTTS and found that VTTS is underestimated when SP data are used. They concluded that more intensive investigations on the difference between RP and SP estimates of VTTS are required in the future. Hensher (2006) investigated SP data and found that the dimensionality of the stated choice design affects the decision rules of respondents, with the result that VTTS might be underestimated if the dimensionality is not accounted for.

Other Applications of Mixed Logit Models

MMNL models also find application in areas other than VTTS. One area in which MMNL models can successfully represent choice situations is spatial correlations. Miyamoto et al. (2004) applied mixing distributions to represent spatial correlations among alternatives, where both the error term and systematic utility is assumed to be spatially autocorrelated. In contrast, Bhat and Guo (2004) developed a version of a GEV model to represent the spatial correlations and used random distributions of certain coefficients to represent unobserved heterogeneity among households using an MMNL structure. The GEV component avoids the higher dimensions of numerical integration that would be required if the MMNL structure were used to represent the spatial correlations. Dugundji and Walker (2005) developed a mode choice model that incorporates spatial network interdependencies using the MMNL structure.

Mode choice behavior has also been analyzed by Lee et al. (2004) and Bhat and Sardesai (2006). Both studies use a combination of RP data and SP data, while the MMNL framework accommodates the scaling difference between RP and SP data. MMNL models have been applied to activity analysis as well. Bhat and Gossen (2004) applied the MMNL model to choice of recreational episode type using RP data. Error components were introduced in order to account for error correlation and heteroscedasticity. Bhat and Lockwood (2004) also applied the MMNL model to choice of activity episode using panel data. Activity scheduling was analyzed using the MMNL model by Mohammadian and Doherty (2005). The alternatives allowed in this model were for scheduling weeks/months ago, the same week, the same day, and impulsive.

Antonini et al. (2006) analyzed pedestrian movements using the CNL and MMNL models. In this study, the next step to be taken by a pedestrian is treated as the dependent variable and it includes alternatives composed of categorized speed and direction. Cross nesting is represented by the CNL and MMNL models. Finer disaggregation of direction is used in the MMNL model than in the CNL model. The results suggest that the two proposed specifications are robust. The parameters of the systematic utility functions are similar to each other in both cases.

In the above applications, models of spatial choice, activity scheduling, and pedestrian movement are based on arbitrary alternatives. In fact, though, location, time, direction, and speed are actually continuous. Any artificial categorization is possible, as long as the categorizations are not inconsistent with the decision maker's decision-making process. For these types of application, consistency in the aggregation of alternatives should be theoretically and empirically investigated as future research into the MMNL model as well as the MNL and NL models examined by Ivanova (2005). Moreover, it is not reasonable to assume that the decision maker considers all available alternatives as the choice set in cases where the size of the choice set is huge. Thus, although some studies have incorporated bounded rationality into the choice modeling process (recently, e.g., Başar and Bhat, 2004; Cantillo and Ortúzar, 2005; Cantillo et al., 2006), more research effort is needed to gain a better understanding of the decision-making process in cases where the definition of alternatives is not obvious.

Other Types of Econometric Choice Modeling

Other types of econometric choice modeling recently examined include: ordered-response models, discrete–continuous choice models, and hazard-based duration models.

Bhat and Srinivasan (2005) developed a multidimensional mixed ordered-response logit model, where an error component structure is introduced into the multidimensional ordered-response logit model. A multivariate ordered-response probit model is feasible if the dimensions are not more than three. In this study, seven dimensions representing different types of activities were adopted and a Halton sequence was used for the multidimensional numerical integrations.

Multiple discrete–continuous choice models were formulated by Kim et al. (2002) and by Bhat (2005), extending the classical discrete–continuous choice model to incorporate the choice of multiple alternatives simultaneously. A Bayesian approach with the Metropolis–Hasting method was used by Kim et al. (2002) to obtain a posterior distribution of model parameters, including unobserved heterogeneity among individuals. A GHK simulator has also been used to evaluate the multivariate normal integral. Bhat (2005), however, assumed extreme value distributions for the random part of the utility function and derived a simple closed-form expression. This is referred to as the multiple discrete–continuous extreme value (MDCEV) model. A simulated maximum likelihood with a scrambled Halton sequence is used to take into account heteroscedasticity and error correlations across alternative utilities. The MDCEV model has been applied for the analysis of discretionary activity engagement and duration (Bhat, 2005; Bhat et al., 2006) and holdings of household vehicle type and annual mileage (Bhat and Sen, 2006). Bhat et al. (2006) further extended the MDCEV model to include a nested structure, which facilitates the joint analysis of imperfect and perfect substitute patterns among the alternatives.

Hazard-based duration models have been applied for the analysis of time use (Bhat et al., 2004, 2005; Mohammadian and Doherty, 2006) and vehicle holding duration (Yamamoto et al., 2004; Chen and Niemeier, 2005). Bhat et al. (2004) examined the duration between successive shopping participations. Nonparametric baseline hazard and parametric unobserved heterogeneity using normal distributions are applied. The latent class structure is incorporated to represent the different characteristics exhibited by regular shoppers and erratic shoppers; the latter are assumed to have a constant baseline hazard. Bhat et al. (2005) also examined the durations between successive activity engagements. In this study, the multiple types of activities are analyzed jointly. Nonparametric baseline hazard, parametric intraindividual heterogeneity with a gamma distribution, and parametric interindividual heterogeneity and covariance among interepisode hazards are incorporated into the model structure simultaneously. Mohammadian and Doherty (2006) examined the duration between planning and execution of preplanned activities. They compared a semiparametric model using the Cox proportional hazard model with parametric models based on exponential, Weibull and log-logistic distributions. Their results suggest that a parametric model with a Weibull distribution is preferred. They also compared the parametric model with a Weibull distribution incorporating parametric unobserved heterogeneity expressed with a gamma distribution and also one without unobserved heterogeneity. This confirmed the existence of unobserved heterogeneity. Yamamoto et al. (2004) and

Chen and Niemeier (2005) examined household vehicle holding duration. A parametric baseline hazard with a Weibull distribution was applied in both studies. Yamamoto et al. (2004) incorporated parametric unobserved heterogeneity using a gamma distribution, while Chen and Niemeier (2005) applied a mass point model to represent nonparametric unobserved heterogeneity.

Challenges of Choice Modeling in Asia

Since the late 1970s, many Asian researchers have been developing and applying travel choice models for transportation project evaluations. It might be supposed that certain characteristics of the Asian situation would require new developments so as to maintain the accuracy or applicability of the choice models. In this section, we summarize these particularly Asian characteristics and describe the empirical issues involved. In particular, economic growth in Asia has led to many big transportation projects and the accuracy of demand models is one important issue. Several case studies and research results are discussed in the section "Inaccuracy in Transport Demand Models".

Characteristics of Transport Modeling in Asian Cities

Asian cities have certain quite extreme features compared with other large cities in the world. Here we summarize these characteristics and review papers related to them by Asian researchers.

Highly Dense and Concentrated Populations

Besides the Tokyo Metropolitan Area (TMA, population: 34 million), there are many other "megacities" in Asia. The UN has reported that 11 Asian cities will be ranked among the top 20 megacities of the world by 2015. Rapid population growth causes serious transportation problems: hypercongestion, increased traffic accident rate, and associated environmental issues. The Eastern Asia Society for Transportation Studies (EASTS), established in 1994, has already held six biannual conferences and many of the papers presented have reported on the issues faced. Morichi (2005) described the characteristics of the Asian megacity and gave a future perspective by comparing detailed statistics from countries in other parts of the world (Figure 2). Fujiwara et al. (2005) collected macro statistics for 46 cities at three different times (1970, 1980, 1990) and estimated the cause–effect relationships between "Land Use," "Environmental Load," "Transportation Demand," and "Transportation Supply" using the LISREL model. Some insights to maintain sustainability in developing countries are suggested in the paper.

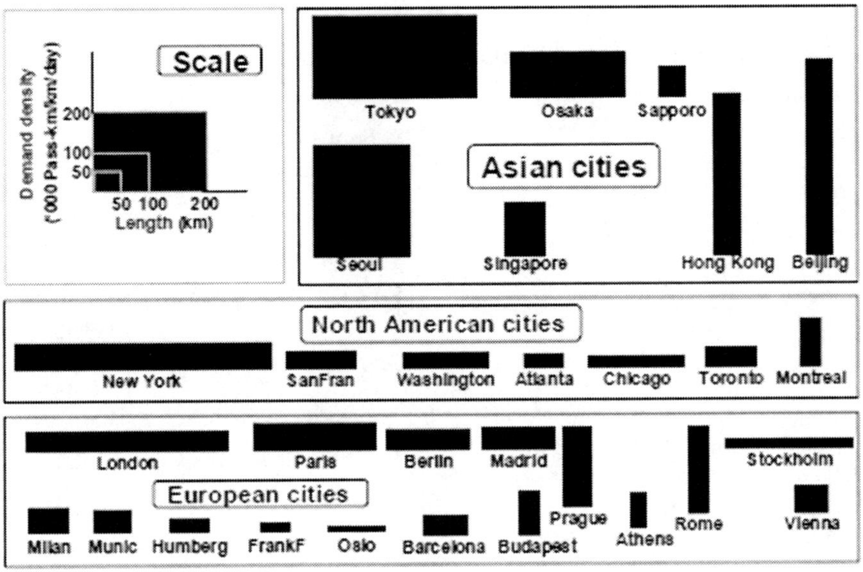

Figure 2
Network Length and Demand Density of Subways
Source: Morichi (2005)

Diversity of Transportation Modes

One of the features of the Asian transportation market is the diversity of modes. Recently, Japan International Cooperation Agency (JICA) collated and summarized existing household interview survey (HIS) data from cities in 11 developing countries and opened up the data for use in academic research. An outline of individual trip data was presented in Hyodo et al. (2005), who provided comparative aggregation results among the 11 cities. They also listed the transportation modes given on each HIS questionnaire sheet (see Table 1). These included some paratransit modes, such as Pedicab, Jeepney, Tricycle, Bajaj, etc. This diversity causes some difficulty in attempting to describe travel behavior using demand models. For example, it is not possible to clearly define the choice set among many alternatives nor their hierarchy. Moreover, some modes do not make regular stops and it is very difficult to develop appropriate level of service (LOS) data.

Demand Models for Big Projects in Asia

There has been substantial investment in transportation facilities over the past decade in the Asian region, while future investment projects are also in planning. The bullet

Table 1
Examples of Transportation Modes Listed on Survey Sheets

Kuala Lumpur	Manila	Jakarta	Cairo
1. Foot	1. Foot	1. Foot to final destination	1. On foot
2. Bicycle	2. Pedicab	2. Foot for transfer	2. Bicycle
3. Motorcycle	3. Bicycle	3. Bicycle	3. Motorcycle
4. Car	4. Motorcycle	4. Motorcycle	4. Private car driver
5. Small van (for passengers)	5. Tricycle	5. Sedan, jeep, Kijang	5. Private car passengers
6. Taxi	6. Jeepney	6. Colt, minicab	6. Pickup for passengers
7. Minibus	7. Minibus	7. Pickup	7. Taxi
8. Feeder bus to/from station	8. Standard bus	8. Truck	8. Shared taxi
9. Intrakota	9. Taxi	9. Rail (express)	9. Public minibus
10. Park Mmay/City Liner	10. HOV taxi	10. Rail (economy)	10. Public bus
11. Other stage bus (with AC)	11. Car/jeep	11. Patas AC	11. Public AC bus
12. Other stage bus (non-AC)	12. School/company/ tourist bus	12. Large bus (patas, regular)	12. Cooperative minibus
13. Factory bus	13. Utility vehicle	13. Medium bus	13. Company (work) car
14. School bus	14. Truck	14. Minibus (Angkot, etc.)	14. Factory/ company bus
15. Other bus	15. Trailer	15. Taxi	15. School bus
16. Small lorry (light; 2-axles)	16. LRT	16. Bajaj	16. Truck for passengers
17. Other lorry	17. PNR	17. Ojek	17. Nile bus
18. STAR (LRT)	18. Water transport	18. Becak	18. Tram
19. KTM train		19. Omprengan	19. Heliopolis metro
		20. Company bus, school bus	20. Underground metro
			21. ENR train
			22. Animal drawn

train (Shinkansen) system in Korea, one of the larger investments, is already in partial operation. A similar system will begin operation in Taiwan this autumn. These systems have a great impact on alternative transportation modes and on the regional economy as well. Demand models for analyzing the modal split between the bullet train and inter-regional bus services have been investigated by Wen (2003), Yang et al. (2003), and Yang (2005). Wen (2003) applied the GNL model proposed previously in Wen and Koppelman (2001). Yang (2005) also analyzed inter-regional travel demand in Taiwan and conducted a comparative analysis of several models: the MMN logit model, the heterogeneous logit model, the latent class model, and the competing destinations model.

Another area of major projects is airport development. Many airports have been constructed in the past decade because of the huge international demand brought by rapid economic growth. These include Incheon airport in Korea (2001), New Hong Kong International Airport (1998), Shanghai Pudong International Airport (1999), Kuala Lumpur International Airport (1998), and others. Some academics have followed this trend and developed econometric transportation demand models. Hiramatsu and Yai (2003) established a demand model system based on a four-step procedure for the North Asian international air market. They examined the feasibility of a regional jet (RJ) service for the mid-size market. Tam et al. (2005) applied a linear structural relationships (LISREL) model to grasp the gap between "perception" and "expectation" on airport access mode choice and suggested appropriate transportation policies for visitors and frequent users.

Advanced Modeling for Dense Transit Networks in Asia

The TMA has quite an extensive transit network. The network of subways and railways, in particular, is very dense (Figure 3). Because of the features of this network, some advanced travel demand modeling methods are required.

First, the number of stations and lines leads to an enormous number of alternatives. In the early 1980s, researchers made efforts to test the discrete choice model for accurate results. Yai (1989) introduced a series of disaggregate behavioral models in Japan. In 1985, the first practical application, a demand model with disaggregate modal split and route choice models, was developed for TMA's future railway and subway network plan. The plan was revised in 2000 and a new modeling method with the structured probit route choice model was applied (Yai et al., 1997). This model was able to overcome the "overlapping problem" among the enormous choice of routes. Hibino et al. (2004) also carried out a comparative analysis of the TMA railway network using a Probit model, an MMNL model and a C-logit model, ultimately proposing a revised C-logit model as an applicable method. This model was used in Hibino et al. (2005) to calculate the network equilibrium assignment for TMA's railway network.

Second, railway and subway stations are supported by several entry and egress modes, so hierarchal modeling techniques should be applied. Since the late 1980s, the most popular approach has been the NL model. During past decade, however, other

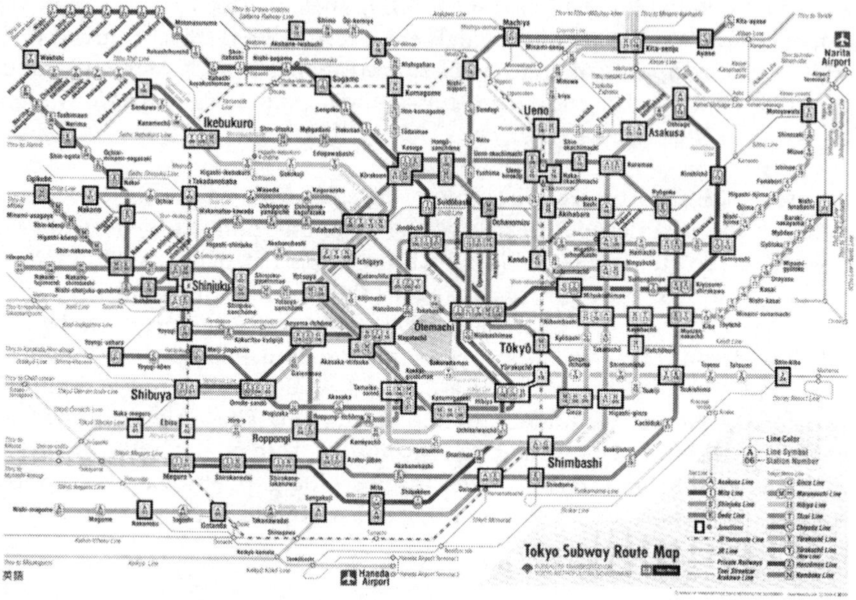

Figure 3
Dense Railway and Subway Network in Tokyo

advanced methods have been examined. Muromachi (2003) introduced a GNL model for a route and parking location choice model. It describes the complicated relationship between route and parking alternatives by defining an "allocation parameter" in the GNL. Mizokami (2003) also estimated a GNL or CNL model and a C-logit model for park-and-ride behavior. It treated a "car" as a common mode for park-and-ride and driving alone and the overlapping effects of different alternatives were explained.

Third, new transportation policies such as peak load pricing and variable (flexible) fare structures have been analyzed by several researchers. Iwakura et al. (2003) developed a departure time choice model. In this model, the error covariance structure among departure time utility was studied using a MMNL model. A peak load pricing policy for the TMA railway network was investigated. The possibility of a temporal demand shift or a movement in the period of peak congestion was reported. Kato et al. (2002) estimated price elasticity using a discrete choice model and clarified the relationship between elasticity and payment mode. The implementation of a new payment mode comprising a post-pay common e-card for all railway companies may open a way to flexible fare structure in the near future.

Inaccuracy in Transport Demand Models

While improving transport demand models theoretically is one thing, to properly institutionalize the best available models is another. Flyvbjerg et al. (2005) investigated 210 road and rail projects worldwide and found that the number of cases where there was a large difference between predicted and observed demand was not insignificant. They also concluded that accuracy in transport demand forecasting has not improved over time, a finding that might lead to undervaluing of the theoretical development of transport demand modeling to date. If planners are to get forecasts right, according to Flyvbjerg et al., a new forecasting method called "reference class forecasting" will be necessary to reduce inaccuracy and bias. Reference class forecasting requires that the following steps are followed for each individual project: identifying a relevant reference class among past projects that is broad enough to be statistically meaningful and comparable with the target project; establishing a probability distribution for the selected reference class; and comparing the target project with the reference class distribution in order to establish the most likely outcome. The British Department for Transport (2004) has already issued guidance to the effect that "reference class forecasting should be used" to overcome optimism bias in the forecasting of transport project costs. The method might also be useful for minimizing similar problems in forecasts of transport demand.

The outputs produced by transport demand models are the major inputs into the process of cost–benefit analysis for transport infrastructure projects in Japan, as is in most other countries. For some projects, the discrepancy between predicted and observed demand has incurred severe criticism. For example, the new bridge and tunnel crossing for Tokyo Bay, the Aqualine, carried only about 40% of the predicted number of vehicles when it opened in 1997. The inaccuracy of transport demand forecasting even became a major item on the agenda during the process of privatizing the Japan Highway Public Corporation. Hyodo (2003) discussed recent issues with transport demand forecasting and its future prospects. The public suspected the government, which is responsible for transport infrastructure planning, was manipulating transport demand models so that projects would nicely meet the cost–benefit criteria. Coupled with a number of cases of corruption by government officials and the long economic slump of the 1990s, the inaccuracy of transport demand forecasts for certain large transport infrastructure projects resulted in a loss of public trust in transport demand models. In response, certain institutions and researchers made serious efforts to find the main factors leading to large differentials between predicted and observed transport demand in the case of past projects.

The Ex-post Evaluation of Transportation Planning Group (EETPG) (1987) conducted one of the earliest studies of this kind. They targeted one metropolitan area transport study in Hiroshima, two public transport projects in Tokadai and

Yukarigaoka, and one road project in Otaru, all implemented during the 1960s and 1970s, and investigated them from the viewpoint of social need, impact, and feasibility. Following Friend and Jessop (1969), they considered three types of uncertainty in relation to transport planning: UE (uncertainty about the related planning environment), UR (uncertainty about the related decisions), and UV (uncertainty about value judgments). For example, uncertainty with regard to major inputs such as future population and economic growth is categorized as UE; uncertainty with regard to decisions made exterior to the transport project, such as major suburban development decisions, is categorized as UR; and uncertainty with regard to the surge of interest in environmental issues in the late 20th century, for example, is UV. While all four cases studied were generally affected by UE during the 1970s when a period of high economic growth came to an end, the road project was most seriously compromised by an uncertainty of type UV, a drastic change in public attitude toward historic sites. The two public transport projects were built in conjunction with large suburban housing developments. Both were exposed to a UE uncertainty, reduced demand for housing, but the private project was able to respond flexibly to the UE uncertainty while the only response possible by the public project was to prolong the project life and no effective steps were taken. One of the objectives of the metropolitan transport study was to reduce UR uncertainty by a comprehensive treatment of the relationship between land use and transport and the interaction between road and public transport, but ultimately it only achieved technical progress with regard to planning and there was no institutional restructuring aimed at implementation.

EETPG (1987) also investigated the discrepancy between predicted and observed demand for the same metropolitan transport study and the road project cases, looking for the major factors that resulted in the discrepancies. Regarding four-step transport demand models, they concluded that one of the most important estimates was that of total transport demand, or control total. A better estimate of total transport demand minimized prediction errors in the final outputs even if major variables such as zonal population were input into the model erroneously. They also found that the root mean square error at the trip distribution step was the largest among the four-step transport demand models and needed further study. As for transport planning, they proposed five areas of improvement: first, a change from static master planning to dynamic strategic planning in order to reduce UR; second, the institutionalization of monitoring; third, drawing a distinction between predicted and planned demand, with predicted demand in the form of a distribution with a lower bound used for financial analysis and a higher bound used for environmental assessment; fourth, the setting of alternatives provided with robustness and adaptability in response to environmental changes; and fifth the introduction of "implementation analysis" by which the capabilities of implementing bodies such as strength, ability, and resources should be evaluated.

The Institution for Transport Policy Studies (ITPS) (2001) conducted a study on better demand forecasting methods for urban railways. Predicted and observed demand was

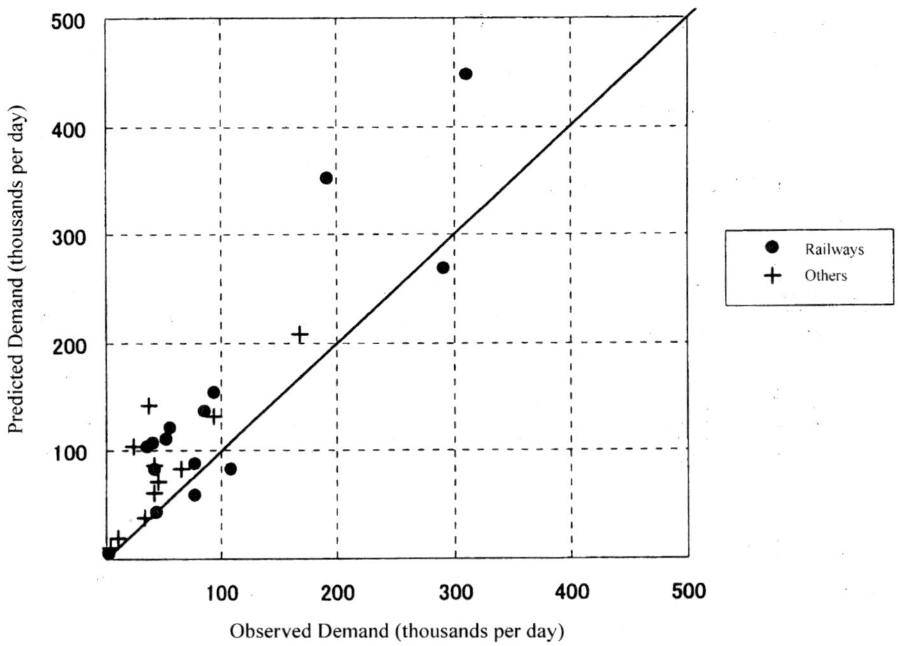

Figure 4

The Comparison between Predicted Demand when the Government Licensed the Segment of Urban Railway Project and Observed Demand when the Project Opened

Note: In case expected opening year when the government licensed the segment of urban railway project differed from actual opening year, adjustments were made based on actual opening year of whole segments of the project

investigated for 26 recently opened railway segments. Figure 4 compares predicted demand at the time of government licensing for the segment with observed demand upon opening.

ITPS found that prediction error, defined as predicted demand divided by observed demand minus one, was within 20% in the case of 5 rail segments, between 20 and 100% for 10 segments, and more than 100% for 10 segments. They also found that predicted demand just before opening was better than that when the government licensed the project, usually several years before opening. They studied the effect of overestimating the population input into railway demand forecasting methods, which were mostly four-step transport demand models, and found that while the prediction error in some cases could be ascribed primarily to the population overestimate, in the case of other segments it might derive from other factors such as the demand forecasting method.

Regarding four-step transport demand models, ITPS concluded that prediction errors resulting from the modal split and route choice steps were greater than the errors caused by the other steps. Inappropriate premises regarding the LOS provided by railways and cars and the restructuring of bus networks also caused large prediction errors. Looking at demand forecasting methods in general, ITPS offered some pointers as to possible approaches to methodological improvement. First, the premises for demand forecasting such as the LOS and development plans should be carefully examined and sensitivity to the setting of these premises should be investigated. Second, an effort to obtain transport data of higher quality is needed. Third, regarding the elaboration of existing models, the models for short trips and for dynamic demand accumulation after project opening need further study, among others. ITPS also considered methods for ensuring a neutral standpoint in conducting demand forecasting, as well as for providing estimates in the form of a distribution as suggested by EETPG (1987).

Doi and Shibata (1997) studied past demand forecasting for the Tokaido Bullet Train (Shinkansen), concluding that the premises made regarding national income and Shinkansen fares, failure to consider competition by air transport and the delay in switching to the new mode immediately after opening made the difference between predicted and observed demand. Doi and Shibata also found difficulty in representing trends during the early 1990s, a period of significant structural change (the bubble economy). Sugie et al. (1997) attempted to improve the modeling of the modal split among car, bus, and new public transport systems through SP/RP modeling, inclusion of state dependence and correction of attrition bias in panel data. After investigating a case where predicted demand was about 14.5 times higher than observed demand for a new public transport system, Morikawa et al. (2004) concluded that, in four-step transport demand models, the generation step during which the population is input resulting in a difference of about 1.7, the modal split step of about 6.6–7.3 and the other steps of about 1.2–1.3 times. They also pointed out that failure to consider competing railways and the use of less temporally stable modal split curves resulted in inaccuracy in the modal split step. In place of modal split curves with only a time variable at the modal split step, they tried discrete choice models with time, money, and several socio-economic variables. The results showed that discrete choice models over predicted the share of the new transport system by about 10 points while the modal split curves over predicted by about 30 points. Discrete choice models estimated from a data set consisting of selected areas similar to those served by the new transport system performed better than those obtained from the entire data set.

Transport demand models for on-going and future projects now face further challenges. The Japanese population started decreasing in 2005. At the same time, as Maruyama et al. (2001) suggested by re-examining future demand for a new monorail, more precise transport demand forecasting will be required to save resources. Public trust in transport demand models and transport infrastructure planning must be recovered. In this regard, Yai et al. (2006) proposed that predicted demand figures should be given in the form of a distribution (rather than a single value) and studied the acceptability of this practice to the public.

Conclusions and Future Studies

This paper comprises a review of recent methodological developments in travel behavior analysis, especially choice modeling, a summary of the particular characteristics of travel behavior in Asia and a review of Asian research efforts to tackle these unique characteristics. Inaccuracy in transport demand forecasting is also discussed.

Since Bhat (2006) wrote that "the field of discrete choice has seen a quantum jump," steady progress has been made both in MMNL and GEV models. While GEV models maintain a closed form in representing choice probability, MMNL models are vulnerable to simulation error, which suggests a preference for GEV models whenever feasible though the interpretation of the covariance parameters is unclear in some cases. Recent developments in relation to GEV models include a practical generating method of flexible covariance matrix, consistent aggregation of alternatives, and ASC in the RP/SP modeling context. The simulation techniques used for numerical integration in the estimation of MMNL models have progressed markedly from pseudorandom sequences to quasirandom sequences and combinations of the two methods. As for other types of choice model, the classical discrete–continuous model has been extended to include multiple cases, while recent hazard-based duration models incorporate rigorously unobserved heterogeneity.

Developments in discrete choice models have revived studies on fundamental factors in transport infrastructure planning such as the VTTS. While MMNL models allow VTTS to be given in the form of a distribution, further intensive investigation is required to determine an appropriate VTTS distribution to use, and the difference between RP and SP estimates. The issue of setting alternatives has also been revisited for cases of large choice sets or where the definition of alternatives is not obvious, with studies including spatial choice, scheduling timing and pedestrian movement models. The diversity of modes and the density of the transit network in some Asian cities require particular attention to the setting of the alternatives available to each decision maker in the choice modeling context.

The premises of conventional discrete choice models, such as a clear definition of alternatives, perfect perception of the attributes of these alternatives, and utility maximization behavior, are often challenged when the inaccuracy of transport demand models is discussed. However, it is inappropriate to ascribe discrepancies between predicted and observed demand in some large transport infrastructure projects solely to deficiencies in transport demand models. However, it is also inappropriate to find transport demand models innocent of any charges of responsibility for discrepancies. Future studies still need to provide more insight into human (travel) behavior on which any good transport demand model depends.

References

Amador, F. J., R. M. González and J. de D. Ortúzar (2005). Preference heterogeneity and willingness to pay for travel time savings. *Transportation* 32, 627–647.

Antonini, G., M. Bierlaire and M. Weber (2006). Discrete choice models of pedestrian walking behavior. *Transportation Research Part B* 40, 667–687.

Bastin, F., C. Cirillo and S. Hess (2005). Evaluation of optimization methods for estimating mixed logit models. *Transportation Research Record* 1921, 35–43.

Bastin, F., C. Cirillo and P. L. Toint (2006). Application of an adaptive Monte Carlo algorithm to mixed logit estimation. *Transportation Research Part B* 40, 577–593.

Başar, G. and C. Bhat (2004). A parameterized consideration set model for airport choice: an application to the San Francisco Bay Area. *Transportation Research Part B* 38, 889–904.

Bhat, C. and A. Lockwood (2004). On distinguishing between physically active and physically passive episodes and between travel and activity episodes: an analysis of weekend recreational participation in the San Francisco Bay area. *Transportation Research A* 38, 573–592.

Bhat, C. R. (2005). A multiple discrete–continuous extreme value model: formulation and application to discretionary time-use decisions. *Transportation Research Part B* 39, 679–707.

Bhat, C. R. (2006). Econometric choice formulations: alternative model structures, estimation techniques, and emerging directions. In K. W. Axhausen (Ed.), *Moving Through Nets: The Physical and Social Dimensions of Travel*, Amsterdam, Elsevier, pp. 45–80.

Bhat, C. R., T. Frusti, H. Zhao, S. Schönfelder and K. W. Axhausen (2004). Intershopping duration: an analysis using multiweek data. *Transportation Research Part B* 38, 39–60.

Bhat, C. R. and R. Gossen (2004). A mixed multinomial logit model analysis of weekend recreational episode type choice. *Transportation Research Part B* 38, 767–787.

Bhat, C. R. and J. Guo (2004). A mixed spatially correlated logit model: formulation and application to residential choice modeling. *Transportation Research Part B* 38, 147–168.

Bhat, C. R. and R. Sardesai (2006). The impact of stop-making and travel time reliability on commute mode choice. *Transportation Research Part B* 40, 709–730.

Bhat, C. R. and S. Sen (2006). Household vehicle type holdings and usage: an application of the multiple discrete–continuous extreme value (MDCEV) model. *Transportation Research Part B* 40, 35–53.

Bhat, C. R. and S. Srinivasan (2005). A multidimensional mixed ordered-response model for analyzing weekend activity participation. *Transportation Research Part B* 39, 255–278.

Bhat, C. R., S. Srinivasan and K. W. Axhausen (2005). An analysis of multiple interepisode durations using a unifying multivariate hazard model. *Transportation Research Part B* 39, 797–823.

Bhat, C. R., S. Srinivasan and S. Sen (2006). A joint model for the perfect and imperfect substitute goods case: application to activity time-use decisions. *Transportation Research Part B* 40, 827–850.

Bierlaire, M. (2002). The network GEV model. *Proceedings of the 2nd Swiss Transportation Research Conference*. Ascona, Switzerland.

Brownstone, D. and K. A. Small (2005). Valuing time and reliability: assessing the evidence from road pricing demonstrations. *Transportation Research Part A* 39, 279–293.

Cantillo, V. and J. de D. Ortúzar (2005). A semi-compensatory discrete choice model with explicit attribute thresholds of perception. *Transportation Research Part B* 39, 641–657.

Cantillo, V., B. Heydecker and J. de D. Ortúzar (2006). A discrete choice model incorporating thresholds for perception in attribute values. *Transportation Research Part B* 40, 807–825.

Chen, C. and D. Niemeier (2005). A mass point vehicle scrappage model. *Transportation Research Part B* 39, 401–415.

Cherchi, E. and J. de D. Ortúzar (2006). On fitting mode specific constants in the presence of new options in RP/SP models. *Transportation Research Part A* 40, 1–18.

Cherchi, E. and J. W. Polak (2005). Assessing user benefits with discrete choice models: implications of specification errors under random taste heterogeneity. *Transportation Research Record* 1926, 61–69.

Cirillo, C. and A. W. Axhausen (2006). Evidence on the distribution of values of travel time savings from a six-week diary. *Transportation Research A* 40, 444–457.

Daly, A. (2001). Recursive nested EV model. ITS Working Paper 559, Institute for Transport Studies, University of Leeds, Leeds, UK.

Daly, A. and M. Bierlaire (2006). A general and operational representation of generalised extreme value models. *Transportation Research Part B* 40, 285–305.

Doi, T. and Y. Shibata (1997). Study on effectiveness of demand forecasting methods applied to Tokaido Shinkansen. *Journal of Infrastructure Planning and Management* 562/IV-35, 121–131 (in Japanese).

Dugundji, E. R. and J. L. Walker (2005). Discrete choice with social and spatial network interdependencies: an empirical example using mixed generalized extreme value models with field and panel effects. *Transportation Research Record* 1921, 70–78.

Ex-post Evaluation of Transportation Planning Group (EETPG) (1987). Ex-post evaluation of transportation planning-prediction errors in planning. The Toyota Foundation Research Grant Program Report I-022.

Faure, H. (1982). Discrepance de suites associatees a un systeme de numeration (en dimensions). *Acta Arithmetica* 41, 337–351.

Flyvbjerg, B., M. K. Skamris Holm and S. L. Buhl (2005). How (in)accurate are demand forecasts in public works projects? *Journal of the American Planning Association* 71, 131–146.

Fosgerau, M. (2006). Investigating the distribution of the value of travel time savings. *Transportation Research Part B* 40, 688–707.

Friend, J. K. and W. N. Jessop (1969). *Local Government and Strategic Choice.* London, Tavistock.

Fujiwara, A., J. Zhang, B. Lee and M. R. M. Da Cruz (2005). Evaluating sustainability of urban development in developing countries incorporating dynamic cause–effect relationship over time. *Journal of EASTS* 6, 4349–4364.

Greene, W. H., D. Hensher and J. Rose (2006). Accounting for heterogeneity in the variance of unobserved effects in mixed logit models. *Transportation Research Part B* 40, 75–92.

Hensher, D. A. (2006). Towards a practical method to establish comparable values of travel time savings from stated choice experiments with differing design dimensions. *Transportation Research Part A* 40, 829–840.

Hensher, D. A., J. Rose and W. H. Greene (2005). The implications on willingness to pay of respondents ignoring specific attributes. *Transportation* 32, 203–222.

Hess, S., M. Bierlaire and J. W. Polak (2005). Estimation of value of travel-time savings using mixed logit models. *Transportation Research Part A* 39, 221–236.

Hess, S., K. E. Train and J. W. Polak (2006). On the use of a modified latin hypercube sampling (MLHS) method in the estimation of a mixed logit model for vehicle choice. *Transportation Research Part B* 40, 147–163.

Hibino, N., T. Hyodo and H. Uchiyama (2004). A study on characteristics of non-IIA route choice models on high density railway network. *Journal of Infrastructure Planning and Management* 765/IV-64, 131–142 (in Japanese).

Hibino, N., H. Uchiyama and Y. Yamashita (2005). A study on evaluation of level of railway services in Tokyo Metropolitan Area based on railway network assignment analysis. *Journal of EASTS* 6, 342–355.

Hiramatsu, T. and T. Yai (2003). Analysis of international air passenger demand for regional jet service in northeast Asia. *Journal of EASTS* 5, 511–525.

Hyodo, T. (2003). Issues and prospects of transportation demand forecasting, B-101, Japan Research Center for Transport Policy (in Japanese).

Hyodo, T., C. M. Montalbo, Jr., A. Fujiwata and S. Soehodho (2005). Urban travel behavior characteristics of 13 cities based on Household Interview Survey data. *Journal of EASTS* 6, 23–38.

Institution for Transport Policy Studies (ITPS) (2001). Better Demand Forecasting Method for Urban Railways, ITPS.

Ivanova, O. (2005). A note on the consistent aggregation of nested logit demand functions. *Transportation Research Part B* 39, 890–895.

Iwakura, S., C. Harada and S. Suzuki (2003). Comparative analysis of choice set for commuting time of day choice model in urban railway networks. *Infrastructure Planning Review* 20, 477–483 (in Japanese).

Kato, H., H. Ieda and Y. Nakajima (2002). Analysis on price elasticity of urban railway users in terms of payment modes. *Journal of Infrastructure Planning and Management* IV-54, 149–158 (in Japanese).

Kim, J., G. M. Allenby and P. E. Rossi (2002). Modeling consumer demand for variety. *Marketing Science* 21, 229–250.

Koppelman, F. S. and V. Sethi (2005). Incorporating variance and covariance heterogeneity in the Generalized Nested Logit model: an application to modeling long distance travel choice behavior. *Transportation Research Part B* 39, 825–853.

Lee, J.-H., K.-S. Chon and C. Park (2004). Accommodating heterogeneity and heteroscedasticity in intercity travel mode choice model: formulation and application to Honam, South Korea, high-speed rail demand analysis. *Transportation Research Record* 1898, 69–78.

Maruyama, T., Y. Muromachi, N. Harata and K. Ohta (2001). The evaluation of influence of aged society with fewer children and decreasing population upon urban public transportation. *Paper on City Planning* 36, 541–546 (in Japanese).

Miyamoto, K., V. Vichiensan, N. Shimomura and A. Paez (2004). Discrete choice model with structuralized spatial effects for location analysis. *Transportation Research Record* 1898, 183–190.

Mizokami, S. (2003). Application of GEV family modal choice models to park and ride system demand forecasting. *Journal of the City Planning Institute of Japan* 38(1), 40–45 (in Japanese).

Mohammadian, A. and S. T. Doherty (2005). Mixed logit model of activity-scheduling time horizon incorporating spatial-temporal flexibility variables. *Transportation Research Record* 1926, 33–40.

Mohammadian, A. and S. T. Doherty (2006). Modeling activity scheduling time horizon: duration of time between planning and execution of pre-planned activities. *Transportation Research Part A* 40, 475–490.

Morichi, S. (2005). Long-term strategy for transport system in Asian megacities. *Journal of EASTS* 6, 1–22.

Morikawa, T., Y. Nagamatsu and N. Sanko (2004). Post-project evaluation of the demand forecast for a new transit system. *Transport Policy Studies' Review* 7(2), 20–29. (in Japanese)

Muromachi, Y. (2003). Inter-relationship between route and parking location choice behavior in downtown. *Journal of EASTS* 5, 1476–1486.

Papola, A. (2004). Some developments on the cross-nested logit model. *Transportation Research Part B* 38, 833–851.

Sándor, Z. and K. Train (2004). Quasi-random simulation of discrete choice models. *Transportation Research Part B* 38, 313–327.

Sivakumar, A., C. R. Bhat and G. Ökten (2005). Simulation estimation of mixed discrete choice models with the use of randomized quasi-Monte Carlo sequences: a comparative study. *Transportation Research Record* 1921, 112–122.

Sobol, I. (1967). On the distribution of points in a cube and the approximate evaluation of integrals. *Zhurnal Vychislitelnoi Matematiki i. Matematicheskoi Fiziki* 7, 784–802.

Sugie, Y., A. Fujiwara and T. Kozasa (1997). Prediction accuracy of mode choice models based on panel data. *Journal of Infrastructure Planning and Management* 576/IV-37, 11–22 (in Japanese).

Tam, M. L., M. L. Tam and W. H. K. Lam (2005). Analysis of airport access mode choice: a case study in Hong Kong. *Journal of EASTS* 6, 708–723.

The British Department for Transport (2004). Procedures for Dealing with Optimism Bias in Transport Planning: Guidance Document.

Train, K. and G. Sonnier (2004). Mixed logit with bounded distributions of correlated partworths. In R. Scarpa and A. Alberini (Eds.), *Applications of Simulation Methods in Environmental and Resource Economics*, Kluwer Academic Publishers, pp. 117–134.

Wen, C.-H. (2003). A covariance heterogeneity generalized nested logit model of new bus services. *Journal of EASTS* 5, 1366–1376.

Wen, C.-H. and F. S. Koppelman (2001). The generalized nested logit model. *Transportation Research Part B* 35, 627–641.

Yai, T. (1989). Disaggregate behavioral models and their applications in Japan. *Transportation Research Part A* 23, 45–51.

Yai, T., D. Fukuda and K. Nehashi (2006). An attitudinal analysis of citizens' credibility gap for travel demand forecasting. *Journal of Infrastructure Planning and Management* 62(1), 131–144 (in Japanese).

Yai, T., S. Iwakura and S. Morichi (1997). Multinomial probit with structured covariance for route choice behavior. *Transportation Research Part B* 31, 195–207.

Yamamoto, T., J.-L. Madre and R. Kitamura (2004). An analysis of the effects of French vehicle inspection program and grant for scrappage on household vehicle transaction. *Transportation Research Part B* 38, 905–926.

Yang, C.-W. (2005). Modeling multiple sources of heterogeneity in mode choice model. *Journal of EASTS* 6, 2031–2045.

Yang, C.-W., L.-S. Duann, W.-P. Fang and Y.-C. Chen (2003). Intercity bus choice models with choice set generation and heterogeneity. *Journal of EASTS* 5, 1518–1533.

2.7 Advances in Activity Analysis

The Expanding Sphere of Travel Behaviour Research
Selected Papers from the 11th International Conference on Travel Behaviour Research

12

Challenges and Opportunities in Advancing Activity-Based Approaches for Travel Demand Analysis

Ram M. Pendyala

Abstract

Activity-based approaches continue to receive much attention in the field of travel behaviour as the wave of the future for travel demand analysis and modelling. Although some progress has been made in moving activity-based approaches to practice using microsimulation modelling frameworks, there are several challenges that have inhibited wider and faster adoption in practice. Recent advances in understanding and modelling human activity–travel patterns, and experience gained with recent implementation of activity-based models in practice offer opportunities for overcoming the challenges and advancing these approaches further. This paper attempts to highlight some recent advances in activity-based modelling, present a manifesto for defining activity-based model systems and identify several issues that remain to be resolved for accelerating the adoption of activity-based methods.

Introduction

The era of activity-based analysis of travel demand has arrived. Activity-based approaches to travel demand analysis have long been recognized as rigorous frameworks for analysing, modelling and representing complex travel behaviour patterns that emerge from the human need to participate in activities that are distributed in time and space (Kitamura, 1988; Axhausen and Garling, 1992). The notion that travel demand is a derived demand has played a key role in the development and formulation of activity-based frameworks for travel demand analysis (Bowman and Ben-Akiva, 2001). Activity-based approaches explicitly recognize the derived nature of travel demand and offer a robust behavioural framework for accounting for time–space constraints, linkages across trips in a trip chain or tour and interactions among individuals in a household (Ettema and Timmermans, 1997). Activity-based model systems entail the use of microsimulation techniques wherein activity–travel patterns of individuals and households are simulated at the level of the individual decision-maker or behavioural unit (Kitamura et al., 2000). This framework allows one to consider intra-household interactions and group decision-making including vehicle allocation among household members, and task allocation and joint activity participation (Timmermans, 2005). In essence, the activity-based approach provides the ability to consider the myriad interactions and constraints that define and characterize human activity–travel behaviour.

The notions of time and space lie at the heart of activity-based analysis. The recognition that activities are distributed in time and space (thus necessitating travel) allows one to explicitly incorporate concepts of time–space geography in understanding and modelling travel behaviour (Pendyala, 2003; Kwan, 2000). In the temporal dimension, one considers time constraints, activity and travel durations (time use), and activity and travel timing (time of day choice). In the space dimension, one is concerned with travel distances, residential and workplace location choices, and activity destination (location) choices, and modal accessibility measures associated with various locations. By combining the time and space dimensions into a multi-dimensional continuum, one can account for time–space interactions and constraints that govern activity–travel patterns (Hagerstrand, 1970). For these reasons, time-use research (and, by extension, time–space geography) has played a central role in activity-based analysis of travel behaviour (Miller, 2005; Bhat and Koppelman, 1999).

The rapid progress in development and application of activity-based analysis methods and models has largely occurred along three lines of inquiry. The first line of inquiry has seen a plethora of research concerned with a fundamental understanding of activity and travel behaviour. Activity-based frameworks have been used to understand activity-scheduling processes (Ettema et al., 1993; Garling et al., 1994; Miller and Roorda, 2003), time-use allocation patterns (Goulias, 2002), intra-household interactions (Bhat and Pendyala, 2005; Kang and Scott, 2008), time–space prism constraints (Pendyala et al., 2002), activity durations and timing decisions (Pendyala and Bhat, 2004), trip chaining behaviour (tour formation) (Golob, 2000) and activity location choices (Kitamura, 1984). The second line of inquiry has largely focused on the development of activity-based model systems for travel demand forecasting. These model systems incorporate (to varying degrees) the fundamental behavioural paradigms and relationships that have emerged from the first line of inquiry. A range of activity-based model systems have been developed over the past decade; several, such as AMOS (Pendyala et al., 1998, 2005), CEMDAP (Bhat et al., 2004), MATSIM

(Balmer et al., 2005), SMASH (Ettema et al., 1996), ILUTE (Salvini and Miller, 2005) and ALBATROSS (Arentze and Timmermans, 2004), have remained largely in the research arena. However, there are several tour-based model systems that have made their way into practice in several metropolitan areas of United States and Europe (Vovsha et al., 2005). The tour-based model systems represent a middle ground between the traditional trip-based approaches to travel forecasting and the more advanced continuous time activity-based models that have largely remained in the research and development arena. Tour-based model systems have been implemented in the United States in several areas including San Francisco, New York, Columbus and Sacramento, with several additional metropolitan areas in various stages of model development and implementation (e.g. Atlanta, Puget Sound, Denver, Phoenix, Tampa). The third line of inquiry involves the use of activity-based approaches to conduct policy analysis and assess quality-of-life issues/impacts (Pendyala et al., 1997; Kitamura et al., 1997b). As activity-based approaches explicitly consider interactions and constraints that characterize activity–travel patterns, it is possible to estimate the secondary and tertiary impacts of a range of policy options on individual and household activity–travel patterns (Pendyala et al., 1998). For example, a telecommuting-oriented policy may impact not only the work trip (primary impact) but also other trips (such as shopping, personal business, social–recreation, eat meal and serve child) due to interactions among trips and individuals in a household. These secondary and tertiary impacts are important considerations when evaluating the overall impacts of a policy on travel demand and greenhouse gas emissions. Similarly, activity- and time-use-based approaches have provided a strong framework for analysing quality-of-life impacts of various policies and infrastructure investments based on time-use utility measures (Pendyala et al., 2007). Thus, activity-based approaches have seen a few applications in the policy planning arena as well.

These advances have clearly been aided and made possible by a series of methodological, computational, technological, and theoretical (behavioural) advances. There has been much work over the past decade in the econometric formulation and estimation of advanced discrete choice models that account for taste variations (Hensher and Greene, 2000), flexible substitution patterns (Bhat, 1998) and heterogeneity in the population (Srinivasan and Mahmassani, 2003; Bhat, 2000) and simultaneous equations model systems that accommodate a variety of endogenous variable types including discrete, continuous and truncated/censored dependent variables (Ye et al., 2007b; Pendyala and Bhat, 2004). New simulation-based (Bhat, 2003; Hess et al., 2006; Train, 2003) and Bayesian estimation approaches (Janssens et al., 2005) coupled with advances in software and hardware systems have provided the analytical and computational capabilities to estimate complex model systems with ease and efficiency. Improved understanding of activity–travel behaviour processes has contributed to enhanced specifications of model systems that reflect the various interactions, constraints and cognitive learning processes (Arentze and Timmermans, 2005) that influence the formation of activity–travel agendas and emergent patterns.

The primary objective of this paper is to highlight some of the recent advances that have taken place in the activity and time-use analysis arena with particular emphasis on six broad themes. These themes are

- Behavioural processes: Decision hierarchies and causal relationships
- Time-use allocation and resource consumption
- Time–space geography: Constraints and interactions
- Agent-based simulation
- Methodological advances
- Policy and planning applications

The intent of covering these six broad themes is to present a manifesto that describes the activity-based approach to travel demand analysis. There are a few additional themes related to activity-based analysis that are not covered in detail in this paper, primarily because there are other resource papers specifically dedicated to these topics. These include

- Data needs and data collection (survey) methods for activity analysis (including GPS-based data collection methods)
- Activity-based and tour-based model systems in practice
- Intra-household interactions and group decision-making

These topics will be discussed within the scope of this paper only to the extent that they play a role within the broader six themes that fall within the scope of this paper.

After presenting a discussion on these six themes and identifying a few advances that have taken place in each area, the paper provides an extensive discussion on the challenges and prospects for the advancement of activity-based approaches in travel behaviour analysis. There are several challenges in and opportunities for accelerating activity-based approaches into mainstream practice and the latter section of the paper is intended to help identify a research agenda in this field for the next several years.

Progress in Activity-Based Analysis

The progress in activity-based approaches to travel analysis has occurred on several fronts and it would be a daunting task to try and cover the entire range of advances within the scope of this paper. This section therefore focuses on the six themes identified in the previous section. Although these concepts are discussed separately, it should be noted all of these themes are interrelated in many respects. For example, behavioural decision processes play an important role in the simulation of agent behaviour. Similarly, behavioural decision processes are often related to the allocation of time among activities and individuals and the time–space interactions and constraints that influence activity–travel behaviour. Methodological advances cut across all themes of activity-based analysis.

It should also be noted that there is an abundance of literature devoted to activity-based analysis of travel demand. Presenting a comprehensive literature review of the field is beyond the scope of this paper and the field has matured to such an extent that the literature is now too vast to be reviewed in a single paper.

Behavioural Decision Processes: Decision Hierarchies and Causal Relationships

A major motivation for the activity-based approach to travel analysis is the ability to represent complex behavioural phenomena, relationships and decision processes. Virtually all activity-based model systems have an underlying behavioural structure that implies the presence of a decision process or hierarchy among activity–travel variables of interest. Activity-based model systems consider the formation of tours or trip chains, location choices for activities, time of day choices for stops in tours and mode choices for tours. All of these decision variables are linked in a behavioural decision structure that is considered to replicate the behavioural decision processes of travellers. The decision structure may also be formulated in such a way that model estimation is tractable and model application is feasible in large-scale planning studies; in other words, behavioural theory may not be the sole factor driving the structure of activity-based model systems.

There are many questions with regard to the behavioural decision structure that should be incorporated into model systems. Advances in the understanding of activity-scheduling decisions provide the ability to develop activity agendas at the household and individual level (Miller and Roorda, 2003; Garling et al., 1994; Ettema et al., 1993). With the increasing use of mobile technologies, it is possible for individuals and households to schedule activities on an impromptu basis. In other words, activity schedules and agendas can change on the fly, tasks can be reallocated among individuals and days of the week without extensive planning a priori, and stops can be inserted and removed from tours/chains with ease (Joh et al., 2005; Mohammadian and Doherty, 2005; Venter and Hansen, 1998). New activities can be generated on the fly depending on the constraints and opportunities prevalent at any moment. New computer-assisted data collection techniques have proved valuable in gaining insights into activity-scheduling processes, particularly in understanding the extent to which certain activities are planned a priori and others occur spontaneously (Doherty and Miller, 2000). As expected, routine activities that have greater levels of temporal and spatial fixity tend to be planned in advance (serve as pegs), while other discretionary activities tend to occur with less advance planning (Chen et al., 2004). Recent work has focused on the development of activity schedules or agendas while recognizing these differences in planning horizons and the need to resolve conflicts that might arise, both within and between person's activity agendas when activity episodes are inserted or removed (Ruiz et al., 2005).

The decision hierarchy assumed among the range of activity–travel choices and variables included in an activity-based model system may be considered to be representative of the behavioural process underlying travel demand. Some choices may be made simultaneously or jointly, while others may be made sequentially with one choice conditional on the other (Kitamura et al., 1997a). The causal relationships among various activity–travel variables are of considerable interest and importance in the specification and development of activity-based model systems (Pendyala and Ye, 2005). The nature of the causal relationships may differ across market segments in the population leading to considerable heterogeneity in the population. Recent advances in simultaneous equations modelling involving mixed dependent variables have provided the ability to estimate systems where multiple travel characteristics are modelled jointly (Pendyala and Bhat, 2004; Ye et al., 2007b). Recent work in this area has examined relationships between timing and duration of activities (Pendyala and Bhat, 2004), vehicle-type choice and utilization (Bhat and Sen, 2006), trip chaining and mode choice (Ye et al., 2007b), mode choice and departure-time choice (Tringides et al., 2004), and residential location choice and a host of travel choices (Pinjari et al., 2007; Bhat and Guo, 2007; Kitamura et al., 1997c; Handy et al., 2005; Mokhtarian and Cao, 2008). These efforts have provided valuable insights into the nature of the relationships that exist between these travel dimensions and have shown that there are substantial differences across market segments defined by gender, car ownership and commuting status. What is also noteworthy is that the constrained choices generally tend to be made first and the less-constrained choices tend to be made conditional on the more-constrained choice (Pendyala and Ye, 2005). For example, it has been found that commuters tend to make mode choice decisions conditional on departure-time choice decisions, while non-commuters tend to make departure-time decisions conditional on mode choice decisions (although this latter relationship is rather weak). This is presumably because commuters are more time constrained due to rather rigid work schedules and hours. More recently, it has been found that strong simultaneity exists among multiple travel-choice dimensions including residential location choice, vehicle and bicycle ownership, and mode choice; this finding suggests that households make choices as a lifestyle package, calling for the joint modelling of multiple activity–travel variables in a simultaneous equations framework as opposed to a more traditional sequential structure (Pinjari et al., 2008).

There are several other aspects of behaviour that have received considerable attention in activity–travel analysis. Attitudes, preferences, perceptions and values have all been shown to be significant factors influencing activity–travel demand and behavioural response to policy measures and modal system changes (Kitamura et al., 1997c). In some instances, it has been found that personal attitudes and preferences are even more significant than demographic and socio-economic characteristics (Kuppam et al., 1999). The jointness in the relationship among multiple activity–travel variables often arises due to common unobserved factors simultaneously influencing several activity–travel characteristics. These common unobserved factors are likely to be personal attitudes and preferences that are rarely measured in household travel surveys and/or incorporated into model systems, presumably due to the inherent difficulty in forecasting such variables (Pinjari et al., 2008).

One of the key paradigms that has defined the activity-based analysis arena is the typology used to characterize activity types. Activities such as work and school are often referred to as mandatory or fixed activities due to the presumably lower levels of spatial and temporal flexibility associated with these activities. Shopping and personal business type activities are considered flexible maintenance activities, that is they have to be undertaken with a certain frequency, but have some level of flexibility with respect to the temporal and spatial dimensions. Finally, social–recreational activities are considered discretionary activities because they offer a potentially high level of temporal and spatial flexibility and it is conceivable that the activity could be foregone entirely at the discretion of the traveller. However, this traditional definition of activity typology is being challenged (Doherty, 2006). Work schedules and locations are becoming increasingly flexible and variable (work at home, flexible work hours, satellite offices, client locations), while social–recreational activities are often quite rigid (going to a sports event at a fixed location at a fixed time). Instead of defining trip purposes or categories based on these traditional definitions, it may be prudent to categorize trips based on a set of criteria that define the true level of spatial and temporal flexibility associated with various trips. Such a typology can go a long way in truly capturing temporal and spatial constraints that exist in activity–travel patterns (Doherty, 2006).

Time-Use Allocation and Resource Consumption

The notion of time is central to the activity-based approach to travel demand analysis (Pendyala, 2003). All activities involve the consumption of time (and money) and, as a consequence, a certain amount of time (and money) is allocated to each activity episode and to each activity type in the course of a day, a week, a month or any period of time that might be considered. Time and money are resources that serve as constraints. There is limited time available (24 hours in a day) to any human being and therefore only a limited amount of time can be allocated to travel and activities. Similarly, households and individuals have monetary budgets and can allocate only a certain amount of money to transportation and activity engagement (notwithstanding the ability to borrow money). In general, activity-based analysis has focused more on time-use allocation or expenditures as opposed to monetary expenditures. This is likely due to two reasons. First, time is truly a limited resource and cannot be borrowed on credit.

On the other hand, although money is a limited resource as well, it is theoretically feasible to borrow money on credit, thus making monetary constraints fuzzier than time constraints. Second, household travel surveys provide detailed temporal information associated with travel and activities, but provide virtually no information about monetary expenditures. In the absence of any data about monetary expenditures, it is virtually impossible to consider monetary resource consumption in activity–travel behaviour analysis. Also, individuals are generally less inclined to disclose income and monetary expenditure information than time-use expenditure information in the course of a household survey.

Time-use research has clearly taken centre stage in activity-based analysis (Kitamura et al., 1997b). Models of daily time allocation to various activity types and duration models of time allocation to individual activity episodes have been developed and estimated using a variety of econometric formulations, largely using utility maximization frameworks (Bhat, 1996; Hensher and Mannering, 1994). Although tour-based model systems implemented in practice do not explicitly consider durations and time allocation measures, most activity-based model systems in the research domain include duration models to explicitly estimate activity durations (Pendyala et al., 2005). The availability of time-use data sets in various countries of the world has made it possible to explicitly consider time allocation behaviour in activity analysis of travel demand. Time-use data sets often include information about both out-of-home and in-home activity engagement for all household members, thus providing a powerful resource for considering trade-offs and complementary relationships between in-home and out-of-home activities and between individuals within the same household.

Historical evidence suggests that individuals are allocating increasing amounts of time to travel and various activities outside the home (Toole-Holt et al., 2005; Banerjee et al., 2007). The increases are largely seen in travel time expenditures and activity durations for flexible and discretionary activities such as shopping, personal business and social–recreation or leisure. This phenomenon is being seen worldwide, particularly in the rapidly developing economies of the world where standards of living are rising at a torrid pace. Unfortunately, traditional travel demand models are not able to reflect the per capita increases in travel time expenditures that occur due to increased participation in flexible and discretionary activities. More importantly, traditional travel demand model specifications do not appear to include the types of factors that are contributing to increases in travel time expenditures and trip frequencies over time (Toole-Holt et al., 2005). This is an issue that merits further research and is discussed again later in the paper.

The issue of time allocation to travel is further exacerbated by recent evidence that at least some travel may offer travellers a positive utility (Redmond and Mokhtarian, 2001). The positive utility of travel, which has been found both in quantitative and qualitative studies in the recent past, implies that individuals enjoy the actual travel experience in addition to the activity episode that is pursued at the destination. This phenomenon may at least partially explain the rising average travel time expenditures seen in many countries around the world. The notion that there is a constant travel time expenditure or budget is being challenged (Banerjee et al., 2007; Toole-Holt et al., 2005). In many countries around the world, rising standards of living, transition to a service-oriented economy, greater activity participation opportunities and loosening constraints (facilitated by modern technology, labour productivity gains, outsourcing, 24/7 business establishments and transportation system improvements) have provided the impetus for increasing travel time expenditures and activity engagement (Pendyala and Kitamura, 2007). Recent work in trying to determine how high travel time expenditures could potentially go suggests that people are spending only about 50 percent of their perceived maximum travel time expenditure, termed a travel time frontier. In other words, evidence suggests that people would be able to allocate about twice the amount of time for travel compared to what they are allocating now. This means that individuals have not yet 'hit' the temporal constraint in terms of the amount of time that they can allocate to travel. It is also plausible that this temporal constraint (or frontier) can shift or loosen over time in light of the reasons mentioned previously.

The discussion here has focused on time-use allocation and travel time expenditures mainly due to the larger body of literature dedicated to time use in the context of activity analysis. However, there is an increasing realization that monetary expenditures and constraints play an important role in shaping activity–travel patterns. As mentioned earlier, the increase in monetary resources in rapidly developing economies is contributing to greater levels of out-of-home activity engagement. Quality of life can be viewed in terms of the ability of individuals and households to participate in activities that they desire. Not only does this require time and activity destination opportunities that are accessible, but this also requires the ability of the individual to afford and allocate monetary resources to activities. This calls for the development of unified theories of time and monetary resource allocation to activities. Recent work in this arena appears to be promising and the availability of disaggregate consumer expenditure data should provide the ability to develop and estimate such unified model systems (Anas, 2007).

Time–Space Geography: Constraints and Interactions

At the heart of activity-based modelling is the explicit consideration of time–space interactions and constraints that influence activity–travel patterns (Miller, 2005; Pendyala et al., 2002). If one considers the time–space continuum, it is possible for an individual to travel to or reach a finite number of destinations within a limited amount of time. This 'action space' is dictated not only by the amount of time available to an individual, but also by the speed of travel. If the speed of travel is higher, then the action space expands and vice versa. The feasible action space of an individual has been represented in various ways with the most common being the time–space prism (Hagerstrand, 1970; Pendyala et al., 2002). The time–space prism represents the domain in which an individual may pursue activities and engage in travel without violating constraints. Destination choice for an activity is dependent on the current location of an individual, the time available to travel and engage in the next activity, the speed of travel, and the location and temporal constraint of the next fixed activity (e.g. having to be at work at a certain time). For these reasons, time–space interdependencies need to be explicitly recognized and incorporated into activity-based models of travel demand. There has been considerable work in the research arena to model or measure time–space prisms. It has been found that the nature and size of time–space prisms varies by residence and work location choices, commuting status, gender, household and individual attributes such as age, number of children, vehicle ownership and day of the week. One of the most powerful applications of the time–space prism concept is the ability to address the notion of induced or latent travel (Noland, 2001). A time–space prism represents the action space within which an individual can travel and engage in activities. If a time–space prism expands (because speed of travel has been improved by a modal investment), then an individual may engage in additional activities and/or additional travel to visit more preferred destinations for existing activities. In traditional travel demand models, while one may be able to capture additional travel due to changes in destination choice, route choice or mode choice, there is virtually no ability to reflect the generation of new activities as a consequence of a supply change. The time–space prism concept offers a robust framework for evaluating induced travel impacts of capacity expansion projects.

The analysis of time–space interactions and the representation of time–space prisms have generally been undertaken by time–space geographers who are interested in understanding the role of time and space in human activity–travel patterns (Miller, 2005; Kwan, 2000). The measurement and understanding of time–space interactions has been further facilitated by rapid advances in computer visualization and animation technology. Over the past decade, these technologies have advanced to such an extent that it is now possible to dynamically visualize human activity and travel patterns in time and space and thus graphically depict the time–space prisms or action spaces of an individual during the course of a day. The use of global positioning systems (GPS) technologies to collect detailed position and time data associated with human movements in transportation networks has further provided the ability to accurately measure and represent time–space interactions and human action spaces (Wolf et al., 2001). Geographic information systems (GIS) platforms are used to plot the trajectories of trips in time and space, determine locations of individuals by time of day and analyse route and location choices (using spatial statistics).

The use of GIS technologies to map and analyse activity–travel patterns has also allowed the study of the relationships between humans and their built and natural environments. GIS platforms allow one to assemble layers of databases representing land use, land cover, buildings and facilities, transportation networks and activity–travel patterns or trajectories. By examining relationships among these different layers of data, one can understand how these entities interact with one another; more importantly, by assembling a series of these databases over time, it is possible to study emergent behaviour in urban systems as the built and natural environment evolves over time along with transportation networks and activity–travel patterns (Waddell, 2000).

Agent-Based Simulation

Within the activity-based analysis arena, the profession has generally treated all of the entities encountered as agents that interact with one another. This has been made possible largely due to the advent of agent-based simulation methods wherein the behaviour of individual travellers or decision-makers is modelled (Arentze and Timmermans, 2004; Salvini and Miller, 2005; Bhat et al., 2004; Pendyala et al., 2005; Waddell, 2000). Households and individuals, business establishments, and modal service providers are treated as agents, while activities and trip are treated as objects. Simulation is performed at the level of the individual traveller, that is the actual behavioural decision-making unit. Disaggregate microsimulation where the behaviours of millions of agents can be modelled and simulated along the continuous time axis has been made possible by major advances in computational power and parallel computing capabilities.

The advantages of agent-based microsimulation methods are quite obvious in the activity analysis context. First, simulation of behaviour is done at the level of the individual decision-maker. Second, agent-based simulation allows one to account for interactions among agents. There has been much research recently into understanding interactions among household members with respect to solo and joint activity participation (Gliebe and Koppelman, 2002; Chandrasekharan and Goulias, 1999), altruism and egoism in activity engagement (Goulias and Henson, 2006), task allocation and assignment (Zhang et al., 2005), vehicle allocation and use (Petersen and Vovsha, 2006), and group decision-making (Bhat and Pendyala, 2005). A special issue of *Transportation* dedicated to this topic was published in 2005 and there have been several additional studies examining interactions among household members. A separate resource paper dedicated to the topic of intra-household interactions and group decision-making has been included in this volume. It is conceivable that there are household constraints that manifest themselves in the form of interactions that must be taken into account for accurately representing activity–travel patterns of individuals within a household. Previous research has shown that there is strong interaction among household members with respect to activity agenda formation (Golob and McNally, 1997). A key interaction that is one of the most obvious is that represented by the dependency of a child on adults in the household for meeting mobility needs. Parents or caregivers must often transport children to school, shopping, play and sports/hobby activities. Many of these activities are constrained in time and space; as a consequence, the adult's activity–travel patterns are shaped by the temporal and spatial characteristics of the child's activities. On the other hand, the locations and timings of children's activities may be determined by the activity and travel constraints of the parent or caregiver who must transport the child. In other words, there are two-way causal influences that shape activity–travel patterns of individuals in a household. It is plausible to expect that strong interaction also exists with respect to longer-term choices such as household location choice, work location choice, vehicle ownership and school location choice (Pinjari et al., 2008).

Integrated models of agent behaviour that purport to capture the entire continuum of choice behaviour are being developed in the field. In a recent study examining relationships between residential location choice (long-term choice), car ownership (medium-term choice), bicycle ownership (medium- to short-term choice) and mode choice (short-term choice), it was found that there is a high degree of simultaneity or jointness in these choice phenomena (Pinjari et al., 2008). There are unobserved factors that simultaneously impact these four choice dimensions and it was concluded that households (and individuals within households) make multiple choices spanning multiple time horizons as an integrated lifestyle package as opposed to a sequence of choices that are made conditional on or independent of one another. The lifestyle package concept has people residing in neighbourhoods with built environments consistent with their lifestyle preferences (residential self-selection) and choosing travel options consistent with that lifestyle preference as well. Integrated land use—transportation models that involve the simulation of individual households from longer-term residential and workplace location choices to shorter-term mode and route choice decisions are under development and take advantage of the ability to simulate individual agents over time within the agent-based simulation frameworks.

Agent-based simulation methods involve the generation of synthetic population of households and individuals that match known population attribute distributions (Pendyala et al., 2005; Guo and Bhat, 2007). The emergent behaviour of each agent in the synthetic population is then simulated using a series of models that represent the decision hierarchy or behavioural process that is assumed to exist for the market segment under consideration. Research is ongoing to incorporate models of agent interactions into these model systems with particular focus on intra-household interactions. Game theory approaches, utility maximization frameworks and structural equations modelling methods have been used to model these interactions.

Methodological Advances in Activity Analysis

The field of activity analysis has greatly benefited from an array of methodological developments that allow the formulation and estimation of model systems that can represent complex behavioural phenomena and relationships among activity–travel variables. Methodological advances have been occurring on several fronts, especially in the past decade that has proven to be an extremely fertile period for these developments. Many of these developments have been made possible by the advent of simulation-based estimation approaches (Train, 2003) allowing the computation of multi-dimensional integrals of multivariate normal distributions and other mixed distributions where closed form solutions do not exist or the derivation of first-order and second-order conditions for optimality is prohibitive (Bhat, 2003; Hess et al., 2006). These simulation-based estimation approaches have been found to be computationally efficient and robust.

Travel behaviour researchers have long recognized the presence of taste variations, heterogeneity in the population and flexible substitution patterns in human activity–travel choices. The generalized extreme value (GEV) family of models leading to the development of the mixed multinomial logit model (or mixed logit model) has provided a methodological breakthrough in the representation of taste variations and population heterogeneity (Walker, 2002). In most traditional choice models, a single coefficient is assumed to represent the sensitivity of individuals to an attribute (say, travel time or cost). Where variation in sensitivity is assumed to exist, market segmentation methods have been adopted to at least partially accommodate the population heterogeneity. However, the mixed logit model provides a robust methodology for accounting for taste variations across the population (Hensher and Greene, 2003). If one were to consider sensitivity to travel time or cost, it is very plausible that different individuals will react to changes in travel time or cost differently (Fosgerau, 2006). While some of these variations may be captured by systematic factors such as demographic and socio-economic attributes, it is also likely that a substantial portion of the variability may be due to random taste variations across individuals. If one does not account for these random taste variations, policy impacts estimated from models are likely to be erroneous. The development of advanced discrete choice models such as the mixed logit model and its variants constitutes one of the most significant advances in recent times.

Another major methodological advance recognizes that individuals may choose multiple discrete alternatives and that several behavioural phenomena need to be considered when modelling multiple discrete choice behaviour (Bhat, 2008). For example, individuals may participate in multiple activities in a time–space prism, own several different cars or use several different modes in a tour. Traditional choice models often restrict the number of chosen alternatives to be equal to 1, thus making it nearly impossible to model multiple discrete choice phenomena. The development of the multiple discrete continuous extreme value (MDCEV) model has provided a significant breakthrough in modelling these phenomena. This method not only allows one to account for the choice of multiple discrete alternatives but it also allows one to estimate the continuous dimension associated with each discrete choice. For example, in the case of vehicle ownership, one can model the fleet of vehicles that a household will own (multiple discrete alternatives) and the amount of miles that each vehicle in the fleet will be driven or utilized (continuous dimension associated with each discrete alternative) (Bhat and Sen, 2006). Similarly, one can model the set of activities that will be pursued by an individual (multiple discrete alternatives) and the amount of time that will be allocated to each activity (continuous time dimension). Within the context of this advance, one also needs to consider the concept of satiation and flexible substitution patterns. The concept of satiation accounts for potential marginal diminishing returns as one consumes an increasing quantity of a certain good. Flexible substitution patterns account for the potential to substitute one alternative with the consumption of another. By introducing parameters that represent satiation and flexible substitution patterns, the model systems are able to capture complex behavioural phenomena of much interest to the profession (Pinjari et al., 2008).

The development and estimation of simultaneous equations models of travel demand that allow one to jointly model several activity–travel variables of interest has also seen rapid progress in the recent past. Econometric model systems that include mixtures of discrete and continuous endogenous variables can now be estimated; thanks to advances in simulation-based estimation approaches (Pendyala and Bhat, 2004; Ye et al., 2007b). In addition to traditional econometric formulations of simultaneous equations systems, structural equations methods have also been used extensively in activity–travel analysis (Golob and McNally, 1997; Lu and Pas, 1999). Structural equations methods offer a computationally tractable approach of estimating simultaneous equations systems involving a large number of dependent variables while accounting for error correlations; however, they are unable to accommodate unordered multinomial discrete choice variables, which often limits their application in travel demand analysis contexts (Kuppam and Pendyala, 2001). Mode choice, departure-time choice, vehicle-type choice, activity-type choice and destination choice are all key examples of unordered discrete choice variables that one cannot model using structural equations modelling methods. On the other hand, econometric formulation of simultaneous equations systems become computationally cumbersome and challenging in the presence of a large number of mixed dependent variables. Models examining relationships between time of day choice and mode choice, trip chaining type and mode choice, timing and duration of activities and time allocation to different types of activities have been estimated and reported in the literature. These model systems shed light on the degree of jointness in activity–travel behaviour and the nature of the causal relationship that may exist between sets of activity–travel variables.

As mentioned earlier, activity–travel analysis has been characterized by an explicit recognition of the role of constraints and interactions in the shaping of human activity–travel patterns. When one is dealing with constraints and interactions, qualitative aspects of behaviour merit consideration in the formulation of model systems. Many qualitative aspects of behaviour can be reduced to sets of rules or heuristics that define constraints, opportunities and interactions (Pendyala et al., 1998; Arentze and Timmermans, 2004). For example, a personal vehicle cannot be abandoned on a tour, a child must be transported between locations by an adult and an individual cannot visit an establishment when it is closed. Similarly, transit must be available for an individual to access a destination using that mode. Many household, situational, modal, institutional and time–space constraints can be represented by a set of rules and heuristics that, in turn, can be programmed into activity-based model systems (Pendyala et al., 1998). These rules and heuristics can be identified through logic and through data collected using qualitative survey methods that shed light on behavioural processes. Rules and heuristics can govern how activity agendas are formed, activity schedules are modified and conflicts are resolved. There have been considerable advances in understanding qualitative aspects of behaviour and identifying rules and heuristics that represent these aspects of behaviour.

More recently, there has been considerable interest in the use of Bayesian approaches for modelling complex activity–travel patterns (Janssens et al., 2005). Bayesian networks offer the ability to represent complex decision processes and develop a set of rules that govern activity schedule formation. Bayesian networks have been found to perform better than traditional decision tree methods in identifying patterns of activity behaviour. Bayesian approaches can be used to model how individuals update their perceptions of activities and travel based on prior experience. These approaches appear to be promising directions in modelling complex activity–travel demand while simultaneously maximizing the utilization of a priori information. Machine learning algorithms and artificial intelligence approaches such as neural network modelling have also been applied in the context of activity–travel demand analysis (Pendyala et al., 1998). These methods are capable of representing and replicating complex relationships among activity and travel variables; however, their use and application has been limited by the inability of these models to provide parameter estimates with intuitive behavioural interpretation and the overall challenge of using these models in application contexts. Finally, in an attempt to relax the rigid distributional assumptions associated with traditional econometric modelling formulations, semi-parametric and non-parametric approaches are being explored for their applicability to activity–travel demand modelling (Fosgerau, 2006). Finally, multilevel modelling approaches (Goulias, 2002) and latent segmentation approaches (Waddell et al., 2007) have also proven useful in the context of analysing behavioural processes and foundations to various choice phenomena.

Policy and Planning Applications of Activity Analysis

The major motivating factor behind the surge in activity-based analysis is the ability of activity-based approaches to offer robust behavioural frameworks for policy analysis and planning studies. There are a number of policy considerations that directly lend themselves to the activity-based paradigm of travel behaviour. This section highlights several application areas where activity-based analysis approaches have been or are likely to be used.

As mentioned earlier, one of the key elements of an activity-based approach is the explicit recognition of time–space prism constraints. The use of time–space prisms allows one to account for the potential induced travel effects of capacity expansion (Noland, 2001). When capacity expansion projects are undertaken, speed of travel improves and time–space prisms are likely to expand. The expanded time–space prisms allow individuals to pursue additional activities without violating the boundaries of the prism. These additional activities constitute induced travel. Similarly, one can deal with the issue of suppressed travel, that is travel that is forgone as a result of worsening transportation supply conditions and the consequent shrinkage of the time–space prism.

There has been considerable interest in the recent past on the influence of the built environment on residential location choice and engagement in physically active travel and activity episodes (Mokhtarian and Cao, 2008; Handy et al., 2005). Concerns have been expressed that the design of the transportation system, particularly in the United States, has promoted a sedentary auto-dominated lifestyle where one must drive or ride in a vehicle for even short trips. Activity-based analysis of travel demand offers the ability to analyse the influence of built environment attributes on travel choices and physically active recreational episode participation, while accounting for residential self-selection whereby households may choose to locate in neighbourhoods that match their lifestyle preferences with regard to walking, bicycling, exercising and transit use (Pinjari et al., 2008).

Modern technology has and continues to transform the way people work, travel, shop, conduct personal business and engage in social communication and recreation (Mokhtarian, 2002). Mobile technology, e-commerce and other technology applications (intelligent transportation systems) have made it possible for individuals to substitute many out-of-home activities with easy online activities. Telecommuting, teleshopping, telebanking and other electronic means of conducting business are just a few of the examples where traditional travel can be replaced by electronic means of communication. However, telecommunications use can also lead to additional travel (complementary relationship) or can influence the nature of travel patterns (transformative relationship). Technology allows impromptu scheduling of activities and trips, and model systems need to be able to accommodate such occurrences. Activity-based analysis approaches have been used to understand the interactions between telecommunications and travel by examining time use and participation rates in different types of activities (Ye et al., 2007a). In general, it appears that telecommunication fosters both substitution and complementary effects in activity engagement.

One of the major thrusts of transportation planning in recent years has been the development of systems to respond quickly and effectively in the event of a major catastrophe such as Hurricane Katrina and the 9/11 terrorist attacks. Emergency-response planning requires knowledge of the locations of people by time of day (Jha et al., 2004). An accurate knowledge of people's locations by time of day will allow the development of effective evacuation plans, route diversion and closure strategies, and emergency service and goods delivery. Activity-based analysis approaches have been used to develop strategies for emergency response, identify vulnerable pieces of the transportation network and prepare evacuation plans (Henson and Goulias, 2006). GIS tools are used to plot thematic maps showing the density of individuals across space along the continuous time axis.

There is increasing recognition that capacity expansion is not the sole solution to transportation problems such as congestion and greenhouse gas emissions. Travel demand management strategies and transportation control measures must be implemented together with modal investments to better manage and control growth in travel demand. These strategies may include telecommuting and flexible work hours, congestion pricing that varies by time of day according to the congestion level, carpool lanes, high-occupancy toll lanes, parking pricing, promotion of mixed land use developments, and provision of transit- and pedestrian-oriented developments. All of these strategies impact the entire daily activity–travel pattern of multiple individuals in a household. Not only does one need to consider the primary impact of the strategy, but one must also consider the secondary and tertiary impacts of the strategy on the entire activity–travel pattern of the individual and other individuals in the household or workplace that the individual interacts with (Pendyala et al., 1997, 1998; Garling et al., 2002). Activity-based approaches offer a rigorous conceptual framework for analysing behavioural response to a range of policies because of their sensitivity to a range of policy variables and because of their explicit recognition of interactions among objects—thus capturing the secondary and tertiary impacts associated with policy implementation (Kitamura et al., 1997b). Activity-based approaches consider how activity schedules and agendas may be modified by individuals in order to effectively respond to a policy intervention.

Individuals often travel to engage in social interaction. The size and nature of an individual's social network will influence his or her activity–travel patterns. There has been considerable interest in the recent past to characterize and describe the nature of an individual's social network with the idea that such knowledge will shed additional light on explaining the manifested activity–travel patterns (Larsen et al., 2006; Axhausen, 2007). There is also considerable concern about social exclusion where certain market segments face a higher likelihood of not being able to engage in social interaction due to limited ability to use the transportation system (Schonfelder and Axhausen, 2003). Activity-based approaches offer the ability to analyse social interactions and networks, or the lack thereof. Social networks are also becoming increasingly fuzzy with modern technology that allows one to communicate and interact with individuals around the world using Internet tools and software that focus on social networking sites. Older individuals and those without cars and living in low-income households are likely to face social exclusion if they are not able to engage in or access activities; by comparing activity–travel patterns between these market segments and other market segments, it is possible to determine the extent of social exclusion that may exist. Environmental justice issues and social equity analysis can also be done using activity-based approaches that focus on activity engagement patterns.

One of the key advantages of the activity-based approach is its close connection with the notion of time use. Activity participation rates and time-use allocation measures offer the potential to study quality of life for various market segments in different locations (Kitamura et al., 1997b; Pendyala et al., 2007; Pendyala, 2003). If one were to consider discretionary activity engagement as a desirable activity, then it may be conjectured that individuals who are able to engage in more discretionary activities (both in frequency and duration) have a higher quality of life. Using activity and time-use data reported in household travel surveys, it is possible to develop time-use utility measures or profiles that shed light on the quality of life of individuals. These time-use utility measures can be used to determine the extent to which a policy intervention adversely or positively impacts an individual's quality of life. The time-use utility measures can be used to assess the quality of life of different market segments and develop strategies that would further enhance people's quality of life. Recent work in this arena has examined the differences in quality-of-life measures (time-use utilities) across market segments defined by gender, working status, income level and presence of children (Pendyala et al., 2007). The ability to assess quality of life that is provided by a built environment and transportation system also lends itself to analysis of urban sustainability. The design of the transportation network should be such that quality of life can be sustained even in the presence of shocks, incremental growth in population and natural or artificial perturbations. The activity-based approach to travel analysis therefore offers much potential in identifying sustainable and resilient development patterns and transportation system configurations.

Finally, activity-based approaches to travel analysis are slowly but surely finding their way into mainstream travel demand forecasting and planning studies. Tour-based model systems, that represent a half-way point between a traditional four-step travel model and a full-fledged activity-based travel model, are being increasingly implemented in urban areas around the world (Vovsha et al., 2005). These model systems are computationally tractable and have some of the desirable features associated with activity-based models. These model systems are being integrated with land-use microsimulation models, incorporate population synthesizers and provide outputs that can be used with static or dynamic traffic assignment techniques. The model systems are being used to develop long-range transportation plans and analyse major infrastructure projects such as new light rail projects and other large-scale modal investments. In addition, these model systems are being used to analyse the potential impacts of ITS and pricing-based strategies for managing travel demand.

Although the above discussion points to the increasing application of activity-based approaches in the policy and planning arena, it is clear that activity-based policy analysis remains in its infancy. The applications of activity-based approaches in real-world policy and planning contexts remain few and far between. Most of the policy simulations involving activity-based approaches have appeared in the research literature where the viability of activity-based approaches for answering a certain policy question is being explored (Pendyala et al., 1997). As additional metropolitan areas adopt activity-based approaches for travel analysis, it is likely that further mainstream applications of these approaches will take place.

Challenges and Future Prospects

The previous section has highlighted several areas in which activity-based approaches have seen major progress in the recent past. Indeed, over the past several years, the insights gained into behavioural foundations of human activity–travel choices, the methodological advances made in econometric formulations, and the additional evidence in the policy and planning arena, suggest that activity-based approaches are here to stay and hold great promise for the future. The question is no longer 'if' activity-based approaches will be adopted, but a question of 'when' and 'how fast' will activity-based approaches be adopted. In conjunction with advances in GPS-based data collection methods and time-use survey design and administration, the profession now has the data necessary to analyse, model and understand behavioural processes underlying the formation of human activity and travel patterns. This, however, does not mean that challenges do not remain. This section aims to identify a series of challenges and unanswered questions that, if addressed, would no longer inhibit the advancement of activity-based approaches in mainstream planning practice.

Knowledge of Behavioural Paradigms

There is no doubt that much has been learned about activity and travel behaviour over the past few decades. The previous section and the literature cited in this paper serve as evidence of the advances made in understanding behavioural theories that constitute the foundation of activity–travel demand. Although much has been learnt, there is much yet to be learned as well. Although there is ample evidence on the role of attitudes and preferences in shaping location choices and activity–travel behaviour, little has been achieved in terms of actually incorporating such variables into activity–travel demand model systems. The collection of such information remains a challenge; more importantly, forecasting such variables into the future in a planning context remains a greater challenge. It is clear that traditional socio-economic and demographic variables are playing an increasingly smaller role in explaining changes in activity–travel behaviour over time. Lifestyle packages are chosen by households and individuals based on their attitudes, values, perceptions, preferences and experiences. Behavioural responses to policies are likely to be shaped substantially by these types of variables. Despite the clear recognition of their significance, behavioural researchers have dismissed the use of such variables under the pretext that such information is difficult to collect and variables are impossible to forecast.

The formation and dissolution of social networks, particularly in today's information age, are not well understood. Although much work has been done in analysing intra-household interactions, virtually no work has been done to understand inter-household and inter-person (outside household) interactions. There has been recent attention paid to the understanding of the formation and extent of social networks; however, much work remains to be done in this arena. This has important implications for activity–travel behaviour analysis as many trips involve interactions among entities that do not belong to the same household or workplace. Even carpool formation and dissolution may often involve individuals from different households (but with other common attributes) coordinating or interacting with one another.

The role of information and communication technologies (ICT) in shaping activity–travel patterns and social networks has been of much interest to the profession. However, detailed data about ICT use and its role in shaping activity–travel patterns is rarely collected. Technology has become so ubiquitous that its influence on activity–travel behaviour needs to be incorporated in mainstream models of travel demand. Activities are scheduled and eliminated on the fly using mobile technology.

There needs to be a continued focus on understanding the jointness of activity–travel choices and behavioural decision processes or causal mechanisms that drive travel demand. Most activity-based model systems are implicitly assuming certain causal decision mechanisms and decision hierarchies without considering the possibility that there may be multiple decision hierarchies present in the same population (population heterogeneity) and that the decision structures may be completely misspecified. Additional focus group and intensive data collection efforts need to be undertaken to obtain insights into the decision hierarchies that would best describe the processes in play.

Finally, many metropolitan areas express the inability to transition to activity-based approaches because they do not have the resources to collect data and implement model systems based on locally collected data. It would be useful to undertake studies of spatial transferability of activity–travel data and activity–travel model systems to help facilitate the wider adoption of activity-based approaches to travel forecasting.

Understanding and Modelling Dynamics

Activity–travel behaviour is dynamic in nature. Activity–travel patterns change from one period to the next, regardless of whether one considers a period to be a day, a month or a year. Virtually all activity-based model systems focus on simulating activity–travel patterns for a single day or 24-hour period and all models are inevitably based on cross-sectional data sets. Although there are a few examples of panel or repeated cross-sectional data sets being collected in various jurisdictions (e.g. Dutch National Mobility Panel of the 1980s, the Puget Sound Transportation Panel of the 1990s), there is virtually no example of a dynamic model of travel demand being developed in practice. There are examples of dynamic models (based on panel data or repeated cross-sectional data) in the research literature, but very little has been done to move these models to mainstream practice.

Studies of temporal transferability would help understand the stability and change in activity–travel patterns over time. The fixation with the 24-hour period needs to be shed as activity–travel patterns are characterized by history dependency, intra-person and inter-person variability, and feedback loops over time. Unfortunately, most activity–travel survey data sets collect information for just 1 or 2 days, providing virtually no ability to consider day-to-day or week-to-week dynamics and inter-dependencies in activity–travel demand. More importantly, the absence of repeated cross-sectional data and panel data has forced the profession to use static model systems for forecasting over time. It is time to move towards the collection of longitudinal data sets that would allow the explicit modelling of "change" in activity–travel patterns over time.

Unified Theory of Time and Resource Consumption

Much of activity-based analysis has focused on the notions of time and space and time–space interactions/constraints. Time-use research has played a central role in activity-based analysis as researchers have strived to understand time allocation to activity episodes and types. While the consumption of time has been studied extensively, very little attention has been paid to monetary expenditures. Travel time and activity duration expenditures constitute one major component of activity engagement. However, monetary expenditures also constitute an important component of activity engagement as they serve as indicators of the quality of an activity, the utility derived from an activity and the ability of an individual to afford to participate in an activity for a certain duration of time. Including variables that capture income and cost effects constitutes a first step in accounting for monetary aspects of activity engagement and travel behaviour. However, it is not sufficient as these variables give very little indication of the monetary expenditure at the activity location that goes together with the time expenditure. A unified theory of time and money expenditures in the context of activity engagement, based on sound behavioural paradigms, is needed to analyse environmental justice issues, quality of life and sustainability. Initial efforts at developing such unified theories appear promising and can shed considerable light on quality-of-life issues. However, the paucity of monetary expenditure data (collected in conjunction with activity–travel data) makes the development of such unified model systems extremely challenging.

Addressing Data Needs

Travel surveys are increasingly being designed to serve as activity surveys wherein all information about out-of-home activities is collected in a detailed manner. These surveys are becoming commonplace in metropolitan areas around the world. However, the travel behaviour field has not yet fully embraced the collection of time-use information that is often collected in time-use surveys. Those surveys collect detailed information about in-home time-use and activity patterns and offer the ability to understand and model interactions between in-home and out-of-home activities and among persons in a household with respect to in-home and out-of-home task allocation and joint activity engagement. Time-use survey design and administration is a mature field and there should be little difficulty in adapting time-use survey designs in the travel survey arena. This has already been done with considerable success in a few contexts and the time is ripe to make this a widespread practice in the field.

As mentioned earlier, the profession needs additional data about dynamics and variability in activity–travel patterns. This means that data would have to be collected for periods far exceeding a 24- or 48-hour period and that data would have to be collected repeatedly at different points in time. Respondent burden is an issue associated with collecting activity–travel data for longer periods of time and this is where GPS- and other technology-based methods can be brought to bear to minimize respondent burden. GPS-based technologies can offer rich data about route choices and spatio-temporal action spaces as well. They provide precise location information without the need for cumbersome geocoding procedures. Longitudinal data collection efforts, such as panel surveys, should be incorporated into planning processes so that jurisdictions can measure and model change over time as a function of changes in system characteristics.

Finally, secondary data needs to be collected and integrated with activity–travel survey data sets to provide the ability to undertake comprehensive activity-based model development and activity-based policy analysis. Data about technology availability and use would allow the analysis of ICT and travel interactions. Data about monetary expenditures would provide the ability to analyse consumption of time and money in a unified framework. Data about health and nutrition would allow the analysis of the health impacts of activity–travel patterns. Detailed parcel-level land use and transportation network supply data would allow the integrated modelling of land use and transportation demand and supply in an appropriate microsimulation framework. Qualitative data sets (based on focus groups and in-depth surveys) would provide the ability to design quantitative studies, specify model systems based on sound knowledge of behavioural processes and interactions/constraints, and understand the role of attitudes and preferences in shaping behavioural response to policies.

Integrated Modelling of the Choice Continuum

Activity-based analysis of travel demand has generally focused on the generation and scheduling of activities, location choices for activities, linking or chaining of activities, timing and duration of activities, and the modes of transportation used to travel to and fro activities. Activity-based analysis has done very little in terms of linking these aspects of travel to route choice and transportation network characteristics. In other words, activity-based analysis has focused on the demand side of activity–travel behaviour and paid very little attention to the supply side of activity–travel demand. Transportation network modellers have been working on the development of dynamic traffic assignment models that recognize the nature of time-varying networks and dynamic route choice behaviour of individuals. Unfortunately, although activity-based model systems offer individual activity–travel records as outputs that dovetail perfectly into dynamic traffic assignment models, there has been little success in the integration of demand- and supply-side model systems. These two streams of research and development activities have largely remained in their respective domains.

A similar situation is encountered in the context of land-use microsimulation models. Land-use microsimulation models have focused on residential location and business location choice modelling by examining economic processes underlying land and property transactions, household and business location choices, and zoning and regulatory processes. Thus, an integration of the three domains of urban systems modelling needs to take place. Land-use microsimulation systems, activity-based microsimulation model systems and dynamic traffic microsimulation model systems need to be integrated to present a true model of the urban continuum—from long-term choices to short-term choices. Recent attempts at integrating these model systems have been promising, although there are a range of unresolved issues in accomplishing a seamless integration. Appropriate feedback loops need to be incorporated to recognize the inter-relationships among these three entities. More importantly, the spatial and temporal resolution and the nature of the behavioural unit tend to differ across these three model enterprises. While dynamic traffic assignment models deal with network links and nodes and movements on a second-by-second basis, land-use microsimulation models deal with parcels and location decisions that occur over much longer periods of time (usually in years). Appropriate protocols and methods need to be developed to resolve these inconsistencies across model architectures.

Software Architecture and Computational Performance

Activity-based microsimulation model systems are computationally intensive. In microsimulation model systems, one is usually starting the process with the generation of a synthetic population of households and individuals within households. The generation of a synthetic population is itself an iterative process that requires one to generate households and persons such that population distributions of several attributes are matched simultaneously. Then, activity-based model systems involve the microsimulation of activity–travel patterns and location choices for all individuals and households in the synthetic population. Usually, one run of the microsimulation model systems offers one realization of the stochastic process underlying the microsimulation. It is necessary to run the model system many times to achieve stability in the results of the simulation. Added to this is the need to undertake feedback; information from the transportation supply or network model needs to be fed back to the land-use microsimulation model as accessibility measures influence land-use development patterns. Network supply measures need to be fed back into the activity-based microsimulation model system as well because congestion or unexpected travel delays may change the activity schedule/agenda, trip chaining pattern and destination choices. So, not only does the entire model system have to be run multiple times, but each run involves multiple iterations involving feedback loops and mechanisms.

First, it is necessary to make sure that the profession clearly defines the terminology associated with activity-based model systems. What constitutes a run, an iteration and a feedback loop? How many iterations are needed to achieve convergence in any single model run? What are convergence criteria and how is convergence defined? How many model runs are needed to achieve stability in model outputs? What constitutes stability in model outputs? Then, once these terms are clearly defined, then it should be necessary to report computational performance for each of these items in the context of activity-based model systems. With a clear definition of these terms and clear documentation about the structure and performance of activity-based model systems, one can determine how to apply model systems in different contexts. Advances in computational power and parallel computing are likely to result in enhanced computational performance in the future; yet, the profession needs to document computational statistics in a detailed and transparent manner and every effort must be made to introduce computational efficiency in algorithms.

Moving Away from Focus on Personal Vehicle

One of the challenges associated with a microsimulation model system is the desire to simulate movements of individual persons on multimodal transportation networks.

Progress is being made in performing such multimodal simulations of person activities and trips, yet most activity-based model systems remain oriented towards simulation of vehicular movements. The activity-based model systems start with simulating household and personal activity agendas, but then transition to vehicle trip simulation somewhere in the model chain or process. This limits the ability to perform true multimodal systems analysis and to microsimulate individuals through the networks.

In a microsimulation-based framework, it is possible to move away from the traditional focus on the vehicle. Activity-based model systems should focus on the microsimulation of individuals and their activity–travel patterns in multimodal networks. By focusing on individuals (as opposed to vehicles), one can trace people walking, bicycling, getting on and off buses and other transit vehicles, and accessing locations where vehicles may be parked off-site. There is an increasing interest in the use of microsimulation model systems to understand transit usage patterns, non-motorized transportation, and physical activity and healthy lifestyles. The spatial, temporal and network resolution must be enhanced to facilitate the microsimulation of pedestrian movements along the continuous time axis.

Proof of Concept in Application (Policy) Contexts

As mentioned in the previous section of this paper, there are many application contexts where activity-based model systems offer unique advantages over traditional trip-based approaches to travel forecasting. What has been lacking is the systematic comparison of four-step trip-based model systems and activity-based model systems in different application and policy contexts. A series of studies must be undertaken to perform rigorous comparisons of model systems whereby one can examine the policy indications provided by trip-based model systems, tour-based model systems and activity–time-use-based model systems. Pricing strategies, flexible work hours and telecommuting strategies, carpool and transit incentives, bicycle- and pedestrian-oriented development strategies, and other travel demand management initiatives constitute a range of transportation policy options against which model systems can be compared and evaluated with respect to the reasonableness of predictions. Activity-based model systems should be used to address environmental justice issues, measure quality of life under a variety of scenarios and measure sustainability and global climate change impacts of alternative development patterns. Such systematic comparisons would provide valuable information on the appropriateness of using different model systems in different application contexts.

As activity-based model systems become increasingly adopted in metropolitan areas, it is likely that these model systems will be used for long-range forecasting, transportation planning studies and modal investment analysis. These studies need to be carefully documented so that the profession can learn from these experiences and enhance future implementations of activity-based model systems. Unfortunately, in the absence of a plethora of real-world applications of activity-based model systems, many jurisdictions remain hesitant to transition to the new model systems. In many areas, existing model systems provide forecasts that meet federal regulatory requirements with respect to air quality and there is a natural hesitation to transition to a new model system that may not meet the regulatory requirements. For this reason, systematic and rigorous comparisons of model outputs need to be made and documented so that metropolitan areas have the information necessary to make a successful transition. Regulatory agencies should encourage the transition to new tools in recognition of the capabilities offered by activity-based model systems.

Validation and Assessment of Activity-Based Model Systems

In connection with the point made above regarding proof of concept of activity-based model systems, additional attention needs to be paid to the validation and assessment of activity-based model systems. Traditional trip-based model systems are often validated with respect to field traffic counts. At a minimum, one would expect activity-based model systems to be also validated to field traffic counts. Presumably, activity-based model systems should be able to replicate ground counts with less adjustment and use of calibration factors than in the case of trip-based models. This is because activity-based models capture the interactions and constraints that are prevalent in activity–travel behaviour while trip-based approaches do not account for such phenomena. Validation criteria need to be established for activity-based model systems. It is not clear if the same criteria used for trip-based model systems would be applicable for activity-based model systems as well.

However, it is not sufficient to stop at replicating ground counts. In general, it is theoretically possible to replicate ground counts using any model system if the model is sufficiently calibrated and adjusted. What is necessary is a comprehensive evaluation and assessment of the sensitivity and policy capabilities of the activity-based model system. Any activity-based model should be subjected to a series of tests where the sensitivity of the model system is evaluated with respect to changes in population, land use and transportation system characteristics. The policy capabilities of the model need to be examined by introducing a range of travel demand management strategies or transportation control measures and changing the inputs that would be affected by these initiatives. The elasticity estimates and travel demand response predictions offered by the activity-based model system need to be assessed for their reasonableness and, where feasible, compared using real-world data where interventions or changes of a similar magnitude may have occurred.

Accounting for Key Drivers of Activity–Travel Demand

One of the points made earlier in the paper is that travel time expenditures and out-of-home activity engagement frequencies have been consistently increasing in many countries around the world. It has been found that traditional demographic and socio-economic factors are not able to adequately explain the changes in travel demand that are being observed. It appears that the profession is missing some of the key drivers of travel demand related to the transition of lifestyles and economies in many societies. The adoption of technology has made it possible for individuals to undertake virtual activities, use travel time productively, and schedule and plan activities on-the-fly. The outsourcing of many activities (lawn care, house cleaning, pool maintenance, dry cleaning, ready-to-eat meals, etc.) has provided additional discretionary time that can now be used to undertake additional activities and travel. Rising standards of living and the transition to knowledge- and service-based economies around the world have made it possible for people to be aware of opportunities for engaging in activities within their monetary budgets. However, travel demand model systems have continued to include only traditional socio-economic and demographic variables as explanatory factors of travel demand. Many of these key changes in societies are not adequately captured and not adequately measured in surveys of activity–travel demand. It would be prudent to collect data on phenomena of this nature and start attempting to include such factors in models of activity–travel demand. Otherwise, it appears that the profession is missing several key drivers of travel demand that are critical to forecasting.

In summary, the field of activity-based travel analysis has seen much progress and maturation over the past decade and the profession has made great strides in understanding and modelling activity–travel patterns in rigorous econometric and microsimulation frameworks. However, the transition of these approaches to practice has been limited and there are several challenges and opportunities associated with this transition that have been identified in this paper. It is believed that this list of challenges and prospects constitutes an ambitious research agenda for the field of activity-based travel analysis.

References

Anas, A. (2007). A unified theory of consumption, travel and trip chaining. *Journal of Urban Economics* 62, 162–186.

Arentze, T. A. and H. J. P. Timmermans (2004). A learning-based transportation oriented simulation system. *Transportation Research B* 38, 613–633.

Arentze, T. A. and H. J. P. Timmermans (2005). Representing mental maps and cognitive learning in micro-simulation models of activity–travel choice dynamics. *Transportation* 32, 321–340.

Axhausen, K. W. (2007). Activity spaces, biographies, social networks and their welfare gains and externalities: some hypotheses and empirical results. *Mobilities* 2, 15–36.

Axhausen, K. W. and T. Garling (1992). Activity-based approaches to travel analysis: conceptual frameworks, models, and research problems. *Transport Reviews* 12, 323–341.

Balmer, M., K. W. Axhausen and K. Nagel (2005). An agent based demand modeling framework for large scale micro-simulations. Working Paper 329, Institute for Transport Planning and Systems (IVT), ETH Zurich, Switzerland. Available at: http://matsim.org/uploads/ab329.pdf (accessed April 28, 2008).

Banerjee, A., X. Ye and R. M. Pendyala (2007). Understanding travel time expenditures around the world: exploring the notion of a travel time frontier. *Transportation* 34, 51–65.

Bhat, C. R. (1996). A hazard-based duration model of shopping activity with nonparametric baseline specification and nonparametric control for unobserved heterogeneity. *Transportation Research B* 30, 189–207.

Bhat, C. R. (1998). Accommodating flexible substitution patterns in multi-dimensional choice modeling: formulation and application to travel mode and departure time choice. *Transportation Research B* 32, 455–466.

Bhat, C. R. (2000). Incorporating observed and unobserved heterogeneity in urban work mode choice modeling. *Transportation Science* 34, 228–238.

Bhat, C. R. (2003). Simulation estimation of mixed discrete choice models using randomized and scrambled Halton sequences. *Transportation Research B* 37, 837–855.

Bhat, C. R. (2008). The multiple discrete continuous extreme value (MDCEV) model: role of utility function parameters, identification considerations, and model extensions. *Transportation Research B* 42, 274–303.

Bhat, C. R. and J. Y. Guo (2007). A comprehensive analysis of built environment characteristics on household residential choice and auto ownership levels. *Transportation Research B* 41, 506–526.

Bhat, C. R., J. Y. Guo, S. Srinivasan and A. Sivakumar (2004). Comprehensive econometric microsimulator for daily activity–travel patterns. *Transportation Research Record* 1894, 57–66.

Bhat, C. R. and F. S. Koppelman (1999). A retrospective and prospective survey of time use research. *Transportation* 26, 119–139.

Bhat, C. R. and R. M. Pendyala (2005). Modeling intra-household interactions and group decision-making. *Transportation* 32, 443–448.

Bhat, C. R. and S. Sen (2006). Household vehicle type holdings and usage: an application of the multiple discrete-continuous extreme value (MDCEV) model. *Transportation Research B* 40, 35–53.

Bowman, J. L. and M. E. Ben-Akiva (2001). Activity-based disaggregate travel demand model system with activity schedules. *Transportation Research A* 35, 1–28.

Chandrasekharan, B. and K. G. Goulias (1999). Exploratory longitudinal analysis of solo and joint trip making using the Puget Sound transportation panel. *Transportation Research Record* 1676, 77–85.

Chen, C., T. Garling and R. Kitamura (2004). Activity rescheduling: reasoned or habitual. *Transportation Research F* 7, 351–371.

Doherty, S. T. (2006). Should we abandon activity type analysis? Redefining activities by their salient attributes. *Transportation* 33, 517–536.

Doherty, S. T. and E. J. Miller (2000). A computerized household activity scheduling survey. *Transportation* 27, 75–97.

Ettema, D. F., A. Borgers and H. Timmermans (1996). SMASH (simulation model of activity scheduling heuristics): some simulations. *Transportation Research Record* 1551, 88–94.

Ettema, D. F., A. Borgers and H. J. P. Timmermans (1993). Simulation model of activity-scheduling behavior. *Transportation Research Record* 1413, 1–11.

Ettema, D. F. and H. J. P. Timmermans (Eds.) (1997). *Activity-Based Approaches to Travel Analysis*. London, UK, Pergamon.

Fosgerau, M. (2006). Investigating the distribution of the value of travel time savings. *Transportation Research B* 40, 688–707.

Garling, T., D. Eek, P. Loukopoulos, S. Fujii, O. Johansson-Stenman, R. Kitamura, R. M. Pendyala and B. Vilhelmson (2002). A conceptual analysis of the impact of travel demand management on private car use. *Transport Policy* 9, 59–70.

Garling, T., M.-P. Kwan and R. G. Golledge (1994). Computational-process modeling of household activity scheduling. *Transportation Research B* 28, 355–364.

Gliebe, J. P. and F. S. Koppelman (2002). A model of joint activity participation between household members. *Transportation* 29, 49–72.

Golob, T. F. (2000). A simultaneous model of household activity participation and trip chain generation. *Transportation Research B* 34, 355–376.

Golob, T. F. and M. McNally (1997). A model of activity participation and travel interactions between household heads. *Transportation Research B* 31, 177–194.

Goulias, K. G. (2002). Multilevel analysis of daily time use and time allocation to activity types accounting for complex covariance structures using correlated random effects. *Transportation* 29, 31–48.

Goulias, K. G. and K. M. Henson (2006). On altruists and egoists in activity participation and travel: who are they and do they live together? *Transportation* 33, 447–462.

Guo, J. Y. and C. R. Bhat (2007). Population synthesis for microsimulating travel behavior. *Transportation Research Record* 2014, 92–101.

Hagerstrand, T. (1970). What about people in regional science? *Papers in Regional Science* 24, 6–21.

Handy, S., X. Cao and P. L. Mokhtarian (2005). Correlation or causality between the built environment and travel behavior? Evidence from Northern California. *Transportation Research D* 10, 427–444.

Hensher, D. and W. H. Greene (2003). The mixed logit model: the state of practice. *Transportation* 30(2), 133–176.

Hensher, D. A. and W. H. Greene (2000). The mixed logit model: the state of practice. *Transportation* 30, 133–176.

Hensher, D. A. and F. L. Mannering (1994). Hazard-based duration models and their application to transport analysis. *Transport Reviews* 14, 63–82.

Henson, K. M. and K. G. Goulias (2006). Preliminary assessment of activity analysis and modeling for homeland security applications. *Transportation Research Record* 1942, 23–30.

Hess, S., K. E. Train and J. W. Polak (2006). On the use of a modified Latin hypercube sampling (MLHS) method in the estimation of a mixed logit model for vehicle choice. *Transportation Research B* 40, 147–163.

Janssens, D., G. Wets, T. Brijs, K. Vanhoof, T. Arentze and H. J. P. Timmermans (2005). Integrating Bayesian networks and decision trees in a sequential rule-based transportation model. *European Journal of Operational Research* 175, 16–34.

Jha, M., K. Moore and B. Pashaie (2004). Emergency evacuation planning with microscopic traffic simulation. *Transportation Research Record* 1886, 40–48.

Joh, C.-H., S. T. Doherty and J. W. Polak (2005). Analysis of factors affecting the frequency and type of activity schedule modification. *Transportation Research Record* 1926, 19–25.

Kang, H. and D. M. Scott (2008). An integrated spatio-temporal GIS toolkit for exploring intra-household interactions. *Transportation* 35, 253–268.

Kitamura, R. (1984). Incorporating trip chaining into analysis of destination choice. *Transportation Research B* 18, 67–81.

Kitamura, R. (1988). An evaluation of activity-based travel analysis. *Transportation* 15, 9–34.

Kitamura, R., C. Chen, R. M. Pendyala and R. Narayanan (2000). Microsimulation of daily activity–travel patterns for travel demand forecasting. *Transportation* 27, 25–51.

Kitamura, R., C. Chen and R. M. Pendyala (1997a). Generation of synthetic daily activity–travel patterns. *Transportation Research Record* 1607, 154–162.

Kitamura, R., S. Fujii and E. I. Pas (1997b). Time-use data, analysis, and modeling: toward the next generation of transportation planning methodologies. *Transport Policy* 4, 225–235.

Kitamura, R., P. L. Mokhtarian and L. Laidet (1997c). A micro-analysis of land use and travel in five neighborhoods in the San Francisco Bay Area. *Transportation* 24, 125–158.

Kuppam, A. R. and R. M. Pendyala (2001). A structural equations analysis of commuters' activity and travel patterns. *Transportation* 28, 33–54.

Kuppam, A. R., R. M. Pendyala and S. Rahman (1999). Analysis of the role of traveler attitudes and perceptions in explaining mode choice behavior. *Transportation Research Record* 1676, 68–76.

Kwan, M.-P. (2000). Interactive geovisualization of activity–travel patterns using three-dimensional geographical information systems: a methodological exploration with a large data set. *Transportation Research C* 8, 1–6.

Larsen, J., K. W. Axhausen and J. Urry (2006). Geographies of social networks: meetings, travel and communications. *Mobilities* 1, 261–283.

Lu, X. and E. I. Pas (1999). Socio-demographics, activity participation and travel behavior. *Transportation Research A* 33, 1–18.

Miller, H. J. (2005). A measurement theory for time geography. *Geographical Analysis* 37, 17–45.

Miller, E. J. and M. J. Roorda (2003). Prototype model of household activity–travel scheduling. *Transportation Research Record* 1831, 114–121.

Mohammadian, A. and S. T. Doherty (2005). Mixed logit model of activity scheduling time horizon incorporating spatial-temporal flexibility variables. *Transportation Research Record* 1926, 33–40.

Mokhtarian, P. L. (2002). Telecommunications and travel: the case for complementarity. *Journal of Industrial Ecology* 6, 43–57.

Mokhtarian, P. L. and X. Cao (2008). Examining the impacts of residential self-selection on travel behavior: a focus on methodologies. *Transportation Research B* 42, 204–228.

Noland, R. B. (2001). Relationships between highway capacity and induced vehicle travel. *Transportation Research A* 35, 47–72.

Pendyala, R. M. (2003). Time use and travel behavior in space and time. In K. G. Goulias (Ed.), *Transportation Systems Planning: Methods and Applications*, New York, CRC Press, pp. 2-1–2-37.

Pendyala, R. M. and C. R. Bhat (2004). An exploration of the relationship between timing and duration of maintenance activities. *Transportation* 31, 429–456.

Pendyala, R. M. and R. Kitamura (2007). The rapid motorization of Asia: implications for the future. *Transportation* 34, 275–279.

Pendyala, R. M., R. Kitamura, C. Chen and E. I. Pas (1997). An activity-based microsimulation analysis of transportation control measures. *Transport Policy* 4, 183–192.

Pendyala, R. M., R. Kitamura, A. Kikuchi, T. Yamamoto and S. Fujii (2005). Florida activity mobility simulator: overview and preliminary validation results. *Transportation Research Record* 1921, 123–130.

Pendyala, R. M., R. Kitamura and D. V. G. P. Reddy (1998). Application of an activity-based travel demand model incorporating a rule-based algorithm. *Environment and Planning B* 25, 753–772.

Pendyala, R. M., T. Yamamoto and R. Kitamura (2002). On the formulation of time–space prisms to model constraints on personal activity–travel engagement. *Transportation* 29, 73–94.

Pendyala, R. M. and X. Ye (2005). Contribution to understanding joint relationships among activity and travel variables. In H. J. P. Timmermans (Ed.), *Progress in Activity-Based Analysis*, Vol. 1–24. Amsterdam, The Netherlands, Elsevier.

Pendyala, R. M., X. Ye and K. Konduri (2007). Time use, constraints, and quality of life of women: making the connection. Paper presented at *the 2007 Annual Meeting of the International Association for Time Use Research*, Washington, DC, October.

Petersen, E. and P. Vovsha (2006). Intrahousehold car-type choice for different travel needs. *Transportation Research Record* 1985, 207–219.

Pinjari, A. R., R. M. Pendyala, C. R. Bhat and P. A. Waddell (2007). Modeling residential sorting effects to understand the impact of the built environment on commute mode choice. *Transportation* 34, 557–573.

Pinjari, A. R., R. M. Pendyala, C. R. Bhat and P. A. Waddell (2008). Modeling the choice continuum: an integrated model of residential location, auto ownership, bicycle ownership, and commute tour mode choice decisions. Working Paper, Department of Civil, Architectural, and Environmental Engineering, University of Texas, Austin, TX. Available at: http://www.ce.utexas.edu/prof/bhat/ABSTRACTS/Clean_Revised_MultidimIntegratedChoiceModel_May7.pdf (accessed May 7, 2008).

Redmond, L. S. and P. L. Mokhtarian (2001). The positive utility of the commute: modeling ideal commute time and relative desired commute amount. *Transportation* 28, 179–205.

Ruiz, T., J. W. Polak and C.-H. Joh (2005). Empirical analysis of factors affecting the resolution of activity-scheduling conflicts. *Transportation Research Record* 1926, 50–60.

Salvini, P. and E. J. Miller (2005). ILUTE: an operational prototype of a comprehensive microsimulation model of urban systems. *Networks and Spatial Economics* 5, 217–234.

Schonfelder, S. and K. W. Axhausen (2003). Activity spaces: measures of social exclusion? *Transport Policy* 10, 273–286.

Srinivasan, K. K. and H. S. Mahmassani (2003). Analyzing heterogeneity and unobserved structural effects in route-switching behavior under ATIS: a dynamic kernel logit formulation. *Transportation Research B* 37, 793–814.

Timmermans, H. J. P. (Ed.). (2005). *Progress in Activity-Based Analysis*. Amsterdam, The Netherlands, Elsevier.

Toole-Holt, L., S. E. Polzin and R. M. Pendyala (2005). Two minutes per person per day each year: exploration of growth in travel time expenditures. *Transportation Research Record* 1917, 45–53.

Train, K. E. (2003). *Discrete Choice Methods with Simulation*. Cambridge, UK, Cambridge University Press.

Tringides, C. A., X. Ye and R. M. Pendyala (2004). Departure time choice and mode choice for non-work trips: alternative formulations of joint model systems. *Transportation Research Record* 1898, 1–9.

Venter, C. and M. Hansen (1998). Flexibility and time dependence in activity scheduling models. *Transportation Research Record* 1645, 120–126.

Vovsha, P., M. Bradley and J. L. Bowman (2005). Activity-based travel forecasting in the United States: progress since 1995 and prospects for the future. In H. J. P.

Timmermans (Ed.), *Progress in Activity-Based Analysis*, Amsterdam, The Netherlands, Elsevier, pp. 389–414.

Waddell, P. A. (2000). A behavioral simulation model for metropolitan policy analysis and planning: residential location and housing market components of UrbanSim. *Environment and Planning B* 27, 247–263.

Waddell, P. A., C. R. Bhat, N. Eluru, L. Wang and R. M. Pendyala (2007). Modeling interdependencies in household residence and workplace choices. *Transportation Research Record* 2003, 84–92.

Walker, J. (2002). Mixed logit (or logit kernel) model: dispelling misconceptions of identification. *Transportation Research Record* 1805, 86–98.

Wolf, J., R. Guensler and W. Bachman (2001). Elimination of the travel diary: experiment to derive trip purpose from global positioning system travel data. *Transportation Research Record* 1768, 125–134.

Ye, X., K. Konduri and R. M. Pendyala (2007a). A time use analysis of work, play, and other activities to assess the role of ICT in promoting sustainable mobility patterns. Paper presented at *the 2007 Annual Meeting of the International Association for Time Use Research*, Washington, DC, October.

Ye, X., R. M. Pendyala and G. Gottardi (2007b). An exploration of the relationship between mode choice and complexity of trip chaining patterns. *Transportation Research B* 41, 96–113.

Zhang, J., H. J. P. Timmermans and A. Borgers (2005). A model of household task allocation and time use. *Transportation Research B* 39, 81–95.

The Expanding Sphere of Travel Behaviour Research
Selected Papers from the 11th International Conference on Travel Behaviour Research

13

Synthesis Report for the Workshop for Advances in Activity Analysis—Approaches for Advanced Activity Analysis in Japan

Kuniaki Sasaki and Kazuo Nishii

Abstract

This chapter is to overview the activity analysis in today's Japan. It focuses on three aspects. The first one is the progress in the technology to collect more precise and easier-to-answer data. The second one is the progress in formulating analytical models that help understand behavioral code along with the change of social circumstances. The last one is the progress of the simulation approach as a tool for policy evaluation. At the end, this chapter will discuss the perspective of this issue in future.

Introduction

The activity analysis has been mainly used to understand travel behavior. The assumption that travel stems from a demand to do something in other location plays an important role in understanding the travel behavior. The concept of prism constraints also helps understand travel behavior. For example, the concept explains the restraint by the availability of transportation. The capacity-constraints, the coupling-constraints and the authority-constraints are all the extensions of prism constraints. By now, researchers know well that the travel mode is largely related to these constraints, which ordinary trip surveys cannot provide. In contrast, the activity analysis has not been used effectively in the practical transportation planning. A lot of researches are now trying to demonstrate that it is easy to apply such analysis and is effective. This chapter shows some approaches and mentions their backgrounds, so that we categorize the current approaches of activity analysis from their features. The categorized approaches are activity data collecting, modeling of activity and application to transportation planning.

The Development of Technology to collect Activity Diary Data in Japan

This section focuses on the development of activity diary survey. One of the reasons why technology for this survey has developed is the decreasing responses to this type of surveys because of more burdens that the activity diary survey generally presents to respondents. Technological development was sought out to cope with such decline of responses. Another reason is the declining cost of using GPS and some related devices, for data collection, as the prevalence of GPS cell phone indicates. Our specific focus here is the development of survey using mobile phone and GPS. First, collecting individual geographical information adopted personal handy phone systems (PHS) (Asakura et al., 2000; Ohmori et al., 1999). Nowadays, most of the cell phones have not only GPS, but also acceleration, temperature, atmosphere and so on (Asakura et al., 2001; Hato et al., 2005). The data collected by those devices are an indirect measurement of the activity. The assumption in converting these data into activity data is that a certain activity takes place in specific environment and will indicate some data. So far, the data collected by those devices are used mainly to identify the route and mode of the trip. The algorithms to identify exact route have been studied for more than 10 years to apply for car navigation systems, and the travel mode can be detected from the route identification to some extent. Nonetheless, effective methods to identify the activity from the data from GPS and multiple sensors are still under development (Hato et al., 2005). In most cases, the precise activities are collected largely by questionnaire as the only available method. The survey normally uses the paper sheets or the Web-based diary system (Nakazato et al., 2004). Another problem is about the information security and the privacy of respondents, in addition to the cost of ICT-based survey (Arimura and Takano, 2000). The price for multiple sensor devices with GPS costs over $1,000 per device (as of year 2006), much higher than the cost of paper survey, though the price may drop in time. Because of these shortcomings of the technique we have so far, developing a technique for surveys which can get more information and analyze it is necessary (Ohmori, 2002). Nonetheless, we have not had such a technique because of the lack of definition by a behavioral model of relationship of multiple data. So far, what we have are the data mining and the advanced analysis of multiple-day data source (Axhausen et al., 2002).

Another issue over the collection of activity diary data is the on-line survey with Web technology (Ohmori et al., 2006), which became possible by the penetration of

Internet connection. Though this type of survey is basically the same as those in the other countries (e.g. Lee et al., 2000), the Japanese one is characterized by the popular cell phone usage to access Internet. Out of a total of 9 million, most of the cell phones provide Internet connection, making both activity diary survey and the positioning survey possible in one device (Endo et al., 2005). The activity diary survey via Internet is frequently used in mobility management experiment, because such survey makes the communication between a participant and an administrator of a survey easier than a paper-based questionnaire. In addition, it can differentiate information given to individuals in a travel feedback program (TFP) experiment (Endo et al., 2006; Daito et al., 2005), an advantage Internet survey in mobility management program can provide. Further, flexibility of the Internet survey yields more advantages just as a computer can do for any survey. For example, individual designing of questionnaires up to their response is possible without being recognized by the respondent (Kitagawa et al., 2006). Automatic coding and screening of data allows warning the respondents who answer inconsistently. The advantage of interactivity becomes more useful through its real-time nature if the survey is conducted through cell phone, because the respondents always have cell phone.

The innovation in collecting data can be a turning point, because it will allow missing activities which do not appear in the paper survey to be recorded and it will find such missing activities. A new analytical method should be developed to examine the abundant data from fewer respondents, that is, continuous and consecutive data from the same respondents. Although such an analysis is generally not used in Japan, except for before-and-after survey of new transportation facility (Nishii et al., 2004), analysis of data from multiple-day activity diary usually is simplified.

Several items are added to support activity analysis. One good example is information about a person accompanying the respondent, which is important to understand actual prism constraint of the activity. A series of the research by Zhang and Fujiwara (e.g. Zhang and Fujiwara, 2004; Zhang et al., 2005a) mentions the importance of interaction among the family members. Another item is the question about the intention of an activity, which is necessary to understand the activity allocation and to analyze the group behavior. Attitudinal indicator about lifestyle or the usage of intellectual tools is another supportive item (Nishii et al., 2002a). Social and technological changes bring about some items to support activity analysis. One of such changes is the diffusion of ICT tools that influence both communication and travel. They made it possible to do, say, shopping or meeting with other people on Internet or mobile phone network (Senbil and Kitamura, 2003; Sasaki et al., 2004a). The effect of ICT technology has been studied particularly for the telecommuters in travel behavior research (Mokhtarian, 1998). Recent diffusions of mobile and IP technology also change the social network and communication, which particularly affect joint activity (Sasaki et al., 2004a, b). As meaningful additional indicator of the activity analysis, there are some necessary cases to collect indexes of telecommunication. For example, the use of telecommunication is a meaningful item in analyzing social exclusion from activity analysis (Ohmori, 2004; Izumiyama et al., 2004).

The Approaches of Activity Diary Data Analysis in Japan

This chapter focuses on the three approaches to activity diary data analysis. The way to analyze the activity diary data is diverse because of their complexity. Which method should be taken depends on the purpose, the object or the expected output of analysis. Mainly, activity analysis has three approaches listed as follows (these are the same as worldwide stream):

1. microeconomic approach;
2. rule-based approach;
3. descriptive analysis approach.

Microeconomic approach is a general approach to analyze the activity. It is used mainly for the ordinary or developing discrete choice models to explain choices in daily activities. It has been applied to discrete choice model activity location choice a number of times. This microeconomic approach was used as the main formula to the development of Prism-Constrained Activity–Travel Simulator (PCATS; Yamamoto et al., 1999; Iida et al., 2000; Kitamura et al., 2005), as well as to departure time choice (Nishino et al., 1999; Iwakura et al., 2003) and activity pattern choice (Fujii et al., 1997). In addition, the activity pattern analysis, the time use analysis (Takao et al., 1998) and duration of activity (Yamamoto et al., 1999; Sasaki and Morikawa, 1997) have been using this approach. Since the joint activity analysis will be mentioned in the 'group behavior' workshop, this chapter will not mention much about it. Nonetheless, the group behavior analysis often uses the activity schedule and its adjusting process to apply their utility-maximizing theory (Zhang et al., 2005a, b). The group behavior analysis assumes group utility (Zhang et al., 2005a, b), and the recent development in the econometric models has made the formulation of the complex choice situation, such as joint decision making of activity type, location, scheduling and duration of activity, easier.

The second approach to activity analysis is rule-based approach. For three reasons, the number of the travel behavior modeling that use this approach has increased in the last decade. One of the reasons is the assumption that the discrete choice models are not really compatible with actual behavior. The view of bounded rationality (Simon, 1996) pointed out that both assumptions of the perfect information and the unlimited resource to optimize for each choice are too ideal. That is, the concept is to assume that decision makers follow a rule that minimizes resources for decision making, and, consequently that they do not make optimized decisions but satisfactory decisions. Developed along with the cognitive psychology and artificial intelligence technology, the rule-based approach can be a powerful tool to analyze activity data (Garling et al., 1989). Having no key theory like 'utility maximization', the approach is more analytical in dealing with a chain of activities. However, if it can replicate precisely the actual behavior or describe the choice probability of a behavior under certain conditions, this approach will be tremendously useful in understanding behaviors. This approach can also possibly find out a new behavioral code, as well as provide a useful alternative to the discrete choice model because the model is too complex in dealing with the multiple-day activity data. While the Western researchers have developed the rule-based approach and tested its validity (e.g. Arentze and Timmermans, 2002), few researches have been done in Japan and researches that try to find and define rules for this approach have just started. A research (Sasaki et al., 2005) calculates the probability by decomposing the activity chain into each activity choice and estimating the activity transfer from one to the other. Other researches adopt the neural network model to find the rules of activity chain (Kato et al., 2002). The selection of the relationship from the existing algorithms generally depends on the goodness-of-fit of real activity. The validity and stability of rules of this approach should be carefully examined in predicting activity changes. Some of the researches using this approach adopt data-mining method to find the rules (e.g. Sasaki et al., 2005). Generally, the volume of data is bigger than the ordinary trip data and the relationship among the data is more complicated than that. These features fit the thinking of data mining. The algorithms in these researches are the clustering of large-scale data, the neural network and the decision tree algorithm.

The third approach of activity diary data analysis is the statistical description approach. While some of the analyses that adopt this approach look similar to analyses based on the microeconomic approach, the assumption of a priori utility divided the two approaches. The statistical description approach mainly focuses on the correlation of activity and environments including prism constraints. This approach chooses models depending on the objectives of the analysis. It usually uses general statistical models such as ANOVA, cluster analysis and principle component analysis to understand activity (e.g. Nishii et al., 2002b). The approach is used to identify the correlation of one activity to the one whose behavioral code is unclear such as ICT. In analyzing the relationship between multivariate indicators and explanatory variables, the structural equation model is commonly used (Watanabe et al., 2002; Fujii and Kitamura, 2000). The structural equations model, a general model of statistical description approach, is common in analyzing the complex relationship among activity data.

Besides modeling the activity and travel, to evaluate transportation policies such as TDM, activity analysis can show some indicators other than travel demands. This approach, if adopted in transportation policies considering environmental improvement, encourages people to change some behaviors and lifestyle. To be successful in such an attempt, the data analysis must cover not only traffic volume, but also the changes in type, location and time of activities to evaluate the effect of the policy. In fact, several activity analyses have been done in Japan considering such a situation (Fujii et al., 1998; Hayashi et al., 2004; Zhang et al., 2005a, b; Yamane et al., 2006). Since the final goal of the transportation planning is the promotion of welfare of the citizens, the welfare of daily life ought to be measured by the daily activity and its psychological indicators which are based on psychological factors like satisfaction level and attitudes. Such an integration of psychological factors and activity is one of the important issues not developed enough in Japan.

Simulation Approach as Practical Applications of Activity Analysis in Transportation Planning in Japan

The transportation policies such as TDM and mobility management should be based on the detailed travel behavior data, because they can bring changes in not only where to go, but also what to do. These policies also require activity analyses of interdependency between trip and activity as well as between travelers. The models used in this forecasting system are generally individual-based microeconomic models or rule-based model mentioned in the section 'The Development of Technology to collect Activity Diary Data in Japan', because the transportation policy making must know how individuals behave in reducing CO_2 emission or in avoiding the peak hours. Activity simulation works well to meet these demands and has become the main evaluation tool for transportation policies (Vovsha et al., 2005; Bradley and Bowman, 2006). In Japan, Kitamura's work known as PCATS represents this method (e.g. Kitamura et al., 2005). This system is based not on activity data, but on trip diary data in simulating out-of-home activity. Introducing the prism constraint, this approach is expected to make the destination choice model more accurate, because the prism constraint can reduce the number of alternatives the destination choice has. The Kitamura's group created another simulator called PCATS-RUM (Fujii et al., 1998). While the PCATS assumes sequential activity decisions, PCATS-RUM assumes simultaneous decision making about time distribution of each activity.

Although no other activity simulator has been developed so far in Japan, we need to develop more in Japan, if the simulator is to be the major next generation tool for transportation planning. Such a simulation is not active in Japan mainly because the Japanese transportation authority has little will to use activity simulation to practical transportation planning. More complicated than trip-based approach, the simulation approach analysis has difficulty in being applied in practical. In spite of this difficulty, this approach must demonstrate its usefulness in replicating base year as well as its superiority to alternative approach (Pendyala and Bhat, 2006). Since using the anticipation of each activity as evaluation indicator is difficult (Sasaki et al., 2004a, b), we had better propose proper indicator to demonstrate the usefulness of activity simulation.

The so-called multiagent simulation, originally developed in the field of artificial intelligence science, and gaming simulation have been used in activity analysis to analyze interaction among agents (Nagal and Marchal, 2002; Rosald and Ronghui, 2005). In Japan, Ohmori et al. (2000) adopted gaming simulation with the prism constraints to analyze the aged people's travel activity. The main purpose of Ohmori's analysis is to grasp the aged people's mobility in terms of the prism constraints and interaction. This analysis provides insights about the whole society that cannot be understood through analyzing the behavior of one agent, because interactions among agents and between the environment and the agents sometimes produce an unimaginable happening in a society. This agent-based simulation is suitable for two conditions. One of them is when agents can be assumed to play the same in reality. The activity analysis fits better here than trip-based analysis. Another is when the agents are simplified to be a metaphor of the real world to be used to analyze a specific behavior. In this case, the agents are supposed to behave along with only a few behavioral codes.

How to integrate the land-use model and that of travels is a hot topic among the students/researchers of the travel behavior analysis (e.g. Miller and Salvini, 2001). Activity analysis gives a fertile insight to this theme. While simulation is generally a very useful way to integrate complicating models, no practical result of any simulation application to this theme has been reported in Japan so far.

Practical Issues of Activity Analysis in Japan

The issues of the research of activity analysis in Japan are to solve the problems we have pointed out in this chapter. They are: proposing data-oriented analysis method, developing the indicators of quality of life based on activity and psychological data, and the validating simulation. Although the technology of data acquisition and the data analysis method have been developing rapidly, the relation between them has not been conjunctive yet. When activity analysis becomes a standard tool of transportation planning, the activity analysis, indicators and data acquisition must be integrated to allow the practitioner to treat them easily. One must prove the usefulness of the simulation approach in spite of its complexity and massive size when it is based on the activity data to analyze the travel demand.

Recently the mobility management policies based on activity analysis have been introduced in Japan. These policies take into account the psychological analysis of the relationship between the change in attitude and that in activity. Some relationships, including the relationship between changes in multidimensional activity and those in multidimensional attitude, are not clear. If transportation planners have knowledge of this relationship, the mobility management policies would be more effective.

References

Arentze, T. A. and H. J. P. Timmermans (2002). *ALBATROSS: A Learning-based Transportation oriented Simulation System.* Eindhoven, EIRASS, Eindhoven University of Technology.

Arimura, M. and K. Takano (2000). A consideration of the traffic survey by using location information of portable device and recognition of privacy. *Infrastructure Planning Review* 21, 10019–11026 (in Japanese).

Asakura, Y., E. Hato, T. Daito and J. Tanabe (2000). Monitoring travel behavior using PHS based location data. *Journal of Infrastructure Planning and Management* 653(IV-48), 95–104 (in Japanese).

Asakura, Y., A. Okamoto, A. Suzuki, Y. H. Lee and J. Tanabe (2001). Monitoring individual travel behavior using PEAMON: a cellular phone based location positioning instrument combined with acceleration sensor. *Proceedings of 8th World Congress on ITS.* ITS, Sydney (CD-ROM).

Axhausen, K. W., A. Zimmermann, S. Schonfelder, G. Rindsfuser and T. Haupt (2002). Observing the rhythms of daily life: a six-week travel diary. *Transportation* 29, 95–124.

Bradley, M. and J. Bowman (2006). A summary of design features of activity-based microsimulation models for US MPOs. Presented at the *Conference on Innovations in Travel Demand Modeling*. Austin, TX.

Daito, T., K. Matsuba, H. Inoue and N. Matsumura (2005). An experience of applying web based TFP (travel feedback program) to some corporation. *Proceedings of Infrastructure Planning*, Vol. 31, JSCE, Higashihiroshima (CD-ROM, in Japanese).

Endo, A., K. Maruishi, K. Sasaki and K. Nishii (2006). A basic study for efficient TFP by using supplementally the Internet-based survey and paper-based survey. *Proceedings of Infrastructure Planning*, Vol. 34, JSCE, Takamatsu (CD-ROM).

Endo, A., K. Sasaki, K. Nishii and M. Ohi (2005). Basic analysis of survey characteristic of activity diary using computer based interview. *Proceedings of Infrastructure Planning*, Vol. 32, JSCE, Miyazaki (CD-ROM, in Japanese).

Fujii, S. and R. Kitamura (2000). Evaluation of trip-inducing effects of new freeways using a structural equations model system of commuters' time use and travel. *Transportation Research* 34B(5), 339–354.

Fujii, S., R. Kitamura and T. Monma (1998). A utility-based micro-simulation model system of individuals' activity–travel patterns. Paper presented at TRB 77th Annual Meeting. Washington, DC.

Fujii, S., R. Kitamura and K. Seto (1997). Development of model system for individuals' daily activity–travel patterns that accounts for the utility of daily activities. *Journal of Infrastructure Planning and Management* 562, 83–96 (in Japanese).

Garling, T., K. Brannas, J. Garvill, R. G. Golledge, S. Gopal, E. Holm and E. Lindberg (1989). Household activity scheduling. *Proceedings of the 5th WCTR*, Vol. 4, WCTR, Yokohama, pp. 235–248.

Hato, E., H. Ojima and K. Yokota (2005). Behavioral context estimation using BCALs. *Proceedings of Infrastructure Planning*, Vol. 31, JSCE, Higashihiroshima (CD-ROM, in Japanese).

Hayashi, A., K. Nishii, K. Sasaki, R. Kitamura and H. Sakai (2004). A basic analysis of activity & travel patterns in relation to uses of cars. *Proceedings of Infrastructure Planning*, Vol. 30, JSCE, Ube (CD-ROM, in Japanese).

Iida, Y., M. Iwabe, A. Kikuchi, R. Kitamura, K. Sasaki, Y. Shiromizu, D. Nakagawa, M. Hatoko, S. Fujii, T. Morikawa and T. Yamamoto (2000). Travel demand forecasting system for urban transportation planning by micro simulation approach. *Infrastructure Planning Review* 17, 841–848 (JSCE, in Japanese).

Iwakura, S., C. Harada and S. Suzuki (2003). Comparative analysis of choice set for commuting time of day choice model in urban railway networks. *Infrastructure Planning Review* 20(3), 485–492 (JSCE, in Japanese).

Izumiyama, H., N. Ohmori, T. Maruyama and N. Harata (2004). Mobility-related social exclusion of older people focused on space–time accessibility. *Proceedings of Annual Meeting of JSCE*. No. 59, JSCE, Toyota (CD-ROM, in Japanese).

Kato, K., S. Matsumoto and K. Sano (2002). Micro-simulation for commuters' mode and discretionary activities by using neural network. *The Third International Conference on Traffic and Transportation Studies* (ICTTS). Guilin.

Kitagawa, T., G. Ooi, N. Shinmori, F. Hara, N. Okoshi and H. Sasaki (2006). Development of a travel feedback program by using the web system. *Proceedings of Infrastructure Planning*, Vol. 33, JSCE, Sendai (CD-ROM, in Japanese).

Kitamura, R., A. Kikuchi, S. Fujii and T. Yamamoto (2005). An overview of PCATS/DEBNETS micro-simulation system: its development, extension and application to demand forecasting. In R. Kitamura and M. Kuwahara (Eds.), *Simulation Approaches in Transportation Analysis: Recent Advances and Challenges*, New York, Springer, pp. 371–399.

Lee, M. S., S. Doherty, R. Sabetishraf and M. G. McNally (2000). iCHASE: an internet-based computerized household activity scheduling elicitor. Presented at the *79th Annual Meeting of the Transportation Research Board*. Washington, DC.

Miller, E. J. and P. A. Salvini (2001). The integrated land use, transportation, environment micro-simulation modeling system: description and current status. In D. Hensher (Ed.), *The Leading Edge in Travel Behavior Research*, Amsterdam, Pergamon, pp. 711–724.

Mokhtarian, P. L. (1998). A synthetic approach to estimating the impacts of telecommuting on travel. *Urban Studies* 35(2), 215–241.

Nagal, K. and F. Marchal (2002). Computational method for multi-agent simulations of travel behavior. *Proceedings of 10th IATBR Conference*. Lucerne, Switzerland.

Nakazato, M., N. Ohmori, T. Maruyama and N. Harata (2004). A study on activity diary survey using GPS mobile phone. *Proceedings of Annual Meeting of JSTE*. No. 24, Tokyo, pp. 261–264 (in Japanese).

Nishii, K., K. Sasaki and T. Imao (2002a). Activity diary survey as a supplement of person trip survey—activity and travel pattern properties of aged people. *Journal of Infrastructure Planning and Management* 702(IV-55), 31–38 (in Japanese).

Nishii, K., K. Sasaki, R. Kitamura and H. Sakai (2004). The advantage of panel activity diary survey for the measurement of effects of the regional HI-SPEC road. *Proceedings of Annual Meeting of JSCE*. No. 59, Toyota (CD-ROM, in Japanese).

Nishii, K., K. Sasaki and Y. Suzuki (2002b). Categorization of activity pattern based on activity diary survey using multivariate analysis. *Proceedings of Annual Meeting of JSTE*, 149–152 (in Japanese).

Nishino, I., S. Fujii and R. Kitamura (1999). Developing a model of time allocation and ARA selection in tourists' excursion activity. *Infrastructure Planning Review (JSCE)* 16, 681–687 (in Japanese).

Ohmori, N. (2002). Data collection and application of activity diary in an era of information technology. *Proceedings of Infrastructure Planning*, Vol. 25, JSCE, Nagoya (CD-ROM, in Japanese).

Ohmori, N. (2004). Transportation and social exclusion: the possibility of virtual mobility. *Transport Policy Studies Review* 7(1), 57–58 (in Japanese).

Ohmori, N., Y. Muromachi, N. Harata and K. Ohota (1999). One week activity diary survey of elderly persons using PHS location information services. *Proceedings of Annual Meeting of JSTE*. No. 19, Tokyo, pp. 113–116 (in Japanese).

Ohmori, N., Y. Muromachi, N. Harata and K. Ohta (2000). Development of GIS-based gaming simulation tool and its application to activity-travel analysis of the elderly. *Infrastructure Planning Review (JSCE)* 17, 667–676.

Ohmori, N., M. Nakazato, N. Harata, K. Sasaki and K. Nishii (2006). Activity diary surveys using GPS mobile phones and PDA. Paper presented at the 85th Annual Meeting of Transportation Research Board. Washington, DC.

Pendyala, R. M. and C. R. Bhat (2006). Validation and assessment of activity-based traveling demand modeling systems. Presented at the *Conference on Innovations in Travel Demand Modeling*. Austin, TX.

Rosald, J. F. and L. Ronghui (2005). Activity-based analysis of travel demand using cognitive agents. In H. Timmermans (Ed.), *Progress in Activity-based Analysis*, Oxford, Elsevier, pp. 139–160.

Sasaki, K. and T. Morikawa (1997). Dynamic choice model revising attrition and non-response biases of panel data. *Proceedings of 8th Meeting of International Association for Travel Behavior Research*. Austin, pp. 147–160.

Sasaki, K., K. Nishii, R. Kitamura and K. Kondo (2004a). The use of mobile communication tools and its influence to joint activities—empirical analysis of personal communication and household activities. Paper presented at TRANSTEC 2004. Athens, Greece.

Sasaki, K., K. Nishii and I. Nishino (2004b). A study on micro-simulation of tour behavior and evaluation of the simulation system based on a classification of travel patterns. Paper presented at 10th WCTR Conference. Istanbul, Turkey.

Sasaki, K., K. Nishii and J. Yamamoto (2005). An analysis of joint activity using household activity diary data in weekend. *Proceedings of Infrastructure Planning*, Vol. 31, JSCE, Higashihiroshima (CD-ROM, in Japanese).

Senbil, M. and R. Kitamura (2003). Simultaneous relationships between travel and telecommunications. *Proceedings of 10th International Conference on Travel Behavior*. Lucerne, Switzerland, IATBR.

Simon, A. H. (1996). *The Sciences of the Artificial*, 3rd edn. Cambridge, MIT Press.

Takao, M., T. Morikawa, S. Kurauchi and K. Sasaki (1998). A time allocation model and its application to work time shift. *Proceedings of Infrastructure Planning*, Vol. 21, Kusatsu, pp. 783–786 (in Japanese).

Vovsha, P., M. Bradley and J. L. Bowman (2005). Activity-based travel forecasting models in the United States: progress since 1995 and prospects for the future. In H. Timmermans (Ed.), *Progress in Activity-based Analysis*, Oxford, Elsevier, pp. 389–414.

Watanabe, K., K. Kato, A. Kondo and Y. Hirose (2002). Analysis of individuals' activity that incorporate house-work. *Proceedings of Infrastructure Planning*, Vol. 26, JSCE, Morioka (CD-ROM, in Japanese).

Yamamoto, T., M. Abe, S. Fujii and R. Kitamura (1999). A simultaneous choice model of monetary and time expenditures, location, and frequency of discretional activities. *Infrastructure Planning Review* 16, 561–567 (JSCE, in Japanese).

Yamane, K., A. Fujiwara and J. Zhang (2006). An evaluation method for local city policy-making focusing on travel behavior patterns and its application. *Proceedings of Annual Meeting of JSTE* 26, 137–140.

Zhang, J. and A. Fujiwara (2004). Basic study on evaluation of living environments and analysis of household residential attitude considering intra-household interaction. *City Planning Review* 39, 619–624 (Institute of City Planning, Japan, in Japanese).

Zhang, J., A. Fujiwara, Y. Sugie and T. Yamada (2005a). Applicability of household time allocation model with heterogeneous intra-household interaction to the analysis of transportation policies for the elderly. *Journal of Infrastructure Planning and Management* 786(IV-67), 53–65 (in Japanese).

Zhang, J., H. Timmermans and A. Borgers (2005b). A model of household task allocation and time use. *Transportation Research Part B* 39, 81–95.

2.8 Integrated Models

The Expanding Sphere of Travel Behaviour Research
Selected Papers from the 11th International Conference on Travel Behaviour Research

14

Integrated Urban Models: Theoretical Prospects

Eric Miller

Abstract

This chapter provides an overview of the theoretical foundations and prospects for integrated land use – transportation modelling ("integrated urban models"). Its starting point is a critique of operational models presented at the 2003 Lucerne IATBR conference by Harry Timmermans. It also builds upon well-known criticisms of the integrated modelling paradigm by Douglas Lee. The chapter briefly defines what an integrated model is, why such models are needed for urban policy analysis and why integrated urban modelling is, in principle, a feasible undertaking. The second half of the chapter then sketches a conceptual framework for integrated modelling that attempt to tie together "what we know" about urban systems in a coherent, "integrated" manner. Implications for model building are discussed throughout. The paper concludes with the identification of significant gaps in integrated modelling theory/practice that should be addressed through new research and, where possible makes some suggestions concerning how the paper's theoretical construct can be used in addressing these research gaps.

Introduction

At the 2003 Lucerne IATBR conference, Harry Timmermans presented the integrated modelling workshop keynote paper. In this paper, he directly confronted integrated modellers with the 'dreams' that they have been dreaming for the past 40 years and challenged them to 'wake up' and take on the serious challenges facing the field if it is to significantly improve its models (Timmermans, 2003). While acknowledging that progress had been made in some respects, Timmermans argued that, overall, we have not advanced the field as far as we need to if integrated models are to be generally adopted as useful decision-support tools. Many possible reasons for this exist, but Timmermans emphasized the lack of a solid theoretical foundation underpinning these models, which inevitably are ad hoc in a variety of ways and overly dependent on statistical rather than behavioural representations. In particular, he identified four key weaknesses in the field:

- Our models of spatial choice processes (residential location choice, trip destination choice, etc.) are extremely weak. In particular, they are overly dependent on distance–decay functions of dubious behavioural validity.
- Our models are not sufficiently context- and domain-specific to capture decision processes adequately: better models of residential location processes, activity/travel choice and firm (as opposed to aggregate employment) location processes are clearly needed (among others).
- We do not really know how to 'integrate' travel and longer term spatial decisions within our so-called 'integrated models'. Current procedures tend to be very ad hoc, inconsistent and overly dependent on logit 'logsum' terms of questionable provenance.
- An over-emphasis on 'forecasting' as our modelling objective, as opposed to 'policy analysis', leads to a striving for a level of precision (especially spatially) in our models that simply may not be achievable and forces a focus on short-run operationalization of models at the expense of longer run model improvements.

In his paper Timmermans was very clearly trying to be confrontational, and therefore deliberately presented a 'glass is half empty' view of integrated modelling practice. There is, however, a 'half full' view that can observe that integrated models are being increasingly used in the US, Europe and elsewhere, that there is an increasing interest in integrated modelling within planning agencies and that technically and methodologically we are better positioned now than ever before to take on the challenge of comprehensively modelling urban regions.

Timmermans' challenge concerning the theoretical foundations of our models, however, remains, and is one that is elaborated on in this chapter. For surely his central thesis is correct: without a coherent and consistent conceptual framework (which has implicit within it a proper regard for behavioural fidelity and context), progress on developing a model system that 'integrates' a variety of socio-economic processes, a multiplicity of actors and a continuum of spatial–temporal scales stands little chance of being anything other than ad hoc in nature and difficult to defend, in either research or application contexts.

Lee's (1973) devastating critique of first-generation land use models identified the 'seven deadly sins' of large-scale models: hypercomprehensiveness, grossness, (data) hungriness, wrongheadedness, complicatedness, mechanicalness and expensiveness. He also, notably, critiqued these early models for their lack of theory. Twenty years later, Lee (1994) similarly criticized large-scale urban models for their lack of theory and for falling between the cracks in the sense of being neither scientific in their foundation nor overly useful in practical application. Again, one can argue that progress has been made during the 12 years since Lee's last critique, but the extent that the charge that integrated models are neither very good science nor good engineering holds true should be a matter of considerable concern to integrated modellers.

Miller et al. (1998) attempted to sketch an 'ideal' integrated modelling system, to provide both design guidelines for model development and an evaluation framework for assessing current models. While reasonably comprehensive, this specification was still primarily operationally oriented and somewhat a-theoretic in nature. This chapter takes a step back from operational models and focuses on the theoretical content of integrated models, both as it currently exists and what it should be if integrated models are to address Timmermans' and Lee's concerns.

In addition to this introductory section, the chapter is divided into two primary parts. The first part provides a foundation for the discussion in terms of briefly defining what we mean by an integrated urban model (see the section 'What is an Integrated Model?'), why integrated models are useful tools to construct and use (see the section 'Why Integrated Models?') and whether integrated modelling is, in principle, a feasible thing to undertake (see the section 'Can We Successfully build Integrated Urban Models?')—as opposed to accepting Lee's critique in its extreme form as a basis for rejecting the exercise all together.

The second part of the chapter then takes up the issue of the theoretical foundation/content of integrated models (both current and desired). The section 'Space, Time and Human Activity' discusses the three fundamental physical elements with which these models deal: space, time and human activity. The section 'Elements of a Theory of Urban Systems' continues with a brief summary of some of the key theoretical building blocks for constructing integrated urban models. Much of this may be 'old hat' to everyone, but we often forget what we know, and it is certainly arguable that we do not always exploit what we know in our models. The section 'Tools for Model Implementation' similarly and even more briefly reviews our methodological toolkit for model building. The section 'What do We need to Know?' then looks at the gaps in our conceptual framework that must be addressed and suggests ways that we might at least begin to address these gaps. Finally, the section 'Final Thoughts' concludes the chapter with some summary comments and final thoughts.

What is an Integrated Model?

The models under discussion in this chapter go by many names: land use models, integrated transportation–land use models, large-scale models, etc. In this chapter, we will simply use the term *integrated urban model*, or, even more simply, integrated model.

Regardless of name, what is it that such models are trying to do? Fundamentally, they are trying to model the spatial evolution of a given study region system state over time as a function of various socio-economic, demographic and political processes. The region's system state is highly multi-dimensional and usually includes:

- the spatial distribution of the region's resident population;
- the spatial distribution of the region's employment and other out-of-home activities;
- the travel that occurs from point to point within the region over the course of a representative time period (usually a single 'typical' weekday);
- the flows of goods and services from point to point within the region over the course of a representative time period.

Key words in this definition include:

- *Spatial*: We are interested in constructing a two-dimensional[1] representation of a study region[2] and, at some level of spatial detail, to describe this region in terms of where people live, where jobs and other 'activity attractors' are located, and the travel that goes on between activity locations. This need to work explicitly in two-dimensional space undoubtedly is one of the key factors contributing to the complexity of the modelling task. This complexity occurs in many aspects, including—determining appropriate representations of space and spatial objects within the computer; computational burden; data requirements (a major source for Lee's 'data hungriness'); and the challenge of representative human cognitive and decision-making processes within an explicit spatial context.
- *Time and evolution*: The model must be able to describe how the spatial system state will evolve over time. The point of the model is to estimate future systems as a function of the known base system state and the forces acting upon it over time that cause this initial state to change. As such, it should be a dynamic model of *process*, rather than a model of *static structure*.
- *Socio-economic, demographic and political*: Urban regions are constructed and evolve over time as the intended and unintended consequences of human actions. Actions that act upon and change the spatial urban system state over time are usually assumed to be primarily social, economic, demographic and political in nature, although potentially the full range of human activity could play a role (religious, cultural, war, etc.). Motivations and behaviours of the study region's residents vary by their socio-economic–demographic characteristics, as do the

[1]To the extent that densities are explicit or implicit in the model, there is an implicit third spatial dimension of height/coverage in these models.

[2]Although usually applied to a contiguous urban region (and hence the label 'integrated *urban* model', they do not need to be. The Oregon TLUMIP project has developed a statewide model system, for example. The approach being discussed here could also be applied to a strictly rural area, if the desire/need existed to do so.

impacts (costs, benefits) incurred by these residents due to spatial state changes. Thus, the heterogeneity in the resident population must be accounted for in the model if the system state evolution is to be properly represented and if the consequences of this evolution are to be adequately assessed.

Why Integrated Models?

The world has been in the process of continuous urbanization since the dawn of the Industrial Revolution. In Canada, for example, the 2001 Census reports that 80% of the nation's population lived in urban 'Census Metropolitan Areas' (CMAs). Further, 51% of the 2001 population resided in the nation's 10 largest urban regions.[3] Continuing urbanization is also a worldwide trend, with 50% of the world's population now living in urban regions,[4] with 25 urban regions of 10 million persons or more (5 of over 20 million) and 438 regions of a million or more people in the world.[5] These statistics, dramatic as they are, actually underestimate the importance of urban regions and their growth. To take but one example: the influence of the urbanized region known as the Greater Toronto Area (GTA) on land development, travel patterns, economic development, loss of natural habitat and farmland, and quality of life extends well beyond the boundary of the Toronto CMA (or even the boundaries of the adjacent Hamilton and Oshawa CMAs), into surrounding 'non-CMA' areas, as 'urban sprawl', employment 'commuter sheds', the search for 'affordable housing', etc., extend further and further into what have traditionally been considered 'rural' areas and/or relatively autonomous regions. Similar examples can be cited for other major urban centres worldwide.

This continuing growth of our urban areas poses immense challenges in terms of:

- environmental and ecological impacts;
- energy sustainability;
- global economic competitiveness;
- safety, security and public health;
- physical infrastructure investment and maintenance;
- social infrastructure investment and maintenance.

The extent to which we successfully address these challenges will determine to a significant extent the quality of life, the healthiness and the economic well-being of the majority of the world's inhabitants in the 21st century.

---

[3]All Canadian Census data are from various Statistics Canada tables found at http://www40.statcan.ca/l01/cst01/

[4]http://www.unis.unvienna.org/unis/pressrels/2004/pop899.html

[5]http://www.citypopulation.de/

Urban policy analysis and decision-making is severely limited in most urban regions by the lack of good decision-support tools and computer-based models of urban systems that would enable planners and decision-makers to explore 'what if' questions concerning alternative urban policies and their likely consequences (both intended and unintended) on urban form and urban spatial processes. The complexity of urban systems derives, to a large extent, from the complex socio-economic behaviours that occur each day within it, and from the diversity of available policy instruments that may influence interactions within the system and, through them, its evolution. It is very difficult to plan, develop and operate the urban system without adequate forecasting methods that are capable of providing timely, credible and policy-sensitive estimates of how the system is likely to respond to changes in the wide variety of urban policies that are potentially applicable within a given urban region. In the absence of such forecasting/policy analysis tools, it is often the case that 'policy gridlock' occurs in which different communities, agencies, interest groups and levels of governments advance conflicting visions and plans for the future, compete (rather than cooperate) for the investment of scarce public funds, and lack adequate mechanisms for assembling coherent, comprehensive and effective plans for evolution of our urban areas.

The motivation for the development of integrated urban models is thus very simple: to improve our ability to assess transportation and land use policies in terms of their contribution towards achieving societal goals and objectives. This statement holds even if we believe that it is rarely possible to achieve full consensus on what those goals and objectives are (Lindblom, 1959). The ability to identify cost–benefit tradeoffs and the distribution of impacts across the population under alternative scenarios and courses of action lies at the heart of transportation planning (Meyer and Miller, 2001). The valid critiques of Lee and others notwithstanding, *if* credible integrated urban models were available for use as another 'voice at the table' within the planning process, it is difficult to see why it would not be advantageous for them to be used.

Can We Successfully Build Integrated Urban Models?

From the foregoing discussions, it is clear that, to be useful, an integrated urban model must be sufficiently comprehensive to incorporate the 'full' range of processes that determine urban system evolution over time, while it must also be sufficiently detailed, both to capture the heterogeneities and non-linearities within the system and to provide outputs with sufficient precision to be of policy use. Given this very challenging mandate, it is easy to see how such models can easily fall prey to any or all of Lee's seven sins.

Lee's first 'sin' of large-scale models is hypercomprehensiveness: the attempt to include too much within one model and to try to build one model that addresses a wide variety of issues. He argues in favour of simpler models of reduced scope that are problem-specific in design and application. One can, however, argue the other side of the coin: without sufficient comprehensiveness, 'simple' models can be very erroneous in their predictions in that they miss critical feedbacks and underestimate or ignore critical secondary and tertiary effects of policies and processes (Vanderburg, 2000). This is particularly the case if we are interested in exploring policies that will change trends away from the status quo and towards more sustainable development paths. Without sufficient complexity that captures key processes and interactions, models are unlikely to be sufficiently flexible to 'discover' emergent new trends in response to new policies. Put another way, models must be sufficiently fundamental and behaviourally sound to capture the full set of system responses to a given set of policies. Both simple and complex models may fit this description, depending on the problem at hand. But certainly complex models need not be ruled out as being a priori infeasible or inappropriate.

In particular, complexity is not the same thing as complicated (Lee's fifth sin). Over the past 30 years, complex systems theory has emerged to show us the complexity inherent in even 'simple' systems,[6] while at the same time showing that pattern can exist within 'chaos' (Gleick, 1987). A complex model also need not be a 'black box' whose workings are incomprehensible to all but the initiated few involved in the model's construction. To the extent that (particularly older) models are 'complicated' in ad hoc, arbitrary, counter-productive and hard to understand/explain ways is surely a reflection of inadequate technology available at the time of model development rather than an attribute that is intrinsic to models per se. To the extent that 'complicated' is pejorative in intent, it tends to connote messy and arbitrary, an indicator of a lack of theory, less than clear/parsimonious thinking, etc. In this sense, 'complicated' is a structural attribute. This is different from complexity, which can be (and often is) elegant in concept, emergent out of simplicity and is an attribute of process. In other words, 'complexity' is not an antonym of 'simplicity', whereas 'complicated' is.

If as a species we threw our hands up at complexity, we would not be unravelling DNA or plumbing the depths of the universe or making progress in countless other areas of scientific endeavour. Are cities really more complex than these examples? In some sense, perhaps they are, since cities are the emergent outcomes of actions of sentient beings possessing free will rather than the direct product of biological or chemical or physical processes per se. The *act* of a single *individual* is, indeed, inherently unpredictable (Arendt, 1958). But the *behaviour* of *people* exhibits regularities[7] that both make *social* science conceivable and provide the basis for the development of

[6]Try predicting the root of (x^4-1) that the Newton–Raphson root-finding method will find from an arbitrary initial starting point.

[7]The distinction between the individual act and behaviour of a group is also Arendt's.

models of socio-economic processes. And so, again, there is no intrinsic reason to believe that city regions cannot be successfully analysed and modelled.

Much of the practical problem with constructing and using integrated models lies with their data hungriness (sin 3) and their cost (sin 7). There is no doubt that these models require significant amounts of data, and that they are costly in time, skilled personnel and money, to construct and to use. These constraints, however, to a large extent simply reflect the priority that has been given to developing these models, which historically has been very small in most urban regions worldwide. A variety of institutional and other reasons exist for this historical record that will not be revisited here.[8] Overall, however, the cost of constructing and maintaining such a model is very small compared to the magnitude of the investments and the flows of benefits and costs that the model might influence if it is skilfully employed. As but one example of this, the 'Generation 1' Oregon statewide integrated modelling system was used to develop a multi-year bridge reconstruction program for Oregon State. The plan developed using the model reduced the cost of the proposed program by $2 billion and will generate considerable additional statewide economic benefits relative to the base plan (Knudsen, 2006).

Despite the very chequered history of integrated urban modelling, the fact remains that urban regions in increasing numbers worldwide are implementing and using integrated models of one form or another. This chapter will not attempt to review the current state of operational models[9]; the key point for present purposes is simply that there is increasing willingness to invest in such models and, hence, the 'expensiveness' of such models is viewed as somewhat less of a 'sin'/obstacle to their implementation than perhaps has been the case in the past, and that, yes, indeed, operational models are feasible to build and useful to apply.

The concern of this chapter, however, is the theoretical underpinning of these models. Having argued that such models are of practical relevance and are feasible to build, the question remains concerning their behavioural and scientific content. This question must address Lee's sins of wrongheadedness, mechanicalness and grossness (among the others) and, of course, is the same fundamental question raised by Timmermans. The remainder of this chapter attempts to take up this question in some detail.

---

[8]In addition to the critiques of Timmermans (2003) and Lee (1973, 1994) that have already been discussed, Miller et al. (1998) discuss in some detail institutional, technical and other factors that historically have limited the development and application of integrated urban models.

[9]For reviews and discussions of operational models, see, among others, Wegener (1994), Miller et al. (1998), Timmermans (2003) and Hunt et al. (2005).

Space, Time and Human Activity

Introduction

In the definition of integrated urban models, three key elements were identified: we are modelling socio-economic activities of *human beings*, and these activities occur in both *space* and *time*. In the following sub-sections, key elements and concerns associated with each of these basic 'building blocks' are discussed in terms of their ramifications for the conceptualization and modelling of urban systems.

Space

We can attach geo-coordinates to any point in physical space for the purposes of referencing one point versus another or for delineating various spatial aggregations (zones, etc.). The concept of 'space' is not very meaningful outside of the context of the human activities we are modelling and of the 'content' (buildings, activities, people, etc.) that is situated within the space. Zones, raster cells, etc., are organizing tools for data storage/display/accounting purposes, but have no behavioural content per se.

'Space' is operationalized in two ways within integrated models. The first is as land and the built environment situated upon the land. Space quà land is transformed into utilitarian[10] activity locations through the action of man. We cannot exist without acting upon and altering our environment. It is this process of 'developing' and 'redeveloping' landscapes into urban regions that lies at the heart of 'land use models'. Once land has distinguishable activity points located over its surface, the second fundamental spatial attribute of interest is the distance between these points. Distance per se, however, has little 'behavioural content'. It is the *time* that is required to travel from one point to another in space—that is, distance mediated by travel mode/level of service—that gives behavioural meaning to distance (a 10 km trip is perceived very differently depending on whether I am walking, taking transit or driving). Thus, space (land) is what we make of it. It is neither fixed nor given. It evolves and is purposefully designed.[11] Our perception of it is mediated by transportation technologies—the fundamental origin of 'the transportation–land use interaction'. And each point in physical space is unique.

Our need to model the spatial dimension of socio-economic activities adds enormous behavioural complexity, data requirements (much of the source of Lee's concern about data hungriness) and computational burden to the problem of modelling urban

[10]Here, 'utilitarian' is interpreted in the broadest possible sense of anything we make use of. A park, a factory, a place of worship, etc., are all purposeful places that we build to 'use' in different ways.

[11]That is not say that there are not unintended consequences that emerge—this too is why we model, in order to try to identify at least some of these.

regions. Constructing a demand function for toothpaste generally does not require knowing anything about where the toothpaste is consumed. Each plot of land, each building or each trip, however, is spatially differentiated from all other plots, buildings or trips. This spatial differentiation is critical both to understand how the urban system works and to assess the implications of our planning policies.

Time

Socio-economic processes play out over time as well as space. Urban regions are inherently dynamic, open systems in which 'forces' (people, money, policies, etc.) are constantly at work shaping and reshaping the urban system. Just as we must somehow aggregate space into some manageable, computable representation, time similarly must be aggregated in various ways to be computationally representable. This typically involves the assumption of a basic *time step*, with which the model 'moves' the urban system through time. Part of the grossness of early models involved the use of very large time steps (often 10 years or more). Current land use models typically employ one-year time steps. Shorter time steps are conceivable if model precision requirements dictate and computational burden permits. Regardless of time step adopted, the two key points to note concerning time steps are that they do, indeed, represent a form of aggregation and, given this, that a given model is 'tied' in a variety of ways (parameter values, algorithmic structure, conditioning of behavioural processes, etc.) to the assumed time step and cannot readily be applied using a different time step. In particular, if a model is indifferent to the time step selected (either for an entire run or permitting time steps to vary within in a run), then serious questions exist concerning the sorts of aggregation problems that might exist within the model.

Miller et al. (1998) and Miller and Salvini (2002) discuss temporal issues in modelling in greater detail, while Litwin (2005) provides a deeper inquiry into the nature of time and its role in behavioural processes. Perhaps the most important temporal concern within a given model is its assumption concerning system equilibrium. Virtually all early models and most current operational models assume that urban land markets, etc., are in equilibrium at each time step (or, they are in a quasi-equilibrium in response to lagged inputs from the previous time period). Given, as noted above, that this system is an open, dynamic one and that many processes of interest (e.g. land development, residential and job location choice, etc.) are relatively 'slow' relative to many of the driving factors (interest rates, government policies, market prices, etc.), the equilibrium assumption is highly questionable at best. It also encourages a static view of the model as being one of urban *structure* rather than a dynamic view of modelling urban *processes*. It would appear that a more theoretically defensible approach is to assume the urban system is a dynamic, path-dependent, open system that may be equilibrium-chasing but not to insist on enforcing equilibrium as an inherent feature of the theory/model.

Human Activity

As is argued at greater length in the next section, human activity is what we are fundamentally trying to model. This is clearly an extraordinarily difficult and complex task. Much of this complexity comes from the fact that different people have different tastes and preferences and, possibly, different decision processes. This inherent *heterogeneity* of the population that we wish to model must be addressed explicitly throughout our models in a variety of ways, including:

- appropriate disaggregation of the population (to capture systematic differences in behaviour from one person to another);
- accounting for heterogeneity in the stochastic components of the model (to account for idiosyncratic, unobservable person-to-person differences in behaviour);
- disaggregating model outputs to identify the distribution of benefits and costs of a given plan or scenario across the different groups of people within the population.

Population heterogeneity would be much less of a problem if behavioural response functions were linear in nature. In general, however, *non-linear response* functions are the rule. Given this, it is well known that serious *aggregation bias* can be built into models (during both estimation and application) if proper disaggregation of the population is not maintained within the model system. Early land use models were particularly susceptible to Lee's sin of grossness. This situation has been improved in many current operational models (particularly with respect to spatial representation), but most remain relatively aggregate with respect to household's or person's socio-economic attributes. This is clearly a weakness in such models since it is well known that socio-economic and demographic attributes (income, auto ownership, lifecycle stage, household structure, etc.) play primary roles in spatial behaviours of all types (location choices, travel demand, etc.).

Indeed, integrated models should be models of demographic evolution as well as of spatial and (as is discussed below) economic evolution. Few current models, however, have a strong demographic component. There does not appear to be any particularly strong technical reason preventing significant improvement in this regard, and in the theoretical construct developed in this chapter it is assumed that a strong demographic component (internal population growth, household formation and evolution, in- and out-migration, etc.) exists within the integrated model system.

Elements of a Theory of Urban Systems

Introduction

As defined in the section 'What is an Integrated Model?' and elaborated in the section 'Space, Time and Human Activity,' integrated urban models attempt to model selected socio-economic activities of human beings in terms of how these activities play out in time and space. At a very fundamental level, there are two ways to approach this problem: *holistic* and *reductionist*. In the holistic approach, we view the urban region as an entity that exhibits behaviour in response to stimuli and we attempt to replicate/predict the behaviour of this entity *as a whole* over time. In the reductionist approach, we observe that the urban region evolves through the actions of the individual agents that are operative within the system and that the system state evolves as the emergent outcome of the actions of these individuals: the whole is defined by the sum of the parts.

The holistic approach often has considerable intellectual and practical appeal. It can be elegant and parsimonious in design; it typically avoids the need for excessive amounts of data and insights into microlevel processes; and it often works very well in practice. We adopt holistic models in a wide variety of engineering and other applications, from Hooke's Law for elastic springs (which does not care about the details about coil structure let alone the microdynamics of how the steel molecules are interacting within the coil) to many/most artificial intelligence methods (IBM's 'Big Blue' does not attempt to replicate the thinking process of a human chess master but is able to play a very fine game of chess nevertheless) to many models (game-theoretic or otherwise) of the response of commercial organizations, nations, etc., to rewards/threats/stimuli, among many others.

The key assumptions of the holistic approach are that the underlying microprocesses within the system are *stable* over time (e.g. the laws of physics determining the behaviour of springs do not change), and that only the *macro*-system state (outcome) is of interest (e.g. the net displacement of the spring given an applied force).

Unfortunately in the case of urban systems, neither of these assumptions usually holds. First, the 'inner workings' of the system typically change over time due to a variety of reasons, including:

- changing population demographics, which change the tastes, preferences, etc., of the decision-making actors;
- changing 'rules of the game' as laws, external constraints, technology, etc., change what is feasible, attractive, etc., to undertake;
- learning/adaptation among people who are free agents to alter their behaviour in response to their environment.

This is of particular importance in planning, given that planning seeks ways in which system behaviour *can* be changed over time so as to move society in a more 'sustainable' direction.

Second, the system state is inherently highly multi-dimensional and disaggregate in nature. We need to know the spatial distribution of people, jobs and trips; we need to know the socio-economic–spatial distribution of policy impacts in detail. In addition to this need for disaggregated *outputs*, we also need a similar level of disaggregation within the system representation itself (the 'inner workings' of the model) in order to capture the key heterogeneities and non-linearities inherent in the system. That is, it is argued that these heterogeneities and non-linearities *cannot* be adequately abstracted away into a more holistic representation.

This last point is clearly an assertion that is not wholly testable. It is conceivable at some philosophical level to suppose that some form of holistic model of urban regions might be constructible that is of practical planning relevance. The argument being advanced here is that this does not seem to be a feasible proposition given our current understanding of urban systems, current modelling methods and the non-negotiable requirement for spatially and socio-economically disaggregated outputs from the model.

If these arguments or propositions are accepted, then one is left with the reductionist approach as the only practical way forward for building models of urban systems, at least at this point in time. The reductionist approach clearly 'works' *if* one has sufficient data, understanding of the microprocesses at work, etc., to construct a credible model. It is, however, clearly susceptible to Lee's seven sins. Like their developers, models are never free from sin: the over-arching question with respect to the credibility/practicality of all models is the extent to which they balance behavioural fidelity, data needs, computability, theoretical soundness and so on.[12] As a practical matter, no model should be more detailed than is needed to answer the question at hand, nor should it be more detailed than available data, theory and methodology can support. In this regard, there is no argument with Lee.

In speaking of holistic and reductionist models, one needs to differentiate these terms from the terms commonly used in transportation modelling of *aggregate* and *disaggregate*. *All* common travel demand, land use and integrated models are reductionist in nature in that they divide the urban system into procedural components, they divide space into some form of zone system and they divide time into steps. They thus are also neither 'aggregate' nor 'disaggregate' but rather sit somewhere along a continuum of aggregation/disaggregation. All models are simplifications and abstractions of reality and hence inevitably involve some level of 'aggregation' (i.e. loss of fidelity with the real world) along all three fundamental dimensions of space, time and human attributes and activities.[13] The art of model building is to find the 'right' level of abstraction/fidelity for the problem at hand.

[12]Note that Lee's critique of models holds equally well for holistic models. Indeed, the argument presented above about why the holistic approach is infeasible for modelling urban systems could be couched in terms of 'grossness', 'wrongheadedness', etc.

[13]Again note that these comments hold equally well for holistic models.

To what extent can a reductionist model of urban systems be based on theory? Indeed, does a 'reductionist theory' of urban systems exist (or is constructable) that can guide model development, testing and evolution? The remaining sub-sections in this section attempt to address this question. Like the reductionist approach itself, the answer presented below consists of inter-related parts, with the whole hopefully merging out of the interaction of these parts.

Human Agency

Behaviourally, the reductionist approach requires a fundamental commitment to the *person* as the fundamental unit of analysis in any conceptual/theoretical representation of the urban system. Land does not develop itself, buildings are not self-erecting and zones do not interact with one another. People provide the sentience and the mental and physical actions that cause 'the city' to be a self-organizing, emergent, dynamic system. Thus, any 'theory of urban systems' must be a theory of the socio-economic processes in which people engage.

A key feature of human beings is that we are social creatures.[14] We form into various groups in response to various motivations. In both theory and modelling application, it is a 'useful fiction' (Salvini and Miller, 2005) to treat certain key groups as if they themselves are sentient beings that are capable of perceiving their environment and acting autonomously within the environment (just as individual persons do), rather than modelling all group behaviour as the emergent outcome of the individual motivations and aspirations of all the persons interacting within the group. This is an obvious example of an abstraction/aggregation that simplifies the modelling problem in a very useful way.[15] Groups of particular interest within integrated models include:

- households;
- firms and/or business establishments[16];
- governments and other public sector agencies.

In constructing a theory of urban spatial processes, a few obvious but fundamental starting points exist that can be taken as being axiomatic, but hopefully meet with universal agreement. The first is that, as either an individual or a group, *as sentient creatures we perceive the world around us, respond to stimuli, and learn and adapt based on our experiences*. Thus, any model of spatially based socio-economic behaviour must deal with:

[14]A characteristic that we share, of course, with many other species on this planet.

[15]It also represents a holistic approach for modelling the behaviour of the group.

[16]A business establishment is an economic unit of production that is located at single point in space. A firm consists of one or more business establishments.

- *Perception*: What information do the actors in the system have about the system and how do they obtain it?
- *Response*: What actions can the actors take in response to their environment and what are the rules or decision processes that determine these responses?
- *Learning*: What new knowledge do actors obtain through their perception of the system and through their observation of the outcomes of their actions that may influence subsequent actions?
- *Adaptation*: To what extent do actors change their 'decision rules', 'choice sets', etc., in response to their experience with their environment?[17]

The second key axiom is that most (if not all) of the behaviour of interest within integrated models is *motivated by our desire to fulfil needs*, explicitly as is discussed in the seminal work of Maslow (1970). As discussed in greater detail in Miller (2005b), decisions about housing, labour force participation and job location, schooling, automobile transactions, travel to participate in activities, etc., are all motivated by a variety of needs. As such, there is self-interest in our actions to meet these needs (at least relatively) efficiently and effectively. We do not, in general, act at random or deliberately to our disbenefit (literally pathological cases aside). This axiom is critical to model building, for without some systematic relationship between environment and response (between cause and effect) we have no starting point upon which to build either theory or operational models. Operationalizing this axiom may lead to utility-based models, prospect theory or many other models of decision-making, but all share this fundamental assumption that decision *rules* do exist and that they possess some level of 'rationality' that can be tied back to the fundamental principle of motivated behaviour.

Given that we engage in motivated behaviour, the third axiom is that we generally (or at least often) plan our activities in advance of their execution. Planning is clearly a rational approach to maximizing need fulfilment; it is also clear that not all people plan to the same extent or as successfully as others. Nor does this assume that the future is knowable with certainty and that things always turn out as planned. Nevertheless, the fourth axiom is that *we can and do envision the future*, and that we can and do make future commitments (contracts to show up at work at 9 a.m. most weekdays, a dentist appointment next Wednesday, etc.), plan future actions (vacations, retirement plans), save for the future and so on. In the limit, every action requires a prior decision to undertake the action and hence, in some abstract sense at least, 'planning'.

In travel demand modelling, we have become very used to talking about *activity-based* models, in which travel emerges out of the activity scheduling process. The key point

[17]In these definitions, learning is associated with building a knowledge base, while adaptation is associated with changing the rules governing the actor's behaviour (responses) in the future.

being made here is that a critical aspect of developing an 'integrated' theory/model of spatial processes is to view *all* our actions as 'activity based'. Indeed this is a tautology in that obviously any action is an activity and hence 'activity based'. That this seems to need to be said, however, points to the fact that we do not tend to think about residential location processes, labour market processes, etc., as 'activities' in the same way as shopping, the journey to work, etc. Adopting a holistic activity-based view of *all* actions/processes, however, provides a useful starting point for an integrated theory of these processes. Miller (2005a, b, c) provides an in-depth discussion of one approach to developing such an integrated theory in terms of defining *all* human activity as occurring within a set of *projects* that encapsulate both short- and long-run behaviour within a consistent decision-making framework. The purpose of this chapter is not to revisit the project-based approach in detail, but rather to simply observe that something like this is required, and the starting point for this 'something' is to adopt an 'activity-based' approach in its broadest and most consistent sense within the integrated theory or model.

The final axiom is that *all actions actually occur in the short run*: we can only act in the present. The difference between the short and the long run is that over the long run we change our resources available for use in the short run, wherein our case 'resources' include dwelling units, jobs (and hence income), cars, education level, etc. (Miller, 2005a). Daily activity and travel occurs within a fixed set of household resources in terms of home, work and school locations, disposable income, cars, driver licences, transit passes, knowledge about the urban area, etc. These resources can stay fixed for arbitrary periods of time. But *at any point in time*, it is conceivable that a decision might be made to alter one or more elements of the *resource set*: to buy a new home, to purchase a second car, to change jobs, to leave school and enter the labour force, etc. What we usually very loosely characterize as 'land use models' are actually dealing with these longer term processes of 'resource change' (residential mobility, workplace location, etc.). Long-run change occurs through specific activities (tying back to the activity-based argument) that occur at specific points in time that are *motivated* by the perceived opportunity/need to alter the actor's resource set (so as to facilitate future actions/need fulfilment).[18]

Thus, it is argued, that 'integration' in the modelling of spatial socio-economic processes is achieved by recognizing that we act in the short run (the day-to-day) within the constraints of the current resource set, where, in particular, these actions include travel to participate in out-of-home activities. But, as part of our perception–response–learn–adapt process, we also over time monitor the effects of these constraints on our

[18]Note that this change in resource set can be either a 'gain' (such as the purchase of a larger house in response to increased income) or a 'loss' (having to sell the car because of losing one's job) in resources. It can also be either opportunistic/voluntary in nature (trade-up to a larger house because 'the market is good') or forced (moving into the region and so must find a dwelling unit somewhere).

well-being, and we alter this resource set as need and opportunity warrant. And both our day-to-day activities and our monitoring/adjusting of our resource set flow from (are motivated by) the same set of needs and aspirations.

Inter-Personal Interactions

The discussion to this point has been 'ego-centric' in that it has focused on the behaviour of the individual actor (whether this be a single person or a group acting as a single actor) acting and reacting within its environment. The 'environment', however, is not 'just' a physical system that is 'passive' from a human agency sense. The 'environment' includes other humans, and much of the behaviour of interest involves the interaction among people. While these interactions are incredibly rich and multi-faceted, for present purposes it is assumed that we can simplistically categorize these interactions as being either *collaborative* or *competitive* in nature.

Collaborative interactions of potential interest within the scope of integrated urban models include:

- within-household decision-making;
- interactions within social networks (friends, extended family, etc.);
- inter-household travel collaboration (car-pooling).

Space does not permit an extensive review of theories and models of inter-personal collaboration within the integrated modelling umbrella. An extensive literature in 'household economics' exists that deals with intra-household decision-making from a microeconomic and/or game-theoretic viewpoint (e.g. Jara-Diaz, 2003), while increasing attention is being paid to household-level modelling in integrated modelling (Miller, 2005a, b, c), which has always recognized the household as an important decision-making unit for location choice processes, as well as in the activity/travel literature (e.g. Gliebe and Koppelman, 2002). As one example of the latter, our experience with the development of the household-based TASHA model (Miller and Roorda, 2003; Miller et al., 2006) is that household-based modelling of individual and inter-personal decision-making is very much a practical proposition, simplifies and improves the representation of travel mode choice (among other decisions being modelled) and provides the basis for the development of the integrated activity-based modelling system discussed in the previous section. As one example of the last point, we now have a prototype auto transactions model (a longer term 'resource change model') that includes inputs from the TASHA daily activity/travel scheduler (Roorda et al., 2006).

Similarly, the application of social network theory to activity/travel analysis is very much emerging as a new and promising field of inquiry (Axhausen, 2005; Dugundji and

Walker, 2005; Páez and Scott, 2007; Carrasco and Miller, 2006) and is undoubtedly an essential step in developing operational models of inter-household interactions. This work is in its early days, and it is likely to be some time before research translates into particularly operational implementations. Thus, for the time being it is important to note that inter-household inter-personal interactions remain a particularly challenging problem, both theoretically and practically. Inter-household car-pooling is a particularly important practical case in point. It is very arguable that good models of this behaviour are very rare currently (if they exist at all). This state-of-the-art largely reflects the current immature theory of inter-household/person interaction.

Competitive interactions for our purposes largely occur within the framework of *market interactions*. These are critical to integrated modelling and are discussed in the next sub-section.

Markets

Most spatial processes possess an economic component (buying and selling). As with all economic activities, the exchange of goods and services (including land, buildings and travel) occurs within a *market*. Thus, *spatial markets must be explicitly modelled* if integrated models are to possess any face validity. Demand and supply processes and the endogenous determination of prices through demand–supply interactions *must* be explicit within the model. A major weakness of early models and a major source of Lee's seven sins was the absence of both an explicit supply process and prices in the model. It simply is not conceivable that the distribution of a region's resident population and economic activities can be credibly generated without accounting for the supply of housing and commercial real estate and the prices/rents that must be paid in order to occupy this building stock.

A major improvement in subsequent generations of integrated models is the incorporation of land markets into the modelling system. Building on the pioneering work of the National Bureau of Economic Research in the US (Ingram et al., 1972) and the less well-known but more successful Communities Analysis Model (Birch et al., 1974), most models that have been developed and applied over the past >20 years have explicitly represented both demand and supply processes (at least in the housing market) and have some form of 'market clearing' procedure to reconcile demand with supply through some type of pricing mechanism.

As usual, a variety of methods have been employed to model housing markets (and, to a lesser extent, commercial real estate markets). Miller et al. (1998) provide a reasonably detailed discussion of modelling spatial markets and common approaches for undertaking this task. Housing demand is typically modelled in more detail and with somewhat greater behavioural fidelity than housing supply, which is often modelled in a very simplistic fashion (discussed further in the section 'What do We need to Know?'). Of the various approaches adopted to represent spatial markets, it is arguable that the strongest theoretically is the *bid choice* theory developed by Martinez (1992, 1996), building on a rich heritage in microeconomics dating all the way back to Ricardo and von Thunen and the more modern work of Alonso (1964) and Ellickson (1981), among others.

Bid choice provides a compelling theoretical foundation for modelling housing and commercial real estate markets. It recognizes that the exchange of land or building stock inherently involves an *auction* process in which the current owner sells[19] to the highest bidder (thereby trying to maximize his profit) while the bids generated by potential buyers emerge out of an attempt to maximize their consumer surplus (given a desired utility level). This is a very powerful approach, which generates not only a distribution of population given housing supply, but also the associated bid rent (hedonic price) functions associated with this distribution and consumer surplus measures that can be used in the evaluation of alternative scenarios.

Martinez' implementation of the theory in MUSSA involves the extensive use of logit models (thereby drawing the ire of Timmermans) and strong assumptions concerning system equilibrium. The fundamental theory, however, works equally well in disaggregate, disequilibrium settings, and, indeed, provides a strong theoretical foundation for microsimulating markets (Miller and Haroun, 2000; Hunt and Abraham, 2001; Salvini and Miller, 2005).

Urban Macroeconomics

In addition to land/floorspace markets, urban regions are massive economic engines that encompass a complex and intertwined system of economic markets associated with all aspects of goods and services associated with a modern economy.[20] Whether one subscribes to Jacobs (1969) theory that cities were invented as economic machines or acknowledge that cities are the outcome of a variety of needs and processes (Lynch, 1981; Mumford, 1961), there is no doubt that the economic function of cities is a primary one, and is growing in importance as urbanization continues and as urban regions increasingly become the primary drivers of the economies of post-industrial nations and primary competitors with other urban regions within the global economy. The urban economy is also a primary determinant of the spatial distribution of

[19]The model can be expressed in terms of landlords renting leased space to occupants as well.

[20]Although industries located in urban areas are largely secondary and tertiary in nature, primary industries also are present in urban areas. As but one example: although no gold is mined in the Toronto region, the City of Toronto is the world administrative and financial capital for the industry.

activities and of flows of people, goods and services within (as well as into, out of and through) the urban region.

Thus, just as it was earlier argued that, from an individual person and household point of view, a 'land use' model was really a 'resource set choice' model, from the more macroview of the city qua economic engine, a 'land use' model should really be a model of the urban region's economy. That is, the place of residence–place of work relationship (and the associated journey to work), shopping travel and the flows of goods and services within the region are all just physical manifestations of regional economic production and consumption processes.

This view of the city as an economic system is a powerful one for organizing the non-household-based elements and processes of the urban region.[21] Most integrated models make at least some assumptions about connections to a more 'macro'-model of the urban economic system or 'control totals' for total employment by sector, etc., although these linkages are typically ad hoc and dependent, at best, on exogenously generated inputs that do not have any linkage to more detailed sets of flows, interactions, etc., generated within the integrated model per se.

A very notable exception to this generalization is the family of models that trace their heritage back to MEPLAN (Echenique et al., 1990; Hunt and Simmonds, 1993): MEPLAN, TRANUS (de la Barra, 1989) and PECAS (Hunt and Abraham, 2003). In this family of models, various forms of a spatially disaggregate input–output (or social accounting) table are used to explicitly model the economic interchanges that occur in the urban region that give rise to the consumption of land (by activity type) and the flows of persons (to/from jobs, shopping, etc.) and goods (to/from business establishments and households).

As originally implemented in early MEPLAN and TRANUS models, the social accounting framework necessitated the use of very large zones (typically 50–100 zones for a large urban region). Limitations also exist in terms of being able to construct a social accounts matrix specifically for an urban region (often state/provincial or even national technical coefficients must be borrowed), and the stability of this matrix over time is, of course, a classic concern of any input–output model. Nevertheless, the 'organizing principle' of the social accounts matrix, and the recognition that the urban economy must be explicitly modelled as part of an 'integrated' approach, represents a significant contribution to the conceptual representation of the urban system that we are trying to build. And, as always, alternative implementation options potentially exist if the social accounts approach is ultimately found to be inadequate. In particular,

[21] Again, this is not to say that there are not other processes and functions at play within the city (social, cultural, religious, etc.) that do not comfortably fit into the economic model.

'firmographic', microsimulation approaches are being experimented with that hold at least some promise to eventually replace current more aggregate representations (see, e.g. Maoh and Kanaroglou, 2005).

Tools for Model Implementation

Introduction

Regardless of available theory, models are only as good as the methods and data available to support their implementation. There is no doubt, for example, that a major part of the failure of the early large-scale models documented by Lee (1973) was due to the fact that the databases, computers and econometric methods (as well as theory) of the day were simply inadequate for the task at hand. There is also no doubt that models will always be limited by available data. Computing and methodological limitations also still exist, but are steadily becoming less critical in terms of dictating what is feasible to undertake. Indeed, it is arguable that the primary barrier to model development currently is our theoretical understanding of the processes to be modelled (and, possibly, our ability to observe and quantify these processes) rather than the methods available for use in model building.

This chapter cannot possibly review in any detail the methods available to support integrated modelling. Instead, it is restricted to brief comments concerning three elements of modelling methodology that are particularly important for the implementation of improved integrated models[22]:

- econometric modelling;
- information theory;
- agent-based microsimulation.

Econometric Modelling

The advances in econometric methods that have occurred over the past several decades are really quite staggering. Most familiar to transportation modellers are, of course, random utility models, but a much wider econometric toolkit exists and is increasingly

[22]This short list hardly does justice to the question of methodological advances of relevance to integrated models. Perhaps the most glaring omission is that of Geographic Information Systems (GIS), which have clearly revolutionized modellers' ability to store, manipulate, analyse and display spatial data. The importance of access to such powerful tools for data analysis and model construction on the one hand and for model output management and display on the other should not be underestimated in terms of its substantive impact on the quality and performance of integrated models.

finding applications in transportation-related research, including structural equation models and multi-level models, among others. As our theory of spatial processes matures, it becomes essential that we have appropriate and sophisticated tools to model the disaggregate and complex behaviours that are of interest to us.

While agreeing with Timmermans' critique of the over-dependence of current operational models on simple logit structures and of the apparent tardiness of integrated modellers to exploit cutting-edge methods, one cannot over-emphasize the importance that random utility theory has played and will continue to play in the development of not just activity/travel models, but also of integrated models as a whole. The key, seminal contribution of pioneers such as McFadden and Willumsen and of all who have followed in their footsteps is the recognition that as observers of human actions we will never capture with certainty people's motivations, utilities or decision processes. As a result, there will always be an 'error term' in our models that results in them being inherently probabilistic in formulation. Having lived with this insight for well over 30 years, we now perhaps take it for granted and do not see it for the strong theory that it is. Without trying to be too grandiose about it, it is somewhat akin to quantum theory in physics in the sense that it places fundamental limits on what is knowable about socio-economic systems, while at the same time providing us with an elegant and powerful architecture within which useful, predictive models are possible to build.

As we continue to disaggregate our models and come closer to the high-fidelity representation implicit in the theory sketched in the previous section, the ability to deal in sophisticated ways with the error structures of our models becomes increasingly important. Heterogeneity is inherent in any theory of human behaviour, as is state-dependency, among other concerns. Without powerful probabilistic modelling methods at our disposal, it is likely that Lee's concerns about wrongheadedness, complicatedness and mechanicalness will, indeed, overwhelm our attempts to build improved, behaviourally sound integrated models.

Information Theory

It is well known that the theoretical foundation of classic models of the gravity/entropy family derives from statistical concepts drawn from entropy maximization (Wilson, 1967) or, equivalently, information minimization (Webber, 1977) based on Shannon's (1948) information theory. The equivalence of multinomial logit models and entropy models in both functional form and estimated parameter values (under proper formulation and estimation of both models) is also well known (Anas, 1983). What is less clear is the extent to which the implications of these findings are for most modelling applications (integrated or otherwise), in particular for the understanding and use of multinomial logit models.

On the one hand, the Anas' insight that a logit model is exactly an entropy model by another name provides a powerful justification for the use of logit models *in the absence of additional information concerning microlevel error structures.* The key strength of entropy models is that information theory shows that they *are* the least biased, most likely estimates of a given system state, given limited known 'macro'-information about the system (e.g. average origin–destination travel time for the journey to work) and given the assumption that all 'micro'-system states (e.g. the permutations of the allocation of all workers in an urban region to specific cells in a place of residence–place of work matrix) are equally likely. Thus, in situations in which this holds, information theory states that a logit-type model is *the* statistically best model that can be justified.

At the same time, this same finding indicates that, despite its random utility theory trappings, the logit model 'merely' defines the statistically most likely set of state probabilities that are consistent with observed system averages (i.e. the model parameters are determined by matching predicted system average values for the explanatory variables to the observed averages in the estimation dataset). Random utility theory is not required in order to generate or justify this particular model.

Indeed, from this point of view, random utility theory in general is itself relatively sparse in its 'behavioural content'. In its most minimal form, 'all' that random utility theory provides is a simple decision rule: a decision-maker chooses the maximum utility alternative from a set of feasible, discrete alternatives. What distinguish one behavioural process from another and one theory/model from another are the modeller's assumptions concerning the definition of the choice set, the specification of the systematic component of the utility function and the assumption of the distribution of the utility function error term. It is in these assumptions that 'behavioural theory' is introduced into the mechanistic utility-maximization decision rule. This in some ways is not dissimilar to the entropy model formalism, in which 'behaviour' is introduced by the modeller through the choice of constraints ('known information') that are assumed to condition the entropy-maximizing/information-minimizing state probabilities. And, in the special case of iid Type I Extreme Value error terms and a linear-in-the-parameters systematic utility function, the random utility and entropy maximizing approaches yield identical results.

The reason that this apparently somewhat esoteric set of observations is raised here is that it ties back to earlier discussions concerning model (dis)aggregation/fidelity and, specifically, to the role of logit models in our modelling systems. In any model system we inevitably reach a point at which further disaggregation of actors, processes, etc., simply is not feasible, given data, theory or computational constraints (among others), or because more microlevel outcomes simply are not of interest and are assumed not to be critical to the determination of the outcomes of interest. At such a point, we inevitably make the assumption that all more microlevel outcomes are equally likely and that the actors being modelled are homogeneous with respect to unmodelled attributes, that is, we make 'entropy model'-type assumptions. At this point, we are acknowledging the furthest reach of our theory and our information about the system that we are trying to model: we cannot go 'deeper' even if we wished to do so. At this point, the best we can do is to generate 'most likely' probabilities as a function of whatever explanatory variables are at hand and are believed to be statistically helpful.

This may be a perfectly fine outcome, given the problem at hand (e.g. a simple choice among uncorrelated alternatives). Implicit in the thrust of this chapter's discussions and explicit in Timmermans' concerns with the 'over-reliance' on simple logit models in many current integrated models is that often this is *not* sufficient, that our preferences for alternatives are, in fact, correlated, that utility specifications are complex and that decision rules other than 'simple' utility maximization may be operative. In all such cases, the call for 'more/better theory' reflects the need to bring additional behavioural insight to the specification of the decision process than is inherent in the simple logit formulation. In particular, as Timmermans eloquently notes, the predominance of typically quite simple logit/entropy models to explain spatial processes such as residential location choice, trip destination choice, etc., is worrisome, given the critical role these models play in the overall model system and given that we know that these decisions depend on many factors over and above those typically included in many operational models. This issue is returned to in the section 'What do We need to Know?'.

Agent-Based Microsimulation

Arguably the single biggest methodological advance over the past >10 years that will continue to play out for some time to come and that will make the high-fidelity behavioural theory sketched in this chapter feasible to implement is the emergence of *agent-based microsimulation* as a viable modelling approach.

An *agent* is an intelligent object that is capable of autonomous action. It perceives its environment and responds to this environment according to a set of decision rules. It may be capable of learning and adapting based on its experiences. This definition could describe a thermostat or an adaptive traffic signal controller, but it also clearly and perfectly describes our theoretical model of the person and the group, as defined in the section 'Elements of a Theory of Urban Systems'. Thus, the agent-based approach provides a potentially one-to-one correspondence between the decision-making entities/agents in the theoretical framework and their computational representation as implemented within a computer-based model.

Stated this way, this may seem like an obvious approach, but it represents a major step forward in terms of our modelling capability: the agent is a powerful and parsimonious object within which a decision-maker can be computationally represented in terms of his/her characteristics, knowledge and behaviours (motivations and decision rules). As such, it is the mechanism by which complex models of agent actions and multi-agent inter-actions (either collaborative/social or competitive/market based) can be constructed, potentially without falling prey to wrongheadedness (because the agent's behaviour has high fidelity with reality), complicatedness (because the behaviour of the agent itself is readily explainable; complexity arises out of the interplay of agent's actions) and mechanicalness (because the system state emerges out of the behaviours of agents rather then from aggregate, correlative statistical functions).

Microsimulation simply refers to a simulation model that operates at a very fine level of disaggregation ('microlevel'), typically involving the stochastic evolution of a system state as the emergent outcome of interactions of microlevel elements that comprise the system being modelled. Microsimulation as a modelling method and its potential strengths as a means for implementing disaggregate behavioural models have been discussed in detail elsewhere (Goulias and Kitamura, 1992; Miller, 1996, 2003; Miller and Salvini, 2002). Microsimulation is clearly the obvious method of choice for agent-based modelling, but not all microsimulation models are agent based. Operational activity/travel microsimulation models are now rapidly becoming the state-of-the-art and even the state of best/advanced practice worldwide. It is clear that they work.[23] They provide a method for avoiding grossness (Lee's second sin) and managing comprehensiveness without incurring the sin of hypercomprehensiveness. Microsimulation, simply put, is what makes agent-based modelling feasible.

Note that in speaking of random utility models, agent-based models and microsimulation, we are not discussing substitutes but rather complementary elements of the overall integrated model. The agent-based approach deals with how to represent decision-making actors and to encapsulate their behaviour (whatever that behaviour might be). That is, it is a model of 'form' or 'entity' and is relatively indifferent to what entity and what behaviour is being modelled. Random utility theory is one approach for modelling behaviour/decision-making. It is relatively indifferent to the representation of the decision-maker. Thus, it can be implemented as the behavioural rule within an agent-based representation of the decision-maker, but it also need not be implemented in this way. And microsimulation is a computational method for representing the system state within which agents exist and act and interact, keeping track of these actions and interactions, handling the flow of information within the system to and among agents and evolving the system state over (simulated) time as an outcome of these actions/interactions. As such, a microsimulator is an *evolutionary engine* that is the

[23]The 23 million trips in the New York metropolitan area are currently operationally modelled using a microsimulation model (Vovsha et al., 2002).

computational representation of the system state and its dynamic evolution (emergent macrosystem 'behaviour') over time. The microsimulator is the 'agent' that 'sums the parts' to create the whole. Or, in other words, the microsimulator is the computational representation of the 'world' within which decision-making agents 'live' and 'behave' as a function of whatever behavioural rules (random utility or otherwise) they have.

It is argued that this nexus of advanced methods for representing decision processes, agent-based representation of decision-making entities and microsimulation as a method for representing and evolving system states (i.e. the collective state of the decision-making agents and their environment), all implemented within cost-effective, readily accessible, high-performance computing systems, substantially changes both the theoretical and operational environment for integrated urban modelling. This means that we can usefully posit theory at the disaggregate level at which we know it occurs, and that we have a way forward towards implementing this theory in practical models.

This represents a substantial shift in worldview from that presented by Lee (1994) just 12 years ago, and indicates to a considerable degree the extent to which the field is rapidly evolving. Returning to the concerns expressed by Timmermans (2003), however, it is clearly the case that the potential outlined in this chapter has not yet translated in large measure into operational models. In particular, within the general (and still quite abstract) framework sketched in this chapter, significant issues of both theory and practical implementation remain to be addressed if the full potential of the general framework is to be realized. These issues are briefly enumerated and discussed in the next section.

What do We Need to Know?

While an arguably strong general theoretical framework has been sketched in the previous sections to support integrated modelling, a number of very critical issues remain for which current theory is inadequate and, as a result, operational models are particularly weak. Several of these were previously discussed by Timmermans (2003) and are revisited here.

Most critical is our *lack of a good, implementable theory of spatial choice*, with respect to both location choices (homes, employment, etc.) and activity destination choice. Timmermans is absolutely correct of his critique of existing models in this regard. The over-reliance on 'spatial interaction' models in which distance (or even a loosely defined 'accessibility' term) is the primary explanatory variable for location or destination choice—and the fact that this reliance has not changed substantially in over 40 years of modelling—is indicative of a significant lack of deep understanding of spatial decision processes.[24] This is very troublesome, to say the least, given that the raison d'etre of integrated models is to model spatial processes!

The disaggregate agent-based conceptual framework outlined in this chapter provides some starting points for developing improved theory/models of spatial behaviour. Elements of an improved approach include:

- Work 'trip distribution' must be replaced by a model (or models) of residential and job location choices, out of which the journey to work is emergent. This is not a new concept: it lies at the heart of 1960s technology Lowry models (Lowry, 1964).[25] Similarly, school 'trip distribution' should reflect a school location choice (or allocation) process.
- Residential locations must be determined within a proper residential housing market model, as sketched above. It may reference access to the known workplaces of household members as one explanatory variable, but it must also incorporate housing prices, neighbourhood attributes, accessibilities to activities other than work and household attributes (income, household size, etc.) that are known to influence residential location choice.
- Similarly, labour markets need to be explicitly modelled in terms of the demand and supply of labour. From this will come the employment locations of workers. Choice of employment location (or the 'dual problem' of choice of workers by firms) can reference known worker locations, but, again, the model must be more than just one of 'spatial interaction', that is, it must include more than just distance/ travel time in its explanatory variable set.
- Improved models of shopping and other location choices must be developed that are sensitive to people's daily schedules and trip chains, non-home 'anchor points' (e.g. work), etc.

A second major weakness of current models identified by Timmermans is the *lack of a theoretical understanding of how short-run activities* (e.g. daily trip making) *influence long-run decisions* concerning residential and job locations, auto ownership levels, etc. This, again, is very troubling given that this linkage between the short run (i.e. travel) and the long run (i.e. location choices) is what the 'integrated' in integrated models is supposed to connote. Many current models are at best loosely 'connected' via a 'logsum' feedback term from the travel model to the 'land use' model. While nominally

[24]The same comment holds true for conventional travel models. The use of gravity models in the trip distribution stage of the modelling system is by far the theoretically weakest link of the model system. This weakness is usually 'covered up' by massive over-fitting of the model during model calibration. The effects of this over-calibration of a behaviourally inadequate model within travel demand forecasting can only be guessed at, since very little systematic investigation into this problem seems to have occurred.

[25]This is also the foundation for the regional travel demand modelling system used in the Greater Toronto Area (Miller, 2001).

motivated by random utility theory, such logsums are in practice rather ad hoc in their implementation. At the other extreme, strongly integrated models, such as the Lowry and MEPLAN families of models, typically are strongly dependent on simple gravity/logit spatial interaction models to establish the integration, and so are susceptible to the criticisms discussed above.

Tied to this question of 'feedback' or 'integration' is the treatment of time and associated assumptions concerning system equilibrium and lags/leads in the system. Most operational models make the reasonable assumption that current decisions depend on the prior system state, since an agent's knowledge can only be based on what she/he has experienced in the past and an agent clearly *cannot* know the current 'instantaneous' system state, since this current state is in the process of emerging as an outcome of this (and other) agent's current decisions. The problem arises in that very arbitrary assumptions are typically made concerning the nature of lagged responses, and, in particular, the time step between decision points. The time step assumed in any simulation model is a critical design parameter and represents a form of temporal aggregation. As a result, a model based on a given time step has embedded within its parameters, etc., artefacts of this temporal aggregation and so cannot be readily applied to a different time step.

Thus, current models tend to be arbitrary with respect to both the nature of the 'feedback' between the short and the long run and the definition of the temporal unit of analysis defining 'short' and 'long' runs and the flow of information between these two time frames. The issue of time step is one that for the foreseeable future will probably remain a matter of model design, although this design assumption can be informed by our best understanding of the 'natural rhythms' of temporal processes.[26] The nature/content of the 'feedback', however, is something that can be improved through improved conceptualization of the problem.

As one example of this, one can build on the concepts presented in this chapter to develop the concept of *stress* as a 'feedback' measure. The concept of stress in spatial modelling is, of course, not new, dating back to at least Rossi's (1955) seminal work concerning residential location stress. As discussed in detail elsewhere (Miller and Sarjeant, 1987; Miller, 2005b; Salvini and Miller, 2005), stress can be defined as the difference between the utility of a current system state and the utility of some desired or 'expected' system state. These stresses are determined within daily life, given current resource constraints. If stress reaches some threshold value, the agent may decide to

[26]Note that much of this problem of 'time step' would be eliminated if one adopted an *event-driven* simulation framework rather than the conventional *time-driven* approach assumed here (Litwin, 2005). Although a promising approach (and very compatible with the overall conceptual framework sketched in this chapter), implementation details remain to be resolved before large-scale event-driven simulators will be operationally viable.

search for ways to change its resource set so as to reduce stress (improve its system state). Thus, for example, stress due to excessive commuting time might be reduced by changing mode or time of day of travel, by purchasing another car, by changing residential location, by changing employment location or by some combination of these options. Thus, within this conceptualization, 'long-run' changes in resources are the behavioural response of agents to the lack of need fulfilment within their daily lives. Two recent papers present preliminary first-cuts at stress-based models of household residential mobility (Habib et al., 2006) and automobile transactions (Roorda et al., 2006) that illustrate this approach to the problem.

A third major limitation of current models is their *weak treatment of land development and building supply processes*. Housing demand typically receives the bulk of modelling attention, with land development models tending to be behaviourally quite simplistic (at best simple profit-maximization assumptions) and aggregate.[27] Although almost inevitably referred to as 'land use' models, most operational models actually are primarily models of *location* choice given land use, with the actual land use component typically being a very weak link in the model system.

The land development and building industries are not particularly well understood, and much more conceptual and empirical research is required into developer/builder behaviour before improved models of building supply will be operationally available (Haider, 2003). The agent-based approach advocated in this chapter provides a possible framework for conceptualizing and eventually operationalizing improved building supply models, but it is clear that this is an area for considerable new and innovative research and development work if such improved models are to be developed.

A somewhat related point is that *'activity supply' representation must be significantly improved in integrated models* if the full benefits of activity-based travel models are to be achieved. Even more so than in the case of housing markets, by far most of the effort to date has gone into the modelling of the *demand* for activity participation, assuming known locations, amounts and types of 'activity sites' (stores, recreational facilities, etc.). The ability to model the evolution of these activity sites over time is very limited at this point in time. This concern obviously ties back to the issue of modelling activity location choice: without detailed representations of the 'activity location choice set', it is difficult to build improved activity location choice models. One approach to improving this situation begins with improving the modelling of the urban region's spatial economy, as discussed in the section 'Urban Macroeconomics'. Note however,

[27]Alternatively, cellular automata models are employed in which each spatial cell/zone 'chooses' the development that will occur within its area. While possessing some theoretical foundation (the cell is a proxy for the developer/owner of the land contained within the cell) and being relatively practical given current computational capabilities, data availability, etc., this approach is a highly abstracted one and is not fully consistent with the human-agent approach recommended in this chapter.

that, while conceptually appealing, this approach involves significant data issues and theoretical concerns with respect to improving the fidelity of both our spatial precision and activity typing.

This chapter has glossed over *household- and social network-based modelling of 'collaborative' agent interactions*. It has noted that significant recent progress in household-based modelling has occurred and is expected to continue for some time to come. Operational modelling of more general agent interactions within social networks is a much longer term research and development project, although it does hold promise for understanding inter-household interactions and decision-making.

Household mobility decisions (auto ownership, possession of driver's licences and transit passes, bicycle ownership, etc.) typically are absent from or at best included in a very rudimentary way in current integrated models. As Ben-Akiva (1974) observed 30 years ago, however, 'mobility bundle' decisions are intermediate between 'short-run' day-to-day travel dynamics and 'long-run' location choices, and have critical interfaces with both. Given, this, they represent an important integrating component within an 'integrated model'. In the framework presented within this chapter, they represent resource set decisions that need to be dealt with as stress-based behaviour within the unified household decision-making process (Roorda et al., 2006).

Finally, we are far from being able to operationalize substantive concepts of *learning and adaptation* in our model systems. This, however, should be a definite research and development goal, since these processes are clearly fundamental to human agency and so must play a substantial role in urban systems dynamics. Again, the conceptual framework outlined in this chapter accommodates learning and adaptation, but it is at the moment essentially a 'blank slate' in this regard and much work is required if appropriate theories of these processes can be developed and tested.

Final Thoughts

This chapter has attempted to sketch a conceptual framework for integrated urban models. It has argued that considerable theory does, indeed, exist to support such models, in particular:

- an understanding of human agency, which includes processes of perception, decision-making, learning and adaptation;
- an understanding of economic processes (micro and macro) that shape urban socio-economic interactions.

Powerful methods for model implementation exist, including:

- GIS for the management, display and analysis of spatial data;

- random utility choice models and other econometric models for implementing disaggregate behavioural models;
- agent-based microsimulation as a modelling paradigm for model implementation.

A number of significant gaps in our theoretical and practical understanding of urban systems, however, exist that limit current models and that require concerted research and development efforts to fill. These include:

- lack of strong theory concerning spatial choice (locations and destinations);
- lack of a consistent representation of how short- and long-run processes actually do 'integrate' within urban system processes;
- weak treatment of land development and building supply processes;
- poor representation of 'activity supply';
- the need for improved models of inter-agent collaboration, within both households and social networks;
- the need to incorporate mobility decisions (auto ownership, transit pass ownership, etc.) within the integrated modelling framework;
- the long-run need to incorporate learning and adaptation explicitly within the integrated modelling framework.

This is quite a 'shopping list' of needed improvements. Some suggestions were made within the chapter in terms of how the chapter's conceptual framework might provide a starting point for addressing a number of these concerns. But it is clear that we have much work ahead of us as we continue to develop integrated urban models that are adequate to meet the policy challenges of urban regions in the 21st century.

References

Alonso, W. (1964). *Location and Land Use*. Cambridge, MA, Harvard University Press.

Anas, A. (1983). Discrete choice theory, information theory, and the multinomial logit and gravity models. *Transportation Research B* 17, 13–23.

Arendt, H. (1958). *The Human Condition*. Chicago, The University of Chicago Press.

Axhausen, K. W. (2005). Social networks and travel: some hypotheses. In K. Donaghy (Ed.), *Social Aspects of Sustainable Transport: Transatlantic Perspectives*, Ashgate, Farnham, UK, pp. 90–108.

Ben-Akiva, M. E. (1974). Structure of passenger travel demand models. *Transportation Research Record* 526, 26–42.

Birch, D., R. Atkinson, S. Sandstrom and L. Stack (1974). *The New Haven Laboratory: A Test-Bed for Planning*. Lexington, MA, D.C. Heath.

Carrasco, J. A. and E. J. Miller (2006). Exploring the propensity to perform social activities: a social networks approach. *Transportation* 33(5), 463–480.

de la Barra, T. (1989). *Integrated Land Use and Transport Modelling*. Cambridge, MA, Cambridge University Press.

Dugundji, E. and J. Walker (2005). Discrete choice with social and spatial network interdependencies: an empirical example using mixed GEV models with field and "panel" effects. *Transportation Research Record* 1921, 70–78.

Echenique, M. H., A. D. J. Flowerdew, J. D. Hunt, T. R. Mayo, I. J. Skidmore and D. C. Simmonds (1990). The MEPLAN models of Bilbao, Leeds and Dortmund. *Transport Reviews* 10, 309–322.

Ellickson, B. (1981). An alternative test of the hedonic theory of housing markets. *Journal of Urban Economics* 9, 56–79.

Gleick, J. (1987). *Chaos: Making a New Science*. New York, Viking.

Gliebe, J. P. and F. S. Koppelman (2002). A model of joint activity participation between household members. *Transportation* 29, 49–72.

Goulias, K. G. and R. Kitamura (1992). Travel demand forecasting with dynamic microsimulation. *Transportation Research Records* 1357, 8–17.

Habib, K. M. N., E. I. Elgar and E. J. Miller (2006). Stress triggered household decision to change dwelling: a simultaneous dynamic approach. *11th International Association for Travel Behaviour Research Conference*. Kyoto.

Haider, M. (2003). Spatio-temporal modelling of housing starts in the Greater Toronto Area. Ph.D. Thesis, Department of Civil Engineering, University of Toronto, Toronto.

Hunt, J. D. and J. A. Abraham (2001). Heterogeneous agents in land use transport interaction modelling. *WEHIA 2001 Conference*. Honolulu.

Hunt, J. D. and J. A. Abraham (2003). Design and application of the PECAS land use modelling system. *8th Computers in Urban Planning and Urban Management Conference*. Sendai, Japan.

Hunt, J. D., E. J. Miller and D. S. Kriger (2005). Current operational urban land-use transport modeling frameworks. *Transport Reviews* 25(3), 329–376.

Hunt, J. D. and D. C. Simmonds (1993). Theory and application of an integrated land-use and transport modelling framework. *Environment and Planning B* 20, 221–244.

Ingram, G. K., J. F. Kain and J. R. Ginn (1972). *The Detroit Prototype of the NBER Urban Simulation Model*. New York, National Bureau of Economic Research.

Jacobs, J. (1969). *The Economy of Cities*. New York, Random House.

Jara-Diaz, S. R. (2003). Allocation and valuation of time savings. In D. A. Hensher and K. J. Button (Eds.), *Handbook of Transportation Modelling*. Amsterdam, Elsevier Science Ltd.

Knudsen, B. (2009). The path to a staged implementation of integrated models. *TRB Innovations in Travel Modeling Conference*. Austin.

Lee, D. B. (1973). Requiem for large scale models. *Journal of the American Institute of Planners* 39, 163–178.

Lee, D. B. (1994). Retrospective on large scale urban models. *Journal of the American Planning Association* 60, 35–40.

Lindblom, C. (1959). The science of muddling through. *Public Administration Review* 19, 79–88.

Litwin, M. (2005). Dynamic household activity scheduling processes. Ph.D. Thesis, Department of Civil Engineering, University of Toronto, Toronto.

Lowry, I. S. (1964). *A Model of Metropolis*. RM-4035-RC. Santa Monica, CA, Rand Corp.

Lynch, K. (1981). *A Theory of Good Urban Form*. Cambridge, MA, MIT Press.

Maoh, H. F. and P. S. Kanaroglou (2005). Agent-based firmographic models: a simulation framework for the City of Hamilton. *PROCESSUS Second International Colloquium on the Behavioural Foundations of Integrated Land-use and Transportation Models: Frameworks, Models and Applications*. Toronto.

Martinez, F. J. (1992). The bid-choice land-use model: an integrated econometric framework. *Environment and Planning A* 24, 871–875.

Martinez, F. J. (1996). MUSSA: land use model for Santiago City. *Transportation Research Record* 1552, 126–134.

Maslow, A. H. (1970). *Motivation and Personality*, 2nd edn. New York, Harper & Row.

Meyer, M. D. and E. J. Miller (2001). *Urban Transportation Planning*, 2nd edn. New York, McGraw-Hill.

Miller, E. J. (1996). Microsimulation and activity-based forecasting. In Texas Transportation Institute (Ed.), *Activity-Based Travel Forecasting Conference, Summary, Recommendations, and Compendium of Papers*. June 2–5, Travel Model Improvement Program, US Department of Transportation and US Environmental Protection Agency, Washington, DC, pp. 151–172.

Miller, E. J. (2001). *The Greater Toronto Area Travel Demand Modelling System, Version 2.0, Volume I: Model Overview*. Joint Program in Transportation. Toronto, University of Toronto.

Miller, E. J. (2003). Microsimulation. In K. G. Goulias (Ed.), *Transportation Systems Planning Methods and Applications*, Vol. 12. Boca Raton, FL, CRC Press, pp. 12-1–12-2.

Miller, E. J. (2005a). Propositions for modelling household decision-making. In M. Lee-Gosselin and S. T. Doherty (Eds.), *Integrated Land-use and Transportation Models: Behavioural Foundations*, Oxford, Elsevier, pp. 21–60.

Miller, E. J. (2005b). An integrated framework for modelling short- and long-run household decision-making. In H. Timmermans (Ed.), *Progress in Activity-based Analysis*, Oxford, Elsevier, pp. 175–202.

Miller, E. J. (2005c). Project-based activity scheduling for household and person agents. In H. S. Mahmassani (Ed.), *Transportation and Traffic Theory, Flow, Dynamics and Human Interaction, Proceedings of the 16th International Symposium on Transportation and Traffic Theory*. Elsevier, Oxford, pp. 565–584.

Miller, E. J. and A. Haroun (2000). A microsimulation model of residential housing markets. *9th International Association for Travel Behaviour Research Conference*. Gold Coast, Queensland, Australia.

Miller, E. J., D. S. Kriger and J. D. Hunt (1998). Integrated urban models for simulation of transit and land-use policies. Final Report, Transit Cooperative

Research Project H-12, University of Toronto Joint Program in Transportation, Toronto. Available at: http://www4.nas.edu/trb/crp.nsf

Miller, E. J. and M. J. Roorda (2003). A prototype model of household activity/travel scheduling. *Transportation Research Record* 1831, 114–121.

Miller, E. J., M. J. Roorda, C. A. Kennedy, A. S. Shalaby and H. MacLean (2006). Activity-based, multi-modal modelling of travel behaviour for urban design. Final Project Report to Transport Canada Transportation Planning and Modal Integration Initiatives, Joint Program in Transportation, University of Toronto, Toronto.

Miller, E. J. and P. A. Salvini (2002). Activity-based travel behavior modeling in a microsimulation framework invited resource paper. In H. S. Mahmassani (Ed.), *Perpetual Motion, Travel Behavior Research Opportunities and Application Challenges*, Vol. 26. Amsterdam, Pergamon, pp. 533–558.

Miller, E. J. and P. M. Sarjeant (1987). A model of continuous intra-urban residential search. *34th North American Meeting of the Regional Science Association*. Baltimore.

Mumford, L. (1961). *The City in History*. New York, Harcourt, Brace & World.

Páez, A. and D. Scott (2007). Social influence on travel behavior: a simulation example of the decision to telecommute. *Environment and Planning A* 39(3), 647–665.

Roorda, M. J., J. A. Carrasco and E. J. Miller (2006). A joint model of car ownership and activity scheduling. *11th International Association for Travel Behaviour Research Conference*. Kyoto.

Rossi, P. (1955). *Why Families Move*. New York, McMillan.

Salvini, P. A. and E. J. Miller (2005). ILUTE: an operational prototype of a comprehensive microsimulation model of urban systems. *Networks and Spatial Economics* 5, 217–234.

Shannon, C. E. (1948). A mathematical theory of communication. *Bell System Technical Journal* 27, 379–423.

Timmermans, H. (2003). The saga of integrated land use-transport modeling: how many more dreams before we wake up? Conference keynote paper. *10th International Conference on Travel Behaviour Research*. Lucerne.

Vanderburg, W. H. (2000). *The Labyrinth of Technology*. Toronto, University of Toronto Press.

Vovsha, P., E. Peterson, and R. Donnelly (2002). Micro-simulation in travel demand modelling: lessons from the New York "best practices" model. *81st Annual Meeting of the Transportation Research Board*. Washington, DC.

Webber, M. (1977). Pedagogy again: what is entropy? *Annuals of the Association of American Geographers* 67, 254–266.

Wegener, M. (1994). Operational urban models: state of the art. *Journal of the American Planning Association* 60, 17–29.

Wilson, A. G. (1967). A statistical theory of spatial distribution models. *Transportation Research* 1, 253–269.

2.9 Application to Policy Analysis and Planning

The Expanding Sphere of Travel Behaviour Research
Selected Papers from the 11th International Conference on Travel Behaviour Research

15

Application to Policy Analysis and Planning

Konstadinos G. Goulias

Abstract

In this paper, an evolving paradigm for modeling and simulation is described. It is emerging from a need to understand and analyze travel behavior and to develop travel demand forecasting procedures in facets that emerge from three sources: (a) dynamic planning practice; (b) sustainable and green visions, and (c) new research and technology. The typical aspects of data collection, modeling, and simulation considered for transportation policy analysis and planning are in this way examined from perspectives that raise many questions about our ability to make programmatic assessments. More sophisticated tools are needed to account for direct and indirect effects of behavior, procedures for behavioral change, and to provide finer resolution in the four dimensions of geographic space, time, social space, and jurisdictions. Dynamic planning is also stressing the need to examine trends, cycles, but to also invert the time progression and develop paths that lead to visions about the future and derive actions needed today. We also find a need for field testing that resembles experimental settings and a research program to design suitable experimental or quasiexperimental methods. Many issues remain to be solved in the modeling areas of scale in time and space, as well as error tolerance and their mapping to strategy evaluations. Three additional needs are a better understanding of perceptions of time and space, consideration of the multiple dimensions of time, and human interaction.

Introduction

The impressive program of this conference emerges from three related but distinct sources (Figure 1). At the very center of Figure 1 is the evolving paradigm of modeling and simulation. It is on the one hand influenced by a tendency to build comprehensive simulation models that attempt to mimic the real world but on the other hand aims

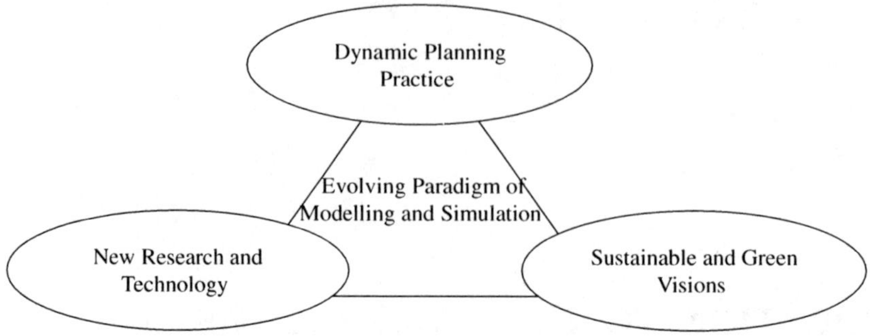

Figure 1
The Evolving Modeling and Simulation Paradigm and its Sources

also to provide special purpose applications designed for limited scope, horizons, and very specific policy questions. We can imagine there are three major sources that influence and define the core paradigm. The first source is a fundamental change in planning practice that moves us toward strategic planning and performance-based planning. The more comprehensive term *dynamic planning* is preferred here to indicate the existence of bidirectional time (from the past to the future and from the future to today), as well as, policy assessment cycles and adjustments taking place within the short-term, medium-term, and long-term horizons. These cycles are also bidirectional in time. Within dynamic planning we find three fundamental directions of practice that are: (a) inventory creation and maintenance; (b) strategy measurement and evaluation; and (c) forecasting and backcasting.

The second source is a vision that generates the substantive problems we need to solve and the specific policies we need to examine. It is named *sustainable and green visions* herein. Problems and solutions in this general area motivate and inspire contemporary substance and content of policies throughout the world and they do not seem to have found solutions. One can identify three complementary and mutually strengthening directions in the economy, environment, and society.

The third source is the never-ending research for improved understanding of the world surrounding us. This source is named *new research and technology* to capture the two most important elements of new discovery and new techniques enabling new discovery. Key directions of inquiry within research and technology are: (a) theory building; (b) modeling and simulation; and (c) enabling technologies.

Dynamic Planning Practice

Dynamic thinking means that time and change are intrinsic in the thought processes underlying planning activities. In the past, assumptions about the existence of a tenable equilibrium and our ability to build the infrastructure needed to meet demand did not require careful orchestration of actions. This was radically changed in the industrialized world to meet specific goals using available resources to maximize benefits. Together with our inability to build at will and a tendency to the preservation of nonrenewable resources (e.g., land and open space, fossil fuels, time), we are much more motivated today to think strategically and to consider in a more careful way the performance of the overall anthropogenic system as we plan, design, operate, and manage transportation systems. Any action of this type, however, requires that we have a detailed and accurate picture of our facilities, their interconnectedness, their status within the hierarchy of movements, their conditions, and their evolving role. An accurate and more complete picture like this is called an inventory herein.

Inventory Creation and Maintenance

Many planning activities at all geographical levels are preceded by data gathering steps of identifying all the sources of data and information. When planning for a specific area, this includes data about the specific area but also data about its relationship with the rest of the world. These inventories include the typical information about the resident population—demographics and employment, land and land uses, economic development and growth, and so forth. Data gathered are also about the flow of people, goods, and communication that takes place at a given period. Inventories may also include data and information about cultural and historical factors. For example, in a statewide plan for Pennsylvania (called PennPlan, Goulias et al., 2001), we identified a variety of corridors as buffers of land and communities around major routes of the movement of people and goods. Some of these routes were created in the 1800s when pioneers were still exploring uncharted lands. These routes experienced a major change when waterways were the main links among economic and military centers, and they are still evolving. Today these same routes contain as backbones railways, freeways, rivers, and often they surround major distribution locations such as ports and airports. Their nature is heavily influenced by their historical and cultural context. Travel behavior analysts are familiar with inventories created for the regional long-range plans, which in the United States subdivide the study area in traffic analysis zones with data from the US Decennial Census suitably reformatted and packaged for use in a specific application (i.e., the long-range regional plan). Then, additional data are assigned to these same subdivisions to build a richer context for modeling and simulation. Thus, the result for a typical long-range metropolitan transportation plan is an electronic map of where people live and work, the network(s) that connect different locations, availability of different modes on each segment of the network, as well as information about travel network performance (e.g., link capacities, speeds on links, congestion, and connectivity). Today the tool of choice for data storage and visualization is a Geographic Information System (GIS) used as a spatio-temporal relational database but other relational databases are also widely used and interfaced with GIS.

One of the thorniest problems within this context is maintaining an up to date inventory (e.g., characteristics of the population in each zone, presence of certain types of businesses). This is a particularly important issue for periods within the interval between decennial censuses. Many of these updates are becoming widely available and much less expensive than in the past. For example, the inventory of the highway network, with suitable additions and improvements, is available from the same private providers of in-vehicle navigation systems. In a similar way, inventories of businesses and residences can also be purchased from vendors. Census data, however, are required even when one uses data from private providers because they contain complementary data (e.g., the age distribution of the resident population). An agency is usually collecting ready-made databases and adds to the inventory other locally available information. This activity reaches its peak when a new long-range plan is created and when some sort of major investment is studied.

Although the need for inventories is undoubtedly extremely important many important issues are yet to be resolved (see the two transportation Research Board conference proceedings on the National Household Travel Survey http://www.trb.org/Conferences/NHTS/Program.pdf and the US Census and the Census American Community Survey http://www.trb.org/conferences/censusdata/. A selection of unanswered questions includes and it is not limited to:

- What levels of detail should we use in updating the data we have?
- Unavoidably data contain errors—what error tolerance are we building into models and policies?
- How often should we update the data and what methods should we use to fuse old with new data?
- Some policies require detail at the level of individuals, establishments, and parcels of land and others could be examined by more aggregate studies—what are some optimal techniques to merge data from different aggregation scales?

Obviously, the answers to these questions are in the form of "it depends." It depends on the budget (time and money) available, consequences of errors in the data, and the use of models in decision making. In fact, one particular type of data collection is strategy measurement and some of these questions become even more important.

Strategy Measurement and Evaluation

Strategic planning and performance-based planning changed the way we plan for the future. This has been a 15-year-long process in United States as its transportation policy at the Federal, State, and Metropolitan levels is shaped by three consecutive legislative initiatives (ISTEA, TEA-21, and SAFETEA-LU). Under all three legislative frameworks and independently of role, location, and perceived need for investment, the overall goal of funding allocation has been to maximize the performance of the transportation system in its entirety and avoid major new infrastructure building initiatives. As a result, planning practice at all geographical levels is becoming heavily performance based and designed in a way that motivates the measurement of policy and program outcomes and judging these outcomes for funding allocation. Two examples of performance-based planning are the Program Assessment Rating Tool (PART) at the federal level and performance-based transportation planning at the state level. PART is used to assess the management and performance of individual programs from homeland security to education, employment, and training. This is a tool that offers assessments about programs based on 25 questions divided into sections to analyze: (a) purpose and design of a program; (b) strategic planning and an agency's ability to define outcome-oriented yearly and longer term goals; (c) management and quality assurance; and (d) ability of a program to report accurately and consistently outcomes. For each program, a tailored analysis yields summaries that receive a rating from 0 to 100 (0–49 is ineffective, 50–69 is adequate, 70–84 is moderately effective, and 84–100 is effective). Programs requiring longer time frames to achieve higher scores are flagged and programs that are consistently underperforming are eliminated. Every year these reports are given to decision makers before budget preparation and they are used in budget allocations (US Government, 2006). Transportation related programs are for airport improvement, highway planning and construction, fixed guideway modernization capital investments, and the federal transit formula grants and research. Key to PART is a yearly update and evaluation.

In a different way but in the same spirit many states have created long-range plans that are strategic and they measure transportation performance (see Figure 2 for Minnesota and Figure 3 for California). Another example is PennPlan that includes yearly evaluative updates used for the first few years of a statewide strategic transportation plan in Pennsylvania. After a comprehensive public involvement campaign, a few themes capturing the desires of the resident population were first identified. To these themes technical requirements based on planners and agency inputs were added, a large number of objectives were created and then a variety of measures of performance were developed. These measures were given target levels that evolved over time to a desired future performance for the entire state and for a finite number of corridors of statewide significance. The yearly evaluation contained measures of target achievement and they were used to guide the Pennsylvania Department of Transportation in its investments.

Many infrastructure improvement projects in the United States are selected from lists of projects that regions (called Metropolitan Planning Organizations) submit to their state to be included in a list of Transportation Improvement Program (TIP) and become candidates for funding. Under statewide performance-based planning, these projects are evaluated with respect to their contribution in meeting the statewide performance measures and in the case of Pennsylvania the performance measures

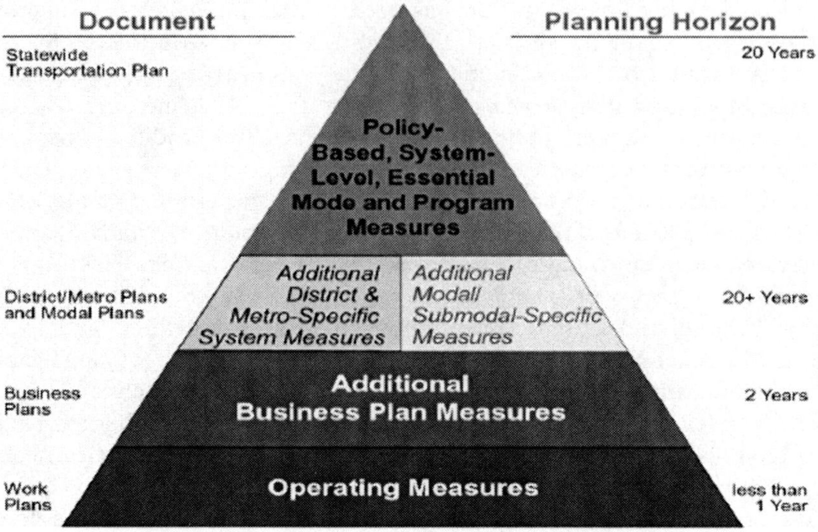

Figure 2
The Minnesota Performance Based Pyramid
Source: http://www.dot.state.mn.us/dashboards/plan-n-prog1.html

of the relevant corridor. Interestingly performance-based planning forces another important issue to move to forefront. Most transportation projects have implications that span their entire life including the period of construction/improvement that can take many years to complete. In fact, a list of transportation projects proposed for funding (named the Transportation Improvement Program) is a collection of short-, medium-, and long-term projects. Although, these projects are blended together very little discussion goes into their joint construction and implementation, relationship of scheduling these projects, and the timeline of impacts caused by that.

Although these examples are far ranging in time and space, they contain operations components and yearly evaluations that: (a) require data collection, modeling, and simulation at finer spatial and temporal scales than their counterpart planning feedbacks used in the long-range transportation planning practice, and (b) need a method that is able to coordinate the short-, medium-, and long-term impacts.

Equally important is also the method employed in making assessments about impacts. One can identify many methods for program assessment such as randomized controlled trials, direct controlled experiments, quasiexperimental, nonexperimental direct analysis, and nonexperimental indirect analysis. A *randomized controlled trial* identifies

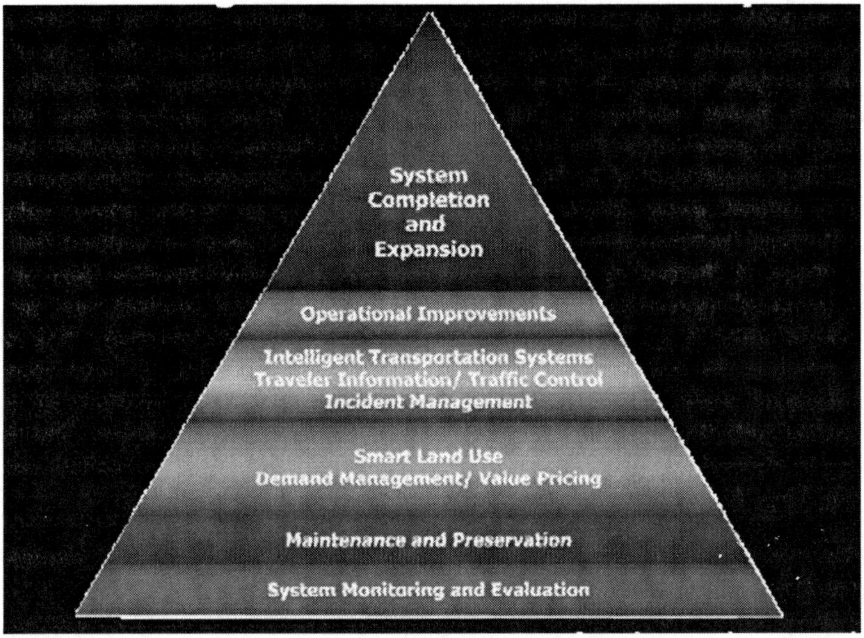

Figure 3
The GoCalifornia Initiative Pyramid
Source: CALTRANS (2007), http://www.dot.ca.gov/hq/tpp/offices/osp/ctp2025_files/ctp01.pdf

the universe of subjects (a person, household, group of persons, firms or establishments, geographic areas, and so forth). Then, a random assignment classifies these units into two groups: one that is subjected to an intervention and another that is not. A before and after measurement of the relevant variables produces measures of program impact and effectiveness. From a measurement viewpoint, this is the ideal method to evaluate impacts. However, it is also very hard to apply in transportation policy and planning due to legal, ethical, and cost-related reasons. Another method called the *direct controlled trials* is an inquiry of the different factors that determine the impact. In this approach, a before intervention survey creates the baseline information. Then, the intervention is implemented and a variety of measurements are made on the variables of interest. Intelligent transportation systems (ITS) evaluations follow this approach to examine the effectiveness of their deployment. A third method that attempts to approximate a randomized controlled trial is the *quasiexperimental group comparison*. In this method, two groups are selected by the analyst that are comparable in their base characteristics. One group is subjected to the intervention and the other is not. Selection is not random and for this reason many control groups and many control variables need to be included to minimize selection bias but to also control for other intervening factors. Many transportation applications use this type of design and data analysis leaving the door always open for doubts about the validity of the findings. A fourth method is the *nonexperimental direct analysis* that examines exclusively the group subject to intervention (e.g., employing a panel analysis approach with baseline considered to be the first occasion of measurement). Unfortunately, the lack of a control group allows for speculation and many doubts about validity of impact findings. In-laboratory experiments are also in this group of methods but in this design, theory is limited by ad-hoc investigations of action–reaction type of trials. A fifth group of approaches are the *nonexperimental indirect analysis* such as poling of an expert panel (e.g., Delphi methods used in land use forecasting). This method is best suited as the last resource. To the best of my knowledge, we have never seen a well-designed study that identifies the best impact assessment method for each of the planning activities and polices considered by transportation analysts. The method seems to be dictated by budgetary circumstances and habit. Some interesting questions emerging from these considerations are:

- What types of consistency do we need among geographic scales for planning and operations actions to perform evaluations?
- Are there policy requirements for coordination among planning activities to ensure consistency?
- Are there suitable methods to coordinate smaller projects in broader contexts (either of policy assessment or geographical area)?
- Do we have all the tools required to perform measurement of impacts and program evaluation at the newly defined assessment cycles?
- Which planning activity is better matched with which evaluation method?
- Are we excluding the randomized controlled experiments when we could perform them?

Some answers to the questions above are offered by the TRANSLAND project (Greiving and Kemper, 1999). Within the context of integration between land use and transportation planning and the context of the European union some of the conclusions include a call to strengthen regional plans, a stronger emphasis on public transport, strategic planning involving all actors, and the packaging of policies aiming at the same objectives. These themes are very similar to statewide and federal/union levels of planning. Very little, however, is said about the assessment methods and the choices we make in impact estimation.

Performance assessment and evaluation of program effectiveness requires the use of the inventory discussed before and a battery of models to forecast future expectations as well as to identify the actions required today to achieve desired futures. We call this forecasting when it departs from the past and the present to extrapolate the future in a prospective view and it is called backcasting when the view is reversed.

Forecasting and Backcasting

The Center for Urban Transportation Studies at the University of Wisconsin (1999), in its state-of-the-practice of travel demand forecasting review for the Federal Highway Administration (US DOT) describes the basic forecasting method used by Metropolitan Planning Organizations and State Departments of Transportation. This state-of-the-practice typical model is a reworked version of the four-step model that Metropolitan Planning Organizations are using for the past 40 years with the addition of freight (goods movement) forecasting. Emerging from that review is a tendency to modeling and simulation that employees simplified procedures, uses data available that are merged with local data sources, and targets a very limited repertory of policies. This approach is clearly inadequate for the contemporary strategic planning approaches used by all levels of government. The report also provides a review from a variety of innovative approaches that illustrate a movement toward the replacement of large traffic analysis zones by a more detailed geographic zonal system and the replacement of models applied to entire geographic areas by models applied to individuals. Contrary to this cautious approach to modeling and simulation by the states, forecasting activities at the regional level are moving rapidly toward an activity-based and microsimulation approach (see the most recent conference documenting the state of the practice in the United States and Europe at http://www.trb.org/Conferences/TDM/Program.asp).

Under this approach, models of discrete choice are applied to individual decision makers that are then used to (micro)simulate most of the possible combinations of choices in a day. The result is in essence a synthetic generation of people and their schedules (trip making and/or activities and trip making). When the microsimulation includes activities and the duration of stay at activity locations it becomes a synthetic schedule. In parallel, for forecasting purposes a synthetic population is first created for each land subdivision with all the relevant characteristics and then models are applied to the individuals in this population to represent areawide behavior. Changes are then imposed on each individual and based on all this predictive scenarios are developed. The evolution of individuals, their groups, and the entire study area can be used for trend analysis that includes details at the level of decision makers (either for passenger travel and/or for freight). In addition, progression in time happens from the present to the future and one could identify paths of change by individuals and groups (e.g., keeping detailed accounting of individuals as they move in time, using models that are designed for transitions over time and so forth). In a forecasting setting progression in time follows calendar time, temporal resolution is most often a year, and the treatment of dynamics is an one way causal stream to the future.

Within the broader study of futures, forecasting is the method we use to develop projective scenarios. Under strategic planning, however, we also need (retro)prospective studies that start from the desirable future and move backwards to identify specific actions that will lead us to that prospect. Backcasting has been used to do exactly this (see Sadek et al., 2002 that derived land use from travel demand using a four-step model). Authors attribute the term *backcasting* to Robinson (1982) in a study of future energy options. Scenarios in backcasting are the "images" of the future and the possible paths that will take us to that future. A typical application includes the stages shown in Figure 4. An open question, however, remains with respect to scenario construction and assessment. This is particularly important when one considers the serious issues mentioned earlier with inadequate design of experiments/trials in the forecasting setting.

Forecasting and backcasting have some important differences in their objectives. On one hand, forecasting is employed to identify likely futures and to develop methods to help us identify small changes in our policies. It is also a method to extrapolate past trends into the future and possibly identify paths of changes that are heavily influenced by habit and inertia. Backcasting, one the other hand, is designed to discover new ways to build desirable futures. It is perfectly aligned with strategic planning and it is a better-suited method for developing a program of conditions to meet targets.

Many of the models presented in this conference and many other conferences appear to be designed for forecasting applications (either to inform the design of forecasting model systems or to create necessary components in the model systems). Yet, planning

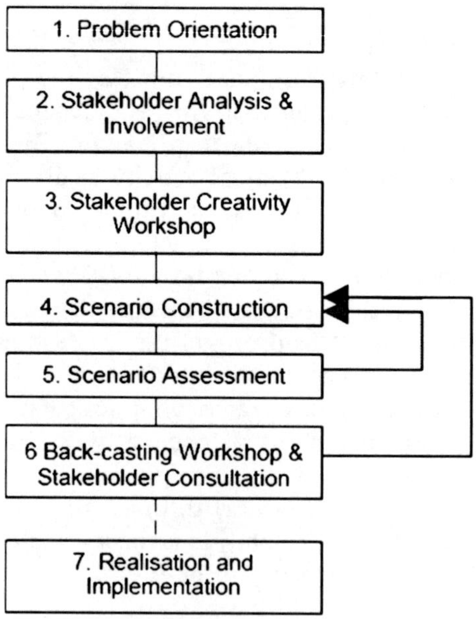

Figure 4

Stages in Backcasting

Source: Quist and Vergragt (2006)

practice is moving toward strategy development and therefore needs model components that fit within a backcasting scenario building that integrates resident attitudes within the scenario building and use of the simulation models.

Sustainable and Green Visions

Contemporary policy actions also view the world surrounding us as an integral ecosystem placing more emphasis on its overall survival by examining direct and indirect effects of individual policy actions and entire policy packages or programs (see the examples in Meyer and Miller, 2001). This trend is not limited to transportation. Lomborg (2001) shows that a sustainable and green vision encompasses the entire range of human activity and the entirety of the ecosystem we live in. Although these are good news, because the approach enables analyses and policies that are consistent in their vision about futures, comprehensive views also reveal that the pace of economic growth and development is in clear conflict with the biological pace of evolution with unknown consequences (Tiezzi, 2003) strengthening the view that more comprehensive analytical frameworks are required.

In fact, a few of the most recent studies on research needs, which addresses the transportation and environment relationship by the Transportation Research Board of the National Academies (TRB, 1999, 2002), expand the envelope to incorporate ecology and natural systems and address human health in a more comprehensive way than in the past reiterating the urgency to address unresolved issues about environmental damage. As a result, we also experience a clear shift to policy analysis approaches that have an expanded scope and domain and they are characterized by explicit recognition of transportation system complexity and uncertainty.

Reflecting all this, *sustainable transportation*, is now often used to indicate a shift in the mentality of the community of transportation analysts to represent a vision of a transportation system that attempts to provide services that minimize harm to the environment. In fact, in one of the most comprehensive reviews of policies in North America, Meyer and Miller (2001) contrast the nonsustainable to the sustainable approaches. They provide a compelling argument about the change in these policies and how we are moving toward a more sustainable path. In the United States during the past 10 years, the need, to examine these new and more complex policy initiatives, has also become increasingly pressing due to the passage of a series of legislative initiatives (Acts) and associated Federal and State regulations on transportation policy, planning, and programming. The multimodal character of the new legislation, its congestion management systems and the taxing air quality requirements for selected US regions have motivated many new forecasting applications that in the early years were predominantly based on the Urban Transportation Planning System and related processes but during the last 5 years motivated a shift to richer conceptual frameworks.

In point of fact, air quality mandates motivated impact assessments of the so-called transportation control measures and the creation of statewide mobile source air pollution inventories (Stopher, 1994; Loudon and Dagang, 1994; Goulias et al., 1993) that require different analytical forecasting tools than in any pre-1990 legislative initiatives (Niemeier, 2003). An added motivation is also lack of substantial funding for transportation improvement projects and a shift to charge the entities that benefit the most from transportation system improvements creating a need for impact fee-assessment for individual private developers. These assessments create the need for higher resolution in the three dimensions of geography (space), time (time of day), and social space (groups of people with common interests and missions, households, individuals) used in typical regional forecasting models but also the domain of jurisdictions where major decisions are made. They also create a pressing need for interfaces with traffic engineering simulation tools that are approved and/or endorsed in legislation (e.g., see Paaswell et al., 1992). Another push for new tools is the assessment of technologies under the general name of ITS (i.e., bundles of technological solutions in the form of user services attempting to solve chronic problems such as congestion, safety, and air pollution). These policies, assessments, and the models developed to support their assessment should not be examined and usually are not studied in isolation from past initiatives. Policy frameworks thus defined emphasize also the market nature of these controls (a carrot–and-stick approach to implementation) and an air quality framework that in essence enriched our policy "tools" (see Meyer and Miller, 2001; Niemeier, 2003).

Today, these tools are becoming even more wide-ranging as the list in Table 1 demonstrates. As Garrett and Wachs, 1996, discuss in the context of a lawsuit against a regional planning agency in the Bay Area, traditional four-step regional simulation models (Creighton, 1970; Hutchinson, 1974; Ortuzar and Willumsen, 2001) are outpaced by the same legislative stream of the past 20 years that defined many of the policies described above. Unlike the "energy crisis" of the 1970s, the urgency and timeliness of modeling and simulation is becoming more urgent, more complex, and requires an "integrated" approach. Under these initiatives, forecasting models, in addition to long-term land use trends and air quality impacts, need to also address issues related to technology use and information provision to travelers in the short and medium terms. Similarly, the European Union focuses on issues such as: increasing citizen participation, intra-European integration, decentralization, deregulation, privatization, environmental concern, mobility costs, congestion management by population segments, and private infrastructure finance (see van der Hoorn, 1997).

These new policy initiatives place more complex issues in the domain of regional policy analysis and forecasting and amplify the need for methods that produce forecasts at the individual traveler and her/his household levels instead of the traffic analysis zone level. In addition to the long-range planning activities and the typical traffic management activities, analysts and researchers in planning need to also evaluate the following: (a) traveler and transportation system manager information provision and use

Table 1
Examples of Policy Tools

Type of policy tool	Brief description	Source of information*
Land use growth and management programs	Legislation that controls for the growth of cities in sustainable paths	www.smartgrowth.org www.awcnet.org www.fhwa.dot.gov/planning/ppasg.htm www.compassblueprint.org http://www.ecoiq.com/onlineresources/center/listoflinks/sustainability/communities/
Land use design and attention to neighborhood design for nonmotorized travel	Similar to the previous but with attention paid to individual neighborhoods	www.sustainable.doe.gov/landuse/luothtoc.shtml www.planning.dot.gov/Documents/DomesticScan/domscan2.htm
City annexations and spheres of influence	City boundaries are divided into incorporated, within the sphere of influence, and external to manage growth	countypolicy.co.la.ca.us/BOSPolicyFrame.htm www.ite.org/activeliving/files/Jeff_Summary.pdf
Accelerated retirement of vehicles programs	Programs to eliminate high emitting and older technology vehicles	ntl.bts.gov/DOCS/SCRAP.html
Public involvement and education programs	Programs aiming at defining goals based on the public's desires	www.fhwa.dot.gov/reports/pittd/contents.htm
Health promoting programs	Programs that promote physical activity in travel to benefit health	www.activelivingbydesign.org
Safety measures	A process to incorporate safety considerations in transportation planning	tmip.fhwa.dot.gov/clearinghouse/docs/safety/ www.fhwa.dot.gov/planning/scp/ www.safetyanalyst.org/
Emission control, vehicle miles traveled, and other fee programs (including carbon taxes and trading)	Programs that shift taxation from traditional sources toward pollutant emissions and natural-resource depletion agents	www.fresh-energy.org/ www.fhwa.dot.gov/environment/ www.fightglobalwarming.com/
Congestion pricing and toll collection programs	A premium is charged to travelers that wish to travel during the most congested periods	www.vtpi.org/london.pdf

Table 1: (Continued)

Type of policy tool	Brief description	Source of information*
Parking fee management	Parking pricing used as a tool to restrict access by space and time	www.gmu.edu/depts/spp/programs/parkingTaxes.pdf
Nonmotorized systems	Programs to support walking and biking	www.vtpi.org/tdm/tdm25.htm www.psrc.org/projects/nonmotorized
Telecommuting and Teleshopping	The employment of telecommunications to substitute–complement–enhance travel	www.telework-mirti.org www.vtpi.org/tdm/tdm43.htm
Flexible and staggered work programs	Programs that change the workweek of individuals and firms	www.its.dot.gov/JPODOCS/REPTS_PR/13669/section05.htm
Goods movements (freight) programs to improve operations	A variety of programs to facilitate and minimize the damage for freight movement	ntl.bts.gov/DOCS/harvey.html
Highway system improvements in traffic operations and flow	Improved data collection, monitoring, and traffic management	www.transportation.org ite.org/mega/default.asp
Intelligent Transportation Systems (ITS)	Use of telecommunications and information technology to manage and control travel	www.itsa.org/ www.ertico.com/ www.its.dot.gov/index.htm
Special event planning and associated traffic management	Enhanced procedures to handle the demands of a special event	http://.ops.fhwa.dot.gov/eto_tim_pse/index.htm
Security preparedness through metropolitan planning processes	A process to incorporate safety considerations in transportation planning	www.planning.dot.gov/Documents/Securitypaper.htm
Individualized marketing techniques with improved information and communication with the "customer"	Public programs to provide personal help in changing travel behavior in favor of environmentally friendly modes	www.local-transport.dft.gov.uk/travelplans/index.htm http://www.travelsmart.gov.au/

*Accessed August 2007.

(e.g., location based services, smart environments providing real-time information to travelers, vehicles, and operators); (b) combinations of transportation management actions and their impacts (e.g., parking fee structures and city center restrictions, congestion pricing), and (c) assessment of combinations of environmental policy actions (e.g., carbon taxes and information campaigns about health effects of ozone).

These also need to have forecasting and backcasting capabilities and they need to be more accurate and detailed in space and time than the usual four-step models. In fact, planning initiatives are moving toward parcel-by-parcel analysis and yearly assessments. It is also conceivable that we need separate analyses for different seasons of a year and days of the week to capture seasonal and within a week variations of travel. Echoing all this and in the context of the Dutch reality Borgers et al. (1997) have identified five information need domains for policy analysis and they are (in a somewhat modified format from the original list):

(a) social and demographic trends that may produce a structural shift in the relationship between places and time allocation by individuals invalidating existing travel behavior model systems;
(b) increasing scheduling and location flexibility and degrees of freedom for individuals in conducting their every day business leading to the need to consider additional choices (e.g., departure time from home, work at home, shopping by the Internet, shifting activities to the weekend) in modeling travel behavior;
(c) changing quality and price of transport modes based on market dynamics and not on external to the travel behavior policies (e.g., the effect of deregulation in public transport);
(d) shifting of attitudes and potential cycles in the population outlook about modes; and
(e) changing scales/jurisdictions (scale is the original term used to signify the different jurisdictions)—different policy actions in different sectors have direct and indirect effects on transportation and different policy actions in transportation have direct and indirect effects in the other sectors (typical example in the United States is the welfare to work program).

New Research and Technologies

The planning and policy analysis discussion identified many requirements for modeling and simulation. Planning and policy have expanded the context of travel behavior models to entire life paths of individuals and for this reason a more general modeling framework is emerging. In fact, modeling made tremendous progress toward a comprehensive approach to, in essence, build simulated worlds on computer enabling the study of complex policy scenarios. The emerging framework in passenger travel demand, however, contains many gaps and it is incomplete (Miller, 2006; Timmermans, 2003). It is, however, rich in the directions taken and potential for scientific discovery, policy analysis, and more comprehensive approaches in dealing with sustainability issues. Although, passenger travel received the bulk of the attention, similar contributions to new research and technology are found in modeling of goods movement (freight transportation) that lag behind passenger planning and modeling (Southworth, 2003). There are four dimensions that one can identify in building taxonomies of policies and models. The first is the *geographic space* and its conditional continuity, the second is the *temporal scale* and calendar continuity, the third is interconnectedness of *jurisdictions*, and the fourth and most important is the set of relationships in *social space* for individuals and their communities. These four dimensions very often cannot be disengaged from each other. For example, when one considers issues associated with a change in propulsion fuels and energy consumption for transportation, the planning horizons are very often 25 or more years. This may also be accompanied by planning that expands beyond the borders of a single country because producers and consumers may be organized in market unions (Organization of Petroleum Exporting Countries—OPEC, European Union—EU) and planned actions involve governments and private companies. Issues of this type are long term, encompass larger geographic regions, and involve a complex network of organizations. These are in the realm of grand visions and policies. In contrast, at the other end of the spectrum we find measures and actions aiming at resolving a very localized problem such as access to facilities for disabled persons. In this case, the time horizon is a few months and the solutions can be achieved locally, for example, access to persons with disabilities via installation of ramps in buildings to meet the Americans with Disabilities Act requirements.

The first dimension, *geographic space* here is intended as the physical space in which human action occurs. This dimension has played important roles in transportation planning and modeling because the first preoccupation of the transportation system designers has been to move persons from one location to another. Initial applications considered the territory divided into large areas (traffic analysis zones), represented by a virtual center of gravity (centroid), and connected by facilities (higher level highways). The centroids were connected to the higher level facilities using a virtual connector summarizing the characteristics of all the local roads within the zone. As computational power increased and the types of policies/strategies required increased resolution the zone became smaller and smaller. Today is not unreasonable to expect software to handle zones that are as small as a parcel of land and transportation facilities that are as low in the hierarchy as a local road (the centroid becomes the housing unit and the centroid connector the driveway of the unit and they are no longer virtual). As we will see later in this chapter in analyzing behavior we are interested in understanding human action. For this reason in some applications geographic space needs to consider more than just physical features (Golledge and Stimson, 1997, p. 387) moving us into the notion of place and social space (see also below). The second dimension is *time* that is intended here as continuity of time, irreversibility of the temporal path, and the associated artificiality of the time period considered in many models. For example, models used in long-range planning applications use typical days (e.g., a Summer day for air pollution). In many regional long-range models, the unspoken assumption is that we target a typical work weekday in developing models to assess policies. Households and their members, however, may not always (if at all) obey this strict definition of a typical weekday to schedule their activities and they may follow very different decision-making horizons in allocating time to activities within a day, spreading activities among many days including weekends, substituting out of home with in home activities in some days but doing exactly the opposite on others, and using telecommunications only selectively (e.g., on Fridays and Mondays more often than on other days). Obviously, taking into account these scheduling activities is by far more complex than what is allowed in existing transportation planning models. The third dimension is *jurisdictions* and their interconnectedness. The actions of each person are "regulated" by jurisdictions with different and overlapping domains such as federal agencies, state agencies, regional authorities, municipal governments, neighborhood associations, trade associations and societies, religious groups, and formal and informal networks of families and friends. In fact, the federal government defines many rules and regulations on environmental protection. These may end up being enforced by a local jurisdiction (e.g., a regional office of an agency within a city). On one hand, we have an organized way of governance that clearly defines jurisdictions and policy domains (e.g., tax collection in the United States). On the other hand, however, the relationships among jurisdictions and decision making about allocation of resources does not follow always this orderly governance principle of hierarchy. A somewhat different and more "bottom up" relationship is found in the social network and for this reason requires a different dimension. The fourth and final dimension is *social space* and the relationships among persons within this space. For example, individuals from the same household living in a neighborhood may change their daily time allocation patterns and location visits to accommodate and/or take advantage of changes in the neighborhood such as elimination of traffic and the creation of pedestrian zones. Depending on the effects of these changes on the pedestrian network, we may also see a shift within the neighborhood social behavior. In contrast, increase in traffic to surrounding places may create outcry by other surrounding neighborhoods, thus, complicating the relationships among the residents. The most important domain and entity within this social space is the household. This has been a very popular unit of analysis in transportation planning recognizing that strong relationships within a household can be used to capture behavioral variation (e.g., the simplest method is to use a household's characteristics as explanatory variables in a regression model of travel behavior). In this way, any changes in the household's characteristics (e.g., change in the composition due to birth, death, or children leaving the nest or adults moving into the household) can be used to predict changes in travel behavior. In fact, new model systems are created to study this interaction within a household looking at the patterns of using time in a day and the changes across days and years. It is, therefore, very important in modeling and simulation as well as other types of policy analysis to incorporate in the models used for policy analysis not only the interactions described above but also interactions among these four fundamental dimensions. The typical example is long-range planning that is usually defined for larger geographical areas (region, states, and countries) and addresses issues with horizons from 10 to 50 years. In many instances, we may find that large geographic scale means also longer time frames applied to wider mosaics of social entities and including more diverse jurisdictions. On the other side of the spectrum issues that are relevant to smaller geographic scales are more likely to be accompanied by shorter term time frames applied to a few social entities that are relatively homogeneous and subject to the rule of a very few jurisdictions. This is one important organizing principle but also an indicator of the complex relationships we attempt to recreate in our computerized models for decision support. In developing the blueprints of these models one can choose from a variety of theories (e.g., neoclassical microeconomics, home production models, cooperative bargaining) and conceptual representations of the real world that help us to develop these models (e.g., a person representing a household or individual household members competing for resources). At the heart of our understanding of how the world (as an organization, a household, or an individual human being) works are models of decision making and conceptual representations of relationships among entities making up this world.

Theory Building

Transportation planning applications are about judgment and decision making of individuals and their organizations. There are different settings of decision making that we want to understand. Two of these settings are: (a) the travelers and their social units from which motivations for and constraints to their behavior emerge; and (b) the transportation managers and their organizations that serve the travelers and their social units (note that we exclude from the discussion here goods movement that contains a few additional actors (Southworth, 2003) and land use, see www.urbansim.org). Both settings have received considerable attention in transportation planning and its modeling of the decision-making process. Conceptual models of this process are transformed into computerized models of a city, a region, or even a state in which we utilize components that are in turn models of human judgment and decision making, for example,, travelers moving around the transportation network and visiting locations where they can participate in activities. Models of this behavior are simplified versions of strategies used by travelers when they select among options that are directly related to their desired activities. In some of these models, we also make assumptions about hierarchies of motivations, actions, and consequences. Some of these assumptions are explicit, for example, when deriving the functional forms of models as in the typical disaggregate choice models, and in other models these assumptions are implicit. When designing transportation planning model interfaces for transportation planners and managers we also implicitly make assumptions about the managers' ability to understand the input, agent representation, internal functioning, and output of these computerized models. Our objective should be not only to understand travel behavior and build models that describe and predict human behavior but also to devise tools (e.g., decision support systems) that allow transportation managers to understand the assumed behavior in the models, study scenarios of policy actions, and define and explain policy implications to others. This, in essence, implies that we, the model system designers, create a platform for a relationship between planners and travelers. A similar but more direct relationship also exists between travelers and transportation managers when we design the observation methods that provide the data used for modeling but also the data used to measure attitudes and opinions such as travel surveys. In fact, this relationship is studied in much more detail in the survey design context and linked directly to the image of the agency conducting the survey and the positive or negative impression of the travelers about the sponsoring agency (Dillman, 2000). Most transportation research for modeling and simulation, however, has emphasized traveler behavior when building surveys and models neglecting the interface with the planners. The summary below, however, applies to individuals traveling in a network but also to organizations and planners in the sense used by H. A. Simon in his Administrative Behavior (1997).

Modeling and Simulation

In spite of the issues raised in the previous section, in transportation modeling and simulation, we have experienced a few tremendously progressive steps forward. Interestingly, these key innovations are from nonengineering fields but very often transferred and applied to transportation systems analysis and simulation by engineers. These are listed here in a somewhat sequential chronological order merging technological innovations and theoretical innovations. At exactly the time that the Bay Area Rapid Transit system was studied and evaluated in the 1960s, Dan McFadden (the Year 2000 Nobel Laureate in Economics) and a team of researchers produced practical mode choice regression models at the level of an individual decision maker (see http://emlab.berkeley.edu/users/mcfadden/, accessed August 2007). The models are based on random utility maximization (of the SEU family) and their work opened up the possibility to predict mode choice rates more accurately than ever before. These models were initially named *behavioral travel–demand models* (Stopher and Meyburg, 1976) and later the more appropriate term of *discrete choice models* (Ben-Akiva and Lerman, 1985) prevailed. Although restrictive in their assumptions, these models are still under continuous improvement and they have become the standard tool in evaluating alternative transportation mode options. Some of the most notable and recent developments advancing the state of the art and practice are: (a) better understanding of the theoretical and particularly behavioral limitations of these models (Gärling et al., 1998; McFadden, 1998; Golledge and Gärling, 2003); (b) more flexible functional forms that resolve some of the problems raised in Williams and Ortuzar (1982) allowing for different choices to be correlated when using the most popular discrete choice regression models (Koppelman and Sethi, 2000; Bhat, 2000, 2003); (c) combination of revealed preference, stated choices by travelers, with stated preferences and intentions, answers to hypothetical questions by travelers, availability of data in the same choice framework to extract in a more informative way travelers willingness to use a mode and willingness to pay for a mode option (Ben-Akiva and Morikawa, 1989, Louviere et al., 2000). This latter "improvement" enables us to assess situations that are impossible to build in the real world; (d) computer-based interviewing and laboratory experimentation to study more complex choice situations and the transfer of the findings to the real world (Mahmassani and Jou, 1998). This direction, however, is also accompanied by a wide variety of research studies aiming at more realistic behavioral models that go beyond mode choice and travel behavior (Golledge and Gärling, 2003); (e) expansion of the discrete choice framework using ideas from *latent variable models* with covariates that were first developed by Lazarsfeld in the 1950s and their estimation finalized by Goodman in the 1970s (see the review in Goodman (2002) and discrete choice applications in Bockenholt, 2002). This family of models was used in Goulias (1999) to study the dynamics of activity and travel behavior and in the study of choice in travel behavior (Ben-Akiva et al., 2002). Two related subjects are also the choice set formation and the perception of alternatives (see Golledge and Stimson, 1997, pp. 33–34).

The most important development in modeling and simulation is the creation of activity-based approaches. Under this label, we find a variety of methods to forecast travel demand with common roots in the 1970s. Chapin's research (1974), providing one of the first comprehensive studies about time allocated to activity in space and time, is also credited for motivating many foundations of activity-based approaches. His focus has been on the propensity of individuals to participate in activities and travel linking their patterns to urban planning. In about the same period, Becker also developed his theory of time allocation from a household production viewpoint (Becker, 1976) applying economic theory in a nonmarketing sector and demonstrating the possibility of formulating time allocation models using economics reasoning (i.e., activity choice). In parallel another approach was developing in geography and Hagerstrand's seminal publication on time geography (1970) provides the third base about constraints in human paths in time and space for a variety of planning horizons. These are *capability* constraints (e.g., physical limitations such as speed); *coupling* constraints (e.g., requirements to be with other persons at the same time and place); and *authority* constraints (e.g., restrictions due to institutional and regulatory contexts such as the opening and closing hours of stores). Cullen and Godson (1975) appear to be the first researchers attempting to bridge the gap between the motivational (Chapin) approach to activity participation and the constraints (Hagerstrand) approach by creating a model that depicts a routine and deliberated approach to activity analysis. Most subsequent contributions to the activity-based approach emerge in one way or another from these initial frameworks with important operational improvements (for reviews see Kitamura, 1988; Bhat and Koppelman, 1999; Arentze and Timmermans, 2000; McNally, 2000). The basic ingredients of an activity-based approach for travel demand analysis (Jones et al., 1990; Arentze and Timmermans, 2000) are: (a) explicit treatment of travel as derived demand (Manheim, 1979), i.e., participation in activities such as work, shop, and leisure motivate travel but travel could also be an activity as well (e.g., taking a drive). These activities are viewed as episodes (starting time, duration, and ending time) and they are arranged in a sequence forming a pattern of behavior that can be distinguished from other patterns (a sequence of activities in a chain of episodes). In addition, these events are not independent and their interdependency is accounted for in the theoretical framework; (b) the household is considered to be the fundamental social unit (decision-making unit) and the interactions among household members are explicitly modeled to capture task allocation and roles within the household, relationships, and change in these relationships as households move along their life cycles and the individual's commitments and constraints change and these are depicted in the activity-based model; and (c) explicit consideration of constraints by the spatial, temporal, and social dimensions of the environment is given. These constraints can be explicit models of time–space prisms or reflections of these constraints in the form of model parameters and/or rules in a production system format (Arentze and Timmermans, 2000). The input to these models are the typical regional model data of social, economic, and demographic information of potential travelers and land use information to create schedules followed by people in their everyday life. The output are detailed lists of activities pursued, times spent in each activity, and travel information from activity to activity (including travel time, mode used, and so forth). More recent reviews of research and practice of activity-based models (Miller, 2006; Timmermans 2003, 2006; Henson and Goulias, 2006) show a movement to a second-by-second and person-by-person simulation but also an attempt of integration with other behavioral models.

Consideration of Behavioral Dynamics

At the heart of behavioral change are questions about the process followed in shifting from a given pattern of behavior to another. In addition to measuring change and the relationships among behavioral indicators that change in their values over time, we are also interested in the timing, sequencing, and staging of these changes. Moreover, we are interested in the triggers that may accelerate desirable or delay undesirable changes and the identification of social and demographic segments that may follow one time path versus another in systematic patterns with systemwide impacts. Knowledge about all this is required to design policies but it is also required to design better forecasting tools. Developments in exploring behavioral dynamics and advancing models for them have progressed in a few arenas. First, in the data collection arena with panel surveys, repeated observation of the same persons over time, that are now giving us a considerable history in developing new ideas about data collection but also about data analysis (Golob et al., 1997; Goulias and Kim, 2003) and interactive and laboratory data collection techniques (Doherty, 2003) that allow a more in-depth examination of behavioral process followed by decision makers. The second arena is in the development of microeconomic dynamic formulations for travel behavior. These include stochastic process formulations (Kitamura, 2000), staged development processes (Goulias, 1999), or outcomes from multiple processes operating at different levels (Goulias, 2001, 2002a). Experimentation with new theories from psychology emphasizing development dynamics is a potential fourth area that is just beginning to emerge (Goulias, 2003).

Integration of Transportation with other Models

The examples of studies in the previous section focus more on the paths of persons in space and time within a somewhat short-time horizon such a day, week, or maybe a month. The consideration of behavioral dynamics has expanded the temporal horizons to a few years. However, regional simulation models are very often designed for long-range plans spanning 25 years or even longer time horizons. Within these longer horizons, changes in the spatial distribution of activity locations and residences (land use) are substantial, changes in the demographic composition and spatial distribution of demographic segments are also substantial, and changes in travel patterns, transport facilities, and quality of service offered can be extreme. Past approaches in modeling and simulating the relationship among land use, demographics, and travel in a region attempted to disengage travel from the other two treating them as mutually exogenous. As interactions among them became more interesting and pressing, due to urban sprawl and suburban congestion, for policy analysis, increasing attention was paid to their complex interdependencies. This led to a variety of attempts to develop "integrated model systems" that enable the study of scenarios of change and mutual influence between land use and travel. An earlier review of these models with heavy emphasis on discrete choice models can be found in Anas (1982). Miller (2003a) and Waddell and Ulfarsson (2003, 2004) 20 years later provide two comprehensive reviews of models that have integrated many aspects in the interdependent triad of demographics-travel-land use models. Both reviews trace the history of some of the most notable developments and both link these models to the activity-based approach above. Both reviews also agree that a microeconomic and/or macroeconomic approach to modeling land and transportation interactions are not sufficient and more detailed simulation of the individuals and their organizations "acting" in a time–space domain need to be simulated in order to obtain the required output for informed decision making. They also introduce the idea of simulating interactive agents in a dynamic environment of other agents (multiagent simulation). A review from a healthy skeptic viewpoint raises some important issues in this integration (Timmermans, 2003) and a rebuttal to this skepticism by Miller (2006) warns us of the difficult path to true integration. Creation of integrated systems is further complicated by the emergence of an entire infrastructural system as another layer of human activity—telecommunication.

Today telecommunication and transportation relationships are absent from regional simulation planning and modeling as well as from the most advanced land use and transportation integrated models. Considerable research findings, however, have been accumulating since the 1970s. Telecommunication here is intended as a much larger system of services and technologies that are named "information and (tele)communication technologies" (ICT). The definition by Cohen et al. (2002) is very appropriate in this case: "(ICT is) a family of electronic technologies and services used to process, store and disseminate information, facilitating the performance of information-related human activities, provided by, and serving the institutional and business sectors as well as the public-at-large." Consider, for example, advanced traveler information systems (ATIS). It is a very good example of a direct impact on travel behavior because it may affect many aspects of daily life including time allocation and related decisions by a household and its members and the type of goods a household considers and acquires. ATIS started as one of the many services offered by ITS and over time expanded beyond the roadside migrating into vehicles, offices, and homes (Weiland and Purser, 2000). This movement took place in all four main media of television, radio, Internet, and telephone expanding the interaction between transportation and telecommunications (see http://www.geo.uu.nl/mobilizingICT/, accessed August 2007). For this reason, when assessing the effects of this technology, we need a wider and more comprehensive framework, than the single trip information acquisition and information use framework adopted by traffic simulation applications (for an overview of these applications, see http://ops.fhwa.dot.gov/trafficanalysistools/ngsim.htm, accessed August 2007).

Salomon (1986) sketched one such framework where he recognized four possible effects of ICT on travel and they are: *substitution*, *modification*, *enhancement*, and *neutrality*. *Substitution* means, that ICT can actually eliminate trips. Telecommuting, teleshopping, and teleconferencing, are some examples. *Modification* indicates ICT can alter the travel behavior of individuals changing the order of trips (sequencing), the travel mode, or the timing of the trip (e.g., departure time). From an operations standpoint, this is particularly important when a shift of commute trips to off-peak hours occurs or a switching to public transportation and/or car-pooling happens because of ICT use. The third category, *enhancement*, reflects those trips that would not have been generated without ICT. For example, when there is more information available for particular activities, one would expect an increase in the desire to travel and participate in these activities. Also, people are able to save time by better planning of their schedules (thanks to ICT) and by communicating while traveling. The saved time is often used to make other trips. The last category, *neutrality*, reflects those instances of ICT that have no remarkable effect on travel behavior. There are, however, many gaps in our knowledge about ICT and transportation interactions that require additional research before policies can be defined in such a way that ICT can play a significant role in changing travel behavior. Ultimately, these changes should also benefit the level of service offered by the transportation system. Mokhtarian (1990) expanded the telecommunications–transportation framework further and the ideas of *substitution*, *modification*, *enhancement*, and *neutrality*, served as the basis for identifying new relationships. Her conceptual framework reflects the impacts of ICT on travel and contains the reverse causality of the effect of travel on ICT. In one of the most recent summaries about this interaction, Krizek and Johnson (2003) map the terrain of research recognizing the many complexities of interaction and expand the Salomon–Mokhtarian framework one step further considering a triad of dimensions that are: (a) nature of the activity pursued using ICT (borrowing the categorization of subsistence, maintenance, and leisure from activity analysis in travel behavior); (b) the effect of ICT on travel (using the four Salomon effects); and (c) the effect of "subtasks" when pursuing an ICT action. This latter aspect of multiple activities at locations is also becoming particularly interesting for research that goes beyond telecommunications and land use. The example above demonstrates that key in understanding the interaction between telecommunications and transportation is also understanding the evolution of the technology as discussed, for example, in Golob (2001), where evidence concerning the usage of personal computers, the Internet, mobile phones, and other new technologies may indicate that there are generational differences among the users. This can be expanded to include awareness of technologies in which different segments of the population may approach the services in different ways (Goulias et al., 2003) and the need to develop market penetration models (Kim and Goulias, 2007). In addition to ICT the last two decades have produced a variety of enabling technologies for modeling and simulation opening the gateways to tremendous improvements. A few of the most important for modeling and simulation are stochastic approaches to simulation, production systems, GIS, interactive and technology-aided data collection approaches, and more flexible data analysis techniques.

Enabling Technologies

Stochastic (dynamic) microsimulation, as intended here, is an evolutionary engine software that is used to replicate the relationships among social, economic, and demographic factors with land use, time use, and travel by people. As discussed above the causal links among these groups of entities are extremely complex, nonlinear, and in many instances unknown or incompletely specified. This is the reason that no closed form solution can be created for such a forecasting model system. An evolutionary engine, then, provides a realistic representation of person and household life histories (e.g., birth, death, marriages, divorces, birth of children, etc.), spatio-temporal activity opportunity evolution, and a variety of models that account for uncertainties in data, models, and behavioral variation (see Miller, 2003b; Goulias, 2002b, for overviews and Sundararajan and Goulias, 2003 for a more recent application that also includes ICT market penetration). Dynamic microsimulation is mainly process and event simulation of microbehavior. When more detailed behavioral processes is the main target of simulation, production systems may be a better option. *Production systems* were first developed by Newell and Simon (1972) to explicitly depict the way humans go about solving problems. These are a series of condition–action statements in a sequence. From this viewpoint, they are search processes that may never reach an absolute optimum and they replicate (or at least attempt to) human thought and action. Models of this kind are called *computational process models* (CPM) and through the use of IF ... THEN ... rules have made possible first the creation of a planning framework in Rand corporation (Hayes-Roth and Hayes-Roth, 1979) who have also linked their framework to alternative planning strategies. Subsequently and based on a decade of work by Gärling et al. (1994), operational model for activity scheduling was developed. In parallel, two applications named PCATS and AMOS (Kitamura and Fujii, 1998) were also developed using this simulation technique and the most complete of all these models named Albatross was developed in the Netherlands (Arentze and Timmermans, 2000). It should also be noted that all new model implementations of CPM today employ some kind of hybrid model (see Henson et al., 2009). All transportation models need spatial representation and the premier technology is *GIS*. GIS are software systems that can be used to collect, store, analyze, modify, and display large amounts of geographic data. They include layers of data that are able to incorporate relations among the variables in each layer and allow to build relationships in data across layers. One can visualize a GIS as a live map that can display almost any kind of spatio-temporal information. Maps have been used by transportation planners and engineers for long time and they are a natural interface to use in modeling and simulation and for this reason their evolution is extremely important for transportation modeling and simulation. These information systems are evolving rapidly and an entire scientific field aims at their next developmental stages including incorporation of time and behavioral dynamics as well as perception (see http://www.ncgia.ucsb.edu/giscc/, accessed August 2007).

There are also two other technologies that merit a note, although, not strictly for modeling. The first is about data collection and particularly data collection using Internet technologies to build complex interviews that are interactive and dynamic (Doherty, 2003). In the same line of development, we also see the use of geographic positioning systems (GPS) that allow one to develop a trace of individual paths in time and space (Wolf et al., 2001; Doherty et al., 2001). Very important development is also the emergence of devices that can record the bulk of environmental data surrounding a person movement, classify the environment in which the individual moves, and then ask simplified questions. In fact, the integration of all these devices and GIS to support modeling and simulation should be one of our ultimate objectives in creating enabling technologies (see the workshop reports and technologies examined in http://www.csiss.org/events/meetings/time-geography/, accessed August 2007). The second technology is data mining and artificial intelligence-borne techniques used to extract travel behavior patterns and to develop modular components for stochastic micro-simulation and/or CPMs (Teodorovic and Vukadinovic, 1998; Wets et al., 2000; Yamamoto et al., 2002; Mohammadian and Miller, 2002; Pribyl, 2007).

The Evolving Paradigm and Some Questions

Policies are dictating to create and test increasingly more sophisticated policy assessment instruments that account for direct and indirect effects of behavior, procedures for behavioral change, and to provide finer resolution in the four dimensions of geographic space, time, social space, and jurisdictions. Dynamic planning is also stressing the need to examine trends, cycles, but to also invert the time progression and develop paths that lead to visions about the future. The demands on new model developments are also becoming increasingly urgent. Although, tremendous progress has been observed in the past 20 years, development requires a faster pace to create the policy tools needed. These policy tools need to disentangle the actions of persons under different policy actions and the impact of policy actions on aggregates to identify conflicts and resolutions. Supporting all this is a rich collection of decision paradigms that are already used and a few new ideas are starting to migrate to practice. The plethora of advances includes: (a) models and experiments to create computerized virtual worlds and synthetic schedules at the most elementary level of decision making using microsimulation and CPM; (b) data collection techniques and new methods to collect extreme details about behavior and to estimate, validate, and verify models using advanced hardware, software, and pattern recognition techniques; and (c) integration of models from different domains to reflect additional interdependencies such as land use and telecommunications. However, much more work remains to be done in order to develop models that can answer the policy questions we face today. For this reason, a few steps are outlined here.

In *policy and program evaluation*, transportation analysis appears to be narrowly applied to only one method of assessment that does not follow the ideal of a randomized controlled trial and does not explicitly define what experimental setting we are using for our assessments. Unfortunately this weakens our findings about policy analysis and action. There are many possibilities to create experimental and quasi-experimental procedures to guide us in data collection as well as guidelines for field studies. However, there is no systematic approach and there is no research program to support this type of policy analysis setting except for very limited lab experiments. In *model building* many issues remain unresolved in the areas of scale in time and space, error tolerance of policy questions and their mapping to strategy evaluations. This is partially due to the lack of methodologies that are able to make these assessments but also due to lack of scrutiny of these issues and their implications on impact assessment.

Regarding *strategic planning and evaluation*, we also lack models designed to be used in scenario building exercises such as backcasting and related assessments. The models about change are usually defined for forecasting and simple time inversion may not work to make them usable in backcasting. Backcasting as a method does not have the long tradition of forecasting modeling and simulation to help us develop suitable models. For this reason more attention should be paid to scenario creation, possibly using a combination of techniques including qualitative research methods, and the interface between this aspect and the experimental methods questions in program evaluation. In the new research and technology area, as many papers in this conference show, we need to consider perceptions of time and space, consideration of the multiple dimensions of time such as tempo, duration, and clock time, and human interaction.

References

Anas, A. (1982). *Residential Location Markets and Urban Transportation: Economic Theory, Econometrics and Policy Analysis with Discrete Choice Models*. New York, Academic Press.

Arentze, T. and H. Timmermans (2000). *ALBATROSS—A Learning Based Transportation Oriented Simulation System*. Eindhoven, The Netherlands, European Institute of Retailing and Services Studies (EIRASS), Technical University of Eindhoven.

Becker, G. S. (1976). *The Economic Approach to Human Behavior*. Chicago, IL, The University of Chicago Press.

Ben-Akiva, M. E. and S. R. Lerman (1985). *Discrete Choice Analysis: Theory and Application to Travel Demand*. Cambridge, MA, MIT Press.

Ben-Akiva, M. E. and T. Morikawa (1989). Estimation of mode switching models from revealed preferences and stated intentions. Paper presented at the International Conference on Dynamic Travel Behavior at Kyoto University Hall, July. Kyoto, Japan.

Ben-Akiva, M. E., J. Walker, A. T. Bernardino, D. A. Gopinath, T. Morikawa and A. Polydoropoulou (2002). Integration of choice and latent variable models. In H. S. Mahmassani (Ed.), *Perceptual Motion: Travel behavior Research Opportunities and Application Challenges*. Amsterdam, The Netherlands, Pergamon.

Bhat, C. R. (2000). Flexible model structures for discrete choice analysis. In D. A. Hensher and K. J. Button (Eds.), *Handbook of Transport Modelling*, Amsterdam, The Netherlands, Pergamon, pp. 71–89.

Bhat, C. R. (2003). Random utility-based discrete choice models for travel demand analysis (Chapter 10). In K. G. Goulias (Ed.), *Transportation Systems Planning: Methods and Applications*, Boca Raton, FL, CRC Press, pp. 10-1–10-30.

Bhat, C. R. and F. Koppelman (1999). A retrospective and prospective survey of time-use research. *Transportation* 26(2), 119–139.

Bockenholt, U. (2002). Comparison and choice: analyzing discrete preference data by latent class scaling models. In J. A. Hagenaars and A. L. McCutcheon (Eds.), *Applied Latent Class Analysis*, Cambridge, UK, Cambridhe University Press, pp. 163–182.

Borgers, A. W. J., F. Hofman and H. J. P. Timmermans (1997). Activity-based modelling: prospects. In D. F. Ettema and H. J. P. Timmermans (Eds.), *Activity-Based Approaches to Travel Analysis*, Oxford, UK, Pergamon, pp. 339–351.

California Department of Transportation (CALTRANS) (2007). California Transportation Plan 2030. Final Draft. July, California Department of Transportation, Sacramento, CA.

Chapin, F. S., Jr. (1974). *Human Activity Patterns in the City: Things People do in Time and Space*. New York, Wiley.

Cohen, G., I. Salomon and P. Nijkamp (2002). Information-communications technologies (ICT) and transport: does knowledge underpin policy? *Telecommunications Policy* 26, 31–52.

Creighton, R. L. (1970). *Urban Transportation Planning*. Urbana, IL, University of Illinois Press.

Cullen, I. and V. Godson (1975). Urban networks: the structure of activity patterns. *Progress in Planning* 4(1), 1–96.

Dillman, D. A. (2000). *Mail and Internet Surveys: The Tailored Design Method*, 2nd edn. New York, Wiley.

Doherty, S. (2003). Interactive methods for activity scheduling processes (Chapter 7). In K. G. Goulias (Ed.), *Transportation Systems Planning: Methods and Applications*, Boca Raton, FL, CRC Press, pp. 7-1–7-25.

Doherty, S. T., N. Noel, M. Lee-Gosselin, C. Sirois and M. Ueno (2001). Moving beyond observed outcomes: global positioning systems and interactive computer-based travel behavior surveys. Transportation Research Circular, E-C026, March 2001, Transportation Research Board, Washington, DC.

Gärling, T., M. Kwan and R. Golledge (1994). Computational-process modeling of household travel activity scheduling. *Transportation Research Part B* 25, 355–364.

Gärling, T., T. Laitila and K. Westin (1998). Theoretical foundations of travel choice modelling: an introduction. In T. Garling, T. Laitila and K. Westin (Eds.), *Theoretical Foundations of Travel Choice Modelling*. Oxford, Pergamon, ISBN 0-08-043062-7.

Garrett, M. and M. Wachs (1996). *Transportation Planning on Trial. The Clean Air Act and Travel Forecasting*. Thousand Oaks, CA, Sage Publications.

Golledge, R. G. and T. Gärling (2003). Spatial behavior in transportation modeling and planning (Chapter 3). In K. G. Goulias (Ed.), *Transportation Systems Planning: Methods and Applications*, Boca Raton, FL, CRC Press, pp. 1–27.

Golledge, R. G. and R. J. Stimson (1997). *Spatial Behavior: A Geographic Perspective*. New York, The Guilford Press.

Golob, T. F. (2001). Travelbehaviour.com: activity approaches to modeling the effects of information technology on personal travel behaviour. In D. Hensher (Ed.), *Travel Behavior Research: The Leading Edge*, Kidlington, Oxford, Elsevier Science/ Pergamon, pp. 145–184.

Golob, T. F., R. Kitamura and L. Long (Eds.) (1997). *Panels for Transportation Planning: Methods and Applications*. Boston, Kluwer.

Goodman, L. A. (2002). Latent class analysis: the empirical study of latent types, latent variables, and latent structures. In J. A. Hagenaars and A. L. McCutcheon (Eds.), *Applied Latent Class Analysis*, Cambridge, UK, Cambridhe University Press, pp. 3–55.

Goulias, K. G. (1999). Longitudinal analysis of activity and travel pattern dynamics using generalized mixed Markov latent class models. *Transportation Research* 33B, 535–557.

Goulias, K. G. (2001). A longitudinal integrated forecasting environment (LIFE) for activity and travel forecasting. In Y. Villacampa, C. A. Brebbia and J.-L. Uso (Eds.), *Ecosystems and Sustainable Development III*, Southampton, UK, WIT Press, pp. 811–820.

Goulias, K. G. (2002a). Multilevel analysis of daily time use and time allocation to activity types accounting for complex covariance structures using correlated random effects. *Transportation* 29(1), 31–48.

Goulias, K. G. (2002b). Forecasting the inputs to dynamic model systems (Chapter 23). In H. S. Mahmassani (Ed.), *In Perpetual Motion. Travel Behavior Research Opportunities and Application Challenges*, Amsterdam, The Netherlands, Pergamon, pp. 480–503.

Goulias, K. G. (2003). Transportation Systems Planning (Chapter 1). In K. G. Goulias (Ed.), *Transportation Systems Planning: Methods and Applications*, Boca Raton, FL, CRC Press, pp. 1-1–1-45.

Goulias, K. G. and T. Kim (2003). A longitudinal analysis of the relationship between environmentally friendly modes, weather conditions, and information-telecommunications technology market penetration. In E. Tiezzi, C. A. Brebbia and J. L. Uso (Eds.), *Ecosystems and Sustainable Development, Volume 2*. Southampton, WIT Press, pp. 949–958.

Goulias, K. G., T. Kim and O. Pribyl (2003). A longitudinal analysis of awareness and use for advanced traveler information systems. *Journal of Intelligent Transportation Systems: Technology, Planning, and Operations* 8(1), 3–17.

Goulias, K. G., T. Litzinger, J. Nelson and V. Chalamgari (1993). A study of emission control strategies for Pennsylvania: emission reductions from mobile Sources, cost effectiveness, and economic impacts. Final Report to the Low Emissions Vehicle Commission. PTI 9403. The Pennsylvania Transportation Institute, University Park, PA.

Goulias, K. G., K. Viswanathan and T. Kim (2001). Pennsylvania's statewide long range transportation plan (PennPlan): performance based planning in the US. In L. J. Sacharov and C. A. Brebbia (Eds.), *Urban Transport VII, Urban Transport and the Environment for the 21st Century*, Southampton, UK, WIT Press, pp. 43–52.

Greiving, S. and R. Kemper (1999). Integration of transport and land use policies: state of the art. Deliverable 2b of the Project TRANSLAND, 4th RTD Framework Programme of the European Commission.

Hagerstrand, T. (1970). What about people in regional science? *Papers of the Regional Science Association* 10, 7–21.

Hayes-Roth, B. and F. Hayes-Roth (1979). A cognitive model of planning. *Cognitive Science* 3, 275–310.

Henson, K. and K. G. Goulias (2006). Preliminary assessment of activity and modeling for homeland security applications. Transportation Research Record: Journal of the Transportation Research Board, No. 1942, Transportation Research Board of the National Academies, Washington DC, pp 23–30.

Henson, K., K. G. Goulias and R. Golledge (2009). An assessment of activity-based modeling and simulation for applications in operational studies, disaster preparedness, and homeland security. *Transportation Letters* 1(1), 19–39.

Hutchinson, B. G. (1974). *Principles of Urban Transport Systems Planning*. Washington, DC, Scripta.

Jones, P., F. Koppelman, J. Orfeuil (1990). Activity analysis: state-of-the-art and future directions, In P. Jones (Ed.), *Developments in Dynamic and Activity-Based Approaches to Travel Analysis. A Compendium of Papers from the 1989. Oxford Conference*. Avebury, UK, pp. 34–55.

Kim, T.-G. and K. G. Goulias (2007). A multivariate multilevel analysis of information technology choice. In K. G. Goulias (Ed.), *Transport Science and Technology*. Amsterdam, Elsevier, pp. 233–246.

Kitamura, R. (1988). An evaluation of activity-based travel analysis. *Transportation* 15, 9–34.

Kitamura, R. (2000). Longitudinal methods. In D. A. Hensher and K. J. Button (Eds.), *Handbook of Transport Modelling*, Amsterdam, The Netherlands, Pergamon, pp. 113–128.

Kitamura, R. and S. Fujii (1998). Two computational process models of activity-travel choice. In T. Garling, T. Laitila and K. Westin (Eds.), *Theoretical Foundations of Travel Choice Modeling*. Oxford, Pergamon, pp. 251–279.

Koppelman, F. S. and V. Sethi (2000). Closed-form discrete–choice models. In D. A. Hensher and K. J. Button (Eds.), *Handbook of Transport Modelling*, Amsterdam, The Netherlands, Pergamon, pp. 211–225.

Krizek, K. J. and A. Johnson (2003). Mapping of the terrain of information and communications technology (ICT and household travel, Transportation Research Board Annual Meeting CD-ROM, Washington, DC.

Lomborg, B. (2001). *The Skeptical Environmentalist: Measuring the Real State of the World*. Cambridge, UK, Cambridge University Press.

Loudon, W. R. and D. A. Dagang (1994). Evaluating the effects of transportation control measures. In T. F. Wholley (Ed.), *Transportation Planning and Air Quality II*. New York, American Society of Civil Engineers.

Louviere, J. J., D. A. Hensher and J. D. Swait (2000). *Stated Choice Methods: Analysis and Application*. Cambridge, UK, Cambridge University Press.

Mahmassani, H. S. and R.-C. Jou (1998). Bounded rationality in commuter decision dynamics: incorporating trip chaining in departure time and route switching decisions (Chapter 9). In T. Garling, T. Laitila and K. Westin (Eds.), *Theoretical Foundations of Travel Choice Modeling*. Oxford, Pergamon, pp. 201–229.

Manheim, M. L. (1979). *Fundamentals of Transportation Systems Analysis, Volume 1: Basic Concepts*. Cambridge, MA, MIT Press.

McFadden, D. (1998). Measuring willingness-to-pay for transportation improvements. In T. Garling, T. Laitila and K. Westin (Eds.), *Theoretical Foundations of Travel Choice Modeling*. Oxford, Pergamon, pp. 339–364.

McNally, M. G. (2000). The activity-based approach. In D. A. Hensher and K. J. Button (Eds.), *Handbook of Transport Modelling*, Amsterdam, The Netherlands, Pergamon, pp. 113–128.

Meyer, M. D. and E. J. Miller (2001). *Urban Transportation Planning*, 2nd edn. Boston, MA, McGraw-Hill.

Miller, E. J. (2003a). Land use: transportation modeling (Chapter 5). In K. G. Goulias (Ed.), *Transportation Systems Planning: Methods and Applications*, Boca Raton, FL, CRC Press, pp. 5-1–5-24.

Miller, E. J. (2003b). Microsimulation (Chapter 12). In K. G. Goulias (Ed.), *Transportation Systems Planning: Methods and Applications*, Boca Raton, FL, CRC Press, pp. 12-1–12-22.

Miller, E. J. (2006). *Resource Paper on Integrated Land Use-Transportation Models.* Kyoto, Japan, IATBR.

Mohammadian, A. and E. J. Miller (2002). Nested logit models and artificial neural networks for predicting household automobile choices. Comparison and performance. Transportation Research Record, 1807, TRB, Washington DC.

Mokhtarian, P. L. (1990). A typology of relationships between telecommunications and transportation. *Transportation Research A* 24(3), 231–242.

Newell, A. and H. A. Simon (1972). *Human Problem Solving.* Englewood Cliffs, NJ, Prentice Hall.

Niemeier, D. A. (2003). Mobile source emissions: an overview of the regulatory and modeling framework (Chapter 13). In K. G. Goulias (Ed.), *Transportation Systems Planning: Methods and Applications*, Boca Raton, FL, CRC Press, pp. 13-1–13-28.

Ortuzar and Willumsen (2001). *Modelling Transport*, 3rd edn. Chicester, UK, Wiley.

Paaswell, R. E., N. Rouphail and T. C. Sutaria (Eds.) (1992). *Site Impact Traffic Assessment. Problems and Solutions.* New York, ASCE.

Pribyl, O. (2007). Computational intelligence in transportation: short user-oriented guide. In K. G. Goulias (Ed.), *Transport Science and Technology*, Amsterdam, The Netherlands, Elsevier, pp. 37–54.

Quist, J. and P. Vergragt (2006). Past and future of backcasting: the shift to stakeholder participation and a proposal for a methodological framework. *Futures* 38, 1027–1045.

Robinson, J. (1982). Energy backcasting: a proposed method of policy analysis. *Energy Policy* 10(4), 337–344.

Sadek, A. W., W. M. El Dessouki, and J. I. Ivan (2002). Deriving land use limits as a function of infrastructure capacity. Final Report, Project UVMR13-7, New England Region One University Transportation Center, MIT, Cambridge, MA.

Salomon, I. (1986). Telecommunications and travel relationships: a review. *Transportation Research A* 20A(3), 223–238.

Simon, H. A. (1997). *Administrative Behavior*, 4th edn. New York, The Free Press.

Southworth, F. (2003). Freight transportation planning: models and methods. In K. G. Goulias (Ed.), *Transportation Systems Planning: Methods and Applications*, Boca Raton, FL, CRC Press, pp. 4.1–4.29.

Stopher, P. R. (1994). Predicting TCM responses with urban travel demand models. In T. F. Wholley (Ed.), *Transportation Planning and Air Quality II.* New York, American Society of Civil Engineers.

Stopher, P. R. and A. H. Meyburg (Eds.) (1976). *Behavioral Travel–Demand Models.* Lexington, MA, Lexington Books.

Sundararajan, A. and K. G. Goulias (2003). Demographic microsimulation with DEMOS 2000: design, validation, and forecasting (Chapter 14). In K. G. Goulias (Ed.), *Transportation Systems Planning: Methods and Applications*, Boca Raton, FL, CRC Press, pp. 14-1–14-23.

Teodorovic, D. and K. Vukadinovic (1998). *Traffic Control and Transport Planning: A Fuzzy Sets and Neural Networks Approach.* Boston, MA, Kluwer.

Tiezzi, E. (2003). *The End of Time.* Southampton, UK, WIT Press.

Timmermans, H. (2003). The saga of integrated land use-transport modeling: how many more dreams before we wake up? Conference keynote paper at the Moving through net: The physical and social dimensions of travel. *10th International Conference on Travel Behaviour Research.* Lucerne, Switzerland, 10-15 August 2003. In *Proceedings of the Meeting of the International Association for Travel Behevaior Research (IATBR).* Lucerne, Switzerland, 2003.

Timmermans, H. (2006). Analyses and models of household decision making processes. Resource paper in the CD ROM. In *Proceedings of the 11th IATBR International Conference on Travel Behaviour Research.* Kyoto, Japan.

Transportation Research Board. (1999). Transportation, energy, and environment. Policies to promote sustainability. Transportation Research Circular 492. TRB, Washington DC.

Transportation Research Board. (2002). *Surface Transportation Environmental Research: A Long-Term Strategy.* Washington, DC, Transportation Research Board.

US Government. (2006). *Analytical Perspectives. Budget of the United States Government, Fiscal year 2007.* Washington, DC, US Government printing Office.

van der Hoorn, T. (1997). Practitioner's future needs. Paper presented at the Conference on Transport Surveys, Raising the Standard, May 24–30. Grainau, Germany.

Waddell, P. and G. F. Ulfarsson (2003). Dynamic simulation of real estate development and land prices within an integrated land use and transportation model system. Presented at the 82nd Annual Meeting of the Transportation Research Board, January 12-16 2003. Washington, DC (also available in http://www.urbansim.org/papers/ accessed August 2007).

Waddell, P. and G. F. Ulfarsson (2004). Introduction to urban simulation: design and development of operational models. In B. Stopher and K. Hensher (Eds.), *Handbook in Transport, Volume 5: Transport Geography and Spatial Systems.* Oxford, Pergamon Press, pp. 203–236.

Weiland, R. J. and L. B. Purser (2000). Intelligent transportation systems. In *Transportation in the New Millennium. State of the Art and Future Directions.* Perspectives from Transportation Research Board Standing Committees.

Transportation Research Board, National Research Council, The National Academies, Washington, DC, p. 6 (also available at http://nationalacademies.org/trb/).

Wets, G., K. Vanhoof, T. Arentze and H. Timmermans (2000). Identifying decision structures underlying activity patterns. An exploration of data mining algorithms. Transportation Research Record 1718, TRB, Washington, DC.

Williams, H. C. W. L. and J. D. Ortuzar (1982). Behavioral theories of dispersion and the mis-specification of travel demand models. *Transportation Research B* 16B(3), 167–219.

Wolf, J., R. Guensler, S. Washington and L. Frank (2001). Use of electronic travel diaries and vehicle instrumentation packages in the year 2000. Atlanta Regional Household Travel Survey. Transportation Research Circular, E-C026, March 2001, Transportation Research Board, Washington, DC.

Yamamoto, T., R. Kitamura, and J. Fujii (2002). Drivers' route choice behavior. Analysis by data mining algorithms. Transportation Research Record, 1807. TRB, Washington, DC.

PART 3

Workshop Reports

The Expanding Sphere of Travel Behaviour Research
Selected Papers from the 11th International Conference on Travel Behaviour Research

16

Behaviour Under Uncertainty

André de Palma and Nathalie Picard

Abstract

Most decisions in the transport area involve human behaviour facing risky or uncertain situations. The economic and statistical literature has evolved a lot during the last decades. Empirical work, natural experiments and experimental economics have started to influence the researcher in the transportation area. However, much has still to be done to incorporate, in the standard frameworks developed in the transportation areas, the standard theory (expected utility) or the less standard one (non-expected utility including perception biases, and asymmetry between gains and losses). Most research areas investigated were concerned with the best manner to accommodate findings from non-expected utility theory in transportation: what is the meaning of optimism or pessimism in evaluating travel time? What are the tradeoffs between efficiency and equity when risk matters? Or, should one use such approaches for normative or descriptive analysis?

> *Today choice under uncertainty is a field in flux: the standard theory is being challenged on several grounds from both within and outside economics.*
>
> (J. Machina, 1987, p. 121)

Objectives and General Framework

The workshop was devoted to the modelling of human behaviour under risk and uncertainty. The scope of the workshop was to (1) identify the *literature* dealing with risk in (theoretical and experimental) economics, psychology, mathematics and finance, which can be selectively used in transportation; (2) exchange *research* experiences and identify future *cross-fertilization* (within transportation and across disciplines); and (3) identify key research questions for coming years.

There is a growing literature in many disciplines/domains in the study of risks (banking and insurance, decision theory, environment etc.) and their impacts.[1] The study of risk provides a common theme that plays a crucial role, too often ignored, in different applications in transportation such as:

- Travel behaviour: Route and departure-time choice, mode choice, parking choice and driver behaviour are risky choices since travel time and parking slots availability are often only partially known.
- Safety: driving behaviour: Speed, over passing etc. are functions of the perceived probability of accident.
- Residential location: Amenities, housing price, probability of divorce are only partially known.
- Activity pattern: Opportunities, travel conditions, connection penalties are subject to risk.

There are two major approaches (methods) to improve the quality of service. *Hard methods* which involve, for example the development of transport infrastructure, often rely on very costly long-term investments. By contrast, in short run, *soft methods* involve policies (pricing, schedules, comfort etc.) based on psychological and sociological studies that aim at improving the perceived quality of service. The idea here is to better understand and measure demand, needs and preferences in order to improve the perception and satisfaction of current users (keeping the infrastructure unchanged). Note that hard methods are much more costly and far less reversible than soft methods.

Reducing risk is one of the key elements, too often neglected, in drivers' preferences. This is not to say that risk should be banned. Reducing risk has costs but also benefits for users (computed by engineers or by economists or estimated via market research); the optimal level of risk is the outcome of these two opposing forces.

The sources of risk are driven by the variability in system performance, by the environment, by incomplete or erroneous knowledge of the system, and possibly by the uncertainty inherent to the human interactions (lack of knowledge of other people's beliefs, intentions and behaviour).

The study of risk incorporates *four dimensions* (supply and demand driven): (1) the actual probability distributions of stochastic events; (2) the individual perception of these distributions; (3) the importance of consequences of events; (4) the individual risk tolerance.

[1]See, for example http://www.RiskAttitude.eu

Along these lines, D. McFadden (1999) suggested '3 dimensions along which risky choice theory must absorb psychological insights:

- Treatment of perceptions
- Conception of preferences
- Processes of choice'.

Many participants discussed the need for clear definitions of the terms used when discussing risk. (A first attempt was done in the resource paper.) Such task is briefly presented below, but would naturally require more time and effort. Let also note that the same term: 'uncertainty' for example is used in different ways in different disciplines (or even specialties) which adds a considerable layer of difficulties.

Risk aversion: An individual is risk averse when (s)he prefers a deterministic payoff to any random payoff, with the same expected value. In the expected utility framework this means that individual utility function is concave.

Uncertainty: Agents face uncertainty when payoffs occur with unknown probabilities, or when the set of payoffs is unknown.

Expected utility theory (von Neumann and Morgenstern): In this framework, individual preferences can be described by utility functions. In risky situations, the agents maximize the utility of the payoffs weighted by their probabilities (mean utility).

Risk premium: Amount of money that an agent is ready to pay in order to avoid a risky payoff and get instead the mean expected payoff.

Absolute risk aversion: Let $U(x)$ be the individual utility derived from payoff x. The absolute aversion is given by: $\mathrm{AR}(x) = -U''(x)/U'(x)$ (where $U'(x)$ and $U''(x)$ are the first and second derivatives, respectively). Empirically, AR is decreasing with wealth.

Relative risk aversion: Let $U(x)$ be the individual utility with payoff x. The absolute aversion is given by: $\mathrm{RR}(x) = -xU''(x)/U'(x)$. Empirically RR is increasing with wealth.

Non-expected utility theory: Experimental evidence often suggests violations of the expected utility theory. This occurs, in particular, when probabilities are very small.[2] Alternative theories which question, in particular, the linearity in probabilities assumption have been proposed (see in particular the 'Prospect theory').

---

[2]See, for example http://www.ExtremRisk.com or http://www.RiskToleranceOnLine.com

Prospect theory: This theory was proposed by Kahneman and Tversky (1979), who treat differently gains and losses. For example, an individual may overestimate small probabilities of losses. In this case, the weights in the objective functions are non-linear function of the probabilities (or of the cumulative probabilities that are used in the cumulative prospect theory, which extends the original prospect theory).

Optimism bias: Systematic tendency to overweight the probability of positive outcome.

Pessimism bias: Systematic tendency to overweight the probability of negative outcomes.

Experimental economics: Test under laboratory conditions (and often using financial incentives) the predictions of economic theories on individual or collective behaviour.[3]

Three papers ware presented: A resource paper 'Modelling travel behaviour in risky and uncertain situations' was presented by J. Polak; 'Modelling risky choice behaviour: evaluating alternatives to expected utility theory', by A. Michea and J. Polak; and 'Learning and risk attitudes in route choice dynamics', by R. Chen and H. Mahmassani.

Debate

Several strong suggestions were made during the workshop, starting with the need to clarify the terminology. The expected utility (EU) and non-expected utility (NEU) theories were presented as different modelling perspectives. The former is more amenable to analytical computation (see, e.g. de Palma and Picard, 2006) and to estimation (see, e.g. de Palma and Picard, 2005 or Small et al., 2005), while the latter is more robust and closer to experimental findings. The standard EU approach was presented more as a *normative* theory, rather than a positive one (though there was no consensus about that in the workshop). Several possible deviations from standard EU were identified in laboratory experiments studying user behaviour. NEU (such as *cumulative prospect theory* or *rank-dependent expected utility theory*) were proposed as possible ways to deal with such deviations. Others involve the use of *non-linear utility* (or cost) functions in EU framework. The possibility to integrate random utility models (RUM) with EU was also advocated as a possible way to reconcile EU theory with data (see de Palma et al., 2008). Finally, last resort methods involving more *drastic* deviations such as adding uncertainty (e.g. ambiguity, vagueness, imprecision) in EU or NEU were discussed. However, it was noted that when using standard revealed preference (RP) or

[3]Other experiments use other vehicles. See, for example http://www.RiskToleranceOnLine.com which is used with or without financial incentives in order to measure the individual levels of risk aversion as well as to elicitate the utility functions.

stated preference (SP) data, it is generally (very) difficult to disentangle value (or utility) components and perception (deviation to EU) components.

One key challenge will be to investigate how it is possible to integrate attitude towards risk in the standard framework of linear random utility (LRU) models. As it stands, the standard LRU model implicitly assumes risk neutrality since the utility functions are additive linear in the error term.

New types of data collection, including those in cognitive science (*neuro-science*) are emerging and may become relevant in transportation during the coming years. Other competing models (such as *fuzzy* set theory or *Choquet* probabilities) were mentioned, but were disregarded in the discussion. In relation with RP and SP data (surveys and experimentation), but also in real life, participants stressed the need to take into account the following aspects (well documented in the risk and uncertainty literature): (1) *bias in the perception* of probabilities (optimism or pessimism); (2) *context-dependent* perception; (3) *reference point*, regret and loss aversion; and (4) *framing effects*.

Research Perspectives

We conclude this brief summary with a short list of topics and research priorities which were identified during the workshop. Some of these topics are discussed in a Special Issue in progress (see de Palma and Picard, 2009).

- Develop models to describe temporal and spatial *learning* (using Bayesian and non-Bayesian approaches) and investigate how active individual learning can reduce uncertainty (see de Lara et al., 2007)
- Integrate *(N)EU* and *RUM* in a consistent and tractable way amenable to econometric estimation
- Theoretical and empirical relation between risk and *equity*
- *Multi-dimensional* aspect of attitude towards risk
- *Bias in perception*, framing, reference point
- Statistics of rare events
- Develop a typology of the different types of risk, from micro to macro, and develop a methodology to introduce risk and uncertainty in cost–benefit analysis
- *Transferability* of the results on attitudes towards risk for the same individual in different contexts or different individuals in similar contexts
- *Interpretation of error term in RUM*: as a lack of knowledge from modeller point of view, or from individual perspective or even as an intrinsic stochastic component
- *Monetarization* of risk and value of information
- Psychologists discovered *new phenomena* (mentioned above), which can be captured in a NEU framework: more can be done to understand the implications of those mechanisms *for safety analysis*, inter alia.

ACKNOWLEDGMENT

We would like to thank all the participants to the workshop who greatly contributed to its success. The participants were Erel Avineri, University of the West of England, UK; Moshe Ben-Akiva, Massachusetts Institute of Technology, USA; Enide Bogers, Delft University of Technology, the Netherlands; Piet Bovy, Delft University of Technology, the Netherlands; Roger Chen, University of Maryland, USA; Caspar Chorus, Delft University of Technology, the Netherlands; André de Palma (chair), University of Cergy-Pontoise and Ecole Nationale des Ponts et Chaussées, France; Mogens Fosgerau, Danish Transport Research, Denmark; Emma Frejinger, Ecole Polytechnique Fédérale de Lausanne, CH; Karst Geurs, Netherlands Environmental Assessment Agency, the Netherlands; Kriste Henson, Los Alamos National Laboratory, USA; Ozbay Kaan, Rutgers University, NJ, USA; Ryuichi Kitamura, Kyoto University, Japan; Goulias Kostas, University of California, Santa Barbara, USA; Hani Mahmassani, University of Maryland, USA; Shoichiro Nakayama, Kanazawa University, Japan; Nathalie Picard, University of Cergy-Pontoise and Institut national d'études démographiques, France; John Polak, Imperial College, UK; Gerd Sammer, Universität für Bodenkultur, Wien, Austria; Joan Walker, Boston University, USA

References

de Lara, M., J.-P. Chancelier and A. de Palma (2007). Road-choice and the one-armed bandit problem. *Transportation Science* 41(1), 1–14.

de Palma, A., M. Ben-Akiva, D. Brownstone, C. Holt, T. Magnac, D. McFadden, P. Moffatt, N. Picard, K. Train, P. Wakker and J. Walker (2008). Risk, uncertainty and discrete choice models. *Marketing Letters* 19(3–4), 269–285.

de Palma, A. and N. Picard (2005). Route choice decision under travel time uncertainty. *Transportation Research Part A: Policy and Practice* 39(4), 295–324.

de Palma, A. and N. Picard (2006). Equilibria and information provision in risky networks with risk averse drivers. *Transportation Science* 40(4), 393–408.

de Palma, A. and N. Picard (Eds.) (2009). Special issue on transport, risk and individual choices. *Journal of Intelligent Transportation Systems: Technology, Planning, and Operations* (under progress).

Kahneman, D. and A. Tversky (1979). Prospect theory: an analysis of decision under risk. *Econometrica* 47(2), 263–291.

Machina, M. (1987). Choice under uncertainty: problems solved and unsolved. *Journal of Economic Perspectives* 1(1), 121–154.

McFadden, D. (1999). Rationality for economists. *Journal of Risk and Uncertainty* 19(1–3), 73–105.

Small, K., C. Winston and J. Yan (2005). Uncovering the distribution of motorists' preferences for travel time and reliability. *Econometrica* 73, 1367–1382.

The Expanding Sphere of Travel Behaviour Research
Selected Papers from the 11th International Conference on Travel Behaviour Research

17

Social Networks and Telecommunications

Patricia L. Mokhtarian

Abstract

The intersection of the three fields of social networking, impacts of information and communication technologies (ICT), and travel behavior generates exciting and important research questions. Challenges include the rapidity with which technology is changing, and our own preconceived ideas about its impacts. Nevertheless, it is clear that current travel behavior models are deficient in taking into account the social context in which travel takes place, and the role that ICT plays in constraining as well as facilitating options. New conceptualizations, methodologies, and datasets are needed to address a plethora of research issues.

Introduction

The workshop on social networks and telecommunications represents the nexus of three important areas of research: social networks, the adoption and impacts of new information and communication technologies (ICT), and travel behavior. Each of these areas has a sizable, and burgeoning, literature behind it, and each pair among the three has also been the subject of considerable scholarly attention. The study of the intersection of all three areas, however, is a relatively recent phenomenon, and much is yet to be learned. The resource paper (Dijst, this volume), synthesis paper (Ohmori, this volume), and three contributed papers presented in this workshop (Andreev et al., forthcoming; Carrasco et al., 2006; Schwanen and Kwan, 2008), together with the free-ranging discussion that occurred, provided a great deal of food for thought. The brief summary below focuses primarily on the workshop discussion, since the papers are separately available in this volume or through the authors. The comments are divided into two groups: those addressing what we currently know and those dealing with what we need or want to know.

What do We know? Observations on the Current State of Knowledge

This short report is not the place to summarize what is known about social networks, ICT, and travel behavior, but participants in the workshop had an assortment of comments about our state of knowledge, and about the conduct of research to extend that knowledge. These comments can be loosely classified as relating to the novelty of this area, critiques of research approaches, and paradoxes inherent in the subject of interest.

The Novelty of this Area

It was readily agreed that technological changes are outpacing the ability of research to keep up. As a result, there is almost always a lag of some years between the introduction and/or modification of new technologies, and an evidence-based understanding of their effects. With respect to earlier ICTs, the social impacts of the telephone were also only slowly understood (de Sola Pool, 1977), and the same is true of many other technologies—automobility being one extremely pertinent example (Wachs and Crawford, 1992).

When it comes to understanding the social impacts of technology, we need both a "ground-level" and a "bird's-eye" view. We obtain the ground-level view from individual, specifically focused studies, and that tends to be the almost inevitable approach in times of rapid change. Some passage of time is probably essential to providing a proper perspective from which to see trends in their broad form—the bird's-eye view.

Although in the early stages of a new phenomenon some purely exploratory research is natural, it is still just as important as ever to clearly articulate one's purpose in conducting a study. The answers obtained will certainly depend on the questions that are asked, which in turn are dictated by the values and interests of the analyst.

Critiques of Research Approaches

It was remarked that transportation researchers tend to be unaware of relevant literatures in other fields—while the converse is also true. This is quite ironic, in view of (1) the vastly improved ability to *find* relevant literature using the same ICTs we are studying and (2) the increasingly globally networked and increasingly interdisciplinary world of academia from which most researchers come. It strikes this author as offering informal evidence of the persistent importance of social networks together with technological ones. Purely technology-based searches can be effective when conscientiously and knowledgeably conducted, but whether through busyness, laziness, ignorance of the "right" vocabulary, or other reasons, many scholars fall short on undertaking systematic literature reviews. By contrast, perhaps the most *practically* effective way of identifying diverse literatures with relevance to one's subject is to meet people and/or hear presentations exposing one to that literature—which highlights the importance of making an effort to mix different disciplines at conferences such as IATBR, and at any other opportunity. In any case, with respect to the present topic, it was noted that the literatures on social capital, network capital, science and technology studies, computer-supported cooperative work (CSCW), and conversation analysis can usefully inform research on the transportation-related impacts of ICT on social networks.

Participants commented on the tendency to approach the study of the impacts of ICT on social networks with preconceptions that often reflect one of two extremes. Some people believe that "there is nothing new under the sun" (in broad terms, the new technologies are continuing the patterns of the old), whereas others perceive that the new technologies are revolutionizing everything. An overemphasis on the revolutionary character of ICT can arise through an understandable focus on what is changing because of it, to the neglect of what is staying the same. For example, punctuality has not now become completely irrelevant, contrary to what some commentators might suggest—the plane will still leave without you, even if you call on your mobile to say you are running late, and you still do not want your child to have to wait for you after school (Schwanen and Kwan, 2008). On the other hand, it seems fair to say that the impact of ICT on the distribution of music and the sale of travel-related services has indeed been paradigm-shifting. Our ongoing challenge as researchers is to avoid being too heavily wedded to our preconceived ideas, and to steer an open-minded course between extremes—going "where the science takes us."

With respect to traditional transportation models, participants felt that we have focused too much on the traveler as an individual rational actor, who primarily wants to minimize travel time and cost. By contrast, we should see travelers more as networked actors, and trips not just in terms of places, but also in terms of place–people bundles (Kwan, 2007; Schwanen, 2008). Sometimes the people may be as important as, or far more important than, the place. For example, one may go to Kyoto, Japan, not just because it is a beautiful and interesting place, but also because a beloved colleague lives there. Or one may go to Dothan, Alabama, not for the place at all, but because one's parents happen to live there. Such *travel* decisions cannot be captured by any conventional measure of place attractiveness, but require an understanding of the individual's social connections. The same can be true of much of daily local travel as well—social considerations may frequently motivate us to choose destinations farther away, or otherwise less attractive, than appears to be rational from a pure cost-minimization standpoint.

Paradoxes

Through the workshop papers and discussion, a number of paradoxes related to ICT were identified. Some instances include:

1. We can have virtual presence in many far-flung places simultaneously, yet corporeality still matters. Distance in some ways is irrelevant, while in others it is still paramount.
2. ICTs relax some constraints while imposing others (Table 1). Thinking of Hagerstrand's (1970) tripartite classification of constraints, Dijst's resource paper notes *capability* constraints such as computer capacity, speed, and size; *coupling* constraints which are still present for synchronous communication modes such as the telephone and videoconferencing; and *authority* constraints such as restrictions on using ICTs in certain places (mobile phones in theaters; laptops during airplane takeoffs and landings), and expectations of constant availability (similar notes are sounded in the contribution by Schwanen and Kwan).
3. To continue this line of thinking with respect to capability constraints in particular, while ICTs enable the dematerialization of many formerly physical objects (audio CDs, paper), they still require a material infrastructure: from towers and transmission and reception devices at the system level down to mobile phones, computers, batteries and chargers, and the like at the individual user level.

Table 1
The Impact of ICTs on Hagerstrand's Constraint Categories

Constraint	Definition (Dijst, this volume)	Example of Relaxation by ICT	Example of Imposition by ICT
Capability	Biological, mental, and instrumental restrictions	ICT-facilitated multitasking "creates time"	Lack of computer/Internet literacy can contribute to social exclusion
Coupling	Synchronization of individuals, instruments, and materials	Do not have to be at a fixed location to make or receive a phone call	Must have physical products and services in place (phones, electricity, transmission equipment, etc.)
Authority	Regulation of access to space	Do not have to shop when the store is physically open	Prohibition on mobile phone use under certain circumstances (in theater, while driving, in flight, and so on)

We are still constrained by the availability and functionality of this physical infrastructure (Graham and Marvin, 2001).

4. The Schwanen and Kwan paper notes that although ICT has been hailed as a utopian liberator for women and other historically disadvantaged sectors of society, it is in many ways actually *perpetuating* gendered roles. At the same time, dystopian visions on the social implications of Internet use—the Web turning youngsters into social nerds with few communicative skills—are equally suspect (cf. Gershuny, 2003). This point is a reminder that technology itself is neutral—it is how humans apply it that can be positive or negative.
5. The role and impacts of ICT can differ by geographic scale, and operate in different directions simultaneously. For example, Townsend (2001) notes that at the national/global level, San Francisco is a major hub of Internet connectivity, but within the region there are marked differences between, say, Oakland and Berkeley. It has also been observed that ICTs facilitate both decentralization and concentration (de Sola Pool, 1980), and that spatial inequities may be accentuated rather than attenuated by ICTs (Gillespie and Robins, 1989).
6. ICT is creating a variety of social network connections which may be invisible to those in physical proximity. Our next-door neighbor may be running an online pornography business; our children may have friends around the world of which we are ignorant.

What do We Want to Know? Some Research Questions, and Observations on Data Needs and Methodological Issues

Some areas for further research are implicitly embedded in the preceding discussion. Below, we sketch some additional issues that arose in the course of the workshop. Some relate to our fundamental conceptualization of the topic. Others relate to methodological concerns and data needs, while still others are simply some specific questions of interest.

Conceptualizations

One comment was that a focus on faithful correspondence to some geographic reality may not always be best. In some contexts, understanding a detailed physical geography may be less important than understanding human flows. Mobile phone navigation screens support this observation in that they may provide only very minimal landmark information.

Perhaps most fundamentally, we need a deeper understanding of the nature of communication itself, including useful dimensions along which it can be categorized (e.g., synchronous versus asynchronous as just one example), and a typology which is relevant to transportation studies. The communication mode choice literature, among others, has tackled this question, so it may simply be a matter of the transportation community absorbing that literature. On the other hand, there may still be contributions that the transportation community can make in terms of expanding and streamlining a set of existing classification dimensions to focus on those most relevant to transportation.

Methodologies and Data

As always, but especially when a field is new, research is hampered by a lack of data that include new variables of interest. For example, with respect to the topic at hand, participants commented that we need more cohort-specific studies of the adoption of ICT in a social networking context. In particular, we should learn more about the adoption and use of ICT by children, teens, and young adults. It is also imperative, however, to conduct more longitudinal studies as well. We often assume that changes in the uses and implications of ICTs occur rather swiftly (because technologies become more sophisticated, we get more used to using them, prices have gone down, and so on). However, we know surprisingly little about how the use of ICTs—and the implications for travel behavior—changes over time for a given individual.

In some cases, new data can be analyzed with methodologies conventional to the field, while in other cases, revised or entirely new methodologies may be called for. A good example of a subject requiring both new data and new methodologies is multitasking. This appears to be an increasingly important phenomenon, greatly facilitated by ICT. Focusing on its role in travel, one's (dis)utility for traveling may be greatly affected by the ability to conduct useful or pleasant activities on the trip, which in turn can affect trip frequency, length, and mode (see, e.g., Lyons and Kenyon, 2007). Thus, such information is important to travel behavior models including trip generation, duration, and mode choice.

So far, however, our models are oblivious to this factor, nor do we have the data to support incorporating this factor into our models. Most activity/time use diaries do not do a good job of collecting data on multitasking (secondary and even tertiary activities conducted simultaneously), and we have little understanding of how multitasking decisions are made and their impacts on other behavior. How can we collect the needed data without imposing too great a burden on the respondent? Direct observation? ICT-enabled automatic data collection? Self-reports?

Multitasking is a good example of a context in which ethnographic methodologies can be useful. In general, such qualitative methodologies can complement more quantitative methods, and play a valuable role in deepening our understanding of the heterogeneity of behavioral choices, motivations, and experiences. Yet few transportation professionals, even travel behavior researchers, are trained in the use of these techniques.

On a related question, to what extent is the ability to multitask while traveling affecting the value of travel time savings? If it is having a significant impact, what are the implications for the valuation of transportation infrastructure improvement investments?

The preponderance of studies on the travel-related impacts of ICT use relatively simple statistical methods such as single-equation regressions or discrete response models. With issues like those above, more sophisticated techniques are needed. For example, the question regarding the impacts of multitasking on the value of travel time savings calls for advanced discrete choice models such as mixed logit and its later variations. Such models allow for the (dis)utility of travel time to be randomly distributed over the population, but issues remain, including how best to approximate that distribution with empirical data (see, e.g., Hess et al., 2005; Mokhtarian, 2005).

Finally, we need data that could enable us to explore relationships between the characteristics of travelers' social networks and their travel and communication behavior in a more explicit way. Recent attempts to capture the role of personal networks in travel and ICT are promising, showing that collecting social network data and travel patterns is a feasible and useful proposition (Larsen et al., 2006; Carrasco et al., 2008a). However, these tools still heavily rely upon experiences from the sociological field, and we need to adapt them further, to answer these and other related questions.

Specific Research Questions/Issues

1. Which broad patterns are different, and which are similar, to those we have seen with earlier communication technologies? For example, recent studies on the role of ICT in the spatial patterns of social networks (e.g., Carrasco et al., 2006, 2008b; Mok et al., 2008) have found that distance still plays a relevant role in the frequency of contact, similar to the way it did 25 years ago in the pre-Internet era (Fischer, 1982; Mok and Wellman, 2007).
2. To what extent are the differences we are seeing important (to the nature of relationships, to transportation and other social impacts)? Are the impacts of new ICT too small to matter much (just more of the same as we have seen with older technologies), dramatic in scope, or somewhere in between?
3. How has the influence of ICTs on social networks affected quality of life, and satisfaction with life? To what extent and under what circumstances are ICTs a

burden? When do their costs outweigh their benefits? What are their implications for privacy?

4. Ohmori's synthesis paper (this volume) gave a fascinating glimpse into differences in the adoption of ICTs among Japan, South Korea, and China. In general, how does the adoption of ICTs, and their impacts on social networks, differ across cultures, including between developed and developing countries? How do they differ between large metropolitan areas, smaller towns, and rural areas of a given country?
5. In a number of developing countries today, rapid economic growth is driving the simultaneous development of transportation and ICT infrastructures. To what extent can the lessons learned by developed countries with respect to progress toward sustainability in transportation and urban planning/policy be transferable to developing countries? In what ways will developing countries be able to leapfrog the legacy technologies and planning approaches of the developed countries?
6. What are some of the second- and third-order, longer term and more indirect, impacts of ICT on social networks? These include impacts on the spatial distribution of travel and activities, and environmental/resource consumption impacts.
7. We need to better understand the nature of the digital divide and potential social exclusion impacts. For example, is it still true that physical mobility-limited individuals also have lower virtual mobility, or have they been able to harness the technology to compensate in part for their limitations?

Conclusions

The convergence of these three individually-and pairwise-exciting fields of inquiry—social networking, impacts of ICT, and travel behavior—poses a number of especially fascinating questions. Although we will in some ways always be playing catch-up with technological developments, we need not—and really, must not—let that prevent us from tackling these issues. On the other hand, it is imperative to keep an open mind with respect to what is to be learned, and to bring considerable creativity to the table as the circumstances call for new thinking, methods, and data. Our reward will be fresh and important insights into some of the most vital manifestations of human life—sociality, communication, and travel—and how they relate to each other.

ACKNOWLEDGMENTS

Thoughtful comments from Tim Schwanen, Nobuaki Ohmori, and Juan Antonio Carrascas improved an earlier draft of this report.

References

Workshop Resource Paper:

Dijst, M. (this volume). ICT and social networks: Towards a situational perspective on the interaction between corporeal and connected presence.

Workshop Synthesis Paper:

Ohmori, N. (this volume). Connected anytime: Telecommunications and activity–travel behavior from an Asian perspectives.

Workshop Contributed Papers:

Andreev, P., I. Salomon and N. Pliskin (forthcoming). Review: State of tele-activities. *Transportation Research Part C*.

Carrasco, J. A., E. J. Miller and B. Wellman (2006). Spatial and social networks: The case of travel for social activities. Available from the authors.

Schwanen, T. and M.-P. Kwan (2008). The Internet, mobile phone and space–time constraints. *Geoforum* 39(3), 1362–1377.

Other References:

Carrasco, J. A., B. Hogan, B. Wellman and E. J. Millar (2008a). Collecting social network data to study social activity–travel behaviour: an egocentred approach. *Environment and Planning B* 35(6), 961–980.

Carrasco, J. A., E. J. Miller and B. Wellman (2008b). How far and with whom do people socialize? Empirical evidence about distance between social network members. *Transportation Research Record* 2076, 114–122.

de Sola Pool, I. (Ed.). (1977). *The Social Impact of the Telephone*. Cambridge, MA, MIT Press.

de Sola Pool, I. (1980). Communications technology and land use. *The Annals of the American Academy of Political and Social Science* 451, 1–12.

Fischer, C. (1982). *To Dwell among Friends: Personal Networks in Town and City*. Chicago, IL, University of Chicago Press.

Gershuny, J. (2003). Web use and net nerds: a neofunctionalist analysis of the impact of information technology in the home. *Social Forces* 82(1), 141–168.

Gillespie, A. and K. Robins (1989). Geographical inequalities: the spatial bias of the new communications technologies. *Journal of Communication* 39(3), 7–18.

Graham, S. and S. Marvin (2001). *Splintering Urbanism: Networked Infrastructures, Technological Mobilities and the Urban Condition*. New York, Routledge.

Hagerstrand, T. (1970). What about people in regional science? *Regional Science Association Papers* 24(1), 7–21.

Hess, S., M. Bierlaire and J. W. Polak (2005). Estimation of value of travel-time savings using mixed logit models. *Transportation Research Part A* 39A(2 & 3), 221–236.

Kwan, M.-P. (2007). Mobile communications, social networks, and urban travel: hypertext as a new metaphor for conceptualizing spatial interaction. *The Professional Geographer* 59(4), 434–446.

Larsen, J., J. Urry and K. W. Axhausen (2006). *Mobilities, Networks, Geographies*. London, Aldershot.

Lyons, G. and S. Kenyon (2007). Introducing multitasking to the study of travel and ICT: examining its extent and assessing its potential importance. *Transportation Research A* 41(2), 161–175.

Mok, D. and B. Wellman (2007). Did distance matter before the Internet? Interpersonal contact and support in the 1970s. *Social Networks* 29, 430–461.

Mok, D., B. Wellman and J. A. Carrasco (2008). Does distance matter in the age of the Internet: are cities losing their comparative advantage? *103rd Annual Meeting of the American Sociological Association*. Boston, August 1–4.

Mokhtarian, P. L. (2005). Travel as a desired end, not just a means. *Transportation Research A* 39A(2 & 3), 93–96.

Schwanen, T. (2008). Managing uncertain arrival times through sociomaterial associations. *Environment and Planning B* 35(6), 997–1011.

Townsend, A. M. (2001). The Internet and the rise of the new network cities, 1969–1999. *Environment and Planning B* 28(1), 39–58.

Wachs, M. and M. Crawford (Eds.) (1992). *The Car and the City: The Automobile, the Built Environment, and Daily Urban Life*. Ann Arbor, MI, University of Michigan Press.

The Expanding Sphere of Travel Behaviour Research
Selected Papers from the 11th International Conference on Travel Behaviour Research

18

Retrospectives and Perspectives on Travel Behavioral Modification Research: A Report of the "Behavior Modification" Workshop

Satoshi Fujii

Abstract

The issues we discussed included theories, methods, and programs for travel behavior modification. Behavior modification has become an important issue in transportation research and practice, especially in mobility management policy. Modifying the behavior of car drivers so that they use their cars less is required to reduce traffic congestion, lower CO_2 emissions, and improve air quality. The theories are important to understand how and why people change their travel behavior. The behavioral theory implies that essential ingredients in any method of changing behavior are *money, power*, and *words*. Actually, words-type methods such as travel feedback programs have been demonstrated to be effective. The behavioral theory could be also used for effective selection of targeting individuals and for designing communicative measures regarding public acceptance of coercive transport measures such as road pricing.

Objective

Behavior modification has become an important issue in transportation research and practice. Modifying the behavior of car drivers so that they use their cars less is required to reduce traffic congestion, lower CO_2 emissions, and improve air quality. This behavior modification includes changing travel modes from car to environmentally sustainable transportation modes such as bicycle, bus, and train; changing travel destinations to points closer to the origin; changing living areas from those without to those with public transit; and changing car ownership patterns to include fewer cars or perhaps none at all. Mobility management and transportation demand management have been proposed and applied to modifying behavior in these areas. More research on behavior modification is required to make these transportation measures more effective and efficient. In this workshop, we discussed issues concerning travel behavior modification research after the presentation of a resource paper (Gärling and Fujii, 2006) and two oral presentations (Behrens and Del Mistro, 2006; Lanzendorf, 2006).

Theories for Behavior Modification

The issues we discussed included theories, methods, and programs for travel behavior modification. The theories are important to understand how and why people change their travel behavior. Such understanding is useful in developing methods of actually changing people's travel behavior. In particular, the theory to describe a process of behavior modification could be used for identifying psychological variables to be targeted in behavior modification interventions; this could include such aspects as attitude, perceived behavioral control, behavioral intention, implementation intention, moral obligation, and habit. These variables are all psychological constructs that are assumed in psychological theories such as the theory of planned behavior, norm activation theory, and theories of implementation intention and habit (Gärling and Fujii, 2006).

Once target psychological variables have been identified, we can select appropriate types of intervention that would be effective for behavior modification. For example, implementation intention could be formed through requests to make a behavioral plan of how to modify travel behavior while behavioral intention could be formed through messages suggesting behavior modification. Moral obligation could be activated through messages on the seriousness of negative consequences of CO_2 emissions from cars.

The theory of behavior modification processes could be also used for effective selective targeting of individuals. Some people may be in the early stages of the behavior modification process. For them, increasing awareness of the negative impact of car use on global warming by providing information on such impacts might be necessary to move them to the more advanced stages of behavior modification. However, for those already at the advanced stages, a more effective method of promoting behavior change would be to provide them information on actually how to use alternatives to the car. Such information programs would be even more effective if they were customized to the individual.

Practical Interventions

The discussions on behavior change theories were followed by discussions on practical interventions for behavior modification. The resource paper showed that the essential ingredients in any method of changing behavior are *money*, *power*, and *words*. These ingredients were all used in mobility management for behavioral modification. *Money* in this context refers to economic factors including not only money, but also goods and services that can be traded for money. Transport mobility management measures using money include road pricing and congestion charging as "push" measures, and discounts or monetary rewards of public transport as "pull" measures. Improvement of public transit service was another example of this because economic theory sometimes converts the level of service into monetary terms. *Power* refers to physical power (barriers) as well as political power (regulation). Legal policies such as prohibiting car traffic in city centers and parking control are two methods of power. *Words* refer to various types of communication including information and education measures.

We then discussed that while methods based on the money and power concepts were the basis of traditional transport policy in many areas, methods based on words had not been extensively used. Even so, words-type methods have been recently tried in some European countries as well as in Australia and Japan. Typical communication measure is travel feedback program (TFP; Fujii and Taniguchi, 2005) such as individualized marketing (Brög et al., 2003), travel blending (Rose and Ampt, 2001), and personal travel planning (Jones and Sloman, 2006). TFPs are individualized communications that provide car users with information or messages that are tailored to their attitude or actions concerning travel behavior. Previous research has shown that TFPs can successfully reduce the car use of targeted individuals or households by 5–20%. For example, a meta-analysis of the reduced use of cars due to TFPs in Japan showed reductions of 18% for residential area TFPs and 9% for workplace TFPs (Taniguchi et al., 2007).

Requesting participants to make plans on how to reduce their car use and having them set specific reduction goals were also reported to be especially effective measures. These findings were obtained through a meta-analysis of TFP cases (Taniguchi et al., 2007). We then discussed that such meta-analysis of successful TFP cases would be effective for the improvement of TFP effectiveness, and that analysis and measurement of behavior modification in TFP cases are essential. In addition, such meta-analysis would be useful in the development of psychological theories for behavior change. This is because such analysis could be used for tests of psychological theory with high ecological validity. Psychological theory for behavior modification should be exposed to actual behavioral data in the real world, in addition to well-designed and well-controlled experimental situations. This analysis of real-world data may highlight phenomena that cannot be explained by existing psychological theories, providing opportunities for substantial improvement in existing theory or the development of new ones.

Measurement of Behavioral and Psychological Modification

Thus, for the practical improvement of communication measures and theoretical development of psychological theories for behavioral modification, measuring the effectiveness of interventions for behavior modification such as TFPs is extremely important. We discussed how a control group was crucial for measuring the effectiveness as a baseline to experimental groups. A control group is composed of participants not subject to interventions such as TFPs, while the experimental groups are composed of those exposed to the interventions. With participants randomly assigned to groups, and the only difference between the groups being the existence of interventions, any difference in behavioral and psychological measurements of the participants can be attributed to the interventions. Thus, the *causal* effect of interventions on measurements can be tested through a comparison between the control and experimental groups.

If transport policy makers can easily assign target individuals or households randomly to control and experimental groups, the aforementioned method of evaluating interventions could be easily applied. This is generally not so easy in the real world because cross-contamination between the experimental and control groups occurs through voluntary social communication. Specifically, TFP messages provided to experimental groups may reach control group members through personal communication. To reduce such contamination, the zone system could be used where one geographical zone is assigned to the control group and others are assigned to experimental groups. However, finding homogenous zones is sometimes difficult. Any zone has its own characteristics that may have some effects on the psychological and behavioral measurement of participants. Even so, since creating a control group for comparison with experimental groups is the highly preferred method for evaluating behavior modification interventions, we discussed the importance of creating a random control group with the least contamination bias possible.

Another method for assessing interventions includes aggregated measures such as traffic volume or the number of passengers using public transit, as opposed to disaggregated measurements such as individuals' attitudes and behavior. Although aggregated measures seem promising for practical evaluations in policy making, it is not always easy to isolate the effects of the interventions from the effects of other concurrent changes such as seasonal differences. We discussed how it would helpful to reduce such biases due to the seasons by, for example, implementing changes during the same period as in the previous year, or by making changes in different areas during the same times of the year.

Timing of Interventions

The effectiveness of an intervention on behavior modification is dependent on its timing as well as its content. Effective timings target life events such as changing residence, obtaining employment, changing jobs, getting married, having children, and reaching driving age (Lanzendorf, 2006). Since these life events are all ones in which people reconsider their travel routines, it would be much easier to modify their attitudes and behavior at these times with interventions such as provision of information about alternatives to the car, and persuasive messages about reducing car use.

For example, many municipalities require new residents to register in person at some administrative office location. This registration would be a good opportunity to provide persuasive messages about reducing car use in the area, especially when accompanied by information about using public transit or riding bicycles. A previous study (Taniguchi and Fujii, 2007) showed that such communication to new residents led to a significant reduction in car use and a considerable increase in the use of public transit. Another study concerned communication to young nondrivers to not obtain their driver licenses (Fujii, 2007). However, research on interventions timed to coincide with life events has not yet been well implemented. Further research on this issue is required.

Public Acceptance Issues

Although the above-mentioned issues are related to mobility management measures utilizing words, other types of mobility management measures based on the power and money approaches, such as road pricing or car regulation, require different types of attitudinal research. A big issue in these types of measures is public acceptance of policies such as road pricing and car regulation because drivers usually have negative attitudes toward such coercive transport policies. Previous research on public acceptance of such coercive measures showed that perceptions of fairness, infringement on freedom, and effectiveness of such measures were crucial factors in their acceptance. While psychological research has been conducted mainly to understand why people accept or reject such coercive measures, practical communication on attitude change should be carried out through, for example, public campaigns or individualized communication. If such coercive measures are really necessary in the public interest, then measures to increase public acceptance are definitely required as well. Therefore, research to explore what communication measures have positive effects on public attitude toward the coercive measures is also important.

Summary and Concluding Remarks

In this workshop, we discussed various aspects of policy measures, as well as behavioral and psychological theories and models for travel behavior modification. The discussion included various issues and indicated further research that is required. This future research includes more theoretical development on behavior and attitudinal modification, research on improvement in behavioral interventions such as TFPs, a meta-analysis of the effectiveness of interventions such as TFPs, methodological research on the evaluation of these interventions, research to investigate effectiveness dependent on timing, and research on practical interventions for public acceptance of coercive measures required for the public interest.

In the tradition of travel behavior research, numerous studies have been carried out on measuring, describing, and modeling travel behavior. However, little work has focused on actually modifying travel behavior itself as noted earlier. The existing studies on measuring, describing, and modeling behavior have incorporated many concepts and methodologies mainly drawn from behavioral econometrics. However, it would seem that based on our discussions in this workshop, studies on behavior modification need to incorporate psychological theories and methodologies. The lines of travel behavior research on behavior modification based on psychology could be described as a new approach, but psychology itself has a long history of understanding and modifying behavior. Therefore, we can easily anticipate that incorporating psychological theories and concepts into travel behavior research would be a useful approach in the future.

We should not forget, however, that travel behavior research is essential for transport policy making in its contribution to social welfare. Therefore, incorporating psychology into travel behavior research is expected to produce a solid bridge between theory and practice in the field of transportation. Such a bridge is critical for further theoretical development based on psychology or behavioral sciences as well as for effective transport policy making. Even though the bridge has not been built, its construction has clearly started. The agreement of the workshop participants was that we should not halt construction of this bridge between theory and practice, and that we should continue the research in travel behavioral modification, which is important from the perspective of transport practice as well as the psychological and behavioral sciences.

References

Behrens, R. and R. Del Mistro (2006). Shocking habits: methodological issues in analysing changing personal travel behaviour over time. CD-ROM of the *Proceedings for the 10th International Association for Travel Behavior Research Conference*. Kyoto, Japan, August 16–20.

Brög, W., E. Erl and N. Mense (2003). Individualised marketing: changing travel behaviour for a better environment. Paper presented at the TRIP Research Conference: The Economic and Environmental Consequences of Regulating Traffic. Hillerød, February 2–3.

Fujii, S. (2007). Communication with non-drivers for promoting long-term pro-environmental travel behaviour. *Transportation Research D* 12, 99–102.

Fujii, S. and A. Taniguchi (2005). Reducing family car use by providing travel advice or requesting behavioral plans: an experimental analysis of travel feedback programs. *Transportation Research D* 10, 385–393.

Gärling, T. and S. Fujii (2006). Travel behavior modification: theories, methods, and programs. CD-ROM of the *Proceedings for the 10th International Association for Travel Behavior Research Conference*. Kyoto, Japan, August 16–20.

Jones, P. and L. Sloman (2006). Encouraging behavioral change through marketing and management: what can be achieved? In K. W. Axhausen (Ed.), *Moving through Nets: The Physical and Social Dimensions of Travel*. Oxford, Elsevier.

Lanzendorf, M. (2006). Key events and their effect on mobility biographies. The case of child birth. CD-ROM of the *Proceedings for the 10th International Association for Travel Behavior Research Conference*. Kyoto, Japan, August 16–20.

Rose, G. and E. Ampt (2001). Travel blending: an Australian travel awareness initiative. *Transportation Research D* 6, 95–110.

Taniguchi, A. and S. Fujii (2007). Mobility management through communication for new residents. Presented at the *17th European Transport Conference*. Leeuwenhorst Conference Centre, The Netherlands, October.

Taniguchi, A., H. Suzuki and S. Fujii (2007). Mobility management in Japan: its development and meta-analysis of travel feedback programs. *Transportation Research Record* 2021, 100–117.

The Expanding Sphere of Travel Behaviour Research
Selected Papers from the 11th International Conference on Travel Behaviour Research

19

Advances in Data Acquisition

Juan de Dios Ortúzar and Piotr Olszewski

Abstract

Positioning technologies using GPS or mobile phones are now mature enough to supplement the traditional travel diary methods on a large scale. The advantages are: less respondent burden, better accuracy and more data being captured, for example, route choice information. The challenges of using this technology are: high cost, privacy and acceptance issues and possible sample bias. Intensive data processing is required but data sets with tracking information create new research opportunities for exploring the dynamics of travel behaviour.

Introduction

Recent developments in geographical positioning and communication technologies bring the possibility of facilitating, enriching and improving the accuracy of travel behaviour surveys by automated tracking of people movements. This can be achieved with the help of dedicated GPS devices as well as mobile phones. So far, positioning technologies have only been applied in small-scale surveys and pilot studies—several such applications have been documented in the literature (e.g. Asakura and Hato, 2000; Draijer et al., 2000; Murakami et al., 2000; Doherty et al., 2001; Wolf et al., 2001; Stopher et al., 2003; Forrest and Pearson, 2005). A good review of recent technological developments is given by Asakura and Hato (2009).

After almost 10 years of experiments and pilot studies, there are now plans to use positioning technologies on a larger scale. However, this approach brings about several methodological and practical problems. These issues were explored and discussed at the recent Kyoto conference in a special workshop dedicated to this theme. The ideas expressed at the workshop have been the inspiration for this paper.

GPS devices are becoming increasingly popular and less expensive, creating the possibility of using them more routinely in large-scale travel surveys. There is now a spectrum of technologies and 'tracking' survey possibilities:

- using GPS-equipped in-vehicle data loggers to capture car movements over several days (e.g. Lexington survey; Murakami and Wagner, 1999);
- electronic travel diaries (requiring respondent's input) with GPS person tracking capability (e.g. Atlanta survey; Wolf et al., 2001);
- limited-scale/long-period passive personal GPS tracking devices supplemented by questionnaire (e.g. French National Travel Survey, 2007–2008; Madre et al., 2007);
- large-scale anonymous tracking using mobile phones (e.g. probe person survey in Japan; Asakura and Hato, 2004).

There are many potential advantages of incorporating positioning technologies in the travel data collection process. The most important benefits seem to be:

- *Reducing respondent burden*: A passive automated tracking system does not require any effort on the part of respondents—other than looking after the equipment (battery charging, etc.). It is well known that respondent burden is one of the biggest problems with the traditional travel diary approach—as it reduces response rates as well as the amount of data captured due to respondents' survey fatigue and lack of patience (Ortúzar and Lee-Gosselin, 2003).
- *Increasing survey accuracy*: Traditional surveys rely on respondents' ability to remember and recall spatial and temporal details of their trips. It is well known that in travel diaries a significant proportion of trips are not reported—it is estimated that in French surveys as much as 30% of short trips are missing. In an American study (Forrest and Pearson, 2005), half of non-work trips were not reported. Trip under-reporting has serious implications on total mileage and travel time estimates (Wolf et al., 2003). This problem which is due to respondents' poor memory or carelessness is eliminated with automated tracking. In addition, trip start and end times are captured much more accurately.
- *Enriching the data collected*: Tracking enables us to capture trip routing information as well as the exact trip distances, travel speeds, delays, waiting times at transfer points, etc. Multi-day data sets can easily be obtained, thus providing some insight into the temporal variability of travel behaviour of individuals (Zhou and Golledge, 2000; Madre et al., 2007).
- *Improving the transport models*: With increased quantity and quality of travel data, it should be possible to improve current transport models. One example is route choice models which have been very difficult to calibrate due to scarcity of data.

Given the longitudinal travel data, collected over longer periods of time, it would be possible to analyse the mobility pattern of individuals and its regularity. Among other things, it would make the estimation of long-term travel elasticities possible.

Challenges in Using the New Technology

Although the use of positioning technologies has undisputed advantages as discussed above, it also creates certain problems, concerning both the technology and the organization of surveys and their subsequent data processing.

Technical Issues

There has been significant advancement of GPS positioning equipment technology in terms of its accuracy, sensitivity and memory capacity. Also, devices are becoming smaller and less obtrusive, but powering them can still be an issue—GPS data loggers used for multi-day surveys may require battery recharging every day.

Notwithstanding, the biggest technical problem with GPS devices is signal loss whenever at least three satellites are not in clear view. This happens when vehicles equipped with positioning data loggers enter tunnels or multi-storey car parks. Signal loss can also occur in city centre streets due to tall buildings (this is known as the 'urban canyon' effect). It is more difficult to capture public transport trips with GPS devices due to poor reception inside trains and trams (Draijer et al., 2000). Finally, personal GPS data loggers may become useless when people enter buildings.

On the other hand, while GPS devices work best in the open, outside urban areas, mobile phones are the opposite: they work best in cities where cell density is the highest. Mobile phones establish their location based on the relative signal strength of nearby cell transmitters. Thus, the positioning method is most accurate in urban conditions where the cells are relatively small and dense. Also, mobile phones of course work inside buildings, so the signal loss problem does not occur. However, the accuracy of positioning with mobile phones is several times worse than for GPS.

Survey Organization Issues

While travel surveys conducted with the help of positioning technology have undisputed advantages, they also create several problems, listed as follows:

- *Cost (equipment and communication)*: Although the cost of GPS receivers is decreasing, it could still be significant for large-scale surveys. In addition to equipment cost, there are operational costs of data transmission (mobile phones) or data retrieval during long surveys such as Automated Travel Diaries (ATD).

- *Privacy*: Generally, people are apprehensive at the idea of being tracked. In the case of mobile phones, consent of the owner is needed for tracking to be legal. To resolve this issue, there are methods of *anonymizing* data so that the identity of travellers is not associated with the travel records.
- *Acceptability*: As with any new technology, there are barriers to the use of positioning devices being accepted by the whole population. Acceptability varies from country to country as it depends on technical literacy and cultural aspects. Apparently, it is not a problem in Japan. Methods to increase acceptability range from financial incentives (Japan) to free gifts for participants (France).
- *Sampling bias*: Use of active devices (ATD) requires a certain level of computer literacy and thus would create a sample bias. The probe person approach which has been used in Japan relies on mobile phone tracking and is, therefore, biased against people not using (or always carrying) mobile phones. Furthermore, post-interviews carried over the Internet further limit the sample. Thus, it appears that to minimize sampling bias, the best approaches are using passive positioning devices and telephone post-interviews.

Data Analysis Issues

Regardless of the type of technology, surveys making use of positioning devices generate large amounts of data. These data typically consist of strings of time–space 'dots' (time plus position coordinates), representing path traces of individual trips. These data need to be cleaned, processed and analysed to extract meaningful travel information. The process can be summarized as follows:

- *Data cleaning*: It is important that dot data should be first cleaned of errors which occur due to GPS signal loss, poor reception, reflections, etc. Erroneous position fixes can be eliminated by statistical analysis.
- *Tracking dot data processing*: The first step in processing cleaned data is 'stay and move' dot identification (Asakura and Hato, 2009). The separation of dots representing movement (move dots) and stops (stay dots) is not a trivial issue; for example, due to positioning errors, a slow movement can be mistaken for a stop and vice versa.
- *Segmentation of tracking data into trips*: After the data have been cleaned, the next step is deciding which stops represent trip ends (activities) and which are involuntary stops en route (e.g. a stop at a traffic signal or in a traffic jam). This task is even more difficult for trips by public transport—a stop can mean a transfer to another mode or a change to another bus service, for example. Generally, it may be impossible to identify these correctly if not aided by post-interview questionnaires.

- *Data fusion*: Dot data analysis can be greatly enhanced by map-matching, that is, superimposing path traces over electronic GIS maps showing the transport network. For example, in a car path trace, dots which fall off the road network are likely to be erroneous position fixes. Knowing the location characteristics can obviously help to identify correctly the type of stops: a stop at a road junction is likely to represent a traffic signal delay while a stop at a train station is most probably a mode transfer.

The process outlined above should be automated as much as possible, especially when dealing with multi-day surveys where the size of the data set can become huge. Several methods have already been proposed for automatically correcting GPS traces, reconstructing trips, identifying road links and modes used, and even imputing trip purposes from destinations (Doherty et al., 2001; Stopher et al., 2003; Axhausen et al., 2004; Chung and Shalaby, 2005).

Research Issues

The richness of travel information collected with positioning data creates opportunities for new travel behaviour research. One example is using longitudinal (multi-day and multi-period) data sets to explore the variability of trip making and stability of travel patterns. Possible analysis and modelling directions have been outlined, for example, by Zhou and Golledge (2000) and Schönfelder et al. (2002). Some of the questions concerning the dynamics of travel which could be answered with such data are:

- Are there cycles in individual travel behaviour?
- To what degree are day-to-day travel patterns correlated?

Efficient processing and extracting useful information from large data sets containing traces of thousands of individual trips is going to present a real research challenge (Limoges et al., 2000). Such data can be explored directly using data mining techniques instead of building traditional trip choice models. This would make it possible to study the topology of travel (time–space characteristics of trip making). There is also a possibility for a new approach to studying land-use transport interactions.

Given the limited funds available for travel surveys and relatively high positioning equipment costs, the obvious trade-off is between sample size and survey duration. Is it better to capture travel of a smaller sample of individuals over longer period of time or of a large sample over a short period? The answer depends on the main purpose of the survey: a large sample would give a better representation of the travel pattern in the area surveyed, while a ‘long sample’ would capture the dynamics of travel behaviour better.

A further research question is: to what extent movement tracking data collection methods may affect the travel behaviour of those being observed? In the Japanese probe person survey, individuals can see their daily travel path traces on the Internet. Is this likely to change their travel behaviour? To answer this question, it is possible to use a reference sample—some participants who will not be able to see their traces. This brings a possibility of using surveys with feedback mechanism to intentionally change peoples' behaviour—for example, for inducing more 'green trips'.

Possible Future Directions

Continuing development and proliferation of car computers and navigational systems will make vehicle tracking surveys even easier in the future. One day, obtaining a full record of vehicle's daily movements will simply be a matter of downloading data from the car's computer. In addition, information such as engine start and stop times, fuel consumption, etc., can easily be appended. These data will be very useful for calibration of vehicle pollutant emission and environmental impact models (Limoges et al., 2000).

For person travel surveys, we will witness further development and miniaturization of both passive tracking devices as well as electronic travel diaries with positioning capabilities. For example, an ATD (AHMCT, 2007) is being developed and tested for the next Caltrans longitudinal travel survey for both person and vehicle tracking. It will have the capability to log continuously 30 days of travel.

Acquisition of tracking data from individuals can be made easier by trading information through ITS systems. In exchange for their consent to being tracked, drivers could be offered real-time information about the road network traffic conditions. This would create a win–win situation: enhanced traffic information service for the users and more data for the traffic management centre to be used for short-term traffic predictions as well as for creating a travel data base. It can be envisaged that one day traffic management centres will have real-time information about the current positions and intended destinations of most of vehicles on the road network under their supervision.

Wider use of mobile phone data for travel data acquisition can also be expected in the future. The progress in positioning accuracy using mobile phones will also be driven by commercial applications such as location-based services, navigation services and the need to pin-point the location of users making emergency calls. A similar information-trading arrangement to the one described above can be envisaged: mobile phone users agreeing to being tracked in exchange for the ability to use commercial navigation or location-based services.

Conclusions

Positioning technology is quickly becoming mature enough to supplement—and possibly even replace—the traditional travel diary methods of travel data acquisition. Both vehicle and person movements can now be tracked with GPS devices, mobile phones or a combination of these technologies. The undisputed advantages of using such tracking methods are less respondent burden, improved trip reporting, better accuracy of time and distance information and improved richness of the data being captured, for example, route choice information.

Before positioning technologies can be used for travel surveys on a large scale, however, some issues and problems need to be resolved including: high equipment costs, privacy and acceptance issues and possible sample bias. Transition to the new technology should be gradual. Tracking data require intensive automated analysis and although several methods have already been proposed, further development is required in this area. On the other hand, data sets with tracking information create new research opportunities for exploring the dynamics of travel behaviour.

Market forces will be driving further development of navigational and location-based services, potentially creating a wealth of travel data. The challenge is how to use these forces for the benefit of travel behaviour research.

ACKNOWLEDGMENTS

The authors would like to thank the following individuals for their contributions to this discussion: Yasuo Asakura, Shlomo Bekhor, Eiji Hato, Laurent Hivert, Shinji Itsubo, Masao Kuwahara, Jean Loup Madre, Philippe Marchal, Elaine Murakami, Voula Psaraki, Vincent Tabak and Kazutaka Takao. Thanks are also due to the FONDECYT, through project 1050672, and to the Millennium Institute on Complex Engineering Systems (Project P05-004F) for having supported this work.

References

AHMCT (2007). GPS Automated travel diary (GPS-ATD) enhances to travel behaviour surveys. Department of Mechanical and Aeronautical Engineering, University of California, Davis. Available at: http://www.ahmct.ucdavis.edu

Asakura, Y. and E. Hato (2000). Analysis of travel behaviour using positioning function of mobile communication devices. Paper presented at the 9th IATBR. Gold Coast, Australia.

Asakura, Y. and E. Hato (2004). Tracking survey for individual travel behaviour using mobile communication instruments. *Transportation Research* 12C, 273–291.

Asakura, Y. and E. Hato (2009). Tracking individual travel behaviour using mobile phones: recent technological development. In R. Kitamura, T. Yoshii and T. Yamamoto (Eds.), *The Expanding Sphere of Travel Behaviour Research*. Bingley, UK, Emerald.

Axhausen, K. W., S. Schönfelder, J. Wolf, M. Oliveira and U. Samaga (2004). 80 weeks of GPS-traces: approaches to enriching the trip information. *Transportation Research Record* 1870, 46–54.

Chung, E. H. and A. Shalaby (2005). A trip reconstruction tool for GPS-based personal travel surveys. *Transportation Planning and Technology* 28, 381–401.

Doherty, S. T., N. Noel, M. Gosselin, C. Sirois and M. Ueno (2001). Moving beyond observed outcomes: integrating global positioning systems and interactive computer-based travel behaviour surveys. Transportation Research Circular E-C026—Personal Travel: The Long and Short of it. TRB, Washington, DC.

Draijer, G., N. Kalfs and J. Perdok (2000). Global positioning system as data collection method for travel research. *Transportation Research Record* 1719, 147–153.

Forrest, T. L. and D. F. Pearson (2005). Comparison of trip determination methods in household travel surveys enhanced by a global positioning system. *Transportation Research Record* 1917, 63–71.

Limoges, E., C. L. Purvis, S. Turner, M. Wigan and J. Wolf (2000). Future of urban transportation data: transportation in the new millennium. Millennium Paper presented to the Transportation Research Board Annual Meeting. Washington, DC.

Madre, J.-L., J. Armoogum, P.-O. Flavigny, J.-P. Hubert, P. Marchal and S. Yuan (2007). Person-based GPS subset in the French National Travel Survey (ENTD 2007–2008). INRETS Working Paper, Arcueil.

Murakami, E. and D. P. Wagner (1999). Can using global positioning system (GPS) improve trip reporting?. *Transportation Research* 7C, 149–165.

Murakami, E., D. P. Wagner and D. M. Neumeister (2000). Using global positioning systems and personal digital assistants for personal travel surveys in the United States. Transportation Research Circular E-C008: Transport Surveys: Raising the Standard. TRB, Washington, DC.

Ortúzar, J. de D. and M. Lee-Gosselin (2003). From respondent burden to respondent delight. In P. R. Stopher and P. M. Jones (Eds.), *Transport Survey Quality and Innovation*, Oxford, Pergamon, pp. 523–528.

Schönfelder, S., K. W. Axhausen, N. Antille and M. Bierlaire (2002). Exploring the potentials of automatically collected GPS data for travel behaviour analysis-a Swedish data source. In J. Möltgen and A. Wytzisk (Eds.), *GI-Technologien für Verkehr und Logistik*, Vol. 13. Münster, Universität Münster, IfGIprints, pp 155–179.

Stopher, P. R., P. Bullock and Q. Jiang (2003). Visualising trips and travel characteristics from GPS data. *Road & Transport Research Journal* 12, 3–14.

Wolf, J., R. Guensler, S. Washington and L. Frank (2001). Use of electronic travel diaries and vehicle instrumentation packages in the year 2000 Atlanta Regional Household Travel Survey. Transportation Research Circular E-C026—Personal Travel: The Long and Short of it. TRB, Washington, DC.

Wolf, J., M. Oliveira and M. Thompson (2003). Impact of underreporting on mileage and travel time estimates: results from global positioning system-enhanced household travel survey. *Transportation Research Record* 1854, 189–198.

Zhou, J. and R. Golledge (2000). An analysis of variability of travel behaviour within one-week period based on GPS. Paper presented at IGERT Conference. UC Davis.

The Expanding Sphere of Travel Behaviour Research
Selected Papers from the 11th International Conference on Travel Behaviour Research

20

Advances in Activity Analysis

Kay W. Axhausen

Abstract

This note summarizes the discussion of the workshop on 'Advances in Activity Analysis' organised during the 11th International Conference on Travel Behaviour Research in Kyoto held in August 2006. It adds a more detailed list of questions which can be used to characterise the activity-based models for their practical application.

Introduction

The parallel workshops of recent IATBR conferences were an opportunity to discuss and develop key issues of interest to travel behaviour research. The starting point was a set of presentations and papers which grounded the discussions with both reviews and new results.[1] Twenty attendees came together in Kyoto under the heading of 'Advances in Activity Analysis'. The progress made across a range of issues is large and was ably surveyed by the background and the synthesis presentations: adoption of passive observation techniques with ever more sophisticated monitors based on GPS and GSM

[1]Background presentation by Ram Pendyala, Arizona State University and synthesis report by Kuniaki Sasaki and Kazuo Nishii, University of Yamanashi and the following papers: Modelling Activity Generation: A Utility Based Model for Activity-Agenda Formation, Khandker M. Nurul Habib and Eric J. Miller, University of Toronto; A Practical Policy Sensitive Activity-Based Model, Yoram Shiftan, Technion and Moshe Ben-Akiva, MIT; The Evolution of Perceived Spatio-Temporal Flexibility in Activity Patterns, Martin E. H. Lee-Gosselin, Pierre Rondier and Luis Miranda-Moreno, Universite de Laval.

location tracking, the availability of semi-automatically processes to enrich these traces in combination with automatically generated web-based surveys; further advances in our ability to extract the structures behind the observed choices and behaviours using both parametric and non-parametric modelling approaches, but especially with discrete choice modelling and rule-based approaches. Finally, the workshop noted with satisfaction that models in the activity-based tradition are crossing the line, even if slowly at this time, between explorations with research-scale tools to policy applications with production-scale tools (see Bradley and Bowman, 2006 for a comparison of the US applications).

Discussion

The discussion revolved around four themes, two each associated with the basic goals of activity analysis and the practical demands of production-scale tools:

- Should we aim for process models or models assuming strictly optimising agents?
- How should we understand activity scheduling?
- What (choice) model structures are practicable in production-scale tools?
- What is an appropriate time frame to obtain a steady-state solution?

Since its inception activity analysis has understood that the *Homo Oeconomicus* is a convenient fiction needed to obtain models, which have desirable properties for policy analysis: a strong link to welfare economics and welfare assessment, stable and reproducible results and most importantly a view of human actors, which is morally defensible; a view which sees travellers as aiming to improve their condition constantly in small and sometimes big steps. Since its inception, the field has also understood that humans are neither able to perform the optimisations stipulated error free, nor have they the necessary individual control over the planning horizons assumed, say their working day. Recent empirical work on the planning horizon of activities performed (Doherty, Axhausen and many others) has consistently shown that a large share of activities are performed ad hoc by using up buffer times, as well by adjusting other activities and plans. In Löchl et al. (2005), for example, 12% of all reported activities are conducted spontaneous and 40% of these involve destinations, which had never been visited before. Models of the process of activity scheduling or models of the processes behind the observed daily patterns would, therefore, be the desirable goal, but the demands of project evaluation (precision and replicability of the results) limit their use at this point.

Tied to the previous question was the discussion of activity scheduling. It was clear, that models employing closed optimisation approaches to derive daily schedules trade tractability for realism (see above). Unfortunately, there is currently too little practical comparative experience with models of activity scheduling to see how big a trade-off this is. How much realism do we trade for how much consistency and computational speed? While models derived from Becker's (1965) work—leisure trade-off model, see scheduling as a knapsack problem of optimal packaging, this is not the only perspective. It can equally be seen as a route choice (delivery) problem with time windows and duration constraints in a capacitated system with externalities between the actors. It became clear, that it is not possible at this point to decide which of the two view points will become the preferred framework to model and to understand scheduling.

The second set of questions concern the current implementations of the activity–analysis idea in practical use. Most of these employ variants of the model structure suggested by Bowman (1995), with the notable exceptions of CEMDAP and MATSIM. While the list of dimensions (see below), which should be addressed, is clear, currently only a subset is addressed. Again, there is not enough comparative experience to see, if one or the other of the approaches is preferable.

The workshop returned repeatedly to the question of the running time of the models, an item which is normally not reported, or with so little detail that conclusions and comparisons are difficult. While there was consensus, that it would be desirable for the models to reach steady state within 14–16 hours (the overnight run), the additional qualities and details of the results of an activity-based model can justify somewhat longer computational times, especially as long as competing aggregate dynamic-assignment models take multiple days to reach equilibrium for comparable networks. Still, the discussion showed that there was a growing awareness of the need to implement fast-running activity-based models, as their adoption in practise would otherwise be undermined. The switch to the new paradigm should not be too expensive for the adopters, in particular those behind the typical early adopters.

Comparing Models

The discussions in Kyoto, but also elsewhere, did show, that the different activity-based models are difficult to place for the interested readers, as the relevant papers skip details, which are often irrelevant to the topic of the paper at hand, but crucial for a comparative understanding of the scope of the models and of their performance. The set of questions proposed below is meant to start the discussion about this short set of questions, which would permit a better understanding of the progress made in the scope, detail and performance of the different modelling streams pursued around the world. It is incomplete, in need of improvement, maybe biased, but a start.

The key issues are performance, the scope of the scheduling model, the modelling of the physical interaction between the agents, the mechanism to reach steady state and the degrees of freedom of the schedule during this process and finally the detail in terms of networks, facilities and the description of the household, agents and their activities.

The *activity scheduling model* has to select a value for each of the following dimensions:

- Number and type of activities
- Sequence of activities
  - Start and duration of the activity
  - Composition of the group undertaking the activity
  - Expenditure for the activity and its allocation to the participants
  - Location of the activity
    - Movement between activities
      - (Type of) vehicle used
      - Point of access to the vehicle
      - Route
      - Point of departure from the vehicle
      - Composition of the group travelling together on purpose
      - Expenditure for the movement and its allocation to the participants.

The description should clarify, which of these are addressed and which are ignored. It should state, which are computed only once during the initialisation of the agent population and which are updated during search for the steady state. Finally, the sub-models and their respective reach should be specified, or example, for the movement between the locations: no modelling of parking, dynamic shortest path routing from door-to-door in each iteration; mode choice at the tour level during the initialisation, which is kept fixed during the iterations; no modelling of group compositions and expenditure allocation.

The scale of the spatial and temporal resolutions has impacts throughout the model structure and its application. It needs to be stated explicitly. For example, a model structure which works with four or five time periods will produce other within-day dynamics then a model which resolves all durations at a second-by-second level. The same holds for the difference between zonally based models and parcel-based models which account for each facility (building, unit) separately.

For a specific application of the model structure one would wish to know, how many and which types of households, agents, activities and facilities are distinguished and how and with what data the parameters of the various imputation and choice models were parameterised. For the agents, this involves the list of variables available to other models in the overall structure, in particular:

- Age
- Sex

- Hours worked and working hours
- Type of employment
- Personal income
- Location of the place of work or education
- Licence holding
- Car ownership/availability
- Public transport season tickets.

As detailed modelling of individual facilities is still unusual, it would be helpful if a model description, specifies the dimensions included and the way in which the relevant data was obtained or imputed, for example:

- Number of types
- Size
- Capacity
- Opening hours
- Price level.

The agents *compete for slots* on the networks, on the transport services and at the facilities, where they want to conduct their activities. The description needs to clarify which networks are covered by the structure and how the competition for slots affects the generalised costs of using the networks and which elements of the generalised costs are endogenous to the model system. For car-based travel, the following questions need to be answered in particular:

- How do you calculate link congestion effects?
- How do you calculate link travel time changes due to the congestion?
- How do you treat junctions? What interactions/controls are accounted for?

Traditionally transport modelling has ignored congestion at the destination. The higher spatial resolution aimed for in many recent implementations does not allow this anymore and the description should be explicit about how crowding effects at the destinations are captured and accounted for.

For the specific application one would need to know the network statistics, that is number of nodes, number of links and in the case of public transport number of stops, number of lines and number of services run (i.e. the way in which the timetable is specified). The source and the quality of the network data would be useful, but not strictly required information.

The model results will not be consistent after the first iteration, that is assumed and realised generalised costs will not be the same. The approach taken to achieve a *steady-state* needs, therefore, to be spelled carefully, if the model structure is aiming for such a state at all. The crucial questions are:

- What is the stopping criterion and how is it calculated across the agent population?
- How do the agents/the system learn from iteration to iteration?
- What share of agents is updated in each iteration?

For the specific application one should report the target value of the stopping criterion and how many iterations were required to achieve this value.

Computing times are meaningless unless the specific configuration of the computer employed is specified in terms of CPU, available RAM, type of hard disk, type of communication infrastructure for parallel computing. Even with these items there remain uncertainties. It is, therefore, useful to specify both the absolute and relative shares of the computing effort is taken by each of these steps:

- Initialisation of the networks and faculties (specifying the I/O share)
- Initialisation of the households and agents (specifying the I/O share)
- Initialisation of the first activity schedules (see above) (specifying the I/O share)
- Iterative process and across all iterations the shares
  - I/O
  - Updating of the schedules (by the sub-models identified in the description above)
  - Calculation of the competition effects by mode (i.e. the traffic flow simulation)
  - Calculation of the steady-state criterion

Outlook

The workshop at the 2006 Kyoto conference concluded optimistically. The move of the first generation of applications into policy practice is a validation of 40 years of research and development work. The increasing speed of adoption needs to be supported by further work on the basics of the approach, but also on the seemingly mundane task of making the models easy to use, robust and fast in the hands of the practicing consultants, local authorities and commercial users of the activity approach. We were looking forward to an update of the workshop and new promising results at the 2009 International Conference on Travel Behaviour Research.

References

Becker, G. S. (1965). A theory of the allocation of time. *Economic Journal* 75, 493–517.

Bowman, J. L. (1995). Activity based travel demand model system with daily activity schedules. Dissertation, MIT, Cambridge.

Bradley, M. A. and J. L. Bowman (2006) A summary of design features of activity-based microsimulation models for US MPOs. Paper presented at the TRB Conference on Innovations in Travel Demand Modeling. Austin.

Löchl, M., S. Schönfelder, R. Schlich, T. Buhl, P. Widmer and K. W. Axhausen (2005) Stabilität des Verkehrsverhaltens. Final Report for SVI 2001/514, Schriftenreihe, 1120, Bundesamt für Strassen, UVEK, Bern.

The Expanding Sphere of Travel Behaviour Research
Selected Papers from the 11th International Conference on Travel Behaviour Research

21

Group Behavior Modeling

Junyi Zhang and Andrew Daly

Abstract

Even though research on group behavior is still a comparatively new field in transportation, rapid progress has been made since the beginning of the 21st century. Up to now, a multiple-member household has been primarily considered as a decision-making unit under the principle of utility maximization with multilinear and iso-elastic household utility functions to represent intrahousehold interactions in household task and time allocation, joint activity participation and ride-sharing, car ownership and residential choice behavior, etc. A few exceptions have been observed to use a rule-based approach. The workshop on "Group Behavior" invited five papers, including the resource paper by Harry Timmermans, who gave a comprehensive review of existing studies and discussed unsolved research issues at the time of writing. The five papers introduced group behavior modeling in Japan, new modeling developments in the context of household timing decision behavior, social network, and pro-social behavior in network. However, existing studies have mainly focused on decision outcomes rather than the processes. Further developments, however, might explore more interpersonal interactions with respect to multifaceted behavior aspects, reflecting the need to bring more consistency in predicting travelers' genuine responses under policy interventions, from both modeling and survey perspectives. It is worth representing context and situation effects as well as temporal effects (e.g., day-to-day dynamics and learning). Group decision theories from other fields could be helpful; for example, game theory could serve as a promising tool but more empirical studies are required. The stated choice approach should be applied to investigate the process of negotiation among decision-makers. As a whole, further efforts in both modeling and survey are required to explore the behavior of more general group units in transportation.

Introduction

Observing travel behavior, it is not difficult to find that decisions are usually made with the involvement of two or more persons. These persons either jointly make decisions or impose direct/indirect influences on the decisions by some of the other persons.

As argued in the resource paper by Timmermans (2009), modeling such travel behavior has in part been motivated by the need to bring more consistency in predicting the various choice facets underlying transport decisions with the coordination and synchronization of activity–travel patterns of individuals belonging to the same household. In the context of transportation policies, ignoring such interpersonal interactions could overestimate the effects of policies and might lead to inappropriate investments. However, the dominating travel behavior models have been mainly built upon individual decision-making theories, which assume that an individual can decide his/her behavior only based on his/her own preference. In this sense, research on group behavior is still a comparatively new field in transportation. Fortunately, substantial achievements have been made since the beginning of the 21st century.

The workshop on "Group Behavior" invited five papers that covered major new modeling developments. Timmermans (2009) presented a resource paper to provide a comprehensive review of existing studies and discussed unsolved research issues by looking at the relating research in other fields at the time of writing. Zhang and Fujiwara (2009a) gave a synthesis report about the research progress in Japan, including the topics of household time/timing decisions, telecommunication and activity participation, joint trip-making, car ownership, and residential choice behavior. Hackney and Axhausen (2006) presented a multiagent model of social network and travel behavior interdependence to study linked geographical and social spaces by defining social-networking visits as travel activities. Having a doubt about the assumption that travelers' behavior is selfish by nature, Avineri (2006) illustrated some basic concepts of pro-social behaviors. Based on these concepts, Avineri extended the traditional user equilibrium to a social equilibrium in the context of transport network models and investigated the sensitivity of the social equilibrium to pro-social values. Finally, Zhang et al. (2006) developed a multidimensional household timing decision model by endogenously incorporating coupling constraints under the principle of utility maximization. The derived household timing model could also be used to flexibly reflect other timing constraints such as opening hour of a shop, the designated start time of a meeting, and departure time of a flight.

The above five papers and the discussions at the workshop reveal that even though relevant models have been developed to incorporate multifaceted behavioral interdependencies and interpersonal interactions, there are still many unsolved research issues about group behavior in transportation. This report summarizes the discussions at the workshop.

State of the Art

Up to now, group behavior modeling in transportation has mainly focused on the multiple-member household by explicitly recognizing the existence and different preferences of household members during decision-making process. The modeling approach relies on the principle of utility maximization and assumes that a household attempts to maximize its utility, defined as a function of its members' utilities. Multilinear and iso-elastic household utility functions have mainly been adopted (Zhang et al., 2002, 2005b; Zhang and Fujiwara, 2006). Such household utility functions allow us to incorporate relative influences of different members and their interactions into the modeling process. The two types of utility functions commonly include additive-, compromise-, capitulation-, and autocratic-type of utility as special cases. Max–max, max–min, and Nash-type utilities are further the special cases of the iso-elastic utility. These utilities have been applied to represent household task and time allocation with joint activity participation, timing decisions with coupling constraints, car ownership, residential choice, and so on. The approach could be directly applied to represent ride-sharing behavior that has not been satisfactorily modeled in the literature. Theoretically, it seems that the approach could also be applied to describe other types of group behavior as long as group members can be clearly identified. In this sense, it might be worth exploring its applicability in describing social network behavior. As another type of utility-maximizing model, Vovsha et al. (2005) conceptually proposed some discrete choice models of generalized extreme value (GEV) class, aiming at the development of a new generation of regional travel demand models with three principal levels of intrahousehold interactions, that is, coordinated principal daily pattern types, episodic joint activity and travel, and allocation of maintenance activities.

Another research stream is the rule-based approach. ALBATROSS (Arentze and Timmermans, 2000, 2004) and TASHA (Miller and Roorda, 2003) are excellent examples. In the ALBATROSS, activity selection of one household member depends on the activity schedule of the other adult, if any, in the household. Choice heuristics are used to assign a car to one of the household members. Joint activity participation, ride-sharing, escorting and chauffeuring are endogenously generated by the model in an implicit way. In the TASHA, activity–travel patterns of household members are generated simultaneously to allow for possible interaction between members with respect to joint activities, which require that the activity has the same start time, duration, and location for each household member participating in that activity.

Other models like FAMOS and CEMDAP do incorporate intrahousehold interaction effects, even though they are built upon individual decision-making theory. Timmermans (2009) gives a detailed discussion about these models.

Note that the above-mentioned modeling approach mainly deals with decision outcomes, rather than processes. They could be good enough for practical applications. In case of understanding group behavior mechanisms, however, modeling the processes is required in the future.

Current Developments

At the workshop, three types of group-related studies were introduced with respect to household, social network, and pro-social behavior in network. The household studies mainly apply time-use and activity diary data from Japan and the Netherlands. The social network study deals with a microsimulation model of social networks in geographic space, in which maintaining social contacts is regarded as a trip-generating activity. The pro-social behavior study describes a social equilibrium model that is used to analyze the performance of an overall network system and its sensitivity to pro-social values. These studies are summarized below.

Household Behavior Modeling

It seems that a turning point of group behavior research in transportation appears at the beginning of the 21st century when two groups of researchers, Gliebe and Koppelman (2002) and Zhang et al. (2002), developed two types of household time allocation models independently. Gliebe and Koppelman developed a proportional shares model of daily time allocation for the analysis of joint activity participation between adult household members. The share model is analogous to the familiar multinomial logit model. In contrast, Zhang et al. developed the household time allocation model by using the multilinear utility function. Since then, group behavior research has been attracting more and more researchers to develop alternative modeling approaches. At the workshop, studies of household behavior modeling were reported by the researchers in Japan. Although researchers in Japan have started the relevant research later than their American and European colleagues, recently an increasing number of studies on household decisions can be observed, covering household time and task allocation, car ownership behavior, joint trip-making behavior, and telecommunication and activity participation (Zhang and Fujiwara, 2009a).

Household time and task allocation models developed based on the above-mentioned multilinear and iso-elastic utility functions were empirically compared by separately using a small-scale activity diary data and a large-scale national time-use data from Japan (Zhang et al., 2005a; Zhang and Fujiwara, 2009b). Model estimation results suggest that similar decision outcomes might result from different decision-making mechanisms. Some special cases of the above-mentioned models were further conceptually extended by incorporating the influence of monetary constraints (Nepal et al., 2005). In addition, the additive-type household utility function is applied to develop a household multidimensional timing model with endogenous coupling constraints, in which the concept of timing utility is applied to reflect the heterogeneous preferences for different moments in time across the population, and coupling constraints are modeled by reflecting the fact that the timings of joint activity–travel are the same for all the involved members (Zhang et al., 2006).

Related to car ownership and residential choice behavior, a new discrete choice model with intrahousehold interaction is developed by directly introducing the household utilities used in the modeling of the above household time allocation behavior as a metautility. Such a modeling approach is very attractive in the sense that it allows for the representation of household decision-making mechanisms under the widely applied GEV modeling framework without imposing any additional assumption about error terms. To represent different types of decision-making mechanisms, an additional group discrete choice model with heterogeneous intrahousehold interaction is built upon latent class modeling framework to integrate three types of MNL-like models with different household utility functions: multilinear, max–max, and max–min utilities (Zhang et al., 2009). The proposed modeling approach provides a promising way to combine different decision rules in the same model structure.

In the context of joint trip-making behavior, focusing on pick-up/deliver choice behavior, Kobayashi et al. (1996) proposed a random matching model to represent pick-up/deliver behavior within a two-member household in transportation. They define the utility of each member in a travel party as a linear function of another member's utility. In other words, altruistic behavior is incorporated into the model. In this sense, the Kobayashi et al.'s approach is similar to that of Browning and Chiappori (1998). Different from the approach by Browning and Chiappori, Kobayashi et al. recognize that choice behavior is conditional on consensus between two members, but such consensus is in fact unobservable.

Studies of telecommunication and activity participation in Japan based on a combined activity and communication diary survey (Sasaki et al., 2004) reveal that joint activities may be activated by mobile communication. It is found that if members with low mobility are present in households, joint activities and mobile communication are significantly interrelated.

A Social Network Study

Axhausen and his colleagues have contributed a lot to this research stream. At this workshop, to study the influence of social network on activity planning, Hackney and Axhausen (2006) presented a multiagent simulation model to generate a global set of interhousehold relationships based on dynamic ego networks that develop with respect to travel opportunities. The agents make trips in their activity space to socialize with their friends and are assumed to have a limited ability or desire to maintain relationships and thus each additional relationship carries a cost. An MNL model is applied to represent the choices of staying at home, random exploration, visiting friends, or visiting friends of friends by trading off socializing utility versus the generalized travel cost. The simulation system represents the dynamics of meeting, learning about space, and therefore the dynamics of the social network by the feedback through activity choice set.

Pro-Social Behavior in Network

Taking the transport system as a social system with pro-social values, Avineri (2006) defines the utility of an agent as a weighted function of its own utility and other agents' utilities, in which travel time is the only explanatory variable. The weight of other agents' utilities is used to classify the agents by their social values: selfish agent, altruistic agent, ultra-altruistic agent, and so on. Different social values lead to different network equilibriums. Selfish behavior results in the traditional user equilibrium. An altruistic agent weighs his/her own utility the same as he/she weighs others' utilities, and a system with such altruistic value converges to the system optimum (pure altruism). In case of ultra-altruistic behavior, all actions taken by the agent are done in order to improve other agents' utilities without consideration of his/her own utility and as a result, the system does not necessarily converge to the system optimum. The equilibrium obtained from these social values is called social equilibrium. In this study, it is assumed that other agents' utilities are weighted the same. The efficiency of the overall transport system, defined as a function of travelers' social values, is evaluated in a numerical analysis, which applies the MNL model to represent the probability of choosing different paths at different time periods.

Research Needs

Timmermans gave a good summary about future research needs and suggests that further studies are required to model more interactions or interdependencies that characterize activity–travel behavior across episodes and space, over time, and among decision-makers from context to context, given a set of dynamic constraints. Such modeling requirements come from the need to bring more behavioral consistency in predicting travelers' responses under policy interventions, especially focusing on the context and situation effects, and temporal (e.g., week-to-week and day-to-day) effects. For this purpose, more theories are required, some of which could be drawn on from other research fields. Game theory could serve as a powerful tool, but needs to be examined based on more empirical studies.

Current model developments and empirical analyses mainly focus on decision outcomes, rather than the processes. Thus, future studies should pay more attention to exploring group decision-making processes that are closely linked with policy instruments. In line with such consideration, stated choice experiments could be a promising way to, for example, represent interpersonal negotiation. Methodological breakthroughs are expected to deal with the complexity resulting from the consideration of the above-mentioned consistency, balancing between policy requirements and operational applicability. But it is not clear at this moment if the utility concept could still provide the solutions desired. Representing heterogeneity is still worth challenging in the sense that the heterogeneity could exist in not only travelers' tastes but also in other behavioral aspects such as decision rules, learning behavior, constraints, contexts, and situations.

Social network and pro-social behavior researchers need to properly answer the following questions:

(1) What kinds of additional information should be included in activity–travel surveys to reflect the influence of social network and pro-social behavior for practical applications?
(2) What are the policy instruments that could contribute to improve the performance of the social network from both individual needs and social needs?
(3) Do anti-car policies lead to any damage of social capital built upon the social network? If there is any, how should it be prevented?
(4) It is expected that social network and pro-social behavior could be more important than demographics in explaining activity–travel behavior. But, what are appropriate variables representing pro-social behavior and how to realize socially desirable equilibrium?

It is expected that more innovative models would be developed in the near future, but better understanding of group decision-making mechanisms requires more observation surveys, focusing on both decision outcomes and processes.

References

Arentze, T. A. and H. J. P. Timmermans (2000). *ALBATROSS: A Learning Based Transportation Oriented Simulation System*. Eindhoven, the Netherlands, European Institute of Retailing and Services Studies.

Arentze, T. A. and H. J. P. Timmermans (2004). *ALBATROSS 2.0: A Learning Based Transportation Oriented Simulation System*. Eindhoven, the Netherlands, European Institute of Retailing and Services Studies.

Avineri, E. (2006). Measuring and simulating altruistic behaviour in group travel choice decisions. Paper presented at the *11th International Conference on Travel Behaviour Research*. Kyoto, August 16–20 (CD-ROM).

Browning, M. and P. A. Chiappori (1998). Efficient intra-household allocations: a general characterization and empirical test. *Econometrica* 66, 1241–1278.

Gliebe, J. P. and F. S. Koppelman (2002). A model of joint activity participation between household members. *Transportation* 29, 49–72.

Hackney, J. and K. W. Axhausen (2006). An agent model of social network and travel behavior interdependence. Paper presented at the *11th International Conference on Travel Behaviour Research*. Kyoto, August 16–20 (CD-ROM).

Kobayashi, K., H. Kita and H. Tatano (1996). A random matching model for joint trips production within households. *Journal of Infrastructure Planning and Management* 536(IV-31), 59–68 (in Japanese).

Miller, E. J. and M. J. Roorda (2003). A prototype model of household activity–travel scheduling. Paper presented at the *82nd Annual Meeting of Transportation Research Board*, Washington, DC.

Nepal, K. P., D. Fukuda and T. Yai (2005). Microeconomic models of intra-household activity time allocations. *Journal of Eastern Society for Transportation Studies* 6, 1637–1650.

Sasaki, K., K. Nishii, R. Kitamura and K. Kondo (2004). The use of mobile communication tools and its influence to joint activities—empirical analysis of personal communication and household activities, *Selected Proceedings of TRANS-TEC (The Transport Science & Technology Congress)*, Athens.

Timmermans, H. (2009). Household decision making in travel behaviour analysis. In R. Kitamura, T. Yoshii and T. Yamamoto (Eds.), *The Expanding Sphere of Travel Behaviour Research*. Bingley, UK, Emerald.

Vovsha, P., J. Gliebe, E. Petersen and F. Koppelman (2005). Sequential and simultaneous choice structures for modeling intra-household interactions. In H. J. P. Timmermans (Ed.), *Progress in Activity-Based Analysis*, Amsterdam, Elsevier, pp. 223–258.

Zhang, J. and A. Fujiwara (2006). Representing household time allocation behavior by endogenously incorporating diverse intra-household interactions: a case study in the context of elderly couples. *Transportation Research Part B* 40(1), 54–74.

Zhang, J. and A. Fujiwara (2009a). Models of household activity and travel behavior with group decision-making mechanisms in Japan. In R. Kitamura, T. Yoshii and T. Yamamoto (Eds.), *The Expanding Sphere of Travel Behaviour Research*. Bingley, UK, Emerald.

Zhang, J. and Fujiwara, A. (2009b). A comparative modeling analysis of household time allocation behavior using a large-scale national time use data in Japan. Compendium of papers CD-ROM, the *88th Annual Meeting of the Transportation Research Board*, January 11–15, Washington, DC.

Zhang, J., A. Fujiwara, H. J. P. Timmermans and A. Borgers (2005). An empirical comparison of alternative models of household time allocation. In H. J. P. Timmermans (Ed.), *Progress in Activity-Based Analysis*, Amsterdam, Elsevier, pp. 259–283.

Zhang, J., A. Fujiwara, H. J. P. Timmermans, B. Lee and T. A. Arentze (2006). Multi-dimensional timing decision model of household activity–travel behavior with endogenous coupling constraints. Paper presented at the *11th International Conference on Travel Behaviour Research*. Kyoto, August 16–20 (CD-ROM).

Zhang, J., M. Kuwano, B. Lee and A. Fujiwara (2009). Modeling household discrete choice behavior incorporating heterogeneous group decision-making mechanisms. *Transportation Research Part B* 43, 230–250.

Zhang, J., H. J. P. Timmermans and A. Borgers (2002). A utility-maximizing model of household time use for independent, shared and allocated activities incorporating group decision mechanisms. *Transportation Research Record* 1807, 1–8.

Zhang, J., H. J. P. Timmermans and A. Borgers (2005). A model of household task allocation and time use. *Transportation Research Part B* 39, 81–95.

The Expanding Sphere of Travel Behaviour Research
Selected Papers from the 11th International Conference on Travel Behaviour Research

22

Seven Critical Directions for Integrated Land Use–Transport Models

Joan L. Walker and Sarah Bush

Abstract

This paper summarizes the workshop discussion on "Integrated Models" organized during the 11th International Conference on Travel Behaviour Research in Kyoto in August 2006. The workshop focused on urban land use models and their integration with transport and activity models. As the companion resource paper offers an excellent and detailed summary of the state of the field and literature, our report primarily summarizes the discussion at the workshop. Historical critiques of land use models, which framed the workshop discussion, are briefly reviewed, and seven critical research directions that emerged are highlighted.

Introduction

The workshop discussion was framed by a few key papers. The first is the workshop's resource paper by Miller (2009) entitled "Integrated urban models: theoretical prospects," which provides a thorough review of the state of the art, the literature, and the research issues. Miller referred to previous critiques of land use models by Lee (1973, 1994) and by Timmermans (2003). As much of the discussion in the workshop responded to these critiques, below we summarize their criticisms, comment briefly on the current state of the art as reflected in the workshop discussion (refer to Miller, 2009 for further detail), and finally highlight the critical research directions that were emphasized by workshop participants.

Framing the Discussion: The Critiques

Lee (1973) framed his early critique of urban land use models in terms of seven deadly sins:

1. *Hypercomprehensiveness*: There is a tendency to attempt to do too much with one model, resulting in a model that does not serve any specific purpose very well.
2. *Grossness*: The models are built at too high a level of aggregation.
3. *Hungriness*: The models require oppressively large amounts of data, making them impractical for practitioners to implement.
4. *Wrongheadedness*: The models are wrong, both theoretically and practically. They are not grounded in theory, and they do not serve the needs of urban policy makers.
5. *Complicatedness*: The models are far too complicated for practitioners to understand or work with, and the benefit of the complexity is often unclear.
6. *Mechanicalness*: The models are ad hoc with no theoretical basis.
7. *Expensiveness*: The cost of developing a model far exceeds available resources at planning agencies.

Two decades later, Lee (1994) updated and further summarized his original seven deadly sins, emphasizing the importance of asking and answering the following two fundamental questions (paraphrased by Miller, 2009):

1. *Are we doing good science?* Are the models based on sound theory? Are we making systematic progress in the field?
2. *Are we doing good engineering?* Are we answering the questions that are asked by urban planners? Are we producing tools that are useful?

More recently, Timmermans' (2003) critique similarly emphasized the lack of behavioural underpinnings for the models. Additionally, he highlighted the reluctance of researchers to take on the following major challenges in the field: spatial choice processes, context and domain specificity, integration of decisions made in different time horizons, and emphasis on policy analysis rather than forecasting.

Finally, Miller (2009) provided detail on how progress in the field has addressed the Lee and Timmermans critiques. Significant progress has been made. Grossness has been tackled most successfully, albeit at the cost of complicatedness and expensiveness. With respect to the question of good science, there is still need for improvements in theoretical grounding: key behavioural components, such as spatial choice, integration over time, and the supply side, have not been adequately addressed. With respect to the question of good engineering, still at issue are hypercomprehensiveness, hungriness, and complicatedness. In general, the critiques offer conflicting objectives requiring balance and trade-offs: making progress along one dimension is often costly along another.

Looking Forward: Seven Critical Directions (and Seven Memorable Quotes)

In terms of future research directions, among workshop participants, there was general agreement that Lee's questions regarding good science and good engineering should motivate and direct future progress in the field. Furthermore, as many of Lee's critiques are fundamental to integrated modelling, they are still in the forefront today. Nevertheless, the workshop discussion highlighted seven specific critical directions to pursue in the development of integrated transport–land use models. We characterize them using seven "deadly" quotes from workshop participants:

1. "*Who meets who in what bar leads to marriage.*" With theories of human agents and agent-based frameworks, the field is rapidly progressing in terms of behavioural realism. Important areas of emphasis include the integration of joint decisions (e.g., travel with work and residential location), the incorporation of psychological factors (e.g., motivation, triggers, attitudes, learning, adaptation, and social influences), and moving beyond naive spatial choice models. However, in pursuit of this finer level of detail, it is important to avoid a "downward spiral of disaggregation." What is gained in terms of policy analysis? Is it necessary to model couples meeting in a bar? Clearly not. The research question remains of where to draw the line. This balancing act between complexity and practicality requires more attention as we incorporate more behavioural detail in our models.
2. "*I don't get up in the morning and decide where I'm going to work.*" A complicating factor of integrated models is the presence of a wide variety of decisions made over diverse time scales. The interactions across short-term (e.g., departure time), medium-term (e.g., non-work destinations), and long-term (e.g., mobility bundle and residential location) decisions have been, at best, weak and ad hoc in existing models. Theories need to be developed to frame the interactions, for example, considering short-term decisions as actions that occur *now* with fixed resources and long-term decisions as those that change those fixed resources.
3. "*Have you ever heard of demand AND SUPPLY?*" Toward the end of the workshop, it was noted that the supply side of the equation had not been mentioned. As in our discussion, the focus of the field has been predominantly on household behaviour. However, the behaviour of supply side firms and developers is just as critical when attempting to accurately forecast urban trends. There are deficiencies in our understanding of the drivers of land development and building supply. Furthermore, the interaction between supply and demand in price setting mechanisms tends to be either non-existent or ad hoc, rather than based on

economic theory. Such economic aspects are one of the weakest links in transport–land use models.

4. "*I'm glad SOMETHING is exogenous.*" A key decision in developing integrated models is where to draw the model boundary. This includes both the geographic boundary and the boundary of integrated components (e.g., demand/supply, households/firms/developers, transport/land use, passenger/freight, highway/transit, microeconomics/macroeconomics, etc.). The research question is what types of integrations are worthwhile and for what purposes. The issue is one of "combinatorics" versus payoff: broader geographic areas and more components significantly increase model complexity and the resulting benefits are often nebulous. Workshop participants agreed to draw the geographic boundary around the urban area, excluding inter-urban interactions. In terms of the components, discussion highlighted the desire to break from a one-size-fits-all mentality and have the model purpose drive model specification. This would result in simpler, more transparent models. However, concern was expressed that a piecemeal approach would work against objectives of collaboration, standardization, and scientific progression.
5. "*When I finish the model, I'll name it MYMODEL.*" The participants noted the issue of competition versus cooperation in the field. Because model development is so resource intensive, it is associated with tremendous start-up costs and often results in propriety models. As a community we need to learn and progress in a more open and systematic way, and infrastructure needs to be developed that facilitates such progress. One push in this direction is Opus (see www.urbansim.org), an open source platform using the R programming language that aims for plug and play components and contributions from a host of researchers. While software infrastructure is one key component to systematic progress, another is having a common dataset (or datasets) that can be used to directly compare different model formulations.
6. "*If we require 20 years of detailed panel data to get where we want to be, then we all need to get a new career.*" The discussion noted the common lament that we are always inhibited by the limitations of available data. We need to reconcile with the fact that we will never have the perfect dataset and employ more creative uses of extant data, for example: accessing data from web sources (e.g., trolling real estate sites), using imputation and data mining, and archiving data to ensure we save what we gather.
7. "*Integrated models are the holy grail.*" In the workshop, we repeatedly returned to the question of "so what?!" Why do we need such complexity? Why do we need the models at all? As a community, it is important that we clearly define the value of integrated models and demonstrate their worth to urban planners and policy makers. For success, the workings of the models need to be such that they can be made transparent to this intended audience. Relevance to urban planners and policy makers must drive development for the models to have real impact.

Conclusion

Although historical critiques of integrated models have been harsh, the feeling at the workshop was that the glass is half full, not half empty. Progress has been made, and a bounty of research opportunities remains. Furthermore, there are methods and theories available to more fundamentally ground our models. The workshop discussion highlighted seven critical directions for future research: balancing the level of behavioural detail with practical use, integrating temporal decision-making scales, incorporating supply mechanisms, defining model boundaries, increasing research collaboration, overcoming data limitations, and demonstrating value. In pursuing these directions, as a community, our work must be informed by the fundamental questions of: Are we doing good science? Are we doing good engineering? Integrated models address all issues of importance in urban areas, including the environment, air quality, climate change, congestion, economy, infrastructure development, and quality of life. Therefore, "while the task may be difficult, the reward is great!"

References

Lee, D. B. (1973). Requiem for large scale models. *Journal of the American Institute of Planners* 39, 163–178.

Lee, D. B. (1994). Retrospective on large scale urban models. *Journal of the American Planning Association* 60, 35–40.

Miller, E. J. (2009). Integrated urban models: theoretical prospects. In R. Kitamura, T. Yoshii and T. Yamamoto (Eds.), *The Expanding Sphere of Travel Behaviour Research*. Bingley, UK, Emerald.

Timmermans, H. (2003). The saga of integrated land use–transport modelling: how many more dreams before we wake up? Conference keynote paper. *10th International Conference on Travel Behaviour Research*. Lucerne.

The Expanding Sphere of Travel Behaviour Research
Selected Papers from the 11th International Conference on Travel Behaviour Research

23

Application to Policy Analysis and Planning

Yoram Shiftan

Abstract

This report presents the main issues and future research directions discussed by the Application to Policy Analysis and Planning Workshop at the 11th International Conference on Travel Behavior Research in Kyoto, Japan. The focus was on various methodological issues, including a combination of various approaches, integrated models, and data issues; evaluation and appraisal issues, including methods, benefits and costs covered, equity, and uncertainty; and finally the dissemination of our modeling and evaluation tools to policy makers, and making sure they understand and use them. The report summarizes the main issues that workshop participants found to be important for application to policy analysis and planning.

Background

Policy analysis and planning constitute the main objectives of travel behavior studies and travel-demand models. A better understanding of travel behavior is critical for implementing new policies and planning for better transportation systems.

Modern life has brought about various changes in travel behavior, among them more travel, more leisure time, and more engagement in non-work and out-of-home activities. Work hours have become more flexible, and more women are in the labor market. Residential, commercial, and work places are being decentralized. The total number of trips has increased, trip chaining is more frequent, and traffic peaks are becoming smoother. These changes significantly increase congestion and air pollution from motor vehicles, necessitating the development of new policy and planning objectives for the purposes of sustainable transportation. Indeed, the various policies we have to deal with provided one of the topics discussed in the workshop: from various auto-restraint policies, such as congestion pricing and parking polices, through emission-control programs to a wide array of urban design and land-use policies.

The growing complexity of travel patterns and the need to estimate changes in travel behavior in response to new policies call for a better understanding of travel behavior. This includes responding to such issues as how travel behavior is affected by new information and communication technologies, how land use and growth management affect travel behavior, and how travelers respond to auto-restraint policies? An understanding of such effects is essential for better design of new policies. In this regard, travel behavior stands at the core of procedures for the analysis and evaluation of transportation-related measures aimed at improving urban mobility, environmental quality, and a wide variety of social objectives.

In order to implement any policy, the responsible planning agency and policy makers need to know the following:

- How will travelers respond to such a policy?
- What travel and emission-reduction effects can be expected from the implementation of a given policy, and what are its broader impacts on safety, land use, and regional development?
- What are the full benefits and costs of this policy?

The main issues discussed in relation to the application to policy analysis and planning may be divided into two main categories: better understanding of travel behavior, including various methodological issues that are important for the practical application of a policy, and the appraisal and evaluation of various policy measures. A third category, though located on a different dimension, is related to outreach, or to making the modeling and evaluation tools known and available to policy makers. In this regard, it is also important to find the right balance between behavioral realism, which tends to complicate our models and tools, and practicality, which makes sure these tools are applicable and being used for policy-making decisions. Although all these issues are quite broad and well covered in the literature and much more can be written about them, the purpose of this report is to highlight the main issues and future needs that the workshop participants felt to be the most important for policy analysis and planning practice.

The workshop discussion was based on the resource paper presented by Konstadinos Goulias (in this book) and three contributed papers by Geurs et al. (in this book), Franklin (2006), and Olszewski and Xie (2006).

Goulias emphasized three main sources for an evolving paradigm for modeling and simulation to support policy analysis and planning: (a) dynamic planning practice, including strategic planning and performance-based planning; (b) a sustainable and green vision as the source of specific policies that need to be examined; and (c) new research and technology, including various advancements in our tools to evaluate policies, such as theory building, modeling and simulation, and enabling technologies. The reader is encouraged to read Goulias' paper, which is found in this volume and provides excellent coverage of these topics, detailing all the issues and raising the critical questions with regard to policy analysis and planning. These issues and questions served as the basis for the workshop discussion, which is summarized below.

The three other papers that were presented at the workshop provide examples of some of the main issues of application to policy analysis and planning. The paper by Geurs et al. presented the "option value" concept in evaluating transport projects, specifically the added benefits that can be obtained from a public transport project through this concept and that are usually not included in current evaluation procedures. Public transport services may have an option value when car owners value the opportunity to use the public transport service if their car for whatever reason is unavailable (breakdown, bad weather, etc.) or if they cannot drive (loss of ability to drive a car). Transport option values can be interpreted in terms of a risk premium that individuals with uncertain demand are willing to pay over and above their expected user benefit for the continued availability of a transport facility. Geurs et al. described a methodology for measuring the option value of public transport services and its application to two regional railway links in the Netherlands.

Congestion pricing is one of the policies most concern to policy makers and transportation professionals today. The two other workshop papers provided good examples of combined issues of methodology and evaluation in regard to this policy. Franklin (2006) showed how roadway tolling can easily be potentially Pareto improving, presuming that the winners compensate the losers. There is substantial evidence, however, that without such compensation or without a deliberately progressive plan to refund toll revenues, the burden and benefits tend to be regressive. Franklin, who compared approaches with and without income effects, showed that omitting income effects will tend to under estimate the regressiveness of tolling. The results also indicate that a toll alone, even *without* the redistribution of the revenues, may still be potentially Pareto improving because the highest income range places a high monetary value on travel-time savings.

Finally, Olszewski and Xie (2006) proposed a method of using Singapore's actual electronic road-pricing (ERP) transaction data to calibrate a discrete choice model of drivers' trip-timing decisions. Their method was used to revise the time-variable charges to enable a better spread of the morning peak traffic. Their method records individual motorists' arrival times at a particular ERP gantry. However, no direct information is available on these individuals' preferred arrival time (PAT), which is a key variable in the trip-timing model. Olszewski and Xie proposed a method of estimating a maximum likelihood PAT value for each individual and of jointly calibrating the trip-timing model to estimate the most likely PATs.

The intensive discussion identified a series of issues affecting the implementation of various transport policies—issues that are important for good planning practice—as well as the barriers to such implementation and the use of travel behavior studies for policy analysis and planning. The discussion closed with an attempt to identify research issues for the immediate future.

Methodological Issues

Other workshops dealt with various methodological issues. The focus of this workshop was on the development of new tools for policy makers. Policy making requires today more sophisticated tools, and these are developed in terms of advanced models, most of them activity based, that go into levels of detail on various scales: geographic, time, and social space. Among the issues that workshop participants raised as needing attention in the new models were those of better capturing attitudes and assessing their impact on travel behavior and better perception of various variables, such as time, distance, and accessibility. The expectations are that the new tools will be able to show how individuals respond to the various policies and how these responses impact policy effectiveness and ensure a good policy-decision process. The main methodological issues discussed can be grouped into three main categories: a combination of approaches, integrated models, and data issues.

Combination of Approaches

One of the main methodological areas identified was the combination and application of various methods and tools, such as a combination of econometric and psychological and social behavior insights, and qualitative and quantitative methods for an analysis of travel behavior. Combining various data sources and approaches, such as aggregate and disaggregate, or revealed and stated preference and intentions, can achieve more efficient use of the data and provide better forecasting results. Within the econometric approach, a mixture of various models, such as the mixed logit combining logit and probit elements, provides more flexibility for model formulation and estimation. It is also important to develop complementary measures or indicators using additional data to check and verify the results of travel-demand models, as well as to gather evidence based on the performance of various policies as will be discussed in more detail in the section "Evidence Base."

Use of backcasting as a complementary approach was also discussed as an important additional element for planning purposes. Most planning practices use forecasting approaches; however, as Goulias notes, "under strategic planning we also need prospective studies that start from a desirable future and move backward to identify specific actions that will lead us to that prospect." Participants agreed that backcasting should indeed be considered good practice when one engages in policy analysis and planning.

Integrated Models

Combining various approaches is one way of building integrated models. However, in addition to integrating various approaches and data sources, models should also combine the various upper- and lower-level models to better explain travel behavior and their interrelationships with the urban system and traffic flow. This includes the integration of transportation, demographic, and economic models and land-use models, as well as the combination of advanced travel behavior models with traffic microsimulation, emission, and dispersion models, to better evaluate the traffic and air-quality effects of various policies. More elements of individual decision should be integrated into the models in more details, one such element being the choice of time when to travel. This choice, which is important for an understanding of many of the new policies, such as congestion pricing, has received somewhat less emphasis in traditional models; however, research and practice have presented this challenge, and new models are being developed for time choice.

Data

Data supply the core building blocks of our models and analytical tools. There are, though, many issues related to data, such as: What data do we need to collect? At what level of detail? How frequently should we collect these data? There is a trend to move from traffic-analysis zones to more detailed parcel and individual-level-based models; how important is this level of detail? For what planning analysis are such details important and for what purposes do they represent an unneeded complication? What data collection methods should we use? How much should we invest, in terms of effort and budget, in data collection, and how much in modeling? There are many other questions. As Goulias states in his paper, the tool of choice for data storage and visualization is a Geographic Information System (GIS), but what is the role of other tools and how can they best be combined? The participants agreed that building a good data inventory is both a research and a practical priority that needs to be addressed for better policy analysis and planning practice.

Appraisal and Evaluation

Improved appraisal and evaluation methods that are well understood and accepted by policy makers are essential for the implementation of new policies. Policy makers have to understand and be convinced of the full costs and benefits of a particular policy or planning program in order to move ahead with its implementation and also secure the public's support. Various issues regarding appraisal and evaluation were discussed at the workshop, from methods and the various benefits included in an appraisal to more specific issues, such as the consideration of equity and uncertainty.

Methods of Appraisal and Evaluation

Most appraisals and evaluations are based on cost–benefit analysis, with more and more elements of multi-criteria analysis (MCA) added to reflect various impacts that are difficult to monetize, such as landscape and severance, and to allow the assignment of different weights to various impacts, such as air quality and safety. The use of MCA is very helpful when presenting the various impacts of projects and policies. Impact summary tables are being developed (for example, in Great Britain and Japan) in order to present to policy makers in a concise, clear manner a one- or two-page summary of the different impacts of a project. There are many other methods, such as an expert panel using Delphi methods, the results of various experiments, and the evidence-based performances of various policies. There are still questions regarding these other methods that should be addressed: Can these various methods be used together, and how? What is the role of more qualitative assessment methods? How can those methods be combined with the more formal qualitative methods? And which method should be used for each policy analysis?

Full Coverage of Benefits and Costs

Appraisal methodology should cover the full range of benefits and costs associated with a specific policy or planning action. The issue of option value raised by Geurs et al. suggests only one of many potential benefits and costs that are neglected in most current appraisal practices. The elimination of such benefits actually under-estimates the full benefits of transit programs. There is some discussion that most of the problems in today's practice are actually biased against public transport projects and exhibit partiality toward highway projects; one example is the failure to fully account for all external effects of air quality, noise, and other environmental parameters. This lack is of major concern to the policies and planning objectives of the "green vision" mentioned by Goulias, since many of the new policies aim at affecting these same impacts not fully accounted for in current practice.

Equity Issues

A central problem raised in the paper by Franklin (2006) concerns how well we can deal with equity issues in our evaluation. Although many of the new policies involve various pricing mechanisms, such as congestion pricing, much of the opposition toward different policies is the result of equity issues. Therefore, to make the implementation of such policies more acceptable, there is need for a systematic way of dealing with equity issues and of evaluating the distribution effects of various policies. This solution should emanate from research into the best distribution of income collected from such policies.

Uncertainty

Another problem that was raised in regard to current evaluation procedures is the lack of treatment of uncertainty. There are numerous sources of uncertainty in the evaluation process, from the travel-demand modeling output to the prediction of external factors, such as population and workforce growth and the transportation network that will be in place in a future year. Dealing with such uncertainties in the appraisal phase can decrease criticism that may eliminate policy implementation because of such uncertainties.

Outreach

In order for modeling tools and appraisal methods to be efficiently used, they must be known and understood by policy makers. There was agreement among workshop participants that the tools are used neither sufficiently nor efficiently and that there is need to better communicate them to policy makers so that they can more readily visualize the new research tools. We need to develop better ways to disseminate our tools to policy makers and to make sure these tools are understood and used. One such development, as discussed in the section "Methods of Appraisal and Evaluation," is an evaluation summary table that offers policy makers a one-page, easy-to-understand table of the different impacts of various projects. The two other main outreach issues discussed at the workshop, and which can also be considered methodological issues, are essentially complementary: (1) showing policy makers the tools that are available and appropriate for each policy; (2) providing policy makers with evidence-based examples of performance. Finally, there was some discussion about the role of public participation in the planning process. These three outreach issues are briefly discussed below.

Sufficiency of Our Tools for Policy Analysis and Planning

One of the main questions that arose in the course of discussions was whether our modeling and evaluation tools and our understanding of travel behavior are sufficient for policy analysis and planning. Travel behavior and travel-demand models have significantly improved in recent years, especially with the development of activity-based models. However, in an effort to enhance behavioral realism, some of these models have reached a significant level of complexity that puts their practical use, which is their main objective, at risk (Shiftan and Ben-Akiva, 2006). Therefore, we need to find the right balance between behavioral realism and model complexity and to provide policy makers with the right tool for the right purpose. There is a need to define objectives and to tailor the tools and models to these objectives. The models have to be sensitive to the policy in question and to produce the required policy indicators. The tools should be capable of predicting and evaluating path-dependence outcomes and dynamic planning as discussed above. Finally, models and results have to be understood by policy makers, who must be provided with the "right" amount of detail needed for decision making.

Evidence Base

For policy analysis and planning, case studies and ex-post studies are of critical importance. Policy makers want to see evidence of the effect of various polices; thus, policy making is much more performance based when the outcome of various impacts affects the future funding of transportation programs. Therefore, more case studies and policy experiments, such as the Stockholm congestion-pricing experiment, should be initiated, and more pre-post- and ex-post-evaluation studies of the effects of various implemented policies should be conducted.

Public Participation

Public participation and input into planning practice is important for the successful implementation of new policies. Public participation is important both because the planning process can reflect the public's values and because the implementation of new policies can secure public support. Policy makers are very concerned with public support when it comes to controversial measures, such as congestion pricing. Getting the public involved and building alliances with various green organizations will help move policies out of committees and into actual practice. Therefore, there is need to develop community and public involvement in the planning process in a more effective manner.

Future Directions—A Research Agenda

Future directions and a research agenda composed the last main subject of the workshop. Discussion of the research agenda and future research directions evolved naturally from the various issues considered above. Therefore, the following points summarize, and somewhat prioritize, the issues identified as needing future research:

- Development of multilateral approaches and combining qualitative and quantitative methods. Specifically, it is important for practical purposes to develop complementary measures using additional data and informal indicators to confirm and extend the present comprehensive models. Such models will be of special importance for building trust among policy makers in the potential impact of various policies.
- Development of more tools for backcasting and promoting their use for policy analysis and planning.
- Conducting more ex-post studies, case studies, and policy experiments to build an evidence-based inventory as a tool to show policy makers evidence and examples of good policies and planning practice.
- Development and promoting the use of better evaluation practices, including better treatment of all externalities, equity issues, uncertainty, and other neglected benefits, such as option value. Better tools should also be developed to present the multiple aspects of projects and policies individually and to allow policy makers to choose the level of detail they want to see in the evaluation process.
- Development and promoting better community and public involvement.
- Finding ways to better disseminate our tools and to have planning agencies and policy makers make better use of them. The gap between research, on the one hand, and practice and decision making, on the other, needs to be identified and recommendations made as to what we should communicate to decision makers. The limitations of current practice and data must be identified and recommendations made as to the methods and tools that should be used for each planning purpose.
- There is continuous need to improve our understanding of travel behavior, and issues in this regard are discussed in more detail in this book. Some of the specific items that arose from this workshop included the need to gain a better understanding of travel behavior attitudes and of perceptions of time, distance, and accessibility.
- Finally, more research is necessary into how to better collect, manage, and use data for modeling and evaluation process. What type of data should we collect? At what level of detail? How frequently? These and other related questions require answers.

In general, all the issues discussed during this workshop are relevant and, being quite general, overlap subjects debated in other workshops. Many papers can be written on each of the points raised at this workshop, and the list of issues considered is far from comprehensive. One example not discussed at the workshop is goods transport, which is of major and growing concern in policy analysis and planning. The purpose of this report was to highlight the main issues and future needs that workshop participants felt to be the most important for policy analysis and planning practice.

References

Franklin, J. P. (2006). The equity effects of roadway tolls: An application of Hicksian welfare measures with income effects. Paper presented at the 11th International Conference on Travel Behavior Research. Kyoto, Japan.

Geurs, K., R. Haaijer and B. van Wee (in this book). The option value of public transport services: empirical evidence from the Netherlands. In R. Kitamura, T. Yoshii and T. Yamamoto (Eds.), *The Expanding Sphere of Travel Behaviour Research*. Bingley, UK Emerald.

Goulias, K. G. (in this book). Application to policy analysis and planning.

Olszewski, P. and L. Xie (2006). Using Singapore ERP transaction data to model trip timing decisions. Paper presented at the 11th International Conference on Travel Behavior Research. Kyoto, Japan.

Shiftan, Y. and M. Ben-Akiva (2006). A practical policy-sensitive activity-based model. Paper presented at the 11th International Conference on Travel Behavior Research. Kyoto, Japan.

The Expanding Sphere of Travel Behaviour Research
Selected Papers from the 11th International Conference on Travel Behaviour Research

24

Advances in Econometric Methods

Chandra Bhat

Background and Presentations

The workshop on "Advances in Econometric Methods" was well attended (about 35 participants) and had several researchers who have contributed in important ways to the econometric field.

The session had one resource paper entitled "Advances in Choice Modeling and Asian Perspectives," by T. Yamamoto, T. Hyodo, Y. Muromachi, and four supplementary papers:

(1) Testing the choice of a mixing distribution in discrete choice models (M. Fosgerau, M. Bierlaire)
(2) Random covariance heterogeneity in discrete choice models (S. Hess, D. Bolduc, J. W. Polak)
(3) The multiple discrete-continuous extreme value (MDCEV) model: role of utility function parameters, identification considerations, and model extensions (C. R. Bhat)
(4) Discrete choice theory with constrained demand (A. de Palma, N. Picard, P. Waddell).

The resource paper examined several key developments in the econometric field since IATBR 2003, focusing on the increasing application of advanced models (especially the mixed logit model and its many variants) in Asian countries. The paper introduced the richness and complexity in the choice alternatives, as well as the diversity in decision mechanisms, that exist in Asian countries in the context of activities and travel choices.

The four supplementary papers focused on specific aspects of recent methodological developments. The first paper examined the issue of testing alternative mixing distributions in mixed logit choice models. This is an important issue, since different mixing distributions can, and generally will, lead to quite different trade-off values among variables, among other things. The paper introduces nonparametric and semi-parametric ways to address this issue. The second paper extended Bhat's (1997) paper on systematic covariance heterogeneity in the nested logit model to more general discrete choice models, as well as includes randomness in the covariance heterogeneity. The paper indicates that there is no reason for randomness to be confined in the parameters or in the variance terms associated with individual utilities, but that it can also exist in covariance terms. The third paper introduces a new MDCEV model that can be used to model the choice of multiple alternatives simultaneously, along with the continuous choice that corresponds to each discrete alternative. The paper formulates such a model based on variety seeking and imposing specific assumptions on the stochastic terms of utility. The resulting model has closed-form expressions for the choice probabilities. The final paper focuses on theoretical developments in discrete choice theory with constrained demand.

Summary

The workshop acknowledged the exciting developments that have happened, and that continue to happen, in the use of simulation techniques for econometric model development. In particular, simulation techniques can be used to formulate and estimate advanced models that can be used as diagnostic tools to assess simpler models, can help in formulation of single and multiple discrete models with supply constraints, and can aid in developing a closer nexus between economic theory and econometric models. In the latter context, one can start model development from the primitives of economic theory and then develop models based on the theory. Many such models may not have a closed-form expression but can be estimated using efficient simulation techniques.

However, the workshop group also cautioned about getting carried away with the simulation developments of the day. In particular, simulation techniques should not be used as a general panacea for specification ills or used as a "black box." The analyst must have a clear understanding of the process being modeled, and the identification issues and implied competition patterns of open-form models. The analyst must also strive to collect good data and know the data well through exploratory analysis. In addition, the first order of business is to attribute as much differences in choice making across decision agents to systematic effects before superimposing random effects. Besides, one should be cautious in how much one can extract by way of structure among factors that are fundamentally unobserved.

The workshop identified several techniques, research topics, and other efforts that need attention in the coming years. First, studies need to estimate not only point values of such parameters as elasticity effects and trade-off values, but also estimate the uncertainty in these parameters. Well-established bootstrap techniques may be used for such computations. Second, the field would benefit from exploring theories and formulations associated with non-compensatory decision mechanisms and other nonrandom utility maximizing models. Third, there is a need for disseminating information on econometric model development and innovations in a way that avoids the use of these developments without a clear understanding of the underlying theories and assumptions. This may be achieved by holding more workshop-style events. Fourth, while there is good documentation of models and results in the literature, the documentation regarding "tricks" and "problem issues" in model estimation and forecasting is almost nonexistent. Developing a repository of such experiences would be valuable to the field. Fifth, there is a continuing need to focus on theory, process, and dynamics that underlie model formulation and estimation.

Reference

Bhat, C. R. (1997). Covariance heterogeneity in nested logit models: Econometric structure and application to intercity travel. *Transportation Research Part B* 31(1), 11–21.

PART 4

Session Papers

4.1 Measurement and Quantification

The Expanding Sphere of Travel Behaviour Research
Selected Papers from the 11th International Conference on Travel Behaviour Research

25

Designing Stated Choice Experiments: State of the Art

Michiel C.J. Bliemer and John M. Rose

Abstract

Data from stated choice experiments has become increasingly popular allowing researchers to investigate choice behavior in the presence of alternatives and their attributes that may not exist in current markets. This paper describes the different steps in creating a stated choice experiment. Underlying each experiment is a design with attribute levels, determining the choice situations presented to respondents. Two types of designs are discussed in more detail, namely orthogonal designs and efficient designs. While primarily orthogonal designs have used in practice for many years, it is shown that these designs can be far from optimal. Efficient designs require more knowledge to generate them, but they are superior in terms of yielding smaller standard errors in estimation.

Introduction

Stated choice (SC) experiments, as proposed by Louviere and Woodworth (1983) and Louviere and Hensher (1983), have received increasing attention in many different fields, including marketing, transportation, health economics, environmental economics, and resource economics. Theoretical advances in and estimation of discrete choice models has had a large impulse from the transportation community, where many state-of-the-art publications on this topic have appeared. In contrast, the main research in design of choice experiments has been in marketing and economics. Lately, the interest in the design of choice experiments has increased in the transportation field as well, and the purpose of this paper is to present a state of the art in designing choice experiments using the knowledge gained over the years till present from all disciplines. While there exist good books with overviews for discrete choice modeling and estimation (Ben-Akiva and Lerman, 1985; Hensher et al., 2005; Louviere et al., 2000; Train, 2003), no such books exist for designing SC experiments. In this paper, we aim to provide an overview of techniques for determining designs for SC experiments and state the current state of the art.

The generation of SC experiments has evolved to become an increasingly important, but complex component of SC studies (see e.g., Bunch et al., 1994; Burgess and Street, 2005; Carlsson and Martinsson, 2003; DeShazo and Fermo, 2002; Ferrini and Scarpa, 2007; Huber and Zwerina, 1996; Kanninen, 2002; Kessels et al., 2006; Kuhfeld et al., 1994; Lazari and Anderson, 1994; Sándor and Wedel, 2001, 2002, 2005; Street and Burgess, 2004; Street et al., 2001; Toner et al., 1999). Typically, SC experiments present sampled respondents with a number of hypothetical scenarios (known as choice situations) consisting of a universal but finite number of alternatives that differ on a number of attribute dimensions. These respondents are then asked to specify their preferred alternative from the set of alternatives presented within each choice situation based on the attribute levels shown. These responses are then pooled both over hypothetical choice scenarios and respondents before being used to estimate parameter weights for each of the design attributes (or in some cases, even attribute levels). Depending on the type of experiment conducted, researchers may obtain estimates of the direct or cross elasticities (or marginal effects) of the alternatives as well as the marginal rates of substitution respondents are willing to make in trading between two attributes (i.e., willingness to pay measures).

In the transportation field, discrete choice models have been used extensively to derive forecasts for new and existing modes (Cherchi et al., 2002; Hensher and Rose, 2005; Jovicic and Hansen, 2003), to understand and model route choice behavior (e.g., Jou, 2001; Lam and Xie, 2002), to model influence on travel behavior (e.g., Peeta et al., 2000), to determine the viability of new infrastructure projects such as proposed toll roads (e.g., Hensher, 2001; Ortúzar et al., 2000), to test the implications on transport systems of proposed policies (e.g., Hensher and King, 2001), to forecast effects of road-pricing measures and uncertainty on departure-time choice (e.g., Van Amelsfort and Bliemer, 2005), etc. Other fields use similar discrete choice models. However, in general, the discrete choice models used in the transportation field are econometrically more advanced than the ones used in other areas due to a wide range of possible sequential, simultaneous, or hierarchical choices. Many other examples can be found in other fields, such as in marketing (e.g., modeling of demand for consumer package goods, see Allenby et al., 2004), health economics (e.g., vaccine choice, see Hall et al., 2002), and environmental and resource economics (e.g., Scarpa et al., 2005a, b).

Traditionally, researchers have relied upon the use of orthogonal experimental designs to populate the hypothetical choice situations shown to respondents (see Louviere et al., 2000, for a review of orthogonal designs). More recently however, some researchers have begun to question the relevance of orthogonal designs when applied to

SC experiments (e.g., Huber and Zwerina, 1996; Kanninen, 2002; Kessels et al., 2006; Sándor and Wedel, 2001, 2002, 2005). Generally, the argument against the use of orthogonality as a design criterion in the construction process is that the property of orthogonality is unrelated to the desirable properties of the econometric models used to analyze SC data (i.e., logit and probit models). The orthogonality (or otherwise) of an experimental design relates to the correlation structure between the attributes of the design; designs in which all correlations between attributes are zero are said to be orthogonal.[1] While orthogonality is an important criterion to determine independent effects in linear models, discrete choice models are not linear (Train, 2003). In models of discrete choice, the correlation structure between the attributes is not what is of importance. Rather, given the usual derivation of the models, it is the correlations of the differences in the attributes which should be of concern.

Huber and Zwerina (1996) took the important step of relating the statistical properties of the SC experiments to the econometric models estimated on such data. In their paper, Huber and Zwerina showed that designs that let go of orthogonality but instead attempt to reduce the asymptotic standard errors of the parameter estimates (i.e., the square roots of the diagonal elements of the asymptotic variance–covariance (AVC) matrix) will generally result in designs that either (i) improve the reliability of the parameters estimated from SC data at a fixed sample size or (ii) reduce the sample size required to produce a fixed level of reliability in the parameter estimates with a given experimental design. The linking of the experimental design generation process to attempts to reduce these asymptotic standard errors has resulted in a class of designs known as efficient or optimal designs, where designs that produce smaller asymptotic standard errors are thought of as being more efficient. With the introduction of efficient designs, a whole new research area was started, and more advanced discrete choice models and designs are currently subject of research.

The paper is outlined as follows. Steps for Creating a Stated Choice Experiment section presents the three main steps in creating an SC experiment, in which determining the experimental design is the most important and complex step and will therefore be subject of the remainder of the paper. Notation section introduces the notation used in the paper. Rest of the sections discuss different design types, such as full and fractional factorial designs (Full and Fractional Factorial Designs), orthogonal designs (Orthogonal Designs), efficient designs (Efficient Designs), and some more advanced designs (Advanced Designs). The paper concludes with a brief discussion of the main results.

---

[1]In some cases, this definition of an orthogonal design may be relaxed to define orthogonality as occurring when all attribute correlations are zero within alternatives but not necessarily between alternatives; see Louviere et al. (2000) for a discussion on sequential versus simultaneous generation of orthogonal designs.

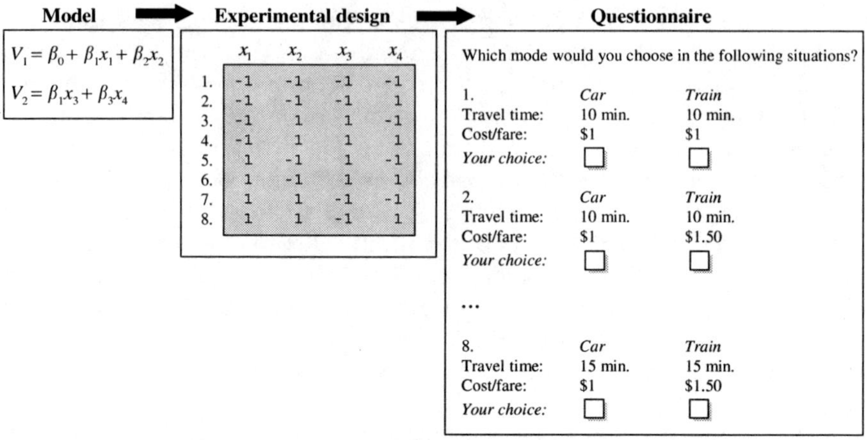

Figure 1
Steps in Designing a Stated Choice Experiment

Steps for Creating a Stated Choice Experiment

The aim is to determine an SC experiment. In creating an SC experiment, three main steps have to be taken, as illustrated in Figure 1. First of all, a complete *model specification* with all parameters to be estimated has to be determined. Based on this model specification, an *experimental design* type has to be selected and then the design can be generated. Finally, a questionnaire (on paper, Internet, CAPI, etc.) is created based on the underlying experimental design and data can be collected. The three steps will be elaborated below. The main part of the paper will be dedicated to the generation of experimental designs (step 2).

Step 1: Model Specification

Each SC experiment is specifically created for estimating a specific model (or sometimes a range of models). Therefore, one needs to specify the model and the parameters to be estimated before creating an experimental design.

First, the problem studied should be refined and hypotheses developed. Secondary data search, focus groups, and in-depth interviews can assist in this. Then the stimuli need to be refined, in which at least the following choices need to be addressed:

- Which alternatives need to be included?
- Which attributes to include for each alternative?

For example, *alternatives* can be existing or not-yet-existing transport modes in the area of interest. Each mode can have different *attributes* (travel time, waiting time, comfort, etc.). Additionally, the *model type* has to be chosen, appropriate to the problem. In other words, is the multinomial logit (MNL) model, the nested logit (NL) model, or perhaps the mixed logit (ML) model suitable?

Essentially, the complete specification of the utility functions needs to be known. For the example shown in Figure 1, the chosen MNL model consists of two utility functions (hence two alternatives are considered), and each alternative has two attributes (the first alternative has attributes x_1 and x_2, while the second alternative has attributes x_3 and x_4).

Another important decision to make is whether an attribute is *generic* over different alternatives, or *alternative specific*. In the example, x_1 and x_3 are assumed to be generic, as they share the same (generic) parameter β_1, while the constant β_0 and the parameters β_2 and β_3 are alternative specific. For example, the attribute travel time can be differently weighted in the utility functions of different mode alternatives, while it is typically weighted equally in case of different route alternatives. If one is not certain about parameters being generic or alternative specific, then it is best to make them alternative specific, as then this can be tested afterward when estimating the parameters. However, each additional parameter in the model represents an extra *degree of freedom*,[2] meaning that the experimental design may become larger (although this is typically not substantial). To be precise, the number of choice situations in the experimental design must be equal to or greater than the degrees of freedom (see also Step 2: Generation of Experimental Design section).

Furthermore of importance is to decide if any *interaction effects* (such as x_1x_2) besides the *main effects* will be included in the model. Finally, the decision has to be made if *nonlinear effects* are taken into account, either estimated using dummy-coded or effects-coded variables.[3] These will introduce extra parameters to be estimated and also impact the number of attribute levels used in the experimental design.

Once the model has been completely specified, the experimental design can be generated. It is important to note that the experimental design will be specifically determined for the specified model and may be suboptimal if other models are

---

[2]A degree of freedom is defined here as the total number of parameters (excluding the constants) plus 1. All constants are accounted for in the "plus 1."

[3]Suppose that attribute X is dummy coded with three levels. Then we introduce two variables (always one less than the number of levels), let us say X1 and X2, each with its own parameter to estimate. In case of dummy coding, the three levels are represented by (X1, X2) = (1,0) for the first level, (0,1) for the second, and (0,0) for the third, while for effects coding the third level is different, namely (−1,−1) instead of (0,0). Effects coding has some theoretical advantages, although interpretation is slightly more complicated.

estimated using the data obtained from the SC experiment. Hence, estimating an ML model is done best using data from an SC experiment using a design generated based on the same ML model. Adding extra variables to the utility functions later in estimation, such as socioeconomic data (age, gender, income, etc.), may make the experimental design again suboptimal, hence if possible they should be taken into account from the beginning (see also Designs with Covariates section).

Step 2: Generation of Experimental Design

Once the model specification is known, the experimental design can be created. An experimental design describes which hypothetical *choice situations* the respondents are faced with in the SC experiment. It typically consists of a table of numbers (as illustrated in Figure 1) in which each row represents a choice situation. The numbers in the table correspond to the *attribute levels* for each attribute (e.g., −1, 1) and are replaced by their actual attribute levels later on in the questionnaire (e.g., \$1, \$1.50). In the example, there are in total eight choice situations and four different columns for each of the four attributes. Different coding schemes can be used for representing the attribute levels in the experimental design. The most common ones are design coding (0, 1, 2, 3, etc.), orthogonal coding ({−1,1} for two levels, {−1,0,1} for three levels, {−3,−1,1,3} for four levels, etc.),[4] or coding according to the actual attribute-level values. In this paper, we will mainly use orthogonal coding or code using the actual values.

There are many experimental designs possible, and the aim here is to determine the best one. Before finding the best design, some design decisions have to be made. These include:

- Should the design be labeled or unlabeled?
- Should the design have the property of attribute-level balance?
- How many attribute levels are used?
- What are the attribute-level ranges?
- What type of design to be used?
- How many choice situations to use?

If the model specification has alternatives with alternative-specific parameters, then these alternatives need to be *labeled* (e.g., car, train, bus) in the experiment. If alternatives have generic parameters, they can be *unlabeled* (e.g., route A, route B, route C).

---

[4]For five levels, we use {−3,−1,0,1,3}, for six levels {−7,−3,−1,1,3,7}, for seven levels {−7,−3,−1,0,1,3,7}, for eight levels {−9,−7,−3,−1,1,3,7,9}, etc. The reason for skipping the even and also some odd numbers is purely mathematical, enabling computations to easily show orthogonality (see Definition of Orthogonality section).

Almost all experimental designs created in practice satisfy the *attribute-level balance* property, which means that each attribute level appears an equal number of times for each attribute. In the example, in each column −1 and 1 both appear exactly four times. Although imposing attribute-level balance may restrict the design to be suboptimal (see also Discussion of Efficient Designs section), it is generally considered a desirable property. Having attribute-level balance ensures that the parameters can be estimated well on the whole range of levels, instead of just having data points at only one or a few of the attribute levels. For the remainder of the paper, we will assume that the design should have the property of attribute-level balance.

The *number of attribute levels* to use depends on the model specification. If nonlinear effects are expected for a certain attribute, then more than two levels need to be used for this attribute in order to be able to estimate these nonlinearities. If dummy and/or effects-coded attributes are included, then the number of levels to use for these attributes is predetermined. However, the more levels used, the higher the number of choice situations will be. Also, mixing the number of attribute levels for different attributes may yield a higher number of choice situations (because of attribute-level balance). For example, if there are 3 attributes with 2, 3, and 5 levels, respectively, then the minimum number of choice situations will be 30 (since this is divisible by 2, 3, and 5). On the other hand, if one would use 2, 4, and 6 levels, then only a minimum of 12 choice situations would be enough. Therefore, it is wise not to mix too many different numbers of attribute levels, or at least have all even or all odd numbers of attribute levels.

Regarding the *attribute-level range*, using a wide range (e.g., \$1–\$6) is statistically better than using a narrow range (e.g., \$3–\$4) as this will theoretically lead to better parameter estimates (i.e., parameter estimates with a smaller standard error). Furthermore, the model estimated is only applicable on the data range it was estimated on. Hence, a wide range has a broader application area. We have to emphasize that this is a pure statistical property and that one should take into account the practical limitations of the attribute levels. The attribute levels shown to the respondents have to make sense. Therefore, there is a trade-off between the statistical preference for a wide range and practical considerations that may limit the range.

Several different *design types* can be considered. A full *factorial design* (see Full and Fractional Factorial Designs section) consists of all possible different choice situations and with this design all possible effects (main and interaction effects) can be estimated. However, for a practical study, the number of choice situations in a full factorial design is typically too large. Therefore, most people rely on so-called *fractional factorial designs* (see Full and Fractional Factorial Designs section), and within this class there exist many different types of designs. One could randomly select choice situations from the full factorial, but clearly this is not the best way of doing it. Rather, one selects choice situations in a structured manner, such that the best data from the SC experiment will be produced for estimating the model. A fractional factorial design consists of a subset of choice situations from the full factorial. The best known fractional factorial design type is the *orthogonal design* (see Orthogonal Designs section), which aims to minimize the correlation between the attribute levels in the choice situations. As will be shown in Orthogonal Designs section, these orthogonal designs have limitations and cannot avoid choice situations in which a certain alternative is clearly more preferred over the others (hence not providing much information). More recently, several researchers have suggested another type of fractional factorial designs; the so-called *efficient designs* (see Efficient Designs section). Instead of merely considering the correlation structure between the attribute levels, they aim to find designs that are statistically as efficient as possible in terms of predicted standard errors of the parameter estimates. Essentially, these designs try to maximize the information from each choice situation. Efficient designs should be able to outperform orthogonal designs; however, prior parameter estimates need to be available. Therefore, efficient designs rely on the accuracy of the prior parameter estimates. In order to obtain more stable designs that rely less on the accuracy of the priors, *Bayesian efficient designs* have been proposed in the last few years (see Efficient Designs section). Instead of assuming fixed prior parameters, the priors are considered to be (uncertain) random parameters. Some other design types have been considered recently, in which attribute-level balance is abandoned, in which constraints on attribute levels are imposed, in which attribute levels are pivoted around realistic values for each respondent, or in which covariates (such as socioeconomics data) are already considered when creating the design. These design types, being at the frontier of the current state of the art, will be briefly discussed in Advanced Designs section.

Already mentioned above is that the *number of choice situations* is bounded from below by the number of degrees of freedom, and the number of choice situations required to ensure attribute-level balance. Also, the design type may restrict the number of choice situations. An orthogonal design sometimes needs (many) more choice situations than the minimum number determined by the number of degrees of freedom and attribute-level balance, merely because an orthogonal design may not exist or may be unknown for these dimensions. A full factorial design has a predetermined number of choice situations, only influenced by the total number of attributes and the number of attribute levels.

How to generate each of these designs will be discussed in Full and Fractional Factorial Designs through Advanced Designs. It should be noted that determining a "good" experimental design is not a simple task, as there are generally billions of possible designs and it is impossible to evaluate all of them. Typically, computer software is used to assist in this process.

Step 3: Construction of Questionnaire

Using the underlying experimental design, the actual questionnaire instrument can be constructed (see Figure 1). Obviously, the experimental design represented by a table of numbers is meaningless to a respondent; hence it needs to be transformed somehow so as to become meaningful. Each row in the experimental design is translated into a choice situation as illustrated for the first three rows in Figure 1. In this example, all four attributes have two levels each, denoted by -1 and 1 in the experimental design. These numbers are replaced by meaningful values for each attribute, for example, 10 and 15 minutes for the travel time attribute for the car and train alternatives, and \$1 and \$1.50 for the cost/fare attribute for both alternatives. Furthermore, for each respondent the order of the choice situations should be randomized in order to rule out any possible effects the ordering may have on the estimation.

At the end, the questionnaire can be either written down on paper, can be programmed into software for computer-aided personal interviewing (CAPI), or implemented as an Internet survey. Of course, CAPI and Internet surveys are much more flexible (choice situations can be responsive to earlier responses or automatically be tailor-made for each respondent), enable more advanced surveys, and make the data readily available without human data entry errors. Therefore, most SC surveys nowadays are computer based.

NOTATION

Let each alternative j, $j = 1, \ldots, J$, have K_j associate attributes. Let the number of choice situations be denoted by S, and the number of respondents by N. Suppose that each respondent n, $n = 1, \ldots, N$, faces all S choice situations. In each choice situation s, $s = 1, \ldots, S$, each alternative has attributes with different attribute levels x_{jks}, $k = 1, \ldots, K_j$. The objective is to determine the experimental design matrix $\mathbf{X}_n = [x_{jksn}]$ for each respondent n with $x_{jksn} \in \Lambda_{jkn}$, where Λ_{jkn} is the set of possible attribute levels for each attribute for respondent n. Let $\ell_{jk} = |\Lambda_{jkn}|$ denote the number of levels for this attribute. In classical experimental designs, each respondent faces the same attribute levels in the same choice situations, hence, the subindex n can be omitted from the variables describing the attribute levels. However, in some cases (as we will see in Pivot Designs and Designs with Covariates sections) a different design for each respondent is created, such that this subindex n is important.

The choice behavior of each respondent is modeled using random utility theory in which we assume that each respondent is trying to maximize his or her utility. Let each alternative j in choice situation s have an associated observed utility V_{jsn}. This observed utility is composed of linear combination of attribute values x and associated parameters (weights) β. Suppose that there are N respondents facing the S choice situations. The utility U_{jsn} perceived in choice situation s by each respondent n is given by

$$U_{jsn}(\mathbf{X}, \beta) = V_{jsn}(\mathbf{X}_n, \beta) + \varepsilon_{jsn}, \quad \text{with } V_{jsn}(\mathbf{X}_n, \beta) = \sum_{k=1}^{K_j} \beta_k x_{jksn} \tag{1}$$

where ε_{jsn} is the unobserved utility. Using the assumption that respondents select the alternative with the highest utility, the probability can be computed if the probability distribution of the unobserved components is known. Depending on the assumptions of ε_{jsn}, different model types result (e.g., MNL, NL, or ML model, see e.g., Train, 2003). The most well-known assumption is that all ε_{jsn} are independently and identically extreme value type I distributed, which yields the following MNL probabilities P_{js} for selecting alternative j in choice situation s (McFadden, 1974):

$$P_{jsn}(\mathbf{X}, \beta) = \frac{\exp(V_{jsn}(\mathbf{X}, \beta))}{\sum_{i=1}^{J} \exp(V_{isn}(\mathbf{X}, \beta))}, \quad j = 1, \ldots, J;\ s = 1, \ldots, S;\ n = 1, \ldots, N \tag{2}$$

Full and Fractional Factorial Designs

A *full factorial design* considers each possible choice situation, that is, each possible combination of the attribute levels. Table 1 shows the full factorial design in case of three attributes (A, B, and C) with 2, 2, and 3 levels, respectively (using orthogonal coding). In total there are 12 (2 × 2 × 3) choice situations.

In general, if there are J alternatives, each with K_j attributes, where attribute $k \in k_j$ has ℓ_{jk} levels, then the total number of choice situations in the full factorial design is

$$S^{ff} = \prod_{j=1}^{J} \prod_{k=1}^{K_j} \ell_{jk} \tag{3}$$

Table 1
Example Full Factorial Design

s	A	B	C
1	−1	−1	−1
2	−1	−1	0
3	−1	−1	1
4	−1	1	−1
5	−1	1	0
6	−1	1	1
7	1	−1	−1
8	1	−1	0
9	1	−1	1
10	1	1	−1
11	1	1	0
12	1	1	1

In case of two alternatives, each having three attributes with four attribute levels each, the total number of combinations is $(4 \times 4 \times 4) \times (4 \times 4 \times 4) = 4^{2 \times 3} = 4{,}096$. Clearly, this number increases rapidly, and it is not feasible to let a single respondent face all these choice situations. Therefore, only for the smallest problems the full factorial design can be used. However, generating the full factorial design may be useful for determining other designs, such as certain fractional factorial designs (e.g., constrained designs, see Constrained Designs section).

In the more practical *fractional factorial designs*, each respondent is only shown a subset of S choice situations from the total number of choice situations. One option is to randomly select choice situations from the full factorial. Another option is to give the first S choice situation to the first respondent, the second S choice situation to the second respondent, and so on. But both options can lead to biased outcomes as, for example, a respondent may face only low or only high values of a certain attribute. This could be avoided by choosing the subsets in such a way that attribute-level balance is satisfied. *Orthogonal designs* and *efficient designs* select subsets in a more structured way, as will be outlined in the next sections.

Orthogonal Designs

Orthogonal designs have been used in the experimental design literature for a long time, but it should be noted that optimal/efficient designs (described in the next section) are gaining popularity among researchers. However, for reasons of history and inertia, orthogonal designs still remain the main form of designs used today.

Definition of Orthogonality

A design is said to be *orthogonal* if it satisfies attribute-level balance and all parameters are independently estimable. This translates into the definition that the attribute levels for each attribute column in the design need to be uncorrelated. In case of using orthogonal coding (see Step 2: Generation of Experimental Design section), an orthogonal design satisfies the property that the sum of the inner product of any two columns is zero:

$$\sum_{s=1}^{S} x_{j_1 k_1 s} x_{j_2 k_2 s} = 0, \quad \forall (j_1, k_1) \neq (j_2, k_2) \tag{4}$$

This is illustrated by the orthogonal design in Table 2. The design in Table 3 is not orthogonal, as the sum of the inner product of columns B and C is not equal to zero.

Table 2
Orthogonal Design with Three Attributes Having Two Levels

s	A	B	C	AB	AC	BC		Correlation matrix		
1	−1	−1	−1	1	1	1		**A**	**B**	**C**
2	−1	1	1	−1	−1	1	**A**	1	0	0
3	1	−1	1	−1	1	−1	**B**	0	1	0
4	1	1	−1	1	−1	−1	**C**	0	0	1
				$\Sigma = 0$	$\Sigma = 0$	$\Sigma = 0$				

Table 3
Nonorthogonal Design with Three Attributes Having Two Levels

s	A	B	C	AB	AC	BC		Correlation matrix		
1	−1	1	−1	−1	1	−1		**A**	**B**	**C**
2	−1	−1	1	1	−1	−1	**A**	1	0	0
3	1	−1	1	−1	1	−1	**B**	0	1	−1
4	1	1	−1	1	−1	−1	**C**	0	−1	1
				$\Sigma = 0$	$\Sigma = 0$	$\Sigma = -4$				

As can be observed from its correlation matrix,[5] columns B and C are perfectly (negatively) correlated.

Orthogonality is preserved if columns are removed, however not when rows are deleted. Therefore, if an orthogonal array exists with more columns than needed, one can randomly select columns to enter the design, and rearrange them in any preferred order. Also, multiplying one or more columns by −1 preserves orthogonality. Therefore, from the orthogonal design in Table 2, in total eight different orthogonal designs can be generated using all possible combinations of column multipliers: (1,1,1), (−1,1,1), (1,−1,1), (1,1,−1), (−1,−1,1), (−1,1,−1), (1,−1,−1), and (−1,−1,−1). Furthermore, when replacing the orthogonal codes with the actual attribute levels when constructing the questionnaire, one is not restricted to assign the attribute levels in the same order as the orthogonal coded levels. For example, one is free to choose the replacement {−1,0,1}→{\$1,\$2,\$3} or {−1,0,1}→{\$2,\$1,\$3}, again preserving orthogonality.

[5]For each combination of variable scales (ratio, interval, ordinal, dichotomous, nominal) a different correlation formula needs to be applied (see Hensher et al., 2005, Table 2A.1). The correlation matrix computed in Microsoft Excel is the Pearson product moment correlation coefficient.

Generating Orthogonal Designs

The problem of finding an orthogonal design can be described as follows:

Given feasible orthogonal coded attribute levels Λ_{jk} for all j and k, given a minimum number of choice situations S, determine the smallest level balanced design X with $x_{jks} \in \Lambda_{jk}$ such that equation (4) is satisfied.

Locating orthogonal designs is not a straightforward task. Suppose that one searches for an orthogonal design with five attributes each with three levels. The smallest number of choice situations possible that satisfy the degrees of freedom requirement (in case of all alternative-specific parameters (the maximum) is 5+1) and attribute-level balance (number of choice situations must be divisible by 3) is 6. However, in this case an orthogonal design with six choice situations does not exist. Even in 9 or 12 choice situations can an orthogonal design be located for the design dimensions required. Indeed, we are only able to locate an orthogonal design with 18 choice situations for this problem. Tables of orthogonal arrays have been derived mathematically for different numbers of columns and levels. These tables are limited and there may not be an orthogonal array known for the problem at hand. There are many lists with two, three, or even four levels, but higher levels become rare, and when mixing different numbers of levels it becomes even harder to find an orthogonal design. For example, Hahn and Shapiro (1966) have published tables with orthogonal designs for certain instances of numbers of attributes and attribute levels, but these are restricted to fairly small models. Computer programs can try to find near-orthogonal designs that can be used.

If an orthogonal design has been found, it may still be too large to give all choice situations to a single respondent. An often used procedure called *blocking* can split the orthogonal design into smaller designs. Each block is not orthogonal by itself, only the combination of all blocks is orthogonal. Blocking mainly ensures that attribute-level balance is satisfied within each block, such that respondents do not just face only low or high attribute levels for a certain attribute. Blocks are typically determined by using an extra uncorrelated column with a number of levels equal to the number of blocks. This is illustrated in Table 4. One can check that the design for attributes A, B, and C is orthogonal, and that also the blocking column is orthogonal to all other columns. The orthogonal design with nine choice situations is blocked into three blocks, such that each respondent now only has to face three choice situations instead of nine. Note that attribute-level balance is satisfied within each of the blocks. Special algebra, used to construct *alias structures*, can be used to create blocks (see e.g., Galilea and Ortúzar, 2005).

Orthogonal designs can be created manually, or can be found in documents such as Hahn and Shapiro (1966), or can be created automatically using computer software

Table 4
Blocking an Orthogonal Design in Three Blocks

s	A	B	C	Block	
1	−1	−1	−1	−1	Block 1
2	0	0	1	−1	
3	1	1	0	−1	
4	−1	0	0	0	Block 2
5	0	1	−1	0	
6	1	−1	1	0	
7	−1	1	1	1	Block 3
8	0	−1	0	1	
9	1	0	−1	1	

such as SPSS (only for simple designs), Ngene,[6] SAS, or one of the many software programs developed by consultants.

Discussion of Orthogonal Designs

It is important to understand that parameters are estimated from data sets underlined by SC experiments, not from the design itself. As we will demonstrate, only under exceptional circumstances will orthogonality be preserved within the data used to estimate discrete choice models, even if the experimental design is orthogonal. Indeed, with regard to choice data sets, one would expect orthogonality to be the exception rather than the rule. Further, even under circumstances where orthogonality is retained in a data set, as we show, orthogonality will likely be lost in the estimation process.

In case of nonresponse, in which a few choice situations are missing, the data will not be orthogonal. In case of blocking, if not all blocks are equally represented in the data set, then orthogonality will be lost. For example, consider again the blocked orthogonal design in Table 4. If blocks 1 and 2 appear twice in the data set and block 3 only once, then the data are correlated as indicated by the correlation matrix in Table 5. Removing data to preserve orthogonality is not common, as extra data are preferred above preserving orthogonality.

Further, it is common practice to collect socio-demographic and contextual variables and to include these in the utility functions for estimating discrete choice models. Even assuming equal representation of each choice situation of a design in the data, the

[6]Developed by Econometric Software, currently in prototype status.

Table 5
Correlation Matrix with Missing Block

	Correlation matrix*		
	A	B	C
A	1	0.1	0.2
B	0.1	1	−0.1
C	0.2	−0.1	1

*Computed using the Pearson product moment correlation coefficient in Microsoft Excel, see also footnote 5.

current standard of sampling is such that analysts fail to ensure orthogonality between the design attributes and other variables within the data set. For example, if age, gender, or income is added as a variable in the utility function for estimation, then the variable will be constant over all choice situations for each respondent, creating correlations between the variable and the attributes in the design.

Another reason that orthogonality may be lost is due to a poor transition between the design codes and the attribute-level labels used within the experiment. Orthogonality of a design will only be maintained if the (quantitative) attribute-level labels used are spaced equally along the range of that attribute. If unequal points are used along the attribute-level range, then orthogonality will be lost. For example, if the orthogonal codes {−1,0,1} are replaced with quantitative attribute-level labels {$2, $5, $15}, then the attribute levels are not equidistant in spacing. Therefore, the data will not be orthogonal.

To summarize, a carefully determined orthogonal experimental design is likely to produce non-orthogonal data. Therefore, the question arises if orthogonality is that important? In the next section optimal or efficient designs will be introduced, which seem to be outperforming orthogonal designs easily, although such designs have not been used much in practice yet.

Efficient Designs

In contrast to orthogonal designs, so-called *optimal* or *efficient* designs do not merely try to minimize the correlation in the data for estimation purposes, but aim to result in data that generate parameter estimates with as small as possible standard errors. These designs make use of the fact that the AVC matrix (the roots of the diagonal of this matrix are the asymptotic standard errors) of the parameters can be derived if the parameters are known. Unfortunately, since the objective of the SC experiment is to estimate these parameters, they are unknown. However, if some prior information about these parameters is available (e.g., parameter estimates available in the literature from similar studies, or parameter estimates from pilot studies), then this AVC matrix can be determined, assuming that the priors are correct. It can be argued that an orthogonal design is efficient only in cases where there is no knowledge about the parameters, but whenever there is any prior parameter information is available (perhaps just knowledge of the sign of the parameter) then the design can be improved.

Definition of Efficiency

An experimental design is called *efficient* if the design yields data that enable estimation of the parameters with as low as possible standard errors. These standard errors can be predicted by determining the AVC matrix based on the underlying experiment and some prior information about the parameter estimates. The following section will first briefly describe how to obtain this AVC matrix. Then, we will present several proposed efficiency measures for expressing the efficiency of an experimental design into a single value.

Deriving the Asymptotic[7] Variance–Covariance Matrix

Let Ω_N denote the AVC matrix given a sample size of N respondents (each facing S choice situations). This AVC matrix depends in general on the experimental design, $\mathbf{X} = [\mathbf{X}_n]$, the parameter values, β, and the outcomes of the survey, $Y = [y_{jsn}]$, where y_{jsn} equals 1 if respondent n chooses alternative j in choice situation s and is zero otherwise. Since the parameter values β are unknown, prior parameter values $\tilde{\beta}$ are used as best guesses for the true parameters.

The AVC matrix is the negative inverse of the expected Fisher information matrix (e.g., see Train, 2003), where the latter is equal to the matrix of second derivatives of the log-likelihood function:

$$\mathbf{\Omega}_N(\mathbf{X}, Y, \tilde{\beta}) = -[E(\mathbf{I}_N(\mathbf{X}, Y, \beta))]^{-1} = -\left[\frac{\partial^2 L_N(\mathbf{X}, Y, \tilde{\beta})}{\partial\beta\partial\beta'}\right]^{-1} \tag{5}$$

where $\mathbf{I}_N(\mathbf{X}, Y, \beta)$ is the Fisher information matrix with N respondents, and $L_N(\mathbf{X}, \tilde{\beta})$ is the log-likelihood function in case of N respondents defined by

$$L_N(\mathbf{X}, Y, \tilde{\beta}) = \sum_{n=1}^{N}\sum_{s=1}^{S}\sum_{j=1}^{J} y_{jsn} \log P_{jsn}(\mathbf{X}, \tilde{\beta}) \tag{6}$$

This formulation holds for each model type (MNL, NL, or ML), only the choice probabilities $P_{jsn}(\mathbf{X}, \tilde{\beta})$ are different. For the MNL model, the choice probabilities

[7]The term asymptotic refers to the fact that it is consistent in large samples, or it is representative as an average for small samples when the survey would be repeated many times.

given in equation (2) apply. It is important to note that MNL and NL models assume S independent responses from each individual, which is clearly not the case. Although this inconsistency is known, all but very few researchers consider the MNL model when constructing an efficient SC experiment due to the time-consuming computational complexity of the (panel) ML model.

There are two ways of determining the AVC matrix, either by Monte Carlo simulation, or analytically. Many researchers have relied on *Monte Carlo simulation*. In this case, a sample of size N is generated and parameters are estimated based on simulated choices (by simply computing the observed utilities using some prior parameter estimates, adding random draws for the unobserved utilities, and then determine the chosen alternative by assume that each respondent selects the alternative with the highest utility). Such as estimation also provides the results for the variance–covariance matrix. This procedure is repeated a large number of times and the average variance–covariance matrix yields the AVC matrix.

Many have not realized that the AVC matrix can be determined *analytically*, as suggested for MNL models with all generic parameters by McFadden (1974). In this case, the second derivative of the log-likelihood function in equation (5) is determined and evaluated analytically. A potential problem is that the vector of outcomes, Y, is part of the log-likelihood function, the reason why most researchers perform Monte Carlo simulations. However, it can be shown that the outcomes Y drop out when taking the second derivatives in case of the MNL model. This has been shown by McFadden (1974) for models with all generic parameters, and in Rose and Bliemer (2005a) for models with alternative-specific parameters, or a combination. Furthermore, Bliemer et al. (2009) have also derived analytical expressions for the second derivatives for the NL model. The outcomes Y do not drop out, but as shown in their paper, they can be replaced with probabilities leading to exactly the same AVC matrix, which has been confirmed by Monte Carlo simulation outcomes. Although more tedious, the second derivatives can also be derived for the ML model and a similar procedure holds for removing the outcome vector Y (see Sándor and Wedel, 2002). Note that the ML model will always require some simulations, as the parameters are assumed to be random and therefore expected probabilities need to be approximated using simulation. However, these simulations have no connection with the simulations mentioned earlier for determining the AVC matrix. To conclude, $\mathbf{\Omega}_N$ can be determined without knowing simulated outcomes Y, hence the dependency on Y disappears in equation (5).

In the special (and most considered) case that all respondents face exactly the same choice situations, that is, $X_n = X$ for all n, it can be shown that (see Rose and Bliemer, 2005a)

$$\mathbf{I}_N(\mathbf{X}, \tilde{\beta}) = N \cdot \mathbf{I}_1(\mathbf{X}, \tilde{\beta}), \quad \text{hence} \quad \mathbf{\Omega}_N(\mathbf{X}, \tilde{\beta}) = \frac{1}{N}\mathbf{\Omega}_1(\mathbf{X}, \tilde{\beta}) \tag{7}$$

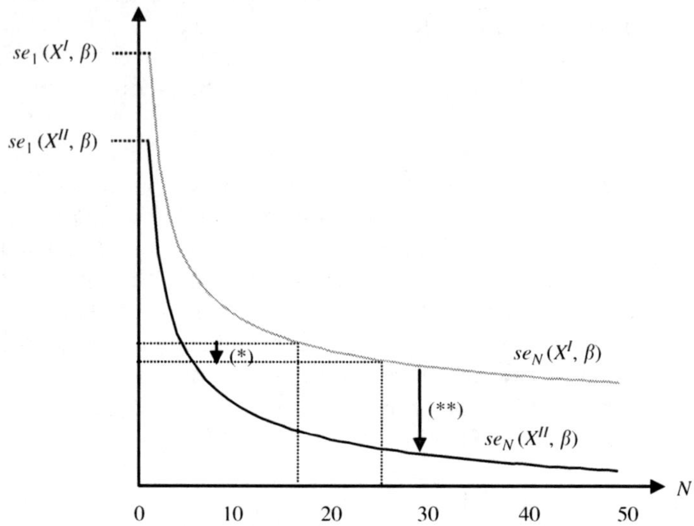

Figure 2
Asymptotic Standard Error as a Function of the Sample Size

where $\mathbf{I}_1$ and Ω_1 are the Fisher information matrix and AVC matrix in case of a single respondent, respectively. In other words, the AVC matrix corresponding to a sample size of N can be derived directly from the AVC matrix from a single respondent using a rate of $1/N$. This means that the impact of sample size on the design can readily be investigated (under all assumptions made so far). The asymptotic standard errors $se_N(\mathbf{X}, \tilde{\beta})$ are the roots of the diagonal of the AVC matrix, therefore these standard errors decrease with a rate of $1/\sqrt{N}$ of the sample size N. This is also illustrated in Figure 2 for a single parameter, clearly indicating a diminishing decreasing asymptotic standard error when the sample size increases. This is an important result, as it suggests that spending (much) more money on collecting data using a larger sample size does in the end not lead to significantly better parameter estimates, indicated by (*) in the figure. As the figure also suggests, it pays off much more to determine a design with a higher efficiency (design with attribute levels X^{II} instead of X^I), in which the standard error can decrease significantly, indicated by (**) in the figure, without spending any extra money!

Efficiency Measures

The efficiency of a design can be derived from the AVC matrix. Instead of assessing a whole AVC matrix, it is easier to assess a design based on a single value. Therefore, efficiency measures have been proposed in the literature in order to calculate such an efficiency value, typically expressed as in efficiency "error" (i.e., a measure for the inefficiency). The objective then becomes to minimize this efficiency error.

The most widely used measure is called the *D-error*, which takes the determinant of the AVC matrix Ω_1, assuming only a single respondent.[8] A design with the lowest *D*-error is called *D-optimal*. In practice, it is very difficult to find the design with the lowest *D*-error, therefore we are satisfied if the design has a sufficiently low *D*-error, called a *D-efficient* design. Different types of *D*-error have been proposed in the literature, depending on the available information on the prior parameters $\tilde{\beta}$. We will distinguish three cases:

(a) No information is available;
If no information is available (not even the sign of the parameters), then set $\tilde{\beta} = 0$. This leads to a so-called D_z-error ("z" from "zero").

(b) Information is available with good approximations of β;
If the information is relatively accurate, $\tilde{\beta}$ is set to the best guesses, assuming they are correct. This leads to a so-called D_p-error ("p" from "priors")

(c) Information is available with uncertainty about the approximations of β;
Instead of assuming fixed priors $\tilde{\beta}$, they are assumed to be random following some given probability distribution to express the uncertainty about the true value of β. This Bayesian approach leads to a so-called D_b-error ("b" from "Bayesian").

The *D*-errors are a function of the experimental design *X* and the prior values (or probability distributions) $\tilde{\beta}$, and can be mathematically formulated as:

$$D_z\text{-error} = \det(\mathbf{\Omega}_1(\mathbf{X}, 0))^{1/H} \tag{8}$$

$$D_p\text{-error} = \det(\mathbf{\Omega}_1(\mathbf{X}, \tilde{\beta}))^{1/H} \tag{9}$$

$$D_b\text{-error} = \int_{\tilde{\beta}} \det(\mathbf{\Omega}_1(\mathbf{X}, \tilde{\beta}))^{1/H} \, \phi(\tilde{\beta}|\theta)\mathrm{d}\tilde{\beta} \tag{10}$$

where *H* is the number of parameters to be estimated. Note that the AVC matrix is an $H \times H$ matrix. In order to let the *D*-error be independent of the size of the problem, the

[8] The assumption of single respondent is just for convenience and comparison reasons and does not have any further implications. Any other sample size could have been used, but it is common in the literature to base it on a single respondent.

D-error is normalized by the power $1/H$. We recommend removing the rows and columns corresponding to the model constants in the AVC matrix as these parameters in general do not have a clear meaning in an SC experiment (in contrast to revealed choices). As the standard errors of these model constants can become fairly large, they could dominate the D-errors, therefore we advise to remove them before taking the determinant (and at the same time also adjust the value of H).

Equation (10) needs some more explanation. In the Bayesian D-error computation, the priors $\tilde{\beta}$ are assumed to be random variables with a joint probability density function $\phi(\cdot)$ with given parameters θ. For example, these priors could follow normal distributions $\tilde{\beta} \sim N(\mu, \Sigma)$, or uniform distributions $\tilde{\beta} \sim U(u, v)$, or a mix, or other distributions. Normal and uniform distributions seem to be the only ones used in the literature so far.

Besides the D-error, other inefficiency measures have been proposed as well. Another well-known efficiency error is called the *A-error*, and the design with the lowest A-error is called *A-optimal.* Instead of taking the determinant, the A-error takes the trace of the AVC matrix, which is the summation of all diagonal elements of the matrix. Therefore, the A-error only looks at the variances and not at the covariances. In order to normalize the A-error it is divided by H (the same recommendation about the model constants applies). Similar to the D-error, different A-errors can be determined based on the availability of information on the parameters. The A_{p}-error is mathematically formulated as

$$A_{\mathrm{p}}\text{-error} = \frac{\mathrm{tr}(\mathbf{\Omega}_N(\mathbf{X}, \tilde{\beta}))}{H} \tag{11}$$

The A_{z}-error and A_{b}-error can be derived using formulations equivalent to equations (8) and (10). The A-error should be used with caution in case not all parameter values are of equal scale. By the simple summation of the variances it is likely that parameters with large values will overshadow the other parameters. Therefore, we suggest using a weighted summation. Using weights it is also possible to give more importance to certain parameters, that is, enable the estimation of these parameters more accurate than others.

A completely different efficiency measure has been introduced in Bliemer and Rose (2005a) and Rose and Bliemer (2005b). They propose a measure that is related to the sample sizes required to estimate each parameter significantly. If the null hypothesis is that $\beta_k = 0$ for a certain parameter, then this hypothesis is rejected if

$$\frac{\beta_k}{\mathrm{se}_{N,k}(\mathbf{X}, \beta)} \geq t_\alpha \tag{12}$$

where t_α is the t-value corresponding to the $(1-\alpha)$-confidence interval (e.g., $t_{0.05} = 1.96$). Assuming that the priors are correct estimates for the true parameters and assuming that all respondents face the same choice situations, that is, equation (7) holds, then equation (12) can be rewritten as

$$N \geq \left(\frac{\text{se}_{1,k}(\mathbf{X}, \tilde{\beta}) t_\alpha}{\tilde{\beta}_k} \right)^2 \tag{13}$$

This number provides a lower bound on the necessary magnitude of the sample size in order to obtain significant estimates for parameter β_k. The measure proposed by Bliemer and Rose (2005a) is derived from the observation that if some parameters need much higher sample sizes than others, it may be better in the experiment to focus more on the parameters that are difficult to estimate significantly. By spreading the information obtained from each choice situation in the design over all parameters, the design can be optimized for sample size, and this is termed *S-optimality*.

Note that equation (13) typically provides a lower bound and does not guarantee significant parameter estimates due to random choice behavior and due to the fact that for the MNL model it is assumed that all random components are independent, even if a single respondent faces multiple choice situations. This will lead to some biases, yielding higher necessary sample sizes. The problem of dependent observations in an SC experiment is a known problem to which unfortunately no simple solution exists, besides putting the correlation structure in a random components model. Therefore, the *S*-optimality measure merely gives an indication in order to compare different designs on lower bounds for the sample sizes.

Several other efficiency criteria have been proposed (see e.g., Kessels et al., 2006) and many others can be formulated. As mentioned, the *D*-error is used in most research and should be preferred over the *A*-error, which may have scaling problems.

Orthogonal Versus Efficient Designs

In case any information about the parameters is available, then efficient designs will always outperform orthogonal designs. This is due to the fact that efficient designs use the knowledge of the prior parameters to optimize the design in which the most information is gained from each choice situation (e.g., dominant alternatives can be avoided as the utilities can be computed). We will come back to dominant alternatives when discussing the (un)importance of utility balancing in Utility Balance section.

What happens in the case no information about the parameters is available? In other words, which design is better, an orthogonal design, or a D_z-optimal design (which assumes $\tilde{\beta} = 0$)? As mentioned in Bliemer and Rose (2005b), there is a close correspondence between orthogonal designs and D_z-optimal designs. In fact, in case all model parameters are alternative specific, a D_z-optimal design is orthogonal. In case all model parameters are generic, it is not necessary to choose between either orthogonality or D_z-efficiency as it is possible to determine *orthogonal* D_z-optimal designs. Street et al. (2001) and Street and Burgess (2004) demonstrate how to create such D_z-optimal designs for generic designs with only two alternatives and where each attribute has a number of levels equal to the power of two (hence, two, four, eight, etc.). In Street et al. (2005) a nice overview is given for determining D_z-optimal (or nearly optimal) designs with multiple alternatives and different levels. However, these remain limited to models with generic parameters.

The design principles in Street et al. (2005) have some limitations. First of all, they are limited to the MNL model. Second, they are only optimal in case all parameters are equal to zero, which is clearly not the case. The fact that their designs are suboptimal under the nonzero parameter case is because that they assume all equal probabilities in the MNL model (see equations 1 and 2). Finally, if alternative-specific parameters are present, then a simple principle that will lead to a D_z-optimal design does not exist.

If correlations in the design have a negative impact on the parameter estimates, then this should implicitly be reflected in the AVC matrix of the design, instead of explicitly in an orthogonal design. Hence, an efficient design will to a certain degree implicitly minimize the correlations in a design, hence it is not necessary to include orthogonality as an additional condition to efficiency.

Importance of Prior Parameter Values

The purpose of the SC experiment is to estimate the parameters of the specified model. But even without estimating them, some information and/or educated guesses regarding parameters are usually available. Again, we would like to stress that D_p-optimal designs will always outperform D_z-optimal designs in case any information about the parameters (even only the sign of the parameters) is available. We argue that it is always possible to obtain some information on the priors.

Just using reasoning alone, it should at least be possible to determine the signs of most parameters. For example, price attributes are typically negatively perceived, while comfort and service are attributes that will receive positive attitudes. Instead of assuming zero priors, assuming a slightly positive or negative prior parameter value would already improve the design.

Many surveys have been conducted around the world, and it is likely to find at least a few similar parameters. If no such studies can be found, then it may be very useful to conduct a small pilot study in order to get an initial idea about the parameter values. With the same amount of money, one could (i) conduct a large survey using an experimental design based on priors equal to zero (no information case), or (ii) conduct a slightly smaller survey using an experimental design based on priors obtained from a pilot study. As Figure 2 also suggested, the second option is preferred, since it can lead to significantly more reliable parameter estimates.

Obviously, a D_p-optimal design is sensitive to the chosen prior parameters. If they are not correct, then the design is suboptimal (note that D_z-optimal will therefore always be suboptimal). Fortunately, the design can be tested for robustness in case one or more prior parameter values are not correct. By taking a fixed design X and computing the AVC matrix as in equation (5) (recall that the outcomes Y drop out) for different values of $\tilde{\beta}$, a sensitivity analyses of the design can be performed. Once the sensitivity of the efficiency of the design to each prior parameter is known, one can decide to either put more effort in determining the prior values for the most sensitive priors, or determine a new design (which may be less efficient, but more robust).

Another way of dealing with uncertainty about prior parameters was already mentioned when describing the Bayesian efficient designs. A Bayesian efficient design optimizes the expected efficiency of the design over a range of prior parameter values, thereby making it more robust to mis-specifying the priors. Priors with a higher uncertainty should see this uncertainty reflected into a larger standard deviation or spread of its probability distribution.

Utility Balance

A couple of times the words "dominant alternatives" or "more information from choice situations" have been used. Here the concept of utility balancing as suggested in Huber and Zwerina (1996) will be described.

As a simple example, consider two choice situations in an unlabeled SC experiment as illustrated in Figure 3. In the first choice situation, route A has both a lower travel time as well as a lower toll cost, making it clearly the preferred alternative. The route A alternative therefore clearly dominates in this choice situation, therefore no information will be gained. In contrast, in the second choice situation there is no clear dominant alternative and the respondent has to make a clear trade-off between travel time and toll cost, hence this will provide information.

The example illustrates that balancing the utilities of alternatives (i.e., having no alternatives that are clearly dominating the others) is of some importance. At least, if it is very unbalanced, the choice situation does not provide information for estimating the parameters. This could lead to the understanding that in the most efficient design, all the choice situations are perfectly utility balanced. This is however not the case. If all alternatives have an equal observed utility, then the random unobserved component dominates. In other words, then the respondent has no clear preference for any of the

Which route would you choose in the following situations?

1.	*Route A*	*Route B*
Travel time:	10 min.	15 min.
Toll cost:	$1	$2
Your choice:	☐	☐
2.	*Route A*	*Route B*
Travel time:	15 min.	10 min.
Toll cost:	$1	$2
Your choice:	☐	☐

Figure 3
Dominant Alternative in Choice Situation 1

alternatives and randomly selects one. This too does not give information. Therefore it can be concluded that an efficient design has some degree of utility balance, but not too much, and not too little. Toner et al. (1999) and Kanninen (2002) have established some optimal utility balance levels, expressed in optimal choice probabilities of each alternative in each choice situation (depending on the dimensions of the experiment), which are for a two-alternative choice situation typically closer to (80%, 20%) or (70%, 30%) than (50%, 50%).

The example shown in Figure 3 represents a particular form of choice experiment where respondents are required to select one of the alternatives presented to them. This type of experiment is known as a forced choice experiment. In some instances, the analyst may wish to allow respondents to elect not to choose one of the alternatives on offer, or even stick with some status quo option. In other cases, analysts may wish to allow respondents to indicate that they are indifferent between the alternatives on offer. The design of SC experiments in the presence of such alternatives has been addressed within the literature (see e.g., Ferrini and Scarpa, 2007; Rose et al., 2008); however, it is important to note that, depending on the objective of the study, the inclusion of such alternatives may represent best practice (see e.g., Dhar and Simonson, 2003; Kontoleon and Mitsuyasu, 2003; Olsen and Swait, 1998).

Utility balance of a choice situation and a whole design can be expressed in a percentage. Consider an SC experiment with J alternatives. Consider a certain choice situation s. This choice situation would have perfect utility balance if all alternatives j have an equal probability, that is, $P_{js} = 1/J$. The utility balance of choice situation s can be defined as:

$$B_s = \prod_{j=1}^{J} \left(\frac{P_{js}}{1/J} \right) \times 100\% \qquad (14)$$

For example, if $J = 3$ and all three alternatives have a probability of 1/3, then $B_s = 100\%$. If the probabilities are 1/2, 1/3, and 1/6, respectively, then the utility balance is $B_s = 75\%$. If one or more of the probabilities is equal to zero, then the utility balance is 0%. The overall utility balance of the design, B, can be determined by averaging over all choice situations (Kessels et al., 2006):

$$B = \frac{1}{S}\sum_{s=1}^{S} B_s \tag{15}$$

The optimal value for utility balance of a design cannot be given, but observations of the utility balance of efficient designs suggest that it lies in the range of 70–90%. Utility balance can be examined for each choice situation, thereby investigating if the design contains choice situations with clearly dominant alternatives, which should not occur in an efficient design. Hence, utility balance could be used in the algorithms for generating efficient designs.

Generating Efficient Designs

The problem of finding an efficient design can be described as follows:

Given feasible attribute levels Λ_{jk} for all j and k, the number of choice situations S, and the prior parameter values $\tilde{\beta}$ (or probability distributions of $\tilde{\beta}$), determine a level balanced design X with $x_{jks} \in \Lambda_{jk}$ that minimizes the efficiency error in equations (8), (9), (10), or (11).

Note that in this formulation attribute-level balance is added as a requirement, consistent with current state of practice. It should be stressed that an efficient design does not necessarily require attribute-level balance. In fact, a more efficient design may be found by removing the level balance requirement as will be discussed in Discussion of Efficient Designs section.

In order to solve the problem of determining the most efficient design, one could determine the full factorial design and then evaluate each different combination of S choice situations from this full factorial. The combination with the lowest efficiency error is the optimal design. However, this procedure is not feasible in practice due to an extremely high number of possible designs to evaluate. For example, consider the problem of determining an efficient design for a hypothetical case with three alternatives as shown in Table 6. The full factorial design has $2^1 \times 3^8 \times 4^2 = 209{,}952$ choice situations. Suppose that we would like to find an efficient design with $S = 12$ choice situations. Selecting 12 choice situations from this set of 209,952 different choice situations yields 7.3×10^{63} possible different designs. Clearly, it is not

Table 6
Example Dimensions for Generating an Efficient Design

Attributes	Alternatives		
	Car (route A)	Car (route B)	Train
Travel time (minimum)	{10, 20, 30}	{15, 30, 45}	{15, 25, 35}
Delay/waiting time (minimum)	{0, 5, 10}	{5, 10, 15}	{5, 10}
Toll cost/fare ($)	{2, 4, 6, 8}	{0, 1, 2, 3}	{4, 6, 8}

feasible to evaluate all possible designs, hence a smart algorithm is necessary to find an efficient as possible design.

There are row-based algorithms and column-based algorithms for finding an efficient design. In a *row-based algorithm* choice situations are selected from a predefined candidature set of choice situations (either a full factorial or a fractional factorial) in each iteration. *Column-based algorithms* create a design by selecting attribute levels over all choice situations for each attribute. Row-based algorithms can easily remove bad choice situations from the candidature set at the beginning (e.g., by applying a utility balance criterion), but it is more difficult to satisfy attribute-level balance. The opposite holds for column-based algorithms, in which attribute-level balance is easy to satisfy, but finding good combinations of attribute levels in each choice situation is more difficult. In general, column-based algorithms offer more flexibility and can deal with larger designs, but in some cases (for unlabeled designs and for specific designs such as constrained designs, see Constrained Designs section) row-based algorithms are more suitable.

The *modified Federov algorithm* (Cook and Nachtsheim, 1980) is a row-based algorithm. First, a candidature set is determined, either the full factorial (for small problems) or a fractional factorial (for large problems). Then, a (attribute-level balanced) design is created by selecting choice situations from the candidature set. After that, the efficiency error (e.g., *D*-error) is computed for this design. Finally, if this design has a lower efficiency error than the current best design, the design is stored as the most efficient design so far, and one continues with the next iteration, repeating the whole process again. The algorithm terminates if all possible combinations of choice situations have been evaluated (which is in general not feasible), or after a predefined number of iterations. Construction of D_z-optimal as described in Street et al. (2005) is also row based, in which in a smart way combinations of choice situations are made.

Relabeling, swapping and cycling (*RSC*) *algorithms* (Huber and Zwerina, 1996; Sándor and Wedel, 2001) are column-based algorithms. In each iteration, different columns for each attribute are created, which together form a design. This design is evaluated and if it has a lower efficiency error than the current best design, then it is stored. The columns are not created randomly, but—as the name suggests—are generated in a structured way using relabeling, swapping, and cycling techniques. Starting with an initial design, each column could be altered by relabeling the attribute levels. For example, if the attribute levels 1 and 3 are relabeled, then a column containing the levels (1,2,1,3,2,3) will become (3,2,3,1,2,1). Swapping means that some attribute levels switch place, for example, if the attribute levels in the first and fourth choice situation are swapped then (1,2,1,3,2,3) would become (3,2,1,1,2,3). Finally, cycling replaces all attribute levels in each choice situation at the time by replacing the first attribute level with the second level, the second level with the third, etc. Since this impacts all columns, cycling can only be performed if all attributes have exactly the same sets of feasible levels (e.g., in case all variables are dummy coded). Sometimes only swapping is used, sometimes only relabeling and swapping is used, as special cases of this algorithm type.

A genetic algorithm, also a column-based algorithm, has been proposed recently by Bliemer (2006). In this algorithm, a population of designs is (randomly) created, and new designs are determined by cross-over of designs in the population (combining columns of two designs, called the parents, creating a new design, called the child). The fittest designs in the population, measured by their efficiency, will most likely survive in the population, while less fit designs with a high efficiency error will be removed from the population (die). Mutation in the population takes place by randomly swapping attribute levels in the columns. Genetic algorithms seem to be quite powerful in finding efficient designs relatively quickly.

If for some reason orthogonality is required in a D_p-efficient design, one could construct a single orthogonal design, from this design easily create a large (but not huge) number of other orthogonal designs, and then evaluate all these orthogonal designs and select the most efficient one. Creating other orthogonal designs from a single orthogonal design is relatively simple, as discussed in Definition of Orthogonality section.

Evaluating each design for the efficiency error is the most time-consuming part of each algorithm, therefore the number of D-error or other efficiency error evaluations should be kept to a minimum by putting more intelligence into the construction of the designs. In determining Bayesian efficient designs this becomes even more important, as the integral in equation (10) cannot be computed analytically, but only by simulation. Mainly pseudo-random Monte Carlo simulations have been performed for determining the Bayesian D-error for each design, which enables the approximation of this D-error by taking the average of all D-errors for the same design using pseudo-random draws for the prior parameter values. This is clearly a computation-intensive process, such that finding Bayesian efficient designs is a very time consuming task. Bliemer et al. (2008) have proposed to use quasi-random draws (such as Halton or Sobol sequences) or preferably Gaussian quadrature methods instead of pseudo-random draws, which require less simulations and therefore enable the evaluation of more designs in the same amount of time.

Manually determining efficient designs is only possible for the smallest hypothetical experiments. Computer software such as SAS and Ngene are able to generate efficient designs. SAS, however, is limited to MNL models and does not include Bayesian efficiency measures, while Ngene is able to determine efficient designs for the MNL, NL, and ML models, including Bayesian efficient designs.

Discussion of Efficient Designs

Efficient or optimal designs have been embraced by more and more researchers as the current best way of designing SC experiments. Practitioners are still somewhat hesitant to deviate from orthogonal designs, which have been claimed to be best for a long time, but there is a growing support for and understanding of efficient designs to which this paper hopefully contributes.

Do the chosen feasible levels, determined before generating an efficient design, impact the potential efficiency of the design? The answer is "yes," they have a significant impact on the efficiency. Broadly speaking, the less attribute levels and, more importantly, the wider the attribute level range, the higher the efficiency of the design can be. A wide attribute level range usually translates into smaller asymptotic standard errors. Therefore, the highest efficiency can theoretically be obtained using so-called *endpoint designs*, which are two-level designs with extreme (wide range) levels. The disadvantage of this kind of designs is that nonlinearities cannot be estimated (more levels are needed for this purpose). Furthermore, the extreme levels should be realistic.

The number of choice situations does not seem to have a large impact on the efficiency of a design, as long as the number of choice situations is not smaller than the number of degrees of freedom. Clearly, more choice situations yield more data per respondent, hence the efficiency will automatically increase with more choice situations. Compensating for this effect by normalizing the efficiency error (i.e., assuming the same amount of data), it does not seem to make much difference how many choice situations are chosen. Therefore, the number of choice situations does not have to be very high (blocking as in orthogonal designs is therefore not necessary) and should mainly depend on the intuition how many choice situations respondents can handle. A higher number of choice situations means a higher level of effort for the respondent. The maximum number of choice situations depends of course on the complexity of each choice situation, but roughly 10–20 choice situations should be possible.[9]

Still, the efficient designs discussed in this section may be improved due to the somewhat restrictive assumptions commonly imposed. First of all, attribute level balanced has been imposed for efficient designs, which is typically only required for orthogonal designs. Attribute-level balance is viewed as a desired property ensuring that all attribute levels appear equally in the data set, which intuitively provides a good basis for estimation. However, the attribute-level balance requirement is mathematically speaking merely imposing another constraint on the problem of minimizing the efficiency error, thereby always leading to less-efficient designs. By relaxing this assumption a more efficient design may be found. An optimal design without the restricting of level balance is likely to be (close to) an endpoint design using just the two extreme levels.

Another assumption made in this section is that of independent observations, that is, the outcomes of all choice situations from the same respondent are assumed independent. This assumption makes it easy to derive analytical expressions of the AVC matrix. However, it is likely that the data does not consist of independent observations, as the random unobserved utilities are correlated within each respondent, and this has to be taken into account. Using an error components structure one could simulate these correlations, but then the AVC matrix has to be computed by simulation instead of analytically (see Scarpa et al., 2005b; Ferrini and Scarpa, 2007).

Some other assumptions normally made are that all respondents face the same choice situations, and that socioeconomic data are ignored. These assumptions are relaxed in the next section. Instead of relaxing some assumptions, it is also discussed how to deal with more constraints.

Advanced Designs

So far we discussed orthogonal designs as still the mainstream design type used by practitioners, and efficient or optimal designs that have theoretical and practical advantages and are envisaged to be used more and more by practitioners. In this

[9]The maximum number of choice situations that a respondent can handle remains one of the most controversial topics in the area of discrete choice modeling to date. For example, research conducted by Brazell and Louviere (1996) found no significant differences in either internal reliability or model variability for models estimated from instruments involving differing numbers of choice situations. Hensher (2006) reports similar findings. On the other hand, research such as that conducted by Caussade et al. (2005) demonstrated that the number of choice situations a respondent reviews has a significant impact upon the error variance of discrete choice models. Careful consideration is therefore advised on the issue.

section, several advanced designs will be discussed. These designs are actually special efficient designs in which some of the assumptions are relaxed to allow more flexibility in the design, or in which more constraints are added, both for practical reasons. It is important to note that the designs discussed in this section are the current state of the art and certainly not state of the practice, although practitioners are highly interested in these advanced designs. There is still a significant amount of research to be done in this area.

First, constraints on combinations of attribute levels are imposed in order to rule out infeasible combinations in choice situations, leading to *constrained designs* (Constrained Designs section). Second, the assumptions that all respondents face the same choice situations will be relaxed. Instead, the choice situations presented to the respondents will depend on their actual situation, for example, their current revealed preference. Pivoting attribute levels around these personal values creates more realistic choice situations specific for each respondent. This leads to efficient *pivot designs* (Pivot Designs section). Third, we will discuss inclusion of covariates (i.e., socio-demographic variables), which are different from the attribute variables in the model. If covariates are not considered when creating a design, then the efficiency in the design will be lost in the data when estimating the model with covariates. By determining a *design with covariates* one can optimize the design for each group of respondents, and maybe even select optimal sample sizes within each of these groups (see Designs with Covariates section).

Constrained Designs

Sometimes certain combinations of attribute levels in a choice situation are not feasible. These infeasible choice situations need to be avoided by adding constraints.

Level-constrained designs are most apparent in applications in health economics. For example, consider two alternatives, treating and not treating a patient. Then the attribute "age of death" in these alternatives should be such that in each choice situation this age for the treating alternative is never lower than the nontreating alternative, and the attribute "current age" cannot be higher than the "age of death." In transportation, one could think of route alternatives with different departure times, free-flow travel times, and arrival times. Clearly, the arrival times should be later than the departure times, and the difference between the arrival and departure time should be greater than or equal to the free-flow travel time.

There are different ways of including above-mentioned constraints. A straightforward way, implemented in Ngene, is using an extended version of the modified Federov algorithm by adding an extra step. After having determined the candidature set, choice situations that do not satisfy the constraints are removed from this set. This ensures that all designs generated from this candidature set will be feasible.

Note that it may be hard or even impossible to find an attribute-level balanced design satisfying the constraints, especially when the constraints impose many restrictions. Also note that in theory also RSC algorithms can be used, but that after each relabeling, swapping, or cycling all choice situations need to be checked for feasibility. Ensuring that all choice situations are feasible could be difficult hence RSC algorithms may not be suitable.

Pivot Designs

So far we have assumed that all respondents face the same choice situations. From a cognitive and contextual point of view, this may not be optimal. The use of a respondent's *knowledge base* to derive the attribute levels of the experiment has come about in recognition of a number of supporting theories in behavioral and cognitive psychology, and economics, such as prospect theory, case-based decisions theory, and minimum-regret theory. This leads to the notion of so-called *reference alternatives*, which may be different for each respondent. As Starmer (2000, p. 353) remarks "While some economists might be tempted to think that questions about how reference points are determined sound more like psychological than economic issues, recent research is showing that understanding the role of reference points may be an important step in explaining real economic behavior in the field." Reference alternatives in SC experiments act to frame the decision context of the choice task within some existing memory schema of the individual respondents and hence make preference revelation more meaningful at the level of the individual.

In a pivot design, the attribute levels shown to the respondents are pivoted from reference alternatives of each respondent. In Table 7 an example is shown, where for compactness only the first alternative is presented. The actual underlying design is

Table 7

Designs Pivoted from a Reference Alternative

	Design		Respondent 1 (travel time = 10, toll = 2)		Respondent 2 (travel time = 30, toll = 3)	
	Travel time (minimum)	Toll costs ($)	Travel time (minimum)	Toll cost ($)	Travel time (minimum)	Toll cost ($)
1.	−10%	+2	9	4	27	5
2.	+10%	+1	11	3	33	4
3.	+30%	+0	12	2	36	3
4.	+10%	+2	11	4	33	5
5.	−10%	+0	9	2	27	3
6.	+30%	+1	12	3	36	4

shown in gray, where the attributes are either a relative pivot (as in the travel time) or an absolute pivot (as in the toll cost). The attribute levels shown in the SC experiment are based on the reference alternative of the respondents. For example, suppose that respondent 1 has answered in an earlier question in the survey that he or she currently has a travel time of 10 minutes and pays \$2 toll, then the attribute levels for the first alternative in the first choice situation will be determined as 10–1 = 9 minutes (10% less travel time), and a toll cost of 2+2 = \$4 (\$2 extra). Therefore, this choice situation will be different from the choice situation presented to respondent 2 (facing a travel time of 27 minutes and a toll of \$5 for the first alternative in the first choice situation).

Hence, instead of creating a design with the actual attribute levels, a pivot design is created with relative or absolute deviations from references. Suppose that a single pivot design is created. The efficiency of this design depends on the references of the respondents, as these determine the actual attribute levels in the choice situations and therefore the AVC matrix. However, in advance the references of the respondents are typically not available. Rose et al. (2008) have compared several different approaches for finding efficient pivot designs:

(a) Use the population average as the reference (yields a single design);
(b) Segment the population based on a finite set of different references (yields multiple designs);
(c) Determine an efficient design on the fly (yields a separate design for each respondent);
(d) Use a two-stage process in which the references are captured in the first stage and the design is created in the second stage (yields a single design).

Intuitively, approach (a) should give the lowest efficiency (individual reference alternatives may differ widely from those assumed in generating the design), while the last approach should yield the highest efficiency (likely to produce truly efficient data). This was also the outcome of the study. Approach (a) worked relatively well, and approach (b) only performed marginally better. Approach (c) and (d) performed best. The outcomes were also compared with an orthogonal design, which performed poorly. Pivot designs for approaches (a) and (b) are relatively easy to generate, for approaches (c) and (d) more effort is needed. Approach (c) requires a CAPI or Internet survey, and an efficient design is generated while the respondent is answering other questions. Approach (d) is sensitive to dropouts, as the design will only be optimal if all respondents in the second stage participate again in the survey.

Designs with Covariates

Including covariates (e.g., socioeconomic data such as income, gender, car-ownership, etc.) in the model estimation may result in loss of efficiency when the design was determined ignoring these covariates. So far, only attributes have been considered in the model specification, but it is common to include covariates in the estimation process. Analysts should primarily be interested in the efficiency of the SC data collected rather than being concerned about the efficiency of the underlying SC design. Designs should be constructed in a manner that will reflect the final data to be collected, including any possible covariates.

Rose and Bliemer (2006) demonstrate how efficient SC experiments may be constructed to account for covariates, and how minimum quotas may be established in order to retain a fixed level of efficiency. The procedures for doing this are not much different for construing efficient designs without considering any covariates. Assuming categorical covariates (or continuous covariates coded categorically), it is possible to calculate the AVC matrix for an SC study by constructing a set of segments based on combinations of covariates, and assigning to each segment one or more SC designs. If multiple covariates are to be analyzed, the analyst may wish to construct a full factorial or fractional factorial of the possible combinations formed by the covariates and assign to each the generated design. Next the analyst may generate segment-specific efficient designs that minimize the AVC matrix for the pooled data. Procedures similar to those discussed in this paper may be used to do this; however, rather than having one design, the analyst now has to deal with multiple "stacked" or pooled designs.

If the covariates are continuous in nature, then the above methods cannot be handled easily. If the above procedure is to be employed, then the number of segments that can be formed may be so large as to not be computationally possible to handle. If this is the case, then the analyst may have to resort to Monte Carlo simulations to simulate the likely data that are expected to be collected.

Discussion

The generation of SC experiments has evolved to become an increasingly significant but complex component of SC studies. Unfortunately, this has meant that as with much of the discrete choice modeling literature, the construction of SC designs has very much become the domain of the specialist. The need to share to a wider audience the technical skills required to correctly construct SC experiments, in a manner that can be readily understood, remains one of the most challenging aspects for those working in this area. While we do not claim that we have successfully done this here, this paper represents what we believe to be the first step in attempting to meet this challenge.

We contend that the generation of SC experiments is critical to the success of any SC study. Failure to correctly construct an appropriate design may result in erroneous findings. This is not so much because a particular design may bias the answers given by respondents (though this may be the case), but more so that a particular design may require greater sample size in order to detect statistical significance of parameter estimates. This is precisely the interpretation that one could give to Figure 2; that one possible objective of selecting a particular design from all other possible designs is to decrease the number of observations required to locate statistically significant parameter estimates. This objective is bourn not only out of science, but also out of practical necessity. Increasing survey costs and a growing awareness of the impacts of greater "complexity" in survey questions on respondents completing SC tasks, appear to be at growing odds with the impetus to capture greater levels of information from sampled respondents.

One of the principal messages we wish to promote is that despite devoting significant space discussing the concept of orthogonality, orthogonality is not a desirable property for discrete choice studies. In linear models, were multicollinearity is a major concern, orthogonality remains a property that analysts should seek out when generating experimental designs. Unfortunately, models of discrete choice are rarely, if ever, linear. As argued by Train (2003), for models of discrete choice, what is important is the differences in the utility functions (and hence parameter estimates as well as attributes) of the alternatives within the data, and not the actual values observed for each of the attributes. Given that it is the differences in the utilities which are of importance, if one is truly concerned about orthogonality within the context of discrete choice models, then that concern should be turned toward the correlations between these differences, and not the correlations between the variables in the data set.

Acknowledgment of the fact that orthogonality is not an appropriate property to the class of models estimated using discrete choice data has resulted in an active area of research examining the generation and construction of statistically more efficient experiments designed specifically for the types of models to be estimated. Unfortunately, more work in this area is required. Most of these methods require that prior information on the parameter estimates may be used to calculate the expected utilities for each of the alternatives present within the design, which in turn may be used to calculate the likely choice probabilities. Given knowledge of the attribute levels, expected parameter estimate values and choice probabilities, it becomes a straightforward exercise to calculate the AVC matrix for the design. By manipulating the attribute levels of the alternatives, for fixed parameter values, the analyst is able to minimize the elements within the AVC matrix, which in the case of the diagonals means lower standard errors and hence greater reliability in the estimates, at a fixed sample size. As such, unlike orthogonal designs, this class of designs addresses our objective of reducing the number of observations required for discrete choice studies.

Once accepted, the use of efficient designs, however, creates their own challenges. A critical issue in the use of efficient designs is what constitutes the best source for determining the priors used in generating the designs. Should the analyst conduct a pilot study, and if so, what represents a sufficient sample size to obtain the priors? Alternatively, should the analyst rely upon managers' and other practitioners' beliefs and how best should such beliefs be captured? These questions remain unanswered and are in urgent need of examination.

Further, the requirement that efficient designs be constructed such that they relate to the final model likely to be estimated as part of the study (otherwise they loose their efficiency) makes generating such designs difficult. First, the analyst may not know the final model form until after the data have been collected. Second, the rapid increase in the econometric modeling available to the analyst has left the experimental design literature well and truly behind. What is urgently required from the literature is a detailed study to determine the likely consequences of mis-specifying not only the priors but also the model form used in generating efficient SC experiments. It is imperative that orthogonal designs not be immune from such a study.

Finally, we conclude by suggesting that SC methods are now an accepted methodology of capturing individual's preferences for goods and services. Such an acceptance has largely arisen due to the methods' ability to emulate real behavior and produce empirically sensible estimates. In this paper, we have concentrated on the processes and statistical properties of SC designs but in doing so have ignored the role of the most important player in SC studies: the respondent. While there has been a steady stream of research addressing the impact upon cognitive burden of varying aspects of SC designs, there also needs to be a direct link made between respondent's ability to partake in SC studies in a meaningful manner given various dimensions of the experiment. It is our opinion that the link between these properties and other important issues, such as the information-processing strategies used by respondents in completing SC tasks, that future research should concentrate. It is only through the combining of knowledge of respondent's behavior and statistical design theory that SC methods can reach their full potential.

References

Allenby, G. M., T. S. Shively, S. Yang and M. J. Garratt (2004). A choice model for packaged goods: dealing with discrete quantities and quantity discounts. *Marketing Science* 23, 95–108.

Ben-Akiva, M. and S. R. Lerman (1985). *Discrete Choice Analysis: Theory and Application to Travel Demand.* Cambridge, USA, MIT Press.

Bliemer, M. C. J. (2006). Genetic algorithm for determining efficient design for stated choice experiments. Working Document, Delft University of Technology.

Bliemer, M. C. J. and J. M. Rose (2005a). Efficiency and sample size requirements for stated choice studies. Report ITLS-WP-05-08, Institute of Transport and Logistics Studies, University of Sydney.

Bliemer, M. C. J. and J. M. Rose (2005b). Efficient designs for alternative specific choice experiments. Report ITLS-WP-05-05, Institute of Transport and Logistics Studies, University of Sydney.

Bliemer, M. C. J., J. M. Rose and D. A. Hensher (2009). Efficient stated choice experiments allowing for estimating nested logit models. *Transportation Research Part B* 43(1), 19–35.

Bliemer, M. C. J., J. M. Rose and S. Hess (2008). Approximation of Bayesian efficiency in experimental choice designs. *Journal of Choice Modelling* 1, 98–127.

Brazell, J. D. and J. J. Louviere (1996). Helping, learning, and fatigue: an empirical investigation of length effects in conjoint choice studies. Working Paper, Department of Marketing, Sydney University.

Bunch, D. S., J. J. Louviere and D. Anderson (1994). A comparison of experimental design strategies for choice-based conjoint analysis with generic-attribute multinomial logit models. Working Paper, Graduate School of Management, University of California, Davis.

Burgess, L. and D. J. Street (2005). Optimal designs for choice experiments with asymmetric attributes. *Journal of Statistical Planning and Inference* 134, 288–301.

Carlsson, F. and P. Martinsson (2003). Design techniques for stated preference methods in health economics. *Health Economics* 12, 281–294.

Caussade, S., J. deD. Ortúzar, L. Rizzi and D. A. Hensher (2005). Assessing the influence of design dimensions on stated choice experiment estimates. *Transportation Research B* 39, 621–640.

Cherchi, E., I. Meloni and J. de D. Ortúzar (2002). Policy forecasts involving new train services: application of mixed RP/SP models with interaction effects. Presented at *XII Panamerican Conference on Transport and Traffic Engineering*, Quito, Ecuador.

Cook, R. D. and C. J. Nachtsheim (1980). A comparison of algorithms for constructing exact *D*-optimal designs. *Techometrics* 22, 315–324.

Dhar, R. and I. Simonson (2003). The effect of forced choice on choice. *Journal of Marketing Research* 40, 146–160.

DeShazo, J. R. and G. Fermo (2002). Designing choice sets for stated preference methods: the effects of complexity on choice consistency. *Journal of Environmental Economics and Management* 44, 123–143.

Ferrini, S. and R. Scarpa (2007). Designs with a-priori information for nonmarket valuation with choice-experiments: a Monte Carlo study. *Journal of Environmental Economics and Management* 53, 342–363.

Galilea, P. and J. deD. Ortúzar (2005). Valuing noise level reductions in a residential location context. *Transportation Research D* 10, 305–322.

Hahn, G. J. and S. S. Shapiro (1966). *A Catalog and Computer Program for the Design and Analysis of Orthogonal Symmetric and Asymmetric Fractional Factorial Experiments*. Schenectady, NY, General Electric Research and Development Center.

Hall, J., P. Kenny, M. King, J. Louviere, R. Viney and A. Yeoh (2002). Using stated preference discrete choice modelling to evaluate the introduction of varicella vaccination. *Health Economics* 11, 457–465.

Hensher, D. A. (2001). Measurement of the valuation of travel time savings. *Journal of Transport Economics and Policy* 35, 71–98.

Hensher, D. A. (2006). Revealing differences in behavioural response due to the dimensionality of stated choice designs: an initial assessment. *Environmental and Resource Economics* 34, 7–44.

Hensher, D. A. and J. King (2001). Parking demand and responsiveness to supply, pricing and location in the Sydney central business district. *Transportation Research A* 35, 177–196.

Hensher, D. A. and J. M. Rose (2005). Development of commuter and non-commuter mode choice models for the assessment of new public transport infrastructure projects: a case study. *Transportation Research A* 41, 428–433.

Hensher, D. A., J. M. Rose and W. H. Greene (2005). *Applied Choice Analysis: A Primer*. UK, Cambridge University Press.

Huber, J. and K. Zwerina (1996). The importance of utility balance in efficient choice designs. *Journal of Marketing Research* 33, 307–317.

Jou, R. (2001). Modelling the impact of pre-trip information on commuter departure time and route choice. *Transportation Research B* 35, 887–902.

Jovicic, G. and C. O. Hansen (2003). A passenger travel demand model for copenhagen. *Transportation Research A* 37, 333–349.

Kanninen, B. J. (2002). Optimal design for multinomial choice experiments. *Journal of Marketing Research* 39, 214–217.

Kessels, R., P. Goos and M. Vandebroek (2006). A comparison of criteria to design efficient choice experiments. *Journal of Marketing Research* 43, 409–419.

Kontoleon, A. and Y. Mitsuyasu (2003). Assessing the impacts of alternative 'opt-out' formats in choice experiment studies: consumer preferences for genetically modified content and production information in food. *Journal of Agricultural Research Policy* 5, 1–43.

Kuhfeld, W. F., R. D. Tobias and M. Garratt (1994). Efficient experimental design with marketing research applications. *Journal of Marketing Research* 21, 545–557.

Lam, S. H. and F. Xie (2002). Transit path models that use RP and SP data. *Transportation Research Record* 1779, 58–65.

Lazari, A. G. and D. A. Anderson (1994). Designs of discrete choice experiments for estimating both attribute and availability cross effects. *Journal of Marketing Research* 31, 375–383.

Louviere, J. J. and D. A. Hensher (1983). Using discrete choice models with experimental design data to forecast consumer demand for a unique cultural event. *Journal of Consumer Research* 10, 348–361.

Louviere, J. J., D. A. Hensher and J. D. Swait (2000). *Stated Choice Methods—Analysis and Application*. UK, Cambridge University Press.

Louviere, J. J. and G. Woodworth (1983). Design and analysis of simulated consumer choice or allocation experiments: an approach based on aggregated data. *Journal of Marketing Research* 20, 350–367.

McFadden, D. (1974). Conditional logit analysis of qualitative choice behaviour. In P. Zarembka (Ed.), *Frontiers of Econometrics*, New York, Academic Press, pp. 105–142.

Olsen, G. D. and J. D. Swait (1998). Nothing is important. Working Paper, Faculty of Management, University of Calgary.

Ortúzar, J. de D., A. Iacobelli and C. Valeze (2000). Estimating demand for a cycle-way network. *Transportation Research A* 34, 353–373.

Peeta, S., J. L. Ramos and R. Pasupathy (2000). Content of variable message signs and on-line driver behavior. *Transportation Research Record* 1725, 102–103.

Rose, J. M. and M. C. J. Bliemer (2005a). Constructing efficient choice experiments. Report ITLS-WP-05-07, Institute of Transport and Logistics Studies, University of Sydney.

Rose, J. M. and M. C. J. Bliemer (2005b). Sample optimality in the design of stated choice experiments. Report ITLS-WP-05-13, Institute of Transport and Logistics Studies, University of Sydney.

Rose, J. M. and M. C. J. Bliemer (2006). Designing efficient data for stated choice experiments. Paper presented at the *11th International Conference on Travel Behaviour Research*, Kyoto, Japan.

Rose, J. M., M. C. J. Bliemer, D. A. Hensher and A. C. Collins (2008). Designing efficient stated choice experiments in the presence of reference alternatives. *Transportation Research Part B* 42, 395–406.

Sándor, Z. and M. Wedel (2001). Designing conjoint choice experiments using managers' prior beliefs. *Journal of Marketing Research* 38, 430–444.

Sándor, Z. and M. Wedel (2002). Profile construction in experimental choice designs for mixed logit models. *Marketing Science* 21, 455–475.

Sándor, Z. and M. Wedel (2005). Heterogeneous conjoint choice designs. *Journal of Marketing Research* 42, 210–218.

Scarpa, R., D. Campbell and G. Hutchinson (2005a). Individual benefit estimates for rural landscape improvements: the role of sequential Bayesian design and response rationality in a choice study. Presented at *14th Annual Conference of the European Association of Environmental and Resource Economics*, Bremen.

Scarpa, R., S. Ferrini and K. G. Willis (2005b). Performance of error component models for status-quo effects in choice experiments. In R. Scarpa and A. Alberini (Eds.), *Applications of Simulation Methods in Environmental and Resource Economics*, Dordrecht, The Netherlands, Springer, pp. 247–274.

Starmer, C. (2000). Development in non-expected utility theory: the hunt for a descriptive theory of choice under risk. *Journal of Economic Literature* 18, 332–382.

Street, D. J., D. S. Bunch and B. J. Moore (2001). Optimal designs for 2^k paired comparison experiments. *Communications in Statistics, Theory, and Methods* 30, 2149–2171.

Street, D. J. and L. Burgess (2004). Optimal and near-optimal pairs for the estimation of effects in 2-level choice experiments. *Journal of Statistical Planning and Inference* 118, 185–199.

Street, D. J., L. Burgess and J. J. Louviere (2005). Quick and easy choice sets: constructing optimal and nearly optimal stated choice experiments. *International Journal of Research in Marketing* 22, 459–470.

Toner, J. P., S. D. Clark, S. M. Grant-Muller and A. S. Fowkes (1999). Anything you can do, we can do better: a provocative introduction to a new approach to stated preference design. *Proceedings of the 8th World Conference on Transport Research*, Antwerp, 3, pp. 107–120.

Train, K. (2003). *Discrete Choice Methods with Simulation*. UK, Cambridge University Press.

Van Amelsfort, D. H. and M. C. J. Bliemer (2005). Uncertainty in travel conditions related travel time and arrival time: some findings from a choice experiment. *Proceedings of the European Transport Conference (ETC)*, Strassbourg, France.

The Expanding Sphere of Travel Behaviour Research
Selected Papers from the 11th International Conference on Travel Behaviour Research

26

Modelling Interdependent Behaviour as a Sequentially Administered Stated Choice Experiment: Analysis of Variable User Charging and Agent Influence in Freight Distribution Chains ☆

Sean M. Puckett and David A. Hensher

Abstract

Many key economic decisions are made by interdependent agents, yet researchers tend to focus on the behaviour of independent decision makers. This is not necessarily due to a lack of interest in interdependent decision making, but rather may be due to difficulties in designing or administering empirical frameworks suitable to the task. This paper discusses a new method to administer group-based stated choice (SC) experiments to interdependent decision makers when other available methods are infeasible for a given application. Named *minimum information group inference* (MIGI), the method builds upon extant SC and econometric methods to allow researchers to administer SC experiments to interdependent decision makers sequentially, yielding estimates of both independent and interdependent preferences, and of group influence structures that are obtained in a cost- and time-efficient manner. This paper outlines the econometric framework and survey methodology utilised in MIGI analysis, and offers estimates of influence structures within transporter-shipper dyads under a hypothetical road user charging system. These MIGI model estimates demonstrate the potential for MIGI to yield desired behavioural estimates when extant methods are infeasible.

☆ Paper presented in the workshop on experimental approaches for the August 2006 Conference of the International Association of Travel Behaviour Research, Kyoto, Japan.

Introduction

Road freight transport commonly involves interactions between decision makers, whether within the same organisation or across organisations (e.g. between a manager of a freight transport company and the manager of a company that is paying the freight transport company to move goods). This interdependent nature of freight leads to significant obstacles when attempting to undertake an empirical study of freight stakeholders. It may be both difficult to design appropriate research frameworks for quantifying behaviour and welfare effects for interdependent stakeholders, and financially prohibitive to utilise extant techniques to carry out the empirical task.

An appropriate research framework for interdependent stakeholders must reflect the nature of transactions made within interactions amongst decision makers (i.e. the unit of analysis must incorporate interactivity). This is not impossible from a conceptual standpoint, yet it necessitates the development of research frameworks that expand either on extant frameworks that are centred on independent decision makers or are unique to the state of practice. Hence, there is a degree of burden placed upon the analyst that is greater than that within an independent decision-making setting when developing the appropriate theoretical and econometric models.

Our motivation is to develop an appropriate interdependent research framework relating to road freight centred on a desire to investigate the potential behaviour of road freight stakeholders under road pricing. Due to a lack of market data on the preferences of supply chain members under road pricing, it was our challenge to build upon existing stated preference techniques within an interdependent setting. The specific road pricing policy instrument we examined was the use of variable user charges (VUCs, i.e. distance-based charges that vary with traffic conditions), utilised in conjunction with reductions in fuel taxes. The main research goal was to gauge the preferences of road freight stakeholders across trip alternatives, each of which offered different mixes of travel time, trip quality and cost (including VUCs) relative to a revealed preference (i.e. experienced in the market) trip.

To quantify the preferences of road freight stakeholders and their clients, one appealing method is interactive agency choice experiments (IACEs), developed by Hensher (see Brewer and Hensher, 2000). IACEs involve an iterative technique by which interdependent respondents have the opportunity to amend their stated preferences within choice menus based on the preferences of other members of the group. The observed process of preference revision enables the analyst to quantify the effects of interactivity whilst maintaining the desirable empirical properties of discrete choice data obtained through stated choice (SC) experiments. Unfortunately, it is often infeasible, especially in a freight distribution chain context, to conduct a non-case-based IACE with a meaningful sample size due to the high level of resources required, including difficulties in matching agents.

Given these constraints, we investigated ways to make behavioural inferences for interdependent decision makers within discrete choice analysis. We first developed a general model, named the *inferred influence and integrative power* (IIIP) model, to accommodate a range of feasible empirical tasks (Hensher et al., 2007). Within this broad model, we selected the minimum information group inference (MIGI) method to obtain our desired behavioural estimates. MIGI enables the analyst to model the influence structures within decision-making groups, such as the freight transport buyer–seller dyads of key interest within our research application (see Hensher and Puckett, 2007; Puckett et al., 2006 for a detailed justification), by inferring the effects of interactivity based upon the stated willingness of respondents to concede towards the preferences of the other member of their respective sampled groups. Whilst we do not contend that MIGI is preferable to the direct observation of interactions amongst interdependent decision makers, we suggest that MIGI represents a means of gaining meaningful inference with respect to group decision making when other methods are infeasible.

The following section discusses the MIGI framework, which forms the centrepiece of the empirical analysis. Section 'Empirical Survey' discusses the empirical survey instrument and data collection process. The empirical evidence is given in the section 'Empirical Results', offering MIGI model results to identify the influence structures between transporters and shippers. The paper concludes with suggestions for future research into interdependent decision-making settings.

Minimum Information Group Inference

The Role of Influence in Group Decision-Making Outcomes

A significant, yet intangible factor in group decision making is the role of influence. Influence can be most parsimoniously presented as an outcome-related quantity (i.e. the extent to which an agent gets his or her way in a negotiation—see Corfman, 1991). Without varying levels of influence across members of a group, the path to agreement would likely go one of two ways: either a middle-of-the-road compromise would be struck, or a stalemate would be reached, as there would be no impetus to accommodate one agent's preferences over another. In this regard, influence may be a useful commodity; rather than being simply a force that enables one agent to get his or her way (at least to an extent) over the wishes of another, influence may play a role as an equilibrative force in negotiations.

The marketing literature offers a rich discussion of how to quantify influence in various settings. We refer the reader to Corfman and Lehmann (1987), Menasco and Curry (1989), Dellaert et al. (1998), Arora and Allenby (1999) and Aribarg et al. (2002) for an introduction to experimental approaches for measuring influence. Dosman and

Adamowicz (2003) offer an innovative method of measuring influence within groups that lends itself particularly well to stated preference techniques, which were our preferred methodology for this application. Power within relationships is measured by comparing the independent preferences of decision makers, estimated using SC data, with observed real-market joint choices of holiday activity. Dosman and Adamowicz estimate the relative power of a focal agent as the proportion of his or her independent preferences that are represented within the group outcome. Based on household resource allocation models (see Vermuelen, 2002 for a thorough review), group utility maximisation is modelled as a function of both independent utility maximisation, which enters the group choice analysis exogenously, and the power structure within the relationship.

Estimates of power are found by first analysing SC data that involved the same attributes as the holiday location decision; this analysis yields estimates of independent utility for each agent. Once these estimates are available, Dosman and Adamowicz reconcile these preferences with the revealed joint choice of holiday location with the following equation:

$$V_{jn} = \delta(\boldsymbol{s}_n)(\boldsymbol{x}_j^n \times \boldsymbol{\beta}) + (1 - \delta(\boldsymbol{s}_n))(\boldsymbol{x}_j^n \times \boldsymbol{\beta}') \quad (1)$$

where V_{jn} is the conditional indirect utility of household n for alternative j, $\boldsymbol{s}_n$ a vector of household and individual characteristics, $\boldsymbol{x}_j^n$ the vector of household attributes in j faced by n, and $\boldsymbol{\beta}$ and $\boldsymbol{\beta}'$ are the vectors of independent marginal utilities held by the two agents for the attributes in j.

Hence, the relative power of a focal agent is specified as a function of both the degree to which the preferences of the focal agent are accommodated within the group decision, and of socio-demographic characteristics. A value of δ between zero and one implies that some degree of bargaining takes place between the decision makers, whilst a value of zero or one implies that one decision maker chooses for the group independently.

Fundamentals of MIGI Analysis

MIGI models augment the standard SC format to incorporate an interactive setting within an experiment. Each experiment is administered to an individual respondent, rather than simultaneously to a group. As with IACEs, each respondent within a sampled group is given a set of identical choice sets. The resulting choice observations are coordinated across respondents, and analysed to infer the effects of interdependency among the sample of interest, without requiring direct interaction among respondents. That is, the effects of interactive agency are inferred *ex post*, by projecting group outcomes based upon the preference rankings given by respondents within an algorithm designed to coordinate these rankings.

Similarly to IACEs, MIGI experiments are framed in terms of an interactive setting, within which respondents are asked to indicate their preferences amongst the given alternatives. Specifically, MIGI experiments prompt respondents to indicate how they would rank the alternatives if they had to attempt to reach agreement with the other member(s) of the sampled group. Importantly, the ranking process includes the option of denoting an alternative as unacceptable, to avoid inferring cooperative outcomes that would not likely be observed under direct interaction. Allowing respondents to indicate that they would not concede towards other respondent(s) to a specified degree within a given choice set preserves the potential to infer non-cooperative outcomes for a sampled group.

Unlike IACEs, MIGI does not involve an iterative process in which respondents are both presented with information about the preferences of the other respondent(s) in the group and given the opportunity to revise their preferences. Rather, the influence of each respondent in a sampled group is inferred through the coordination of the preference rankings given by each respondent in a particular sampled group for a particular choice set. Influence is hypothesised to be represented within the preference rankings, in that respondents who are relatively more willing to accept less favourable alternatives are modelled as though they would be willing to offer relatively more concession within a direct interaction with the other group member(s).

Utilising the preference rankings of each respondent in a sample group, group preferences and influence structures are estimated through 'power models' described in the section 'Empirical MIGI Modelling Structure'. The power models offer a means of quantifying group influence structures consistent with the manner proposed by Dosman and Adamowicz (2003). MIGI analysis builds upon the econometric structure offered by Dosman and Adamowicz by enabling the analyst to estimate attribute-specific measures of influence.

The motivation for proposing this methodology is that the most essential information to the analyst in a group decision-making setting may simply be the degree to which respondents are willing to offer concession within a real-market- or representative sampled group. If the use of power models within a group-based choice setting are sufficient for this task, similar results may be achieved through having the agents in a sampled group responding independently as to having the group interact directly.

The process begins with gathering background information about the relationship among group agents. This information is used to establish the choice scenario as representatively as possible. Once this scenario is established, the respondents are hypothesised to act in accordance with the elements that they feel are governing the relationship.

Coordinating Independent Responses towards Projected Group Outcomes

Although MIGI choice experiments are administered to one single respondent at a time, to estimate a model of joint choice we must match respondent pairs in some meaningful way, and then coordinate the preferences of the respondents towards projected group outcomes. To accomplish this, we have developed the following four-stage sampling strategy:

Stage 1: *Initially sample respondents who have the information required to establish the choice scenario and reference alternative.* We satisfied the elements of Stage 1 by first interviewing freight transport providers. These respondents offered the required information for specifying elements of both the choice setting (i.e. offering details of a revealed preference freight trip) and the relationship between their organisations and the clients involved in the revealed preference trip.

Stage 2: *Fix the attribute levels and relationship characteristics in the subsequent SC design to correspond exactly to those in the choice sets answered by respondents from Stage 1.* To allow for a projection of group choice, we must ensure that all respondents within a sampled group are given the identical choice sets and contextual setting. Hence, the choice setting and choice sets generated through surveying the initial respondent must be stored and designated for the appropriate subsequent respondent(s).

Stage 3: *Recruit appropriate respondents to complete the sampled groups, and administer the survey to them.* To find appropriate respondents for this stage, the analyst must establish selection criteria to distinguish among candidate respondents. The ideal solution is to recruit the real-market counterpart(s) indicated by the initial respondent. However, if the analyst is unable to secure the cooperation of the real-market counterpart, the analyst must rely on the selection criteria to recruit an appropriate sampled group counterpart.

Stage 4: *Project group choice outcomes for each choice set.* MIGI utilises a series of *concession models* to project group choice outcomes based on the stated preferences of each respondent in a sampled group. Each concession model centres on the first preferences of a focal type of decision makers (e.g. shippers). The first preferences of the focal agent in a given concession model are compared with the stated willingness of other agents to accept that alternative as a group choice outcome as follows:

Step 1. For each choice set p faced by group g in a concession model centring on agent type t denote the first preference of the respondent of agent type t as J_t.

Step 2. If alternative J_t was acceptable to the respondent not of agent type t (i.e. not the focal agent), designate the group choice as J_t.

Step 3. If alternative J_t was unacceptable to the respondent not of agent type t (i.e. not the focal agent), designate the group choice as an impasse. When impasse occurs, the analyst can choose one of two decision rules for specifying the final group choice: (1) designate the group choice as the alternative most plausible to occur under impasse; or (2) designate the group choice as a non-coincident choice across decision makers, involving the first preferences of each decision maker.

By estimating concession models that focus on all agents in the group, cases of non-coincident choice projection are smoothed out parsimoniously. That is, if the available information reveals that the projected group choice is sensitive to the choice of focal respondent in Step 3, and there is no further information about the general structure of interactions within the sampled relationships, the fairest projection available is to model the interactive setting as though it is carried out multiple times with varying results.

Consider a case where two agents q and q' in group g face three alternatives A, B and C in choice set p, and where both agents find A and B to be acceptable group outcomes. If both agents prefer A to B, then the projection of group choice is trivial. However, if q prefers A to B and q' prefers B to A, no group choice agreement would be found when only using the first preferences of each agent in the analysis. Given the information about the preferences of the agents, the failure of the procedure to project a group preference appears to be a waste of choice data (and a loss of useful behavioural information on preferences). Identifying rank order beyond rank 1 is a way of taking into account some amount of likely negotiation that would have occurred if a first preference IACE approach were implemented. Under MIGI, A would be projected as the group choice in the concession model in which q' concedes towards q, whilst B would be projected as the group choice in the concession model in which q concedes to q'.

With the experimental procedure now outlined, the following section formalises the way in which relative influence is integrated into a joint agency choice model that is conditioned on the independent utility estimates of each respondent, in a manner consistent with Dosman and Adamowicz (2003). This procedure utilises the projected group choices described in Stage 4 above to calibrate relative influence based upon the independent utility estimates.

Empirical MIGI Modelling Structure

The first stage of econometric analysis in MIGI modelling involves the estimation of individual preferences for each agent type. As with standard SC experiments, individual preferences are estimated through discrete choice models, in which respondents are hypothesised to maximise utility in their designation of their preferred alternative. Once independent utility estimates have been obtained for each respondent in the sample and a range of group choices have been projected for each choice set commonly faced by each group, we may estimate group preferences using a procedure that is consistent with empirical modelling structures that are utilised for the analysis of interactive agency SC data or revealed preference data (e.g. Dosman and Adamowicz, 2003; Hensher and Knowles, 2006). That is, for a given choice set, the projected chosen alternative of the group is compared to the unchosen alternatives in order to estimate a vector of attribute-specific power measures, $\boldsymbol{\tau}_{qk}$.

To accomplish this, estimates of the individual preference parameters for respondents in a group are carried forward as constant exogenous terms into the following *power model*, and multiplied by the corresponding attribute levels for each of the K attributes in each alternative j in choice set p faced by all respondents q in group g. For each simulated group interaction gp, the alternative designated as the choice is the group choice projected using the choice coordination algorithm. The previously estimated independent marginal utilities derived by each q in each j, the vector of attribute levels in each alternative $\boldsymbol{x}_{jk}$ and any covariates of interest are the exogenous variables used to calculate the vector $\boldsymbol{\tau}_{qk}$, which, along with any alternative-specific constants are the only free parameters in the model. Whilst the most general two-agent case is offered here, this calculation can be augmented through the inclusion of interaction terms and additional respondents:

$$
\begin{aligned}
U_{11} &= \alpha_{11} + (\boldsymbol{\tau}_{qk} \times \boldsymbol{\beta}_{qk})' \boldsymbol{x}_{1k} + ((1 - \boldsymbol{\tau}_{qk})\boldsymbol{\beta}_{q'k})' \boldsymbol{x}_{1k} + \varepsilon_{11} \\
&\dots \\
U_{1J} &= \alpha_{1J} + (\boldsymbol{\tau}_{qk} \times \boldsymbol{\beta}_{qk})' \boldsymbol{x}_{1k} + ((1 - \boldsymbol{\tau}_{qk})\boldsymbol{\beta}_{q'k})' \boldsymbol{x}_{Jk} + \varepsilon_{1J} \qquad (2) \\
&\dots \\
U_{JJ} &= \alpha_{JJ} + (\boldsymbol{\tau}_{qk} \times \boldsymbol{\beta}_{qk})' \boldsymbol{x}_{Jk} + ((1 - \boldsymbol{\tau}_{qk})\boldsymbol{\beta}_{q'k})' \boldsymbol{x}_{Jk} + \varepsilon_{JJ}
\end{aligned}
$$

where U_{jm} is the estimated utility the group g derives from the joint choice of alternative j by agent q and alternative m by agent q' in simulated group interaction gp, α represents an alternative-specific utility component for the joint choice alternative, $\boldsymbol{\tau}_{qk}\boldsymbol{\beta}_{qk}$ represents a vector of the product of relative influence measures for a focal agent type and the independent marginal utility derived by q for attribute k in j, $\boldsymbol{x}_{jk}$ represents the vector of levels of each k present in j, $((1 - \boldsymbol{\tau}_{qk})\boldsymbol{\beta}_{q'k})'$ represents a vector of the product of relative influence measures for the other agent $(1-\boldsymbol{\tau}_{qk})$ and the independent marginal utility derived by q' for k in m, $\boldsymbol{x}_{mk}$ represents the vector of levels of each k present in m, and ε_{jm} represents the unobserved effects for the joint choice alternative.

The above general case includes all possible non-agreement outcomes (i.e. those where the choice of one agent does not coincide with the choice of another agent). We refer to it as the first pass group model for cooperation and non-cooperation. It may, however, be preferable behaviourally to restrict the analysis to cases of agreement, in that the ultimate group decision outcome should involve a consensus choice across group members. That is, the final decision of a group should involve either agreement across all members, or impasse. When restricting the analysis to cases of agreement, the model reduces to the subset of equation (2) in which the choices made by both decision makers are coincident (i.e. each agent chooses the same alternative *j*). We refer to this context as group equilibrium, under which one can estimate influence structures under cooperative outcomes.

As the power measures for agents q (τ_{qk}) and q' ($1-\tau_{qk}$) sum to unity for each attribute k, comparisons of influence across agent types are straightforward. If the two power measures are equal for a given attribute k (i.e. $\tau_{qk} = (1-\tau_{qk}) = 0.5$), then group choice equilibrium is not governed by a dominant agent with respect to attribute k. In other words, regardless of the power structure governing other attributes, agent types q and q' tend to reach perceptively fair compromises when bridging the gap in their preferences for k. If the power measures are significantly different across agent types (e.g. $\tau_{qk} \gg (1-\tau_{qk})$), then τ_{qk} gives a direct measure of the dominance of one agent type over the other with respect to attribute k; as τ_{qk} increases, so does the relative power held by agent type q over q' for k.

For example, the power measures may reveal that one agent type tends to get its way with regard to monetary concerns, whereas the other agent type tends to get its way with regard to concerns for levels of service. These relationships can be examined further within subsets of agent groups (by decomposition of the random parameter specification of τ_{qk}), in order to reveal deviations from the inferred behaviour at the sample level that may be present for a particular type of relationship (Figure 1).

The distribution of power measures across a given set of decision makers can be decomposed, and hence explained, by both objective and subjective descriptors of the relationship between members of groups within a sample. That is, mixed logit models can be utilised within MIGI analysis, allowing the analyst to model relative influence with respect to a given attribute as a function of characteristics within the relationship

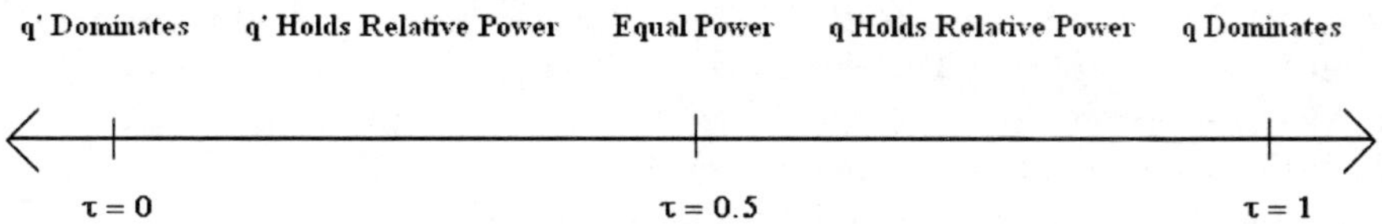

Figure 1
Interpretation of Values of τ_{qk}

between interdependent decision makers. Objective descriptors include tangible factors such as measures of market power and the length of the relationship, whilst subjective descriptors include attitudinal statements about the importance of elements within the relationship, and the effectiveness of the relationship in achieving those elements.

Empirical Survey

In 2005, we administered a MIGI survey to representatives of freight transport firms and their customers in the Sydney Metropolitan Area to gauge respondents' preferences and potential supply chain behaviour under a variable user charging system. The first step in the data collection process was administering the experiment to representatives of freight firms. Centred on a CAPI survey with a d-optimal experimental design (discussed in Puckett et al., 2007), the MIGI experiment involves three distinct procedures: (1) non-stated-choice questions intended to capture the relevant deliberation attributes and other contextual effects; (2) choice menus corresponding to an interactive (i.e. freight-contract-based) setting; and (3) questions regarding the attribute processing strategies enacted by respondents within each choice set. Once data were collected from representatives of freight transport firms, corresponding survey instruments were administered to representatives of customers of freight transport firms.

Preliminary in-depth interviews with shippers of goods, transporters and receivers of goods, suggested that the majority of decisions on distribution are made by, at most, two agents (Puckett et al., 2007). The agency set was defined as the freight transport provider carrying the goods, and the organisation paying the freight transport provider for those services. Any additional party (e.g. a recipient of the goods which does not interact with the freight transport provider) was treated as an exogenous force, setting some constraints on the interaction within the two-member group.

Capturing Relevant Deliberation Attributes and Contextual Effects

The set of relevant deliberation attributes and contextual effects were partitioned into those that describe freight activity and those that describe the experience or familiarity of respondents with the elements of the interactive setting, including the types of firms and transactions involved. The combination of these attributes and effects allows the modeller to accomplish three goals: (1) the rich description of the choice setting, enabling the respondent to make choices within a familiar and plausible setting; (2) capturing a sufficient amount of information regarding the other agent in the choice setting, such that an appropriate corresponding respondent can be located and (3) capturing a sufficient amount of information on these attributes and effects, such that analysis can be carried out with respect to key relationships of interest.

Respondents from freight firms were asked to provide a range of information that is used to set the context of the choice setting and to recruit appropriate clients of freight firms. These respondents were asked to recall the details of a series of goods movements carried out for a client of their choosing. The information about freight activity includes details on the commodities being carried, the spatial profile of the goods movement, the magnitude of freight activity for the relationship in question, and appropriate measures of performance and cost. Respondents from freight firms were also asked to provide corresponding information about the appropriate interactive setting, including a classification of the client involved and a description of the contractual basis under which the two firms interact (i.e. whether the two firms operate under rigid contracts, or whether soft, letter-of-rate-based interactions govern the relationship). A series of attitudinal questions (on a 7-point Likert scale) were included to establish the perceived importance and effectiveness of specific business relationships between transporters and shippers on 12 criteria. The interaction between 'importance' and 'effectiveness' highlights the extent to which specific issues that are important to an agent have been effective or ineffective in building a business relationship with another agent in the distribution chain.

Designing the Stated Choice Experiment

Given the interest in evaluating a range of trip attribute profiles in terms of dimensions of time and money, especially VUCs that do not currently exist in real markets, we selected a SC framework (Louviere et al., 2002) within which the transporter defined a recent reference trip in terms of its time and cost attributes (detailed below), treating fuel as a separate cost item to the VUC. A pivot design, using principles of d-optimality in experimental design, was developed to vary the levels of existing attributes around the reference levels plus to introduce a VUC based on distance travelled but with varying rates per kilometre.

The SC alternatives were kept generic to one another, representing various options of re-routeing and re-scheduling; however, these alternatives are inherently different to the reference alternative, which does not involve variable road user charges. We selected two SC alternatives, found to be sufficient to offer the desired variation in attribute bundles, giving a total of three alternatives from which to choose.

Selecting the set of attributes for the choice sets involved an iterative process of finding candidate attributes and determining how they could fit intuitively into the choice sets. Whilst in-depth interviews and literature reviews revealed myriad attributes that influence freight decision making (Puckett et al., 2006; Hensher and Puckett, 2007), we focussed on the subset of these attributes that were most likely to be directly affected by congestion-centred variable road user charges. The attributes that defining the choice sets are: free-flow travel time, slowed-down travel time, time spent waiting to unload at the final destination, likelihood of on-time arrival, fuel cost and distance-based road user charges.

The levels and ranges of the attributes were chosen to reflect a range of coping strategies under a hypothetical congestion-centred road user charging regime. The reference alternative was utilised to offer a base, around which the SC design levels were pivoted. The resulting mixes represent coping strategies including: taking the same route at the same time as in the reference alternative under new traffic conditions, costs or both; and taking alternative, previously less favourable routes, departing at alternative, previously less-favourable times, or both, with corresponding levels of traffic conditions and costs.

Congestion charging presently does not exist in Sydney, the empirical setting, hence we needed to utilise available information to set realistic levels for the distance-based charges. Literature reviews revealed that fuel taxes are currently set as a second-best instrument to recover externality costs caused by heavy goods vehicle movements. Furthermore, the literature revealed that policy makers acknowledge that distance-based or mass-distance-based road user charging may be a more efficient method of internalising externality costs. Hence, we decided to specify the empirical study in terms of potential policy adjustments, in which fuel taxes may be amended in preference of direct road user charges reflecting vehicle tonne kilometres travelled and congestion costs caused. To accomplish this, we utilised the fuel costs within the reference alternative as a base for the hypothetical road user charges. As fuel costs (and hence fuel taxes) increase with vehicle load and distance travelled, they form a useful, market-linked base for these hypothetical charges.

One potential complication is that changes in levels of service and operating costs (i.e. changes in fuel costs and new road user charges) could lead to upward or downward adjustments in the freight rate charged by the transport company. Whilst this is clearly within the set of possible strategies to be enacted by the transporter, incorporating an endogenous (at least to the freight transport provider) choice into the experimental design that could swamp the changes in costs is not a simple matter. To combat this, we developed a method to internalise this endogeneity and uncertainty, making it exogenous to the final choice. For each SC alternative involving a net change in direct operating costs (i.e. the change in fuel costs is not equal to the (negative) value of the new road user charges), respondents from freight firms were asked to indicate by how much of the net change in costs they would like to adjust their freight rate. Hence, the freight rate, which is not a design alternative, yet is clearly an important contextual effect, is allowed to vary across SC alternatives under changes in net operating costs.

The reference alternative within each choice set for respondents from freight firms is created using the details specified by the respondent for the recent freight trip. In all cases except for the variable charges, the attribute levels for each of the SC alternatives are pivoted off of the levels of the reference alternative, as detailed below. The levels are expressed as deviations from the reference level, which is the exact value specified in the corresponding non-SC questions, unless noted:

(1) *Free-flow time*: −50%, −25%, 0, +25%, +50%
(2) *Congested time*: −50%, −25%, 0, +25%, +50%
(3) *Waiting time at destination*: −50%, −25%, 0, +25%, +50%
(4) *Probability of on-time arrival*: −50%, −25%, 0, +25%, +50%, with the resulting value rounded to the nearest 5% (e.g. a reference value of 75% reduced by 50% would yield a raw figure of 37.5%, which would be rounded to 40%). If the resulting value is 100%, the value is expressed as 99%. If the reference level is >92%, the pivot base is set to 92%. If the pivot base is greater than 66% (i.e. if 1.5* the base would be greater than 100%), let the pivot base equal X, and let the difference between 99% and X equal Y. The range of attribute levels for on-time arrival when X>66% are (in percentage terms): X−Y, X−0.5*Y, X, X+0.5*Y, X+Y. This yields five equally spaced attribute levels between X−Y and 99%.
(5) *Fuel cost*: −50%, −25%, 0, +25%, +50% (representing changes in fuel taxes of −100%, −50%, 0, +50%, +100%)
(6) *Distance-based charges*: Pivot base equals 0.5*(reference fuel cost), to reflect the amount of fuel taxes paid in the reference alternative. Variations around the pivot base are: −50%, −25%, 0, +25%, +50%.

The attribute levels include positive and negative deviations from the pivot bases to both cover a range of levels of service and costs that may exist for a given trip option in the future, and to represent alternative means of routing and scheduling a given trip option at one point in time. This makes the choice data sufficiently rich to allow for inference under a range of scenarios.

The choice experiment focuses on the reaction of firms to the introduction of a VUC system in the context of trip service levels, other trip costs, freight rates and time loading and unloading goods. The survey was conducted via a computer-aided personal interview (CAPI). This was essential to seed each choice set faced by respondents with the RP information they specify within the pre-choice-set phase of the questionnaire.

Figures 2 and 3 reproduce the relevant CAPI screens related to the description of VUCs and the SC experiment in which each sampled respondent has to review the attribute packages and make a choice. To familiarise respondents with VUCs, we provided an example trip situation of travel times and costs associated with taking a particular hypothetical trip during peak hours, contrasted with the travel times and costs of taking the same trip during the off-peak (Figure 2). The same trip is then discussed under hypothetical VUCs, revealing altered travel times and costs for both the peak and off-peak options.

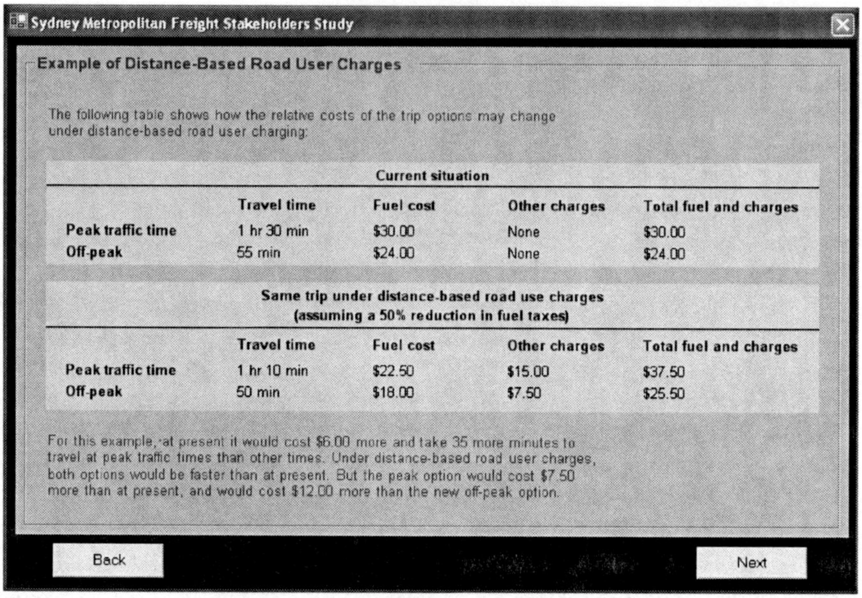

Figure 2
CAPI Screen Offering an Example of the Effects of Variable User Charges (VUCs)

Respondents were faced with four choice sets if representing a freight firm and with eight choice sets if representing a client of a freight firm. The difference is due to the relatively larger burden placed on respondents from freight firms, in that they must supply the trip- and relationship-specific details required to establish the choice setting and reference alternative. The exact four choice sets answered by a given respondent from a freight firm are given to the corresponding sampled client. The additional four choice sets faced by the sampled client use the same reference alternative as the other four choice sets.

Respondents were asked to assume that, for each of the choice sets given, the same goods need to be carried for the same client, subject to the same constraints faced when the reference trip was undertaken. Respondents are then informed that the choice sets involve three alternative methods of making the trip (Figure 3): their stated trip[1] and two SC alternatives that involve VUCs. The choice tasks are described to respondents

[1]The summary of trip details that appears when clicking on 'Trip Details' includes: the name of the client or freight firm involved, the type of truck used, the primary contents of the truck, the amount paid for delivery of the goods, kilometres travelled, the last location of loading before delivery, the total number of locations at which the truck delivered goods, the allowable lead time, the time from request of delivery to departure of truck and, in the case of questionnaires given to sampled clients, the value of the cargo. This last element is omitted from questionnaires given to representatives of freight firms, as they are not prompted for this information.

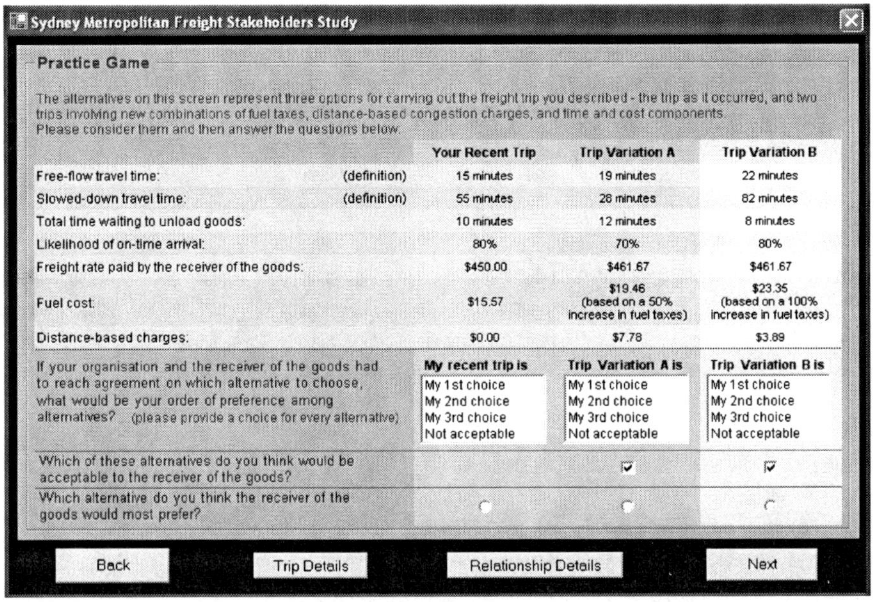

Figure 3
Main Choice Set Screen

Note: The summary of relationship details that appears when clicking on 'Relationship Details' includes: the length of the relationship between the two organisations, their contractual arrangement, the organisations that have input into the routing and scheduling of the trip, and, in the case of respondents representing freight firms, the proportion of business represented by the relationship with the client. This last element is omitted from questionnaires involving sampled clients, as they may not know this information in the marketplace.

as two steps. The first step is to indicate which alternatives would be preferable if the two organisations had to reach agreement, whilst the second step is to indicate what information mattered when making each choice.[2]

Respondents have the option to click to find a definition for the two travel time attributes, each of which includes an illustrative photograph. The specific choice task on the initial screen is, 'If your organisation and the client had to reach agreement on

[2]As the tasks are likely to involve some unfamiliar terms, respondents are given definitions of the terms 'attribute' and 'alternative,' and informed that a showcard is available for any unfamiliar terms in the choice sets. Respondents were also informed that any details relating either to the trip or to the relationship between the two firms that are not shown in the choice sets can be found by clicking on the buttons labelled 'Trip Details' and 'Relationship Details', respectively.

which alternative to choose, what would be your order of preference among alternatives?' Respondents are asked to provide a choice for every alternative. The available options for each alternative are: (Name of the alternative) is: {My 1st choice; My 2nd choice; My 3rd choice; Not acceptable}. At least one of the alternatives must be indicated as a first choice, which was not found to be restrictive, given that the reference alternative represents the status quo, which was clearly acceptable in the market. We focus herein on the first preference choice.[3]

The resulting estimation sample, after controlling for outliers and problematic respondent data,[4] includes 108 transporters and 102 shippers, yielding 1,248 observations (432 choice sets faced by transporters and 816 choice sets faced by shippers). The transporters response rate was 45% whilst that of the shippers was 72%.

Coordination of the Sample and Analysis

After a sampled respondent from a freight firm completed the survey, a client of a freight firm matching the classification offered by the respondent was recruited and given a survey involving the identical series of choice sets faced by the corresponding

[3]Two further tasks are given relating to the role of the other decision maker. Firstly, respondents are asked to indicate which of the two SC alternatives they feel would be acceptable to the other decision maker. Secondly, respondents are asked to indicate which of the three alternatives is likely to be most preferred by the other decision maker. These supplementary tasks serve two purposes: (1) reminding the respondent of the likely preferences of the other decision maker; and (2) allowing the analyst to compare the perceived preferences of the other agent type with the actual preferences of that agent type. That is, the supplementary questions both reinforce the interdependent nature of the choice setting by explicitly asking respondents to consider the preferences of the other decision maker in the choice setting, and serve as a check of the degree of accuracy with which decision makers gauge the preferences of other classes of decision makers with which they interact.

[4]Preliminary analysis revealed that the degree of heterogeneity in reference trips was sufficiently high that some outliers obscured the inferential power of the data. After careful consideration, the following observations were removed from the final sample: (a) trips based on a fuel efficiency over 101 l/100 km (or approximately twice the average fuel consumption for the larger trucks in the sample); (b) trips based on a probability of on-time arrival less than 33%; (c) round trips (or tours) of less than 50 km and (d) round trips of more than 600 km. The trips eliminated, based on low fuel efficiency, may have obscured the results due to significantly prohibitive values for fuel cost and variable charges, reflecting reference trips that are too atypical to be pooled with other trips. An alternative source of obscuring effects via low fuel efficiency may be that the implied values of fuel efficiency were inaccurate, and hence either made the trade-offs implausible to respondents or reflect an inability of the respondent to offer meaningful information on which to base the alternatives. The trips eliminated, based on low probability of on-time arrival, are likely to have obscured the results because the trips involved travel quality significantly worse than the remainder of the sample, making the pooling of these trips into the sample problematic. Similarly, extremely short or long trips may have involved trade-offs that are significantly different to the trade-offs made by respondents in the sample at large.

freight firm. The surveys responded to by representatives of clients of freight firms (i.e. shippers) include the same set of attribute processing questions after each choice set that are included in the surveys responded to by representatives of freight firms. However, the non-stated-choice questions faced by the respondent's shipper were a subset of the non-stated-choice questions faced by the respondents from freight firms. This occurred because details regarding the corresponding freight firms are taken as given (i.e. they are directly observed when a freight firm agent participates in the survey), and hence there is no need for the shipper to offer a reciprocal description of the freight firm.

The main task to satisfy when collecting data for MIGI models is to carry forward the identical choice sets faced by a given respondent q to a respondent $-q$ that fulfils the characteristics of $-q$'s agent type specified in the choice sets faced by q. The participation of a given class of respondent indicated by q is not guaranteed a priori. Hence, the analyst cannot be assured of achieving the required sample. Careful specification of eligible agent types must be coupled with a sound recruitment strategy to maximise the ability of the analyst to obtain the desired sample.

Empirical Results

There are two types of power models that can be estimated within the (MIGI) framework, representing the temporal endpoints of an interactive choice setting. The first model type, the *initial pass model*, involves the estimation of all possible joint first preferences of decision makers. The initial pass model serves to represent the prevailing power relationships that decision makers bring to the table when interacting with one another. Power is represented in the initial pass model through the parameterisation of the proportion of the independent preferences of each decision maker that would be preserved if the joint first preferences of each agent were observed for a particular choice set faced by members of a sampled group.

The second type of model that can be estimated within the MIGI framework is the *concession model*. The concession models centre on the projection of group choice equilibrium based on the stated willingness of each respondent to concede towards the first preference of his or her partner. Power is represented in the concession model through the parameterisation of the proportion of the independent preferences of each decision maker that would be preserved under the group choice equilibria projected within the analysis. Hence, the concession model serves to represent the group influence structures leading to joint choice equilibrium. However, due to the inability of the analyst to project group choice equilibrium with perfect confidence in cases where the first preferences of sampled group members coincide, we must project group choice equilibrium in a parsimonious manner. This is accomplished by estimating parallel models, each specifying one type of agent (i.e. shippers or transporters) as the focal agent towards whom the other agent may or may not offer concession. The resulting range of power measures across the concession models offers insight into the range of relative influence transporters and shippers may hold over each attribute within the choice sets.

There are nine possible outcomes in our initial pass model (i.e. transporter chooses alternative A–shipper chooses alternative A, transporter chooses A–shipper chooses alternative B, through to transporter chooses alternative C–shipper chooses alternative C), and three possible outcomes in the concession model (i.e. transporter and shipper agree to choose A, transporter and shipper agree to choose B, transporter and shipper agree to choose C). The specification of the joint choice is trivial in the initial pass model, as the first preference of each decision maker is observed directly. However, the specification of the joint choice is complex in the concession model, as transporters and shippers do not always hold coincident first preferences.

The explanatory variables in the MIGI framework are the (dis)utilities of each decision maker for each attribute in each alternative for a given choice set. The joint utility of a given outcome *ij* in which agent *q* chooses alternative *i* and agent *q*′ chooses alternative *j* is specified as:

$$U_{ij} = \alpha_{ij} + (\boldsymbol{\tau}_{qk} \times \boldsymbol{\beta}_{qk})' \boldsymbol{x}_{ik} + ((1 - \boldsymbol{\tau}_{qk})\boldsymbol{\beta}_{q'k})' \boldsymbol{x}_{jk} + \varepsilon_{ij} \tag{3}$$

Rearranging terms, this can be expressed as:

$$U_{ij} = \alpha_{ij} + \boldsymbol{\tau}_{qk}((\boldsymbol{\beta}_{qk} \times \boldsymbol{x}_{ik}) - (\boldsymbol{\beta}_{q'k} \times \boldsymbol{x}_{jk})) + \boldsymbol{\beta}_{q'k} \times \boldsymbol{x}_{jk} + \varepsilon_{ij} \tag{4}$$

where the vector of relative power measures $\boldsymbol{\tau}_q$ is equal to $(1 - \boldsymbol{\tau}_{q'})$ and is parameterised based upon the difference in utilities between transporters and shippers for each attribute for a given outcome *ij*. A power measure around 0.5 implies that transporters and shippers hold similar power with respect to the attribute, whilst a power measure significantly greater than (less than) 0.5 implies that transporters (shippers) hold relatively more power with respect to the attribute. Hence, the analysis must frame comparisons of results in reference to values of 0.5 (including tests of statistically significant difference to 0.5), in order to make meaningful inferences.

The differences in utilities were found by carrying forward the marginal utility estimates from independent preference models, taking the product of these estimates and their corresponding attribute levels in each alternative, and then subtracting the resulting (dis)utility measures for shippers from the corresponding measures for transporters in each sampled group. We refer the reader to Hensher et al. (2007) for a detailed discussion of the estimates from the independent preference models utilised within this analysis.

Initial Pass Model Results

As shown in Table 1, the initial pass model reveals that, with a mean power measure insignificantly different from 0.5, transporters and shippers tend to hold balanced power with respect to free-flow travel time. This may represent a shared preference for freight stakeholders to seek ways to minimise the amount of time trucks spend in transit. However, transporters appear to hold strong power with respect to slowed-down travel, with a mean power measure greater than unity. This is intuitive, in that, once arrival reliability is accounted for, the transporter is the agent directly impacted by congested travel conditions; hence, transporters hold a relatively stronger motivation to influence the degree to which trucks travel in congested conditions. Transporters also appear to dominate with respect to on-time arrival reliability, with a mean power measure significantly greater than 0.5. This is an important result, as both transporters and shippers value on-time reliability (see Hensher et al., 2007), yet transporters appear to be the decision makers who hold the bulk of power with respect to strategies that may achieve improved reliability.

Whilst transporters reveal a general tendency to hold power over temporal elements, the power structure is more complex with respect to monetary measures. Indeed, transporters appear to hold strong power with respect to fuel cost (mean power measure above unity), which is a direct operating cost. However, transporters and shippers appear to share power with respect to variable charges (mean power measure insignificantly different from 0.5), which would also be an operating cost borne at least initially by transporters. This may reflect an opportunity for freight stakeholders to work together to implement strategies that improve efficiency by optimising with respect to variable charges. Lastly, shippers appear to hold strong power with respect to the freight rate (mean power measure less than zero). The ultimate implication of this, in tandem with the other estimates of power, is that shippers appear to be able to negotiate the price that they want, whilst allowing transporters to operate as they see most effective. Given the apparent ability of transporters and shippers to share power with respect to free-flow travel time and variable charges, shippers may have the opportunity to work with transporters to utilise variable charges in order to achieve reduced travel times. To achieve this, however, shippers may have to absorb enough of the charges (i.e. increase the effective freight rate) to make a change in distribution strategy sufficiently favourable to transporters.

Power measures can be interpreted utilising several methods, each of which is complementary. Hence, rather than looking solely at the mean and standard deviation of the estimates, it is useful to take a more holistic approach when analysing the results. Table 2 offers a summary of the mixed logit model results.

Shippers appear to hold relative power over the predominant component of transit time, free-flow time. This power is offset through the transporter's relative power over

Table 1
Mixed Logit Model Results: Initial Pass Model

Attribute	Parameter (t-statistic relative to 0) [t-statistic relative to 0.5]
Mean power measures (>0.5 represents relative power to transporter; <0.5 represents relative power to shipper)	
Free-flow time	0.3714 (1.74) [−0.60]
Slowed-down time	1.0140 (3.20) [1.62]
Probability of on-time arrival	0.7101 (7.32) [2.16]
Fuel cost	1.1509 (4.81) [2.72]
Variable charges	0.6793 (2.59) [0.68]
Freight rate	−0.1041 (−0.76) [−4.43]
Constant (transporter chooses A, shipper chooses B)	−0.3666 (−1.62)
Constant (transporter chooses A, shipper chooses C)	−1.1059 (−3.14)
Constant (transporter chooses B, shipper chooses A)	−1.0475 (−2.89)
Constant (transporter chooses B, shipper chooses B)	−0.3758 (−1.41)
Constant (transporter chooses B, shipper chooses C)	−3.4944 (−3.85)
Constant (transporter chooses C, shipper chooses A)	−0.7014 (−2.12)
Constant (transporter chooses C, shipper chooses B)	−3.5601 (−3.78)
Constant (transporter chooses C, shipper chooses C)	−2.1050 (−3.07)
Standard deviation of random parameters	
Free-flow time	0.7429 (1.74)
Slowed-down time	2.0281 (3.20)
Probability of on-time arrival	1.4203 (7.32)
Fuel cost	2.3018 (4.81)
Variable charges	1.3585 (2.59)
Freight rate	0.2082 (0.76)
Constant (transporter chooses A, shipper chooses B)	0.7332 (1.62)
Constant (transporter chooses A, shipper chooses C)	−1.1059 (3.14)
Constant (transporter chooses B, shipper chooses A)	2.0950 (2.89)
Constant (transporter chooses B, shipper chooses B)	0.7516 (1.41)
Constant (transporter chooses B, shipper chooses C)	6.9889 (3.85)
Constant (transporter chooses C, shipper chooses A)	1.4029 (2.12)
Constant (transporter chooses C, shipper chooses B)	7.1212 (3.78)
Constant (transporter chooses C, shipper chooses C)	4.2099 (3.07)
Model fits	
Number of observations	404
LL(B)	−709.195
Adjusted pseudo-R^2	0.20

300 Halton draws used to estimate the random parameters; all random terms distributed triangularly with spread equal to twice the mean

Table 2
Descriptive Statistics of Power Measures: Initial Pass Model

	Free-flow time	Slowed-down time	On-time reliability	Variable charges	Fuel cost	Freight rate
Mean	0.3710	1.0147	0.7169	0.6795	1.1345	−0.1041
Standard deviation	0.0244	0.1169	0.1624	0.0046	0.1236	0.2863
95% range of values	0.3176–0.4288	0.7452–1.3045	0.3754–1.1263	0.3669–0.8694	0.4281–1.5693	−0.1102–0.0922
95% confidence interval	0.3232–0.4188	0.7856–1.2438	0.3986–1.0352	0.6705–0.6885	0.8922–1.3768	−0.6652–0.4570
Minimum	0.2897	0.5364	0.2744	0.3085	−0.3696	−0.1157
Maximum	0.5089	1.8033	1.3120	0.9200	1.7442	−0.0771
Values below 0.5	100%	0%	8.9%	11.6%	4.0%	100%
Values above 0.5	0%	100%	91.1%	88.4%	96.0%	0%

slowed-down time and on-time reliability. In the case of the two transit time measures, these power relationships appear to be essentially absolute for the entire sample: only one observation was found where a transporter's power measure is above 0.5 for free-flow time, whilst the entire range of observed values for slowed-down time is above 0.5. Transporters' power over on-time reliability is less absolute, with 8.9% of the estimated values indicating relative power held by the shipper.

Whilst the general distributions of these measures are important, their relative magnitudes are of critical significance, as well. The power measures for free-flow time indicate that shippers are not able to have their preferences for free-flow time accommodated entirely; at the mean, an estimated power measure of 0.371 indicates that transporters are willing to accommodate some, but not all, of shippers' preferences for free-flow time. Conversely, transporters demonstrate a tendency to get their way with respect to slowed-down time, with a mean power measure of 1.01. The results are more mixed in terms of the magnitude of the power measure for on-time reliability, with a mean value indicating that shippers are willing to accommodate some, but not all, of transporters' preferences for slowed-down time.

Differences in magnitude play a central role in the evaluation of power and transporters' costs. Although the distributions of power measures for variable charges and fuel cost indicate the same general behaviour (i.e. shippers tend to hold relative power with respect to the cost measures), the relative magnitudes of the two measures indicate unique behavioural relationships. In the case of variable charges, the estimated power measures are clustered around 0.68, indicating a tendency for the transporter to hold minor relative power with respect to the charges; the range of values shows that some shippers do hold relative power with respect to the charges (i.e. a strategic input that could benefit shippers through increased efficiency), whilst some transporters hold near-absolute power, as well. Conversely, transporters demonstrate a tendency to hold near-absolute power with respect to fuel cost (i.e. a non-strategic input, with respect to which optimisation may be best left to the agent in charge of utilising the input), with 96% of power measures above 0.5, clustered around a mean of 1.13.

Shipper Concession Model Results

In the *shipper concession model*, the model estimates the relative power held by each decision maker with respect to each attribute that would be observed if shippers offered their maximum stated willingness to concede with respect to the first preference of the transporter. If the shipper did not indicate such a willingness to concede, the joint choice is projected as the status quo (i.e. the reference alternative). Hence, the concession models frame power structures in terms of the influence that would be present when transporters and shippers jointly determined whether to move away from their current agreement (i.e. the reference alternative), towards an alternative distribution strategy involving a positive level of variable charges (i.e. one of the SC alternatives). This strategy for accommodating cases where the conceding agent is unwilling to accept the focal agent's first preference was selected because it is a behaviourally plausible representation of the consequences of impasse within a negotiation: if the parties cannot agree on how best to make a change from the status quo, then the status quo will be preserved.

Table 3 presents the findings for the shipper concession model.

Table 3
Shipper Concession Model (Mixed Logit)

Attribute	Parameter (*t*-statistic relative to 0) [*t*-statistic relative to 0.5]
Mean random power measures	
Probability of on-time arrival	1.1048 (7.54) [1.29]
Fuel cost	1.3343 (2.55) [1.59]
Variable charges	3.1636 (5.33) [4.49]
Freight rate	0.5647 (3.27) [0.37]
Fixed power measure	
Free-flow and slowed-down time	1.1703 (2.50) [1.43]
Heterogeneity around means of parameters	
Free-flow and slowed-down time*	
Number of years the companies have been working together	−0.0979 (−2.42)
Variable charges*	
Number of years the companies have been working together	−0.0325 (−1.60)
Fuel cost*	
Number of years the companies have been working together	0.0701 (2.03)
Standard deviation of random parameters	
Probability of on-time arrival	2.2095 (7.54)[a]
Fuel cost	4.7091 (3.20)[b]
Variable charges	4.6392 (2.43)[b]
Freight rate	1.1295 (3.27)[a]
Model fits	
Number of observations	404
LL(B)	−335.385
Adjusted pseudo-R^2	0.23

300 Halton draws used to estimate the random parameters; all random terms distributed triangular. Power >0.5 represents relative power to transporter; <0.5 represents relative power to shipper

[a]Denotes range constrained to be twice the mean parameter estimate

[b]Denotes range unbounded

Within the concession models, transit time measures had to be combined into one variable, in order to yield a superior model. This aggregate measure was the only explanatory variable to have all explicable heterogeneity captured through decomposition by the number of years the transporter has been carrying goods for the shipper. Both cost measures for transporters were also decomposed by this covariate, yet still display significant unobserved heterogeneity after accounting for these effects. The power measure for the transit time aggregate has a low mean value, implying a tendency for shippers to hold relative power with respect to transit time. However, as shown in Table 4, the distribution of values is split fairly evenly (51.5% in favour of shippers, 48.5% in favour of transporters). With mean power measures above unity, the concession that shippers are willing to offer implies that transporters have the potential to hold significant relative power over on-time reliability, variable charges and fuel cost, in addition to the strong potential to hold relative power with respect to the freight rate.

The relative power of shippers with respect to transit time and variable charges are shown to increase as the length of the relationship increases. That is, the longer the transporter has been carrying goods for the shipper, the more likely the shipper is to hold relative power with respect to transit time, whilst the relative power of the transporter with respect to variable charges falls. Conversely, the dominance of the transporter with respect to fuel cost increases as the length of the business relationship increases.

The model implies that transporters have the potential to hold a degree of relative power with respect to the freight rate, with a mean power measure slightly above 0.5. As shown in Table 4, almost one-fifth of shippers are estimated to hold relative power over the freight rate after conceding towards transporters. Table 4 underscores the potential for transporters to control decisions with respect to on-time reliability, variable charges and fuel cost, with 94% or greater of the estimated power measures for each attribute >0.5.

Table 4

Descriptive Statistics of Power Measures (Mixed Logit, Shipper Concession Model)

	FF/SD time	On-time reliability	Variable charges	Fuel cost	Freight rate
Mean	0.1444	1.0991	2.8233	2.0539	0.5656
Standard deviation	1.2476	0.2918	0.8543	1.0985	0.1005
95% range of values	−3.7267–1.1214	0.3518–1.7618	0.7786–3.7367	−0.0328–4.8589	0.4457–0.8798
Minimum	−8.6238	0.0372	−1.3056	−1.2558	0.3709
Maximum	1.1704	1.9294	4.0049	8.4883	0.9800
Values below 0.5	51.5%	3.7%	1.2%	5.9%	19.6%
Values above 0.5	48.5%	96.3%	98.8%	94.1%	80.4%

Transporter Concession Model

As demonstrated in Table 5, the transporter concession model identifies significant unobserved and observed sources of heterogeneity.

Specifically, power measures for the transit time aggregate and the freight rate reveal a systematic relationship with multiple covariates; after accounting for these impacts, no significant unobserved heterogeneity could be found. Conversely, although no systematic influences on the remaining power measures could be found, significant unobserved heterogeneity was found for power measures for on-time reliability, and variable charges. Due to the peculiar nature of power models (i.e. the most important reference for significance is difference to 0.5 rather than zero), significant unobserved heterogeneity is difficult to gauge for variables with mean power measures that imply total dominance by shippers (i.e. mean power measures close to zero). When combining the above model results with supplementary results for the distributions of the power measures shown in Table 6, an interesting picture emerges.

Transporters appear most resistant to yielding power over on-time reliability and variable charges when conceding towards shippers. This resistance appears absolute with respect to on-time reliability, with a mean power measure greater than unity, and with no estimated power measures below 0.5. Transporters' relative power with respect to variable charges under concession is strong, as well; the mean power measure is well above unity, with only 2.2% of estimated values below 0.5.

However, shippers appear to have the potential to hold relative power with respect to the remaining variables. This relative power is weakest for transit time, with approximately one-third of estimated power measures above 0.5; the mean power measure for transit time is close to zero, however, implying a strong potential for the shipper to hold significant power over transit time. The relative power represented by shippers in this model is strongest for fuel cost and freight rate. In the case of the former, shippers have the potential to dominate, with a mean power measure below zero and no estimated values above 0.5. In the case of the latter, the mean power measure is near zero, with only 3% of estimated power measures above 0.5.

The power measures for transit time demonstrate a positive relationship with the amount of time the decision maker for the shipper has been working with his or her organisation (i.e. the greater the experience of the decision maker for the shipper, the greater the relative power of the transporter). Transit time displays a negative relationship with the length of the relationship and the importance the transporter places on being in charge of decision making. That is, the longer the transporter has been carrying goods for the shipper, and the more important it is to the transporter to be in charge of decision making, the greater the power of the transporter with respect to transit time. The length of the relationship also has a positive relationship

Table 5

Transporter Concession Model (Mixed Logit)

Attribute	**Parameter (*t*-statistic relative to 0) [*t*-statistic relative to 0.5]**
Mean random power measures	
Probability of on-time arrival	1.1075 (10.98) [6.02]
Fuel cost	−0.1231 (−0.69) [−3.51]
Variable charges	1.6617 (4.94) [3.45]
Fixed power measure	
Free-flow and slowed-down time	0.2118 (0.53) [−0.71]
Freight rate	−0.0478 (−0.30) [−3.48]
Heterogeneity around means of parameters	
Free-flow and slowed-down time* Number of years the companies have been working together	−0.0561 (−2.34)
Free-flow and slowed-down time* Years shipper has been working with one's organisation	0.0672 (1.85)
Free-flow and slowed-down time* Importance of being in charge of decision making (transporter)	−0.0234 (−2.29)
Freight rate* Years shipper has been working with one's organisation	0.0250 (1.88)
Freight rate* Number of drivers employed by the transporter	−0.0011 (−1.64)
Standard deviation of random parameters	
Probability of on-time arrival	1.1075 (10.98)*
Fuel cost	0.1231 (0.69)*
Variable charges	3.3234 (4.94)[a]
Model fits	
Number of observations	404
LL(B)	−293.054
Adjusted pseudo-R^2	0.25

300 Halton draws used to estimate the random parameters; all random terms distributed triangular. Power >0.5 represents relative power to transporter; <0.5 represents relative power to shipper

*Denotes range constrained to be equal to the mean parameter estimate

[a]Denotes range constrained to be twice the mean parameter estimate

with power measures for the freight rate. Power measures for the freight rate are negatively related to the scale of the transporter; the more drivers utilised by the transporter, the greater the ability of the shipper to keep the freight rate relatively low.

Table 6

Descriptive Statistics of Power Measures (Mixed Logit, Transporter Concession Model)

	FF/SD time	On-time reliability	Variable charges	Fuel cost	Freight rate
Mean	0.1473	1.1087	1.6735	−0.1231	0.0275
Standard deviation	1.0131	0.0944	0.4229	0.0011	0.3339
95% range of Values	−1.9890–1.7416	0.8599–1.3114	0.5136–2.2087	−0.1256–−0.1211	−1.0728–0.5998
Minimum	−5.0044	0.8037	−2.2275	−0.1292	−0.1292
Maximum	2.3480	1.5787	2.5112	−0.1192	0.7374
Values below 0.5	65.3%	0%	2.2%	100%	97.0%
Values above 0.5	34.7%	100%	97.8%	0%	3.0%

Table 7

Summary of Power Measures across Model Specifications

	FF/SD time	On-time reliability	Variable charges	Fuel cost	Freight rate
Shipper concession					
Mean	0.1444	1.0991	2.8233	2.0539	0.5656
Standard deviation	1.2476	0.2918	0.8543	1.0985	0.1005
Transporter concession					
Mean	0.1473	1.1087	1.6735	−0.1231	0.0275
Standard deviation	1.0131	0.0944	0.4229	0.0011	0.3339

>0.5 represents relative power to transporter; <0.5 represents relative power to shipper

Comparison of Results under Shipper Concession and Transporter Concession

By comparing the results from the shipper concession and transporter concession models, one has the capability of inferring the range of power structures that are likely to be observed amongst road freight transport operators and their customers under variable charging. There are three main types of power structures that are likely to be observed at the variable level: relative power held by transporters, relative power held by shippers and balanced power (either on average, with power depending upon relationship characteristics, or overall, with a general tendency for power to be balanced). All three types of relationships are observed. Table 7 presents the mean and standard deviation of each power measure from the concession models.

This information, when considered along with the initial pass model results, paints an interesting picture. Transporters appear to hold strong power with respect to on-time reliability and variable charges, regardless of the degree of concession offered by either type of decision maker. That is, in both concession models, the estimated power measures have means greater than one and with small standard deviations relative to the mean, making transporters appear to hold strong power over supply chain decisions with respect to both determining the level of reliability offered and the degree to which variable charges are utilised. Hence, the model infers that policy measures centred on the implementation of variable charges are likely to impact urban goods movement most directly through the influence of the preferences of transporters. Despite the interdependent nature of urban goods movement, transporters appear to hold considerable relative power over the response of supply chains to a variable charging system. Likewise, the model infers that policy measures affecting the reliability of the road network are likely to involve supply chain responses based on the preferences of transporters. Still, although the relative power held by transporters appears to be dominant with respect to on-time reliability, it should be noted that shippers still may hold enough power to influence supply chain responses to variable charges. Hence, the preferences of shippers are likely to influence the group response to variable charges to at least some degree.

However, shippers' preferences are inferred to dominate the supply chain response to policy measures influencing transit time, rather than the transporter, on average, with mean power measures close to zero in both concession models. Likewise, shippers may be more likely than transporters to influence supply chain responses to factors impacting the freight rate. The shipper concession model showed that shippers are generally only willing to move towards equitable outcomes regarding the freight rate (power measures clustered around 0.5), whilst the transporter concession model showed that transporters may ultimately be willing to yield to downward price pressure from shippers (mean power measure of 0.028). Respondents indicated that both transporters and shippers are potentially willing to concede relatively more towards the preferences of their partners with respect to the freight rate and fuel cost. Ultimately, it appears that the response of supply chains with respect to these variables is relationship-specific, with no strong tendency for one type of decision maker to hold relative power.

The initial pass model is consistent with the findings above with respect to travel time, on-time reliability and the freight rate, yet differs with respect to variable charges and fuel cost. This implies that, throughout the process of interacting with one another, shippers are capable of preserving their relative power over travel time and the freight rate. Likewise, transporters appear capable of preserving their relative power over on-time reliability. However, transporters appear to have the opportunity to achieve more favourable results with respect to variable charges than one would expect based upon the estimate of relative power that transporters carry at the onset of interacting with shippers. Similarly, shippers appear to have the opportunity to achieve more favourable results with respect to fuel cost than one would expect based upon the estimate of relative power that shippers carry at the onset of interactions with transporters.

Concluding Remarks and Future Research

The method of inference in MIGI modelling has been designed as a parsimonious estimation procedure used to gain a measure of understanding for group interaction processes and outcomes. It is not designed as a perfect substitute for direct observation of group interaction processes. However, MIGI is offered as a powerful and straightforward improvement on models of group choice behaviour that model each agent within a group solely in isolation. That is, it is posited here that this modelling technique is an improvement on models that abstract from interaction, offering a positive step towards establishing a framework that allows the analyst to maximise his or her inferential power with respect to group choice behaviour, subject to constraints that restrict the analyst from directly observing interactions within sampled groups.

The MIGI methodology offered within this paper is not meant as a definitive structure by which to analyse group decision making when direct experimental interaction is infeasible. Rather, it is offered as a base off of which to develop more powerful means of estimating group decision-making behaviour and influence structures when direct experimental interaction is infeasible. Future research may demonstrate that a MIGI variant is sufficiently effective to utilise in cases where direct experimentation is feasible, yet considerably more cost- or labour-intensive than MIGI.

Of great importance is the utilisation of the behavioural results in physical transport models. One context to investigate is the influence of changes in the level of service of the traffic infrastructure and relative costs of trip options on the departure time choices of road freight stakeholders. That is, ceteris paribus, to what extent will the temporal distribution of freight trips be affected by changes in private passenger flows and distribution costs relating to candidate transport policies? The information presented offers a valuable tool for the calibration of physical transport models, by offering insight into the degree to which freight stakeholders would value the relative benefits presented by each departure time alternative (e.g. prior to the morning peak, during the morning peak, mid-day, during the evening peak, following the evening peak).

ACKNOWLEDGMENTS

Support for this research has been provided by the Australian Research Council Discovery Program under Grant DP0208269 on Freight Transport and the Environment. The comments of two referees are appreciated.

References

Aribarg, A., N. Arora and H. O. Bodur (2002). Understanding the role of preference revision and concession in group decisions. *Journal of Marketing Research* 39(August), 336–349.

Arora, N. and G. M. Allenby (1999). Measuring the influence of individual preference structures in group decision making. *Journal of Marketing Research* 37(November), 476–487.

Brewer, A. and D. A. Hensher (2000). Distributed work and travel behaviour: the dynamics of interactive agency choices between employers and employees. *Transportation* 27(1), 117–148.

Corfman, K. P. (1991). Perceptions of relative influence: formation and measurement. *Journal of Marketing Research* 28(May), 125–136.

Corfman, K. P. and D. R. Lehmann (1987). Models of cooperative group decision-making and relative influence. *Journal of Consumer Research* 14(1), 1–13.

Dellaert, B. G. C., M. Prodigalidad and J. J. Louviere (1998). Family members' projections of each other's preference and influence: a two-stage conjoint approach. *Marketing Letters* 9(2), 135–145.

Dosman, D. and W. Adamowicz (2003). Combining stated and revealed preference data to construct an empirical examination of intrahousehold bargaining. Working Paper, Department of Rural Economy, University of Alberta.

Hensher, D. A. and L. Knowles (2006). Spatial alliances of public transit operators: establishing operator preferences for area management contracts with government. In R. Macario, J. Viega and D. A. Hensher (Eds.), *Competition and Ownership of Land Passenger Transport*, Oxford, Elsevier, pp. 517–546.

Hensher, D. A. and S. M. Puckett (2007). Theoretical and conceptual frameworks for studying agent interaction and choice revelation in transportation studies. *International Journal of Transport Economics* XXXIV(1), 17–47.

Hensher, D. A., S. Puckett and J. Rose (2007). Agency decision making in freight distribution chains: revealing a parsimonious empirical strategy from alternative behavioural structures. *Transportation Research B*.

Louviere, J., R. Carson, A. Ainslie, T. Cameron, J. R. DeShazo, D. Hensher, R. Kohn and T. Marley (2002). Dissecting the random component of utility. *Marketing Letters* 13(3), 163–176.

Menasco, M. B. and D. J. Curry (1989). Utility and choice: an empirical study of wife/husband decision making. *Journal of Consumer Research* 16(1), 87–97.

Puckett, S., D. A. Hensher and H. Battellino (2006). The adjustment of supply chains to new states: a qualitative assessment of decision relationships with special reference to congestion charging. *International Journal of Transport Economics* XXXIII(3), 313–339.

Puckett, S. M., D. A. Hensher, A. Collins and J. Rose (2007). Design and development of a stated choice experiment in a two-agent setting: interactions between buyers and sellers of urban freight distribution services. *Transportation* 34(4), 429–451.

Vermuelen, F. (2002). Collective household models: principles and main results. *Journal of Economic Surveys* 16(4), 533–564.

The Expanding Sphere of Travel Behaviour Research
Selected Papers from the 11th International Conference on Travel Behaviour Research

27

Choice Models Using Matching Data

Nobuhiro Sanko and Takayuki Morikawa

Abstract

Stated preference (SP) data are frequently used for travel behaviour analysis. In terms of the response formats of the data, *choice* has dominated due to the ease of answering and the development of an appropriate modelling technique called discrete choice modelling. Even when other response formats, such as *ranking* and *rating*, are employed, the data are often converted into choice data. Since choice offers an alternative with the highest priority, researchers use the priority information for SP analysis.

One of the tasks of this study is to examine the possibility of using preference indifference information (matching data) rather than priority information. Preference indifference is a condition in which more than one alternative has the same preference level (also considered a boundary where a behaviour changes from one alternative to another) and can contain wealth of information other than priority information.

The aims of this study are to: (i) propose a methodology to utilise matching data (i.e. a response format for obtaining reliable matching data) and a corresponding model formulation in the framework of a discrete choice model; and (ii) show that the proposed methodology for the SP and revealed preference (RP)/SP models has higher estimation efficiency than models using choice data.

Matching data are obtained through a family of double-bounded (DB) response formats, which is relatively common in the contingent valuation method (CVM). Data are collected in the *Keihanshin* (Kyoto–Osaka–Kobe) and *Chukyo* (Nagoya) metropolitan areas in Japan. In both sets of data, two commuting alternatives, auto and transit, are considered.

Estimation efficiency is evaluated based on *t*-statistics and standard errors of estimates. A family of DB formulations brought higher efficiency not only for both the SP and RP/SP models but also for both the *Keihanshin* and *Chukyo* data sets. A discussion on parameter equality between the RP and SP models revealed further insights and identified topics for future research.

Introduction

Stated preference (SP) data of observations of respondents' preferences under hypothetical conditions have complementary relationships with revealed preference (RP) data of observations of their actual behaviours. SP data are widely used in the field of travel behaviour analysis. As the use of SP data spread, the world's researchers and practitioners improved their methodology, but a general consensus has yet to be achieved on either this or the SP response format for surveys, which is an element of SP experiment design. Researchers continue to use a process of trial and error.

While the *ranking* and *rating* response formats were used in the past, these days, the *choice* format is often used. The main reasons for this include: (1) the choice format allowing for simple answering, which ensures high data reliability, and (2) development of a discrete choice model that is appropriate for the analysis of choice data. Actually, the data obtained from response formats other than choice are often converted into choice data for analytical purposes. Since the alternative with the highest priority is selected in the choice format, researchers use the priority information in the SP analysis.

One task of this study is to examine the possibility of using preference indifference information rather than the priority information. Preference indifference is a condition in which more than one alternative has the same preference level (also considered a boundary where a behaviour changes from one alternative to another) and can contain wealth of information other than priority information. To obtain the preference indifference information, the *matching* format is sometimes used. In the matching format, a respondent faces two alternatives, the second of which is missing a value for one attribute. The respondent is asked to fill in the missing value so that the two alternatives are preference indifferent. Matching data are not often used for analyses, however, due to the lack of both data reliability and an appropriate modelling technique. The aims of this study are to: (i) propose a methodology for utilising matching data (i.e. a response format for obtaining reliable matching data, or preference indifference information) and a corresponding model formulation in the framework of a discrete choice model; and (ii) show that the proposed methodology for the SP and RP/SP models has higher estimation efficiency than models using choice data.

In 'SP Data Revisited' section, SP response formats used in the transport research are revisited briefly. In addition, the formats used in the field of contingent valuation method (CVM) are investigated to gain insights into obtaining matching data. In 'Matching Data in Transport Research: Methodology' section, the response formats of CVM that were explained in 'SP Data Revisited' section are applied to transport research and a corresponding model is formulated. In 'Data' section, the data used in this paper are explained, focusing on how to obtain matching information. In 'Estimates' section, the estimation results are presented and a model using matching data is compared with a model using choice data. In 'Parameter Equality Between the

RP and SP Models' section, the estimation results are further discussed from the viewpoints of parameter equality between the RP and SP models. Finally in 'Conclusions' section, the concluding remarks are presented.

SP Data Revisited

SP Data in the Field of Transport Research

SP data began to be used for transport research in the 1970s and have been widely used since then. The response formats used in transport research include ranking, choice, rating and matching. A special case of matching is transfer price (TP). In TP response format, a respondent faces two alternatives in which the price of the second alternative has a missing value. The respondent is asked to fill in the price so that the two alternatives are preference indifferent. Response formats are explained in greater detail in some books and papers, including Pearmain et al. (1991), Payne et al. (1993), Hensher (1994) and Louviere et al. (2000).

Matching or TP formats might seem appropriate for obtaining matching data, but the data obtained with these formats are of low reliability. This is one reason why matching and TP formats are not used more frequently.

SP Data in the CVM

The response formats used in the CVM are reviewed in order to find a way to more easily obtain highly reliable matching data. The CVM measures environmental resources in monetary terms. However, there is no market to trade environmental resources, and the only way to measure them is to ask the respondents. In the CVM, respondents are asked their willingness to pay (WTP) or willingness to accept compensation (WTA) when presented with hypothetical environmental improvement or hypothetical environmental deterioration. The monetary value of the environmental resources is then calculated based on their WTP or WTA.

The response formats for the CVM are summarised in Table 1. In the open-ended CVM, respondents are asked to fill in the price freely, and the open-ended CVM is similar to the matching and TP formats of SP. In the bidding game CVM, the price is determined through an auction sale. Respondents are asked to choose between paying and not paying the price written on a card, and the prices are presented from the lower price, for example. The bidding game CVM is similar to the repetition of the SP choice format. In the payment card CVM, researchers present several cards in order of prices (written on the cards) at the same time, and respondents are asked to choose one card from them. The payment card CVM is similar to the SP ranking format, since the task

Table 1
CVM Response Formats

Response format	Explanation	Characteristics	Similar SP
Open-ended CVM	Fill in the price freely	Many non-responders; appearance of too high or too low prices	Matching, TP
Bidding game CVM	Determine price as in an auction sale	Time consuming; influenced by an initial bid	Repetition of choice
Payment card CVM	Choose a price from those set by a researcher	Influenced by a range of prices	Ranking
Dichotomous choice CVM	Answer 'yes' or 'no' to the price set by a researcher	Easier to answer; less bias	Choice
DB CVM[a], 1.5B CVM[b]	The 2nd price is set by a researcher based on the response to the 1st dichotomous choice	The price set in the 1st choice influences the 2nd response; inaccurate price set in the 1st choice is covered by the price set in the 2nd choice	Repetition of choice

Source: Modified from Kuriyama (1998, p. 62).
[a]Double-bounded dichotomous choice CVM.
[b]1.5 bound CVM.

can be similar to rank the cards shown and an additional virtual card written 'will not pay'. (In the payment card format, the card chosen is a next to the card of 'will not pay'.) The dichotomous choice CVM is exactly the same as the SP choice format. The double-bounded dichotomous choice CVM (DB CVM) and 1.5 bound CVM (1.5B CVM) are special cases of the repetition of SP choice. In DB, a respondent is first asked if he/she is willing to pay price T. If he/she is willing to pay T, then he/she is asked if he/she is willing to pay price T^{U} ($>T$). If he/she is not willing to pay T, then he/she is asked if he/she is willing to pay price T^{L} ($<T$). In 1.5B, the second question is given either to those who are willing to pay price T or to those who are not willing to. Hanemann et al. (1991) compared the DB CVM with the dichotomous choice CVM, and concluded that the DB CVM was better from the viewpoints of parameter estimation efficiency, goodness of model fit and efficiency of WTP.

Matching Data in Transport Research: Methodology

Methodology for Obtaining Matching Data from Transport Research

This section proposes a methodology for obtaining matching data from transport research. The CVM response formats considered in Section 'SP Data in the CVM' are the basis of the discussion here. However, the open-ended format is not discussed due to its low reliability. The dichotomous choice format is also not examined because of the difficulty of obtaining matching information without repeating dichotomous choices. The bidding game, payment card, DB and 1.5B formats are examined. A binary situation comprising auto and transit is examined as an example. The questionnaire asks respondents their intentions to change their current transport mode. (It is possible to ask respondents their intentions to change their transport mode chosen under hypothetical conditions.)

Bidding Game Format

Those who currently use auto are asked their intentions when, for instance, the travel time by auto increases by 5, 10 and 15 minutes. The questioning is continued until they choose transit. Matching information exists between the level of service at which they chose transit and the level of service at which they last chose auto. Other attributes can be changed and those who currently use transit can be respondents.

Payment Card Format

Those who currently use auto are shown some cards at the same time. For example, the respondents are shown five cards listing auto travel times increase ('by 5 minutes', 'by 10 minutes', 'by 15 minutes', 'by 20 minutes' and 'by 25 minutes'). They are asked to choose a minimum auto travel time change so that they choose transit. Matching information exists between the chosen level of service and the level of service next to the chosen card (in favour of the auto user). Other attributes can be changed and those who currently use transit can be respondents.

Double-Bounded (DB) and 1.5 Bound (1.5B) Formats

The DB format is discussed first. Those who currently use auto are asked to choose between auto and transit when one level of service (here, e.g. auto travel time) is changed. (a) They are asked to make choices when the travel time by auto becomes longer (1st bound, or 1st B). (b) If they continue to choose auto in the 1st bound, they are asked to make choices when travel time by auto becomes much longer. (c) If they change to transit in the 1st bound, they are asked to make choices when the travel time by auto is longer than that in the current situation but shorter than that in the 1st bound ((b) and (c) are called the 2nd bound, or 2nd B). Other attributes can be changed, and those who currently use transit can be respondents. In the 1.5B format, only '(a) and (b)' or '(a) and (c)' are used. DB or 1.5B are response formats that increase the chance of obtaining matching information (preference indifference information) by repeating reliable choice formats (responses in each bound can be considered choices).

Table 2
Response Patterns of DB and 1.5B Formats

No.	RP	SP (1st bound)	SP (2nd bound)
1	Auto (*i*)	Auto (*i*)	Transit (*j*)
2	Auto (*i*)	Auto (*i*)	Auto (*i*)
3	Auto (*i*)	Transit (*j*)	Transit (*j*)
4	Auto (*i*)	Transit (*j*)	Auto (*i*)
5	Transit (*j*)	Transit (*j*)	Auto (*i*)
6	Transit (*j*)	Transit (*j*)	Transit (*j*)
7	Transit (*j*)	Auto (*i*)	Auto (*i*)
8	Transit (*j*)	Auto (*i*)	Transit (*j*)

Note: *i* and *j* will be explained in a later part of this paper.

Table 2 lists the response patterns for the DB and 1.5B formats. For the DB format, matching information lies between 1st and 2nd bounds in Nos. 1, 4, 5 and 8, and between the RP and the 2nd bound in Nos. 3 and 7. Matching information cannot be identified or bounded by two responses in Nos. 2 and 6. If matching information must be identified by SP responses, then it cannot be bounded by two responses in Nos. 3 and 7.

In 1.5B, the 2nd bounds of either Nos. 3, 4, 7 and 8 or Nos. 1, 2, 5 and 6 are omitted. Supposing that the 2nd bounds of Nos. 3, 4, 7 and 8 are not obtained, then matching information lies between the 1st and 2nd bounds in Nos. 1 and 5, and between the RP and the 1st bound in Nos. 3, 4, 7 and 8. Matching information cannot be identified or bounded by two responses in Nos. 2 and 6. If matching information must be identified by SP responses, then it cannot be bounded by two responses in Nos. 3, 4, 7 and 8.

In all response formats discussed in Sections 'Bidding Game Format', 'Payment Card Format' and 'Double-Bounded (DB) and 1.5 Bound (1.5B) Formats', matching information can be identified by being bounded by two responses. Therefore, these types of response formats are generically called a family of DB formats.

Methodology of Model Formulation

In this section, data obtained through the response formats discussed in section 'Methodology for Obtaining Matching Data from Transport Research' (bidding game, payment card, DB and 1.5B formats) are modelled in the discrete choice modelling framework. The model is developed based on the DB format with two alternatives, *i* and *j*. Data obtained through other formats can be modelled in the same manner, and these models are generically called a family of DB models.

Let U_{in}^{B} be a utility of individual n choosing alternative i in bound B (B: 1st or 2nd) and assume that U_{in}^{B} can be divided into the systematic component, V_{in}^{B}, and the error component, ε_{in}^{B}.

$$U_{in}^{B} = V_{in}^{B} + \varepsilon_{in}^{B} \tag{1}$$

Suppose also that ε_{in}^{1st} and ε_{in}^{2nd} are the same as ε_{in}^{SP} (ε_{jn}^{1st} and ε_{jn}^{2nd} are the same as ε_{jn}^{SP}), and that $\varepsilon_{jn}^{SP} - \varepsilon_{in}^{SP}$ is standard normally distributed. The model is formulated as follows using data from the 1st and 2nd bounds (Equations (2a) and (2b) are described in greater detail, and (2c) and (2d) are derived similarly.):

Nos. 1 and 8 in Table 2

$$\begin{aligned}
\text{prob}(d_n^{1st} = i, d_n^{2nd} = j) &= \text{prob}(U_{in}^{1st} > U_{jn}^{1st} \text{ and } U_{in}^{2nd} < U_{jn}^{2nd}) \\
&= \text{prob}(V_{in}^{1st} - V_{jn}^{1st} > \varepsilon_{jn}^{SP} - \varepsilon_{in}^{SP} \text{ and } V_{in}^{2nd} - V_{jn}^{2nd} < \varepsilon_{jn}^{SP} - \varepsilon_{in}^{SP}) \\
&= \text{prob}(V_{in}^{1st} - V_{jn}^{1st} > \varepsilon_{jn}^{SP} - \varepsilon_{in}^{SP} > V_{in}^{2nd} - V_{jn}^{2nd}) \\
&= \Phi(V_{in}^{1st} - V_{jn}^{1st}) - \Phi(V_{in}^{2nd} - V_{jn}^{2nd})
\end{aligned} \tag{2a}$$

Nos. 2 and 7 in Table 2

$$\begin{aligned}
\text{prob}(d_n^{1st} = i, d_n^{2nd} = i) &= \text{prob}(U_{in}^{1st} > U_{jn}^{1st} \text{ and } U_{in}^{2nd} > U_{jn}^{2nd}) \\
&= \text{prob}(U_{in}^{1st} > U_{jn}^{1st} | U_{in}^{2nd} > U_{jn}^{2nd})\text{prob}(U_{in}^{2nd} > U_{jn}^{2nd}) \\
&= \text{prob}(U_{in}^{2nd} > U_{jn}^{2nd}) \text{ (since prob}(U_{in}^{1st} > U_{jn}^{1st} | U_{in}^{2nd} > U_{jn}^{2nd}) = 1) \\
&= \text{prob}(V_{in}^{2nd} - V_{jn}^{2nd} > \varepsilon_{jn}^{SP} - \varepsilon_{in}^{SP}) \\
&= \Phi(V_{in}^{2nd} - V_{jn}^{2nd})
\end{aligned} \tag{2b}$$

Nos. 3 and 6 in Table 2

$$\text{prob}(d_n^{1st} = j, d_n^{2nd} = j) = 1 - \Phi(V_{in}^{2nd} - V_{jn}^{2nd}) \tag{2c}$$

Nos. 4 and 5 in Table 2

$$\text{prob}(d_n^{1st} = j, d_n^{2nd} = i) = \Phi(V_{in}^{2nd} - V_{jn}^{2nd}) - \Phi(V_{in}^{1st} - V_{jn}^{1st}) \tag{2d}$$

where $\Phi(\cdot)$ is standardised cumulative normal distribution and d_n^{B} is response in bound B of individual n.

The formulation above uses matching information obtained through the responses of the 1st and 2nd bounds. If matching information is obtained not only through the responses of the 1st and 2nd bounds but also through the RP responses, then another assumption is required. The assumption is that ε'^{RP}_{in} is the same as ε^{SP}_{in} (ε'^{RP}_{jn} is the same as ε^{SP}_{jn}). ($\varepsilon'^{RP}_{\bullet n}$ is an error component of the SP model, where all attributes' levels are exactly the same as those of the RP model.) It may be difficult to accept this assumption that the RP and SP error components are the same. If, however, we assume that the error component of SP models, where all attributes' levels are exactly the same as those of RP models, is the same as the error component of 1st and 2nd bound SPs, then this assumption can be justified. Here $\varepsilon'^{RP}_{\bullet n}$ is used instead of $\varepsilon^{RP}_{\bullet n}$, since the authors consider not the error component of the RP model but that of the SP model, where all attributes' levels are the same as those of the RP model. In Sections 'Estimates' and 'Parameter Equality Between the RP and SP Models', the RP model uses the data in the RP column in Table 2. The SP model uses the data in the SP (1st Bound) and SP (2nd Bound) columns when $\varepsilon'^{RP}_{\bullet n}$ and $\varepsilon^{SP}_{\bullet n}$ are assumed to be different; the SP model uses the data in the RP, SP (1st Bound) and SP (2nd Bound) columns when $\varepsilon'^{RP}_{\bullet n}$ and $\varepsilon^{SP}_{\bullet n}$ are assumed to be the same.

Data

Keihanshin (Kyoto–Osaka–Kobe) Data

The data in the *Keihanshin* metropolitan area were from a supplementary survey of a person trip survey (household travel survey) taken in 2000. Besides the RP mode choice for commuting, the SP survey is based on the 1.5B format in a commuting situation in which both auto and transit are available. An example of a 1.5B question is shown in Figure 1. Only those who do not change their commuting mode in the 1st bound participate in the 2nd bound.

Question 1
If the cost of parking near your working place were to increase, would you commute by bus or rail? (For those who do not pay for parking, assume that you must pay the fee shown below.)
(I) If the cost of parking increased by 1,000 JPY per month,
1. you would commute by bus or rail → go to **Question 2**
2. you would commute by auto → go to **Question 1** (II)
(II) If the cost of parking increased by 3,000 JPY per month,
1. you would commute by bus or rail
2. you would commute by auto

Figure 1
An Example of 1.5B SP in the *Keihanshin* Survey
Note: This is a question for those who currently commute by auto.

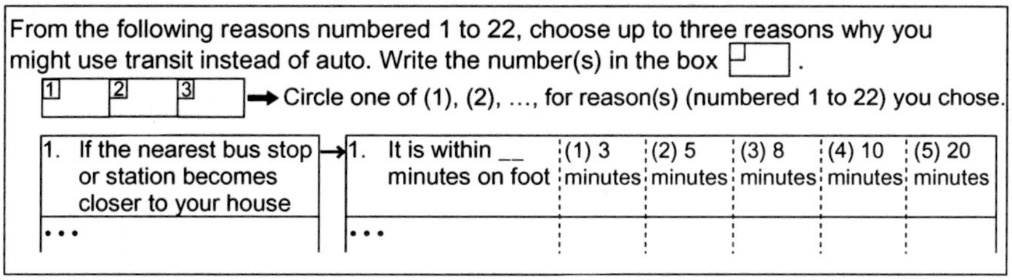

Figure 2

An Example of a Payment Card SP in the *Chukyo* Survey

Note: This is a question for those who commute by auto and who answered 'yes' to the question, 'if the level of public transit service increased or the level of auto service decreased, would you stop commuting by auto and start commuting by public transit?'

Chukyo (Nagoya) Data

The data in the *Chukyo* metropolitan area were collected in cooperation with a small-scale person trip survey (household travel survey) in 1997. In addition to the RP mode choice for commuting, the SP survey is based on a payment card format for commuting situations in which auto and transit are available. An example of a payment card SP is shown in Figure 2.

Those who commute by auto but have an intention to use the bus or rail instead of auto are asked for their reasons (up to three reasons, e.g. 'if the nearest bus stop or station becomes closer to your house') and the necessary change in the level of service (e.g. choose one from within '3 minutes', '5 minutes', '8 minutes', '10 minutes' and '20 minutes' on foot from your house) so that they choose the bus or rail. Note that those who currently commute by bus or rail do not have SP questions.

ESTIMATES[1]

Keihanshin Data

Estimates from the *Keihanshin* data are shown in columns RP and (i)–(iii) of Table 3. For the RP model, the binary probit model is adopted. The details of the RP/SP model and the RP/SP model with serial correlation can be found in the Appendix.

[1]In the RP/SP model with serial correlation estimated in Sections 'Estimates' and 'Parameter Equality Between the RP and SP Models', a standard normal distribution is assumed for λ (see Appendix 'RP/SP Combined Estimation Method with Serial Correlation'). A standard normal distribution is assumed for $v_{jn}^{SP} - v_{in}^{SP}$ (see Appendix 'RP/SP Combined Estimation Method with Serial Correlation').

Table 3
Estimates from the *Keihanshin* Data

Variable name[a]	RP	(i) 1st bound choice			(ii) 1st and 2nd bound choice			(iii) 1.5B			(iv) 1.5B difference		
		SP	RP/SP	RP/SPsc[b]	SP	RP/SP	RP/SPsc[b]	SP	RP/SP	RP/SPsc[b]	SP	RP/SP	RP/SPsc[b]
RP constant (T)	1.04	–	0.984	1.42	–	0.914	1.23	–	0.305	0.755	–	0.836	1.21
	(3.85)		(3.70)	(3.91)		(3.62)	(3.77)		(1.65)	(2.97)		(3.26)	(3.36)
SP constant (T)	–	−1.46	−7.59	−1.04	−1.18	−4.34	−0.184	−1.09	−0.961	0.624	−1.54	−4.63	−0.667
		(−6.77)	(−1.91)	(−1.36)	(−8.25)	(−3.39)	(−0.43)	(−6.52)	(−4.08)	(2.18)	(−8.16)	(−3.62)	(−1.24)
Scale parameter μ	–	–	0.147	0.468	–	0.206	0.545	–	0.592	1.86	–	0.242	0.617
			(2.29)	(4.03)		(4.34)	(5.58)		(8.21)	(7.16)		(4.58)	(5.63)
Inertia (T)*	–	2.79	18.0	5.53	2.36	11.0	3.30	1.79	2.73	0.796	3.14	12.5	4.63
		(15.30)	(2.14)	(3.59)	(20.44)	(4.03)	(4.40)	(12.98)	(6.80)	(2.99)	(16.53)	(4.10)	(4.44)
Travel time [hours]	−2.05	−0.323	−2.04	−2.82	−0.252	−1.91	−2.42	−0.757	−1.55	−2.11	−0.465	−2.04	−2.99
	0.304	*0.203*	*0.299*	*0.423*	*0.135*	*0.292*	*0.381*	*0.122*	*0.221*	*0.285*	*0.166*	*0.291*	*0.413*
	(−6.75)	(−1.59)	(−6.82)	(−6.68)	(−1.87)	(−6.53)	(−6.37)	(−6.20)	(−7.02)	(−7.41)	(−2.80)	(−7.02)	(−7.24)
Cost (out of pocket) [1,000JPY]	−1.27	−0.180	−1.27	−1.84	−0.425	−1.43	−2.19	−1.22	−1.85	−2.84	−0.492	−1.45	−1.97
	0.240	*0.147*	*0.235*	*0.316*	*0.0977*	*0.222*	*0.295*	*0.0899*	*0.201*	*0.242*	*0.113*	*0.223*	*0.313*
	(−5.30)	(−1.23)	(−5.40)	(−5.83)	(−4.35)	(−6.43)	(−7.44)	(−13.59)	(−9.22)	(−11.73)	(−4.35)	(−6.52)	(−6.30)
Civil servant (T)	0.652	0.304	0.718	0.862	0.178	0.676	0.769	0.232	0.492	0.579	0.105	0.607	0.731
	(2.01)	(1.48)	(2.27)	(1.97)	(1.17)	(2.27)	(1.84)	(1.32)	(2.25)	(1.50)	(0.58)	(2.04)	(1.71)
Seat (T)**	0.354	0.147	0.382	0.515	0.0091	0.294	0.402	0.166	0.297	0.278	0.0710	0.344	0.539
	(1.90)	(1.20)	(2.09)	(2.12)	(0.11)	(1.73)	(1.96)	(2.17)	(2.70)	(2.39)	(0.69)	(2.01)	(2.20)
Under the age of 30 (T)	0.482	0.391	0.589	0.746	0.163	0.526	0.621	0.324	0.550	0.692	0.151	0.507	0.608
	(1.78)	(2.28)	(2.22)	(2.04)	(1.30)	(2.15)	(1.87)	(2.19)	(3.02)	(2.20)	(0.99)	(2.05)	(1.76)

Transfers more than twice (T)	−2.22	−0.0083	−2.08	−2.28	−0.382	−2.18	−2.36	−0.450	−1.31	−2.08	−0.715	−2.55	−3.44
	(−2.02)	(−0.02)	(−1.98)	(−1.65)	(−1.07)	(−2.37)	(−2.19)	(−1.12)	(−2.31)	(−2.21)	(−1.65)	(−2.72)	(−2.70)
Car with free use (A)***	1.51	−0.170	1.43	2.02	−0.0645	1.30	1.73	0.0303	0.888	1.58	−0.125	1.30	1.83
	(6.92)	(−0.95)	(6.46)	(6.59)	(−0.54)	(5.94)	(5.87)	(0.21)	(5.01)	(5.95)	(−0.86)	(5.93)	(6.10)
Free parking (A)****	0.347	0.233	0.410	0.640	0.220	0.464	0.739	0.0974	0.204	0.358	0.102	0.331	0.402
	(1.75)	(1.89)	(2.12)	(2.69)	(2.59)	(2.61)	(3.90)	(0.96)	(1.62)	(3.59)	(0.86)	(1.81)	(1.54)
D Travel time [hours]	–	–	–	–	–	–	–	–	–	–	−1.97	−8.39	−5.22
											(−6.68)	(−4.06)	(−5.18)
D Cost (out of pocket) [1,000JPY]	–	–	–	–	–	–	–	–	–	–	−4.83	−19.4	−11.4
											(−14.36)	(−4.57)	(−6.27)
D Seat (T)**	–	–	–	–	–	–	–	–	–	–	0.284	1.15	0.668
											(1.75)	(1.64)	(1.82)
D Free parking (A)****	–	–	–	–	–	–	–	–	–	–	0.488	1.87	0.936
											(3.44)	(2.85)	(3.05)
Scale parameter θ (T)	–	–	–	2.72	–	–	1.93	–	–	1.77	–	–	2.29
				(5.25)			(8.09)			(11.61)			(7.28)
N	326	960	1,286	326	1,737	2,063	326	948	1,274	326	948	1,274	326
Initial log-likelihood	−225.97	−665.42	−891.39	−891.39	−1,204.00	−1,429.96	−1,429.96	–	–	–	–	–	–
Final log-likelihood	−124.07	−268.29	−398.50	−376.65	−587.19	−721.37	−687.80	−684.24	−826.48	−711.61	−550.52	−682.43	−647.51
Adjusted ρ^2	0.411	0.582	0.539	0.563	0.504	0.487	0.510	–	–	–	–	–	–

Note: *t*-statistics are in parentheses. Standard errors are in italics. Standard errors other than travel time and cost are omitted. Column (iv) is mentioned in Section 'Parameter Equality Between the RP and SP Models'.
'D' before a variable name indicates a difference term.
[a]T and A in parentheses are alternative specific to transit and auto, respectively. Variable names without such indications are generic.
[b]RP/SP models with serial correlation.
*1: RP choice result is transit; 0: otherwise.
**Seat always or sometimes available.
***Having a car that is free to use.
****Free parking near your working place.

The estimates from the SP models are: (i) Only 1st bound responses are modelled as choice data using binary probit (Table 3, column (i)); (ii) The 1st and 2nd bound responses are modelled as independent choice data using binary probit (Table 3, column (ii)); and (iii) The 1st and 2nd bound responses are modelled as 1.5B data using the formulation discussed in Section 'Methodology of Model Formulation' (Table 3, column (iii)).

Accordingly, it is possible to compare the analyses of the 1st and 2nd bound SPs as 1.5B (Table 3, column (iii)) and as independent choices (Table 3, column (ii)). 1st bound SP model (Table 3, column (i)) is also modelled for comparison purposes, since assuming that 1st and 2nd bound SPs are independent can be questionable.

Concerning (iii), the 1.5B model, when all values of the explanatory variables are the same in the 1st and 2nd bounds (all values of explanatory variables may be the same even when the attributes' levels are not the same), the 1.5B model cannot be estimated due to the zero probability in equation (2). This is why some portions of the data used in models (i) and (ii) are not included in model (iii). Additionally, in the 1.5B model, only matching information bounded by 1st and 2nd bound SPs is used, since the authors assume that the error component of the SPs, where all attributes' levels are exactly the same as those of the RP, and the error components of the 1st and 2nd bound SPs are not always the same.

An estimate from the RP model (binary probit model) is shown in the first column of Table 3. Travel time and cost estimates are significant.

Estimates from the SP models were also investigated. For comparison purposes, the same set of explanatory variables is employed in models (i)–(iii). Socio-economic characteristics such as 'civil servant', 'under the age of 30' and 'car with free use' have the same values in both the RP and the SP conditions. One of the variables for level of service, 'transfers more than twice', also has the same values in both the RP and the SP conditions. The investigation is focused more on travel time, cost, seat and free parking for which the attribute levels in the SP can differ from those in the RP.

In the 1st bound choice model (Table 3, column (i)), the travel time and cost estimates are not significant. *t*-statistics indicate that seat dummy and free parking dummy estimates are less significant and a little bit more significant, respectively, compared to those for the RP model. In the 1st and 2nd bound choice model (Table 3, column (ii)) the cost estimate is significant, but the travel time estimate is insignificant. *t*-statistics indicate that, compared to the RP model, the seat dummy estimate is less significant, while the free parking dummy estimate is significant.

In the 1.5B SP model (Table 3, column (iii)), the travel time and cost estimates are significant. *t*-statistics indicate that the seat dummy estimate is significant, while the free parking dummy estimate is less significant compared to RP model. Comparing the three SP models, the *t*-statistics for travel time and cost are best in the 1.5B model (excluding the relatively less significant dummy variables). Standard errors for travel time and cost are smallest in the 1.5B model, suggesting the highest estimation efficiency. The constant and inertia terms are the closest to zero in the 1.5B model, suggesting that the other variables provide a better explanation.

Estimates from the RP/SP models were also examined. Four explanatory variables, the attribute levels of which can differ in the RP and SP conditions, are discussed here. In the 1st bound RP/SP model (Table 3, column (i)), the *t*-statistics for the four estimates are slightly better than those in the RP model, but in reality, the *t*-statistics are almost the same as those in the RP model. In the 1st and 2nd bound RP/SP model (Table 3, column (ii)), the *t*-statistics for cost and free parking dummy are better than they are in the RP model, but the *t*-statistics for travel time and seat dummy are worse.

In the 1.5B RP/SP model (Table 3, column (iii)), the *t*-statistic for cost is greatly improved over that in the RP model, while the *t*-statistics of travel time and seat dummy are improved. However, the *t*-statistic for free parking is worse than that in the RP model. Comparing the three models, the *t*-statistics for travel time and cost are best in the 1.5B model (excluding the relatively less significant dummy variables). Standard errors for travel time and cost are smallest in the 1.5B model, suggesting the highest estimation efficiency. The constant and inertia terms are closest to zero in the 1.5B model, suggesting that the other variables provide a better explanation. The scale parameter estimate is closest to unity in the 1.5B model, suggesting that the RP and 1.5B SP models differ little.

In addition, the RP/SP models with serial correlation were estimated (Table 3, columns (i)–(iii)). Some of the advantages of the RP/SP model with serial correlation over RP/SP model without serial correlation are summarised below:

- The SP constant and inertia terms are closer to zero, suggesting that the other variables provide a better explanation.
- The scale parameter is larger, suggesting that the variance of error component in the SP model is smaller. Particularly for the 1.5B model, the variance of error component is smaller in the SP than that in the RP, suggesting that the SP data are more reliable.

Parameter equality between the RP and SP models was also statistically tested. The results are summarised in Table 4. In the 1st bound choice model, parameter equality is not rejected at a 5% level of significance. On the other hand, both in the 1st and 2nd bound choice model and in the 1.5B model, parameter equality is rejected at a 1% level of significance. This means the assumption that the parameters for the RP and SP models are the same is not justified statistically.

Table 4
χ^2 Test of the Parameter Equality (*Keihanshin*)

Model	χ^2 value
1st bound choice model (Table 3, column (i))	12.27
1st and 2nd bound choice model (Table 3, column (ii))	20.22
1.5B model (Table 3, column (iii))	36.33

Note: Seven degrees of freedom, $\chi^2_7(.05) = 14.07$, $\chi^2_7(.01) = 18.48$.

Chukyo Data

Estimates from the *Chukyo* data are shown in columns RP and (i)–(iii) of Table 5. For the RP model, the binary probit model is adopted. Details of the RP/SP model and the RP/SP model with serial correlation can be found in the Appendix. In this section, for the purposes of explanation, the card chosen is called 1st bound and the next card chosen (in the auto user's favour) is called 2nd bound.

The estimates from the SP models are: (i) only 1st bound responses are modelled as choice data using binary probit (Table 5, column (i)); (ii) the responses of the 1st and 2nd bounds are modelled as independent choice data using binary probit (Table 5, column (ii)); and (iii) the responses of the 1st and 2nd bounds are modelled as payment card data using the formulation discussed in Section 'Methodology of Model Formulation' (Table 5, column (iii)).

Accordingly, it is possible to compare the analyses of the 1st and 2nd bound SPs as payment card (Table 5, column (iii)) and as independent choices (Table 5, column (ii)). The 1st bound SP model (Table 5, column (i)) is also modelled for comparison purposes, since assuming that the 1st and 2nd bound SPs are independent can be questionable.

Concerning (iii), the payment card model, when all values of the explanatory variables are the same in the 1st and 2nd bounds, the payment card model cannot be used for estimations due to the zero probability in equation (2). This is why the data excluded in model (iii) are also excluded in models (i) and (ii). Moreover, the payment card model uses matching information bounded not only by 1st and 2nd bound SPs but also by the RP and the SP. For example, in Figure 2, if a respondent chooses reason number 1 and '(5) 20 minutes', then the matching information, which lies between '20 minutes' and the current access time (usually greater than 20 minutes), is used. If it is equal or greater than the current access time, or if this causes zero probability, then the data are excluded from the analysis. In the *Chukyo* payment card data, levels of services are listed in rows, and the authors assume that the respondents have a current level of service explicitly in their mind when choosing one of the listed level of services. In other

Table 5
Estimates from the *Chukyo* Data

Variable name[a]	RP	(i) 1st bound choice			(ii) 1st and 2nd bound choice			(iii) Payment card			(iv) Payment card difference		
		SP	RP/SP	RP/SPsc[b]	SP	RP/SP	RP/SPsc[b]	SP	RP/SP	RP/SPsc[b]	SP	RP/SP	RP/SPsc[b]
RP constant (A)	−0.403	–	–	–	–	−0.401	−0.564	–	−0.286	−0.406	–	−0.424	−0.601
	(−3.85)					(−3.85)	(−3.86)		(−3.11)	(−3.12)		(−4.16)	(−4.20)
SP constant (A)	–	–	−0.553	−0.826	−0.155	−1.03	−1.51	−1.39	−0.954	−1.41	0.643	1.35	1.21
			(−6.70)	(−6.82)	(−1.29)	(−2.93)	(−3.07)	(−13.01)	(−9.10)	(−9.41)	(3.65)	(2.08)	(2.05)
Scale parameter μ	–	–	–	–	–	0.184	0.137	–	1.45	3.20	–	0.513	0.436
						(2.30)	(2.35)		(9.29)	(7.05)		(3.97)	(5.09)
Travel time [hours]	−1.78	–	−1.27	−2.15	−0.393	−1.79	−2.52	−1.98	−1.44	−1.77	−0.740	−1.72	−2.45
	0.209		*0.144*	*0.208*	*0.179*	*0.207*	*0.290*	*0.135*	*0.158*	*0.215*	*0.204*	*0.221*	*0.287*
	(−8.49)		(−8.81)	(−10.33)	(−2.20)	(−8.63)	(−8.67)	(−14.67)	(−9.15)	(−8.20)	(−3.64)	(−7.76)	(−8.53)
Cost [1,000JPY]	−0.292	–	0.134	0.0417	0.134	−0.281	−0.398	−1.40	−0.754	−1.42	−0.240	−0.300	−0.432
	0.144		*0.128*	*0.187*	*0.259*	*0.143*	*0.201*	*0.160*	*0.0892*	*0.142*	*0.298*	*0.141*	*0.196*
	(−2.03)		(1.05)	(0.22)	(0.52)	(−1.97)	(−1.98)	(−8.74)	(−8.45)	(−10.01)	(−0.80)	(−2.12)	(−2.21)
Head [hours] (T)	−1.36	–	−0.903	−1.50	−0.268	−1.36	−1.90	−1.26	−0.975	−1.17	−0.979	−1.47	−2.06
	0.289		*0.198*	*0.290*	*0.271*	*0.284*	*0.397*	*0.194*	*0.154*	*0.188*	*0.310*	*0.261*	*0.376*
	(−4.72)		(−4.57)	(−5.17)	(−0.99)	(−4.78)	(−4.79)	(−6.49)	(−6.32)	(−6.21)	(−3.16)	(−5.64)	(−5.48)
D Travel time [hours]	–	–	–	–	–	–	–	–	–	–	−5.13	−10.0	−12.5
											(−16.71)	(−4.12)	(−5.81)
D Cost [1,000JPY]	–	–	–	–	–	–	–	–	–	–	−12.3	−24.0	−29.7
											(−11.93)	(−3.80)	(−5.15)
D Head [hours] (T)	–	–	–	–	–	–	–	–	–	–	−4.12	−7.78	−9.47
											(−9.02)	(−3.95)	(−5.01)
Scale parameter θ (A)	–	–	–	–	–	–	0.254	–	–	0.896	–	–	0.813
							(0.51)			(9.42)			(2.45)
N	679	–	887	679	416	1,095	679	208	887	679	208	887	679
Initial log-likelihood	−470.65	–	−614.82	−614.82	−288.35	−759.00	−759.00	–	–	–	–	–	–
Final log-likelihood	−335.79	–	−548.65	−557.04	−285.27	−621.34	−623.10	−684.33	−1,029.00	−936.03	−420.60	−756.95	−757.81
Adjusted ρ^2	0.278	–	0.101	0.0875	−0.00320	0.173	0.170	–	–	–	–	–	–

Note: *t*-statistics are in parentheses. Standard errors are in italics. Standard errors other than travel time, cost and head are omitted. Column (iv) is mentioned in Section 'Parameter Equality Between the RP and SP Models'.

'D' before a variable name indicates a difference term.

[a]T and A in parentheses are alternative specific to transit and auto, respectively. Variable names without such an indication are generic.

[b]RP/SP models with serial correlation.

words, the authors assume that the error component of the SP, where all attributes' levels are exactly the same as those of the RP, and the error components of the 1st and 2nd bound SPs are the same.

An estimate from the RP model (binary probit model) is shown in the first column of Table 5. Estimates for travel time, cost and head are significant.

Estimates from the SP models were also investigated. For comparison purposes, the same set of explanatory variables is employed in models (i)–(iii). In the 1st bound choice model (Table 5, column (i)), the SP model is not estimated since, in *Chukyo* survey, only current auto users were respondents. That is, all SP responses in the 1st bound are transit. In the 1st and 2nd bound choice model (Table 5, column (ii)), the *t*-statistics for three of the level of service variables are less significant than those in the RP model. The cost estimate has a positive sign.

In the payment card SP model (Table 5, column (iii)), the *t*-statistics of three of the level of service variables are better than those in the RP model. Compared with those of the 1st and 2nd bound choice model (Table 5, column (ii)), the *t*-statistics of three of the estimates are better in the payment card model (Table 5, column (iii)). Standard errors for three of the estimates are smaller in the payment card model, suggesting higher estimation efficiency. The inertia term is not included in the model because all of the respondents currently use auto.

Estimates for the RP/SP models were also examined. In the 1st bound RP/SP model (Table 5, column (i)), the *t*-statistics for travel time and head are almost the same as those in the RP model. However, the cost estimate has a positive sign. Note that the scale parameter cannot be estimated and only one constant (the same constant term in the RP and SP models) is estimated.[2] In the 1st and 2nd bound RP/SP model (Table 5, column (ii)), the *t*-statistics of the three level of service estimates are almost the same as those in the RP model. The scale parameter indicates that the variance of error component is larger in the SP model.

In the payment card RP/SP model (Table 5, column (iii)), the *t*-statistics of three of the level of service variables are better than those in the RP model. The scale parameter

[2](1) Since the SP constant includes an SP-specific bias, different constants are estimated in the RP and SP models. (2) The scale parameter μ is introduced in order to share parameters between the RP and SP models after adjusting the variances of error components in the two models. (3) The scale parameter θ is introduced, since there is no guarantee that the scale of the systematic component of error terms is the same in both the RP and SP models (discussed in the RP/SP models with serial correlation). However, none of the above is considered in this model. Since in the *Chukyo* data, the 1st bound choice result is transit only, and the SP-specific constant and scale parameters are not reasonably estimated. For comparison purposes only, a simplified model is estimated here.

Table 6
χ^2 Test of the Parameter Equality (*Chukyo*)

Model	χ^2 value
1st bound choice model (Table 5, column (i))	–
1st and 2nd bound choice model (Table 5, column (ii))	0.57
Payment card model (Table 5, column (iii))	17.76

Note: Two degrees of freedom, $\chi_2^2(.01) = 9.21$, $\chi_2^2(.50) = 1.39$.

indicates a smaller variance of error component in the SP model. Comparing the three models, the *t*-statistics of three of the level of service variables are best in the payment card model. The standard errors for these three variables are smaller than in the 1st and 2nd bound choice model, in which the sign for cost is correctly estimated, suggesting better estimation efficiency in the payment card model.

The RP/SP models with serial correlation were also estimated (Table 5, columns (i)–(iii)). The scale parameter in the payment card model is larger, suggesting that the SP is more reliable.

Parameter equality between the RP and SP models was tested statistically. The results are summarised in Table 6. In the 1st and 2nd bound choice model, parameter equality is not rejected at a 50% level of significance. In the payment card model, however, parameter equality is rejected at a 1% level of significance. This means the assumption that parameters of RP and SP models are the same is not justified statistically.

Parameter Equality Between the RP and SP Models

Parameter Equality Between the RP and SP Models, and a Proposal

In the previous section, the DB model family offered the highest estimation efficiency not only for both the SP and RP/SP models but also for both the *Keihanshin* and *Chukyo* data. However, in the DB model family, parameter equality between the RP and SP models is not justified statistically. Two interpretations of this are explored in this section.

In the first interpretation, each individual is assumed to follow the same behavioural norm in both the RP and SP models, and a rejection of the parameter equality can be caused by SP response bias. Since only one level of service has changed from the RP condition, exaggerated responses can be observed and can include a bias.

In the second and a little bit more interesting interpretation, each individual is assumed to have a different behavioural norm in the RP and SP models. Parameters obtained from the RP model describe the behaviour of the whole sample and express average relationships among the variables. However, a specific individual has a chance to change his/her behavioural norm in accordance with a change in the level of service, especially when only one level of service is changed. In other words, when an individual faces a situation where only one level of service is changed, he/she can be forced to restructure his/her preference, leading to a change in preference. In marketing science, Mizuno and Katahira (2003) pointed out that a consumer can be forced to reconstruct his/her preference, which can be a cause of a preference change, when the product space expands thanks to a technological innovation.

Parameter equality is evaluated by statistical testing and the equality is rejected in a DB model family. However, many studies justify the equality when more than one level of service is changed from the current situation. In our data, where only one level of service is changed from the current situation, the equality is justified in the 1st bound choice model in the *Keihanshin* data and in the 1st and 2nd bound choice model in the *Chukyo* data. The justification for parameter equality can depend on the response formats and/or model formulation.

In any case, parameter equality is rejected in the DB model family and the problem remains. To solve this problem, the authors present the following proposal:

The formulation of the traditional RP/SP model is shown in equations (3a)–(3c).

RP model

$$U_{in}^{\mathrm{RP}} = \boldsymbol{\beta}'\mathbf{x}_{in}^{\mathrm{RP}} + \boldsymbol{\alpha}'\mathbf{w}_{in}^{\mathrm{RP}} + \varepsilon_{in}^{\mathrm{RP}} \tag{3a}$$

SP model

$$U_{in}^{\mathrm{SP}} = \boldsymbol{\beta}'\mathbf{x}_{in}^{\mathrm{SP}} + \boldsymbol{\gamma}'\mathbf{z}_{in}^{\mathrm{SP}} + \varepsilon_{in}^{\mathrm{SP}} \tag{3b}$$

Ratio of variances between the RP and SP error components

$$\mathrm{Var}(\varepsilon_{in}^{\mathrm{RP}}) = \mu^2 \mathrm{Var}(\varepsilon_{in}^{\mathrm{SP}}), \quad \forall i, n \tag{3c}$$

where U_{in}^{M} is total utility of individual n choosing alternative i in M model; $\varepsilon_{in}^{\mathrm{M}}$ is error component of total utility U_{in}^{M}; $\mathbf{x}_{in}^{\mathrm{M}}$, $\mathbf{w}_{in}^{\mathrm{M}}$ and $\mathbf{z}_{in}^{\mathrm{M}}$ are explanatory variable vectors of deterministic utility of individual n choosing alternative i in M model; $\boldsymbol{\alpha}$, $\boldsymbol{\beta}$ and γ are unknown parameter vectors to be estimated; M is type of model; μ is scale parameter explaining the differences of variances between the RP and SP error components.

By introducing scale parameter, parameter $\boldsymbol{\beta}$ can be shared between the RP and SP models. On the other hand, the model proposed here separates the explanatory variables for the SP into an 'RP part' and a 'difference from the RP part'. Here, equation (3b) is replaced by (3d).[3]

SP model

$$U_{in}^{SP} = \boldsymbol{\beta}'\mathbf{x}_{in}^{RP} + \tilde{\boldsymbol{\beta}}'(\mathbf{x}_{in}^{SP} - \mathbf{x}_{in}^{RP}) + \boldsymbol{\gamma}'\mathbf{z}_{in}^{SP} + \varepsilon_{in}^{SP} \quad (3d)$$

In the SP model, the SP attributes are divided into an 'RP part' ($\mathbf{x}_{in}^{RP}$) and a 'difference from the RP part' ($\mathbf{x}_{in}^{SP} - \mathbf{x}_{in}^{RP}$), and parameters $\boldsymbol{\beta}$ and $\tilde{\boldsymbol{\beta}}$ are set, respectively. The parameter vector for the 'RP part', that is, $\boldsymbol{\beta}$, is shared between the two models. The parameter vector for the 'difference part', ($\mathbf{x}_{in}^{SP} - \mathbf{x}_{in}^{RP}$), that is, $\tilde{\boldsymbol{\beta}}$, is interpreted as a respondent's contingent preference when facing the SP question in the first interpretation, and as a respondent's preference change when facing the SP question in the second interpretation. The parameter vector for the 'RP part' ($\mathbf{x}_{in}^{RP}$), that is, $\boldsymbol{\beta}$, is interpreted as a respondent's core preference in the first interpretation and as an average preference of the whole sample in the second interpretation.

When the proposed model is used for forecasting, parameter vector $\boldsymbol{\beta}$, which explains the core preference, must be used in the first interpretation. In the second interpretation, only parameter vector $\boldsymbol{\beta}$, which explains the average preference of the whole sample, can be used. Preference change can occur when a level of service is changed, but not all respondents can make this preference change. However, when all respondents make a preference change, parameter vectors $\boldsymbol{\beta}$ and $\tilde{\boldsymbol{\beta}}$ must be used. This must be concluded through empirical analysis using, for example, panel data.

Keihanshin Data

The estimates from the *Keihanshin* data are shown in Table 3 (column (iv)). The chi-squared value is 15.70 and the parameter equality is not rejected at a 2.5% level of significance, suggesting that parameter equality is justified statistically.

An estimate for the SP model was also examined. The estimated parameters for the 'difference from the RP part' are generally larger (about 4–10 times the size of the 'RP part') and more significant than the 'RP part'. The *t*-statistics of the 'RP part's' cost and time parameters are better compared to the 1st bound choice model (Table 3, column (i)) and 1st and 2nd bound choice model (Table 3, column (ii)). Compared to the 1st bound choice model (Table 3, column (i)), in which the parameter equality is

[3]Instead of (3d), the following formulation is available. The same estimate of $\boldsymbol{\beta}$ as in equation (3d) is obtained, but the different estimate of $\tilde{\boldsymbol{\beta}}$ from equation (3d) is obtained.

$$U_{in}^{SP} = \boldsymbol{\beta}'\mathbf{x}_{in}^{SP} + \tilde{\boldsymbol{\beta}}'(\mathbf{x}_{in}^{SP} - \mathbf{x}_{in}^{RP}) + \boldsymbol{\gamma}'\mathbf{z}_{in}^{SP} + \varepsilon_{in}^{SP}$$

justified, the standard errors of 'RP part' are smaller in the time and cost variables, suggesting higher estimation efficiency in the proposed model.

An estimate for the RP/SP model was also examined. Compared with Table 3 columns (i) and (ii), the *t*-statistics for the time and cost estimates in the 'RP part' are improved. Compared with the 1st bound RP/SP model (Table 3, column (i)), in which the parameter equality is justified, standard errors of the 'RP part' are smaller in the time and cost estimates, suggesting that the proposed model has higher estimation efficiency.

An estimate of the RP/SP model with serial correlation was also examined. Compared with the RP/SP model in Table 3 column (iv), the SP constant and inertia terms are again approaching zero. The scale parameter is approaching unity, suggesting reliable SP data. The usefulness of the models with serial correlation is also suggested.

Chukyo Data

Estimates for the *Chukyo* data are shown in Table 5 column (iv). The chi-squared value is 1.13 and parameter equality is not rejected at a 50% level of significance, suggesting that parameter equality is statistically justified.

An estimate for the SP model was also examined. Parameters for the 'difference from the RP part' are generally larger (about 4–50 times the size of the 'RP part') and more significant than the 'RP part'. The *t*-statistics for the 'RP part' are better than those for the 1st and 2nd bound choice model (Table 5, column (ii)) and the signs are as expected.

An estimate for the RP/SP model was also examined. The *t*-statistics are generally improved (or at least remain at the same level) and the signs are as expected, as compared to the 1st bound choice model and the 1st and 2nd bound choice model (Table 5, columns (i) and (ii)). Compared to model (ii), where the parameter signs are reasonable, standard errors for three variables generally remain almost at the same level or are improved, suggesting higher or at least the same level of estimation efficiency.

An estimate for the RP/SP model with serial correlation was also examined. Compared with the RP/SP model in Table 5 column (iv), the SP constant is smaller, suggesting that the other variables provide a better explanation. Generally speaking, the merits of models with serial correlation are limited in the *Chukyo* data as compared to the *Keihanshin* data. A possible reason for this is that only those who commute by auto have the maximum three SP data, leading to a relatively smaller number of SP responses per respondent.

Summary

In 'Estimates' section, parameter equality is not justified in a DB family formulation. A model dividing the SP variable into the 'RP part' and the 'difference from the RP part' is developed, and parameter equality in the 'RP part' is justified. The formulation described in 'Parameter Equality Between the RP and SP Models' section indicates at least the same or a higher level of estimation efficiency compared to the traditional choice model, suggesting the usefulness of the proposed formulation. In Section 'Parameter Equality Between the RP and SP Models, and a Proposal', this formulation is interpreted from two points of view: SP bias and preference change.

In the transport behaviour model demonstrated in this paper, the validity of parameter equality can be statistically tested. In some cases of CVM, however, RP data is impossible to obtain, and validation cannot be performed. This is why detailed guidelines for CVM surveys have been developed (e.g. Arrow et al., 1993). For transport behaviour modelling, however, few comprehensive guidelines for SP surveys exist. The required level of SP survey design again must be discussed.

Conclusions

The results of this study can be summarised as follows:

- The value of obtaining matching data is discussed.
- Matching data are effectively obtained in a DB family format and formulated within the framework of discrete choice modelling.
- Estimates using the *Keihanshin* and *Chukyo* data show increased estimation efficiency in a DB model family formulation.
- In a DB family formulation, however, parameter equality between the RP and SP models is not justified statistically. A model formulation in which the SP level of service is divided into the 'RP part' and the 'difference from the RP part' is proposed. The estimates justify parameter equality in the 'RP part' in the proposed model. The proposed model has at least the same or a higher level of estimation efficiency compared to traditional choice formulation. The proposed model is interpreted from two aspects: SP bias and preference change. (Another specification, noted in footnote 3, is available.)

Topics for further research:

- When applying a DB family format to actual demand forecasting, compare the results with the results of the traditional choice format.
- Matching information can be obtained through the payment card, bidding game, DB and 1.5B formats, and a better response format for obtaining matching information must be discussed.

- The validity of dividing the SP level of service into the 'RP part' and the 'difference from the RP part' must be verified through more case studies.

ACKNOWLEDGMENTS

The authors wish to thank the anonymous reviewers for their comments. The authors also wish to thank Dr. Toshiyuki Yamamoto (Associate Professor at Nagoya University, Japan) for his valuable comments. This study is supported by Grant-in-Aid for Scientific Research from the Ministry of Education, Culture, Sports, Science and Technology (Japan).

APPENDIX

RP/SP Combined Estimation Method

The RP/SP combined estimation method is briefly explained. More details are available from Morikawa (1989), Ben-Akiva and Morikawa (1990) and others. The RP and SP models and the ratio of variances between the RP and SP error components are formulated in equations (A1)–(A3).

RP model

$$U_{in}^{RP} = \boldsymbol{\beta}'\mathbf{x}_{in}^{RP} + \boldsymbol{\alpha}'\mathbf{w}_{in}^{RP} + \varepsilon_{in}^{RP},\ i = 1,\dots,I_n^{RP} \text{ and } n = 1,\dots,N^{RP} \tag{A1}$$

SP model

$$U_{in}^{SP} = \boldsymbol{\beta}'\mathbf{x}_{in}^{SP} + \boldsymbol{\gamma}'\mathbf{z}_{in}^{SP} + \varepsilon_{in}^{SP},\ i = 1,\dots,I_n^{SP} \text{ and } n = 1,\dots,N^{SP} \tag{A2}$$

Ratio of variances between the RP and SP error components

$$\mathrm{Var}(\varepsilon_{in}^{RP}) = \mu^2 \mathrm{Var}(\varepsilon_{in}^{SP}), \quad \forall i, n \tag{A3}$$

where U_{in}^{M} is total utility of individual n choosing alternative i in M model; ε_{in}^{M} is the error component of total utility U_{in}^{M}; $\mathbf{x}_{in}^{M}$ and $\mathbf{w}_{in}^{M}$ and $\mathbf{z}_{in}^{M}$ are explanatory variable vectors of deterministic component of individual n choosing alternative i in M model; $\boldsymbol{\alpha}$, $\boldsymbol{\beta}$ and $\boldsymbol{\gamma}$ are unknown parameter vectors to be estimated; I_n^{M} is number of alternatives included in the choice set of individual n in M model; N^{M} is number of observations in M model; M is type of model; μ is scale parameter explaining the ratio of variances between the RP and SP error components.

RP/SP Combined Estimation Method With Serial Correlation

The RP/SP combined estimation method with serial correlation is briefly explained. More details are available from Morikawa (1994) and others. Unlike Section 'RP/SP Combined Estimation Method', the error components are divided into λ (which is common to each individual and alternative) and ν (which is truly random for researchers (white noise)), and λ is shared between the two models.

$$\varepsilon_{in}^{RP} = \lambda_{in} + \nu_{in}^{RP} \tag{A4}$$

$$\varepsilon_{in}^{SP} = \theta_i \lambda_{in} + v_{in}^{SP} \tag{A5}$$

The RP and SP models and the ratio of variances between the RP and SP error components are then formulated using equations (A6)–(A8).

RP model

$$U_{in}^{RP} = \boldsymbol{\beta}'\mathbf{x}_{in}^{RP} + \boldsymbol{\alpha}'\mathbf{w}_{in}^{RP} + \lambda_{in} + v_{in}^{RP},\ i = 1, \ldots, I_n^{RP} \text{ and } n = 1, \ldots, N^{RP} \tag{A6}$$

SP model

$$U_{in}^{SP} = \boldsymbol{\beta}'\mathbf{x}_{in}^{SP} + \boldsymbol{\gamma}'\mathbf{z}_{in}^{SP} + \theta_i \lambda_{in} + v_{in}^{SP},\ i = 1, \ldots, I_n^{SP} \text{ and } n = 1, \ldots, N^{SP} \tag{A7}$$

Ratio of variances between the RP and SP error components

$$\mathrm{Var}(v_{in}^{RP}) = \mu^2 \mathrm{Var}(v_{in}^{SP}), \quad \forall i, n \tag{A8}$$

where λ_{in} is systematic component of error component of individual n choosing alternative i; v_{in}^{M} is white noise of error component; θ_i is unknown parameter to be estimated.

References

Arrow, K., R. Solow, P. R. Portney, E. E. Leamer, R. Radner and H. Schuman (1993). Report of NOAA Panel on Contingent Valuation. 58 Federal Register 4601 (January 15).

Ben-Akiva, M. and T. Morikawa (1990). Estimation of travel demand models from multiple data sources. In M. Koshi (Ed.), *Transportation and Traffic Theory (Proceedings of the 11th International Symposium on Transportation and Traffic Theory)*. New York, Elsevier, pp. 461–476.

Hanemann, M., J. Loomis and B. Kanninen (1991). Statistical efficiency of double-bounded dichotomous choice contingent valuation. *American Journal of Agricultural Economics* 73(4), 1255–1263.

Hensher, D. A. (1994). Stated preference analysis of travel choices: the state of practice. *Transportation* 21, 107–133.

Kuriyama, K. (1998). *Environmental Value and Valuation Method.* Sapporo, Hokkaido University Press, (in Japanese).

Louviere, J. J., D. A. Hensher and J. D. Swait (2000). *Stated Choice Methods: Analysis and Application.* Cambridge, Cambridge University Press.

Mizuno, M. and H. Katahira (2003). Expanding product space and the formation of preferential decision rules: an evolutionary process of products and consumer preferences. *Journal of Marketing Science* 11(1–2), 1–21 (in Japanese).

Morikawa, T. (1989). Incorporating stated preference data in travel demand analysis. Ph.D. dissertation, Department of Civil Engineering, MIT.

Morikawa, T. (1994). Correcting state dependence and serial correlation in the RP/SP combined estimation method. *Transportation* 21, 153–165.

Payne, J., J. Bettman and E. Johnson (1993). *The Adaptive Decision Maker*. Cambridge, Cambridge University Press.

Pearmain, D., J. Swanson, E. Kroes and M. Bradley (1991). *Stated Preference Technique: A Guide to Practice*, 2nd edn. Richmond, Steer Davies Gleave and Hague Consulting Group.

4.2 Behavioral Change

The Expanding Sphere of Travel Behaviour Research
Selected Papers from the 11th International Conference on Travel Behaviour Research

28

Location Choice vis-à-vis Transportation: The Case of Recent Home Buyers

Michelle Bina and Kara M. Kockelman

Abstract

An understanding of residential location choice is fundamental to behavioral models of land use, and, ultimately, travel demand. A survey of over 900 recent home buyers in the Austin, Texas area offers valuable data on movers and their reasons for moving. This paper examines priorities in location selections and tradeoffs from such decisions. Predictive models of home value, amenities, and location offer important insights, while controlling for many key factors. For example, while younger persons are more likely to rate bus service as important, they are still more likely to choose larger lots and shopping access over transit access, relative to other recent movers. Men, Caucasians, and persons of low income tend to be less concerned with accessibility during the housing search process. And homes near significant shopping centers or within walking distance of any level of commercial center tend to fetch lower values than those enjoying a more moderate level of shopping opportunity, everything else constant. These results and many others are explained by various model specifications.

Introduction

Households are a key actor in the theater of urban development. An understanding of when, why, and where households move is critical to predicting future land use and activity patterns. In order to generate a model of residential location choice, a survey of recent home buyers was undertaken in the Austin, Texas region. It asked such households about their primary reasons for moving, the importance of various housing and location attributes, their current location, current travel patterns, and basic demographic information. This paper positions this study within the context of prior work, describes the data collected, and investigates determinants of residential location (in terms of the reasons for moving, priorities during the housing search process, and tradeoffs in choosing a home). It provides the empirical results of a variety of regression models, including logit models of neighborhood choice.

Before continuing, it should be noted that 33.8% of all US households do not own their dwelling unit. For this reason, a similar survey was conducted of apartment dwellers, and those results are discussed in a related paper (Bina et al., 2006). This paper focuses on the decisions of those residing in homes that were recently purchased.

Literature Review and Motivation

Economic tradition presents the household location problem in a utility-maximization framework, where choices depend on tradeoffs between transport costs and housing prices (Guiliano, 1989). After Alonso's (1964) monocentric city model, Mills (1967) and Muth (1969) pioneered improvements to this model. By using simplified models of spatial equilibrium, these authors argue that when people move farther from their center of employment, greater commuting costs are counterbalanced by less expenditure on land (Wheaton, 1977).

Rosen (1974) first presented a theoretical work on hedonic prices that has motivated the specification of models to relate housing market prices to housing characteristics (see, e.g., Huh and Kwak, 1997; Orford, 2000; Kockelman, 1997). However, it has been argued that hedonic price functions offer limited information regarding consumer behavior (Ellickson, 1981). A need to reflect taste variations among households has motivated the application of logit models in the analysis of housing markets (Cho, 1997). Numerous studies have applied logit models to predict individual households' housing choices (see, e.g., Weisbrod et al., 1980; Friedman, 1981; Ben-Akiva and Bowman, 1998; Sermons and Seredich, 2001; Zondag and Pieters, 2005). Studies most relevant to this work have incorporated transport choices and access variables into the analysis.

Since accessibility is a major theme in residential location theories, transportation has been a focus of many models. Such studies provide a good basis for understanding the connections between transportation and land use; however, empirical data suggest that many models are incomplete (Guiliano, 1989). Two key weaknesses in many older studies include the assumption of a single-worker household and a monocentric city (in which all jobs occupy the central business district) (Guiliano, 1989). Feminization of the workforce, decentralization, and emergence of multiple centers have invalidated these assumptions (Waddell, 1996). Efforts to model dual-worker households include the studies by Waddell (1996), Sermons and Koppelman (2001), Freedman and Kern (1997), and Van Ommeren et al. (1998), among others.

Also, many studies are based on the data of static households (see, e.g., Bhat and Guo, 2004). Surveys of recent movers can provide better data since such respondents can more accurately recall their motivations for moving and their characteristics at the time of the move. Since household location models seek to identify the determinants of the move decision, and the chosen dwelling unit (including location), there is strong interest in identifying priorities during the search process, and in quantifying all tradeoffs.

In response to such interests, the US Census Bureau recently published a couple Current Population Reports that contain only cross-tabulations and raw distributions of the 2000 Current Population Survey (CPS) and the 2003 Annual Social and Economic Supplement to the CPS (Schachter, 2001, 2004). Over 30 years ago, Murie (1974) explored the reasons for movement and related them to a few housing and demographic variables, but his data are outdated and only summarize basic variable statistics. Filion et al. (1999) addressed households' reasons for moving, but they did not relate these reasons to home qualities or demographic characteristics.

Another important aspect of residential location choice involves the housing search process, particularly the importance of factors that determine household priorities. Filion et al. (1999) and the 2004 American Community Survey (ACS) present some raw statistics regarding the importance associated with accessibility and other, neighborhood variables. However, these studies do not explore explanatory variables that affect these relationships (such as income and household size).

Moves are costly with sellers generally paying 6% (of their home's value) in realtor fees and 1–2% in other transaction costs, and all parties typically paying several hundreds to thousands of dollars for transport of furnishings. Households often tradeoff a variety of location, size, quality, and cost factors when selecting a home and location. Weisbrod et al. (1980) examined several tradeoffs between transportation and other factors for recent movers in Minnesota, but did not quantify these or tie them to demographic characteristics. The 2004 ACS explored a few tradeoffs, but provided only raw statistics (Belden Russonello and Stewart Research and Communications, 2004). This paper links residential location and home attributes to key demographic variables. It relies on logit and ordered probit models of location choice, attribute preferences, and other survey responses.

Data Acquisition

A *survey of realtors* in the Austin area was distributed in order to ascertain key characteristics and preferences of Austin movers. Three realtors were interviewed at length, and then a formal survey instrument was developed and distributed to 229 Austin-area realtors via electronic mail (including 3 reminder emails). This effort yielded just 22 complete responses but provided valuable insights and impressions. Its results were used to aid in the development of the more extensive *recent-mover survey*, which was designed as a mail-out mail-back (self-completion) survey. It was offered in both English and Spanish, following pilot tests and several rounds of formal revision. The resulting instrument contains 37 questions and can be found at www.ce.utexas.edu/prof/kockelman/public_html/RecentMoverSurvey.htm.

USA Data Inc. assembled the sample frame of all home buyers identified (via deed purchases and transfers) in the Austin three-county region between March 2004 and February 2005 (a one-year period). A random sample of just over half of these identified households was purchased, providing 4,451 names and addresses.[1] Surveys were mailed to all 4,451 households in April 2005, and reminders were sent four to six weeks later. (The survey was available on-line as well, for those who had not retained the original survey form, but the reminders generated only 100 or so responses, so no further reminders were sent.) By the end of June 2005, the sample had yielded 965 complete surveys, or a 21.7% response rate. Since some households were not appropriate for the sample frame,[2] the actual response rate, from the pool of qualified survey recipients, is believed to be somewhat higher (25% or higher). Those who did respond but did not qualify as "recent movers" were not included in the final data set used for analysis. The following section describes this final data set and results of the analysis.

Data Sets and Basic Results

The *results of the realtors' surveys* were used to familiarize the researchers with movers' preferences. For example, realtors indicated that movers are believed to have a hierarchy of needs when searching for a home and neighborhood. The survey asked realtors to rank which housing and location characteristics are most important to their clients. The results revealed that realtors view housing cost/value, quality of schools, and distance to work as most important to their clients. Among all the attributes believed to be relevant (and thus offered on the survey form), pedestrian/bike accommodations and transit access were felt to be least important. Yet realtors

[1]USA's Data Inc.'s sampling frame included 8,541 households. This is believed to be appropriate for the 1.2-million population region, since Texas A&M Real Estate Center (2005) estimated that 9,613 homes were sold in the Austin Metropolitan Statistical Area (MSA) five-county region (Bastrop, Caldwell, Hays, Travis, and Williamson counties) between June 2004 and May 2005.

[2]In this analysis, "neighborhood" refers to the region's traffic serial zones (TSZs) as defined by the Capital Area Metropolitan Planning Organization (CAMPO). CAMPO provided information on zonal areas, population, number of households, and employment. Zonal housing characteristics came from the 2000 Census of Population census tract data sets, which were apportioned uniformly to the smaller TSZs, on the basis of area.

generally indicated that attributes of both housing and location were *equally important* to their clients. These results are consistent with NCHRP Report 423A's (Parsons Brinkerhoff Quade & Douglas, Inc., 1999) summary of influential factors, which states that housing cost comes first (and is related to home size, quality, type, and age), and accessibility comes second.

Another survey question asked realtors to rate various categories of clients according to their concerns for access. The results suggest that central-city dwellers are most concerned, which may be because downtown dwellers are more exposed to congestion and/or because they have chosen their central locations in order to maximize access. Lower income clients and renters also were identified as classes of people most concerned about access. Clients that are perceived by realtors as being least concerned are high-income, childless, and residing in suburban locations. Clients without children may be less subject to time constraints and those with high incomes may enjoy more flexibility in work hours. These results seem fairly intuitive and provide a basis for expected results of the household survey, which offers many more observations.

The first step in analysis of the *recent-mover data set* involves looking at the raw data. Table 1 provides a variety of summary statistics. Respondents were asked to indicate their "*primary reason(s) for moving*" to their current home. Although most other surveys (e.g., Murie (1974) and the CPS) ask respondents to indicate a single primary reason for moving, it is believed that many households move for multiple reasons. The results of the survey confirm this hypothesis: almost half of all respondents (48.23%) indicated more than one "primary" reason for moving. Table 2 provides these sample results. Simple bivariate correlations indicate statistically significant associations between (1) birth/adoption and wanting a newer/bigger/better home and one that is closer to quality schools, as well as (2) retirement and wanting a change of climate, closer access to family and medical facilities, and having an "other" reason for moving. Multivariate models of this and other decisions are discussed in the following section.

Households were also asked to consider various housing and location attributes and its significance while they were searching for a new home. Table 3 offers summary statistics of these results. Consistent with the realtor survey results, price is the most important. The quality and distance to local public schools were less important, which is contradictory to what was expected from the results of the realtor survey. However, only 31% of responding households had children (age 16 years or under) at home. In contrast, the average realtor surveyed indicated that 71% of his/her clients have children at home. (The US Census suggests that 36% of all households include members under the age of 18 years. Thus, the 22 surveyed realtors may represent a rather biased sample of home buyers.) Ordered probit models offer a multivariate look at such priorities, simultaneously controlling for the presence of children and a variety of other household characteristics.

Table 1
Sample Characteristics of Recent-Mover Data Set

Variable	Minimum	Maximum	Mean	Standard deviation	Number of observations
Home features					
Number of bedrooms	1	3	2.13	0.58	964
Number of bathrooms	1	4	3.11	0.73	965
Number of living areas	0	4	1.79	0.77	962
Age of dwelling (years)	1	147	25.25	19.98	919
New home	0	1	0.03	0.17	919
Home value ($)	50,000	500,000	219,605	118,526	913
Down payment (%)	1	25	12.10	8.93	828
Interior size (sq. ft.)	1,000	5,000	2,071.78	914.43	909
Lot size (acres)	0	1	0.39	0.20	844
Neighborhood and location features					
All or most friends/family live nearby	0	1	0.03	0.18	964
Travel time to grocery store (min)	5	38	8.58	5.24	963
Travel time to mall (min)	5	76	14.53	8.35	962
Rural	0	1	0.12	0.33	909
Suburban	0	1	0.53	0.50	909
Urban	0	1	0.33	0.47	909
CBD	0	1	0.02	0.12	909
Median income (dollars)	0	169,590	51,031	28,735	909
Median number of housing units	0.00	3,605.00	1,147.38	877.02	909
Ratio of median home value to income of the surveyed household	0.32	19.92	2.30	1.80	909
Housing units' median number of rooms	2.5	8.4	5.64	1.31	909
Number of bus stops (stops per square mile)	0	5,234	57.99	286.63	909
Distance to CBD (miles)	0.16	23.35	7.82	4.26	909
Population density (people per square mile)	0	23,540	3,280	2,809	909
Overall density (number of jobs and households per square mile)	6	14,3175	3,297	9,226	909
Aggregated logsums (home-based work trips)	4,362.74	10,336.11	5,451.74	887.94	909

Table 1: (Continued)

Variable	Minimum	Maximum	Mean	Standard deviation	Number of observations
Aggregated logsums (home-based non-work trips)	4,533.44	12,076.92	5,874.06	1,084.52	909
Commercial center is within walking distance	0	1	0.67	0.47	933
High-quality public schools are nearby.	0	1	0.75	0.43	741
Household/respondent information					
Number of children in household	0	4	0.51	0.88	961
Presence of children (at least one child)	0	1	0.31	0.46	961
Married	0	1	0.54	0.50	921
Age (years)	19	87	39.56	12.18	897
Male	0	1	0.56	0.50	915
Non-Caucasian	0	1	0.16	0.36	914
Full-time student	0	1	0.04	0.19	962
Retired	0	1	0.05	0.21	962
Number of vehicles available in household	0	8	1.95	0.81	900
Number of vehicles per licensed driver	0	4	1.08	0.37	900
Household has no vehicles	0	1	0.01	0.09	900
Bus use (times per month)	0	30	0.99	4.64	965
Household income ($ per year)	11,080	200,000	93,199	51,994	965

Model Results

Four different types of models were used to analyze the recent-mover data set. An ordinary least squares (OLS) hedonic regression model of home value reveals marginal market valuations of various housing features, as well as effects of several location characteristics. Logit models were used to analyze stated preferences in binary experiments, and ordered probit models were used to track levels of associated importance in search criteria. A multinomial logit model helps explain significant factors in choosing a particular location within the region. (For statistical discussions of all these models, see Green (2003).)

Table 2

Primary Reason(s) for Moving

Primary reason for moving	Frequency	Percent
Wanted to own home	486	50.4
Newer/bigger/better home	227	23.5
Other reason	216	22.4
New job/job transfer	207	21.5
Easier commute	182	18.9
Marriage or divorce	96	9.9
Higher quality schools	87	9.0
Less expensive housing	52	5.3
Birth/adoption in household	44	4.6
Change of climate	40	4.1
Attending or graduating from college	33	3.4
Retiring	29	3.0
Member of household moving out of home/need smaller home	12	1.2
Health reasons	10	1.0

Table 3

Mean Rank of Importance of Housing and Location Attributes (Ranks range from 1 to 5, with 1: Not at all Important and 5: Very Important)

Housing/location attributes	Mean rank	Very important or important (%)
Price	3.72	99.3
Attractive neighborhood appearance	3.58	96.2
Investment potential or resale	3.40	89.6
Perception of crime rate in the neighborhood	3.36	89.7
Number of bedrooms	3.28	89.7
Commute time to work (or school for full-time students)	3.12	79.1
Noise levels	3.07	80.2
Lot size or yard size	2.86	69.0
Access to major freeway(s)	2.70	64.9
Social composition of the neighborhood	2.69	60.7
Distance/travel time to shopping	2.54	52.7
Quality of local public schools	2.52	50.6
Views	2.49	45.3
Neighborhood amenities, such as recreational facilities	2.45	49.5
Closeness to friends or relatives	2.24	39.4
Distance to medical services	2.12	31.8
Distance to local public schools	2.04	33.7
Access to bus services	1.57	14.6
Physical disability accommodations	1.47	9.7

Linear Regression Analysis of Home Price

The OLS hedonic model of home purchase prices allows one to quantify (in dollars) many tradeoffs that households make in home selection, across home and location attributes. Responses to attitudinal questions also were used as explanatory indicator variables (taking a value of 1 if the respondent agreed to certain statements), to represent features that are not easily measured (e.g., proximity to high-quality schools). Table 4 provides the final model specification, which was developed based on a process of stepwise addition and deletion and a maximum p-value of 0.10 (although slightly greater thresholds were allowed for those of practical significance).

As expected, many physical features of the home are statistically and practically significant. Everything else constant—including square footage—the number of bedrooms is found to reduce value. Perhaps this is because having more bedrooms without increasing home size results in smaller, cramped bedrooms, and smaller

Table 4
Final Specification for Linear Regression of Home Value

Variables	β	Standardized β	p	Elasticities
Home features				
Constant	240,537.11		0.001	
(Number of bedrooms)^2	−1,505.79	−0.052	0.079	−0.07
(Number of bathrooms)^2	11,339.83	0.227	0.000	0.25
Number of living areas	10,709.55	0.067	0.014	0.09
(Age of dwelling)^2	10.21	0.139	0.000	0.05
Interior size (sq. ft)	46.71	0.361	0.000	0.44
Lot size (acre)	50,264.53	0.085	0.001	0.09
Neighborhood features				
Travel time to grocery store (min)	−1,124.28	−0.047	0.072	−0.04
Travel time to mall (min)	669.40	0.043	0.112	0.04
Urban or CBD	17,195.03	0.065	0.032	0.03
Median income (dollars)	1.38	0.337	0.000	0.42
ln(Distance to CBD)	−58,635.61	−0.302	0.000	−0.50
ln(Population density)	−10,659.58	−0.114	0.002	−0.37
Aggregated logsums (home-based work trips)	165.56	1.176	0.012	4.11
Aggregated logsums (home-based non-work trips)	−134.84	−1.169	0.009	−3.61
Commercial center is within walking distance	−12,094.48	−0.046	0.048	−0.04
High-quality public schools are nearby	12,061.14	0.042	0.057	0.04
Number of observations	568			
Adjusted R^2	0.753			

kitchen, bathroom, and other areas. Another somewhat surprising result is that older homes enjoy higher values. This may be attributed to quality of construction (including hard wood floors, crown molding, or other attributes), maturity of trees, and neighborhood design diversity. It also may result from age proxying for other key variables, such as location. Older homes are more central, and the network-distance-to-CBD and other variables somehow may not capture all these effects. Access considerations are not easy to quantify.

Many neighborhood (TSZ)[3] and other location features also are significant. Results indicate that homes in urban areas and the CBD (as classified by CAMPO) are worth approximately $17,200 more than rural and suburban homes. Travel time to the resident's most frequented grocery store and major shopping center (i.e., a mall) is found to be statistically significant. Their coefficients suggest that homeowners pay more for proximity to a grocery store but less for proximity to a major shopping center. Certainly, households are likely to require food more frequently than other types of goods, so such convenience may be more valued. Moreover, the presence of a grocery store does not necessarily change the character of a neighborhood, whereas large shopping centers may be associated with large areas of parking, traffic, and access roads, which are not valued by homeowners. However, those who have commercial centers within walking distance of their residences tend to have lower valued homes. At first, this may seem counter-intuitive; however, if living in a CBD and distance to CBD are already controlled for, perhaps this variable is controlling for those living in suburban areas and close to commercial centers. One can imagine, in a suburban or rural area, homes that are located next to commercial facilities might be worth less than those with more privacy.

The neighborhood's median income level is estimated to have a positive effect on home value, which is intuitive. Higher income households tend to live in nicer areas, so this variable may proxy for neighborhood appearance, views, the quality of public infrastructure, as well as other variables that are difficult to control for. Distance to the CBD and population density variables both have negative coefficient estimates, as expected. Yet the most practically significant variables are the logsum measures of regional accessibility (which are based on discrete-choice models of travel demand (as calibrated by Kalmanje and Kockelman, 2004)). Higher access for home-based work (HBW)-type trips is estimated to increase home value (elasticity of +4.1%), but this is offset to some extent by the home-based non-work (HBNW)-trip accessibility index's effect (elasticity of −3.6%). Of course, these accessibility terms are correlated with one another as well as with the other measures of CBD and shopping access,

---

[3]Several survey recipients called to report that they had recently refinanced, rather than purchased their home. Others indicated that they were not actually living at the property but had purchased it as an investment.

creating issues of multicollinearity in interpretation (and thus some negative coefficient signs). That is fine, as long as the analyst recognizes that it may be very difficult to hold "everything else constant" when interpreting the coefficient values in isolation.

Finally, to control for the school quality, respondents were asked if (they believed that) their home is located in a high-quality school district. Those who agreed with the statement have homes that were valued at \$12,100 more, on average. Surprisingly, investment potential, noise, safety, recreational amenities, and freeway access are estimated to play statistically insignificant roles in home value. The market may be neglecting these features, even though investment potential, safety, and noise were priorities for movers (according to Table 3). Less subjective measures of school quality, more comprehensive measures of access and land use patterns, and additional information on home structure (such as the presence of stone or brick, landscaping, and garage size) could prove helpful to this model. However, its predictive power is quite reasonable (adjusted $R^2 = 0.753$), except in the case of high-valued homes (especially for those valued around \$1,000,000 or more) due to the coding of the data. The survey contained categorical responses for home value, and homes valued at \$500,000 or more were coded as \$500,000 for analysis. Additionally, it seems that the predictive power of the structural aspects (adjusted $R^2 = 0.664$) is higher than the location information (adjusted $R^2 = 0.524$), when examined separately.

Binary Logit Models of Home–Location Tradeoffs

While the hedonic model for home value offers valuable metrics of revealed preferences using market prices, a great many factors are at play. Stated preference scenarios allow one to control for a host of such potentially confounding variables. Six hypothetical scenarios, each offering two home-choice options, were presented in the survey. (And all other features of each respondent's current residence were assumed to apply, in order to permit a clear and relatively realistic choice situation.) The scenarios compared pairs of the following attributes: easy freeway access (i.e., being within 1 mile of one of Austin's two major freeways and a 50% commute-time reduction), increased home size (a larger kitchen and living room), toll road access (within 1 mile of a major toll road and a 50% commute-time reduction), transit access (bus stops within (1/4) mile from the home and workplace, or any other frequent destination), larger lot/yard, and easy access to shopping facilities (i.e., within 1 mile of a shopping center). Binary logit models were calibrated to ascertain household preferences, as a function of a variety of demographic and other control variables, including information concerning their current residence (since these characterized the choice alternatives). Table 5 shows the final specifications for all six scenarios. Several variables are not shown in the final specifications, because they were not statistically (or practically) significant, but these were considered initially. (These include occupation and type of dwelling unit, for example.)

Table 5
Final Specifications for Scenario Questions

Variable	Final estimates											
	Freeway access vs. increased home size		Increased home size vs. toll road access		Toll road access vs. bus access		Bus access vs. larger lot size		Larger lot size vs. shopping access		Shopping access vs. freeway access	
	β	p	β	p	β	p	β	p	β	p	β	p
Home features												
Constant	0.5015	0.032	0.1921	0.674	0.5317	0.202	0.4439	0.362	−0.6336	0.092	−0.4846	0.089
Number of bedrooms							−0.4723	0.003				
Number of bathrooms							0.3928	0.089				
Age of dwelling (years)			1.250E−02	0.029	−1.664E−02	0.000						
Home value ($)	−2.261E−06	0.041					−4.179E−06	0.000	−1.462E−06	0.080		
Down payment (%)	0.0240	0.011	−0.0192	0.073			0.0227	0.040				
Interior size (sq. ft)	2.332E−04	0.109	−2.443E−04	0.089	3.307E−04	0.005						
Lot size (acres)									1.4336	0.002		
Neighborhood features												
Commute time to grocery store									0.0462	0.006		
All or most friends/ family live nearby	−1.1158	0.036										
Rural							0.4955	0.108				
Suburban	0.3197	0.066							0.3274	0.049	−0.4756	0.002
Distance to CBD	−0.0799	0.000	0.0773	0.006			−0.1073	0.000	0.0718	0.001	0.0470	0.010
Median income of neighborhood	−6.396E−06	0.074	6.109E−06	0.108								

Household/respondent information												
Number of children in household									0.2723	0.008		
Number of licensed drivers					−0.5063	0.000						
Married							0.4113	0.046				
Age (years)					−1.324E−02	0.054	2.590E−02	0.002	−3.779E−02	0.000		
Male			0.3855	0.043					0.2468	0.136	0.2784	0.066
Number of vehicles available in household			0.2037	0.111			−0.2848	0.034	0.2507	0.021		
Number of vehicles per licensed driver											−0.4260	0.049
Bus use (times per month)			6.004E−02	0.090	−0.0555	0.012	0.0895	0.000				
HH income			−3.657E−06	0.099	6.882E−06	0.000						
Number of workers in household											1.5614	0.000
Non-White	−0.5250	0.021	0.6545	0.036	−0.4426	0.051					0.4819	0.019
Number of observations	721		667		768		699		711		819	
Cox and Snell R^2	0.050		0.059		0.113		0.122		0.118		0.057	
Nagelkerke R^2	0.066		0.086		0.239		0.171		0.157		0.077	
Market shares (home 1 vs. home 2)	47% vs. 53%		72% vs. 18%		48% vs. 52%		32% vs. 68%		48% vs. 52%		38% vs. 62%	

In examining the results of the models, there appear to be many similarities between those who favor commute-time reductions via freeway and toll road access. They include those who live in homes in which the physical structure is larger, newer, and less expensive homes. Those who live in suburban areas that are relatively close to the CBD, as well as those in lower income neighborhoods, tend to favor commute reductions. Demographically, men, higher income households, and those making a larger down payment are estimated to be less concerned with such access. In terms of transit access, demographic distinctions seem more apparent. Women, older persons, and frequent bus riders are more likely to prefer bus access over toll road access and increased lot size. And non-Caucasians, rural or CBD residents, and older persons are more likely to prefer easy shopping access, as opposed to larger lot size and/or easy freeway access. Those living closer to the CBD are more likely to choose shopping access over lot size—but not over freeway access. This is as expected, since persons living in the CBD are less likely to use/need freeways.

Overall, the two scenarios related to transit access provide the highest predictive power. In both these cases, household income and vehicle ownership are very helpful predictors of response.

Ordered Probit Models of the Importance of Access

Ordered probit models were calibrated in order to ascertain the importance of access attributes during the housing search process. Only demographic/personal control variables were used (rather than home/structural attributes), and Table 6 provides parameter estimates for final specifications. For model results of other, non-access attributes, readers may refer to Bina et al. (2006).[4]

As hypothesized earlier, knowing the reason(s) for a household's move can provide insight into the movers' final home choices (e.g., retirees may locate closer to children or medical facilities, and expecting parents may be interested in a larger home and good schools). As one would expect, those who moved for an easier commute are more likely to indicate that access (of all types) is a priority. Those who move for a new job (or job transfer) view commute time and shopping access as important but are estimated to be less likely to value transit access.

Demographically, several characteristics were estimated to play important roles in respondents' valuations of access. For example, in every one of the three models, men are estimated to be less concerned with access than women. Higher income households

[4]A model for the importance of freeway access also is not discussed here, since this model offered almost no predictive power (adjusted LRI = 0.009).

Table 6

Ordered Probit Results for Importance of Commute Time, Distance/Travel Time to Shopping, and Access to Bus Services

Variable	Commute time		Distance/travel time to shopping		Access to bus services	
	Final Estimates		Final Estimates		Final Estimates	
	β	p	β	p	β	p
Constant	2.021	0.000	0.835	0.000	0.395	0.029
Reasons for move						
New job/job transfer	0.453	0.000	0.233	0.018	−0.230	0.054
Easier commute	1.010	0.000	0.481	0.000	0.186	0.118
Retiring	−0.972	0.012				
Member of household moving out of home/need smaller home						
Newer/bigger/better home			0.280	0.002		
Health reasons					1.138	0.001
Employment status						
Two full-time workers or one part-time worker						
One full-time, one part-time worker, or two part-time workers	0.181	0.116			0.334	0.009
One full-time worker					−0.240	0.029
No workers			0.471	0.006		
Full-time student	0.891	0.015			1.036	0.000
Household/respondent information						
Presence of children (at least one child)						
Married			0.369	0.000		
Age (years)	−6.02E−03	0.153	7.93E−03	0.025	−3.74E−03	0.026
Male	−0.310	0.000	−0.341	0.000	−0.167	0.077
Number of vehicles available in household			−1.14E−01	0.017	−2.70E−01	0.000

Table 6. (*Continued*)

Variable	**Commute time**		**Distance/travel time to shopping**		**Access to bus services**	
	Final Estimates		**Final Estimates**		**Final Estimates**	
	β	p	β	p	β	p
Household has no vehicles					1.242	0.002
Household income ($ per year)	1.13E−06	0.196	1.97E−06	0.015		
Non-Caucasian	0.184	0.117			0.414	0.000
Thresholds						
$\mu(0)$	0	N/A	0	N/A	0	N/A
$\mu(1)$	1.139	0.000	1.301	0.000	0.852	0.000
$\mu(2)$	2.465	0.000	2.697	0.000	1.646	0.000
Number of observations	808		860		723	
Log-likelihood	−845.868		−985.485		−675.385	
Log likelihood: constants only	−914.099		−1032.326		−737.556	
Adjusted LRI	0.065		0.037		0.069	

tend to place greater value on access (with the exception of transit). This seems to contradict the realtor survey results, which indicated that lower income households are more concerned with accessibility.

Married persons are estimated to place greater value on shopping access (than unmarried persons). Those owning more vehicles are less likely to value shopping and transit access, while those owning no vehicles place greater value on bus access, as expected. In contrast to full-time students, older persons are estimated to be less likely to value commute time and transit access. Even retirees are less likely to value transit access, which is disconcerting to see, since such persons may need to start considering other travel options (as age takes its toll on driving abilities).

While these models' results suggest it is difficult to predict the level of importance that recent movers assign to various access features (all three likelihood ratio index values lie below 0.07), they do illuminate some of the general trends at play. And these trends play a role in location choice, as described in the following section.

Multinomial Logit Model of Location Choice

A location choice model was calibrated for recent movers, using the three-county (Travis, Williamson, and Hays) region's 1,074 TSZs. The movers' choice set consisted of 10 alternatives: 9 randomly drawn from the set of TSZs, plus the chosen option. Zonal attributes were obtained by matching geocoded home addresses to several data sources including CAMPO's zonal file (which provided information on zone's areas, population, number of households, and employment), the 2000 Census of Population (which provided information on median home values, housing units, housing units' median number of rooms, and average commute times for employed people), and the work by Kalmanje and Kockelman (2004). It is this last work that provided accessibility indices, calibrated from logsums emerging from travel demand models of HBW and HBNW trips.[5] Zone "size" was quantified via a natural-log-of-number-of-housing-units control variable (in order to help ensure proportionality between choice probabilities and home availability, everything else constant).

First, a pooled model was calibrated, recognizing all sampled households at once. Then the households were segmented, based on a number of demographic attributes, resulting in a series of models for purposes of parameter comparisons. Table 7 presents the pooled model results.

[5]The logsum used here is the expected maximum utility derived across all mode, departure time, and destination combinations available to a trip maker. Kalmanje and Kockelman (2004) calibrated nested logit models for Austin-area trips using the 1996 Austin Travel Surveys. They considered four modes and five times of day, along with the 1,074 TSZ destinations.

Table 7
MNL Location Choice Model (Pooled)

Explanatory variables	*β*	Standard error	*t*-Ratio	*p*
Distance to CBD (mile)	−0.1856	0.0154	−12.0	0.000
Aggregated logsums (home-based work trips)	−0.0003628	8.30E−05	−4.37	0.000
Number of bus stops per square mile	−0.0006955	0.000310	−2.24	0.024
Natural logarithm of the number of housing units in a TSZ	1.094	0.0528	20.7	0.000
Ratio of median home value in a TSZ to income of the surveyed household	−0.2733	0.0381	−7.17	0.000
Zoned density (number of jobs plus number of households per square mile)	4.49E−05	1.12E−05	4.03	0.000
Housing units' median number of rooms in each TSZ	0.7294	0.0437	16.7	0.000
Likelihood ratio index	0.3640			
Log-likelihood at convergence		−1,259		
Log-likelihood equal proportions		−1,980		
Number of observations		860		

The pooled results suggest that central locations (closer to the CBD) are preferred, everything else constant—including the logsum measures of regional accessibility. This indicates that centrality offers something more than travel preferences alone reveal.[6] However, it also counteracts, to some extent, the negative coefficient on the HBW-trip logsum term. That term implies a proximity to jobs may not be so desirable for many households, particularly those with few workers and/or making relatively few trips each day. While access is no doubt valued by many households, so is a quiet residential neighborhood. The need for balance between these competing objectives is a challenge for planners, policymakers, developers, and others who want to meet households' preferences—while mitigating congestion, emissions, car dependence, and other associated impacts of longer distance trip-making.

Median home values, divided by respondent household incomes, were used to describe neighborhood affordability. As expected, more expensive locations are less likely. Also, as expected, neighborhoods offering larger homes (a higher median number of rooms per home) are preferred. In addition, the results suggest that locations with a higher presence of bus service (i.e., zones with more bus stops per square mile) are less likely.

[6]Though simple in nature, distance to CBD measures almost always proves helpful, even in the face of other, more comprehensive variables. See, for example, hedonic models by Kockelman (1997) and land use change models by Zhou and Kockelman (2008).

Finally, the coefficient on the natural logarithm of housing units in a zone is very close to one, as anticipated on theoretical grounds (as mentioned earlier).

Elasticities were calculated for the case of an average medium-income two-worker household with one child and two vehicles. In this particular case, a 1% increase in distance to the CBD is found to be highly elastic, reducing the probability of location choice by 3.3%, while a 1% increase in home values (normalized with respect to income, of course) results in a 0.80% demand reduction. Also, a 1% increase in the median number of rooms in a zone results in a 4.6% increase in the location choice probability, whereas an increase of 1% in zone density is found to increase the probability of choosing a location by 0.36%.[7]

Household Segmentation

Data segmentation permits a closer look at behavioral tendencies across demographic groups. Due to space limitations, tables of the numeric results are not provided here, but key results are described. Variations in parameter values across segmented models suggest that higher income households (i.e., those with annual incomes over $100,000) are more sensitive to centrality (preferring zones closer to the Austin CBD) and to home size (preferring larger homes)—everything else constant. CBD access and home affordability are estimated to be more important for households with children than those without. A higher density of bus stops, however, makes a zone less likely for those with children. (This variable may be proxying for the prevalence of busy streets in a zone, rather than simply bus service provision.)

As a household's size increases, accessibility, affordability, and home size become more important, as expected. The value of access also appears to rise with vehicle ownership, which is interesting to detect. Perhaps those with more vehicles travel more frequently and thus desire shorter trips; they also may be wealthier, everything else constant (including income, which is used in the denominator of a neighborhood's median home value). As vehicle ownership increases, households are more likely to prefer locations near the CBD.

Segmentation according to age of the heads of households suggests that middle-aged household heads (ages 35–55 years) are more likely to value access as well as CBD proximity. Segmentation according to age and the number of workers suggests no additional distinctions, however.

[7]For elasticity equations, please see Green (2003).

Conclusions and Extensions

The survey of almost 1,000 recent movers in the Austin region enhances our understanding of the relationship between home choices and transportation. Top reasons for these moves are a desire to own one's home, wanting a newer/bigger/better home, facing a new job or job transfer, and wanting an easier commute. Once the decision to move was made, price, neighborhood appearance, and investment potential were top priorities.

Respondents also indicated the level of importance they placed on a variety of home attributes. Ordered probit models of accessibility ratings and stated preferences across pairs of housing alternatives revealed that a variety of demographic characteristics, including recent reasons for moving, factor prominently. For example, women, non-Caucasians, and those who move to be closer to work or to have an easier commute place a higher value on accessibility (of various types). Younger persons, full-time students, and higher income households tended to place greater importance on commute time, while married persons, older persons, and those with fewer vehicles and/or higher incomes rated shopping access rather highly. Bus access was a greater concern for full-time students, younger persons, and households with fewer vehicles.

Home price is a key consideration for buyers, and this was found to rise with proximity to minor shopping, such as a grocery store (by $1,100 per minute saved in travel time), but fall with proximity to a major shopping center (such as a mall) (by $670 per minute saved in travel time) and fall for homes within walking distance of a commercial center (by $12,100). (The design of such centers was not controlled for, but may play a key role in this result.) More densely populated locations and those further from the CBD suffered reductions. For example, a home located 5 mile from the CBD is worth approximately $64,000 more than a home located 15 mile from the CBD, everything else constant.

A logit model of location choice was calibrated for recent movers. Segmentation based on a number of demographic attributes allowed parameter comparisons. Results suggest that as income increases, households are more sensitive to centrality (preferring zones closer to the Austin CBD) and to home size (preferring larger homes)—everything else constant. CBD access and home affordability are estimated to be more important for households with children than those without. Segmentation according to age of the heads of households suggests that middle-aged household heads (ages 35–55 years) are more likely to value access as well as CBD proximity. Segmentation according to age and the number of workers suggested no additional distinctions.

While the home-choice decision is very complex, this new data set and its many associated behavioral models offer many insights. The reasons for a move and priorities in home selection, the hedonic models of home value, the paired comparisons of potential home enhancements, the importance scores of various attributes, and the logit models of location choice allow researchers, planners, and developers to more accurately characterize the tradeoffs households make in their home/location choices. When coupled with models of life cycle changes, land development, and population growth, as well as travel demand, vehicle ownership, and other behaviors, such models facilitate a more integrated look at our communities and their futures.

ACKNOWLEDGMENTS

We would like to thank the following persons for their invaluable help in mailing the surveys as well as entering the results into a database: Annette Perrone, Laura Narat, Kristin Donnelly, Caroline Soo, Robin Lynch, and Prenon Islam. We also acknowledge the many contributions of Mr. David Suescun, Graduate Student Researcher, Department of Civil, Architectural and Environmental Engineering at the University of Texas at Austin. This research effort was funded by the Southwest University Transportation Center (SWUTC).

References

Alonso, W. (1964). *Location and Land Use*. Cambridge, MA, Harvard University Press.

Belden Russonello and Stewart Research and Communications (2004). 2004 American Community Survey: National Survey on Communities. Washington, DC. Available at: http://www.realtor.org/SG3.nsf/files/NAR-SGA%20Final%20(2004).pdf/$FILE/NAR-SGA%20Final%20(2004).pdf

Ben-Akiva, M. and J. L. Bowman (1998). Integration of an activity-based model system and a residential location model. *Urban Studies* 35, 1131–1153.

Bhat, C. R. and J. Y. Guo (2004). A mixed spatially correlated logit model: formulation and application to residential choice modeling. *Transportation Research Part B* 38(2), 147–168.

Bina, M., V. Warburg and K. Kockelman (2006). Location choice vis-à-vis transportation: the case of apartment dwellers. *Transportation Research Record* 1977, 93–102.

Cho, Ch.-J. (1997). Joint choice of tenure and dwelling type: a multinomial logit analysis for the city of Chongju. *Urban Studies* 34(9), 1459–1473.

Ellickson, B. (1981). An alternative test of a joint model of residential mobility and housing choice. *Journal of Urban Economics* 9, 56–79.

Filion, P., T. Bunting and K. Warriner (1999). The entrenchment of urban dispersion: residential preferences and location patterns in the dispersed city. *Urban Studies* 36(8), 1317–1347.

Freedman, O. and C. R. Kern (1997). A model of workplace and residence choice in two-worker households. *Regional Science and Urban Economics* 27, 241–260.

Friedman, J. (1981). A conditional logit model of the role of local public services in residential choice. *Urban Studies* 18, 347–358.

Green, W. (2003). *Econometric Analysis*, 5th edn. New Jersey, USA, Prentice Hall.

Guiliano, G. (1989). New directions for understand transportation and land use. *Environment and Planning A* 21, 145–159.

Huh, S. and S.-J. Kwak (1997). The choice of a functional form and variables in the hedonic price model in Seoul. *Urban Studies* 34(7), 989–998.

Kalmanje, S. and K. Kockelman (2004). Credit-based congestion pricing: travel, land value, and welfare impacts. *Transportation Research Record* 1864, 45–53.

Kockelman, K. (1997). The effects of location elements on home purchase prices and rents: evidence from the San Francisco Bay Area. *Transportation Research Record* 1606, 40–50.

Mills, E. (1967). An aggregate model of resource allocation in a metropolitan area. *American Economic Review* 57, 197–210.

Murie, A. (1974). *Household Movement and Housing Choice*. Birmingham, UK, Centre for Urban and Regional Studies, University of Birmingham.

Muth, R. F. (1969). *Cities and Housing*. Chicago, The University of Chicago Press.

Orford, S. (2000). Modelling spatial structures in local housing market dynamics: a multilevel perspective. *Urban Studies* 37(9), 1643–1671.

Parsons Brinkerhoff Quade & Douglas, Inc. (1999). NCHRP Report 423A: Land Use Impacts of Transportation: A Guidebook, National Academy Press, Washington, DC.

Rosen, S. (1974). Hedonic prices and implicit markets: product differentiation in pure competition. *Journal of Political Economy* 82, 34–55.

Schachter, J. (2001). Why People Move: Exploring the March 2000 Current Population Survey. US Census Bureau, Washington, DC. Available at: http://www.census.gov/prod/2001pubs/p23-204.pdf

Schachter, J. (2004). Geographic Mobility: 2002 to 2003. US Census Bureau, Washington, DC. Available at: http://www.census.gov/prod/2004pubs/p20-549.pdf

Sermons, M. W. and F. S. Koppelman (2001). Representing the differences between female and male commute behavior in residential location choice models. *Journal of Transport Geography* 9, 101–110.

Sermons, M. W. and N. Seredich (2001). Assessing traveler responsiveness to land and location based accessibility and mobility solutions. *Transportation Research Part D* 6, 417–428.

Van Ommeren, J. N., P. Rietveld and P. Nijkamp (1998). Spatial moving behavior of two-earner households. *Journal of Regional Science* 38, 23–41.

Waddell, P. (1996). Accessibility and residential location: the interaction of workplace, residential mobility, tenure, and location choice. Presented at the *Lincoln Land Institute TRED Conference*. Cambridge, MA.

Weisbrod, G., M. Ben-Akiva and S. Lerman (1980). Tradeoffs in residential location decisions: transportation versus other factors. *Transportation Policy and Decision-Making* 1, 13–26.

Wheaton, W. (1977). Income and urban residence: an analysis of consumer demand for location. *The American Economic Review* 67(4), 620–631.
Zhou, B. and K. Kockelman (2008). Neighborhood impacts on land use change: a multinomial logit model of spatial relationships. *Annals of Regional Science* 42(2), 321–340.
Zondag, B. and M. Pieters (2005). Influence of accessibility on residential location choice. *Transportation Research Record* 1902, 63–70.

The Expanding Sphere of Travel Behaviour Research
Selected Papers from the 11th International Conference on Travel Behaviour Research

29

Does the Release from Household Responsibilities lead to More Out-of-home Activities? The Case of hiring Live-in Maids in Hong Kong

Donggen Wang

Abstract

Household responsibilities such as maintenance and childcare not only induce activities and travel, but also impose time constraints on individuals' participation in discretionary activities and associated travel. Instead of sharing household responsibilities, household members may hire live-in maids to take some or most of the household maintenance activities and childcare. This is a common practice in some Asian cities such as Singapore and Hong Kong. The presence of live-in maids in households may lead to changes in many aspects of households and individuals' activity–travel behavior: destination, timing, duration, etc. Would the release from household maintenance activities lead to more out-of-home activities and travel? Despite the significance of this issue, to my knowledge, there is hardly any research on this topic reported in the literature. In an attempt to answer this research question and to make a contribution to the literature on the relations between household responsibilities and activity travel behavior, this paper presents some empirical evidence on how the presence of live-in maids in households affects the activity–travel behavior of the male and female household heads. The data are derived from the 2002 Travel Characteristic Survey of Hong Kong. The structural equation modeling framework is used to study the effects of live-in maids on the participation in out-of-home activities. It is found that the presence of live-in maids significantly increases the time spent for subsistence activities by female head. As expected, it significantly reduces the undertaking of maintenance activities by both male and female heads. Apart from these generation and replacement effects, the presence of live-in maid is also found to increase the joint activities but reduce the individual discretionary activities of the two household heads. The findings of this research provide a new perspective to the understanding of the relationships between household responsibilities and activity and travel behavior.

Introduction

Household responsibilities such as maintenance and childcare not only induce activities and travel, but also impose time constraints on individuals' participation in discretionary activities and associated travel. There is an obvious linkage between household responsibilities and activity–travel patterns. A number of studies have examined the allocation of household responsibilities such as maintenance activities and travel among household members (Townsend, 1987; Golob and Mcnally, 1997; Gliebe and Koppelman, 2002; Srinivasan and Bhat, 2005). These studies have contributed greatly to our understanding of the mechanism of task allocation and its implication for individuals' activity and travel patterns.

However, instead of sharing household responsibilities, households may hire live-in maids to take some or most of the household maintenance activities and childcare. This is a common practice in some Asian cities such as Singapore and Hong Kong. According to the Census and Statistics Department of the Hong Kong Special Administrative Region (SAR) government, there were 218,430 foreign domestic helpers or live-in maids working in Hong Kong in 2004 (Census and Statistics Department, 2005, p. 32). The major responsibilities of live-in maids include childcare, house works, preparing meals, shopping, etc. The presence of live-in maids may change the activity–travel behavior of household members, in particular, household heads who usually shoulder most household maintenance duties. On the one hand, because maintenance activities are taken by live-in maids, household members' maintenance activities and associated travel may be reduced; on the other hand, because of the release from household maintenance duties, members should have more free times for discretionary activities and travel. Thus, individuals of households with live-in maids may engage more in out-of-home activities and travel. Apart from these possible addition and substitution effects, the presence of live-in maids may also lead to changes in other aspects of activity–travel. For example, because of the release from house works such as preparing meals, members are more flexible in arrival times; because children are taken care of by live-in maids, husband and wife are more likely to engage in out-of-home joint activities; similarly, because of the release from escorting child, husband and/or wife may not need to chain trips. These examples show that the presence of live-in maids in households may lead to changes in many aspects of individuals' activity–travel behavior such as destination, timing, duration, etc. Despite the significance of this issue, to my knowledge, there is hardly any research on this topic reported in the literature.

In an attempt to answer these questions and to make a contribution to the literature on the relations between household responsibilities and activity travel behavior, this paper develops a structural equation model to examine how the presence of live-in maids in households affects the activity–travel behavior of household members. The data are derived from the 2002 Travel Characteristic Survey of Hong Kong, which provides activity and trip diaries of about 1.4% of households in Hong Kong. Given the fact that most household responsibilities lie on the household head and his/her spouses and thus the presence of live-in maids more likely impacts on their activity–travel patterns, this study will focus on the male and female household heads. The structural equation modeling framework is applied because the presence of live-in maids may generate direct and indirect effects on household heads' activity–travel behavior and interactions between household heads and between different activities need to be taken into account. It is assumed that the presence of live-in maids may result in the re-allocation of responsibilities and duties among household members. In order to accurately derive the indirect effects, it is important to consider the interactions between household members in activity participation and travel.

The rest of the paper is structured as follows. The next section will review the literature on household activity–travel interactions. This is followed by the introduction of hiring live-in maids in Hong Kong and the hypotheses about the impacts of live-in maids. The section "Modeling the Impacts of Live-in Maids on Out-of-home Activity Patterns of Household Heads" presents the model specification, introduces the data, and lists the modeling results. Implications of the research findings and future research directions are discussed in the last section.

Intrahousehold Activity–Travel Interactions: Literature Review

Activity and travel interactions between household members have recently received increasing research attentions. Quite a number of attempts have been made to develop models accounting for interactions between household members in activity participation and tradeoffs between joint and individual engagement in activities.

Townsend (1987) proposed a framework conceptualizing household interactions in activity participation into substitution, companion, and complementary relationships between household members. The study reveals that the presence of children increases maintenance activities for females and employment status reduces females' undertaking of leisure activities (Golob and McNally, 1997). Golob and McNally (1997) develop a structural equations model to examine the interactions in activity participation and travel between household heads. The model studies both within- and cross-person activity and travel interactions. It is found that the male head's participation in work activities decreases his maintenance and discretionary activities and travel, and also the female head's discretionary activities and travel, but increases the female head's maintenance activities and travel. On the other hand, more participation in work activities by the female head reduces her maintenance and discretionary activities but causes no change to the male head's maintenance and discretionary activities. The model does not explicitly model joint activities. Fujii et al. (1999) use the structural equations model to study time allocation to in-home and out-of-home joint activities with family members and non-family members. They find that individuals in general are more likely to perform out-of-home independent activities rather than joint activities with family members. They prefer to spend more time with family members for in-home activities.

Gliebe and Koppelman (2002) develop a so-called proportional shares model for daily time allocation. The model accounts for interpersonal linkages between adult household members by examining their decisions concerning the participation and time allocation to independent and joint activities. The empirical results show that employment levels and presence of children significantly influence the tradeoffs between independent and joint activities. A similar attempt is made by Scott and Kanaroglou (2002), who estimate trivariate-ordered probit models for couples of three household types: non-worker, one-worker, and two-worker households. They find significant interactions between household heads and more interestingly the nature of these interactions varies by household types. In non-worker households, access to vehicle is conducive to joint activities; in one-worker households, the presence of children (younger than 6 years) is found to be a contributing factor to joint participation in out-of-home activities; in two-worker households, however, the presence of children seems to be a negative factor to joint out-of-home activities. The impacts of the presence of children on joint activities have also been reported elsewhere. Couples without children living at home are found to be more likely to pursue joint out-of-home non-work activities than couples with children living at home; most joint activities for couples with children are in-home activities (Kostyniuk and Kitamura, 1983).

Zhang et al. (2002, 2004) assume that the allocation of activities to household members is a group decision-making process, which maximizes household utility and incorporates individuals' preferences and household needs, subject to resource constraints. Household members contribute to household utilities by conducting independent, shared, or allocated activities. The relative influences of household members in the group decision-making process are explicitly modeled. They find that male members have larger influence on the joint decision-making; male members in younger households (measured by the age of the oldest member in the household) tend to conduct more allocated and shared activities than those in older households. Female members in younger households tend to perform more allocated activities, but fewer shared activities than those in older households.

Vovsha et al. (2004) develop a model for the allocation of maintenance activities to household members. The model consists of two linked discrete choices: the former concerns the generation of maintenance activities (shopping, escorting, and other maintenance activities) for the entire household and the latter allocates these activities to household members for implementation. The study finds that the size of household increases the number of maintenance activities and there is strong substitution between joint and individual maintenance activities. Household members with available time window more likely implement individual maintenance activities. On the other hand, participation in any type of household joint activities reduces the probability to undertake individual maintenance activities. Similarly, Srinivasan and Athuru (2005) investigate the allocation of maintenance activities among household members. Their study, however, does not model the generation of maintenance activities but takes them as given. Two interrelated decisions are studied: whether the maintenance activities should be conducted individually or jointly and who should conduct the activities if they are to be performed individually. They find that the household head seems more likely to conduct maintenance activities than his/her spouse and children do. The more employed members the household has, the less likely those maintenance activities are performed jointly. Females are more likely to perform maintenance activities than males. Full-time workers have lower probability to perform home-based maintenance activities. Working and commuting duration negatively impact on the probability of full-time workers to perform maintenance activities. Household head and spouse tend to share maintenance responsibilities on a more equal basis in higher income households than in lower income households. On the other hand, lower income households are more likely to engage in joint maintenance activities than medium- and high-income counterparts. Household heads are more likely to engage in joint maintenance activities during weekend days than weekdays.

Gliebe and Koppelman (2005) adopt the tour-based approach to study interactions between household heads. The study differentiates fully and partially joint tours in five spatial arrangements of tours involving joint activities and ride. A so-called structural discrete choice model is developed to model the effects of household and personal attributes on the choice of different types of tours. It is found that households with zero or one worker more likely engage in fully joint tours; the total number of children in the household is found to have significant negative effect on not only fully, but also partially joint tours.

The study by Srinivasan and Bhat (2005) focuses on the generation of in-home and out-of-home maintenance activities. The former is simulated by the so-called seemingly unrelated regression system, while the latter is treated as a discrete–continuous decision, which is modeled by a so-called joint mixed-logit hazard-duration model structure. Household/individual characteristics (e.g., gender) and the characteristics of mandatory activities (e.g., work duration) are found to be significant factors influencing in-home as well as out-of-home maintenance activities. For example, non-working female household heads more likely shoulder a large burden of household maintenance task. Households with only one car conduct more joint grocery shopping than those with more cars. Srinivasan and Bhat (2006) adopt a similar modeling approach to study intrapersonal tradeoffs between in-home and out-of-home discretionary activities and interpersonal tradeoffs between solo and joint discretionary activities. The empirical results show that the decision on participation in discretionary activities is influenced by the mandatory and maintenance activity participation characteristics of the spouse. They also find that the vehicle availability contributes positively to the undertaking of independent out-of-home discretionary activities. The presence of children has a negative impact on joint discretionary activities between couples.

Potential Effects of hiring Live-in Maids on Household Heads' Activity–Travel Behavior: Hypothesis

Hiring Live-in Maids in Hong Kong

Hiring live-in maids from foreign countries, or domestic helpers, as they are often called in Hong Kong, has become popular in Hong Kong since the 1970s when Hong Kong's economy started to take off (Constable, 1997). The rapid expansion of the manufacturing sector in the 1960s and 1970s generated enormous demand for factory labors. As a result, local female workers who used to take up the jobs of domestic helpers changed to factory jobs with more pay. Many vacancies for domestic helpers became available. This trend continued when Hong Kong's economy transformed from manufacturing to service dominated and female workers experienced general upward job mobility (e.g., more educated females moved to the service sector). At the same time, Hong Kong's family structure was also dramatically changed. The share of nuclear families increased from 54% in 1981 to 62% in 1991 (Census and Statistics Department, 1995; Constable, 1997). This trend resulted in the shortage of family members who may share household maintenance duties, in particular, childcare. All these factors contributed to the growth of demand for domestic helpers in Hong Kong. On the other hand, countries like the Philippines and Indonesia faced a different problem. Take the Philippines, a country that contributes the majority of domestic helpers to Hong Kong today, as an example. After her independence in 1946, the government adopted the import-substitution strategy, which meant "firms import labor-saving machinery and used capital-intensive production techniques more appropriate to industrialized countries" (Constable, 1997). As a result, the development of the country became "growth without jobs" and had "massive labor surpluses" (Constable, 1997). Since the 1970s, many young Filipinos began to look for jobs in the rapid growing economies like Singapore and Hong Kong. This generated a great supply for domestic helpers to Hong Kong and other places.

According to Constable (1997), the number of foreign domestic helpers in Hong Kong was only a few hundred in the early 1970s. It then rapidly increased to around 41,500 in 1987, 63,300 in 1990, and 120,700 in 1995 (Census and Statistics Department, 1995, p. 70). In the year 2004, Hong Kong's households employed about 218,430 foreign domestic helpers from the Philippines (119,711), Indonesia (90,045), Thailand (4,922), Nepal (1,398), India (1,294), Sri Lanka (885), and others (Census and Statistics Department, 2005, p. 32). Table 1 presents the socio-demographic characteristics of the

Table 1
Socio-demographics of Filipinos and Indonesians in Hong Kong

Socio-demographics	**'000 (percentage)**	
	Filipinos	**Indonesians**
Gender		
Male	5.5 (3.5%)	2.0 (4.9%)
Female	152.7 (96.5%)	38.2 (95.1%)
Age (years)		
<15	0.8 (0.5%)	0.5 (1.3%)
15–24	15.4 (9.8%)	14.6 (36.5%)
25–34	81.8 (51.7%)	20.1 (50.1%)
35–44	50.9 (32.2%)	4.3 (10.6%)
>45	9.3 (5.8%)	0.6 (1.5%)
Marital status		
Married	69.3 (43.8%)	23.7 (59.0%)
Single/divorced/widowed	88.8 (56.2%)	16.5 (40.9%)
Education attainment		
University or above	50.5 (31.9%)	1.7 (4.3%)
Senior high school	60.5 (38.3%)	12.7 (31.5%)
Junior high school or lower	47.1 (30.8%)	25.7 (64.1%)
Occupation		
Unskilled	144.4 (94.4%)	37.6 (96.8%)
Others	8.6 (5.6%)	1.3 (3.2%)
Monthly income (Hong Kong dollars)		
<6,000	143.5 (93.8%)	37.3 (96.3%)
>6,000	8.7 (5.7%)	1.3 (3.1%)
Language ability		
English		
Fluent	108.7 (68.7%)	6.5 (16.4%)
Middle or low	43.1 (27.3%)	17.4 (43.5%)
No	6.4 (4.0%)	16.1 (40.1%)
Chinese (Cantonese)		
Fluent	9.1 (5.8%)	7.7 (19.1%)
Middle or low	66.0 (41.7%)	24.7 (61.7%)
No	83.0 (52.5%)	7.7 (19.1%)
Total	158.1	40.1

Source: A survey on Hong Kong's minority groups commissioned by Home Affairs Bureau and Census and Statistics Department of Hong Kong SAR government and conducted in the year 2000. Website: http://www.legco.gov.hk/yr00-01/chinese/panels/ha/papers/590c01.pdf

people from the Philippines and Indonesia who live in Hong Kong, the two countries that provide the largest number of domestic helpers to Hong Kong. As the table shows, more than 95% of these two minority populations are females and more than 90% of them are employed as unskilled labors or domestic helpers with a monthly salary less than 6,000 Hong Kong dollars. The Filipinos have much higher education attainment (more than 30% of them have university education or above and more than 70% have senior high school education or above) than the Indonesians (only 4.3% of them have university education and more than 60% of them have junior high school education or lower). The main duties of the live-in maids often include cleaning, cooking, washing, as well as taking care of children or the elderly. As many domestic helpers, particularly those from the Philippines, have high education attainment and speak fluent English, some of them also take the duties of tutoring children.

Potential Effects of Hiring Live-In Maid on Task Allocation and Household Heads' Activity–Travel Behavior: Hypothesis

Hiring live-in maids may impact on the task allocation among household members and on the activity–travel patterns of household heads. These impacts may be direct and indirect. We may classify them into the following types:

(a) *Substitution/replacement*: By substitution or replacement effects, we mean that household members are replaced by live-in maids in conducting maintenance activities. As explained earlier, live-in maids are hired for undertaking household maintenance activities including grocery shopping, escorting children, in-home maintenance, etc. As a result, household members should have fewer maintenance activities and associated travel; substitution or replacement effects may thus be present.
(b) *Generation*: Because of the release from household task, members should have more free time for out-of-home discretionary or even subsistence activities. Thus, we assume that members of households with live-in maids may engage more in out-of-home activities.
(c) *Modification*: Apart from these possible generation and substitution effects, the presence of maid may also lead to changes in other aspects of activity–travel. For example, because of the release from house works such as preparing meals, members are more flexible in arrival times; because the child is taken care of by the maid, husband and wife are more likely to engage in out-of-home joint activities; similarly, because of the release from the activities of escorting child, husband and/or wife may not need to chain trips.

Further, because of the traditional gender-based task allocation with female head being more likely to undertake household maintenance activities such as grocery shopping, we assume that the impacts of hiring live-in maid may be different to the male and female household heads. Previous studies have revealed that the traditional gender roles continue to exist (Scott and Kanaroglou, 2002; Srinivasan and Bhat, 2005; Srinivasan and Athuru, 2005). Srinivasan and Bhat (2005) find that non-working female household heads more likely shoulder a large burden of household maintenance task. Thus, when the maintenance task is taken over by the maid, the female household heads may be released from these responsibilities and their activity–travel patterns are more likely to change. For example, female heads may get back into the work force and get employed. Thus, we suspect that the female heads of households with live-in maids may spend more time on subsistence activities than those without live-in maids. Similarly, they may spend more time on discretionary activities than those female heads of households without live-in maids.

Modeling the Impacts of Live-in Maids on Out-of-home Activity Patterns of Household Heads

Model Specification

Because household maintenance activities are mostly shouldered by the two heads of households (Srinivasan and Athuru, 2005) and live-in maids are in general hired to take up maintenance activities, it is appropriate to limit our study objects to household heads and choose households as the analytical unit. Since in-home activities do not have explicit and direct implication for travel, our focus will be on out-of-home activities. Following the activity typology proposed by Reichman (1976) and adopted by Bhat and Koppelman (1993) and Bhat and Mirsa (1999), we categorize three activity types, namely subsistence activities which concern mainly work and work-related activities, maintenance activities which include grocery shopping, escorting children, etc., and discretionary activities which consist of social and recreation activities motivated by cultural and psychological needs.

Because of the interactions between the two household heads and between different types of activities, the presence of live-in maids may impact not only directly but also indirectly on the undertaking of out-of-home activities. To accurately model these impacts, it is appropriate to apply the Structure Equations Modeling (SEM) approach, which has been proved useful in disentangling the interrelations in activity–travel behavior (Golob and McNally, 1997; Lu and Pas, 1999). For more details about SEM, readers are referred to Golob (2003). In addition to the variable on the presence of live-in maids, we use the two opposite genders, three activity types defined earlier, and two participation modes (joint or independent) to define eight more endogenous variables: male subsistence activities, male maintenance activities, male discretionary activities, female subsistence activities, female maintenance activities, female discretionary activities, joint maintenance activities, and joint discretionary activities.

Based on the hypotheses made in the previous section, it is postulated that the presence of live-in maids will reduce female heads' undertaking of maintenance activities but increase the time spent for subsistence activities and probably the probabilities of conducting discretionary activities. Similarly, it is assumed that as a result of hiring live-in maids, male heads' sharing of maintenance activities will be reduced but their discretionary activities may be increased. For the same token, the presence of live-in maids may lead the couples to engage in more joint discretionary activities, but fewer joint maintenance activities.

Apart from the hypothesized effects of live-in maids, interactions between activities of the two household heads are also included in the model. Specifically, it is assumed that more time spent for subsistence activities by the male head will impact on not only his undertaking of independent as well as joint maintenance and discretionary activities, but also the female head's probability of conducting maintenance and discretionary activities; similarly, more time spent for subsistence activities by the female head will impact on not only her undertaking of independent as well as joint maintenance and discretionary activities, but also the male head's probability of conducting maintenance and discretionary activities. The postulated effects of live-in maids and interactions between activities of the two household heads are illustrated in Figure 1.

Based on the data availability and the literature, the following exogenous variables are included: variables related to the needs of household maintenance—household size in terms of the number of members, the presence of child aged 1–5 years as well as the presence of child aged 6–17 years; variables on resource availability for activity participation—household monthly income and the availability of car in the household;

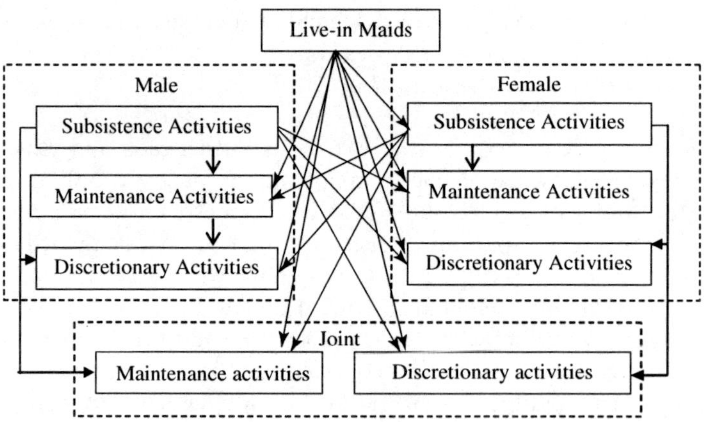

Figure 1

The Postulated Direct Effects of Live-in Maids on and Interactions between Out-of-Home Activities of Male and Female Household Heads

and others—age of household head (the head declared in the interview) and type of housing. Type of housing is included because the housing system in Hong Kong consists of various types of housing, including "public rental housing" which is owned by the government, "subsidized sale flats" which are subsidized by the government, and private housing. For the convenience of analysis, the first two types are combined and referred as "public housing," which are generally inferior to private housing in terms of size, quality, and facilities. According to the housing department of Hong Kong SAR government, in 2005, about 46.3% households lived in public housing, while 52.4% lived in private housing (http://www.housingauthority.gov.hk/en/aboutus/resources/figure/0,,3-0-13893–2005,00.html, accessed on June 8, 2006). We assume that all exogenous variables may impact on all endogenous variables. Thus, every exogenous variable is connected to every endogenous variable.

Data

The data are derived from the Hong Kong Travel Characteristics Survey conducted in 2002. This survey is conducted for every 10 years. Major items in the survey include activity and trip making characteristics as well as personal and household demographic, social, and economic variables. Among other socio-economic variables, there is a piece of information on whether households have live-in maids. Information about all activities and trips made on a reference weekday was collected. The 2002 survey successfully interviewed 30,005 households (about 1.4% of households of Hong Kong in 2002) involving 89,974 individuals. Information on the duration, timing, destination, etc., of the activities and associated travel conducted within 24 hours is provided by the survey. A total of 27 activity types are differentiated in the survey.

As our focus is on the effects of live-in maids on activity allocation between the two household heads, we select only households that have married couples. After removing the cases with missing values, the final sample used for this study involves 13,322 households. Perhaps because of its large size, the sample is very representative of the society. About 9.9% of the households in the sample have live-in maids; a total of 15.9% of them have private car or company car that may be used for private purposes; about 17.0% of the households have the presence of child aged 1–5 years and 45.4% have child aged 6–17 years; 48.2% of the households live in private apartment or house and 51.8% live in dwellings of either publicly owned or subsidized; 76.1% of male heads are employed and 49.2% of female heads are employed.

Results

Golob and McNally (1997) suggest that whenever sample size permits, the asymptotically distribution free, weighted least squares estimation method should be used to estimate the SEM model and because the normal distribution assumption cannot be assumed for most of the variables in the present study, the weighted least square estimation method is used to estimate the model in this study. We started by estimating a model by using the variables on time use for various activities. It did not result in a reasonable model in the sense that the standard errors of the coefficients are extremely large. We examined the reasons and discovered that the major cause is that these variables are extremely skewed to the zero value, because of the large percentages of zero values particularly on maintenance and discretionary activities (due to the non-participation in these activities). We then recoded the six variables on time use for maintenance and discretionary activities into dichotomous variables (with "1" representing participation in those activities and "0" not) and those on male and female heads' time use for subsistence activities into ordinal variables (i.e., "0" = 0 minutes; "1" = 1–200 minutes; "2" = 201–400 minutes; … "7" = >800 minutes). In other words, instead of the time use, we model the participation in maintenance and discretionary activities either jointly or individually by male or female head.

After the transformation of the variables, we first estimated a model with the links postulated earlier. The modification indices suggest that adding the following two links on interperson interactions will significantly improve the Chi-square value of the model: the female head's maintenance activities on the male head's discretionary activities and the female head's discretionary activities on the male head's discretionary activities. In addition, it is also indicated that a major improvement in Chi-square value may be obtained if the link from joint discretionary activities to joint maintenance activities is added. This implies that the competition between different types of joint activities should be considered. The overall fit of the final model to the data is well by most of the indicators. The goodness-of-fit index and the adjusted goodness-of-fit index of the final model are, respectively, 0.9996 and 0.9983, both larger than 0.9. The standardized root mean square residual is 0.019, which is smaller than 0.05. These three indicators show that the model fits the data well. However, the associated p-value of the Chi-square value 119.53 with 33 degree of freedom is not larger than 0.05, as required by a good fitted model. Nevertheless, as Chi-square measure is sensitive to sample size and large sample size tends to produce large Chi-square value (Jöreskog and Sörbom, 2001), a large Chi-square value may be expected for the present study which involves 13,322 samples. As a piece of evidence, we did estimate a model with similar specification but for only 3,000 samples. The model has a Chi-square value of 23.5 (33 degree of freedom) and a p-value of 0.86. This approves that the small p-value of the present model is the result of a large sample.

Table 2 presents the total, direct, and indirect effects of endogenous variables on each other and Table 3 lists the total, direct, and indirect effects of exogenous variables on endogenous variables. In the following, these effects will be reported, interpreted, and discussed.

Table 2

Total, Direct, and Indirect Effects of Endogenous Variables on each other

	Presence of live-in maid	Male subsistence activity duration	Male maintenance activities	Male discretionary activities	Female subsistence activity duration	Female maintenance activities	Female discretionary activities	Joint maintenance activities	Joint discretionary activities
Male maintenance activities									
Total	−0.4227	−0.3766			1.3007				
Direct	−4.1512	−0.3766	–	–	1.3007	–	–	–	–
Indirect	3.7284	–			–				
Male discretionary activities									
Total	−0.4311	−0.4793	−0.2816		1.2095	*−0.4370*	*−0.0446*		
Direct	−8.6431	−0.4785	−0.2816	–	2.1833	*−0.6031*	*−0.0446*	–	–
Indirect	8.212	*−0.0008*	–		*−0.9738*	*0.1661*	–		
Female subsistence activity duration									
Total	2.8664								
Direct	2.8664	–	–	–	–	–	–	–	–
Indirect	–								
Female maintenance activities									
Total	−2.9194	0.1721			0.9744				
Direct	−5.7125	0.1721	–	–	0.9744	–	–	–	–
Indirect	2.7931	–							
Female discretionary activities									
Total	−1.6623	0.0687			0.4442	−3.7228			
Direct	−24.2019	0.7093	–	–	4.0717	−3.7228	–	–	–
Indirect	22.5396	−0.6406			−3.6276	–			

Table 2. (Continued)

	Presence of live-in maid	Male subsistence activity duration	Male maintenance activities	Male discretionary activities	Female subsistence activity duration	Female maintenance activities	Female discretionary activities	Joint maintenance activities	Joint discretionary activities
Joint maintenance activities									
Total	*0.1764*	−0.4818			−2.4791				*−4.3063*
Direct	*31.6590*	*−2.1420*	–	–	*−10.9010*	–	–	–	*−4.3063*
Indirect	*−31.4826*	*1.6602*			*8.4219*				–
Joint discretionary activities									
Total	*0.0548*	−0.3855			−1.9557				
Direct	5.6606	−0.3855	–	–	−1.9557	–	–	–	–
Indirect	−5.6058	–							

Note: Figures in italics are not significant at the 0.05 level; all others are significant at the 0.05 level or below. (–) Cases where no link is postulated.

Table 3

Total, Direct, and Indirect Effects of Exogenous Variables on Endogenous Variables

	Household income	Type of housing	Household size	Age of household head (years)	Presence of child aged 1–5 years	Presence of child aged 6–17 years	Availability of car
Presence of live-in maid							
Total	0.5189	0.3003	0.1769	0.3171	0.5354	0.2871	0.0793
Direct	0.5189	0.3003	0.1769	0.3171	0.5354	0.2871	0.0793
Indirect	–	–	–	–	–	–	–
Male subsistence activity duration							
Total	*0.0305*	*0.0344*	0.2860	−0.6249	−0.3145	−0.1500	−0.0721
Direct	*0.0305*	*0.0344*	0.2860	−0.6249	−0.3145	−0.1500	−0.0721
Indirect	–	–	–	–	–	–	–
Male maintenance activities							
Total	0.1752	−0.1002	−0.3068	0.2600	0.2795	0.3328	*0.0104*
Direct	2.2050	1.0290	*−0.1935*	2.2795	3.2293	2.2824	0.4729
Indirect	−2.0298	−1.1292	*−0.1133*	−2.0195	−2.9498	−1.9496	−0.4625
Male discretionary activities							
Total	*−0.0149*	−0.0800	*−0.1144*	0.3990	*0.1353*	*−0.0081*	0.1111
Direct	4.3485	2.1683	*−0.0568*	4.7189	6.4293	4.2433	1.0391
Indirect	−4.3634	−2.2483	*−0.0576*	−4.3199	−6.2940	−4.2513	−0.9280
Female subsistence activity duration							
Total	0.1044	0.1002	0.5603	−0.7216	−0.6503	−0.6258	−0.1232
Direct	−1.3830	−0.7606	*0.0532*	−1.6304	−2.1849	−1.4489	−0.3507
Indirect	1.4875	0.8607	0.5071	0.9089	1.5346	0.8231	0.2274
Female maintenance activities							
Total	0.0624	−0.1820	−0.4600	0.3518	0.4967	0.6046	*−0.0019*
Direct	2.9198	1.4299	*−0.0445*	2.9737	4.2428	2.8806	0.5839
Indirect	−2.8574	−1.6119	*−0.4155*	−2.6219	−3.7461	−2.2760	−0.5858
Female discretionary activities							
Total	0.1043	−0.1549	−0.4792	0.3975	0.4294	0.3694	0.1311
Direct	12.4488	6.0028	*−0.3940*	12.7619	18.1066	12.2244	2.5973
Indirect	−12.3445	−6.1577	*−0.0852*	−12.3645	−17.6772	−11.8551	−2.4663
Joint maintenance activities							
Total	−0.1984	0.0571	*−0.0368*	0.3153	*−0.0022*	−0.2262	0.1869
Direct	*−15.3743*	*−8.2700*	*−1.0609*	*−16.2843*	*−23.1103*	*−15.8339*	*−3.7120*
Indirect	*15.1759*	*8.3270*	*1.0241*	*16.5996*	*23.1081*	*15.6078*	*3.8989*
Joint discretionary activities							
Total	*0.0114*	*0.0033*	−0.4978	0.6137	0.3724	*0.1455*	*0.0258*
Direct	−2.7101	−1.4874	*−0.2932*	−2.8332	−4.0512	−2.7617	−0.6922
Indirect	2.7215	1.4906	*−0.2046*	3.4469	4.4236	2.9072	0.7179

Note: Figures in italics are not significant at the 0.05 level; all others are significant at the 0.05 level or below.
(–) Cases where no link is postulated.

The Effects of Live-in Maids on Household Heads' Participation in Out-of-Home Activities

We first examine how the presence of live-in maids impacts on the participation of the two household heads in out-of-home activities and on the interactions between them. As Table 2 shows, the presence of live-in maids has generation, substitution, and modification effects on out-of-home activity participation of the two household heads.

Generation Effects The presence of live-in maids has a very significant positive direct effect on the time spent for subsistence activities by female head. Its *t*-value (not shown in the table) is the second largest, which suggests that this direct effect is one of the most significant ones among the endogenous variables. This finding supports our hypothesis that the presence of a live-in maid leads female head to join the work force and spend more time for subsistence activities. One may argue that it is probably another way around, that is, the households with employed female heads are more likely to hire live-in maids. This is probably true as well. However, from this research's point of view, which is the real cause does not really matter, what matters is the finding that female heads of households with live-in maids spend more time for subsistence activities. The importance of this effect goes beyond itself because the fact that female heads spend more time for work may totally restructure the activity–travel pattern of the female heads. We will discuss this later. The generation effect is also evident for the joint discretionary activities. Table 2 shows that the direct effect of live-in maids on joint discretionary activities is also positive and highly significant. This implies that the presence of live-in maids may lead to more joint discretionary activities by the two household heads. Nevertheless, the total effect seems not significant. This is because the positive direct effect is largely canceled out by a similar magnitude but negative indirect effect. This negative indirect effect (−5.6058) is mediated by female heads' time use for subsistence activities, to which the presence of live-in maids has a positive direct effect (2.8664) but which negatively impacts on the joint discretionary activities (−1.9557). In other words, on the one hand, the presence of live-in-maids leads the two household heads to engage in more joint discretionary activities; on the other hand, this same variable increases female heads' time for subsistence activities which in turn reduces the probability for joint discretionary activities. The total effect thus becomes insignificant.

Substitution/Replacement Effects Apart from the generation effect, the substitution effects of live-in maids are also evident. As Table 2 shows, the presence of live-in maids has negative and significant total and direct effects on the undertaking of maintenance activities by both male and female heads. In other words, the hiring of live-in maids leads to fewer maintenance activities undertaken by either male or female household head. This is as expected, because the domestic helpers are employed to take up the household maintenance duties. To our surprise, the variable has also negative and significant direct effects on discretionary activities of both male and female heads. This seems to be in contradiction to our assumption that hiring live-in maids may allow the household heads to have more free time for discretionary activities. However, an examination of the lifestyle of Hong Kong people may suggest a possible explanation: households with live-in maids likely spend more time at home partly because they have someone to serve meals and others. This may reduce the chance for them to go out to have meals and thus chances for other discretionary activities.

Modification Effects As an example of the modification effects, we may examine how the presence of live-in maids leads to the change of the maintenance and discretionary activities of the female head. Earlier it was mentioned that as direct effects, the presence of live-in maids reduces the female head's undertaking of maintenance and discretionary activities. However, Table 2 also shows that its indirect effect is positive, that is, indirectly the presence of live-in maids increases female heads' maintenance activities. This indirect effect (2.7931) is resulted from the product of its positive effects toward time use for subsistence activities (2.8664), which in turn stimulates more maintenance activities (0.9744) (later, it will be explained that for female heads, more time spent for subsistence activities may induce some maintenance activities such as personal business, shopping activities, etc.). The net effect, as indicated by the negative total effect, is thus resulted from a negative direct effect offset partially by a smaller but positive indirect effect. In other words, on the one hand, the presence of live-in maids reduces female heads' maintenance activities through substitution effect; on the other hand, it also increases maintenance activities through modification effect. The final outcome is that the presence of live-in maids reduces female heads' maintenance activities, though to a less extent because of the modification effect. Similarly, as indirect effects, the presence of live-in maids contributes positively to female heads' participation in discretionary activities. This indirect effect (22.5396) comes from three sources [22.5396 = 2.8664*4.0717+(−5.7125)*(−3.7228)+2.8664*0.9744*(−3.722*)]:

(a) the product of its positive effects toward time use for subsistence activities (2.8664) which in turn stimulates more discretionary activities (4.0717);
(b) the product of its negative effects toward maintenance activities (−5.7125) which in turn reduces the probability for discretionary activities (−3.7228);
(c) the product of its positive effects toward time use for subsistence activities (2.8664) which in turn stimulates more maintenance activities (0.9744) which further reduces the undertaking of discretionary activities (−3.7228). The modification effect is also evident for the joint discretionary activities as discussed earlier.

The Effects of More Mandatory Activities on Less Ones

Previous studies have demonstrated that mandatory activities impose time constraints, or define the time windows for less mandatory or discretionary activities (e.g., Lu and Pas, 1999). This is also evident in this study. As Table 2 shows, more time spent for subsistence activities reduces the probability for male heads to conduct maintenance and discretionary activities. It also diminishes male heads' likelihood to participate in joint discretionary as well as maintenance activities. Further, by taking maintenance duties, male heads conduct fewer discretionary activities. However, the story is somehow different for female heads. More time spent for subsistence activities is found to increase female heads' maintenance as well as discretionary activities. A possible explanation is that by joining the work force, female heads may need more personal maintenance, such as personal business, shopping for items that are needed at work place (e.g., clothes), etc. Further, they are exposed to more opportunities for discretionary activities and thus more participation in these types of activities. Nevertheless, more time spent for subsistence activities also seems to reduce the probabilities for female heads to participate in joint discretionary and maintenance activities. This is likely because it is difficult to coordinate their schedules for the two heads if they are both employed. Similar to the finding for male heads, the conduct of maintenance activities by female heads reduces their probabilities of undertaking discretionary activities.

Interactions between the Two Household Heads

A number of interaction effects between the two household heads can be observed from Table 2. First, time spent for subsistence activities by male heads has a positive and significant direct effect on the probability of female heads to undertake maintenance activities. In other words, maintenance activities are more likely to be taken by the female head if the male head has to work longer. Similar findings have been reported by Golob and McNally (1997). On the other hand, more time spent for subsistence activities by female heads also increases the probability of undertaking maintenance activities by male heads. Similarly, more time spent for subsistence activities by male heads increases the participation of female heads in discretionary activities; more time spent for subsistence activities by female heads increases male heads' engagement in discretionary activities. These findings echo those of earlier studies by Srinivasan and Athuru (2005) and Srinivasan and Bhat (2006), who suggest that household heads' participation in discretionary activities is influenced by the mandatory and maintenance activity participation characteristics of the spouse. An explanation to these results is that if one of the heads is committed to work activities, the coupling constraints are relaxed and the other head may thus have time to engage in discretionary activities (Hägerstrand, 1970).

What Households' Socio-Demographic Variables determine their Probability of hiring Live-in Maids?

Table 3 shows that household income, type of housing, and the presence of child aged 1–5 years all have positive and very significant impact on the probability of hiring live-in maids. These three variables measure, respectively, households' affordability, room availability, and needs for hiring domestic helpers. The modeling results are within our expectation: more household income means higher affordability and thus more likely to hire domestic helpers. The positive effect of the type of housing suggests that households living in private apartments or houses are more likely to hire live-in maids. Since private housing is usually larger than public housing in Hong Kong, households living in private houses have more space to accommodate live-in maids than those living in public houses. The presence of children, in particular, young children, generates enormous maintenance duties and thus increases the practical needs for hiring domestic helpers. Apart from these three variables, the availability of car, which is another indicator of household affordability, contributes also positively to the probability of hiring live-in maids. The age of household head, a variable of family cycle, is also found to be influential on the hiring of live-in maids.

Effects of Socio-Demographics on Activity Allocation between the Two Household Heads

Household socio-demographic variables are found in previous studies to be influential to activity allocation between the two household heads. Table 3 shows that household income has a positive total effect on male as well as female heads' undertaking of maintenance activities but a negative total effect on joint maintenance activities. This suggests that the higher the household income, the more likely the two household heads will conduct maintenance activities individually rather than jointly. Similar findings are reported by an earlier study (Srinivasan and Athuru, 2005). On the other hand, household income seems not effective on joint discretionary activities and on male heads' independent participation in discretionary activities, though it contributes positively to female heads' engagement in discretionary activities. The presence of both younger and older children is found to favor the conduct of maintenance activities individually, though the presence of younger child (aged 1–5 years) seems to stimulate more joint discretionary activities, a finding that is different from that of an earlier study (Srinivasan and Bhat, 2006). On the other hand, the availability of private car promotes the joint implementation of maintenance activities but seems to encourage individual conduct of discretionary activities. Household size is found to impact negatively on female heads' discretionary activities and the joint participation of the two heads in discretionary activities. Age of household head (the head declared in the survey) has positive total effect on individual as well as joint participation in maintenance activities, suggesting that heads of older households conduct more maintenance activities either jointly or individually than those of younger households.

Conclusions and Discussion

This paper studied the impacts of live-in maids on the participation of household heads in out-of-home activities. It was postulated that the presence of live-in maids might generate, substitute, or modify the out-of-home activity patterns of the two household heads. We further assumed that the impacts might be different for male and female heads, because of the different family roles they take. The hypotheses were tested to a sample derived from the 2002 Travel Characteristics Survey of Hong Kong. The structural equations model system was applied to identify the direct and indirect effects of live-in maids on household heads' participation in out-of-home activities and to model the interactions between the two household heads and between different activity types.

As expected, the presence of live-in maids was found to reduce the undertaking of maintenance activities by both female and male household heads. Most importantly, it was discovered that female heads of households with domestic helpers spent more time for subsistence activities than those without. This is an important piece of evidence of the generation effect of live-in maids. This finding also supports an argument put forward by a previous study: releasing home makers from burdens of household work, the domestic helpers help to "allow more Hong Kong people to work, rather than looking after children or the elderly"[1] and lead to the "dramatic shifts in patterns of women's employment in Hong Kong" (Constable, 1997). To our surprise, the presence of live-in maids did not increase but reduced household heads' participation in discretionary activities. The presence of live-in maids was also found to trigger the restructuring of activity patterns of household heads through indirect effects. In other words, the modification effects were also evident. The findings of this study support the argument that the domestic helpers have contributed a great deal not only to the local economy by increasing the working hours of female heads (Collier, 2004), but also to Hong Kong people's quality of life by facilitating household heads' adjustment of activity patterns so that a balance between maintaining a career and a happy family life can be reached (Constable, 1997).

The present study may be improved by explicitly modeling both the discrete and continuous components of activity participation. Moreover, it might be desired to develop a theoretical model that considers how households tradeoff between spending money to hire a maid and shoulder the maintenance responsibilities.

ACKNOWLEDGMENT

This research is sponsored by a research grant from Hong Kong Research Grant Council (RGC) (HKBU2441/05H).

[1]http://www.ordinarygweilo.com/2004/10/helping_the_eco.html

References

Bhat, C. R. and F. S. Koppelman (1993). A conceptual framework of individual activity program generation. *Transportation Research* 27A(6), 433–446.

Bhat, C. R. and R. Mirsa (1999). Discretionary activity time allocation of individuals between in-home and out-of-home and between weekdays and weekends. *Transportation* 26, 193–209.

Census and Statistics Department. (1995). Domestic helpers. Social Data Collected by the General Household Survey: Special Topics Report No. 14, Government Printer, Hong Kong, p. 70.

Census and Statistics Department. (2005). *Hong Kong Annual Digest of Statistics*, 2005 edn. Hong Kong, Government Printer, p. 32

Collier, A. (2004). Maids' $13b lift for Hong Kong. *The Standard*, September 27, Hong Kong.

Constable, N. (1997). Sexuality and discipline among Filipina domestic workers in Hong Kong. *American Ethnologist* 24(3), 539–558.

Fujii, S., R. Kitamura and K. Kishizawa (1999). Analysis of individuals' joint activity engagement using a model system of activity–travel behavior and time use. *Transportation Research Record: Journal of the Transportation Research Board* (1676), 11-19 (TRB, National Research Council, Washington, DC).

Gliebe, J. P. and F. S. Koppelman (2002). A model of joint activity participation between household members. *Transportation* 29, 49–72.

Gliebe, J. P. and F. S. Koppelman (2005). Modeling household activity–travel interactions as parallel constrained choices. *Transportation* 32, 449–471.

Golob, T. and M. G. McNally (1997). A model of activity participation and travel interactions between household heads. *Transportation Research B* 31(3), 177–194.

Golob, T. F. (2003). Review structural equation modeling for travel behavior research. *Transportation Research Part B* 37, 1–5.

Hägerstrand, T. (1970). What about people in regional science? *Papers of the Regional Science Association* 23, 7–21.

Jöreskog, K. and D. Sörbom (2001). *LISREL 8: User's Reference Guide*. Lincolnwood, USA, Scientific Software International, Inc.

Kostyniuk, L. P. and R. Kitamura (1983). An empirical investigation of household space–time paths. In S. Carpenter and P. M. Jones (Eds.), *Recent Advances in Travel Demand Analysis*. Aldershot, UK, Gower.

Lu, X. and E. I. Pas (1999). Socio-demographics, activity participation and travel behaviour. *Transportation Research Part A* 33, 1–18.

Reichman, S. (1976). Travel adjustments and life styles: a behavioral approach. In P. Stopher and A. Meyburg (Eds.), *Behavioral Travel Demand Models*. Lexington, MA, Lexington Books.

Scott, D. M. and P. S. Kanaroglou (2002). An activity-episode generation model that captures interactions between household heads: development and empirical analysis. *Transportation Research B* 36, 875–896.

Srinivasan, K. K. and S. R. Athuru (2005). Analysis of within-household effects and between-household difference in maintenance activity allocation. *Transportation* 32, 495–521.

Srinivasan, S. and C. R. Bhat (2005). Modelling household interactions in daily in-home and out-of-home maintenance activity participation. *Transportation* 32, 523–544.

Srinivasan, S. and C. R. Bhat (2006). A multiple discrete–continuous model for independent- and joint-discretionary–activity participation decisions. *Transportation Research Board 85th Annual Meeting Pre-Print*. Washington, DC. (CD-ROM).

Townsend, T. A. (1987). The effects of household characteristics on the multi-day time allocations and travel–activity patterns of households and their members. Unpublished Ph.D. Dissertation, Northwestern University.

Vovsha, P., E. Peterson and R. Donnelly (2004). A model for allocation of maintenance activities to the household members. Paper presented at the 83rd Annual Conference of the Transportation Research Board, Washington, DC.

Zhang, J., H. J. P. Timmermans and A. Borgers (2002). A utility-maximizing model of household time use for independent, shared, and allocated activities incorporating group decision mechanisms. *Transportation Research Record: Journal of the Transportation Research Board* (1807), 1-8 (TRB, National Research Council, Washington, DC).

Zhang, J., H. J. P. Timmermans and A. Borgers (2004). Model structure kernel for household task allocation incorporating household interaction and inter-activity dependency. *Transportation Research Board 83rd Annual Meeting Pre-Print*. Washington, DC (CD-ROM).

The Expanding Sphere of Travel Behaviour Research
Selected Papers from the 11th International Conference on Travel Behaviour Research

30

Role of Minority Influence on the Diffusion of Compliance with a Demand Management Measure

Yos Sunitiyoso, Erel Avineri and Kiron Chatterjee

Abstract

This study utilizes an agent-based approach to simulate behaviours of individuals. It is aimed to obtain some informed insights about the role of social interaction, social learning and social influence on travellers' decision making to comply with a policy measure. A multi-agent model which incorporates these social aspects is developed. The social interaction includes consideration of various interaction domains (e.g. neighbourhood, workplaces, or non-work activity clubs) and two sequential processes of interaction: meeting and communicating. In the social learning and influence, an investigation of the role of minority influence on the spread of compliance with a policy measure becomes a primary consideration. Aspect like inertia in decision making is also considered. An explorative behavioural survey has been conducted to obtain initial information regarding mechanisms of social interaction and social learning. Based on the survey, parameters and initial values of variables required for the simulation model have been estimated. The survey suggests that some individuals may be influenced by other people, who are relatively close to them, regarding travel-related decision. These close persons of an individual may have an opinion/expectation which can be important for the individual. Both empirical and theoretical findings are combined to develop a multi-agent simulation model. The results of simulation experiments suggest that the model is able to provide some informed insights about the spread of compliance with a 'soft' measure from an individual to other individuals and the diffusion from a group to other groups. Social interaction has been shown to have a major role in spreading compliance with the measure. The role of minority influence on eliciting compliance has been demonstrated in the experiments. A small number of influential individuals with consistency of choice on complying with the measure were able to diffuse their choice to others. Also, a group that consists of influential agents was able to diffuse their compliance to other individuals from different groups. The results have also shown that a social club domain with a high frequency of repeated interactions between its members have an important role on the spread of compliance. Overall, the study has fulfilled its objectives and has also shown how we can incorporate social aspects, such as social interaction, social learning, and social influence, into modelling travellers' change of behaviour.

Introduction

Demand management measures are utilized to address the problem of people's car dependence by incorporating structural interventions ('hard' measures) as well as psychological interventions ('soft' measures). 'Hard' measures include policy interventions that alter the objective features of the decision situation by changing the incentive patterns associated with cooperation and non-cooperation. Examples of 'hard' measures may include changing payoff structure (e.g. congestion charging), reward-punishment (e.g. incentives for public transport users, restriction on car parking) and situational change (e.g. residential or workplace relocation). 'Soft' measures can be defined as policy interventions that are aimed at influencing attitudes and beliefs that may guide people's cooperative and non-cooperative behaviours. 'Soft' measures, which are more persuasive than 'hard' measures, can be implied by increasing individuals' awareness of the environmental impacts of excessive car use (e.g. travel awareness campaign) and providing advice and information to encourage the use of alternative modes than car (e.g. travel plan, individualized marketing) and alternative way of using car (e.g. car sharing).

In this study, we argue that the effectivenesses of 'soft' measures may be enhanced if more consideration and emphasis is given to the support of social aspects of human behaviour. Given the fact that behavioural change does not take place in a social vacuum, broader society and its social values have important roles to play. Social aspects, including *social interaction*, *social learning/imitation* and *social influence*, may influence travellers' decision making and behaviour. Within social influence, emphasis shall be put on *minority influence* as this type of social influence may have an important role in spreading compliance with a soft measure. In the minority influence, a few individuals (independently or in group) have influencing power built on their reputation to induce compliance in the population (Sampson, 1991, pp. 151–163). Better understanding of these aspects will provide us with some informed insights about the potential for utilizing them to encourage travellers' compliance.

The idea of utilizing a simulation model to better understand the impact of a demand management measure on travellers' behaviours has not been given much consideration until recently, despite its potential to provide a different 'flavour' on travel behaviour studies by deriving informed insights from simulation experiments (e.g. Kitamura et al., 1999; Sunitiyoso and Matsumoto, 2009). In studying the effects of a treatment/intervention on individuals, a simulation experiment offers extension to a laboratory experiment since it is able to handle the interactions of a large number of individuals with each other and with a transport system. It also makes possible for conducting a large number of repetitions (time periods), which enable the researcher to observe whether individuals' choices converge to an equilibrium point or not, how they converge and the dynamics before convergence, and how many repetitions are required to reach the convergence point. A simulation approach may also give predictive benefit to forecast travellers' behaviour in different kind of situations and to know how robust the results of the laboratory experiments are in other parametric conditions.

The diffusion process of compliance with a demand management measure has become our interest as it may have important role in encouraging behavioural change. Jones and Sloman (2003) argued that the existence of the 'snowball effect', a phenomenon where long-term effects may be greater than short-term ones, would increase the effectiveness of 'soft' measures over time. They stated that there is some evidence that the change may be very slow at first, but then accelerates as people see their colleagues and neighbours changing their travel behaviour. In the implementation of voluntary travel behaviour change programs, Ampt (2003) argued that strategies that require households to diffuse information both between households and ultimately across communities are likely to be sustainable. Spreading information by 'word-of-mouth' has been argued to be most effective way for diffusion and reinforcement (Stern et al., 1987). When a person tells someone about what she is doing, she is both reinforcing her own behaviour in the process and giving a level of commitment. Involving key people (not necessarily traditional leaders, but 'trusted others' in the community) will provide more advantages since people are more willing to hear from someone who is trusted, respected or perceived to have similar values. This is related with the idea of minority influence where a few influential agents are able to influence the opposing majority to the minority's way of thinking. Stopher (2005) added the importance of diffusion effects in the implementation of voluntary programs by stating the need to measure the effects in schools, workplaces, and other locations. A study by Shaheen (2004) also considered this word-of-mouth communication as a means to diffuse the change of behaviour in a car-sharing programme. Taniguchi and Fujii (2007) in their study of promoting community bus service found that word-of-mouth advertising through recommendations to friends and family plays an important role in promoting bus use. This interaction process may have begun a chain of bus use and recommendations. In modelling, Ellison and Fudenberg (1995) developed a formal model of the influence of word-of-mouth communication structure in social learning. Their paper discusses the way that word-of-mouth communication aggregates the information of individual agents. They found that word-of-mouth communication may lead all agents to adopt the action that produces socially efficient outcomes. This tends to occur when each agent receives limited information about other agents.

A way of spreading information which is commonly used is by media (e.g. newspaper, radio, TV, etc.), as often used in social norms media campaigns (e.g. DeJong, 2002). However, this study does not address this way of communicating. It is looking at the diffusion of information directly from person to person.

The structure of this chapter consists of seven sections. Following an introduction in this section, the hypotheses underlying the research as well as the research objectives are discussed in the section 'Hypotheses'. The section 'General Framework and Main Concepts' presents the general framework of the study and the main concepts such as social interaction, social learning and influence, and individuals' decision making process. The section 'Simulation Model' provides discussions about the simulation model, followed by the section 'Setting Values To The Model's Parameters And Variables' which discusses model's parameters and variables. Simulation results are analysed and discussed in the section 'Simulation Results and Discussion'. The chapter is closed with conclusions and future research in the sections 'Conclusions' and 'Future Research', respectively.

Hypotheses

The study aims at investigating the following hypotheses:

a. Social aspects, mainly *social interaction*, *social learning/imitation* and *social influence*, may influence travellers' decision making and behaviour.
b. *Repeated social interactions* between individuals generate a high propensity for communicating which later give more opportunity to induce compliance in the population, since communication enables exchanges of information between individuals and provides a means of social learning/imitation.
c. *Minority influence*, a type of social influence, may have an important role in spreading compliance with a soft measure. A few influential individuals with a good reputation derived from their consistency on complying with the policy measure may influence other individuals' decision of whether to comply or not.

Based on those hypotheses, research objectives are derived. The main objective of this study is to obtain informed insights on the influence of social interaction and social learning in travellers' decision making to comply with a soft measure by utilizing an agent-based approach to simulate behaviours of individuals.This primary objective can be splitted into two sub-objectives:

a. To provide a model of *social interaction* with respect to travel decision making, which includes the consideration of:
   - various interaction domains: neighbourhood, workplaces/schools, non-work/non-study activity clubs;
   - processes of interaction: meeting and communicating.
b. To develop a model of *social learning and social influence* in the context of travel-choice behaviour, which primarily includes the investigation of the role of minority influence on spreading compliance with a soft measure. Aspect like inertia in decision making is also considered.

General Framework and Main Concepts

Figure 1 presents the general framework of the study. Two main focuses are *social interaction,* which consists of the process of meeting and communicating, and *social learning/imitation* and *social influence*, where imitating/learning and influencing process may occur between individuals. Individual's own experience is also being considered, however it is rather simplified. Social learning and social influence, together with individual's experience-based learning, affect the individual's preference that later influence her behaviour. Other factors, such as costs, values, attitudes, social norms, habit, personality traits and constraints, may also influence individuals' preference. However, since not being the scope of this study, these factors are not included in the research framework.

The framework is a snapshot of an individual's dynamic responses. The processes in the framework are iterative processes of adaptation to the changes of decision-making environment caused by own experience and other people decisions/behaviours, as well as changes in travel environment caused by a policy intervention. In this study, we focus on the period of time where a policy measure is being applied, particularly a 'soft' measure. However, it is not restricted to a 'soft' measure. It is also applicable to a situation where a structural change produced by a 'hard' measure has been applied and the effects of cost change have been minimized (e.g. people has already got used to a new travel cost resulting from the structural change and become less sensitive to the cost difference).

Social Interaction

In this study, we consider that social interactions occur beyond residential neighbourhoods. There may be multi-dimensional relationships between individuals,

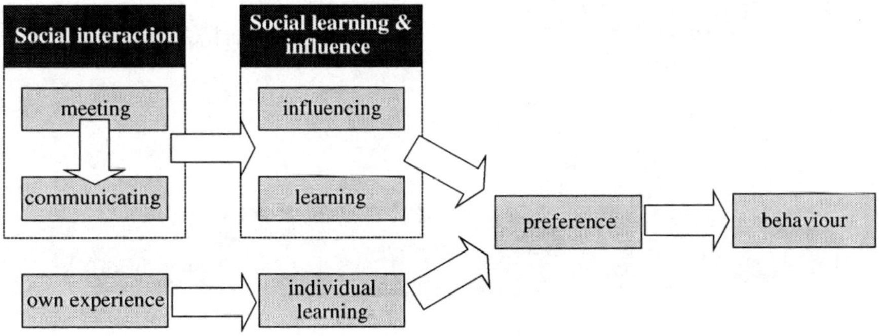

Figure 1
General Framework

which are built based on similarities of 'social club' domains, including workplace, non-work activity club and also within a household. Since this study does not focus on intra-household interactions, interactions within members of a household are not included in the model. Social club membership may be initiated by some key events during a life course (for reference about key events, see Van der Waerden et al., 2003; Stanbridge et al., 2004). For example, moving house initiates new neighbourhood relationship, a new workplace or a new school implies the probability of repeated interactions with schoolmates, etc. Becoming a new member of a group such as family, work or other social clubs, automatically creates social links between the new and existing members of the group. Arentze and Timmermans (2006) argued that the links exist as long as the membership holds and may or may not sustain beyond the membership period depending on the extent they are being reinforced over time. In this Internet era, the 'online' social network domain has also arisen and is used in some research studies (e.g. Tian et al., 2003).

The possibility of repeated and frequent interactions between individuals differs from one social club to another. For example, a workplace gives more opportunity for interaction than a sport/leisure club since colleagues in the same workplace spend around 5 days a week, whereas members of sport/leisure club may only meet less frequently. With each individual involved in various interaction domains, compliance in a group may diffuse to other groups during repeated processes of interaction. Figure 2 shows an illustration of multi-domain interactions between three individuals

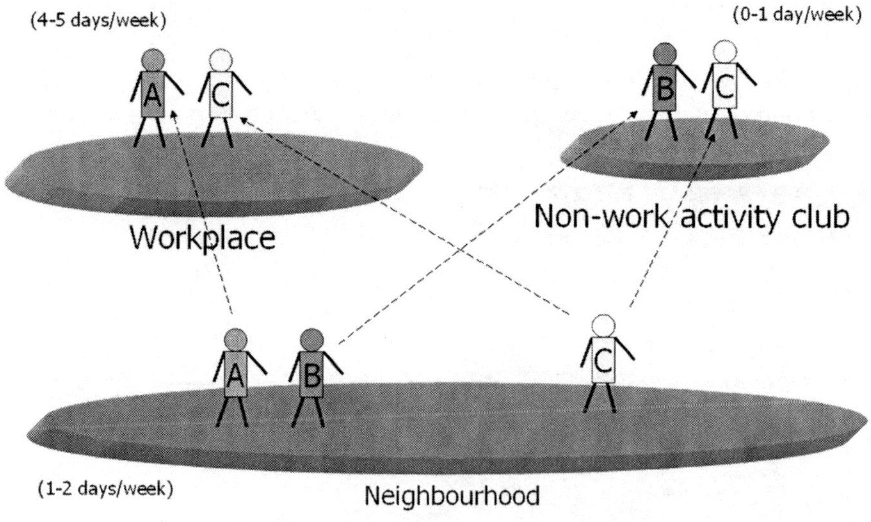

Figure 2
Illustration of a Multi-Domain Social Interaction and Social Learning/Influence

(A, B and C) as well as possible frequencies of interactions within each domain. Domains of interactions are not limited to those which are illustrated in the figure. Social interactions with friends or relatives in other domains may also exist and exert influence.

In the simulation model developed in this study, social interaction is represented by two processes: *meeting* and *communicating*. These processes may occur in any social club domain depending on the day of the week whenever agents (who represent individuals) involve with activities in the domain. Meeting is defined as a process where two agents meet each other without engaging in an intensive communication involving an exchange of information. Communication may follow the meeting if there is a 'mutual agreement' between them, which depends on whether they are both closely connected or not (represented by the value of perceived degree of relationship) and on whether a threshold for communicating has been exceeded or not. Arentze and Timmermans (2006) described different criteria to achieve mutual agreement. They argued that the agreement can be achieved if both agents consider that the expected utility of the interaction (communication) compensates for the loss in discretionary time and the effort involved. The criteria used in this study are simpler and probably more realistic since individuals may not be too 'rational' regarding social interaction (meeting and communicating) for the sake of utility gained from the interaction, instead a simple reason, such as the feeling that they are closely related, may start communication. Table 1 shows the possibility for communicating which depends on the value of perceived degree of relationship and threshold and relationship. The higher the threshold is, the lower the possibility for an individual to have a communication with another individual. The higher the perceived degree of relationship is, the higher the possibility for communicating.

As social network may affect the spread of influence (Kempe et al., 2003), the structure of network has an important role to determine a successful diffusion of compliance. There are many kinds of communication structure that may exist between individuals. In this study, it is assumed that within the neighbourhood domain individuals may meet (but not necessarily followed by communication) their neighbours in a lattice-structured network. Imagine that each individual occupies a cell in a 2D plane,

Table 1
Possibility for Communicating

	Threshold for communicating	
	Low	**High**
Perceived degree of relationship		
Low	Medium	Low
High	High	Medium

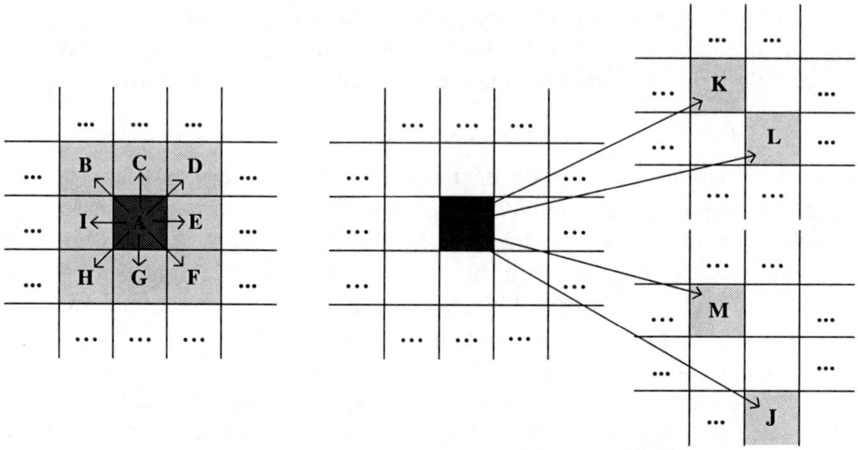

(a) lattice-structured network **(b) complete mixing network**

Figure 3
Illustration of Social Interactions through Lattice-Structured and Complete Mixing Networks

Figure 3a illustrates a lattice-structured social network between an individual (called A) and her/his immediate neighbours (B, C, D, E, F, G, H and I). While in other types of social club (e.g. workplace, non-work social club), they meet any other member in random manner (complete mixing). This is illustrated in Figure 3b where individual A has a complete mixing network with individual J, K, L and M which are located in dispersed cells on the 2D plane.

A study by Blonski (1999), which utilized the Case-Based Decision Theory (CBDT) developed by Gilboa and Schmeidler (1995) for investigating social learning process through different communication structures, reported an important finding in relation to the effects of communication structure on the spread of influence. There is a communication structure called 'star' structure, where each individual is informed only about his own actions and the action of one distinguished agent, called the 'star'. There is no communication between agents except with the star. This distinguished agent has the power of manipulating the direction of social learning. The agent does not face a choice problem and is not subject to any stochastic shocks. It has been reported that the star communication structure was able to generate a high level of cooperation. This study is in line with our proposed study on investigating minority influence, since the 'stars' may represent a minority with high influencing power. However, agents do not necessarily communicate with stars only, but they may also communicate with other common agents.

Social Learning and Social Influence

An agent may learn individually from her own experience and learn socially from information gained during communication with other agents. The concept of learning suggests that individuals learn from their past experience and acquire an adaptive decision-making process to cope with uncertain nature of environment (Arentze and Timmermans, 2005). In transport field, individual learning concept has been utilized in the context of mode choice, route choice and departure time choice (e.g. Akiyama and Tsuboi, 1996; Verplanken et al., 1997; Fujii et al., 2001; Nakayama et al., 2001; Srinivasan and Guo, 2003; Avineri and Prashker, 2005). On contrary, incorporation of the social learning concept in travel behaviour studies is still a challenge as it has not been investigated intensively, although evidences from other disciplines (e.g. Pingle, 1995; Pingle and Day, 1996; Offerman and Sonnemans, 1998; Smith and Bell, 1994; Kameda and Nakanishi, 2002, 2003) have shown that this kind of learning is influential and important. In social learning, decision makers may have the opportunity to observe the behaviours or preferences of others prior to making a choice.

There is a slight difference that can be drawn between social learning and social influence. In social learning, the change of judgments, opinions and attitudes of an individual is a result of active search for information by the individual, where as in social influence, the change is a result of being exposed to those of other individuals (Van Avermaet, 1996).

Social influence is more than the majority's efforts to produce conformity on the part of a minority; it is also a minority's effort to convert the majority to its own way of thinking (Sampson, 1991). In this research, minority influence becomes the point of interest. Minority influence is investigated by introducing a situation where a few influential agents (independently or in group) have more power to influence others whom they communicate with. The strength of their influence is derived from the reputation built from their consistency of choice to comply with the measure (Van Avermaet, 1996; Sampson, 1991, p. 155). An influential individual is not necessarily a traditional leader, but she can be a 'trusted person' with a respected reputation in the social club. Individuals are more willing to hear from someone who is trusted and respected as a consistent person. For example, a suggestion to car share by a consistent car sharer, who has been car sharing regularly in a considerable period of time, would have more influence than that of other individuals' who have not done so.

Latané and Wolf (1981), in the first principle of their Theory of Social Impact-Principle of Social Forces, argued that social impact is a multiplicative function of three factors: strength (e.g. power, expertise), immediacy (proximity in space and time) and size (number of the influence sources). The principle shares the same idea with Tanford and Penrod's (1984) Social Influence Model (SIM). However, Tanford and Penrod's theory is more formal and it is based on certain features presumed to exist in any majority and minority influence situation, such as group size, number of influence sources, probabilities that a majority member will choose the minority position without any influence attempted by the minority, and individual differences in members' susceptibility to persuasion. The minority influence may have smaller number of influence sources than majority, but it may still rely on strength (power to influence derived from reputation) and immediacy (closeness of relationships between individuals).

Decision-Making Process

The decision of whether to comply with a demand management measure is made based on the individual *i*'s preference value (P_i). Each individual learns individually from past decisions, learns/imitates other agents' decisions and is influenced by 'influential' individuals, and then updates her preference value in a reinforcement process. The higher the preference to comply is, the more the probability that the individual will comply with the measure.

The decision making of each agent is based on a social influence model with each agent takes into consideration previous choices and choices of other people. The model is based on Gordon et al.'s (2004) social influence model. Considering difficulties on measuring some of the original model's parameters, assumptions are used to simplify the model. We modify and extend the Gordon et al.'s model by adding an individual experience term, so that the model can be formulated as:

$$C_{it+1} = f\left(\frac{1}{\|\vartheta_i\|}\sum_{j\in\vartheta_i}\beta_{ij}C_{jt}, \beta_{ii}C_{it}\right) \tag{1}$$

where C_{it} is the decision/choice of individual i at time t (binary choice, $C_{it}\in\{0,1\}$; multiple n choice, $C_{it}\in\{0,1, \ldots, n\}$); ϑ_i the set of individual *i*'s neighbours/colleagues/friends ($\vartheta_i \subseteq S$); S a set of agents in the population; β_{ij} a weight given by individual i to the recent choice of individual j ($\beta_{ij}\in[0,1]$); β_{ii} a weight given by individual *i*'s to her own recent choice ($\beta_{ii}\in[0,1]$; $\sum\beta_{ij} + \beta_{ii} = 1$).

In the model, interactions between two or more agents are treated in one-to-one interaction basis. For example, interactions between individuals i, j and k are considered as three interaction processes: $i\leftrightarrow j$, $i\leftrightarrow k$ and $j\leftrightarrow k$. So that, there will be only a pair of individuals in each interaction ($N = 2$). The number of individual *i*'s neighbours/colleagues/friends in each single interaction is only 1 ($\|\vartheta_i\| = 1$), since the interaction is one-to-one. Then equation (1) becomes:

$$C_{it+1} = f(\beta_{ij}C_{jt}, \beta_{ii}C_{it}); i\neq j \tag{2}$$

where j is a single individual with whom individual i interacts.

This research considers that every single choice of own and other individuals contributes to the change of individual i's preference at time t (P_{it}) in an individual learning process from time to time. Since the processes of individual and social learning may take place at the same time, there are two processes of updating P_i by using a simple weighted updating mechanism in this equation:

$$P_{it+1} = \begin{cases} (1-\beta_{ij})P_{it} + \beta_{ij}C_{jt} \Leftarrow i \neq j \\ (1-\beta_{ii})P_{it} + \beta_{ii}C_{it} \Leftarrow i = j \end{cases} \tag{3}$$

The first part of equation (3) applies whenever individual i interacts with individual j and puts the choice of individual j into consideration following a process of social learning or social influence. The other part represents a simple individual learning process of individual i's whenever she makes a decision/choice. The choice of individual i at time $t+1$ (C_{it+1}) depends on her preference value at that time (P_{it+1}). A uniform-distributed $U[0,1]$'s random number x is generated and then compared with the preference value using equation (4) to decide whether to comply ($C_{it+1} = 1$) or not to comply ($C_{it+1} = 0$).

$$C_{it+1} = \begin{cases} 1 \Leftarrow P_{it+1} > x \\ 0 \Leftarrow P_{it+1} \leq x \end{cases} \tag{4}$$

The decision-making process of each individual is repeated from time to time. The preference to comply with a demand measure (P_{it}) is also updated when the individual makes decision as well as when she/he learns from (is influenced by) other individuals. However, the population of individuals also displays inertia, where only a number of them make a decision and the others continue with their previous choice. And also each individual does not have perfect information about the choice of all other individuals in the population. She/he only knows the choice of other individuals whom she communicates with.

As the emphasis of this study is on exploring the spread of compliance during the implementation of a 'soft' policy measure, which may not incur any economic cost to the travellers, we do not assume any specific utilities or payoff consequences (e.g. cost, earning or other outcomes in amount of money) of every choice made by an agent. In some studies, payoff or cost consequences are not used in order to avoid a cost-driven situation which may hinder the investigation of the social aspects being studied, as well as to avoid too many complications (e.g. Axelrod, 1997; Nakamaru and Levin, 2004). Moreover, in some situations, people may not economically rational to make a travel-choice decision. As the choice in the model is a binary choice of whether to comply or not to comply, for simplicity, a score of one ($C_{it} = 1$) is given to compliance and zero ($C_{it} = 0$) to non-compliance.

The model is a simple social influence model where each agent only takes into consideration previous choices and choices of other people, without considering the outputs of the choices. The model is neither based on reinforcement-learning theory nor utility theory. It contains a process where preferences are updated based on choices, which deviates from an assumption of reinforcement-learning theory that the value of an action is updated each time an action is chosen based on perceived rewards (not based on choice of the action). Utilities are also not represented in the model, only tendencies to repeat earlier behaviour or behaviour of others. However, for future development, utilities of agent's action (e.g. cost, earning) shall be considered in the model. In addition, reinforcement-learning models (e.g. heuristic, weighted-return and average-return) may be incorporated into the modelling of agents' decision-making algorithms.

Simulation Model

The model consists of three main sections: social interaction, social learning and influence, and decision making. Figures 4a and b presents the algorithm of the developed model. The algorithm starts with initialization process of assigning a number of agents into the social interaction domains (also referred as 'social clubs'), such as *residential neighbourhood, workplace/school* and *other activity clubs.*

In the initialization process, a value of global parameters (e.g. size of the minority N_{m}) and an initial value of global variables (e.g. level of compliance LC) are set. A population of agents (S) is then generated (virtually in a grid space) and given attributes (parameters and initial variables). A value of individual parameters (TH_i, REP_i, β_{ij}, α_{ij} and γ_{ij}; see Table 2 in the section 'Setting Values to the Model's Parameters and Variables' for description of these parameters) and an initial value of individual variables (P_i, R_{ij}, $t\mathrm{Dec}_i$ and C_i; see Table 3 for description) are assigned to every single agent i.

There are two types of agents: an influential agent (which is a member of the minority) and a common agent. An influential agent is given reputation $\mathrm{REP}_i = 1$ and a common agent is given $\mathrm{REP}_i = 0$. REP is used to decide the direction of learning/influence during the process of social influence. In the model, it is assumed that the direction of learning is from the partner to the initiator. However, individuals with a high REP (minority agents) are able to force the direction of learning from them to other (common) agents. The number of influential agents is according to size of minority (N_{m}). Each simulation run is a period of T days, which on each day an agent may involve in one or more interaction within one or more domains of interaction.

A social interaction process starts when an agent (e.g. agent i) involves in an activity within a 'social club' domain on day t. Agent i, who is the initiator, chooses a partner (agent j) randomly from its neighbours (for lattice-structured network) or anyone of other agents (for complex mixing network). Technically, it is conducted one by one,

(a)

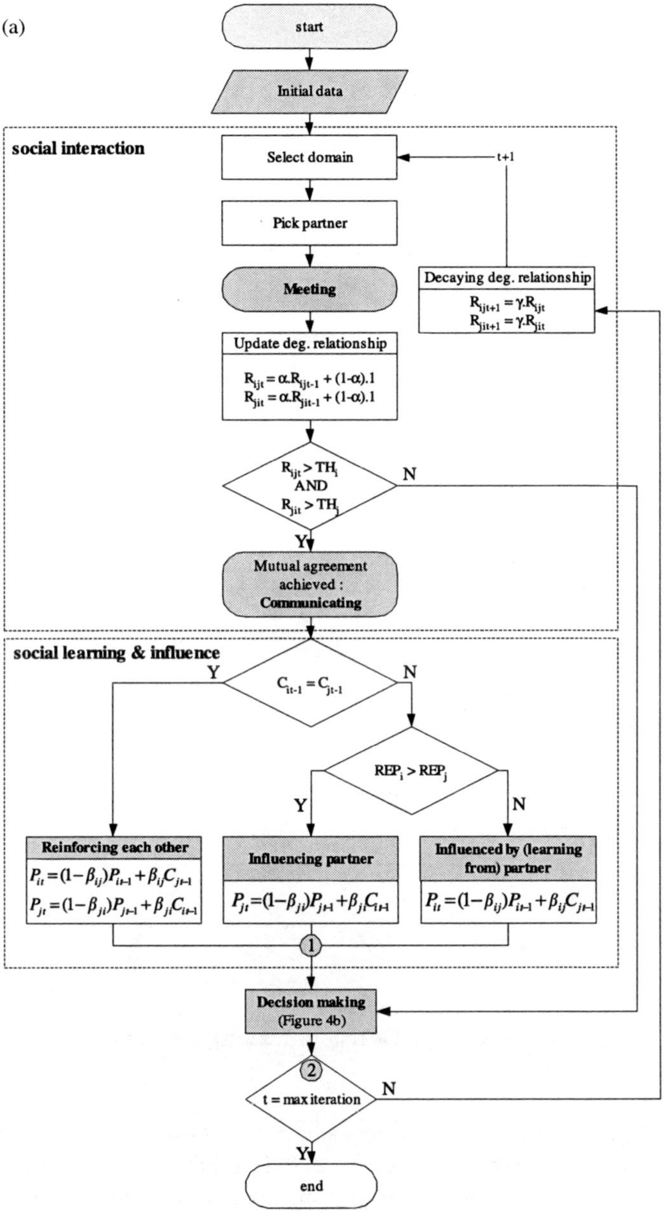

Figure 4a

Flowchart of Social Interaction, Social Learning and Social Influence

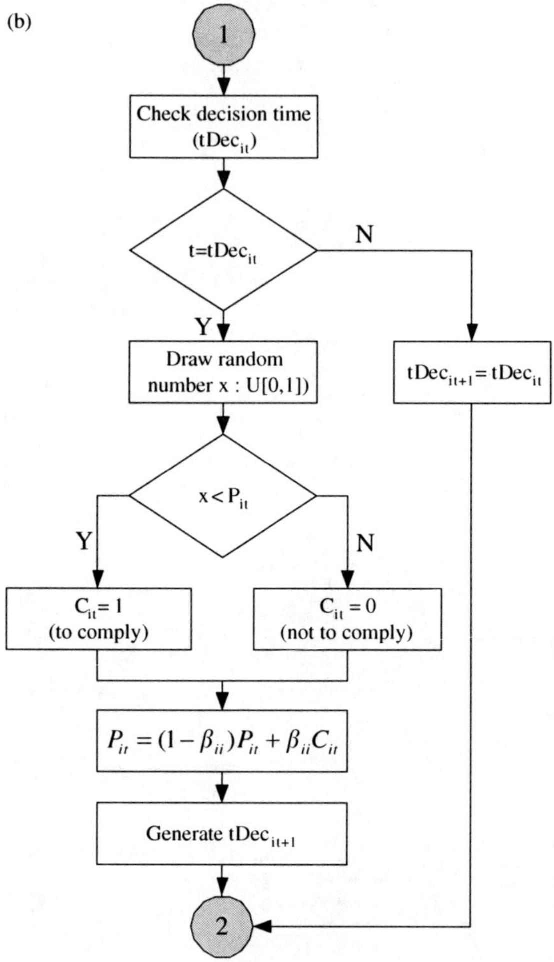

Figure 4b
Flowchart of Decision-Making Process

from $i = 1$ to N. They are then meeting each other. Perceived degree of relationship (R_{ijt}) of two interacting agents is then updated. Each meeting reinforces perceived degree of relationship of both agents with reinforcement factor $\alpha = 0.9$ ($R_{ijt} = \alpha R_{ijt-1} + (1-\alpha)1$). On the next day ($t+1$), it decays over time with decaying factor $\gamma = 0.999$ ($R_{ijt+1} = \gamma R_{ijt}$).

Both agents i and j check whether or not their perceived degree of relationship (R_{ijt}) exceeds their thresholds for communicating (TH_i and TH_j) in order to decide whether

Table 2
Model Parameters

Parameter	Description	Source	Value assigned to model
TH_i	Threshold for communicating of agent *i*	Randomly assigned	$TH_i \in U[0,1]$
REP_i	Reputation of agent *i*	Survey results	$REP_i \in \{0,1\}$ 0, common individual; 1, influential individual
β_{ij}	Weight of the influence of agent *j*'s choice on agent *i*'s preference	Survey results	$\beta_{ij} \in [0,1]$
α_{ij}	Reinforcement factor of R_{ij} (see Table 3)	Assumed	$\alpha_{ij} \in [0,1]$; $\alpha_{ij} = \alpha$ For experiment, $\alpha = 0.9$
β_{ii}	Weight of influence of agent *i*'s previous choice on its preference	Assumed	$\beta_{ii} \in [0,1]$; $\beta_{ii} = \beta_i$ For experiment, $\beta_i = 0.1$
γ_{ij}	Decaying factor of R_{ij}	Assumed	$\gamma_{ij} \in [0,1]$; $\gamma_{ij} = \gamma$ For experiment, $\gamma = 0.999$
N_m	Size of minority	Survey results	$N_m \in (0.50\%)$ From survey, $N_m = 6.18\%$

Table 3
Model Variables

Variable	Description	Source	Value assigned to model
P_{it}	Preference of agent *i* at time *t*	Survey results (initial value)	$P_{it} \in [0,1]$
R_{ijt}	Perceived degree of relationship by agent *i* about its relation with agent *j* at time *t*	Randomly assigned (initial value)	$R_{ijt} \in U[0,1]$
$t\mathrm{Dec}_{it}$	Timing of decision making of agent *i* at time *t*	Assumed exponentially distributed	$\lambda = 0.0714$ $t\mathrm{Dec}_{it} = -\ln(x)/\lambda + t$
C_{it}	Decision/choice of agent *i* at time *t*	Survey results (initial value)	$C_{it} \in \{0,1\}$ 0, not to car share; 1, to car share
LC_t	Level of compliance at time *t*	Survey results (initial value)	$LC_t \in [0\%,100\%]$ Initial value = 17.41% ($= \Sigma$ initial C_i/N_s)

Note: $i \neq j$; $i, j \in S$ (*i*, subject (initiator); *j*, partner; *S*, population of agents) or not they will communicate about travel-related decision. Thresholds are assumed to be randomly $U[0,1]$ distributed. If $R_{ijt} > \mathrm{TH}_i$ and $R_{jit} > \mathrm{TH}_j$, then communication involving exchange of information will follow. Otherwise, they will not communicate about their travel decision. On the same day, agent *i* may then have another interaction with another agent (say, agent *k*) which takes place in the same or another domain of interaction.

The process of social learning and social influence may exist during a process of communication between two agents, *i* and *j*. If both of communicating agents have the same choice on day $t-1$ ($C_{it-1} = C_{jt-1}$) then they are reinforcing each other ($P_{it} = (1-\beta_{ij})P_{it-1} + \beta_{ij}C_{jt-1}$ and $P_{jt} = (1-\beta_{ji})P_{jt-1} + \beta_{ji}C_{it-1}$). If they have different choices, there are two possibilities. First, if one of communicating agents has a higher reputation than the other ($\mathrm{REP}_i > \mathrm{REP}_j$ or $\mathrm{REP}_i < \mathrm{REP}_j$) then the exchange of information will only be one way, from the agent with higher reputation to the other with lower reputation ($P_{it} = (1-\beta_{ij})P_{it-1} + \beta_{ij}C_{jt-1}$ or $P_{jt} = (1-\beta_{ji})P_{jt-1} + \beta_{ji}C_{it-1}$). The process is called social influence. Second, if they both have the same reputation, then only the agent who initiates the social interaction learns from partner's choice by updating its preference ($P_{it} = (1-\beta_{ij})P_{it-1} + \beta_{ij}C_{jt-1}$), since the initiator is considered as the one who is looking for information.

The decision-making process considers that the population of agents may display inertia, where only a fraction of agents considers changing decision at the same time. The other fraction of agents continues with their previous choices. The time between each decision making ($t\mathrm{Dec}_i$) of each agent follows an exponential distribution with mean $\lambda = 0.0714$. The mean value of the distribution is derived from the assumption that in average each agent considers changing its decision twice in a month (4 weeks) or one in 14 days ($1/14 = 0.0714$). In every iteration, each agent checks whether or not the current iteration is the time to make a decision, which may result in the same choice as previous decision or a different choice. If this is the case ($t = t\mathrm{Dec}_{it}$), then the agent proceeds to a process of decision making based on preference using a random utility model of decision making. A uniform-distributed $U[0,1]$'s random number x is then generated. If $P_{it} > x$ then agent *i* chooses to comply ($C_{it} = 1$), otherwise, choose not to comply ($C_{it} = 0$). Preference at time t (P_{it}) is again updated ($P_{it} = (1-\beta_{ii})P_{it} + \beta_{ii}C_{it}$). After making a decision, the timing for next decision is generated and the process loops back to the beginning of social interaction. If it is not a decision-making time ($t \neq t\mathrm{Dec}_{it}$), then the process loops back to the starting process of social interaction and the decision time will be checked again at $t+1$ ($t\mathrm{Dec}_{it+1} = t\mathrm{Dec}_{it}$).

Based on this simulation model, a numerical experiment is conducted to demonstrate how the model works and provide some informed insights about changes of travellers' decision and behaviour on complying with a 'soft' measure, in this case, a car-sharing programme within a university.

Setting Values to the Model's Parameters and Variables

Before developing the model, a university-based behavioural survey with students as respondents ($N = 178$) has been conducted to obtain information regarding mechanisms of social interaction and social learning in addition to those derived from literatures, as well as to set values of parameters and variables required for the simulation model. The respondents are students in the Faculty of the Built Environment, University of the West of England, Bristol. Car sharing, as a 'soft' demand management measure, was used as a case study in the survey and is used in the simulation model. The survey suggests that some individuals may be influenced by other people, who are relatively close to them, regarding travel-related decision. These close persons of an individual may have an opinion/expectation which may have some level of importance to the individual. The initial level of compliance with a soft measure is also estimated from the survey results.

Examples of the survey results are given in Figures 5 and 6. Figure 5 shows respondents' expectation that the persons that are particularly close to them may have an opinion about the way they travel to the University. In the family category, around 80 respondents (44%) have a close person in her family who may have at least a weak opinion about her travel choice. A similar trend happens in the housemate, coursemate and other friend category. Although in each category the majority of respondents (more than 100 persons) do not expect that a close person in each category has any opinion, there are actually 41% of respondents who answer no opinion to all

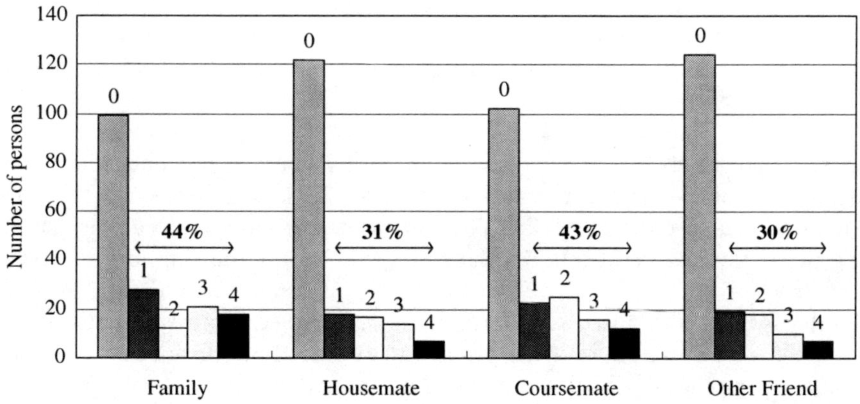

Figure 5

Close Persons may have Opinion

Note: 0, no opinion; 1, weak opinion; 2, somewhat strong; 3, quite strong; 4, strong opinion

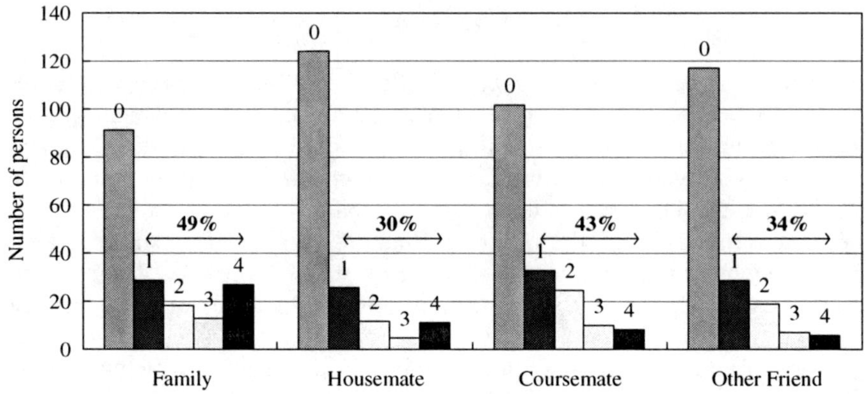

Figure 6
Importance of Close Persons' Opinion

Note: 0, unimportant; 1, slightly important; 2, somewhat important; 3, quite important; 4, important

categories. So that there are 59% of respondents have at least a close person who may have (at least) a weak opinion about their choice of travel.

When respondents are asked about the importance of other people's opinion, at least in one category there are 30–49% of respondents consider close people's opinion (at least) slightly important on their decision about the way to travel to the University (Figure 6). Around 37% of respondents consider that their close persons' opinion about their travel mode choice is unimportant for them in all categories, so that majority of respondents (63%) have at least a close person whose her/his opinion is (at least) slightly important.

The behavioural survey has provided some of model's parameters and initial values for the variables, while others are based on theoretical assumptions, as they are very difficult to be measured empirically. The following explanations highlight the way of deriving the parameters and initial values of variables for the simulation model.

Initial values of an individual's preference (P_i) is derived from the question of 'how inclined are you to join a car-sharing programme?' Based on the answers (definitely not join, probably not join, possibly not join, neutral, possibly join, probably join and definitely join), a 7-level of preference is obtained (0, 1/6, 1/3, 1/2, 2/3, 5/6 and 1). The average preference to car share is 0.47. Respondents who 'regularly car share but have only begun to do so in the last 6 months' or 'regularly car share and have been doing so regularly for 6 months' are considered to have a decision to car share ($C_i = 1$) as an initial value. There are 31 respondents satisfy one of these criteria, so that the initial LC is 17.41%. The LC is simply calculated as a percentage of the number of car sharers in the population of respondents (or agents in the simulation).

The size of minority (N_m) in the survey is defined as the number of individuals who are 'regularly car share and have been doing so for 6 months' and have initial preference value (P_i) from 5/6 to 1. From the survey, we found that $N_m = 6.18\%$. Respondents who are members of the minority are given a reputation value of one ($\text{REP}_i = 1$). Others are given zero value of reputation ($\text{REP}_i = 0$). Weight of the influence of agent j's choice on agent i's preference (β_{ij}) is derived from respondents answer about 'the importance of a close person' opinion/expectation on their travel choice to get to the university'. Five-level of weight is obtained (0, 1/4, 1/2, 3/4 and 1).

Tables 2 and 3 highlights parameters and variables of the simulation model, respectively.

Simulation Results and Discussion

In the simulation model, a number of agents (N_s = 4,096) are generated and given attributes (parameters and initial variables) according to the attributes of respondents (N = 178) in the survey. So that approximately each respondent has 23 'clones' ($N_s/N = 4096/178 \approx 23$) in the population of agents. Each simulation run is a period of T = 1,460 days (4 years). The interaction domains ('social clubs') used in the model is limited to the domains used in the university context used in the behavioural survey. They are *residential neighbourhood, course of study* and *non-study activity club.*

There are 4×7 possible scenarios based on the existence and location of influential minority: (a) no minority, (b) minority spread in the population, (c) minority exist only in a particular course of study and (d) minority exist in several non-study activity clubs; and based on the domain of interactions: (a) neighbourhood, (b) course, (c) non-study activity club, (d) combination of neighbourhood and course, (e) combination of neighbourhood and non-study activity club, (f) combination of course and non-study activity club and (g) all three domain together. Another scenario where social interaction does not exist will also be presented. In this study, the setting of simulation is limited into eight scenarios as in Table 4.

In the neighbourhood domain, agents interact in a lattice structure network where each agent has eight neighbours surrounding it. Agents who are located on the edges of the plane have less than eight neighbours. Interactions in a course of study and a non-study activity club are in a *complete mixing network* (random manner), where an agent can meet any other agent within similar course or club. The average frequency of interaction in each domain per week is: 2/7 within neighbourhood, 4/7 within course of study and 1/7 within non-study activity club. There are 16 courses of study having

Table 4
Scenarios of Simulation Run

Scenario	Existence and location of influential minority	Interaction domain (neighbourhood, course of study, non-study activity club)
1	No	No social interaction
2	No	All domains
3	Yes, spread in population	All domains
4	Yes, spread in population	Neighbourhood only
5	Yes, spread in population	Course of study only
6	Yes, spread in population	Non-study activity club only
7	Yes, only in a course of study	All domains
8	Yes, only in several non-study activity clubs	All domains

approximately 256 students per course and 64 non-study activity clubs having approximately 64 members per club. Each scenario is repeated for 10 runs.

Effects of Social Interaction and Influential Minority Agents (Scenarios 1–3)

Figure 7 presents the results of Scenarios 1–3. The results presented in the figure is only for the first 365 days (1 year) of simulation run, since the system is static after that until the end of the run (1,460 days = 4 years). Each point in the graph is an average of 10 simulation runs. In Scenario 1, where social interaction between agents does not exist, the number of car sharers goes up gradually up to 2008 agents (LC = 49.0%) at the last 90 days the simulation run. (Note: Results of all scenarios can be found in Table 5.) When social interactions (in all domains of interactions: neighbourhood, course of study, and non-study activity club) exist between agents (Scenario 2), the number of car sharers increases with a slower trend than in Scenario 1. However, the level of compliance in this scenario is higher than in Scenario 1 with 2,290 car sharers (LC = 55.9%). The situation becomes better for car sharing when a number of influential minority agents (6.18% of total) exist in the population as seen in Scenario 3. These influential minority agents are able to increase the level of compliance up to in average of 2,514 car sharers (LC = 61.4%).

Average preferences of agents (Figure 8) in Scenarios 1–3 reach almost similar points to their levels of compliance (Figure 7), since they are highly correlated based on the fact that the decision of each agent is made based on its preference. In Scenario 1, where social interaction does not exist, the average of preference is stable day to day with an average of 0.49 in the last 90 days of simulation runs. This result is close to the

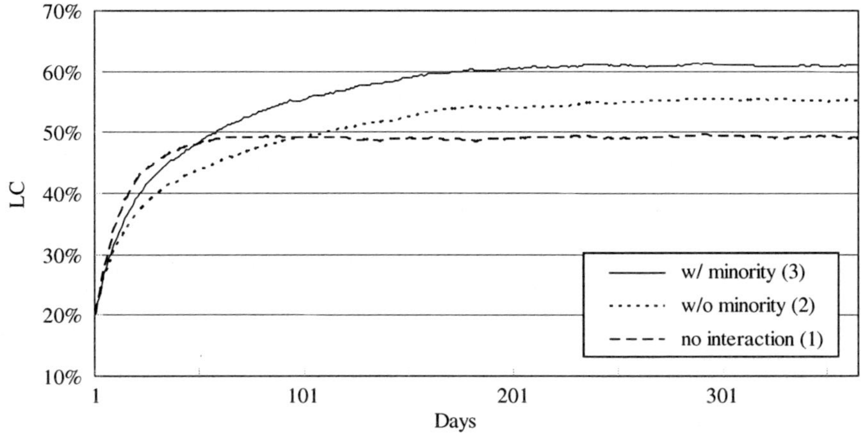

Figure 7
Level of Compliance (LC) in Scenarios 1–3
Note: Scenario Numbers in Parentheses

Table 5
Results of Simulation Runs (Average of the Last 90 Days)

Scenario	Number of Car Sharers	LC (%)
1	2,008	49.0
2	2,290	55.9
3	2,514	61.4
4	2,289	55.9
5	2,395	58.5
6	2,285	55.8
7	2,425	59.3
8	2,481	60.6

initial average preference based on survey results, which is 0.47. Scenarios 2 and 3 have similar patterns of changes. In early interactions, average preferences in these scenarios decrease since majority of agents, who have a low preference to car share, decide not to car share causing the decrease of average preference. After the effects of initial condition can be minimized, as agents involve in interactions with each other, the average preferences in Scenarios 2 and 3 increase higher than that of Scenario 1. When influential minority agents are in charge, a higher level of compliance can be achieved in Scenario 3 (with minority) than that of Scenario 2 (without minority).

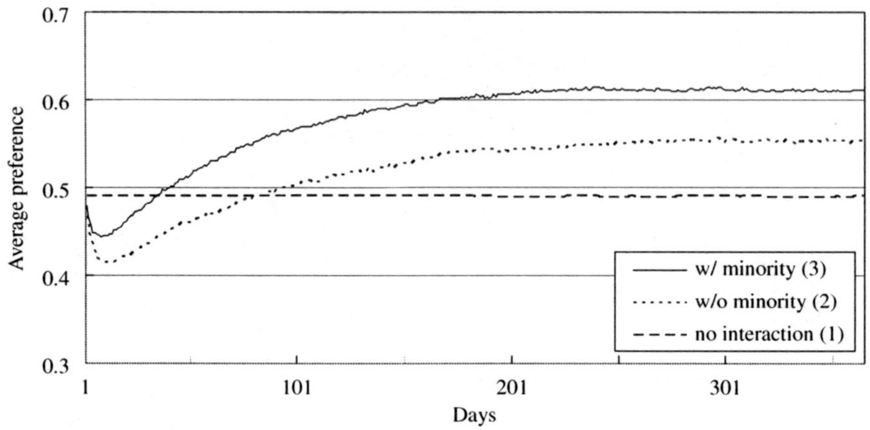

Figure 8
Average Preferences to Car Sharing in Scenarios 1–3

Effects of Interaction Domains (Scenarios 3–6)

Similar to Scenario 3, Scenarios 4–6 represent a situation where influential minority agents exist in the population of agents (Figure 9). The effects of interaction domains are studied by comparing the system's behaviour whenever interactions happen in different sets of domains. Level of compliance has the highest level in Scenario 3 where all domains of interaction (neighbourhood, course of study and non-study activity club) are in use. It is followed by Scenario 5 where the domain is course of study. In this scenario, the level of compliance has almost similar path to Scenario 3 in the first 100 days, but then the rate of increase in Scenario 3 is faster than in Scenario 5. Scenario 5 ends up with 2395 car sharers (LC = 58.5%). Neighbourhood domain (Scenario 4) and non-study activity club domain (Scenario 6) have similar paths in the first 100 days of simulation and almost similar levels of compliance, 55.9 and 55.8% respectively.

Effects of Interaction Domains (Scenarios 3, 7 and 8)

We investigate the effect of location of influential minority agents to the results of simulation by running simulation runs with a scenario where minority agents are located within a course of study (Scenario 7) and another scenario where they are located in several non-study activity clubs (Scenario 8). In Scenario 7, all influential minority agents (6.18% $\approx$ 254 agents) are allocated in a course of study, whereas in Scenario 8, they are allocated in 4 non-study activity clubs with 64 members each. Figure 10 shows the results of simulation runs with these two scenarios compared with a scenario where minority agents spread in the population (Scenario 3).

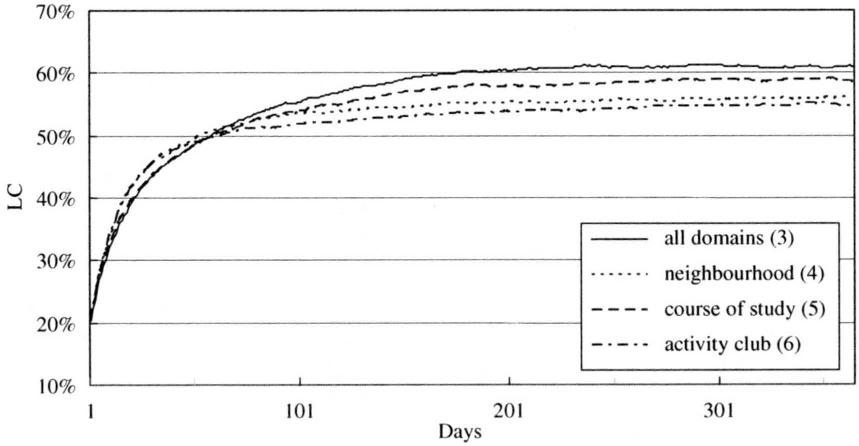

Figure 9
Level of Compliance (LC) in Scenarios 3–6

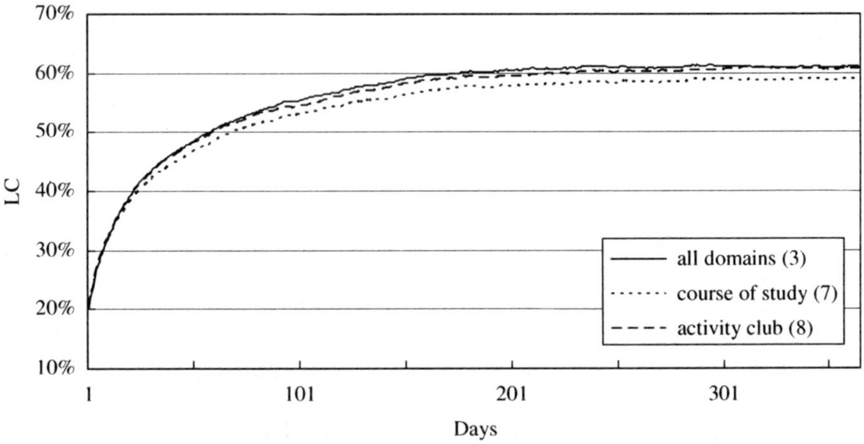

Figure 10
Level of Compliance (LC) in Scenarios 3, 7 and 8

Scenario 3, 7 and 8 give almost similar results. Only small differences in the dynamics can be seen in these scenarios, in terms of the pattern of changes as well as the end results. However, when minority agents only exist in a course of study as in Scenario 7, the level of compliance is slightly lower than that of Scenario 8.

Overall, there is no significant effect of the minority agents' location that can be reported based on the results in these scenarios.

CONCLUSIONS

The results of simulation experiments suggest that the model is able to provide some informed insights about the spread of compliance with a 'soft' measure from an individual to other individuals through various kinds of interaction domain. Social interaction has been shown to have a major role in spreading compliance with the measure. It is also found that the existence of influential minority agents in the model increases the level of participation within population of agents.

A small number of influential individuals, who were located randomly in the population, with consistency of choice on complying with the measure were able to diffuse their choice to others. Also, a group that consists of influential agents was able to diffuse their compliance to other individuals from different groups. A 'social club' domain with a high opportunity of repeated interactions between its members, like course of study, has been reported to have an important role on the spread of compliance. Neighbourhood is a domain which has often been used in existing simulation models, however it may have smaller role than course of study since the interactions between neighbours are mostly incidental and not as frequent as interactions within a course of study. These findings show that repeated interactions between individuals would generate higher propensity for communicating which later give more opportunity for social learning and social influence to induce compliance in the population.

One of the elements that can be transferred from the model into real systems is behaviour insights obtained from the simulation experiment. The insights obtained in this study may be useful for understanding and finding possibilities for influencing travellers' change of behaviour during the implementation of a demand management measure in practice. For example, the simulation shows that involving 'key people' in diffusing compliance with the measure into population would increase the level of participation. It supports the importance of 'key people' involvement in promoting a soft measure, which is one of tools for changing behaviour suggested by Ampt (2003).

The model developed in this study is still limited to be able to derive any conclusions in terms of substantial 'quantitative' findings from the results. However, we may consider that the findings produced by the model is more in 'qualitative' sense than 'quantitative', since the model is used to explore or to understand causal relationships of interaction between people in real-world society. Much elaboration is needed to produce sufficient sensitivity and accuracy in order to ensure that the findings are substantially important.

Finally, the model has shown how we can incorporate social aspects, such as social interaction, social learning and social influence, into modelling travellers' decision making and behaviour. The use of an agent-based simulation model is also expected to have implications for travel behaviour modelling practice as some potential benefits can be gained from this tool.

Future Research

The simulation experiment presented in this study is a demonstration of how we can predict the changes of travellers' behaviour when social interaction, social learning/imitation and social influence exist. The way these aspects may increase effectiveness of a 'soft' demand management measure is an informed insight obtained from this study. To make the prediction of the model more reliable, more credible parameters for the model are highly required. These can be done by conducting intensive behavioural survey and laboratory experiments in order to evaluate these parameters. More reliable parameters will give better understanding about behavioural mechanisms and causal relationships between individuals in the society. The understanding is important for developing a model which is able to represent individuals in real society as agents in the model. Hence, better qualitative understanding can be produced.

The development of a method to measure diffusion effects in the implementation of a 'soft' measure, as identified by Stopher (2005), would provide a benefit in obtaining empirical data that can be used to validate the results of the simulation model. Empirical data from a longitudinal study with several waves before and after the implementation of a 'soft' measure would serve best for validation purpose.

The concepts and model presented in the paper may be applicable to other situational contexts, with some modifications and customizations to fit with specific characteristics of each situational context. There are also possibilities to run different kinds of scenario using the model in order to gain some informed insights for formulating and evaluating effective policy interventions.

Studies on predicting the effects of diffusion process in the implementation of 'soft' measures, such travel blending, individualized marketing and car sharing, may benefit from this study. However, applications of the model into real-world practice still requires further development as the model is relatively simple and the factors involved in the practice would be much more complicated and beyond the scope of this study. There are also interrelationships between the social aspects with other individual aspects, such as personality, attitude, habit, etc.; as well as complexity of travel environment that need to be considered in the further development.

ACKNOWLEDGMENTS

The authors would like to thank two anonymous referees for their constructive and useful comments and suggestions for improving this article.

References

Akiyama, T., H. Tsuboi (1996). Description of route choice behavior by multi-stage fuzzy reasoning. *Highways to the Next Century Conference*. Hongkong.

Ampt, E. (2003). Voluntary household travel behaviour change: theory and practice. *10th International Conference on Travel Behavior Research*. Lucerne.

Arentze, T. and H. Timmermans (2005). Modelling learning and adaptation in transportation context. *Transportmetrica* 1, 13–22.

Arentze, T. and H. Timmermans (2006). Social networks, social interactions and activity-travel behavior: a framework for micro-simulation. *85th TRB Annual Meeting*. Washington, DC.

Avineri, E. and J. N. Prashker (2005). Sensitivity to travel time variability: travellers' learning perspective. *Transportation Research C* 13(2), 157–183.

Axelrod, R. (1997). *Complexity of Cooperation*. Princeton, NJ, Princeton University Press.

Blonski, M. (1999). Social learning with case-based decisions. *Journal of Economic Behavior & Organization* 38, 59–77.

DeJong, W. (2002). The role of mass media campaigns in reducing high-risk drinking among college students. *Journal of Studies on Alcohol* (Suppl. 14), 182–192.

Ellison, G. and D. Fudenberg (1995). Word-of-mouth communication and social learning. *Quarterly Journal of Economics* 110(1), 93–125.

Fujii, S., T. Gärling and R. Kitamura (2001). Changes in drivers' perceptions and use of public transport during a freeway closure. *Environment and Behavior* 33(6), 796–808.

Gilboa, I. and D. Schmeidler (1995). Case-based decision theory. *Quarterly Journal of Economics* 110(3), 605–639.

Gordon, M. B., J. P. Nadal, D. Phan and V. Semeshenko (2004). How to choose under social influence. *1st European Conference on Cognitive Economics (ECCE 1)*. Gif-sur-Yvette.

Jones, P. and L. Sloman (2003). Encouraging behavioural change through marketing and management: what can be achieved? *10th International Conference on Travel Behavior Research*. Lucerne.

Kameda, T. and D. Nakanishi (2002). Cost/benefit analysis of social/cultural learning in a nonstationary uncertain environment: an evolutionary simulation and an experiment with human subjects. *Evolution and Human Behavior* 23, 373–393.

Kameda, T. and D. Nakanishi (2003). Does social/cultural learning increase human adaptability? Rogers's question revisited. *Evolution and Human Behavior* 24, 242–260.

Kempe, D., J. Kleinberg and E. Tardos (2003). Maximizing the spread of influence through a social network. *9th ACM SIGKDD International Conference on Knowledge Discovery and Data Mining*. Washington, DC.

Kitamura, R., S. Nakayama and T. Yamamoto (1999). Self-reinforcing motorization: can travel demand management take us out of the social trap? *Transport Policy* 6, 135–145.

Latané, B. and S. Wolf (1981). The social impact of majorities and minorities. *Psychological Review* 88, 438–453.

Nakamaru, M. and S. A. Levin (2004). Spread of two linked social norms on complex interaction networks. *Journal of Theoretical Biology* 230, 57–64.

Nakayama, S., R. Kitamura and S. Fujii (2001). Drivers' route choice rules and network behavior: do drivers become rational and homogeneous through learning? *Transportation Research Record* 1752, 62–68.

Offerman, T. and J. Sonnemans (1998). Learning by experience and learning by imitating successful others. *Journal of Economic Behavior and Organization* 34, 559–575.

Pingle, M. (1995). Imitation versus rationality: an experimental perspective on decision making. *The Journal of Socio-Economics* 24(2), 281–315.

Pingle, M. and R. H. Day (1996). Modes of economizing behavior: experimental evidence. *Journal of Economic Behavior & Organization* 29, 191–209.

Sampson, E. (1991). Innovation and the minority-influence model. In E. Sampson (Ed.), *Social Worlds Personal Lives: An Introduction to Social Psychology*. San Diego, USA, Harcourt Brace Jovanovich, Inc.

Shaheen, S. (2004). Dynamics in behavioral adaptation to a transportation innovation: a case study of Carlink-a smart carsharing system. Ph.D. Thesis Report, Institute of Transportation Studies, University of California, Davis, CA.

Smith, J. M. and P. A. Bell (1994). Conformity as a determinant of behavior in a resource dilemma. *The Journal of Social Psychology* 134(2), 191–200.

Srinivasan, K. and Z. Guo (2003). Day-to-day evolution of network flows under departure time dynamics in commuter decisions. *Transportation Research Record* 1831, 47–56.

Stanbridge, K., G. Lyons and S. Farthing (2004). Travel behaviour change and residential relocation. *3rd International Conference on Traffic and Transport Psychology*. Nottingham.

Stern, P. C., E. Aronson, J. M. Darley, W. Kempton, D. H. Hill, E. Hirst and T. J. Wilbanks (1987). Answering behavioral questions about energy efficiency in buildings. *Energy* 12(5), 339–353.

Stopher, P. (2005). Voluntary travel behavior change. In K. J. Button and D. A. Hensher (Eds.), *Handbook of Transport Strategy, Policy and Institutions*. Oxford, UK, Elsevier, pp. 561–578.

Sunitiyoso, Y. and S. Matsumoto (2009). Modelling a social dilemma of mode choice based on commuters expectations and social learning. *European Journal of Operational Research* 193(3), 904–914. 10.1016/j.ejor.2007.10.058

Tanford, S. and S. Penrod (1984). Social influence model: a formal integration of research on majority and minority influence processes. *Psychological Bulletin* 95, 189–225.

Taniguchi, A. and S. Fujii (2007). Promoting public transport using marketing techniques in mobility management and verifying their quantitative effects. *Transportation* 34, 37–49.

Tian, Y. H., Z. Mei, T. J. Huang and W. Gao (2003). Incremental learning for interaction dynamics with the influence model. *9th ACM SIGKDD International Conference on Knowledge Discovery and Data Mining*. Washington, DC.

Van Avermaet, E. (1996). Social influence in small groups. In M. Hewstone, W. Stroebe and G. Stephenson (Eds.), *Introduction to Social Psychology: A European Perspective*, 2nd edn. Oxford, UK, Blackwell.

Van der Waerden, P., H. Timmermans and A. Borgers (2003). The influence of key events and critical incidents on transport mode choice switching behaviour: A descriptive analysis. *10th International Conference on Travel Behaviour Research*. Lucerne.

Verplanken, B., H. Aarts and A. V. Knippenberg (1997). Habit, information, acquisition, and the process of making travel mode choice. *European Journal of Social Psychology* 27, 539–560.

4.3 Behavior and Values

The Expanding Sphere of Travel Behaviour Research
Selected Papers from the 11th International Conference on Travel Behaviour Research

31

The Influence of Trip Length on Marginal Time and Money Values: An Alternative Explanation

Andrew Daly and Juan Antonio Carrasco

Abstract

The objective of this work was to investigate whether heterogeneity in valuation existed in transport choice data and whether this heterogeneity might be responsible—through a range of mechanisms—for the observed increase in values of time with trip length. The methodology developed in the paper allows the estimation of random utility choice models with error components included in the utility functions to represent heteroskedastic variation. The results of the analyses confirm that significant heterogeneity of preference—represented as heteroskedasticity in time or cost, but not both simultaneously—exists in all the data sets analysed. Our main conclusion is therefore that the increase in values of time with trip length is very likely to be due to heterogeneity (in the data studied), leading to self-selection, rather than to non-linearity in the functions, so that the underlying value of time does not necessarily increase with distance at an individual level. At the same time, the substantial differences in the results obtained from different model formulations suggest that analysts need to exercise care concerning the key values implied by their models, such as elasticity and implied values of time.

Introduction

The work described in this paper is motivated by the strong empirical finding that the marginal trade-off between time and money in travellers' decision making appears to vary with the length of the trip. Specifically, travellers over longer distances appear to have a higher 'value of time'[1] (VOT). General intuition does not indicate that VOT should increase in this way, indeed there seem to be good reasons to expect an opposite trend, so that interest in this issue is natural.

Although there is a general correlation between income and trip length, this is not sufficient to explain the strength of the positive relationship between VOT and trip length, which has been observed in many contexts. For example, VOT studies in several countries (Accent and HCG, 1996; Algers et al., 1996; Ramjerdi et al., 1997; HCG, 1998; Fosgerau et al., 2006) have found such an effect. Large-scale modelling studies in Paris (Hague Consulting Group, 1994), Sydney (Milthorpe et al., 2000), the Netherlands (Daly and Gunn, 1985; Bakker et al., 2000), and the West Midlands (RAND Europe, 2004) show VOT increasing with trip length. Similarly, some long-distance corridor studies (unpublished work) show a similar effect, so that the increase can be observed over trip lengths from a few kilometres to thousands of kilometres.

An important characteristic of the empirical findings on this issue is that the increase of VOT with trip length appears to be caused by a declining marginal disutility of cost, not an increasing marginal disutility of time. The issue of increasing VOT was considered in the context of large-scale modelling by Ben-Akiva et al. (1987) who described and justified the way in which the effect was modelled in the then current version of the Netherlands National Model. Specifically, while the marginal disutility of travel time in that model was kept constant, the marginal disutility of travel cost was allowed to decline with increasing trip cost by the use of a logarithmic function. A similar device has been used in many of the other large-scale models that have found this effect (e.g. Paris, Sydney and West Midlands, mentioned above); the log cost function appears in many cases to give a satisfactory approximation of the effect, within the accuracy of estimation achievable in those models. Certainly the log cost function fits the data much better than a function with linear cost.

An important difficulty with a formulation that allows the marginal impedance of cost to decrease with trip length—whether by a log function or by any other non-linear transformation—is that it is difficult to explain in the context of an economic theory of utility maximisation subject to a budget constraint. An increasing marginal disutility of money expenditure could be explained, in terms of an approach to the ultimate budget constraint, but the empirical results point strongly to decreasing marginal disutility.

The explanation that is suggested in this paper is based on the insight that unobserved heterogeneity in the population can have important effects on the variation of VOT over different choice contexts. Additionally, information is presented from the modelling

[1]This convenient phrase will be used to denote the marginal trade-off ratio of time to money.

analysis which exploits the insights of unobserved heterogeneity to improve understanding of the variation of VOT with income on a cross-sectional basis and over time.

In order to obtain a broad range of information on the extent of this effect, three data sets have been analysed, varying by location (Paris, Sydney and the Netherlands), by data type (revealed preferences and stated choices) and by date within the Sydney and Dutch data. Income information is also available in these data sets, so that the impact of income variation within the cross-sectional data and between years can be contrasted.

To formulate appropriate modelling solutions to the problem, it is first necessary to determine how the effect might operate. In the following section of the paper, therefore, a series of possible mechanisms are considered and a number identified which are plausible explanations for the evidence that has been assembled. The plausible mechanisms that are found all operate on the basis that the observed effect is caused by unobserved heterogeneity in the travelling population.

In the third section, the methods of analysis available for unobserved heterogeneity are considered and an error components implementation of the 'mixed logit' model is selected as the appropriate approach. The three data sets to be analysed are discussed and a number of the necessary technical issues are explained.

The fourth section presents the results of the analysis of the three data sets and summarises them. Finally, an overview of the conclusions of the research from all three data sets is given, with recommendations for further research.

Possible Explanations of the Effect

In searching for solutions to the apparent inconsistency of theory and empirical evidence, a number of explanations can be advanced. Several of these were suggested in the paper of Ben-Akiva et al. (1987) and others have been proposed more recently. The approach of the present work is to consider a number of these suggestions, determine how these might affect travellers' behaviour, and test the formulation of the more promising suggestions on a number of data sets.

The Paper of Ben-Akiva et al.

Ben-Akiva et al. (1987) speculate on a number of potential causes for the non-linear effects that they had observed, which at that time were not so widely confirmed as now but which were already becoming apparent in those authors' empirical work.

- First, they suggested that non-linearities in disutility with respect to trip length might be caused by risk aversion. If travellers disliked variation in travel time, presumably increasing with the trip length, this could cause a non-linearity in the disutility curve.

- Second, non-linearity could be caused by a lack of awareness among travellers, particularly relating to more distant travel opportunities and not necessarily directly related to the time and cost of travel to reach those opportunities.
- Third, travellers may feel that a given marginal time or cost increase is 'less important' on a longer journey than on a shorter journey. It is relatively easy to imagine interview data supporting this idea.
- Fourth, the effect could be caused by the fact that travel over longer distances consumes more of the travellers' time and money budgets. As the relevant budget is approached, the marginal disutility of both time and money will increase. Because money can be transferred between periods, it is reasonable to suppose that the relative increase in marginal utility for time would be greater than that for money.
- Fifth, since the main concern of Ben-Akiva et al. was with commuter travel, they suggested that there may be a connection between housing and travel costs. In general, it might be expected that travellers coming to employment centres from more distant locations would be paying less for their housing to compensate for their increased journey cost. This mechanism would imply that the sum of housing and travel cost increased less rapidly than the travel cost alone, giving rise to the effect observed.

The suggestions of Ben-Akiva et al. are summarised in Table 1. While each of the postulated causes could have an impact in the 'right' direction, it is necessary to explain why each would apply to one of the time and cost variables and not to the other.

As outlined in the introduction, more recent results have made clear that, whichever explanation or combination of explanations was responsible, the effect had to be such that VOT would increase, and probably because the disutility of cost decreased. Of the

Table 1

Hypotheses of Ben-Akiva et al. to Explain Increased Value of Time with Trip Length

Hypothesis number	Nature of mechanism	Change in marginal utility with increasing trip length	
		Cost	Time
1.1	Risk aversion	Increasing	Increasing
1.2	Non-awareness of distant opportunities	Increasing	Increasing
1.3	Proportionate valuation	Decreasing	Decreasing
1.4	Impact of budgets	Increasing	Increasing
1.5	Influence of housing costs (commuting only)	Decreasing	Decreasing

Notes: Light shading indicates mechanisms that could cause the observed increase in values of time, heavy shading those that could cause this increase by a decrease in the marginal utility of cost.

explanations suggested by Ben-Akiva et al., the first, second and fourth indicate an *increasing* marginal disutility of cost with trip length and are therefore not immediate candidates to explain the totality of the empirical observations. The third and fifth suggestions would account for decreasing marginal disutility, but do not explain why this should be more applicable to cost than to time, while the fifth suggestion does not explain the impact on non-commuter purposes. Only by a combination of mechanisms, for example increasing uncertainty about cost or time of travel together with a budget mechanism operating more strongly on time than on cost could explain the observations.

Alternative Explanations

It is possible to devise further possible explanations for the increase of VOT with trip length in addition to those suggested by Ben-Akiva et al.

- One such way in which the observed effect of increasing VOT with trip length might be brought about is by choice on the part of the travellers. It is clearly the case that, on the whole, faster modes are more expensive and this would lead travellers with higher VOT to choose these modes to gain time at the expense of increased cost. Since these modes are also more suitable for longer distances, travellers with higher VOT would thus be observed travelling further.
- A second idea is that some types of cost are less clearly perceived or are less disliked than other types of cost. In particular, car running costs are known to be poorly perceived and are in any case difficult to allocate clearly between trips.
- A third possibility is that the behaviour is generally heteroskedastic. This could lead to a range of different effects when behaviour is modelled using a homoskedastic model.
- A fourth possibility is that the effect is linked to travel frequency, with more frequent (i.e. shorter) trips having higher marginal impacts on the traveller because their frequency makes it more difficult to transfer money or time between days.
- A postulation is that the effect is caused by the incidence of multiple destinations on trips. If there are such destinations, then the marginal disutility of the journey could decline as the traveller takes advantage of the journey to undertake other important activities.
- A further possibility is that the increase in willingness to pay with trip length is related to car occupancy. Generally, car occupancy increases with increasing trip length, and this mechanism would explain part of the observed increase in willingness to pay.
- A seventh potential cause of the observed effect is that it is caused by a positive correlation of trip length with income.
- A final suggestion is that the effects that have been observed are due to a general correlation with unmeasured variables.

Table 2

Further Possible Explanations of Increasing Value of Time with Trip Length

Hypothesis number	Nature of mechanism	Change in marginal utility with increasing trip length	
		Cost	Time
2.1	Self-selection by choice of mode	Decreasing	Increasing
2.2	Poor perception of costs	Decreasing	None
2.3	General heteroskedasticity	Uncertain	Uncertain
2.4	Link to travel frequency	Decreasing	Decreasing
2.5	Multiple activities	Decreasing	Decreasing
2.6	Car occupancy	Decreasing	None?
2.7	Correlation with income	Decreasing?	None
2.8	Correlation with unmeasured variables	Uncertain	Uncertain

Notes: Light shading indicates mechanisms that could cause the observed increase in values of time, heavy shading those that could cause this increase by a decrease in the marginal utility of cost.

The eight alternative hypotheses of this section are summarised in Table 2.

Clearly, the most promising hypothesis here is 2.1, which operates on both time and cost in the appropriate way, with numbers 2.2 and 2.6 also promising and numbers 2.4 and 2.5 being possible additional sources of explanation.

The Influence of Heteroskedasticity

The most promising hypotheses listed in Table 1 (1.3) and Table 2 (2.1 and 2.2) that could cause the observed properties involve heteroskedasticity, in that the variability of trip disutility increases with trip length. To test empirically whether such mechanisms could explain the observed effects requires the development of methods that can handle this form of heteroskedasticity. Further, should heteroskedasticity be indicated as the cause of the observed effect, it would still not be possible to identify which of the postulated causes was actually responsible. Nevertheless, the demonstration that heteroskedasticity, and not a true decline in the marginal disutility of money, was the cause of the observed effect would be very useful in helping to understand travel behaviour and develop more reliable forecasting models.

Heteroskedasticity can be introduced by including variables in the model which postulate that error variance increases with increasing trip length. The measure of length can be specified to be the distance, cost or time taken on the journey, or the variance can be defined to depend on combinations of these variables. The theoretical specification of models which achieve appropriate heteroskedastic forms is not difficult

Table 3
Implications of Findings of Heteroskedasticity for Hypotheses

Hypothesis number	Nature of mechanism	Heteroskedasticity related to length measured as	
		Cost	Time
1.1	Risk aversion	Reject	Accept
1.2	Non-awareness of distant opportunities	Reject	Accept
1.3	Proportionate valuation	Accept	Reject
2.1	Self-selection by choice of mode	Accept	Accept
2.2	Poor perception of costs	Accept	Uncertain
2.3	General heteroskedasticity	Uncertain	Uncertain
2.8	Correlation with unmeasured variables	Uncertain	Uncertain

Note: Shading and numbering of the hypotheses repeat those of Tables 1 and 2.

when working within the random utility framework, as discussed in the following section of the paper.

Two basic questions have to be asked of the model:

- Is there significant heteroskedasticity relating to trip length?
- Does a model with heteroskedasticity and constant marginal utility explain travel choices well or better than a model with non-constant marginal utilities?

The finding of a significant heteroskedastic term could indicate the presence of one or more mechanisms that would explain the effect of increasing VOT with trip length. The possible conclusions that could be drawn from the finding of significant results are set out in Table 3. The research conducted will in principle not be able to distinguish fully between these mechanisms, as illustrated by Table 3, although it may well give indications as to which of them may be more likely.

Methods for an Empirical Investigation

In order to deal with variation in preference between individuals and between repeated choices of the same individual, and to incorporate the fact that the analyst is not able to observe or model all of the relevant variables and mechanisms, the framework of 'random utility' is commonly used. In this framework, a traveller is postulated to choose the alternative that maximises his or her utility, where utility is modelled as a random variable, that is the choice is alternative j if that alternative has the maximum utility U_j:

$$j = \arg\max (U), \quad \text{where } U_j = V_j + \eta_j$$

where V represents the analyst's best estimate of the traveller's utility and η the error in the analyst's estimate and is treated as a random number with zero mean.

Usually, V is represented by a function linear in unknown parameters:

$$V_{ij} = \sum_r \beta_r x_{ijr}$$

where x_{ij} represents the characteristics of the journey to destination j by mode i and β the parameters to be estimated.

In this present context, it would be possible for a variable x to represent either cost or log cost as appropriate to test the success of each formulation of that variable.

Representation of Heteroskedasticity

The heteroskedastic mechanism that is postulated is that the variance of utility increases with trip length. A suitable formulation is then

$$\eta_j = \gamma x_j^* \xi + \varepsilon_j$$

where γ is a parameter to be estimated; x^* the variable (cost, time, etc.) used to measure the length of the trip; ξ a normalised random variable and ε an independent random variable, accounting for a residual error in the model that is *not* related to the trip length.

The formulation using a normalised random variable for ξ (i.e. mean zero and standard deviation 1) means that the mean and variance of the heteroskedastic mechanism can be estimated. The coefficient β of x^* appearing in V gives the mean effect, while the standard deviation is estimated as γx^*, increasing proportionally with the trip length x^*. Clearly, if γ is zero, the heteroskedastic component disappears from the model, so that a test whether γ is significantly different from zero is thus a test for significant heteroskedasticity.

Note that the same random variable ξ and coefficient γ are used for each alternative j. This means that the marginal value of x^* is assumed to be the same over the alternatives, introducing a correlation between the utilities of the alternatives. When considering the VOT, it is natural to think that a traveller with a high VOT for one alternative will also have a high VOT for another alternative, but it is possible to test independent ξ variables for each alternative to determine whether this natural supposition is in fact correct.

Most of the heteroskedastic models to be considered contain a single random term in each utility function. However, tests are sometimes made of heteroskedasticity relating to two variables (e.g. time and cost). The complete formulation of the utility function which is used for the models described in this paper is then

$$U_j = \sum_r \beta_r x_{jr} + \sum_s \gamma_s x_{js} \xi_s + \varepsilon_j \tag{1}$$

A model form that has recently become popular and which allows for the structures of variance required in this context is the mixed logit model, also known as logit kernel, random parameters or error components logit (among the early references is Ben-Akiva and Bolduc, 1991). In the present context, we shall use the error components presentation, with occasional reference to random parameters.

Error components logit takes as its starting point the multinomial logit model, which attributes an independent, identically distributed Gumbel distribution as the sole random term in the utility function of each alternative, and extends that by adding further error components in the form of random terms with non-identical, possibly correlated distributions. In the model framework indicated by equation (1), ε is used as the Gumbel term and the additional error components are those containing ξ.

Most of the base models against which the testing was conducted were multinomial logit in form, in which only the Gumbel term was present alongside the non-random components. Equation (1) is therefore a proper generalisation of these models, a feature which is convenient for testing the advantage given by the error components.

It is in principle possible to consider a number of possibilities for specifying the ξ distribution. In the present work, the normal distribution, which is the most commonly used distribution in this context, was used. The support of the normal distribution is unbounded and therefore in principle not suited as a distribution of a parameter whose sign is known a priori. However, it is not thought that importantly different conclusions on the specific points studied in this work, which are not directly related to the values of the parameters, would have been reached if an alternative distribution had been used.

Estimation Procedure

The main task undertaken in the work described in this paper was the estimation of the unknown parameters β and γ in equation (1). In order to base the estimation on data of observed choices among alternatives for which utility functions (1) could be defined, the probability of observing each of the possible choices must be calculated:

$$\begin{aligned}\Pr\{\text{choice} = j\} &= Pr\{U_j \geq U_k, \quad \text{for all alternatives } k\} \\ &= \Pr\left\{\sum_r \beta_r x_{jr} + \sum_s \gamma_s x_{js} \xi_s + \varepsilon_j \geq \sum_r \beta_r x_{kr} + \sum_s \gamma_s x_{ks} \xi_s + \varepsilon_k \forall k\right\} \end{aligned} \tag{2}$$

Given that the distributions of ε and ξ are specified to be independent and standard, this probability of choosing j for a given observation, that is with given values of x, depends only on β and γ. The overall likelihood function for the observed data can then be calculated as a function of β and γ and maximised to find the maximum likelihood values of those parameters. However, the specific function is difficult to evaluate and involves multiple integration.

To make these calculations, use is made of a procedure set out by Ben-Akiva and Bolduc (1991). Ben-Akiva and Bolduc note that, in equation (2), if ξ is fixed then

$$\Pr\{\text{choice} = j|\xi\} = L_j\left(\sum\nolimits_r \beta_r x_r + \sum\nolimits_s \gamma_s x_s \xi_s\right) \tag{3}$$

where $L_j(W) = \exp W_j / \Sigma_k \exp W_k$, for a vector W, i.e. the multinomial logit function.

The advantage of this formula is that it can be evaluated very quickly, so that part of the problem of evaluating the probability in equation (2) is solved. The speed advantage has particular relevance in conjunction with the ALOGIT software used in the work, because ALOGIT has a highly efficient algorithm for evaluating multinomial logit.

The remainder of the calculation of the probability is performed by a Monte Carlo process, as proposed by Ben-Akiva and Bolduc. The essence of this procedure is that calculations are made of the probability (3) for different values of ξ and these results are averaged. In principle, the values of ξ are drawn randomly from the standard normal distribution. However, a development which was very recent in 2000 was the use of 'quasi-random' numbers for making the Monte Carlo integration (Bhat, 2001; Train, 1999). As shown by Bhat and Train, the use of 'carefully crafted' sequences of numbers can substantially reduce the run time relative to pseudo-random draws by ensuring that a given number of draws gives a better coverage of the space.

At the time this work was done, in 2000, the problems of computer run time and storage space represented a substantial problem. Careful planning of the computer resources was therefore essential to completing the work within a reasonable time. A number of tests were performed to test the stability of the quasi-random sampling and these are reported in the section below describing the results of the Paris model.

Data Sets for Testing

To investigate the hypotheses set out in the section above entitled 'Possible Explanations of the Effect', it is necessary to analyse real data to determine whether the suggestions that have been made can be supported empirically. For the present work, data was conveniently available from three countries: France (Île de France, i.e. the region containing Paris), Australia (Sydney area) and the Netherlands (a national database). The data sets were chosen as giving a range of the types of situation in which the effect of increasing VOT with trip length had been encountered and which were conveniently available for analysis. The Sydney and Paris data was collected by home interviews in the form of travel diaries. The Dutch data was also collected by home interviews, but in the form of stated choices in response to hypothetical alternatives presented to respondents.

The analysis was restricted to commuting. This was done to restrict the scope of the analysis to a reasonable extent and to maximise the comparability between data sources. A number of the suggested mechanisms causing VOT to increase with trip length apply specifically to commuting.

Of course, the results presented remain dependent on the data sets which have been analysed. However, by basing the analysis on three different data sets, collected in different countries and in different ways, it is hoped that the generality of the results is substantially more than would be the case with a single data set.

Results of the Model Estimation

In this section of the paper, the results of the analyses of the three data sets are presented in turn.

Results from Sydney Model

The Sydney model selected for analysis in this study was the commuter mode-destination choice model, a component of the new Strategic Transport Model (STM) developed in a study by Hague Consulting Group for the New South Wales Department of Transport (Milthorpe et al., 2000). The model predicts choice among seven modes and 800–900 destinations in the Sydney area.

Base Model

For the present work a multinomial logit model was used; this multinomial model does not differ greatly from the nested model implemented, but does permit a consistent estimation of the parameters with a reduced set of destinations, based on McFadden's (1978) positive conditioning criterion. The set of alternatives considered is all of the available modes for each of the sampled destinations, that is the modes are not sampled.

The data on which the model is based was collected in two household interview surveys:

- 5,099 home-work return journey records were available for modelling from the 1991/1992 survey;
- 2,298 records were available from the continuous survey process which started in July 1997, data for this work was available up to December 1998.

To take account of the rapid development in the Sydney area in the relevant period, the number of zones was slightly increased between the two surveys. In addition, data was available describing the transport networks and distribution of activities.

In the base model, a total of 46 parameters were estimated, all but one of which were statistically significant:

- 12 year-specific mode-specific constants (i.e. two year-specific sets of six mode-specific constants);
- 4 year-specific constants for tours remaining within the origin zone or with destination in the central business area;
- 8 socio-economic dummy variables;
- 6 distance adjustment terms;
- 5 dummy variables representing mode-destination interactions;
- 4 log cost coefficients for four income groups;[2]
- 6 time coefficients for travel time spent in different circumstances (in car, bus, train, accessing public transport, initial wait time and subsequent wait time);
- 1 scale parameter reflecting the slightly more accurate data of 1997/1998 relative to 1991.

In the original model specification, the logarithmic formulation for the cost variable was clearly superior to the linear variant, giving a likelihood improvement of 62.6 units with the same number of degrees of freedom.

When separate runs were made for the two years of data, the 1997/1998 data showed a loss from the log to the linear cost formulation of only 6.9 units, while the 1991/1992 data showed a loss of 50.3 units. In each of these models, 37 parameters are estimated, omitting six year-specific mode-specific constants, two year-specific destination-specific constants and the scaling applied between the two years of data. The gain from logarithmic modelling is established clearly for each of the years.

[2]The function was formulated as log (max(cost, 0.10)), that is setting a cost minimum of 10 Australian cents (about € 0.06), on a consistent (1996) basis. Income was defined as personal pre-tax income.

Table 4

Sydney Error Components Models Log Likelihood Results

Year	1991/1992	1997/1998	Total
Base, linear cost	−20,012	−8,391	−28,403
Base, log cost	−19,965	−8,385	−28,350
EC time, linear cost	−19,947	−8,379	−28,326
EC time, log cost	−19,929	−8,382	−28,311
EC cost, linear cost	−19,973	−8,381	−28,354
EC cost, log cost	−19,929	−8,383	−28,312

Notes: Shading indicates the best model(s) in each column. In the four last models, 'EC' indicates to which variable a random coefficient was applied.

Error Component Models

To investigate the impact of heteroskedasticity using mixed logit models, it was first necessary to improve the model run time by reducing the rate at which the destinations were sampled. In the original modelling work, an average of 188.6 destinations were sampled for each observation (20–25% of the total) and covering 85% of the likely destinations.[3] For this work, a different sampling scheme was implemented which gave an average of 31.5 sampled destinations per observation (i.e. 3.5–4% of the total, a run time reduction of a factor of nearly 6) but covering 60% of the likely destinations.

With this reduced sampling rate, none of the significant coefficients in the initial logarithmic model changed by as much as 5%. McFadden's (1978) theory assures us that, because of the positive conditioning property and the fact that these are multinomial logit models, the estimates are all consistent.

Error component models were then estimated for each year, including an error component reflecting a normally distributed dispersion of preference attached either to the total cost or to the total time of each variable.[4] The overall likelihood results of these models are set out in Table 4.

From Table 4, it can be seen that the introduction of heteroskedasticity (with respect to either time or cost) improves the models and that this improvement is a lot more for the

[3]The measure of coverage used is the sum of the predicted probabilities of the sampled destinations, using the simplified model on which the sampling is based. This is believed to be a good measure of the accuracy of the sampling procedure.

[4]Strictly, the McFadden correction procedure has been proved to apply only to MNL models and not to mixed logit. Nevertheless, the changes to the models resulting from the addition of the error component are relatively small, suggesting that the approximation involved here is modest.

models with linear cost than with log cost. However, for the 1991/1992 data set, the improvement is not sufficient to overcome the difference between the linear and log cost formulations, although it is sufficient in the 1997/1998 data. The larger size of the 1991/1992 data means that it dominates the 'total' column, but it should be noted that the higher quality of the 1997/1998 data is not represented in this analysis. In the 1991/1992 data, when using a linear cost formulation, it is better to attach the error component to the time variable than to the cost variable and this is also true for 1997/1998, though to a much smaller extent.

Other investigations were made on the 1997/1998 data only.

- One such investigation showed that it was possible to improve the linear cost model further (to −8,377) by adding error components for *both* time and cost, but that this gave only a small improvement (to −8,381) to the log cost model.
- A further investigation showed that associating the heteroskedasticity with distance was not as successful as either time or cost, whether the log or the linear formulation of cost was used.
- A final investigation showed that treating the error components as being independent across the alternatives, that is general noise rather than the variation of preference of the individual, gave consistently worse results.

Application of the Models

In order to assess the importance of distinguishing carefully between the models presented in the previous section, a series of analyses were made of the elasticities given by the models and of the VOTs that they indicated. Elasticities were calculated with respect to car cost and public transport time, using a sample enumeration method applied to the estimation data, and in each case only the 'own' elasticities are presented, that is the elasticities of demand for the mode whose cost or time has been changed. The elasticity values are set out in Table 5.

From Table 5, it can be seen that the issue of model formulation can be crucial to the appraisal of a policy. The models with a linear cost formulation give own-cost elasticities 2.5–3 times higher than the models with log cost formulation, presumably because of the much greater impact predicted for longer-distance trips. In contrast, the results for public transport times are much more stable.

Extracting the VOTs implied by these models is complicated by:

- the estimation of six separate coefficients for different time components—we therefore present results for car time only (the best determined of the time coefficients);

Table 5

Sydney 'Own' Elasticities for Car Cost and PT Time, Kilometrage, 1997/1998 Models

Variable	Car cost	PT time (train)
Base, linear cost	−0.25	−0.76
Base, log cost	−0.10	−0.83
EC time, linear cost	−0.27	−0.60
EC time, log cost	−0.09	−0.76
EC cost, linear cost	−0.26	−0.65
EC cost, log cost	−0.09	−0.82

Notes: Results given in the final column are the elasticity of train kilometres to changes in *all* public transport times. Thus, for a public transport time increase, apart from the strict 'own' effect, train travel would be reduced because of an increase in bus access time but increased because of an increase in competing bus times. These results ignore any 'second-order' effects arising because of changed congestion on the networks.

- the estimation of four separate cost coefficients for different income groups—we therefore present the most detailed results for the group with third highest incomes (the best determined of the cost coefficients);
- the complication of calculating a VOT for models with a log cost formulation.

VOT can be calculated from the utility functions appearing in the model as the ratio of the marginal utilities of time and cost,

$$\mathrm{VOT} = \frac{\partial U}{\partial t}\frac{\partial U}{\partial c} \approx \frac{\partial V}{\partial t}\frac{\partial V}{\partial c}$$

the latter approximation following because, where it appears, the expectation for ξ is zero.[5] When the model is linear in cost, we obtain

$$\mathrm{VOT} = \frac{\beta_t}{\beta_c}$$

simply the ratio of the coefficients, but when the model has a log cost formulation, we get

$$\mathrm{VOT} = \frac{\beta_t}{\beta_c/(c+0.10)}$$

The presence of the cost in the formula means that we need to assign a value to cost in order to make a calculation for comparative purposes. In principle we need to make an integration over the entirety of possible relevant values of c, taking into account the

[5] In this approximation, we neglect any bias caused by the distribution of the denominator.

Table 6

Sydney Values of Car Time, Income Group 2, AUD Per Hour*

Year	1991/1992	1997/1998
Base, linear cost	16.93	13.49
Base, log cost	2.56	3.08
EC time, linear cost	15.66	13.09
EC time, log cost	3.48	3.44
EC cost, linear cost	8.55	8.23
EC cost, log cost	3.18	3.26

*The income groups are numbered from 1 (lowest) to 4 (highest). We have not converted VOT values to a standard currency (e.g. Euro) basis because of the considerable fluctuations in currency rates in the relevant period. These results are presented at 1996 price levels.

fact that c appears in the denominator of $(\partial V/\partial c)$. For the presentation in Table 6, we have assumed a standard cost of AUD 1.00 (about € 0.60).

Once again, we see that the specification of the model can have a dramatic impact on the outputs. The models with linear cost and no random valuation of cost give VOT that is clearly too high in most cases. In contrast, the models with log cost give more reasonable or slightly low results, but this is entirely a function of the input average cost that is assumed. The most reasonable results, which do not depend on the assumed cost, are those for linear cost with a random variation in the cost coefficient.

Comparing the results for different income groups is again complicated, in this case by the fact that the cost coefficients do not always decrease monotonically with increasing income. Clearly one could not propose such models for use in practice, but in the present study, it is not desirable to introduce inconsistencies in model specification. VOTs for the four income groups are shown for the base model (log cost, no random effect) and for the candidate replacement model (linear cost with random effect), for the two years of data, in Figure 1.

The results in the figure show, broadly, an increase of VOT with income in the cross-sectional data, but it is not consistent or even always monotone. There is an increase in VOT between the two years in the base model, consistent with the increase in real incomes in the period, but not in the alternative model.

Conclusions from Sydney Models

The main considerations are the fit of the models to the data, the reasonableness of the models themselves and considerations of modelling intuition and forecasting.

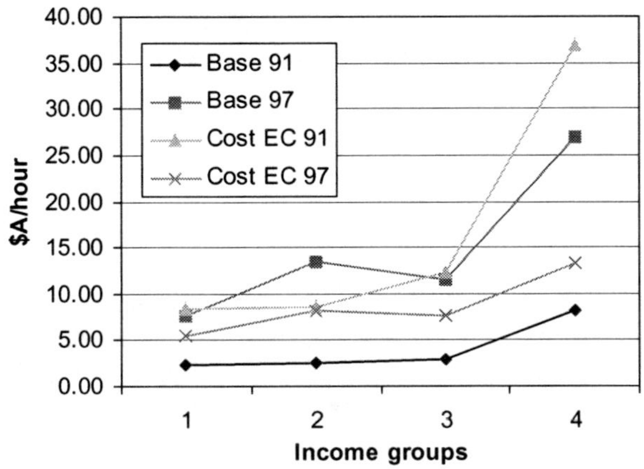

Figure 1
Sydney Values of Car Time from Base Log Cost and Linear Random-Cost Model

- In terms of fit to the data, the introduction of random cost or time valuation improves the fit, more for linear cost than for log cost, but the better performance of log cost relative to linear cost on the (less good) earlier data, whatever the random component, dominates these assessments.
- In terms of elasticity, there is little to choose on time elasticities, but the car cost elasticity of the linear cost models is substantially higher than that of the log cost models. However, both results would be within a generally accepted range of values.
- The VOT values themselves are not easy to understand, since they do not vary consistently between model specifications, income groups or years.
- It seems that the base model and a candidate alternative model cannot be clearly distinguished in terms of their overall reasonableness.

We conclude that it is possible to formulate a model with an intuitively more acceptable linear cost function, providing a random cost or time valuation is included, which is competitive with the base model.

Results from Paris Model

The Paris model selected for analysis in this study was the commuter mode-destination choice model, a component of the ANTONIN Model developed in a study during 1994–1995 by Hague Consulting Group for the Syndicat des Transports Parisiens (STP) and covering the Île de France, essentially the enlarged Paris region, with a particular focus on public transport.

Because of this focus, the model represents 13 separate mode alternatives, of which 10 are public transport combinations; mode availability is incorporated into the model specification. A very detailed segmentation of the working population is used, facilitated by the sample enumeration procedure used for applying the model.

Base Models

The base models describe mode and destination choice for home-based tours to work, separately for 'professional' and other workers, following classical French analysis procedures.[6] The models are of the multinomial form and estimation and application are based on a sample of alternatives, again using all of the modes for each sampled destination but in this case using just 16 destinations, selected by stratified sampling among the 984 zones of the study area. McFadden's (1978) relevant theory assures us that the estimates remain consistent, provided the appropriate correction is made, while the large databases give quite accurate estimates of the model coefficients.

The estimation was based on the Enquête Globale de Transport, conducted in 1991–1992, which yielded 4,210 home-work tours for the higher income group and 5,230 tours for the lower income group. This data gave a rich description of the workers, who made these tours, and of their households, including vehicle ownership. Additionally, detailed network data was available for both highway and the extensive public transport systems of the Paris region. Finally, zonal data on employment and population was used to describe the attraction of each zone.

A particular feature of these models is the way in which the attractiveness of the zones is described. Following the methods set out by Daly (1982), a term is included in the utility functions V for each alternative in the model, additional to the ordinary time, distance and socio-economic variables, in logarithmic form:

$$V = \sum_r \beta_r x_r + \gamma \log a$$

where x represents the ordinary variables (time, cost, etc.) and β their coefficients; a an attraction variable (in this case employment); γ the coefficient of the entire attraction term.

The coefficient γ must lie between 0 and 1. A value less than 1 implies that the zone boundaries have some meaning for travellers, i.e. that there is some unobserved utility component which applies to all the possible destinations in a zone. Given the way in

[6]These groups are described rather approximately as high and low income, respectively, in the remainder of this section.

which the zones are defined in Paris, based on the historical *arrondissements* and *quartiers*, it is very likely that such components do indeed exist.

A total of 35 coefficients were estimated for the high-income models and 38 for the low-income models, all of which were statistically significant except for the mode-specific constants:

- 12 mode constants;
- 5 destination-specific dummy terms (of which three in both models, two in the low-income model only);
- 9 origin or destination and mode-specific interaction terms (of which five in both models, one in high-income only, three in low-income only);
- 1 log cost coefficient;[7]
- 5 time coefficients for travel time spent in different circumstances (in car as driver, in car as passenger, in train, accessing the train, time waiting for trains);
- 1 coefficient for the number of train transfers;
- 3 socio-economic dummy variables;
- 1 distance variable for slow modes;
- 3 employment density variables (of which two in the high-income model only, one in the low-income model only);
- 1 attraction term coefficient, that is γ.

In the original model, the logarithmic formulation of the cost variable was clearly superior to the linear formulation. The difference was 14.6 units in the high-income model and 24.4 units in the low-income model.

Error Component Models

As for the Sydney models, the possible impact of heteroskedasticity was investigated using mixed logit models. Models were estimated for each income group; the results for overall likelihood are set out in Table 7.

From Table 7, it can be seen that the introduction of heteroskedasticity with respect to time does not give an important improvement in the models, but that heteroskedasticity with respect to cost gives substantial improvements in the log cost case and large improvements in the linear cost case. These improvements have the effect that the log formulation is no longer better than the linear formulation. Adding both forms of heteroskedasticity does not give significant further improvements. All of these results apply consistently for the two income groups.

[7]The function was formulated as log (3+ cost in FF). FF 3 is approximately € 0.45.

Table 7

Paris Error Component Model Log Likelihood Results

Employment	Low income	High income	Total
Base, linear cost	−16,636	−12,965	−29,601
Base, log cost	−16,612	−12,950	−29,562
EC time, linear cost	−16,635	−12,962	−29,597
EC time, log cost	−16,611	−12,949	−29,560
EC cost, linear cost	−16,594	−12,940	−29,534
EC cost, log cost	−16,605	−12,944	−29,550
EC time and cost, linear cost	−16,592	−12,940	−29,532
EC time and cost, log cost	−16,604	−12,944	−29,548

Note: Shading indicates the best models in each column.

Table 8

Paris 'Own' Elasticities for Car Cost and PT Time, Kilometrage, Low-Income Group

Variable	Car cost	PT time (train)
Base, linear cost	−0.18	−0.89
Base, log cost	−0.18	−0.88
EC cost, linear cost	−0.20	−0.87
EC cost, log cost	−0.18	−0.88

Note: These results ignore any 'second-order' effects arising because of changed congestion on the networks.

Application of the Models

To investigate the importance of the choice of model formulation, elasticities and VOTs for the various specifications were calculated. The key elasticity results for the low-income group are set out in Table 8.

As for Sydney, we see that the public transport time elasticities are stable with respect to model specification, but in this case stability also applies to the car cost elasticities.

VOTs are set out in Table 9. As in the Sydney case, these are calculated for the log cost case based on an assumed standard trip cost, in this case FF 10 (about € 1.50).

Once again, we see the importance of the model specification in its impact on the outputs of the model. It is difficult to compare the log and linear formulations with each other and the ratio of high- to low-income VOT changes from about 1.5 to 2 as we change the cost specification. However, we see that the introduction of heteroskedasticity reduces the VOT in the linear model but increases it in the log cost model.

Table 9
Paris Values of Car Time, FF Per Hour

Group	High income	Low income
Base, linear cost	142	60
Base, log cost	48	34
EC cost, linear cost	61	36
EC cost, log cost	62	41

Conclusions from Paris Models

The conclusions from these models are clearer than those from Sydney.

- In terms of fit to the data, it is clear that the introduction of heteroskedasticity with respect to cost gives a better explanation of the data and completely reverses the preference of linear and log cost.
- Heteroskedasticity with respect to time has no significant impact, either separately or in association with cost heteroskedasticity.
- Elasticity is not noticeably affected by these changes in model specification and the values appear reasonable.
- VOT does depend significantly on model specification. It is difficult to say whether the original base model has a reasonable time value, but the candidate replacement model is clearly acceptable in this respect.

In summary, the heteroskedastic linear cost model clearly dominates the original base model in terms of consistency with theory and fit to the data.

Additional Testing on Paris Data

Two further series of tests were made on the Paris data.

Non-Linear Time Variables The first series of tests investigated whether the effect of increasing VOT with trip length could be explained without heteroskedasticity by introducing a non-linear effect in time. The fit of these models to the data is illustrated with reference to the original base and candidate new models in Table 10.

It was not possible to obtain comparable results for models with log time, as some records had to be removed because times by some modes were zero. However, in these models with reduced numbers of observations, the log time coefficient was not significant. Similarly, the models containing time-squared terms did not improve the original base model.

Table 10

Fit of Models with Non-Linear Time, Log Likelihood Values, High-Income Group

Group	Base model	Time squared	Log time	Cost EC
Base, linear cost	−12,965	−12,965	*	−12,940
Base, log cost	−12,950	−12,950	*	−12,944

*These values were not calculated, see the text.

It may be concluded that a good fit to this data is obtained by representing a decreasing marginal utility of cost rather than by introducing a non-linear utility of time.

Stability with Respect to Random Sampling The second series of tests was to test the stability of the results with respect to the random sampling of the quasi-random numbers (ξ) used in the model estimations. Three tests were made:

- changing the signs of the coefficients of the random terms;
- changing the number of draws made and
- changing the prime number which is used as the basis for generating the quasi-random numbers.

These tests were made using the high-income group.

The tests made indicated that sign change had little impact.

Changing the number of draws from the initial value of 100 to 125, 200 and 300 would generally be expected to worsen the apparent fit to the data, because of a bias in the calculation of the likelihood function for small numbers of draws. This change had little impact in the model with linear cost and cost EC, with losses of log likelihood of up to 0.4 units. In the model with log cost and cost EC, about 2 likelihood units were lost for all three runs with an increased number of draws, so that it is possible that the runs analysed above were unduly optimistic with respect to this specification. Clearly, the conclusions would not be changed by increasing the number of draws.

Finally, an investigation was made of the impact of changing the sequence of quasi-random draws, implemented by changing the prime number on which the quasi-random series was based. Once again, this change had little impact on the results.

It appeared reasonable to conclude that the results obtained, which focus on likelihood values, were not significantly influenced by noise surrounding the random sampling process, although that process might have had more impact on the values of specific coefficients.

Results from Dutch data

The Dutch data analysed for this study was collected by Hague Consulting Group in two studies for the Transport Research Centre (AVV) of the Rijkswaterstaat, part of the Netherlands Ministry of Transport and Public Works. The data comprises stated preference (SP) interviews conducted in 1988 and 1997. The first study was intended to establish VOT values for motorised travel in the Netherlands, while the second was aimed specifically at investigating changes in those values and therefore replicated as far as possible the survey instruments and methods used in the first study (HCG, 1998).

In this paper, consistent with the Sydney and Paris work, we analyse commuter data only. Further, in contrast to the original work, no correction is made for the fact that up to 12 responses are obtained from each individual in the survey, so that the assumption of independence of the observations is not reasonable. Conclusions from the present work, in particular the assessment of the significance of results, must then be drawn with care.

Base Models

Two base model specifications were used. The first, 'old', specification was developed for the 1988 data and was subsequently applied to the 1997 data. However, in the application of the old specification to the later data, it was found that a number of the coefficients were no longer significantly different from zero, and a reduced 'new' specification was developed in which all of the coefficients could be estimated significantly on the 1997 data. These two specifications from the original work were both used in the present study.

In contrast to the Sydney and Paris models, the log cost variable was not a feature of the VOT models. Instead, two series of modifiers were introduced, one series modifying the coefficient of the (linear) cost variable, the other modifying the coefficient of the time variable. This structure implied that the cost variable had coefficients:

- 1 which applied to all respondents;
- 4/3 (old/new specification) which modified the cost coefficient if the respondent had income higher than the lowest group.

The time variable had a more extensive series of modifiers:

- 1 which applied to all respondents;
- 3/1 relating to the household structure;
- 1 for part-time workers;

- 3/2 relating to the age of the respondent;
- 1 relating to sex;
- 2/1 relating to the amount of free time that the respondent had;
- 2/0 modifying the VOT for public transport users;
- 4/1 modifying the VOT as a function of the type of road being used (for car travellers);
- 0/1 modifying the VOT for morning peak travel.

These specifications gave a total of 22 (old) and 13 (new) parameters for estimation. In addition, when runs were made to combine the data from the two surveys, a further time conditioner was added to the model.

Error Component Models

Models were estimated using both old and new specifications, applying heteroskedasticity to either time or cost coefficients. Because the 1997 data was more substantial than the 1988 data, runs were made for the 1997 data on its own (17,787 responses) and for the data sets combined (23,122 responses). The results of these runs are set out in Table 11.

In the results of Table 11, it can be seen that the addition of error components gives very large improvements to the models. The gains in the combined data are substantially larger than in the 1997 data alone, so that the improvement also applies to the 1988 data. It must be concluded that there is a large amount of unobserved heterogeneity in the data, despite the conditioning variables that have been included.

Next, we see that a cost error component performs substantially better than a time EC, in both specifications and for both data sets.

Comparing the specifications, we see then that new specification is little worse than the old, despite using nine fewer parameters; the likelihood difference is significant on a χ^2

Table 11
Dutch Error Component Model Log Likelihood Values

		1997 data	Gain from base	Combined data	Gain from base
Old specification	Base	−9,790		−12,834	
(22 degrees of freedom)	EC cost	−9,561	229	−12,523	311
	EC time	−9,653	137	−12,653	181
New specification	Base	−9,797		−12,839	
(13 degrees of freedom)	EC cost	−9,569	228	−12,531	308
	EC time	−9,665	104	−12,672	167

test at about the 5% level. Given also the presence of insignificant parameter estimates in the old specification, we may conclude that the cost EC result with the new specification (shaded) is the most reasonable interpretation of this data.

Application of the Models

Application of the Dutch models presents greater difficulty than the Sydney and the Paris cases. First, in the nature of VOT data, the calculation of elasticity values from this analysis is not relevant: the choices presented to respondents concern abstract trading. Second, the calculation of VOT itself requires enumeration of the sample to obtain the average, and this processing was beyond the resources available for the present study. Because the modification of the cost coefficient is relatively simple, it is possible to take this into account, and we can obtain indications of the overall VOT by looking at the base time coefficient without reference to the modifiers.

Figure 2 presents the results for the base and cost EC models (new specification), showing the unmodified time coefficient divided by the modified cost coefficient for each income group in guilders per hour.[8] The modified values (HCG, 1998) are also presented. It can be seen that in this case, there is very little difference in VOT as a result of the model specification or between the years of the survey.

HCG (1998) goes further into the reasons for this apparent lack of increase in VOT between the two years of the survey, finding that the sample was biased in different ways in the two years, so that when expanded an increase in value of 5% was found, still substantially less than the increase in real income.

Conclusions from the Netherlands Models

The evidence from this work is that it is clear that unobserved heterogeneity exists in VOT, despite the numerous observed qualifiers incorporated in these models, and that this heterogeneity is most closely related to the marginal utility of cost, although the marginal utility of time is also not homogenous. These findings are very strong in both years of data analysed.

In this case, where the original model was linear rather than logarithmic in cost, the introduction of heterogeneity does not appear to change the VOT, although this analysis is not complete because of the complexity of the model used.

---

[8]One guilder was worth approximately € 0.45 at the time of introduction of the Euro in 2000. However, the graph is presented in 1988 prices.

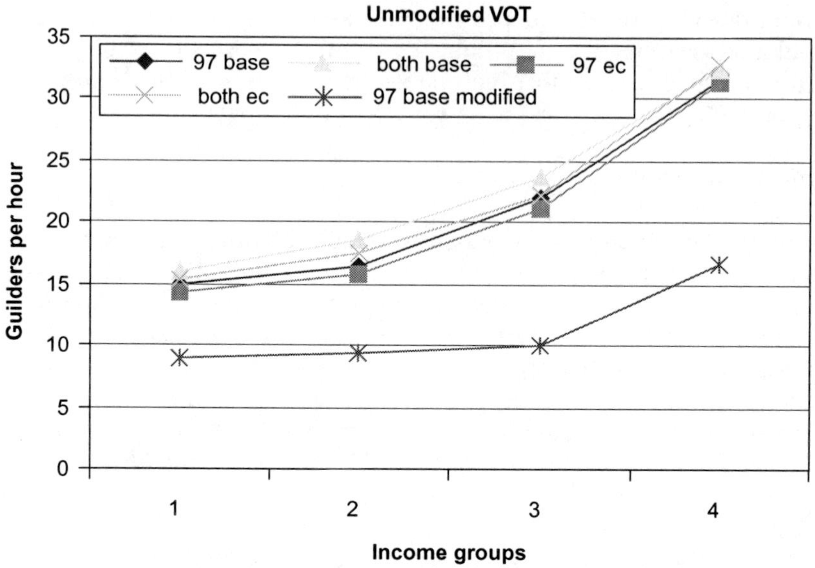

Figure 2
Base (Unmodified) VOT by Income Group

Conclusions, Implications and Recommendations for Further Research

The objective of this work was to investigate whether heterogeneity in valuation existed in transport choice data, and whether this heterogeneity might be responsible—through a range of mechanisms—for the observed increase in VOT with trip length. An analysis methodology was developed which allowed the estimation of choice models with error components representing heteroskedastic variation.

The results of the analyses confirm that significant heterogeneity of preference exists in all the data sets analysed. This heterogeneity can be represented as heteroskedasticity in time or in cost and either is found to be significant in most of the models tested. Heteroskedasticity in both time and cost was tested only for the Paris models and gave little further improvement.

Alternative means of representing non-linear responses to cost were present in the original models of the Sydney and Paris studies (log cost), and non-linear time variables were tested on the Paris data. However, the log cost formulation was found to be inferior to heteroskedasticity in cost as a way of introducing heterogeneity in nearly all of the models tested and to be a close competitor in the other models. Non-linear time variables (tested for the Paris data only) were not found to be significant.

For all the models with linear cost functions and three of the four models with log cost functions, heteroskedasticity with respect to cost gave a greater improvement than introducing heteroskedasticity with respect to time. For the models with log cost functions, heteroskedasticity with respect to time was more competitive, but these models were generally inferior to those with linear heteroskedastic cost. In terms of fit to the data, the best model overall was that with linear heteroskedastic cost.

In terms of the hypotheses of Table 3 which could explain the observed increase in time value with trip length, these results tend to undermine hypotheses 1.1 and 1.2 which depend on heteroskedasticity in time but not cost. Hypotheses 1.3, 2.1 and 2.2 are supported by the results, although for hypothesis 1.3 it has to be supposed that proportionate valuation applies much more strongly to cost than to time. Hypotheses 2.3 and 2.8 remain uncertain. The most likely mechanisms causing the increase are therefore in order of support by the present results:

2.1	Self-selection by choice of mode
2.2	Poor perception of costs
1.3	Proportionate varying valuation of cost (but not of time)

General heteroskedasticity or correlation with unmeasured variables, which would be relevant if (e.g.) the measured variables were actually partially proxy for other variables, are supported by the results but do not obviously explain an increase in VOT with trip length.

Our main conclusion is therefore that the increase in VOT with trip length is more likely to be due to heteroskedasticity (in the data studied) and the underlying VOT is therefore not increasing with distance at an individual level.

The results obtained from the alternative formulations are often substantially different. For this reason, analysts should ensure they are happy with the values implied by the models they are using. Key model properties such as elasticity and implied VOT need to be considered in choosing a model for application.

The results are somewhat different for the three data sets considered, although all three are believed to be of good quality. This variation is typical of the variation in specification that is found when estimating models across a range of areas and suggests that there exist further influences on choice that are not incorporated in the models. Clearly, tests of this approach on other data sets would be useful in clarifying the extent to which these findings are transferable to a wide range of contexts.

For further research, there are two apparent avenues for improving the current results.

- First, a search could be made for alternative functional forms, perhaps intermediate between the linear and logarithmic forms, that might improve the fit to the data.

- Second, means could be sought to improve the run time for mixed logit models in forecasting, rather than estimation, or to find effective approximations to those models.
- Third, further work of this type on data sets of different type and quality might help in understanding the impact of data quality and type on heteroskedasticity.

None of these approaches, however, would immediately solve all of the problems.

ACKNOWLEDGMENTS

The first author acknowledges the help of Denis Bolduc during 1992–1993 in making operational the first implementation of the mixed logit version of the ALOGIT software used in this work. However, responsibility for any errors in this work remains ours.

The analytical work was undertaken in 2000, during a student placement of the second author at Hague Consulting Group (which was incorporated in RAND Europe in 2001); both authors acknowledge the support provided by Hague Consulting Group. The description of the work in this paper was largely written by the first author in 2005 through support provided to the Institute for Transport Studies, University of Leeds, by the UK Department for Transport. Any views presented here are those of the authors and do not necessarily represent the views of the Department.

References

Accent Marketing and Research and Hague Consulting Group (1996). The value of time on UK roads, The Hague.

Algers, S., J. Lindqvist and S. Widlert (1996). The national Swedish value of time study. Paper presented to Value of Time Seminar, Easthampstead Park, Berkshire.

Bakker, D., P. Mijjer, A. Daly and F. Hofman (2000). Updating the Netherlands national model. Paper presented to ETC Conference.

Ben-Akiva, M. and D. Bolduc (1991). *Multinomial Probit with Autoregressive Error Structure, Cahier 9123.* Canada, Département d'Économique, Université Laval.

Ben-Akiva, M., A. Daly and H. Gunn (1987). Destination choice models: Design and appraisal. Paper presented to PTRC Summer Annual Meeting.

Bhat, C. R. (2001). Quasi-random maximum simulated likelihood estimation of the mixed multinomial logit model. *Transportation Research* 35B, 677–693.

Daly, A. and H. Gunn (1985). Cost-effective methods for national-level demand forecasting. Paper presented to Conference on Behavioural Research for Transport Policy, Noordwijk.

Daly, A. J. (1982). Estimating choice models containing attraction variables. *Transportation Research* 16A, 663–670.

Fosgerau, M., K. Hjort and S. Vincent Lyk-Jensen (2006). The Danish value of time study, final report. DTF Report.

Hague Consulting Group (1994). Modèles de choix de mode et de destination. Report HCG 423, Paris, December 1994.

Hague Consulting Group (1998). Value of Dutch travel time savings in 1997—Final report. Report HCG 6098, The Hague, February 1998.

McFadden, D. (1978). Modelling the choice of residential location. In A. Karlqvist, L. Lundqvist, F. Snickars and J. Weibull (Eds.), *Spatial Interaction Theory and Residential Location*. Amsterdam, North-Holland.

Milthorpe, F., A. J. Daly, and C. Rohr (2000). Re-estimation of the Sydney travel model. In: IATBR 2000 Conference.

Ramjerdi, F., L. Rand, I. Sætermo and K. Sælensmide (1997). *The Norwegian Value of Time Study*. Oslo, Institute of Transport Economics.

RAND Europe (2004). Tour based mode destination modelling. Available at: www.prism-wm.com

Train, K. (1999). Halton Sequences for Mixed Logit. Berkeley, CA, University of California, unpublished.

The Expanding Sphere of Travel Behaviour Research
Selected Papers from the 11th International Conference on Travel Behaviour Research

32

Controlling for Sample Selection in the Estimation of the Value of Travel Time

Stefan L. Mabit and Mogens Fosgerau

Abstract

It is often found that the value of travel time (VTT) is higher for car drivers than for public transport passengers. Here we investigate whether self-selection into transport mode on the basis of unobserved individual VTT can explain this finding. We use a mixed logit model to estimate VTT together with a probit model to account for the possible self-selection using instrumental variables. We find that self-selection seems to explain at least part of the difference in VTT between modes. The investigation highlights that it is difficult to find appropriate instruments and that the results on self-selection are highly dependent on the specification of the mixed logit model.

Introduction

This paper investigates how value-of-travel-time (VTT) estimates are affected by self-selection into transportation modes. The term self-selection means that individuals choose a specific mode partly based on their VTT. Self-selection has implication for the interpretation of VTT estimates, for example, a relatively high VTT for a sample of car drivers may reflect either discomfort of traveling by car or a self-selection effect whereby individuals with high VTT are more likely to choose to travel by car. We find that accounting for self-selection can reduce the difference in VTT obtained for car and public transport (PT). Our ability to account for self-selection depends of course on the availability of good instruments. Such instruments are generally hard to find and our case is no exception. With better instruments, we conjecture that result can be correspondingly stronger.

The VTT can be estimated within the framework derived from DeSerpa (1971) together with a general theory on discrete choices (see, e.g., Train, 2003). This framework has shown its use with both revealed-preference (RP) data and stated-preference (SP) data (for recent applications and references, see, e.g., Hensher, 2001; Axhausen et al., 2004; Sillano and Ortúzar, 2005). The VTT is found as the ratio of the estimated time and cost coefficients in the discrete choice model.

Much research has been devoted to the specification of discrete choice models and in the case of mixed logit (ML) models to the choice of distribution for the coefficients. Very little research has focused on the role of the sample except for the case of choice-based sampling (see Manski and Lerman, 1977), and efficiency concerns (see Rose and Bliemer, 2006). A general question concerning the effect of the sample would be the following: If we want to estimate the average VTT for a given population, which part of the population do we sample and how do we correct the results if we sample a subpopulation that is not representative?

Suppose our interest is to estimate the average VTT in car for some population, based on SP data. Then we would choose a subpopulation and have them make SP choices, for example, route choices by car. Two possible ways of choosing the subpopulation would be either a random sample from the general population or a sample of people using car. The first sample fulfills the statistical condition of random sampling that is often assumed in most applied work but raises the effort needed to assure realism in the choice task. This happens because we do not know what experience a person never using a car refers to when choosing between alternative car trips. The second sample has the opposite characteristics because every individual has a reference trip but the sample is not necessarily random in the population. The second sample is necessary for SP samples based on pivoting (see Train and Wilson, 2008 for references).

The problem that could arise from using the second sample is best illustrated by an example. Suppose everybody in a population has the same VTT in both car and bus. But the population is divided into two equal-sized groups: one with high VTT and one with low. Suppose that for this population car is fastest and the only thing that matters in a mode choice is travel time and cost. Furthermore, suppose costs are such that half of the population travels by car. In this population, everybody with high VTT uses car and everybody with low VTT uses bus. Hence, an SP experiment to infer VTT based on a sample of car users would not yield the average VTT in car for the population. The above is a simplified illustration of user type effects. As discussed by Wardman (2004), these are often confounded with mode effects in applications.

One indication that this might be a real problem is the fact that VTT in car is often estimated to be higher than VTT in PT for individuals who have identical observable characteristics (see references in Axhausen et al., 2004 or results in the section "VTT estimation results"). This is counter-intuitive following the theory on VTT as the difference between modes mainly should reflect differences in comfort. According to the theory, higher VTT in car implies that people should feel less comfortable in car than in PT.

Self-selection has been investigated in a different context in the transportation field. In the case of choice-based sampling, the problem is to estimate a discrete choice model describing some choice of interest based on a sample influenced by the same choice. Hence, individuals self-select into a choice-based sample. It has been shown that random sample estimation procedures lead to inconsistent estimates on choice-based samples (Manski and Lerman, 1977). So if self-selection is present in the VTT context, it may also lead to inconsistent estimates.

Self-selection resembles the mechanism behind certain endogeneity issues. Train and Wilson (2008) discuss the endogeneity that arises when SP choices are designed based on RP choices, for example, some pivoted SP designs. The endogeneity they discuss arises when SP choices on mode choice are based on an RP mode choice. The self-selection we describe arises when SP choices on route choice are based on an RP mode choice.

In the field of labor supply, the problem of self-selection has been studied for many years (see Heckman, 1979 for an early reference). In a labor supply model, the interest is to estimate a wage equation, that is, the mean log(wage) as a function of some explanatory variables. The problem is that the expected wage affects participation in the labor market and that inference on wage equations is based on individuals observed in the labor market. Thus, individuals select to be part of the labor market, and hence the sample population, based on their expected wage. The model described by Heckman consists of a selection model describing whether an individual participates in the labor market and a wage equation. In the original model, the selection model is a probit model and the wage equation is a linear regression model. So the standard model is enlarged by a selection model to capture the process of self-selection. Self-selection corresponds to correlation between these two equations. Central to this model are the explanatory variables that enter the selection equation and not the wage equation. These variables act as instruments for the selection. The approach by Heckman has also been applied to the case where both the selection and the main equation are discrete (see Vella, 1992). In both cases, the models are connected through correlation of the error terms. This approach has also been used in contingent valuation where sample selection was seen to have significant effect on willingness-to-pay estimation (see Eklof and Karlsson, 1999).

Here we adapt the approach from labor supply to the VTT context. We use an ML model as VTT model together with a probit model to model the selection into modes. The VTT model allows for random VTT reflecting unobserved heterogeneity. Since interest is on VTT, the concern is whether the sampling is connected with the coefficients in the model and not the additive error. Therefore, our model, though resembling the model discussed by Vella, is different since the correlation is captured as an interaction between the selection equation and the random coefficients of the ML model.

The remainder of this paper is organized as follows. In the section "Selection Model" the selection model is presented and in the section "VTT Models" the VTT model is presented with several specifications. The simultaneous model is described in the section "Simultaneous Model" and calculation of the mean VTT is discussed in the section "VTT Estimation." The section "Data" contains a discussion of the data and the section "Instruments" discusses the choice of explanatory variables in both models. The section "Estimation Results" discusses the estimation of the models. The resulting VTT estimates are presented in the section "VTT Estimation Results" with a discussion of results in the section "Discussion." The final section "Summary and Conclusions" contains some concluding remarks.

Model Formulation

This section presents the general model. The model estimates VTT from a panel ML model and simultaneously estimates a probit model that controls for the effect of sampling. The probit model will be referred as the selection model and the ML model as the VTT model.

Selection Model

The selection model is a binary probit model describing choice between car and PT. Let n denote a given individual. Then the binary outcome of the selection, Y_n, depends on a latent variable U_{1n}

$$Y_n = 1\{U_{1n} > 0\}$$

where 1{} denotes the indicator function and U_{1n} a latent variable determining the choice. Let $Y_n = 1$ denote that the individual chooses car. Then U_{1n} denotes the utility of car minus the utility of PT. We assume that conditional on explanatory variables and coefficients, the latent variable is the sum of a deterministic part and an independent random error term:

$$U_{1n} = \gamma' x_{1n} + u_{1n}$$

where $u_{1n} \sim N(0, 1)$ and x_{1n} denote the explanatory variables including a constant. From these assumptions, we find that

$$P(Y_n = 1 | \gamma, x_{1n}) = \Phi(\gamma' x_{1n})$$

We require that x_{1n} contains at least one variable that does not enter the VTT model and, at the same time, is uncorrelated with the random part of VTT. It is through such variables, generally known as instruments, the model derives its ability to control for the effect of self-selection. The choice of instruments depends on the data available; therefore, this is discussed in the section "Instruments."

VTT Models

The VTT model is an ML model for panel data. The model applies to a panel of binary choices; in our case, we have unlabeled route choices. We introduce the notation where each alternative has just two attributes: cost and time. The model allows for repeated choices from each individual:

$$Z_{nt} = 1\{U_{2nt} > 0\}$$

$$Z_n = \{Z_{n1}, \ldots, Z_{nT_n}\}$$

Each choice depends on the latent variable U_{2nt} that corresponds to the difference in utility between the two alternatives. The latent variable is decomposed into a random term and a systematic term conditional on random taste coefficients

$$U_{2nt} = V_{nt} + e_{nt} = a_n^C\, \Delta C_{nt} + a_n^T\, \Delta T_{nt} + \varepsilon_{nt}$$

where ε_{nt} is independent mean zero logistic and we have omitted the alternative specific constants because the SP experiment is unlabeled. The ΔC_{nt} and ΔT_{nt} refer to the difference in the cost attributes and time attributes between the two alternatives in the SP choice. Under the above assumptions, we have

$$P(Z_{nt} = z_{nt} | V_{nt}) = \frac{\mathrm{e}^{z_{nt} V_{nt}}}{1 + \mathrm{e}^{V_{nt}}}$$

and

$$P(Z_n = z_n | V_n) = \prod_{t=1}^{T_n} \frac{\mathrm{e}^{z_{nt} V_{nt}}}{1 + \mathrm{e}^{V_{nt}}} \tag{1}$$

Here V_n denotes the vector $\{V_{nt}\}$. An important question in an ML model is which distribution to choose for the coefficients. In this paper, the parameters α_n^C and α_n^T are chosen so that the VTT is lognormally distributed, that is, the fraction α_n^T/α_n^C follows a lognormal distribution. This distribution ensures positive VTT, and that the VTT as well as the inverse VTT has a well-defined mean. Another reason for the choice is that on the same data set it has been shown to perform well in a non-parametric investigation of VTT (see Fosgerau, 2006). The model allows for parameterization of VTT with explanatory variables. This induces heterogeneity in VTT.

It is seen from equation (1) how the probabilities depend on V_n. We will use different specifications of V_n that all lead to lognormal VTT. For all specifications, the following notation is used:

$$\text{VTT} = \frac{\alpha_n^T}{\alpha_n^C} = \mathrm{e}^{\beta+\sigma u_n}$$

where $u_n \sim N(0,1)$ signifies that VTT follows a lognormal distribution such that $\log \text{VTT} \sim N(\beta, \sigma^2)$.

We investigate three different specifications. The first is a classical specification in preference space with independent coefficients:

$$V_{nt} = \mathrm{e}^{-\beta_C' x_{2n} - \sigma_2 u_{2n}}\, \Delta C_{nt} + \mathrm{e}^{\beta_T + \sigma_3 u_{3n}}\, \Delta T_{nt} \tag{2}$$

where the coefficients are independently lognormally distributed and explanatory variables, x_{2n}, enter the cost coefficient. Implicitly in this is the standard, but strong, assumption that u is independent of x. The choice to enter x_{2n} in the cost coefficient is discussed in the section "Model I Estimation Results." The signs on the coefficients are chosen to ease comparison of coefficients across specifications. This specification is denoted Model I.

The second specification is an inverse VTT space specification:

$$V_{nt} = \mathrm{e}^{-\beta' x_2 - \sigma_2 u_2}\, \mathrm{e}^{\beta_T + \sigma_3 u_3}\, \Delta C_{nt} + \mathrm{e}^{\beta_T + \sigma_3 u_3}\, \Delta T_{nt} \tag{3}$$

The name comes from the fact that we parameterize directly with the inverse of VTT (see Train and Weeks, 2005, for a discussion of VTT space). Reasons for doing this are discussed in the section "Model II Estimation Results."[1] For another account of VTT space, see Fosgerau (2007), where the estimation in VTT space performs well when compared with alternative specifications. In the VTT space specification, correlation between selection and VTT can be modeled directly, whereas it will only be indirectly through correlation with the cost or time coefficient in the model in equation (2).

Models I and II are quite similar. The only difference is in the specification of the correlation structure between the coefficients. A different model is obtained by a log

[1]To our knowledge, this is the first application of an inverse VTT specification.

transformation of the data together with a change from an additive ε to a multiplicative ε relative to VTT. This leads to an ML model in log VTT space. This model is investigated in more detail in Fosgerau (2007). The specification becomes:

$$V_{nt} = -\log\left(\frac{-\Delta C_{nt}}{\Delta T_{nt}}\right) + \beta' x_{2n} + \sigma_2 u_{2n} \tag{4}$$

where $u_{2n} \sim N(0, 1)$. In this model, $\text{VTT} = e^{\beta' x_{2n} + s_2 u_{2n}}$. We refer to the model as Model III.

We will later refer to a standard estimation of VTT. This refers to estimation of the above models ignoring selection. The VTT calculated from the standard model estimation will be denoted VTT_s.

Simultaneous Model

The model for selection from the section "Selection Model" and the model for VTT estimation above allow for interaction through correlation of the different normally distributed random terms. This gives a model where it is possible to test whether the selection equation influences the VTT estimation. Assuming that u_{1n} and u_{2n} follow a joint normal distribution, we can use a Choleski factorization to write

$$u_{1n} = v_{1n}, \quad \sigma_2 u_{2n} = s_1 v_{1n} + s_2 v_{2n}, \quad \text{and} \quad \sigma_3 u_{3n} = s_3 v_{3n} \tag{5}$$

where v's are iid normal with mean zero and variance one. The model captures correlation between u_{1n} and u_{2n} which is natural for Models II and III. For Model I, it means that correlation is captured in the cost coefficient. This issue is discussed in the section "Model I Estimation Results."

Now we can derive the simultaneous likelihood for the selection and the SP choices. We observe a vector of choices Z_n when $Y_n = 1$. We condition on x_n, ΔT_n, and ΔC_n, but leave this out of the notation

$$\begin{aligned} P(Z_n = z_n, Y_n = 1) &= E(P(Z_n = z_n, Y_n = 1|v_n)) \\ &= E(P(Z_n = z_n|Y_n = 1, v_n)P(Y_n = 1|v_n)) \\ &= E\left(\prod_{t=1}^{T_n} \frac{e^{z_{nt}V_{nt}}}{1 + e^{V_{nt}}} 1\{v_{n1} > -\gamma' x_{1n}\}\right) \\ &= \int\int\int_{-\gamma' x_{1n}}^{\infty} \prod_{t=1}^{T_n} \frac{e^{z_{nt}V_{nt}}}{1 + e^{V_{nt}}} \phi(v_{n1}, v_{n2}, v_{n3}) \mathrm{d}v_n \end{aligned}$$

where we parameterize by $v = (v_1, v_2, v_3)$ and V_{nt} is given by equations (2)–(4) with the factorization in equation (5). Together with $P(Y_n = 0) = \Phi(-\gamma' x_1)$, the above expression can be used to form the partial likelihood necessary for estimation. It is seen from the simultaneous model that s_1 captures the correlation between the selection and the VTT estimation. It is also seen that $s_1 > 0$ corresponds to positive correlation between VTT and Y.

We have focused on the case $Y = 1$ (car) in the above calculations. The equivalent model for a panel of binary choices for individuals with $Y = 0$ (PT) can be deduced in a similar way.

Even though the two models are estimated simultaneously, the causal interpretation is that selection occurs prior to the SP choice.

VTT Estimation

The VTT is lognormally distributed in all the models. To evaluate the models with selection and compare them to the standard estimation without selection, we evaluate the mean VTT. This can be done either by averaging VTT over the sample or by choosing a representative individual. The first is appropriate in many applications but for the purpose at hand where we compare different models the second approach is more useful since model differences are not confused with sample characteristics. Therefore, we evaluate the mean VTT using an individual with mean socio-economic variables, that is, $\bar{x}_k = (1/N)(\sum_n x_{kn})$ and $\bar{x} = (\bar{x}_k)$.

We will describe the mean VTT calculation based on Model II. The calculations are similar for the other models. So assume that the systematic utility is given by equation (3). First suppose that we estimate a model using a standard model without selection. Then we have

$$\frac{\alpha_T^s}{\alpha_C^s} = e^{\beta_s' x_2 + s_s u_2}$$

From this, the mean VTT evaluated at x is

$$E\left(\frac{\alpha_T^s}{\alpha_C^s} | \bar{x}\right) = e^{\beta_s' \bar{x}_2 + (1/2)(s_s^2)} \tag{6}$$

From the model with selection in equation (3), we have

$$\frac{\alpha_T}{\alpha_C} = e^{\beta' x_2 + s_1 v_1 + s_2 v_2}$$

where v_1 and v_2 are independent normal. Therefore, we get

$$E(\text{VTT}|\bar{x}) = E\left(\frac{\alpha_T}{\alpha_C}|\bar{x}\right) = e^{\beta'\bar{x}_2+(1/2)(s_1^2+s_2^2)} \tag{7}$$

In the same way, we can estimate the mean conditional on the individual $\bar{x}$ being a car user, that is

$$E\left(\frac{\alpha_T}{\alpha_C}|\bar{x}, Y=1\right) = \frac{\Phi(\gamma'\bar{x}_1 + s_1)}{\Phi(\gamma'\bar{x}_1)} e^{\beta'\bar{x}_2+(1/2)(s_1^2+s_2^2)} \tag{8}$$

The expression is found by integration over the truncated lognormal distribution. Conditional on being a PT user, the expression becomes:

$$E\left(\frac{\alpha_T}{\alpha_C}|\bar{x}, Y=0\right) = \frac{\Phi(-\gamma'\bar{x}_1 - s_1)}{\Phi(-\gamma'\bar{x}_1)} e^{-\beta'\bar{x}_2+(1/2)(s_1^2+s_2^2)} \tag{9}$$

These expressions depend on γ, β, and s. We could use the point estimates for these, but this ignores the fact that they are estimates (Hensher and Greene, 2003). It is more appropriate to use the estimated asymptotic distribution of (γ, β, s). To do this for the model in equation (7), we draw M times (β_m, s_m) and calculate

$$E(\text{VTT}_m|\bar{x}) = e^{\beta'_m\bar{x}_2+(1/2)(s_{1m}^2+s_{2m}^2)}$$

Then we use the average

$$E(\text{VTT}|\bar{x}) = \frac{1}{M}\sum_m E(\text{VTT}_m|\bar{x})$$

as the mean VTT estimate from the model with selection. As an estimate of the variation in the mean VTT, we calculate

$$\text{std} = \left(\frac{1}{M}\sum_m (E(\text{VTT}_m|\bar{x}) - (\text{VTT}|\bar{x}))^2\right)^{1/2}$$

and report this as the standard deviation of the estimated mean. Equations (6), (8), and (9) are simulated in the same way.

Data and Estimation

Data

The data are from the 2004 Danish VTT study known as DATIV (see Fosgerau et al., 2006). We use observations of commuters using car or PT, giving us 1,425 individuals.

Table 1
Statistics on the Attributes

Variable	Mean	Standard deviation	Minimum	Maximum	Mean(PT)	Mean(car)
ΔT	−7.24	6.9	−60	−1	−7.77	−6.42
ΔC	6.94	11.2	0.5	200	7.11	6.68

Each individual was asked nine SP choices in an unlabeled experiment referring to a current commute trip, that is, car users only make car choices. Every choice was a binary choice where the alternatives were only described by travel time and cost. One of the SP choices was a check question, that is, a choice where one alternative is slower and more expensive than the other. A total of 177 persons chose this dominated alternative. Since we could not be sure that these people understood the SP task, they were taken out of the sample. Of the remaining 1,248 individuals, 3 had unrealistic reported travel times, 5 had unrealistically large travel costs, 24 had unrealistic travel speeds, and 1 did not complete all of his choices. This left 1,216 individuals of which 739 used PT and 477 used car.

We exclude the dominant check question from the estimations since the information given by this choice is uninformative in the framework of DeSerpa (1971) that implies non-negative VTT.

To estimate the model, the alternatives have been arranged such that alternative 1 is the fastest. With this rearrangement, the differences between the attributes of the SP choices can be seen in Table 1, where ΔT denotes the time attribute of the first alternative minus the time attribute of the second, etc.

Table 2 summarizes the 0–1 dummies used as explanatory variables.[2] The reason why a few car users have no cars in household is that they are car passengers.

Descriptions for the continuous variables are shown in Table 3. Here x_{age} is the age and x_{dis} the log of the distance in kilometers between origin and destination. If distance was set to zero, x_{dis} is set to zero. The variable x_{inc} is the log of gross personal income for the people with reported income (income is not continuous, but discrete with 11 levels). The variable x_{time} is the log of reported travel time in minutes. Each alternative in the SP choices concerning car also included the attribute congested time. Since this attribute in all SP choices had a fixed ratio to the total time depending on reported congestion, we choose to use only total travel time and include the congestion ratio as

[2] 1 Euro = 7.5 DKK.

Table 2
Descriptive Statistics, 0–1 Indicators, Share = 1 in Percent

Variable	All	PT	Car	Description
x_{area}	37.9	47.8	22.6	Residence in Copenhagen
x_{area2}	34.2	24.5	49.5	Residence in small town (<10,000)
x_{carno}	21.5	33.6	2.7	No cars in household
x_{cars}	16.5	8.3	29.4	More than one car in household
x_{carsin}	8.8	5.3	14.3	One car in single-adult household
x_{child}	10.7	10.7	10.7	Child in household
x_{grp2}	6.0	2.0	12.2	Travel with family
x_{grp3}	5.9	4.3	8.4	Travel with non-family
x_{hinc}	32.2	33.7	29.8	Household income >600,000 DKK
x_{noinc}	5.5	5.0	6.3	Income unknown
x_{lic}	91.0	85.5	99.4	Holding a driver's license
x_{lug}	11.7	10.0	14.3	Travel with large luggage
x_{female}	53.4	49.8	58.9	Female
x_{tripf}	41.9	53.2	24.3	Travel less often than daily
$x_{weekend}$	4.7	2.8	7.6	Travel on weekend
x_{workh}	80.8	81.9	79.3	Work home less than once a week
x_{occup}	98.1	97.2	99.6	Wage earner or self-employed

Table 3
More Descriptive Statistics

Variable	Mean	Standard deviation	Minimum	Maximum	Mean(PT)	Mean(car)
x_{age}	42.8	11.2	16	73	41.4	45.0
x_{dis}	3.02	1.13	0	6.40	2.98	3.08
x_{inc}	1.26	0.51	0	2.4	1.25	1.27
x_{time}	3.22	0.80	1.10	5.86	3.25	3.17
x_{cong}	0.10	0.13	0	0.49	–	0.10

an explanatory variable. The statistics for congestion is only calculated over car users. This approach was also used in Fosgerau (2006).

It is worth noting that car users are older and travel longer distances in shorter time but income is the same in the two segments. The fact that income is similar in the two segments is somewhat unusual. In this data set, the explanation could be that people working in central Copenhagen have higher income in general together with better service by PT.

Instruments

Now we will return to the question of instruments introduced in the section "Selection Model." In the selection equation, we have a vector of explanatory variables. These are divided into two groups: the variables that also enter the VTT equation and the instruments. The first choice to make is which explanatory variables to include in both equations. These variables should have a causal effect on VTT to avoid endogeneity. As explanatory variables in the VTT equation, we choose to include income and time, since it is restrictions on these two resources that cause the VTT to exist. Furthermore, we choose to include age and sex since the causality between these variables and VTT is clear.[3] The inclusion of these two variables has the same purpose as segmentation.

For the remaining variables, we do not have theory to support their inclusion in the VTT equation. Some of them, like car ownership, are clearly correlated with VTT but since it is very probable that higher VTT leads to higher car ownership it would violate the assumptions of the model to enter car ownership in the VTT equation. The remaining variables are therefore used as instruments in the selection equation. Since these variables are not collected for a mode choice model but as background variables in an SP experiment, special care has to be taken. They must be independent of the chosen mode. A variable indicating if working on the reference trip is an example of a variable that cannot be used based on these criteria.

The instruments used are area, number of cars, travel group, license, luggage, trip frequency, weekend, work home, and occupation. An ideal instrument would be a variable having a large influence on selection of mode but being uncorrelated with VTT. None of the instruments above are obvious candidates. The number of cars is very likely to affect mode selection but it is doubtful if it is uncorrelated with VTT. Luggage and license seem like the best candidates but they have low variation in the population.

Estimation Results

Estimation was performed using a program written in Ox (Doornik 2001). The program used maximum simulated likelihood (see Train, 2003), and Halton draws where the first 20 periods were removed from each series. The final results were based on 1,500 Halton draws.

For each of the three specifications discussed in the section "VTT Models," two models were estimated—one with correlation between the selection equation and the VTT equation and one without correlation. Since each model is estimated for both car and PT users, this gives a total of 12 models. The model fits are summarized in Table 4.

[3]The VTT does not affect age and sex.

Table 4
Model Fits

	Car			PT		
	Model I	**Model II**	**Model III**	**Model I**	**Model II**	**Model III**
Sequential selection	−509.6	−509.6	−509.6	−509.6	−509.6	−509.6
Sequential VTT equation	−2110.9	−2028.3	−2040.4	2821.7	−2712.7	−2689.5
Simultaneous	−2619.7	−2536.6	−2550.0	−3330.8	−3221.7	−3198.9

Table 5
Estimation Result for the Selection Equation

	Estimate	***t*-Test**
γ_0	−3.11	−4.27
γ_{age}	0.12	2.77
γ_{area}	−0.40	−3.42
γ_{area2}	0.33	2.89
γ_{carno}	−1.42	−8.15
γ_{cars}	0.87	7.02
γ_{carsin}	0.54	3.54
γ_{child}	−0.27	−1.93
γ_{dis}	−0.15	−3.69
γ_{grp2}	1.53	7.21
γ_{grp3}	0.59	3.10
γ_{hinc}	−0.24	−2.30
γ_{lic}	1.70	4.60
γ_{lug}	0.44	3.05
γ_{sex}	−0.32	−3.43
γ_{tripf}	−1.08	−10.96
γ_{week}	0.66	2.77
γ_{occup}	1.88	3.14
γ_{workh}	−0.28	−2.32

In Table 4, Model I refers to the specification in preference space, Model II refers to the specification in inverse VTT space, and Model III refers to the specification in log VTT space. Now we will comment on the estimations for each of the three specifications. For the sequential selection models, the results are in Table 5. The results for these coefficients in the simultaneous models are similar, so they are not reported. The VTT model estimates are given in Table 6.

Table 6
Estimation Results for the VTT Equations

	Car		PT		Car		PT	
	Estimate	***t*-Test**	**Estimate**	***t*-Test**	**Estimate**	***t*-Test**	**Estimate**	***t*-Test**
Model I								
β_T	−1.42	−15.73	−1.01	−18.45	−1.43	−16.26	−1.01	−18.28
β_0	−0.61	−1.46	−1.80	−6.34	−0.57	−1.40	−1.84	−7.14
β_{age}	−0.23	−3.86	−0.12	−2.61	−0.23	−3.96	−0.09	−2.14
β_{inc}	0.24	1.29	0.69	5.70	0.22	1.32	0.67	5.58
β_{ninc}	1.03	2.90	1.02	3.88	1.12	3.35	1.03	4.12
β_{sex}	−0.29	−2.19	0.06	0.60	−0.34	−2.72	0.04	0.46
β_{time}	0.71	8.11	0.51	9.18	0.67	9.03	0.52	10.27
β_{cong}	1.07	2.21			1.07	2.31		
s					0.23	2.00	0.17	1.21
s_1	1.00	14.70	0.98	20.40	0.98	14.68	0.96	19.70
s_2	0.91	10.86	0.66	13.83	0.94	13.30	0.68	13.59
Model II								
β_T	−1.21	−10.41	−0.79	−10.12	−1.19	−10.41	−0.79	−10.14
β_0	−1.45	−5.50	−2.37	−15.16	−1.34	−6.03	−2.35	−14.04
β_{age}	−0.27	−7.50	−0.15	−4.59	−0.27	−7.73	−0.15	−4.47
β_{inc}	0.43	4.44	0.84	10.70	0.41	5.40	0.85	10.07
β_{ninc}	0.94	4.60	1.24	7.12	0.94	5.41	1.32	8.01
β_{sex}	−0.25	−3.72	0.04	0.49	−0.20	−2.54	0.00	0.02
β_{time}	0.50	16.39	0.36	7.53	0.46	9.12	0.38	8.44
β_{cong}	1.82	7.21			1.71	4.99		
s					0.10	3.13	0.12	4.10
s_1	1.06	18.09	1.01	22.58	1.07	21.56	1.01	30.06
s_2	1.66	9.27	1.23	11.34	1.65	9.71	1.23	11.11
Model III								
β_0	−1.58	−3.67	−2.32	−8.66	−1.61	−3.68	−2.33	−8.67
β_{age}	−0.31	−5.03	−0.16	−3.82	−0.31	−4.95	−0.16	−3.59
β_{inc}	0.55	2.97	0.88	7.64	0.54	2.89	0.88	7.66
β_{ninc}	0.87	2.40	1.34	5.43	0.86	2.39	1.36	5.44
β_{sex}	−0.20	−1.49	0.05	0.57	−0.22	−1.58	0.05	0.54
β_{time}	0.46	5.26	0.29	5.24	0.46	5.20	0.29	5.26
β_{cong}	2.14	4.21			2.13	4.20		
s					0.08	0.49	0.07	0.60
s_1	1.18	15.67	1.02	23.22	1.18	15.59	1.02	22.97
m	1.18	20.28	1.88	29.44	1.18	20.28	1.88	29.45

Model I Estimation Results

Model I without correlation consists of two independent models: a probit model describing selection and an ML model for the SP experiment. The dependent variable is choosing car for both segments in the probit model. Remember that the selection only uses socio-demographic variables, so the parameters are differences in the effect of a variable on utility of car and PT.

The estimation of the probit is based on all 1,216 individuals. All estimates are significant at the 5% level except for γ_{child} which comes very close. One sees that γ_{age}, γ_{area2}, γ_{cars}, γ_{carsin}, γ_{grp2}, γ_{grp3}, γ_{lic}, γ_{lug}, $\gamma_{weekend}$, and γ_{occup} all are positive. This is expected for γ_{age}, γ_{area2}, γ_{cars}, γ_{carsin}, γ_{lic}, and γ_{lung}. For the others, it is less obvious but also reasonable, for example, the effect of γ_{occup} is possibly derived from higher income and car ownership. The other variables have negative signs. This is expected for γ_{area}, γ_{carno}, and γ_{female}. Of the remaining, the most surprising is that γ_{hinc} has a negative sign. A possible explanation for this is the fact mentioned earlier that high-income individuals tend to work in the Copenhagen area where PT service is better.

The VTT estimation is based on equation (2). For this VTT equation, we allow β_C to be parameterized by x, that is, age, income, dummy for unknown income, dummy for female, time, and congestion. The choice of parameterizing the cost coefficient is based on initial estimation suggesting higher significance of the explanatory variables and better fit. Furthermore, estimation without explanatory variables showed larger variance in the cost coefficient than in the time coefficient.

From the estimation of the car VTT equation, we get the expected signs on the parameters, that is, VTT rises with income, time, and congestion; it is lower for females and declines with age. The most surprising result is the size of β_{inc} and the fact that it is insignificant. For the PT segment, we get different sizes for the estimates but the same signs. Except for β_{female}, all parameters are significant in the PT segment. This is more in line with what one would expect.

The simultaneous model consists of the selection and VTT equation connected through correlation as described in the section "Simultaneous Model," otherwise the models are unchanged. The results for the car segment resemble the sequential model. The signs are the same and the same parameters are seen to be significant with the only exception being that γ_{child} is now significant. So β_{inc} is still insignificant. The correlation, s_1, is seen to be significant and positive. For the PT segment, all signs are the same as for the sequential model and the only change is that γ_{child} becomes significant. The correlation is not significant but keeps the positive sign. The sign is positive for both segments. Since the dependent variable in the selection model is an indicator for car, the positive sign is equivalent to positive correlation between higher VTT and choosing car for both segments.

There were problems with the convergence of the above simultaneous models. Using 500, 1,000, 1,500, and 2,000 Halton draws, the *t*-test on the correlations changed between 1 and 3. Therefore, we will not put too much emphasis on this model in the discussion and conclusion later.

Model II Estimation Results

Model II is the specification using equation (3) in the VTT model. The model is specified in inverse VTT space instead of VTT space for the same reasons that the cost coefficient is parameterized in Model I.

The probit results for the sequential model are the same as for Model I. The VTT estimation for the car segment is seen to outperform Model I based on log-likelihood. This is an indication that Model II is better than Model I at describing the data. Since the models are non-nested, we cannot perform a formal likelihood ratio test. Concerning the signs, we get the expected ones and all coefficients are significant. In general, the estimates are more significant and it is very comforting that income is now significant.

For the PT segment, we get similar results. Model II is again seen to clearly outperform Model I based on log-likelihood. All signs are the expected ones and except for β_{female} all estimates are more significant.

The two simultaneous models repeat the pattern from the sequential models. The parameters are all significant with expected signs for the car segment and for the PT segment only γ_{child} and β_{female} are insignificant. Both models are seen to outperform Model I. Now the correlation in both models is significant. This confirms that it is more appropriate to model correlation between the VTT and selection directly as in Model II. Again we see that the sign is positive for both segments with the same interpretation as before that VTT is higher conditional on an individual being a car user.

Model III Estimation Results

Model III uses the specification in log VTT space. For the results of the probit models, the same comments apply that were mentioned for Model I. Looking at the VTT specification in equation (4), the coefficient on the first variable is set to 1. Therefore, it is possible to estimate the scale of the logistic error. The scale is reported as *m* in the results. The two sequential VTT estimations are seen to give the same signs as Model II. The only difference is that β_{female} is now insignificant for both segments and in general all coefficients are less significant. Compared to Model II, the car model is seen to have a lower log-likelihood, whereas the PT model has a higher one. In this comparison, it should be noted that Model III has one less mixed variable. Again one has to remember that the models are non-nested.

The simultaneous models correspond to the sequential. In both segments, the correlation is seen to be insignificant with a positive sign.

VTT Estimation Results

The mean VTT is simulated for each of the three models. The results are seen in Tables 7–9 with standard deviation of the mean in parenthesis. All means are evaluated at the mean value of the explanatory variables, x, in the sample, except for congestion that is set to zero to allow for comparison across modes. For all models, we have evaluated

Table 7
VTT for Average Individual from Model I in DKK per Minute

Model/segment	Car	PT
$E(\mathrm{VTT_s}\|x)$	1.54 (0.21)	0.97 (0.07)
$E(\mathrm{VTT}\|x)$	1.39 (0.19)	1.06 (0.10)
$E(\mathrm{VTT}\|x,\ Y=1)$	1.79 (0.27)	1.30 (0.29)
$E(\mathrm{VTT}\|x,\ Y=0)$	1.23 (0.22)	0.97 (0.07)

Table 8
VTT for Average Individual from Model II in DKK per Minute

Model/segment	Car	PT
$E(\mathrm{VTT_s}\|x)$	1.08 (0.07)	0.83 (0.04)
$E(\mathrm{VTT}\|x)$	1.07 (0.06)	0.89 (0.04)
$E(\mathrm{VTT}\|x,\ Y=1)$	1.21 (0.07)	1.02 (0.07)
$E(\mathrm{VTT}\|x,\ Y=0)$	1.02 (0.06)	0.84 (0.04)

Table 9
VTT for Average Individual from Model III in DKK per Minute

Model/segment	Car	PT
$E(\mathrm{VTT_s}\|x)$	0.93 (0.11)	0.70 (0.04)
$E(\mathrm{VTT}\|x)$	0.90 (0.14)	0.72 (0.05)
$E(\mathrm{VTT}\|x,\ Y=1)$	0.97 (0.14)	0.79 (0.14)
$E(\mathrm{VTT}\|x,\ Y=0)$	0.87 (0.19)	0.69 (0.04)

the four different means described in the section "VTT Estimation." The first mean is the mean calculated from the model not taking selection into account, that is, $E(\text{VTT}_s)$. The second mean is the population mean calculated from the model with selection. The third mean is calculated conditional on the average individual being a car user, that is, it is the second mean conditional on $Y = 1$. This is possible since the model taking selection into account can condition on this choice. The fourth mean corresponds to the third mean but instead we condition on using PT.

Looking at Table 7, we see that the standard mean $E(\text{VTT}_s|x)$ in car is much higher than in PT. The pattern is similar for the model with selection. Again $E(\text{VTT}|x)$ is higher in car, but looking at the two means one sees that they are now closer. They have both moved toward one another. So part of the gap between VTT in car and PT has been explained by the selection.

The value of $E(\text{VTT}|x, Y = 1)$ for car should be compared with $E(\text{VTT}_s|x)$ for car since they represent the same mean for the two models. They are somewhat different, but the large standard deviations make it impossible to say anything about bias. In the same way, $E(\text{VTT}|x, Y = 0)$ for PT should be compared to $E(\text{VTT}_s|x)$ in PT. They are seen to be similar as both equal 0.97.

For Model II, the remarks are similar for the PT segment. The model with selection has higher mean. Furthermore, the mean VTT_s is similar to mean VTT conditional on $Y = 0$. They are 0.83 and 0.84. For the car segment, it is seen that the mean with and without selection are close. They are 1.07 and 1.08. This is somewhat surprising since the correlation is significant.

For Model III, we see that the effects are small which corresponds to the fact that the correlation is insignificant. The patterns though are similar to the patterns for Model II.

We can draw one immediate conclusion: in the standard case, VTT_s, one would conclude that the VTT in car is higher than in PT. This conclusion is not so obvious when taking selection into account for the models with significant correlation.

Discussion

Three model specifications have been estimated. All three gave reasonable parameter estimates with the exception of the income parameter in Model I for car which turned out insignificant. Both Models II and III outperform Model I based on log-likelihood. Therefore, the remaining discussion will concentrate on these two models. The correlation has the same sign in both models, and it is significant in Model II. The sign shows that there is a positive correlation between choosing car and having a higher VTT.

The main difference between the two model types is that the logistic error is multiplicative in Model III and additive in Model II relative to the VTT. This means that in Model III the logistic error affects the choice behavior relatively depending on the VTT of the individual. For Model II, the logistic error becomes dominant for small values of ΔT and ΔC and disappears for large values. A second difference is that the scale is lognormal in Model II, whereas it is constant in Model III.

These model differences aside, it is still sound to conclude based on the estimation that on our sample Models II and III should be preferred to Model I. Hence, we are left to conclude that either we discard the standard structure with additive errors or we have to acknowledge the significant self-selection.

Of course, it is also possible to do both. Since both models depend on our instruments, we are left with the concern whether we have used appropriate instruments. As mentioned in the section "Instruments," a good instrument must have a large impact on the selection of mode. From the estimates, car ownership, travel group, license, trip frequency, and occupation have a high impact on selection. This supports that we actually have good instruments. But since they do not result in stronger correlation, we have to look critically at the selection model. The assumption that the error term is normal is very restrictive. Furthermore, it is very probable that car ownership should be treated as endogenous. Hence, a more flexible selection model could be worth pursuing. The above also highlights that besides careful design of the SP choices in future VTT experiments, it would be fruitful to design background questions in the questionnaire with the search for appropriate instruments in mind.

Summary and Conclusions

This paper has presented a discrete choice model that investigates the effect of self-selection on VTT estimates through the unobserved heterogeneity in the VTT model. The model is an addition both to the literature on ML models and on self-selection in the way it incorporates the self-selection into an ML model.

The model has led to reasonable VTT estimates with significant correlation in half of the models. This partial evidence of correlation should be seen as an indication that more work is needed. Moreover, we would expect the possible effects of self-selection to be larger in a sample where the income differences are larger between modes. An important question is if we have used appropriate instruments and whether they can be found. This is a challenge for future SP questionnaire designs.

There are several ways to continue the present investigation. One immediate extension would be to estimate everything jointly for the car and PT segment as opposed to here where we estimate models separately for each segment.

A second extension would be the methodological challenge to relax the assumption of joint normality of log VTT and the error in the selection equation. This has been done in the case of labor supply models (see, e.g., Vella, 1998).

Instead of extensions of the model, a different approach to the central problem of the effect of self-selection on VTT estimates could be to carefully design an across-mode SP experiment. In such an experiment, it would be possible to compare VTT for PT passengers and car users in car directly. The SP experiment would have to ensure that both reference trips were carefully described to capture any mode bias in the sample not related to VTT.

The main conclusion from this paper is that the sample selection affects VTT estimates and that the effect can alter the final output from the model. A second conclusion is that self-selection should be looked at more seriously in the transportation field especially now that researches have moved away from the robust multinomial logit model. So more research is needed to investigate if it is just a sample and/or model-specific selection effect we have found.

ACKNOWLEDGMENT

The authors would like to thank two anonymous referees for valuable comments.

References

Axhausen, K. W., A. König, G. Abay, J. J. Bates and M. Bierlaire (2004). Swiss value of travel time savings. Paper presented at the European Transport Conference. Strasbourg.

DeSerpa, A. (1971). A theory of the economics of time. *The Economic Journal* 81, 828–846.

Doornik, J. (2001). *Ox: An Object-oriented Matrix Language*. London, Timberlake Consultants Press.

Eklof, J. and S. Karlsson (1999). Testing and correcting for sample selection bias in discrete choice contingent valuation studies. SEE/EFI Working Papers Series in Economics and Finance, No. 171.

Fosgerau, M. (2006). Investigating the distribution of the value of travel time savings. *Transportation Research Part B: Methodological* 40(8), 688–707.

Fosgerau, M. (2007). Using nonparametrics to specify a model to measure the value of travel time. *Transportation Research Part A* 41, 842–856.

Fosgerau, M., K. Hjorth and S. V. Lyk-Jensen (2006). An integrated approach to the estimation of the value of travel time. Paper presented at the European Transport Conference. Strasbourg.

Heckman, J. J. (1979). Sample selection bias as a specification error. *Econometrica* 47(1), 153–162.
Hensher, D. A. (2001). Measurement of the valuation of travel time savings. *Journal of Transport Economics and Policy* 35(1), 71–98.
Hensher, D. A. and W. H. Greene (2003). The mixed logit model: the state of practice. *Transportation* 30, 133–176.
Manski, C. and S. Lerman (1977). The estimation of choice probabilities from choice based samples. *Econometrica* 45(8), 1977–1988.
Rose, J. and M. Bliemer (2006). Designing efficient data for stated choice experiments: accounting for socio-demographic and contextual effects in designing stated choice experiments. Paper presented at IATBR. Kyoto.
Sillano, M. and J. de D. Ortúzar (2005). Willingness-to-pay estimation with mixed logit models: some new evidence. *Environment & Planning A* 37(3), 525–550.
Train, K. and M. Weeks (2005). Discrete choice models in preference space and willingness-to-pay space. In R. Scarpa and A. Alberini (Eds.), *Applications of Simulation Methods in Environmental and Resource Economics*, Dordrecht, Netherlands, Springer, pp. 1–16.
Train, K. and W. Wilson (2008). Estimation on stated-preference experiments constructed from revealed-preference choices, *Transportation Research B* 42(3), 191–203.
Train, K. E. (2003). *Discrete Choice Methods with Simulation*. New York, NY, Cambridge University Press.
Vella, F. (1992). Simple tests for sample selection bias in censored and discrete choice models. *Journal of Applied Econometrics* 7(4), 413–421.
Vella, F. (1998). Estimating models with sample selection bias: a survey. *The Journal of Human Resources* 33(1), 88–126.
Wardman, M. (2004). Public transport values of time. *Transport Policy* 11, 363–377.

The Expanding Sphere of Travel Behaviour Research
Selected Papers from the 11th International Conference on Travel Behaviour Research

33

Social Value Orientation and the Efficiency of Traffic Networks

Erel Avineri

Abstract

Transport models include the mathematical and logical abstractions of real-world systems. It is common to describe the traffic system as a non-cooperative agents' game, assuming travellers' behaviour is selfish by nature (focus on optimizing outcomes for themselves, without considering much others' benefits). In this paper, some basic concepts of pro-social behaviour are illustrated. Adding to the individual user's utility function, a component to represent social value, the user equilibrium is extended to a social equilibrium. The sensitivity of the social equilibrium to social values is investigated. Also introduced here is a dynamic travel-choice model of travel behaviour which considers social value orientation. The potential for incorporating social aspects in the development of transport modelling is demonstrated by a numeric example.

Introduction

Traffic network models are designed to emulate the behaviour of travellers in the traffic network over time and space, and to predict changes in system performance, when influencing conditions are changed. Such models include the mathematical and logical abstractions of real-world systems implemented in computer software. In many of the applied models each traveller is formulated as an individual agent, making independent decisions about his or her desired use of the transport system (travel mode, route, departure time, etc.).

Social aspects of travel behaviour (such as social value orientation) are commonly omitted from the formal modelling process, quite often treated as (unbiased) random errors or qualitative caveats. Travel behaviour research in recent years has tended to focus on normative models, which tend to represent the individual traveller as a *homo economicus*, a rational economic human being, rather than on descriptive models to represent and measure travel behaviour without making an explicit value judgement. A clear distinction between normative modelling and descriptive modelling of travel behaviour is not always made. As stated by Gärling (1998), the behavioural assumptions in travel demand models are almost always made without reference to the existing theories in behavioural sciences.

Many transport problems can be defined as social dilemmas. A *social dilemma* problem represents a situation in which (voluntary) contributions are needed to attain some common and shared social payoff, and where the rational choice of the individual is to not to cooperate. It is common to represent the performance of a traffic network as the aggregate behaviour of the individual agents, not taking into consideration the social interactions and the social values they may have towards each other. This approach is based on an implicit assumption that social aspects can be neglected.

Recently, there have been signs of increased interest in the study of social influence in the context of travel, mainly in activity-based modelling (see, e.g. Vovsha et al., 2003; Salvini and Miller, 2005; Arentze and Timmermans, 2006; Goulias and Henson, 2006). However, socio-psychological aspects of dynamic choice behaviour have not gained much attention from researchers of the more traditional travel behaviour models (such as equilibrium models, microsimulation and discrete choice analysis). Understanding and modelling the behaviour of the individual traveller, influenced by his/her social values, may be considered to be a new territory in travel behaviour that has not been much explored.

This paper presents an investigation of the effect of social value orientation on choice behaviour in a path-choice situation, simulating a social dilemma. The sensitivity of the traffic equilibrium to the travellers' social value orientation is demonstrated, followed by a discussion on the importance of incorporating social value orientation into transport modelling.

Social Value Orientation and the Social Equilibrium

In congested traffic networks, the optimal route choice for an individual depends on the congestion on alternative routes and on the route choices made by other individuals. Under *system optimum* (SO) conditions traffic should be arranged in congested networks such that the total travel cost is minimised. This implies that each agent behaves cooperatively in choosing his/her own route to ensure the most efficient use of the whole system. However, in such networks, patterns of traffic flow may differ from the socially efficient state of SO, as individual travellers attempt to minimize their own travel cost without taking into consideration the effects of their actions on other travellers, thus without considering the system externalities.

A typical equilibrium of a traffic network with a finite number of non-cooperative agents (players) is the Nash non-cooperative optimum. It represents a situation where no agent can receive any benefit by changing his/her own route decision. When players are symmetric (i.e. they are identical in all respects and share the same origin and destination) and the number of players becomes infinitely large, the Nash equilibrium converges to the Wardrop equilibrium (Haurie and Marcottet, 1985).

Each network user non-cooperatively seeks to minimize his/her cost of transport. This leads to Wardrop's (1952) principle of route choice, which states that the journey times (or costs) in all routes actually used are equal and less than those that would be experienced by a single vehicle on any unused route. The traffic flows that satisfy this principle are usually referred to as *user equilibrium* (UE) flows, since each user chooses the route that is the best for him or herself. Specifically, a user-optimized equilibrium is reached when no user can decrease his/her route travel time (or cost) by unilaterally switching routes. This well-known equilibrium became accepted by transport modellers as a sound and simple behavioural principle to describe the spreading of trips over alternate routes due to congested conditions.

Every transport system may be described as a social system, composed of individuals who interact and influence one another's behaviour. While in most of the transport applications, we are interested in studying the behaviour of the totalistic system as the prime focus, the tools used by transport modellers tend to focus on the behaviour of the individual traveller. The analysis of travel behaviour is typically disaggregated, meaning that common models represent the choice behaviour of individual decision-making entities, whether these are individual travellers or households. However, merely aggregating individuals' choices means that the functions and the characteristics of the social system are ignored. Attention should be given to interactions between individuals who are part of a social system, and to other social aspects of travel behaviour that may influence the system equilibrium and the system dynamics.

Assuming travellers behave in a completely non-cooperative and selfish way might be too extreme. The paradigm that selfish motives always underlie the choices travellers make may be questioned (Gärling, 1998). A certain level of collaboration, which may result from social interactions, information sharing and considering others' utilities, may change the system equilibrium and the network's overall dynamics. The importance of understanding the social aspects of travel-choice behaviour is not only relevant to the measurement and the prediction of such behaviour. It may also be important in terms of influencing and changing travel behaviour.

There is also a valuable line of intended enquiry in studying altruism, which is defined by behaviourists as 'being costly acts that confer economic benefits on other individuals' (Fehr and Fischbacher, 2003). Many definitions of altruism also include what is often considered a critical component of such behaviour: that the behaviour must have some cost for the actor. According to Sorrentino and Rushton (1981, p. 427), altruism is 'behavior directed toward the benefit of others at some cost to the self where no extrinsic or intrinsic benefit is the primary intent of the behavior'. Fehr and Fischbacher (2003) distinguish between *reciprocal altruism*, whereby people help in return for having been helped, and *strong reciprocity*. They define strong reciprocity as a combination of altruistic rewarding and altruistic punishment. Strong reciprocators bear the cost of rewarding cooperators or punishing defectors even if it confers no personal benefit, whereas reciprocal altruists only reward or punish if this is in their long-term self-interest. Many behavioural scientists debate the existence of pure altruism in humans (Skinner, 1978). There are alternative explanations to individuals' pro-social behaviour and motivation to cooperate, rather than pure altruism. For example, where gains to the beneficiary are not perceived to be meaningfully larger than the costs to the benefactor, cooperative players may not be regarded as altruistic.

This work looks at *pro-social behaviour* which is a broader term than altruism. It comprises helpful actions intended to benefit another person, which are not undertaken through professional obligation. Altruism is a narrower category of pro-social behaviour, in which the motivation for helping is, in addition, characterised by empathy and the ability to understand the perspective of the help-recipient. Pro-social behaviour can be categorised as either egoistically motivated (helping someone in order, ultimately, to benefit oneself) or altruistically motivated (intended only to benefit the other person) (Bierhoff, 2001).

In their work on interdependence theory, Thibaut and Kelley (1978) propose that interdependent persons may find it mutually beneficial to perform a pro-social transformation, in which each person starts to take decisions on the basis of what benefits the other person, rather than him/herself. One of the factors determining whether or not such a transformation takes place is *social value orientation* (McClintock, 1972). Essentially, social value orientation determines one's preference for a particular allocation of common resources between oneself and others, referred to as 'self and other'. According to McClintock's model, the importance a person attaches to outcomes for self may be used to categorize people to those having a pro-self value orientation who focus on optimizing outcomes for themselves, and to others with a pro-social value orientation who focus on optimizing outcomes for others. A distinction is made between pro-socials and pro-selves in the study of social dilemmas (See, e.g. Van Vugt et al., 1995; Gärling, 1999).

Over the last decade, the study of social interactions, social value orientation and collaborative behaviour has attracted much research in behavioural sciences and economic decision-making (see a review in Soetevent, 2006). In research into social dilemmas it has been found that some people cooperate even when they are anonymous and unaware of others' choices. These people (*pro-socials*) are assumed to have a pro-social value orientation (Liebrand and McClintock, 1988). It is possible to encourage people with a more individualistic social value orientation (*pro-selfs*) to make choices that take into consideration the system's negative externalities.

Structural interventions can alter the objective features of the decision situation by changing the incentive patterns associated with cooperation and non-cooperation (see, e.g. Yamagishi, 1986). Providers and managers of transport systems have introduced structural interventions that include a change of the incentive patterns associated with cooperation and non-cooperation. Typical examples of such interventions may include changing the payoff structure (e.g. congestion charging), reward–punishment (e.g. incentives for public transport users, restriction on car parking) and situational change (e.g. residential or workplace relocation). Recently, there has also been increasing interest in the influence of psychological and social aspects on the behaviour of travellers. This so-called 'softer' side of transport policy is relatively new in the UK and Australia (see, e.g. Cairns et al., 2004 and Stopher, 2005). Such soft measures are aimed at influencing travellers' attitudes and beliefs rather than making physical or economic changes in the transport system. Sunitiyoso et al. (2006) argued that the effectiveness of 'soft' measures may be enhanced if more consideration and emphasis is given to the support of social aspects of human behaviour. Goulias and Henson (2006) considered pro-social behaviour and altruism as a powerful determinant of travel behaviour, and as a motivator to use in changing travel behaviour. They provide two main reasons to study the potential of altruistic behaviour modelling in such a context: (a) understand altruism as a value to use in motivating people to move towards the common good and (b) understand altruism expressed in specific activity and travel behaviours. They suggest that social interactions should be the core of activity-based approaches to travel demand forecasting.

Laboratory experiments simulating route-choice situations (Rapoport et al., 2006, 2008, 2009; Morgan et al., 2009) revealed that aggregated route choices and resulting travel times are significantly closer to the predictions of UE rather than to the predictions of SO. In all of the above works, participants were not familiar with each other, communication between participants during the experiment was forbidden and the participants were paid based on their individual performance. Morgan et al. (2009) did not provide participants with information on the choices of others. One may argue that these aspects of experimental design do not encourage participants to exhibit pro-social value orientation, and that there is not much reason to expect pro-social behaviour by the participants.

Other important factors that might influence the degree of pro-social value orientation may be the size and complexity of the transport network (e.g. the number of alternative routes), and the size of the social group an individual traveller is identified with. A small group of individuals is more likely to secure voluntary compliance than a larger group (Olson, 1971). Common traffic networks are quite large, and individual travellers may have only little social interactions with each other; neither do they have much '*group identification*', thus might not identify themselves with the larger group (or society) values and interests. One may argue that due to the social characteristics of the traffic situations which travellers are faced with, it is unlikely that common users of the traffic network exhibit strong pro-social behaviour. Indeed, experimental work on route-choice (Rapoport et al., 2006, 2008, 2009; Morgan et al., 2009) does not provide any evidence of pro-social behaviour in small groups of participants, varying in size from 10 to 40.

The translation of social responsibility to economic behaviour can be done by adding the attitude towards the policy or the community to the utility function (see Train et al., 1987; Rabin, 1993). Following this concept, an n-agents system in which social values influence travel choice is considered. Agent i's social utility at time period t is defined as follows:

$$U_i(x^t) = -k_{ii}tt_i(x^t) - \sum_{i \neq j}^{n} k_{ij}tt_j(x^t); \quad k_{ii} + \sum_{i \neq j}^{n} k_{ij} = 1 \tag{1}$$

The first component of equation (1) represents agent i's individual utility, which is defined as the negative value of his travel time (tt_i), weighted by the parameter k_{ii}. The weighted utilities of other agents, in the mind of agent i, are represented by the second component of equation (1). Each agent's travel time tt_i is a function of the choices made by all agents at time period t, x^t. Other externalities, related to the travel choices made by the network users, are not explicitly represented in equation (1); however, equation (1) (and mainly its second component) can be generalised in order to represent them as well.

For simplicity, it is assumed that other agents' utilities are weighted the same, that is

$$k_{ij} = \frac{1 - k_{ii}}{n - 1} \quad \forall j \neq i \tag{2}$$

Agent i's social value is defined by the ratio

$$k_i = \frac{k_i'}{k_{ii}} \tag{3}$$

Agents may be classified into types according to their social values (k_i). A selfish agent, who does not consider others' utilities at all, is represented by $k_i = 0$. A system in which $k_i = 0$, $\forall i$ converges to the UE. $k_i = 1$ represents a high pro-social value orientation by agent i, who weights his own utility the same as he/she weights others' utilities. A system in which $k_i = 1$, $\forall i$ (i.e. $k_{ii} = k_i' = 0.5; \forall i$) converges to the SO. $k_i > 1$ represents an altruistic behaviour by agent i, where actions taken by him are done mainly in order to improve other agents' utilities, without considering his own utility. A system in which $\exists i$, $k_i > 1$ does not necessarily converge to the SO. The situations where $k_i < 0$ may be considered to be less realistic in a travel behaviour context; an agent with a negative k_{ii} value aims to minimise his own utility, while an agent with a negative k_i' value is interested in reducing others' utilities ('aggression'). However, in some contexts of travel behaviour (mainly car driving) we may find some evidence of users who fail to acknowledge the courtesy of others, aggressive driving, road rage, and even physical violence among travellers.

The change in the utility of agent i at time $t+1$, assuming he/she made a choice x_{it} at time t, and other agents do not change the choices they made at time t, is represented in equation (4).

$$\Delta u_{it+1} | (x_{it+1}; x_{jt+1} = x_{jt}, \forall j \neq i) = -k_{ii}A - k_i' B \tag{4}$$

where $A = (tt_{it+1} - tt_{it})$, $B = \sum_{j \neq i}(tt_{jt+1} - tt_{jt})$, and tt_{jt} is the travel time of agent j at time period t (tt_{jt} is a function of the choice made by agent j at time period t, x_{jt}, and the choices made by other agents at time period t, x').

Assuming the system has converged to a social equilibrium state ($t \to \infty$), the change in the utility of agent i at time $t+1$ cannot be positive, regardless of the decision he/she makes at time $t+1$, x_{it+1}; thus

$$-k_{ii}A - k_i' B < 0 \quad \forall i, \quad \forall x', t \to \infty \tag{5}$$

Equations (4) and (5) are derived from the definition of agent i's social utility function as defined in equation (1), and the generalisation of Wardrop's principle.

There are two applications of equation (5): (i) observing travellers' behaviour and the network performance, it is possible to estimate travellers' social value (k_i) and (ii) assigning different values to k_i, different states of social equilibrium can be explored. This may be useful in the study of the effect of demand management measures, where structural and/or psychological interventions are introduced.

Combining the applications (i) and (ii), it provides a potential tool to evaluate the required change in travellers' social values in order to change the social equilibrium to a different (more efficient) one.

The two extreme cases of traffic equilibrium, SO ($k_i = 1$) and UE ($k_i = 0$), are studied much in the transport literature; however, other degrees of social value ($0 < k_i < 1$) may lead to other social equilibria. This is demonstrated by the numeric example given in the next section.

Numerical Example

In this section, a simple path-choice numerical example, featuring Braess' Paradox, is investigated in order to demonstrate how a measure of travellers' social value orientation can be incorporated into modelling of multi-agents traffic systems. The concept of social UE is illustrated in the section 'The Social Value User Equilibrium' and the sensitivity of this equilibrium to travellers' social value orientation is investigated. In the section 'Experiment' group travel choice decisions are studied in the laboratory environment, featuring the same numerical example. A methodology to derive the social value from participants' choices is demonstrated. Finally, a simulation model to represent the dynamics of social agents' choices is developed in the section 'Simulation Model of Agents with Social Value Orientation' and its results are compared with the results of the static equilibrium model in the section 'The Social Value User Equilibrium'.

The Social Value User Equilibrium

In order to illustrate the traffic assignment process, and to demonstrate some of the concerns related to the choice of scale when representing a traffic network, the following numeric problem is considered.

Assume that the link volume-travel time functions are linear, and given by

$$T_{ij} = \alpha_{ij} + \beta_{ij} f_{ij} \tag{6}$$

where T_{ij} is the travel time on link ij, α_{ij} the free flow time on link ij, β_{ij} the delay parameter for link ij (the increase in travel time per unit increase in the flow on link ij) and f_{ij} the flow on link ij.

Let us consider a simple network problem, presented in Figure 1. There are three possible paths to get from origin 'a' to destination 'd', and the total traffic Q is equal to the sum of traffic volumes on paths 1, 2 and 3 (represented by F_1, F_2 and F_3, accordingly).

$$Q = F_1 + F_2 + F_3 \tag{7}$$

where

$$f_{ab} = F_1 + F_3;\ f_{bd} = F_1;\ f_{ac} = F_2;\ f_{cd} = F_2 + F_3;\ f_{bc} = F_3 \tag{8}$$

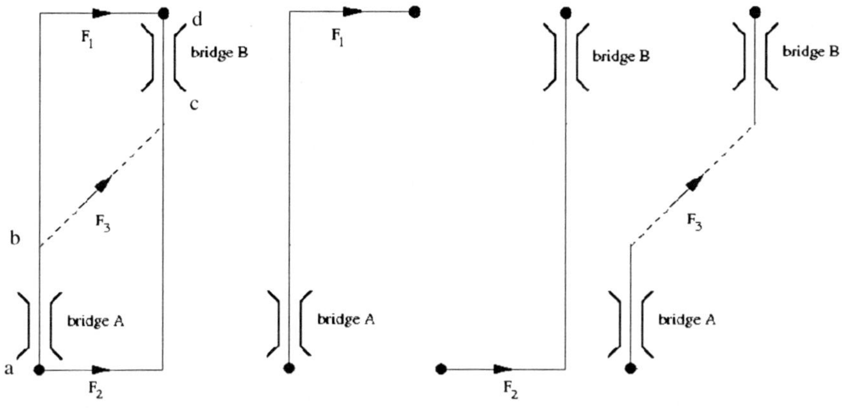

Figure 1
The Traffic Network and Three Possible Paths

Table 1
Parameter Values of the Road Segments

Link (*ij*)	α_{ij}	β_{ij}
ab	0	1/3.5
bd	15	0
ac	15	0
cd	0	1/3.5
bc	7.5	0

and the travel times on paths 1, 2 and 3 (represented by T_1, T_2 and T_3, accordingly) are

$$T_1 = T_{\mathrm{ab}} + T_{\mathrm{bd}};\ T_2 = T_{\mathrm{ac}} + T_{\mathrm{cd}};\ T_3 = T_{\mathrm{ab}} + T_{\mathrm{bc}} + T_{\mathrm{cd}} \tag{9}$$

The parameter values used in this numeric example are presented in Table 1.

Following Wardrop's principles, in a UE state, no user can decrease his/her route travel time by unilaterally switching routes. This condition may be represented by

$$T_1 = T_2 = T_3 \tag{10}$$

Setting Q (the total volume) to 32, the UE solution for this three-path network is $F_1 = F_2 = 6$; $F_3 = 20$ and the resulting travel time is $T_1 = T_2 = T_3 = 22.4$ minutes. The SO of the same network is $F_1 = F_2 = 16$; $F_3 = 0$, and the resulting travel time is $T_1 = T_2 = 19.6$ minutes. This illustrates the Braess' paradox (Braess, 1968): 'adding new capacity (such as an extra link) in a congested network does not necessarily reduce congestion and can even increase it'. This situation happens because the network users do not face the true social cost of an action; in a situation where all travellers exhibit pro-social travel behaviour, no traffic is assigned to path 3.

The UE and the SO are not the only possible equilibrium states, and other social equilibrium states may be present as well. Seventeen different equilibrium states result by taking into consideration travellers' social value orientation, and assigning different weights to k_i ($0 \leq k_i \leq 1$). The sensitivity of the system performance to travellers' social value orientation was investigated by calculating the possible social equilibrium volumes. Figure 2 presents the proportion of path choices as a function of travellers' social value (k_i).

The system efficiency of a social equilibrium as a function of travellers' social value orientation is defined as

$$E(k_i) = 1 - \frac{\sum_{j=1}^{n} tt_j^{k_i} - \mathrm{Min}_{k_i} \sum_{j=1}^{n} tt_j^{k_i}}{\mathrm{Max}_{k_i} \sum_{j=1}^{n} tt_j^{k_i} - \mathrm{Min}_{k_i} \sum_{j=1}^{n} tt_j^{k_i}} \tag{11}$$

where $\sum_{j=1}^{n} tt_j^{k_i}$ is the total travel time at a social equilibrium resulting from assigning all agents with k_i as the social value; $\mathrm{Min}_{k_i} \sum_{j=1}^{n} tt_j^{k_i}$ is the minimal travel time at the SO, resulting from assigning a value of 1 to k_i; $\mathrm{Max}_{k_i} \sum_{j=1}^{n} tt_j^{k_i}$ is the maximal travel time at a social equilibrium (this value does not necessarily result from the UE); and n is the number of agents (in this numerical example, $n = 32$).

For example, by assigning all agents a social value $k_i = 0.1$, the system efficiency of the resulting social equilibrium is 74%.

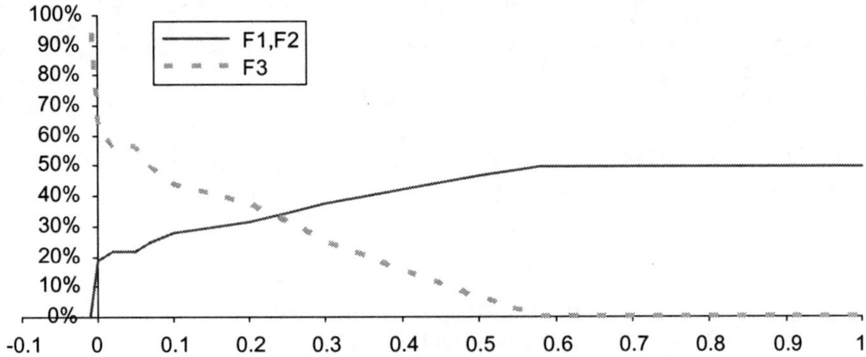

Figure 2
Proportion of Path Choices as a Function of the Social Value (k_i)

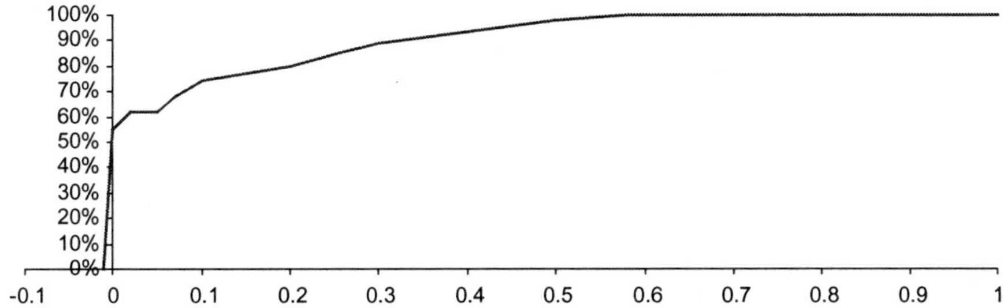

Figure 3
The System Efficiency as a Function of the Social Value (k_i) (Based on Analysis of Static Equilibrium States)

The system efficiency as a function of travellers' social value is presented in Figure 3.

Based on the above sensitivity analysis, several observations can be made: (i) the maximum efficiency (system equilibrium) can be achieved with social value less than 1 ($E = 100\%$ for $k_i \geq 0.58$); (ii) assigning k_i with a negative value, a static equilibrium which is worse than the UE becomes possible, but this might be a less realistic situation in a travel behaviour context; (iii) as can be seen from Figures 1 and 2, the social equilibrium is very sensitive to the social value in the range $0 \leq k_i \leq 0.1$. Thus, making a small adjustment to travellers' social value in the above range may make a noticeable change to the system efficiency. On the other hand, motivating agents with higher social values may not make much impact on the resulting social equilibrium and the system efficiency.

Experiment

Based on the numeric example described in the section 'The Social Value User Equilibrium', a path-choice experiment was conducted in order to demonstrate how terms of social value orientation can be estimated and used.

Thirty-two undergraduate students from the Ben-Gurion University of the Negev, Israel took part in the experiment. The participants knew each other before the experiment. They had basic background in operational research, but have never been introduced before to concepts of network theory or concepts of equilibrium. The participants were introduced to the simple network problem shown in Figure 1, and were provided with the functions to calculate the different path travel times. On each trial, each participant was asked to choose one of the two alternative paths. The participants were given about 30 seconds to write down their choices. They were not allowed to discuss their choices with their colleagues or inform them of their decision.

After all the participants made their choices, they were provided with the travel time on each of the paths. Following this information, they were asked to make another choice. This stage was repeated four times.

The average proportion of path 1, 2 and 3 choices during the experiment were $P_1 = 32\%$, $P_2 = 34\%$ and $P_3 = 35\%$, respectively. The resulting system efficiency is 74% (average value). The proportion of path 3 choices is much lower than the choice proportion predicted by the UE (63%, see Figure 2). The experimental results do not provide evidence in support for the existence and significance of pro-social behaviour. But they do not necessarily support the opposite, but they are close to the predictions of UE. However, one should be careful in explaining the experimental results by the existence of pro-social values: it is rather likely that some of the deviation from the SO is due to confusion, inexperience with the network, and the small number of iterations. Due to the small scale of the experiment, these results do not provide clear evidence of the existence and significance of pro-social values. Following the methodology described in equations (4) and (5), the social value of travellers during the experiment is evaluated as $k_i = 0.17$. Taking into account the small size of the group and correlated effects due to group identification, this can be considered to be a low social value.

A value of $k_i = 0.17$ is far from representing any sign of pro-social behaviour. However, as been illustrated above, in order to have a maximum efficiency a social value of $k_i = 0.58$ would be enough. Thus, a partial representation of the network externalities (in this example, $\Delta k_i = 0.41$) may be sufficient in order to have a strong effect on the social equilibrium and the overall efficiency of the network.

The experimental design neither supported direct cooperation, nor encouraged pro-social behaviour. However, the participants, who knew each other before the experiment took place, could have had some group identification and the social distance between group members may have been smaller than in the overall population of the users of a typical network. This, together with the small group size, may have some effect on the revealed behaviour and the derived social value, which may be assumed to be higher than a value derived from travellers' behaviour in real-life situations. In future experiments of group travel behaviour, it may be important to control (but not necessarily reduce) as much as possible the endogenous and exogenous (contextual) interactions, as well as correlated effects, between subjects, due to the possibility that some of them may be familiar with each other, or have some group identification.

The participants in this experiment were provided with complete information about others' choices and resulting travel time. In real-life scenarios, information on the choices of other travellers and the travel time outcomes are quite limited, and travellers may be informed only about their own travel costs. In the presence of uncertainty, providing complete information does not necessarily lead to higher system efficiency, which can be explained by the bounded rationality of Bayesian-learning travellers (Avineri and Prashker, 2005). The dynamic processes of travellers' behaviour in different information schemes may have a considerable effect on the aggregated route choices and the performance of the overall network. This limits the generalisability of the numeric example studied here.

Simulation Model of Agents with Social Value Orientation

Taking into consideration travellers' social value orientation, as discussed in the section 'The Social Value User Equilibrium' and described by equations (1–5), a state of social equilibrium is assumed. Such equilibrium may not hold due to measurement errors, bounded rationality, dynamic fluctuations in aggregate choice or over-sensitivity of users to the alternative utility values. Thus, the aggregated behaviour of travellers with social values may not be converged to a social equilibrium. As an alternative to the equilibrium model presented in the previous sections, and in order to address perception errors and the dynamic process of learning and adaptation, we introduce a dynamic model of travellers' choice with components of social value orientation.

Travellers' choices are represented by the Multinomial Logit model; it implies that each probability to choose a route is non-negative, and the sum of the probabilities of any route to be chosen is unity ($\sum_{k=1}^{m} p_k = 1$). Specifically, the probability that path l will be chosen by agent i at time period t is

$$p_{li}^{t} = \frac{e^{\lambda u_i(x^t | x_i^t = l;\; x_j^t = x_j^{t-1} \forall j \neq i)}}{\sum_{k=1}^{m} e^{\lambda u_i(x^t | x_i^t = k;\; x_j^t = x_j^{t-1} \forall j \neq i)}} \tag{12}$$

where $u_i(x^t)$ is agent i's utility value of path l at time period t, as defined in equation (1). $\lambda \geq 0$ is a free parameter that determines the 'extremeness' of the choice probabilities, and the sum is over m route alternatives. Assigning λ a value of 0 represents an agent who is indifferent between choices and will have similar propensity to choose each of the alternative choices, while assigning λ with a high value represents an agent who will very rarely choose an alternative which has low utility value.

The system efficiency of the network described in the section 'The Social Value User Equilibrium' was estimated based on the aggregated behaviour of 32 agents simulated over a time period of 10 iterations. In order to demonstrate the sensitivity to social value k_i and the extremeness of choice probabilities λ, 16 scenarios, each of them representing a different set of parameter values (k_i and λ), were studied. The system efficiency as a function of these two parameters is represented in Figure 4. Also presented in this figure is the sensitivity of the social equilibrium to the social value k_i, as defined in the section 'The Social Value User Equilibrium'.

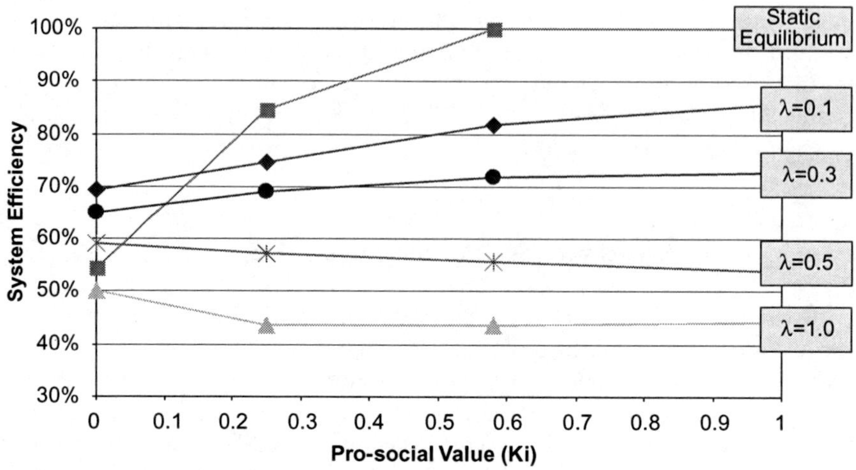

Figure 4

The System Efficiency as a Function of the Social Value (k_i) and the Extremeness of Choice Probabilities (λ) (Based on Simulated Results of Dynamic Choice Behaviour and on Analysis of Static Equilibrium States)

As can be seen from Figure 4, the efficiency of the overall system is highly sensitive to the value of λ; low value of λ, reflecting high sensitivity of agent's choice to experienced travel times on the previous time period, leads to much dynamic fluctuation between the alternative paths. Even with high social value, the pattern of aggregate choices for paths 1 and 2 is far from being stable.

It is assumed that all agents adopt a strategy based on the decision rule described in equation (12): each agent makes his/her choice at time period t based on the assumption that other agents will repeat the choices they made at time $t-1$. Since all agents make their choices at the same time, this strategy may lead to a 'herd behaviour', where agents avoid tactical decision making and follow rather simple rules, such as Thorndike's law of effect (1898). This law states that good outcomes, associated with selecting a particular strategy, increase the probability that this strategy would be chosen again. Fluctuations revealed in the simulation model (as well as in the experiment described in the section 'Experiment') may be explained by Thorndike's law of effect or other reinforcement learning models—an overestimation of travellers' propensity to choose the alternative which was more attractive in the recent turn. The low level of stability may be explained by these fluctuations. Observations of route choices in the laboratory environment revealed fluctuations in travellers' choices (see, e.g. Selten et al., 2004 and Morgan et al., 2009). It has been argued in these works that the fluctuations about the mean are persistent, and that the UE provides good prediction of mean traffic flows. On the other hand, it has been shown by simulation studies that social learning in route choice situations and other situations that can described as 'stochastic fictitious games' may lead to oscillating aggregated behaviour, where traffic volumes are not converged to a single equilibrium (Horowitz, 1984). Moreover, in a small group of network users, any small change of choices may generate high fluctuations in the group behaviour and may destabilise the equilibrium or convergence. *Overreaction* may happen when too many travellers respond to the information producing oscillations at aggregate level or instability of choices at individual level and is a consequence of the fact that travellers' have only limited ability to forecast the behaviour of others (Ben-Akiva et al., 1991).

Although the decision-making strategy represented in equation (12) was not validated by empirical research, and might be too simplistic, it may provide us with a possible explanation to the system efficiency revealed in the experiment. In a system where all agents have a social value orientation of zero, it is still possible to achieve an efficiency level higher than the one resulting from the UE. The aggregated choices of users who are motivated to maximize their individual utilities, without considering the system externalities, may deviate from UE simply because they fail to maximise outcomes for themselves.

In situations where travellers are provided with complete information on the travel-time functions and the choices previously made by other individuals, some travellers may adopt more sophisticated choice strategies. While such strategies may be possible in small-size groups of travellers, they are not expected in relatively large-size group of travellers (where $n = 32$ in the example presented in this work may be considered to be a reasonably large group).

Assuming all travellers have the same social value ($k_i = k_j \quad \forall i, j$) may be too simplistic. The heterogeneity of pro-social values in a social group may influence the dynamics of the individual agent behaviour and the overall behaviour of the system; the level of agents' compliance and the social equilibrium the system is converged to might be very sensitive to the distribution of social value orientations among the network users.

Summary and Conclusions

The importance of social value orientation and its influence on travel behaviour as a measure to analyse, predict and improve the performance of the overall system was demonstrated in the numerical example presented in the section 'Numerical Example'. First, it was argued that besides the extreme cases of UE (representing complete selfishness) and SO (representing pro-social behaviour), other states of social equilibrium, based on mid-values of social parameter values, may result as well. The social equilibrium model described in the section 'The Social Value User Equilibrium' provides us with one possible tool to analyse the performance of the overall system and its sensitivity to social value orientation. Using such models, policy makers can estimate the effectiveness of structural and psychological interventions to motivate a change in travel behaviour, and to better understand the reasons for the success or failure of such schemes.

The lack of existence of a pro-social value in the experiment described in the section 'Experiment' is not surprising. Moreover, there is no reason to believe that in many common real-life situations travellers will exhibit pro-social values, unless demand management measures will be utilized to address situations of transport social dilemmas. This can be done by influencing travellers' social value orientation and incorporating structural approaches that offer material reward or punishment (such as congestion charging) as well as psychological approaches ('soft measures') to influence attitudes.

Incorporating social aspects such as social values orientation in the analysis and modelling of travel choice behaviour may help in setting the perspective on the social system, and not only on the individual. There is a need for experimental and empirical work in order to investigate the existence of social value orientation in a transport-related context, and the influence of pro-social values on travellers' behaviour. Further research may assess the degree to which beliefs and attitudes towards travel behaviour affect an individual's propensity to take a pro-social travel decision, and the dynamics of this process.

ACKNOWLEDGMENTS

The author would like to thank Professor Amnon Rapoport from the University of Arizona and Caroline Bartle from the University of the West of England, Bristol for their comments and suggestions on an early draft of this paper.

References

Arentze, T. and H. Timmermans (2006). Co-evolutionary dynamics in social networks and activity-travel repertoires: A framework for micro-simulation. Paper presented at the 85th Transportation Research Board Annual Meeting, Washington, DC.

Avineri, E. and J. N. Prashker (2005). Sensitivity to travel time variability: Travelers' learning perspective. *Transportation Research C* 13, 157–183.

Ben-Akiva, M., A. de Palma and I. Kaysi (1991). Dynamic network models and driver information system. *Transportation Research A* 25, 251–266.

Bierhoff, H. W. (2001). Prosocial behaviour. In M. Hewstone and W. Stroebe (Eds.), *Introduction to Social Psychology*, Oxford, UK, Blackwell Publishing, pp. 285–314.

Braess, D. (1968). Über ein Paradoxon aus der Verkehrsplanung. *Unternehmensforschung* 12, 258–268.

Cairns, S., L. Sloman, C. Newson, J. Anable, A. Kirkbridge and P. Goodwin (2004). *Smarter Choices: Changing the Way We Travel* (2 volumes). Department for Transport, London, UK, ISBN 1-904763-46-4.

Fehr, E. and U. Fischbacher (2003). The nature of human altruism. *Nature* 425, 785–791.

Gärling, T. (1998). Behavioural assumptions overlooked in travel-choice modelling. In J. de Dias Ortúzar, D. Hensher and S. Jara-Diaz (Eds.), *Travel Behaviour Research: Updating the State of Play*. Oxford, UK, Pergamon, Elsevier.

Gärling, T. (1999). Value priorities, social value orientations and cooperation in social dilemmas. *British Journal of Social Psychology* 38, 397–408.

Goulias, K. G. and K. M. Henson (2006). On altruists and egoists in activity participation and travel: Who are they and do they live together? *Transportation* 33(5), 447–462.

Haurie, A. and P. Marcottet (1985). On the relationship between Nash-Cournot and Wardrop equilibria. *Networks* 15, 295–308.

Horowitz, J. L. (1984). The stability of stochastic equilibrium in a two-link transportation network. *Transportation Research B* 18, 13–28.

Liebrand, W. B. G. and C. G. McClintock (1988). The ring measure of social values: A Computerized procedure for assessing individual differences in information processing and social value orientation. *European Journal of Social Psychology* 2, 217–230.

McClintock, C. G. (1972). Social motivation – a set of propositions. *Behavioural Science* 17, 438–454.

Morgan, J., H. Orzen and M. Sefton (2009). Network architecture and traffic flows. *Games and Economic Behavior* 66, 348–372.

Olson, M. (1971). *The logic of collective action: public goods and the theory of groups*, 2nd ed. Cambridge, MA, Harvard University Press.

Rabin, M. (1993). Incorporating fairness into game theory and economics. *American Economic Review* 83, 1281–1302.

Rapoport, A., T. Kugler, S. Dugar and E. Gisches (2008). Braess paradox in the laboratory: an experimental study of route choice in traffic networks with asymmetric costs. In T. Kugler, J. C. Smith, T. Connolly and Y. J. Son (Eds.), *Decision Modeling and Behavior in Uncertain and Complex Environments*. Springer.

Rapoport, A., T. Kugler, S. Dugar and E. Gisches (2009). Choice of routes in congested traffic networks: experimental tests of the Braess paradox. *Games and Economic Behavior* 65(2), 538–571.

Rapoport, A., V. Mak and R. Zwick (2006). Navigating congested networks with variable demand: experimental evidence. *Journal of Economic Psychology* 27, 648–666.

Salvini, P. and E. J. Miller (2005). ILUTE: An operational prototype of a comprehensive microsimulation model of urban systems. *Networks and Spatial Economics* 5(2), 217–234.

Selten, R., M. Schreckenberg, T. Chmura, T. Pitz, S. Kube, S. F. Hafstein, R. Chrobok, A. Pottmeier and J. Wahle (2004). Experimental investigation of day-to-day route-choice behavior and network simulations of Autobahn traffic in North Rhine-Westphalia. In M. Schreckenberg and R. Selten (Eds.), *Human Behavior and Traffic Networks*, Berlin, Springer, pp. 1–21.

Skinner, B. F. (1978). The ethics of helping people. In L. Wispé (Ed.), *Altruism, Sympathy and Helping: Psychological and Sociological Principles*. New York, Academic Press.

Soetevent, A. R. (2006). Empirics of the identification of social interactions: an evaluation of the approaches and their results. *Journal of Economic Surveys* 20, 193–228.

Sorrentino, R. M. and J. P. Rushton (1981). Altrusim and helping behaviour: current perspectives and future possibilities. In J. P. Rushton and R. M. Sorrentino (Eds.), *Altruism and Helping Behavior: Social, Personality and Development Perspectives*, Hillsdale, NJ, Lawrence Erlbaum Associates, Inc., pp. 425–440.

Stopher, P. (2005). Voluntary travel behavior change. In K. J. Button and D. Hensher (Eds.), *Handbook of Transport Strategy, Policy and Institutions*, Oxford, UK, Elsevier, pp. 561–580.

Sunitiyoso, Y., E. Avineri and K. Chatterjee (2006). Role of minority influence on the diffusion of compliance with a demand management measure. Paper presented at the 11th International Conference on Travel Behaviour Research, Kyoto.

Thibaut, H. H. and J. W. Kelley (1978). *Interpersonal Relations: A Theory of Interdependence*. New York, Wiley.

Thorndike, E. L. (1898). Animal intelligence: an experimental study of the associative processes in animals. *Psychological Monographs* 2(8).

Train, E. K., D. L. McFadden and A. A. Goett (1987). Consumer attitude and voluntary rate schedules for public utilities. *The Review of Economics and Statistics* 69, 383–391.

Van Vugt, M., R. Meertens and P. van Lange (1995). The role of social value orientations in a real-life social dilemma. *Journal of Applied Social Psychology* 25(3), 258–278.

Vovsha, P., E. Peterson and R. Donnelly (2003). Explicit modelling of joint travel by household members: statistical evidence and applied approach. *Transportation Research Record* 1831, 1–10.

Wardrop, J. G. (1952). Some theoretical aspects of road traffic research. *Proceedings of the Institution of Civil Engineers* 1(PART II), 325–378.

Yamagishi, T. (1986). The provision of a sanctioning system as a public good. *Journal of Personality and Social Psychology* 51, 110–116.

The Expanding Sphere of Travel Behaviour Research
Selected Papers from the 11th International Conference on Travel Behaviour Research

34

Towards a Multi-Activity Multi-Person Accessibility Measure: Concept and First Tests

Joyce K.L. Soo, Dick Ettema and Henk F.L. Ottens

Abstract

This paper presents a multi-activity multi-person accessibility measure (MAMPAM). With changes in lifestyles and activity patterns, the limitations that are inherent to traditional accessibility measures that focused on describing the accessibility of a single activity for a single person need to be addressed. First, an accessibility framework that combines the space-time prism concept and utility theory in time allocation is developed to incorporate multi-activity and multi-person effects. This is followed by a numerical example to test the sensitivity of the measure to household interaction types and spatio-temporal changes. The MAMPAM can be used to enhance decision-making with regards to land use and transportation planning.

Introduction

Accessibility measures are useful tools for the assessment of both land use and transportation policies (e.g. Geurs and van Eck, 2001). On the one hand, they provide information regarding the quality of locations in terms of how well they enable people to engage in activities or allow access to markets. On the other hand, they may serve as explanatory factors in understanding why household or firms settle down at certain locations. Traditional accessibility measures, for example, contour and potential measures, score well in the ease of operation and interpretation but have difficulties in accounting for temporal and individual constraints (Geurs and van Wee, 2004).

Furthermore, traditional accessibility measures have been unidimensional in the sense that they describe the accessibility of a single activity for a single person. With changes in life styles and activity patterns, the limitations that are inherent to traditional accessibility measures need to be addressed. In particular, accessibility measures need to reflect the opportunity on the household level to engage in multiple activities subject to spatio-temporal constraints, such as opening hours of facilities and fixed work hours.

An important motivation to develop a multi-activity accessibility measure is that people in urbanised societies tend to combine multiple tasks in their daily activity patterns; thus, accessibility to activities should be regarded in the context of the total activity pattern. In addition, the opportunities to engage in an activity at some location very much depend on constraints set by other activities. For example, if one works from 9 a.m. to 5 p.m. and stores are opened from 9 a.m. to 6 p.m., store accessibility will be affected in terms of the number of stores one can reach within an hour and the time available for shopping at each of the chosen stores. For countries such as Germany and Spain, opening hours for stores and services are still restricted, and an accessibility assessment on the extension of opening hours will be relevant for policy makers.

Accounting for multi-person interactions is another way to make improvements in accessibility measurements. Trends, such as increased female labour force participation, have resulted in increasingly interwoven activity patterns of household members. Certain activities such as shopping or childcare can be performed by either spouse, depending on the occasion. Therefore, from a household perspective, accessibility should describe how well the household as a whole can engage in all activities required to maintain the household and derive personal satisfaction. For instance, the accessibility situation of a household may be improved if both spouses have stores in the vicinity of their work location, so that maintenance activities can be transferred from one spouse to another.

This paper describes extensions to existing accessibility measures, which aim to provide better tools to account for the interdependence between activities and between household members. Such multi-activity multi-person accessibility measures (MAMPAMs) can provide better insight into the quality of the residential location of households with particular activity programmes (e.g. two-worker households or households with children). Also, MAMPAMs may improve our understanding of why households reside in certain locations.

Although the literature describes some activity-based accessibility measures, we feel that these efforts are limited in that they do not account for the effect of the duration of activities (Dong et al., 2005) or are limited to conceptual frameworks (Ashiru et al., 2004). This paper is organised as follows. The next section will discuss MAMPAM with respect to traditional, space-time and activity-based accessibility measures. The third section will present an alternative approach based on the integration of time-geography with utility theory. Section four includes a numerical example of the household accessibility. The paper concludes with the applicability of the MAMPAM to policy analysis and avenues for further research.

Accessibility Measurement

Accessibility measures can be broadly classified into area-based and person-based accessibility measures. Distance, contour and potential accessibility measures are examples of area-based measures. Space-time and activity-based accessibility measures are person-based measures that have been shown to accommodate multiple activities. Hägerstrand's (1970) work on the space-time prism has been the starting point for accessibility measurement by Lenntorp (1976) and Burns (1979). Their method of accessibility measurement was based on the volume of the space-time prism and the utility derived from activity participation as facilitated by the prism. The operational form of space-time accessibility was facilitated through the use of GIS (Miller, 1991; Kwan, 1998). Many improvements were made to the space-time accessibility measurement by accounting for travel time and its variation in the transport network, facility opening hours, location attractiveness and activity duration (Miller, 1999; Wen and Koppelman, 2000; Kim and Kwan 2003; Ettema and Timmermans, 2007).

Gender differences in space-time accessibility were highlighted in Kwan (1999a, b), and it was noted that the observed spatial–temporal behaviour is the outcome of several adaptive strategies that can be engaged at different levels: individual, household or social network. In addition, Kwan (1999a) remarks that individual accessibility is determined not only by the number of opportunities in proximity to the base locations, but these opportunities have to be evaluated in the context of the individual's background and adaptive capacity. Although Dong et al. (2005) developed an activity-based accessibility measure that could account for a larger range of socio-demographic factors through the use of utility functions, the activity patterns may not conform to the boundaries of the space-time prism. Miller (1999) integrates the utility-based accessibility measure with the space-time approach, but the measurement is confined to an individual. Thus, there still lacks an accessibility measure that can reflect the opportunities within the space-time prism while accounting for the social-demographic profile of the individual and the individual's and household's adaptive strategies.

Three adaptive strategies were outlined in Kwan (1999b). The first strategy is by social means—task sharing or reallocation to social networks or other household members. The second strategy is by temporal means—rearranging the timing of the activities within a time frame. The third strategy is by spatial means—changing the location of activities, residence or workplace. By incorporating aspects of these strategies, household time allocation and pattern generation to account for the opportunities within the space-time prism, a MAMPAM can be developed.

Framework of MAMPAM

The basic contention underlying the MAMPAM is that it should represent how well a given spatial configuration of destinations facilitates household activity patterns in given residential and work locations. That is to say, the accessibility will be higher if all persons in the household can engage in activity patterns with higher utilities. Hence, the accessibility will be higher if the spatial configuration allows them to undertake all required activities, and if they can be undertaken with a longer duration.

At the household level, MAMPAM aims to reflect interactions within the household and to account for the flexibility within the household to reallocate activities between household members. Greater flexibility within the household to reallocate activities means that the household interaction, residential location and spatial configuration of facilities allow the household to have more options to perform its intended activities and reach more attractive patterns of task and time allocation. In other words, the more flexible the household task reallocation, the more the opportunities for the household to carry out its intended agenda, the better the accessibility of the household. The optimisation of task and time allocation, however, takes place subject to constraints such as available time windows, travel speeds and opening hours of facilities.

Following the principle of more traditional accessibility measures, the MAMPAM enumerates (combinations of) locations where activities can take place, determines the attractiveness of these locations, and aggregates these into an accessibility level of a residential location. Given the scope of the MAMPAM, and the adaptive strategies that need to be incorporated, several extensions are needed. This leads to the following steps in specifying the MAMPAM:

1. identifying the independent tasks and tasks that can be transferred to other household members and generating task allocation combinations for household members
2. generating locations for activities
3. generating activity and trip patterns for each household member, given the locations
4. determining which activity patterns are feasible
5. determining the utility of feasible activity patterns on the individual level
6. aggregating the individual utilities to form the household utility
7. aggregating the household utilities across sets of locations to achieve the household utility.

Formally, the MAMPAM can be specified as:

$$A_h = \otimes_l V_l \tag{1}$$

$$V_l = \otimes_c V_{lc} \tag{2}$$

$$V_{lc} = \otimes_{p_1} \otimes_{p_2} V_{lcp_1p_2} \tag{3}$$

$$V_{lcp_1p_2} = \frac{1}{1-\alpha} \sum_p w_p V_{lcp}^{1-\alpha} \tag{4}$$

where A_h is the accessibility level of household h; V_l the aggregate utility from a set of locations at which discretionary and maintenance activities can take place; V_{lc} the aggregate utility from a set of activity allocation patterns c, given a set of locations l; $V_{lcp_1p_2}$ the joint utility from trip patterns p_1 and p_2, given allocation pattern c and set of locations l; p_x the trip pattern of household member x; V_{lcp} the utility derived from trip pattern p, given allocation pattern c and set of locations l; $\otimes_{\mathrm{d}}$ a general expression for aggregating across dimension d. Note that the aggregation includes summation, multiplication or logsum formulations.

These steps will be discussed in more detail in the remainder of this section, preceded by an overview of the relevant household interactions and exogenous factors.

Overview of Household Interactions and Exogenous Factors

Household interactions can take many forms, for example, joint activities, task (re)allocation or task sharing, time allocation, car allocation and rideshare. Regarding joint activities, there are models on joint maintenance activities (Srinivasan and Athuru, 2005), fully or partially joint activities in different patterns (Gliebe and Koppelman, 2005), and joint leisure and maintenance activities (Gliebe and Koppelman, 2002).

Task (re)allocation, task sharing, car allocation and rideshare are featured mainly in time allocation and activity pattern generation models to reflect the dynamics in the household. Task allocation models have been mainly developed for maintenance activities between household heads, as these tasks could in principle be transferred between household members. Models of maintenance task allocation have focused on how task allocation (including separate or joint allocation) varies with socio-demographics and in-home maintenance activities (Srinivasan and Athuru, 2005; Srinivasan and Bhat, 2005). More extensive models of task allocation between spouses that extend to various in-home and out-of-home activities were proposed by Ettema et al. (2007).

Activity pattern generation is usually the next step after task allocation. Many activity-based models have been proposed that describe activity pattern generation processes (e.g. Arentze and Timmermans, 2002; Ben-Akiva and Bowman, 1998). Most of these models avoid dealing with the full combinatorial set of all activity patterns, specified by location, sequence, trip pattern etc. by using heuristic or nested approaches. While this is understandable from the viewpoint of behavioural realism and computational efficiency, accessibility measures should typically (ideally) deal with the full set, to properly reflect accessibility. Therefore, we limit the discussion to models that include enumeration procedures in their model structure.

Activity pattern generation has been modelled as the number of activity episodes (Scott and Kanaroglou, 2002), and as work, non-work or home patterns, fully or partially joint for different interdependent social groups (Bradley and Vovsha, 2005). Wen and Koppelman (2000) developed a model with activity patterns and its permutations as possible outcomes of maintenance task allocation, car allocation for workers and non-workers. As these models did not establish a direct relationship to the individual's space-time prism, it is unclear which of the patterns are feasible. An earlier study of activity patterns, PESASP by Lenntorp (1976), generated all activity patterns and its permutations at the individual level within the constraints of the space-time prism. Thereafter, studies of activity patterns expanded from the individual level to the household level. Recker et al. (1986) developed a household interaction and activity generation model, STARCHILD, which includes unplanned activities, activity patterns and permutations, choice set reduction and final pattern choice. In this study, activity duration and locations are predetermined. Recker (1995) further pursued the household activity pattern problem and proposed a general solution that identifies the optimal schedule subject to constraints including time window, travel cost budget and travel time budget, and minimises household travel disutility. However, it assumes activity durations at the outset and thus does not allow for behavioural adaptation from the individual to adjust activity durations.

Another aspect of activity patterns in which household interactions can manifest is in the time allocation of activities. Household time allocation has been explored by several authors. Golob and McNally (1997) used structural equations to model the time allocation between different activity types for each spouse, and the time allocation interaction of these activity types between the couple. Borgers et al. (2002) modelled the time allocation between spouses by first deriving the time spent on joint activities. The time left for individual pursuit is then allocated to different activity types. Zhang et al. (2005) presented a range of household utility functions for time allocation and demonstrated the use of multi-linear utility functions. Zhang and Fujiwara (2006) extended the work on household utility functions by using a more general form, the iso-elastic class of social welfare. An advantage of using household utility functions is that it incorporates the individual's and household's socio-demographic profile in its formulation and provides a measure of welfare which can, in line with economic theory, be used as a measure of accessibility. This would put the household utility and thus the household accessibility measurement into their specific context, as emphasised by Kwan (1999a).

Given the above range of behavioural options on the household level, decisions need to be made regarding which adaptive strategies are included in the MAMPAM, and which ones are assumed to be exogenous. This decision is necessary since enumerating all theoretically feasible activity patterns on the household level would computationally not be feasible. In particular the following decisions were made. First, the MAMPAM calculates the accessibility level for two working spouses. Effectively, this divides the working day into five distinct periods:

1. a period at home before going to work
2. a time window between leaving home and being at work
3. the time spent at the work place
4. a time window between leaving work and arriving home
5. the time after arriving home from work.

It is assumed that periods 1, 3 and 5 are defined by given start and end times, so that the two time windows 2 and 4 define the available time slots for engaging in out-of-home discretionary and maintenance activities. To define the time remaining for activity participation, we assume that travel times between locations are known and constant, and that the travel mode is predetermined. In the numerical example, we have assumed the travel mode to be a car. Within this structure, spouses can allocate maintenance activities to one or the other spouse (see also the section 'Locations'), decide about the timing and sequence of maintenance and discretionary activities and decide about the duration of these activities. It is assumed in this stage of development that spouses engage in either one or two maintenance and or discretionary activities.

For task allocation, MAMPAM will incorporate the various maintenance activity allocation options within the household. Next, the activity pattern generation for individuals by Lenntorp (1976) will be applied to household members, and the activity durations will be derived for each pattern, using household time allocation procedures.

Locations

As noted before, MAMPAM generates the set of feasible activity patterns, given a set of locations for the maintenance and discretionary activities, and comes up with an aggregated measure of overall utility. By repeating this for many different sets of locations, a good indication of the accessibility is obtained. Ideally, this procedure would be repeated for all combinations of locations. However, given that we include two activities for each spouse, this would lead to n^4 sets of locations. For large n, this would lead to unacceptable long computing times. Therefore, a sampling-based method was chosen. In particular, we randomly sample locations for the two activities of each spouse and repeat this for a large number of times, such that an adequate representation of the spatial variation is obtained.

Household Task Allocation

Here, flexibility in household task allocation relates to possibilities to reallocate a maintenance activity to another household member, or to share the load of a maintenance activity with another household member. Only maintenance activities are transferable, as mandatory activities such as work are tied to specific individuals and their capabilities, and discretionary activities are meant for the specific individual's enjoyment, which is unlikely to be a vicarious experience if transferred to another member.

From observed activities of household members, it is possible to extract maintenance activities and generate different task allocation patterns that account for flexibility. Figure 1 shows an example of the different task allocations possible of a couple that each performs one maintenance activity and one discretionary activity, on top of their work (mandatory) activity. In this example, the combinations of task allocation include the following:

- one person doing the maintenance activities or
- both persons doing both maintenance activities.

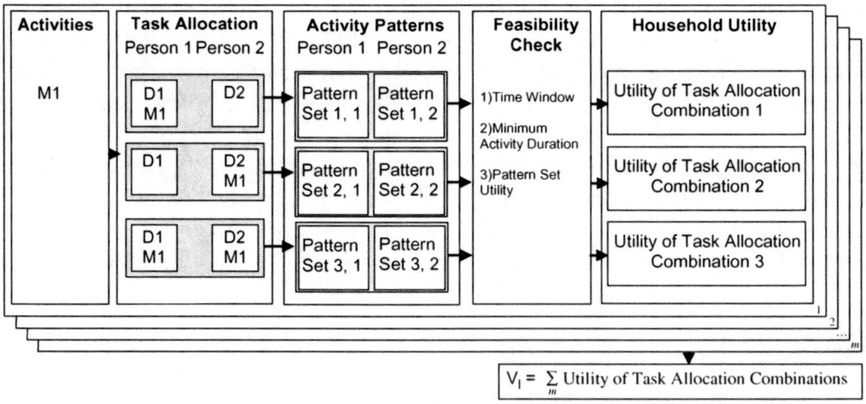

Figure 1
An Example of Flexible Task Allocation and Household Accessibility

In this way three allocation variants are defined, which are all further specified in terms of activity patterns and time allocation. Random sample locations for the two activities of each spouse were repeatedly generated for *m* number of times (see Figure 1).

Activity and Trip Patterns

For each household task allocation combination, activity patterns at the individual level can be generated. The household maintenance tasks will be combined with the individual's maintenance and discretionary activities to create activity patterns. Such an enumeration is based on decisions regarding the sequence to perform activities, the time window to perform activities and whether the activities are to be performed as single purpose trips or as part of trip chains. Figure 2 shows an example of activity patterns extending from the household described in the section 'Household Task Allocation' and Figure 1.

Accounting for every activity pattern here will ensure that MAMPAM captures the flexibility of an individual to perform activities. The reasoning behind the activity pattern generation is similar to the household task allocation. The more ways the individual can accomplish the intended activities, the better the ability of the individual to carry out his or her personal and household agenda, the better the accessibility of the household.

Feasible Activity Patterns

The activity patterns described in the above section undergo two checks. The first check is to ensure that the pattern can adhere to the time window. The second check filters out patterns in which the activity duration does not fulfil the minimum duration criterion. For instance, if the pattern adheres to the time window but only has 1 minute of activity duration, the individual is unlikely to consider this pattern. Thus, the minimum activity duration criterion is to allow only patterns with reasonable levels of activity duration to contribute to the individual's utility. The sections below will describe in detail how feasible activity patterns are obtained.

Time Windows

As departure and arrival times are not completely fixed, the observed time windows are only an indication of the actual time window. One method to derive the time windows is to use stochastic frontier modelling to obtain the vertices of the space-time prism (Pendyala et al., 2002; Nehra et al., 2004; Yamamoto et al., 2004; Kitamura et al., 2006). Another method is to derive the time allocation for different categories of activities, differentiating for the time episode before work and after work. By using

Pattern Set (1,1) (2,2) (3,1) (3,2)

$b_1 - D - b_1 - M - b_1 - b_2 - b_1$
$b_1 - M - b_1 - D - b_1 - b_2 - b_1$
$b_1 - D - b_1 - b_2 - M - b_1$
$b_1 - D - b_1 - b_2 - b_1 - M - b_1$
$b_1 - M - b_1 - b_2 - D - b_1$
$b_1 - M - b_1 - b_2 - b_1 - D - b_1$
$b_1 - D - b_2 - M - b_1$
$b_1 - D - b_2 - b_1 - M - b_1$
$b_1 - M - b_2 - D - b_1$
$b_1 - M - b_2 - b_1 - D - b_1$
$b_1 - b_2 - b_1 - D - b_1 - M - b_1$
$b_1 - b_2 - b_1 - M - b_1 - D - b_1$
$b_1 - D - M - b_1 - b_2 - b_1$
$b_1 - M - D - b_1 - b_2 - b_1$
$b_1 - D - M - b_2 - b_1$
$b_1 - M - D - b_2 - b_1$
$b_1 - b_2 - D - M - b_1$
$b_1 - b_2 - M - D - b_1$
$b_1 - b_2 - b_1 - D - M - b_1$
$b_1 - b_2 - b_1 - M - D - b_1$

Pattern Set (1,2) (2,1)

$b_1 - D - b_1 - b_2 - b_1$
$b_1 - D - b_2 - b_1$
$b_1 - b_2 - D - b_1$
$b_1 - b_2 - b_1 - D - b_1$

Key:
b_1 home
b_2 work
D discretionary activity
M maintenance activity

Figure 2
An Example of Activity Patterns in the Pattern Set from Figure 1

separate models for workers and non-workers, the time windows will better reflect the different constraints facing these groups. However, as the derivation of time windows is beyond the scope of this study, they are exogenously determined by the authors. Using a scenario-based approach the effect of changes in the time window will be evaluated.

Travel Time Ratio and Travel Time Price

Using the time windows, and spatial and temporal characteristics of the base activities, locations of activity participation are identified using the travel time ratio (TTR) (Dijst and Vidakovic, 2000) and travel time price (Chen and Mokhtarian, 2006). The TTR identifies a locus of points that represents the trade-off between travel time and activity duration. Travel time price incorporates the effect of socio-demographics on the trade-off between travel time and activity duration. Here, an extension of the travel time price will be used that will also account for the inter-activity trade-off of travel time in multiple-purpose trips (Soo et al., 2008).

One could argue that limiting the choice set of locations is not necessary, since the procedure of calculating the MAMPAM also includes a check on the feasibility of the final activity pattern. However, drawing locations randomly from the set of all locations in a study area would result in numerous infeasible draws, which greatly increases computation times. Since the TTR reflects the outcome of individuals' destination decisions made under the space-time constraints used to check the feasibility of patterns, it constitutes a realistic approach to limiting the number of infeasible patterns at later stages. In this respect, the question can be raised as to what activity duration the TTR is applied to derive maximum travel times for activity locations. We suggest deriving durations from observed activity patterns, using for instance the 75th percentile instead of the mode or mean, so as not to limit the search space too much, and allow relatively remote locations to be included in the choice set.

Random selections of these locations arising from the TTR and travel time price are allocated to the set of activity patterns. At this point, using the locations of the bases and activities and the sequence of activities in the pattern, relevant travel times from origin–destination matrices can be retrieved. By subtracting the travel times from the time window, the total time for activities can be obtained.

An added advantage of using of locations from the random draws is that it can be related to the spatial adaptation strategies in Kwan (1999b). These random activity locations can be treated as alternatives to the original choice, where they would reflect the extent to which spatial adaptation strategies can be engaged by the individual and the household, given their home and work locations.

Minimum Activity Duration

A minimum level of activity duration can be imposed here to ensure that there is a reasonable amount of time left for activity participation. Kim and Kwan (2003) noted that it is important to impose lower and upper limits for activity and travel duration respectively, to obtain a realistic locus of points for space-time accessibility calculation. Following Kim and Kwan (2003), the minimum activity duration will be assumed to be 10 minutes.

Utility of Activity Pattern of the Individual

If only one activity is performed in a time slot, its duration will be determined by the length of the time slot minus the required travel time. If multiple activities are performed in a time slot, a decision is needed on how to allocate the available time between the activities. It is assumed that this is done such as to maximise utility as follows. Each activity j in a feasible activity pattern will contribute a utility V_{ij} to person i, which would take the form of

$$V_{ij} = \rho_{ij} \ln t_{ij} \tag{5}$$

where ρ_{ij} indicates the factors influencing the utility of activity j of household member i; and t_{ij} is the time allocated to activity j by household member i.

The coefficient ρ_{ij} includes the individual's socio-demographic characteristics that will put the utility measurement and consequently the accessibility measurement into the context of the individual's and household's background.

Following Zhang and Fujiwara (2006), the utility of an activity pattern p, V_{ip}, is expressed in terms of the utilities of the activities in the pattern

$$V_{ip} = \sum_{j} \gamma_{ij} V_{ij} + \sum_{j} \sum_{j'>j} \delta_{ij} \gamma_{ij} \gamma_{ij'} V_{ij} V_{ij'} \tag{6}$$

where δ_{ij} is the inter-activity dependency parameter for member i; and γ_{ij} is household member i's weight parameter for activity j.

Household Utility

The household utilities from each task allocation combination would require the utilities of feasible patterns for that combination of each household member. Note that for each task allocation combination to be feasible, all household members must have feasible activity patterns stemming from that combination. In the case where one household member has no feasible activity pattern from that combination, that task allocation and its corresponding utilities from other household members will not be counted.

Logically, the household utility is some form of aggregation of the individual utilities, but the way in which the aggregation takes place may reflect household preferences or priorities. The general form of a household utility function (HUF) is

$$\text{HUF} = H(V_{lcp_1}, V_{lcp_2}, \ldots, V_{lcp_n}) \tag{7}$$

Following Atkinson (1970) and Zhang and Fujiwara (2006) and extending their formulation to the context of MAMPAM, the iso-elastic class of social welfare function as the household utility function is expressed as

$$V_{lchh} = \frac{1}{1-\alpha}\sum_i w_i V_{lcp_i}^{1-\alpha}, \quad w_i \geq 0 \quad \text{and} \quad \sum_i w_i = 1 \tag{8}$$

where w_i is household member i's weight parameter and indicates the member's relative influence parameter; and α is a parameter indicating intra-household interaction.

As descibed in Zhang and Fujiwara (2006), the outcomes of α from the model will indicate the type of household interaction, which is divided into four types. First, if α is larger than 1, the increase in household utility is more dependent on the member with the smallest individual utility. Another type of interaction is present when α tends to 1. In this case the household members decide on the personal optimal solution before making adjustments at the household level. The third type of interaction is identified when α is equal to zero. This implies that household members enact an alternative with the utilities of the other household members in mind. The fourth type of interaction revealed when α is negative. This would describe a household in which members with relatively higher individual utilities having stronger influence on the household utility.

Numerical Example

To illustrate the ability of MAMPAM to reflect household interactions, and temporal and spatial changes, an activity travel diary of a household is used. This household comprises of two working adults, each engaging in one discretionary activity (shopping), and both having to juggle or share one maintenance activity (banking) between them. The task allocation options and the following steps in household accessibility calculation are as previously shown in Figure 1. The different activity pattern permutations for one and two activities in Figure 2 are used here. The base scenario for this household assumes that Person 1 in the household has two time windows, once between 7 a.m. and 9 a.m. and the second between 5 p.m. and 7 p.m. The time windows for Person 2 are between 7 a.m. and 10 a.m., and between 5 p.m. and 7 p.m. The weights w_i are assigned the value 0.5 for both persons, and the household interaction parameter α is set at 0.5. Household accessibility is calculated for each possible household location in the spatial context of the province of Utrecht in the Netherlands, as highlighted in Figure 3. The Utrecht province is divided into postal code zones, for which the number of employees for the retail and banking sectors are known for each zone. This household is allocated work locations for each person, at zones 2 and 200. Although there are slight variations when using different sampling sizes for the location sets, Figure 4 shows a consistent trend in the basic scenario of

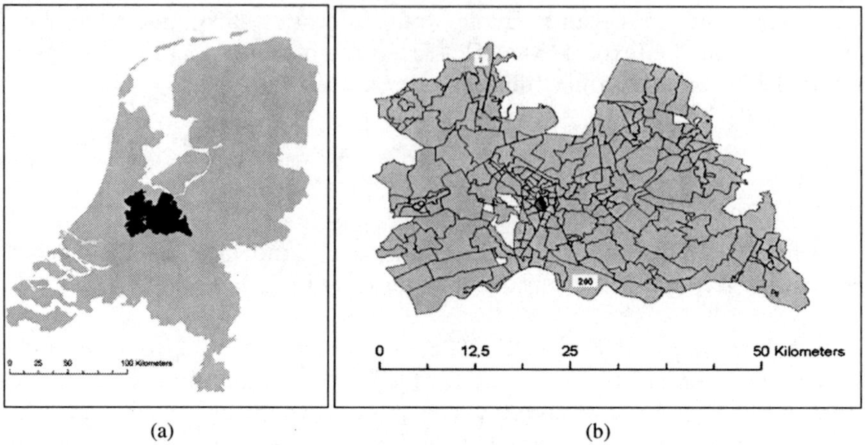

Figure 3

(a) Utrecht Province in Netherlands and (b) Enlargement of the Utrecht Province Divided into Postal Code Zones with Zones 2, 45 (Dark Gray), 46 (Black) and 200 Highlighted

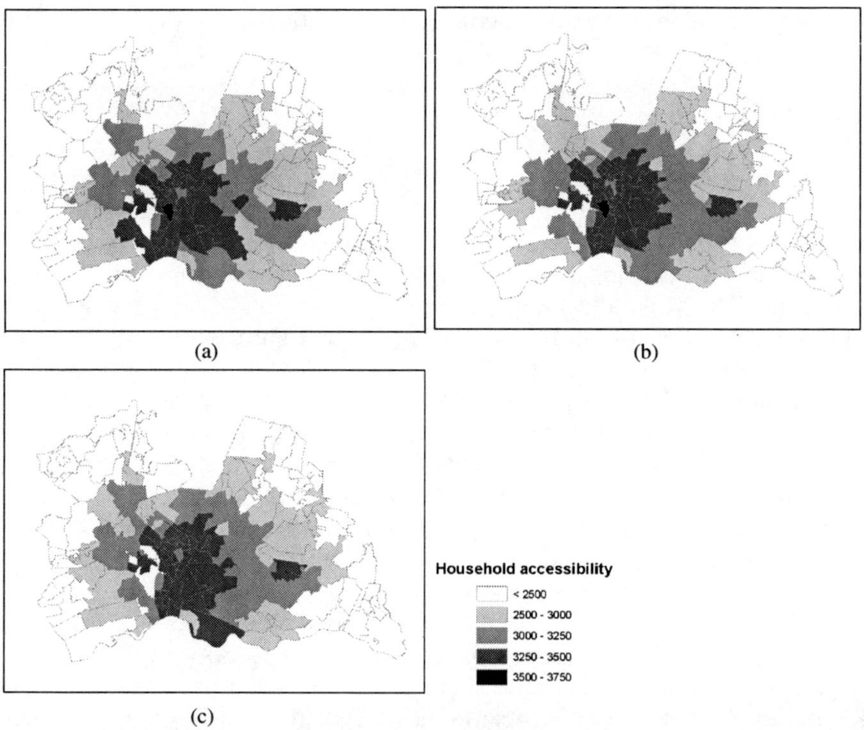

Figure 4

Base Scenario with Different Location Set Sampling Sizes: (a) 100, (b) 250, and (c) 1,000

higher accessibility for residential locations in the central region of Utrecht than the outskirts due to the concentration of shops and services. The sampling size is set at 100 for the rest of the analysis.

To test the temporal sensitivity of MAMPAM, changes were made to the time windows of Person 1 and Person 2. First, time windows for both persons were extended by 30 minutes from 5 p.m. to 7.30 p.m. A comparison of Figure 5a and b shows that this increase in household accessibility across the zones is reflected by MAMPAM. Next, the time window was only extended for Person 1 by 30 minutes from 5 p.m. to 7.30 p.m. Figure 5c reveals that household accessibility also increases across the zones when compared to the base scenario, but the increase is not the same or as much when compared to extended time windows of 30 minutes for both persons. In the third case, the time windows for both persons were extended by 60 minutes from 5 p.m. to 8 p.m. Figure 5d shows that the 60 minute extension in the time window translates to a higher

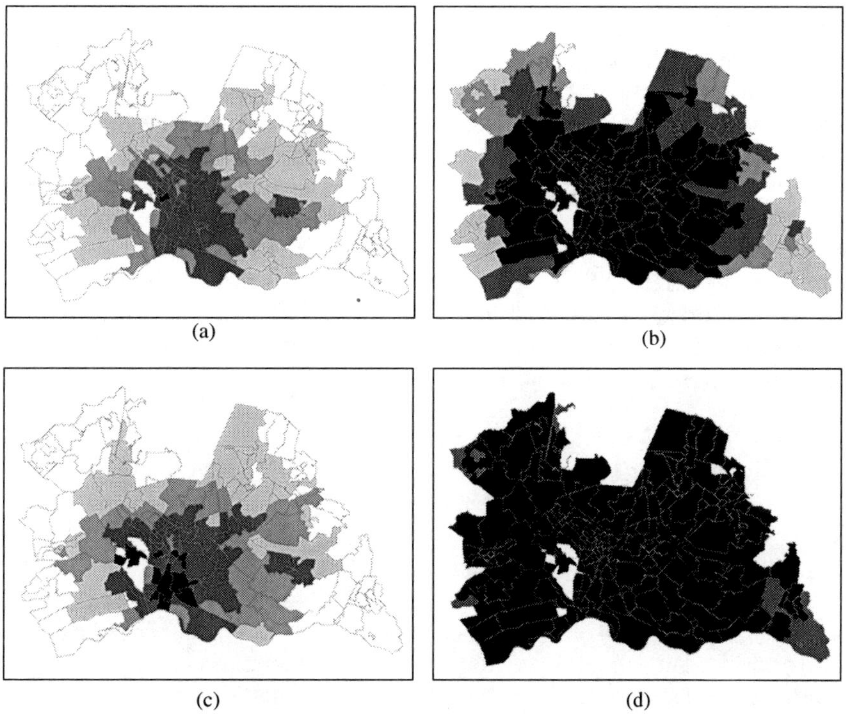

Figure 5

Household Accessibility under Different Time Windows: (a) Base Scenario, (b) Time Window Extension of 30 Minutes for Both Persons, (c) Time Window Extension of 30 Minutes for One Person and (d) Time Window Extension of 60 Minutes for Both Persons

household accessibility across the study area as compared to a 30 minute extension in the time window or the base scenario. However, the first extension of 30 minutes results in a greater number of zones increasing in household accessibility than the next 30 minutes.

MAMPAM is also able to differentiate between households having the same spatial and temporal settings but different household interactions. By altering the household interaction parameter α, diverse household accessibility outcomes are generated. Figure 6a–c illustrates the different household accessibility when α is 0.5 (base scenario), α is 0 and α is -0.5 respectively. This implies that in a study with large numbers of households a classification of households would be required so that household interaction parameters can be derived for each category. Meaningful analyses of accessibility are obtained through a comparison of scenarios of the same household interaction type, followed by a comparison of accessibility gains or losses across household interaction types for that scenario.

Apart from testing MAMPAM's sensitivity to temporal variation and household interactions, three spatial scenarios regarding the quantity and quality of services and shops and changes to the work locations of the couple were applied and contrasted to the base scenario (Figure 7a). First, MAMPAM was adjusted to account for the quality of services and shops by increasing the ρ_{ij} term for zones that have more people employed in retail and services. The resulting accessibility in Figure 7b reveals a more differentiated accessibility landscape than in Figure 7a where the quality of services and shops were not accounted for. The second scenario involves a change in the work locations of both persons from zones 2 and 200 to zones 45 and 46, which are located in the central city of Utrecht. Figure 7c shows that more zones around zone 45 and 46 allow for higher household accessibility than before in Figure 7a. Thus, with a set of known work locations for a particular household, it is possible to identify home locations that give rise to better accessibility outcomes.

Discussion and Conclusions

Criteria for Accessibility Measurement

This section will discuss the four main criteria of accessibility measurement raised by Geurs and van Wee (2004) with respect to MAMPAM. The first criterion is its theoretical basis. The second is the ease to understand and to impart that understanding, while the third is the difficulty to acquire the data to evaluate accessibility. The final criterion is its usefulness in social and economic assessments.

The theoretical cornerstones of accessibility measurement are its ability to reflect the difficulty to travel from one point to another; mirror the modification to the quantity, value and geographical spread of possibilities; echo the timing limitations of these

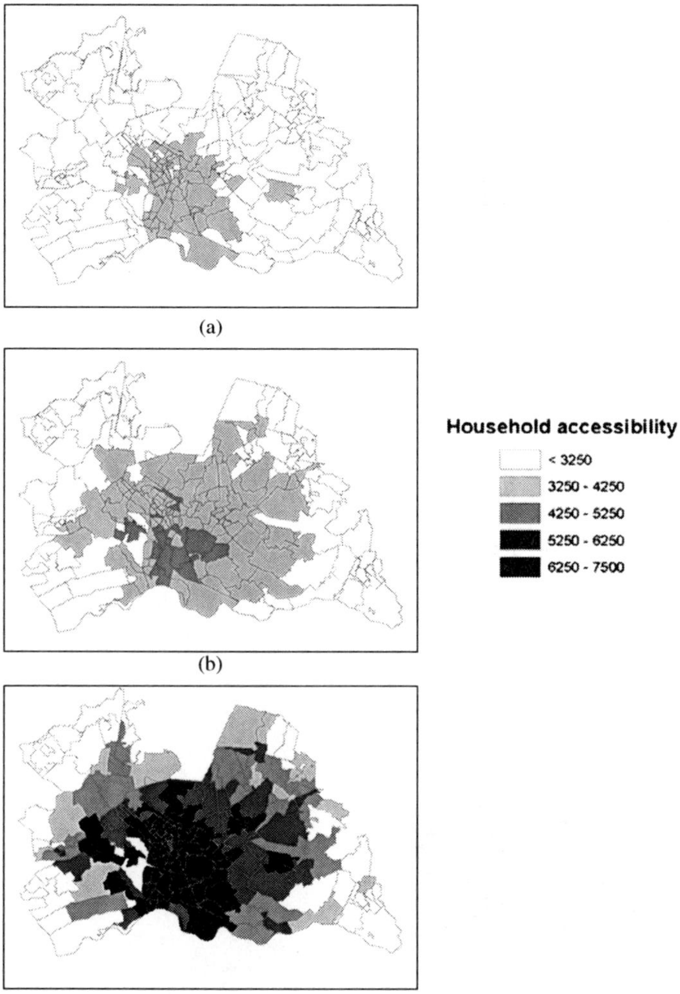

(c)

Figure 6
Household Accessibility under Different Interaction Parameters. Base Scenario (a) $\alpha = 0.5$, (b) $\alpha = 0$ and (c) $\alpha = -0.5$

opportunities and to reflect the individual's background (Geurs and van Wee, 2004). These issues have been embodied in MAMPAM's formulation, where the ρ_{ij} term not only accounts for the individual's socio-economic background, but for travel impedance and activity characteristics too. In addition, the quantity and spatial distribution of opportunities will be reflected in the number of activity locations in the feasible activity patterns through the use of TTR and travel time price. As one of the

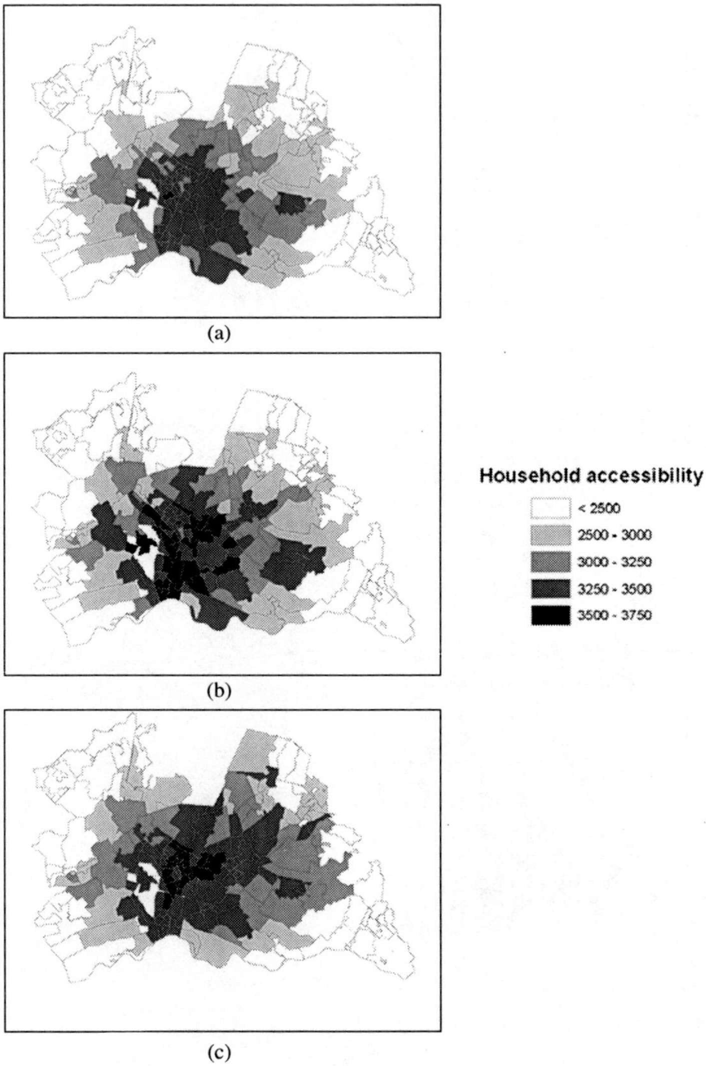

Figure 7

Household Accessibility under Different Spatial Settings: (a) Base Scenario, (b) Accounting for Varying Shopping and Service Quality and (c) Changing the Work Locations of Both Persons to Utrecht City Centre

feasibility checks, limitations on the time at which certain shops and services operate are imposed on the activity patterns. The numerical example gives further proof of the theoretical basis of MAMPAM. The temporal, household and spatial sensitivity are displayed in Figures 4–6 respectively.

Another approach to evaluate theoretical basis can be found in Weibull's (1976) axiomatic framework for accessibility measures. Using the axioms, Miller (1999) demonstrated how a space-time accessibility measure could be confirmed as a standard attraction-accessibility measure. In the same way, MAMPAM is shown to be a standard attraction-accessibility measure in the Appendix.

In terms of the second criteria of the ease to understand and to convey that understanding, the formulation of MAMPAM makes that straightforward. From the α parameter, the household interaction can be deduced. From the coefficients in the ρ_{ij} term, the relative impact that socio-economic factors, travel impedance and activity characteristics have on household accessibility can be seen. Furthermore, by visualising the accessibility outcomes for each zone as shown in Figures 4–6, the accessibility landscape for a particular household is apparent.

The third criterion is the data requirements for the accessibility measurement. In this respect, MAMPAM enjoys the advantage of using hypothetical travel diaries and spatial configuration. This also means that MAMPAM can be used for scenario analysis, which extends MAMPAM's advantage to the next criterion of usefulness in social and economic assessments.

Limitations of MAMPAM

Since this study is a first attempt to develop a MAMPAM, there are aspects that can be improved upon. First, the time frame for investigating household accessibility should be extended to a longer period covering other essential household activities. This would involve determining all the time windows within that period for the household members, possibly generating a set of weekly activity patterns that contains all relevant activities and their permutations, and testing to see which activity patterns are feasible within the time windows. In addition, MAMPAM can be refined to include submodels that replace the exogenous inputs of work locations, number and type of activities, time windows and mode choice.

Conclusions

This paper has contributed to the existing pool of accessibility measures by developing a measure that accounts for the effects of multiple activities and multiple persons.

MAMPAM is unique as it borrows the advances in household time allocation models and applies in a space-time prism framework. Despite MAMPAM's limitations, it can potentially be used to investigate the change in accessibility for different policy interventions. For example, the accessibility change across household types residing in the same spatial configuration and the accessibility change across spatial configurations for the same household type can be explored. Another possible application of MAMPAM would be to test the influence of household accessibility on residential locations for different household types.

Appendix

In this appendix, the Weibull conditions for a standard attraction-accessibility model will be applied to the household accessibility formulation proposed in this article. In particular, the equivalents of equations (19)–(22) of Miller's (1999) paper will be calculated to see if the derivatives have the correct sign.

As previously seen in equation (8), the household utility function is

$$V_{lchh} = \frac{1}{1-\alpha}\sum_i w_i V_{lcp_i}^{1-\alpha}$$

$$= \frac{1}{1-\alpha}\sum_i w_i \left[\sum_l \sum_c \sum_p \left(\sum_j \gamma_{ij} u_{ij} + \sum_j \sum_{j'>j} \delta_{ij}\gamma_{ij}\gamma_{ij'} u_{ij} u_{ij'}\right)\right]^{1-\alpha}$$

where $u_{ij} = \rho_{ij}\ln(t_{ij}+1)$; and $t_{ij} + \tau_{ij} = T_{ij}$ implying that τ_{ij} is the decrease in the time available for activity j

$$\sum_j T_{ij} = T_i$$

$$\rho_{ij} = \beta_a x_a + \sum_k \beta_k x_k$$

We assume that $w_i > 0, \gamma_{ij} \geq 0, \delta_{ij} \geq 0, \rho_{ij} \geq 0, \beta_a > 0$, where w_i is household member i's weight parameter in relation to other household members; α the intra-household interaction parameter; γ_{ij} the household member i's weight parameter for activity j; δ_{ij} the inter-activity dependency parameter for member i; u_{ij} the utility due to participating in activity j; t_{ij} the duration of activity j for person i; τ_{ij} the travel duration associated with activity j for person i; T_i the total time available for activities; T_{ij} the sum of duration of activity j and its corresponding travel duration; ρ_{ij} the activity, spatio-temporal, individual and household attributes; x_a the variable representing attractiveness of activity location; β_a the coefficient of the variable representing attractiveness of activity location; x_k the activity, spatio-temporal, individual and household factors in the ρ_{ij} term; and β_k the coefficients for the x_k terms.

Substitute attraction at zero distance equals the original attraction

For zero distance, $\tau_{ij} = 0$

Using $u_{ij} = \rho_{ij}\ln(T_{ij} - \tau_{ij} + 1)$ we get:

$$u_{ij} = \rho_{ij}\ln(T_{ij}+1)$$

Inserting this formulation into the equation of V_{clhh}, the maximum utility is obtained without any loss of utility due to distance decay. It should be noted here that, different from Miller (1999, equation 19), MAMPAM does not treat attractiveness and distance decay in a separate manner. Instead, distance decay is accounted for by a shorter activity duration resulting in a lower utility. In this structure, it is by definition the case that for a zero distance, the maximum utility (or attractiveness) is achieved, which is equivalent to requirement 1.

Accessibility is non-increasing with respect to travel time

$$\frac{\partial V_{lchh}}{\partial \tau_{ij}} = \sum_i w_i \left[\sum_l \sum_c \sum_p \left(\sum_j \gamma_{ij} u_{ij} + \sum_j \sum_{j'>j} \delta_{ij} \gamma_{ij} \gamma_{ij'} u_{ij} u_{ij'} \right) \right]^{-\alpha}$$
$$\times \sum_i w_i \left[\sum_l \sum_c \sum_p \left(\sum_j \gamma_{ij} \frac{\partial u_{ij}}{\partial \tau_{ij}} + \sum_j \sum_{j'>j} \delta_{ij} \gamma_{ij} \gamma_{ij'} u_{ij'} \frac{\partial u_{ij}}{\partial \tau_{ij}} \right) \right]$$

$$\frac{\partial u_{ij}}{\partial \tau_{ij}} = \frac{-\rho_{ij}}{T_{ij} - \tau_{ij} + 1}$$

For any feasible activity pattern, $T_{ij} - \tau_{ij} > 0$

$$\frac{\partial u_{ij}}{\partial \tau_{ij}} = \frac{-\rho_{ij}}{T_{ij} - \tau_{ij} + 1} \leq 0$$
$$\frac{\partial V_{lchh}}{\partial \tau_{ij}} \leq 0$$

If the available time interval for activity *j* decreases, the utility will decrease as well. Thus, accessibility is non-increasing with respect to travel time.

Accessibility is non-decreasing with respect to attractiveness

$$\frac{\partial V_{lchh}}{\partial x_a} = \sum_i w_i \left[\sum_l \sum_c \sum_p \left(\sum_j \gamma_{ij} u_{ij} + \sum_j \sum_{j'>j} \delta_{ij} \gamma_{ij} \gamma_{ij'} u_{ij} u_{ij'} \right) \right]^{-\alpha}$$
$$\times \sum_i w_i \left[\sum_l \sum_c \sum_p \left(\sum_j \gamma_{ij} \frac{\partial u_{ij}}{\partial x_a} + \sum_j \sum_{j'>j} \delta_{ij} \gamma_{ij} \gamma_{ij'} u_{ij'} \frac{\partial u_{ij}}{\partial x_a} \right) \right]$$

$$\frac{\partial u_{ij}}{\partial x_a} = \beta_a \ln(t_{ij} + 1)$$

Since $\beta_a > 0$ and $t_{ij} \geq 0$,

$$\Rightarrow \frac{\partial u_{ij}}{\partial x_a} \geq 0$$
$$\Rightarrow \frac{\partial V_{lchh}}{\partial x_a} \geq 0$$

The household utility and also the accessibility increases with increasing utility gained from an equal amount of time spent in an activity. Thus, accessibility is non-decreasing with respect to attractiveness.

Accessibility is non-decreasing with activity duration

$$\frac{\partial V_{lchh}}{\partial t_{ij}} = \sum_i w_i \left[\sum_l \sum_c \sum_p \left(\sum_j \gamma_{ij} u_{ij} + \sum_j \sum_{j'>j} \delta_{ij} \gamma_{ij} \gamma_{ij'} u_{ij} u_{ij'} \right) \right]^{-\alpha}$$

$$\times \sum_i w_i \left[\sum_l \sum_c \sum_p \left(\sum_j \gamma_{ij} \frac{\partial u_{ij}}{\partial t_{ij}} + \sum_j \sum_{j'>j} \delta_{ij} \gamma_{ij} \gamma_{ij'} u_{ij'} \frac{\partial u_{ij}}{\partial t_{ij}} \right) \right]$$

$$\frac{\partial u_{ij}}{\partial t_{ij}} = \frac{\rho_{ij}}{t_{ij}+1} > 0$$

$$\Rightarrow \frac{\partial V_{lchh}}{\partial t_{ij}} \geq 0$$

With more time spent on an activity, the household utility and the accessibility increases. Thus accessibility is non-decreasing with respect to activity duration.

References

Arentze, T. and H. Timmermans (2002). *Albatross: A learning based transportation oriented simulation system*. Eindhoven, European Institute of Retailing and Services Studies.

Ashiru, O., J. W. Polak and R. B. Noland (2004). The utility of schedules: a theoretical model of departure time choice and activity time allocation with application to individual activity schedules. *Transportation Research Record* 1894, 84–98.

Atkinson, A. B. (1970). On the measurement of inequality. *Journal of Economic Theory* 2, 244–263.

Ben-Akiva, M. and J. L. Bowman (1998). Integration of an activity-based model system and a residential location model. *Urban Studies* 35, 1131–1153.

Borgers, A., F. Hofman and H. Timmermans (2002). Conditional choice modelling of time allocation among spouses in transport settings. *European Journal of Transport and Infrastructure Research* 2, 5–17.

Bradley, M. and P. Vovsha (2005). A model of joint choice of daily activity pattern types of household members. *Transportation* 32, 545–571.

Burns, L. D. (1979). *Transportation, Temporal, and Spatial Components of Accessibility*. Lexington, Massachusetts Heath.

Chen, C. and P. L. Mokhtarian (2006). Tradeoffs between time allocations to maintenance activities/travel and discretionary activities/travel. *Transportation* 33, 223–240.

Dijst, M. and V. Vidakovic (2000). Travel time ratio: the key factor of spatial reach. *Transportation* 27, 179–199.

Dong, X., M. E. Ben-Akiva, J. L. Bowman and J. Walker (2005). Moving from trip-based to activity-based measures of accessibility. *Transportation Research Part A* 40, 163–180.

Ettema, D., T. Schwanen and H. Timmermans (2007). The effect of location, mobility and socio-demographic factors on task and time allocation of households. *Transportation* 34, 59–105.

Ettema, D. and H. Timmermans (2007). Space-time accessibility under conditions of uncertain travel times: theory and numerical simulations. *Geographical Analysis* 39, 217–240.

Geurs, K. T. and R. van Eck (2001). *Accessibility Measures: Review and Applications.* Bilthoven, RIVM.

Geurs, K. T. and B. van Wee (2004). Accessibility evaluation of land use and transport strategies: review and research directions. *Journal of transport geography* 12, 127–140.

Gliebe, J. P. and F. S. Koppelman (2002). A model of joint activity participation between household members. *Transportation* 29, 49–72.

Gliebe, J. P. and F. S. Koppelman (2005). Modeling household activity-travel interactions as parallel constrained choices. *Transportation* 32, 449–471.

Golob, T. F. and M. G. McNally (1997). A model of activity participation and travel interactions between household heads. *Transportation Research Part B* 31, 177–194.

Hägerstrand, T. (1970). What about people in regional science?. *Papers of the Regional Science Association* 24, 7–21.

Kim, H. M. and M. P. Kwan (2003). Space-time accessibility measures: a geocomputational algorithm with a focus on the feasible opportunity set and possible activity duration. *Journal of Geographical Systems* 5, 71–91.

Kitamura, R., T. Yamamoto, Y. O. Susilo and K. W. Axhausen (2006). How routine is a routine? An analysis of the day-to-day variability in prism vertex location. *Transportation Research Part A* 40, 259–279.

Kwan, M. P. (1998). Space-time and integral measures of individual accessibility: a comparative analysis using a point-based framework. *Geographical Analysis* 30, 191–216.

Kwan, M. P. (1999a). Gender and individual access to urban opportunities: a study using space-time measures. *Professional Geographer* 51, 210–227.

Kwan, M. P. (1999b). Gender, the home-work link, and space-time patterns of nonemployment of activities. *Economic Geography* 75, 370–394.

Lenntorp, B. (1976). *Paths in Time-Space Environments: A Time Geographic Study of Movement Possibilities of Individuals.* Lund, Department of Geography, Royal University of Lund.

Miller, H. J. (1991). Modelling accessibility using space-time prism concepts within geographic information systems. *International Journal of Geographical Information Systems* 5, 287–301.

Miller, H. J. (1999). Measuring space-time accessibility benefits within transportation networks: basic theory and computational procedures. *Geographical Analysis* 31, 187–212.

Nehra, R. S., A. Banerjee, R. M. Pendyala and S. L. Dhingra (2004). Analysis of personal time-space prism vertex locations: a developing country context. *Transportation Research Record* 1898, 19–27.

Pendyala, R. M., T. Yamamoto and R. Kitamura (2002). On the formulation of time-space prisms to model constraints on personal activity-travel engagement. *Transportation* 29, 73–94.

Recker, W. W. (1995). The household activity pattern problem: general formulation and solution. *Transportation Research Part B* 29, 61–77.

Recker, W. W., M. G. McNally and G. S. Root (1986). A model of complex travel behavior: part II – an operational model. *Transportation Research Part A* 20, 319–330.

Scott, D. M. and P. S. Kanaroglou (2002). An activity-episode generation model that captures interactions between household heads: development and empirical analysis. *Transportation Research Part B* 36, 875–896.

Soo, J., D. Ettema and H. F. L. Ottens (2008). Analysis of travel time in multiple-purpose trips. *Transportation Research Record* 2082, 56–62.

Srinivasan, K. K. and S. R. Athuru (2005). Analysis of within-household effects and between-household differences in maintenance activity allocation. *Transportation* 32, 495–521.

Srinivasan, S. and C. R. Bhat (2005). Modeling household interactions in daily in-home and out-of-home maintenance activity participation. *Transportation* 32, 523–544.

Weibull, J. W. (1976). An axiomatic approach to the measurement of accessibility. *Regional Science and Urban Economics* 6, 357–379.

Wen, C. and F. S. Koppelman (2000). A conceptual and methodological framework for the generation of activity-travel patterns. *Transportation* 27, 5–23.

Yamamoto, T., R. Kitamura and R. M. Pendyala (2004). Comparative analysis of time-space prism vertices for out-of-home activity engagement on working and non-working days. *Environment and Planning B* 31, 235–250.

Zhang, J. and A. Fujiwara (2006). Representing household time allocation by endogenously incorporating diverse intra-household interactions: a case study in the context of elderly couples. *Transportation Research Part B* 40, 54–74.

Zhang, J., H. J. P. Timmermans and A. Borgers (2005). A model of household task allocation and time use. *Transportation Research B* 39, 81–95.

4.4 Decision Dynamics

The Expanding Sphere of Travel Behaviour Research
Selected Papers from the 11th International Conference on Travel Behaviour Research

35

Schedule-based Dynamic Assignment Models for Air Transport Networks

Umberto Crisalli and Fiorella Sciangula

Abstract

This paper presents a class of dynamic assignment models specified through a schedule-based approach that can be used to compute flows on air transport networks. They can be considered an extension to air transport of the schedule-based approach specified by the author for transit networks (Nuzzolo, A., F. Russo and U. Crisalli (2003). Transit network modelling. The schedule-based dynamic approach. In *Collana Trasporti*. Milano, Franco Angeli). This assignment model has been applied to the Italian national air transport network in order to verify the specification and implementation of the proposed approach.

Introduction

This paper presents a dynamic assignment model specified by the schedule-based approach. It allows us to estimate the number of passengers on each flight of the air transportation network as the result of user choices in a behavioural framework where the difference between the user arrival/departure time and that of flights is explicitly taken into account.

Earlier papers on air traffic assignment can be really referred to 1980s: until this period the literature is rather scarcely and namely refers to operational research tools (constrained optimization) applied to scheduling problems. The increase of air transportation demand and the greater and greater competition among airlines (mainly induced by the deregulation), as well as the development of aircraft and control system technologies, are some reasons of the new impulse to air transportation research, aiming at improving safety, security and customer satisfaction, as well as minimizing airline operative costs in order to increase competitiveness.

In this period, the assignment problem has not still been approached as demand–supply interaction, but it has been investigated as consequence of the need to have a procedure to estimate traffic flows to be used as input to solve other kind of problems such as localization (Hsu and Wu, 1997), scheduling (Mathaisel, 1997) and seat allocation (Curry, 1990; Zhao and Zheng, 2001; Gosavi et al., 2002). Moreover, the literature can also be investigated in the sphere of low-frequency transit services that can also be used for air transportation models because they take into account some typical features of air transportation system, as the explicit consideration of schedule services, the presence of explicit flight capacity constraints, as well as the presence of a seat-reservation system to access services. Therefore, the state-of-the-art for assignment models to air transportation networks is shortly reported considering two different classes:

- *assignment models*, defined in the traditional framework of transport system engineering, that is, specified through a (behavioural) path choice model and a network loading procedure;
- *assignment methods and procedures*, where the assignment problem is considered in a simplified way, as a sub-model to support other problems solving.

Among traditional assignment models, Hsiao and Hansen (2005) proposed an equilibrium model with rigid demand (i.e. demand is fixed and is independent from transportation costs). This model considers the delay due to airport congestion, and network flows are carried out by considering the users' choices in terms of no-stop flights, or otherwise, and in terms of the choice of airport hub, if a transfer is required to connected the considered O/D pair.

In this particular case, assignment results reflect the interaction between airlines and users: airlines calibrate their services as close as user needs, while users choose the best perceived alternative available on the air market.

The equilibrium represents the state of the system in which airlines (in terms of services) and users (in term of choices) do not perceive additional advantages in considering further alternative choices/strategies.

A class of assignment models that can be adapted for air transportation networks is those specified for low-frequency transit systems by using the schedule-based approach (Nuzzolo et al., 2000). They use path choice models in which each run (vehicle) and each user target time are explicitly considered by using a diachronic network model.

An alternative approach is that proposed by Friedrich and Wekech (2004), who use a branch-and-bound approach to generate paths, and related attributes, using a tree representation of transit services. These models derive from public transport modelling for which congestion usually refers to the phenomenon for which user on-board comfort decreases as the on-board load increases, up to a maximum threshold (vehicle capacity), after which users are not allowed to board and have to wait for the next arriving one.

The use of such models for air transport implies a quite different definition and modelling of congestion, as airplanes have a fixed capacity and the unique variable users perceive is if they are allowed to board a flight or otherwise.

In the literature, congestion has been modelled by using an implicit or an explicit approach. The implicit approach has been derived from road network modelling, for which strictly non-decreasing continuous link-cost functions with respect to link flows are defined for particular links, aiming at discouraging user boarding on overcrowded vehicle (full flights). The explicit approach has been considered congestion by introducing explicit vehicle capacity constrains, for which users board the arriving run according to its residual capacity, and assignment models have to be able to capture changes in user behaviour when oversaturation and fail-to-board events occur.

Among methods and procedures that can be considered as assignment, Hsu and Wu (1997) proposed an optimal airport localization model in order to define an optimal market size for each origin–destination city pair. This market size is function of both the airport influence zone and socio-economic variables, while transportation costs are not explicitly considered.

This model defines the number of optimal markets, as well as the optimal airport location, in order to connect the considered city pairs.

Mathaisel (1997) proposed an assignment method inside a methodology to solve the air transportation scheduling problem. It is based on the definition of a so-called 'desired function', which includes attributes related to minimum and total travel time on the route, some elasticity factors, daily frequency, the desired departure/arrival time, the day choice for travelling, aircraft capacity, the choice of connection with/without intermediate stops, the airline brand (reliability) and the user preference in terms of on-board services (e.g. business or economy class). The demand–supply interaction is carried out as follows: given the flight capacity, the demand is assigned to flights up to capacity. Then, loading procedure allocates market segments according to the desirable function using a deterministic approach (e.g. loading the best desirable alternative only). If demand exceeds aircraft capacity, the demand in excess will be assigned to the next flight.

Mashford and Marksjö (2004) extended the Mathaisel procedure overcoming the deterministic approach approximation by using a stochastic approach in which they optimize the connection between airports minimizing aircraft costs.

Finally, seat-reservation problem can be also considered as a method for the indirect solution of the assignment problem. In the literature, this problem is known as 'seat inventory control' or 'seat allocation' and can be studied by operational research (maximization of expected revenue), games theory (solution of an oligopolistic game into two steps according to Nash theory, in which players are demand and supply), queue theory, Markov processes as well as economics (revenue management problems).

Seat-reservation assignment models can be divided into *leg-based* models, in which different local seat allocation are optimized for a travel that involves a single leg (*one leg*), and *network-based* models, in which global seat allocation is optimized for a travel that involves more than one leg, and in which there are one or more intermediate stops (*multileg*).

In the following, the section 'A Schedule-based Assignment Model' presents a schedule-based assignment model that has been applied to the Italian national air transport network, as shortly reported in the section 'An Application Example: The Italian Air Transport Network'.

A Schedule-based Assignment Model

This section presents an assignment model specified in the framework of the schedule-based approach in order to calculate the on-board loads on each flight of a given air transport network. The used approach refers to the so-called schedule-based approach that was originally developed for transit assignment problems by Tong and Richardson (1984); it has been widely applied in recent years to low-frequency services (e.g. Nuzzolo et al., 2000) and can be also used to simulate air transport networks. The schedule-based approach (Nuzzolo et al., 2003) requires an explicit treatment for:

- temporal segmentation of the origin/destination matrix (as user's departure or arrival target time distribution has to be taken into account);
- supply modelling (as single flights with explicit departure/arrival times at airports have to be considered);
- path choice and assignment models (as they have to consider explicitly within-day time dependence).

The following sub-sections will deal with these three main aspects and their specification for the simulation of air transport networks.

Time-varying Demand

In order to consider the variation of the demand over time, the whole demand has to be split in time slices, according to the user target times defined as follows.

In the sphere of the air transport, as well as for low-frequency services, users have a desired departure time (DDT) from the origin or a desired arrival time (DAT) at destination. Usually DAT is relative to home-living trips, for which users need to arrive in time to start their activities, while DDT concerns returning trips related to the end of user activities and to their desire to come back home.

The segmentation of the reference period usually entails a sub-division into n time slices, whose width $\delta\tau$ depends on the aim of the simulation (e.g. 60 minutes in the case of air transport). The generic time slice i covers time interval $[\tau_i - \delta\tau/2, \tau_i + \delta\tau/2]$ and a DAT and DDT, represented by τ_{Di} and τ_{Ai}, are associated with each interval i. Of course, time intervals are such that

$$\left\| \tau_{Di} - \frac{\delta\tau}{2}, \tau_{Di} + \frac{\delta\tau}{2} \right\| = \left\| \tau_{Di-1} - \frac{\delta\tau}{2}, \tau_{Di-1} + \frac{\delta\tau}{2} \right\|, \quad \forall i = 2, \ldots, n \tag{1a}$$

$$\left\| \tau_{Ai} - \frac{\delta\tau}{2}, \tau_{Ai} + \frac{\delta\tau}{2} \right\| = \left\| \tau_{Ai-1} - \frac{\delta\tau}{2}, \tau_{Ai-1} + \frac{\delta\tau}{2} \right\|, \quad \forall i = 2, \ldots, n \tag{1b}$$

User type can be classified on the basis of their different perception of level of service attributes (e.g. prices). For example, they can be classified according to different classes of gross income and whether their costs are reimbursed or otherwise (e.g. for business or no-business). Demand segments are defined by trip purpose and user type; the demand $d^{\mathrm{od},m}$, relative to the O/D pair od and segment m, will be further divided into DAT and DDT.

So, the whole demand on the O/D pair od for the demand segment m is given by

$$d^{\mathrm{od},m} = \sum_{i=1}^{n} d_{\tau_{Di}}^{\mathrm{od},m} + \sum_{i=1}^{n} d_{\tau_{Ai}}^{\mathrm{od},m} \tag{2}$$

where $d_{\tau_{Di}}^{\mathrm{od},m}$ and $d_{\tau_{Ai}}^{\mathrm{od},m}$ are the parts of $d^{\mathrm{od},m}$ characterized by desired origin departure time (DDT) τ_{Di} and desired destination arrival time (DAT) τ_{Ai}, respectively.

This demand simply represents the average number of users who want to travel during the considered reference period. In the case of air transport, it is the result of a travelling decision process which involves user choices many days in the past

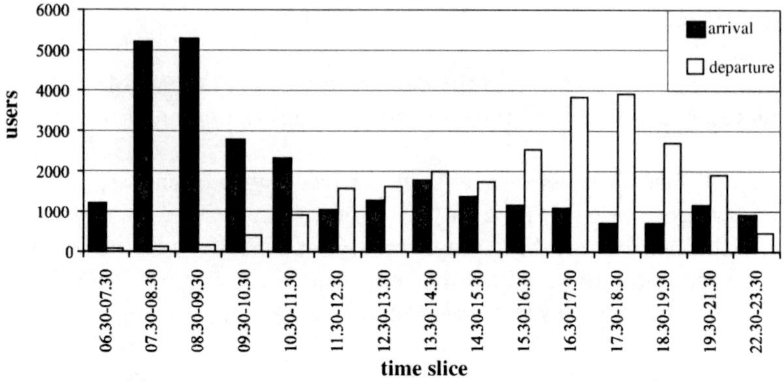

Figure 1
Example of Demand Segmentation in DAT and DDT

according to ticket costs and available seats for a given flight that can be used to reach the destination in the considered reference period. The estimation of the demand is not the aim of this paper and it is considered as an input data of this assignment problem.

In the following, the generic desired origin departure time (DDT) τ_{Di} and the desired destination arrival time (DAT) τ_{Ai} will be defined as target time and indicated by τ_{TT}, while $d[\tau_{TT}]$ represents the demand vector, whose elements are $d^{od,m}_{\tau_{TT}}$ for all O/D pairs, target times τ_{TT} and market segments m.

A typical demand segmentation in DAT and DDT for business trips is reported in Figure 1, where DAT are concentrated in the morning hours, while DDT are mainly located in the afternoon.

Run-based Supply Model

In order to take into account the service time dependence, the supply model has to be specified using the so-called *run-based* approach and a particular graph, known as *diachronic* graph, can be used (Nuzzolo and Russo, 1993). The run-based graph is similar to that traditionally set up to represent transit lines, for which the difference consists of representing each run with explicit consideration of arrival/departure time at stop, according to the timetable. The following sub-sections will describe the graph characteristics (section 'The Diachronic Graph') and the adopted cost functions (section 'Link-cost Function') for the used diachronic supply model.

The Diachronic Graph

The diachronic graph Ω consists of three different sub-graphs (see Figure 2) in which each node has an explicit time coordinate:

- a *service* sub-graph Ω_s, in which each run (flight) is defined both in space, through its stops, and in time, according to its arrival/departure times at stops (airports);
- a *demand* sub-graph Ω_d, in which each node (temporal centroid) represents a DDT or DAT, in order to simulate the space–time characteristics of the trip;
- an *access/egress* sub-graph Ω_{ae}, which allows the demand connection of the demand sub-graph (zones) with access/egress stops (airports).

The *service* sub-graph Ω_s consists, in turn, of different sub-graphs $\Omega_{s,r}$ (one for each run of the transit services). Referring to the generic flight r, the relative sub-graph $\Omega_{s,r}$of nodes representing the arrival ($b^{a}_{rs}$and departure (b^{p}_{rs}) times at airports, and links representing travel from one airport to another (run section) or the dwelling of the flight at a given airport. Other nodes represent the time in which users board or alight from each flight (run) at the stop. These nodes are connected to the nodes representing flight arrival and departure through boarding and alighting links. Finally, the whole sub-graph Ω_s is built by connecting all the sub-graphs $\Omega_{s,r}$ through links representing the users' transfer from one flight to another at the same stop (*stop axis*), which represents an airport.

The *demand* sub-graph Ω_d representing temporal demand segmentation is made up, in turn, by the same number of sub-graphs $\Omega_{d,c}$ as zones. For each spatial centroid c representing a given traffic zone, the sub-graph $\Omega_{d,c}$ consists of temporal centroids $n_o^{\tau_{TTi}}$, that are nodes located spatially in the position of the spatial centroid n_o and temporally according to the user target times τ_{TTi} (τ_{Di} for DDTs and τ_{Ai} for desired arrival ones), representing the demand defined in the section 'Time-varying Demand'.

The *access/egress* sub-graph Ω_{ae} is made up of links representing access (egress) from (to) the centroids. The representation is made of direct links connecting nodes representing arrival/departure times on the demand sub-graph and nodes representing arrival/departure times of flights at airports on the service sub-graphs, as reported in Figure 2. Access/egress attributes are associated with these links; they can be calculated in a more or less complex way by considering access/egress inclusive variables, which take into account the utility of each access/egress mode, or consider only access/egress times and costs.

Finally, the global diachronic graph Ω is obtained through

$$\Omega = \Omega_s \cup \Omega_d \cup \Omega_{ae}$$

in which links connecting the three sub-graphs are properly adopted.

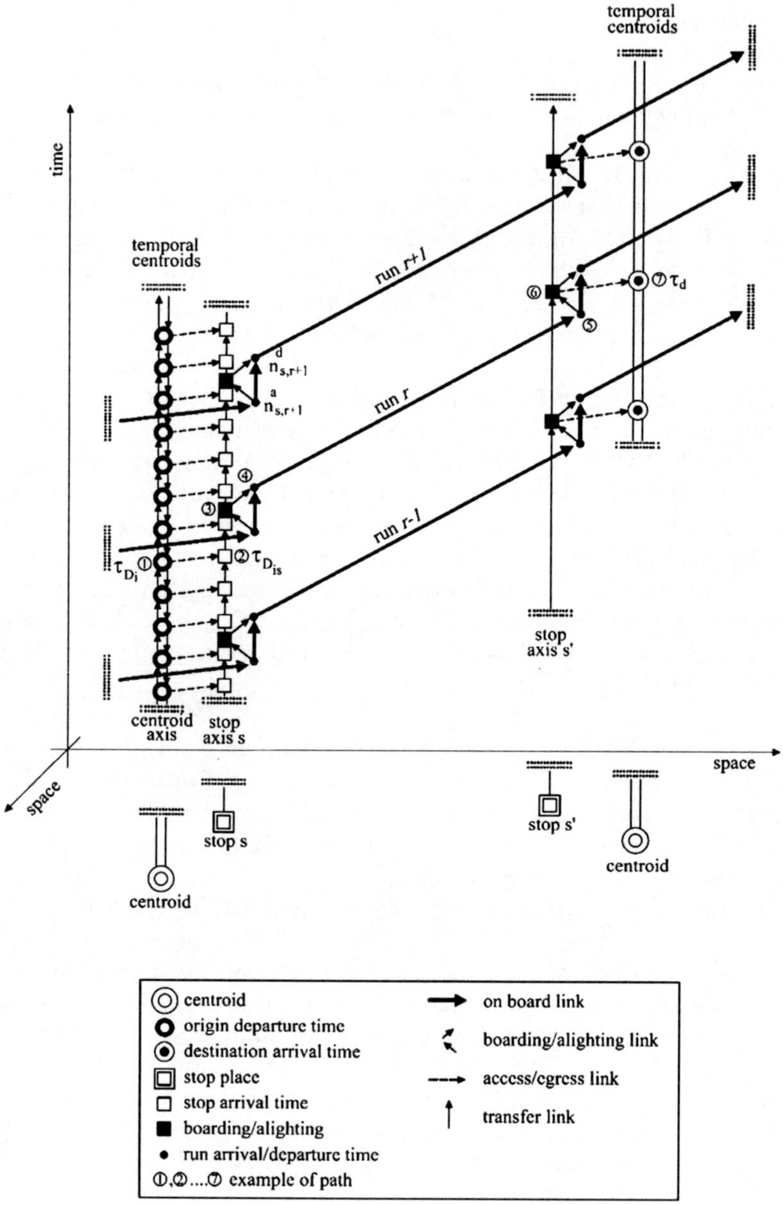

Figure 2
The Diachronic Graph

Link-cost Function

Link costs associated with diachronic graph are calculated on the basis of flow-dependent cost functions, for which the average link cost depends on the number of users on the link and, possibly, on other links of the graph (separable or not-separable cost functions).

Different cost functions for different link types can be considered. As an example, for run and dwell links, we can use separable cost functions as

$$c_i(f_i) = k_1 + k_2 t_i + k_3 \left(\frac{f_i}{\text{cap}_r} \right)^{k_4} \tag{3}$$

where f_i is the load on link i, t_i its own travel time, cap_r the capacity of run r, represented by link i, and $k_1 \geq 0$, $k_2 > 0$, $k_3 > 0$ and $k_4 > 1$ the function parameters.

Value of parameter k_4 is such that link cost c_i goes to infinite when load f_i reaches flight capacity cap_r, leading to not-available alternatives that are sold out.

Performance attributes and generalized transportation cost (disutility) can be extended from links to paths. The path cost $g_k$is generally made up of the link-wise additive cost, g_k^{ADD}, and the non-additive cost, g_k^{NA}:

$$g_k = g_k^{\text{ADD}} + g_k^{\text{NA}} = \sum_a \delta_{ak} c_a + g_k^{\text{NA}} \tag{4}$$

or in matrix terms:

$$\underline{g} = \underline{\Delta}' \underline{c} + \underline{g}^{\text{NA}} \tag{5}$$

where $\underline{g}$ is the path cost vector, $\underline{g}^{\text{NA}}$ the relative non-additive path cost vector, $\underline{c}$ the link-cost vector and $\underline{\Delta}$ the link-path incidence matrix relative to graph Ω, whose element δ_{ak} is 1 if link a belongs to path k and is 0 otherwise. Examples of non-additive cost could be the price structure, that can be non-linear with respect to distance (e.g. based on the O/D pair), or the schedule delays (see the section 'Behavioural Assumptions and Choice Set Generation').

The number of users who follow path k is defined as the path load h_k. A link load f_a can be associated with each link a; it represents the number of travellers who use the link. Note that, using the run-based approach in supply modelling, when we consider users associated with a link, we refer to loads instead of flows as each link is located both in space and in time. Thus, given an absolute value of users associated with each link, it is more consistent to talk of loads instead of flows which traditionally refer to values per time unit. Link loads can be obtained by summing loads on all paths including those links

$$f_a = \sum_k \delta_{ak} h_k \tag{6}$$

or in matrix terms:

$$\underline{f} = \underline{\Delta}\,\underline{h} \tag{7}$$

The diachronic graph is very useful as it allows efficient use of standard network algorithms (as least cost paths) and allows a more straightforward treatment of congestion, if it is considered.

Schedule-based Path Choice Model

Schedule-based path choice models, that are the core of dynamic assignment models, are specified in the framework of the random utility theory (RUM approach) according to air transport characteristics (namely the medium–low service frequency) and user type.

In the schedule-based approach for air transport networks, a path k is defined both in space and in time; it includes the space–time sequence: origin o with origin departure time τ_{Di}, access airport s with relative arrival time τ_{Dis}, flight r (or sequence of flights) and its relative departure time τ_r from access airport, egress airport s' and destination d with relative arrival time at destination τ_d. A path can be defined through a sequence of links of the Ω graph described in the section 'Run-based Supply Model'.

In order to describe the characteristics of the proposed path choice models for air transport networks, the following sub-sections will deepen on the user behaviour assumption, the choice set generation, as well as the specification of the model for the calculation of the choice probability of using each flight of the air transport network for a given O/D pair and user target time.

Behavioural Assumptions and Choice Set Generation

Flight services are usually characterized by *regular* service functioning and users behave considering all information at their disposal before starting the trip, which mainly concerns routes and timetable.

Travelling by air for users, characterized by an origin–destination and a target time, can be modelled within a framework in which the joint choice of departure time, airport and flight is defined in an explicit space–time dimension (schedule-based approach), even if some simplifications in choice dimensions could be considered. In fact, according to the assumptions on demand reported in the section 'Time-varying Demand', the departure time choice is not strictly related to avoid congestion (full flights), but it is considered to define the best perceived flight allowing users to reach their destination. For this reason, departure times are assumed to coincide with target times and the departure time choice cannot be explicitly considered.

Moreover, according to the structure of the air transport network, except for big metropolitan areas for which many access/egress airports are available, it is common that only one access airport as well as a single egress airport is available, so airport choice can be easily simulated, while the flight (run) choice represents a crucial point.

The flight choice is assumed fully pre-trip, in the sense that it is made before departing and includes the comparison of possible flights having a residual capacity, as well as the choice of one of them on the basis of expected characteristics or attributes, including schedule delays that represent the difference between the user desired departure or arrival times and the departure or arrival of scheduled flights.

For what concerns the generation of alternatives (choice set), given an O/D pair and a user target time (DDTs at origin or destination arrival times at destination), is the choice set made of the 'nearest' paths in terms of minimum early and/or late schedules delays, which are represented by particular links of the diachronic supply model in order to consider the possibility to define schedule penalties through non-linear functions with respect to the duration of schedule delays.

Path alternatives can be generated using a selective approach based on the criteria of maximum earliness and lateness values that define a time slice around user target time, within which the path choice set is defined (e.g. at least two flights departing/arriving within 6 hours before/after the user target time).

The availability of early and/or late flights depends on the trip purpose, as well as the maximum earliness/lateness value can be defined according to air service characteristics.

As an example, if users are not strictly allowed to have a little delay in arrival, only the early flights have to be considered, as well as the maximum earliness/lateness can be as close to the target time (e.g. from the entire day up to 2 hours) as the number of available flights is high for the considered O/D pair.

In the framework of RUM, users are assumed rational and behave with the aim of maximizing their perceived utility U_r associated with each alternative.

The probability $p[r|\text{od}, \tau_{\text{TT}i}]$ of choosing flight r, given the O/D pair od and user target time $\tau_{\text{TT}i}$ (DDT $\tau_{\text{D}i}$ or DAT $\tau_{\text{A}i}$), can be written as

$$p[r|\text{od}, \tau_{\text{TT}i}] = \text{prob}(U_r > U_{r'}) = \text{prob}(V_r + \varepsilon_r > V_{r'} + \varepsilon_{r'}) \quad (8)$$

where the perceived disutility U_r associated with flight (or sequence of flights) r can be written as the sum of a systematic utility V_r and a random term ε_r:

$$U_r = V_r + \varepsilon_r = \sum_j \beta_j X_{jr} + \varepsilon_r \quad (9)$$

Systematic utility V_r is a linear combination, through β_j parameters, of attributes X_{jr}. In addition to the usual level of service attributes X_{jr} (access and egress times and costs, on-board times, transfer times, number of transfers, monetary cost), a key role is given by the above-described temporal gap between user DDT and flight scheduled departure time or between user DAT at destination and flight scheduled arrival. This gap (that for air transport can be relevant) induces a further disutility component known as *early schedule penalty* or *late schedule penalty* that can be explicitly calculated considering a schedule-based approach only.

Model Specification

Different path choice models can be specified according to the assumptions on random residuals ε_r.

Some possible model structures are reported in the following. They refer to different logit-family models, whose complexity increases according to the complexity of the air transportation market (national, international, intercontinental) and to the structure of the airline competition and alliances.

In fact, short-range (national) air transportation networks are usually characterized by few airlines that do not strongly compete among them, except for the most important O/D pair. In this case, a simple multinomial logit model, which considers alternative flights for given O/D pair and user target time $\tau_{\text{TT}i}$, can be used (see Figure 3).

More complex air transport networks, as well as the possibility to perceive flight alternatives in a more structured way (e.g. low-cost versus traditional airlines, or airline preferences), requires the specification of nested-logit models characterized by (at least)

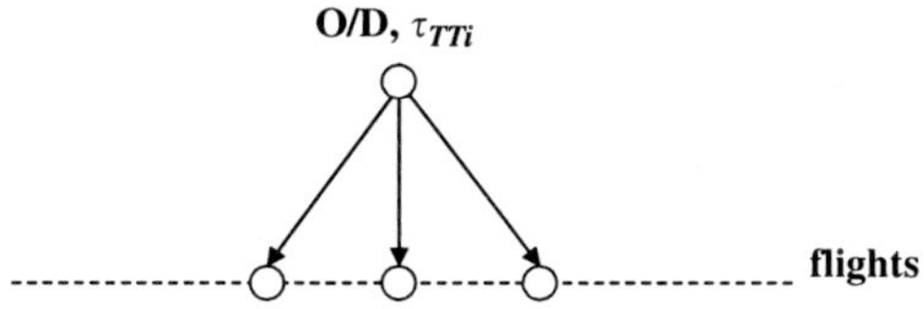

Figure 3
Example of Multinomial Logit Structure

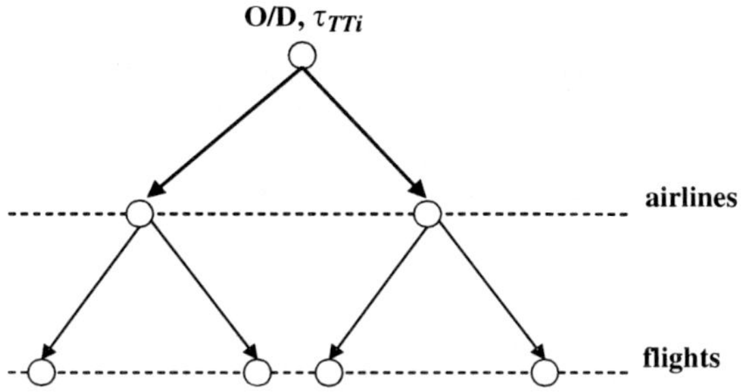

Figure 4
Example of Nested-logit Structure

two choice dimensions, such as that of airline choice and flight one, typical of medium-range (e.g. European) air transport networks, as pictured in Figure 4.

Finally, in the case of the presence of airline alliances (typical of medium–long range air transportation networks), it is possible to adopt more complex modelling structures, as, for example, the cross-nested one pictured in Figure 5, which represents the possibility of considering code-sharing flights for different airlines.

For example, using the nested-logit model of Figure 4, given an O/D pair and a user target time $\tau_{\mathrm{TT}i}$, the probability $p[r, a/\mathrm{od}, \tau_{\mathrm{TT}i}]$ of choosing flight r operated by airline a can be written as

$$p\left(r, \frac{a}{\mathrm{od}}, \tau_{\mathrm{TT}i}\right) = p\left(\frac{a}{\mathrm{od}}, \tau_{\mathrm{TT}i}\right) p\left(\frac{r}{a, \mathrm{od}}, \tau_{\mathrm{TT}i}\right) \tag{10}$$

where the probability of choosing airline a can be written as

$$p\left(\frac{a}{\mathrm{od}}, \tau_{\mathrm{TT}i}\right) = \frac{\exp(\theta_r Y_a/\theta_a)}{\sum_{a'} \exp(\theta_r Y_{a'}/\theta_a)} \tag{11}$$

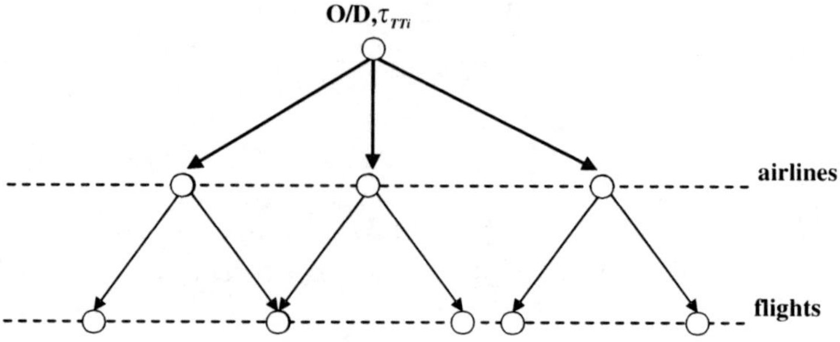

Figure 5
Example of Cross-nested-logit Structure

and the probability of choosing flight r operated by airline a can be written as

$$p\left(\frac{r}{a, \text{od}}, \tau_{\text{TT}i}\right) = \frac{\exp(V_r/\theta_r)}{\sum_{r'} \exp(V_{r'}/\theta_r)} \tag{12}$$

with $Y_a = \ln \sum_{r'} \exp(V_{r'}/\theta_r)$that represents the logsum of available flights r' of airline a, and V_r that represents the systematic utility associated with flight r, made of specific flight attributes (e.g. access and egress times and costs, on-board times, transfer times, number of transfers, monetary cost, early/late schedule delay, O/D distance, income level and so on).

Supply–Demand Interaction Model

The demand–supply interaction is based on a multiclass assignment model that considers different user types (e.g. business and leisure) acting on a congested network, in which each flight has a fixed capacity. It can be classified as a dynamic process model, in which the core is made of a within-day dynamic assignment. A classification of schedule-based assignment models, as well as the formalization of assignment models different from the one described below, can be deepened on Nuzzolo et al. (2003).

Given a simulation period t, an air transportation network represented through a diachronic graph Ω and a demand vector $\underline{d}[\tau_{\text{TT}}]$ (made of the demand for all the od pairs and user target times $\tau_{\text{TT}i}$, for both DAT and DDT), the on-board loads on each flight of the air transport network can be calculated, for each time τ, using the path choice model described in the section 'Schedule-based Path Choice Model'.

It allows us to calculate the path loads, $h_\tau^{\mathrm{od},\tau_{\mathrm{TT}i}}$, relative to flight (or to the sequence of flights) r, generated through demand $d_{\tau_{\mathrm{TT}i}}^{\mathrm{od}}$ relative to the O/D pair od, considering the user target time $\tau_{\mathrm{TT}i}$ and the departure time τ ($=\tau_r$) of flight r, as follows:

$$h_\tau^{\mathrm{od},\tau_{\mathrm{TT}i}} = d_{\tau_{\mathrm{TT}i}}^{\mathrm{od}} p_\tau \left[s, \frac{r}{\mathrm{od}}, \tau_{\mathrm{TT}i} \right] \tag{13}$$

If $\underline{P}_\tau$ is the choice probability matrix at time τ, with a column for each O/D pair od and target time $\tau_{\mathrm{TT}i}$, and a row for each flight (path) r, equation (13) can be written as

$$\underline{h}_\tau = \underline{P}_\tau \, \underline{d}[\underline{\tau}_{\mathrm{TT}}] \tag{14}$$

where $\underline{d}[\underline{\tau}_{\mathrm{TT}}]$ is the above-defined demand vector and $\underline{P}_\tau$ the path choice probability matrix, whose generic element is given by equation (8) for $\tau \leq \tau_r$ and is equal to zero otherwise $(\tau > \tau_r)$.

Given the path loads $\underline{h}_\tau$, if $\underline{\Delta}$ represents the link-path incidence matrix, the link load vector $\underline{f}_\tau$ at time τ can be calculated as:

$$\underline{f}_\tau = \underline{\Delta}\, \underline{h}_\tau \tag{15}$$

which includes on-board loads for each run-link of the diachronic graph that represents each flight of the air transport network.

An Application Example: The Italian Air Transport Network

Finally, aiming at verifying the specification and implementation of the proposed approach, an application of the presented models to the Italian national air transport network has been carried out.

The whole demand for the national air transport market in Italy that has been considered in this study has been carried out by available statistical sources, for which about 76,000 trips have been considered. This demand is divided, at first, in market segments m, according to business trips and non-business ones, and then according to the adopted time segmentation (hourly based) in DDT and DAT.

In relation to the characteristics of the Italian air market, the demand has been divided in four main time periods, as follows

- before 10:30 (morning peak);
- 10:30–14:30 (morning off-peak);
- 14:30–18:30 (afternoon off-peak);
- after 18:30 (afternoon peak).

This segmentation allows us to take into account DAT and DDT for different trip purposes, as mentioned in the section 'Time-varying Demand' that have been further split in hourly time slices, allowing us to define the demand for each of the 24 hours of a workday for each considered trip purpose (business and no-business).

As an example, Figure 6 describes the adopted demand segmentation for business trip purpose, which represents about 80% of the whole air demand in a workday.

For business trips, as pictured in Figure 6, demand related to DAT is concentrated in the early morning for those which have to start their activities in the mid-morning (typical of Italian business meetings), and in the late morning for those who will start their activities in the early afternoon. For all business activities, which typically ends within a workday, the DDT is mainly concentrated in the evening (after 18:30), which represents the peak for DDT trips.

The Italian national air transport network is made of 38 airports (1 for each main town, except for Milan and Rome that have at their disposal 2 different airports) through which 776 national flights are operated in a typical workday. The air services are operated by 20 different airlines, some of which really compete on the main O/D pairs (air markets) which connect the main Italian towns.

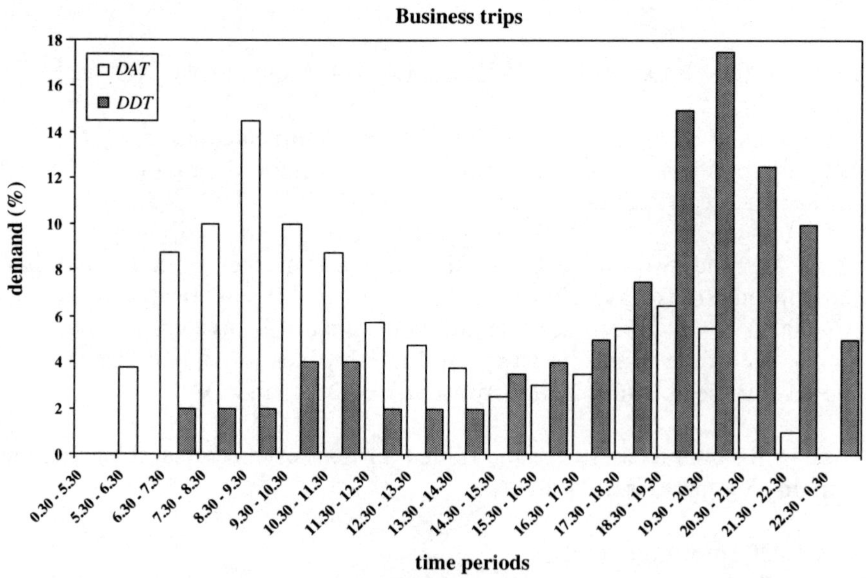

Figure 6
Demand Time Distribution (Business Trips)

Each considered flight is characterized by an aircraft type which defines vehicle capacity to be explicitly considered in the assignment of the demand to the air network.

The representation of the Italian air transport network has been made by a diachronic graph Ω, for which the service sub-graph Ω_s consists of 3,148 nodes and 5,414 links.

Path choice model has been specified using a logit model in which systematic utility has been expressed as

$$V_r[\tau_{TTi}] = \beta_1 \mathrm{TV}_r + \beta_2 C_r + \beta_3 \mathrm{NT}_r + \beta_4 \mathrm{TC}_r + \beta_5 \frac{\mathrm{ESD}_r}{\mathrm{distOD}} + \beta_6 \frac{\mathrm{LSD}_r}{\mathrm{distOD}} + \beta_7 \mathrm{CFW}_r + \beta_8 Y_{\mathrm{AE}} \quad (16)$$

where TV_r is the travel time on flight r, C_r the monetary cost of flight r, NT_r the number of transfers on flight (precisely the sequence of flights) r, TC_r the transfer time, ESD_r the early schedule delay for flight r, LSD_r the late schedule delay for flight r, distOD the distance on the O/D pair, CFW_r the flight load factor, Y_{AE} the access/egress logsum and β_j the model parameters.

Model parameters have been carried out by an aggregate calibration for both business and no-business trip purpose on a set of available data for the Italian transportation market.

Path (flight) alternatives have been generated by a selective approach in which the two closer early and late flights with respect to user target time have been considered. As an example, Table 1 reports flight alternatives and attributes carried out for the

Table 1

Example of Flight Alternatives and Attributes (Catania–Rome DAT = 10.00)

Flight	AZ 1736	AZ 1740	AZ 1738	AP 2867
Origin	Catania	Catania	Catania	Catania
Destination	Rome	Rome	Rome	Rome
Departure	7.10	7.30	9.00	9.15
Arrival	8.30	8.50	10.20	10.30
Early schedule delay (minutes)	90	70	0	0
Late schedule delay (minutes)	0	0	20	30
Distance (km)	370	370	370	370
Travel time (minutes)	80	80	80	75
Monetary cost (€)	245	245	245	230

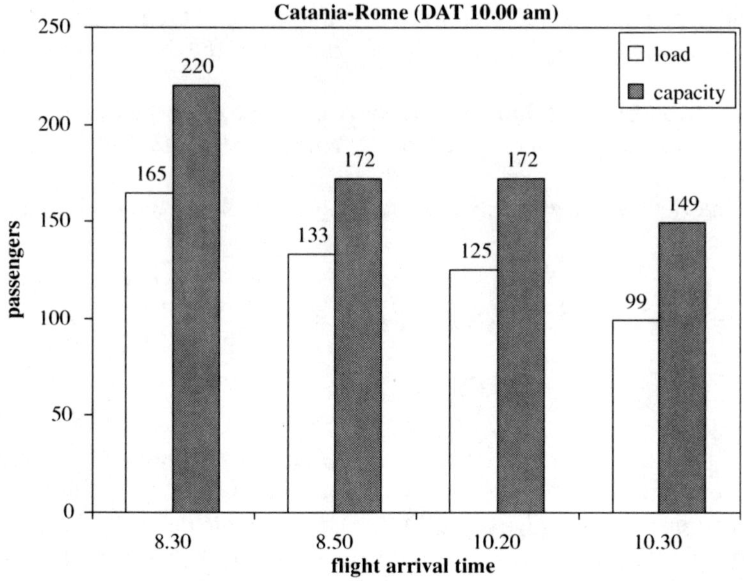

Figure 7
Example of Assignment Results

Catania–Rome O/D pair and DAT at 10:00 a.m., through which flight choice probabilities are calculated.

The application to the whole Italian network allows us to carry out on-board loads on each considered flight. As an example, Figure 7 reports some results of the assignment model in terms of load of each flight, compared with aircraft capacity, for the selected alternatives on the above-described Catania–Rome O/D pair and DAT at 10:00 a.m.

Conclusions

In this paper, a class of schedule-based dynamic assignment models, which can be used to compute flows on air transport networks, has been presented. They can be considered an extension to air transport of the schedule-based approach for transit networks (Nuzzolo et al., 2001).

Path (flight) choice model, that is the core of the assignment model, is specified in the framework of the RUM theory, according to air transport characteristics and user type. This model includes the disutility that occurs because of the difference (that can be considerable) between desired user departure time and flight scheduled departure time or between desired user arrival time at destination and flight scheduled arrival. They are known as early schedule penalty or late schedule penalty and can be calculated explicitly considering a schedule-based approach only.

The demand–supply interaction has been specified by a within-day dynamic assignment model that considers different user types (e.g. business and no-business) acting on a congested network, in which each flight has a fixed capacity.

Finally, an application of the presented models to the Italian national air transport network (38 airports and 776 flights per day) has been shortly described in order to verify the specification and implementation, as well as to show the goodness of the proposed approach.

References

Curry, D. (1990). Optimal airline seat allocation with fare classes nested by origins and destinations. *Transportation Science* 24(3), 193–204.

Friedrich, M. and S. Wekech (2004). A schedule-based transit assignment model addressing the passengers' choice among competing connections. In N. H. M. Wilson and A. Nuzzolo (Eds.), *Schedule-based Dynamic Transit Modeling. Theory and Applications*. UK, Kluwer Academic Publishers.

Gosavi, A., N. Bandla and T. Das (2002). A reinforcement learning approach to a single leg airline revenue management problem with multiple fare classes and overbooking. *IIE Transaction* 34, 729–742.

Hsiao, C. Y. and M. Hansen (2005). Air transportation network flows: an equilibrium model. *TRB 2005 Annual Meeting*. Washington, USA.

Hsu, C. and Y. Wu (1997). The market size of a city-pair route at an airport. *The Annals of Regional Science* 31(4), 391–409.

Mashford, J. S. and B. S. Marksjö (2004). Airline base schedule optimisation by flight network annealing. *Annals of Operation Research* 108, 293–313.

Mathaisel, D. F. X. (1997). Decision support for airline schedule planning. *Journal of Combinatorial Optimization* 1(3), 251–275.

Nuzzolo, A., U. Crisalli and F. Gangemi (2000). A behavioural choice model for the evaluation of railway supply and pricing policies. *Transportation Research* 35A, 211–226.

Nuzzolo, A. and F. Russo (1993). Un modello di rete diacronica per l'assegnazione dinamica al trasporto collettivo extraurbano. *Ricerca Operativa* 67, 37–56.

Nuzzolo, A., F. Russo and U. Crisalli (2001). A doubly dynamic schedule-based assignment model for transit networks. *Transportation Science* 35, 268–285.

Nuzzolo, A., F. Russo and U. Crisalli (2003). Transit network modelling. The schedule-based dynamic approach. In F. Angeli (Ed.), *Collana Transporti.* Milan, Italy.

Tong, C. O. and A. J. Richardson (1984). Estimation of time-dependent origin–destination matrices for transit networks. *Journal of Advanced Transportation* 18, 145–161.

Zhao, W. and Y. S. Zheng (2001). A dynamic model for airline seat allocation with passenger diversion and no-shows. *Transportation Science* 35(1), 80–98.

The Expanding Sphere of Travel Behaviour Research
Selected Papers from the 11th International Conference on Travel Behaviour Research

36

Learning and Risk Attitudes in Route Choice Dynamics

Roger B. Chen and Hani S. Mahmassani

Abstract

This study examines individual risk attitudes and travel time perceptions under different learning mechanisms, and their effect on the day-to-day behaviour of traffic flows. Depending on the behavioural framework, risk attitudes are captured either through the shape of the utility function or in the assessment (subjective weighing) of objective probabilities. Under the decision-making framework proposed in this study, individuals subjectively weigh objective probabilities according to risk attitudes. This framework is used to examine the role of risk attitudes and travel time uncertainty on the day-to-day evolution of network flows. Additionally, three learning types are also considered: (i) reinforcement; (ii) belief and (iii) Bayesian. Depending on the learning type, individual travel time perceptions vary with new experiences. These learning and risk mechanisms are modelled and embedded inside a microscopic (agent-based) simulation framework to study their collective effects on the day-to-day behaviour of traffic flows. These experiments provide an initial exploration of how different learning rules affect individual travel times and the role of risk attitudes. Additionally, the role of risk seekers in driving system-wide properties of traffic networks over time is examined.

Introduction and Background

Learning, from a human perspective, is the process of acquiring information or experiences and relating them with current information to make decisions. In the context of route choice, individuals continually learn about the travel times in a network as they make repeated route choices every day. Many dynamic system-wide properties of traffic networks, such as the convergence, robustness and existence of equilibrium states may result from the learning behaviours of users. Thus, learning plays an important role from a network performance standpoint in driving the day-to-day evolution of flows. In the context of route choice decisions, learning processes allow individuals to relate historical with current travel time experiences, thus shaping their estimates or perceptions of network travel times. Additionally, learning processes may help individuals reduce the perceived uncertainty surrounding these travel time estimates, consequently affecting risk attitudes over time. Learning and risk attitudes are two interrelated parts of a decision-making process. However, the specific mechanisms operating behind their relationship in the context of individual route choice and network traffic flow evolution have not been fully investigated.

Measures of Risk and Risk Attitudes

Measures of risk and risk attitudes have been extensively examined in studies of decision making under uncertainty, which requires an assessment of (i) the desirability (or 'value') of possible outcomes and (ii) their respective likelihoods. Under the classical theory of decisions under uncertainty, the utility of each outcome is weighted by its probability of occurrence (von Neumann and Morgenstern 1947; Bernoulli (1738) [1954]). In expected utility theory (EUT), the decision maker's risk attitudes are reflected in the shape of the utility function. A concave utility function indicates risk aversions, while risk seeking is associated with a convex utility function. The expected utility model lends itself to operational use, and thus underlies many normative applications of decision analysis in practice. However, experimental studies of actual decisions have shown that individuals often violate the expected utility perspective. An alternate perspective is provided by prospect theory (PT), including its extension cumulative PT (Kahneman and Tversky, 1982). Under PT, risk attitudes are reflected through a value function and associated weighing function, which overweighs small probabilities and underweighs moderate and high probabilities, explaining behaviours encountered in experimental data (Kahneman and Tversky, 1979; Payne et al., 1981; Wehrung, 1989). This weighing function has been estimated for gains and losses using median data (Kahneman and Tversky, 1982). Despite its conceptual attractiveness to behavioural decision theorists, PT has not been made operational using datasets collected outside of controlled laboratory settings.

In the context of route choice, a growing number of researchers are focusing on the effects of learning, travel time uncertainty and risk. Both early and more recent laboratory experiments reveal that learning and uncertainty are important determinants of route choice decisions, showing that route switching depends on previously experienced travel time differences and their variance (Mahmassani and Liu, 1999; Nakayama et al., 1999; Srinivasan and Mahmassani, 2000; Mahmassani and Srinivasan, 2004; Avineri and Prashker, 2003, 2005). Many studies have also examined risk and uncertainty in route choice at a more microscopic level, focusing on individual attitudes and perceptions, but not examining the network performance effects. Econometric methods for measuring risk aversion and their application to survey data on route choice were recently examined (de Palma and Picard, 2005). The authors highlight the significance of key socio-economic factors in explaining risk aversion but not risk seeking. Their methodology is consistent with situations where individuals tend to over- or underevaluate the probability of risky events, but confounds risk aversion and biased perceptions of probabilities. Route choice has also been modelled as a one-armed bandit problem (choice between a random and safe route) under different information regimes (Chancelier et al., 2007). Through numerical examples, the authors show that individuals reduce their uncertainty about travel times as a function of their risk aversion. Risk-neutral individuals tend to select the risky route and stick to it, while more risk-averse individuals pick the safe route more frequently. Interestingly, the authors show that users indifferent between the safe and random route after experiencing one or the other value learning more before settling on a final route choice (convergence). The authors' approach allows study of the individual economic benefits of learning, but not the interrelationship between all users' choices, reflected in the congestion resulting from the collective decisions of users.

Learning and Information Integration

Past travel experiences are likely to influence day-to-day perceptions of network performance. Thus, modelling and understanding the mechanisms by which individuals integrate (or learn from) past experiences and information from other sources is important. Several generic theories of learning have been proposed in a variety of fields, such as machine learning, game theory and behavioural decision theory. Behavioural decision theorists (psychologists) have examined learning at the individual level, focusing on information acquisition and integration in decision making in both deterministic and uncertain environments (Einhorn and Hogarth, 1981; Ariely and Camron, 2000; Wallsten et al., 2006). However, psychological studies have typically ignored the effects of other decision makers and different information conditions. Information availability plays an important role in determining the feasibility of theories in different environments. Economists have investigated learning both experimentally and theoretically, studying how simple information adjustment rules drive equilibrium processes in games under different information environments (Roth and Erev, 1993; Crawford, 1995; Camerer et al., 2002). Theoretical work has generally relied on the mathematics of stochastic processes to prove theorems about the limiting properties of different rules (Weibull, 1995; Fudenberg and Levine, 1998). Learning strategies with realistic limiting properties are often regarded as useful models of 'actual' learning, but if limiting behaviours take too long to unfold, these theorems are less useful than modelling the actual path of equilibration over time. Additionally, game theory studies are less concerned with the attributes of the players; thus, learning in their studies does not affect the perceptions of payoffs and related uncertainty. Learning in the context of machine learning looks at determining classification based on new samples, and is more algorithmic than behavioural in nature (Mitchell, 1997; Duda et al., 2001). Their applicability in actual human decision making is limited due to the intense information-processing and calculation requirements of their rules.

Transportation studies that have examined the integration or learning of past experiences or other information sources typically used an averaging rule applied to route or departure time choices (Horowitz, 1984; Tong et al., 1987; Mahmassani and Chang, 1988; Ben-Akiva et al., 1991; Hu and Mahmassani, 1995). Although these studies examined different integration rules and their effect on travel choices and system properties, they do not address travel time perceptions and the learning processes for updating these perceptions and other latent attributes, such as uncertainty or variance associated with travel times, and risk attitudes and perceptions. To account for both the integration of travel times and the associated uncertainty, a Bayesian updating model has been proposed (Kaysi, 1991; Jha et al., 1998). A Bayesian statistical framework can account for updating both the estimate of the mean and variance of a distribution or statistical process in light of new information (DeGroot, 1970). However, Bayesian statistics do not explicitly address the frequency of learning, information sources for updating, or the relationship between the updated parameters (mean and variance) on other latent attributes, such as risk perception. Recently, triggering and terminating mechanisms in the context of travel time learning were addressed, but information availability and risk perceptions were not addressed (Chen and Mahmassani, 2004). Experimental studies on route choice and learning have revealed that learning plays an important role at the aggregate system level by steering traffic networks towards cooperative states (Helbing et al., 2005) and at the individual level by reducing uncertainty (Avineri and Prashker, 2005; Chancelier et al., 2007). Several studies have examined some aspect of learning, uncertainty perception or risk attitudes in the context of route choice. However, the connection between perceived uncertainty, risk attitudes and their aggregate effects in traffic systems where payoffs (travel time savings) are dependent on the decisions of all users has not been fully addressed.

Research Objectives

This study models risk attitudes and travel time perceptions under different learning rules, and examines their effect on the day-to-day behaviour of traffic flows in a network. In this study, risk attitudes are captured through a subjective weighing function applied to objective probabilities, similarly to PT (Tversky and Fox, 1995). Additionally three different types of learning are considered: (i) reinforcement, (ii) belief and (iii) Bayesian. Changes in travel time perception under these learning rules and risk mechanisms are examined in the context of day-to-day route choices.

The learning rules and risk mechanisms are modelled and embedded inside a microscopic (agent-based) simulation framework to study their collective effects on the day-to-day behaviour of traffic flows.

Simulation experiments are conducted using this model to examine the effect of different travel time learning processes and risk mechanisms on (i) travel time perceptions over time, including the degree of uncertainty; (ii) risk attitudes and perceptions of uncertainty over time and (iii) the relationship of the latent attributes described in (i) and (ii) on traffic flow evolution and other dynamic system properties, particularly convergence and stability. This study extends previous work by:

1. further considering the individual travel time learning process;
2. further considering the role of risk perception on route choice and its system-wide effects;
3. further examining the effects of different perception mechanisms on risk perception;
4. determining the relationship across different travel time learning processes and
5. capturing the effect of the above on day-to-day network dynamics, in particular convergence and stability.

Modelling Framework

Network traffic flow results from the interaction between users, their evaluation of past experiences, the resulting travel decisions and the supply-side characteristics of the network. The following section presents different rules by which users integrate past experiences with current ones, including mechanisms that describe route switching decisions. Learning mechanisms determine the role of past experiences in current choices. Route switching or choice mechanisms describe the evaluation and choice of alternatives, given updated individual experiences, perceived uncertainty and risk attitude.

For a given day, an individual's route choice yields an outcome or experience (travel time) that is a function of the individual's decision and those of other system users. This travel experience is integrated with past experiences through some learning mechanism. Based on the acceptability of the experience in light of past experiences, the individual will decide to switch routes or keep the current choice. Acceptability is based on the individual's current perception (judgement) of travel time, which depends on travel times experienced over a number of days, and to some extent an individual's risk attitudes. Different mechanisms for learning determine the effects of prior experiences on perceptions of current ones. Risk mechanisms that capture the perception of likelihoods reflect risk attitudes and their role in evaluating current choices relative to other alternatives. Furthermore, users may perceive each route to have a distribution of travel times that changes with each new experience. Thus, route

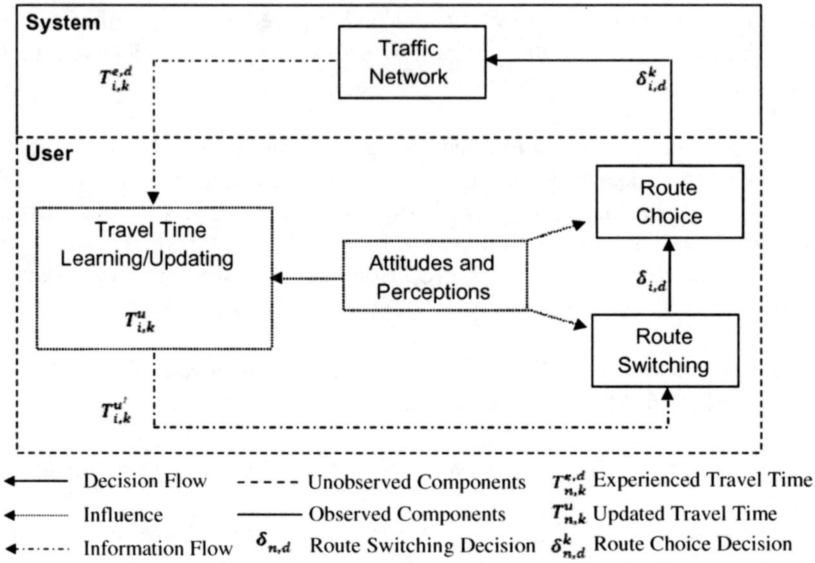

Figure 1
Route Choice Decision Framework

choice is decision between different routes, each with a different perceived (overall) travel time distribution, including associated uncertainty. Figure 1 depicts the framework for route choice decisions. The following sections articulate the individual components of this framework that captures the interaction between risk mechanisms, learning mechanisms, route switching mechanisms and travel time perception.

Travel Time Perception

In this study, individuals base route choice decisions on the perceived travel times for routes in the system. These perceived travel times vary across individuals in the system, and are updated in light of travel times experienced across time. Thus, the perceived travel time is constantly updated, or altered and calibrated, as new travel times are experienced every day. The perceived updated travel time can be stated as follows:

$$T^u_{i,k} = \tau^u_{i,k} + \varepsilon^u_{i,k}, \forall k \in K, i \in I \tag{1}$$

where $T^u_{i,k}$ is the updated perceived travel time for individual i on route k; $T^u_{i,k}$ the mean of the updated perceived travel time; $\varepsilon^u_{i,k}$ the associated error that is distributed Normal $\sim N(0, \sigma^u_{i,k})$; and $\sigma^u_{i,k}$ the standard deviation of the associated error for individual i on route k.

Consequently, $T^{u}_{i,k}$is distributed Normal $\sim N(\tau^{u}_{i,k}, \sigma^{u}_{i,k})$, with the distribution varying across routes and individuals. As individuals experience new travel times, $\tau^{u}_{i,k}$ and $\sigma^{u}_{i,k}$ are updated accordingly. The perceived experienced travel time can be stated as follows:

$$T^{e,n}_{i,k} = \tau^{e,n}_{i,k} + \varepsilon^{e,n}_{i,k}, \forall k \in K, i \in \tag{2}$$

where $T^{e,n}_{i,k}$ is the perceived experienced travel time for individual i on route k; $\tau^{e,n}_{i,k}$ the mean perceived experienced travel time; and $\varepsilon^{e,n}_{i,k}$ the associated error, distributed Normal $\sim N(0, \sigma^{e,n}_{i,k})$.

Consequently, $T^{e,n}_{i,k}$is distributed Normal $\sim N(\tau^{e,n}_{i,k}, \sigma^{e,n}_{i,k})$, with the distribution varying across each route for each individual, and varying across individuals. In this study $\tau^{e,n}_{i,k}$ is assumed to be the objective (actual) travel time on a particular route. The perceived experienced travel time is assumed to have the same error as the perceived updated travel time ($\sigma^{e,n}_{i,k} = \sigma^{u}_{i,k}$). Behaviourally, this implies that individuals perceive their experienced travel times with the same error as the travel time they learn or keep in memory, implying further that the uncertainty associated with the travel times in memory carries over and influences the perception of experienced travel times. Thus, the experienced route travel time users perceive reflects or is correlated with past experienced travel times for a particular route.

Experienced travel times are integrated with updated travel times through learning mechanisms. Additionally, individuals make route switching and choice decisions based on these perceived travel times in conjunction with risk attitudes that affect the perception of gains and losses amongst routes in the choice set. Both learning mechanisms and risk attitudes play important roles in individuals' route choices across time. The next section describes different learning mechanisms considered in this study by which individuals update their travel times in memory.

Learning Mechanisms

Information availability plays an important role in determining which learning mechanisms are feasible under different environments (Duda et al., 2001; Camerer, 2003). In addition to relating experiences with current choices, learning processes may also help reduce uncertainty perceived by individuals, influencing the risk perception of alternatives over time. In the context of day-to-day route choice, individuals update a perceived travel time $T^{u}_{i,k}$ with new travel times $T^{e,n}_{i,k}$ experienced with different learning mechanisms. Since perceived travel times are distributed according to a mean $\tau^{u}_{i,k}$ and associated variance $\sigma^{u}_{i,k}$, learning mechanisms update both of these components, yielding new updated travel time distributions in light of new experienced travel times.

Several generic theories of learning or information updating have been proposed in the psychology, game theory and machine learning literatures, such as reinforcement, belief, sophisticated (anticipatory), directional, Bayesian and Boltzmann learning, each with different information requirements. In this study, three general types of learning are considered: (i) reinforcement, (ii) belief and (iii) Bayesian. Each of these learning types is presented next in the context of day-to-day route choice and discussed. (Note: hereafter the subscripts i (individual) and k (route) are dropped for convenience.)

Reinforcement Learning

Under this learning model, alternatives or routes are 'reinforced' by their previous payoffs only when they are chosen and a positive outcome occurs, possibly 'spilling over' to similar alternatives (routes with overlapping links) (Erev et al., 1999). In terms of perceived travel times, a reinforcement-type learning rule for updating the mean and variance can be expressed as:

$$\tau^{u'} = \left[\frac{\phi C_{\text{prior}}}{\phi C_{\text{prior}} + C_{N_e}}\right](\tau^{u}) + \left[\frac{C_{N_e}}{\phi C_{\text{prior}} + C_{N_e}}\right](\overline{T_{N_e}}) \quad (3)$$

where $\tau^{u'}$ is the updated perceived travel time; τ^{u} the prior perceived travel time; ϕ the parameter reflecting the weight on past experiences; N_e the days from which the travel time experiences have not been integrated into memory; C_{prior} the total number of times a route was chosen in previously, and a lower travel time relative to a reference travel time (travel time gain) was experienced; C_{N_e} the total number of times the route is chosen during period N_e, and a lower travel time relative to a reference travel time (travel time gain) was experienced; and $\overline{T_{N_e}}$ the sample average of travel times experienced by the individual in period N_e that were below a reference travel time (travel time gain).

Under reinforcement learning strategies, individuals make choices based only on their own experiences, requiring only information on received payoffs from actual choices (Roth and Erev, 1993). In the context of day-to-day route choice, travel times for a particular route are updated only when the route is selected and an improved travel time results relative to the updated travel time for that route, thus 'reinforcing' the estimates of these travel times. Thus, the reference travel time used for judging improvements is the updated travel time. Consequently, the only piece of information required by individuals are the travel times experienced for the chosen route. According to the expressions above, reinforcement learning is governed by ϕ, which reflects the 'strength of memory' or 'rate of forgetting'. As the memory weight ϕ increases in value, the rate of forgetting for an individual decreases, and increases the effect of past experiences on current travel time perceptions. Additionally, the reinforcement of chosen routes by their experienced travel times is reflected by the weights corresponding to the prior updated travel time and the recently experienced travel times. Thus, although an individual may have a high strength of memory (high ϕ), if the number of times a route is chosen (and an improvement in travel time results) since updating is high (high C_{N_e}), then the weight on new experiences will be greater compared to the weight on past experiences. C_{N_e} is affected by both the number of times an individual selects a route and the frequency of learning, suggesting a trade-off between the rate of learning, amount of experimentation (how often an individual decides to sample a route) and the success rate (number of times the route choice yields a positive payoff). A second learning mechanism similar to reinforcement that also considers the travel times on alternatives or routes not chosen is belief learning.

Belief Learning

A belief learning mechanism assumes that individuals form and update beliefs about the choices of other individuals, making choices based on these beliefs (Crawford, 1995). One example of belief learning is fictitious play, where individuals keep track of the relative frequency by which other individuals make choices, selecting the alternative with the highest relative frequency of choice. In this case, the relative frequencies are the 'beliefs' individuals use to make their next choices. Belief learning strategies assume that individuals formulate beliefs about other individuals' choices and base their own choices on these beliefs. Thus, belief learning requires information on choices of other and their associated payoffs. In the context of route choice decisions, this can be expressed as:

$$\tau^{u'} = \left[\frac{\phi C_{\text{prior},\, I_e}}{\phi C_{\text{prior},\, I_e} + C_{N_e,\, I_e}}\right](\tau^u) + \left[\frac{C_{N_e,I_e}}{\phi C_{\text{prior},\, I_e} + C_{N_e,\, I_e}}\right](\overline{T_{N_e,I_e}}) \tag{4}$$

where $\tau^{u'}$ is the updated perceived travel time; τ^u the prior perceived travel time; ϕ the parameter reflecting the weight on past experiences; N_e the days from which the travel time experiences have not been integrated into memory; I_e the set of individuals who selected a particular route in N_e days; $C_{\text{prior},\, I_e}$ the total number of times a particular route is chosen previously by users I_e; C_{N_e,I_e} the total number of times a particular route is chosen during period N_e by I_e; and $\overline{T_{N_e,I_e}}$ the sample average of travel times experienced by I_e in period N_e.

Both belief and reinforcement learning are a type of weighted average between past and current experiences. The main departure lies in the source of information used to update past experiences, and that in belief learning both choices that result in gains and losses are used. In reinforcement learning, an individual's own experiences are used, whereas in belief learning, individuals consider the choices of all individuals. Also, the weight used in equations (5) and (6) exhibits a trade-off between 'strength of memory' and frequency of learning, similar to reinforcement learning. Many game theory studies have shown that heterogeneity in beliefs across individuals lead to different equilibria in coordination games (Van Huyck et al., 1991). The adaptive dynamics in coordination games have been shown to produce results similar to experiments with belief learning models (Crawford, 1995; Ho and Wiegelt, 1996; Battalio et al., 2001). Helbing et al. (2005) have shown that day-to-day route choice resembles coordination games, and that after time players learn to take turns on a two-link network. However, the study did not investigate the different mechanisms that lead to coordination.

Bayesian Learning

Similar to both reinforcement and belief learning, Bayesian learning is also a type of 'weighted' average between past and current experiences. More specifically, in Bayesian learning, probability distributions and their parameters are updated in light of new samples taken. Thus, Bayesian learning is amenable to this study since the route travel times in memory are assumed to be normally distributed. In the context of route choice decisions, Bayesian learning is expressed as:

$$\tau^{u'} = \left[\frac{1/\sigma^u}{(1/\sigma^u)+(N_e/\sigma_e)}\right](\tau^u) + \left[\frac{N_e/\sigma_e^u}{(1/\sigma^u)+(N_e/\sigma_e)}\right](\overline{T_e}) \tag{5}$$

$$\sigma^{u'} = \frac{\sigma^u \cdot \sigma_e}{\sigma_e + N_e \cdot \sigma^u} = \frac{1}{(1/\sigma^u)+(N_e/\sigma_e)} \tag{6}$$

where $\tau^{u'}$ is the updated perceived travel time; τ^u the prior perceived travel time; $\sigma^{u'}$ the updated variance in memory; σ^u the prior variance in memory; N_e the number of experienced travel times in the sample; $\overline{T_e}$ the sample mean of experienced perceived travel times; and σ_e the sample variance of the experienced travel times.

Bayesian learning departs from other learning rules in the weight placed on past experiences. Reinforcement and belief learning assume that the weight placed on historic experiences is a characteristic of the individual. Under Bayesian learning, these weights are determined statistically as a function of the parameters of the sample of experiences. If 'confidence' is assumed to be the inverse of variance, then as variance increases, confidence decreases. Three important properties result from Bayesian learning: (i) with every experienced travel time, the variance associated with the travel time in memory always decreases (N_e and σ_e are always positive) and confidence always increases; (ii) as the number of experienced travel time increases, the confidence associated with the posterior travel time in memory increases and (iii) as the confidence associated with the posterior travel time in memory increases such that the confidence in memory is much greater than that of the sample, the effect of newly experienced travel times decreases.

Interestingly, Bayesian, belief and reinforcement learning share two common properties: (i) updated travel times are a weighted average of the (prior) updated travel time and the travel times experienced and ii) these weights imply a trade-off between frequency of updates and size of each update sample. The departure point between the different rules is the source of experiences used in learning. Reinforcement relies on travel times from individual choices. Belief learning considers experiences from other individuals in the population. Bayesian learning does not specify the source of the sample (how the sample is constructed or taken). These similarities and differences suggest, all else being equal, Bayesian learning may lead to a different rate of convergence compared to belief and reinforcement learning since its weights are a function of the actual travel time experienced (through the use of sample variance) and not just the frequency of choice.

Risk and Risk Attitudes

Decision making in environments with uncertainty requires the evaluation of the desirability of outcomes and their likelihood of occurrence. Day-to-day route choice may be framed as a choice between routes with travel times expressed as a distribution with a perceived mean and variance. Given a perceived travel time distribution for each route, the choice of alternatives can be framed as a decision that considers the likelihood of a particular route yielding a travel time less than a reference point. In this study, the reference point is taken to be the updated perceived travel time $\tau^{u'}$. According to EUT, the classical framework for decisions under uncertainty, individuals consider an expected utility that is a weighted sum of alternatives and their probability of occurrence. Risk attitudes are reflected in the shape (concavity or convexity) of an individual's utility curve, where gains and losses are mapped through a function $u(x)$, and x is the value (payoff) of an alternative. Although the EUT has dominated economic studies, experimental studies have shown inconsistent behavioural results with EUT (Kahneman and Tversky, 1979; Payne et al., 1981; Wehrung, 1989). In particular, experimental studies suggest that individuals tend to underweigh outcomes that are merely probable in comparison with those of certainty, depending on gain or loss. An alternative theory to account for these inconsistencies is PT. The prospect of a lottery is determined by summing the values of alternatives weighted by their subjective (or weighted) probabilities of occurrence, and a choice is made based on these prospects. Under PT, individuals exhibit four different patterns of risk-averse and risk-seeking behaviours (Kahneman and Tversky, 1979, 1982; Tversky and Fox, 1995): (i) risk-seeking for gains and (ii) risk aversion for losses of low probabilities; and (iii) risk aversion for gains and (iv) risk-seeking for losses of high probabilities. This fourfold pattern is based on the assumption of overweighing low probabilities and underweighing high probabilities, independent of gain or loss. This study proposes a similar model, under which individuals subjectively weigh objective probabilities of gains and losses, independent of whether the probability is high or low. Risk-averse behaviour is indicated by underweighing probabilities of gains and overweighing probabilities of losses. Risk-seeking individuals exhibit the converse, underweighing probabilities of losses and overweighing probabilities of gains. In this study, a probability weighing function (equation 8) that gives this fourfold pattern is used, along with the following value function (equation 9). Given these functions, this study considers the following model:

$$P = \Omega^{gain}[\Phi(T^{gain})] \cdot v(T^{gain}) + \Omega^{loss}[\Phi(T^{loss})] \cdot v(T^{loss}) \tag{7}$$

$$\Omega(p) = \left\{ \begin{array}{ll} \frac{(1-\pi)}{\pi \cdot p} & p \leq \pi,\ 0 \leq \pi \leq 1 \\ \frac{\pi}{(1-\pi)}p - \left(\frac{1-2\pi}{1-\pi}\right) & p > \pi,\ 0 \leq \pi \leq 1 \end{array} \right\} \tag{8}$$

$$v(\Delta T) = \left\{ \begin{array}{ll} (\Delta T)^{\alpha} & \text{if } \Delta T \geq 0 \\ -\lambda(\Delta T)^{\alpha} & \text{if } \Delta T < 0 \end{array} \right\} \tag{9}$$

$$T^{gain} = \frac{1}{\Phi(\Delta T \geq 0)} \int_0^{\tau^u_{best}} (\Phi(\Delta T) \cdot \Delta T) d\Delta T \tag{10}$$

$$T^{loss} = \frac{1}{\Phi(\Delta T < 0)} \int_{-\infty}^{0} (\Phi(\Delta T) \cdot \Delta T) d\Delta T \tag{11}$$

where ΔT is the difference between a travel time and the best travel time among routes ($\tau^u_{best} - T^u$); $\Phi(\cdot)$ the probability distribution function (pdf) for a Normal distribution; α and λ the parameters that determine the shape of the value function $v(\cdot)$; and π the parameter between 0 and 1 that determines the position of the infliction point of the probability weighing function $\Omega(p)$.

The attractiveness of a route is determined by equation (7) as the weighted sum of the value of a gain (positive ΔT) and the value of a loss (negative ΔT). These values are weighted by their probabilities of occurrence, which are subjectively weighted according to equation (8), plotted in Figure 2. Objective probabilities are weighed subjectively according to parameter π which varies with risk attitude. A risk-averse individual corresponds to a low π for losses (low π^{loss}), resulting in an overweighing of probabilities, and a high π for gains (π^{gain}), resulting in an underweighing of probabilities, where π^{gain} and π^{loss} sum to 1 ($\pi^{gain}+\pi^{loss} = 1$). Risk seekers exhibit the opposite. The value function (equation 9) is assumed to be concave for gains and

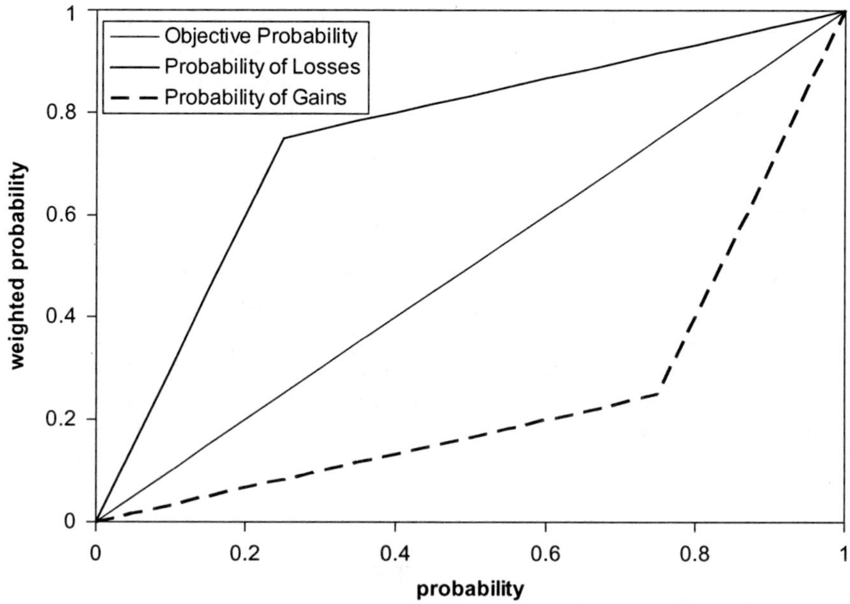

Figure 2
Weighing Functions (equation (8)) for Risk-Averse Individual ($\pi^{loss} = 0.25$; $\pi^{gain} = 0.75$)

convex for losses, determined by the shape parameter α. Given that the shape parameter λ is positive, the function is steeper for losses compared to gains.

Route Switching

Route switching is based on the difference between the best and current routes, following a boundedly-rational rule used in several previous studies (Mahmassani and Jayakrishnan, 1991; Hu and Mahmassani, 1995). Acceptability or tolerance for travel time differences is defined by the difference between the current and best travel times. This tolerance-based switching mechanism can be stated as follows:

$$\delta_{in} = \begin{cases} 1 & \text{if } \dfrac{(\tau_{ik}^{u} - \tau_{ik}^{u,\text{best}})}{\tau_{ik}^{u,\text{best}} \geq \Delta^{i} \cdot \tau_{ik}^{u}}, \text{ where } 0 \leq \Delta^{i} \leq 1 \\ 0 & \text{otherwise} \end{cases} \tag{12}$$

where δ_{in} is a binary variable that takes a value of 1 if the difference between the mean current and best learned travel times is acceptable to individual i, and 0 otherwise; and Δ^{i} is the acceptability or tolerance threshold for the difference in travel times that defines the percentage improvement over the current travel time to warrant switching routes.

As the tolerance for travel time differences increases (Δ^i increases), individuals are more tolerant of travel time differences, and are less willing to switch for only marginal travel time improvements. As the tolerance for travel time differences decreases, individuals are more willing to switch for even small travel time differences.

Route Choice Evaluation

Previously, learning mechanisms for integrating experiences with an updated perceived travel time were presented, in addition to a mechanism for route switching decisions. However, the actual choice among routes was not addressed. Furthermore, given that updating does not occur every day, individuals may base route choice decisions on the travel time experienced previously or the updated perceived travel time. Three possibilities are as follows:

$$T_C = \tau^u_{ik} \tag{13}$$

$$T_C = \begin{cases} \tau^u_{ik} & \text{travel time updating occurs} \\ \beta(\tau^u_{ik}) + (1-\beta)T^{e,n}_{i,k} & \text{otherwise} \end{cases} \tag{14}$$

$$T_C = \begin{cases} \tau^u_{i,k} & \text{travel time updating occurs} \\ T^{e,n}_{i,k} & \text{otherwise} \end{cases} \tag{15}$$

where T_C is the route travel time used for making route choices; and β the weighing parameter.

The expressions above imply different types of route choice evaluations. Under equation (13), route choice each day is only on the basis of perceived updated travel times. If an extremely long travel time for a particular route is experienced on day n, and if this experience has little impact on the updated travel time, perhaps due to a long history of short travel times, route switching would not occur. Equation (15) is the opposite, under which route choice is based on experienced travel times unless updating occurs. The next section describes the simulation experiments conducted using the framework and mechanisms described in the previous sections.

Description of Simulation Experiments

This section describes the system features and related details of the simulation experiments, principal factors investigated, and specific properties and performance descriptors considered in this investigation.

System Features

The network used for this study, shown in Figure 3, consists of 9 nodes and 12 links. Link cost-flow functions were used with a linearly varying cost beyond the value $e_{\text{link}}\text{cap}_{\text{link}}$, according to the following expressions for link l:

$$c_l = \begin{cases} t_l^{\min}\left[\dfrac{1 + b_l f_l}{(\text{cap}_l - f_l)}\right] & f_l \leq e_l \text{cap}_l \\ t_l^{\min}\left[1 + \dfrac{b_l e_l}{(1 - e_l)} + b_l\left(\dfrac{(f_l/\text{cap}_l) - e_l}{(1 - e_l)^2}\right)\right] & f_l > e_l \text{cap}_l \end{cases} \quad (16)$$

where $t_l^{\min}$ is the free-flow travel time; b_l defines the slope of the curve; cap_l the link capacity; and $0 \leq e_l \leq 1$ defines the undersaturation limit.

Links located near the centre of the network have smaller capacities compared with links on the border, and thus their cost-flow functions are more sensitive to varying flows. Links of the border have larger free-flow times compared with the links in the centre. Nodes 1, 4, 5, 8 and 9 are origins and destinations (ODs), and all possible OD pairs are connected. Parameter values and OD pairs and base demand values are given in Tables 1 and 2.

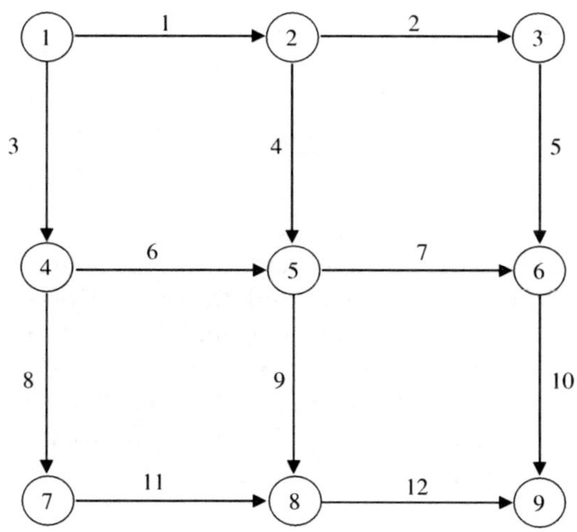

Figure 3
Network Used in Simulation Experiment

Table 1
Link Characteristics and Parameters

Link	t^{min}	Capacity	b	E
1	20	360	0.1	0.95
2	12	360	0.1	0.95
3	15	240	0.12	0.95
4	12	180	0.15	0.95
5	12	360	0.1	0.95
6	10	150	0.15	0.95
7	12	180	0.15	0.95
8	15	240	0.12	0.95
9	10	150	0.15	0.95
10	30	360	0.1	0.95
11	15	240	0.12	0.95
12	15	240	0.12	0.95

Table 2
OD Demand

O–D	Routes	Demand
1–8	6	60
1–9	2	40
9–8	2	10
1–5	1	10
5–8	1	10
1–4	1	10
4–8	1	10

In order to initiate the dynamics of the system, travel times for the initial iteration are specified using the initial loading pattern, using the cost-flow functions. Consequently, the initial mean updated travel time is set to the initial travel time, and the variance set to $\beta\tau_0^u$, where β is interpreted as the initial variance of the perceived travel time over a segment of unit travel time and is the same for all users. Thus, a large β indicates that the initial overall level of uncertainty is high in the system, which is realistic for systems with many 'new' users. The initial perceived updated travel time is represented by τ_0^u. Users are loaded uniformly across ODs and subsequently paths. Different probabilistic loading patterns could also be used. Other specifics that have been varied across simulations are discussed next.

Table 3
Experimental Factors Considered

Factors Relating to Experiments Considering Risk Attitudes	Factors Common to All Experiments
(i) Percentage of risk seekers and avoiders	(i) Demand level (V)
	(ii) Initial uncertainty (β)
(ii) Degree of risk attitude (and)	(iii) Perceived travel times
	(iv) Learning mechanisms

Experimental Factors

The experimental factors investigated are grouped broadly into two categories: (i) factors related to risk and attitudes and (ii) factors relating to learning. Two scenarios were considered: (a) a population with risk seekers and avoiders and (b) a population that does not explicitly consider their risk attitudes. Individuals under the first scenario make use of the subjective weighing of objective probabilities shown in equations (7)–(11). A summary of factors considered is shown in Table 3.

Risk Attitude Factors

Equation (7) states that the score or prospect of an alternative is the weighted average of values of alternatives weighted by their subjective probabilities. Values are evaluated based on differences from a reference point (the best travel time of all routes) and determined according to equation (13). Furthermore, in evaluating alternatives, three possibilities are expressed in equations (13)–(15). The degree of individual's over- and underweigh objective probabilities are governed by parameters π^{loss} and π^{gain}. The parameter was normally distributed across the population of agents using a mean π^{loss} with a variance of π^{loss} v_{pop}. The following values were used: $\pi^{\text{loss}} = \{0.10, 0.2, \ldots, 0.5\}$. Additionally the percentage of risk seekers in the population ($\gamma_{\text{risk}} \times$ total number of users) were varied by setting $\gamma_{\text{risk}} = \{0, 0.1, 0.2, \ldots, 1\}$.

Learning Factors

The main parameter governing the reinforcement and belief learning mechanisms is the weight $\phi_i \in [0,1]$ placed on historical experiences, as shown in equations (3)–(6). As ϕ_i increases, the greater an individual's memory, and more the weight placed on historical experiences. The parameter ϕ is normally distributed across the population with a mean ϕ and a variance of ϕ v_{pop}.

Population Factors

In addition to the factors described previously, two population related factors were also considered:

Demand Level Five different demand levels were considered in this study for each OD (a set number of users was assigned to each OD). The base case was 100 users corresponding to a population factor of 1 ($V = 1$). Other population levels considered were $V = \{0.75, 1.2, 1.5$ and $2\}$. Previous studies have shown that convergence is harder to obtain at higher levels of population.

Initial Degree of Perceived Dispersion Additionally, different levels of initial perceived dispersion or variance in travel times were also considered. Dispersion is measured by the initial β used to determine the initial variance of travel time. Three different values of β were considered: $\beta = \{1, 2$ and $2.5\}$.

Performance Measures and Properties

Day-to-Day Flow Pattern of Traffic, in Particular Convergence

Convergence is reached when users have stopped switching routes for the remainder of the simulation. For cases where a strict convergence is unattainable, a plot of the day-to-day flow is shown to facilitate a qualitative analysis.

Number of Days until Convergence

The number of days till convergence is the number of days from the start of the simulation till convergence is reached. For cases where strict convergence is unattainable, the number of days till convergence is the number of days till the flows on all paths change within an acceptable tolerance.

Simulation Results

The results from three sets of simulation experiments are presented and discussed in this section. First, the effects of varying demand level under Bayesian, reinforcement and belief learning mechanisms are presented. The next set of experiments considers the effects of varying mean π values and different percentages of risk seekers and avoiders within the population. The third set of experiments considers the effects of varying initial travel time perception uncertainty (variance) on the convergence of the system. The final set of experiments examines the effects of the perceived travel time on convergence.

Varying Demand Levels

In traffic systems, demand levels fluctuate over time, due to latent demand for travel and time-varying activity patterns. Past studies have shown that as demand levels increase, convergence is more difficult to obtain (Mahmassani, 1990; Chen and Mahmassani, 2004). In the first set of experiments conducted in this study, demand levels were varied across different learning mechanisms. Demand levels are varied by increasing the base demand level (100 users) through a demand factor (V). Thus, $V = 1$ corresponds to the base demand level, while $V = 2$ corresponds to an increase in demand by a factor of 2. The results from these experiments are shown in Table 4.

Under Bayesian and reinforcement learning, lower usage levels show a greater propensity towards convergence compared to high levels, confirming past results, but under different learning mechanisms. However, under a belief learning which updates using averages of experiences across all users on a particular route, convergence appears less sensitive to demand levels. High demand showed lower propensity towards convergence principally because the travel times are more sensitive to flow with more congestion in the system, as captured in the link flow-cost functions (and would be predicted by virtually all standard queuing or traffic flow models). Under belief learning, since users update using travel times averaged across all user experiences for a particular route, the effects of travel time fluctuation or variation across users may be reduced, leading to similar travel time perceptions across all users on a particular route, all else being equal. Finally, strict convergence under reinforcement learning was more difficult to obtain, relative to other learning mechanisms. One plausible explanation is that reinforcement is a selective updating mechanism that leads to updating only for experienced travel time gains (choices that lead to a reduction in travel times). Thus, under reinforcement learning, updating may occur less frequently and with smaller samples in general compared to other mechanisms. One assumption of the learning rules used in this study is that with each update, the confidence increases (variance decreases), leading to perceived travel time distributions that become tighter around the mean with each update. Thus, new experiences (travel times) have less impact on users' travel time perceptions. Under reinforcement learning, since updating only occurs for travel time gains, the perceived travel time uncertainty (variance) may not

Table 4
Iterations until Convergence for Different Demand Levels (V)

Demand Level (V)	Bayesian	Reinforcement	Belief
1.00	11	16	7
1.50	10	61	7
2.00	15	NC	7
3.00	NC	NC	7

decrease at the same rate as other mechanisms, thus leading to slower convergence compared to Bayesian and belief learning.

Varying Initial Uncertainty

Experiments were also conducted to examine the effects of the initial uncertainty, determined by the value of β, under each of the three learning rules. These results are shown in Table 5 for two demand levels ($V = 1$ and $V = 2$).

The results above indicate that under Bayesian and reinforcement learning, as the initial uncertainty increases, convergence in traffic flows is more difficult to obtain. One possible explanation is that given that users have a higher perceived uncertainty or judgement error, more new experiences are required to decrease this perception error. In general, reinforcement takes more time until convergence relative to Bayesian learning, since the travel time experiences sampled under reinforcement learning only consists of travel time 'gains' (reduction in travel time). Under belief learning, since users update using travel times averaged across all user experiences for a particular route, the effects of travel time fluctuation or variation across users may be reduced, leading to similar travel time perceptions across all users on a particular route, all else being equal. Finally, similar to the results in Table 4, higher demand levels lead to more difficulty with respect to convergence.

Risk Attitudes

Under a decision process that accounts for perceptions of uncertainty, risk attitudes play important roles in the evaluation of travel time likelihoods in route choice. The

Table 5
Number of Iterations until Convergence for Different Initial Perceived Errors (β)

	Bayesian	Reinforcement	Belief
Demand: $V = 1$			
$\beta = 1$	11	16	7
$\beta = 2$	13	22	7
$\beta = 3$	15	38	7
Demand: $V = 2$			
$\beta = 1$	15	NC	7
$\beta = 2$	16	NC	7
$\beta = 3$	16	NC	7

Note: β is the variance associated with a unit of travel time for two demand levels.

parameter π^{loss} indicates the inflection point in equation (12), indicating the degree users' subjectively over- or underweighted objective probabilities. Results show that risk attitudes do affect the convergence of traffic systems. The results for Bayesian and belief learning mechanisms under a decision process that takes into account risk attitudes are presented in Figures 4 and 5.

Figure 4 shows that under Bayesian learning, as π^{loss} increases, the propensity towards convergence is greater, relative to a lower π^{loss}. Furthermore, a high percentage of risk seekers (90%) leads to more propensity towards convergence under Bayesian learning, compared to a low percentage (10%). In the risk framework in this study, risk seekers would underweigh probabilities of losses and overweigh probabilities of gains. Thus, risk seekers may have a higher propensity towards switching to routes with larger perceived variances, unless the travel time gain between the current and alternative routes is huge. Risk avoiders on the other hand show greater propensity towards staying on routes with lower variances, despite the possibility of a travel time gain for switching. One consequence of the Bayesian learning rule is that as users gain travel time experiences over time, their perceived variance decreases; thus, users' perceived travel times are insensitive to new experiences. One plausible explanation for the higher propensity towards convergence exhibited by systems with more risk seekers relative to risk avoiders is that risk seekers switch at a greater frequency due to their propensity

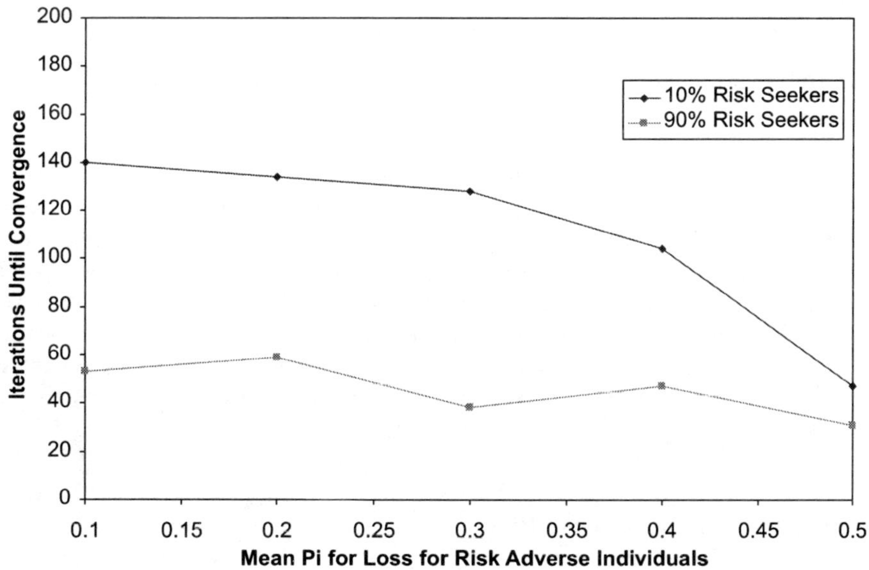

Figure 4

Number of Iterations until Convergence as the Mean π^{loss} Increases for Different Percentages of Risk Seekers in the Population: Bayesian Learning Experiments

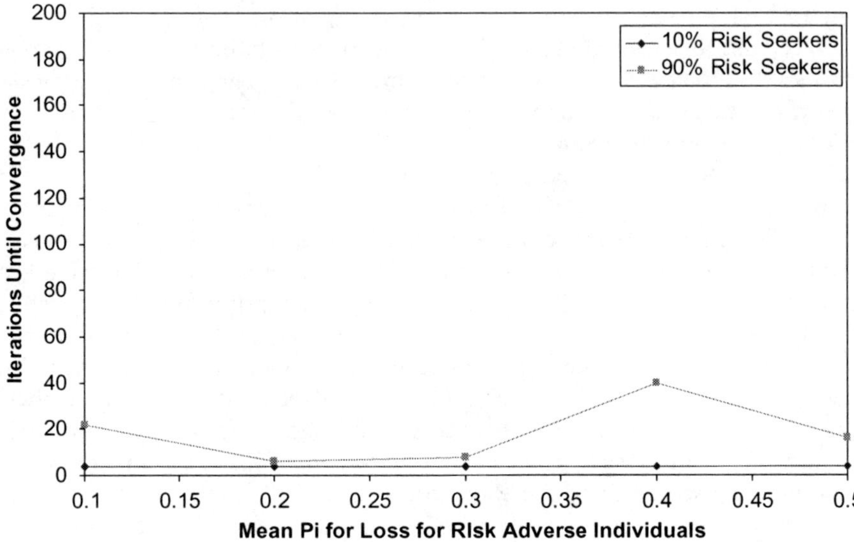

Figure 5

Number of Iterations until Convergence as the Mean π^{loss} Increases for Different Percentages of Risk Seekers in the Population: Belief Learning Experiments

towards routes with huge variances, relative to risk avoiders, thus reducing their perceptions of travel time uncertainty at a greater rate compared to risk avoiders.

The results for belief learning (Figure 5) show that although a system with a low percentage of risk seekers has a greater propensity towards convergence than one with a high percentage of risk seekers, the difference in propensities is less relative to the results from a Bayesian learning rule. Under belief learning, perceived travel times are updated using averaged travel times across all users choosing the same route. Thus, the effects of travel time fluctuations or variation across users are reduced, leading to similar travel time perceptions across all users of a particular route, all else being equal, leading to a greater propensity towards convergence, compared to systems where individuals are perceiving different travel times.

Initial Perceived Variance (β) and Risk

The parameter β indicates the initial dispersion of the perceived travel times. Thus, a higher β indicates greater initial perceived variance in the travel times (low confidence). The number of iterations until convergence for different percentages of risk seekers in the population and different values of initial perceived travel time variance are

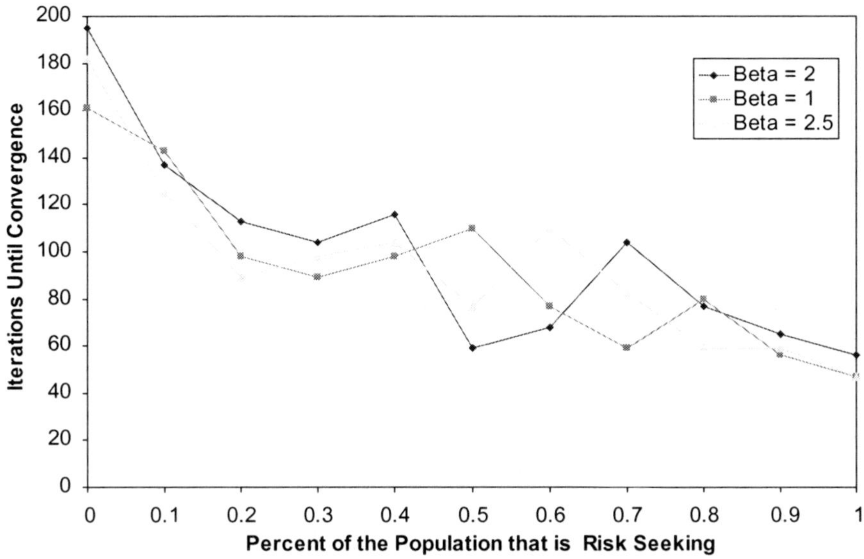

Figure 6

Number of Iterations until Convergence as the Number of Risk-Seeking Individuals in the Population Increases for Different Initial Perceived Variances (β): Bayesian Learning

presented in Figures 6 and 7 for different initial values (β) for perceived travel time uncertainty. The initial perceived dispersion (variance) of travel times seems to have no effect on convergence under Bayesian and belief learning. This departs from previous studies that show that if the initial perceived variance is too low (low β), the system has a lower propensity towards converging since additional learning has marginal effects on the perceived variance (Chen and Mahmassani, 2004). One plausible explanation for this difference is that risk attitudes are explicitly considered in this study. Some users may be very risk seeking, thus switching routes for any small probability of a travel time gain. Thus, a low perceived variance may not have a pronounced effect since some risk-seeking individuals would be switching regardless.

Also note that a low percentage of risk seekers does not necessarily indicate the absence of extreme risk-seeking behaviours (high π^{loss}), since the values are drawn from a normal distribution. Thus, for any percentage of risk-seeking users there would be users with a high degree of risk-seeking behaviour (high π^{loss}).

Finally, under Bayesian learning, as the percentage of users who are risk-seeking increases, convergence appears easier to obtain. Also, convergence is easier to obtain under belief learning compared to Bayesian learning overall. These results are consistent with those observed in Figures 4 and 5. The effects of varying initial

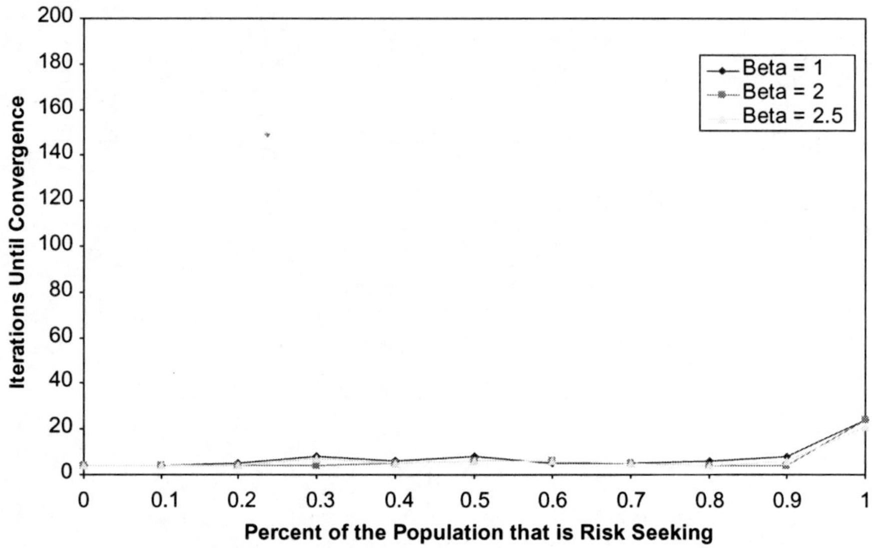

Figure 7

Number of Iterations until Convergence as the Number of Risk-Seeking Individuals in the Population Increases for Different Initial Perceived Variances (*β*): Belief Learning

perceived travel time variance may be reduced due to the presence of risk-seeking (and risk-avoiding) users in the system that may switch routes or stay despite small probabilities of gains or losses.

Reference Travel Time

Finally, the effects of changing the reference point travel time on convergence were examined (equations 13–15). These results show that as users place more weight on updated travel times, the propensity towards convergence increases, compared to users who place more weight on recently experienced travel times. These results are shown in Figure 8.

The results show that under Bayesian learning, as the number of risk seekers in the population increases, convergence is more difficult to obtain in general, similar to other results obtained in this study. Risk seekers may exhibit greater switching, relative to risk avoiders, and leading to a greater spread from iteration to iteration, resulting in higher propensity towards convergence. Additionally, as the experienced travel time is weighed more than the perceived travel time, convergence is more difficult to obtain. Also, as users choose (sample) the same route more frequently from day-to-day, their confidence in the perceived travel time for that route increases (variance decreases), and thus future experiences will have less impact.

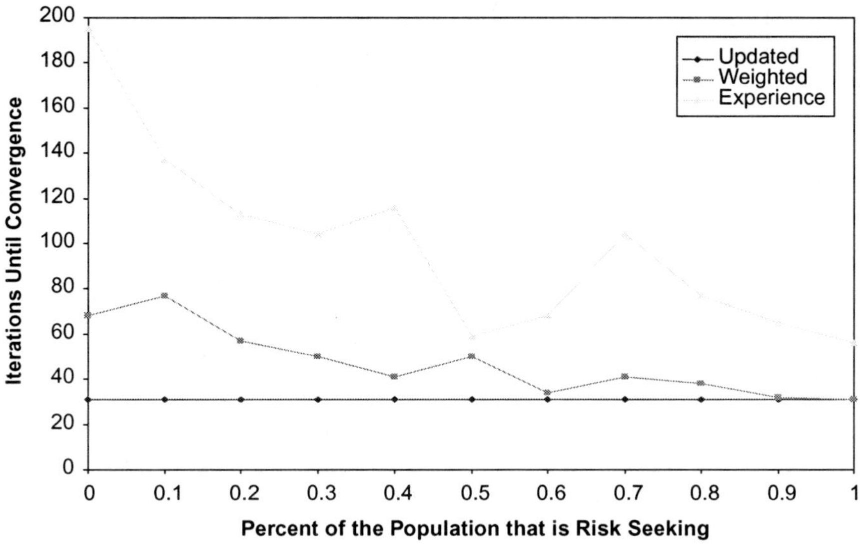

Figure 8

Number of Iterations until Convergence as the Percentage of Risk Seekers Increases for Different Types of Perceived Travel Time: Bayesian Learning

Conclusions

This study examines the role of risk attitudes and individual perceptions of travel time on the day-to-day behaviour of traffic flows. In this study a PT-type decision-making framework is used to examine the role of risk attitudes and travel time uncertainty on day-to-day network flows. Additionally, three learning types are considered: (i) reinforcement; (ii) belief and (iii) Bayesian. These learning and risk mechanisms are modelled and embedded inside a microscopic (agent-based) simulation framework to study their collective effects on the day-to-day behaviour of traffic flows. We also examined the role of risk seekers in driving system-wide properties of traffic networks over time.

The results show that explicitly considering risk attitudes and their effect on an individual's perception of uncertainty does influence the convergence of traffic flows in a network. Additionally, in the case of belief learning, they also affect the spread of individuals across routes at convergence. Risk attitudes affect route choice decisions by influencing how individuals perceive uncertainty and how uncertainty relates to route travel times experienced in the decision-making process. Additionally, the results show that the percentage of risk seekers in the population affects the rate of convergence, possibly by affecting the rate of sampling taken by individuals and by adding variability in travel times for individuals who are not risk seeking. Additionally, for Bayesian learning, any mechanism that affects the rate of sampling will affect the rate of convergence. Convergence under Bayesian learning is a function of both the perceived travel times and the perceived dispersion of these travel times.

Reinforcement learning describes how travel times experienced are integrated, but does not explicitly say anything about how uncertainty changes over time. There is no assumption in reinforcement learning that individuals perceive less dispersion in travel times as more experiences are gained. Thus, unlike a system with Bayesian learners, convergence is more difficult to achieve. Although belief learning faces the same issue, since it considers experiences of all users, this may serve to lead a system to faster convergence compared to reinforcement learning.

Finally, results show that there are system-wide properties that are common to all cases, regardless of learning rule or the explicit consideration of risk attitudes. First, as demand levels increase, convergence is more difficult to achieve. Second, as individuals weigh their perceived updated travel time more, less switching among routes occurs and individuals choose a particular route more consistently.

References

Ariely, D. and Z. Camron (2000). Gestalt characteristics of experiences: the defining features of summarized events. *Journal of Behavioral Decision Making* 13(2), 191–201.

Avineri, E. and J. N. Prashker (2003). Sensitivity to uncertainty: the need for a paradigm shift. *Transportation Research Record* 1854, 90–98.

Avineri, E. and J. N. Prashker (2005). Sensitivity to travel time variability. *Transportation Research Part C* 13, 157–183.

Battalio, R., L. Samuelson and J. van Huyck (2001). Optimization incentives and coordination failure in laboratory stag hunt games. *Econometrica* 69, 749–764.

Ben-Akiva, M., A. De Palma and I. Kaysi (1991). Dynamic network models and driver information systems. *Transportation Research* 25A(5), 251–266.

Bernoulli, D. (1738). Exposition of a new theory on the measurement of risk. *Econometrica* 22(1), 23–36. Translated by Sommer L. (1954).

Camerer, C., T. Ho and K. Chong (2002). Sophisticated experienced-weighted attraction learning and strategic teaching in repeated games. *Journal of Economic Theory* 104, 137–188.

Camerer, C. F. (2003). *Behavioral Game Theory*. Princeton, New Jersey, Princeton University Press.

Chancelier, J.-P., M. de Lara and A. de Palma (2007). Road choice and the one armed bandit. *Transportation Science* 41(1), 1–14.

Chen, R. B. and H. S. Mahmassani (2004). Learning and travel time perception in traffic networks. *Transportation Research Record* 1894, 209–221.

Crawford, V. P. (1995). Adaptive dynamics in coordination games. *Econometrica* 63(1), 103–143.

DeGroot, M. (1970). *Optimal Statistical Decisions*. USA, McGraw-Hill.

de Palma, A. and N. Picard (2005). Route choice under travel time uncertainty. *Transportation Research Part A* 39, 295–324.

Duda, R., P. Hart and D. Stork (2001). *Pattern Classification*. New York, Wiley Science.

Einhorn, H. and R. Hogarth (1981). Behavioral decision theory: processes of judgment and choice. *Annals of Psychology* 32, 53–88.

Erev, I., Y. Bereby-Meyer and A. Roth (1999). The effect of adding a constant to all payoffs: experimental investigation, and implications for reinforcement learning models. *Journal of Economic Behavior and Organization* 39(1), 111–128.

Fudenberg, D. and D. Levine (1998). *The Theory of Learning in Games*. Cambridge, MA, MIT Press.

Helbing, D., M. Schonhof and H.-U. Stark (2005). How individuals learn to take turns: emergence of alternating cooperation in a congestion game and the prisoner's dilemma. *Advances in Complex Systems* 8, 87–116.

Ho, T. and K. Wiegelt (1996). Task complexity, equilibrium selection, and learning: an experimental study. *Management Science* 42, 659–679.

Horowitz, J. L. (1984). The stability of stochastic equilibrium in a two-link transportation network. *Transportation Research* 18B(1), 13–28.

Hu, T.-Y. and H. S. Mahmassani (1995). Evolution of network flows under real-time information: a day-to-day simulation assignment framework. *Transportation Research Record* 1493, 46–56.

Jha, M., S. Madanat and S. Peeta (1998). Perception updating and day-to-day travel choice dynamics in traffic networks with information provision. *Transportation Research* 6C(3), 189–212.

Kahneman, D. and A. Tversky (1979). Prospect theory: an analysis of decision under risk. *Econometrica* 47(2), 263–292.

Kahneman, D. and A. Tversky (1982). Advances in prospect theory: cumulative representation of uncertainty. *Journal of Risk and Uncertainty* 5, 297–323.

Kaysi, I. (1991). Framework and models for provision of driver information system, PhD. Thesis, Department of Civil Engineering, Massachusetts Institute of Technology, Cambridge, MA.

Mahmassani, H. S. (1990). Dynamic models of commuter behavior: experimental investigation and application to the analysis of planned traffic disruptions. *Transportation Research Part A* 24, 465–484.

Mahmassani, H. S. and G.-L. Chang (1988). Travel time prediction and departure time adjustment behaviour dynamics in a congested traffic system. *Transportation Research B* 22B(3), 217–232.

Mahmassani, H. S. and R. Jayakrishnan (1991). System performance and user response under real-time information in a congested traffic corridor. *Transportation Research A* 25A(5), 293–308.

Mahmassani, H. S. and Y.-H. Liu (1999). Dynamics of commuting decision behaviour under advanced traveler information systems. *Transportation Research C* 7, 91–107.

Mahmassani, H. S. and K. K. Srinivasan (2004). Experiments with route and departure time choices of commuters under real-time information: heuristics and adjustment processes (Chapter 4). In M. Schreckenburg and R. Selten (Eds.), *Human Behavior and Traffic Networks*. Berlin, Germany, Springer-Verlag.

Mitchell, T. M. (1997). *Machine Learning*. USA, McGraw Hill.

Nakayama, S., R. Kitamura and S. Fujii (1999). Drivers' learning and network behavior: a systematic analysis of the driver-network system as a complex system. *Transportation Research Record* 1493, 30–36.

Payne, J. W., D. J. Laughhunn and R. Crum (1981). Aspiration level effects in risk behavior. *Management Science* 27, 953–958.

Roth, A. and I. Erev (1993). Learning in extensive-form games: experimental data and simple dynamic models in the intermediate term. *Games and Economic Behavior* 8, 164–212.

Srinivasan, K. K. and H. S. Mahmassani (2000). Modeling inertia and compliance mechanisms in route choice behavior under real-time information. *Transportation Research Record* 1725, 45–53.

Tong, C.-C., H. S. Mahmassani and G.-L. Chang (1987). Travel time prediction and information availability in commuter behaviour dynamics. *Transportation Research Record* 1138, 1–7.

Tversky, A. and C. Fox (1995). Weighing risk and uncertainty. *Psychological Review* 102(2), 269–283.

Van Huyck, J., R. Battalio and R. Beil (1991). Strategic uncertainty, equilibrium, selection, and coordination failure in average opinion games. *Quarterly Journal of Economics* 106, 885–909.

von Neumann, J. and O. Morgenstern (1947). *Theory of Games and Economic Behavior*, 2nd edn. Princeton, NJ, Princeton University Press.

Wallsten, T., T. J. Pleskac and C. Lejuez (2006). Modeling behavior in a clinically diagnostic sequential risk-taking task. *Psychological Review* 112(4), 862–880.

Wehrung, D. A. (1989). Risk taking over gains and losses: a study of oil executives. *Annals of Operations Research* 19, 115–139.

Weibull, J. (1995). *Evolutionary Game Theory*. Cambridge, MA, MIT Press.

The Expanding Sphere of Travel Behaviour Research
Selected Papers from the 11th International Conference on Travel Behaviour Research

37

Stress Triggered Household Decision to Change Dwelling: A Comprehensive and Dynamic Approach

Khandker M. Nurul Habib, Eric J. Miller and Ilan Elgar

Abstract

This paper presents models for residential mobility decisions. The models use the dynamic concept of residential stress and comprehensively model three decisions: dwelling duration, the reason of changing dwelling and tenure change. Latent residential stresses are addressed to model dwelling duration. Two alternative modelling frameworks are proposed. The first framework has two components: the first component uses a parametric competing risk hazard model for dwelling duration and the reason of change simultaneously. This component is followed by a heteroskedastic probit model for tenure change decision. The second framework has three components: the first component considers all stress events as a single general stress event. This component is followed by a multinomial logit model for reason of change and a heteroskedastic probit model for tenure change decision. Second framework is designed to overcome some basic limitations of competing risk hazard model. The logit model in second framework considers the probability of terminating the event of a particular stressor as a function of event duration only, but the effect of the duration is derived from a parametric function of various socio-economic and spatial variables. As for the prototype application, both of the proposed modelling frameworks are estimated using data from a retrospective survey of household spatial search behaviour conducted in the Greater Toronto Area (GTA) in 1998. The prototype estimation results give behavioural insights and better understanding of residential mobility processes. The proposed models are designed to fit within the Integrated Land Use Transportation and Environment (ILUTE) modelling framework.

Introduction

The paper presents econometric and microsimulation-based modelling frameworks for urban residential mobility decisions. The decision outcomes of the models are the *dwelling duration*, the *reason of changing dwelling* and *tenure change*. The models are intended to implement within the Integrated Land Use Transportation and Environment (ILUTE) modelling system as described by Salvini and Miller (2005). These models are an alternative proposal for the first step (mobility decisions) of the three-step process of modelling residential mobility in the sub-model: *Housing Market* of the ILUTE framework. The other two steps are search processes and bid formation. The models proposed in this paper extend the general concept of *stress* in the ILUTE framework to the specific residential *stress* as originally proposed by Rossi (1955). The proposed models handle the three correlated decisions regarding residential mobility in a comprehensive way. Central to the models is the assumption of multiple stress events playing throughout the life cycle of all households in the urban area. Models are designed to accommodate the existence of multiple stress events and their competition to terminate the dwelling duration in a particular location. The dynamic propagation of the stress events triggered by multiple stressors is recognized explicitly.

Two alternative modelling structures are proposed. These are presented in Figures 1 and 2. Empirical estimation of the proposed models is done by using retrospective survey data of household spatial search behaviour collected in the Greater Toronto Area (GTA) in 1998. In addition to microsimulating the behavioural process of residential mobility, the models concentrate on providing necessary input to the residential location choice model. It is conceivable that the mobility decision together with the reason of moving reduces the choice set of the residential location choice models considerably. With a smaller choice set, the location choice model can perform better and incorporate various temporal and spatial autocorrelations in very tractable ways. At the same time, the incorporation of the concept of stress allows the housing market sub-module of ILUTE to have better and meaningful integration with other components. As the stresses mentioned in this paper are originally derived from other elements of urban socio-economic and demographic systems, this effort enhances the comprehensiveness in modelling urban evolution.

The paper is organized as follows: section 'Background and Context' describes the necessary background and context, section 'Concept of Stress in Residential Mobility' discusses the key assumptions and definitions, section 'Proposed Modelling Structures' presents two proposed modelling frameworks, section 'Data for Empirical Application' describes the data used to estimate the proposed models and section 'Discussion on Estimated Parameters' discusses the results of empirical estimations. The paper ends with conclusions and direction to some future research

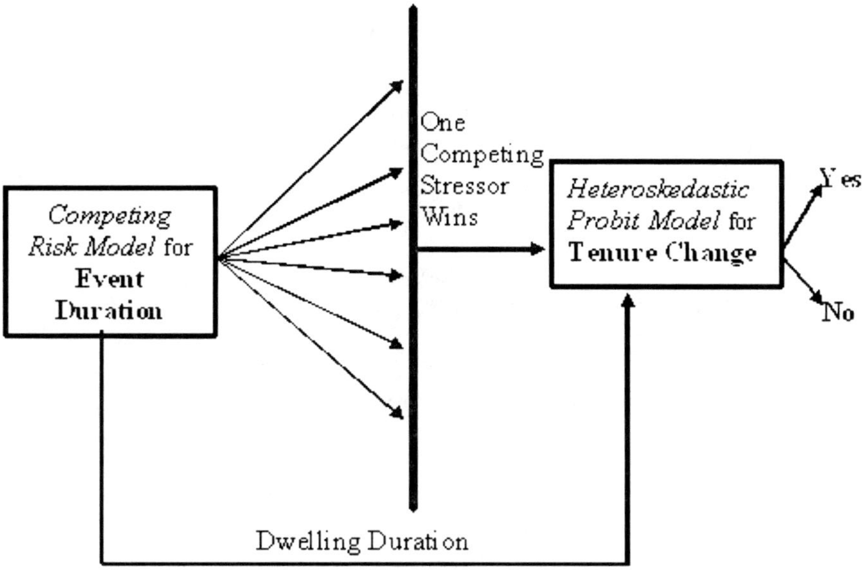

Figure 1
The First Proposed Specification

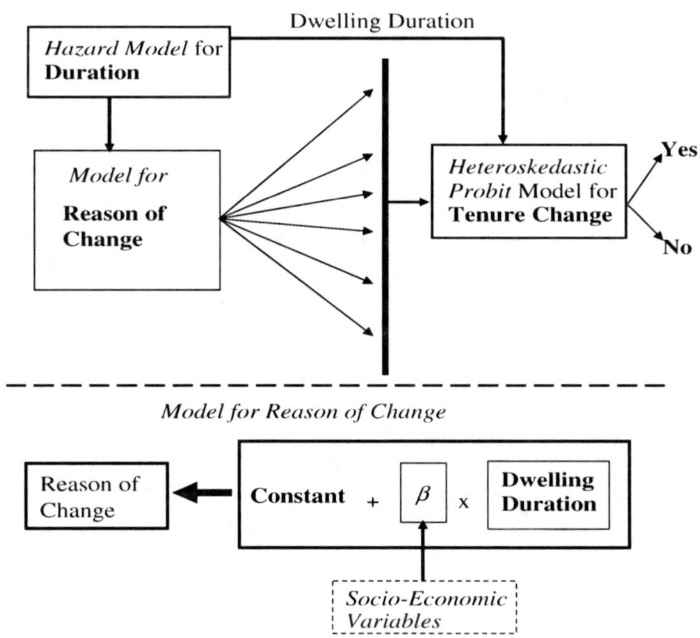

Figure 2
The Second Proposed Specification

Background and Context

Residential mobility decisions are some of the major household-based decisions that are directly or indirectly responsible for urban spatial evolution (Ommeren et al., 1999; Pinto, 2002; Lin and Long, 2006). In particular, the movement of people within urban space is very much influenced by these residential mobility decisions (Meurs and Haaijer, 2001). For these reasons, the capability to model household mobility decisions is recognized as having great potential for improving the forecasting capability of travel demand models (Hollingworth and Miller, 1996). The integrated land use and transportation models do one step further; they integrate both travel demand and residential mobility within an integrated urban framework, for example ILUTE (Salvini and Miller, 2005), ILUMASS (Strauch et al., 2003), UrbanSim (Waddell and Ulfarsson, 2004), etc. The motivation of all integrated models is to entangle the intra-urban sub-modules with different scales of decision dynamics within an integrated framework, so that the interactions among the sub-modules can be structured specifically to ensure the multidirectional interactions and feedback among the sub-modules. These integrated models use microsimulation techniques to model the urban evolution. Microsimulating the urban evolution requires following the time-steps longitudinally. Typically, a yearly time step is used to model the annual process of urban evolution (Waddell, 2002).

It is very important to distinguish the dynamics of the sub-modules and the simulation time step. Different sub-modules, for example residential mobility, auto-ownership, travel demand, etc. may have different behavioural dynamics. To ensure that individual sub-module dynamics are sufficiently modelled, a longitudinal approach within the sub-modules is necessary as opposed to cross-sectional approaches. The longitudinal simulation time step does not necessarily follow the longitudinal urban evolution pattern unless individual sub-modules are considered longitudinal mathematically. To ensure these behavioural dimensions, the ILUTE framework is designed to be an integrated full feedback model where different sub-modules are allowed to have their own dynamics, but higher-level decisions (residential mobility) influence lower-level decisions (such as travel behaviour) and vice versa. So, to conform to this architecture of ILUTE, the sub-modules should also be sufficiently comprehensive and entangle the dynamics of the sub-systems. In such an approach, modelling residential mobility decisions poses a considerable challenge.

Modelling residential mobility decisions can be divided broadly into two types: the cross-sectional approach and the longitudinal approach. The cross-sectional approach (e.g. Borsch-Supan and Pitkin, 1988) concentrates on a particular cross-section of time and models decisions based on the recent mover, thus introduces non-random elements (Henderson and Ioannides, 1987). Such a cross-sectional approach also does not allow exploring properly time-dependent mobility decisions, which are clearly long term (Hollingworth and Miller, 1996). On the other hand, the longitudinal approach refers to approaches that track changes the conditions leading to the particular decisions over time. Various mathematical models can be perceived in such cases and event history analysis is one of them. Event history analysis is inherently dynamic as it tracks the particular event that occurs periodically over time. It conforms to the idea proposed by Scheiner (2006) that residential mobility is not a discrete and cross-sectional decision per se, rather there is some process at work.

Pickles and Davis (1991) first introduced the concept of using event history analysis in a hazard model of residential mobility decisions. Since then the application of hazard models to residential mobility is very common in the literature. Chan (1996); Hollingworth and Miller (1996); van der Vlist et al. (2002); Clark and Huang (2003); Li (2004), etc. all use the hazard modelling approach to model dwelling duration and thereby mobility decisions. Some authors (e.g. Ommeren et al., 1999) extended the univariate hazard model to bivariate hazard model for modelling residential and job mobility decisions together. All of these papers consider the household in a particular dwelling place as an event itself. Various covariates including time-dependent variables are incorporated to model their effect on terminating the dwelling event. However, this household or dwelling event is a derived event that follows the course of underlying psychological inertia of changing places of the members of the household. Sarjeant (1986) argues for the continuous interaction of the household and the environment that creates behavioural inertia (static or dynamic) and influences the household to change or stay in a particular location. To introduce this behavioural issue and thereby add a new dimension to the existing literature, this paper incorporates the concept of residential or household stress that triggers households to change dwelling. The next section discusses the issue of stress in greater detail.

Concept of Stress in Residential Mobility

The concept of stress is mainly derived from the seminal book of Rossi (1955), where he argues that the life cycle factors are major triggers for household relocation decisions. Since then, the stress has been considered a variable that influences dwelling durations and other residential mobility decisions (see Clark and Huang, 2003). In general, stress is defined as the psychological pressure to adjust the current situation. Death and birth of a household member, marriage, job change, income change and many other life cycle factors create such stress. Such stress arises when current position deviates from some alternative desired/expected/optimal state (Miller, 2005). But this psychological dimension of stress requires that stress is continuous or cumulative in nature (Huff and Clark, 1977). Although some of the triggering factors like death, birth, job change, etc. occur at specific points of time, the stress corresponding to these factors is longitudinal (Clark, 1992).

This notion of the continuous nature of stress is also consistent with the psychological explanation that we are not always able to act at the margin. Also in many situations, we are not able to continuously adjust so as to maintain at an optimum state because of incomplete information availability, our limitations in absorbing information, the psychological and monetary cost involved in transactions and many other factors (Miller, 2005). In such situations, stresses work as continuous endogenous psychological traits that build up gradually and lead to the termination of the present situation (e.g. dwelling location) at some discrete point in time. So, residential stress can be an explanatory variable for other modules of an integrated land use and transportation model (see Miller, 2005), but in the case of residential mobility, this stress itself is the psychological process and warranted to be recognized explicitly in the modelling framework. Thus, the stresses act as the reasons for moving from the current location.

These reasons for moving from the current location are often mentioned as "push" factors in residential mobility modelling. On the other hand, the factors that attract people to specific locations are referred to "pull" factors. In the case of long-term decisions like residential mobility, such push and pull factors are not always the same (see Clark and Onaka, 1983). As mentioned before, the ILUTE architecture for residential mobility sub-module is divided into three parts. This paper deals with the first part: decision and cause of moving (the push factor). The matching of the push and pull factors is performed in the other two parts of the process, which are not addressed in this paper: spatial search and bid formation.

The adoption of the stress concept in modelling residential mobility allows us to model the underlying behavioural process of household decisions regarding housing change. The assumption of stresses as individual events as opposed to the dwelling event allows investigating prospective mobility due to various changes in socio-economic conditions. In this paper, we considered various factors that are representative of individual stress types and termed as stressors. The next sub-section discusses these issues more specifically.

Key Assumptions and Definitions

Complying with Salvini and Miller (2005), we use the term stressor to avoid confusion in common use of the term stress. Here *stressor* refers to something that causes stress. The assumption is that multiple stressors are continuously active in our life. The origin of the stressor events is the starting of the household at a particular location. Once the household moves to a new dwelling, all stressor events start from the origin again. The duration of the household at the particular location is basically defined by the duration of the responsible stressor event. At any specific point of time (at the simulation time step), all the stressors present a composite risk set with some probability of termination. Thus, individual stressors work as competing risks throughout the life cycle of occupation of a given dwelling unit. The tenure change decision follows the termination of the stressor event and depends on the total duration of the event, stressor type causing the termination and many other socio-economic factors. The tenure change decision is considered as a binary decision, where the household decides whether to change from owner to renter or *vice versa*. These assumptions are based both on behavioural and mathematical tractability considerations. Based on these assumptions, the next section describes two alternative modelling frameworks and details mathematical formulations.

Proposed Modelling Structures

Based on the concept of stress, two proposed modelling frameworks are presented here. The first model uses a competing risk hazard model to determine the dwelling duration and the stressor that causes the termination of the duration simultaneously. This is presented schematically in Figure 1. Given the dwelling duration and the cause of termination, a heteroskedastic probit model determines the decision to change tenure. In the competing risk hazard model, the individual stressors are considered to be independent. The independent stressor events propagate with time and the termination of the dwelling duration is caused by only one stressor. While termination is caused by one stressor type, the other stressor events remain right censored. That means although multiple stressor events are active throughout the life, we only observe the one transition that occurs first. The time representation in competing risk model is considered continuous. The continuous time, event-driven model allows us to simulate event history for each micro unit (Lancaster, 1990). Such a model assumes a random process that generates the stressor events with the probability density for experiencing the events depending on a set of explanatory variables.

However, in terms of application, the competing risk approach does not allow us to investigate probability of a termination by all individual stressors individually; hence application in microsimulation might be problematic. So, as an alternative to the competing risk model, the second specification proposes a two-step procedure of estimating the dwelling duration and the cause of termination. The schematic diagram of this specification is presented in Figure 2. The first stage is a continuous time hazard model representing all stressor events together as a general stressor event followed by a multinomial logit model to determine the probability set of terminating stressors.

To comply with the basic process of comparable competing risk approach, the logit model used in this paper has a hierarchical parameter structure to ensure that the termination cause is purely duration dependent but the effect of duration on the termination cause is determined by some variables. As opposed to a simple multinomial logit model, this model creates a sequential structure where the same covariates define the duration of stress event and also the effect of duration on the termination cause. The idea is that the household has been under stresses due to a number of stressor types throughout time. The termination of stress events is observed as the dwelling duration and the cause of termination is the end realization. The dwelling duration and the termination cause are directly related to each other and the various covariates influence a particular cause to be the dominating factor of termination. So, firstly, the termination cause is assumed to be a function of duration, but the effect of duration on specific termination cause is determined by household socio-economic structure.

Mathematically, the combined estimation of hazard model and the logit model results in a competing risk type modelling approach, but such combined estimation will also incur considerable computation burden. The two-step assumption simplifies the mathematical formulation but conceptually conforms to the competing risk type structure. Such complex modelling structure is sometimes inevitable in case of complex situations where the same household variables influence different levels of decisions in different ways (Molin and Timmermans, 2003). Thus, the first specification gives the dwelling duration and the name of the stressor that causes the termination of the dwelling duration, whereas the second specification gives the dwelling duration and a probability set of all competing stressors. Both of the specifications are estimated using empirical survey data. The next sub-sections discuss the mathematical issues of the individual modelling components.

In both the specifications described above, the tenure change model is same and is considered as a heteroskedastic probit model. The tenure change decision depends on many factors including durations and the causes of changing dwelling. Considerable heterogeneity exists in tenure decisions across the population. Although a binomial logit model may work well in such a case, the maximum likelihood estimates are inconsistent when heteroskedasticity is present across the population (Greene, 2002). Such inconsistency can be addressed by directly taking into account the heterogeneity of the process under study (Alvarez and Brehm, 1995). Specially, in our case, when we are modelling three residential mobility decisions, it is better to consider the heterogeneity in the individual components.

Hazard Model and Competing Risk Model

The theory of hazard modelling is well developed in the literature, with applications in a variety of areas. Keifer (1988), Lancaster (1990), Kalbfleisch and Prentice (2002) all describe the basic theories of hazard models. Here, the duration of the event T is considered as a positive, continuous and random variable. The probability that the episode terminates within a time interval dt conditional upon survival up to the time t is $\Pr(t \leq T \leq t+dt | T \geq t)$. The average probability per unit of time for terminating the episode duration is then called the hazard rate. Considering the time interval dt is very small, and $\mathbf{x}$ is a vector of covariates, the hazard function of the duration $\lambda(t)$

can be expressed as

$$\lambda(t, x) = \lim_{dt \to 0} \frac{\Pr(t \leq T \leq t + dt | T \geq t, x)}{dt} \tag{1}$$

If the cumulative distribution function of duration is $F(t) = \Pr(T \leq t)$ and the survival function is $S(t) = \Pr(T \geq t) = 1 - F(t)$, the hazard function can be expressed as

$$\lambda(t, x) = \frac{f(t, x)}{S(t, x)} = \frac{-\partial[\log(1 - F(T, x))]}{dt}$$
$$f(t, x) = \lambda(t, x) S(t, x) \tag{2}$$

Based on these principle relationships, three general types of hazard model can be developed: non-parametric, semi-parametric and parametric hazard model. The detailed comparison of these three major hazard model types is available in Habib and Miller (2005). In this paper, we use the parametric approach with accelerated failure time assumption (the time scale is expressed as a direct function of covariates) for both hazard and competing risk models. The parametric hazard models assume a distribution for the baseline hazard rate and the parameters are estimated by using the full information likelihood method. The unobserved heterogeneity of these accelerated time models can be considered using a multiplicative form:

$$\lambda(t, x) = \alpha \lambda(t, x) \tag{3}$$

Here α is any positive distribution. Typically, a gamma or an inverse Gaussian distribution with mean value 1 and variance θ gives a closed form likelihood function. But consideration of heterogeneity in competing risk models is very difficult, where multiple events are modelled together. In the case of competing risk analyses, the number of events is more than 1. Considering J events, according to the law of total probability,

$$\lambda(x, t) = \sum_{j=1}^{J} \lambda_j(t, x) \tag{4}$$

The assumptions that the individual events are independent of each other, the overall termination of life occurs for only one cause, whichever one comes first. Suppose that N observations exist with four variables (t_i, d_i, j_i, x_i) for each observation i, where t_i is the observed failure time, d_i the dummy variable indicating right censoring, j_i the cause of failure and x_i a vector of covariates. For a single hazard model, the likelihood function becomes

$$L = \prod_{i=1}^{N} \lambda_{ji}(t_i, x_i)^{d_i} S(t_i, x_i) \tag{5}$$

The likelihood function indicates that the observations which are right censored at an observed time contribute the probability of being alive at that time in $S(t_i, x_i)$ only, but the observations which terminate for a cause j at the observed time contribute by $\lambda_{ij}(t_i, x_i)\, S(t_i, x_i)$. Now if we consider J distinct type of causes then the overall likelihood function becomes

$$L = \prod_{i=1}^{N} \prod_{j=1}^{J} \lambda_{ji}(t_i, x_i)^{d_i} S(t_i, x_i) \tag{6}$$

This implies that if an observation is due to cause j, it is right censored for all other $(J-j)$ causes. For any observation, the competing risk model defines a set of latent failure times $(T_1, T_2, T_3, \ldots\ T_J)$. But what is observed is the realization of one T which is for the cause j for which T is minimum within the set $\{T_1, T_2, T_3, \ldots\ T_J\}$. So mathematically, we can define the hazard rate or survival rate of the one cause, which causes failure, but the rest are not individually identifiable. Various types of hazard model specifications are possible (for details, see Kalbfleisch and Prentice, 2002). In this paper, we consider parameterization of the baseline hazard rate using cause-specific dummy variables. The goodness of fit statistic for hazard model and competing risk model is pseudo R-square, which indicates 1 minus the ratio of log likelihood of the full model to the log likelihood of the null mode (the constant-only model).

Logit Model for Reason of Change

The model as used in this paper has the following form:

$$\begin{aligned} P(j) &= \beta_0 + \beta'(\text{Duration}) + \varepsilon \\ \beta_0 &= \gamma_0 + \varepsilon' \\ \beta' &= \gamma' + x'\beta'' \end{aligned} \tag{7}$$

where $P(j)$ represents the probability of termination of duration by the cause j; x' a vector of covariates; γ_0, γ', β_0 and β'' the parameters to be estimated; ε and ε' the random variables. Here, ε is assumed as IID type I extreme value distribution and ε' is assumed as multivariate normal distribution with zero mean and non-zero standard deviation. If we consider total $(j = 1, 2, 3, \ldots, J)$ alternatives, in general, the probability functions can be written as

$$\begin{aligned} P(1) &= \varphi((x\beta)_1) \\ P(2) &= \varphi((x\beta)_2) \\ P(3) &= \varphi((x\beta)_3) \\ &\vdots \\ P(J) &= 1 - \varphi((x\beta)_1) - \varphi((x\beta)_2) - \ldots - \varphi((x\beta)_{J-1}) \end{aligned} \tag{8}$$

Equivalently this can be written as

$$g(P(j)) = (x\beta) \tag{9}$$

where $g(\cdot)$ is an inverse function of $\varphi(\cdot)$ and $(x\beta)$ is its linear predictor. This inverse function is usually referred as the *link* function that maps the mean value of the response to the linear predictors. The link function represents the conditional expectation of the observed outcome given the explanatory variables. In our case this link function is a *logit* link function, η, which indicates that the log-odds of falling into the jth category relative to falling into Jth category (considering Jth category as reference category).

$$g(P(j)) = \log\left(\frac{\varphi((x\beta)_j)}{\varphi((x\beta)_J)}\right) \tag{10}$$

Conceptually, the link function connects the linear predictors with the outcome variable (multinomial choice probability), but the linear predictor contains the multivariate normal error term $\varepsilon' \sim N(0, \sigma^2)$, where σ^2 is the variance term of the random variable. Having these random error terms, the likelihood function of the logit model becomes a multiple integral function and for that reason the full information likelihood estimation incurs considerable computational burden.

To overcome these issues, several estimation procedures are proposed in the existing literature. Detailed descriptions of such algorithms are available in McCullagh and Nelder (1989) and Raundenbush and Bryk (2002). In this paper we used the Panelized Quasi Likelihood (PQL) method (Breslow and Clayton, 1993). The PQL method uses joint posterior modes of coefficients (to be estimated) given the variance–covariance matrix. The variance–covariance matrix is estimated using a normal approximation to the restricted likelihood. The model used in this paper is estimated by the software HLM6 (Raundenbush et al., 2006). However, the test for statistical fitness of such hierarchical models is not easy. The Wald test is not fully justified because the null value is on the border of parameter space. On the other hand, for likelihood ratio test, the test statistics no longer have the conventional chi-square distribution under the null hypothesis (Habib and Miller, 2006). The approximate log likelihood values calculated by PQL method can be used to get a reasonable idea of goodness of fit, with this measure being basically a pseudo-likelihood ratio test.

Heteroskedastic Probit Model

The heteroskedastic probit model for tenure change assumes a utility function, U_i, for changing tenure as a latent variable for the individual household i:

$$U = (x_i\beta) + \varepsilon_i \tag{11}$$

Here, x_i indicates a vector of socio-economic variables of the individual household i, β the corresponding parameters and ε_i the unobserved random error term. The observed choice of tenure change is y_i which is a dichotomous variable based on the latent utility function. That is

$$y_i = \begin{cases} 1 & \text{if } U_i > 0 \\ 0 & \text{if } U_i \leq 0 \end{cases} \tag{12}$$

In the heteroskedastic probit model case, the distribution of ε is assumed as univariate normal distribution with mean zero.

$$\begin{aligned} E[\varepsilon_i] &= 0 \\ V[\varepsilon_i] &= \sigma_i^2 = [\exp(z_i\gamma)]^2 \end{aligned} \tag{13}$$

Here, z_i indicates a vector of variables and γ the corresponding parameters. So the probability of changing tenure by the household i is

$$P(y_i = 1) = P(\varepsilon_i > -(x_i\beta)) = 1 - \Phi\left(\frac{-(x_i\beta)}{\exp(z_i\gamma)}\right) = \Phi\left(\frac{(x_i\beta)}{\exp(z_i\gamma)}\right) \tag{14}$$

The log likelihood function of the model becomes

$$\text{Log } L = \sum_i \left(y_i \log \Phi\left(\frac{(x_i\beta)}{\exp(z_i\gamma)}\right) - (1 - y_i) \log\left[1 - \Phi\left(\frac{(x_i\beta)}{\exp(z_i\gamma)}\right)\right]\right) \tag{15}$$

The estimation procedure of the above log likelihood function is available in Corneliben (2005). The goodness of fit statistic for the model is rho-square, where rho-square indicates 1 minus the ratio of log likelihood of the full model to the log likelihood of the null mode (the constant-only model).

Data for Empirical Application

The data used in this study was collected by a retrospective survey of household spatial search behaviour for a sample of 293 households in the GTA. The detail description of the survey design is available in Pushkar (1998). The survey was a mail-back revealed and stated preference survey on the sample of households who moved between 1988 and 1998 within the GTA. The survey area covered five regional municipalities: Toronto, York Region, Peel, Halton and Durham. The areas were selected considering the people who work in Toronto but live and commute from these regions. In addition to the duration and type of the last dwelling unit, a variety of socio-economic and spatial information was collected in this survey including information regarding present and past household conditions. The key parts of the survey that is one of the main concerns of this paper are the duration of dwelling at the last housing location and the reasons of changing dwelling location. The duration is calculated in terms of the total number of months, and the reasons for moving are divided into seven categories. These seven categories as mentioned by the respondents are assumed as seven types of stressors that cause continuous residential stress to change the dwelling. The stressors are:

1. *Stressor01*: The urge to change tenure, this may be renter to owner or owner to owner.
2. *Stressor02*: The pressure due to the household change for marriage/cohabitation, divorce/widowed, birth/death and other household composition change, etc.
3. *Strssor03*: The reason of affordability change, such as wanting less expensive housing or wanting to invest more in housing, etc.
4. *Stressor04*: The urge to improve accessibility, such as wanting to be closer to work place/school/college/university, closer to other activity locations, improve general accessibility, etc.
5. *Stressor05*: The urge to get an improved location, such as desire to move to a safer/desired neighbourhood/community, a better area for children or seniors, wanting to move to a more urbanized area, wanting to move to less urbanized area, etc.
6. *Strssor06*: The urge to improve housing unit, such as wanting more space (yard or units), desire to reduce unnecessary spaces, wanting a different dwelling type/privacy/yard, wanting housing unit in better condition/better layout, reasons of eviction/previous housing is no longer available, etc.
7. *Stressor07*: All other reasons, such as job transfer, good interest/mortgage rate, difficulties with previous landlord/management committee, retirement, etc.

These seven stressors are assumed to play continuously on the households from the time of initial occupation of the dwelling. In terms of variables, a variety of socio-economic, dwelling and spatial variables are considered. The variables are in general:

- Family structure: household size, composition, age and gender of the head of the household, number of children, number of adults, etc.
- Household education level in terms of number of university graduates, number of college graduates, number of high-school graduates and number of primary school students, etc.
- Household automobiles and total number of driving license holders.
- Household employment/school information: total number of full time employee, total number of part time employee, total number of unemployed people, total number of retired people, total number of employee with fixed job locations, total number of employees with flexible job location, total number of full time students and total number of part time students, etc.
- Annual household income in Canadian dollars: the income is classified into six categories: below 15,000 CAD, 15,000–29,000 CAD, 30,000–44,000 CAD, 45,000–59,000 CAD, 60,000–74,000 CAD and above 75,000 CAD.

- Tenure type (owner/renter), change of tenure, total number of rooms, total number of bedrooms, total monthly parking cost, etc.
- Location: City of Toronto (Area1), York Region (Area2), Peel Region (Area3), Halton and Durham regions (these two regions are collectively identified as Area4, due to the low number of observations in the sample).
- The number of activity locations (for work/school, shopping, entertainment, socializing) in terms of the number of regions outside the home region to which the household members need to travel.
- Stated information regarding housing satisfaction: the minimum number of bedrooms required and the maximum number of bedrooms desired.

All of these variables were considered for modelling; however, based on statistical tests and model specification considerations, we could not incorporate all of these in our models. Out of a total of 293 households only 179 households are retained after cleaning for missing and ambiguous information. The minimum observed duration is 2 months and the maximum is 520 months.

Figure 3 shows the non-parametric estimation of competing risk for the seven stressors considered in this study. The non-parametric competing risk function is estimated using the modified Kaplan–Meier estimation method proposed by Gooley et al. (1999). Here, the observed cumulative incidence function is plotted against dwelling durations.

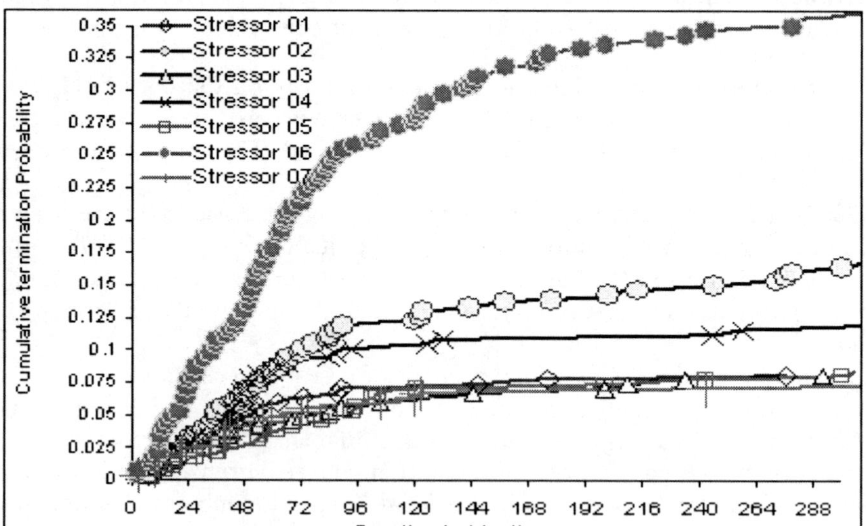

Figure 3
The Non-Parametric Competing Risk Model

The cumulative incidence function estimates the probability of failure of the dwelling duration due to the competing stresses corresponding to the seven stressors. The inherent assumption of this estimation method is that every dwelling duration is equally likely to be failed by any of the seven stressors. The termination occurs for one of the seven competing risks posed by seven stressors. The figure reveals that for the short term (0–24 months), all stressors compete equally, but for the long term, stressor 06 dominates. Stressor 06 represents urges to obtain more space, privacy, moving to a suburban area or coming to urban area from the suburban area, forced evictions, etc. It also indicates the increasing suburbanization of the GTA. Following stressor 06, stressor 02, representing stress due to the changes in household structure, and stressor 04, representing stress to improve accessibility, are also significantly important. On the other hand, over the longer term, the other four stressors compete almost equally with each other. This non-parametric model gives a picture of the observed sample, but we do not obtain the relationships between socio-economic and other policy variables and residential mobility decisions in this model. The parametric models as described in the next section provide more insight into the residential mobility process.

Discussion on Estimated Parameters

The models as described in section 'Proposed Modelling Structures' were estimated using the cleaned sample of size 179 households. The household socio-economic and spatial variables as described in previous sections are considered in all modelling components. Unfortunately in many cases, many variables (household class, employment, description of dwelling units, etc.) were found to be statistically insignificant. The statistical significance of the estimated parameters are measured for 95% confidence limit, the value of '*t*' statistics for which should be more than or equal to 1.64. However, some variables with even lower '*t*' values are retained in some cases (where possible) because they provide significant insight into behavioural process and also we believe that if a larger data set were available, these parameters might show statistical significance.

The overall frameworks of the two proposed model specifications are described in section 'Proposed Modelling Structures". Here we discuss the individual components separately.

Parametric Competing Risk Model

For the parametric competing risk model component of the first specification, we consider several distributional assumptions (exponential, weibull, log-logistic and lognormal) of the baseline hazard rate. For the accelerated failure time assumption, the log-logistic parametric competing risk model gives the highest pseudo *R*-square value;

hence it is retained for discussion. The parametric representation of the accelerated time hazard model starts with the representation of the duration of the event as a log-linear function of covariates:

$$\ln t_{ij} = x_{ij}\beta + \psi_{ij} \tag{16}$$

The distributional assumptions of the error term, ψ_{ij}, give different types of parametric hazard model. For the log-logistic assumption the survival function becomes

$$S = \{1 + (\exp(-x_{ij}\beta)t_{ij})^{1/\gamma}\}^{-1} \tag{17}$$

Here γ is the ancillary parameter. In the competing risk model, we parameterize this ancillary parameter using stressor-specific dummy variables that yields a competing risk model with the same covariate parameters but separate baseline hazard rates.

Table 1 presents the estimated parameters of the model. The goodness of fit of the model is 0.126. In addition to the separate baseline distribution, the model also contains stressor-specific dummy variables as covariates. The model conforms to the non-parametric competing risk model as described in section 'Data for Empirical Application'. Here, it is clear that the ancillary parameter is the highest for stressor 06 followed by stressors 02 and 04. The stressor-specific dummy parameters as covariates also show the same trend.

In terms of the other covariates, 12 variables are retained. It seems that the renters change dwelling less frequently than the homeowners in GTA. Lower income households are more likely to change dwelling compared to higher income households. The age of the head of the family plays a significant role in dwelling duration: older heads are less likely to change dwelling frequently than younger heads. Larger household size also influences longer durations in a particular location. It is intuitive that in larger household, different members have different constraints so it is more likely to stay in a stable location for longer time. Monthly parking cost for the household seems to have positive effect on dwelling duration. The total number of bedroom shows positive effect on dwelling duration, meaning the people with larger dwellings usually stay longer time but like many others this key variable does not show sufficient statistical significance. In terms of dwelling expectation, if the minimum bedroom requirement is higher, it is more likely that the people will change the dwelling sooner and *vice versa*. In terms of the employment characteristics of the household members, it is seen that if the number of employed members whose job location is not fixed is larger, the household is more likely to stay a shorter duration in a particular location. Intuitively for such people, the commuting travels pattern changes more frequently than the people with fixed job location. Less stable commuting travels pattern requires more frequent adjustment indicating frequent change of dwelling place/location. The variable 'number of activity locations' is measured as the number

Table 1
Log-Logistic Competing Risk Model for Seven Competing Stressors

Pseudo *R*-square value: 0.126

	Coefficient	***t*-Statistics**
Covariates		
Home owner	−0.9807	−5.67
Annual income below 15,000 CAD	−0.4886	−1.80
Annual income 75,000+ CAD	−0.0936	−0.52
Total household automobile	0.1792	1.69
Age of the head of family	0.0189	2.78
Household size	0.0311	0.49
Monthly parking cost	0.0084	2.18
Total no. of rooms	0.0134	0.32
Minimum bedroom required	−0.1590	−1.84
No. of household members with flexible work place	−0.0882	−0.50
No. of activity locations	−0.0724	−1.09
Halton and Durham Region	−0.1367	−0.75
Stressor02	0.1472	2.93
Stressor03	0.0177	0.52
Stressor04	0.1004	2.25
Stressor05	0.0207	0.59
Stressor06	0.6787	7.20
Stressor07	0.0316	0.86
Constant	3.8992	8.48
Ancillary parameter (γ)		
Stressor01	0.54	
Stressor02	0.58	
Stressor03	0.52	
Stressor04	0.53	
Stressor05	0.54	
Stressor06	0.63	
Stressor07	0.49	

of cities (outside the own city) the household members need to travel for different activities (shopping, socializing, entertainment, etc.).

It seems that the household of which the members need to travel higher number of places outside their own city for day-to-day activities are more likely to change dwelling place frequently than the household whose members' activity spaces are more or less within the same city. In terms of specific regions of the study area, the people of

Halton and Durham regions change dwelling more frequently than the people of Toronto, York and Peel regions.

This competing risk model presented in the Table 1 models the dwelling duration and the cause of changing duration simultaneously. The accelerated failure time assumption ensures the dynamic modelling of the duration change, but the problem of this model is that for a particular time step, only the highest probability cause (stressor) of the reason of change is considered to be the result, and the values of all other probabilities (of the corresponding stressors) have no practical significance because they are not mathematically identified. If we are concerned about the probability set corresponding to all stressors for terminating dwelling duration at any particular time step, this model does not give it. To overcome this, the second specification proposed dwelling duration modelled as a combined stressor event leading to the logit model, where, in logit model, the probability set of competing stressors are modelled as a function of the dwelling duration. The probability ratio for any competing stressor (to the reference stressor) is expressed as a function of a random intercept and the duration. The slope of duration is explained by various socio-economic variables. Another criticism of the competing risk hazard model presented in Table 1 is that it is very difficult to consider unobserved heterogeneity across the population when the competing stressors are higher in number. But in the second specification, it is easy to consider unobserved heterogeneity in every component. The next section discusses the combined stressors hazard model of the second specification.

Parametric Hazard Model for Combined Stressor Events

Similar to the competing risk model as described in previous section, here we considered an accelerated time assumption. For the baseline distribution, several distributional assumptions are made and the one that gives highest pseudo R-square value is reported here. In this case, the Weibull distribution with gamma heterogeneity is the best one and is presented in Table 2. The survival function for the Weibull distribution is

$$S = \exp(-\exp(-px_{ij}\beta)t_{ij}^{p}) \tag{18}$$

and the hazard rate is

$$h_{ij} = \alpha h_{ij}(t) \tag{19}$$

Here p is the ancillary parameter, and α is considered as inverse Gaussian distributed with mean value 1 and variance θ. Higher values (greater than 1) of θ indicate greater heterogeneity across the population. The estimation results are presented in Table 2. The goodness of fit of this model is higher than that of the competing risk model. The

Table 2
Weibull Hazard Model with Inverse Gaussian Heterogeneity for Combined Stressors

	Coefficient	t-Statistics
Pseudo R-square value: 0.132		
Covariates		
Home owner	−0.9438	−6.19
Annual income 15,000–29,000 CAD	−0.5368	−2.47
Total household automobile	0.1524	1.58
Monthly parking cost	0.0080	2.34
Age of the head of family	0.0162	2.88
Household size	0.0404	0.77
Minimum no. of bedroom required	−0.1811	−2.54
No. of household members with flexible work place	−0.1103	−0.78
No. of activity locations	−0.0820	−1.44
Halton and Durham Region	−0.1858	−1.23
Constant	4.1575	11.15
Ancillary parameter		
p	1.88	
θ	2.92	

value of θ is higher than 1. This indicates that considerable unobserved heterogeneity exists across the household. The sign of the variable parameters are consistent with the competing risk model as described in previous section. In addition to all other variables, the total number of household automobiles variable indicates that households with higher number of automobiles are less likely to change their dwelling frequently. This combined stressor hazard model will give the input to the next logit model as described in the next sub-section.

Logit Model for Competing Risk

Given the dwelling duration determined by the hazard model, the logit model estimates the probability of termination by the specific stressors. The logit model is presented in Table 3. The likelihood ratio value of the estimated model is 79.69 compared to the constant-only model, whereas the standard chi-square value for 32 degrees of freedom (32 parameters in the model) is 62.49 for the p value of 0.001. So the model passes the chi-square test with significant margin. The reference category in this model is stressor 07. The random intercepts are mentioned as γ_{0n} ($n = 1, 2, 3, \ldots, 6$). The random part of the intercepts assumed to be multivariate normal distributed with 0 mean. All variance terms pass the chi-square test.

Table 3
Logit Model For Stressor (Reason of Change)

Likelihood ratio value: 79.69

Covariates	**Coefficient**	***t*-Statistics**
Stressor 01		
γ_{01}	−0.8641	−1.49
Constant, $\gamma_{10(1)}$	0.0067	1.43
Owner of the home	3.2853	3.63
Annual income 15,000–29,000 CAD	−1.3776	−1.27
Age of the head of family	−0.1264	−4.33
Total household size	−0.1787	−1.21
Stressor 02		
γ_{02}	1.1375	3.95
Constant, $\gamma_{10(2)}$	0.0080	2.36
Total driving license holders	−0.3409	−1.50
Age of the head of family	−0.1185	−5.07
Annual income 45,000–59,000 CAD	−0.2485	−1.47
Number of children at home	1.1375	3.95
Stressor 03		
γ_{03}	0.3183	0.91
Constant, $\gamma_{10(3)}$	0.0032	0.87
Annual income 30,000–44,000 CAD	1.1603	2.58
Total household automobile	0.2759	0.95
Age of the head of family	−0.0533	−2.31
Total no. of part time employees	−0.5215	−0.87
Total retired persons	−1.0203	−1.39
Stressor 04		
γ_{04}	0.7111	2.18
Constant, $\gamma_{10(4)}$	0.0050	1.34
Age of the head of family	−0.0748	−3.77
Monthly parking cost	−0.0374	−1.68
Number of full time students	0.5598	1.86
York Region	1.1415	3.00
No. of activity locations	0.2605	1.63
Stressor 05		
γ_{05}	0.3443	1.01
Constant, $\gamma_{10(5)}$	0.0051	1.48
Total household automobile	0.5833	2.34
Age of the head of family	−0.0979	−4.39
Number of adults at home	−0.7037	−1.96
York Region	0.5127	1.13
No. of activity locations	−0.1076	−0.56

Table 3: (Continued)

Likelihood ratio value: 79.69		
Covariates	**Coefficient**	***t*-Statistics**
Stressor 06		
γ_{06}	1.9661	7.36
Constant, $\gamma_{10(6)}$	0.0039	1.27
Age of the head of family	−0.0749	−5.15
Number of children at home	−0.1268	−0.96
Minimum no. of bedroom required	0.1493	1.00

According to the alternate specific constant terms (the intercept), stressor 06 is the most dominant stressor followed by stressors 02 and 04, which are consistent with the findings of the non-parametric and parametric competing risk models. In terms of the slope of the duration variable (the slope of duration variable in logit model for the stressors are explained by variables), the value of the constant term is very low for all stressor. This justifies our modelling structure that though the dwelling duration and cause of termination go hand in hand, the effects of the duration on the cause of termination is fully explainable by various socio-economic variables. In the case of stressor 01, the dummy variable representing homeowner has a large and positive coefficient. This means that people who actually buy a new home, in most cases they have owned a home before. Lower number of renters change dwelling to own home than owners trade one house for another. This finding is consistent with the general findings of the study area (Pushkar, 1998). High-income people are more susceptible to this stress as they desire to own a home more than the low-income people (or, at least are more able to realize their desire to own a home). Young household heads change their dwelling for this reason more than the older household heads. Families with smaller household size change their dwelling for this reason more than the families with larger household size.

Stressor 02 indicates the pressure to change dwelling for changing household structure. The positive and larger coefficient of the variable 'number of children in household' is consistent with this. However, the households with smaller number of auto users (with driving license), younger household head and medium income (45,000–59,000 CAD) are less susceptible to this stressor.

Stressor 03 indicates the pressure due to the changes in affordability. The largest positive coefficient indicates that the households with medium income (30,000–44,000 CAD) are most susceptible to this stressor. Also higher automobile ownership, younger household head, lower number of part time employee and lower number of retired people at home indicate greater susceptibility to this stressor.

Stressor 04 indicates the desire to improve accessibility. People living in York Region are more susceptible to this stressor. York Region is adjacent to the City of Toronto. Many people commute from York Region to Toronto and the lack of accessibility in many cases poses severe stress. Also households with larger activity space and higher number of full time students are susceptible to this stressor.

Stressor 05 indicates desire to move to a better or desired location. It seems that households with higher number of automobiles are more susceptible to this stressor, but the households with smaller activity space, smaller number of household adults and younger household heads are less likely to change dwelling for this reason.

Stressor 06 indicates the urge to change dwelling for wider space, eviction/previous housing is no longer available, etc. It seems that households with younger heads and smaller numbers of children are more likely to change dwelling for this reason. For households with better housing expectation in terms of higher minimum number of bedroom requirement are more likely to change dwelling for this reason.

Heteroskedastic Probit Model for Tenure Change

This section presents the heteroskedastic probit model for tenure change. This component is common for both of the proposed specifications. Tables 4 and 5 present

Table 4
Heteroskedastic Probit Model for Household Tenure Change Decision (Renter to Owner)

Rho-square value: 0.65		
	Coefficient	***t*-Statistics**
Covariates		
Annual income below 35,000–44,000 CAD	0.8905	1.27
Age of the head of family	0.0357	1.13
Household size	0.2480	1.93
Minimum bedroom required	−0.5027	−1.62
No. of activity locations	0.2471	1.93
Dwelling duration in months	0.0028	1.77
Stressor03	0.7715	0.77
Stressor06	0.8548	1.22
Constant	−4.9257	−2.03
Log (variance)		
Dwelling duration in months	−0.0038	−1.67
Stressor02	0.7291	1.76

Table 5
Heteroskedastic Probit Model for Household Tenure Change Decision (Owner to Renter)

Rho-square value: 0.23		
	Coefficient	***t*-Statistics**
Covariates		
Annual income below 45,000–69,000 CAD	0.3441	2.60
Annual income below 60,000–74,000 CAD	0.1418	0.85
Age of the head of family	−0.0241	−2.43
Monthly parking cost	0.0058	2.30
Minimum bedroom required	0.1759	2.49
No. of household members with work location not fixed	0.1501	2.42
Dwelling duration in months	−0.00314	−2.58
Stressor02	−0.3384	−1.84
Stressor06	−0.2214	−2.03
Constant	−0.0241	−0.08
Log (variance)		
Annual income below 45,000–69,000 CAD	−1.1401	−3.23
Household size	−0.0890	−1.20

the estimated parameters of the model for renter-to-owner and owner-to-renter tenure change models. These models are applicable for all households except for those who change dwelling for the stressor 01 because stressor 01 itself indicates the tenure change. The goodness of fit of the renter-to-owner model is higher than the owner-to-renter model. However, the incorporation of the heteroskedastic variance terms improved the goodness of fit of both models as compared to a simple binomial logit model (the model out performs the simple binomial logit model with the same variables). The reason is that the choice of changing tenure is heterogeneous. The heterogeneity across the households is a function of household size, household income, total dwelling duration and types of stressor influencing the change of dwelling. It is clear that different types of variable influence the renter-to-owner and the owner-to-renter tenure change differently. It is evident that effects of household income categories are significantly different in these two types of tenure change. The higher income is influential to owner-to-renter tenure change, whereas the lower income is influential to renter-to-owner tenure change.

Age of head have opposite signs in the two models, indicating that older heads are more willing to own the house than renting. Household size is a significant variable in renter-to-owner model and indicates that larger size influence to change renter to owner. Monthly parking cost is a significant variable in owner-to-renter model indicating that increasing parking cost influence to change owner to renter. Minimum number of bedroom requirement enters into the both tenure change models but with opposite sign. It indicates that higher minimum number of bedroom requirement influence to be renter than owner. Total duration of present dwelling also enters into the both model but with opposite sign. It indicates that dwelling duration positively influence the renter-to-owner tenure change but negatively influence the owner-to-renter tenure change. Stressor 02 has negative effect on owner-to-renter tenure change. Stressor 03 has positive effect on renter-to-owner tenure change. Stressor 06 has positive effect on renter-to-owner tenure change but negative effect on owner-to-renter tenure change. However, it is found difficult to have all stressor types as significant variables in tenure change models.

Conclusions and Future Research

The paper presents integrated frameworks to model residential mobility decisions: dwelling durations, cause of changing dwelling and tenure change. The paper proposes that stress caused by various stressors is continuously active throughout our life. The central theory of the paper is to consider this latent stress variable as a longitudinal continuous function that can result in the termination of the dwelling duration at any point in time. To ensure the longitudinal and continuous nature of stress, the paper considers the duration of a particular household at a particular location as the duration of competing stress events. Household stresses are considered to be derived from seven general stressor types. In brief, these stressors indicate the desire to be a house owner, the pressures of changed household structure, the pressure of changed affordability, the necessity to improve accessibility, the urge to move to a better/desired location, the desire to get more/reduced space or eviction/previous unit is not longer available, and all other factors including job transfer, economic opportunity/disadvantage, retirement, etc. Two modelling frameworks are proposed and estimated using the data from a retrospective survey of household residential search process conducted in the GTA.

The first approach considers a competing risk accelerated failure time hazard model for simultaneous decision of dwelling duration and termination cause followed by a heteroskedastic probit model for tenure change decision. On the other hand, the second specification is a three-step one: first it considers dwelling duration as an event duration that is a function of all stressors in general, followed by a logit model for predicting the probability of each stressor being the termination cause and, finally, a heteroskedastic probit model for tenure change decision. Both of the specifications are comprehensive and dynamic in nature. Although the first specification models the dwelling duration and termination cause simultaneously, in terms of handling the heterogeneity in peoples' behaviour, the second specification is the better one. Empirical estimations of both of the specifications show consistent results with each other and also with the non-parametric distributions of the observed data. It is seen that for the study area, for longer durations, the most dominant cause of changing dwelling is the desire to get more/reduced space or eviction/previous unit is not longer available. The second dominant cause is the pressures due to the changes in household structures and the third one is the desire to improve accessibility. The estimated parameters of the models conform to this observed behaviour.

In terms of variables in the models, a wide range of socio-economic, spatial and characteristics of the dwelling units are considered. In many case, it is seen to be difficult to observe statistical significance of many variables, although all components of both specifications show sufficient goodness of fit to the observed data. The explanation for this is that considering the dynamic behaviour and the processes in an appropriate, tractable and comprehensive way eliminates the necessity of many variables usually assumed to be driving factors.

The proposed models are developed as part of the residential mobility decision component of the ILUTE modelling framework. The models need to be tested with larger data sets. Finally, it is hoped that the use of the concept of stress can provide the necessary and meaningful linkage and feedback for other modules of the ILUTE framework that is designed to handle both short- and medium- to long-term household decisions.

ACKNOWLEDGMENT

This research was funded by the Major Collaborative Research Initiative (MCRI) grant from the Social Science and Humanities Research Council (Canada).

REFERENCES

Alvarez, R. M. and J. Brehm (1995). American ambivalence towards abortion policy: development of a heteroskedastic probit model of competing values. *American Journal of Political Science* 34, 1055–1082.

Borsch-Supan, A. and J. Pitkin (1988). On discrete choice model of housing demand. *Journal of Urban Economics* 24, 153–172.

Breslow, N. and D. Clayton (1993). Approximate inference in generalized linear mixed model. *Journal of American Statistical Association* 88, 9–25.

Chan, S. (1996). Residential mobility and mortgages. *Regional Science and Urban Economics* 26, 287–311.

Clark, W. A. (1992). Comparing cross-sectional and longitudinal analysis of residential mobility and migration. *Environment and Planning A* 24, 1291–1302.

Clark, W. A. V. and Y. Huang (2003). The life course and residential mobility in British housing market. *Environment and Planning A* 35, 323–339.

Clark, W. A. V. and J. L. Onaka (1983). Life cycle and housing adjustment in explanations of residential mobility. *Urban Studies* 20, 47–57.

Corneliben, T. (2005). Standard errors of marginal effects in the heteroskedastic probit model. Discussion Paper No. 320, Institute of Quantitative Economic Research, University of Hanover, Germany, ISSN: 0949-9962.

Gooley, T. A., W. Leisenring, J. Crowley and B. E. Storer (1999). Estimation of failure probabilities in the presence of competing risks: new representations of old estimators. *Statistics in Medicine* 18, 695–706.

Greene, W. H. (2002). *Econometric Analysis*, 5th ed. New Jersey, Prentice Hall.

Habib, K. M. N. and E. J. Miller (2006). Modelling individual's frequency and time allocation behaviour for shopping activities considering household level random effects. *Transportation Research Record* 1985, 78–87.

Habib, K. M. N. and E. J. Miller (2005). Modelling duration of work/school episodes using activity diary data for the specification of activity travel scheduler. *Proceedings of Second International Colloquium on the Behavioural Foundation of Land-Use Transportation Models: Frameworks, Models and Applications*, June 12–15, Toronto.

Henderson, J. and Y. Ioannides (1987). Owner occupancy: investment versus consumption demands. *Journal of Urban Economics* 21, 228–241.

Hollingworth, B. J. and E. J. Miller (1996). Retrospective interviewing and its application in study of residential mobility. *Transportation Research Record* 1551, 74–81.

Huff, J. and W. Clark (1977). Cumulative stress and cumulative inertia: a behavioural model for decision to move. *Environment and Planning A* 10, 1101–1119.

Kalbfleisch, J. D. and R. L. Prentice (2002). *The Statistical Analysis of Failure Time Data*, 2nd ed. Chichester, Wiley.

Keifer, M. N. (1988). Economic duration data and hazard function. *Journal of Economic Literature* XXVI, 646–679.

Lancaster, T. (1990). *The Econometric Analysis of Transition Data*. Cambridge, UK, Cambridge University Press.

Li, S-M. (2004). Life course and residential mobility in China. *Environment and Planning A* 36, 27–43.

Lin, J. and L. Long (2006). What neighbourhood are we in? Empirical findings of relationships between residential location, lifestyle and travel. Paper presented in *85th Annual Meeting of Transportation Research Board*, January 22–26. Washington, DC.

McCullagh, P. and J. A. Nelder (1989). *Genaralized Linear Models*, 2nd ed. London, Chapman & Hall.

Meurs, H. and R. Haaijer (2001). Spatial structure and mobility. *Transportation Research Part D* 6, 429–446.

Miller, E. J. (2005). An integrated framework for modelling short- and long-run household decision-making. In H. J. P. Timmermans (Ed.), *Progress in Activity-Based Analysis*. Oxford, UK, Elsevier.

Molin, E. J. E. and H. J. P. Timmermans (2003). Testing hierarchical information theory: the causal structure of household residential satisfaction. *Environment and Planning A* 35, 43–58.

Ommeren, J. V., P. Roedveld and P. Nijkam (1999). Job moving, residential moving and commuting: a search perspective. *Journal of Urban Economics* 46, 230–253.

Pickles, A. and R. Davis (1991). The empirical analysis of housing careers: a review and general statistical modelling framework. *Environment and Planning A* 23, 465–484.

Pinto, S. M. (2002). Residential choice, mobility and the labor market. *Journal of Urban Economics* 51, 469–496.

Pushkar, A. O. (1998). Modelling household residential search process: methodology and preliminary results of an original survey. Masters Thesis, Department of Civil Engineering, University of Toronto.

Raundenbush, S. W. and A. S. Bryk (2002). *Linear Models: Application and Data Analysis Methods*. New Bury Park, CA, Sage Publication.

Raundenbush, S. W., A. S. Bryk, Y. F. Cheong and R. T. Congdon (2006). *HLM 6: Hierarchical Linear and Nonlinear Modeling*. Lincolnwood, IL, USA, Assessment System Corporation.

Rossi, P. (1955). *Why Families Move*. New York, McMillan.

Salvini, P. and E. J. Miller (2005). ILUTE: an operational prototype of comprehensive microsimulation model of urban systems. *Network and Spatial Econometrics* 5, 217–234.

Sarjeant, P. M. (1986). Continuous search as a basis for residential mobility modelling. M.A.Sc. Thesis, Department of Civil Engineering, University of Toronto.

Scheiner, J. (2006). Housing mobility and travel behaviour: a process-oriented approach to spatial mobility, evidence from a new research field in Germany. *Journal of Transport Geography*, *14*, 287–298.

Strauch, D., R. Moeckel, M. Wegener, J. Grafe, H. Mulhans, G. Rindfuser and K.-J. Beckmann (2003). Linking transport and land use planning: the microscopic dynamic simulation model ILUMASS. Paper Presented at the *7th International Conference on GeoComputation*, September 8–10, UK.

van der Vlist, A. J., C. Gorter, P. Nijkamp and P. Rietveld (2002). Residential mobility and local housing market difference. *Environment and Planning A* 34, 1147–1164.

Waddell, P. (2002). UrbanSim: modelling urban development for land use, transportation and environmental planning. *Journal of American Planning Association* 68, 297–314.

Waddell, P. and G. F. Ulfarsson (2004). Introduction to urban simulation: design and development of operational models. In P. Stopper, J. Kingley and D. Hensher (Eds.), *Handbook of Transport, Volume 5: Transport Geography and Spatial System*. Oxford, UK, Pergamon Press, pp. 203–236.

4.5 Prediction and Application

The Expanding Sphere of Travel Behaviour Research
Selected Papers from the 11th International Conference on Travel Behaviour Research

38

The Option Value of Public Transport Services: Empirical Evidence from the Netherlands

Karst Geurs, Rinus Haaijer and Bert van Wee

Abstract

This paper describes a methodology for measuring the option value of public transport services, and its application to two regional railway links in the Netherlands. Transport option values can be interpreted in terms of a risk premium that individuals with uncertain demand are willing to pay over and above their expected user benefit for the continued availability of a transport facility. These values represent a benefit category not included in conventional transport appraisal. From an Internet-based survey examining the value of regional rail services to residents, option values were concluded to be a potentially relevant benefit category in public transport policy appraisal. This survey included three different stated choice experiments to separate willingness to pay for use, option use and non-use. Significant option values could be obtained from the stated choice experiments for both regional railway links.

Introduction

Public transport serves a number of public interests associated with the actual use of the services. It provides mass transportation in heavily populated areas, and may contribute to a reduction in traffic congestion, environmental pressure and improvement of traffic safety. It also offers a basic level of accessibility to social and economic opportunities for people without a car—particularly important in rural areas. This is the main rationale for governments to subsidise public transport: for example, in the

Netherlands, local, regional and national governments currently pay about 50% of the operational costs of public transport (Advisory Council for Transport, Public Works and Water Management, 2004). Economists have argued, however, that there is little relationship between the size of the funding and the level of public transport provision to the general public or specific user groups (e.g. see Poort et al., 2005; Roson, 2000). An explanation for the high level of subsidisation may be that public transport is not only valued for the actual use of the service but also for the opportunities it offers for unexpected future use (Roson, 2000). For example, car-owners may value having a public transport service 'stand-by' in unexpected situations in which they cannot drive (e.g. due to bad weather or loss of ability to drive a car) or in which their car is unavailable (e.g. due to a breakdown). This 'option value' is a well-known concept in environmental economics for valuating natural assets (e.g. national parks) that offer possibilities for future consumption (Cameron and Englin, 1997; Kling, 1993; Walsh et al., 1984). There have, however, been few attempts to apply the option value concept in the transportation field.

This paper records one of the few empirical studies in the transport field that shows the relevance of option values as an additional benefit category, and represents the first study on transport option values in the Netherlands. The study is exploratory and is concerned as much with identifying and developing the methodology for measuring option values as with the values themselves. An elaborate description of the study can be found in Geurs (2006) and Geurs et al. (2006).

This paper firstly provides a definition and classification of economic-benefit categories for public transport services (Categorisation of Economic Benefits of Public Transport Services section) and a review of existing applications of the option value concept in the transport field (Empirical Evidence on Transport Option Values section). The paper secondly describes the development of a survey instrument to elicit willingness-to-pay (WTP) values for public transport of different service qualities (Development of a Survey Instrument section). Thirdly, describes its application in two case studies to derive a first set of WTP estimates for option use of public transport services in the Netherlands (Case Study Results section). Two railway links were selected as the case study area, one located in a low-density rural area in the eastern Netherlands and one in the highly urbanised western part of the country. Conclusions and Discussion section presents the conclusions and discusses the results of the study, and finally, Where to Direct Further Research section describes possibilities for further research.

Categorisation of Economic Benefits of Public Transport Services

Over the last decades economists have already spent considerable effort in identifying the range of benefits derived by people from transport infrastructure and transport services. Literature on cost–benefit analysis (CBA) provide categorisations of benefit

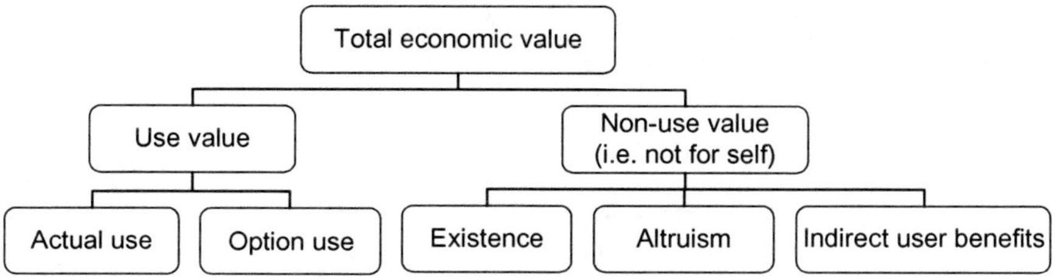

Figure 1
Classification of Economic Benefit Categories
Source: Adapted from Bateman et al. (2002)

categories consistent with welfare economics (e.g. see Bateman et al., 2002; Boardman et al., 2001). In CBA, costs and benefits are expressed in terms of the individual's preferences. WTP is the standard measure to secure benefits in monetary terms (or, alternatively, the willingness to accept compensation to forgo the same). The concept of 'total economic value' is used as the sum of all relevant WTPs for an individual of any change in well-being due to a policy or project (Boardman et al., 2001). Total economic value can first be broken down in to terms of 'use value' and 'non-use value' (Figure 1).

Use value relates to the *actual use* of a good or service in question (here public transport), *planned use* (a trip planned in the future) or *possible use.* Actual use and planned use are fairly obvious concepts, but possible use could also be important. People may be willing to pay to maintain a good in order to preserve the option of using it in the future. Option value thus becomes a form of use value (Bateman et al., 2002). Non-use values represent a category of benefits not attributable to the actual use or consumption of a good or service. The types of non-use value can be classified in several ways, for example existence values, altruistic values and indirect benefits, and can vary. Note that categorisation of option values in the literature on economics is somewhat confusing. In environmental and resource economics, option values are often categorised as a non-use benefit category (e.g. Dietz et al., 1994; Hanley and Spash, 1997). The different categories are shortly described below.

Actual use value relates to benefits accruing from the actual use of a good and service in question (e.g. public transport use, visit to a national park) or planned use (a visit planned in the future) (Bateman et al., 2002). Measurement of actual use benefits is traditionally based on the classical concept of 'consumer surplus', where benefits accrue directly from use since users are prepared to pay more (WTP) than they actually have to pay. Consumer surplus is thus defined as the difference between the WTP for use of a good or service and the actual price (P):

$$\mathrm{CS} = \mathrm{WTP} - P \tag{1}$$

The *option value* concept originates in Weisbrod (1964), who describes the hypothetical case of the closure of a national park and states that individuals who anticipate visiting the park at some time in the future may be willing to pay something for the option of using the commodity in the future. Weisbrod has argued that when demand for a good or service is uncertain, consumer's surplus will underestimate the maximum payment individuals are willing to pay.[1] Literature on CBA (see Boardman et al., 2001; Smith, 1987) distinguishes between the concepts 'option *price*' and 'option *value*'. Option *price* is considered the theoretically correct ex ante measure of the total user benefits in the sense that consumers value policies (here, preventing closure of a public transport service) without knowing if certain contingencies (e.g. car trouble, bad weather) will occur (Boardman et al., 2001; Smith, 1987). Option *values* are thought of as corrections of consumer surplus estimates to account for uncertainties in key parameters faced by them. In the case of public transport, individuals may face fundamental uncertainties related to: (a) their individual situations in the future, for example loss of ability to drive, future housing and job location, and (b) the availability of their primary mode influenced by such contingencies as car trouble, car accidents, bad weather, future car travel time or costs and an energy crisis. In our study, we interpret option values as a risk premium that individuals with uncertain demand are willing to pay over and above their expected user benefit for the continued availability of a transport service. Thus, the option price (OP) can be defined as the sum of expected user benefits (CS; equation 1) and the option value (OV). Rearranging the equation, the option value (OV) can be estimated by subtracting expected consumer surplus (CS) from the option price (OP):

$$OP = CS + OV \tag{2}$$

$$OV = OP - CS \tag{3}$$

Option price can generally be considered the conceptually correct measure of user benefits in circumstances of uncertainty but its measurement is rather difficult. There are few opportunities to infer option prices directly from observable behaviour. Insurance premiums which for example may convey some useful information about people's WTP for reductions in risk for some goods or services (Boardman et al., 2001) are not applicable in the transport field.

---

[1] In environmental economics, the option value concept has been topic of a theoretical debate on the sign of option values under different assumptions of uncertainties and risk aversion (see for an overview Boardman et al., 2001). Theoretical studies suggest that for risk-seeking individuals and inferior goods (when demand decreases with income) the option value should be seen as negative for demand- and supply-side uncertainties. In this study we assume individuals to be averse to risk and rail transport as a normal good. MuConsult (1992) shows that train use in the Netherlands increases with income, controlling for other variables as car ownership, residential location and educational level. Hence, the option value of rail services is treated as positive.

Non-use values can be conveniently classified in terms of existence values, altruistic values and indirect benefits. *Existence values* refer to WTP to keep a good or service in existence in a context where the individual expressing the value has no actual or planned use for himself/herself or for anyone else. In environmental economics there is considerable literature on the measurement of existence values for natural environments and wildlife, although the particular estimates are often controversial (e.g. see Boardman et al., 2001, for an overview). Transport infrastructure is not likely to provide a pure existence value derived from mere contemplation of the value object, similar, for example, to the existence of whales or polar bears. *Altruistic values* arise when individuals are willing to pay to preserve a service which benefits others, for example friends and relatives, or which is regarded as being beneficial to society in general. A mixture of altruistic motives may be related to public transport. Individuals may be willing to pay to subsidise (or preserve) public transport services which benefit others, particularly friends and relatives, specific groups in society (e.g. the poor) or society in general. A *bequest value* is a specific form of altruism, which arises when an individual is concerned that next and future generations have the option of making use of a good or service (Boardman et al., 2001). *Indirect user benefits* can be described as benefits which individuals derive indirectly from the use made of a public transport service by others.[2] For example, they may avoid giving lifts and receiving visits from people who use public transport and who would otherwise not visit in its absence. Individuals may also benefit from the use of public transport by others, if this reduces congestion and/or environmental degradation. Indirect user benefits form a benefit category commonly included in economic appraisal of transport projects and may be positive or negative: for example bus services may create delays, air pollution, noise or other disamenity effects. The other non-use benefit categories raise issues of motivation typically avoided by economists because of the risk of double counting benefits (Boardman et al., 2001).

Empirical Evidence on Transport Option Values

In the literature, some attempts are made to quantify the option value or non-use benefits of public transport services using stated preference techniques. Three empirical studies have so far been conducted in the UK, and two other studies are found in the academic literature examining public transport services in Italy and the United States. Contingent valuation and choice experiments (or conjoint analysis) have been used as stated preference methods. This section briefly describes the studies (see Laird et al., 2006, for an elaborate review).

[2] In the literature, the term indirect benefits is sometimes also used to refer to the wider economic benefits such as productivity gains of firms—benefits not being the direct transport benefits of a project but indirectly related to the project. This is, however, a very different benefit category.

An initial group of studies examined non-use values as a group of benefits, including option values. Bristow et al. (1991a, b) developed a methodology using travel diaries and an iterative bidding contingent valuation technique (in face-to-face interviews) to examine the value of retention of suburban bus services in Leeds; a follow-up study was also conducted to examine values placed on the retention of the Settle–Carlisle rail service (Crockett, 1992). WTP was derived for use (consumer surplus) and non-use as a group of motives, including option values. Furthermore, Painter et al. (2001) examined the non-use benefits of rural bus (transit) services in two rural areas in Washington State (USA) using a contingent valuation questionnaire administered to a panel of randomly selected local residents. These studies, however, do not show the relevance of option values as a benefit category. Firstly, the studies have not estimated option value as a separate benefit category. Secondly, the studies were limited in scope, that is the sample size of the empirical studies ranged from about 50 to 200 respondents. Thirdly, the studies used contingent valuation techniques, which introduce several methodological problems. The most serious problems with contingent valuation (see e.g. Hausman, 1993, and Baarsma, 2000, for overviews) are related to cognitive stress and strategic answers. In contingent valuation studies respondents found it a difficult mental task to assign direct monetary values, and there are very few incentives for people to express their real value, which can lead individuals to respond to surveys with higher WTP values than they would attach in reality.

A second group of studies have explicitly attempted to quantify the option value of public transport services. Roson (2001) estimated WTP for service-level improvements of a bus link and a railway link in two areas in Northern Italy, using choice experiments in face-to-face interviews. Choice experiments have become popular SP-valuation-method techniques in the transport field for evaluating new vehicle types, transport modes, infrastructure or service levels currently not in existence (e.g. see Louviere et al., 2000). In this study, respondents (users and non-users) were asked in face-to-face interviews to choose between pairs of alternatives, varying in service frequency and local property taxation. A service frequency increase was associated with a proportional increase in local taxes on real estate property. The paper presents the impact of socio-economic variables on stated willingness to contribute to subsidisation of the public transport services, but WTP values are not reported in the paper. The author does state that respondents were willing to pay a little more tax to increase the service level; about two-thirds of the respondents prefer the current situation. Another problem with the study is that the author does not distinguish between different motives for WTP for service-level changes; the term option value is used for what is probably a mixture of consumer surplus, option value and non-use values. Moreover, WTP to prevent a complete service withdrawal is not examined, and thus probably strongly underestimates individuals' total WTP values.

Humphreys (2004; Humphreys and Fowkes, 2006) presented the first empirical study which breaks down the different components of the total economic value of the

Edinburgh to North Berwick railway link in Scotland. Humphreys used contingent valuation to quantify train users' consumer surplus, and conducted a choice experiment to quantify option value and non-use value categories. Option value estimates were significant at £150 and £172 per person per year for users and non-users, respectively. However, the study had an exploratory character with limited scope (see section "Validation of the Results" for a further discussion).

In conclusion, the field of measuring transport option values is far from developed. To the authors' knowledge, all applications of the option value concept in the transport field are, however, related to bus or rail services. To date, studies are lacking on other transport modes or facilities, freight transport and option values that firms may place on transport infrastructure or services. Also, existing studies have not included potential users or option users from other parts of the country. Although residents in outlying areas outside the service area of the rail links are generally unlikely to use the train under any condition, a small proportion of residents (possibly with an option value) may be future visitors to the case study areas. All stated preference studies included in the review are exploratory and limited of scope. Only two empirical studies attempted to separate option values from consumer surplus and non-use benefit categories. The results of the different empirical studies are not easily compared due to differences in the case study area, methodology used and scope of the study.

Development of a Survey Instrument

An Internet-based survey instrument was constructed to include stated choice experiments to elicit WTP values for use, option use and non-use of specific rail links. The methodology was applied in two case studies aimed at deriving reliable WTP estimates of residents in the service area of the public transport links for option use, additional to use and non-use. Two railway links with a typical regional transport function were selected: both had relatively low use and cost-coverage levels below 50%. The first one, the Arnhem–Winterswijk light-rail link, is located in a low-density rural area situated in the eastern part of the Netherlands and connecting 10 small- to medium-sized rural towns (5,000–40,000 inhabitants) to the larger town of Arnhem (about 130,000 inhabitants). The second one, the Leiden–Gouda railway link is situated in the highly urbanised western part of the Netherlands and connects three medium-sized towns to the larger towns of Leiden (about 120,000 inhabitants) and Gouda (about 70,000 inhabitants). A light-rail link with a high level of service (4–8 trains per hour; 7 new stops) and cost coverage of 70% is planned to replace the current link by the year 2010. The case study area comprises the municipalities bordering on the selected railway links (see Figure 2). This section describes the main elements in the survey, the design of the stated choice experiments, the data collection method and problems of bias in responses.

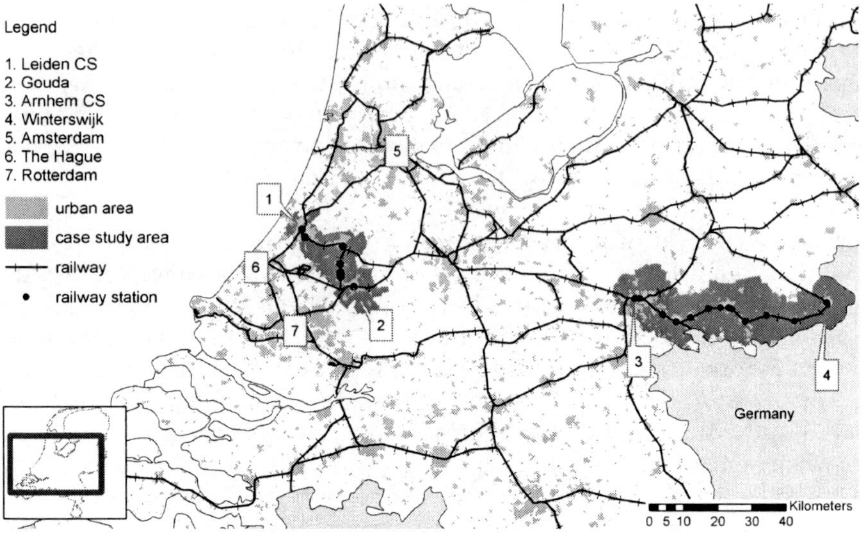

Figure 2
Location of Case Study Areas in the Netherlands

The Main Elements in the Survey

The survey comprised three main elements: (1) introductory questions; (2) questions about travel behaviour and characteristics of the respondent and household; and (3) stated choice experiments to elicit WTP values for public transport at different levels of service quality.

The first element in the survey comprised several introductory questions for the selection of respondents relevant for the study and stratifying the sample into different research groups. Respondents were considered relevant for this study if they were train users of the selected railway links or car users in the railway link area. Respondents were subdivided into four unique groups, that is 'regular train user', 'option user', 'car user' and 'possible option user' (see Table 1 for definitions). This division was made to ensure a sufficient distribution of respondents across the different stated choice experiments to allow reliable estimations of use, option use and non-use values from the choice experiments. The focus was not to achieve a representative sample of the population.

The second element in the survey consisted of questions about the respondents' personal travel behaviour, the travel behaviour of their partner and/or children. The questions on their travel behaviour were different for users and non-users. *Regular train users* and *option users* were asked to give trip origin and destination, frequency, time of day, ticket or train subscription type and trip motive of a (frequently) made trip using the selected

Table 1
Classification of Respondent Groups

	Respondent group	Choice experiment
User of selected rail link	*Regular train user*: a person who used the selected railway link in the past year (not as option user)	'consumer surplus'+('option price' or 'non-use value')
	Option user: a car-owner who used the selected railway link in the past year in unexpected situations when he or she could not drive or the car was not available	'consumer surplus'+('option price' or 'non-use value')
Non-user of selected rail link	*Car user*: a person who made car trips in the research area and did not use the selected railway link in the past year	'non-use value'
	Possible option user: a car user who did not use the selected railway link in the past year, but would consider using the train in future unexpected situations if the car was not available	'option price'+'non-use value'

railway link. *Possible option users* were asked to give trip characteristics of a hypothetical train trip (option trip) which would replace an actual car trip in unexpected situations when the car is not available. These trip data were firstly used to link the stated choice experiments in the survey to actual trips made. Secondly, the trip data were used to estimate train costs per trip (using information on train ticket and subscription costs from the Netherlands Railways). In addition, respondents were asked questions about different types of uncertainty possibly related to option values. Respondents were asked if they expect a change in their personal situation (residential location, job location, car ownership) and car trip characteristics (trip costs and travel times) in the next 2 years. In addition, they were asked about motives for car and train use, and the importance of possible consequences of service withdrawal. Finally, socio-economic characteristics of the respondents (education level, net personal and household incomes) and characteristics of the car used (fuel type, vehicle weight, year of manufacture) were asked. The latter information was used to compute fuel costs per trip, using average fuel consumption data by vehicle type class.

The third element of the survey covered the stated choice experiments. In measuring option values there is a real risk of double counting when trying to separate individuals' WTP for the option of using the service from their WTP for their actual use and/or non-use of the service. This was handled by constructing different stated choice experiments to elicit WTP for use, option use and non-use:

(1) the choice experiment 'consumer surplus' was constructed to elicit the maximum number of train users willing to pay for a trip using the selected railway link.

Combined with information on trip costs from the second part of the survey, consumer surplus can be estimated (equation 1);

(2) the choice experiment 'option price' was constructed to elicit the total WTP for improvement or deterioration of train service levels. Option prices were elicited as the WTP to prevent closure of the railway service. Option values for train users can be estimated by subtracting expected consumer surplus from the option price (equation 3); for possible option users, consumer surplus is zero and option price thus equals option value;

(3) the choice experiment 'non-use value' was constructed to elicit WTP for improvement or deterioration of train service levels when the respondent (and other household members) no longer uses the railway link.

Users of the selected railway links could apply for all experiments, but were selected for only two to reduce the survey length and prevent potential boredom, irritation and fatigue, which may arise when respondents are repeatedly asked to participate in similar choice experiments. These respondents were always selected for the choice experiment 'consumer surplus' and randomly for the choice experiments 'option price' or 'non-use value' (see Table 1).

Design of the Stated Choice Experiments

The most critical dimensions in stated choice experiments are the number of alternatives, attributes and choice sets presented (e.g. see Arentze et al., 2003; Caussade et al., 2005). Too many alternatives and attributes affect the respondent's choice consistency. In this study, the design of the choice experiment 'consumer surplus' differs from the choice experiments 'option value' and 'non-use value' in terms of number of alternatives, variables and payment mechanism. In the choice experiment 'consumer surplus' respondents had to choose from three alternatives (two train alternatives plus the no-choice), whereas the other choice experiments had two alternatives. The no-choice option was included to elicit the maximum amount respondents were willing to pay for a train trip. Train travel times were included as a variable to allow a consistency check with value-of-time values found in other studies (see Validation of the Results section), and train ticket price was included as payment mechanism. The choice experiment 'consumer surplus' comprised the following variables and attribute levels:

- Train travel time: +25%/+10%/current state/−10%/−25%;
- Train frequency (for a working day during busy hours): 1 train per hour (frequency halving)/2 trains per hour (current state)/4 trains per hour (frequency doubling);
- Train ticket price: +25%/+10%/current state/−10%/−25%.

The choice experiments 'option price' and 'non-use value' were identical in design, but differed in the respondent groups selected for the experiments (see Table 1) and the context presented. The choice context in the choice experiment, 'option price', was an actual or hypothetical trip; in the choice experiment 'non-use value' respondents were asked to imagine a situation in which the respondent and other household members would no longer use the railway link, for example the respondent will travel by car from now on, current trip destination has changed (e.g. relocation of work, school), etc.

Since there is no actual market in which actual payments can be made to maintain public transport services, a hypothesised payment mechanism had to be postulated to trade off rail service levels and financial burden. In this study, monthly local property taxes were chosen as payment mechanism. In the Netherlands, municipalities collect property taxes periodically (monthly, yearly) from residents who own or rent houses. The variation in local taxation was computed considering the change in operation and maintenance costs of the railway link when railway stations are introduced/closed or train frequency levels increase/decrease. Operation and maintenance cost figures were taken from the economic analysis of the introduction of a light-rail link between Gouda and Leiden (Ecorys/Prorail, 2003). The change in cost was subsequently distributed among the total number of households in the case study area.[3] Of course, other payment mechanisms are possible to link service quality and costs, but earlier studies successfully used comparable payment mechanisms (Roson, 2001; Painter et al., 2001).

The choice experiments 'option price' and 'non-use value' consisted of the following variables and attribute levels:

- Train frequency (working day, at day): no train/1 train per hour (frequency halving)/current state (2 trains per hour)/4 trains per hour (frequency doubling);
- Railway stations: entire railway link closed/closure of minor railway stations/ current state/introduction of new railway stations;[4]
- Monthly local property taxes: 10 Euro increase/5 Euro increase/current state/ 5 Euro decrease/10 Euro decrease.

An optimal choice design was used for each of the choice experiments. Parameter estimates can be obtained with higher efficiency if the design is optimal. In other words,

[3]This results in the following variation in monthly taxation: a 6 Euro decrease when the entire link is closed and a 7 Euro increase when the rail frequency is doubled and new railway stations are introduced. In the choice experiments a bandwidth among these values was used of 5 and 10 Euro increase or decrease of monthly local taxation.

[4]The attribute 'new railway stations' involved two new stops on the Arnhem–Winterswijk link (i.e. at the villages Westervoort and Gaanderen) and seven new stops on the Leiden–Gouda link (i.e. Leiden Transferium A4, Zoeterwoude, Hazerswoude, Alphen a/d Rijn Lorentzweg, Boskoop Snijdelweg, Waddinxveen Coenencoop, Gouda Goudsepoort). The attribute 'closure of railway stations' involved closure of six stops on the Arnhem–Winterswijk link (i.e. Arnhem Velperpoort, Duiven, Didam, Wehl, Doetinchem de Huet, Varsseveld and Aalten) and three on the Leiden–Gouda link (i.e. Waddinxveen Noord, Boskoop, Leiden Lammerschans).

a lower number of choice sets are needed to obtain these estimates. So, using an optimal design can reduce the task for the respondents in comparison to the situation where 'standard' choice designs were used. An optimal design is characterised by (a) orthogonality: each variable (level) can be estimated independently from other variable (level)s, (b) level balance: each level of a variable occurs with equal frequency, (c) minimal overlap: as few as possible equal variable levels occur in each choice set, and (d) utility balance: the utilities of the choice alternatives are as close to each other as possible in each choice set. In general, choice sets that generate extreme probabilities are less effective in constraining the parameters than moderate ones (Huber and Zwerina, 1996). Since these four criteria in general cannot be met simultaneously, a computerised search algorithm is needed to find an efficient design. We used a program based on Zwerina et al. (1996), which searches for a minimal determinant (D-efficient) covariance matrix. This algorithm was used to create two efficient choice designs: (i) one for the choice experiment 'consumer surplus', which included the no-choice option and (ii) one for the choice experiments 'option price' and 'non-use value', which accounted for the fact that the attribute level 'entire railway link closed' is always combined with the attribute level 'no train frequency'. In each choice experiment the task consisted of 12 choice sets. Each choice task was preceded by instruction on the task. Furthermore, extra information on the attributes and the levels could be obtained through 'pop-up' textboxes in each choice set.

Task, attribute and choice set randomisations were conducted to avoid order effects. The choice experiments were firstly offered in random order, except when the choice experiment 'non-use value' was involved; this experiment was always offered last. Secondly, the choice sets from the efficient design were offered to the respondents in random order. Thirdly, the attributes in the choice sets were offered in random order (between respondents, not individually). For example, for one respondent 'price' may have been listed first in each choice set; for the next respondent this may have been 'frequency'.

Data Collection Method

An Internet-based survey was chosen here as research method. Internet is a cost-effective method in complicated studies which require advanced or tailor-made designs (such as stated choice experiments) and large samples (Nossum, 2005). Respondents were recruited from a large Internet panel in the Netherlands that provides a relatively high spatial coverage of Dutch territory (more than 200,000 panel members, about 2% of the households in each municipality). Internet panel members living in the case study areas were recruited for the study. Data collection using an Internet panel has the advantage that respondents are experienced (respondents can handle complicated SP surveys), highly motivated (respondents are paid for each survey) and reliable (members who have filled in 'suspicious' questionnaires before are periodically removed from the panel).

There were two major disadvantages of the data collection method used. Firstly, data collection via the Internet is still not a satisfactory alternative for all population groups, in particular for elderly. The proportion of people in the Netherlands having access to Internet is very high (about 73% in 2004), but access among elderly people is still relatively low (about 17% of over-65s), especially the elderly with a low education level (5% of over-65s with only primary education) (Statistics Netherlands, 2005). A second disadvantage was that only one person per household was a member of the Internet panel. This complicated the aggregation of option value estimates to the household level. As the purpose of this study is to conduct an initial exploratory study examining the relevance of option values as a benefit category, the advantages of the Internet panel survey method largely outweighed the disadvantages.

Case Study Results

Respondent Groups and Characteristics

About 7,500 panel members living in one of the two case study areas were requested by email to participate in the survey. About 2,665 respondents completed the introductory questions (response of about 35%), of which about 2,450 were users of the selected rail link or car user in the case study area. The results from the introductory questions show that about 40% and 47% of the respondents were users of the Arnhem–Winterswijk and Leiden–Gouda train links, respectively. However, the level of use is relatively low—typical for railway links with a regional transport function. Most train users were infrequent travellers, about 70% used the train less than once per month, only 7% were frequent users, with a frequency of 4–5 times per week. About 25% of the train users in both study areas made use of the train as option user in the past year (the year 2004). The frequency of option use was relatively low: about 45% used the train one or two times per year as option user, 30% three to five times, 10% six to ten times, and 15% more than 11 times per year. Furthermore, more than 75% of car users in the sample are 'possible option users'—they would consider using the rail service in unexpected situations when their car is not available.

About 1,000 respondents were selected to participate in the full survey. The selection of respondents was aimed at a sufficient distribution of respondents across the different stated choice experiments. After cleaning the data, 779 valid questionnaires remained, of which 395 were in the case study area of Arnhem–Winterswijk and 384 in Leiden–Gouda. In the stratified sample, train users were underrepresented in all choice experiments and option users in the Leiden–Gouda area (see further Consumer Surplus, Option Value and Non-Use Value section).

A comparison of the socio-economic characteristics of participants with a sample of (about 4,000) respondents for both study areas taken from the 2004 Dutch National

Travel Survey (Ministry of Transport, Public Works and Water Management, 2005a) revealed—as expected—that elderly people (over 65) and people with a low educational level are underrepresented, that is about 1% and 4% of respondents, respectively, compared to 17% and 14% in the National Travel Survey. Furthermore, the percentage of unemployed/disabled workers and the level of job participation are overrepresented, that is about 8% of respondents are unemployed/disabled and 68% have paid jobs, compared to 3% and 47% in the National Travel Survey. To improve the representativeness of the sample, respondents were weighted in all model estimations to correct for the differences in education level and work situation. Furthermore, elderly people were excluded from the sample. As a result, we were not able to estimate WTP estimates of elderly people.

Consumer Surplus, Option Value and Non-Use Value

Parameter estimates for each choice experiment and respondent group were obtained through maximum likelihood estimation of multinomial or binomial logit models. The logit model estimations result in utility values for each attribute level. In the estimation, effects coding has been used for the highest attribute level for each variable, for example 'frequency doubling', 'train travel time −25%' and 'train ticket price −25%' in the choice experiment 'consumer surplus'. Effect coding has the advantage that non-linear effects in the attribute levels may be measured. Utility functions derived from the survey (with the current situation as reference point) were s-shaped and asymmetric. That is the (dis-)utility of an increase in local property taxes is higher than the utility of a reduction in property taxes by the same amount. This is consistent with the concept of loss aversion from prospect theory widely used in behavioural economics, which explains risk-averse behaviour—people prefer avoiding losses to making equally high gains (Boardman et al., 2001; Kahneman and Tversky, 1979; Van de Kaa, 2008). Monetary values were derived from the model estimations by estimating the ratios between utility values of the train service level attributes and price attributes (ticket price or local property taxes), multiplied by absolute price changes. Absolute price changes were either given (property taxes) or computed from the revealed preference data (train fair actually paid for the selected trip on the railway link).

Consumer Surplus Estimates

Multinomial logit models were estimated to obtain WTP estimates from choice experiment 'consumer surplus'. For each respondent group, separate models were estimated for each case study area and for the whole sample. The number of observations, goodness of fit measures (log likelihood and Nagelkerke's pseudo-R^2), estimated coefficients for each attribute level, T-statistics and estimated monetary values are reported for each model in Annex 1. Consumer surplus estimations were based on the parameter included for the no-choice option in the choice experiment. The no-choice attribute represents the ticket price increase at which a train user decides to stop making trips. Monthly consumer surplus was estimated as the monetary value of the no-choice attribute, multiplied by respondents' average monthly trip frequency.

More than 410 train users participated in the choice experiment 'consumer surplus', resulting in about 5,000 observations, roughly evenly divided between the two case study areas. The number of respondents is sufficient for each respondent group to obtain robust models. Here, a minimum of 50 individuals is used as a rule-of-thumb criterion to obtain robust logit models from choice experiments (Hensher et al., 2005). All models show a decent goodness of fit (see Table A1, Annex 1 for details), that is a pseudo-R^2 of 0.3–0.4 of a discrete choice model equivalent to a R^2 of 0.6–0.8 of a linear regression model (Hensher et al., 2005). Moreover, estimated coefficients for all attribute levels and respondent groups are significant at the 5% level, except for the current frequency and current travel time.

On average, monthly consumer surplus for regular train users is about three times as high as for option users. This is primarily due to the higher trip frequency (4.5 compared to 1.3 trips per month); average WTP is about 40% above the average ticket price of 6 Euro and differs much less between regular train users and option users.

Option Value Estimates

Binomial logit models were estimated to obtain WTP estimates from the choice experiment 'option price'. In total, about 455 respondents participated in this choice experiment, of which about 230 were train users and 225 were possible option users (non-users), roughly evenly divided between the two case study areas. Robust models could, unfortunately, not be obtained for regular train users and option users for each case study area separately, and are not reported here. All models presented show a decent goodness of fit and coefficients significant at the 5% level[5] (see Annex 1 for details).

The average option price estimate for regular train users (about 20 Euro per month) for the whole sample is significantly higher than for option users (on average about 14 Euro per month), which, in turn, is higher than for possible option users (on average about 12 Euro per month). This result agrees with a priori expectations. Option value estimates were obtained as the average option price reduced with average monthly consumer surplus for each respondent group. Train users were willing to pay a significant amount over and above their consumer surplus for the continued availability of the railway link: an average of about 8 Euro for both case study areas.

[5]The attribute level 'current frequency' was not significant for all respondent groups and was excluded from the model specification presented here.

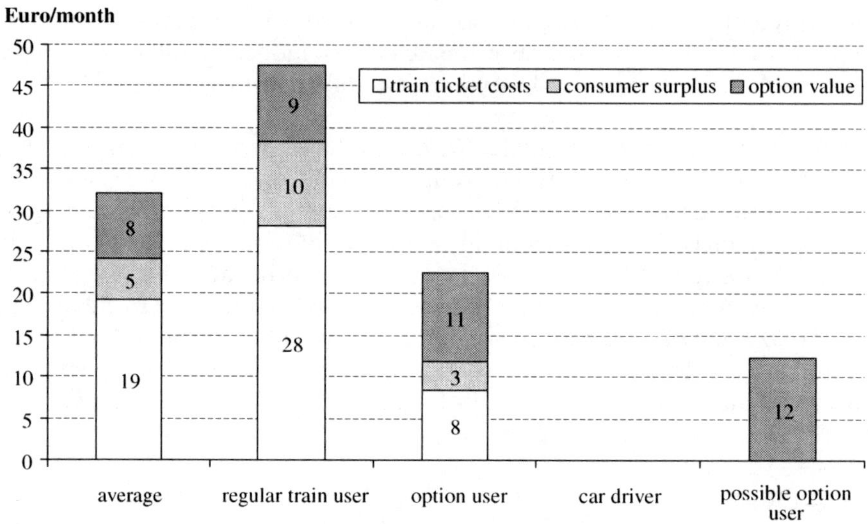

Figure 3

Monthly Train Ticket Costs, Consumer Surplus and Option Value Estimates (Euro per Month) by Respondent Group, Average Values for Both Study Areas

Surprisingly, average option values do not differ strongly between regular train users and option users. A priori it was expected that consumer surplus of regular train users would dominate the option price and option values to be lower than for (frequent) option users. Apparently, train users have a relatively high WTP to preserve the option for trips not yet anticipated or currently undertaken by other modes.

The option value estimates for possible option users are significant (11 and 14 Euro per month for the Leiden–Gouda and Arnhem–Winterswijk link area, respectively) which indicates the importance of the railway links as a backup transport mode for car-owners with uncertain demand. The average option value for non-users is 20–30% lower (8 and 11 Euro per month for the Leiden–Gouda and Arnhem–Winterswijk link area, respectively), accounting for the percentage of car-owners who are unlikely to use the train under any condition and thus have a zero option value. Figure 3 shows that option values are significant compared to average monthly ticket costs and consumer surplus estimates for train users.

Non-Use Value Estimates

Binomial logit models were estimated to obtain WTP estimates from the choice experiment 'non-use value'. About 510 persons participated in this experiment, but were not evenly divided between respondent groups and case study areas. As a result, robust models could not be obtained for regular train users and option users for each case study area separately. All models presented show a decent goodness of fit and coefficients significant at the 5% level, except for car users, where the goodness of fit is somewhat less (see Annex 1 for details).

Respondents seem willing to pay significant amounts to maintain the railway link in a non-use context. This agrees with a priori expectations: that is in an earlier stage of the survey, respondents scored several types of community benefits (availability of the train service to people without a car or visitors, functioning of society in general) and indirect benefits of maintaining the rail service (congestion, environment) as being important or very important (see Geurs, 2006, for an elaborate description). Higher non-use values obtained for users compared to non-users also agreed with a priori expectations—users are more familiar with the train service and may have a stronger positive attitude towards the train service. However, it seems implausible that the non-use value estimates obtained for users are a factor 2–3 higher than those for non-users. For car users and possible option users an average WTP of 6–9 Euro per month for the whole sample was obtained; for option users and regular train users this was 13–19 Euro per month.

Non-use value estimates were firstly hypothesised to be biased by train use by other household members on the WTP of respondents. Indeed, logit model estimates (not reported here; see Geurs et al., 2006) revealed that train use by other household members significantly affects non-use value estimates; for non-users with train-using household members a WTP was obtained which was about 9–10 Euro higher than for non-users with no train-using household members. Train use by household members, however, did not explain the relatively high WTP values for train users. That is, one would expect smaller differences between the WTP estimates for users and non-users when train use by household members is accounted for. The high non-use value for train users may be biased by the difficulty of the mental task train users were presented within the choice experiment, that is having to imagine a situation in which they and other household members would no longer use the railway link. The mental task is obviously much easier for non-users with no train-using household members whose WTP estimates of 6–7 Euro seem reasonable. Thus, non-use values obtained in the study are subject to doubts, and there is a real risk of doubling counting benefits when computing the total economic value as the sum of consumer surplus, option and non-use value estimates.

Validation of the Results

The literature review presented in Empirical Evidence on Transport Option Values section has already revealed the field of measuring option values to be far from developed. There are thus very few possibilities to validate the WTP estimates derived in our study. Humphreys (2004); Humphreys and Fowkes (2006) presented the only empirical effort so far to separate transport option values from consumer surplus and non-use value of the Edinburgh to North Berwick railway link in Scotland. The results of this study are not easily compared with our study due to differences in the case study areas, methodology used and scope of the study. Moreover, the number of participants in the choice experiment was relatively small (about 80 respondents) and results presented were subject to a range of doubts, including the quality of the data which was undermined by the inexperience of the subcontracted market research company. The consumer surplus estimates seem consistent with our study (i.e. WTP is about 30% above fares paid). Humphreys estimated option values at £150 and £172 per person per year (equivalent to about 19 and 21 Euro per month) for users and non-users, respectively, in 2002 prices. These are about twice as high as the estimates from our study. Humphreys breaks down non-use benefits into WTP for road traffic changes (indirect use benefits) and discount rail cards for family members and specific population groups (altruistic value). This resulted in much smaller total non-use value estimates (4 Euro per month for users, negative for non-users) than in our study. Other studies examining non-use values of public transport as a group of benefits seem to obtain higher estimates. For example, Painter et al. (2001) examined the non-use benefits of rural bus (transit) services in two rural areas in Washington state (USA) using contingent valuation. Average WTP per month for an optimal transit system that the respondent could not use was estimated at 4.5 and 10 US dollars for non-users and users, respectively, in 1999 prices.

At the start of the study it was already known that validation of WTP estimates would prove to be difficult. Therefore, a variable 'train travel time' was included in the choice experiment 'consumer surplus' to obtain value-of-time estimates and to allow for a consistency check with estimates from the literature. To allow a comparison with Dutch value of time values from the literature, the attribute levels of the variables 'travel time' and 'ticket costs' were converted to absolute travel time and cost changes and then specified as linear variables in the logit model (detailed estimates are not reported here, see Geurs et al., 2006). The value-of-time estimates seem plausible for the different respondent groups and average values (4.9 Euro per hour) are consistent with national Dutch estimates. That is, value-of-time values of 5.2 and 6.6 Euro per hour are prescribed for use in Dutch CBA for non-work-related train trips and all trip motives, respectively, for the year 2004 (Transport Research Centre, 2005b). As 75% of the train trips reported by respondents are non-work-related trips, average values obtained from the choice experiment (about 4.5–5 Euro per hour) seem realistic. Furthermore, estimates are—as expected—higher for regular train users (6.7 Euro/hour) than for option users with low frequencies of use (3.6 Euro/hour). In conclusion, it is difficult to validate the WTP values obtained in our study, but the consumer surplus and option value estimates seem plausible. Non-use value estimates obtained in our study are clearly higher than the few comparable estimates found in the literature, in particular, for train users, confirming our hypothesis that these estimates may not be plausible.

Conclusions and Discussion

The option value concept is well known in environmental economics for valuating natural assets that offer opportunities for future consumption. The field of measuring transport option values, however, is far from developed. This paper records one of the few empirical studies in the transport field that shows the relevance of option values as a benefit category additional to the traditional use and non-use benefit categories. Here we have shown our development of a survey instrument to quantify option value benefits of public transport services, including three stated choice experiments for separate eliciting of WTP for use, option use and non-use. To derive the first set of WTP estimates for option use of public transport services in the Netherlands, the survey instrument was applied to two regional railway links in the Netherlands—one located in a low-density rural area situated in the eastern Netherlands and one in the highly urbanised western part of the country. Respondents were selected and recruited from a national Internet panel.

The main conclusion from our study is that option values may form a potentially relevant benefit category in public transport policy appraisal, additional to use and non-use benefit categories (e.g. congestion, environmental impacts) typically included. Significant option values could be obtained from the stated choice experiments for both regional railway links. Train users seemed to be willing to pay about 9 Euro per month over and above their consumer surplus for the continued availability of the railway link. Non-users with uncertain demand seemed to be willing to pay about 12 Euro per month to maintain the railway link. These results provide a first indication of the order of magnitude of the option value of regional railway links to users and non-users, but estimates obtained are not directly transferable to other railway links. That is, both railway links were selected because option values would likely form an important benefit category: the links have relatively low use and cost-coverage levels, and no real public transport alternatives are present in the area. Option values are likely to be smaller in railway link areas where residents exhibit higher-use levels (and consumer surplus will dominate total use value) or where good rail or bus alternatives exist.

The survey instrument developed in this study proved to be useful, but a number of issues related to the survey design and data collection method can be improved. Firstly, the survey design allowed the computation of average use and option values for different respondent groups, however, not on the individual level. In other words, the survey included three stated choice experiments, but respondents applicable to all experiments were selected for only two choice experiments. This was to reduce survey length and prevent potential boredom, irritation and fatigue, which can arise when respondents are repeatedly asked to participate in several choice experiments. Secondly, in our study we did not examine different payment mechanisms, which have been shown in the literature to have an impact on WTP. Bateman et al. (2002)

indicate that when asked for a monthly payment, respondents have a tendency to pay more than the corresponding yearly payment. There were also two major issues in using an Internet panel as data collection method. Firstly, data collection via the Internet is still not a satisfactory alternative for collecting data for all population groups. In our study we were not able to address elderly people properly in the study. Secondly, only one person per household was a member of the Internet panel. We were thus not able to examine option values for each household member individually, and could not examine differences in the valuation of public transport services between household members.

Where to Direct Further Research

The first direction to pursue is to incorporate option values in transport appraisal (i.e. CBA) of public transport strategies or projects. To date and to the best of our knowledge there have, however, been no incidences of option and non-use values being monetised and included in transport appraisal. The UK is at this moment the only country where option values are recognised as specific benefit category and where guidance is given on its measurement in transport appraisal guidelines (DfT, 2004). So far, however, qualitative procedures have been followed in transport appraisal studies in the UK to score the effect of changes in public transport provision on option value. There are a number of difficulties that arise in applying the option values derived in this study in a transport appraisal. Firstly, the empirical evidence on option values presented in this paper reflects the absolute level of option value of railway links with a typical regional transport function and a particular level of service. The results of the two case studies are not directly transferable to railway links of national or international importance or the introduction of new railway links. Ideally, a set of WTP estimates would need to be generated (either from a series of small-scale surveys at the project level or from a large-scale national survey) which could then be included as rules of thumb in a CBA guideline. New research would also need to generate WTP values for incremental changes in service provision, for example replacement of a rail service by a bus service, as this is often the concern of transport appraisal. Secondly, at this moment in time there is no evidence on how values vary with distance from access/egress points to the infrastructure/service (stations, bus stops etc.) and whether option and non-use values are held by households outside those catchment areas. Examples of public transport scheme appraisals including monetised option values will be necessary to examine the importance of public transport option values in transport appraisal.

A second direction to pursue in future research is to examine option values of population groups not yet included in our exploratory study. More study on the valuation of public transport on the household level and for elderly is necessary. In addition, we have included residents living in the municipalities bordering on the railway links in our study and have not included potential users or option users from other parts of the country. Although residents in outlying areas outside the service area of the rail links are generally unlikely to use the train under any condition, a small proportion of residents (possibly with an option value) may be future visitors to the case study areas. Furthermore, we have not examined the option value that firms may place on transport infrastructure or services. To our knowledge, no studies have so far attempted to quantify this benefit. Furthermore, more research will be necessary to disentangle non-use values from option and use values, especially for train users and individuals with other train-using household members. There are few efforts in the literature which have attempted to quantify the non-use benefits of public transport.

A third direction that further research might take is to examine the degree to which revealed preference approaches (ex post evaluations) approximate the option value estimates (ex ante evaluations) derived in our study. Firstly, in case of railway closures, the second-best alternative available to train users (e.g., taxi, car rental, a bus service, work at home) may be examined using travel survey data and/or transport models. The difference in travel costs between use of the second-best alternative and the current railway service may then be calculated and compared with option value estimates. Secondly, research may be conducted to examine if the option value that users and non-users attach to transport facilities is reflected in a person's choice of location and housing prices.

ACKNOWLEDGMENTS

This research was partly funded by Prorail, the Dutch national railway infrastructure manager. The authors thank Prorail for making this study possible. We are also grateful to Peter Scheffer, Johan van Dalen and Ruud Thunnissen from Prorail for their valuable comments during the project.

ANNEX 1 DETAILED RESULTS FROM LOGIT MODEL ESTIMATIONS

Table A1. Multinomial Logit Model Estimates Derived From the Choice Experiment 'Consumer Surplus'

	All respondents			Arnhem–Winterswijk link area			Leiden–Gouda link area		
	All train users	Regular train user	Option user	All train users	Regular train user	Option user	All train users	Regular train user	Option user
Respondents (N)	413	232	181	204	92	112	209	140	69
Observations ($N \times 12$)	4,956	2,784	2,172	2,448	1,104	1,344	2,508	1,680	828
−Log likelihood	3,244	1,867	1,363	1,563	746	799	1,658	1,094	558
Pseudo-R^2	0.40	0.39	0.43	0.41	0.38	0.46	0.40	0.41	0.39
Estimated coefficient									
Frequency halving	−0.69	−0.74	−0.62	−0.68	−0.75	−0.65	−0.69	−0.74	−0.58
Current frequency	0.37	0.43	0.27*	0.41	0.63	0.23*	0.32	0.31*	0.33*
Frequency doubling	*0.32*	*0.31*	*0.35*	*0.27*	*0.12*	*0.41*	*0.36*	*0.43*	*0.25*
Travel time +25%	−0.36	−0.39	−0.35	−0.32	−0.25	−0.38	−0.41	−0.48	−0.29
Current travel time	0.23	0.22*	0.27*	0.19*	0.01*	0.35*	0.28	0.35	0.14*
Travel time −25%	*−0.13*	*−0.17*	*−0.08*	*−0.12*	*−0.24*	*−0.03*	*−0.14*	*−0.13*	*−0.15*
Ticket price +25%	−1.53	−1.42	−1.70	−1.36	−1.01	−1.70	−1.72	−1.74	−1.69
Ticket price +10%	−0.55	−0.44	−0.72	−0.48	−0.25	−0.69	−0.63	−0.56	−0.79
Current ticket price	0.39	0.40	0.39	0.31	0.27	0.35	0.48	0.51	0.45
Ticket price −10%	0.74	0.64	0.90	0.68	0.48	0.87	0.82	0.76	0.94
Ticket price −25%	*0.95*	*0.81*	*1.13*	*0.85*	*0.52*	*1.16*	*1.04*	*1.02*	*1.10*
No-choice	−1.94	−1.91	−1.96	−2.34	−2.47	−2.25	−1.64	−1.65	−1.60

T-statistic									
Frequency halving	−17.1	−14.1	−9.9	−12.2	−9.4	−8.0	−12.0	−10.6	−5.8
Current frequency	3.6	3.2	1.7	2.8	3.0	1.1	2.2	1.8	1.3
Travel time +25%	−6.7	−5.4	−4.2	−4.2	−2.3	−3.6	−5.4	−5.1	−2.2
Current travel time	2.5	1.8	1.9	1.4	0.0	1.9	2.1	2.2	0.6
Ticket price +25%	−27.0	−19.5	−18.7	−17.9	−10.0	−14.7	−20.2	−16.6	−11.5
Ticket price +10%	−9.6	−5.8	−7.9	−5.9	−2.2	−5.9	−7.6	−5.6	−5.4
Current ticket price	8.0	6.0	5.3	4.5	2.7	3.7	6.8	5.6	3.9
Ticket price −10%	12.5	8.2	9.5	8.0	4.0	7.1	9.7	7.3	6.4
No-choice	−29.8	−22.2	−19.7	−21.8	−15.0	−15.8	−19.7	−15.9	−11.5
Monetary value (Euro)									
No-choice (= CS/trip)	2.4	2.2	2.5	2.1	1.7	2.5	2.7	2.6	3.0
Monthly CS	7.2	10.2	3.3	6.9	10.8	3.4	7.7	9.6	3.6

Terms in *italic* depict reference attribute level.
*Not significant at the 5% level.

Table A2. Binomial Logit Model Estimates Derived From the Choice Experiment 'Option Price'

	All respondents				Arnhem–Winterswijk link area		Leiden–Gouda link area	
	All train users	Regular train user	Option user	Possible option user	All train users	Possible option user	All train users	Possible option user
Number of respondents (*N*)	228	114	114	226	121	111	107	115
Number of observations ($N \times 12$)	2,736	1,368	1,368	2,706	1,450	1,326	1,286	1,378
−Log likelihood	1,514	733	792	1,506	809	737	696	712
Pseudo-R^2	0.33	0.36	0.31	0.32	0.32	0.32	0.35	0.33
Estimated coefficient								
Frequency halving	−0.44	−0.51	−0.36	−0.31	−0.33	−0.23	−0.57	−0.40
Frequency doubling	*0.44*	*0.51*	*0.36*	*0.31*	*0.33*	*0.23*	*0.57*	*0.40*
Closure of railway stations	0.34	0.45	0.23	0.28	0.21	0.18	0.50	0.40
Railway link closure	−1.33	−1.49	−1.20	−1.19	−1.31	−1.19	−1.38	−1.21
Current railway stations	0.46	0.52	0.42	0.40	0.53	0.55	0.38	0.25
New railway stations	*0.54*	*0.53*	*0.55*	*0.51*	*0.57*	*0.46*	*0.51*	*0.55*
Monthly tax +10 Euro	−1.09	−1.03	−1.15	−1.29	−1.10	−1.28	−1.10	−1.31
Monthly tax +5 Euro	−0.20	−0.17	−0.22	−0.28	−0.14	−0.30	−0.27	−0.25
Monthly tax −5 Euro	0.59	0.65	0.54	0.72	0.55	0.76	0.64	0.68
Monthly tax −10 Euro	*0.69*	*0.55*	*0.83*	*0.85*	*0.68*	*0.83*	*0.72*	0.89
T-statistic								
Frequency halving	−9.8	−8.0	−5.8	−6.8	−5.6	−3.5	−8.4	−6.1
Railway link closure	−22.1	−16.6	−14.6	−20.3	−15.8	−14.1	−15.5	−14.6
Closure of railway stations	6.9	6.4	3.4	5.8	3.1	2.5	6.7	5.6
Current railway stations	9.2	7.1	5.9	7.8	7.7	7.4	5.1	3.5
Monthly tax +10 Euro	−15.2	−10.1	−11.4	−17.5	−11.2	−12.1	−10.3	−12.7
Monthly tax +5 Euro	−4.0	−2.4	−3.3	−5.6	−2.1	−4.3	−3.7	−3.7
Monthly tax −5 Euro	10.0	7.3	6.8	12.1	7.0	8.8	7.2	8.3
Monetary value (Euro/month)								
Frequency halving	7.2	8.3	6.2	5.3	6.8	3.7	7.8	6.1
Frequency doubling	2.8	2.4	3.3	2.2	3.0	1.5	4.4	2.9
Closure of railway stations	3.2	2.0	4.1	2.1	1.5	6.2	−0.9	−1.1
New railway stations	0.7	0.1	1.3	0.7	0.4	−0.4	1.0	2.2
Railway link closure (= option price)	16.5	19.5	14.1	12.4	16.7	13.6	16.0	11.1
Option value (= option price−CS)	9.3	9.3	10.7	12.4	9.8	13.6	8.3	11.1

Terms in *italic* depict reference attribute level.

Table A3. Binomial Logit Model Estimates Derived From the Choice Experiment 'Non-Use Value'

	All respondents					Arnhem–Winterswijk link area			Leiden–Gouda link area		
	All train users	Regular train user	Option user	Car user	Possible option user	All train users	Car user	Possible option user	All train users	Car user	Possible option user
Respondents (N)	189	112	78	105	216	82	70	106	107	35	110
Observations ($N \times 12$)	2,273	1,344	936	1,260	2,592	985	842	1,267	1,288	415	1,321
−Log likelihood	1,217	691	512	735	1,458	546	486	731	663	247	714
Pseudo-R^2	0.36	0.40	0.34	0.26	0.31	0.32	0.28	0.28	0.40	0.24	0.35
Estimated coefficient											
Frequency halving	−0.44	−0.52	−0.32	−0.12*	−0.23	−0.38	−0.11*	−0.19	−0.49	−0.14*	−0.28
Frequency doubling	*0.44*	*0.52*	*0.32*	*0.12*	*0.23*	*0.38*	0.11	*0.19*	*0.49*	0.14	*0.28*
Railway link closure	−1.42	−1.58	−1.23	−0.55	−0.93	−1.24	−0.59	−0.97	−1.58	−0.50	−0.91
Closure of railway stations	0.44	0.39	0.52	0.05*	0.30	0.51	0.09*	0.15	0.39	−0.03*	0.48
Current railway stations	0.47	0.55	0.37	0.18	0.27	0.36	0.22*	0.39	0.56	0.10*	0.14*
New railway stations	*0.51*	*0.64*	*0.34*	*0.33*	*0.36*	*0.37*	*0.28*	*0.43*	*0.63*	*0.42*	*0.29*
Monthly tax +10 Euro	−1.16	−1.12	−1.22	−1.29	−1.31	−1.17	−1.37	−1.12	−1.15	−1.13	−1.53
Monthly tax +5 Euro	−0.36	−0.34	−0.41	−0.32	−0.45	−0.34	−0.27	−0.44	−0.39	−0.42	−0.47
Monthly tax −5 Euro	0.72	0.66	0.82	0.80	0.71	0.77	0.86	0.61	0.69	0.71	0.82
Monthly tax −10 Euro	*0.80*	*0.80*	*0.80*	*0.80*	*1.05*	*0.73*	*0.78*	*0.94*	*0.85*	*0.85*	*1.18*
T-statistic											
Frequency halving	−8.6	−7.8	−4.1	−1.8	−4.8	−5.0	−1.3	−3.0	−7.1	−1.3	−3.9
Railway link closure	−21.1	−17.0	−12.4	−7.1	−16.5	−12.7	−6.1	−12.0	−16.8	−3.7	−11.3
Closure of railway stations	7.9	5.4	5.9	0.7	5.9	6.0	1.1	2.1	5.2	−0.2	6.2
Current railway stations	8.3	7.4	4.2	2.5	5.1	4.3	2.5	5.3	7.3	0.8	1.9
Monthly tax +10 Euro	−14.3	−10.4	−9.8	−12.0	−17.4	−9.8	−10.3	−11.0	−10.4	−6.2	−13.4
Monthly tax +5 Euro	−6.6	−4.8	−4.7	−4.2	−8.7	−4.1	−2.9	−6.0	−5.3	−3.2	−6.3
Monthly tax −5 Euro	10.7	7.4	7.8	10.0	12.2	7.6	8.5	7.6	7.5	5.3	9.6
Monetary value (Euro/month)											
Railway link closure (= non-use value)	16.3	19.0	13.2	5.7	9.1	13.7	5.9	12.1	18.6	(5.2)	6.9

Terms in *italic* depict reference attribute level; ( ), sample size is too small to obtain a reliable estimate.
*Not significant at the 5% level.

References

Advisory Council for Transport Public Works and Water Management (2004). De waarde van het openbaar vervoer [The value of public transport]. Advisory Council for Transport, Public Works and Water Management, The Hague.

Arentze, T., A. Borgers, H. Timmermans and R. DelMistro (2003). Transport stated choice responses: effects of task complexity, presentation format and literacy. *Transportation research part E* 39(3), 229–244.

Baarsma, B. (2000). Monetary valuation of environmental goods. Alternatives to contingent valuation. Tinbergen Institute Research Series 220, Universiteit van Amsterdam, Amsterdam.

Bateman, I. J., R. T. Carson, B. Day, M. Hanemann, N. Hanley, T. Hett, M. J. Lee, G. Loomes, S. Mourato, E. Ozdemiroglu, D. W. Pearce, R. Sugden and J. Swanson (2002). *Economic Valuation with Stated Preference Techniques: A Manual.* Cheltenham, Edward Elgar.

Boardman, A. E., D. H. Greenberg, A. R. Vining and D. L. Weimer (2001). *Cost–Benefit Analysis: Concepts and Practice*, 2nd edn.Upper Saddle River, NJ, Prentice Hall.

Bristow, A. L., P. G. Hopkinson, C. A. Nash and M. Wardman (1991a). Evaluation of the use and non-use benefits of public transport. Report No. 1. Developments of a survey methodology. ITS Working Paper 309, ITS, Leeds.

Bristow, A. L., P. G. Hopkinson, C. A. Nash and M. Wardman (1991b). Evaluation of the use and non-use benefits of public transport. Report No. 2. Application of the method. ITS Working Paper 310, ITS, Leeds.

Cameron, T. A. and J. Englin (1997). Welfare effects of changes in environmental quality under individual uncertainty about use. *Rand Journal of Economics* 28, S45–S70 (cited in Roson, 2000).

Caussade, S., J. de Dios Ortuzar, L. I. Rizzi and D. A. Hensher (2005). Assessing the influence of design dimensions on stated choice experiment estimates. *Transportation Research Part B: Methodological* 39(7), 621–640.

Crockett, D. (1992). *Should Non-Use Benefits be Included in Social Cost Benefit Analysis.* Leeds, Institute for Transport Studies, University of Leeds, (not published).

DfT (2004) The option values sub-objective. TAG Unit 3.6.1. Department for Transport, London. Available at: http://www.webtag.org.uk/webdocuments/doc_-index.htm

Dietz, F., W. Hafkamp and J. van der Straaten (1994). *Basisboek Milieu-Economie [Handbook of Environmental Economics].* Amsterdam, Boom.

Ecorys/Prorail. (2003). *Integrale Business Case Rijn Gouwe Lijn. Volgens LIBRA methodiek [Business Case Rijn Gouwe Rail Link].* Rotterdam, Ecorys/Prorail.

Geurs, K. T. (2006). De optiewaarde van het spoor. De waardering van de aanwezigheid en gebruik van regionale spoorlijnen. Methodiek en case studies [The option value of railways. Valuation of the presence and use of regional railways.

Methodology and case studies]. Rapport 500021002/2005, Netherlands Environmental Assessment Agency, Bilthoven.

Geurs, K. T., R. Haaijer and B. van Wee (2006). Option value of public transport: methodology for measurement and case study for regional rail links in the Netherlands. *Transport Reviews* 26(5), 613–643.

Hanley, N. and C. L. Spash (1997). *Cost Benefit Analysis and the Environment*. Cheltenham, Edward Elgar Publishing Limited.

Hausman, J. A. (1993). *Contingent Valuation. A Critical Assessment*. Amsterdam, North-Holland.

Hensher, D. A., J. M. Rose and W. H. Greene (2005). *Applied Choice Analysis: A Primer*. Cambridge, UK, Cambridge University Press.

Huber, J. and K. Zwerina (1996). The importance of utility balance in efficient choice designs. *Journal of Marketing Research* 33(3), 307–317.

Humphreys, M. (2004). Assessing indirect use and non-use values for rail transport using expressed preference techniques. Ph.D. Thesis. Institute for Transport Studies, University of Leeds, Leeds.

Humphreys, M. and A. S. Fowkes (2006). The significance of indirect use and non-use values in transport appraisal. *International Journal of Transport Economics* XXXIII(1), 17–35.

Kahneman, D. and A. Tversky (1979). Prospect theory: an analysis of decision under risk. *Econometrica* 47, 263–291.

Kling, C. L. (1993). An assessment of the empirical magnitude of option values for environmental goods. *Environmental and Resource Economics* 3, 471–485.

Laird, J., R. Batley, C. Nash and K. Geurs (2006). *Option Values, Non-Use Values and Transport Appraisal*. Leeds, Institute for Transport Studies, University of Leeds.

Louviere, J. J., D. A. Hensher and J. Swait (2000). *Stated Choice Methods. Analysis and Application*. Cambridge, UK, Cambridge University Press.

MuConsult. (1992). *Inkomen en Treingebruik Naar Motief [Income and Train Use by Trip Purpose]*. Amersfoort, MuConsult.

Nossum, A. (2005). Stated preference Surveys on Internet-an Effective Method for Finding Passengers' Preferences? Summary Report. TOI rapport 763/2005, TOI, Oslo.

Painter, K. M., R. D. Scott II, P. R. Wandschneider and K. L. Casavant (2001). Using contingent valuation to measure user and nonuser benefits: an application to public transit. *Review of Agricultural Economics* 24(2), 394–409.

Poort, J., I. Groot, L. Kok, D. de Graaf and B. Hof (2005). Accessibility of public services. SEO Report 775, SEO/Ministry of Economic Affairs, Amsterdam.

Roson, R. (2000). Social cost pricing when public transport is an option value. *Innovation* 13(1), 81–94.

Roson, R. (2001). Assessing the option value of a publicly provided service: the case of local transport. *Urban studies* 38(8), 1319–1327.

Smith, V. K. (1987). Uncertainty, benefit-cost analysis and the treatment of option value. *Journal of Environmental Economics and Management* 14, 283–292.

Statistics Netherlands (2005). Dertig procent van de volwassenen Internet niet [Thirty percent of adults do not use the Internet]. CBS Webmagazine, 13-06-2005, Statistics Netherlands.

Transport Research Centre. (2005). *Mobiliteitsonderzoek Nederland 2004 [Mobility Survey 2004]*. Rotterdam, Ministry of Transport, Public Works and Water Management.

Transport Research Centre (2005b). Value of time personenvervoer: Trein per motief; Basisjaar 2004 [Value of Time: Train by trip purpose; base year 2004]. Rotterdam.

van de Kaa, E. J. (2008). Extended prospect theory. Findings on choice behaviour from economics and the behavioural sciences and their relevance for travel behaviour. Ph.D. Thesis, Delft University, Delft.

Walsh, R. G., J. B. Loomis and R. A. Gillman (1984). Valuing option, existence and bequest demands for wilderness. *Land Economics* 60, 14–29.

Weisbrod, B. A. (1964). Collective consumption services of individual consumption goods. *Quarterly Journal of Economics* 78, 471–477.

Zwerina, K., J. Huber and W. F. Kuhfeld (1996). *A General Method for Constructing Efficient Choice Designs*. Cary, SAS Institute.

The Expanding Sphere of Travel Behaviour Research
Selected Papers from the 11th International Conference on Travel Behaviour Research

39

Longitudinal Simulation of Travel Under Budget Constraints

Dirk Zumkeller, Tobias Kuhnimhof and Christoph Gringmuth

Abstract

With changing societal and economic boundary conditions, new challenges for transport models arise. Models that are based on fixed trip rates from empirical distributions are often not appropriate in these situations. This is because with respect to activity generation, they are not sensitive to budget constraints on the side of the traveler or to rising costs on the supply side. In our paper, we propose a new generation of model that is able to consider budget restrictions. This entails microscopic modeling of entire weekly schedules because travelers do not balance budgets on a day-to-day basis. This in turn involves modeling the right balance of routine and nonroutine, particularly in mode and destination choice. The last section of the paper is dedicated to the discussion of different approaches for activity scheduling under budget restrictions. We found that a relatively simple algorithm (GO-algorithm) was superior to a genetic algorithm. Both algorithms produced realistic weekly activity schedules. However, the GO-algorithm uses much less computation time and is therefore easier to apply in large simulation contexts.

Introduction

In the past decades the development of travel in Germany was largely characterized by growth. Since a few years back, this general growth has come to a standstill. Nevertheless, travel behavior continues to change, for example, driven by the demographic development. However, travel today is characterized by other processes than it used to be in the earlier decades: growth and recession occur at the same time in different places and different segments of travel. At the same time, there are more travelers with increasing modal options because of the decline of captive transit riders due to increasing car availability.

In order to understand traveler's choices and behavioral processes in this situation, multiday and multi-period travel surveys such as the German Mobility Panel (MOP) were established. The findings from analyzing such data form a basis for successfully implementing microscopic simulation models that open up the possibility of addressing new issues with transport modeling with a longitudinal perspective.

One of these new issues is the modeling of transport mode clienteles in an environment where travelers have increasing modal options. Another issue is the limit to traveler behavior that arises from individual time and money budget constraints. This issue is of increasing importance in countries like Germany that undergo economical and societal changes while dealing with an aging population.

With new issues such as these arising, transport models also have to expand their sphere. In the paper on hand, we present the challenges that arise for transport modeling in this situation. Based on this, we present the concept of a model which is currently being developed at the Institute for Economic Policy Research (IWW) and the Institute for Transport Studies (IfV) in Karlsruhe. In the final section of the paper, we present in detail an activity scheduling algorithm that forms the core of our proposed model.

What is new about our presented model is the microscopic approach that considers travel time and travel money budgets of the individual in a longitudinal perspective. With this concept the model is able to evaluate the influence of budget changes on mobility. The concept of limited individual or household budgets involves a modeling time frame of one week. This is because travelers do not balance their budgets on a day-to-day basis. Therefore, when considering budgets the consequence is "the longer the modeling period the better." However, with respect to respondent burden, reporting periods in travel surveys which represent the database for modeling have to be limited (Zumkeller et al., 2004b). A week seems to be a long enough period of time to consider individual budgets for travel—a limitation to the mobility options of the individual—at least for everyday travel.

The fact that the modeling time frame for our longitudinal microscopic model is one week entails a number of consequences. Particularly with respect to destination and mode choice, habitual choices and individual preferences have to be considered. This, in turn, enables the model to reproduce the clientele of transport modes.

After presenting the new challenges for transport modeling, we will discuss the conceptual framework of the entire model. Finally, we focus in detail on presenting the activity scheduling process which forms the core of our behavioral model. In that part of the paper, we concentrate on time budget restrictions even though the model concept is designed for considering other budget restrictions as well.

New Challenges for Modeling Transport

Since a few years back, the general growth of travel demand in Germany has come to a standstill and the extension of the infrastructure has slowed down. There are multilayer reasons for these changes in trends that include the economic development as well as the countries changing demography (Zumkeller et al., 2004a). In this context, the traditional application of transport models that are employed to appraise new parts of infrastructure or infrastructure improvements is no longer the normal case. Aside from traditional tasks new challenges for transport modeling arise. The following issues are some examples of this type of challenge.

Modeling Increased Access and Travel Time Savings

The results of conventional transport modeling when evaluating measures in the transport infrastructure are usually travel time savings. Depending largely on this variable, the prospective value of measures is determined. On the one hand, different studies show that this reflects reality: To a large degree travel time savings, for example, on a particular link in the network, really result in more time spent at home (Fujii et al., 1997). This is also confirmed by the time allocation of travelers who spend much time commuting: Compared to others with similar working times, commuters with long commutes usually hardly reduce their time spent on other out-of-home activities and associated travel. The main source of time for commuting a lot is the time spend at home (Kuhnimhof, 2006). These findings show that there are indeed a number of situations when travel time savings are realized in the sense that travelers gain time for activities other than travel. This particularly applies to individual situations that are characterized by a tight time schedule.

On the other hand, experiences of the past decades show that the aggregate travel time has not fallen despite improvements of the infrastructure that resulted mainly in travel time savings. Instead the distance traveled per passenger and day has risen, that is, activity spaces and access have grown. This observation has led to the call for different transport models that evaluate the increase in access instead of travel time savings while keeping the aggregate travel time constant (Metz, 2004; Mokhtarian & Chen, 2003; Zumkeller et al., 1980).

This leads to the question if the two concepts of transport models are contradictory. From our viewpoint they are not, but they operate on different scales: The concept of travel time savings describes the situation of single travelers under unchanged boundary conditions, for example, with respect to job or residential location. However, as a long-term consequence of the infrastructure improvement, travelers might change their boundary conditions by choosing another work or residential place. The additional access that travelers gain when infrastructure improvements are implemented is probably realized to a large degree through long-term decisions.

Based on these considerations, the following requirements for an integrative transport model can be derived: When evaluating the individual impact of measures in the transport infrastructure under unchanged boundary conditions, the concepts of travel time savings is appropriate, at least for travelers with relatively tight time schedules. When the long-term consequences of measures are taken into consideration, the model result should not be travel time savings. In contrary, the aggregate travel time consumption in a cross-sectional perspective should be the same under before and after conditions. On the other hand, travelers should exhibit larger activity spaces after adapting their life situation and not only their behavior. This is likely to reflect the reality better than the conventional and one-dimensional travel time savings analysis. In both cases, the regime of time plays an important role and limits the possibilities of the individual traveler. An activity-based model aiming at reproducing this interrelationship must consider individual travel time restrictions. A necessary condition for this type of model is the knowledge of individual time budgets in a longitudinal perspective.

Appraisal of a new generation of measures

With the slowdown of the infrastructure extension a new generation of measures has gained importance. These range from road pricing to advanced traveler information. Such information is supposed to help travelers to reconsider and change travel time, mode, and route choice if applicable. Road pricing can help to distribute traffic demand in space and time. Road pricing aims at controlling the demand on the network elements where pricing exists and helps to deliver a guaranteed level of service (Gringmuth et al., 2006).

Based on earlier experiences the impact of such measures on traveler behavior can be roughly estimated. However, conventional models implemented today are largely unable to predict the changes in travel behavior that arise from such measures. In some cases, destination-, mode-, and route-choice models might be sensitive to such measures. Trip or activity generation is usually unaffected. Models that do not operate on the basis of fixed trip or activity generation but consider individual travel budgets will help to understand the impact of such new measures on travel behavior. Such models enable us to perform scenarios in order to simulate and evaluate the effect of such measures.

Changes of Costs and Regimes

While the built infrastructure is unlikely to develop extensively in next future, major changes with respect to the costs of travel and on the side of the travelers are likely to occur. With a globally increasing demand for crude oil, fuel prices have risen significantly and are unlikely to go down again. At the same time economic growth and particularly income growth have come to a slow down in Germany. With the ongoing demographic change, the individual need to invest in private pension is rising. This entails shifting of household budgets from spending to saving. All these developments of framework conditions are likely to affect the household travel money budgets on the one hand and travel costs on the other (Zumkeller et al., 2004a).

Not only the money budget is affected by the ongoing societal and economic changes: While working hours of employees have been decreasing in Germany for decades, this trend has now been broken and working hours are going up again. On the other hand, the share of retirees is rising and therefore also the share of those who have more degrees of freedom to use their time. Altogether it is apparent that the time budget for travel is also undergoing changes.

Only relatively few changes to the transport infrastructure can be expected in the oncoming years but major changes with respect to travel costs as well as budgets on the side of the traveler. The task for transport models therefore shifts toward modeling the implications of such changes on travel behavior. Hence, the connections between budgets and travel not only have to be well understood but also integrated in model of travel behavior.

Modeling Travelers Options and Transport Mode Clienteles

At the same time, more and more travelers continue to have increasing options. This particularly applies to car availability: 17% of the German adult populations do not hold a driving license today. As these are predominantly elder persons, in the long run about 95% of adults will hold a license. In addition, the number of cars per capita in Germany (today: ~0.517) is still rising (Kuhnimhof et al., 2006).

Furthermore, despite belt-tightening, public transport still offers good and in some places improving quality. In fact, we observe that public transport gained ground in the last 10 years by slightly increasing its share in the modal split in terms of kilometers traveled. In scenarios of increasing fuel prices and relatively declining household budgets, the competition between modes is even likely to grow. The reason for this is that with high fuel prices, public transport might be the more economic choice in a lot more situations compared to today. Reciprocally, the clientele of transport modes is likely to change from travelers who are more or less captive toward a clientele that has a number of options and makes pragmatic use of them.

Modeling Trend Changes and Shrinkage

A close look at the current overall stagnation of travel demand in Germany shows growth and shrinkage at the same time. They go on in different places and different parts of the society. Today, particularly rural regions and urban regions with economic difficulties in the eastern German states experience shrinkage. The city of Halle, for example, has lost about 100,000 inhabitants—a third of it's population—in the past 15 years. This exemplifies that shrinkage is an up-to-date topic even today and it is likely to be more important in the future because of Germany's changing demography.

Under conditions of shrinkage, the question of transport planning is no longer whether a planned piece to infrastructure will be worth its money. The problem shifts toward the question which parts of the infrastructure or services are worth to be kept alive because they will be valuable even with a smaller population and less travel going on and which parts have to be given up.

Shrinkage and trend reversals in travel are not necessarily a result of changes of the population with respect to age or number. They can also occur under an unaltered population if regimes such as budgets or costs change. This type of trend change is particularly difficult to predict if transport models are based on trip or activity rates from an empirical study. In order to be able to foresee such changes in mobility, the linkage between budgets and travel behavior has to be incorporated in the modeling process.

Conceptual Framework of the Presented Model

The model we present is designed to perform behavioral scenarios under varying boundary conditions, for example, changing incomes or mobility costs. Therefore, the travelers are assigned a specific agenda of what they intend to do during the modeling period of seven days. In addition, the travelers are given mobility tools as well as individual budgets which can include time and money. Within this framework the individual traveler can perform his activities keeping the restricting budgets.

In the following, we present the background and the concept of the different model components. Figure 1 shows an overview over the different model components prior to the activity scheduling. The focus of the first stage of the model implementation is the restrictions to travel behavior caused by travel time budget constraints. Therefore, the focus in this paper is also on travel time and other issues are discussed with less detail.

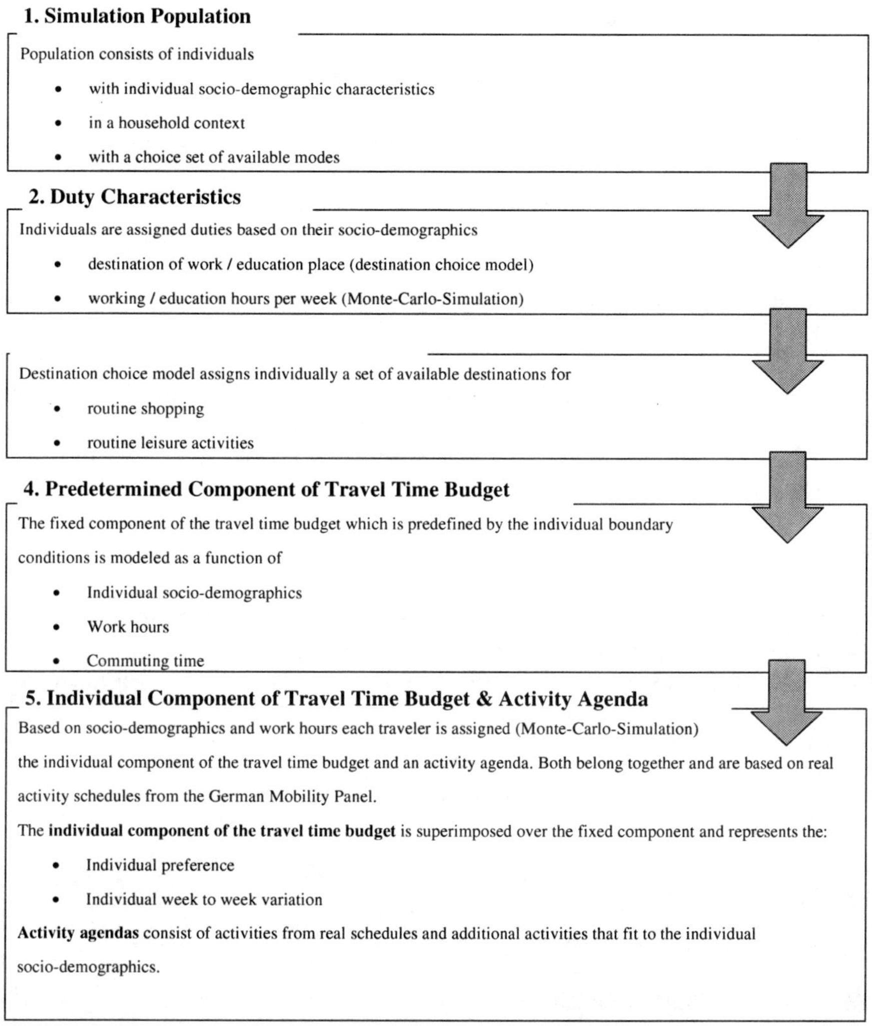

Figure 1

Components of Behavioral Model Previous to the Activity Scheduling in the First Stage of Model Implementation

In the last part of the paper, we discuss different innovative approaches that have been tested for the actual activity scheduling process. The database which represents the empirical background and source of statistics and distributions for our model is the German mobility (Zumkeller et al., 2005).

Individual Travel Time Budget

With respect to modeling, the regime of time has important properties that have to be considered: General time availability, 24 hours a day, is the same for everybody. The possibilities to transfer time are very limited. This applies to transferring time from one day to the other (things that are not done today can be taken care of tomorrow in some cases only). This also applies to transferring time from one person to another (within households tasks can be assigned to different persons). Hence, the natural unit that has to make sure time expenditures do not get out of hand is the individual. The mean travel time per person and day is about 80 minutes, that is, we spend about 5–6% of our total time with travel.

Individuals differ by the duties they have to fulfill—work, education, in-home duties—and the travel time associated with these duties, predominantly commuting time. Beyond these duties individuals have time at their own disposal. This also applies to travel time. Figure 2 shows the distribution of total travel time per person and day. Depicted in Figure 2 are medium-term means (three weeks) of individual travel times. Hence, Figure 2 shows how travelers differ with respect to their means of travel times per person and day.

Once the times for duties (work) and associated travel (commuting) are known, regressions explain about 20–30% of the travel time variance for discretionary activities. This depends on how much is known about the individual's situation

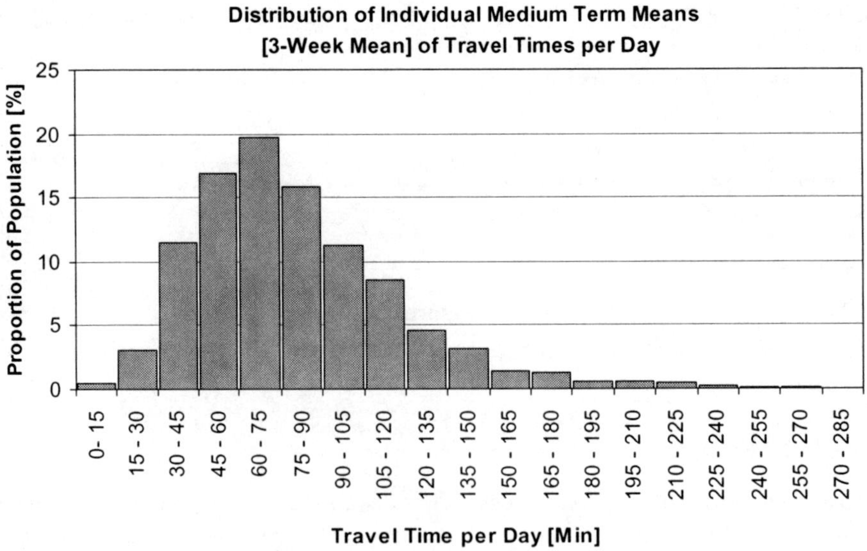

Figure 2
Distribution of Individual Medium-Term Means of Travel Times Per Day

(household context). Hence, even though travel time expenditures are strongly subject to individual preference, a large part can be explained by the life situation. This can be referred to as the predetermined component of the travel time budget.

Hence, in our model, first the life situation is determined. It is characterized by the household context and the work or education duties that a person has to fulfill. The individual locations of work or education are determined as well in a destination choice model. On this basis individual commuting times are assigned. Depending on this life context, every traveler in the model is assigned the predetermined component of the individual travel time budget that only depends on the life situation. In reality, this predetermined component is complemented by the travelers' individual preference of how much daily time he likes to spend with travel. Together this results in the individual mean travel time per day.

The question arises what significance this individual mean travel time has. A desired travel time budget in the sense that we plan our travel according to a subconscious timer appears to be unlikely. However, in the course of everyday life, we have developed our routines. In the context of these routines, we develop habits of how much time is useful to be invested in travel.

We do vary our individual travel times from day to day but much less from week to week (Kunert, 1992). Because of our routines the travel time variations from week to week are limited (Figure 3). Major variations from this practical daily or weekly travel time are unlikely because they put a time pressure on other activities we want or have to engage in: Spending too much time for travel leads to sleeping not enough or cutting back on other activities. From this background the individual mean travel time can be referred to as the individual travel time budget.

However, as shown in Figure 3, the travel time expenditures vary from week to week. The consequence is that individual travel times in particular weeks are not only a function of the predetermined travel time component and the individual preference but also subject to week-to-week variation. Therefore, in our model we use Monte-Carlo simulation to superimpose the predetermined travel time component with a distribution that represents the individual preference and the intrapersonal week-to-week variation of travel times. As a result, each traveler in the model has an individual travel time at his own disposal during the model week. The intra- and interpersonal variations of these model travel times conform to real world distributions.

Household Travel Money Budget

Money budgets generally differ from time in that they are not equally distributed among travelers. This makes money a regime much more difficult to handle in a behavioral model. With all the shortcomings associated with this approach, we use

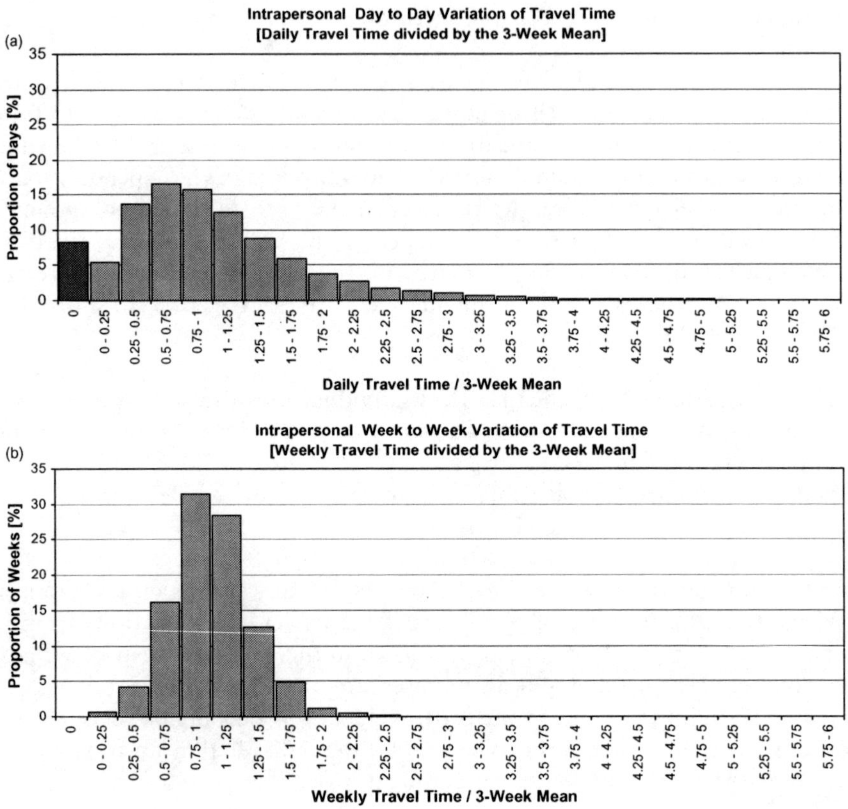

Figure 3

Distribution of Individual Medium-Term Means of Travel Times Per Day

household income as the primary indicator of the general household money budget. The results of the official German income and expenditure statistic EVS (DESTATIS, 2006) and the German MOP match widely with respect to the findings on travel money expenditures: Households in Germany spend about €310 on travel each month (air travel not included). This corresponds with about 14% of the household net income.

Opposed to time, the possibilities to transfer money in time (i.e., save money at one time to spend it another time) and between persons particularly within a household are plenty. This makes the household the natural unit that has to balance the travel money account. This applies to mobility tool ownership as well as to daily travel expenses.

A third important difference between time and money is that on an aggregate level, the largest share of travel money expenditures is fixed costs. About two-thirds of travel spendings are fixed costs for the car or public transport season tickets. The rest are out of pocket travel expenditures, mainly for fuel and public transport single fares.

In terms of money spent for travel, the main distinction has to be made between households with a car and households without a car. While households with car spend about €375 monthly on travel (17% of corresponding household incomes), those without car spend about €25 (2% of corresponding household incomes).

It is obvious that household incomes have paramount significance with respect to mobility tool ownership, that is, car ownership and associated fixed costs. The implications of the money budget on daily out-of-pocket travel expenditures are not that clear. On average, about 5% of household incomes are spent for out-of-pocket travel expenditures. Only 10% of households spend more than 10% of their income for out-of-pocket travel expenses.

In summary, when modeling travel behavior these findings have to be considered as follows: Depending on the household income, households can be assigned a travel money budget. This predominantly impacts on mobility tool ownership, that is, in first instance the number and types of cars in the household. In addition to this, the household out-of-pocket travel expenditures should be in accordance with the travel money budget.

Mobility Tools

Mobility tools predominantly include the car and public transport season tickets. Bicycle or motorcycle ownership is not considered in our model. As illustrated above, the ownership of mobility tools is to a large degree influenced by the household income.

Mobility tool ownership influences the resistance when modeling destination choice: Particularly places that are not accessible without car have a low probability of being chosen if no car is available. Mobility tool ownership also impacts on the costs of specific modes when modeling mode choice: season ticket holders usually use public transport at no additional cost.

Habitual Destination Choice

Longitudinal micro-simulation can only lead to realistic results when habitual behavior is incorporated. Evidently, commuting is the most habitual field of travel. However, other activities are also largely subject to routines: We tend to shop the same supermarkets, meet friends at the same places, etc. In other words, for large parts of our everyday destination choices, we have a limited set of destinations that we actually choose from. In other cases, activities are fixed to particular places. Hence, in our model, activities other than work are classified into two categories:

- *Activities that can be performed at different locations.* The individual choice set of destinations is limited because it is subject to routine. An example for this type of activity is grocery shopping. Each traveler in our model is assigned a set of destinations where he or she can do grocery shopping. Trial runs indicate that three locations for grocery shopping are sufficient to lead to realistic results. The actual destination choice is part of the activity scheduling process: Out of the available destinations, the destination that fits best into the activity schedule is chosen.
- *Activities with a predefined location.* An example for this type of activity is going to the theater. In this case the activity is linked to a particular destination. In our model, the destination is determined in a destination choice model before the activity scheduling process takes place. The choice sets for this destination choice are all available destinations. Once the destination is determined, it becomes part of the agenda because it is a property of the activity which can only be carried out at this place. If the place cannot be reached in a reasonable time (i.e., keeping the time budget) or the activity does not fit into the time schedule because of time conflicts, the activity cannot be performed.

With this simple distinction, we achieve the stability in destination choice that reflects habitual destination choice on the one hand and non-habitual destination choice on the other as it exists in real life.

Assignment of Agenda and Activity Scheduling

After defining the conditions in which the individual travel can unfold, the travelers in our model are assigned an agenda of what they ought to do during the week. This agenda is based on empirical distributions of reported behavior. The individual agendas are selected according to the individual life situation (role of person in household, employment, etc.).

Thereafter, a scheduling approach is applied to transform the agenda into the virtual behavior of each traveler in the model. This scheduling process considers the individual framework of conditions of travel, that is, the traveler disposes of his set of mobility tools and has to keep his travel time budget. Moreover, there are spatial conditions that have to be met, that is, certain activities can only be performed at certain locations. These locations are either predefined or the traveler can choose from a limited set of possible destinations.

Different algorithms have been tested for activity scheduling (see section "Activity Scheduling—Discussion of two Approaches"). The scheduling process produces a feasible but not necessarily optimal (e.g., with respect to time) schedule of activities for the entire week for each traveler in the simulation.

Habitual Mode Choice

The defined individual activity schedule is feasible with the modes available to the traveler, but mode choice decisions have not yet been made in our model. In the case of our model, the issue of mode choice differs from conventional mode choice which is designed for cross-sectional transport models. In a conventional model individuals do not usually chose repeatedly. If so, then only to the extend that they have various tours throughout one day. Routines in mode choice are usually not considered.

This is different when the temporal scope of the model is one week: During one week travelers usually perform about 25 trips or 11 tours. Mode choices in these situations are not independent from each other. Two factors have to be considered here:

- *Travelers have general modal preferences*: They might always choose the car even though other modes seem to be advantageous from an objective perspective. The reason is just a general bias of particular travelers toward a specific mode. This influence on mode choice is not new and has been described in the literature. However, in a longitudinal mode choice model has to be considered particularly because travelers make repeated decisions which are influenced by their preferences.
- *Mode choice is habitual*: For similar or same situations or tours, travelers tend to use the same mode of travel. Independent from the individual modal preference, travelers develop routines that lead to the point where no actual mode choice decision is made but a mode is taken because it has always been used for this type of trip (Kuhnimhof et al., 2006).

In our mode choice model, these routines and preferences in mode choice have to be considered besides the attributes of the alternative modes. This is to make individual mode choice consistent throughout the course to the modeled week.

Activity Scheduling—Discussion of Two Approaches

The problem of activity scheduling addresses the task of creating feasible weekly activity plans based on agendas and framework conditions. An agenda comprises a set of compulsory and discretionary activities a traveler intends to perform during the week. The framework conditions contain budget restrictions on the side of the traveler as well as the environment in which the traveler operates. The environment consists of the opportunities on the one hand and the transport infrastructure on the other. The transport infrastructure comprises the built infrastructure as well as services (public transport, information, etc.). In the model the infrastructure is represented by its properties (travel times, road pricing) (Figure 4).

In different environments and under different budget constraints, the same agendas lead to different schedules. In turn, schedules have to change if the environment changes due to measures or physical changes.

We tested different activity scheduling algorithms in order to examine their applicability in a microscopic modeling environment. The requirement was that the algorithms produce realistic schedules on the one hand and realistic changes to these schedules on the other when environment conditions alter. Additionally, modeling relevant aspects like simulation time were considered.

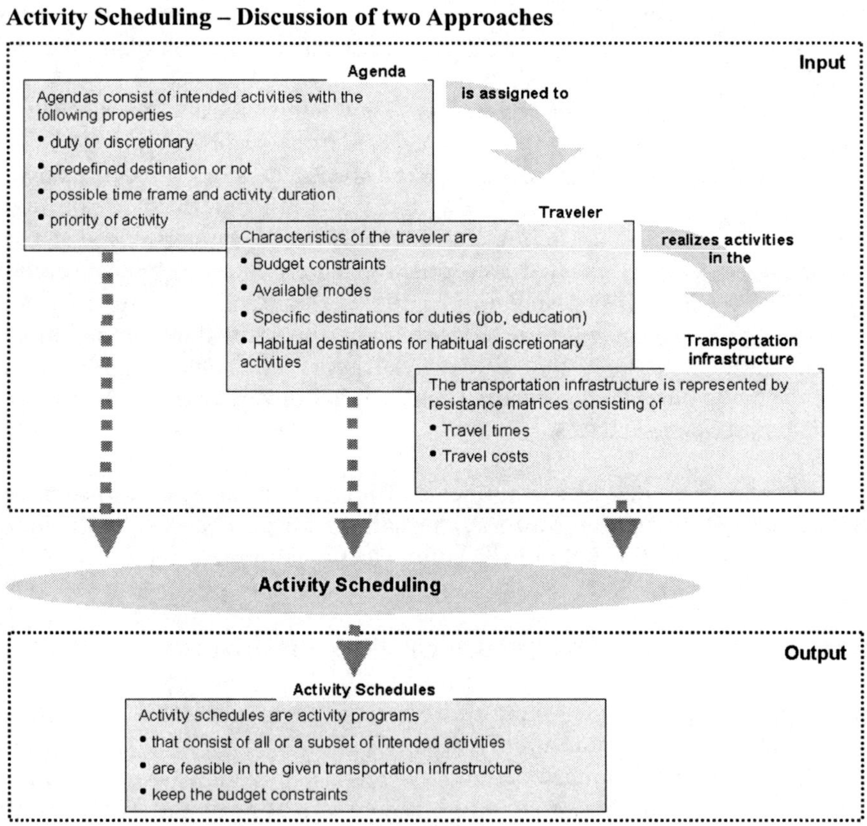

Figure 4
Input, Output, and Problem Formulation of Activity Scheduling

Implementation

Figure 5 shows the graphical user interface of the implemented model consisting of an input and output section. The input section (upper part) consists of the two main sections: template and agenda. For every person type a template can be defined which

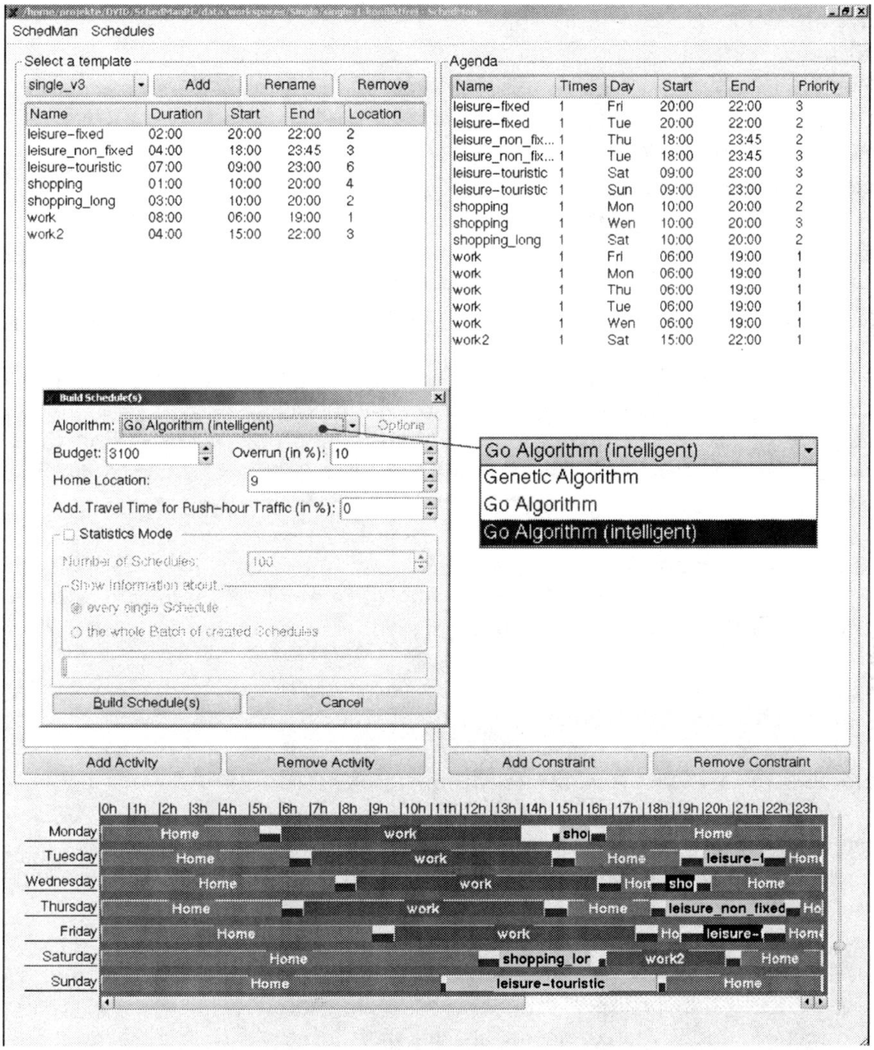

Figure 5
Input and Output Window of the Model

consists of typical activities of this person group. The right side shows the complete agenda. The output section shows a simulated weekly activity plan.

In our model each activity has the following attributes:

- Purpose (Name)
- Activity duration (Duration)
- Start time (Start)
- End time (End)
- Weekday (Day)
- Activity frequency (Times)
- Possible destinations (Location)
- Activity priority (Priority).

In the window "Build schedule," the boundary conditions for the scheduling of the agenda can be defined, for example, as the weekly travel time budget. The travel times during rush hours (6–9 a.m.; 4–7 p.m.) can be increased by a traffic factor.

More than one possible solution exists for each scheduling problem defined by an agenda and boundary conditions. Therefore, the model provides the opportunity to produce one or more schedules. In case of producing only one solution the output window displays the schedule. This one solution is a random selection from all possible solutions.

When producing more than one schedule, the modeling tool allows statistical evaluations of the results. In this case, the mean number of conducted activities and the mean travel time consumption are displayed.

Comparing Scheduling Algorithms

The model provides two types of algorithms to choose from:

- genetic algorithm,
- greedy algorithm (two versions implemented, "Go-Algorithm" and "Go-Algorithm (intelligent)" in Figure 5).

Genetic algorithms follow the idea of evolutionary processes (Russell and Norvig, 2004): At random they produce a number of starting solutions. These are assessed by a fitness function and ordered according to their fitness value. Depending on this assessment and based on the starting solutions, a new generation of solutions is generated by the evolutionary steps selection, recombination or mutation. This process is repeated until one solution fulfils a defined threshold of the fitness function.

In our model the fitness function is fulfilled if all activities of the agenda are scheduled within the budget constraints. If not, one activity is eliminated from the agenda and the process starts again.

Greedy algorithms perform a local search. The decision for each next step depends only on the current situation. Only the benefit of the next step is evaluated, that is, no overall optimization takes place (Russell and Norvig, 2004).

In our model, the greedy algorithm begins the scheduling process by choosing the activity with the highest priority and the fewest alternatives to place the activity. The algorithm tries to find a placement without time conflicts. If this is not possible, the activity is removed from the schedule and the process continues with the next activity. The model repeats this process until

- either all activities are scheduled
- or the time budget is exhausted.

Both types of algorithms, the genetic and the greedy algorithm, produce weekly activity schedules of travelers. While the genetic algorithm performs an overall optimization until the boundary conditions are met, the GO-algorithm produces feasible solutions but no optimal solutions. Both algorithms have in common that they solve time conflicts between the activities to be scheduled. They consider budget constraints, travel times between the locations, and priorities of the activities.

The objective of providing different algorithms was to evaluate their influence on the activity schedules and test their applicability in a model environment. The comparison of the algorithms led to the following conclusions: Both algorithms produce feasible and realistic single schedules. Figure 5 shows an example of a weekly activity plan produced by the Go-algorithm.

The results from both algorithms, genetic and GO, are very similar in most cases. In terms of number of scheduled activities the results differ only from 3% to 5%. This is actually not a surprising result: Since this type of scheduling problem is a natural part of everyday life, it seems that the solution algorithm is simple. Therefore, a back of an envelope-scheduling algorithm seems to be sufficient to solve this everyday problem.

Because the quality of the results is quite similar in both cases, the applicability of the model in a large simulation context is the decisive criteria: The computation time of the GO-algorithm for one activity schedule is less than a millisecond, while the computation time of the genetic algorithm was on the range of several minutes.

For these reasons, the GO-algorithm was chosen for the further development of the overall model. The simulations presented in the following were produced with the GO-algorithm.

Simulation Results under Different Boundary Conditions

The model was tested performing scenarios of road pricing and information services. Their impact was represented by changing travel times in the peak load periods. In the model, the increasing travel times are expressed by traffic factors which multiply travel time in peak load periods.

The results discussed here were produced with the GO-algorithm. Person- and environment-related parameters were varied in order to examine the plausibility of the results. The person-related parameter was the travel time budget, and the environment-related parameter was the travel time in peak load periods. For every agenda, 50 feasible activity schedules were simulated and mean values for key variables (number of activities, number of trips, travel time) were calculated (Figures 6 and 7).

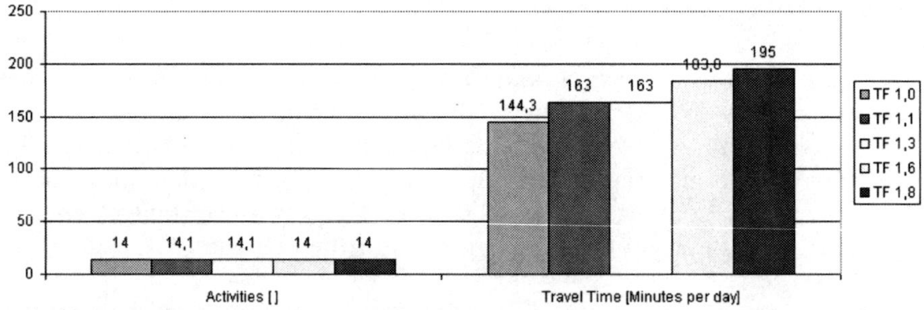

Figure 6

Number of Activities and Travel Time without Travel Time Budget Constraints Under Conditions of Rising Travel Time in Peak Load Periods

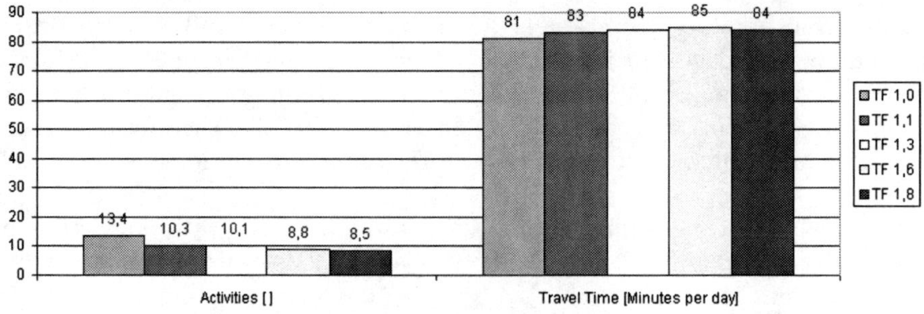

Figure 7

Number of Activities and Travel Time with Travel Time Budget Constraints Under Conditions of Rising Travel Time in Peak Load Periods

The focus of interest was to evaluate the applicability of the model by simulating typical commuters with additional leisure and shopping activities, like employed singles or family men. The simulations emphasized a significant role of the travel time budget. We ran the simulations by simulating schedules with and without travel time budget under increasing travel times in the peak load periods.

Without budget constraints, the total time spent for traveling increases with rising travel times in peak load periods. This is consistent with expectation. However, the number of scheduled activities is almost constant with rising travel times in peak load periods. This result can be interpreted as follows: Even though travel times were rising the travelers were able to schedule all of their activities. This is because they had enough degrees of freedom in scheduling the single activities and the rising travel time did not cause local time conflicts. In the case of local time conflicts single activities would have had to be omitted.

An example for this is shown in Figure 6, which summarizes the simulation results of family men with the same agenda. Their situation was characterized by a long commuting distance. There was no time budget constraint, that is, they had as much time available as they needed. Due to the long commute, the daily travel time was quite high (144 minutes per day) even in the basic case without peak load travel time factor (TF 1.0). When increasing the travel time during rush hour by traffic factor 1.8, the total travel time increased to 195 minutes per day, while the number of activities stayed constant. In this scenario, the increase of travel times in peak load periods resulted in much less time spent at home. The reason is that all out-of-home activities were performed like before with additional time consumed for travel.

With budget constraints, the activity scheduling produced different results: Figure 7 summarizes the simulation results for employed singles assuming time budget constraints. Again it was always the same agenda. In this case, the number of activities decreased from about 14 to 9 activities due to the rising travel time. Five of the remaining nine activities are duty activities (work). This can be interpreted as follows: Under rigid time budget constraints predominantly discretionary activities are reduced if travel time increases significantly.

The first case represents a behavior where a person performs every activity, which he or she is able to schedule without consideration of the amount of travel time. The second case represents a behavior where the time budget determines the possible number of activities in a given environment situation.

First, these results show that under different boundary conditions in terms of budget constraints and travel times, the same agendas lead to different activity schedules. This is a result that conforms to expectation and therefore confirms the chosen approach of activity scheduling.

However, these results must be interpreted interpersonally and not intrapersonally: On the one hand hardly anybody would change his activity agenda at all if commuting times doubled (Figure 6). This is because our everyday life is subject to time restrictions. On the other hand, mobility data analysis shows that commuters with longer commuting times have higher travel time budgets. Therefore, it is unlikely that travelers reduce their discretionary travel time in a one-to-one exchange if commuting times increase.

When applying the above-discussed activity scheduling, one of the crucial tasks is assigning appropriate travel time budgets that relate to the situation of the travelers in the model. This task was discussed in section "Conceptual Framework of the Presented Model" of the paper. Whenever the life situation of traveler changes, for example, due to commuting time increases, the individual travel time budget has to be adapted. When realistic time budget has been assigned to the travelers in the model, the GO-algorithm provides an applicable and fast activity scheduling algorithm that produces realistic results.

The quality of the results relies on the quality of the input of the simulation, that is, the quality of the agenda. If the simulation goal is the reproduction of activity patterns of the German MOP, the agendas must represent the constraints of the activity plans of the panel survey. If the simulation goal is the generation of future scenarios, the boundary conditions of the future scenarios have to be transformed to agenda constraints representing, for example, changed opening hours of shops or longer travel times because of higher travel demand or the use of different modes.

Outlook

Up to now the GO-algorithm was tested in a virtual environment, that is, travel time matrices were not based on a real study area. The next steps will be implementing the GO-algorithm in a larger and lifelike modeling environment, that is, modeling a real population of an investigation area.

So far, the GO-algorithm is only designed to consider travel time budget constraints. This has two reasons: In most cases, the time budget is the budget that impacts stronger on our daily scheduling decisions than the money budget. In addition to this, the travel time budget is a much better explored field than that of travel money expenditures. However, in the next phase of the model implementation, the household context will be considered which opens up the possibility of including travel money budgets in addition to the time budget.

Conclusions

In this paper, we presented the concept for modeling travel in a longitudinal perspective, that is, a microscopic model of weekly travel behavior under budget constraints. The concept is dedicated to transport planning. We discussed the increasing need for such models: The problems in transportation modeling shift from the traditional applications toward the evaluation of a new generation of measures. Moreover, it is foreseeable that budget changes on the one hand and price changes on the other will significantly impact on travel behavior.

Longitudinal micro-simulation like we present in our paper enables new applications for transportation models. That type of model will not only be able to model the travel demand for the different modes but also to predict the clientele of modes. Moreover, modeling one week allows the consideration of individual budgets for travel as basic framework conditions. When modeling shorter periods of time, budgets cannot be taken into account in microscopic simulation. This is because individual travel expenditures vary largely from day to day. This variation does not allow balancing time and financial budgets on a daily basis. A week, however, represents a time span for which travelers start to balance their budgets.

In comparison to cross-sectional model, modeling one week increases the complexity of the model because the right balance between variation and stability of individual behavior during one week (e.g., in mode and destination choice) has to be achieved. In the paper on hand, we discussed concepts of how this balance can be achieved and appropriate budget can be assigned.

In the final section of the paper, we presented two algorithms that were tested with respect to their applicability for activity scheduling under budget constraints. The GO-algorithm, which belongs to the group of "greedy algorithms," and a genetic algorithm were found to produce comparable and realistic results. The GO-algorithm uses an approach that reflects human behavior and is much faster than the genetic algorithm.

In the first phase of the model implementation, only travel time budgets were considered and single schedules in a virtual environment were produced. The results show that the GO-algorithm provides a simple and easy-to-understand tool for producing realistic activity schedules on the basis of empirical distributions for agendas. Moreover, the GO-algorithm realistically reproduces the influence of budget constraints and the infrastructure conditions such as travel times. Therefore, it represents a good and applicable core for the proposed model of longitudinal simulation of travel.

The GO-algorithm as presented in this paper does not incorporate situational changes to the activity schedules that can arise from unforeseen influences such as delays when traveling. This means that at the moment, there is no feedback from the travel situation to activity scheduling, that is, the model is not dynamic. However, the generated activity plans can be used as an input for dynamic microscopic modeling. In this case, the activity schedules can be altered subsequently due to influences from the traffic situation.

The presented algorithm produces weekly activity schedules for all individuals of a simulation population in a given study area. Each of these activity schedules is feasible in the given area under investigation and respects individual constraints. In the aggregate, empirical distributions as surveyed by the German MOP are reproduced. With this functionality the presented model is already useful for many applications in modeling for transportation planning.

References

Destatis, S. B. W. (2006). Webpage of the Federal Statistical Office Germany. Available at: http://www.destatis.de. 6-12-2006

Fujii, S., R. Kitamura and T. Monma (1997). A study of commuters' activity patterns for the estimation of induced trips. *Journal of Infrastructure Planning and Management* 562, 109–120.

Gringmuth, C., T. Batz, J. Mülle, S. Geweke and B. Chlond (2006). Endbericht OVID—Stärkung der Selbstorganisation im Verkehr durch I+K-gestützte Dienste.

Kuhnimhof, T. (2006). Mobilität und Zeit-Längsschnittanalysen auf Basis des MOP und Konzepte zur mikroskopischen Modellierung. Arbeitsberichte des Instituts für Verkehrswesen. Institut für Verkehrswesen, Universität Karlsruhe.

Kuhnimhof, T., S. von der Ruhren and B. Chlond (2006). Users of transport modes and multimodal travel behavior: steps toward understanding travelers' options and choices. *Transportation Research Board Annual Meeting*. Washington, DC.

Kunert, U. (1992). Individuelles Verhalten im Wochenverlauf. DIW Beiträge zur Strukturforschung 130.

Metz, D. (2004). Travel time-variable or constant. *Journal of Transport Economics and Policy* 38(Part 30), 333–344.

Mokhtarian, P. L. and C. Chen (2003). TTB or Not TTB, that is the Question: A Review and Analysis of the Empirical Literature on Travel Time (and Money) Budgets. Davis, California.

Russell, S. and P. Norvig (2004). *Künstliche Intelligenz—Ein Moderner Ansatz. 2. Auflage, 150–155.* Pearson Education Deutschland, München.

Zumkeller, D., M. Poeck and Y. Zahavi (1980). Verkehr und Stadt als Interaktionsmechanismus. Forschungsauftrag des Bundesminister für Verkehr. A 25/16.39.10-1/78. Düsseldorf.

Zumkeller, D., B. Chlond, T. Kuhnimhof and P. Ottmann (2005). Panelauswertung 2004. Datenaufbereitung, Plausibilisierung, erste Auswertungen zu den Erhebungen zur Alltagsmobilität 2004/06 sowie zu den Fahrleistungen und Treibstoffverbräuchen 2005/07 für das Mobilitätspanel. Zwischenbericht. Institut für Verkehrswesen, Universität Karlsruhe TH. FE 70.0753/2004. Karlsruhe.

Zumkeller, D., B. Chlond and W. Manz (2004a). Infrastructure development in Germany under stagnating demand conditions: a new paradigm? *Transportation Research Record: Journal of the Transportation Research Board* 1864, 121–128. Washington, DC, TRB, National Research Council.

Zumkeller, D., J.-L. Madre, B. Chlond and J. Armoogum (2004b). Panel surveys. *Resource Paper for Workshop A8 at the 7th International Conference on Travel Survey Methods*, Costa Rica.

The Expanding Sphere of Travel Behaviour Research
Selected Papers from the 11th International Conference on Travel Behaviour Research

40

A Tour-Based Model for the Simulation of a Distributive Freight System

Armando Cartenì and Francesco Russo

Abstract

Freight demand models differ from passenger models due to the distinction between what is actually transported and the decision-maker, as well as the multitude of agents involved in freight transport. In this work we propose a disaggregate tour-based model for the simulation of a distributive freight system. The flexible structure of the tour-based approach allows simulation of the choices of different decision-makers and, if necessary, of only part of the supply chain which is an aggregation of the choices involved. Furthermore, the choice of using a tour-based approach allows to simulate commodity flows congruently, explicitly considering the simulation of transit destinations and of all the other choices connected with them, such as the choice of loading unit and the mode.

The model system proposed could be used as a decision support system (DSS) by a public administration which needs a tool able to simulate the total commodity flows.

There are various possible fields of application of the model system proposed. The most suitable location of a new logistic centre can be appraised (through a what if approach) or, for example, it is possible to estimate the effects on the freight transport system (hence on traffic congestion) caused by interventions in the socio-economic system.

Another aim was to test the effectiveness of the aggregate calibration technique for estimating freight model parameters. Furthermore, the idea of using aggregate data to estimate the parameters of the disaggregate model has allowed to compare the model proposed with other aggregate models commonly calibrated through aggregate data.

Introduction

Transport and logistics basically need a network of carriers and users jointly operating to transfer people and goods across a region on more than one transport mode, such as road–rail, road–ship and train–ship. This means that in freight transport there is no single decision-maker, as happens in passenger transport, choosing whether to effect a trip, when to effect it, by which transport mode and according to which itinerary, but rather a complex set of decision-makers responsible for all the activities required to move goods from suppliers to consumers. Choices made will observe a hierarchical order and will condition each other; for example, before making a choice about the transport mode it will be necessary to establish the loading unit to use for the transfer; choice of the freight quantity to ship will affect the choice of the loading unit to use and so on.

Following these considerations, an in-depth study is therefore required to conduct logistical research, for the purpose of proposing a useful instrument for planning interventions on a transport and a logistic system.

The results of the study on the European Union (EU) freight mobility show that in the EU more than 75% of the tons/year moved are by road (processing from Eurostat, 2005). Table 1 shows that urban trips (related to distance band 0–50 km) account for about 58% of road mobility, regional trips (related to distance band 50–150 km) for more than 21% with more than 3,000 million tons/year while national trips (longer than 150 km) also account for 21%. With regard to tons × km the percentage for trips longer than 150 km is about 75%, trips on a 50–150 km distance band account for more than 16% while trips shorter than 50 km about 9%.

From these data there emerges the importance of regional trips; about 98% of these trips are made by road. Curiously, this freight band has not been widely investigated in the literature. For this trip type, two transport modes/services are used: heavy goods vehicles (HGVs) and light goods vehicles (LGVs). The first specializes in transporting commodities and semi-manufactured goods using unified loading units, and the second is mainly used by service companies and for light consignments in terms of low weight and/or high frequency.

Table 1

European Union (25 Countries) Road Freight Transport by Distance Band

Trip type	Distance band (km)	Tons/2004 (× 1,000)	Percentage	Tons × Km ($\times 10^6$)	Percentage
Urban	≤50	8,418,508	57.7%	139,857	8.8%
Regional	50–150	3,111,426	21.3%	255,363	16.1%
National	>150	3,066,013	21.0%	1,192,310	75.1%
All	Total	14,595,947	100.0%	1,587,530	100.0%

Source: Eurostat (2005).

Given this context, the University of Salerno (Italy) and the University of Reggio Calabria (Italy) set up a joint research project to study freight transport and logistics as well as model the distributive transport and logistic system to simulate commodity flows (freight demand). The first phase involved information gathering: various interviews with freight sector operators and logistics experts were conducted to understand the complex dynamics of commodity flows as well as the number and identity of the decision-makers involved. This enabled us to define an open and flexible disaggregate modelling architecture to simulate a distributive transport and logistic system based on a tour-based approach (see the section 'General Architecture'). The flexible structure of the tour-based approach allows simulation of the choices of different decision-makers, namely the choices regarding freight transport and, if necessary, of only part of the supply chain which is an aggregation of the choices involved.

Approaches commonly adopted of an aggregate gravitational or behavioural trip-based nature to simulate commodity flows for freight distribution often produce estimation errors caused by the hypothesis that the freight reaches its destination without passing through some transit destinations (e.g. gravitational models simulate commodity flows from an origin to a final destination). This modelling hypothesis produces still larger estimation errors when we wish to estimate the vehicle link flows on the relevant infrastructures through an assignment model. In this case, by assuming that the freight follows a minimum path linking the origin to the final destination, we obtain strongly distorted estimates of path flows (hence link flows) given that there are transit destinations which modify path choices. The choice of using a tour-based approach (which has not yet found applications in the literature) allows us to simulate commodity flows congruently, explicitly considering the simulation of transit destinations and of all the other choices connected with them, such as the choice of loading unit and the mode.

The model system proposed in this paper could be used as a decision support system (DSS) by a public administration which needs a tool able to simulate the total commodity flows (e.g. aggregation of all the supply chains, firms and economic sectors).

To test the applicability of the modelling architecture proposed we carried out an application to estimate commodity flows for the region of Campania (southern Italy). This application also allowed us to investigate commodity flows relative to the 50–150 km distance band which, for Campania, represents more than 35% of tons/year transported. Besides, the model yielded both commodity-based and vehicle-based results, allowing both commodity and vehicle flows to be simulated (see the section 'Application').

Another aim of this paper is to test the use of aggregate data, available for freight demand and/or traffic counts, to estimate the parameters of the models (Hogberg, 1976; Cascetta, 1986; Cascetta and Russo, 1997; Cascetta, 2001; Cascetta and Postorino, 2001). These data can be combined in different ways, obtaining different estimators of unknown parameters of the models, in relation to the classic or Bayesian interpretation of the initial estimation and the assumption of the probability distribution of the measurement, assignment and model errors. In the application proposed, a generalized least squares (GLS) estimator was used. The outputs of the calibration are the same origin–destination (OD) commodity flows and vehicle freight flows on the main infrastructures of the road network. In the literature, this estimation technique has been mainly used to estimate OD flows (see, e.g. Cascetta and Postorino, 2001); such an application generates the problem of estimating many unknowns (OD flows) using a significantly smaller number of aggregate data (e.g. 40,000 unknowns vs. 400 aggregate data available). However, in this paper we use this technique to estimate the model parameters (see, e.g. Hogberg, 1976; Cascetta and Russo, 1997) from a significantly larger number of aggregate data (e.g. 40 unknowns vs. 400 aggregate data available).

Furthermore, the idea of using aggregate data to estimate the parameters of the disaggregate model allow to compare the model proposed with other aggregate models commonly calibrated through aggregate data (e.g. gravitational models).

The second part of our research will consist in conducting a statistically significant number of surveys directly targeting categories of decision-makers involved in the distributive transport and logistic system so as to apply the modelling architecture proposed in a disaggregate way, specifying and calibrating a behavioural demand model. The results of this research will be the subject of a future paper.

The paper is divided into five parts. The first section reports the state-of-the-art of freight demand models, the second summarises the basic definitions and notation used, the third presents the model system architecture, the fourth discusses an application of the model system within Campania, followed by the last section that reports conclusions and research prospects.

State-of The-Art of Freight Demand Models

In spite of the importance of freight transport, research in this sector has developed only recently. There are two main freight system simulation approaches in the literature, deriving from the decision-maker considered.

The first approach allows single supply chains (or parts of them) to be optimised with respect to single firms (see, e.g. Rushton and Oxley, 1993; Tavasszy et al., 1998; Daganzo, 1999; Regan and Garrido, 2000; Ghiani and Musmanno, 2000; Nagurney et al., 2002); maximising firm benefits is the criterion for choosing the best project to develop. Description of such models lies outside the scope of this paper.

The second approach, represented by demand models, allows interventions to be planned on the freight system as a whole as it considers the effects on the whole supply chain through the aggregation of all the firms so as to simulate commodity flows as a whole. This approach is often used by public administration which must, either directly or indirectly, consider the effects of proposed actions on the community. In this paper the second simulation approach is investigated. Freight demand models appear different from passenger models due to the distinction between the subject of the transport and the decision-maker as well as the multitude of agents involved in freight transport.

Many papers have proposed a survey on freight demand models (see, e.g. Crainic, 1987; Mazzarino, 1997; Regan and Garrido, 2000; Cascetta, 2001). There emerge two main classification elements: one concerning the basic hypotheses and functional form of the models, and the other concerning the choice dimension simulated. For the first criterion we may distinguish between:

- *disaggregate or aggregate models*, depending on the variables occurring, concern disaggregate units such as single firms or single shipments, or their aggregations, such as all the firms of a certain category and/or economic sectors;
- *behavioural or non-behavioural models* depending on whether they are based on explicit hypotheses on the behaviour of decision-makers or on empirical relations linking freight transport demand to variables in the economic and/or transportation system (of these, discrete choice models are the most widely used);
- *models differentiated by input data required* and the areal context of application (national, regional, urban models);
- *intersectoral and spatial price equilibrium models* (macroeconomic models).

As regards the second classification criterion we may distinguish between:

- *localisation models*, which simulate industrial location choices;
- *emission/attraction* (some time acquisition) *and distribution models*, which simulate the level and spatial distribution of freight;
- *mode choice models*, which simulate the split of freight flows between the various transportation modes available.

Every model regarding the second classification could be implemented using the basic hypotheses and the functional forms introduced into the first classification.

Localisation Models

As freight transport demand is affected both by business activity in the area and by the characteristics of the transportation system, one of the main problems which often needs tackling concerns the choice of the most appropriate site for production.

Localisation models basically allow the siting of production markets to be optimised, minimising, amongst other things, establishment costs and those of transport (Weber,

1929; Hoover, 1948; Isard, 1960; Alonso, 1967). Though often proving to be aggregate, such models allow medium- and long-term forecasts to be made. In the medium term they allow us to assess the effects that variations in demand have on firms, while in the long term they allow us to analyse the effects that new business has on the transportation system. Although most of these models aim to simulate 'long-range' transportation demand, at times regional models are encountered in the literature which consider attributes of regional economic growth such as: labour migration, regional GDP, changes in the composition and level of regional production etc. (Meyer, 1963). In such studies, the variables proving most significant are the location of natural resources, restocking and accessibility.

Emission/Attraction and Distribution Models

Different approaches may be found in the literature to simulate the level and spatial distribution of freight. Domencich and McFadden (1975) propose two different approaches for this purpose. The first allows us to simulate the quantity of consignment (freight demand) emitted or attracted by each traffic zone considered (emission/attraction models) according to socio-economic variables. Formally, such models may be represented as:

$$\text{emission model}: d_o = f_1(\boldsymbol{SE}_o); \quad \text{attraction model}: d_d = f_2(\boldsymbol{SE}_d, \boldsymbol{LU}_d)$$

The second approach concerns the simulation of the distribution of freight flows between each traffic zone. Formally, such models (often aggregate) may be represented as:

$$\text{distribution models } F_{od} = f_3(\boldsymbol{SE}_o, \boldsymbol{SE}_d, \boldsymbol{T}_{od})$$

where d_o and d_d represent respectively the quantity of consignment from zone *o* and the quantity of consignment attracted by zone *d*; F_{od} is the percentage of the consignment exchanged between the origin *o* and destination *d*; SE_o and SE_d represent the socio-economic variables for zones *o* and *d* respectively; LU_d stands for the land-use variables associated to zone *d*; T_{od} is a cost attribute (e.g. time, distance, monetary cost) between zones *i* and *j*.

The other more common modelling approaches for the distribution of commodity flows between each traffic zone (see, e.g. Bayliss, 1998; Harker, 1985) include:

- Macro-economic models, such as multiregional input–output models (Isard, 1951; Leontief and Costa,1987; Cascetta, 2001; Marzano and Papola, 2004), which allow simulation not only of the level of demand but also freight spatial distribution (such models are generally applied to simulate national mobility);

- Non-behavioural distribution models (Ogden, 1992; Oppenheim, 1995; Cascetta and Iannò, 2000; Cartenì and Russo, 2004), which allow, once the quantity of consignment emitted is known, the simulation of commodity flows between individual traffic zones (the most commonly used are gravitational models);
- Behavioural models (e.g. random utility models), which allow, once the quantity of consignment emitted is known, the destination choice to be simulated, knowing the characteristics of the commodity flows such as the origin, the commodities sector etc. (there are no significant applications to freight transport). The latter include trip-based and tour-based models (for a comparison between the two approaches see the section 'General Architecture'). In recent years, activity-based models have been developed: these simulate trip choices as the last result of more complex choices regarding everyday activities.

Besides the modelling approaches described (which are generally applied at a national or regional scale), specific applications are being developed for the movement and management of urban freight (see, e.g. Ogden, 1992; Oppenheim, 1995; Russo and Comi, 2002; Russo and Comi, 2004) and problems concerned with City Logistics (see Taniguchi et al., 2001; Taniguchi and Thompson, 2006). Such models are found downstream of the previous ones and generally use as input variables the output from the previous models.

Mode Choice Models

The third approach involves modal split models; these models are generally classified in the literature according to the hypotheses characterising some model components such as level of aggregation, the consignment decision-maker, the reference unit for the choice, the functional form of the choice model or attributes used. In this paper we will describe these models by their aggregation level, according to which modal split models may be classified into aggregate and disaggregate (Winston, 1983), depending on whether the basic unit of observation is on an aggregate (national or regional) or disaggregate level (a single decision for each shipment).

There are various aggregate models of modal choice to be found in the literature. The first models that may be mentioned included that proposed by Quandt and Baumol (1966) (and developed by Smith, 1974; Morton, 1969; Boyer, 1977; or Levin, 1978). Aggregate models, albeit more straightforward to apply, have shown limited capacities to analyse and reproduce the phenomenon of freight modal choice, in that many important factors may be attributed to a higher disaggregation level.

The disaggregate modal choice models that have received most attention in the literature are behavioural models. These include random utility models which may be split into: consignment models that simulate modal choice for each consignment, and logistical models which simulate in integrated fashion a sequence of logistical choices comprising size and frequency of consignments, as well as the choice of transportation mode.

Modal choice 'consignment' models are far more widely used in applications. They usually have a functional form belonging to the family of Logit models (Cascetta and Di Gangi, 1996; Cascetta and Iannò, 2000; Cascetta, 2001), more often of a multinomial Logit type, although hierarchical Logit models are not lacking. Introduction of Box–Cox transformations, used in the field of passenger transport, suggested an application to freight modal choice models (Fridstrøm and Madslien, 1994, 1995).

Disaggregate logistical modal choice models (Nuzzolo and Russo, 1997) simulate the choice of transportation mode in the context of logistical decisions made by the firm which decides the transportation mode, which may be either the vending firm or the purchasing firm. In particular, it is hypothesised that modal choice depends on the logistical cost related to its use.

Basic Definitions and Notation

To apply the model system described in the section 'General Architecture', the study area (for instance, an administrative region) is assumed to be divided into zones, and a centroid is associated to each zone to represent origin o or destination d. Moreover, connections are modelled through a transport network.

The following definitions and notation will be adopted in the remaining chapter. For simplicity, only two transit destinations will be considered (extension to the case of three or more transit destinations is straightforward); see the example in Figure 1.

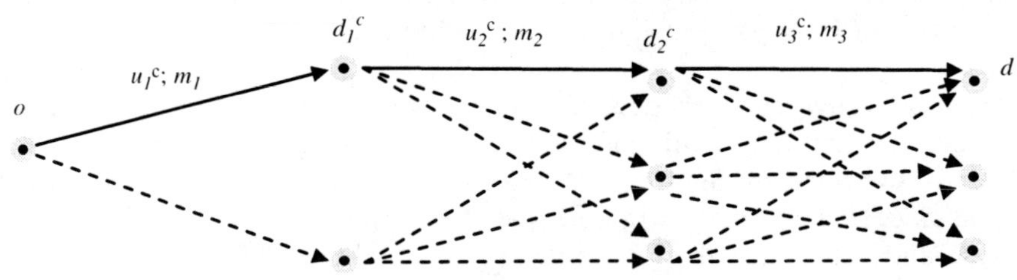

Figure 1
Example of distribution channels

H	reference period of the simulation (e.g. average business day)
DC	generic distribution channel (e.g. supplier–logistic centre–wholesaler–retailer), that could be defined as the number and type of transit destinations between the origin (e.g. the supplier) and the final destination (e.g. the retailer); see the example in Figure 1
c	generic commodity class. A commodity class c is any commodity aggregation which, according to the field of application of the model, can refer to a company class, economic sector, supply chain and so on (e.g. agriculture products, energy products and minerals). For this reason, in this paper we will refer to one of these aggregations without distinction, always using the symbol c
o	origin zone which is the procurement market (e.g. the supplier)
d	destination zone which is the sale market (for example the retailer) and/or the consumer market
$I\mathrm{DC}_c$	set of the distribution channels related to the commodity class c; different commodity classes may use different distribution channels
Ic	set of all the commodity classes c
Ic,o	set of the commodity classes for which the decision-maker at origin o (the supplier) chooses destination d (the retailer) to sell the commodity. Sometimes we need to differentiate whether the supplier (or firm) directly chooses whether to sell the commodity or if the retailer chooses the supplier (or firm) from which to purchase the commodity. In this case, we need to consider two different sets: one with the commodity classes for which the decision-makers are at origin o and another for which the decision-makers are at destination d. These two sets may or may not contain the same types of commodities (economic sectors). It is important to underline that the distinction is related to the decision-maker (origin decision-maker vs. destination decision-maker)
Ic,d	set of the commodity classes for which the decision-maker at destination d chooses the origin o from which to purchase the commodity
Io_c	set of the origin zones; it consists of the zones in which there is at least one supplier related to the commodity class c
Id_c	set of destination zones, comprising the zones in which there is at least one retailer related to commodity class c
$F^c_{od}[H]$	commodity flow between origin o and destination d related to the reference period H and the commodity class c
$d^c_{o\cdot}[H]$	is the total consignment quantity related to the reference period H and the commodity class c that origin o must send towards all the destination zones; this value may be estimated through a macro-economic model and/or an emissions models. Sometimes, the value can also be estimated as the product of consignment frequency and average consignment size

$po[d/H,c,o](\boldsymbol{L},\boldsymbol{T},\boldsymbol{E},\boldsymbol{\beta})$ probability of choosing destination d conditional upon the reference period H, the commodity class c and origin o. The generic choice probability is a function of quantity attributes grouped into the four vectors below:

$\boldsymbol{L}$ vector of logistic attributes relative to the logistic system considered (e.g. total or partial logistic costs). This functional dependence will be omitted for simplicity in the next sections

$\boldsymbol{T}$ vector of transport level of service attributes (travel time, loading time, warehousing time etc.). This functional dependence will be omitted for simplicity in the next sections

$\boldsymbol{E}$ vector of economic attributes (number of firms/retailers/shops or number of operators, number of logistic centres etc.). This functional dependence will be omitted for simplicity in the next sections

$\boldsymbol{\beta}$ vector of coefficients existing in mathematical models used. This functional dependence will be omitted for simplicity in the next sections

$d_d^c[H]$ total demand of commodities related to the reference period H and the commodity class c that destination d must purchase from all the origin zones; this value could be estimated through macro-economic and/or attraction models

$pd[o/H,c,d](\boldsymbol{L},\boldsymbol{T},\boldsymbol{E},\boldsymbol{\beta})$ probability of choosing origin o conditional upon the reference period H, the commodity class c and destination d

hod delivery time slice (e.g. hour) within the reference period H (e.g. average business day) in which the consignment has to be delivered

$Ihod$ set of the delivery time slice

$p[hod/H,c,o,d](\boldsymbol{L},\boldsymbol{T},\boldsymbol{E},\boldsymbol{\beta})$ probability of choosing the time slice hod conditional upon the reference period H, the commodity class c, destination d and origin o

$d1$ first transit destination (such as dry ports and logistic centres)

$Id1_c$ set of the first transit destinations related to the commodity class c; different commodity classes may use different transit destinations

$p[d1/H,c,o,d,hod,\mathrm{DC}](\boldsymbol{L},\boldsymbol{T},\boldsymbol{E},\boldsymbol{\beta})$ probability of choosing the first transit destination $d1$ conditional upon all the preceding choices $H,c,o,d,hod,$DC

$u1$ loading unit/loading quantity (container, semi-trailer, pallet etc.) used for the first trip

$Iu1_c$ set of the loading unit/loading quantity used for the first trip related to the commodity class c

$p[u1/H,c,o,d,hod,\mathrm{DC},d1](\boldsymbol{L},\boldsymbol{T},\boldsymbol{E},\boldsymbol{\beta})$ probability of choosing the loading unit $u1$ for the first trip conditional upon all the preceding choices $H,c,o,d,$ $hod,$DC, $d1$

$h1$ departure time slice for the first trip, between origin o and the first transit destination $d1$

$Ih1_{hod,h1}$ set of the departure time slices for the first trip related to the delivery time slice hod and the departure time slice for the first trip $h1$

$p[h1/H,c,o,d,hod,DC,d1,u1](\boldsymbol{L},\boldsymbol{T},\boldsymbol{E},\boldsymbol{\beta})$ probability of choosing the departure time slice $h1$ for the first trip conditional upon all the preceding choices $H,c,o,d,hod,DC,d1,u1$

$m1$ freight mode or freight service used for the first trip

$Im1_{d1,u1,h1}$ set of the freight mode/service for the first trip conditional upon the first transit destination $d1$, the loading unit $u1$ and the departure time slice $h1$

$p[m1/H,c,o,d,hod,DC,d1,u1,h1](\boldsymbol{L},\boldsymbol{T},\boldsymbol{E},\boldsymbol{\beta})$ probability of choosing the freight mode $m1$ conditional upon all the preceding choices H,c,o,d,hod,DC, $d1,u1,h1$

$d2$ second transit destination (wholesaler, peripheral logistic centre, local warehouse etc.)

$Id2_c$ set of the second transit destinations related to the commodity class c

$p[d2/H,c,o,d,hod,DC,d1,u1,h1,m1](\boldsymbol{L},\boldsymbol{T},\boldsymbol{E},\boldsymbol{\beta})$ probability of choosing the second transit destination $d2$ conditional upon all the preceding choices H,c,o,d,hod,DC, $d1,u1,h1,m1$

$u2$ loading unit/loading quantity (container, semi-trailer, pallet etc.) used for the second trip

$Iu2_c$ set of the loading unit/loading quantity used for the second trip related to the commodity class c

$p[u2/H,c,o,d,hod,DC,d1,u1,h1,m1,d2](\boldsymbol{L},\boldsymbol{T},\boldsymbol{E},\boldsymbol{\beta})$ probability of choosing the loading unit $u2$ for the second trip conditional upon all the preceding choices H,c,o,d,hod,DC, $d1,u1,h1,m1,d2$

$h2$ departure time slice for the second trip, between the first transit destination $d1$ and the second transit destination $d2$

$Ih2_{hod}$ set of the departure time slices for the second trip related to the delivery time slice hod

$p[h2/H,c,o,d,hod,DC,d1,u1,h1,m1,d2,u2](\boldsymbol{L},\boldsymbol{T},\boldsymbol{E},\boldsymbol{\beta})$ probability of choosing the leaving time slice $h2$ conditional upon all the preceding choices H,c,o,d,hod,DC, $d1,u1,h1,m1,d2$, $u2$

$m2$ freight mode or freight service used for the second trip

$Im2_{d2,u2,h2}$ set of the freight service/mode for the second trip conditional upon the second transit destination $d2$, the loading unit $u2$ and the departure time slice $h2$

$p[m2/H,c,o,d,hod,DC,d1,u1,h1,m1,d2,u2,h2](\boldsymbol{L},\boldsymbol{T},\boldsymbol{E},\boldsymbol{\beta})$ probability of choosing the freight mode $m2$ conditional upon all the preceding choices H,c,o,d,hod,DC, $d1,u1,h1,m1,d2$, $u2,h2$

$u3$ loading unit/loading quantity (container, semi-trailer, pallet etc.) used for the third trip

$Iu3_c$ set of the loading unit/loading quantity used for the third trip related to the commodity class c

$p[u3/H,c,o,d,hod,DC,d1,u1,h1,m1,d2,u2,h2,m2](\boldsymbol{L},\boldsymbol{T},\boldsymbol{E},\boldsymbol{\beta})$ probability of choosing the loading unit $u3$ conditional upon all the preceding choices H,c,o,d,hod,DC, $d1,u1,h1,m1,d2$, $u2,h2,m2$

$h3$ departure time slice for the third trip, between the second transit destination $d2$ and destination d

$Ih3_{hod}$ set of the departure time slices for the third trip related to the delivery time slice hod

$p[h3/H,c,o,d,hod,\mathrm{DC},d1,u1,h1,m1,d2,u2,h2,m2,u3](\boldsymbol{L},\boldsymbol{T},\boldsymbol{E},\boldsymbol{\beta})$ probability of choosing the departure time slice for the third trip $h3$ conditional upon all the preceding choices $H,c,o,d,hod,$DC, $d1,u1,h1,m1,d2$, $u2,h2,m2,u3$

$m3$ freight mode or of freight service used for the third trip

$Im3_{d,u3,h3}$ set of the freight service/mode for the third trip conditional upon destination d, the loading unit $u3$and the departure time slice $h3$

$p[m3/H,c,o,d,hod,\mathrm{DC},d1,u1,h1,m1,d2,u2,h2,m2,u3,h3](\boldsymbol{L},\boldsymbol{T},\boldsymbol{E},\boldsymbol{\beta})$ probability of choosing the freight mode for the third trip $m3$ conditional upon all the preceding choices $H,c,o,d,hod,$DC, $d1,u1,h1,m1,d2$, $u2,h2,m2,u3,h3$

$F^{c}_{od}[H,hod,DC,d1,u1,h1,m1,d2,u2,h2,u3,h3,m3]$ commodity flow between origin o and destination d for the reference period H; the commodity class c; delivery time slice hod; distribution channel DC; transit destinations $d1$ and $d2$; loading units $u1$, $u2$ and $u3$; departure time slices $h1$, $h2$ and $h3$; and freight modes $m1$, $m2$ and $m3$

$\mathrm{CV}[H,o,d1,m1]$ vehicle-based model related to reference period H, origin o, transit destination $d1$ and mode $m1$. For example, this model could be used to convert tons/year commodity flows into vehicle/day commodity flow

$F_{od1}[H,m1]$ commodity flow which uses mode $m1$ for the trip from origin o to the first transit destination $d1$ in the reference period H

General Architecture

As stated above, the model system proposed in this paper could be used as a DSS by a public administration requiring a tool which is able to simulate the total commodity flows. For this reason, the choice of the best simulation approach for estimating these freight demand flows is fundamental.

Generally, discrete choice models are the most widely used behavioural demand models; they could be either trip-based or tour-based models. The trip-based approach could be defined as a model that simulates the trips making up a journey (sequence of trips), assuming that the choices for each trip (e.g. choice of destination and/or mode) are independent of those for other possible trips belonging to the same journey. Such assumptions are reasonable when the journey is a single trip. Within freight transport, this approach is generally used for aggregate models to simulate aggregate demand flows (e.g. national demand flows) and the year is the simulation reference period of time (e.g. freight demand flows in tons/year).

When the journeys connecting several activities in different locations, that is journeys consisting of sequences of trips influencing on another, it is necessary to use a tour-based approach which can be defined as a model that simulates the trips making up a journey, assuming that the choices for each trip affect other trips belonging to the same journey. This approach allows us to simulate the dependences existing between successive trips of the same journey congruently respecting, for example, time constraints, the modes of subsequent trips etc. through a spatial–temporal connection among activities of different trips. For this mathematical approach there is no 'standard' structure like the case for trip-based models. This is due both to the recent interest in these models (this approach was developed in the late 1980s and 1990s in the Netherlands) with fewer examples, and to the greater complexity of the phenomenon to be represented. Such models have been developed only to simulate passenger mobility for several years now, but few have been implemented in real situations and mostly in an urban area (see, e.g. Algers et al., 1995; Cascetta et al., 1994).

The tour-based approach adequately reproduces the choice structure of freight transport; this model simulates the dependences existing between successive trips of the same distribution channel. This means that each destination will be chosen according to the preceding and successive destinations by considering the number of transfers as a whole, and so on. In order to implement this model it is essential to understand the constraints linking all the decision-makers' choices and to identify the type of relations linking one decision-maker with another.

For the specification of this type of model, discrete choice models can be used (e.g. a Nested Logit model) which ably match the hierarchical structure chosen. In particular, as there is no single decision-maker in freight strategies but, quite often, several subjects are involved along the transport chain from the manufacturing plants to the retailers, the adoption of such a model allows explicit simulation of single individual choices (which, however, affect one another).

As said above, approaches commonly adopted of a gravitational or behavioural trip-based nature to simulate commodity flows for freight distribution often produce estimation errors caused by the hypothesis that the freight reaches its destination without passing through some transit destinations. This modelling hypothesis produces still larger estimation errors when we wish to estimate the vehicle link flows on the relevant infrastructures through an assignment model. The choice of using a tour-based approach, whether in a behavioural or non-behavioural fashion, allows us to simulate commodity flows congruently, explicitly considering the simulation of transit destinations and of all the other choices connected with them, such as the choice of loading unit and the mode.

The model system proposed is able to simulate a distributive freight system: the freight procurement phase, from suppliers to manufacturers, and the freight distribution phase, from producers to retailers. These two activities are quite similar and, though developed at different moments in the supply chain, may be modelled through the same model architecture. Hence, we will only refer to the activity of freight distribution, though the model structure can easily be transferred to simulation of the freight procurement phase.

To define the model architecture it is important to distinguish between the decision-maker and the nature of the decision. The subjects who take part in the decision-making process are:

- *retailers/manufacturers/suppliers*, choosing where and what to purchase/sell (e.g. for the retailers, the suppliers and type of goods are chosen);
- *shippers*, making choices concerning, for example, the distribution strategy (the number and type of intermediate stops are the choices made), the loading unit to use (e.g. the container, semi-trailer, swap body) and the mode to use (e.g. truck, train, ship, airplane);
- *carriers* who sometimes choose the path to follow (the routes).

As stated above, in freight transport there is no single decision-maker, but rather a complex set of decision-makers responsible for all the activities required to move goods; the choices made observe a hierarchical order and condition each other. The idea of the model architecture proposed is to develop a different macro-model for a different homogeneous group of decision-makers (or a single decision-maker) for example, a macro-model to simulate the choices made by the supplier and/or the retailers and so on. Starting from these considerations, the model system proposed basically consists of three macro-models: the *distribution strategy model* (DSM); the *first trip model* (FTM) and the *subsequent trips model* (STM). The structure of the model system proposed is shown, conditioned by two types of factors: (1) first-level decisions condition the second-level ones and (2) second-level decisions condition first-level ones. An example of how a first-level decision can condition a second-level one is the choice of the departure time slice, according to which if an in-between trip has not been carried out (first level), the subsequent one (second level) cannot be started. An example of how a second-level choice can influence a first-level one might be the choice of loading unit (first level) which undoubtedly has to take into account the freight modes available (second level).

As stated above, assuming two transit destinations in the distribution channel at most (extension to the case of three or more stops is straightforward), the following choice hierarchy can be taken into account for the model proposed; obviously, sometimes, more than one choice may be taken concurrently and the choice hierarchy could be inverted and/or aggregated (see Figure 2):

1. *DSM*, simulating all choices relative to the origin, destination and the distribution channel:
   - choice of destination *d* (the sales market) and/or origin *o* (the procurement market);

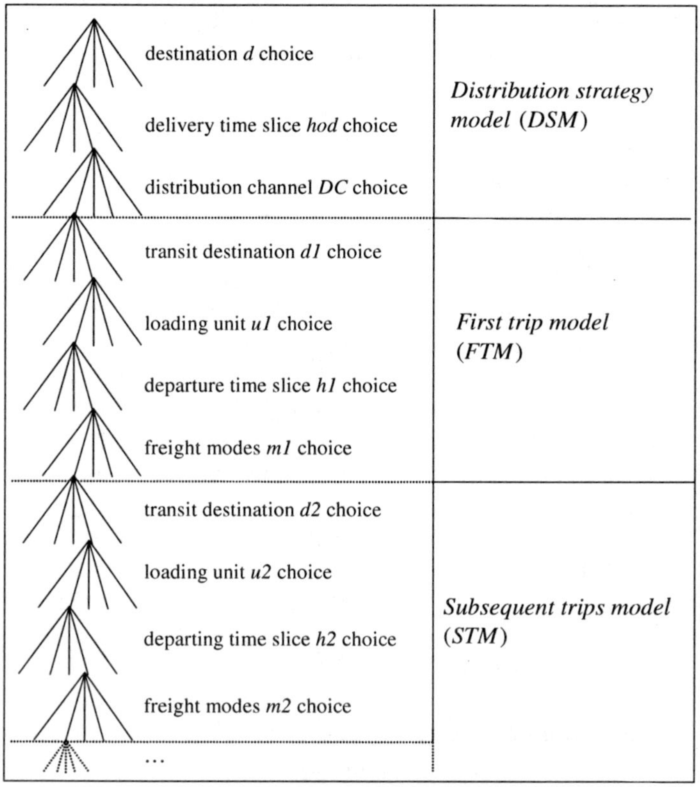

Figure 2
Model choice hierarchy

- choice of the delivery time slice *hod* (e.g. hour) within the reference period *H* (e.g. average business day) on which delivery has to be made;
- choice of the distribution channel DC (e.g. supplier–logistic centre–wholesaler–retailer).

2. *FTM*, simulating all choices relative to trips from the origin to first transit destination, possibly provided in the distribution channel (such as dry ports and regional logistic centres):
   - choice of the first transit destination *d*1;
   - choice of the loading unit/loading quantity *u*1 (container, semitrailer, pallets etc.) for the first trip;
   - choice of the departure time slice *h*1 for the first trip;
   - choice of the freight modes or the freight service *m*1 for the first trip.
3. *STM*, simulating all the choices relative to trips from first transit destination to second transit destination, possibly existing in the distribution channel

(provincial logistic centres, local warehouses etc.) up to the final destination at urban level, the retailer (as stated above for urban distribution, specific models need to be considered):

- choice of the second transit destination $d2$ (wholesaler, peripheral logistic centre, local warehouse etc.);
- choice of the loading unit/loading quantity $u2$ for the second trip;
- choice of the departure time slice $h2$ for the second trip;
- choice of freight modes or freight service $m2$ for the second trip;
- choice of the loading unit/loading quantity $u3$ for the third trip;
- choice of the departure time slice $h3$ for the third trip;
- choice of the freight modes or freight service $m3$ for the third trip.

The model assumes as known (input variable) the total consignment quantity (in tons, TEUs etc.) as referred to a fixed reference period H (day, month, year etc.), grouping firms that act in a similar way, that is firms for which a similar commodity class and a similar supply chain structure may be assumed. This allows for any commodity class c to consider the same choice criteria to be taken into account, as representing the same class of decision-makers. For each class the same set of variables may thus be used. In order to identify these classes of firms, a range of company segmentation criteria has been assumed:

- commodity sector (e.g. perishable/non-perishable goods, high-/low-value goods, high/low packing volume, hazardous/non-hazardous goods and so on);
- company size (e.g. large, medium or small);
- type of manufacturing process (e.g. just in time or on stock);
- choice/non-choice of the sales market (if the firm chooses to sell the commodity directly, or the retailer chooses the firm from which to purchase the commodity).

Thus, any segmentation criterion represents a different commodity class, and for each of them different choice models and/or logistic variables are assumed. Hence, for each commodity class identified, a specific model must be specified, estimated and validated.

The model system proposed allows us to estimate the OD commodity flows for a fixed period of time, a commodity class and an ever possible aggregation of the choice levels introduced; for example, possible OD flows could refer to the commodity class and type of freight vehicles (tons/day moved by the HGVs).

Through the commodity flows using a *vehicle-based model*, vehicle OD flows may be estimated per period of time, as well as an aggregation of the choice levels (e.g. HGVs/day OD flows). Furthermore, through an assignment model we can estimate the freight vehicle link flows on the relevant infrastructures. Assuming non-homogeneous users (with respect to relevant behavioural models and parameters) and a congested network we need to use a *multi-class assignment model*; this hypothesis also needs to consider passenger vehicle OD flows. User classes depend on the type of application. For example, classes may be defined by vehicle type (car, light and heavy commercial vehicles); in this case, motorway tolls, time values and path choice models may differ (Cascetta, 2001).

The model system could be calibrated both with a disaggregate and an aggregate approach. Sometimes, the realisation of a survey for a disaggregate calibration is expensive and difficult (especially for the freight transport). Hence, available aggregate data (both OD commodity flows and link vehicle flows) could be used to estimate model parameters. These data can be combined in different ways, obtaining different estimators in relation to the classic or Bayesian interpretation of the initial estimation and the assumption of the probability distribution of the measurement, assignment and model errors (Hogberg, 1976; Cascetta, 1986, 2001; Cascetta and Russo, 1997; Cascetta and Postorino, 2001).

The following sections are dedicated to a full description of the model system proposed.

Distribution Strategy Model

The market choice model allows us to simulate the commodity flow between origin o and destination d, for the commodity class c in the reference period H. The specification of this model is a function of the field of application and/or of the available input data. The model is formulated as follows:

$$F_{od}^{c}[H] = d_{o}^{c}[H] \cdot po\left[d/H, c, o\right] \quad \forall c \in Ic, \quad \forall o \in Io_{c}, \quad \forall d \in Id_{c} \qquad (1)$$

Equation (1) is valid under the hypothesis that suppliers (or firms) directly choose whether to sell the commodity, as is the case where the decision-maker is at origin o; retailers may sometimes choose the suppliers from which to purchase the commodity, as is the case where the decision-maker is at destination d. If we consider both cases possible, equation (1) becomes:

$$F_{od}^{c}[H] = d_{o}^{c}[H] \cdot po\left[d/H, c, o\right] \quad \forall c \in Ic, o, \quad \forall o \in Io_{c}, \quad \forall d \in Id_{c}$$

and

$$F_{od}^{c}[H] = d_{d}^{c}[H] \cdot pd\left[o/H, c, d\right] \quad \forall c \in Ic, d, \quad \forall d \in Id_{c}, \quad \forall o \in Io_{c}$$

The previous two equations must respect the congruence equation:

$$d_o^c = \sum_d d_d^c \cdot pd[o/H,c,d] \quad \forall c \in Ic, d, \quad \forall o \in Io_c$$

In other words, the total quantity of origin *o* consignment related to the commodity class *c* must be equal to the summation over all the destinations of total demand to purchase from origin *o* related to the commodity class *c*.

According to the model system proposed, to estimate the commodity flows $F_{od}^c[H]$ which, since they are related to the supply chain, are independent of the territorial scale, we also need to know national freight mobility (or European freight mobility, depending on the application scale) as representing the level of materials procurement and the quantity of manufacturing as referred to a reference period of time. Macro-economic models are generally used to simulate national freight mobility. The outputs of these models (such as multi-regional input–output models) are OD flows in monetary units. Generally, in applying macro-economic models, relatively large zones are used. This is due to the availability of statistical information required by the model (typically zones coincide with entire regions). The outputs of the national models are sometimes the inputs of behavioural and non-behavioural distribution models. Starting from these considerations, the input of the model system proposed, d_o^c and d_d^c, could be estimated either through the output of a macro-economic model (at times also through an emission/attraction model) or through aggregate data available, such as freight statistical information (this is the source used for the application).

The delivery time choice model allows us to simulate the choice of *hod*, the time slice by which delivery of the consignment, originating from origin *o*, has to be effected to destination *d* within the reference period *H*. This model gives the probability of choosing the time slice *hod*:

$$p[hod/H,c,o,d] \quad \forall c \in Ic, o, \quad \forall o \in Io_c, \quad \forall d \in Id_c, \quad \forall hod \in Ihod$$

The choice set *Ihod* consists of the *nH* time slices in which the reference period is divided; it requires that $1 \cup 2 \cup \ldots \cup nH \equiv H$ and $1 \cap 2 \cap \ldots \cap nH \equiv 0$; for example, if the reference period *H* is the average business day, the time slices could be represented by hours.

These probabilities (and those introduced below) could be estimates with respect to the systematic utilities associated to the choice alternatives. Such systematic utilities incorporate a *logsum* variable (inclusive variable) which allows successive choice levels to be considered (below, we will not repeat this consideration, which holds for all the next submodels, except the last one).

The *distribution channel choice model* allows us to simulate the choice of the distribution channel DC compatible with the commodity class *c*, origin *o*, destination

d and the *hod* time slice. The choice set $I\text{DC}_c$ consists of all the possible distribution channels considered, depending on commodity class c. For example, assuming at most two in-between stops in the distribution channel, the choice alternatives could be:

- supplier–retailer;
- supplier–wholesaler–retailer;
- supplier–logistic centre–retailer;
- supplier–logistic centre–wholesaler–retailer.

According to the tour-based approach, the simplest formulation simulates the choice between two alternatives: *round trip* (one forward trip; for example, the trip from supplier to the retailer apart from the backward trip: the empty return trip) and more than one trip (one or more intermediate stops between the manufacturer and retailer, apart from the empty return trip). This model gives the probability of choosing the distribution channel DC:

$$p[\text{DC}/H, c, o, d, hod] \quad \forall c \in Ic, o, \quad \forall o \in Io_c, \quad \forall d \in Id_c, \quad \forall hod \in Ihod, \quad \forall \text{DC} \in I\text{DC}_c$$

First Trip Model

The *first transit destination choice model* allows us to simulate the choice of the first transit destination $d1$ conditional upon the distribution strategy $H,c,o,d,hod,$DC. The first transit destination $d1$ choice set $Id1_c$ is a function of the commodity class c: different c company classes could use different $d1$ transit destinations. The choice alternatives are the zones in which there is at least one first-level logistic centre (such as a logistic centre or dry port).

This model gives the probability of choosing the first transit destination $d1$:

$$p[d1/H, c, o, d, hod, \text{DC}] \quad \forall c \in Ic, o, \quad \forall o \in Io_c, \quad \forall d \in Id_c, \quad \forall hod \in Ihod, \quad \forall \text{DC} \in I\text{DC}_c, \quad \forall d1 \in Id1_c$$

By using the *loading unit choice model* for the first trip, we can simulate the choice of the loading unit $u1$ for the first trip, conditional on the first transit destination $d1$ and the distribution strategy $H,c,o,d,hod,$DC. The $Iu1_c$ choice set comprises the available loading unit linking origin o and transit destination $d1$; this set is also a function of the commodity class c as different goods need different loading units.

This model gives the probability of choosing the loading unit $u1$ for the first trip:

$$p[u1/H, c, o, d, hod, \text{DC}, d1] \quad \forall c \in Ic, o, \quad \forall o \in Io_c, \quad \forall d \in Id_c, \quad \forall hod \in Ihod, \quad \forall \text{DC} \in I\text{DC}_c, \quad \forall d1 \in Id1_c, \quad \forall u1 \in Iu1_c$$

The departure time slice choice model for the first trip allows us to simulate the choice of the departure time slice $h1$ between origin o and first transit destination $d1$, conditional upon $d1$, $u1$ and the distribution strategy H,c,o,d,hod,DC. The choice set $Ih1_{hod}$ related to the departure time slices for the first trip comprises $nh1/hod$ possible time slices; it requires that $1 \cup 2 \cup \ldots \cup nh1,hod \equiv hod$ and $1 \cap 2 \cap \ldots \cap nh1,hod \equiv 0$. If, for example $hod = 18{:}00$ (H is the average business day), the $Ih1,hod$ choice set could comprise the 18 hours from 00:00 to 18:00. Obviously from this set we need to eliminate the time slices for which there is no freight mode $m1$ that is able to deliver the consignment within the delivery time slice hod.

This model gives the probability of choosing the departure time slice $h1$ for the first trip:

$$p[h1/H,c,o,d,hod,\mathrm{DC},d1,u1] \quad \forall c \in Ic,o, \quad \forall o \in Io_c, \quad \forall d \in Id_c, \quad \forall hod \in Ihod,$$
$$\forall \mathrm{DC} \in I\mathrm{DC}_c, \quad \forall d1 \in Id1_c, \quad \forall u1 \in Iu1_c, \quad \forall h1 \in Ih1_{hod}$$

The *freight mode choice model* simulates the choice of the freight modes or of the freight service $m1$, conditional upon all the preceding choices H,c,o,d,hod,DC,$d1,u1,h1$. The choice set $Im1_{d1,u1,h1}$ consists of the available modes, conditional upon the first transit destination $d1$, the loading unit $u1$ and time slice $h1$. Indeed, having fixed the destination d, there will only be one possible subset of all the modes, or sequence of modes, to reach the transit destination $d1$ (e.g. the lack of a railway will exclude the train mode). From this set we need to eliminate the modes unable to transport loading unit $u1$ (e.g. if $u1$ = *container*, the mode $m1$ = LGV cannot be considered) and the modes unable to deliver the consignment within the delivery time slice hod starting the trip during the departure time slice $h1$.

This model gives the probability of choosing the freight mode $m1$:

$$p[m1/H,c,o,d,hod,\mathrm{DC},d1,u1,h1] \quad \forall c \in Ic,o, \quad \forall o \in Io_c, \quad \forall d \in Id_c,$$
$$\forall hod \in Ihod, \quad \forall \mathrm{DC} \in I\mathrm{DC}_c, \quad \forall d1 \in Id1_c,$$
$$\forall u1 \in Iu1_c, \quad \forall h1 \in Ih1_{hod}, \quad \forall m1 \in Im1_{d1,u1,h1}$$

Subsequent Trip Model

Using the *second transit destination choice model* we may simulate the choice of the second transit destination $d2$ conditional upon the distribution strategy $H,c,o,d,$ hod,DC and the first trip choices $d1,u1,h1,m1$. The second transit destination $d2$ choice set $Id2_c$ is a function of the commodity class c. The choice alternatives are the zones in which there is at least one second-level logistic centre (wholesaler, peripheral logistic centre, local warehouse etc.).

This model gives the probability of choosing the second transit destination $d2$:

$$p[d2/H, c, o, d, hod, \mathrm{DC}, d1, u1, h1, m1] \quad \forall c \in Ic, o, \quad \forall o \in Io_c, \quad \forall d \in Id_c, \quad \forall hod \in Ihod, \quad \forall \mathrm{DC} \in I\mathrm{DC}_c, \quad \forall d1 \in Id1_c, \quad \forall u1 \in Iu1_c, \quad \forall h1 \in Ih1_{hod}, \quad \forall m1 \in Im1_{d1,u1,h1}, \quad \forall d2 \in Id2_c$$

The loading unit choice model for the second trip allows us to simulate the choice of the loading unit $u2$ for the second trip, conditional on the distribution strategy $H,c,o,d,hod,$DC, the first trip choices $d1,u1,h1,m1$ and the second transit destination $d2$. The choice set $Iu2_c$ comprises the available loading unit linking the first transit destination $d1$ and the second transit destination $d2$; this set is also a function of the commodity class c as different goods require different loading units.

This model gives the probability of choosing the loading unit $u2$ for the second trip:

$$p[u2/H, c, o, d, hod, \mathrm{DC}, d1, u1, h1, m1, d2] \quad \forall c \in Ic, o, \quad \forall o \in Io_c, \quad \forall d \in Id_c, \quad \forall hod \in Ihod, \quad \forall \mathrm{DC} \in I\mathrm{DC}_c, \quad \forall d1 \in Id1_c, \quad \forall u1 \in Iu1_c, \quad \forall h1 \in Ih1_{hod}, \quad \forall m1 \in Im1_{d1,u1,h1}, \forall d2 \in Id2_c, \quad \forall u2 \in Iu2_c$$

By using the *departure time slice choice model* for the second trip we can simulate the choice of the departure time slice $h2$ between the first transit destination $d1$ and the second transit destination $d2$, conditional upon the distribution strategy $H,c,o,d,hod,$DC; the first trip choices $d1,u1,h1,m1$; the second transit destination $d2$ and loading unit $u2$. The choice set $Ih2_{hod,h1}$ consists of all the possible time slices conditional upon the delivery time slice *hod* and the departure time slice for the first trip $h1$. If, for example $h_{od} =$ 18:00 (H is the average business day), $h_1 =$ 12:00 and mode $m1$ requires 1 hour for the first trip between origin o and destination $d1$, the choice set $Ih2_{hod,h1}$ could be represented by the 5 hours from 13:00 to 18:00. Obviously, from this set the time slices for which all the modes $m2$ are unable to deliver the goods within the *hod* time slice must be eliminated.

This model gives the probability of choosing the departing time slice $h2$:

$$p[h2/H, c, o, d, hod, \mathrm{DC}, d1, u1, h1, m1, d2, u2] \quad \forall c \in Ic, o, \quad \forall o \in Io_c, \quad \forall d \in Id_c, \quad \forall hod \in Ihod, \quad \forall \mathrm{DC} \in I\mathrm{DC}_c, \quad \forall d1 \in Id1_c, \quad \forall u1 \in Iu1_c, \quad \forall h1 \in Ih1_{hod}, \quad \forall m1 \in Im1_{d1,u1,h1}, \quad \forall d2 \in Id2_c, \quad \forall u2 \in Iu2_c, \quad \forall h2 \in Ih2_{hod,h1}$$

The *freight mode choice model* for the second trip allows us to simulate the choice of freight mode or freight service $m2$, conditional upon all the preceding choices $H,c,o,d,hod,\mathrm{DC},d1,u1,h1,m1,d2,u2,h2$. The choice set $Im2_{d2,u2,h2}$ consists of the available modes conditional upon the second transit destination $d2$, the loading unit $u2$ and the departure time slice $h2$.

This model gives the probability of choosing the freight mode $m2$:

$$p[m2/H,c,o,d,hod,DC,d1,u1,h1,m1,d2,u2,h2] \quad \forall c \in Ic,o, \quad \forall o \in Io_c,$$
$$\forall d \in Id_c, \quad \forall hod \in Ihod, \quad \forall DC \in IDC_c, \quad \forall d1 \in Id1_c, \quad \forall u1 \in Iu1_c,$$
$$\forall h1 \in Ih1_{hod}, \quad \forall m1 \in Im1_{d1,u1,h1}, \quad \forall d2 \in Id2_c, \quad \forall u2 \in Iu2_c, \quad \forall h2 \in Ih2_{hod,h1},$$
$$\forall m2 \in Im2_{d2,u2,h2}$$

Analogous considerations could be made regarding the *loading unit choice model, departing time slice choice model* and *freight mode choice model* for the third trip, allowing estimation of the corresponding choice probabilities: loading unit $u3$, departure time slice $h3$ and freight mode $m3$ related to the third trip.

The General Model

The commodity flow between origin o and destination d for the reference period H; the commodity class c; delivery time slice hod; distribution channel DC; transit destinations $d1$ and $d2$; loading units $u1$, $u2$ and $u3$; departure time slices $h1$, $h2$ and $h3$; and freight modes $m1$, $m2$ and $m3$ is as follows:

$$\begin{aligned}
F^c_{od}&[H,hod,\mathrm{DC},d1,u1,h1,m1,d2,u2,h2,u3,h3,m3] = F^c_{od}[H]\cdot p[hod/H,c,o,d]\cdot\\
&p[\mathrm{DC}/H,c,o,d,hod]\cdot p[d1/H,c,o,d,hod,\mathrm{DC}]\cdot p[u1/H,c,o,d,hod,\mathrm{DC},d1]\cdot\\
&p[h1/H,c,o,d,hod,\mathrm{DC},d1,u1]\cdot p[m1/H,c,o,d,hod,\mathrm{DC},d1,u1,h1]\cdot\\
&p[d2/H,c,o,d,hod,\mathrm{DC},d1,u1,h1,m1]\cdot p[u2/H,c,o,d,hod,\mathrm{DC},d1,u1,h1,m1,d2]\cdot\\
&p[h2/H,c,o,d,hod,\mathrm{DC},d1,u1,h1,m1,d2,u2]\cdot\\
&p[m2/H,c,o,d,hod,\mathrm{DC},d1,u1,h1,m1,d2,u2,h2]\cdot\\
&p[u3/H,c,o,d,hod,\mathrm{DC},d1,u1,h1,m1,d2,u2,h2,m2]\cdot\\
&p[h3/H,c,o,d,hod,\mathrm{DC},d1,u1,h1,m1,d2,u2,h2,m2,u3]\cdot\\
&p[m3/H,c,o,d,hod,\mathrm{DC},d1,u1,h1,m1,d2,u2,h2,m2,u3,h3]
\end{aligned}$$

$$\forall c \in Ic,o, \quad \forall o \in Io_c, \quad \forall d \in Id_c, \quad \forall hod \in Ihod, \quad \forall \mathrm{DC} \in I\mathrm{DC}_c,$$
$$\forall d1 \in Id1_c, \quad \forall u1 \in Iu1_c, \quad \forall h1 \in Ih1_{hod}, \quad \forall m1 \in Im1_{d1,u1,h1},$$
$$\forall d2 \in Id2_c, \quad \forall u2 \in Iu2_c, \quad \forall h2 \in Ih2_{hod,h1}, \quad \forall m2 \in Im2_{d2,u2,h2},$$
$$\forall u3 \in Iu3_c, \quad \forall h3 \in Ih3_{hod,h2}, \quad \forall m3 \in Im3_{d,u3,h3}$$

As stated above, through commodity flows using a *vehicle-based model*, vehicle flows may be estimated for a reference period of time and an aggregation of the choice levels considered. For example, if CV[H,o,$d1$,$m1$] is the *vehicle-based model* related to a reference period H, origin o, transit destination $d1$ and mode $m1$, tons/year commodity flows can be converted into HGVs/day commodity flows.

Formally, vehicle flow, associated to mode $m1$, from origin o to the first transit destination $d1$ in the reference period H is:

$$\text{Fveich}_{od1}[H,m1] = \text{CV}[H,o,d1,m1]\cdot F_{od1}[H,m1] \quad \forall o \in Io_c, \quad \forall d1 \in Id1_c, \quad \forall m1 \in Im1_{d1,u1,h1}$$

where:

$$F_{od1}[H,m1] = \sum_{c}\sum_{hoc}\sum_{\text{DC}}\sum_{u1}\sum_{h1} F^{c}_{od}[H]\cdot p[hod/H,c,o,d]\cdot p[\text{DC}/H,c,o,d,hod]\cdot p[d1/H,c,o,d,hod,\text{DC}]\cdot p[u1/H,c,o,d,hod,\text{DC},d1]\cdot p[h1/H,c,o,d,hod,\text{DC},d1,u1]\cdot p[m1/H,c,o,d,hod,\text{DC},d1,u1,h1]$$

$F_{od1}[H,m1]$ is the commodity flow which uses mode $m1$ for the trip from origin o to the first transit destination $d1$ in the reference period H.

Through the OD vehicle flow, the vehicle link flows on the relevant infrastructures may be estimated through an assignment model.

There are several possible fields of application of the model system proposed: the most suitable location for a new logistic centre may be assessed (through a *what if* approach) or, for example, the effects on the freight transport system (and hence on traffic congestion) caused by interventions in the socio-economic system may be appraised.

In this study the model system proposed was applied (specified, calibrated and validated) to simulate freight distribution within the southern Italian region of Campania. Some hypotheses were added to the general architecture proposed. The following section is dedicated to a full description of the application.

Application

In this paper we applied the model system described in the section 'General Architecture' to simulate regional freight distribution: in particular, commodity flows within Campania were simulated. Campania is a region in southern Italy comprising five provinces (Naples, Caserta, Avellino, Benevento and Salerno) and about 550 municipal districts (with over 5,600,000 inhabitants as a whole). Most of the population is concentrated along the coastal strip; Naples province has about 3 million inhabitants and has the municipal district with the highest population density in Europe (Portici: 14,726 inhabitants/km^2).

The application proposed in this paper aims to reproduce the procurement phase (from suppliers to manufacturers) and the distribution phase (from manufacturers to retailers). The model system was calibrated in aggregate fashion for two reasons: for freight transport surveys for disaggregate calibration are costly and difficult, and secondly, our aim was to test the effectiveness of the aggregate calibration technique for estimating freight model parameters. Obviously, from the results obtained we can claim that aggregate estimations, outputs of the model system (commodity flows and link vehicle flows), are reliable; but nothing can be asserted regarding the single disaggregate choices (e.g. choice of the delivery lapse of time) for which a very disaggregate calibration would be necessary (this will be one of our future research aims). In this sense, the Nested Logit model was used as a 'descriptive' mathematical formulation without a behavioural interpretation (see the model architecture described in Figure 3).

As stated in the section 'General Architecture', the choice of using a tour-based approach, albeit in a non-behavioural and simplified way like that proposed in this application, allows us to simulate commodity flows congruently, considering explicitly the transit destinations and the modes used for distribution trips. Furthermore, the model applied has been compared with some aggregated models with respect to both validation indicators and model elasticity.

Transportation System Identification

The whole regional area was divided into traffic zones. In this phase, the study of the socio-economic and transport framework of the area is essential. Indeed, knowledge of the location of factories and logistic centres throughout the area, as well as of existing infrastructures, suggested the zoning used. Seventeen zones were introduced according to their business and infrastructure density (smaller areas matching large concentrations of major factories and infrastructures). Relevant infrastructures include the whole motorway network and the main urban and extra urban infrastructures. At the intersection between these main infrastructures and the border of Campania, the external centroids were positioned (external zones are represented by external zone centroids). The main characteristics of the graph are: links = 1,176; nodes = 436; internal centroids = 17 and external centroids = 6.

Concerning the supply model, in this application the cost functions associated to the links of the graph take into account the travel time, tolls, driver costs and driver

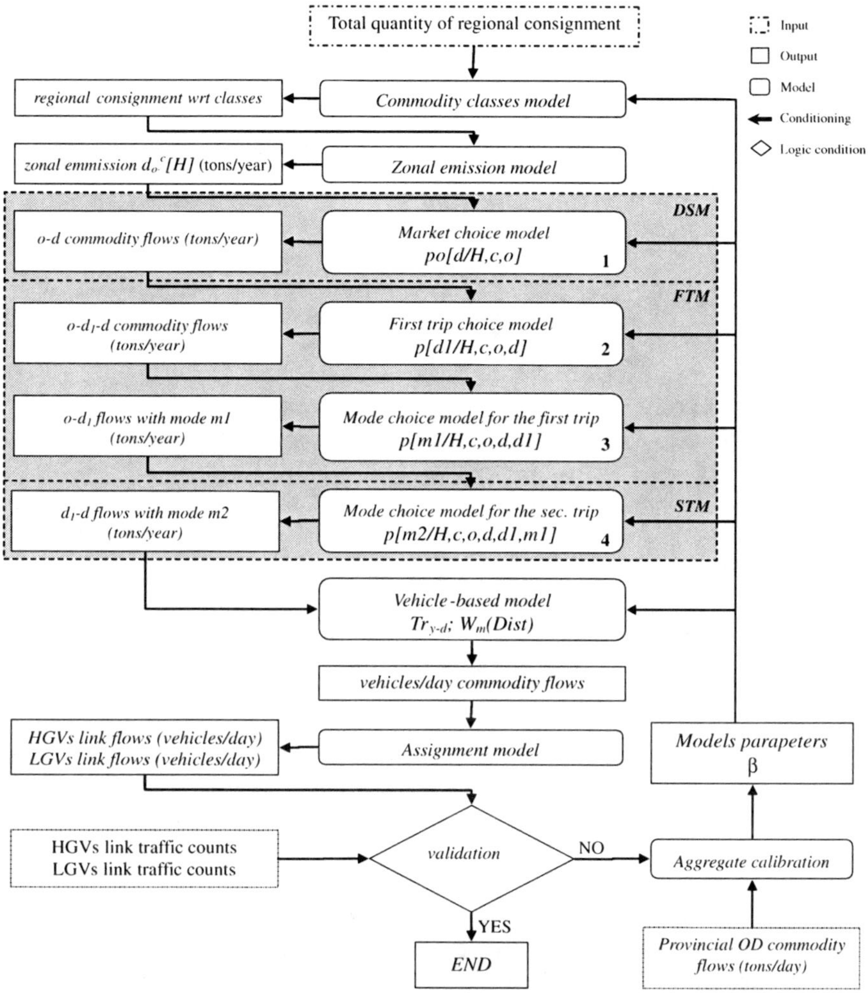

Figure 3

The freight distribution architecture model used in the application

standing times, which are generally the major perceived costs within route choice for inter-provincial trips (0–150 km).

To estimate the freight link travel time we used the function proposed by Russo (2005), estimated for the whole of Italy.

As mentioned above, the model used assumes as known the total $d_o^c[H]$ related to the reference period H and the commodity class c that origin o must send towards all the destination zones. From the Transportation National Count (2001), total exchanges inside Campania and between this region and the other Italian regions were identified. These values are in tons/2001 because the 2001 is the H reference period considered. These quantities of consignments were split into the various commodity classes c through a *commodity class model* (see Figure 3) on the basis of the results of a nationwide survey (Di Gangi, 1996).

The commodity classes considered are:

- agriculture and foodstuffs;
- energy products;
- minerals;
- chemical and pharmaceutical products;
- other products.

For each class, the total regional commodity inflows (from external centroids towards internal destinations) and outflows (from internal centroids towards external destinations) were subsequently identified. The total commodity outflows from Campania were then split among the 17 internal zones through a gravitational model (*zonal emission model*) as a function of attraction and cost variables similar to those used in models 1 and 2 described in the next subsection.

Since the current truck freight commodity flow corresponds to approximately 97% of the aggregate amount of Campania's intra-regional freight flows and to approximately 78% of extra-regional flows (road haulage used to transport 88% tons/year throughout Campania), two transport modes were considered: HGVs (max loading $>$ 3.5 tons) and LGVs (max loading $\leq$ 3.5 tons).

Some provincial commodity flows (in tons/2001) estimated through the Transportation National Count (2001) and some traffic counts (41 traffic sections for the two modes), estimated through an ITER (2002) truck survey (commissioned by the Transportation Department of the University of Naples) are the aggregate data used for the calibration.

Specification

The proposed model simulates freight distribution both for commodity flows entering a zone (inflows) and for commodity flows leaving a zone (outflows). In other words, for the outflows (both from internal and external centroids) with a destination within Campania, the model simulates the choice of the final destination d to sell the commodity, while for the flows entering the external centroids (inflows), the model simulates the choice of origin o from which to purchase the commodity. In both cases, because of the restricted area of Campania and due to the large area of the zones considered, at most one in-between transit destination in the distribution channel was considered and simulated.

Therefore, the choice hierarchy considered in the model is the following:

1. choice of the distribution strategy (i.e. of the final destination d given the origin o of the outflow or of the acquisition market o given the destination d of the inflows);
2. choice of the possible transit destination $d1$ (logistic centre, dry port etc.);
3. choice of the mode $m1$ for the first trip between the origin o and the transit destination $d1$ (HGVs and LGVs);
4. choice of the mode $m2$ for the second trip between the transit destination $d1$ and the final destination d (HGVs and LGVs).

From these choices the model structure represented in Figure 3 was derived. In particular:

- the *market choice model* allows us to simulate the commodity flow between origin o and destination d:

$$po[d/H, c, o] \quad \forall c \in Ic, o, \quad \forall o \in Io_c, \quad \forall d \in Id_c, \quad \text{or } pd[o/H, c, d]$$
$$\forall c \in Ic, o, \quad \forall d \in Id_c, \quad \forall o \in Io_c$$

- the *first trip choice model* allows simulation of the choice of the first transit destination $d1$:

$$p[d1/H, c, o, d] \quad \forall c \in Ic, o, \quad \forall o \in Io_c, \quad \forall d \in Id_c, \quad \forall d1 \in Id1_c$$

- the *mode choice model* for the first trip simulates the modal choice $m1$ for the first trip:

$$p[m1/H, c, o, d, d1] \quad \forall c \in Ic, o, \quad \forall o \in Io_c, \quad \forall d \in Id_c,$$
$$\forall d1 \in Id1_c, \quad \forall m1 \in Im1_{d1,u1,h1}$$

- the *mode choice model* for the second trip allows us to simulate modal choice $m2$ for the second trip:

$$p[m2/H, c, o, d, d1, m1] \quad \forall c \in Ic, o, \quad \forall o \in Io_c, \quad \forall d \in Id_c, \quad \forall d1 \in Id1_c,$$
$$\forall m1 \in Im1d_{1,u1,h1}, \quad \forall m2 \in Im2_{d2,u2,h2}$$

For the specification of this system of models, a Nested Logit model was used. In Table 2 the attributes used in the systematic utilities are reported.

With these models, through the model parameters estimated (Table 3), the mode commodity flows can be estimated in tons/year. To transform the OD tons/year into vehicles/day the *vehicle-based model* must be applied (Figure 3). Each OD tons/year must be transformed into tons/day multiplying each item by the Tr_{y-d} calibrated value (Table 4) and then into vehicles/day by multiplying each single item by a calibrated coefficient. In order to convert from tons/day to vehicles/day, W_m(Dist) average vehicle weight was estimated according to mode m and Dist trip distance (see the results of the

Table 2
Attributes Used in the Systematic Utilities

Model	Attributes
1	T_{od} is the time (in minutes), calculated on the network, for the o–d trip; *Pop* is the logarithm of the population of destination d (or at origin o); *Empc* is the logarithm of the number of employees, in the commodity class c, at destination d (or at origin o); *Firmc* is the number of firms, in the commodity class c, at destination d (or origin o).
2	*Empf* is the logarithm of the numbers of employees in freight firms (haulage, warehousing and storage) belonging to the intermediate destination $d1$; *Firmf* is the number of freight firms (haulage, warehousing and storage) belonging to the intermediate destination $d1$; *FLC* is a dummy variable; it assumes the value of one if there are 'first-level' logistic centres (ports, dry ports etc.) in the intermediate destination $d1$; $T_{o,d1}$ is the time (in minutes), calculated on the network, for the o– $d1$ trip (accessibility attribute); $T_{d1,d}$ is the time (in minutes), calculated on the network, for the $d1$–d trip (accessibility attribute).
3	*Dd*1 (only in LGV systematic utility) is the population density (inhabitants/km^2) of the transit destination $d1$; this attribute allows us to simulate the greater probability of choosing LGVs in high-population density zones; *IZo* (only in HGV systematic utility) is a dummy variable which assumes a value of one if $o = d1$; this attribute allows us to simulate the lower probability of choosing HGVs for intra-zone trips; *Dist* is the trip distance (in km), calculated on the network; this attribute allows simulation of the greater probability of choosing LGVs for short-distance trips or the greater probability of choosing HGVs for long-distance trips.
4	*Dd* (only in LGV systematic utility) is the population density (inhabitants/km^2) of the final destination d; *IZd* (only in HGV systematic utility) is a dummy variable which assumes the value of 1 if $d1 = d$; *Dist* is the trip distance (in km), calculated on the network.

calibration in Table 4). Finally, such vehicle/day commodity flows must be multiplied by an amplifying estimated coefficient to take into account deadheading (to consider the *empty return trip*), and then assigned to the network through an SNL Probit assignment model.

Calibration and Validation

The model was calibrated with aggregate data available (both OD commodity flows and link vehicle flows) through a GLS estimator. In Tables 3 and 4, results in terms of model parameter values are reported.

In order to compare observed (ob) and modelled (md) values, y_i^{ob} and y_i^{md}, a simple analysis through scatter diagrams has been considered enough for the scope of the study. With this aim a linear function: $y_i^{\text{md}} = \alpha + \beta \cdot y_i^{\text{ob}}$ has been calibrated. Exact modelling of observed values occurs with $\alpha = 0$ and $\beta = 1$ (and $\rho^2 = 1$).

Table 3
Results in Terms of Model Parameter Values

Attributes	Class 1	Class 2	Class 3	Class 4	Class 5
T_{od}	−0.0388	−0.0286	−0.062	−0.0884	−0.0206
Pop	0.0847	0.0370	0.0234	0.0406	0.0972
Firmc	0.0044	0.0408	0.0015	0.0278	0.0003
Empc	0.0618	0.0438	0.0143	0.0544	0.0198
Empf	0.0768	0.0981	0.0343	0.0594	0.0581
Firmf	0.0027	0.0068	0.0019	0.0023	0.001
FLC	1.9263	2.6284	1.7873	1.9123	1.7814
$T_{o,d1}$; $T_{d1,d}$	−0.0238	−0.0436	−0.087	−0.099	−0.0356
*Dd*1; *Dd*	2.36E-05	2.36E-05	2.36E-05	2.36E-05	2.36E-05
IZo; *IZd*	−2.2068	−2.2068	−2.2068	−2.2068	−2.2068
Dist(LGV)	−0.1279	−0.1279	−0.1279	−0.1279	−0.1279
Dist(HGV)	−0.0733	−0.0733	−0.0733	−0.0733	−0.0733

Table 4
Average Weight W_m(Dist) Deadheading Amplifying Coefficient

Distance band	LGV	HGV	OD type of trip	LGV	HGV
50–150 km	3.1	8.3	Inside–inside	1.41	1.52
> 150 km	3.1	21.5	Other	1.20	1.25
		$Tr_{\text{y-d}} = 1/296 = 0.00338$			

Table 5 and Figure 4 show main results. Both for the LGVs and the HGVs, β values are close to 1; data α values are close to zero with respect to average observed values and $\hat{y}_i^{ob} \cong 2,500$. Values of ρ^2 are greater than 0.74 for the LGVs data and greater than 0.83 for the HGVs data. In addition, values of β and ρ^2 are only slightly affected by considering a null α; values of β being even closer to 1. All these results allow us to consider the analysed model effective.

The model system was validated also through a *hold-out sample*, consisting in seven traffic sections, for each mode, not used for the calibration (see results in Table 5 and Figure 4). Both for this sample, the β values of LGVs and the HGVs are close to 1; data α values are close to zero with respect to average observed values. Values of ρ^2 are greater than 0.90 for the LGVs data and greater than 0.80 for the HGVs data. In

Table 5

Results in Terms of Performance Indicator Values

Data	ρ^2	α	β	(with $\alpha = 0$)	
				ρ^2	β
Calibration sample					
LGVs	0.747	66.761	0.963	0.745	1.009
HGVs	0.839	155.502	0.872	0.829	0.954
Hold-out sample					
LGVs	0.921	179.701	1.160	0.913	1.063
HGVs	0.874	357.311	0.774	0.831	0.928

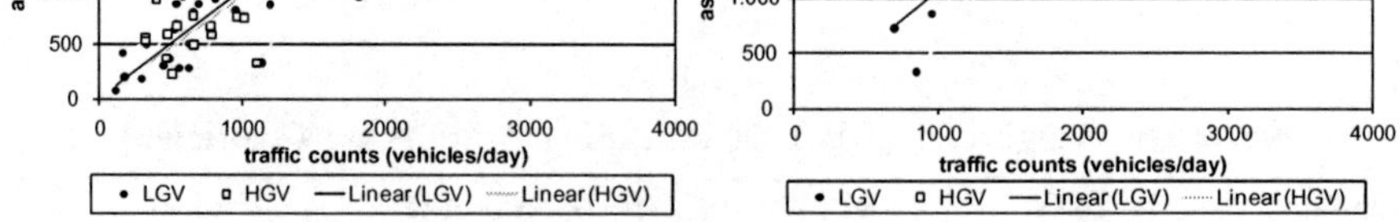

Figure 4

Comparison between traffic counts and assigned flows (calibration sample and hold-out sample)

addition, values of β and ρ^2 are only slightly affected by considering a null α; values of β being even closer to 1.

A more detailed analysis is out of scope of this paper and will be performed to validate the disaggregate calibration, object of a future paper.

The model system previously described was then applied to: the outflows of both the internal zones and the external centroids, with its interpretation as 'choice of final destination'; and the external centroid inflows, with its interpretation as 'choice of the acquisition market'.

Fixing the H reference period of the simulation and the c commodity class, it could be possible to estimate the disaggregate outputs:

- *origin–final destination* commodity flows in tons/year and vehicle/day;
- *origin–transit destination* commodity flows in tons/year and vehicle/day;
- *transit destination–final destination* commodity flows in tons/year and vehicle/day;
- *link* commodity flows in tons/year and vehicle/day.

Even if a calibrated tour-based model allows to estimate more disaggregate outputs than an aggregate distribution model commonly used in literature (e.g. a gravitational model), the idea of using aggregate data to estimate the parameters of the model allows to compare the model proposed with other aggregate models calibrated through a subset of the aggregate data cited above. In particular, different gravitational models have been calibrated testing different model specifications using the logistic, transport level of service and economic attributes described above. The results of these calibrations have allowed to conclude that the tour-based model, even if calibrated through aggregate data, reproduce better data in terms of validation indicators: the tour-based model produces on average a ρ^2 value better than 17% with respect to the best gravitational models estimated.

Furthermore, through a before and after study it has been possible to compare the prediction reliability of the tour-based model with respect to the aggregate calibrated models. As stated in the section 'Transportation System Identification', the reference period of time is 2001; using the available data referring 1996 it has been possible to compare the elasticity of the calibrated models. The results show that the disaggregate model reproduce better the 1996 data with, for example, a ρ^2 value better than 12% with respect to the best gravitational models estimated, with absolute values always greater than 0.65.

From an aggregate point of view, the results of the application show that about 65% of the exchange trips (about 24 million tons/year) effect an intermediate stop before reaching the final destination; this represents about 45% of intra-regional trips. Campania's infrastructures are used daily by about 48,000 LGVs and 26,000 HGVs, amounting to about 74,000 freight vehicles per day. The percentage distribution differs in terms of mode and trip type. In fact, while about 90% of the LGVs (41,630 LGVs/day) effect trips within Campania, the percentage of HGVs that effects the same type of trip falls 65% short (16,420 HGVs/day). In all, 79% of the freight-circulating vehicles undertake internal trips; 6% effect internal–external trips, 9% effect external–internal trips and 6% undertake crossing trips (external–external trips). An interesting comparison may be made among the percentage distribution in terms of freight vehicles/day and tons/year transported by the different freight vehicles. While the LGVs make up about 65% of total vehicles/day, they transport 30% of the tons/year due to their low load capacity. Conversely, while HGVs account for 35% of total vehicles/day, they transport more than 70% of the tons/year.

Freight link flows, the output of the system of models implemented, were compared with passenger mobility link flows; it emerged that freight flows at times accounted for 40% of the total.

Conclusion and Research Prospects

The University of Salerno (Italy) and the University of Reggio Calabria (Italy) set up a joint research project to study freight transport and logistics as well as model the distributive transport and logistic system to simulate commodity flows.

In this paper we enabled to define an open and flexible modelling architecture to simulate a distributive transport and logistic system based on a tour-based approach. The flexible structure of the tour-based approach allows simulation of the choices of different decision-makers, namely the choices regarding freight transport and, if necessary, of only part of the supply chain which is an aggregation of the choices involved. Furthermore, the choice of using a tour-based approach (which has not yet found applications in the literature for freight transport), whether in a behavioural or non-behavioural fashion, allows us to simulate commodity flows congruently, explicitly considering the simulation of transit destinations and of all the other choices connected with them, such as the choice of loading unit and the mode.

The model system proposed could be used as a DSS by a public administration which needs a tool able to simulate the total commodity flows.

There are various possible fields of application of the model system proposed. The most suitable location of a new logistic centre can be appraised (through a *what if* approach) or, for example, it is possible to estimate the effects on the freight transport system (hence on traffic congestion) caused by interventions in the socio-economic system.

To test the applicability of the modelling architecture proposed, we carried out an application to estimate commodity flows for the region of Campania (southern Italy). This application also allowed us to investigate commodity flows relative to the regional trips (50–150 km distance band). Besides, the model yielded both commodity-based and vehicle-based results, allowing both commodity and vehicle flows to be simulated.

Another aim was to test the effectiveness of the aggregate calibration technique for estimating disaggregate model parameters. Furthermore, the idea of using an aggregate calibration allows to compare the model proposed with other aggregate models with respect to both the validation indicators and the elasticity of the model. The results allow to conclude that the tour-based model, even if calibrated through aggregate data, reproduce better the data used for the calibration and has a better prediction reliability with respect to an aggregate model.

The second part of our research will consist in conducting a statistically significant number of surveys directly targeting categories of decision-makers involved in the distributive transport and logistic system so as to apply the modelling architecture proposed in a disaggregate way, specifying and calibrating a behavioural demand model. The results of this research will be the subject of a future paper.

References

Algers, S., A. Daly, P. Kjelmann and S. Wildert, (1995). Stockholm model system (SISM): application. *Proceeding of the Seventh World Conference of Transportation Research*. Sydney, Australia.

Alonso W. (1967). A reformulation of classical location theory and its relation to rent theory. In M. D. Thomas (Ed.), Papers, *The St. Louis Meeting*, Vol. 19. Regional Science Association.

Bayliss, B. (1998). *The Measurement of Supply and Demand in Freight Transport*. Hants, England, Avebury Grower Publishing Company Ltd.

Boyer, K. D. (1977). Minimum rate regulation, modal split sensitivities, and the railroad problem. *Journal of Political Economy* 85, 189–493.

Cartenì, A. and F. Russo (2004). *A Distribution Regional Freight Demand Model, Urban Transport X: Urban Transport and the Environment in the 21st Century*. Southampton, UK, Wessex Institute of Technology.

Cascetta, E. (1986). A class of travel demand estimators using traffic flow. *CRT Publication* 375, Université de Montréal, Montreal, Canada.

Cascetta, E. (2001). *Transportation Systems Engineering: Theory and Methods*. Boston, USA, Kluwer Academic Publishers.

Cascetta, E. and M. Di Gangi (1996). A multi-regional input-output model with elastic trade coefficients for the simulation of the freight transport demand in Italy. *Proceeding of the 24th PTRC*. European Transport Forum.

Cascetta, E. and D. Iannò (2000). Calibrazione aggregata di un sistema di modelli di domanda merci a scala nazionale. In G. E. Cantarella and F. Russo (Eds.), *Metodi e Tecnologie dell'Ingegneria dei Trasporti*. Milan, Italy, Franco Angeli, pp. 156–178.

Cascetta, E., A. Nuzzolo and V. Velardi (1994). *A System of Mathematical Models for the Evaluation of Integrated Traffic Planning and Control Policies*. Salerno, Italy, Laboratorio Ricerche Gestione e Controllo Traffico.

Cascetta, E. and M. N. Postorino (2001). Fixed point models for the estimation of O-D matrices using traffic counts on congested networks. *Transportation Science* 35(2), 134–147.

Cascetta, E. and F. Russo (1997). Calibrating aggregated travel demand models with traffic counts: estimators and statistical performance. *Transportation* 24(3), 271–293.

Crainic, T. G. (1987). Operations research models of intercity freight transportation: the current state and future research issues. *Logistic and Transportation Review* 23.

Daganzo, F. (1999). *Logistics Systems Analysis*. Heidelberg, Springer Verlag.

Domencich, T. A. and D. McFadden (1975). *Urban Travel Demand: A Behavioural Analysis*. New York, McGraw-Hill.

Di Gangi, M. (1996). Modelli per la distribuzione spaziale della domanda merci: Modelli per la stima dei coefficienti di scambio, metodo per la provincializzazione, *F.I.R.S.T. s.r.l.*

Eurostat (2005). Specific aspects of road freight transport. *Statistics in Focus*, Luxembourg. Available at: http://ec.europa.eu/eurostat/

Fridstrøm, L. and A. Madslien (1994). Own account or hire freight: a stated preference analysis. *Proceeding of the 7th International Conference on Travel Behaviour*. Valle Nevado, Chile.

Fridstrøm, L. and A. Madslien (1995). *A Stated Preference Analysis of Wholesaler's Freight Choice*. Oslo, Institute of Transport Economics.

Ghiani, G. and R. Musmanno (2000). *Modelli e metodi per l'organizzazione dei sistemi logistici*. Bologna, Pitagora Editrice.

Harker, P. T. (1985). *Spatial Price Equilibrium: Advances in Theory, Computation and Application*. Heidelberg, Springer Verlag.

Hogberg, P. (1976). Estimation of parameters in models for traffic prediction: a non-linear regression approach. *Transportation Research Part B* 10, 263–265.

Hoover, E. M. (1948). *The Location of Economic Activity*. New York, McGraw-Hill.

Isard, W. (1951). Interregional and regional input-output analysis: a model of space-economy. *The Review of Economics and Statistics* 33(4), 318–328.

Isard, W. (1960). *Methods of Regional Analysis: An Introduction to Regional Science*. Cambridge MIT Press.

ITER (2002). A truck mobility survey commissioned by the Transport Department of the University of Naples, Italy.

Leontief, W. and P. Costa (1987). Il trasporto merci e l'economia italiana. Scenari di interazione al 2000 e al 2015. *Sistemi Operativi*, New York—Venice.

Levin, R. C. (1978). Allocation in surface freight transportation: does rate regulation matter? *Bell Journal of Economics* 9, 18–45.

Marzano, V. and A. Papola (2004). Modelling freight demand at a national level: theoretical developments and application to Italy. *Proceedings of the Annual ETC Conference*. Strasbourg.

Mazzarino, M. (1997). Modelling freight transport demand: a survey. *I quaderni di Trasporti Europei*, Trieste.

Meyer, J. R. (1963). Regional economics: a survey. *American Economic Review* 53, 19–54.

Morton, A. (1969). A statistical sketch of intercity freight demand. *Highway Research Record* 166.

Nagurney, A., J. Dong and D. Zhang (2002). A supply chain network equilibrium model. *Transportation Research Part E: Logistics and Transportation Review* 38(5), 281–303.

Nuzzolo, A. and F. Russo (1997). Modal split at international level: a system of models for Italian-based freight. *Proceeding of the 25th PTRC*. European Transport Forum, London.

Ogden, K. W. (1992). *Urban Goods Movement: A Guide to Policy and Planning*. Farnham, UK, Ashgate.

Oppenheim, N. (1995). *Urban Travel Demand Modeling*. San Francisco, USA, Wiley International Publication.

Quandt, R. E. and W. J. Baumol (1966). The demand for abstract transport modes: theory and measurement. *Journal of Regional Science* 6(2), 13–26.

Regan, A. C. and R. A. Garrido (2000). Modeling freight demand and shipper behaviour: state of the art, future directions. *Proceeding of the IATBR*. IATBR Conference, Sydney.

Rushton, A. and J. Oxley (1993). *Manuale di logistica distributiva*. Milan, Italy, Franco Angeli.

Russo, F. (2005). *Sistemi di trasporto merci*. Milan, Italy, Franco Angeli.

Russo, F. and A. Comi (2002). A general multi-step model for urban freight movements. *Proceeding of the PTRC*. European Transport Forum, London.

Russo, F. and A Comi (2004). A general coordinated model to simulate urban freight distribution. *Proceeding of the Triennial Symposium on Transportation Analysis-TRISTAN V*. Le Gosier, Guadeloupe, French West Indies.

Smith, P. L. (1974). Forecasting freight transport demand—the state of the art. *Logistic and Transportation Review* 10(4), 311–326.

Taniguchi, E. and R. G. Thompson (ed.), (2006). Recent advances in city logistics, *Proceeding of the 4th International Conference on City Logistics*, 12–14 July 2005. Malaysia, Elsevier Science.

Taniguchi, E., R. G. Thompson, T. Yamada and R. van Duin (2001). *City Logistics: Network Modelling and Intelligent Transport Systems*. Oxford, Pergamon.

Tavasszy, L. A., B. Smeenk and C. J. Ruijgrok (1998). A DSS for modelling logistic chains in freight transport policy analysis. *International Transactions in Operational Research* 5(6), 447–459.

Transportation National Count (2001). Ministry of Transport, Rome.

Weber, A. (1929). *Theory of the Location of Industries*. Chicago, IL, University of Chicago.

Winston, C. (1983). The demand for freight transportation: models and applications. *Transportation Research Part A* 17(6), 419–427.